Whitaker's London Almanack 2001

Whitaker's London Almanack (£40.00)
© The Stationery Office Ltd 2000

The Stationery Office Ltd
51 Nine Elms Lane, London SW8 5DR

ISBN 0 11 702243 8

A CIP catalogue record for this book is available in the British Library

All rights reserved. No part of this publication may be reproduced, stored in a retrieval system, or transmitted in any form or by any means – electronic, mechanical, photocopying, recording or otherwise – without prior written permission of the publisher, to be obtained from: the Contracts and Rights Manager, The Stationery Office Ltd, St Crispins, Duke Street, Norwich NR3 1PD.

Crown copyright material is reproduced with the permission of the Controller of Her Majesty's Stationery Office.

Whitaker's Almanack is a registered trademark of J. Whitaker and Sons Ltd. Registered Trade Mark Nos: (UK) 1322125/09; 132212/16 and 1322127/41; (EC) 19960401/09; 16, 41, licensed for use by The Stationery Office Ltd.

Publisher: Tim Probart
Consulting Editor: Gyles Brandreth
Editor: Lauren Hill
Deputy Editor: Vanessa Taylor
Database Co-ordinator: Arlene Zuccolo

Typeset, printed and bound by Unwin Brothers Ltd, Old Woking, Surrey

Contributors: Jon Asworth (**Finance**); Clive Longhurst (**Insurance**); Paul Hammond (**Education**); David Holloway and Tim Hoffman (**Law**); Karen Harries-Rees (**Environment**); David Warwick (**Index**)

Published by The Stationery Office and available from:

The Publications Centre
(mail, telephone and fax orders only)
PO Box 29, Norwich NR3 1GN
Telephone orders/General enquiries 0870 600 5522
Fax orders 0870 600 5533
Web: http://www.thestationeryoffice.com

The Stationery Office Bookshops
123 Kingsway, London WC2B 6PQ
(Tel: 020-7242 6393; Fax: 020-7242 6412)
68–69 Bull Street, Birmingham B4 6AD
(Tel: 0121-236 9696; Fax: 0121-236 9699)
33 Wine Street, Bristol BS1 2BQ
(Tel: 0117-926 4306; Fax: 0117-929 4515)
9–21 Princess Street, Manchester M60 8AS
(Tel: 0161-834 7201; Fax: 0161-833 0634)
16 Arthur Street, Belfast BT1 4GD
(Tel: 028-9023 8451; Fax: 028-9023 5401)
The Stationery Office Oriel Bookshop
18–19 High Street, Cardiff CF1 2BZ
(Tel: 029-2039 5548; Fax: 029-2038 4347)
71 Lothian Road, Edinburgh EH3 9AZ
(Tel: 0870-606 5566; Fax: 0870-606 5588)

The Stationery Office's Accredited Agents
(see Yellow Pages)

and through good booksellers

PREFACE

By Gyles Brandreth, Consulting Editor

Maybe it's because I'm a Londoner that I love London so. I have lived in London all my life. As a child, I was brought up in mansion flats in Earl's Court, South Kensington and Baker Street. When I left university I made a foray to the north (Muswell Hill), returned towards the centre (to Clarence Gate Gardens, Marylebone, to a flat where the poet T. S. Eliot had once lived, adjacent to St Cyprian's, arguably the church with the finest interior in town), then moved west to Notting Hill Gate. Now I have settled south of the river, just over Hammersmith Bridge, by Barn Elms, where Samuel Pepys used to take his family for walks in the 1680s and where you can now take yours to visit the newly-opened Wildfowl and Wetlands Centre. (The Centre's Cafeteria is located on the spot where, on 16 January 1668, the Duke of Buckingham and the Earl of Shrewsbury fought a famous duel 'all about my Lady Shrewsbury' who – according to Pepys – 'is a whore and is at this time, and hath been for a great while been, a whore to the Duke of Buckingham').

I have worked in London all my adult life: in Fleet Street, off Fleet Street (in Gough Square, where Dr Johnson lived and LBC, Britain's first commercial radio station was born), in Enfield (where I was director of Spear's games, makers of Scrabble), in Camden Town, at the Barbican (next door to the Museum of London: if you've not been, go), in the City, at Westminster and in Whitehall, at Canary Wharf and at Nine Elms (the London base of The Stationery Office Ltd, publishers of the book you are now holding). I can claim to have visited more parts of the capital than most: as a child I made it my mission to travel to every station on the London Underground, from Wimbledon in the south-west to Cockfosters in the north-east. When I was studying for my A Levels, I did all my revision on the Circle Line. I spent entire days on the tube: every time I reached Paddington I would get out and reward myself with a cup of British Rail tea.

I am setting out my London credentials in this personal way, simply because I want you to know that, while this is a serious work of reference, hard on fact, comprehensive, authoritative, wide-ranging, its Consulting Editor doesn't just have a soft spot for his subject: he loves it passionately. I go all the way with Samuel Johnson's famous dictum: 'When a man is tired of London he is tired of life; for there is in London all that life can afford.' Of course, these days affording life in London is quite another matter, but if there is a richer, more diverse, more stimulating city on the planet I have yet to discover it. Inevitably, in the fifty years I have known London, the place has changed, and not always for the better ('I don't know what London is coming to – the higher the buildings, the lower the morals' – Noel Coward), but it seems to me that on the whole – and certainly in terms of commercial and cultural opportunities – the nation's capital is a more exciting and rewarding place than it ever has been.

While most of what Dr Johnson had to say about London still holds true ('By seeing London, I have seen as much of life as the world can show'), one of his most notorious utterances would today be considered not only controversial but also wildly politically incorrect: 'Sir, the noblest prospect that a Scotchman ever sees is the high road that leads to London.' In the year 2000, in the new era of devolution, with the Scottish Parliament established in Edinburgh, with *Whitaker's Scottish Almanack* on the bookstands, no self-respecting Scot could accept London as the centre of the universe. It is, however, the centre of my universe and it is, of course, what this book is all about.

The publication of *Whitaker's London Almanack* has been triggered by the latest developments in the governance of the capital. The history of London goes back to Roman times. The ancient city of London has had a mayor since 1189. But the development of the governance of greater London has really taken place over the last two hundred years, since the rapid growth in the size of the metropolitan population around the beginning of the nineteenth century. In 1829 the Metropolitan Police was created. In 1848 a Board of Sewers was established, both to improve the capital's health and hygiene and to co-ordinate flood protection. In 1855 some 300 small, very local authorities, mainly concerned with paving and lighting, were replaced by a series of new bodies who appointed members to a Metropolitan Board of Works. The London Government Act of 1888 introduced the London County Council which survived until the London Government Act of 1963 which, in turn, introduced the Greater London Council, famously led by Ken Livingstone in its heyday, and famously abolished by Margaret Thatcher in hers.

Now, for the new millennium, we have a new governing body, the Greater London Assembly – and a familiar face in a new role: Ken Livingstone as London's first elected mayor. In case you were worried, London is in no danger of being under-governed: we still have thirty-two London boroughs, each with their elected councils, and, of course, the City of London still boasts its traditional Lord Mayor (although, the poor chap – it does still seem to be a man – no longer receives an automatic knighthood).

This book is designed to help you find your way through the maze that is the modern management of London. It aims to do much more besides, covering everything from broadcasting to banking, from the environment to the astronomical and tidal data you would expect to find in an almanac. As Consulting Editor, I want *Whitaker's London Almanack* to be the indispensible, *vade mecum* for anyone who lives or works or does business of any and every kind in this extraordinary city. The book is published by The Stationery Office Ltd, our national publisher, and is part of the family of current affairs reference works created by the London publisher Joseph Whitaker almost one hundred and fifty years ago. *Whitaker's Almanack* itself has been published annually since 1868. I would like to see *Whitaker's London Almanack* living as long and proving as useful. The editorial team – led by Lauren Hill and Vanessa Taylor – have endeavoured to ensure that all the information in the pages that follow is as accurate and up-to-date as possible. I want this book to be useful, practical, authoritative, accessible. If there are any alterations or improvements that you would like to see in future editions, please let me know.

Let me know too if you can come up with a line in praise of London that predates this one. It comes from the pen of the poet William Dunbar, and was written around the year 1500: 'London, thou art the flower of cities all!' Need I say more?

Gyles Brandreth
London, September 2000

INTRODUCTION

By Lauren Hill, Editor, Whitaker's Almanack

Welcome to the first edition of *Whitaker's London Almanack*. As Editor of *Whitaker's Almanack*, the most comprehensive of reference works, I am proud to introduce the first edition of this sister publication. Since the first edition of *Whitaker's Almanack* in 1868, both the publication and the information requirements of its readers have grown and the idea of *Whitaker's London Almanack* was born from a desire to provide information for a changing world and to enhance the expanding *Whitaker's Almanack* range which now includes *Whitaker's Scottish Almanack, Whitaker's Olympic Almanack* and *Whitaker's Almanack Pocket Reference*.

For the first time since the mid-1970s we are witnessing a London governed by a central authority and on 4 May 2000 the capital voted for Ken Livingstone as mayor and his Greater London Assembly. The following pages provide not only a definitive guide to who's who and what's what in the GLA and central and local government but also an abundance of maps, statistics and directory listings covering leisure, business, law, health, education, media, the voluntary sector, the emergency services and the environment in the capital.

Whitaker's London Almanack and The Stationery Office Ltd are pleased to welcome Gyles Brandreth as Consulting Editor of this edition – Gyles has been Consulting Editor on *Whitaker's Almanack* for a number of years.

I would like to take this opportunity to thank the editorial team and the freelancers, contributors and production teams for their hard work in ensuring that Whitaker's London Almanack was published to an extremely tight schedule.

Lauren Hill
Editor
Whitaker's London Almanack
The Stationery Office Ltd
51 Nine Elms Lane
London
SW8 5DR
Tel: 020-7873 8442
Fax: 020-7873 8723
Email: whitakers.almanack@theso.co.uk
Web: http://www.ukstate.com

WHITAKER'S LONDON ALMANACK – NOTES FOR READERS

Whitaker's London Almanack portrays London within 12 categories:

Statistical London
Governed London
Public Services London
Business London
Legal London
Media London
Cultural, Historical and Recreational London
Environmental London
London and the World
Religious London
Societies, Institutions and Charities
Astronomy, Tides, Calendars and Forthcoming Events

As well as the main contents page at the front of the book, each section has a contents page which breaks down the key elements of that section. Readers should note that listings such as 'Public Relations Agencies' will not comprise all the agencies in London as there are just too many to list. Such listings are in no way an endorsement of the quality of the services provided by each company but are purely representative of those companies responding to our enquiries and questionnaires. Other listings such as 'Police Forces' in the Public Services section, are to our knowledge fully comprehensive.

As this is the first edition of Whitaker's London Almanack and as with all the Whitaker's reference books, we are always keen to hear your comments and suggestions. Further, if you have ideas for a subject or entry that could be considered for inclusion in future editions, please get in contact with us.

CONTENTS

Preface	iii
Introduction	v

STATISTICAL LONDON	1
Population	3
Births and Deaths	4
Migration	4
Deprivation	5
Household Expenditure	6

GOVERNED LONDON	7
Greater London Authority	9
Election Results	13
Assembly Members	24
London Borough Councils	27
Members of Parliament	71
Members of the European Parliament	79
Government Departments and Public Offices	80

PUBLIC SERVICES LONDON	89
Education	91
Emergency Services	105
Ambulance	105
Fire	105
Police	105
Health Care	113
Housing	118
Libraries	121
Transport	134
Utilities	145

BUSINESS LONDON	147
Introduction	149
Banking	152
Financial Services Regulation	153
Insurance	155
London Stock Exchange	158
Ombudsmen	159
Business and the Workforce	160
Trade Unions	164
Employers' Associations	166
Training and Enterprise	168
Charity and the Voluntary Sector	170
Conference and Exhibition Venues	176

LEGAL LONDON	183
Legal System	186
Circuit Judges	187
Crown Courts	188
County Courts	188
Magistrates' Courts	189
Coroners' Courts	191
Tribunals	191
Crown Prosecution Service	192
Prison Service	194
Probation Service	195
Legal Bodies	195
Legal Notes	198

MEDIA LONDON	215
Television	217
Radio	218
Press and Publishing	220
Advertising	239
Public Relations	241
Telecommunications	248
Postal Services	252

CULTURAL LONDON	253
History Timeline	255
English Kings and Queens	257
Order of Succession	260
Order of Precedence	261
Scenes and Sights of London	262
Blue Plaques	262
Clubs	287
Museums and Galleries	292
Theatres	299
Sport	305
Cultural, Historical and Recreational Organisations	318
Tourism	322

ENVIRONMENTAL LONDON	323
Introduction	325
Nature Reserves	325
Sights of Special Scientific Interest	326
River Thames	327
Environmental Groups	328
Waste Minimisation and Recycling	330

LONDON AND THE WORLD	335
Tourist Boards	337
Embassies	340
International Organisations	347
European Union	347
Time Zones	348
Air Distances from London	350
International Direct Dialling Codes	352

RELIGIOUS LONDON	355
Christianity	357
Baha'i Faith	358
Buddhism	358
Hinduism	359
Islam	359
Jainism	360
Judaism	360
Sikhism	360
Zoroastrianism	361
Churches	361

SOCIETIES, INSTITUTIONS AND CHARITIES	367
ASTRONOMICAL AND TIDAL DATA	393
FORTHCOMING EVENTS	406
MAPS	408

STATISTICAL
LONDON

POPULATION TRENDS
BIRTHS AND DEATHS
MIGRATION
DEPRIVATION
HOUSEHOLD EXPENDITURE

STATISTICAL LONDON

London is the largest metropolis within the European Union and is culturally diverse. Almost 50 per cent of Britain's ethnic minority population live and work in London. The capital is one of the world's top financial centres and is home to an abundance of businesses, educational establishments, leisure and cultural facilities, transport links, communities...the list is vast.

Within this section you will find a wealth of data aimed at providing a statistical insight into the people, population and work of London.

POPULATION TRENDS AND PROJECTIONS OF LONDON 1961-2011 (000s)

	1961	1971	1981	1983	1991	1997	2001*	2011*
Inner London	3,481	3,060	2,550	2,523	2,627	2,727	2,765	2,863
Outer London	4,496	4,470	4,255	4,242	4,263	4,395	4,450	4,607
London Total	7,977	7,529	6,806	6,765	6,890	7,122	7,215	7,470
UK	52,807	55,928	56,362	56,377	57,808	59,009	59,618	60,929

*1996-based sub-national projections.
Source: Focus on London '99, Office for National Statistics © Crown Copyright 1999

POPULATION OF LONDON BY AGE 1971-2011 (PERCENTAGES AND 000s)

Age	London					UK				
	1971	1981	1991	1997	2011*	1971	1981	1991	1997	2011*
0-4	7.3	5.8	7.0	7.1	6.4	8.1	6.1	6.7	6.3	5.6
5-14	14.0	12.5	11.5	12.5	12.0	15.9	14.5	12.4	13.0	11.6
15-19	6.2	7.7	5.6	6.1	6.2	6.9	8.4	6.5	6.1	6.3
20-24	8.7	8.8	9.1	7.0	7.6	7.7	7.6	7.8	6.1	6.6
25-44	24.9	27.5	33.2	34.2	30.4	24.1	26.2	29.4	29.9	26.3
45-59/64	22.3	19.5	17.2	18.1	23.0	20.9	19.4	18.8	20.4	23.9
60/65-74	11.8	12.1	9.8	8.9	9.0	11.6	12.0	11.4	10.9	12.1
75-84	3.9	4.9	5.1	4.5	3.8	3.9	4.7	5.4	5.4	5.4
85+	1.0	1.2	1.5	1.7	1.5	0.9	1.1	1.5	1.8	2.1
All ages (000)s	7,529	6,806	6,890	7,122	7,470	55,928	56,352	57,808	59,009	60,929

* 1996-based sub-national and national projections.
Source: Focus on London '99, Office for National Statistics © Crown Copyright 1999

POPULATION OF LONDON BY ETHNIC GROUP, 1991 (PERCENTAGES AND 000s)

Ethnic Group	Inner London	Outer London	Total London	Great Britain
White	74.4	83.1	79.8	94.5
Black Caribbean	7.1	2.7	4.4	0.9
Black African	4.4	1.3	2.4	0.4
Black other	2.0	0.7	1.2	0.3
Indian	3.0	6.5	5.2	1.5
Pakistani	1.2	1.4	1.3	0.9
Bangladeshi	2.8	0.4	1.3	0.3
Chinese	1.1	0.7	0.8	0.3
Other Asian	1.8	1.6	1.7	0.4
Other	2.3	1.5	1.8	0.5
All persons (000s)	2,504	4,175	6,680	54,889

Source: Focus on London '99, Office for National Statistics © Crown Copyright 1999

4 Statistical London

BIRTHS AND DEATHS IN LONDON 1971-1997 (PER 1,000 POPULATION)

Year	London Live births	Deaths	UK Live births	Deaths
1971	15.0	11.3	16.1	11.5
1981	13.6	11.4	13.0	11.7
1991	15.4	10.0	13.7	11.2
1992	15.4	9.6	13.5	10.9
1993	15.0	9.9	13.1	11.3
1994	15.1	9.4	12.9	10.7
1995	14.9	9.6	12.5	11.0
1996	14.9	9.2	12.5	10.8
1997	14.8	8.9	12.3	10.7

Source: Focus on London '99, Office for National Statistics © Crown Copyright 1999

AGE-ADJUSTED MORTALITY RATES IN LONDON*, BY CAUSE** AND GENDER, 1997

	Males London	UK	Females London	UK
Circulatory diseases	373	407	381	436
Respiratory diseases	167	147	193	179
Cancer†	255	265	244	245
Injury and poisoning	38	42	20	23
Other causes	124	123	163	173
All causes‡	957	984	1,002	1,056

* Rates are standardised to the mid-1991 UK population for males and females separately
** Data for individual causes exclude death at ages under 28 days occurring in England and Wales as they are not assigned an underlying cause
† Malignant neoplasms only
‡ Including deaths at ages under 28 days
Source: Focus on London '99, Office for National Statistics © Crown Copyright 1999

MIGRATION TO AND FROM LONDON: BY AGE, 1996-7* (000s)

Age	Within the UK To London	From London	International** To London	From London
0-15	16.1	36.8	7.2	4.7
16-24	66.1	45.0	38.1	9.6
25-44	70.3	92.0	35.9	34.5
45-64	11.0	27.2	3.3	3.9
65+	5.1	16.4	0.4	-
All ages	168.5	217.4	84.8	52.7

*Mid-1996 to mid-1997
** Excludes asylum seekers/visitor switchers and movements to and from the Irish Republic
Source: Focus on London '99, Office for National Statistics © Crown Copyright 1999

Statistical London 5

LONDON HOUSEHOLDS, 1996

	Average household	Household Type % Married Couple	Co-habiting Couple	Lone-parent*	One-person	Other	All households (000s)
Inner London	2.19	30.1	7.7	9.8	38.7	13.8	1,209.5
Outer London	2.41	47.4	7.3	5.9	29.8	9.7	1,789.3
Total London	2.33	40.4	7.4	7.5	33.4	11.4	2,998.8

* Lone parents with dependent children
Source: Focus on London '99, Office for National Statistics © Crown Copyright 1999

MOST SEVERELY DEPRIVED DISTRICTS IN ENGLAND, 1998*

Ranking*	Districts	Ranking*	Districts
1	Liverpool	16	Nottingham
2	NEWHAM	17	CAMDEN
3	Manchester	18	HAMMERSMITH & FULHAM
4	HACKNEY	19	Newcastle-upon-Tyne
5	Birmingham	20	BRENT
6	TOWER HAMLETS	21	Sunderland
7	Sandwell	22	WALTHAM FOREST
8	SOUTHWARK	23	Salford
9	Knowsley	24	Middlesbrough
10	ISLINGTON	25	Sheffield
11	GREENWICH	26	Kingston-upon-Hull
12	LAMBETH	27	Wolverhampton
13	HARINGEY	28	Bradford
14	LEWISHAM	29	Rochdale
15	BARKING & DAGENHAM	30	WANDSWORTH

* Based on the Index of Local Deprivation
Source: Focus on London '99, Office for National Statistics © Crown Copyright 1999

WHERE LONDON'S RESIDENTS WORK*, 1991 (PERCENTAGES AND 000s)

Percentage of London's residents working...	
...in central London**	23.1
...elsewhere in London	71.6
...outside London	5.3
Total residents (000s)	2,826

* The figures are derived from 10% data and relate to residents who are employed
** Defined as the West End and the City of London
Source: Focus on London '99, Office for National Statistics © Crown Copyright 1999

6 Statistical London

HOUSEHOLD EXPENDITURE, BY COMMODITY AND SERVICE, 1996-98* (£ PER WEEK AND PERCENTAGES)

	£ per week		As a % of Average Weekly Expenditure	
	London	*UK*	*London*	*UK*
Housing (net)†	64	50	18	16
Fuel and Power	12	13	3	4
Food and non-Alcoholic drinks	59	56	17	17
Alcoholic drinks	12	13	3	4
Tobacco	6	6	2	2
Clothing & Footwear	20	19	6	6
Household Goods & Services	49	44	14	14
Motoring & Fares	51	52	15	16
Leisure Goods & Services	55	52	16	16
Personal Goods & Services	15	12	4	4
Miscellaneous	2	2	1	1
Average Household Expenditure	345	319	100	100

* *Combined data from the 1996-97 and 1997-98 surveys.*
† *Net of Housing Benefit and Council Tax Benefit (rates rebate in Northern Ireland)*
Source: Focus on London '99, Office for National Statistics © Crown Copyright 1999

GOVERNED
LONDON

GREATER LONDON AUTHORITY
LONDON BOROUGH COUNCILS
MEMBERS OF PARLIAMENT
MEMBERS OF EUROPEAN PARLIAMENT
GOVERNMENT DEPARTMENTS

8 Governed London

CONSTITUENCIES OF THE GREATER LONDON AUTHORITY

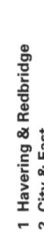

London Constituencies

1. Havering & Redbridge
2. City & East
3. North East
4. Enfield & Haringey
5. West Central
6. Barnet & Camden
7. Brent & Harrow
8. Ealing & Hillingdon
9. South West
10. Merton & Wandsworth
11. Croydon & Sutton
12. Lambeth & Southwark
13. Greenwich & Lewisham
14. Bexley & Bromley

GOVERNED LONDON

GREATER LONDON AUTHORITY (GLA)

Romney House, 43 Marsham Street, London SW1P 3PY (Tel: 020-7983 4000; Press Office: 020-7983 4071/4072/4090/4067/4228;
Email: mayor@london.gov.uk;
Web: http://www.london.gov.uk)

OVERVIEW

On 7 May 1998 London voted in favour of the formation of the Greater London Authority. The first elections to the GLA were on Thursday, 4 May 2000 and the new Authority took over its responsibilities on 3 July 2000.

The structure and objectives of the GLA stem from its eight main areas of responsibility. These are transport, planning, economic development and regeneration, the environment, police, fire and emergency planning and culture and health. The bodies that co-ordinate these functions and report to the GLA are: Transport for London (TfL), London Development Agency (LDA), Metropolitan Police Authority (MPA) and the London Fire and Emergency Planning Authority (LFEPA). The GLA has also absorbed a number of London bodies, such as the London Planning Advisory Committee, the London Ecology Unit and the London Research Centre.

The GLA consists of a directly elected mayor, The Mayor of London and a separately elected assembly, The London Assembly. The Mayor has the key role of decision making with the Assembly performing the tasks of regulating and scrutinising these decisions. In addition, the GLA has around 400 permanent staff to support the activities of the Mayor and the Assembly, which are overseen by a Head of Paid Service. The Mayor may appoint two political advisors but he/she may not appoint the Head of Paid Service, the Monitoring Officer or the Chief Finance Officer. These must be appointed by the Assembly.

The Mayor is also responsible for appointing a Cabinet. The Cabinet functions as part of the Mayor's objective of eliminating barriers to effective decision making and enabling the GLA to speak with one voice on behalf of London. The function of the Mayor's Cabinet is to provide the Mayor with the most sound advice on policy and strategy. Meetings of the Cabinet are designed to be a powerful forum for discussing the issues affecting Londoners. The Cabinet is not intended to fit the Whitehall Cabinet model in that GLA members will not be bound by the convention of collective responsibility, the absence of which does not mean that the Mayor will devolve or federalise his powers. All decisions are made by the Mayor acting on the honest advice of his Cabinet. Cabinet members can be broadly categorised into (a) those with specific policy brief (e.g. in the areas of planning, policing or fire and civil defence and (b) those who have been chosen to give advice and/or reflect political breadth.

The role of the mayor can be broken down into a number of key areas:
- to represent and promote London at home and abroad and speak up for Londoners
- to devise strategies and plans to tackle London-wide issues, such as transport, economic development and regeneration, air quality, noise, waste, bio-diversity, planning and culture
- to set budgets for Transport for London, the London Development Agency, the Metropolitan Police Authority and the London Fire and Emergency Planning Authority
- to control new transport and economic development bodies and appoint their members
- to make appointments to the new police and fire authorities
- to publish regular reports on the state of the environment in London

The role of the Assembly can be broken down into a number of key areas:
- to provide a check and balance on the Mayor
- to scrutinise the Mayor
- to have the power to amend the Mayor's budget by a majority of two-thirds
- to investigate issues of London wide significance and make proposals to the Mayor
- to provide the Deputy Mayor and the members serving on the police, fire and emergency planning authorities.

The GLA will be housed at the temporary address shown above until its new premises are complete. The new GLA building will be built on a brown field site on the south bank of the river Thames, adjacent to Tower Bridge. The building is a distinctive glass globe with a purpose built assembly chamber and offices for 400 people. It will stand fifty metres high, with 21,700 square metres of floor space.

ELECTIONS AND THE VOTING SYSTEMS

The Assembly will be elected every four years at the same time as the Mayor and consists of 25 members. There is one member from each of the 14 GLA Constituencies topped up with 11 London-wide members who are representatives of political parties or individuals standing as independent candidates.

The GLA constituencies are: Barnet and Camden; Bexley and Bromley; Brent and Harrow; City and London East, covering Barking and Dagenham and the City of London; Newham and Tower Hamlets; Croydon and Sutton; Ealing and Hillingdon; Enfield and Haringey; Greenwich and Lewisham; Havering and Redbridge; North East, covering Hackney, Islington and Waltham Forest; Lambeth and Southwark; West Central, covering Hammersmith and Fulham, Kensington and Chelsea and Westminster; South West, covering Hounslow, Kingston upon Thames and Richmond upon Thames; Merton and Wandsworth.

Two distinct voting systems were used to appoint the Mayor and the Assembly. The Mayor was elected using the Supplementary Vote (SV) system. With the SVS

10 Governed London

electors have two votes; one to give the first choice for Mayor and one to give the second choice. Electors cannot vote twice for the same candidate. If one candidate gets more than half of all the first choice votes, he or she becomes Mayor. If no candidate gets more than half the first choice votes, the two candidates with the most first choice votes remain in the election and all the other candidates drop out. The second choice votes on the ballot papers of the candidates who drop out are then counted. Where these second choice votes are for the two remaining candidates they are added to the first choice votes these candidates already have. The candidate with the most first and second choice votes combined would become the Mayor of London.

The Assembly was appointed using the Additional Member (AM) system. With AMS electors have two votes. The first vote is for a constituency candidate. The second vote is for a party list or individual candidate contesting the London-wide Assembly seats. The 14 constituency members were elected under the first-past-the-post system, the same system used in general and local elections. Electors vote for one candidate and the candidate with the most votes wins. The Additional (London) Members were drawn from party lists or were independent candidates who stood as London Members.

The Greater London Returning Officer (GLRO) was the independent official responsible for running the election in London. The GLRO had overall responsibility for running a free, fair and efficient election. He was supported in this by Returning Officers in each of the 14 London Constituencies.

GLRO: Robert V Hughes: CBE

FUNCTIONS AND STRUCTURE

Every aspect of the Assembly and its activities must be open to the view of the public and therefore accountable. Assembly meetings are open to the public and the reports it produces are available to the public. Other measures such as a twice yearly 'people's question time' will also take place. The meetings where the Assembly questions the Mayor will also be open to the public.

Funding

The GLA is responsible for funding Transport for London, the London Development Agency, the Metropolitan Police Authority and the London Fire and Emergency Planning Authority. Budgets are set by the Mayor, and scrutinised by the Assembly. Funds are allocated subject to safeguards on service standards. The GLA inherited its funding from the bodies that it replaced. This is thought to amount to around £3bn. As the GLA did not take up its role until after the start of the financial year, its budget was apportioned appropriately with its 'predecessor' bodies. The GLA also received a government grant to cover the cost of the Mayor, Assembly and additional staff. The contribution of each London taxpayer to the cost of the GLA is around £1.70 a year, (3p per day).

Transport for London (TfL)

The TfL is run by a board of members appointed by the mayor. Its role is:
- to manage the buses, Croydon Tramlink and the Docklands Light Railway (DLR)
- to manage the underground once Public Private partnership contracts are in place
- to manage an important network of roads to be known as the GLA Road Network
- to regulate taxis and minicabs
- to run the London River services and promote the river for passenger and freight movement
- to help to co-ordinate the Dial-a-Ride and Taxicard schemes for door-to-door services for transport users with mobility problems
- to take responsibility for traffic lights

London Borough Councils will maintain the role of highway and traffic authorities for 95 per cent of London's roads. Bodies such as London Transport and London Underground will be wound up and their powers transferred to TfL.

Transitional Chief Executive: Anthony Mayer.

Spatial Development Strategy (SDS)

The Mayor of London is responsible for strategic planning in London in the form of a Spatial Planning Strategy. This sets priorities and provides direction for the future development of London. It replaces regional planning guidance provided by the Secretary of State. The SDS incorporates the key aspects of the many other areas of the Mayor's responsibility including sustainable development, transport, economic development, housing, the built environment, the natural and open environment, waste, town centres, cultural and community facilities, London's Capital and World City roles and the River Thames.

London Borough Councils continue to deal with all planning applications and produce development plans.

London Development Agency (LDA)

The LDA promotes economic development and regeneration. It is one of the eight regional development agencies set up around the country to perform this task. The key aspects of the LDA's role are:
- to promote business efficiency, investment and competitiveness
- to promote employment
- to enhance the skills of local people
- to create sustainable development

The London Boroughs retain powers to promote economic development in their local areas.

The Environment

The mayor is required to formulate strategies to tackle London's environmental issues including: the quality of water, air and land; the use of energy and London's contribution to climate change targets; ground water levels and traffic emissions; municipal waste management.

Metropolitan Police Authority (MPA)

This new body, which oversees the policing of London consists of 12 members of the assembly, including the deputy mayor, 4 magistrates and 7 independents. One of the independents was appointed by the Home Secretary. The role of the MPA is:
- to maintain an efficient and effective police force
- to publish an annual policing plan
- to set police targets and monitor performance
- to be involved in the appointment, discipline and removal of senior officers
- to be responsible for the performance budget

Greater London Authority

The boundaries of the metropolitan police districts have been changed to be in line with the 32 London boroughs. Areas beyond the GLA remit have been incorporated into the Surrey, Hertfordshire and Essex police areas. The City of London has its own police force.

London Fire and Emergency Planning Authority (LFEPA)

In 3 July 2000 the existing London Fire and Civil defence authority became the London Fire and Emergency Planning Authority. It consists of 17 members, 9 drawn from the new assembly and 8 nominated by the London Boroughs. The role of LFEPA is:
- to set the strategy for the provision of fire services
- to ensure that the fire brigade can meet all the normal requirements efficiently
- to ensure that effective arrangements are made for the fire brigade to receive emergency calls and deal with them promptly
- to ensure that information useful to the development of the fire brigades is gathered
- to assist the boroughs with their emergency planning training and exercises.

Health

Healthcare in London will continue to be the remit of the NHS and the London Ambulance Service. The NHS London Regional Office will be supported by the GLA in its development of strategies to improve the health of Londoners.

The Cultural Strategy Group for London (CSGL)

The GLA aims to provide a wide ranging culture strategy, encompassing the arts, sport and tourism. The CSGL will provide advice and guidance to the GLA on this matter. It is envisaged that the GLA will:
- produce a strategy for the cultural development of London
- endorse and bid for major sporting events which London may host
- develop the creative industries' contribution to the London economy
- take over management of Trafalgar Square and Parliament Square
- develop a policy for the development of tourism in London

THE MAYORAL CANDIDATES

In the build up to the election of the Mayor for London, there were a number of controversial issues which dogged the main parties in the nominations of their Mayoral candidate. Each party held an internal ballot to appoint their official candidate, the results for the three main parties are given below. There were also a number of independent candidates running whose details are also given.

Conservative Party
Ballot Date: 17 January 2000
Chosen Candidate: Steven Norris
Rival Candidate: Andrew Boff
Voting System: One member one vote
Result of Ballot: 12,903 in favour; 4,712 rebuff

Labour Party
Ballot Date: 20 February 2000
Chosen Candidate: Frank Dobson
Rival Candidates: Ken Livingstone*; Glenda Jackson
Voting System: Votes split into three sections. One was for the 41,000 London party members. The second was for the unions and societies affiliated to labour; the third was for MPs and MEPs and GLA candidates.
Result of Ballot: Membership vote: Dobson – 35.3%; Jackson – 9.8%; Livingstone - 54.9%; Unions Vote: Dobson - 26.9%; Jackson – 2.1%; Livingstone – 71.0%; MPs, MEPs and GLA candidates: Dobson - 86.5%; Jackson – 1.3%; Livingstone – 12.2%
Totals after reallocation of Glenda Jacksons' votes: Dobson – 51.5%; Livingstone – 48.5%

On the 6 March 2000 Ken Livingstone announced that he would stand as an independent candidate.

Liberal Democrats
Chosen Candidate: Susan Kramer
Rival Candidates: Donnachadh McCarthy; Mike Tuffrey, Keith Kerr.
Percentage of vote won: 62%

CANDIDATES FOR GLA MEMBERSHIP

Labour Party Candidates
Trevor Phillips
Samantha Heath
David Lammy
Jeanette Arnold
Joe Docherty
Diana Johnson
Abdul Asad
Pam Wharfe
Talal Karim
Katy Thorne
Navin Shah
John Biggs

Conservative Candidates
Bob Neill
Eric Ollerenshaw
Syed Kamall
Rhodri Harris
Roger Evans
Tony Arbour
Andrew Pelling
Irene Kimm
Elizabeth Howlett
Lurline Champagnie
Richard Barnes
Victoria Borwick
Bernard Gentry
Michael Flynn
Patti Komlosty
Bob Blackman
Peter Forrest
Diane Henry
Robert Moreland
Harry Stokes
Piers Wauchope
David Williams
Cheryl Potter

12 Governed London

Liberal Democrat Candidates
Sally Hamwee
Graham Tope
Lynne Featherstone
Louise Bloom
Mike Tuffrey
Geoff Pope
Meher Khan
Duncan Borrowman
Chris Noyce
Monroe Palmer
Meral Ece

Green Party Candidates
Darren Johnson
Victor Anderson
Jenny Jones
Noel Lynch
Shane Collins
Hilary Jago
Ashley Gunstock
John Street
Jayne Forbes
Simone Aspis
Catherine Mukhopadhyay

London Socialist Alliance Candidates
Paul Foot
Greg Tucker
Janine Booth
Christine Blower
Theresa Bennett
Anne Murphy
Kate Ford
Tobias Abse
Jean Kysow
George Taylor
Mark Steel

UK Independence Party Candidates
Damian Hockney
Christopher Pratt
Anthony van der Elst
Anthony Scholefield
Gregory Sylsz
John de Roeck
Robert Bryant
Gerald Roberts
James Feisenberger
Mark Lester
Penelope Weald

Socialist Labour Party Candidates
Arthur Scargill
Amanda Rose
Harpal Brar
Margaret Sharkey
Hardev Dhillon
Nicola Hoarau
Geoff Palmer
Novjoy Brar
Robert Siggins
Ella Rule
John Hayball

Natural Law Party Candidates
Geoffrey Clements
Richard Johnson
Judith Thomas
Alexander Hankey
Gerard Valente
Jeanie Livesley
Juliette Taylor-Elwes
Johnathan Hinde
Michael Mears

Campaign Against Tube Privatisation Candidates
Patrick Sikorski
Oliver New
Catherine Effer
Robert Law
Pam Slinger
Enoh Iterjere
Brian Monroe
Arwyn Thomas
Lewis Peacock
Graham Campbell
Davey Lyons

The Christian Peoples' Alliance Party candidates
David Campanale
Sue May
Andrew Farmer
Ellen Greco
Deepak Mahtani
Nigel Poole
Stuart MacPherson
Philippa Berry
Tim Ward
Peter Wolstenholme

British National Party Candidates
David Hill
Peter Hart
Ken Francis
Michael Davidson
Paul Ferguson
Frank Walsh

Communist Party of Britain Candidates
Nick Wright
Sandra Lusk
James Beavis
Monty Goldman
Salvador Urdiales-Antelo
Anita Halpin
Anita Wright
Kevin Halpin
Richard Maybin

Pro-Motorist Small Shop Candidates
Geoffrey Ben-Nathan
Brian Bartle
Russ Conway
Joseph Pronckus

Other Independent Candidates
Peter Tatchell

GLA Election Results

THE MAYORAL AND ASSEMBLY ELECTION RESULTS

BARNET AND CAMDEN
Mayor

Name	Party	1st Pref	%	2nd Pref	%
Ken Livingstone	Ind	51,649	38.88	13,368	12.0
Steven Norris	Con	36,826	27.68	14,858	13.34
Susan Kramer	LD	17,096	12.5	33,144	29.75
Frank Dobson	Lab	16,978	12.76	17,125	15.37
Darren Johnson	Green	3,564	2.8	16,621	14.92
Ram Gidoomal	CPA	2,336	1.6	3,649	3.28
Michael Newland	BNP	1,451	1.09	2,285	2.05
Geoffrey Ben-Nathan	PMSS	1,055	0.79	2,865	2.57
Damian Hockney	UKIP	972	0.73	2,832	2.54
Ashwin Kumar Tanna	Ind	708	0.53	2,938	2.64
Geoffrey Clements	NL	397	0.30	1,388	1.25
Turnout	Total Votes:	133,032	(35.0%)	111,073	

Assembly
First Past the Post

Name	Party	Votes	%
Brian Coleman	Con	41,583	32.9
Helen Gordon	Lab	41,032	32.46
Jonathan Davies	LD	22,295	17.63
Miranda Dunn	Green	14,768	11.68
Candy Udwin	London Socialist Alliance	3,488	2.76
Magnus Nielsen	UKInd	2,115	1.67
Diane Derksen	Maharishi's Natural Prog.	1,081	0.90
Majority	Total Votes: 551 (0.4%)		
Turnout	Total Votes: 136,384 (35.0%)		

Top up seats (London wide)

Name	Votes	%
Conservative	37,795	29.40
Labour	37.352	29.06
Liberal Democrats	19,376	15.07
Green	16,789	13.06
Christian Peoples' Alliance	3,258	2.53
London Socialist Alliance	2,421	1.88
British National Party	2,217	1.72
UK Independence Party	2,037	1.58
Peter Tatchell	1,908	1.48
Campaign Against Tube Privatisation	1,517	1.18
Pro-Motorist Small Shop	1,381	1.07
Socialist Labour Party	1,115	0.87
Natural Law Party	677	0.53
Communist Party of Britain	632	0.49
Turnout	Total Votes: 127,475 (35.0%)	

BEXLEY AND BROMLEY
Mayor

Name	Party	1st Pref	%	2nd Pref	%
Steven Norris	Con	57,193	39.30	18,552	15.29
Ken Livingstone	Ind	41,679	28.63	12,935	10.67
Susan Kramer	LD	20,610	14.16	38,691	31.91
Frank Dobson	Lab	11,975	8.23	14,898	12.30
Michael Newland	BNP	3,785	2.60	5,569	4.59
Ram Gidoomal	CPA	3,678	2.53	5,093	4.20
Darren Johnson	Green	2,673	1.84	13,335	11.00
Damian Hockney	UKInd	2,149	1.48	5,593	4.61
Geoffrey Ben-Nathan	PMSS	749	0.51	1,847	1.52
Ashwin Kumar Tanna	Ind	617	0.42	3,366	2.78
Geoffrey Clements	NL	286	0.20	1,385	1.14
Turnout	Total Votes:	145,391	(37.3%)	121,264	

14 Governed London

Assembly
First Past the Post

Name	Party	1st Pref	%
Bob Neill	Con	64,879	47.20
Charlie Mansell	Lab	30,320	22.06
Duncan Borrowman	LD	29,710	21.61
Ian Jardin	Green	11,124	8.09
Jean Kysow	London Socialist Alliance	1,403	1.02
Majority	Total Votes: 34,559 (25.2%)		
Turnout	Total Votes: 137,436 (35.3%)		

Top up seats (London wide)

Name	Votes	%
Conservative	59,019	41.80
Labour	29,776	21.09
Liberal Democrats	23,302	16.50
Green	11,021	7.81
British National Party	5,060	3.58
Christian Peoples' Alliance	4,621	3.27
UK Independence Party	3,746	2.65
Pro-Motorist Small Shop	1,167	0.83
Peter Tatchell	759	0.54
London Socialist Alliance	721	0.51
Socialist Labour Party	701	0.50
Campaign Against Tube Privatisation	656	0.46
Natural Law Party	443	0.31
Communist Party of Britain	321	0.23
Turnout	Total Votes: 142,072 (36.4%)	

BRENT AND HARROW
Mayor

Name	Party	1st Pref	%	2nd Pref	%
Ken Livingstone	Ind	47,044	43.70	11,847	13.60
Steven Norris	Con	25,293	23.50	11,240	12.90
Krank Dobson	Lab	15,279	14.19	15,372	17.65
Susan Kramer	LD	10,797	10.03	23,718	27.23
Ram Gidoomal	CPA	2,841	2.64	3,902	4.48
Darren Johnson	Green	1,809	1.68	9,959	11.43
Michael Newland	BNP	1,362	1.27	2,022	2.32
Ashwin Kumar Tanna	Ind	1,200	1.11	4,002	4.59
Geoffrey Ben-Nathan	PMSS	905	0.84	2,198	2.52
Damian Hockney	UKInd	788	0.73	1,945	2.23
Geoffrey Clements	NL	424	0.38	1,102	1.27
Turnout	Total Votes:	107,742	(32.5%)	87,307	

Assembly
First Past the Post

Name	Party	Votes	%
Lord Toby Harris	Lab	36,675	37.60
Bob Blackman	Con	32,295	33.11
Chris Noyce	LD	17,161	17.59
Simone Aspis	Green	8,756	9.00
Austin Burnett	London Socialist Alliance	2,546	2.61
Majority	Total Votes: 4,380 (4.5%)		
Turnout	Total Votes: 97,433 (29.4%)		

GLA Election Results

Top up seats (London wide)

Name	Votes	%
Labour	37,818	36.50
Conservative	28,622	27.62
Liberal Democrats	13,551	13.08
Green	9,763	9.42
Christian Peoples' Alliance	3,541	3.42
British National Party	1,955	1.9
UK Independence Party	1,943	1.8
London Socialist Alliance	1,299	1.25
Campaign Against Tube Privatisation	1,267	1.22
Pro-Motorist Small Shop	1,068	1.03
Peter Tatchell	975	0.94
Socialist Labour Party	816	0.79
Natural Law Party	545	0.53
Communist Party of Britain	534	0.52
Turnout	Total Votes: 103,697 (31.3%)	

CITY AND EAST
Mayor

Name	Party	1st Pref	%	2nd Pref	%
Ken Livingstone	Ind	46,236	40.60	13,638	14.70
Frank Dobson	Lab	24,832	21.81	18,998	20.48
Steven Norris	Con	19,026	16.71	12,188	13.14
Susan Kramer	LD	9,919	8.71	20,468	22.06
Michael Newland	BNP	5,081	4.46	4,839	5.22
Ram Gidoomal	CPA	3,009	2.64	3,192	3.44
Darren Johnson	Green	2,383	2.09	10,740	11.58
Damian Hockney	UKInd	1,264	1.11	2,848	3.07
Geoffrey Ben-Nathan	PMSS	1,123	0.99	1,480	1.60
Geoffrey Clements	NL	816	0.72	1,568	1.69
Ashwin Kumar Tanna	Ind	783	0.69	2,832	3.05
Turnout	Total Votes:	114,022	(28.5%)	92,791	

Assembly
First Past the Post

Name	Party	Votes	%
John Biggs	Lab	45,387	45.90
Syed Kamall	Con	19,266	19.48
Janet Ludlow	LD	18,300	18.51
Peter Howell	Green	11,939	12.07
Kambiz Boomla	London Socialist Alliance	3,908	4.0
Majority	Total Votes: 26,121 (26.4%)		
Turnout	Total Votes: 98,800 (24.7%)		

Top up seats (London wide)

Name	Votes	%
Labour	44,329	40.40
Conservative	19,116	17.42
Liberal Democrats	12,526	11.42
Green	10,079	9.18
British National Party	7,763	7.07
Christian Peoples' Alliance	4,001	3.65
UK Independence Party	2,977	2.71
London Socialist Alliance	1,844	1.68
Peter Tatchell	1,835	1.67
Campaign Against Tube Privatisation	1,710	1.56
Socialist Labour Party	1,149	1.05
Pro-Motorist Small Shop	818	0.75
Communist Party of Britain	784	0.71
Natural Law Party	672	0.61
Turnout	Total Votes: 109,603 (27.4%)	

16 Governed London

CROYDON AND SUTTON
Mayor

Name	Party	1st Pref	%	2nd Pref	%
Ken Livingstone	Ind	41,818	32.90	12,935	12.20
Steven Norris	Con	41,794	32.88	15,534	14.65
Susan Kramer	LD	18,331	14.42	32,418	30.58
Frank Dobson	Lab	12,399	9.75	14,223	13.41
Ram Gidoomal	CPA	4,925	3.87	5,911	5.58
Michael Newland	BNP	2,389	1.88	3,686	3.48
Darren Johnson	Green	2,201	1.73	11,322	10.68
Damian Hockney	UKInd	1,578	1.24	4,238	4.00
Ashwin Kumar Tanna	Ind	716	0.56	3,149	2.97
Geoffrey Ben-Nathan	PMSS	647	0.51	1,725	1.63
Geoffrey Clements	NL	309	0.24	1,197	1.13
Turnout	Total Votes:	127,107	(34.8%)	106,338	

Assembly
First Past the Post

Name	Party	Votes	%
Andrew Pelling	Con	48,421	40.60
Anne Gallop	LD	30,614	25.67
Maggie Mansell	Lab	29,514	24.74
Peter Hickson	Green	8,884	7.45
Mark Steel	London Socialist Alliance	1,823	1.53
Majority	Total Votes: 17,807 (14.9%)		
Turnout	Total Votes: 119,256 (32.7%)		

Top up seats (London wide)

Name	Votes	%
Conservative	43,666	35.40
Labour	29,221	23.69
Liberal Democrats	23,837	19.32
Green	9,658	7.83
Christian Peoples' Alliance	6,039	4.90
British National Party	3,206	2.60
UK Independence Party	2,902	2.35
Pro-Motorist Small Shop	1,028	0.83
London Socialist Alliance	907	0.74
Peter Tatchell	803	0.65
Campaign Against Tube Privatisation	779	0.63
Socialist Labour Party	675	0.55
Natural Law Party	440	0.36
Communist Party of Britain	354	0.29
Turnout	Total Votes: 123,515 (33.9%)	

EALING AND HILLINGDON
Mayor

Name	Party	1st Pref	%	2nd Pref	%
Ken Livingstone	Ind	48,192	37.60	13,243	12.79
Steven Norris	Con	34,948	27.27	13,879	13.41
Frank Dobson	Lab	19,566	15.27	17,357	16.77
Susan Kramer	LD	14,011	10.93	29,281	28.30
Ram Gidoomal	CPA	3,127	2.44	4,156	4.01
Michael Newland	BNP	2,679	2.09	3,700	3.57
Darren Johnson	Green	2,612	2.04	12,344	11.93
Damian Hockney	UKInd	1,266	0.99	3,335	3.22
Geoffrey Ben-Nathan	PMSS	841	0.65	1,784	1.72
Ashwin Kumar Tanna	Ind	666	0.52	3,052	2.94
Geoffrey Clements	NL	386	0.30	1,332	1.28
Turnout	Total votes:	128,294	(30.7%)	103,463	

GLA Election Results 17

Assembly
First Past the Post

Name	Party	Votes	%
Richard Barnes	Con	44,850	37.40
Gurcharan Singh	Lab	38,038	31.72
Mike Cox	LD	22,177	18.49
Graham Lee	Green	11,788	9.83
Nick Grant	London Socialist Alliance	2,977	2.48
Majority	Total Votes: 6,812 (5.7%)		
Turnout	Total Votes 119,830 (30.7%)		

Top up seats (London wide)

Name	Votes	%
Labour	40,551	32.70
Conservative	38,191	30.80
Liberal Democrats	16,575	13.37
Green	11,863	9.57
Christian Peoples' Alliance	3,846	3.10
British National Party	3,823	3.08
UK Independence Party	2,387	1.92
Campaign Against Tube Privatisation	1,474	1.19
London Socialist Alliance	1,261	1.02
Peter Tatchell	1,067	0.86
Pro-Motorist Small Shop	973	0.78
Socialist Labour Party	950	0.77
Natural Law Party	531	0.43
Communist Party of Britain	529	0.43
Turnout	Total Votes: 124,021 (30.7%)	

ENFIELD AND HARINGEY
Mayor

Name	Party	1st Pref	%	2nd Pref	%
Ken Livingstone	Ind	50,250	43.00	12,067	12.70
Steven Norris	Con	28,522	24.41	11,691	12.30
Frank Dobson	Lab	16,469	14.09	16,119	16.97
Susan Kramer	LD	12,113	10.37	26,092	27.46
Darren Johnson	Green	2,762	2.36	15,095	15.89
Ram Gidoomal	CPA	2,398	2.05	3,317	3.49
Michael Newland	BNP	1,967	1.68	2,784	2.93
Damian Hockney	UKInd	928	0.79	2,524	2.66
Geoffrey Ben-Nathan	PMSS	667	0.57	1,411	1.49
Ashwin Kumar Tanna	Ind	475	0.41	2,552	2.69
Geoffrey Clements	NL	369	0.32	1,216	1.28
Turnout	Total Votes:	116,920	(33.6%)	94,868	

Assembly
First Past the Post

Name	Party	Votes	%
Nicky Gavron	Lab	34,509	32.24
Peter Forrest	Con	31,207	29.15
Sean Hooker	LD	14,319	13.38
Richard Course	Ind Pro-Livingstone	12,581	11.75
Peter Budge	Green	10,761	10.05
Weyman Bennett	London Socialist Alliance	3,671	3.43
Majority	Total Votes: 3,302 (3.1%)		
Turnout	Total Votes: 107,048 (30.8%)		

18 Governed London

Top up seats (London wide)

Name	Votes	%
Labour	37,191	33.95
Conservative	29,807	26.41
Green	14,673	12.99
Liberal Democrats	13,824	12.25
Christian Peoples' Alliance	3,277	2.90
British National Party	2,634	2.33
London Socialist Alliance	2,564	2.27
UK Independence Party	2,278	2.02
Peter Tatchell	1,803	1.60
Campaign Against Tube Privatisation	1,424	1.26
Socialist Labour Party	1,213	1.07
Pro-Motorist Small Shop	895	0.79
Communist Party of Britain	718	0.64
Natural Law Party	571	0.51
Turnout	Total Votes: 112,872 (32.5%)	

GREENWICH AND LEWISHAM
Mayor

Name	Party	1st Pref	%	2nd Pref	%
Ken Livingstone	Ind	47,522	45.87	11,413	12.90
Steven Norris	Con	19,822	19.13	10,204	11.53
Frank Dobson	Lab	15,124	14.60	15,365	17.37
Susan Kramer	LD	10,880	10.50	23,439	26.49
Darren Johnston	Green	2,679	2.59	14,335	16.20
Ram Gidoomal	CPA	2,668	2.58	3,105	3.51
Michael Newland	BNP	2,562	2.47	2,987	3.38
Damian Hockney	UKInd	932	0.90	2,285	2.58
Ashwin Kumar Tanna	Ind	570	0.55	2,934	3.32
Geoffrey Ben-Nathan	PMSS	531	0.51	1,106	1.25
Geoffrey Clements	NL	302	0.29	1,144	1.29
Turnout	Total Votes:	103.592	(31.6%)	88,317	

Assembly
First Past the Post

Name	Party	Votes	%
Len Duvall	Lab	40,386	42.66
Rhodri Harris	Con	22,401	23.66
David Buxton	LD	16,290	17.20
Terry Liddle	Green	11,839	12.50
Ian Page	London Socialist Alliance	3,981	4.20
Majority	Total Votes: 17,985 (19.0%)		
Turnout	Total Votes: 94,697 (29.0%)		

Top up seats (London wide)

Name	Votes	%
Labour	37,200	36.98
Conservative	20,450	20.33
Green	13,269	13.19
Liberal Democrats	12,704	12.63
Christian Peoples' Alliance	3,729	3.71
British National Party	3,487	3.47
London Socialist Alliance	2,274	2.26
UK Independence Party	2,117	2.10
Peter Tatchell	1,592	1.58
Socialist Labour Party	1,215	1.21
Campaign Against Tube Privatisation	903	0.89
Pro-Motorist Small Shop	798	0.79
Natural Law Party	464	0.46
Communist Party of Britain	390	0.39
Turnout	Total Votes: 100,592 (30.7%)	

GLA Election Results   19

HAVERING AND REDBRIDGE
Mayor

Name	Party	1st Pref	%	2nd Pref	%
Ken Livingstone	Ind	39,277	33.80	10,927	11.50
Steven Norris	Con	38,088	32.78	13,903	14.63
Frank Dobson	Lab	14,549	12.52	14,355	15.09
Susan Kramer	LD	12,719	10.95	27,913	29.38
Michael Newland	BNP	3,938	3.39	5,231	5.51
Ram Gidoomal	CPA	2,784	2.40	3,579	3.77
Darren Johnston	Green	1,815	1.56	9,934	10.4
Damian Hockney	UKInd	1,619	1.39	3,865	4.15
Geoffrey Ben-Nathan	PMSS	618	0.53	1,670	1.76
Ashwin Kumar Tanna	Ind	511	0.44	2,726	2.87
Geoffrey Clements	NL	287	0.25	1,179	1.24
Turnout	Total Votes:	116,205	(32.9%)	95,282	

Assembly
First Past the Post

Name	Party	Votes	%
Roger Evans	Con	40,919	37.55
Chris Robbins	Lab	32,650	29.96
Geoffrey Seeff	LD	14,028	12.87
Ian Wilkes	Residents' Association	12,831	11.77
Ashley Gunstock	Green	6,803	6.24
George Taylor	London Socialist Alliance	1,744	1.60
Majority	Total votes: 8,269 (7.6%)		
Turnout	Total votes: 108,975 (30.8%)		

Top up seats (London wide)

Name	Votes	%
Conservative	40,350	36.03
Labour	32,717	29.21
Liberal Democrats	13,691	12.23
Green	8,280	7.39
British National Party	5,170	4.62
Christian Peoples' Alliance	3,658	3.27
UK Independence Party	2,974	2.70
Campaign Against Tube Privatisation	1,087	0.97
London Socialist Alliance	967	0.86
Pro-Motorist Small Shop	939	0.84
Socialist Labour Party	740	0.66
Peter Tatchell	678	0.61
Natural Law Party	384	0.34
Communist Party of Britain	345	0.31
Turnout	Total Votes: 111,980 (31.7%)	

LAMBETH AND SOUTHWARK
Mayor

Name	Party	1st Pref	%	2nd Pref	%
Ken Livingstone	Ind	52,028	47.63	12,769	13.70
Steven Norris	Con	18,437	16.88	9,651	10.35
Frank Dobson	Lab	15,863	14.52	16,073	17.24
Susan Kramer	LD	13,139	12.03	25,497	27.36
Darren Johnson	Green	3,061	2.80	15,974	17.14
Ram Gidoomal	CPA	2,917	2.67	3,416	3.67
Michael Newland	BNP	1,572	1.44	2,050	2.20
Ashwin Kumar Tanna	Ind	815	0.75	3,654	3.92
Damian Hockney	UKInd	616	0.56	1,723	1.85
Geoffrey Ben-Nathan	PMSS	469	0.43	1,028	1.10
Geoffrey Clements	NL	323	0.30	1,116	1.20
Turnout	Total Votes:	109,240	(31.3%)	92,951	

20 Governed London

Assembly
First Past the Post

Name	Party	Votes	%
Valerie Shawcross	Lab	37,985	53.51
Peter Facey	LD	22,492	31.68
Irene Kimm	Con	19,238	27.10
Storm Poorun	Green	13,242	18.65
Theresa Bennett	London Socialist Alliance	6,231	8.77
Tony Robinson	Humanist	1,261	1.77
Jonathan Silberman	Communist League	536	0.75
Majority	Total Votes: 15,493 (15.3%)		
Turnout	Total Votes: 70,983 (29.0%)		

Top up seats (London wide)

Name	Votes	%
Labour	35,957	33.80
Liberal Democrats	18,065	16.98
Conservative	17,245	16.21
Green	16,130	15.16
Christian Peoples' Alliance	4,237	3.98
London Socialist Alliance	3,305	3.11
Peter Tatchell	3,241	3.05
British National Party	2,412	2.27
UK Independence Party	1,700	1.60
Campaign Against Tube Privatisation	1,264	1.19
Socialist Labour Party	1,123	1.06
Pro-Motorist Small Shop	705	0.66
Natural Law Party	507	0.48
Communist Party of Britain	486	0.46
Turnout	Total Votes: 106,377 (30.5%)	

MERTON AND WANDSWORTH
Mayor

Name	Party	1st Pref	%	2nd Pref	%
Ken Livingstone	Ind	46,218	38.77	12,530	12.40
Steven Norris	Con	36,237	30.40	13,928	13.78
Frank Dobson	Lab	14,436	12.11	16,330	16.16
Susan Kramer	LD	13,752	11.53	29,863	29.55
Ram Gidoomal	CPA	3,162	2.65	4,310	4.27
Darren Johnson	Green	2,713	2.28	14,049	13.90
Michael Newland	BNP	1,468	1.23	2,259	2.24
Damian Hockney	UKInd	979	0.82	2,931	2.90
Geoffrey Ben-Nathan	PMSS	502	0.42	1,320	1.31
Ashwin Kumar Tanna	Ind	496	0.42	2,673	2.65
Geoffrey Clements	NL	325	0.27	1,265	1.25
Turnout	Total Votes:	119,197	(35.5%)	101,458	

Assembly
First Past the Post

Name	Party	Votes	%
Elizabeth Howlett	Con	45,308	39.53
Maggie Cosin	Lab	32,438	28.30
Siobhan Vitelli	LD	12,496	10.90
Mark Thompson	Ind Lab Pro-Livingstone	11,918	10.40
Rajeev Thacker	Green	8,491	7.41
Syeed Manzoor	Ind Pro-Motorist	1,465	1.28
Sarbani Mazumdar	London Socialist Alliance	1,450	1.27
Terence Sullivan	Ind Pro-Transport	1,049	0.92
Majority	Total Votes: 12,870 (11.2%)		
Turnout	Total Votes: 114,615 (34.1%)		

GLA Election Results

Top up seats (London wide)

Name	Votes	%
Conservative	38,122	33.04
Labour	34,167	29.61
Liberal Democrats	14,199	12.31
Green	13,631	11.81
Christian Peoples' Alliance	3,969	3.44
British National Party	2,176	1.89
UK Independence Party	2,122	1.84
Peter Tatchell	1,703	1.48
Campaign Against Tube Privatisation	1,393	1.21
London Socialist Alliance	1,264	1.10
Socialist Labour Party	863	0.75
Pro-Motorist Small Shop	843	0.73
Natural Law Party	494	0.43
Communist Party of Britain	441	0.38
Turnout	Total Votes: 115,387 (34.3%)	

NORTH EAST
Mayor

Name	Party	1st Pref	%	2nd Pref	%
Ken Livingstone	Ind	63,333	47.98	14,422	13.30
Steven Norris	Con	21,676	16.42	11,632	10.73
Frank Dobson	Lab	20,075	15.21	19,708	18.12
Susan Kramer	LD	14,731	11.16	28,230	26.03
Darren Johnson	Green	4,253	3.22	20,678	19.07
Ram Gidoomal	CPA	2,791	2.11	3,472	3.20
Michael Newland	BNP	2,454	1.86	3,078	2.84
Damian Hockney	UKInd	986	0.75	2,331	2.15
Geoffrey Ben-Nathan	PMSS	720	0.55	1,367	1.26
Geoffrey Clements	NL	494	0.37	1,443	1.33
Ashwin Kumar Tanna	Ind	463	0.35	2,372	2.19
Turnout	Total Votes	131,976	(32.3%)	108,733	

Assembly
First Past the Post

Name	Party	Votes	%
Meg Hillier	Lab	42,459	36.11
Paul Fox	LD	24,856	21.14
Eric Ollerenshaw	Con	20,975	17.84
Yen Chit Chong	Green	18,382	15.63
Cecelia Prosper	London Socialist Alliance	8,269	7.03
Paul Shaer	Ind Universal Justice	1,501	1.28
Erol Basarik	Reform 2000	1,144	0.97
Majority	Total Votes: 17,603 (15.0%)		
Turnout	Total Votes: 117,586 (28.7%)		

Top up seats (London wide)

Name	Votes	%
Labour	43,382	33.87
Conservative	20,923	16.34
Green	20,449	15.97
Liberal Democrats	19,790	15.45
London Socialist Alliance	5,556	4.34
Christian Peoples' Alliance	3,869	3.02
British National Party	3,515	2.74
Peter Tatchell	2,981	2.33
UK Independence Party	2,156	1.68
Campaign Against Tube Privatisation	1,572	1.23
Socialist Labour Party	1,435	1.12
Communist Party of Briatin	979	0.76
Pro-Motorist Small Shop	817	0.64
Natural Law Party	644	0.50
Turnout	Total Votes: 128,068 (31.3%)	

22 Governed London

SOUTH WEST
Mayor

Name	Party	1st Pref	%	2nd Pref	%
Ken Livingstone	Ind	52,457	36.29	15,974	13.00
Steven Norris	Con	41,618	28.79	17,525	14.26
Susan Kramer	LD	23,745	16.43	38,124	31.03
Frank Dobson	Lab	15,719	10.87	18,033	14.68
Ram Gidoomal	CPA	3,195	2.21	5,000	4.07
Darren Johnson	Green	2,916	2.02	15,154	12.33
Michael Newland	BNP	1,862	1.29	2,977	2.42
Damian Hockney	UKInd	1,397	0.97	3,962	3.22
Ashwin Kumar Tanna	Ind	658	0.45	3,209	2.61
Geoffrey Ben-Nathan	PMSS	637	0.44	1,689	1.37
Geoffrey Clements	NL	356	0.25	1,466	1.19
Turnout	Total Votes:	144,560	(37.6%)	123,113	

Assembly
First Past the Post

Name	Party	Votes	%
Tony Arbour	Con	48,248	35.41
Geoff Pope	LD	41,189	30.23
Jagdish Sharma	Lab	31,065	22.80
Judy Maciejowska	Green	13,426	9.85
Danny Faith	London Socialist Alliance	2,319	1.70
Majority	Total Votes: 7,059 (5.2%)		
Turnout	Total Votes: 136,247 (35.4%)		

Top up seats (London wide)

Name	Votes	%
Conservative	43,258	30.59
Labour	35,538	25.13
Liberal Democrats	31,585	22.30
Green	14,966	10.58
Christian Peoples' Alliance	4,115	2.91
UK Independence Party	2,772	1.96
British National Party	2,625	1.86
Peter Tatchell	1,257	0.89
London Socialist Alliance	1,251	0.88
Campaign Against Tube Privatisation	1,089	0.77
Pro-Motorist Small Shop	1,029	0.73
Socialist Labour Party	906	0.64
Natural Law Party	583	0.41
Communist Party of Britain	459	0.32
Turnout	Total Votes: 141,433 (36.7%)	

WEST CENTRAL
Mayor

Name	Party	1st Pref	%	2nd Pref	%
Steven Norris	Con	44,954	38.8	13,256	14.10
Ken Livingstone	Ind	40,176	34.7	10,741	11.42
Susan Kramer	LD	11,609	10.0	27,937	29.72
Frank Dobson	Lab	11,070	9.6	14,139	15.04
Darren Johnson	Green	2,680	2.3	13,224	14.07
Ram Gidoomal	CPA	2,229	1.9	4,387	4.67
Michael Newland	BNP	999	0.9	1,870	1.99
Damian Hockney	UKInd	850	0.7	3,260	3.47
Geoffrey Ben-Nathan	PMSS	495	0.4	1,531	1.63
Geoffrey Clements	NL	396	0.3	1,384	1.47
Ashwin Kumar Tanna	Ind	337	0.3	2,307	2.45
Turnout	Total Votes:	115,795	(30.9%)	94,036	

GLA Election Results

Assembly
First Past the Post

Name	Party	Votes	%
Angie Bray	Con	47,117	44.20
Kate Green	Lab	28,838	27.05
Jon Burden	LD	14,071	13.20
Julia Stephenson	Green	12,254	11.50
Christine Blower	London Socialist Alliance	2,720	2.55
Stephen Smith	Homeless and Addicted	1,600	1.50
Majority	Total Votes: 18,279 (17.2%)		
Turnout	Total Votes: 106,600 (30.9%)		

Top up seats (London wide)

Name	Votes	%
Conservative	44,489	39.62
Labour	27,675	24.65
Green	13,339	11.88
Liberal Democrats	12,530	11.16
Christian Peoples' Alliance	3,032	2.70
Peter Tatchell	2,260	2.01
UK Independence Party	1,943	1.73
British National Party	1,627	1.45
London Socialist Alliance	1,439	1.28
Campaign Against Tube Privatisation	1,266	1.13
Socialist Labour Party	789	0.70
Pro-Motorist Small Shop	787	0.70
Natural Law Party	604	0.54
Communist Party of Britain	517	0.46
Turnout	Total Vote: 112,279 (17.2%)	

OVERALL RESULTS

First Pref	Party	Votes	%
Ken Livingstone	Ind	667,877	39.00
Steven Norris	Con	464,434	27.12
Frank Dobson	Lab	223,884	13.07
Susan Kramer	LD	203,452	11.88
Ram Gidoomal	CPA	42,060	2.46
Darren Johnson	Green	38,121	2.23
Michael Newland	BNP	33,569	1.96
Damian Hockney	UK Ind	16,234	0.95
Geoffrey Ben-Nathan	PMSS	9,956	0.58
Ashwin Kumar Tanna	Ind	9,015	0.53
Geoffrey Clements	Natural Law Party	5,470	0.32

Second Pref	Party	Votes	%
Susan Kramer	LD	404,815	28.50
Frank Dobson	Lab	228,095	16.06
Darren Johnson	Green	192,764	13.57
Steven Norris	Con	188,041	13.24
Ken Livingstone	Ind	178,809	12.59
Ram Gidoomal	CPA	56,489	3.98
Michael Newland	BNP	45,337	3.19
Damian Hockney	UK Ind	43,672	3.07
Ashwin Kumar Tanna	Ind	41,766	2.94
Geoffrey Ben-Nathan	PMSS	23,021	1.62
Geoffrey Clements	Natural Law Party	18,185	1.28

24 Governed London

THE MAYOR AND ASSEMBLY
The Mayor: Ken Livingstone
Political and Career History: Member of Lambeth LBC 1971–8; Member of Camden LBC 1978–1982; Member of the Regional Executive of the Greater London Labour Party 1974–1986; became a member of the GLC in 1973; Elected leader of the GLC in 1973; Labour Candidate for Hampstead and Highgate at the 1979 general election; Elected MP for Brent East 1987.

CONSTITUENCIES AND MEMBERS
Constituency: Barnet and Camden
Member: Brian Coleman (Conservative)
Political and Career History: Councillor, Barnet LBC (Totteridge Ward) 1998 – date.

Constituency: Bexley and Bromley
Member: Bob Neill (Conservative)
Political and Career History: Barrister (specialising in criminal law) since 1975; Councillor, Havering LBC 1974–1990; Chairman of Environment and Social Services Committees, Havering LBC; GLC Member (Romford) 1985-1986; Leader, London Fire and Civil Defence Authority 1985–1987; Parliamentary Candidate, Dagenham 1983–1987; Chairman, Greater London Conservatives 1996-1999.

Constituency: Brent and Harrow
Member: Lord Toby Harris (Labour)
Political and Career History: Labour Councillor since 1978; Leader, Haringey LBC 1987-1999; Chair, Association of London Government; Director, Association of Community Health Councils 1987-1998; Appointed 'working peer' in 1998.

Constituency: City and East
Member: John Biggs (Labour)
Political and Career History: Councillor, Tower Hamlets LBC, 1988 – date; Opposition Council Leader, Tower Hamlets LBC, 1991–1995; Labour spokesperson on Transport, GLA.

Constituency: Croydon and Sutton
Member: Andrew John Pelling (Conservative)
Political and Career History: Croydon LBC Councillor 1982–date; Chairman of Croydon Education Committee 1988-1994; Deputy Leader, Croydon Council Conservative Group 1996–date; President, Oxford University Conservative Association 1980; Secretary and Librarian of Oxford Union Society Autumn 1979–Spring 1980.

Constituency: Ealing and Hillingdon
Member: Richard Barnes (Conservative)
Political and Career History: Conservative leader of Hillingdon LBC; Vice-Chairman of Hillingdon Health Authority; Member of the Metropolitan Police Authority and the GLA Standing Order Committee.

Constituency: Enfield and Haringey
Member: Nicky Gavron (Labour)
Political and Career History: Councillor, Haringey LBC, 1986; Labour leader of the London Planning Advisory Committee and Chair since 1994; Vice-chair of the Planning Committee of the Local Government Association; Chair of the National Planning Forum; Member of Commission for Integrated Transport; Advisor to the Government's Urban Task Force.

Constituency: Greenwich and Lewisham
Member: Len Duvall (Labour)
Political and Career History: Deputy Leader, Greenwich LBC 1990; Leader, Greenwich LBC 1992-2000; Deputy Chair of the Association of London Government; Member of the London Fire and Civil Defence Authority; Chair, Thames Gateway London Partnership; Vice-chair, Local Government Information Unit 1994-1996; Non-executive Director of New Millennium Experience Forum; awarded OBE in 1998 for contribution to London local government.

Constituency: Havering and Redbridge
Member: Jeremy Roger Evans (Conservative)
Political and Career History: Waltham Forest LBC councillor 1980–date; Waltham Forest LBC Opposition Deputy Leader 1993-1994; Waltham Forest LBC Opposition Leader 1994-1998

Constituency: Lambeth and Southwark
Member: Valerie Shawcross (Labour)
Political and Career History: Former Leader of Croydon LBC; former Chair of the Education Service of Croydon LBC; former Labour Party National Women's Officer.

Constituency: Merton and Wandsworth
Member: Elizabeth Howlett (Conservative)
Political and Career History: Professional opera singer 1961-1988; Professor, Royal College of Music 1988 – date; Deputy Chairman, Putney Conservative Association 1984-1986; Elected Councillor for Wandsworth LBC 1986; Chairman–Social Services, Wandsworth LBC; Chairman–Education, Wandsworth LBC 1992-1998; Mayor, Wandsworth LBC 1998-1999; Chief Whip, Wandsworth LBC 1999-2000; Freeman of the City of London 1999.

Constituency: North East
Member: Meg Hillier (Labour)
Political and Career History: Reporter, *Yorkshire Times*, 1991; Petty Officer, P&O Ferries, 1992; Newlon Housing Group, 1993; Reporter, *Housing Association Weekly*, 1999; Features Editor, *Housing Today*, 1995-1998; Councillor, Islington LBC, 1994-date; Mayor, Islington LBC 1998-9.

Constituency: South West
Member: Anthony Arbour (Conservative)
Political and Career History: Councillor, Richmond upon Thames LBC 1968; Magistrate, Richmond upon Thames 1975; Chairman, Hampton Wick United Charity 1975; Vice-chairman, Kingston and Richmond Family Health Services Authority 1990-1996; Leader Conservative Group, Richmond upon Thames 1994; Senior Lecturer, Kingston University Business School, 1983.

Constituency: West Central
Member: Angie Bray (Conservative)
Political and Career History: Radio presenter/reporter for British Services Broadcasting 1979 – 1980 and for LBC 1980-1988; Head of Broadcasting for Conservative Central Office 1989-1991; Press Secretary to Chairman of the Conservative Party (The Rt. Hon Chris Patten) 1992-1992; Manager of Media Unit, IGA 1992-1995; Senior Consultant for APCO Ltd 1995-2000.

GLA Committees 25

LONDON LIST MEMBERS

Member: Victor Anderson (Green)
Political and Career History: Protestor against the dominance of the car in London; researcher for Plaid Cymru at the Houses of Commons and Welsh Assembly.

Member: Louise Bloom (Liberal Democrat)
Political History: Researcher to Liberal Democrat Candidates, Royal Borough of Kingston 1991-93; Voluntary Sector Employment 1994-97; Information Officer, Richmond Advice and Information on Disability 1998-2000; Vice Chair, Green Liberal Democrats 1995 – present.

Member: Lynne Featherstone (Liberal Democrat)
Political and Career History: Director of an electrical company; former strategic design consultant to a transport consultancy; Leader of the Opposition, Haringey LBC.

Member: Baroness (Sally) Hamwee (Liberal Democrat)
Political and Career History: Councillor, London Borough of Richmond upon Thames (Palewell ward) 1978-98; Chair, London Planning Advisory Committee 1986-87; Member of Joseph Rowntree Foundation Inquiry, Planning for Housing, 1991; Appointed Life Peer 1991 (Liberal Democrat Lords spokesperson, Environment Transport and the Regions); Member of Liberal Democrat General Election Team 1992 and 1997; Appointed Deputy Chair of Greater London Assembly, May 2000.

Member: Samantha Heath (Labour)
Political and Career History: Trained as a civil engineer; former lecturer in design and construction management at the University of Greenwich; Councillor, Wandsworth LBC; has served on Education, Housing and Environment Committees at Wandsworth LBC since 1994.

Member: Darren Johnson (Green)
Political and Career History: Green Party National Executive 1993-1995; organiser of European Elections in 1994.

Member: Jennifer Jones (Green)
Political and Career History: joined Green Party in 1988; Chair of the Green National Executive 1995 1997; qualified as an archaeologist; recently worked as a financial controller.

Member: David Lammy (Labour)
At the time of going to press, David Lammy had just been elected MP for Tottenham. His status as GLA Member had not been finalised. Please contact the GLA for further details.

Member: Eric Ollerenshaw (Conservative)
Political and Career History: Chairman of Hackney North and Stoke Newington Conservative Association 1991-1999; Leader of Hackney LBC Conservative Group; Member of the Inner London Education Authority 1986-1990.

Member: Trevor Phillips (Labour)
Political and Career History: former President of the National Union of Students; worked for London Weekend Television and the BBC on current affairs programmes; owner of a television production company; awarded an OBE in 1999.

Member: Graham Tope (Liberal Democrat)
Political and Career History: Leader of the European Liberal Democrat and Reform Group on the Committee of the Regions; Vice-president of the Local Government Association; Liberal Democrat MP for Sutton and Cheam in 1972; Sutton LBC Councillor in 1974; Leader of Sutton LBC 1986-1999; Deputy General Secretary for Voluntary Action Camden 1975-1990; awarded CBE in 1991; made Life Peer in 1994.

COMMITTEE MEMBERSHIP OF THE GLA

Appointments Committee
Brian Coleman
Len Duvall
Lynne Featherstone
Samantha Heath
Elizabeth Howlett
Darren Johnson
Eric Ollerenshaw
Graham Tope

London Development Agency
Victor Anderson
Len Duvall
Andrew Pelling

London Fire and Emergency Planning Authority
Louise Bloom
Brian Coleman
Lynne Featherstone
Samantha Heath
Bob Neill
Eric Ollerenshaw
Trevor Phillips
Valerie Shawcross

Metropolitan Police Authority
Tony Arbour
Richard Barnes
John Biggs
Roger Evans
Lynne Featherstone
Nicky Gavron
Elizabeth Howlett
Darren Johnson
Graham Tope

Standards Committee
Tony Arbour
Toby Harris
Meg Hillier
Valerie Shawcross
Graham Tope

Standing Orders Committee
Victor Anderson
Richard Barnes
John Biggs
Angie Bray
Sally Hamwee

Salaries as at July 2000
Mayor: £86,832*
Assembly member: £34,438

*Reduced by one third if Mayor is also an MP.

LONDON BOROUGH COUNCILS

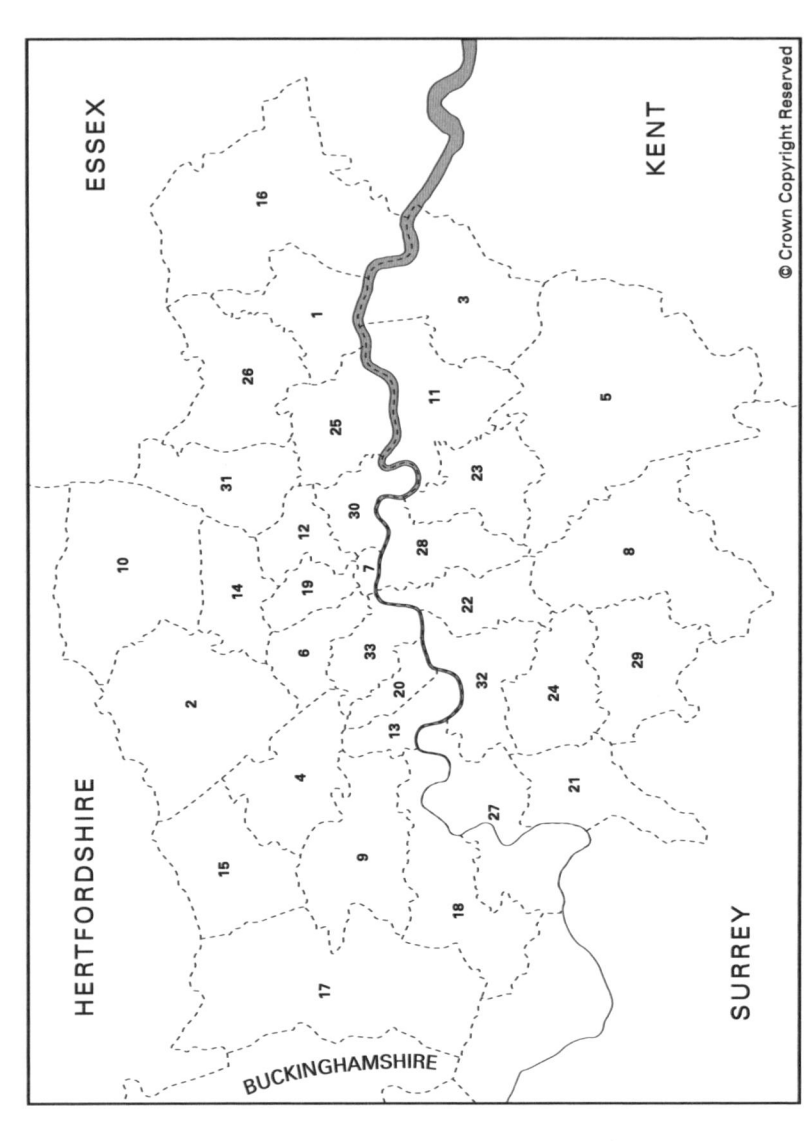

London Boroughs

1. Barking & Dagenham
2. Barnet
3. Bexley
4. Brent
5. Bromley
6. Camden
7. City of London
8. Croydon
9. Ealing
10. Enfield
11. Greenwich
12. Hackney
13. Hammersmith & Fulham
14. Haringey
15. Harrow
16. Havering
17. Hillingdon
18. Hounslow
19. Islington
20. Kensington & Chelsea
21. Kingston upon Thames
22. Lambeth
23. Lewisham
24. Merton
25. Newham
26. Redbridge
27. Richmond upon Thames
28. Southwark
29. Sutton
30. Tower Hamlets
31. Waltham Forest
32. Wandsworth
33. Westminster

LONDON BOROUGH COUNCILS

By virtue of the London Government Act 1963 the Greater London Council and 32 chartered boroughs came into existence in April 1965. The GLC ceased to exist in 1986 by virtue of the Local Government Act 1985. Currently in London there are 32 boroughs plus the Corporation of London. In this section we have provided maps and contact information for each borough along with listings of the chief officers and councillors. Political composition, parliamentary constituency and council tax details are also included. London borough councillors have four year terms of office retiring together – the next elections will be held in May 2002. The listings of councillors are correct as at May 2000.

BARKING AND DAGENHAM

Civic Centre, Dagenham RM10 7BN (Tel: 020-8592 4500)
Director of Housing and Health: 2 Stour Road, Dagenham RM10 7JF
Education Officer: Town Hall, Barking IG11 7LU
Contracts Services: Valence Depot, Becontree Avenue, Dagenham RM8 3BU
Librarian: Central Library, Barking IG11 7NB
Valence House Museum: Valence House, Becontree Avenue, Dagenham RM8 3HT
Registration of Births, Deaths and Marriages: Arden House, 198 Longbridge Road, Barking IG11 8SY (Tel: 020-8270 4742)

CHIEF OFFICERS

Chief Executive: Graham Farrant
Borough Finance Officer: Barry Pummell
Borough Officer for Community Learning and Chief Inspector of Schools: Roger Luxton
Borough Officer for Democratic Support and Legal Services: Roy Cottle
Borough Officer for Policy and Review: John Tatam
Borough Personnel Officer: Alan Beadle
Controller of Development and Technical Services: Jack Knowles
Director of Housing and Health: David Woods
Director of Social Services: Julia Ross

MEMBERS OF THE COUNCIL

Councillor	Ward
Mayor: P. J. Manley, Lab.	Eastbury
Deputy Mayor: W. Dale, Lab.	Village
Leader of the Council: C. J. Fairbrass, Lab.	Heath
J. L. Alexander, Lab.	Abbey
M. G. Baker, Lab.	Longbridge
D. F. Best, Lab.	Village
J. Blake, Lab.	Parsloes
E. E. Bradley, Lab.	Becontree
G. J. Bramley, Lab.	Abbey
S. Bramley, Lab.	Longbridge
J. E. Bruce, Lab.	Valence
L. E. Bunn, Lab.	Eastbrook
H. J. Collins, Lab.	Fanshawe
L. A. Collins, Lab.	Eastbrook
J. Conyard, Lab.	Manor
A. Cooper, LD	Eastbury
V. W. Cridland, Lab.	Valence
R. J. Curtis, R.	Chadwell Heath
J. Davis, Lab.	Triptons
M. A. R. Fani, Lab.	Abbey
K. J. Flint, Lab.	Gascoigne
C. Geddes, Lab	Triptons
A. Gibbs, R.	Chadwell Heath
N. S. S. Gill, Lab.	Longbridge
S. P Gill, Lab.	Parsloes
K. A. Golden, Lab.	Village
I. Jamu, Lab.	River
R. J. E. Jeyes, R.	Chadwell Heath
F. C. Jones, Lab.	Fanshawe
S. Kallar, Lab.	Heath
J. H. Lawrence, Lab.	Heath
M. E. McKenzie, Lab.	Gascoigne
B. M. Osborne, Lab.	Valence
R. B. Parkin, Lab.	Fanshawe
R. A. J. Pateint Lab.	Thames
C. T. W. Pond, Lab.	Marks Gate
J. W. Porter, Lab	Campbell
J. E. Rawlinson, Lab.	Campbell
R. P. Rogers, Lab.	Manor
V. M. Rush, Lab.	Gascoigne
G. H. Shaw, Lab.	Thames
L. A. Smith, LD.	Goresbrook
S. Summerfield, Lab.	Eastbrook
A. G. Thomas, Lab.	Goresbrook
P. A. Twomey, Lab.	River
J. M. Van Roten, Lab.	Campbell
T. G. W. Wade, Lab.	Alibon
J. P. Wainwright, Lab.	Becontree
M. M. West, Lab.	Triptons
E. J. White, Lab.	Alibon
M. M. Worby, Lab.	Marks Gate

Political Composition: Lab. 46; R. 3; LD. 2.
Parliamentary Constituencies: Barking; Dagenham.
Population: 154,786
Area: 3,611 hectares.

ABOUT BARKING AND DAGENHAM

Barking and Dagenham lies on the north side of the River Thames to the east of the City. It is a mainly residential area, however, a variety of industries are based in the borough, notably Ford Motor Company's factory in

28 Governed London

Dagenham. Barking Town Centre is home to the Vicarage Field Shopping Centre which has a large pedestrianised area and the Borough has nearly 1000 acres of parks and open spaces and two nature reserves – The Chase Nature Reserve and Barking Reach Nature Reserve. There are numerous leisure and sporting facilities in the borough including a theatre, swimming pools, leisure centres and community halls.

COUNCIL TAX BANDS 2000-2001

Band	Market Value of the Property in 1991	Council Tax
A	Up to £40,000	£522.95
B	£40,001 to 52,000	£610.10
C	£52,001 to 68,000	£697.26
D	£68,001 to 88,000	£784.42
E	£88,001 to 120,000	£958.74
F	£120,001 to 160,000	£1133.05
G	£160,001 to 320,000	£1307.37
H	£320,001 or more	£1568.84

BARNET

Town Hall, The Burroughs, Hendon NW4 4BG. (Tel: 020 8359 2000; Fax: 020-8359 2480; Email: info.centre@barnet.gov.uk; Web: http://www.barnet.gov.uk)
Chief Executive: Town Hall, The Burroughs, Hendon NW4 4BG (Tel: 020-8359 2021; Fax: 020-8359 2579).
Strategic Director of Community Development: Town Hall, The Burroughs, Hendon NW4 4BG (Tel: 020-8359 2462; Fax 020 8359 2025).
Strategic Director of Education and Children: Town Hall, The Burroughs, Hendon NW4 4BG (Tel: 020-8359 2283; Fax 020 8359 2284).
Strategic Director of Environment: Town Hall, The Burroughs, Hendon NW4 4BG (Tel: 020-8359 2116; Fax 020 8359 2561).
Strategic Director of Resources: Town Hall, The Burroughs, Hendon NW4 4BG.
Strategic Director of Social Affairs: Town Hall, The Burroughs, Hendon NW4 4BG (Tel 020-8359 2714; Fax 020-8359 2284).
Registration of Births, Deaths and Marriages: 29 Wood Street, Barnet EN5 4BD and 182 Burnt Oak Broadway, Edgware, Middlesex HA8 0AU (Tel: 020-8731 8731).

CHIEF OFFICERS

Chief Executive: vacant
Strategic Director, Community Development: Rita Dexter
Strategic Director, Education and Children: Martyn Kempson
Strategic Director, Environment: Anne Lippitt
Strategic Director, Resources: Jeremy Jaroszek
Strategic Director, Social Affairs: Brian Reynolds

MEMBERS OF THE COUNCIL

Councillor	Ward
Mayor: Gill Sargeant, Lab.	Colindale
Deputy Mayor: Ansuya Sodha, Lab.	West Hendon
Leader of the Council: Alan Williams, Lab.	Burnt Oak
Roger Axworthy LD	Mill Hill
Steven Blomer, Lab.	Hale
Maureen Braun, C.	Hendon
Anita Campbell, Lab.	Arkley
Wayne Casey, LD	Mill Hill
James Chapman, C.	Friern Barnet
Danish Chopra, Lab.	Colindale
Usha Chopra, Lab.	East Barnet
Pauline Coakley Webb, Lab.	Arkley
Jack Cohen, LD	Childs Hill
Melvin Cohen, C.	Golders Green
Brian Coleman, C.	Totteridge
Pam Coleman, Lab.	Arkley
Geoff Cooke, Lab.	Brunswick Park
Katia David, C.	Hadley
Jeremy Davies, LD	Mill Hill
Aba Dunner, C.	Golders Green
Kevin Edson, C.	Totteridge
Olwen Evans, C.	East Barnet
Anthony Finn, C.	Hendon
Arun Ghosh, Lab.	West Hendon
Brian Gordon, C.	Hale
Helen Gordon, Lab.	East Finchley
Eva Greenspan, C.	Finchley
Christopher Harris, C.	Golders Green
Lynne Hillan, C.	Brunswick Park
Anne Jarvis, Lab.	East Barnet
Barbara Langstone, C.	Finchley
Malcolm Lester, C.	Edgware
Victor Lyon, C.	Totteridge
Kitty Lyons, Lab.	St. Paul's
Liz Mammatt, C.	Hadley
John Marshall, C.	Garden Suburb
Linda McFadyen, Lab.	Burnt Oak
Katherine McGuirk, Lab.	St. Paul's
Alison Moore, Lab.	East Finchley
Jazmin Naghar, C.	Garden Suburb
Ruth Nyman, Lab.	Hale
Monroe Palmer, LD	Childs Hill
Susette Palmer, LD	Childs Hill
Kanti Patel, C.	Hadley
Beverley Pearce, Lab.	Woodhouse
Barry Rawlings, Lab.	Woodhouse
Paul Rogers, Lab.	Woodhouse
Nathaniel Rudolf, Lab.	Colindale
Brian Salinger, C.	Friern Barnet
Joan Scannell, C.	Edgware
Andrew Sherling, C.	Hendon
Peter Skolar, C.	Garden Suburb
Agnes Slocombe, Lab.	West Hendon

London Borough Councils 29

Anthony Spencer, C. — Edgware
Leslie Sussman, C. — Finchley
Andreas Tambourides, C. — Brunswick
Jim Tierney, Lab. — St. Paul's
John Tiplady, C. — Friern Barnet
Allan Turner, Lab. — Burnt Oak
Philip Yeoman, Lab. — East Finchley

Political Composition: C: 28; Lab. 26; LD. 6.
Parliamentary Constituencies: Chipping Barnet, Finchley and Golders Green, Hendon.
Population: 331,548
Area: 8,663 hectares.

ABOUT BARNET

Barnet is one of the largest local authorities in London. It was created in 1965 from the former urban districts of Chipping Barnet and East Barnet, previously in Hertfordshire and Friern Barnet and the boroughs of Finchley and Hendon, previously in Middlesex. It lies on the edge of London's green belt and contains 14 conservation areas. It is crossed by three major roads from London to the North, The Edgware Road, Watling Street or A5 and the Great North Road renamed the A1000 after a bypass was built in the 1920s. Barnet has a number of areas of architectural and historical interest including the RAF Museum at Hendon and the Jewish Museum in Finchley.

COUNCIL TAX BANDS 2000-2001

Band	Market Value of the Property in 1991	Council Tax
A	Up to £40,000	£543.26
B	£40,001 to 52,000	£633.80
C	£52,001 to 68,000	£724.35
D	£68,001 to 88,000	£814.89
E	£88,001 to 120,000	£995.98
F	£120,001 to 160,000	£1177.07
G	£160,001 to 320,000	£1358.15
H	£320,001 or more	£1629.78

Bexley Civic Offices, Broadway, Bexleyheath, DA6 7LB (Tel: 020-8303 7777; Fax: 020-8301 2661; Web: http://www.bexley.gov.uk)
Environmental Services: Wyncham House, 207 Longlands Road, Sidcup, DA15 7JH
Education, Leisure, Social and Community Services: Hill View, Hill View Drive, Welling, DA16 3RY
Registration of Births, Deaths and Marriages: Manor House, The Green, Sidcup DA14 6BW (Tel: 020-8300 4537)

CHIEF OFFICERS

Chief Executive and Director of Finance: Christopher Duffield
Chief Educational Services Officer: Ms. Pauline Maddison
Chief Engineer: Peter Morley
Chief Works and Contract Officer: David Coleman
Controller of Finance and Personnel Services: D. Berry
Controller of Legal Services: Alan Short
Director of Environmental Services: Melvyn Checketts
Director of Social and Community Services: Paul McGee
Head of IT: Steve Ripley

MEMBERS OF THE COUNCIL

Councillor	Ward
Mayor: J. P. Wilkinson, C.	Bostall
Deputy Mayor: P. Cammish, C.	Blackfen
J. Antenbring, C.	Blendon and Penhill
R. F. Ashmole. C.	Upton
G. A. Bacon, C.	Sidcup West
Linda Bailey, C.	Christchurch
C. Ball, Lab.	Thamesmead East
A. M. Beckwith, C.	Lamorbey
N. P. Betts, C.	Falconwood
G. Blowers, Lab.	St. Michaels
Beryl Brand, LD.	St. Michaels
Donna Briant, Lab.	Thamesmead East
Joel Briant, Lab.	Cray
M. Brooks, C.	Barnehurst
J. Browning, Lab.	Erith
Doreen Cameron, Lab.	Belvedere
D. B. Cammish, C.	Upton
C. E. Campbell, C.	St. Mary's
A. W. Catterall, C.	St. Mary's
I. S. Clement, C.	Bostall
J. W. Eastaugh, Lab.	North End
W. Flint, C.	Sidcup East
Sylvia Fortune, LD.	Danson
Liz French, Lab.	Barnehurst North
Mick French, Lab.	Thamesmead East
R. H. French, C	Brampton
C. J. Garland, C.	Blackfen
R. M. Gillespie, C.	Barnehurst
G. Hacker, Lab.	Northumberland Heath
C. F. Hargrave, Lab.	North End
P. Hollamby, Lab.	Belvedere
G. R. Holland, C.	Lamorbey
D. N. Ives, Lab.	North End
G. Johnson, C.	Christchurch
R. J. Justham, Lab.	Cray
Tonya Kelsey, Lab.	Crayford
M. Ketley, C.	Sidcup West
J. Lawrenson, Lab.	East Wickham
Ann Lucas, Lab.	Northumberland Heath
Richard Lucas, Lab.	Belvedere
Sharon Massey, C.	Christchurch
K. McAndrew, C.	Sidcup West
R. A. Morgan, C.	Bostall
L. S. Newton, C.	Upton

30 Governed London

N. O'Hare, LD	East Wickham
B. W. Oliver, LD	East Wickham
Mrs M. A. O'Neill, Lab.	Erith
Teresa O'Neill, C.	Brampton
Ann Partington, C.	Blendon and Penhill
R. J. Passey, C.	Lamorbey
Teresa Pearce, Lab.	Erith
Wendy Perfect, Lab.	St. Michael's
T. Perrin, Lab.	Crayford
Cheryl Potter, C.	Brampton
N. Sayers, C.	Blendon and Penhill
J. D. Shepheard, Lab.	Crayford
E. J. Shrimpton, LD.	Danson
June E. Slaughter, C.	Sidcup East
M. A. Slaughter, C.	Sidcup East
Kathryn Smith, Lab.	Northumberland Heath
B. C. Standen, LD.	Danson
C. L. Tandy, C.	St. Mary's

Political Composition: C. 32; Lab. 24; LD. 6.
Parliamentary Constituencies: Old Bexley and Sidcup, Bexleyheath and Crayford, Erith and Thamesmead.
Population: 219,311 (Mid 1996 Est.)
Area: 6,065 hectares.

ABOUT BEXLEY

Bexley is situated in the south east of London. It is within easy reach of the major road, rail, air and sea networks including the M25, A2 and A20; Heathrow, Gatwick, Stansted and City airports all within an hours distance away. Links to Europe via the Channel Tunnel and Dover are also around an hour away. The borough is home to more than 4,000 businesses ranging from large-scale manufacturers to small and medium scale commercial ventures. Bexley contains over 90 parks and gardens which are open to the public. Sites of architectural and historical interest include Hall Place at Bexley and Danson Mansion and the Red House at Bexleyheath.

COUNCIL TAX BANDS 2000-2001

Band	Market Value of the Property in 1991	Council Tax
A	Up to £40,000	£534.86
B	£40,001 to 52,000	£624.00
C	£52,001 to 68,000	£713.15
D	£68,001 to 88,000	£802.29
E	£88,001 to 120,000	£980.58
F	£120,001 to 160,000	£1158.86
G	£160,001 to 320,000	£1337.15
H	£320,001 or more	£1604.56

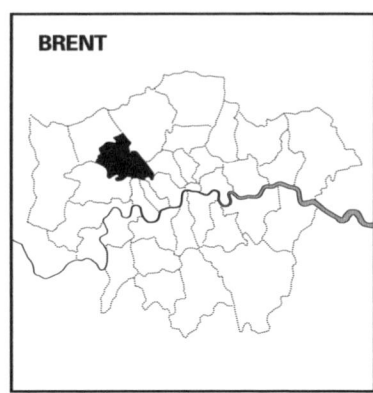

BRENT

Brent Town Hall, Forty Lane, Wembley, HA9 9HX (Tel: 020-8937 1234; Fax: 020-893 1202; Web: http://www.brent.gov.uk)
Chief Executive and Corporate Services: Brent Town Hall, Forty Lane, Wembley, HA9 9HX (Tel: 020-8937 1007)
Education Office: Chesterfield House, 9 Park Lane, Wembley, HA9 7RW (Tel: 020-8937 3130)
Environmental Services: Brent House, 349-357 High Road, Wembley, HA9 6BX (Tel: 020-8937 5006)
Trading Standards: 249 Willesden Lane, London, NW2 (Tel: 020-8937 5500)
Housing: Mahatma Gandhi House, 34 Wembley Hill Road, Wembley, HA9 8AD (Tel: 020-8937 2341)
Corporate Finance: Town Hall, Forty Lane, Wembley, HA9 9EZ (Tel: 020-8937 1423)
Libraries Service: Chesterfield House, 9 Park Lane, Wembley, HA9 7RW (Tel: 020-8937 3146)
Principal Curator: Grange Museum, Local History Library, Neasden Lane, London, NW10 1QB (Tel: 020-8937 3600)

CHIEF OFFICERS

Chief Executive: Gareth Daniel
Director of Corporate Services: Bernard Diamant
Director of Education: Jacky Griffin
Director of Environmental Services: Richard Saunders
Director of Housing: Deborah Ward
Director of Social Services: Jenny Goodall

MEMBERS OF THE COUNCIL

Councillor	Ward
Mayor: Joyce Bacchus, Lab.	Roundwood
Deputy Mayor: Ramesh Patel, Lab.	Queensbury
Leader of the Council: Paul Daisley, Lab.	Harlesden
Andrew Ammerlaan, Lab.	Manor
Mary Arnold, Lab.	Carlton
Ian Bellia, Lab.	Mapesbury
Lincoln Beswick, Lab.	Wembley Central
Nicola Blackman, C.	Tokyngton
Robert J. Blackman, C.	Preston
Daniel Brown, LD	Alperton
Dr. Alec Castle, Lab.	Tokyngton
Reg Colwill, C.	Kingsbury
David Coughlin, Lab.	St. Raphael's
Mary Cribbin, Lab.	Kilburn
Orugbani Douglas, Lab.	Tokyngton
William Dromey, Lab.	Roe Green
John Duffy, Lab.	Roe Green
Uma Fernandes, C.	Sudbury
Keith Ferry, Lab.	Brondesbury Park
Gideon Fiegel, C.	Sudbury Court
Ralph Fox, Lab.	Brentwater
Moore Giwa, Lab.	Manor
Helga Gladbaum, Lab.	Kensal Rise
John Godfrey, Lab.	Chamberlayne
Robert Hamadi, Lab.	Stonebridge
Richard Harrod, Lab.	St. Andrew's

London Borough Councils 31

Vanessa Howells, C.
Havard Hughes, LD
Ann John, Lab.
Lesley Jones, Lab.
Bertha Joseph, Lab.
Gabrielle Kagan, Lab.
Suresh Kansagra, C.
John Lebor, Lab.
Peter Lemmon, Lab.
Dorman Long, Lab.
Janice Long, Lab.
Paul Lorber, LD
Michael Lyon, Lab.
Eric McDonald, C.
Colum Moloney, Lab.
Cormach Moore, C.
Neil Nerva, Lab.
James O'Sullivan, C.
Sean O'Sullivan, C.
Lawrence Pardoe, Lab.
Harshadbhai Patel, C.
Kantibhai J. Patel, Lab.
Tullah Persaud, Lab.
Neil Rands, C.
John Rattray, LD
Ann Reeder, Lab.
Akber Sarguroh, Lab.
Abdui Sattar-Butt, Lab.
Jack Sayers, C.
Carupiah Selvarajah, C.
Asish Sengupta, Lab.
Ahmad Shahzad, Lab.
Carol Anne Shaw, C.
Arthur Steel, C.
Tom Taylor, C.
Bobby Thomas, Lab.
Noel Thompson, Lab.
Irwin Van Colle, C.
Sarah Walker, Lab.
Mohammad Zakriya, Lab.

Sudbury Court
Barham
St. Raphael's
Willesden
Kensal Rise
Brondesbury Park
Barnhill
Carlton
Chamberlayne
Church End
Mapesbury
Barham
Gladstone
Queensbury
Stonebridge
Sudbury
Queens Park
St. Andrew's
Kenton
Fryent
Preston
St. Raphael's
Wembley Central
Sudbury
Alperton
Harlesden
Brentwater
Gladstone
Cricklewood
Kingsbury
Fryent
Willesden
Cricklewood
Kenton
Preston
Church End
Kilburn
Barnhill
Queens Park
Roundwood

Political Composition: Lab. 43; C. 19; LD.4.
Parliamentary Constituencies: Brent North, Brent South, Brent East.
Population: 249,551
Area: 4,421 hectares.

ABOUT BRENT

Brent is situated in the north west of London. It is connected to the West End of London and the City by a network of 26 over and underground railway stations. Heathrow airport is also around 30 minutes away by car or train. Brent is home to the world famous Wembley Stadium which has hosted an array of events including the World Cup and Olympic Games. Regeneration is the key objective of Brent LBC. The Borough consists of a number of deprived regions and has received investment in recent years in order to achieve the aim of long term social and economic revival. Projects that have evolved include the Wembley Park Single Regeneration Budget, The Park Royal Partnership and Brent Reading Recovery Project.

COUNCIL TAX BANDS 2000-2001

Band	Market Value of the Property in 1991	Council Tax
A	Up to £40,000	£493.21
B	£40,001 to 52,000	£575.41
C	£52,001 to 68,000	£657.61
D	£68,001 to 88,000	£739.81
E	£88,001 to 120,000	£904.21
F	£120,001 to 160,000	£1068.62
G	£160,001 to 320,000	£1233.02
H	£320,001 or more	£1479.62

BROMLEY

Civic Centre, Stockwell Close, Kentish Way, Bromley, BR1 3UH (Tel: 020-8464 3333);
Web: http://www.bromley.gov.uk)
Director of Leisure Services: Central Library, High Street, Bromley, BR1 1EX (Tel: 020-8460 9955)

CHIEF OFFICERS

Chief Executive: M. Blanch
Director of Education: Ken Davis
Director of Environmental Services: G. N. Hayward
Director of Social Services and Housing: Ms. Clare Marchant
Director of Leisure and Community Services: R. Stoakes
Borough Secretary: W. Million
Borough Treasurer: D. Bartlett

MEMBERS OF THE COUNCIL

Councillor	Ward
Mayor: David Crowe, LD	Clock House
Deputy Mayor: Bill Hawthorne, LD	St. Paul's Cray
Co-Leaders of the Council: John Holbrook, Lab. and Chris Maines, LD	St. Mary Cray Orpington
Graham Arthur, C.	Hayes
Peter Ayres, LD	Martins Hill and Town
Peter Bloomfield, C.	Darwin
Katy Boughey, C.	Chislehurst
Tara Bowman, C.	Petts Wood and Knoll
Joan Bryant, C.	Chislehurst
I. A. Buckley, C.	Bickley
Cathy Bustard, C.	Plaistow and Sundridge

32 Governed London

Stephen Carr, C.	Bromley Common and Keston	
Alan Carter, LD	Bromley Common and Keston	
Gill Charmarette, LD	Chelsfield and Goddington	
Martin Curry, LD	St. Paul's Cray	
Ernest Dyer, Lab.	Mottingham	
Chris Elgar, C.	Kelsey Park	
Peter Fookes, Lab.	Penge	
John Gallop, C.	Bickley	
Chris Gaster, LD	Anerley	
Jamie Gillespie, LD	Plaistow and Sundridge	
Steve Gosling, LD	Plaistow and Sundridge	
Geoff Gostt, LD	Biggin Hill	
John Gray, C.	West Wickham South	
Jane Green, LD	Eden Park	
Mike Hall, LD	Chelsfield and Goddington	
Jenny Hillier, C.	Farnborough	
Carole Hubbard, C.	West Wickham North	
Brian Humphrys, C.	West Wickham North	
Malcolm Hyland, C.	Shortlands	
John Ince, C.	Petts Wood and Knoll	
Gordon Jenkins, C.	Bickley	
Philip Jones, C.	Lawrie Park and Kent House	
John Lewis, C.	Lawrie Park and Kent House	
Martin Lockwood, LD	Clock House	
Bill MacCormick, LD	Anerley	
Anne Manning, C.	Hayes	
David McBride, LD	St. Mary Cray	
Russell Mellor, C.	Copers Cope	
Alexa Michael, LD	Bromley Common and Keston	
Mike Norris, LD	Orpington	
Graem Peters, LD	Chelsfield and Goddington	
Tony Phillips, LD	Eden Park	
Sue Polydorou, Lab.	St. Mary Cray	
Helen Rabbatts, LD	Crofton	
Neil Reddin, C	Hayes	
Karen Roberts, Lab.	Penge	
Viv Ross, LD	Crofton	
Bob Shekyls, LD	Biggin Hill	
George Taylor, C.	Shortlands	
Michael Tickner, C.	Kelsey Park	
Len Tutt, C.	West Wickham South	
R. P. Warner, LD	Martins Hill and Park	
Tony Wilkinson, C.	Copers Cope	
Colin Willetts, Lab.	St. Paul's Cray	
Peter Woods, C.	Petts Wood and Knoll	
Joan Wykes, C.	Chislehurst	
Rob Yeldham, Lab.	Mottingham	

Political Composition: C. 28; LD. 24; Lab. 7.
Parliamentary Constituencies: Beckenham, Bromley and Chislehurst.
Population: 295,600
Area: 14,964 hectares.

ABOUT BROMLEY

Bromley is geographically the largest of the London Boroughs and is home to many commuters, especially as London train stations can be reached in under half an hour. The borough has considerable historic pedigree – Scadbury Park Estate in Chislehurst was the home to Sir Thomas Walsingham and Charles Darwin wrote his renowned book 'On the Origin of Species' at Downe. Shopping and leisure facilities are diverse in the borough with The Glades shopping centre being rated amongst the best in the country. There are numerous recreation centres, sports courses, libraries and theatre-goers can visit the borough's Churchill Theatre.

COUNCIL TAX BANDS 2000-2001

Band	Market Value of the Property in 1991	Council Tax
A	Up to £40,000	£490.44
B	£40,001 to 52,000	£572.18
C	£52,001 to 68,000	£653.92
D	£68,001 to 88,000	£735.66
E	£88,001 to 120,000	£899.14
F	£120,001 to 160,000	£1062.62
G	£160,001 to 320,000	£1226.10
H	£320,001 or more	£1471.32

CAMDEN

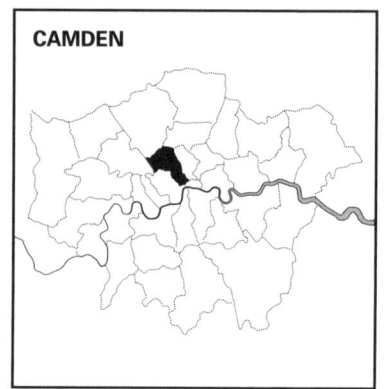

Camden Town Hall, Judd Street, London, WC1H 9JE
For all Departments (Tel: 020-7278 4444;
Web: http://www.camden.gov.uk)
Register Office: (Tel: 020-7974 6002)
Financial Services Branch: Town Hall Extension, Argyle Street, London WC1H 8NL
Environment Department: Town Hall Extension, Argyle Street, London WC1H 8EQ
Housing Department: 20 Mabledon Place, London, WC1H 9BF
Leisure and Community Services: Crowndale Centre, 218-220 Eversholt Street, London, NW1 1BD
Social Services Department: 79 Camden Road, London, NW1 9ES
Education Department: The Crowndale Centre, 218-220 Eversholt Street, London, NW1 1BD

CHIEF OFFICERS

Chief Executive: Steve Bundred
Assistant Chief Executive (Communications): Deirdre Colledge
Assistant Chief Executive (Personnel): Ms. Tracey Dennison

London Borough Councils 33

Assistant Chief Executive (Policy and Partnership): Dennis Skinner
Borough Solicitor: Alison Lowton
Controller of Financial Services: John Mabey
Director of Education: R. J. Litchfield
Director of Environment: Mark Gilks
Director of Housing: Neil Litherland
Director of Leisure and Community Services: Ian McNicol
Director of Social Services: Simon White

MEMBERS OF THE COUNCIL

Councillor	Ward
Mayor: Heather Johnson, Lab.	Kilburn
Deputy Mayor: Roger Robinson, Lab.	St. Pancras
Leader of the Council:	
Richard Arthur, Lab.	Highgate
Penelope Abraham, Lab.	St. John's
Bill Budd, Lab.	Chalk Farm
Patricia Callaghan, Lab.	Bloomsbury
Ewan Cameron, C.	Belsize
Pam Chesters, C.	Frognal
Maggie Cosin, Lab.	Highgate
Edward Cousins, Lab.	Brunswick
Martin Davies, C.	Fitzjohn's
John Dickie, Lab.	Grafton
Julian Fulbrook, Lab.	Holborn
Dermot Greene, Lab.	Camden
Janet Guthrie, Lab.	South End
Bob Hall, Lab.	Swiss Cottage
Aileen Hammond, Lab.	Belsize
Gerry Harrison, Lab.	South End
Charlie Hedges, Lab.	Kilburn
Stephen Hocking, C.	Swiss Cottage
Dave Horan, Lab.	St. John's
Peter Horne, C.	Adelaide
Barbara Hughes, Lab.	King's Cross
Ernest James, Lab.	Somers Town
Bernard Kissen, Lab.	Caversham
Deirdre Krymer, Lab.	Castlehaven
Gloria Lazenby, Lab.	St. Pancras
Margaret Little, LD	Hampstead Town
Sidney Malin, LD	Hampstead Town
Andrew Marshall, C.	Adelaide
Andrew Mennear, C.	Fitzjohn's
John Mills, Lab.	Gospel Oak
Keith Moffitt, LD	West End
Honora Morrissey, C.	Swiss Cottage
Pat Nightingale, Lab.	Camden
Richard Olszewski, Lab.	Regent's Park
Judith Pattison, Lab.	Gospel Oak
Flick Rea, LD	Fortune Green
John Rolfe, Lab.	Priory
Nirmal Roy, Lab.	Bloomsbury
Jane Schopflin, LD	Fortune Green
Roy Shaw, Lab.	Grafton
Sybil Shine, Lab.	Somers Town
Nick Smith, Lab.	King's Cross
Dawn Somper, C.	Frognal
Huntly Spence, C.	Belsize
Anne Swain, Lab.	Caversham
John Thane, Lab.	Highgate
Heather Thompson, LD	West End
Jake Turnbull, Lab.	Bloomsbury
Jim Turner, Lab.	Regent's Park
Phil Turner, Lab.	Priory
Tim Walker, Lab.	Kilburn
Barbara Ward, Lab.	Regent's Park
Piers Wauchope, C.	Adelaide
Brian Weekes, Lab.	Brunswick
John White, Lab.	Chalk Farm
Brian Woodrow, Lab.	Holborn

Political Composition: Lab. 42; C. 11; LD. 6.
Parliamentary Constituencies: Hampstead and Highgate; Holborn and St. Pancras.
Population: 192,000
Area: 2,200 hectares.

ABOUT CAMDEN

The London Borough of Camden stretches from Covent Garden to Hampstead and Highgate. It is home to numerous famous museums, historic houses and contemporary art galleries including the British Museum, the British Library, Kenwood House and London Zoo. It also contains a number of parks and open spaces including Regent's Park, Waterlow Park and Hampstead Heath.

COUNCIL TAX BANDS 2000-2001

Band	Market Value of the Property in 1991	Council Tax
A	Up to £40,000	£604.13
B	£40,001 to 52,000	£704.82
C	£52,001 to 68,000	£805.82
D	£68,001 to 88,000	£906.19
E	£88,001 to 120,000	£1107.56
F	£120,001 to 160,000	£1308.94
G	£160,001 to 320,000	£1510.32
H	£320,001 or more	£1812.38

CORPORATION OF LONDON

CITY OF LONDON

PO Box 270, Guildhall, London EC2P 2EJ (Tel: 020-7606 3030; Web: http://www.cityoflondon.uk).

CHIEF OFFICERS

Town Clerk: T. C. Simmons
Chamberlain: P. Derrick
City Solicitor: A. J. Colvin

34 Governed London

The City of London is the historic centre at the heart of London known as 'the square mile' around which the vast metropolis has grown over the centuries. The City's residential population is 5,500. The civic government is carried on by the Corporation of London through the Court of Common Council.

The City is an international financial centre, generating over £20 billion a year for the British economy. It includes the head offices of the principal banks, insurance companies and mercantile houses, in addition to buildings ranging from the historic Roman Wall and the 15th-century Guildhall, to the massive splendour of St Paul's Cathedral and the architectural beauty of Wren's spires.

The City of London was described by Tacitus in AD 62 as 'a busy emporium for trade and traders'. Under the Romans it became an important administrative centre and hub of the road system. Little is known of London in Saxon times, when it formed part of the kingdom of the East Saxons. In 886 Alfred recovered London from the Danes and reconstituted it a burgh under his son-in-law. In 1066 the citizens submitted to William the Conqueror who in 1067 granted them a charter, which is still preserved, establishing them in the rights and privileges they had hitherto enjoyed.

THE MAYORALTY

The Mayoralty was established c.1189, the first Mayor being Henry Fitz Ailwyn who filled the office for 23 years and was succeeded by Fitz Alan (1212-14). A new charter was granted by King John in 1215, directing the Mayor to be chosen annually, which has ever since been done, though in early times the same individual often held the office more than once. A familiar instance is that of 'Whittington, thrice Lord Mayor of London' (in reality four times, 1397, 1398, 1406, 1419); and many modern cases have occurred. The earliest instance of the phrase 'Lord Mayor' in English is in 1414. It was used more generally in the latter part of the 15th century and became invariable from 1535 onwards. At Michaelmas the liverymen in Common Hall choose two Aldermen who have served the office of Sheriff for presentation to the Court of Aldermen, and one is chosen to be Lord Mayor for the following mayoral year.

LORD MAYOR'S DAY

The Lord Mayor of London was previously elected on the feast of St Simon and St Jude (28 October), and from the time of Edward I, at least, was presented to the King or to the Barons of the Exchequer on the following day, unless that day was a Sunday. The day of election was altered to 16 October in 1346, and after some further changes was fixed for Michaelmas Day in 1546, but the ceremonies of admittance and swearing-in of the Lord Mayor continued to take place on 28 and 29 October respectively until 1751. In 1752, at the reform of the calendar, the Lord Mayor was continued in office until 8 November, the 'New Style' equivalent of 28 October. The Lord Mayor is now presented to the Lord Chief Justice at the Royal Courts of Justice on the second Saturday in November to make the final declaration of office, having been sworn in at Guildhall on the preceding day. The procession to the Royal Courts of Justice is popularly known as the Lord Mayor's Show.

REPRESENTATIVES

Aldermen are mentioned in the 11th century and their office is of Saxon origin. They were elected annually between 1377 and 1394, when an Act of Parliament of Richard II directed them to be chosen for life.

The Common Council, elected annually on the first Friday in December, was, at an early date, substituted for a popular assembly called the Folkmote. At first only two representatives were sent from each ward, but the number has since been greatly increased. The Corporation is reducing the number of Common Councilmen from 130 to 100 through natural wastage. The Government has introduced legislation to remove anomalies from the election system and to extend the non-resident franchise.

OFFICERS

Sheriffs were Saxon officers; their predecessors were the wic-reeves and portreeves of London and Middlesex. At first they were officers of the Crown, and were named by the Barons of the Exchequer; but Henry I (in 1132) gave the citizens permission to choose their own Sheriffs, and the annual election of Sheriffs became fully operative under King John's charter of 1199. The citizens lost this privilege, as far as the election of the Sheriff of Middlesex was concerned, by the Local Government Act 1888; but the liverymen continue to choose two Sheriffs of the City of London, who are appointed on Midsummer Day and take office at Michaelmas.

The office of Chamberlain is an ancient one, the first contemporary record of which is 1237. The Town Clerk (or Common Clerk) is mentioned in 1274.

ACTIVITIES

The work of the Corporation is assigned to a number of committees which present reports to the Court of Common Council. These Committees are: City Lands and Bridge House Grants Estates, Policy and Resources, Finance, Planning and Transportation, Central Markets, Billingsgate and Leadenhall Markets, Spitalfields Market, Police, Port and City of London Health and Social Services, Libraries, Art Galleries and Records, Board of Governors of City of London Freemen's School, Music and Drama (Guildhall School of Music and Drama), Establishment, Housing and Sports Development, Gresham (City side), Hampstead Heath Management, Epping Forest and Open Spaces, West Ham Park, Privileges, Barbican Residential and Barbican Centre (Barbican Arts and Conference Centre).

The City's estate, in the possession of which the Corporation of London differs from other municipalities, is managed by the City Lands and Bridge House Grants Estates Committee, the chairmanship of which carries with it the title of Chief Commoner.

The Honourable the Irish Society, which manages the Corporation's estates in Ulster, consists of a Governor and five other Aldermen, the Recorder, and 19 Common Councilmen, of whom one is elected Deputy Governor.

The Lord Mayor 1999-2000
The Rt. Hon. the Lord Mayor, Clive Martin, OBE, TD
*Note that the Lord Mayor assumes office in November each year. Elections for the Lord Mayor 2000-2001 take place at the end of September.

The Sheriffs 1999-2000
R. Aggutter (Alderman, Castle Baynard) and N. Branson; elected, 26 June 2000; assumed office, 28 September 2000

London Borough Councils 35

THE ALDERMEN

Alderman	Ward
Nicholas Anstee	Aldersgate
The Rt. Hon. The Lord Mayor Clive Martin, OBE, TD	
David Brewer	Aldgate
John Hughesdon	Bassishaw
Michael Oliver	Billingsgate
Michael Savory	Bishopsgate
Sir David Rowe-Ham, GBE	Bread Street
	Bridge and Bridge Without
Sir Christopher Colett, GBE	Broad Street
Richard Nichols	Candlewick
Richard Agutter	Castle Baynard
Anthony Bull	Cheap
Robert Finch	Coleman Street
Sir Brian Jenkins, GBE	Cordwainer
David Howard	Cornhill
Gavyn Arthur	Cripplegate
Sir Christopher Leaver, GBE	Dowgate
Sir Christopher Walford	Farringdon Within
Vacant	Farringdon Without
Sir Alan Traill, GBE	Langbourn
Michael Everard	Lime Street
Lord Levene of Portsoken, KBE	Portsoken
Sir Alexander Graham, GBE	Queenhithe
Sir Roger Cork	Tower
Sir John Chalstrey	Vintry
Sir Paul Newall, TD	Walbrook

THE COMMON COUNCIL

Councillor	Ward
Absalom, J. D.	Farringdon Wt.
Altman, L. P., CBE	Cripplegate Wn.
Andrade, P.	Farringdon Wt.
Angell, E. H.	Cripplegate Wt.
Archibald, W. W.	Cornhill
Ayers, K. E.	Bassishaw
Balls, H. D.	Castle Baynard
Barker, J. A.	Cripplegate Wn.
Barnes-Yallowley, H. M. F.	Coleman Street
Barter, S.	Langbourn
Beale, M. J.	Lime Street
Bird, J. L., OBE	Bridge
Bowman, J. C. R.	Aldgate
Bradshaw, D. J.	Cripplegate Wn.
Bramwell, F. M.	Langbourn
Brewster, J. W., OBE	Bassishaw
Brighton, R. L.	Portsoken
Brooks, W. I. B.	Billingsgate
Byllam-Barnes, J. C. F. B.	Cheap
Caspi, D. R.	Bridge
Cassidy, M. J.	Coleman Street
Catt, B. F.	Farringdon Wn.
Chadwick, R. A. H.	Tower
Challis, G. H., CBE	Langbourn
Charkham, J. P.	Farringdon Wt.
Cohen, Mrs C. M.	Lime Street
Cole, Lt.-Col. Sir Colin, KCB, KCVO, TD	Castle Baynard
Cotgrove, D.	Lime Street
Currie, Miss S. E. M.	Cripplegate Wt.
Daily-Hunt, R. B.	Cripplegate Wt.
Darwin, G. E.	Farringdon Wt.
Davis, C. B.	Bread Street
Dove, W. H., MBE	Bishopsgate
Dunitz, A. A.	Portsoken
Eskenzi, A. N.	Farringdon Wn.
Eve, R. A.	Cheap
Everett, K. M.	Candlewick
Falk, F. A., TD	Broad Street
Farr, M. C.	Walbrook
Farrow, M. W. W.	Farringdon Wt.
Farthing, R. B. C.	Aldgate
FitzGerald, R. C. A.	Bread Street
Forbes, G. B.	Bishopsgate
Fraser, S. J.	Coleman Street
Fraser, W. B.	Vintry
Galloway, A. D.	Broad Street
Gillon, G. M. F.	Cordwainer
Ginsburg, S.	Bishopsgate
Gowman, Miss A. J.	Dowgate
Graves, A. C.	Bishopsgate
Green, C.	Aldersgate
Hall, B. R. H.	Farringdon Wn.
Halliday, Mrs P.	Walbrook
Hardwick, Dr P. B.	Aldgate
Harris, B. N.	Broad Street
Hart, M. G.	Bridge
Haynes, J. E. H.	Cornhill
Henderson-Begg, M.	Coleman Street
Holland, J., CBE	Aldgate
Holliday, Mrs E. H. L.	Vintry
Horlock, H. W. S.	Farringdon Wn.
Jackson, L. St J. T.	Bread Street
Kellett, Mrs M. W. F.	Tower
Kemp, D. L.	Coleman Street
King, A.	Queenhithe
Knowles, S. K.	Candlewick
Lawrence, G. A.	Farringdon Wt.
Lawson, G. C. H.	Portsoken
Leck, P.	Aldersgate
Littlechild, Mrs V.	Cripplegate Wt.
Luder, I. D.	Farringdon Wt.
McGuinness, C.	Castle Baynard
MacLellan, A. P. W.	Walbrook
McNeil, I. D.	Lime Street
Malins, J. H., QC	Farringdon Wt.
Martinelli, P. J.	Bassishaw
Mayhew, Miss J.	Queenhithe
Mayhew, J. P.	Aldersgate
Mead, Mrs W.	Farringdon Wt.
Mitchell, C. R.	Castle Baynard
Mobsby, D. J. L.	Billingsgate
Mooney, B. D. F.	Queenhithe
Montgomery, B.	Dowgate
Moss, A. D.	Tower
Nash, Mrs J. C.	Aldersgate
Newman, Mrs P. B.	Aldersgate
O'Ferrall, P. C. K., OBE	Aldgate
Owen, Mrs J.	Langbourn
Owen-Ward, J. R.	Bridge
Parmley, A. C., Ph.D.	Vintry
Pembroke, Mrs A. M. F.	Cheap
Platts-Mills, J. F. F., QC	Farringdon Wt.
Price, E. E.	Farringdon Wt.
Pulman, G. A. G.	Tower
Punter, C.	Cripplegate Wn.

36 Governed London

Quilter, S. D. — Cripplegate Wt.
Regan, R. D. — Farringdon Wn.
Revell-Smith, P. A., CBE — Vintry
Rigby, P. P., CBE — Farringdon Wn.
Robinson, Mrs D. C. — Bishopsgate
Roney, E. P. T., CBE — Bishopsgate
Samuel, Mrs I., MBE — Portsoken
Sargant, K. A. — Cornhill
Saunders, R. — Candlewick
Scriven, R. G., CBE — Candlewick
Scott, J. — Broad Street
Sellon, S. A., OBE, TD — Cordwainer
Shalit, D. M. — Farringdon Wn.
Sharp, Mrs I. M. — Queenhithe
Sherlock, M. R. C. — Dowgate
Snyder, M. J. — Cordwainer
Spanner, J. H., TD — Broad Street
Stevenson, F. P. — Cripplegate Wn.
Taylor, J. A. F., TD — Bread Street
Thompson, S. — Bassishaw
Thorp, C. R. — Billingsgate
Trotter, J. — Billingsgate
Walsh, S. — Farringdon Wt.
Warner, D. W. — Cripplegate Wn.
Willoughby, P. J. — Bishopsgate
Wilmot, R. T. D. — Cordwainer
Wixley, G. R. A., CBE, TD — Coleman Street

COUNCIL TAX BANDS 2000-2001

Band	Market Value of the Property in 1991	Council Tax
A	Up to £40,000	£371.18
B	£40,001 to 52,000	£433.04
C	£52,001 to 68,000	£494.91
D	£68,001 to 88,000	£556.77
E	£88,001 to 120,000	£680.50
F	£120,001 to 160,000	£804.23
G	£160,001 to 320,000	£927.95
H	£320,001 or more	£1113.54

THE CITY GUILDS
(Livery Companies)

The constitution of the livery companies has been unchanged for centuries. There are three ranks of membership: freemen, liverymen and assistants. A person can become a freeman by patrimony (through a parent having been a freeman); by servitude (through having served an apprenticeship to a freeman); or by redemption (by purchase).

Election to the livery is the prerogative of the company, who can elect any of its freemen as liverymen. Assistants are usually elected from the livery and form a Court of Assistants which is the governing body of the company. The Master (in some companies called the Prime Warden) is elected annually from the assistants.

THE CITY GUILDS

The Worshipful Company of Mercers
Ironmonger Lane, London, EC2V 8HE (Tel: 020-7726 4991; Fax: 020-7600 1158; E-mail: mail@mercers.co.uk; Web: http://www.mercers.co.uk)
Clerk: C. H. Parker
Master: R. C. Cunis

The Worshipful Company of Grocers
Princes Street, London, EC2R 8AD (Tel: 020-7606 3113; Fax: 020-7600 3082; E-mail: beadle@grocershall.co.uk; Web: http://www.grocershall.co.uk)
Clerk: Brig. P. P. Rawlins, MBE
Master: T. N. N. Guinness

The Worshipful Company of Drapers
Throgmorton Avenue, London, EC2N 2DQ (Tel: 020-7588 5001; Fax: 020-7628 1988; E-mail: mail@thedrapers.co.uk)
Clerk: A. L. Lang, MBE
Master: J. M. F. Padovan

The Workshipful Company of Fishmongers
London Bridge, London, EC4R 9EL (Tel: 020-7626 3531; Fax: 020-7929 1389)
Clerk: K. S. Waters
Prime Warden: The Earl of Erroll

The Worshipful Company of Goldsmiths
Foster Lane, London, EC2V 6BN (Tel: 020-7606 7010; Fax: 020-7606 1511;
E-mail: the.clerk@thegoldsmiths.co.uk;
Web: http://www.thegoldsmiths.co.uk)
Clerk: R. D. Buchanan-Dunlop, CBE
Prime Warden: The Rt. Hon. Sir Adam Butler, DL

The Worshipful Company of Merchant Taylors
30 Threadneedle Street, London, EC2R 8JB (Tel: 020-7450 4440; Fax: 020-7588 2776)
Clerk: D. A. Peck
Master: Alderman Sir Brian Jenkins, GBE

The Worshipful Company of Skinners
8 Dowgate Hill, London, EC4R 2SP (Tel: 020-7236 6590; Fax: 020-7236 6590)
Clerk: Capt. D. Hart Dyke, CBE, LVO, RN
Master: P. Attenborough, CBE

The Worshipful Company of Haberdashers
39-40 Bartholomew Close, London, EC1A 7JN (Tel: 020-7606 0967; Fax: 020-7606 5738;
E-mail: enquiries@haberdashers.co.uk)
Clerk: Capt. R. J. Fisher, RN
Master: M. D. G. Wheldon, FRICS

The Worshipful Company of Salters
4 Fore Street, London, EC2Y 5DE (Tel: 020-7588 5216; Fax: 020-7638 3679;
E-mail: company@salters.co.uk)
Clerk: Col. M. P. Barneby
Master: The Hon. A. H. Todd

The Worshipful Company of Ironmongers
Shaftesbury Place, Barbican, London, EC2Y 8AA (Tel: 020-7606 2726; Fax: 020-7600 3519;
E-mail: beadle@ironhall.co.uk;

London Borough Councils 37

Web: http://www.ironhall.co.uk)
Clerk: J. A. Oliver
Master: S. D. Apsley

The Vintners' Company
Upper Thames Street, London, EC4V 3BG (Tel: 020-7236 1863; Fax: 020-7236 8177;
E-mail: theclerk@the-vintners-livery-co.org.uk)
Clerk: Brig. M. Smythe, OBE
Master: D. B. Butler-Adams

The Worshipful Company of Clothworkers
Dunster Court, Mincing Lane, London, EC3R 7AH (Tel: 020-7623 7041; Fax: 020-7283 1289;
E-mail: enquiries@clothworkers.co.uk)
Clerk: M. G. T. Harris
Master: J. C. Hutchins

The Worshipful Company of Actuaries
81 Worrin Road, Shenfield, Brentwood, Essex CM15 8JN (Tel: 01277-261110; Fax: 01277-261110)
Clerk: Mrs J. V. Evans
Master: S. J. Green

The Guild of Air Pilots and Air Navigators
Cobham House, 9 Warwick Court, Gray's Inn, London, WC1R 5DJ (Tel: 020-7404 4032; Fax: 020-7404 4035; E-mail: gapan@gapan.org; Web: http://www.gapan.org)
Grand Master: HRH The Prince Philip, Duke of Edinburgh, KG, KT, OM, GBE, PC
Clerk: Air Vice-Marshal R. G. Peters, CB
Master: A. G. Thorning

The Society of Apothecaries
14 Black Friars Lane, London, EC4V 6EJ (Tel: 020-7236 1189; Fax: 020-7329 3177)
Clerk: Lt.-Col. R. J. Stringer
Master: R. J. Parker

The Company of Armourers and Brasiers
81 Coleman Street, London, EC2R 5BJ (Tel: 020-7606 1199; Fax: 020-7606 7481)
Clerk: Cdr. T. J. K. Sloane, OBE, RN
Master: The Venerable C. Wagstaff

The Worshipful Company of Bakers
Harp Lane, London, EC3R 6DP (Tel: 020-7623 2223; Fax: 020-7621 1924; E-mail: clerk@bakers.co.uk;
Web: http://www.bakers.co.uk)
Clerk: R. E. B. Sawyer
Master: J. W. Tompkins

The Worshipful Company of Barbers
Barber and Surgeons' Hall, Monkwell Square, Wood Street, London, EC2Y 5BL (Tel: 020-7606 0741; Fax: 020-7606 3857; E-mail: clerk@barbers.org.uk;
Web: http://www.barbers.org.uk)
Clerk: Brig. A. F. Eastburn
Master: G. G. Macdonald

The Worshipful Company of Basketmakers
48 Seymour Walk, London, SW10 9NF (Tel: 020-7351 2918; Fax: 020-7351 6559)
Clerk: Maj. G. J. Flint-Shipman, TD
Prime Warden: Deputy G. A. G. Pulman

The Worshipful Company of Blacksmiths
48 Upwood Road, London, SE12 8AN (Tel: 020-8318 9684; Fax: 020-8318 9687;
E-mail: hammerandhand@supanet.com)
Clerk: C. Jeal
Prime Warden: H. A. E. Adams

The Worshipful Company of Bowyers
11 Aldermans Hill, London, N13 4YD (Tel: 020-8882 3055; Fax: 020-8882 5851;
E-mail: john@owen-ward.u-net.com;
Web: http://www.bowyer.com)
Clerk: J. R. Owen-Ward
Master: E. J. Burnett

The Worshipful Company of Brewers
Aldermanbury Square, London, EC2V 7HR (Tel: 020-7606 1301; Fax: 010-7796 3557)
Clerk: C. W. Dallmeyer
Master: J. H. Wells

The Worshipful Company of Builders Merchants
4 College Hill, London, EC4R 2RB (Tel: 020-7329 2189; Fax: 020-7329 2190; E-mail: wcobm@aol.com)
Clerk: Miss S. M. Robinson, TD
Master: C. G. A. Latham

The Worshipful Company of Butchers
Butchers Hall, 87 Bartholomew Close, London, EC1A 7EB (Tel: 020-7606 4106; Fax: 020-7606 4108)
Clerk: G. J. Sharp
Master: G. A. Jackman

The Worshipful Company of Carmen
35-37 Ludgate Hill, London, EC4M 7JN (Tel: 020-7489 8289; Fax: 020-7236 3313)
Clerk: Cdr. R. M. H. Bawtree, OBE, RN
Master: B. H. Owen

The Worshipful Company of Carpenters
1 Throgmorton Avenue, London, EC2N 2JJ (Tel: 020-7588 7001; Fax: 020-7638 6286;
Web: http://www.thecarpenterscompany.co.uk
Clerk: Maj.-Gen. P. T. Stevenson, OBE
Master: N. B. C. Evelegh, MBE

The Worshipful Company of Chartered Secretaries and Administrators
3rd Floor, Sadler's Hall, 40 Gutter Lane, London, EC2V 6BR (Tel: 020-7726 2955; Fax: 020-7600 5699)
Hon. Clerk: C. H. Grinsted
Master: W. C. Hammond, MBE

The Worshipful Company of Chartered Surveyors
16 St Mary-at-Hill, London, EC3R 8EE
Clerk: Mrs A. L. Jackson
Master: Miss D. F. Patman

The Worshipful Company of Clockmakers
Room 66-67, Albert Buildings, 49 Queen Victoria Street, London, EC4N 4SE (Tel: 020-7236 0700; Fax: 020-7236 0800; E-mail: clerk: @clockmakers.org;
Web: http://www.clockmakers.org)
Clerk: Gp Capt. P. H. Gibson, MBE
Master: Prof. A. Boksenberg, CBE, FRS

38 Governed London

The Worshipful Company of Constructors
181 Fentiman Road, London, SW8 1JY (Tel: 020-7735 1459; Fax: 020-7735 1459)
Clerk: L. L. Brace
Master: D. A. Hutchison, MBE

The Worshipful Company of Cooks
Registry Chambers, The Old Deanery, Deans Court, London, EC4V 5AA (Tel: 020-7593 5043; Fax: 020-7248 3221)
Clerk: M. C. Thatcher
Master: P. D. Herbage

The Worshipful Company of Coopers
13 Devonshire Square, London, EC2M 4TH (Tel: 020-7247 9577; Fax: 020-7377 8061; E-mail: clerk@coopers-hall.co.uk)
Clerk: J. A. Newton
Master: W. M Heath

The Worshipful Company of Cordwainers
8 Warwick Court, Gray's Inn, London, WC1R 5DJ (Tel: 020-7242 4411; Fax: 020-7242 3366)
Clerk: Lt.-Col. J. R. Blundell, RM
Master: Rear-Adm. J. F. T. G. Salt, CB

The Worshipful Company of Cutlers
Warwick Lane, London, EC4M 7BR (Tel: 020-7248 1866; Fax: 020-7248 8426)
Clerk: K. S. G. Hinde, OBE, TD
Master: C. M. L. Evans

The Worshipful Company of Distillers
71 Lincoln's Inn Fields, London, WC2A 3JF (Tel: 020-7405 7091; Fax: 020-7405 1453)
Clerk: C. V. Hughes
Master: R. H. Nicholson

The Worshipful Company of Dyers
10 Dowgate Hill, London, EC4R 2ST (Tel: 020-7236 7197)
Clerk: J. R. Chambers
Prime Warden: R. A. Leuchars, FRACS, BSC

The Worshipful Company of Farmers
Chislehurst Business Centre, 1 Bromley Lane, Chislehurst, Kent, BR7 6LH (Tel: 020-8467 2255; Fax: 020-8467 2666)
Clerk: Miss M. L. Winter
Master: J. H. Cossins, CBE

The Worshipful Company of Fletchers
3 Cloth Street, London, EC1A 7LD (Tel: 020-8882 3055; Fax: 020-8882 5851; E-mail: john@owen-ward.u-net.com)
Clerk: J. R. Owen-Ward
Master: H. R. Vogt

The Worshipful Company of Founders
Number One, Cloth Fair, London, EC1A 7JA (Tel: 01273-858700; Fax: 01273-858900)
Clerk: A. J. Gillett
Master: (until October 2000) L. W. Kemp; (from October 2000) Sir Ian Ley, Bt

The Worshipful Company of Framework Knitters
Whitegarth Chambers, 37 The Uplands, Loughton, Essex, IG10 1NQ (Tel: 020-8502 1964; Fax: 020-8502 5237; E-mail: clerk@frameworkknitters.co.uk; Web: http://www.frameworkknitters.co.uk)
Clerk: H. W. H. Ellis
Master: J. M. Dean

The Worshipful Company of Fuellers
22 Broadfields, Headstone Lane, Hatch End, Middx, HA2 6NH (Tel: 020-8421 6616; Fax: 020-8421 6616; E-mail: fuellers@aol.com)
Clerk: R. A. Riley
Master: F. B. Harrison, CBE

The Worshipful Company of Furniture Makers
Painters' Hall, 9 Little Trinity Lane, London, EC4V 2AD (Tel: 020-7248 1677; Fax: 020-7248 1688; E-mail: clerk@furnituremkrs.co.uk; Web: http://www.furnituremkrs.co.uk)
Clerk: Mrs J. A. Wright
Master: S. F. Brown

The Worshipful Company of Gardeners
25 Luke Street, London, EC2A 4AR (Tel: 020-7739 8200; Fax: 020-7613 3412)
Clerk: Col. N. G. S. Gray
Master: The Venerable P. Delaney

The Worshipful Company of Girdlers
Girdlers Hall, Basinghall Avenue, London, EC2V 5DD (Tel: 020-7638 0488; Fax: 020-7628 4030; E-mail: girdlers@lineone.net)
Clerk: Lt.-Col. R. Sullivan
Master: S. V. Straker

The Worshipful Company of Glaziers and Painters of Glass
9 Montague Close, London, SE1 9DD (Tel: 020-7403 3300; Fax: 020-7407 6036)
Clerk: Col. D. W. Eking
Master: P. R. Batchelor

The Worshipful Company of Glovers of London
71 Ifield Road, London, SW10 9AU (Tel: 020-7351 4006; Fax: 020-7351 4006; E-mail: gloverslondon@aol.com)
Clerk: Mrs M. Hood
Master: Mrs M. Linton

The Worshipful Company of Gold and Silver Wyre Drawers
Twizzletwig, The Ballands South, Fletcham, Leatherhead, Surrey, KT22 9EP (Tel: 01372-374952)
Clerk: T. J. Waller
Master: (until 8 January 2001) K. P. Kirby; (from 8 January 2001) Sir Peter S. Yarraton

The Worshipful Company of Gunmakers
The Proof House, 48-50 Commercial Road, London, E1 1LP (Tel: 020-7481 2695; Fax: 020-7480 5102)
Clerk: J. M. Riches
Master: D. T. C. Caldow

London Borough Councils 39

The Worshipful Company of Information Technologists
39A Bartholomew Close, London, EC1A 7JN (Tel: 020-7600 1992; Fax: 020-7600 1991;
E-mail: assistant@wcit.org.net;
Web: http://www.wcit.org.uk/)
Clerk: Mrs G. Davies
Master: P. Cropper

The Worshipful Company of Innholders
30 College Street, London, EC4R 2RH
Clerk: J. R. Edwardes Jones
Master: Dr R. Glover

The Worshipful Company of Insurers
20 Aldermanbury, London, EC2V 7HY (Tel: 020-7600 4006; Fax: 020-7972 0153)
Clerk: L. J. Walters
Master: M. J. Pickard

The Worshipful Company of Launderers
Launderers' Hall, 9 Montague Close, London Bridge, London, SE1 9DD (Tel: 020-7378 1430; Fax: 020-7407 6036)
Clerk: Mrs J. Polek
Master: P. C. Crane

The Worshipful Company of Leathersellers
15 St Helen's Place, London, EC3A 6DQ (Tel: 020-7330 1444; Fax: 020-7330 1445;
E-mail: enquiries@leathersellers.co.uk;
Web: http://www.leathersellers.co.uk)
Clerk: Capt. J. G. F. Cooke, OBE, RN
Master: D. R. Curtis

The Worshipful Company of Lightmongers
Crown Wharf, 11A Coldharbour, Blackwall Reach, London, E14 9NS (Tel: 020-7515 9055; Fax: 020-7538 5466)
Clerk: D. B. Wheatley
Master: E. H. Ring

The Worshipful Company of Loriners
8 Portland Square, London, E1W 2QR (Tel: 020-7709 0222; Fax: 020-7709 0222)
Clerk: G. B. Forbes
Master: J. R. A. Allison

The Worshipful Company of Masons
22 Cannon Hill, Southgate, London, N14 6LG (Tel: 020-8882 9520; Fax: 020-8882 9520;
E-mail: clerk@masonslivery.co.uk;
Web: http://www.masonslivery.co.uk)
Clerk: P. F. Clark
Master: B. J. Rushton

Honourable Company of Master Mariners
HQS Wellington, Temple Stairs, Victoria Embankment, London, WC2R 2PN (Tel: 020-7836 8179; Fax: 020-7240 3082; E-mail: hcmm@clara.co.uk)
Admiral: HRH The Prince Philip, Duke of Edinburgh, KG, KT, OM, GBE, PC
Clerk: J. A. V. Maddock
Master: Capt. L. A. Holder

The Worshipful Company of Musicians
75 Watling Street, London, EC4M 9BJ
Clerk: S. F. N. Waley
Master: Sir Alan Traill, GBE, QSO

The Worshipful Company of Needlemakers
5 Staple Inn, London, WC1V 7QH
Clerk: M. G. Cook
Master: Sir Anthony Wilson

The Worshipful Company of Painter-Stainers
Painters' Hall, 9 Little Trinity Lane, London, EC4V 2AD (Tel: 020-7236 6258; Fax: 020-7236 0500)
Clerk: Col. J. W. Chesshyre
Master: The Hon. M. Robson

The Worshipful Company of Paviors
3 Ridgemount Gardens, Enfield, Middx, EN2 8QL (Tel: 020-8366 1566; Fax: 020-8366 1566)
Clerk: J. L. White
Master: J. E. Cruse

The Worshipful Company of Pewterers
Oat Lane, London, EC2V 7DE (Tel: 020-7606 9363; Fax: 020-7600 3896; E-mail: clerk@pewterers.org.uk;
Web: http://www.pewterers.org.uk)
Clerk: Cdr. A. St. John Steiner, OBE, RN
Master: W. Grant

The Worshipful Company of Plaisterers
1 London Wall, London, EC2Y 5JU (Tel: 020-7606 1361; Fax: 020-7796 1408)
Clerk: R. Vickers
Master: P. J. Cook

The Worshipful Company of Plumbers
Room 28, 49 Queen Victoria Street, London, EC4N 4SA (Tel: 020-7236 7816; Fax: 020-7236 7816)
Clerk: Lt.-Col. R. J. A. Paterson-Fox
Master: (until October 2000) J. H. Mayfield; (from October 2000) A. H. M. Moir

The Worshipful Company of Saddlers
40 Gutter Lane, London, EC2V 6BR (Tel: 020-7726 8661; Fax: 020-7600 0386;
E-mail: clerk@saddlersco.co.uk;
Web: http://www.saddlersco.co.uk)
Clerk: Gp Capt. W. S. Brereton Martin, CBE
Master: M. F. S. Bullen

The Scientific Instrument Makers
9 Montague Close, London, SE1 9DD (Tel: 020-7407 4832; Fax: 020-7407 1565;
E-mail: theclerk@wcsim.co.uk;
Web: http://www.locsim.co.uk)
Clerk: F. G. Everard
Master: J. M. T. Hilton

The Worshipful Company of Scriveners
HQS Wellington, Temple Stairs, Victoria Embankment, London, WC2R 2PN (Tel: 020-7240 0529; Fax: 020-7497 0645;
Web: http://www.scriveners.co.uk)
Clerk: G. A. Hill
Master: P. H. Grove

The Worshipful Company of Shipwrights
Ironmongers Hall, Barbican, London, EC2Y 8AA (Tel: 020-7606 2376; Fax: 020-7600 3515;

40 Governed London

E-mail: clerk@shipwrights.co.uk)
Permanent Master: HRH The Prince Philip, Duke of Edinburgh, KG, KT, OM, GBE, PC
Clerk: Capt. F. R. Channon, RN
Prime Warden: Dr T. J. Parker

The City of London Solicitors' Company
4 College Hill, London, EC2R 2RB (Tel: 020-7329 2173; Fax: 020-7329 2190; E-mail: mail@citysolicitors.org.uk; Web: http://www.citysolicitors.org.uk)
Clerk: Miss S. M. Robinson, TD
Master: Mr Alderman and Sheriff R. G. Finch

The Worshipful Company of Spectacle Makers
Apothecaries' Hall, Black Friars Lane, London, EC4V 6EL (Tel: 020-7236 2932; Fax: 020-7329 3249; E-mail: clerk@spectaclemakers.com; Web: http://www.spectaclemakers.com)
Clerk: Lt.-Col. J. A. B. Salmon, OBE, LLB
Master: B. J. Mitchell, FCA, FRSA

The Worshipful Company of Stationers and Newspaper Makers
Ave Maria Lane, London, EC4M 7DD (Tel: 020-7248 2934; Fax: 020-7489 1975; E-mail: admin@stationers.org)
Clerk: Brig. D. G. Sharp, AFC
Master: R. T. H. Harrison

The Worshipful Company of Tallow Chandlers
4 Dowgate Hill, London, EC4R 2SH (Tel: 020-7248 4726; Fax: 020-7236 0844)
Clerk: Brig. W. K. L. Prosser, CBE, MC
Master: Brig. N. H. Thompson, CBE

The Worshipful Company of Turners
182 Temple Chambers, Temple Avenue, London, EC4Y 0HP (Tel: 020-7353 9595; Fax: 020-7353 9933; E-mail: clerk@turnerscompany.demon.co.uk)
Clerk: E. A. Windsor Clive
Master: Maj.-Gen. C. Tyler, CB

The Worshipful Company of Upholders
Hall in the Wood, 46 Quail Gardens, Selsdon Vale, Croydon, CR2 8TF (Tel: 020-8656 6811; Fax: 020-8656 6814)
Clerk: J. P. Cody
Master: B. E. Chapman, CBE

The Worshipful Company of Water Conservators
16 St Mary-at-Hill, London, EC2R 8EF (Tel: 020-7621 0414; Fax: 020-7621 0414; E-mail: waterlco@aol.com; Web: http://www.waterlco.co.uk)
Clerk: R. A. Riley
Master: P. N. Paul

The Worshipful Company of Wax Chandlers
Gresham Street, London, EC2V 7AD (Tel: 020-7606 3591; Fax: 020-7600 5462; E-mail: waxchandlershall@ukonline.co.uk; Web: http://www.waxchandlershall.co.uk
Clerk: Cdr. J. Stevens, RN
Master: R. A. Blaxland

The Worshipful Company of Weavers
Saddlers' House, Gutter Lane, London EC2V 6BR (Tel: 020-7606 1155; Fax: 020-7606 1119; E-mail: weavers@weaversco.co.uk)
Clerk: Mrs F. Newcombe
Upper Bailiff: (until October 2000) R. H. W. Graham-Palmer; (from October 2000) R. D. B. Mynors

The Worshipful Company of World Traders
36 Ladbroke Grove, London, W11 2PA (Tel: 020-7792 3410; E-mail: clerk@world-traders.org; Web: http://www.world-traders.org)
Clerk: N. R. Pullman
Master: Miss S. Hughes

The Company of Firefighters
The Insurance Hall, 20 Aldermanbury, London, EC2V 7GF (Tel: 020-7600 1666; Fax: 020-7600 1666)
Clerk: G. P. Ellis
Master: Prof. D. E. Bland, OBE, Ph.D., FCA

The Company of Parish Clerks
c/o 1 Dean Trench Street, London, SW1P 3HB (Tel: 020-7222 1138; Fax: 020-7233 1913)
Clerk: Lt.-Col. B. J. N. Coombes
Master: W. H. Dove, MBE

The Company of Watermen and Lightermen
16 St Mary-at-Hill, London, EC3R 8EF (Tel: 020-7283 2373; Fax: 020-7283 0477; E-mail: info@watermenshall.org; Web: http://www.watermenshall.org)
Clerk: C. Middlemiss
Master: L. G. Barrow

CROYDON

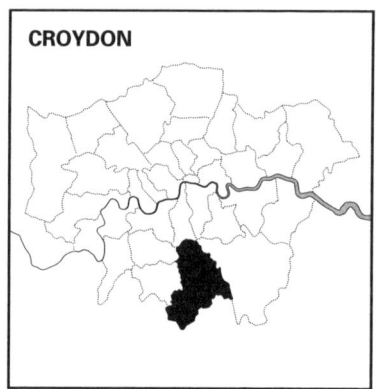

Taberner House, Park Lane, Croydon, CR9 3JS (Tel: 020 8686 4433; Fax 020 8760 5657; Web: http://www.croydon.gov.uk)
Director of Finance: Municipal Offices, Fell Road, Croydon, CR9 1BQ (Tel: 020 8686 4433; Fax 020 8686 7405)
Libraries and Museums: Central Library, Katherine Street, Croydon, CR9 1ET.
Registration of Births, Deaths and Marriages: Register Office, Mint Walk, Croydon CR0 1EA (Tel: 020-8760 5617)

London Borough Councils 41

CHIEF OFFICERS

Chief Executive: D. Wechsler
Director of Corporate Services: Miles Smith
Director of Education: Dr. David Sands
Director of Environmental Health and Trading Standards: Don Boon
Director of Finance and IT: Jan Willis
Director of Housing: Mike Davis
Director of Leisure Services: Steve Nalsey
Director of Planning and Development: Philip Goodwin
Director of Public Services and Works: K. C. Ollier
Director of Social Services: Hannah Miller
Head of Corporate Construction: K. Herriott
Head of Information Technology: D. Fitze
Head of Policy and Executive Office: Will Tuckley

MEMBERS OF THE COUNCIL

Councillor	Ward
Mayor: Mary Walker, Lab.	Fieldway
Deputy Mayor: P. Hopson, Lab.	Norbury
Leader of the Council: Hugh Malyan, Lab.	Beulah
D. Adamson, C.	Selsdon
E. Arram, C.	Ashburton
Ian Atkins, LD	Coulsdon East
Jane Avis, Lab.	South Norwood
Gavin Barwell, C.	Woodcote and Coulsdon West
G. Bass, C.	Purley
Gee Bernard, Lab.	West Thornton
C. Burling, Lab.	Waddon
Alex Burridge, Lab.	Bensham Manor
Jan Buttinger, C.	Kenley
John Calvert, C.	Waddon
Amanda Campbell, Lab.	Addiscombe
P. Cambell, C.	Monks Orchard
R. Chandarana, Lab.	West Thornton
Pat Clouder, Lab.	Thornton Heath
R. Coatman, C.	Fairfield
S. Collins, Lab.	Broad Street
Graham Dare, C.	Waddon
A. Dennis, Lab.	Thornton Heath
B. Finegan, Lab.	Woodside
Mike Fisher, C.	Spring Park
J. Fitzpatrick, Lab.	Addiscombe
S. Fitzsimons, Lab.	Addiscombe
C. Fraser, Lab.	South Norwood
Wally Garratt, Lab.	Thornton Heath
R. Grantham, Lab.	Beulah
Lynne Hale, C.	Sanderstead
Anna Hawkins, C.	Woodcote and Coulsdon West
Steve Hollands, C.	Kenley
Maureen Horden, C.	Heathfield
Karen Jewitt, Lab.	Rylands
M. Jewitt, Lab.	South Norwood
Nick Keable, C.	Croham
Shafi Khan, Lab.	Norbury
Pat Knight, C.	Fairfield
T. Laffin, Lab.	New Addington
Toni Letts, Lab.	Whitehorse Manor
Derek Loughborough, C.	Monks Orchard
H. Maylan, Lab.	Beulah
Maggie Mansell, Lab.	Norbury
Janet Marshall C.	Spring Park
R. Matlock, Lab.	Broad Street
Paul McCombie, C.	Croham
C. McKenzie, Lab.	West Thornton
D. Mead, C.	Selsdon
Margaret Mead, C.	Heathfield
P. Mee, Lab.	Bensham Manor
D. Millard, C.	Purley
T. Newman, Lab.	Woodside
D. Osland, C.	Woodcote and Coulsdon West
Ian Payne, Lab.	Upper Norwood
A. Pelling, C.	Heathfield
J. Perry, C.	Coulsdon East
Gerry Ryan, Lab.	Whitehorse Manor
Pat Ryan, Lab.	Upper Norwood
E. Shaw, C.	Sanderstead
Paula Shaw, Lab.	Bensham Manor
A. Slipper, C.	Ashburton
P. Spalding, Lab.	Broad Street
Mark Stockwell, C.	Croham
Phil Thomas, C.	Purley
Martin Tiedemann, Lab.	Whitehorse Manor
J. Walker, Lab.	Fieldway
Christopher Ward, Lab.	New Addington
Louisa Woodley, Lab.	Rylands
C. Wright, C.	Coulsdon East
M. Wunn, C.	Fairfield

Political Composition: Lab. 38; C. 31; LD. 1
Parliamentary Constituencies: Croydon Central; Croydon North; Croydon South.
Population: 333,800
Area: 8,662 hectares.

ABOUT CROYDON

Croydon is the largest of the London boroughs in terms of population. There are approximately 128,000 households in the borough. Outside of central London Croydon is the largest office centre in the south of England and has nearly 3 million square feet of retail space. Many of the borough's residents commute into London with journeys into London's Victoria Station taking less than 15 minutes.

COUNCIL TAX BANDS 2000-2001

Band	Market Value of the Property in 1991	Council Tax
A	Up to £40,000	£538.48
B	£40,001 to 52,000	£628.23
C	£52,001 to 68,000	£717.98
D	£68,001 to 88,000	£807.72
E	£88,001 to 120,000	£987.21
F	£120,001 to 160,000	£1166.71
G	£160,001 to 320,000	£1346.20
H	£320,001 or more	£1615.44

42 Governed London

Town Hall, London W5 2BY (Tel: 020 8579 2424; Fax: 020-8579 5224; Email: webmaster@ealing.gov.uk; Web: http://www.ealing.gov.uk)
Director of Corporate Resources: Town Hall Annex, London, W5 2BY.
Perceval House: 14-16 Uxbridge Road, London, W5 2HL.

CHIEF OFFICERS

Chief Executive: Ms. Gillian Guy
Director of Corporate Resources: Clyde E. Green
Director of Education: Alan Parker
Director of Environment Group: John Birch
Director of Regeneration and Housing: Chris Dallison
Director of Social Services: Prof. Norman Tutt

MEMBERS OF THE COUNCIL

Councillor	Ward
Mayor: Ranjit Dheer, Lab.	Mount Pleasant
Deputy Mayor: David Bond, Lab.	West End
Leader of the Council: John Cudmore, Lab.	Heathfield
Jasbir Anand, Lab.	Glebe
Joan Ansell, C.	Argyle
Mohammad Aslam, Lab.	Dormers Wells
Tej Ram Bagha, Lab.	Mount Pleasant
Martin Beecroft, Lab.	Walpole
Elizabeth Brooks, Lab.	Heathfield
Anthony Brown, C.	Ealing Common
Brian Castle, C.	Argyle
Umesh Chander, Lab.	Glebe
Julia Clements-Elliott, Lab.	Elthorne
Edward Coleman, Lab.	Elthorne
Katherine Crawford, Lab.	Vale
John Delaney, Lab.	Springfield
Kamaljit Dhindsa, Lab.	Waxlow
Steven Donnelly, Lab.	Springfield
Peter Downham, C.	Mandeville
Fred Dunckley, Lab.	West End
Laurence Evans, Lab.	Costons
Kieron Gavan, Lab.	Northfield
Ian Gibb, C.	Argyle
Richard Gordon, Lab.	Wood End
Tony Gray, Lab.	Victoria
Ian Green, C.	Ealing Common
Phyllis Greenhead, Lab.	Hobbayne
Brenda Hall, C.	Wood End
Eileen Harris, C.	Ealing Common
Joy Hetherington, C.	Costons
Audrey Hider, C.	Pitshanger
Frank Impey, Lab.	West End
Yvonne Johnson, Lab.	Heathfield
Swarn Singh Kang, Lab.	Costons
Manjit Keith, Lab.	Waxlow
Manjit Singh Mahal, Lab.	Northcote
Margaret Majumdar, Lab.	Elthorne
Rajinder Sing Mann, Lab.	Dormers Wells
Shital Manro, Lab.	Horsenden
Andrew Mitchell, LD	Southfield
Glenn Murphy, C.	Mandeville
Diane Murray, Lab.	Ravenor
Inderjeet Singh, Nijhar Lab.	Perivale
Joseph O'Neill, Lab.	Northfield
Diane Pagan, C.	Pitshanger
Rabindara Pathak, Lab.	Glebe
Madhav Patil, Lab.	Mount Pleasant
Christopher Payne, Lab.	Perivale
Margaret Payne, Lab.	Springfield
Ram Perdesi, Lab.	Northcote
Richard Porter, Lab.	Wood End
Philip Portwood, Lab.	Victoria
Ian Potts, C.	Hanger Lane
Royston Price, Lab.	Hobbayne
Rev. N. Richardson, Lab.	Mandeville
Harvey Rose, LD	Southfield
Kieran Ryan, LD	Southfield
Gurdip Singh Sahota, Lab.	Northcote
Stephen Sears, Lab.	Hobbayne
Virendra Sharma, Lab.	Walpole
Gurcharan Singh, Lab.	Waxlow
Jill Stokoe, Lab.	Ravenor
Nigel Sumner C.	Hanger Lane
Leonora Thomson, Lab.	Ravenor
Frederick Varley, Lab.	Hosenden
Surinder Varma, Lab.	Dormers Wells
Peter Wicks, Lab.	Walpole
Paul Woodgate, Lab	Vale
Simon Woodroofe, Lab.	Northfield
Barbara Yerolemou, C.	Hanger Lane
Anthony Young, C.	Pitshanger

Political Composition: Lab. 52; C. 16; LD. 3
Parliamentary Constituencies: Ealing-Acton and Shepherds Bush, Ealing-Southall; Ealing-North.
Population: 298,000
Area: 5,550 hectares.

ABOUT EALING

Ealing encompasses the areas of Ealing, Acton, Hanwell, Southall, Northolt, Perivale and Greenford. Southall is home to one of the major centres in Asian population in the country and there is a substantial African-Caribbean community in Acton. There are nearly 2000 acres of parks and open spaces in Ealing and there is a leisure complex in Park Royal.

London Borough Councils

COUNCIL TAX BANDS 2000-2001

Band	Market Value of the Property in 1991	Council Tax
A	Up to £40,000	£504.10
B	£40,001 to 52,000	£588.12
C	£52,001 to 68,000	£672.13
D	£68,001 to 88,000	£756.15
E	£88,001 to 120,000	£924.18
F	£120,001 to 160,000	£1092.22
G	£160,001 to 320,000	£1260.25
H	£320,001 or more	£1512.30

ENFIELD

Civic Centre, Silver Street, Enfield, EN1 3XA (Tel: 020-8366 6585; Web: http://www.enfield.gov.uk)
Occupational Health Service: Kimberley Gardens, Enfield, London EN1 3ST (Tel: 020-8351 8051; Fax 020-8351 8018)
Trading Standards Officer: Gentleman's Row, Enfield, London, EN2 6PS (Tel: 020-8379 8515)
The Register Office: Public Offices, Gentleman's Row, Enfield EN2 6PS (Tel: 020-8367 5757)

CHIEF OFFICERS

Chief Executive: David Plank
Director of Corporate Services and Solicitor to the Council: Paul Hart
Director of Education: Ms. Liz Graham
Director of Finance: Guy Ware
Director of Housing Services: Donald Graham
Director of Leisure Services: Ms. Christine Neyndorff
Executive Director of Environmental Services: John Pryor
Executive Director of Social Services: Mervyn Eastman

MEMBERS OF THE COUNCIL

Councillor	Ward
Mayor: A. Constantinides, Lab.	Weir Hall
Deputy Mayor: Yasemin Brett, Lab.	Arnos
Leader of the Council: Doug Taylor, Lab.	Green Street
Pamela Adams, C.	Southgate Green
Daniel Anderson, Lab.	Southgate Green
Neil Aves, Lab.	Palmers Green
Brian Barford, Lab.	Huxley
Alan Barker, C.	Highfield
Chris Bond, Lab.	Ponders End
R. Buckley, Lab.	Enfield Wash
David Burrowes, C.	Trent
Stanley Carter, Lab.	Southbury
Bambos Charalambous, Lab.	Palmers Green
Christopher Cole, Lab.	Highfield
J. A. Connew, Lab.	Angel
Betty Costello, Lab.	Angel
Wendell Daniel, Lab.	St. Mark's
Don Delman, C.	Merryhills
Tony Dey, C.	Worcester
John Egan, C.	Town
Graham Eustance, C.	Willow
Foston Fairclough, Lab.	Ponders Green
M. Fenton, Lab.	Craig
Peggy Ford, C.	Chase
Jonathan French, C.	Grovelands
Achilleas Georgiou, Lab.	Bowes
Vivien Giladi, Lab.	Arnos
N. Gilmore, C.	Grange
Derek Goddard, Lab.	Jubilee
J. Gorton, Lab.	Bullsmoor
B. Grayston, Lab.	Enfield Wash
Verna Horridge, Lab.	Hoe Lane
J. W. E. Jackson, C.	Village
Dennis Keighley, C.	Winchmore Hill
Bernadette Lappage, Lab.	Enfield Lock
Michael Lavender, C.	Oakwood
Alasdair MacPhail, C.	Town
Alex Mattingly, Lab.	Craig
Joanne McCartney, Lab.	Weir Hall
Clive Morrison, Lab.	St. Alphege
Christopher Murphy, Lab.	St. Alphege
Danny Neary, Lab.	Bullsmoor
Terence Neville, C.	Winchmore Hill
Ayfer Orhan, Lab.	Green Street
Anne Pearce, C.	Trent
Irene Richards, Lab.	Southbury
Colin Robb, Lab.	St. Peter's
J. Rodin, Lab.	Bowes
Lyn Romain, Lab.	Oakwood
Peter Rust, C.	Grovelands
Michael Rye, C.	Willow
George Savva, Lab.	Huxley
Toby Simon, Lab.	Raglan
Edward Smith, C.	Merryhills
Eric Smythe, Lab.	St. Peter's
Rita Smythe, Lab.	Jubilee
Geoff Southwell, Lab.	Hoe Lane
Phill Sowter, Lab.	Latymer
Austin Spreadbury, C.	Worcester
Andrew Stafford, Lab.	Latymer
M. Sutters, Lab.	Enfield Lock
Glynis Vince, C.	Grange
Mark Walton, Lab.	Raglan
Ivor Wiggett, Lab.	St. Mark's
John Wyatt, C.	Village
J. M. Yates, C.	Chase

Political Composition: Lab. 43; C. 23.
Parliamentary Constituencies: Edmonton; Enfield-North; Enfield-Southgate.
Population: 265,000
Area: 8,218 hectares.

44 Governed London

ABOUT ENFIELD

Enfield is located some 12 miles north of the City on the northern outer edge of the capital. There are numerous parks and open spaces in the borough and there are fourteen conservation areas. Enfield has approximately 113,000 residential dwellings and a substantial number of these are owner-occupied. There are five main shopping centres in the borough along with several out of town superstores and the area is well served by public transport with four overland train services to central London and the Piccadilly underground line.

COUNCIL TAX BANDS 2000-2001

Band	Market Value of the Property in 1991	Council Tax
A	Up to £40,000	£531.53
B	£40,001 to 52,000	£620.12
C	£52,001 to 68,000	£708.71
D	£68,001 to 88,000	£797.30
E	£88,001 to 120,000	£974.48
F	£120,001 to 160,000	£1151.66
G	£160,001 to 320,000	£1328.83
H	£320,001 or more	£1594.60

GREENWICH

Town Hall, Wellington Street, London, SE18 6PW (Tel: 020-8854 8888; Fax: 020-8312 5110; Web: http://www.greenwich.gov.uk)
Chief Executive: Town Hall, Wellington Street, London SE18 6PW (Tel: 020-8921 5000)
Head of Legal Services: 29-37 Wellington Street, London SE18 6PW.
Chief Finance Officer: 45-53 Wellington Street, London, SE18 6RA.
Head of Planning and Regeneration: Peggy Middleton House, 50 Woolwich New Road, London, SE18 6HQ.
Director of Strategic Planning, Director of Public Services, Director of Housing: Peggy Middleton House, 50 Woolwich New Road, London SE18 6HQ.
Director of Social Services: Nelson House, 50 Wellington Street, London, SE18 6HQ (Tel: 020 8854 8888).

CHIEF OFFICERS

Chief Executive: David Brooks
Chief Finance Officer: Paul Dale
Director of Education Services: George Gyte
Director of Housing Services: Ms. Joanna Simons
Director of Social Services: David Behan
Director of Strategic Planning: David McCollum

MEMBERS OF THE COUNCIL

Councillor	Ward
Mayor: J. Sekhon, Lab.	West
Deputy Mayor: T. Malone, Lab.	Tarn
Leader of the Council: C. Roberts, Lab.	St. Alfege
N. R. Adams, Lab.	Kidbrook
D. Austen, Lab	Glyndon
B. Barwick, Lab.	Lakedale
M. Best, Lab.	Ferrier
C. Boothe, Lab.	Lakedale
G. E. Brighty, C.	Blackheath
P. Brooks, Lab.	Thamesmead Mooring
P. M. Challis, Lab.	Slade
A. Cornforth, Lab.	Rectory Field
J. A. Cove, Lab.	Kidbrook
I. A. Danesi, Lab.	Eynsham
M. Devaux, Lab.	Coldharbour
G. S. Dhillon, Lab.	Woolwich Common
L. L. Duvall, Lab.	St. Mary's
John Fahy, Lab.	St. Mary's
W. Freeman, Lab.	Well Hall
J. J. Gillman, Lab.	Trafalgar
J. Gillman, Lab.	Hornfair
A. H. W. Grant, Lab.	Vanbrugh
D. I. Grant, Lab.	Charlton
B. Groves, Lab.	Eynsham
T. Hales, Lab.	Woolwich Common
H. R. Harris, Lab.	Middle Park
R. C. Harris, C.	Blackheath
M. R. Hayes, Lab.	Sherard
Mick Hayes, Lab	Shrewsbury
A. Hills, C.	New Eltham
A. C. Hutchinson, Lab.	Slade
S. Jawaid, Lab.	Charlton
B. A. Jones, Lab.	Herbert
J. Kelly, Lab.	Coldharbour
P. J. H. King, C.	Palace
P. Kotz, Lab.	Thamesmead Mooring
R. E. Lewis, Lab.	Hornfair
A. T. Macrae, Lab.	St. Nicholas
C. Mardner, Lab.	Abbey Wood
Q. Marsh, Lab.	Sherard
N. C. McShee, Lab.	St. Mary's
D. O. Mepsted, C.	New Eltham
A. G. Miles, C.	Deansfield
V. E. Morse, Lab.	Plumstead Common
M. O'Mara, Lab.	West
B. R. O'Sullivan, Lab.	Arsenal
G. Parker, Lab.	Rectory Field
K. M. Patel, Lab.	St. Alfege
M. S. Pattenden, LD	Avery Hill
D. J. Picton, Lab.	Vanbrugh
D. D. Poston, C.	Eltham Park
K. Scott, Lab.	Nightingale
R. Sidhu, Lab.	Herbert

London Borough Councils

J. M. Simpson, C.
C. Slee, Lab.
D. J. Smith, Lab.
D. Steedman, Lab.
B. Taylor, Lab.
J. Wakefield, Lab.
R. Walker, Lab.
B. J. Woodcraft, LD

Eltham Park
St. Nicholas
Ferrier
Abbey Wood
Middle Park
Glyndon
Well Hall
Sutcliffe

Political Composition: Lab. 51; C. 8; LD. 2.
Parliamentary Constituencies: Greenwich and Woolwich; Eltham; Erith and Thamesmead.
Population: 212,073
Area: 5,043 hectares.

ABOUT GREENWICH

Greenwich is the reference point for the World's Time. Set on the banks of the river Thames, Greenwich and is a popular tourist destination outside of central London with attractions such as the Meridian line at the Royal Observatory, The Millennium Dome, The Royal Park, The Royal Naval College and the Cutty Sark Tea Clipper. Greenwich is served by the Docklands Light Railway (DLR) as well as the Jubilee line extension of the London Underground. The Council has introduced a number of projects to regenerate the Borough including a series of developments along the waterfront from Deptford creek to the Greenwich peninsula and Woolwich. These, it is hoped, will bring new employment opportunities, tourism, business as well as housing and leisure facilities.

COUNCIL TAX BANDS 2000-2001

Band	Market Value of the Property in 1991	Council Tax
A	Up to £40,000	£588.90 (£624.00)
B	£40,001 to 52,000	£687.05 (£728.00)
C	£52,001 to 68,000	£785.20 (£832.00)
D	£68,001 to 88,000	£883.35 (£936.00)
E	£88,001 to 120,000	£1079.65 (£1144.00)
F	£120,001 to 160,000	£1275.95 (£1352.00)
G	£160,001 to 320,000	£1472.25 (£1560.00)
H	£320,001 or more	£1766.70 (£1872.00)

Figures in brackets to represent the amount of Council Tax set for dwellings situated in the area surrounding Gloucester Circus Garden Square.

HACKNEY

Town Hall, Mare Street, London, E8 1EA (Tel: 020-8356 5000; Fax: 020-8356 3202;
Web: http://www.hackney.gov.uk)
Haggerston Park, Queensbridge Road, London E2 8PB (Tel: 020-7739 9725)
Emergency Service (Out of Hours) (Tel: 020-8356 2300/2301/2302/2303)
First Stop Shop: Shoreditch Library, Hoxton Street, London, N1 6LP (Tel: 020-8356 4360)
Revenues and Benefits: Dorothy Hodgkins House, Reading Lane, London, E8 1DS (Tel: 020-8356 5000)
Commercial Standards Unit: 205 Morning Lane, London E9 6LG (Tel: 020-8986 4929)
Core Finance: 298 Mare Street, London, E8 1HE (Tel: 020-8356 2618)

Environmental Health Service Unit: 205 Morning Lane, London, E9 6LG (Tel: 020-8356 4771)
Architecture and Planning: 161 City Road, London, EC1V 1NR (Tel: 020-8356 8062)
Leisure and Learning: Edith Cavell Building, Enfield Road, London, N1 5AZ (Tel: 020-8356 5000)
Education: Edith Cavell Building, Enfield Road, London, N1 5AZ (Tel: 020-8356 7341)
Customer and Advice Services: Christopher Addison House, Wilton Way, London, E8 1BJ (Tel: 020-8356 3665)
Estate Management and Development: Christopher Addison House, Wilton Way, London, E8 1BJ (Tel: 020-8356 3671)
Adult Community Services; Services for Older People; Children and Family Services: 205 Morning Lane, London E9 6LG (Tel: 020-8356 5000)

CHIEF OFFICERS

Managing Director: Max Caller
Borough Secretary and Solicitor: Christopher Hinde
Borough Treasurer: George Jenkins
Democratic Services Manager: Peter Loveday
Director of Education: Elizabeth Reid
Executive Director: Joe Duckworth
Executive Director: Lorraine Langham
Head of Communications: vacant

MEMBERS OF THE COUNCIL

Councillor	Ward
Mayor: J. Lobenstein, C.	Springfield
Deputy Mayor: L. Oleforo, Lab.	Rectory
S. M. Achhala, LD	Northwold
Sylvia Anderson, LD	Clissold
D. Bentley, LD	Dalston
A. Bridgewater, LD	Wick
D. Candlin, C.	Moorfield
J. Carswell, Lab.	North Defoe
Y. C. Chong, Ind.	North Defoe
R. Cornell, Lab.	Homerton
P. Corrigan, Lab.	Eastdown
Jessica Crowe, Lab.	Rectory
I. Darbyshire, Lab.	Chatham
K. Daws, LD	Wenlock
Meral Ece, LD	Dalston
Lorraine Fahey, C.	Moorfield
A. Gee-Turner, LD	Wick
Julie Grimble, Lab.	Westdown

46 Governed London

J. Grosskopf, LD	New River
J. Hudson, Lab.	Clissold
N. Hughes, LD	Wick
H. Hyman, LD	Victoria
P. Kenyon, Lab.	Brownswood
I. Leibowitz, C.	Springfield
M. Lewis-Spencer, C.	Northfield
Z. Leiberman, LD	Northwold
Samantha Lloyd, Lab.	Rectory
D. Manion, Lab.	Westdown
Patricia McGuinness, LD	Victoria
Maureen Middleton, C.	New River
Bonnie Miller, Lab.	Leabridge
A. Milton, Lab.	Leabridge
Lindsay Montgomery, C.	Victoria
A. Mulla, Lab.	Leabridge
Sally Mulready, Lab.	Chatham
Vicki Munro, Lab.	Clissold
W. Nicholson, Lab.	Haggerston
C. O'Leary, C.	De Beauvoir
E. Ollerenshaw, C.	Springfield
Bharti Patel, Lab.	Eastdown
Sharon Patrick, Lab.	Homerton
I. Peacock, Lab.	South Defoe
F. Pearson, Lab.	De Beauvoir
P. Pearson, LD	Dalston
B. Peretz, C.	Northfield
Hettie Peters, LD	Queensbridge
D. Phillips, Ind.	New River
Jules Pipe, Lab.	South Defoe
Naomi Russell, Lab.	Chatham
S. Sartain, Lab.	Eastdown
I. Sharer, LD	Northwold
S. Siddiqui, Lab.	Kings Park
C. Sills. C.	Northfield
Linda Smith, Lab.	Brownswood
Kay Stone, LD	Wenlock
M. Williams, LD	Queensbridge
V. Williams, C.	Queensbridge
Andrew Windross, Lab.	De Beauvoir
D. Young, Lab.	Haggerston

Political Composition: Lab. 28, LD. 17, C. 12, Ind. 1.
Parliamentary Constituencies: Hackney North and Stoke Newington; Hackney South and Shoreditch.
Population: 193,843
Area: 1,950 hectares.

ABOUT HACKNEY

Hackney runs north from the City of London to Stamford Hill. It is both an inner city borough and part of the East End. The borough of Hackney was created in 1965 when the metropolitan boroughs of Shoreditch, Stoke Newington and Hackney were merged. Hackney is about 30 minutes journey by train from central London with underground stations, Old Street and Manor House and 10 over-ground stations. The borough's first tube line will be the northern extension of the East London Line, from Whitechapel through Dalston to Highbury and Islington. Four new stations will be at Bishopsgate, Hoxton, Haggerston and Dalston Junction. It is expected that they will be open by 2004.

COUNCIL TAX BANDS 2000-2001

Band	Market Value of the Property in 1991	Council Tax
A	Up to £40,000	£467.84
B	£40,001 to 52,000	£545.82
C	£52,001 to 68,000	£623.79
D	£68,001 to 88,000	£701.77
E	£88,001 to 120,000	£857.72
F	£120,001 to 160,000	£1013.67
G	£160,001 to 320,000	£1169.01
H	£320,001 or more	£1403.54

HAMMERSMITH AND FULHAM

HAMMERSMITH & FULHAM

Town Hall, London, W6 9JU (Tel: 020-8748 3020; Web: http://www.lbhf.gov.uk)
Advice Centre: 338 Uxbridge Road, London, W12 7LL (Tel: 020 8743 6953)
Director of Housing: Housing Centre, Glenthorne Road, London, W6 9BR (Tel: 020-8748 3020)
Director of Social Services: 145-155 King Street, London (Tel: 020-8748 3020)
Director of Education: Cambridge House, London (Tel: 020-8748 3020)
Registration of Births, Deaths and Marriages: The Register Office, Nigel Playfair Avenue, London W6 9JY (Tel: 020-8576 5032)

CHIEF OFFICERS

Managing Director: Richard Harbord
Director of Education: Ms C. Whatford
Director of Environment: Peter Bishop
Director of Housing Services: B. Simons
Director of Policy and Information: Henry Peterson
Director of Social Services: Geoff Alltimes

MEMBERS OF THE COUNCIL

Councillor	Ward
Mayor: A. F. Slaughter, Lab.	Gibbs Green
C. Aherne, Lab.	Wormholt
Emile Al-Uzaizi, C.	Palace
A. Alford, C.	Colehill
Chris Allen, Lab.	Grove
B. Bird, Lab.	Sands End
Min Birdsey, Lab.	Magravine
D. Blaney, C.	Eel Brook

N. Botterill, C. — Sulivan
R. E. Browne, Lab. — White City and Shepherds Bush
S. Burke, Lab. — Wormholt
M. Cartwright, Lab. — Broadway
Joan Caruana, Lab. — Normand
Siobhan Coughlan, Lab. — Addison
S. Cowan, Lab. — Grove
H. Davies, Lab. — Broadway
Fiona Evans, Lab. — Ravenscourt
J. Garrett, Lab. — Sherbrooke
I. Gibbons, Lab. — White City and Shepherds Bush
Christine Graham, Lab. — Coningham
A. Gray, Lab. — Crabtree
S. Greenhalgh, C. — Town
A. Ground, C. — Palace
Greg Hands, C. — Eel Brook
W. Harcourt, Lab. — College Park and Old Oak
Polly Hicks, Lab. — Brook Green
J. Hillman, Lab. — Starch Green
Sonya Hilton, C. — Avonmore
Lisa Homan, Lab. — Magravine
G. Johnson, Lab. — Brook Green
Ghassan Karian, Lab. — Addison
T. Kennedy Harper, C. — Sherbrooke
Jafar Khaled, Lab. — White City and Shepherds Bush
A. Lillis, C. — Town
Amanda Lloyd Harris, C. — Crabtree
K. Mallinson, Ind. — Avonmore
R. McLaughlin, Lab. — College Park and Old Oak
C. Pavelin, Lab. — Sands End
Sally Powell, Lab. — Wormholt
Hefin Rees, Lab. — Ravenscourt
C. Round, C. — Colehill
Melanie Smallman, Lab. — College Park and Old Oak
Frances Stainton, C. — Walham
T. Stanley, Lab. — Coningham
C. Treloggan, Lab. — Gibbs Green
Jenny Vaughan, Lab. — Walham
Josie Wicks, Lab. — Coningham
G. Wilkinson, Lab. — Starch Green
D. Williams, Lab. — Normand
G. Wombwell, C. — Sulivan

Political Composition: Lab. 35; C. 14; Ind. 1
Parliamentary Constituencies: Ealing, Acton and Shepherds Bush, Hammersmith and Fulham.
Population: 157,000
Area: 1,617 hectares.

ABOUT HAMMERSMITH AND FULHAM

The Borough of Hammersmith and Fulham is located near the heart of London. Until 1965 the boroughs of Hammersmith and Fulham were separate. It is the fourth smallest London Borough and has the fourth highest population density. There are numerous transport links within the borough including the Metropolitan, Piccadilly and District lines of the underground. The A4 also connects Hammersmith to Heathrow airport and the M4. The borough is served by three road bridges, Hammersmith, Putney and Wandsworth. The BBC is the largest employer in the borough with almost 8,000 staff working at Television Centre and the rest of the White City Complex. Hammersmith and Fulham is also home to companies such as Coca Cola, HarperCollins, Haymarket Publications, EMI, and Seagram. House prices in Hammersmith and Fulham are on average the fourth highest in London. The council has therefore made the provision of affordable rented housing one of its key objectives.

COUNCIL TAX BANDS 2000-2001

Band	Market Value of the Property in 1991	Council Tax
A	Up to £40,000	£551.35
B	£40,001 to 52,000	£643.24
C	£52,001 to 68,000	£735.13
D	£68,001 to 88,000	£827.02
E	£88,001 to 120,000	£1010.80
F	£120,001 to 160,000	£1194.58
G	£160,001 to 320,000	£1378.37
H	£320,001 or more	£1654.84

HARINGEY

All Departments: Civic Centre, PO Box 264, High Road, London, N22 4LF. (Tel: 020 8489 0000; Web: http://www.haringey.gov.uk)

CHIEF OFFICERS

Chief Executive: Gurbux Singh
Assistant Chief Executive (Policy, Planning and Performance Management): Gill Davies
Assistant Chief Executive (Regeneration and Partnership): Chris Shellard
Director of Corporate Services: David Warwick
Director of Education Services: Frances Magee
Director of Environmental Services: Peter Norton
Director of Housing and Social Services: Mary Richardson

MEMBERS OF THE COUNCIL

Councillor	Ward
Mayor: H. Brown, Lab.	Bruce Grove
Deputy Mayor: Mary Neuner, Lab.	Alexandra
Leader of the Council: G. Meehan, Lab.	Woodside

48 Governed London

Gina Adamou, Lab.	Harringay
C. Adje, Lab.	White Hart Lane
June Andersen, LD.	
Lucinda Arnold, Lab.	Bowes
Jane Atkinson, Lab.	South Hornsey
D. Basu, Lab.	Seven Sister
Judy Bax, Lab.	Archway
Sally Billot, Lab.	South Hornsey
R. Blanchard, Lab.	Harringay
S. Brasher, Lab.	Bruce Grove
Jean C. Brown, Lab.	Noel
Jean E. Brown, Lab.	White Hart Lane
N. Canver, Lab.	South Tottenham
N. Cleeveley, Lab.	Green Lanes
Lucy Craig, Lab.	Alexandra
T. Davidson, Lab.	Bowes
Maureen Dewar, Lab.	Coleraine
Isidoros Diakides, Lab.	High Cross
D. Dillon, Lab.	Woodside
R. Dodds, Lab.	Park
P. Droussiotis, Lab.	Alexandra
Susan Eedle, Lab.	Fortis Green
Lynne Featherstone, LD.	Muswell Hill
P. J. Forrest, C.	Highgate
Nicky Gavron, Lab.	Archway
Julia Glenn, LD.	Muswell Hill
B. Haley, Lab.	Green Lanes
B. Harris, Lab.	Tottenham Central
Toby Harris, Lab.	Hornsey Central
S. Horne, Lab.	Hornsey Vale
Josie Irwin, Lab.	Hornsey Vale
H. Jones, Lab.	White Hart
P. Jones, Lab.	West Green
Iris Josiah, Lab.	South Tottenham
A. Knight, Lab.	Seven Sister
W. MacDougall, C.	Highgate
Narendra Makanji, Lab.	Noel
Vivienne Mannheim, Lab.	Bowes
R. Muhal, Lab.	West Green
J. Patel, Lab.	Woodside
Sheila Peacock, Lab.	Park
D. Predergast, Lab.	Fortis Green
G. Rahman Khan, Lab.	West Green
S. Reeve, Lab.	Tottenham Central
R. Reynolds, Lab.	Tottenham Central
R. Rice, Lab.	Coleraine
A. Richardson, Lab.	Fortis Green
Irene Robertson, Lab.	Bruce Grove
C. Sandbach, Lab.	Crouch End
C. Sharp, Lab.	Crouch End
Catherine Stafford, Lab.	Hornsey Central
A. Stanton, Lab.	High Cross
Takki Sulaiman, Lab.	Harringay
Bernice Vanier, Lab.	Coleraine
N. Wilmott, Lab.	Crouch End
A. Zaman, Lab.	Noel

Political Composition: Lab. 54; LD. 3; C. 2.
Parliamentary Constituencies: Hornsey and Wood Green; Tottenham.
Population: 216,000
Area: 11.5 square miles

ABOUT HARINGEY

Haringey was formed in 1965 from the boroughs of Hornsey, Tottenham and Wood Green. Bus and rail networks link Haringey to the rest of London as do the Piccadilly and Victoria lines of the Underground. Haringey largely consists of residential areas although hi-tech industry is a rapidly developing trend, notably at the Lee Park Technopark. The Service sector and cultural industries are also flourishing and clothing and textiles are growth sectors.

COUNCIL TAX BANDS 2000-2001

Band	Market Value of the Property in 1991	Council Tax
A	Up to £40,000	£621.33
B	£40,001 to 52,000	£724.89
C	£52,001 to 68,000	£828.44
D	£68,001 to 88,000	£932
E	£88,001 to 120,000	£1139.11
F	£120,001 to 160,000	£1346.22
G	£160,001 to 320,000	£1553.33
H	£320,001 or more	£1864

HARROW

Civic Centre, Station Road, Harrow HA1 2XF
(Tel: 020-8863 5611;
Web: http://www.harrow.gov.uk)

CHIEF OFFICERS

Chief Executive and Director of Finance: A. G. Redmond
Borough Secretary and Solicitor to the Council: G. Balabanof
Chief Environmental Health Officer: M. Esom
Director of Education: Paul Osburn
Director of Environmental Services: T. Pugh
Director of Social Services: Ms Mary Ney
Head of Children and Families and Provided Services: Ms Jo Blake
Head of Contract Services: A. Trehern
Head of Corporate and Information Technology Services: M. Walklate
Head of Environment, Planning and Transportation: B. Hodgson
Head of Financial and Exchequer Services: Ms C. Cutler

London Borough Councils 49

Head of Housing and Environmental Health: M. Wright
Head of Property and Construction: G. Easton
Head of School and Community Services: M. Hart
Head of Strategy and Care Management: D. Burnell
Head of Strategy and Resources: Ms. S. Ernstoff

MEMBERS OF THE COUNCIL

Councillor	Ward
Mayor: K. Thammaiah, Lab.	Centenary
Deputy Mayor: Jerry J. Miles, Lab.	Roxeth
A. Alexander, LD	Rayners Lane
D. J. Ashton, C.	Wemborough
Marilyn Ashton, C.	Stanmore Park
Anastasia Attaki, Lab.	Greenhill
Camilla Bath, C.	Stanmore Park
Christine Bednell, C.	Stanmore Park
H. S. Bluston, Lab.	Greenhill
S. Brown, Lab.	Stanmore South
K. Burchell, Lab.	Stanmore South
Lurline Champagnie, C.	Pinner
A. Cocksedge, C.	Pinner
Janet Cowan, C.	Canons
John Cowan, C.	Canons
C. Cox, RA	Wemborough
L. Cox, LD	Roxeth
J. Cripps, RA	Roxeth
Bob Currie, Lab.	Roxbourne
C. Davies, Lab.	Kenton West
H. Davies, Lab.	Harrow on the Hill
Margaret Davine, Lab.	Stanmore South
M. Dharmarajah, Lab.	Roxbourne
Anne Diamond, LD	Wemborough
Sanjay Dighe, Lab.	Kenton West
A. T. Foulds, Lab.	Kenton East
P. Fox, Lab.	Ridgeway
R. Frogley, Lab.	Kenton West
B. E. Gate, Lab.	Ridgeway
Mary Graham, LD	Harrow Weald
Mitzi Green, Lab.	Centenary
Ann Groves, Lab.	Marlborough
C. Harrison, Lab.	Wealdstone
G. M. Howard, C.	Pinner West
M. Ingram, Lab.	Roxbourne
Mary John, C.	Hatch End
D. M. Kerr, Lab.	Greenhill
Eileen Kinnear, C.	Harrow on the Hill
A. C. Knowles, C.	Hatch End
J. Lammiman, C.	Hatch End
Nicola Lane, LD	Headstone North
P. Lyne, LD	Harrow Weald
Ahmed Marikar, LD	Harrow Weald
Chris Mote, C.	Pinner West
P. Nandhra, LD	Rayners Lane
J. W. Nickolay, C.	Pinner West
C. D. Noyce, LD	Rayners Lane
P. O'Dell, Lab.	Marlborough
A. R. Olins, C.	Pinner
D. Redford, Lab.	Centenary
R. D. Romain, C.	Canons
C. Scowen, C.	Harrow on the Hill
A. Seymour, C.	Headstone North
N. Shah, Lab.	Kenton East
Bob Shannon, Lab.	Wealdstone
E. Silver, C.	Headstone North
Margaret Sims, Lab.	Marlborough
B. Stephenson, Lab.	Headstone South
N. Stillerman, Lab	Ridgeway
Ann Swain, Lab.	Wealdstone
K. Toms, Lab.	Kenton East
Gillian Travers, Lab.	Headstone South
Anne Whitehead, Lab.	Headstone South

Political Composition: Lab. 32; C. 20; LD. 9; RA. 2.
Parliamentary Constituencies: Harrow East; Harrow West.
Population: 210,000
Area: 5,036 hectares.

ABOUT HARROW

Harrow is situated in the North west of London and is surrounded by green belt land. Harrow Borough Council has been awarded Beacon Status, given in recognition of the achievements of the Council in 'modern service delivery', particularly its system for handling Council Tax and Housing Benefit. The borough is primarily residential with numerous transport links with the rest of London. It contains more that 50 parks and open spaces. Sights of architectural and historical interest include the Harrow Museum and Heritage Centre. This site is a registered ancient monument and contains a 16th Century Tithe barn and a 14th Century moated manor house.

COUNCIL TAX BANDS 2000-2001

Band	Market Value of the Property in 1991	Council Tax
A	Up to £40,000	£568.42
B	£40,001 to 52,000	£663.16
C	£52,001 to 68,000	£757.89
D	£68,001 to 88,000	£852.63
E	£88,001 to 120,000	£1042.10
F	£120,001 to 160,000	£1231.58
G	£160,001 to 320,000	£1421.05
H	£320,001 or more	£1705.26

HAVERING

Havering Town Hall, Romford, RM1 3BD
(Tel: 01708 434343; Fax: 01708 432058;
Email: info@havering.gov.uk;
Web: http://www.havering.gov.uk)

50 Governed London

Environment and Planning, Development Control, Transportation and Engineering: Mercury House, Mercury Gardens, Romford, RM1 3DS.
Children and Lifelong Learning: Broxhill Centre, Broxhill Road, Harold Hill, Romford, RM4 1XN.
Social Services: Whitworth Centre, Noak Hill Road, Harold Hill, Romford, RM3 7YA (Tel: 01708 434343; Fax 01708 433010)
Housing: 71-73 Gooshays Gardens, Harold Hill, Romford, RM3 8AF (Tel: 01708 349200; Fax 01708 349156)
Architectural and Engineering Services: Whitworth Centre, Noak Hill Road, Harold Hill, Romford, RM3 7YA (Tel: 01708 434343; Fax 01708 433010)
Contract Services and Direct Service Organisation: Administrative Offices, Upper Rainham Road, Hornchurch RM12 4ET.
Central Library: Main Road, Romford, RM1 3AR (Tel: 01708 434343; Fax: 01708 432391)
Resources: Havering Town Hall, Romford, RM1 3BD (Tel: 01708 434343)
Legal Services: Ballard Chambers, 26 High Street, Romford, RM1 1HR
Registration of Births, Deaths and Marriages: Langtons, Billet Lane, Hornchurch, Essex RM11 1XL (Tel: 01708 434343; Fax: 01708 432391)

CHIEF OFFICERS

Chief Executive: Harold W. Tinworth
Executive Director (Children and Lifelong Learning): Stephen Evans
Executive Director (Community Services): Anthony Douglas
Executive Director (Enterprise Services): Heather Bonfield
Executive Director (Environment): Jim Paterson
Executive Director (Resources): Barry Arden

MEMBERS OF THE COUNCIL

Councillor	Ward
Mayor: Brian E. Eagling, Lab.	Harold Wood
Deputy Mayor: Harry Webb, Lab.	Rainham
Leader of the Council: Ray Harris, Lab.	Elm Park
Tom Binding, Lab.	South Hornchurch
Edward Cahill, C.	Ardleigh
Eileen Cameron, RA	Hacton
Ivor Cameron, RA	Hacton
Ken Clark, Lab.	Heaton
Jonathan Coles, LD	Harold Wood
Raymond Connelly, Lab.	St. Edward's
Yve Cornell, Lab.	Gooshays
Pam Craig, Lab.	Mawney
Andrew Curtin, C.	Collier Row
Janet Davis, Lab.	Elm Park
Tony Ellis, Lab.	Rainham
Ray Emmett, Lab.	Airfield
Valerie Evans, RA	Gidea Park
Mark Gadd, C.	Ardleigh Green
P. C. Gardner, C.	Emerson Park
Bill Harrison, Lab.	Gooshays
Linda Hawthorn, RA	Upminster
David Hill, Lab.	Hilldene
Jack Hoepelman, Lab.	Elm Park
Brian F. Kent, Lab.	Rainham
Bob Kilbey, Lab.	Mawney
Margaret Latham, Lab.	Heaton
Geoff Lewis, RA	Cranham East
Joan Lewis, RA	Cranham West
Len Long, RA	South Hornchurch
Eamonn Mahon, Lab.	Brooklands
Sheila McCole, Lab.	Mawney
Nigel Meyer, LD	Oldchurch
Wilfrid Mills, Lab.	Hilldene
Jean Mitchell, Lab.	Cranham East
E. A. Munday, C.	Heath Park
John Mylod, RA	St. Andrew's
Patricia Mylod, RA	Upminster
Barry Norwin, Lab.	Airfield
Denis O'Flynn, Lab.	Heaton
Chris Oliver, RA	St. Andrew's
Chris Purnell, Lab.	Airfield
Barbara Reith, RA	Hacton
Ann Roberts, Lab.	Hilldene
Kevin Robinson, Lab.	Gooshays
Paul Rochford, C.	Emerson Park
Andrew Rosindell, C.	Chase Cross
Ray Shaw, Lab.	Hylands
Louise Sinclair, RA	Cranham West
Jeff Stafford, Lab.	Brooklands
Geoffrey Starns, C.	Collier Row
Alby Tebbutt, C.	Chase Cross
Wendy Thompson, C.	St. Edward's
Owen Ware, RA	Upminster
Joseph Webster, C.	Rise Park
Michael White, C.	Heath Park
Maisie Whitelock, Lab.	Hylands
Reg Whitney, RA	South Hornchurch
Ian Wilkes, RA	Gidea Park
Mike Winter, RA	St. Andrew's
Caroline Wood, Lab.	Harold Wood
Mike Wood, Lab.	Hylands
Malcolm Zetter, LD.	Oldchurch

Political Composition: Lab. 31; RA. 16; C. 12; LD. 3
Parliamentary Constituencies: Hornchurch; Upminster; Romford.
Population: 230,000
Area: 40 square miles

ABOUT HAVERING

Havering is the second largest borough in Greater London with an area of 40 square miles, 24 of which are green belt. The Borough was created in 1965 in merger of the former Borough of Romford and the Urban District Council of Hornchurch. The name Havering originates from the village of Havering-atte-Bower, where at one time there was a royal palace. Havering is a successful business and commercial Centre with access to the M25 and River Thames frontage of three miles in the south.

COUNCIL TAX BANDS 2000-2001

Band	Market Value of the Property in 1991	Council Tax
A	Up to £40,000	£568.67
B	£40,001 to 52,000	£663.44
C	£52,001 to 68,000	£758.23
D	£68,001 to 88,000	£853.00

London Borough Councils 51

E	£88,001 to 120,000	£1042.56
F	£120,001 to 160,000	£1232.11
G	£160,001 to 320,000	£1422.67
H	£320,001 or more	£1706.00

HILLINGDON

Civic Centre, Uxbridge, UB8 1UW (Tel: 01895 250111; Fax 01895 273636; Web: http://www.hillingdon.gov.uk)
Borough Information Centre: 14-15 High Street, Uxbridge, UB8 1HD (Tel: 01895 250600)

CHIEF OFFICERS

Chief Executive: Dorian Leatham
Assistant Chief Executive: Tom Moloney
Corporate Director, Corporate Services: Ms. Amanda Kelly
Corporate Director of Education, Youth and Leisure Services: Phillip O'Hear
Corporate Director of Environmental Services: Ruth Willis
Corporate Director of Housing Services: Pam Lockley
Corporate Director of Social Services: Graeme Betts

MEMBERS OF THE COUNCIL

Councillor	Ward
Mayor: A. Kanjee, C.	Colham
Deputy Mayor: Catherine Dann, C.	Eastcote
D. Allam, Lab.	Yeading
Lynne Allen, Lab.	Botwell
Ann Banks, C.	West Drayton
D. Banks, C.	Yiewsley
R. Barnes, C.	Ickenham
Josephine Barrett, C.	Hillingdon West
R. Benson, C.	Northwood
J. Bianco, C.	Northwood Hills
D. Bishop, C.	Northwood Hills
Lindsay Bliss, Lab.	Branhill
Janet Campbell, LD	Cavendish
S. Carey, LD	Cavendish
D. Chand, Lab.	Townfield
G. Cooper, C.	Uxbridge North
P. Corthorne, C.	St. Martin's
G. Courtenay, C.	Cowley
M. C. Craxton, Lab.	Charville
Parmjit Dhanda, Lab.	Yeading
Mahan Dhillon, Lab.	Yeading
Janet Gardner, Lab.	Wood End
Jacqueline Griffith, C.	Ickenham
P. K. Harmsworth, Lab.	Yiewsley
Shirley Harper-O'Neill, C.	Bourne
E. Harris, Lab.	Charville
M. Heywood, C.	Uxbridge North
R. Hill, Lab.	Townfield
G. Horn, C.	Eastcote
D. Horne, Lab.	Hillingdon East
Sandra Jenkins, C.	Harefield
J. Jonas, Lab.	Uxbridge South
Mohammed Khursheed, Lab.	Colham
M. Kilbey, C.	Ruislip
Maurice Lancaster, C.	Ruislip
A. G. Langley, C.	Hillingdon West
J. Major, Lab.	Barnhill
R. Marshall, Lab.	Cowley
I. McIntosh, Lab.	Hillingdon East
D. S. Mills, C.	St. Martin's
M. Miraj, C.	Manor
A. Morrison, Lab.	Colham
J. Morse, Lab.	Bourne
Caroline Mutton, C.	Harefield
B. T. Neighbour, Lab.	Harlington
N. Nunn-Price, Lab.	Botwell
J. O'Neill, C.	Deansfield
A. O'Shea, Lab.	Uxbridge South
J. Oswell, Lab.	Crane
S. Ouseley, Lab.	Charville
D. Patel, C.	West Drayton
C. Pattenden, Lab.	Crane
D. Payne, C.	Eastcote
R. Puddifoot, C.	Ickenham
A. Retter, C.	Northwood Hills
Jill Rhodes, LD	Hillingdon North
Valerie Robins, C.	Hillingdon West
P. M. Ryerson, Lab.	Wood End
S. Seaman-Digby, C.	Northwood
D. Simmonds, C.	Cowley
Jeanne Smith, Lab.	Townfield
Catherine Stocker, Lab.	Heathrow
Solveig Stone, C.	Deansfield
G. R. Tomlin, Lab.	Harlington
M. Usher, Lab.	Heathrow
A. Vernazza, LD	Hillingdon North
A. Way, Lab.	Barnhill
Marion Way, Lab.	Harlington
D. A. Yarrow, C.	Manor

Political Composition: C. 33; Lab. 32; LD. 4.
Parliamentary Constituencies: Hayes and Harlington; Ruislip-Northwood; Uxbridge.
Population: 231,602
Area: 11,240 hectares.

ABOUT HILLINGDON

The London Borough of Hillingdon covers the North west corner of the former County of Middlesex. In 1965 the Borough of Uxbridge and the Urban Districts of Hayes and Harlington, Yiewsley and West Drayton and Ruislip-Northwood were amalgamated to form the Borough.

52 Governed London

COUNCIL TAX BANDS 2000-2001

Band	Market Value of the Property in 1991	Council Tax
A	Up to £40,000	£549.41
B	£40,001 to 52,000	£640.97
C	£52,001 to 68,000	£732.54
D	£68,001 to 88,000	£824.11
E	£88,001 to 120,000	£1007.24
F	£120,001 to 160,000	£1190.38
G	£160,001 to 320,000	£1373.51
H	£320,001 or more	£1648.22

HOUNSLOW

Civic Centre, Lampton Road, Hounslow, TW3 4DN (Tel: 020-8570 2000; Fax: 020-8583 2598; Web: http://www.hounslow.gov.uk)
Registration of Births, Deaths and Marriages: The Register Office, 88 Lampton Road, Hounslow TW3 4DW (Tel: 020-8862 5112)

CHIEF OFFICERS

Chief Executive: Derek Myers
Acting Director of Social Services: Susanna White
Borough Solicitor: Mike Smith
Borough Treasurer: Alan Steele
Director of Cultural and Community Investment: Howard Simmons
Director of Education: Doug Trickett
Director of Environmental Services: John Evans
Director of Housing: Chris Langstaff
Head of Economic Development: Abdul Rashid Craig
Head of Information and Communication: vacant
Head of Members Services: Robert Wearing
Head of Public Services: Simon Caplan
Head of Revenues Services: Ray Keech
Head of Strategic Personnel: Willie Griffin
Head of Strategic Property: Graham Smith

MEMBERS OF THE COUNCIL

Councillor	Ward
Mayor: Devinder Sandhu, Lab.	East Bedfont
Deputy Mayor: Mohinder Gill, Lab.	Heston Central
Govind Agarwal, Lab.	Hounslow South
Philip Andrews, O.	Isleworth South
Norah Atkins, C.	Chiswick Homefields
Ronald Bartholomew, Lab.	Isleworth North
Rajinder Bath, Lab.	Heston West
L. Bawn, Lab.	Feltham South
Premila Bhanderi, C.	Spring Grove
Kamikar Brar, Lab.	Feltham Central
Tristan Bunnell, Lab.	Gunnersbury
Ruth Cadbury, Lab.	Brentford Clifden
Peter Carey, C.	Spring Grove
Michael Carman, Lab.	Brentford Clifden
John Chatt, Lab.	Feltham North
Mohammed Chaudhary, Lab.	Heston West
Dalbir Cheema, Lab.	Hounslow West
Krishan Chopra, Lab.	Hounslow Heath
Roger Clarke, Lab.	Heston West
Melvin Collins, Lab.	Gunnersbury
John Connelly, Lab.	Hounslow West
Samantha Davies, C.	Turnham Green
Sukhbir Dhaliwal, Lab.	Cranford
Ajmer Dhillon, Lab.	Hounslow Heath
Gopal Dhillon, Lab.	Heston Central
Jagir Dhillon, Lab.	Cranford
Colin Driscoll, Lab.	Feltham Central
Colin Ellar, Lab.	Feltham Central
Raymond Fincher, LD	Hanworth
Darshan Grewal, Lab.	Hounslow West
Herbert Ham, Lab.	Feltham South
Christine Hay, Lab.	Hounslow South
Walter Hill, C.	Hounslow South
Peter Hills, LD	Hanworth
David Hopkins, Lab.	Gunnersbury
David Hughes, Lab.	East Bedfont
Michael Hunt, Lab.	Feltham North
Sahm Jassar, Lab.	Hounslow Central
Harbans Kanwal, Lab.	Cranford
James Kenna, Lab.	Heston West
Ilyas Khwaja, Lab.	Hounslow Central
Robert Kinghorn, C.	Chiswick Riverside
Valerie Lamey, Lab.	Brentford Clifden
Josephine Langton, C.	Chiswick Riverside
Adrian Lee C.	Turnham Green
Paul Lynch, C.	Chiswick Riverside
Amritpal Mann, Lab.	Heston East
Andrew Morgan-Watts, LD	Hanworth
John Murphy, LD	Feltham South
Patricia Nicholas, Lab.	Isleworth South
Brian Price, Lab.	East Bedfont
Barbara Reid, C.	Spring Grove
Jagdish Rai Sharma, Lab.	Hounslow Heath
Corinna Smart, Lab.	Isleworth North
Vanessa Smith, Lab.	Isleworth South
Patricia Sterne, Lab.	Chiswick Homefields
Peter Thompson, C.	Turnham Green
Janet Tindall, Lab.	Isleworth North
Stuart Walmsley, Lab.	Feltham North
Pamela Wharfe, Lab.	Hounslow Central

Political Compositon: Lab. 44; C.11; LD. 4; O. 1.
Parliamentary Constituencies: Brentford and Isleworth, Feltham and Heston.
Population: 205,000
Area: 5,852 hectares.

London Borough Councils

ABOUT HOUNSLOW

The borough stretches from Chiswick in the east to Heathrow Airport in the west. The borough has a lot to offer in terms of culture and history and boasts a variety of historic homes and gardens including Osterley Park, Syon House, Chiswick House, Hogarth's House, Boston Manor House and Gunnersbury Park. Other attractions include Waterman's Arts Centre, The Paul Robeson Theatre and the Kew Bridge Steam Museum. The borough benefits from a variety of cultures and communities with over a quarter of residents from ethnic minorities.

COUNCIL TAX BANDS 2000-2001

Band	Market Value of the Property in 1991	Council Tax
A	Up to £40,000	£573.43
B	£40,001 to 52,000	£669.01
C	£52,001 to 68,000	£764.58
D	£68,001 to 88,000	£860.15
E	£88,001 to 120,000	£1051.29
F	£120,001 to 160,000	£1242.44
G	£160,001 to 320,000	£1433.58
H	£320,001 or more	£1720.30

ISLINGTON

Town Hall, Upper Street, London N1 2UD (Tel: 020-7226 1234; Web: http://www.islington.gov.uk)
Education Department: Laycock Street, London N1 1TH (Tel: 020-7457 5753; Fax: 020-7457 5903)
Environment, Leisure, IT, Human Resources, Planning, Finance and Property: Municipal Offices, 222 Upper Street, London, N1 1XR (Tel: 020-7477 4525; Fax: 020-7447 4642)
Housing and Social Services: Highbury House, 5 Highbury Crescent, London N1 1XR (Tel: 020-7477 4293/4294; Fax: 020-7477 4118)
Islington Building Services: Ashburton House, Ashburton Grove, London N7 7AA (Tel: 020-7457 4648; Fax: 020-7457 4948)
Central Library: 2 Fieldway Crescent, London, N5 1PF (Tel: 020-7226 1234)
Play and Youth: Block B Barnsbury Complex, Offord Road, London N1 1TH (Tel: 020-7457 5822; Fax: 020-7457 5547)

CHIEF OFFICERS

Chief Executive: Leisha Fullick
Executive Director: Jonathan Slater
Executive Director: Nick Sharman
Executive Director: Stan Szaroleta
Executive Director: Valerie Vaughan-Dick
Head of Corporate Strategy: Ms Beverly Taylor
Head of Education: Mike Clayden
Head of Environment and Leisure: Lesley Carter
Head of Housing Services: Andy Jenkins
Head of Human Resources Development: Claudette Francis
Head of Information and Customer Services: Jennifer Powell.
Head of Information Technology and Systems: Susan Cahill
Head of Islington Building Services: Peter Hayter
Head of Law and Public Services: Jane Ramsey
Head of Play and Youth: Jane Dixon
Head of Regulatory Planning: Ian Crawley
Head of Social and Economic Regeneration and Partnership: Martin Smith
Head of Social Services: P. Curran
Head of Strategic Finance, Audit and Property Services: Steve Hughes

MEMBERS OF THE COUNCIL

Councillor	Ward
Mayor: Mary Powell, LD	St. Peter
Deputy Mayor: J. Trotter, LD	Bunhill
Leader of the Council: D. Sawyer, Lab.	Tollington
G. Allan, LD	Clerkenwell
Jeanette Arnold, Lab.	Mildmay
D. Barnes, LD	Quadrant
Rosey Blackmore, Lab.	St. George's
D. Bonner, Lab.	Sussex
M. Boye-Annwomah, Lab.	Mildmay
Janet Burgess, Lab.	Junction
Wally Burgess, Lab.	St. George's
Sheila Camp, Lab.	Hillrise
A. Clinton, Lab.	Hillrise
Joan Coupland, LD	St. Mary
Isobel Cox, LD	St. Mary
Mary Creagh, Lab.	Highbury
Mary Dearth, LD	Canonbury East
Margot Dunn, LD	Holloway
E. Featherstone, LD	Hillmarton
Bridget Fox, LD	Barnsbury
Paul Fox, LD	Hillrise
R. Greening, Lab.	Gillespie
Edna Griffiths, Lab.	Thornhill
Pat Haynes, Lab.	Mildmay
R. Heseltine, LD	St. Mary
Meg Hillier, Lab.	Sussex
S. Hitchens, LD	St. Peter
Isabelle Humphreys, LD	Clerkenwell
Talal Karim, Lab.	Junction
J. Kempton, LD	Holloway
Maureen Leigh, Lab.	Highbury
A. Loraine, LD	Barnsbury
Sandy Marks, Lab.	Junction
N. Mason, Lab.	Gillespie
Ruari McCourt, Lab.	Highview
R. McKenzie, Lab.	Tollington

54 Governed London

Shonagh Methven, Lab.
B. Neave, LD
R. Perry, Lab.
Carol Powell, LD
Chris Pryce, LD
Jenny Rathbone, Lab.
Angela Ribezzo, LD
Jenny Sands, Lab.
Doreen Scott, LD
Barbara Sidnell, Lab.
Barbara Smith, LD
D. Taylor, LD
Jyoti Vaja, LD
R. Washington, LD
Laura Willoughby, LD
Rose Wooding, LD.

St. George's
Clerkenwell
Thornhill
Barnsbury
St. Peter
Highbury
Canonbury West
Highview
Hillmarton
Tollington
Canonbury West
Holloway
Bunhill
Canonbury East
Quadrant
Bunhill

Political Composition: Lab. 25, LD. 27.
Parliamentary Constituencies: Islington North, Islington South and Finsbury.
Population: 176,800
Area: 1,489 hectares.

ABOUT ISLINGTON

Situated just north of the City, the borough of Islington has strong historical connections with entertainment and craftsmanship. Sadlers Wells is situated in the borough and the area of Clerkenwell is renowned for crafts such as jewellery and clock-making. There are a number of educational institutions in the borough including the City University and the University of North London and the borough is rich in cultural and leisure facilities. Islington is home to Arsenal Football Club and St John's Gate at Clerkenwell is one of the oldest surviving buildings in the borough which houses a collection of paintings, silverware and furniture highlighting periods in the history of St John of Jerusalem.

COUNCIL TAX BANDS 2000-2001

Band	Market Value of the Property in 1991	Council Tax
A	Up to £40,000	£591.34
B	£40,001 to 52,000	£689.89
C	£52,001 to 68,000	£788.45
D	£68,001 to 88,000	£887.00
E	£88,001 to 120,000	£1084.11
F	£120,001 to 160,000	£1281.22
G	£160,001 to 320,000	£1478.34
H	£320,001 or more	£1774.00

ROYAL BOROUGH OF KENSINGTON AND CHELSEA

Town Hall, Hornton Street, London W8 7NX (Tel: 020-7937 5464; Fax 020-7938 1445; Web: http://www.rbkc.gov.uk)
Central Library: Hornton Street, London, W8 5HX (Tel: 020-7937 2542; Fax 020 7361 2976)
Environmental Services: Council Offices, 37 Pembroke Road, London, W8 6PW
Registration of Births, Deaths and Marriages: The Register Office, Chelsea Old Town Hall, Kings Road, London SW3 5EE (Tel: 020-7361 4100)

KENSINGTON & CHELSEA

CHIEF OFFICERS

Chief Executive and Town Clerk: A. Taylor
Executive Director of Education and Libraries: Roger Wood
Executive Director of Environmental Services: M. Stroud
Executive Director of Housing and Social Services: M. Gibb
Executive Director of Planning and Conservation: M. J. French

MEMBERS OF THE COUNCIL

Councillor	Ward
Mayor: R. Walker-Arnott, C.	Norland
Deputy Mayor: T. Coleridge, C.	Hans Town
Leader of the Council: The Lady Hanham, CBE, C.	Holland
T. Ahern, C.	Campden
J. Atkinson, Lab.	St. Charles
J. Blakeman, Lab.	Colville
S. Blanchflower, Lab.	Avondale
T. Boulton, Lab.	South Stanley
C. Buckmaster, C.	Campden
Barbara Campbell, C.	Pembridge
D. Campion, C.	Pembridge
Elizabeth Christmas, MBE, C.	Abingdon
Anthony Coates, C.	Courtfield
M. Cockell, C.	North Stanley
J. Corbet-Singleton, C.	Cheyne
J. Cox, C.	Courtfield
K. Cunningham, Lab.	Kelfield
A. Dalton, C.	Queen's Gate
I. Donaldson, C.	Royal Hospital
J. Edge, C.	Royal Hospital
T. Fairhead, C.	Earl's Court
M. Field, C.	Abingdon
A. Fitzgerald, C.	Church
Mrs. Ian Frazer, C.	North Stanley
R. Freeman, C.	Campden
Joanna. Gardner, C.	Church
Pat Healy, Lab.	Colville
Bridget Hoier, Lab.	Golborne
S. Hoier, Lab.	Kelfield
L. A. Holt, C.	Courtfield
Rima Horton, Lab.	St. Charles
D. Hudson C.	Brompton
M. Lasharie, Lab.	Avondale

London Borough Councils

B. Levitt, C. — Holland
W. Lightfoot, C. — Holland
P. Mason, Lab. — Golborne
G. Mond, C. — Queen's Gate
D. Moylan, C. — Queen's Gate
Dr. J. Munday, C. — Abingdon
N. Paget-Brown, C. — Hans Town
B. Phelps, C. — Earl's Court
B. Pope, Lab. — Colville
Shireen Ritchie, C. — Brompton
J. Seidler, C. — Redcliffe
S. Shapro, Lab. — Golborne
S. Stanley, Lab. — Avondale
Frances Taylor, C. — Redcliffe
E. P. Tomlin, C. — Norland
P. Warrick, C. — Cheyne
Mary Weale, C. — Hans Town
Doreen M. Weatherhead, C. — Pembridge
A. Whitfield, C. — Redcliffe
A. Wood, Lab. — South Stanley

Political Composition: C. 38; Lab. 15
Parliamentary Constituencies: Kensington and Chelsea, Regents Park and Kensington North, Ealing, Acton and Shepherds Bush.
Population: 164,000
Area: 1,238 hectares

ABOUT KENSINGTON AND CHELSEA

In 1965 the Boroughs of Kensington and Chelsea were united to form the single London Borough of Kensington and Chelsea. It covers five square miles, 70 percent of which is located in conservation areas. It is home to 34 embassies and numerous London Landmarks. The title 'Royal Borough' was granted in 1901 by King Edward VII, in recognition of his mother's (Queen Victoria) wish to recognise her birthplace.

COUNCIL TAX BANDS 2000-2001

Band	Market Value of the Property in 1991	Council Tax
A	Up to £40,000	£410.04
B	£40,001 to 52,000	£478.37
C	£52,001 to 68,000	£546.71
D	£68,001 to 88,000	£615.05
E	£88,001 to 120,000	£751.73
F	£120,001 to 160,000	£888.40
G	£160,001 to 320,000	£1025.09
H	£320,001 or more	£1230.10

ROYAL BOROUGH OF KINGSTON UPON THAMES

Guildhall, Kingston upon Thames, KT1 1EU
(Tel: 020-8546 2121; Fax: 020-8547 5012;
Web: http://www.kingston.gov.uk)
Tourist Information Centre: The Market House, Market Place, Kingston upon Thames, KT1 1JS
(Tel: 020-8547 5592; Fax: 020-8547 5594)
Registration of Births, Deaths and Marriages: 35 Coombe Road, Kingston upon Thames KT2 7BA
(Tel: 020-8546 0920)

KINGSTON UPON THAMES

CHIEF OFFICERS

Acting Chief Executive: Bruce McDonald
Assistant Director (Leisure and Lifelong Learning): Scott Herbertson
Borough Environmental Health Officer: Bob Smart
Chief Planner: Anna Cronin
Chief Trading Standards Officer: Ted Forsyth
Director of Community Services: Roy Taylor, CBE
Director of Education and Leisure: John Braithwaite
Director of Environmental Services: Alan McMillen
Director of Finance: Tony Knights
Director of Personnel: Bruce McDonald
Head of Children and Family Services: Margie Rooke
Head of Corporate Planning: Chris Field
Head of Housing: Michael England
Head of Legal Services: Sue Jackson
Head of Secretariat: Andrew Bessant
Head of Technical Services: Tim Darwen

MEMBERS OF THE COUNCIL

Councillor	Ward
Mayor: Shiraz Mirza, LD	Chessington South
Deputy Mayor: Ian McDonald, LD	Malden Manor
Leader of the Council: D. Edwards, C.	Hill
M. Amson, C.	St. James's
Patricia Bamford, LD	Chessington South
B. Bennett, LD	Chessington North
D. Booth, C.	Tolworth East
Janet Bowen-Hitchings, C.	Surbiton Hill
P. Brill, LD	Cambridge
T. Brown, C.	Berrylands
D. Chester, LD	Grove
P. Codd, C.	Coombe
P. Crerar, C.	Coombe
D. Cunningham, C.	Tudor
Leslie Dale, C.	Berrylands
Marian Darke, Lab.	Tolworth West
Rolson Davies, LD	Malden Manor
K. Davis, C.	Berrylands
D. De Lord, C.	St. Mark's
D. Doe, C.	Tudor
J. Ellin, Lab.	Canbury
W. Evans, LD	Norbiton Park
R. Faulkner, Lab.	Tolworth South

56 Governed London

D. Fraser, C.	St. James's
Julie Haines, LD	Cambridge
A. Hall, Lab.	Tolworth South
Vicki Harris, LD	Chessington North
R. Hayes, LD	Grove
J. Heamon, LD	Cambridge
Chrissie Hitchcock, LD	Grove
E. Humphrey, C.	Hill
Jan Jenner, C.	St. Mark's
P. Johnston, C.	Surbiton Hill
D. Jordan, LD	Norbiton Park
Wendy Malseed, Lab.	Canbury
S. Mama, Lab.	Norbiton
R. Matthews, C.	St. Mark's
A. McLeay, LD	Burlington
E. Naylor, Lab.	Norbiton
D. Osbourne, LD	Burlington
R. Pandya, C.	St. James's
C. Priest, Lab.	Canbury
J. Reay, Lab.	Norbiton
I. Reid, LD	Hook
Mary Reid, LD	Hook
Sally Scrivens, LD	Chessington South
Jane Smith, C.	Surbiton Hill
Gwen Symonds, C.	Tudor
J. Thorn, Lab.	Tolworth West
K. Witham, C.	Tolworth East

Political Composition: C. 21; LD. 19; Lab. 9
Parliamentary Constituencies: Kingston and Surbiton; Richmond Park
Population: 144,313 (Registrar General mid year 1998 Estimate)
Area: 3,756 hectares

ABOUT KINGSTON UPON THAMES

The Royal Borough of Kingston upon Thames is located in South west London on the banks of the river Thames. It is approximately thirty minutes by train to central London and is situated between the two major London airports of Heathrow and Gatwick. The borough consists of the town centre of Kingston and the district centres of New Malden, Surbiton and Tolworth.

COUNCIL TAX BANDS 2000-2001

Band	Market Value of the Property in 1991	Council Tax
A	Up to £40,000	£575.46
B	£40,001 to 52,000	£671.37
C	£52,001 to 68,000	£767.28
D	£68,001 to 88,000	£863.19
E	£88,001 to 120,000	£1055.01
F	£120,001 to 160,000	£1246.83
G	£160,001 to 320,000	£1438.65
H	£320,001 or more	£1726.38

LAMBETH

Lambeth Town Hall, Brixton Hill, London SW2 1RW (Tel: 020-7926 1000; Fax: 020-7926 2255; Web: http://www.lambeth.gov.uk)
Executive Director of Education Services: International House, Canterbury Crescent, Brixton, London SW9 7QE (Tel: 020-7926 1000)
Executive Director of Environmental Services: 1-5 Acre Lane, London SW2 5SD (Tel: 020-7926 1000)
Executive Director of Finance and Corporate Services: International House, Canterbury Crescent, Brixton, London, SW9 7QE (Tel: 020-7926 1000)
Executive Director of Housing and Social Services: Hambrook House, Porden Road, London SW2 1RP (Tel: 020-7926 1000)
Executive Director of Social Services: Mary Seacole House, 91 Clapham High Street, London SW4 7TF (Tel: 020-7926 1000)
Registration of Births, Deaths and Marriages: The Register Office, 361 Brixton Road, London SW9 7DA (Tel: 020-7926 9240)

CHIEF OFFICERS

Chief Executive: Vacant
Acting Executive Director of Education: Alan Wood
Borough Solicitor: Gerard Curran
Executive Director of Finance and Corporate Services: Michael Crich
Executive Director of Housing Services: John Broomfield
Executive Director of Social Services: Lisa Cunstensen

MEMBERS OF THE COUNCIL

Councillor	Ward
Mayor: Clare Whelan, C.	Thurlow Park
Deputy Mayor: Claudette Hewitt, Lab.	Clapham Town
R. A'Court, C.	Gipsy Hill
M. Abu-Bakr, Lab.	Ferndale
D. Anyanwu, Lab.	Angell
R. Bawden, Lab.	Larkhall
C. Bennet, LD	St. Leonard's
L. Boodram, Lab.	Bishop's Ward
A. Bottrall, LD	Stockwell
S. Bourne, Lab.	Bishop's Ward
Judith Brodie, Lab.	St. Martin's

London Borough Councils 57

C. Cattermole, Lab. — Town Hall
Sheila Clarke, LD — Streatham Wells
G. Compton, C. — Gipsy Hill
P. Connolly, Lab. — Knights Hill
K. Craig, Lab. — Larkhall
M. Crichton-Stuart, LD — Oval
C. Crooks, Lab. — Knights Hill
Geraldine Curtis, Lab. — Town Hall
H. David, Lab. — Stockwell
J. Dickson, Lab. — Herne Hill
R. Doven, Lab. — Clapham Park
M. English, Lab. — Clapham Town
J. Feenan, LD — Oval
June Fewtrell, LD — Streatham Hill
K. Fitchett, LD — Princes
T. Franklin, Lab. — St. Martin's
R. Giess, LD — St. Leonard's
T. Goddard, Lab. — Tulse Hill
Esther Green, Lab. — Larkhall
Janet Grigg, C. — Gipsy Hill
Daphne Hayes-Moyon, LD — Streatham Wells
J. Heather, LD — Streatham Wells
C. Henley, Lab. — Clapham Town
P. Hewitt, Lab. — Thornton
A. Hogan, Lab. — Angell
R. Jarman, Lab. — Ferndale
J. Kazantis, Lab. — Streatham South
S. Lawman, LD — Princes
Ruth Ling, Lab. — Clapham Park
A. Lumsden, LD — Streatham Hill
D. Malley, Lab. — Streatham South
R. McConnell, LD — Knights Hill
M. McEwan, Lab. — Clapham Park
P. McGlone, Lab. — Ferndale
Kirsty McHugh, Lab. — Herne Hill
A. McKenna, Lab. — Vassall
Jackie Meldrum, Lab. — Tulse Hill
Abigale Melville, Lab. — Stockwell
Julie Minns, Lab. — Thornton
R. O'Brien, LD — Streatham Hill
P. O'Connell, Lab. — Herne Hill
B. Palmer, LD — St. Leonard's
S. Reed, Lab. — Town Hall
D. Sabbagh, Lab. — Vassall
T. Sargeant, Lab. — Streatham South
A. Sawdon, LD — Oval
Johanna Sherrington, Lab. — Tulse Hill
T. Smith, Lab. — St. Martin's
S. Stevens, Lab. — Angell
P. Truesdale, LD — Bishops Ward
M. Tuffrey, LD — Princes
Kitty Ussher, Lab. — Vassall
J. Whelan, C. — Thurlow Park

Political Composition: Lab. 41; LD. 18; C. 5.
Parliamentary Constituencies: Dulwich and West Norwood; Streatham; Vauxhall
Population: 269,500
Area: 2,727 hectares

ABOUT LAMBETH

Lambeth measures some seven miles north to south and about two and a half miles east to west. There are many important sites and cultural attractions within the borough's boundaries. Lambeth includes the South Bank complex as the most visible element of an expanding arts and leisure industry within the borough. Examples include the Old Vic, the Young Vic, the National Theatre, the Royal Festival Hall and the National Film Theatre. The borough is also home to the Oval Cricket Ground and the Florence Nightingale Museum. Waterloo, Westminster, Lambeth and Wandsworth bridges are all partly located within Lambeth's boundaries, as is Lambeth Palace, the official London residence of the Archbishop of Canterbury. Socially and culturally Lambeth is one of the most diverse communities in Great Britain. Thirty four per cent of Lambeth's population are from ethnic minorities – the seventh highest figure for a London borough.

COUNCIL TAX BANDS 2000-2001

Band	Market Value of the Property in 1991	Council Tax
A	Up to £40,000	£437.33
B	£40,001 to 52,000	£510.22
C	£52,001 to 68,000	£583.11
D	£68,001 to 88,000	£656.00
E	£88,001 to 120,000	£801.78
F	£120,001 to 160,000	£947.56
G	£160,001 to 320,000	£1093.33
H	£320,001 or more	£1312.00

LEWISHAM

Lewisham Town Hall, London SE6 4RU (Tel: 020-8314 6000; Web: http://www.lewisham.gov.uk)
Borough Information Centre: 199-201 Lewisham High Street, London SE13
Education and Culture: 3rd Floor, Lawrence House, 1 Catford Road, London SE6 4RU
Regeneration: 5th Floor, Lawrence House, 1 Catford Road, London SE6 4RU
Registration of Births, Deaths and Marriages: 368 Lewisham High Street, London SE13 6LQ (Tel: 020-8690 2128)
Resources: 3rd Floor, Town Hall, London SE6 4RU
Social Care and Health: 1st Floor, Lawrence House, 1 Catford Road, London SE6 4RU

CHIEF OFFICERS

Chief Executive: B. Quirk
Director for Regeneration: J. Montgomery
Director of Education and Culture: A. Efunshile

58 Governed London

Director of Resources: R. Whiteman
Acting Director of Social Care and Health: Kathryn Hudson

MEMBERS OF THE COUNCIL

Councillor	Ward
Mayor: Dave Sullivan, Lab.	Horniman
Deputy Mayor: Gavin Moore, Lab.	Blackheath
Jackie Addison, Lab.	Forest Hill
Obajimi Adefiranye, Lab.	Drake
Abdeslam Amrani, Lab.	St. Andrew
Barrie Anderson, Con.	St. Mildred
Chris Best, Lab.	Sydenham East
Dave Bodimeade, Lab.	Churchdown
Andrew Brown, Lab.	Blackheath
Joseph Burns, Lab.	Catford
Liam Carlisle, Con.	St. Mildred
Alicia Chater, Lab.	Churchdown
Fiona Crichlow, Lab.	Crofton Park
Liam Curran, Lab.	Sydenham East
Andrew Davies, Lab.	Hither Green
Kate Donnelly, Lab.	St. Margaret
Les Eytle, Lab.	Blythe Hill
Paul Fallon, Lab.	Hither Green
Peggy Fitzsimmons, Lab.	Rushey Green
Gurbakhsh Garcha, Lab.	Crofton Park
Annette Gordon, Lab.	Marlowe
Donovan Green, Lab.	Grove Park
Carl Handley, Lab.	St. Andrew
Roger Harris, Lab.	Sydenham West
Colin Hastie, Lab.	Perry Hill
Jane Hastie, Lab.	St. Margaret
Mike Holder, Lab.	Perry Hill
Matthew Huntbach, LD	Downham
Miriam Iloghalu, Lab.	Ladywell
Carl Kisicki, LD	Whitefoot
Helen Klier, Lab.	Rushey Green
Vanessa Large, Lab.	Grinling Gibbons
Mee Ling, Lab.	Evelyn
Madeliene Long, Lab.	Manor Lee
Jim Mallory, Lab.	Grinling Gibbons
Paul Maslin, Lab.	Marlowe
Alyson McGarrigle, Lab.	Churchdown
Phil Mills, Lab.	Sydenham West
Man Mohan, Lab.	Grinling Gibbons
Paul Morris, Lab.	Grove Park
Pauline Morrison, Lab.	Ladywell
Paul Newing, Lab.	Ladywell
Mark Nottingham, Lab.	Evelyn
Crada Onuegbu, Lab.	Evelyn
John O'Shea, Lab.	Bellingham
Stephen Padmore, Lab.	Marlowe
Ian Page, Soc.	Pepys
Jarman Parmar, Lab.	Drake
John Paschoud, Lab.	Forest Hill
Alan Pegg, Lab.	Sydenham East
Catherine Priddey, LD	Downham
Margaret Sandra, Lab.	Pepys
Sylvia Scott, Lab.	Blythe Hill
Terry Scott, Lab.	Drake
Alan Smith, Lab.	Whitefoot
Eva Stamirowski, Lab.	Sydenham West
Ron Stockbridge, Lab.	Bellingham
Martin Taylor, Lab	Catford
Nicholas Taylor, Lab.	Pepys
Kristine Taylor-Carroll, Lab.	Horniman
Alan Till, Lab.	Perry Hill
Ian Walton, LD	Downham
Ruth Watt, Lab.	Crofton Park
David Whiting, Lab.	Horniman
David Wilson, Lab.	Hither Green
Susan Wise, Lab.	Horniman

Political Composition: Lab. 59; LD. 3; C. 2
Parliamentary Constituencies: Lewisham-Deptford, Lewisham East, Lewisham West.
Population: 241,500
Area: 3,473 hectares

ABOUT LEWISHAM

Lewisham is situated in the south east of London and enjoys influences from the inner city and the borders of Kent. The area is culturally diverse and a considerable percentage of the population are from ethnic minorities. This is demonstrated by festivals such as People's Day, Black History Month and the Irish Festival which are held annually. Lewisham also hosts the South East London Beer Festival. The area is well served by public transport with numerous rail and bus links and a recently opened Docklands Light Railway line.

COUNCIL TAX BANDS 2000-2001

Band	Market Value of the Property in 1991	Council Tax
A	Up to £40,000	£532.17
B	£40,001 to 52,000	£620.86
C	£52,001 to 68,000	£709.56
D	£68,001 to 88,000	£798.25
E	£88,001 to 120,000	£975.64
F	£120,001 to 160,000	£1153.06
G	£160,001 to 320,000	£1330.42
H	£320,001 or more	£1596.50

MERTON

Merton Civic Centre, London Road, Morden SM4 5DX (Tel: 020-8543 2222)
Registration of Births, Deaths and Marriages: Morden Cottage, Morden Hall Road, Morden, Surrey SM4 5JA (Tel: 020-8540 5011)

CHIEF OFFICERS

Chief Executive: Roger Paine
Acting Head of Human Resources: Paul Holmes

London Borough Councils

Acting Head of Legal Services: Mike Cogher
Acting Head of Strategic Policy and Quality: Diane Bailey
Assistant Director (Child Policy and School Effectiveness): Ms. Lorriane O'Reilly
Assistant Director (Community services: Robert Hobbs
Assistant Director (Planning and Resources): Ms. Penny Parker
Director of Education, Leisure and Libraries: Mrs. Jenny Cairns
Director of Environmental Services: Richard Rawes
Director of Financial Services: Mike Parsons
Director of Housing and Social Services: Peter Walters
Head of Audit: Chris Johnson
Head of Communications and Member Services: Gene Saunders
Head of Information Technology: Gurnel Bansal
Head of Revenue and Benefits: Mike Teesdale

MEMBERS OF THE COUNCIL

Councillor	Ward
Mayor: I. Munn, Lab.	Phipps Bridge
Deputy Mayor: A. Samad Chaudhry, Lab.	Longthornton
Leader of the Council: P. Jones, Lab.	Ravensbury
J. B. Abrams, Lab.	Graveney
K. Abrams, Lab.	Trinity
S. Assinen, Lab.	Abbey
Barbara Bampton, Lab.	Dundonald
P. Barasi, Lab.	Trinity
N. Beddoe, C.	Raynes Park
R. Bell, C.	Raynes Park
M. Breirly, C.	Raynes Park
D. Cairns, Lab.	Longthornton
K. Carter, Lab.	Abbey
D. Child, Ind.	Merton Park
J. H. Cole, Lab.	Pollards Hill
D. Connellan, Lab.	Figges Marsh
T. Daniels, C.	Lower Morden
I. Dysart, LD	West Barnes
Samantha George, C.	Village
Chris Grayling, C.	Hillside
Vivien Guy, Lab.	Trinity
P. Harper, Lab.	Phipps Bridge
N. Harris, LD	West Barnes
R. Harwood, C.	Hillside
P. Holt, Lab.	Colliers Wood
C. Housden, C.	Village
A. Jones, C.	Village
A. Judge Lab.	Figges Marsh
M. Karim Lab.	Abbey
Linda Kirby Lab.	Graveney
S. Knight, Lab.	Colliers Wood
Karen Livingstone, Lab.	Longthornton
C. Lucas, Lab.	Connon Hill
Edith Macauley, Lab.	Lavender
R. Makin, Lab.	Pollards Hill
M. Mannion, Lab.	Connon Hill
Maxi Martin, Lab.	St. Helier
P. McCabe, Lab.	Ravensbury
P. Morss, C.	Lower Morden
J. Nelson-Jones, Ind.	Merton Park
Joyce Paton, Lab.	Dunsford
D. Pearce, Lab.	St. Helier
S. Pickover, Lab.	Dundonald
G. Reynolds, Lab.	Colliers Wood
Judy Saunders, Lab.	Phipps Bridge
M. Searle, Lab.	Lavender
Bridget Smith, Ind.	Merton Park
P. Smith, Lab.	Ravensbury
M. Spacey, Lab.	St. Helier
Geraldine Stanford, Lab.	Figges Marsh
M. Syed, Lab.	Pollards Hill
M. Thompson, Lab.	Durnsford
B. White, Lab.	Cannon Hill
D. T. Williams, C.	Hillside
Jenny Willott, LD.	West Barnes

Political Composition: Lab. 38; C. 11; LD. 3; Ind. 3.
Parliamentary Constituencies: Wimbledon; Mitcham and Morden.
Population: 184,315
Area: 3,796 hectares

ABOUT MERTON

The Borough of Merton is located in the South West of London and comprises of the five main towns of Wimbledon, Morden, Mitcham, Raynes Park and Colliers Wood. Merton has a number of large open spaces including Mitcham and Wimbledon Commons with the river Wandle flowing through the Borough. Merton is approximately 13 minutes from Central London and has numerous rail, tube and bus facilities.

COUNCIL TAX BANDS 2000-2001

Band	Market Value of the Property in 1991	Council Tax
A	Up to £40,000	£577.80 (594.17)
B	£40,001 to 52,000	£674.09 (690.46)
C	£52,001 to 68,000	£770.40 (786.77)
D	£68,001 to 88,000	£866.69 (883.06)
E	£88,001 to 120,000	£1059.29 (1075.66)
F	£120,001 to 160,000	£1251.89 (1268.26)
G	£160,001 to 320,000	£1444.29 (1460.86)
H	£320,001 or more	£1733.38 (1749.75)

Figures in brackets are for properties within ³/₄ of a mile of Wimbledon Common. This payment is passed on to the Wimbledon and Putney Common conservators for the upkeep of the common.

60 Governed London

NEWHAM

Town Hall, East Ham, London E6 2RP (Tel: 020-8430 2000; Fax: 020-8557 8662 Web: http://www.newham.gov.uk)
Environment Department: 25 Nelson Street, East Ham, London E6 4EH (Tel: 020-8430 2000; Fax: 020-8472 2284)
Education/Social Services: Broadway House, 322 High Street, London E15 1AJ (Tel: 020-8430 2000)
Housing Department: Bridge House, 320 High Street, London E15 1EW (Tel: 020-8430 2000; Fax: 020-8519 2826)
Environmental Health: Alice Billings House, 2-12 West Ham Lane, London, E15 4SF (Tel: 020-8430 2000; Fax: 020-8557 8869)
Consumer Services: 465 High Street North, Manor Park, London, E12 6TH (Tel: 020-8430 2000; Fax 020-8557 8969)
Leisure Services: 292 Barking Road, East Ham, London, E6 3BA (Tel: 020-8430 2000)
Registration of Births, Deaths and Marriages: Newham Register Office, Passmore Edwards Building, 207 Plashet Grove, East Ham E6 1BT (Tel: 020-8430 2000)

CHIEF OFFICERS

Chief Executive: Dave Burbage
Deputy Chief Executive and Director of Education: Ian Harrison
Director of Environment: M. Smith
Director of Social Services: Ms. Deborah Cameron
Director of Housing: C. Wood
Head of Environmental Health: Mr. S. Miller
Head of Trading Standards: R. Sweeting

MEMBERS OF THE COUNCIL

Councillor	Ward
Mayor: B. Collier, Lab.	Hudsons
Deputy Mayor: Sukhdev Singh Marway, Lab.	Kensington
Leader of the Council: R. Wales, Marway, Lab.	Canning Town and Grange
M. Ahmad, Lab.	Castle
S. Ahmad, Lab.	Forest Gate
Riaz Ahmed-Mirza	Plaistow
N. Ali, Lab.	Upton
S. Ali, Lab.	Kensington
A. Baikie, Lab.	Little Ilford
P. Brickell, Lab.	Forest Gate
L. Brown, Lab.	Canning Town and Grange
W. Brown, Lab.	Monega
G. Cambage, Lab.	West Ham
A. Chaudhary, Lab.	Park
Marie Sylvia Collier, Lab.	Ordnance
I. Corbett, Lab.	Greatfield
R. Crawford, Lab.	Little Ilford
Unmesh Desai, Lab.	St. Stephen's
J. Ejiofor, Lab.	Little Ilford
V. Fone, Lab.	Greatfield
C. Furness, Lab.	Canning Town and Grange
D. Gilles, Lab.	Manor Park
A. Griffiths, Lab.	Park
Megan Harris, Lab.	Ordnance
Patricia Holland, Lab.	Canning Town and Grange
L. Hudson, Lab.	Monega
K. Jenkins, Lab.	Greatfield
A. Kellaway, Lab.	South
Q. Khan, Lab.	Manor Park
M. Knight, Lab.	Beckton
Joy Laguda, Lab.	Plaistow
G. Lane, Lab.	Hudsons
June Leitch, Lab.	Central
K. Mangat, Lab.	Wall End
R. Manley, Lab.	West Ham
A. McAlmont, Lab.	New Town
C. McAuley, Lab.	Forest Gate
D. McGladdery, Lab.	Castle
Rupindra Nandra, Lab.	Plashet
J. Newstead, Lab.	Stratford
Q. Peppiatt, Lab.	South
C. Rackley, Lab.	Canning Town and Grange
J. Riley, Lab.	Stratford
S. Ruiz, Lab.	Beckton
Paul Sathianesan, Lab.	Wall End
J. Saunders, Lab.	Park
C. Seddon, Lab.	South
A. Shakoor, Lab.	St. Stephen's
A. Sheikh, Lab.	Upton
A. Singh, Lab.	Manor Park
Mary Skyers, Lab.	Central
E. Sparrowhawk, Lab.	Wall End
J. Thorne, Lab.	Plashet
V. Turner, Lab.	Bemersyde
W. Vaughan, Lab.	New Town
G. Vincent, Lab.	Bemersyde
Harvinder Singh Virdee, Lab.	Upton
F. Warwick, Ind.	Plaistow
R. Williams, Lab.	Plashet
N. Wilson, Lab.	Hudsons

Political Composition: Lab. 59; Ind. 1.
Parliamentary Constituencies: East Ham, West Ham, Poplar and Canning Town
Population: 226,000
Area: 3,875 hectares

ABOUT NEWHAM

Newham is part of the East End of London, sitting just north of the river Thames. It has a growing population of over 226,000, over half of which comes from more than 30 ethnic minority groups. Transport links in Newham include road links to the city airport, the Jubilee line extension has stations in Canning Town, West Ham and Stratford. An International Channel Tunnel Rail link is scheduled to open in Stratford in 2003.

Newham borough was formed in 1965 from the old county boroughs of East and West Ham. It experienced a serious economic decline with the closure of the Royal Docks. Considerable public and private investment has since taken place with the council placing a firm focus on its urban regeneration strategy to encourage business growth, new investment, higher employment levels and a general increase in the standard of living for residents of Newham.

COUNCIL TAX BANDS 2000-2001

Band	Market Value of the Property in 1991	Council Tax
A	Up to £40,000	£512.09
B	£40,001 to 52,000	£597.43
C	£52,001 to 68,000	£682.78
D	£68,001 to 88,000	£768.13
E	£88,001 to 120,000	£938.83
F	£120,001 to 160,000	£1109.52
G	£160,001 to 320,000	£1280.22
H	£320,001 or more	£1536.26

REDBRIDGE

Town Hall, High Road, Ilford IG1 1DD (Tel: 020-8708 3020; Fax: 020-8478 9525)
First Stop Shop: Lynton House, 255-259 High Road, Ilford IG1 1NN (Tel: 020-8708 3440)
Social Services: Ley Street House, 497/499 Ley Street, Ilford IG2 7QX (Tel: 020-8503 8198)
Housing Advice Centre: 17/23 Clements Road, Ilford, IG1 1AG (Tel: 020-8708 4002)
Community Care Advice Centre: Aldborough Road North, Newbury Park, Ilford IG2 7SR (Tel: 020-8503 8833)
8 Perth Terrace, Perth Road, Ilford IG2 6AT
Olympic House, 28-42 Clements Road, Ilford, IG1 1BD
Registration of Births, Deaths and Marriages: Queen Victoria House, 794 Cranbrook Road, Barkingside, Ilford IG1 1JS (Tel: 020-8708 7171)

CHIEF OFFICERS

Chief Executive: Michael Frater
Acting Chief Education Officer: John Pallet
Acting Chief Leisure Officer: Brian Sangha
Chief Administration Officer: Steve Wastell
Chief Children and Families Officer: John Drew
Chief Communications Officer: Ms Maxine Bradley
Chief Community Care Officer: Ms Anne Bristow
Chief Customer Services Officer: David Muggleton
Chief Finance Officer: Geoff Pearce
Chief Legal Officer: Deborah Holmes
Chief Planning Officer: Paul Clark
Chief Policy Officer: Ms Anne Fisher
Corporate Director: Daniel Zammit
Corporate Director: Ms Lesley Seary
Corporate Director: Roger Hampson

MEMBERS OF THE COUNCIL

Councillor	Ward
Mayor: M. Hoskins, LD	Church End
Deputy Mayor: A. Boyland, LD	Roding
Leader of the Council: K. Axon, C.	Barkingside
F. Banks, LD	Roding
R. I. Barden, C.	Clayhall
I. G. Bond, LD	Roding
G. F. Borrott, C.	Barkingside
J. Brindley, Lab.	Valentines
R. Brunnen, C.	Barkingside
A. Burgess, C.	Wanstead
H. Cleaver, LD	Church End
Vanessa Cole, C.	Aldborough
J. Coombes, Lab.	Aldborough
Claire Cooper, C.	Bridge
G. Corfield, C.	Cranbrook
L. Davies, C.	Fullwell
J. Edelman, Lab.	Wanstead
G. Elgin, Lab.	Snaresbrook
C. Elliman, C.	Cranbrook
R. Emmett, C.	Fairlop
G. Evans, Lab.	Newbury
J. Fairley-Churchill, Lab.	Hainault
G. George, Lab.	Wanstead
R. Golding, Lab.	Mayfield
P. Goody, C.	Snaresbrook
S. Green, Lab.	Clementswood
M. Hickey, C.	Bridge
L. Hilton, Lab.	Mayfield
R. Hoskins, LD	Church End
L. Huggett, C.	Monkhams
A. Hughes, C.	Fullwell
M. Javed, Lab.	Loxford
P. Laugharne, Lab.	Clementswood
P. Lawrence, C.	Bridge
R. Littlewood, Lab.	Seven Kings
J. R. Lovell, C.	Clayhall
F. K. Maravala, Lab.	Loxford
S. Middleburgh, Lab.	Goodmayes
S. Mirza, C.	Cranbrook
A. Moth, C.	Fullwell
R. Newcombe, Lab.	Hainault
G. Nicholson, Lab.	Newbury
S. Nolan, C.	Snaresbrook
F. A. Noor, Lab.	Clementswood
E. Norman, Lab.	Valentines
J. O'Shea, C.	Monkhams

62 Governed London

A. Parkash, Lab.	Mayfield	
M. Patel, Lab.	Seven Kings	
E. Peake, Lab.	Hainault	
E. Pearce, Lab.	Seven Kings	
D. Radford, Lab.	Goodmayes	
J. Ryan, C.	Fairlop	
L. Scott, C.	Fairlop	
R. Scott, LD	Chadwell	
D. Sharma, Lab.	Newbury	
S. Speller, Lab.	Loxford	
G. Staight, LD	Chadwell	
M. Stark, C.	Monkhams	
V. Tewari, Lab.	Valentines	
K. Turner, Lab.	Aldborough	
J. Tyne, LD	Chadwell	
A. Weinberg, C.	Clayhall	

Political Composition: Lab. 28; C. 25; LD. 9.
Parliamentary Constituencies: Ilford North; Ilford South, Leyton and Wanstead, Chingford and Woodford Green.
Population: 231,000 (latest est.)
Area: 5,652 hectares

ABOUT REDBRIDGE

Redbridge was formed in 1964 with the joining of Ilford and Wanstead and Woodford, together with parts of Dagenham and Chigwell. Situated in the North East of London, Redbridge boasts 1,200 acres of forest and 600 acres of green parkland.

COUNCIL TAX BANDS 2000-2001

Band	Market Value of the Property in 1991	Council Tax
A	Up to £40,000	£540.67
B	£40,001 to 52,000	£630.18
C	£52,001 to 68,000	£720.89
D	£68,001 to 88,000	£811.00
E	£88,001 to 120,000	£991.22
F	£120,001 to 160,000	£1171.45
G	£160,001 to 320,000	£1851.67
H	£320,001 or more	£1622.00

RICHMOND UPON THAMES

RICHMOND UPON THAMES

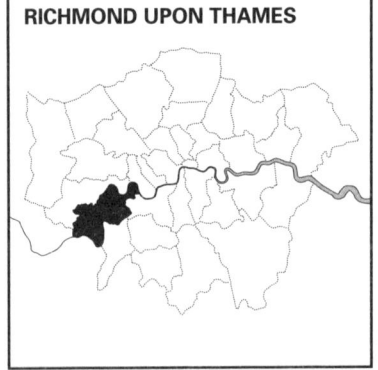

Civic Centre, 44 York Street, Twickenham TW1 3BZ
(Tel: 020-8891 1411;
Web: http://www.richmond.gov.uk)

Leisure Services: Langholm Lodge, 146 Petersham Road, Richmond upon Thames, TW10 6UX (020-8940 8351; Fax 020-8891 7787; E-mail leisure@richmond.gov.uk).
Information Service: Old Town Hall, Whittaker Avenue, Richmond TW9 1TP (Tel: 020-8940 9125; Fax: 020-8940 6899)
Education Department: Regal House, London Road, Twickenham TW1 3QB (020-8891 7500; Fax 020-8891 7714; E-mail education@richmond.gov.uk)
Consumer Advice: (020-8891 7770; Fax 020-8891 7726; E-mail tradingstds@richmond.gov.uk)
Environmental Health: (020-8891 7726; E-mail commercaileh@richmond.gov.uk)
Housing: 44 York Street, Twickenham, TW1 3BZ (020-8891 7400; 020-8891 7717).
Registration of Births, Deaths and Marriages: 1 Spring Terrace, Richmond, Surrey TW9 1LW (Tel: 020-8940 2651)

CHIEF OFFICERS

Chief Executive: Mrs Gillian Norton
Director, Caring for People: Peter Wilson
Director, Environment and Sustainability: Alison Quant
Director of Finance: Mark Maidment
Director, Opportunities for All: Robert Hancock
Head of Personnel and Management Services: R. Wood
Head of Legal Services: R. Mellor
Head of Communications and Media: R. Dividson
Acting Chief Education Officer: P. Lomax
Acting Heads of Planning and Building Control: D. Barnes (*Development Control*); P. Wealthy (*Policy and Design*); D. Batsford (*Building Control*)
Head of Highways and Transport: B. Alker
Head of Client Services: J. Kent
Head of Services for Children: T. Earland
Head of Services for Adults: G. Elford
Head of Housing: D. Done
Head of Health, consumer and Registration Services: P. Mott
Head of Leisure Services: J. Wright
Emergency Planning Office: G. Iles
Head of IT: P. Keane
Head of Revenues and Benefits: M. Gravatt
Head of Construction and Property: W. Dyke
Head of Environmental and Operational Services: D. Streeter

MEMBERS OF THE COUNCIL

Councillor	Ward
Mayor: Barbara Westmorland, LD	Barnes
Deputy Mayor: A. Mollett, LD	Richmond Hill
Leader of the Council: Sir David Williams, LD	Ham and Petersham
Barbara Alexander, LD	Hampton Hill
T. Arbour, C.	Hampton Wick
A. Barnett, LD	Kew
A. Butler, C.	South Twickenham
J. Cardy, LD	Hampton Nursery
N. Carthew, LD	Richmond Town
Alison Cornish, LD	Richmond Town
D. Cornwell, LD	East Twickenham

London Borough Councils 63

M. Daglish, LD — Palewell
M. Elengorn, LD — Teddington
Maria Flemington, C. — East Sheen
Katie Gent, LD — Barnes
M. Gold, Lab. — West Twickenham
Michael Jones, LD — Heathfield
Sue Jones, LD — Ham and Petersham
B. King, LD — Heathfield
S. Knight, LD — Teddington
M. Kreling, C. — Hampton Hill
N. Lait, C. — South Twickenham
Simon Lamb, C. — Central Twickenham
B. Langford, Lab. — Mortlake
Penelope Lee, LD — Richmond Hill
S. Lourie, LD — Kew
Liz Mackenzie, Lab. — West Twickenham
Gina MacKinney, LD — Whitton
K. MacKinney, LD — Whitton
L. Mann, LD — East Twickenham
B. Matthews, Lab. — Mortlake
Jean Matthews, C. — Hampton
B. Miller, LD — Ham and Petersham
Jill Miller, LD — Kew
J. Mumford, LD — Teddington
D. Orchard, C. — South Twickenham
Pat Parsons, C. — Hampton Wick
D. Porter, C. — Central Twickenham
G. M. Rae, LD — Hampton Wick
G. Samuel, C. — Hampton Hill
Eleanor Stanier, LD — Mortlake
Angela Style, LD — Barnes
Anne Summers, LD — Palewell
W. Treble, LD — Heathfield
N. True, C. — East Sheen
N. Urquhart, C. — Palewell
K. Warren, LD — Whitton
Mary Weber, LD — Richmond Hill
J. Whittall, LD — East Twickenham
B. Woodriff, LD — Hampton
Maureen Woodriff, LD — Hampton Nursery
Anne Woodward, C. — Hampton

Political Composition: Lab. 34; C. 14; LD. 4
Parliamentary Constituencies: Richmond Park; Twickenham
Population: 182,766
Area: 5,905 hectares

ABOUT RICHMOND UPON THAMES

The London Borough of Richmond stretches from Hampton Court Palace to Twickenham Rugby Football Ground to Kew Gardens. It contains numerous parks, historic houses, museums and galleries.

COUNCIL TAX BANDS 2000-2001

Band	Market Value of the Property in 1991	Council Tax
A	Up to £40,000	£605.77
B	£40,001 to 52,000	£706.73
C	£52,001 to 68,000	£807.69
D	£68,001 to 88,000	£908.65
E	£88,001 to 120,000	£1110.57
F	£120,001 to 160,000	£1312.49
G	£160,001 to 320,000	£1514.42
H	£320,001 or more	£1817.30

SOUTHWARK

Chief Executive and Director of Finance: Town Hall, Peckham Road, London SE5 8UB (Tel: 020-7525 5000; Web: http://www.southwark.gov.uk)
Director of Regeneration and Environment; Director of Education and Leisure Services: Bradenham Close, London (Tel: 020-7525 5007)
Director of Social Services: Mabel Goldwin House, 49 Grange Walk, London (Tel: 020-7525 3796)
Director of Housing: 9 Larcom Street, London (Tel: 020-7525 7845)
Registration of Births, Deaths and Marriages: 34 Peckham Road, London SE5 8QA (Tel: 020-7525 7669)

CHIEF OFFICERS

Chief Executive and Director of Finance: R. Coomber
Director of Education and Leisure Services: G. Mott
Director of Housing: Michael Irvine
Director of Regeneration and Environment: F. Manson
Director of Social Services: C. Bull

MEMBERS OF THE COUNCIL

Councillor	Ward
Mayor: H. Canagasbey, Lab.	Chaucer
Deputy Mayor: Dora Dixon-Foyle, Lab.	St. Giles
Leader of the Council: N. Duffy, Lab.	Rye
N. Baar, LD	Rotherhithe
M. Barnard, Lab.	Waverley
Beverley Bassom, LD	Rotherhithe
C. Blango, LD	Dockyard
S. Bosch, LD	Cathedral

64 Governed London

Catherine Bowman, LD — Browning
D. Bradbury, C. — Ruskin
R. Bright, LD — Faraday
Denise Capstick, LD — Bricklayers
C. Cherill, Lab. — Barset
C. Claridge, Lab. — Barset
G. Cope, Lab. — Lyndhurst
R. Cornall, Lab. — Lane
N. Dolezal, Lab. — Lyndhurst
T. Eckersley, C. — Ruskin
Mary Ellery, Lab. — Liddle
Stephanie Elsy, Lab. — St Giles
J. Friary, Lab. — Brunswick
Norma Gibbes, Lab. — Alleyn
A. Graham, Lab. — Lane
J. Gurling, LD — Newington
J. Halley, LD, — Burgess
B. Hargrove, Lab. — Friary
Janet Heatley, Lab. — Bellenden
Jeffrey Hook, LD — Rotherhithe
Kim Humphreys, C. — College
W. Kayada, Lab. — Liddle
P. Kelly, Lab. — Bellenden
Joan Khachik, Lab. — Friary
A. L'Estrange, LD — Riverside
Jelli Ladipo, LD — Newington
S. Lanchashire, Lab. — Chaucer
A. Langely, LD — Faraday
H. Latham, Lab. — Alleyn
Linda Manchester, LD — Abbey
D. McInerny, Lab. — Lyndhurst
K. Mizzi, LD — Burgess
Vicki Naish, Lab. — Brunswick
G. Nash, Lab. — Bricklayers
D. Noakes, LD — Faraday
B. Olliffe, LD — Riverside
D. Partridge, LD — Dockyard
Michelle Pearce, Lab. — Ruskin
F. Pemberton, Lab. — Friary
Caroline Pidgeon, LD — Newington
A. Ritchie, Lab. — St Giles
W. Rowe, C. — College
A. Shaha, LD — Chaucer
R. Shannon, LD — Browning
A. Simmons, Lab. — Bellenden
B. Skelly, Lab. — Liddle
H. Stanton, LD — Riverside
R. Thomas, LD — Abbey
D. Thorncroft, Lab. — Rye
Viv Todd, Lab. — Waverley
H. Vahib, Lab. — Consort
N. Watson, LD — Browning
Hilary Wines, LD — Cathedral
I. Wingfield, Lab. — Brunswick
A. Worsley, Lab — Consort
Anne Yates, LD — Dockyard

Political Composition: Lab. 33; LD. 27; C. 4.
Parliamentary Constituencies: Southwark North and Bermondsey, Camberwell and Peckham, Dulwich and West Norwood
Population: 230,500
Area: 2,888 hectares

ABOUT SOUTHWARK

The second oldest London borough after the City of London, Southwark is a borough steeped in history. Southwark's Thames-side location brought commercial wealth to the area in its early days, a location which nowadays forms a number of residential developments. Culturally, the borough is rich and is home to the Globe and Rose Theatres and the Bankside Gallery of Modern Art. Leisure and shopping facilities are good and the borough boasts numerous parks and gardens, East Street and Borough markets and Surrey Quays and Elephant and Castle shopping centres. Transport links are excellent and Southwark is home to London Bridge and Waterloo mainline railway stations as well as four stations on the recent Jubilee line extension and bus routes serving the West End, the City and beyond.

COUNCIL TAX BANDS 2000-2001

Band	Market Value of the Property in 1991	Council Tax
A	Up to £40,000	£563.63
B	£40,001 to 52,000	£657.56
C	£52,001 to 68,000	£751.51
D	£68,001 to 88,000	£843.44
E	£88,001 to 120,000	£1033.31
F	£120,001 to 160,000	£1221.19
G	£160,001 to 320,000	£1409.07
H	£320,001 or more	£1509.88

SUTTON

Civic Offices, St. Nicholas Way, Sutton, SM1 1EA (Tel: 020-8770 5000; Fax: 020-8770 5404; Web: http://www.sutton.gov.uk)
Environment and Leisure: 24 Denmark Road, Carshalton, SM5 2JG
Learning for Life: The Grove, Carshalton, Surrey SM5 3AL
Registration of Births, Deaths and Marriages: The Register Office, Russettings, 25 Worcester Road, Sutton, Surrey SM2 6PR (Tel: 020-8770 6790)

CHIEF OFFICERS

Chief Executive: Patricia Hughes
Strategic Director, Community Services Group: Eleanor Brazil

London Borough Councils 65

Strategic Director, Environment and Leisure Group: Brian Madge
Strategic Director, Finance and Information Group: Anne McMeel
Strategic Director, Learning for Life Group: Dr. Ian Birnbaum

MEMBERS OF THE COUNCIL

Councillor	Ward
Mayor: Lal Hussain, LD	Sutton East
Deputy Mayor: Maggie Woodley, LD	Carshalton Beeches
R. Aitken, LD	Beddington South
Sheila Andrews, LD	Wandle Valley
R. Bailey, LD	Wallington South
Angela Baughan, LD	Carshalton Central
R. Bentley, LD	Carshalton Beeches
D. Biss, LD	Belmont
Wendy Bradley, LD	Worcester Park South
S. Brennan, LD	Sutton Central
D. Brims, LD	Sutton East
Anne Brown, C.	Sutton South
P. Burstow, LD	Rosehill
Leslie Coman, LD	Worcester Park
M. Cooper, LD	Carshalton North
Pamela Cooper, LD	Beddington North
Margaret Court, LD	Wandle Valley
Joan Crowhurst, LD	Sutton West
N. Cull, LD	Sutton South
J. Dodwell, LD	Wallington North
N. Dologhan, LD	Beddington South
J. Freeman, LD	North Cheam
Anne Gallop, LD	Sutton Common
P. Geiringer, C.	Sutton South
Lyn Gleeson, LD	Cheam West
R. Gleeson, LD	Cheam West
C. Hall, LD	Wallington South
P. Hewitt, LD	Carshalton North
J. Keys, LD	Wallington North
J. Leach, LD	Beddington North
S. Lloyd, Lab.	St. Helier South
Janet Lowne, LD	Sutton East
C. Mansell, Lab.	St. Helier South
R. Marvelly, LD	Wallington North
G. Miles, LD	Carshalton Beeches
J. Morgan, Lab.	St. Helier North
Lesley O'Connell, LD	Sutton Common
P. Overy, LD	Worcester Park
Penny Overy, LD	Rosehill
D. Park, C.	Cheam South
R. Roberts, LD	Worcester Park South
I. Ruxton, LD	Worcester Park North
Coleen Saunders, LD	Beddington South
Ruth Shaw, LD	North Cheam
Sheila Siggins, LD	Wrythe Green
Joyce Smith, Lab.	St. Helier North
Sue Stears, LD	Wrythe Green
S. Theed, LD	Wallington South
A. Theobald, Lab.	St. Helier North
R. Thistle, LD	Clockhouse
G. Tope, LD	Sutton Central
E. Trevor, C.	Cheam South
Myfanwy Wallace, LD	Sutton West
T. Wallace, LD	Belmont
G. Whitham, C.	Woodcote
J. Woodley, LD	Carshalton Central

Political Composition: LD. 46; Lab. 5; C. 5.
Parliamentary Constituencies: Carshalton and Wallington; Sutton and Cheam
Population: 177,084
Area: 4,343 hectares

ABOUT SUTTON

On the edge of south London with the North Downs to the south and with more trees than any other London borough, Sutton is a combination of city and country. It boasts more than 1,000 acres of open space, yet lies within a few miles of the heart of London. The borough has attracted major employers such as Reed Business Publishing, the Crown Agents, Canon, Sainsbury's Homebase and Securicor. Caring for the local environment has become a priority and Sutton regularly tops the national statistics for recycling.

COUNCIL TAX BANDS 2000-2001

Band	Market Value of the Property in 1991	Council Tax
A	Up to £40,000	£530.37
B	£40,001 to 52,000	£618.77
C	£52,001 to 68,000	£707.16
D	£68,001 to 88,000	£795.56
E	£88,001 to 120,000	£972.35
F	£120,001 to 160,000	£1149.14
G	£160,001 to 320,000	£1325.93
H	£320,001 or more	£1591.12

TOWER HAMLETS

Town Hall, Mulbery Place, 5 Clove Crescent, London E14 2BG (Tel: 020-7364 5000; Fax: 020-7364 4296; Web: http://www.towerhamlets.gov.uk)
Social Services: 62 Roman Road, London E2 0QJ (Tel: 020-7364 5000)
Planning and Environmental Services: 41-47 Bow Road, London E3 2BS (Tel: 020-7364 5000)
Tower Hamlets Information Service: 18 Lamb Street, London E1 2EA (Tel: 020-7364 4970)
Registration of Births, Deaths and Marriages: The Register Office, Bromley Public Hall, Bow Road, London E3 3AA (Tel: 020-8980 8025)

66 Governed London

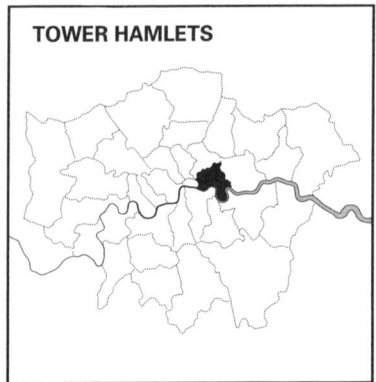

TOWER HAMLETS

CHIEF OFFICERS

Chief Executive: Ms Sylvie Pierce
Acting Director of Housing: Paul Bloss
Corporate Director of Support Services: Ms Eleanor Kelly
Corporate Director, Customer Services: Eric Bohl
Director of Education and Community Services: Ms Christine Gilbert
Director of Social Services: Ian Wilson
Solicitor to the Council: Russell Power

MEMBERS OF THE COUNCIL

Councillor	Ward
Mayor: Denise Jones, Lab.	St. Katherine's
Deputy Mayor: A. Sardar, Lab.	Bromley
Leader of the Council: M. Keith, Lab.	Shadwell
H. Abbas, Lab.	Limehouse
B. Ahmed, Lab.	St. Dunstan's
R. Ahmed, Lab.	East India
M. Ali, Lab.	Weavers
B. Alom, Lab.	Shadwell
S. Alom, Lab.	Limehouse
A. Asad, Lab.	St. Katherine's
Elizabeth Baunton, LD	Park
D. Bayat, Lab.	Redcoat
Jusna Begum, Lab.	St. Peter's
J. Biggs, Lab.	St. Dunstan's
D. Charles, LD	Park
Betheline Chattopadhyay, Lab.	Bromley
C. Creegan, Lab.	Weavers
Barrie Duffey, LD	Holy Trinity
D. Edgar, Lab.	Limehouse
Ray Gipson, LD	Bow
A. Heslop, Lab.	St. Mary's
Catherine Hinvest, Lab.	Bromley
A. Hoque, Lab.	St. Katherine's
Richard Hunn, Ind.	Grove
Diana Johnson, Lab.	Lansbury
M. Keating, Lab.	Lansbury
Janet Ludlow, LD	Grove
J. Mainwaring, Lab.	Millwall
R. Marney, Lab.	St. Peter's
Lorraine Melvin, Lab.	St. James'
R. Miah, Lab.	St. Peter's
S. Mizan, Lab.	Spitalfields
S. Molyneaux, Lab.	Millwall
K. Morton, Lab.	Lansbury
G. Mortuza, Lab.	Spitalfields
K. Murshid, Lab.	Blackwall
A. Rahman, Lab.	Redcoat
A. Shukur, Lab.	Shadwell
J. Snooks, LD	Holy Trinity
B. Son, Lab.	East India
Terry Stacy, LD	Bow
M. Taylor, Lab.	St. James'
Catherine Tuitt, Lab.	Weavers
A. Uddin, Lab.	Spitalfields
M. Uddin, Lab.	St. Dunstan's
S. Ullah, Lab.	Holy Trinity
M. Uz-Zuman, Lab.	St. Mary's
Marian Williams, LD	Bow
S. Wright, Lab.	Blackwall
M. Young, Lab	Millwall

Political Composition: Lab. 41; LD. 8; Ind. 1
Parliamentary Constituencies: Bethnal Green and Bow, Poplar and Canning Town
Population: 179,834
Area: 1980 hectares

ABOUT TOWER HAMLETS

Tower Hamlets is located in the East End of London with the Docklands river bend of the Thames at its southern boundary. It is served by the Central, District and new Jubilee Line of the London Underground. The economy of the borough was severely disrupted by the declining prosperity of the Docklands areas. The area has received over £1 billion in UK government assistance and £5 billion in private investment. This has culminated in the rapid re-growth of the local economy with intensive industrial and commercial development of the 530 acres of previously derelict land. The Docklands area is now home to many companies representing the banking, finance and communication sectors.

COUNCIL TAX BANDS 2000-2001

Band	Market Value of the Property in 1991	Council Tax
A	Up to £40,000	£484.35
B	£40,001 to 52,000	£565.07
C	£52,001 to 68,000	£645.80
D	£68,001 to 88,000	£726.52
E	£88,001 to 120,000	£887.97
F	£120,001 to 160,000	£1049.42
G	£160,001 to 320,000	£1210.88
H	£320,001 or more	£1453.04

London Borough Councils

WALTHAM FOREST

Town Hall, Forest Road, London E17 4JF Tel : 020-8527 5544; E-mail: chief.executive@ce.lbwf.gov.uk Web: http://www.lbwf.gov.uk)
Education, Planning and Economic Development: Municipal Offices, 16 The Ridge, London E4 6PS Tel: 020-8527 5544
Environmental Health Service: 154 Blackhorse Road, Walthamstow, London E17 6NW (Tel: 020-8520 0221; E-mail environmentalhealth@lbwf.gov.uk)
Education and Social Services: Municipal Offices. High Road, London, E10 5QJ **Housing:** Willow House, 869 Forest Road, London E17 4UH (Tel: 020-8527 5544)
Arts and Leisure; Legal Services: Sycamore House, PO Box 416, Forest Road, London E17 4SY (Tel: 020-8527 5544)
Consumer Protection: Cherry Tree House, Town Hall, London, E17 4JF (Tel: 020-8527 5544)
Trading Standards: 8 Buxton Road, Walthamstow, London, E17 7EJ
Registration of Births, Deaths and Marriages: 106 Grove Road, Walthamstow, London E17 9BY (Tel: 020-8520 8617)

CHIEF OFFICERS

Chief Executive: A. Tobias
Acting Director of Finance: R. Cooke
Chief Education Officer: A. Lockhart
Director of Arts and Leisure: C. Small
Director of Planning and Economic Development: A. Bennett
Director of Social Services: R. Wallace

MEMBERS OF THE COUNCIL

Councillor	Ward
Mayor: M. Nasim, Lab.	Hoe Street
Deputy Mayor: S. Poulson, Lab.	Hoe Street
L. Ali, Lab.	High Street
D. Arnold, C.	Chingford
P. Atherton, LD	Chapel End
A. Bean, Lab.	Wood Street
R. Belam, LD	Chapel End
T. Bhogal, Lab.	Grove Green
D. Blunt, Lab.	High Street
L. Braham, C.	Hatch End
M. Broadley, Lab.	Valley
R. Bruni, Lab.	Lea Bridge
A. Buckley, Lab.	Lea Bridge
S. Buckley, Lab.	Lea Bridge
R. Carey, LD	Highham Hill
P. Dawe, Lab.	Wood Street
K. Dhillon, Lab.	Forest
C. Dunn, Lab.	Wood Street
J. Duran, Lab.	Grove Green
R. Evan, C.	Valley
L. Finlayson, C.	Hale End
M. Fish, C.	Chingford
M. Fitzgerald, C.	Hatch End
J. Gover, C.	Valley
J. Gray, Lab.	Leytonstone
P. Herrington, C.	Endlebury
S. Highfield, Lab.	Cathall
L. Hodges, LD	Leyton
Mladen Jovcic, C.	Endlebury
E. Jones, Lab.	Lloyd
T. Kamal, Lab.	St. James Street
C. Kitson, LD	Cann Hall
I. Leslie, Lab.	Leytonstone
M. Lewis, C.	Chingford
C. Loakes, Lab.	Leytonstone
A. Lock, Lab.	Grove Green
M. Martin, Lab.	Cathall
N. Matharoo, Lab.	Lloyd
D. Murray, Lab.	St James Street
D. Norman, C.	Hale End
M. O'Connor, Lab.	Lloyd
E. Phillips, LD	Cann Hall
M. Fazlur Rahman, Lab.	Forest
K. Rayner, LD	Cann Hall
E. Sizer, Lab.	Hoe Street
G. Smith, Lab.	St. James Street
R. Sullivan, LD	Leyton
M. Thompson, Ind.	Larkswood
S. Tucker, Lab.	Forest
C. Tuckley, LD	Leyton
G. Walker, C.	Hatch End
J. Walter, C.	Larkswood
R. Wheatley, LD	High Street
T. Wheeler	Cathall
E. Williams, C.	Larkswood
P. Woollcott, LD	Highham Hill
G. Woolnough, LD	Chapel End

Political Composition: Lab. 29; C. 14; LD. 12; Ind. 1.
Parliamentary Constituencies: Chingford and Woodford; Leyton and Wanstead; Walthamstow
Population: 221,100
Area: 15 square miles

ABOUT WALTHAM FOREST

Waltham Forest is situated in the north east of London. It is mainly a residential borough but contains significant amounts of forest, reservoirs and open spaces. Epping Forest flanks the eastern side of the borough and to the west lies the river Lea and the Lea Valley. The southern areas of Walthamstow, Leyton and Leytonstone contain two thirds of the boroughs total population. The remaining third reside in the northern area of Chingford.

The area is famous for its William Morris Gallery, the only museum dedicated to the Victorian artist and designer and Walthamstow market.

68 Governed London

COUNCIL TAX BANDS 2000-2001

Band	Market Value of the Property in 1991	Council Tax
A	Up to £40,000	£585.06
B	£40,001 to 52,000	£682.57
C	£52,001 to 68,000	£780.08
D	£68,001 to 88,000	£877.59
E	£88,001 to 120,000	£1072.61
F	£120,001 to 160,000	£1267.63
G	£160,001 to 320,000	£1462.65
H	£320,001 or more	£1755.18

WANDSWORTH

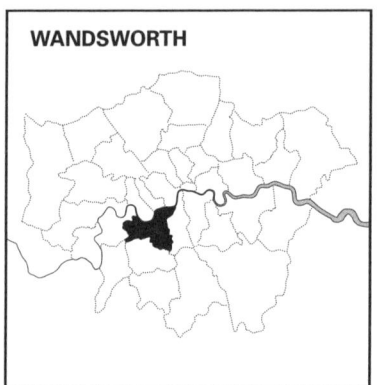

The Town Hall, Wandsworth High Street, London SW18 2PU (Tel: 020-8871 6000; Web: http://www.wandsworth.gov.uk)

CHIEF OFFICERS

Borough Planner: I. Thompson
Borough Solicitor: M. Walker
Chief Executive and Director of Adminstration: G. Jones
Director of Education: P. Robinson
Director of Finance and Deputy Chief Executive: H. Heywood
Director of Housing: R. Sheppard
Director of Leisure and Amenity Services: L. Garrett
Director of Social Services: M. Rundle
Director of Technical Services: W. Myers
Head of Environmental Services: A. R. Waren

MEMBERS OF THE COUNCIL

Councillor	Ward
Mayor: J. Garrett, C.	Springfield
Deputy Mayor: R. Vivian, C.	Queenstown
Leader of the Council: E. Lister, C.	Thamesfield
L. Ayonrinde, C.	Balham
P. Beddows, C.	Shaftesbury
A. Belton, Lab.	Latchmere
T. Beresford, C.	St John
R. Bird, C.	Thamesfield
Jane Briginshaw, Lab.	Furzedown
B. Burn, C.	West Putney
M. Calderbank, C.	West Putney
J. Cousins, C.	Shaftesbury
C. Dawe, C.	Bedford
C. Dixon, C.	Northcote
J. Farebrother, Lab.	Furzedown
S. Finn, C.	Bedford
A. Flook, C.	St Mary's Park
A. Gibbons, Lab.	Graveney
R. Govindia, Lab.	Nightingale
A. Graham, C.	Earlsfield
V. Graham, C.	Fairfield
M. Grimston, C.	West Hill
J. Hallmark, C.	St Mary's Park
T. Harris, C.	Roehampton
I. Hart, C.	Furzedown
M. Heaster, C.	Nightingale
S. Heath, Lab.	Latchmere
D. Hosain, Lab.	Graveney
E. Howlett, C.	Parkside
C. Humphries, C.	Queenstown
G. Hurley, C.	Balham
B. Jeffrey, C.	West Hill
M. Johnson, Lab.	Latchmere
Martin Johnson, C.	Northcote
S. Khan, Lab.	Tooting
S. King, Lab.	Tooting
L. Lees, C.	Thamesfield
Jan Leigh, C.	Southfield
R. Longmore, C.	Balham
N. Longworth, C.	Southfield
S. Lorch, C.	Southfield
H. Lumby, C.	Roehampton
P. McCausland, C.	St John
E. McDermott, C.	Nightingale
Leslie McDonnell, C.	East Putney
C. McNaught-Davis, C.	Earlsfield
M. Mervis, C.	Springfield
G. Passmore, C.	Northcote
B. Prichard, C.	East Putney
G. Senior, C.	Shaftesbury
M. Simpson, C.	Roehampton
T. Strickland, C.	Fairfield
Jeremy Swan, C.	Parkside
Pam Tatlow, Lab.,	Graveney
K. Tracey, C.	Springfield
Jane White, Lab.	Tooting
D. Whittingham, C.	East Putney
S. Wilkie, C.	Bedford
S. Williams, C.	St Mary's Park
N. Zahawi, C.	West Putney

Political Composition: C. 49; Lab. 12
Parliamentary Constituencies: Battersea, Putney, Tooting
Population: 266,300
Area: 3,432 hectares

ABOUT WANDSWORTH

Wandsworth is in the south west of London and houses a number of areas including Battersea, Earlsfield, Putney and Southfields. Much of the borough lies along the Thames and the Oxford and Cambridge boat race starts in the borough at Putney.

London Borough Councils

COUNCIL TAX BANDS 2000-2001

Band	Market Value of the Property in 1991	Council Tax	
A	Up to £40,000	£265.03	£275.95
B	£40,001 to 52,000	£309.02	£321.93
C	£52,001 to 68,000	£353.37	£367.93
D	£68,001 to 88,000	£397.54	£413.91
E	£88,001 to 120,000	£485.88	£505.89
F	£120,001 to 160,000	£574.22	£598.87
G	£160,001 to 320,000	£662.57	£689.86
H	£320,001 or more	£795.07	£827.82

(There are two columns as the borough has two council tax groupings, one for the borough generally and one for areas of the borough which are subject to a Conservative levy (right-hand column)).

WESTMINSTER CITY
WESTMINSTER

Westminster City Hall, Victoria Street, London SW1E 6QP (Tel: 020-7641 6000;
Web: http://www.westminster.gov.uk)
Registration of Births, Deaths and Marriages: Westminster Council House, Marylebone Road, London NW1 5PT Tel: 020-7641 1161

CHIEF OFFICERS

Chief Executive and Director of Finance: Bill Roots
Director of Education: John Harris
Director of Environment and Leisure: Jeff Austin
Director of Housing: Vic Baylis
Director of Legal Services: Colin Wilson
Director of Planning and Transportation: Carl Powell
Director of Policy and Communications: Graham Ellis
Director of Resources: Peter Rogers
Director of Social and Community Services: Mrs. Julie Jones

MEMBERS OF THE COUNCIL

Councillor	Ward
Lord Mayor: M. Brahams, C.	Bayswater
Deputy Lord Mayor: C. Longworth, C.	Belgrave
Leader of the Council: S. Milton, C.	Lancaster Gate
A. Allum, C.	Cavendish
Carol Ann Bailey, C.	Churchill
A. Barns, C.	Bayswater
Pamela Batty	Hyde Park
Jenny Bianco, C.	Bryanston
F. Blois, C.	Belgrave
N. Boles, C.	West End
A. Bradley, C.	St. George's
J. Bull, C.	Bryanston
Susie Burbridge, C.	Maida Vale
M. Caplan, C.	Little Venice
J. Cox, C.	Knightsbridge
C. Cronin, C.	Churchill
R. Davis, C.	Lancaster Gate
P. Dimoldenberg, Lab.	Queen's Park
J. Djanogly, C.	Regent's Park
K. Gardner, C.	Lords
Barbara Grahame, Lab.	Church Street
R. Harley, Lab.	Church Street
D. Harvey, C.	Victoria
A. Hooper, C.	Baker Street
L. Hyams, C.	St. James's
T. Joiner, C.	Regent's Park
A. Lazarus, Lab.	Harrow Road
E. Lazarus, C.	Hyde Park
J. Lord, C.	Little Venice
A. Mallinson, C.	Hyde Park
K. Malthouse, C.	St. George's
H. Marshall, C.	Cavendish
G. Martin, Lab.	Harrow Road
T. Mitchell, C.	Victoria
C. Nemeth, C.	Lords
A. Nicholl, C.	St. James's
R. Nye, C.	Hamilton Terrace
M. Page, C.	Cavendish
J. Powell-Tuck, C.	Millbank
J. Predergast, C.	Maida Vale
Murad Qureshi, Lab.	Church Street
Mushtaq Qureshi, Lab.	Queen's Park
R. Raymond-Cox, C.	Maida Vale
G. Rees-Mogg, C.	Knightsbridge
Glenys Roberts, C.	West End
D. Sandys, C.	Millbank
B. Schmeling, C.	Little Venice
A. Segal, C.	St. George's
Jill Selbourne, Lab.	Harrow Road
L. St. John-Howe, C.	Regent's Park
Simon Stockhill, Lab.	Westbourne
R. Tallboys, C.	Lancaster Gate
B. Taylor, Lab.	Queen's Park
Katy Thorne, Lab.	Westbourne
F. Tombolis, C.	Bayswater
G. Walsh, C.	Churchill
J. Warner, C.	Hamilton Terrace
A. Whitley, Lab.	Westbourne
I. Wilder, C.	Baker Street
P. Wright, Lab.	Millbank

Political Composition: C. 46; Lab. 13
Parliamentary Constituencies: City of London and Westminster, Regents Park and Kensington North
Population: 212,300
Area: 2,204 hectares

ABOUT WESTMINSTER CITY

The City of Westminster occupies an important part of both London and Great Britain as a whole. Buckingham Palace, Downing Street, the Houses of Parliament and most Government departments are within its bound-

70 Governed London

aries. The City is also home to Westminster Abbey, the Roman Catholic Westminster Cathedral and the London Central Mosque. There is culture in the form of the Royal Albert Hall, Royal Opera House and English National Opera and many major theatres and cinemas. There are also countless restaurants, notably in Soho, numerous hotels and many of London's most famous shops. Five major parks and many smaller areas provide light, colour and fresh air.

Over 200,000 people live in Westminster, a figure boosted each day to one million by tourists and workers. Half a million people travel into Westminster to their work helped by the fact that four main railway lines terminate here. All Underground lines pass beneath Westminster's streets and coaches go to and from destinations across the United Kingdom from Victoria Coach Station.

The City of Westminster is administered by a directly elected City Council providing social services, housing (22,000 dwellings), libraries, refuse collection and street cleansing. It is also the main highway and planning authority. Sixty percent of Westminster has been designated conservation areas and overall the city contains 9,000 buildings of architectural and historical significance.

As well as being an important place for residents, tourist, government and culture, the City of Westminster is also a key commercial centre with over 30,000 businesses within its boundaries.

COUNCIL TAX BANDS 2000-2001

Band	Market Value of the Property in 1991	Council Tax
A	Up to £40,000	£250.00
B	£40,001 to 52,000	£291.67
C	£52,001 to 68,000	£333.33
D	£68,001 to 88,000	£375.00
E	£88,001 to 120,000	£458.33
F	£120,001 to 160,000	£541.67
G	£160,001 to 320,000	£625.00
H	£320,001 or more	£750.00

ORGANISATIONS CONNECTED WITH LOCAL GOVERNMENT IN LONDON

ASSOCIATION OF LONDON GOVERNMENT

36 Old Queen Street, London SW1H 9JF (020-7222 7799; Fax 020-7799 2339).

The new Association of London Government was created in April 2000. It combines the Association of London Government, London Borough Grants, Greater London Employers Association, the London Housing Unit and the Transport Committee for London. The new body represents and speaks on behalf of London's 33 councils. Its main committee comprises the elected leaders of all London councils. The objectives of the ALG are to promote economic partnership between the public and private sectors; to develop schemes to improve the environment and quality of life of Londoners; to support local government and to contact Central Government and Europe. Its other functions include the distribution of grants to voluntary organisations in the capital on behalf of the boroughs, and running the London-wide concessionary fares scheme which provides free transport to more than one million elderly and disabled Londoners. The Association of London Government is due to move to new premises in Southwark in March 2001.

Chief Executive: Martin Pilgrim

AUDIT COMMISSION FOR LOCAL AUTHORITIES AND THE NATIONAL HEALTH SERVICE IN ENGLAND AND WALES

1 Vincent Square, London SW1P 2PN (Tel: 020-7828 1212; Fax: 020-7976 6187); Press Office: 26 Grosvenor Gardens, London SW1W 0GT (Tel: 020-7838 4848; Fax: 020-7838 4871)

The Audit Commission for England and Wales is an independent watchdog, promoting proper stewardship of public finance amongst local authorities and local health service bodies. It also has a responsibility to reassure the public and help those responsible for the management and delivery of public services to achieve economy, efficiency and effectiveness through focusing on probity, regularity and value for money.

The Commission carries out work in five principal ways:
- by appointing external auditors to all local authorities - including the GLA – health authorities and hospital trusts in England and Wales;
- by undertaking studies which make recommendations for improving economy, efficiency and effectiveness of service;
- by identifying examples of best practice and encouraging their wider adoption;
- by investigating the impact on local authorities of legislation or central government action or advice;
- by inspecting local authority services in line with Best Value legislation

The Commission has a Chair, Deputy Chair and 18 members drawn from a wide range of backgrounds which include local government, the health service, the civil service, the voluntary sector, academia and the private sector. Members are appointed by the Secretary of

State for the Environment, Transport and the Regions. The Commission's income derives almost entirely from fees charged for audit work and it is required, taking one year with another, to be self-financing. The Commission has about 200 headquarters staff and employs around 1,200 staff in its auditing agency, District Audit. Audit appointments are made either from District Audit or from one of a number of private firms. Additional responsibilities for the Commission include assisting Ofsted with the inspection of Local Education Authorities and joint reviews with the Social Services Inspectorate.

Chair: Dame Helena Shovelton
Deputy Chairman: Jeremy Orme
Members: Sir Peter Soulsby, Mrs Iris Tarry, CBE, J. R. Foster, Sir Ronald Watson, CBE, Rosalynde Lowe, Adrienne Fresko, Cllr Richard Arthur, Cllr David Williams, Prof. Sue Richards, Dr. Judy Curson, Sir Graham Hart, Elizabeth Firkin, Brian Wolfe, Julie Baddeley.

THE LONDON MAYORS' ASSOCIATION
8 Bentinck Street, London W1M 6BJ

The Metropolitan Mayors' and Ex-Mayors' Association was formed in 1901 with the purpose of promoting and discussing general matters affecting the metropolis. Mayors and former Mayors from all the London Boroughs are entitled to join but the chairman is always the Mayor of Westminster.

President: Hon. Alderman Mrs Margaret Calcott-James, (Mayor of Wandsworth 1982-83)
Chairman: Cllr Alex Segal (Lord Mayor of Westminster 1999-2000)

PARLIAMENTARY CONSTITUENCIES IN LONDON

The information below comprises the results of voting in each parliamentary constituency at the last general election which was held on 1 May 1997. The majority in the 1992 general election is given where the constituency covers the same area as in 1992. Where the boundaries of a constituency have changed since 1992, a notional result for 1992 is given. For the constituencies of Beckenham, Uxbridge, Kensington and Chelsea and Tottenham we have also supplied subsequent by-election results.

E. = Total number of electors in the constituency at the 1997 general election
T. = Turnout of electors at the 1997 general election

Barking
E.53,682 T. 61.41%
Mrs M. Hodge, Lab. 21,698
K. Langford, C. 5,802
M. Marsh, LD 3,128
C. Taylor, Ref. 1,283
M. Tolman, BNP 894
D. Mearns, ProLife 159
Lab. majority 15,896
(Boundary change: notional Lab.)

Battersea
E.66,928 T 70.82%
M. Linton, Lab. 24,047
J. Bowis, C. 18,687
Ms P. Keaveney, LD 3,482
M. Slater, Ref. 804
R. Banks, UK Ind. 250
J. Marshall, Dream 127
Lab. majority 5,360
(Boundary change: notional C.)

Beckenham
E.72,807 T. 74.65%
P. Merchant, C. 23,084
R. Hughes, Lab. 18,131
Ms R. Vetterlein, LD 9,858
L. Mead, Ref. 1,663
P. Rimmer, Lib. 720
C. Pratt, UK Ind. 506
J. Mcauley, NF 388
C. majority 4,953
(Boundary change: notional C.)

*(by-election 20 November 1997)
E. 72,807 T. 43.7%
Ms. J. Lait, C. 13,162
R. Hughes, Lab 11,935
Ms R. Vetterlein, LD 5,864
P. Rimmer, Lib 330
J. McAuley, NF 267
L. Mead, New Britain Ref. 237
T. Campion, Social Foundation 69
J. Small, NLP 44
C. majority 1,227

72 Governed London

Bethnal Green and Bow
E.73,008 T. 61.20%
Ms O. King, Lab. 20,697
K. Choudhury, C. 9,412
S. N. Islam, LD 5,361
D. King, BNP 3,350
T. Milson, Lib. 2,963
S. Osman, Real Lab. 1,117
S. Petter, Green 812
M. Abdullah, Ref. 557
A. Hamid, Soc. Lab. 413
Lab. majority 11,285
(Boundary change: notional Lab.)

Bexleyheath and Crayford
E.63,334 T. 76.14%
N. Beard, Lab. 21,942
D. Evennett, C. 18,527
Mrs F. Montford, LD 5,391
B. Thomas, Ref. 1,551
Ms P. Smith, BNP 429
W. Jenner, UK Ind. 383
Lab. majority 3,415
(Boundary change: notional C.)

Brent East
E.53,548 T. 65.87%
K. Livingstone, Lab. 23,748
M. Francois, C. 7,866
I. Hunter, LD 2,751
S. Keable, Soc. Lab. 466
A. Shanks, ProLife 218
Ms C. Warrilo, Dream 120
D. Jenkins, NLP 103
Lab. majority 15,882
(Boundary change: notional Lab.)

Brent North
E.54,149 T. 70.50%
B. Gardiner, Lab. 19,343
Rt. Hon. Sir R. Boyson, C. 15,324
P. Lorber, LD 3,104
A. Davids, NLP 204
G. Clark, Dream 199
Lab. majority 4,019
(Boundary change: notional C.)

Brent South
E.53,505 T. 64.48%
P. Boateng, Lab. 25,180
S. Jackson, C. 5,489
J. Brazil, LD 2,670
Ms J. Phythian, Ref. 497
D. Edler, Green 389
C. Howard, Dream 175
Ms A. Mahaldar, NLP 98
Lab. majority 19,691
(Boundary change: notional Lab.)

Brentford and Isleworth
E.79,058 T. 71.00%
Mrs A. Keen, Lab. 32,249
N. Deva, C. 17,825
Dr G. Hartwell, LD 4,613
J. Bradley, Green 687
Mrs B. Simmerson, UK Ind. 614

M. Ahmed, NLP 147
Lab. majority 14,424
(Boundary change: notional C.)

Bromley and Chislehurst
E.71,104 T. 74.17%
Rt. Hon. E. Forth, C. 24,428
R. Yeldham, Lab. 13,310
Dr P. Booth, LD 12,530
R. Bryant, UK Ind. 1,176
Ms F. Speed, Green 640
M. Stoneman, NF 369
G. Aitman, Lib. 285
C. majority 11,118
(Boundary change: notional C.)

Camberwell and Peckham
E.50,214 T. 56.71%
Ms H. Harman, Lab. 19,734
K. Humphreys, C. 3,383
N. Williams, LD 3,198
N. China, Ref. 692
Ms A. Ruddock, Soc. Lab. 685
G. Williams, Lib. 443
Ms J. Barker, Soc. 233
C. Eames, WRP 106
Lab. majority 16,351
(Boundary change: notional Lab.)

Carshalton and Wallington
E.66,038 T. 73.33%
T. Brake, LD 18,490
*N. Forman, C. 16,223
A. Theobald, Lab. 11,565
J. Storey, Ref. 1,289
P. Hickson, Green 377
G. Ritchie, BNP 261
L. Povey, UK Ind. 218
LD majority 2,267
(April 1992, C. maj. 9,943)

Chingford and Woodford Green
E.62,904 T. 70.66%
I. Duncan Smith, C. 21,109
T. Hutchinson, Lab. 15,395
G. Seeff, LD 6,885
A. Gould, BNP 1,059
C. majority 5,714
(Boundary change: notional C.)

Chipping Barnet
E. 69,049 T. 71.78%
Sir S. Chapman C. 21,317
G. Cooke, Lab. 20,282
S. Hooker, LD 6,121
V. Ribekow, Ref. 1,190
B. Miskin, Loony 253
B. Scallan, ProLife 243
Ms D. Dirksen, NLP 159
C. majority 1,035
(Boundary change: notional C.)

Cities of London and Westminster
E.69,047 T. 58.16%
Rt. Hon. P. Brooke, C. 18,981
Ms K. Green, Lab. 14,100

M. Dumigan, LD 4,933
Sir A. Walters, Ref. 1,161
Ms P. Wharton, Barts 266
C. Merton, UK Ind. 215
R. Johnson, NLP 176
N. Walsh, Loony 138
G. Webster, Hemp 112
J. Sadowitz, Dream 73
C. majority 4,881
(Boundary change: notional C.)

Croydon Central
E.80,152 T.69.62%
G. Davies, Lab. 25,432
D. Congdon, C. 21,535
G. Schlich, LD 6,061
C. Cook, Ref. 1,886
M.-S. Barnsley, Green 595
J. Woollcott, UK Ind. 290
Lab. majority 3,897
(Boundary change: notional C.)

Croydon North
E.77,063 T.68.21%
M. Wicks, Lab. 32,672
I. Martin, C. 14,274
M. Morris, LD 4,066
R. Billis, Ref. 1,155
J. Feisenberger, UK Ind. 396
Lab. majority 18,398
(Boundary change: notional C.)

Croydon South
E.73,787 T.73.45%
R. Ottaway, C. 25,649
C. Burling, Lab. 13,719
S. Gauge, LD 11,441
A. Barber, Ref. 2,631
P. Ferguson, BNP 354
A. Harker, UK Ind. 309
M. Samuel, Choice 96
C. majority 11,930
(Boundary change: notional C.)

Dagenham
E.58,573 T.61.74%
Mrs J. Church, Lab. 23,759
J. Fairrie, C. 6,705
T. Dobrashian, LD 2,704
S. Kraft, Ref. 1,411
W. Binding, BNP 900
R. Dawson, Ind. 349
M. Hipperson, Nat. Dem. 183
Ms K. Goble, ProLife 152
Lab. majority 17,054
(Boundary change: notional Lab.)

Dulwich and West Norwood
E.69,655 T.65.49%
Ms T. Jowell, Lab. 27,807
R. Gough, C. 11,038
Mrs S. Kramer, LD 4,916
B. Coles, Ref. 897
Dr A. Goldie, Lib. 587
D. Goodman, Dream 173
E. Pike, UK Ind. 159

Capt. Rizz, Rizz Party 38
Lab. majority 16,769
(Boundary change: notional Lab.)

Ealing Acton and Shepherd's Bush
E.72,078 T.66.68%
C. Soley, Lab. 28,052
Mrs B. Yerolemou, C. 12,405
A. Mitchell, LD 5,163
C. Winn, Ref. 637
J. Gilbert, Soc. Lab. 635
J. Gomm, UK Ind. 385
P. Danon, ProLife 265
C. Beasley, Glow 209
W. Edwards, Ch. P. 163
K. Turner, NLP 150
Lab. majority 15,647
(Boundary change: notional Lab.)

Ealing North
E.78,144 T.71.31%
S. Pound, Lab. 29,904
H. Greenway, C. 20,744
A. Gupta, LD 3,887
G. Slysz, UK Ind. 689
Ms A. Siebe, Green 502
Lab. majority 9,160
(Boundary change: notional C.)

Ealing Southall
E.81,704 T.66.88%
P. Khabra, Lab. 32,791
J. Penrose, C. 11,368
Ms N. Thomson, LD 5,687
H. Brar, Soc. Lab. 2,107
N. Goodwin, Green 934
B. Cherry, Ref. 854
Ms K. Klepacka, ProLife 473
Dr R. Mead, UK Ind. 428
Lab. majority 21,423
(Boundary change: notional Lab.)

East Ham
E.65,591 T.60.81%
S. Timms, Lab. 25,779
Miss A. Bray, C. 6,421
I. Khan, Soc. Lab. 2,697
M. Sole, LD 2,599
C. Smith, BNP 1,258
Mrs J. McCann, Ref. 845
G. Hardy, Nat. Dem. 290
Lab. majority 19,358
(Boundary change: notional Lab.)

Edmonton
E.63,718 T.70.37%
A. Love, Lab. Co-op. 27,029
Dr I. Twinn, C. 13,557
A. Wiseman, LD 2,847
J. Wright, Ref. 708
B. Cowd, BNP 437
Mrs P. Weald, UK Ind. 260
Lab. Co-op. majority 13,472
(April 1992, C. maj. 593)

74 Governed London

Eltham
E.57,358 T.75.71%
C. Efford, Lab. 23,710
C. Blackwood, C. 13,528
Ms A. Taylor, LD 3,701
M. Clark, Ref. 1,414
H. Middleton, Lib. 584
W. Hitches, BNP 491
Lab. majority 10,182
(Boundary change: notional C.)

Enfield North
E.67,680 T.70.43%
Ms J. Ryan, Lab. 24,148
M. Field, C. 17,326
M. Hopkins, LD 4,264
R. Ellingham, Ref. 857
Ms J. Griffin, BNP 590
Mrs J. O'Ware, UK Ind. 484
Lab. majority 6,822
(April 1992, C. maj. 9,430)

Enfield Southgate
E.65,796 T.70.72%
S. Twigg, Lab. 20,570
Rt. Hon. M. Portillo, C. 19,137
J. Browne, LD 4,966
N. Luard, Ref. 1,342
A. Storkey, Ch. D. 289
A. Malakouna, Mal 229
Lab. majority 1,433
(Boundary change: notional C.)

Erith and Thamesmead
E.62,887 T.66.13%
J. Austin-Walker, Lab. 25,812
N. Zahawi, C. 8,388
A. Grigg, LD 5,001
J. Flunder, Ref. 1,394
V. Dooley, BNP 718
M. Jackson, UK Ind. 274
Lab. majority 17,424
(Boundary change: notional Lab.)

Feltham and Heston
E.71,093 T.65.58%
A. Keen, Lab. Co-op. 27,836
P. Ground, C. 12,563
C. Penning, LD 4,264
R. Stubbs, Ref. 1,099
R. Church, BNP 682
D. Fawcett, NLP 177
Lab. Co-op. majority 15,273
(Boundary change: notional Lab. Co-op.)

Finchley and Golders Green
E.72,225 T.69.65%
R. Vis, Lab. 23,180
J. Marshall, C. 19,991
J. Davies, LD 5,670
G. Shaw, Ref. 684
A. Gunstock, Green 576
D. Barraclough, UK Ind. 205
Lab. majority 3,189
(Boundary change: notional C.)

Greenwich and Woolwich
E.61,352 T.65.85%
N. Raynsford, Lab. 25,630
M. Mitchell, C. 7,502
Mrs C. Luxton, LD 5,049
D. Ellison, Ref. 1,670
R. Mallone, Fellowship 428
D. Martin-Eagle, Constit. 124
Lab. majority 18,128
(Boundary change: notional Lab.)

Hackney North and Stoke Newington
E.62,045 T.52.95%
Ms D. Abbott, Lab. 21,110
M. Lavender, C. 5,483
D. Taylor, LD 3,806
Yen Chit Chong, Green 1,395
B. Maxwell, Ref. 544
D. Tolson, None 368
Miss L. Lovebucket, Rain. Ref. 146
Lab. majority 15,627
(April 1992, Lab. maj. 10,727)

Hackney South and Shoreditch
E.61,728 T.54.67%
B. Sedgemore, Lab. 20,048
M. Pantling, LD 5,068
C. O'Leary, C. 4,494
T. Betts, New Lab. 2,436
R. Franklin, Ref. 613
G. Callow, BNP 531
M. Goldman, Comm. P. 298
Ms M. Goldberg, NLP 145
W. Rogers, WRP 113
Lab. majority 14,980
(Boundary change: notional Lab.)

Hammersmith and Fulham
E.78,637 T.68.70%
I. Coleman, Lab. 25,262
M. Carrington, C. 21,420
Ms A. Sugden, LD 4,728
Mrs M. Bremner, Ref. 1,023
W. Johnson-Smith, New Lab. 695
Ms E. Streeter, Green 562
G. Roberts, UK Ind. 183
A. Phillips, NLP 79
A. Elston, Care 74
Lab. majority 3,842
(Boundary change: notional C.)

Hampstead and Highgate
E.64,889 T.67.86%
Ms G. Jackson, Lab. 25,275
Miss E. Gibson, C. 11,991
Mrs B. Fox, LD 5,481
Ms M. Siddique, Ref. 667
J. Leslie, NLP 147
R. Carroll, Dream 141
Miss P. Prince, UK Ind. 123
R. J. Harris, Hum. 105
Capt. Rizz, Rizz Party 101
Lab. majority 13,284
(Boundary change: notional Lab.)

Parliamentary Constituencies

Harrow East
E.79,846 T.71.37%
A. McNulty, Lab. 29,927
H. Dykes, C. 20,189
B. Sharma, LD 4,697
B. Casey, Ref. 1,537
A. Scholefield, UK Ind. 464
A. Planton, NLP 171
Lab. majority 9,738
(Boundary change: notional C.)

Harrow West
E.72,005 T.72.92%
G. Thomas, Lab. 21,811
R. Hughes, C. 20,571
Mrs P. Nandhra, LD 8,127
H. Crossman, Ref. 1,997
Lab. majority 1,240
(Boundary change: notional C.)

Hayes and Harlington
E.56,829 T.72.31%
J. McDonnell, Lab. 25,458
A. Retter, C. 11,167
A. Little, LD 3,049
F. Page, Ref. 778
J. Hutchins, NF 504
D. Farrow, ANP 135
Lab. majority 14,291
(Boundary change: notional C.)

Hendon
E.76,195 T.65.67%
A. Dismore, Lab. 24,683
Sir J. Gorst, C. 18,528
W. Casey, LD 5,427
S. Rabbow, Ref. 978
B. Wright, UK Ind. 267
Ms S. Taylor, WRP 153
Lab. majority 6,155
(Boundary change: notional C.)

Holborn and St Pancras
E.63,037 T.60.28%
F. Dobson, Lab. 24,707
J. Smith, C. 6,804
Ms J. McGuinness, LD 4,750
Mrs J. Carr, Ref. 790
T. Bedding, NLP 191
S. Smith, JP 173
Ms B. Conway, WRP 171
M. Rosenthal, Dream 157
P. Rice-Evans, EUP 140
B. Quintavalle, ProLife 114
Lab. majority 17,903
(Boundary change: notional Lab.)

Hornchurch
E.60,775 T.72.30%
J. Cryer, Lab. 22,066
R. Squire, C. 16,386
R. Martins, LD 3,446
R. Khilkoff-Boulding, Ref. 1,595
Miss J. Trueman, Third Way 259
J. Sowerby, ProLife 189
Lab. majority 5,680
(April 1992, C. maj. 9,165)

Hornsey and Wood Green
E.74,537 T.69.08%
Mrs B. Roche, Lab. 31,792
Mrs H. Hart, C. 11,293
Ms L. Featherstone, LD 5,794
Ms H. Jago, Green 1,214
Ms R. Miller, Ref. 808
P. Sikorski, Soc. Lab. 586
Lab. majority 20,499
(April 1992, Lab. maj. 5,177)

Ilford North
E.68,218 T.71.60%
Ms L. Perham, Lab. 23,135
V. Bendall, C. 19,911
A. Dean, LD 5,049
P. Wilson, BNP 750
Lab. majority 3,224
(Boundary change: notional C.)

Ilford South
E.72,104 T.69.37%
M. Gapes, Lab. Co-op. 29,273
Sir N. Thorne, C. 15,073
Ms A. Khan, LD 3,152
D. Hodges, Ref. 1,073
B. Ramsey, Soc. Lab. 868
A. Owens, BNP 580
Lab. Co-op. majority 14,200
(Boundary change: notional C.)

Islington North
E.57,385 T.62.49%
J. Corbyn, Lab. 24,834
J. Kempton, LD 4,879
S. Fawthrop, C. 4,631
C. Ashby, Green 1,516
Lab. majority 19,955
(April 1992, Lab. maj. 12,784)

Islington South and Finsbury
E.55,468 T.63.67%
C. Smith, Lab. 22,079
Ms S. Ludford, LD 7,516
D. Berens, C. 4,587
Miss J. Bryett, Ref. 741
A. Laws, ACA 171
M. Creese, NLP 121
E. Basarik, Ind. 101
Lab. majority 14,563
(Boundary change: notional Lab.)

Kensington and Chelsea
E.67,786 T.54.71%
Rt. Hon. A. Clark, C. 19,887
R. Atkinson, Lab. 10,368
R. Woodthorpe Browne, LD 5,668
Ms A. Ellis-Jones, UK Ind. 540
E. Bear, Teddy 218
G. Oliver, UKPP 176
Ms S. Hamza, NLP 122
P. Sullivan, Dream 65
P. Parliament, Heart 44
C. majority 9,519
(Boundary change: notional C.)

76 Governed London

* (by-election 25 November 1999)
E. 65,806 T. 29.7%
Rt. Hon. M. Portillo, C. 11,004
R. Atkinson, Lab. 4,298
R. Woodthorpe Browne, LD 1,831
J. Stevens, ProECP 740
N. Hockney, UK Ind. 450
H. Charlton, Green 446
C. Burford, Dem. 182
C. Paisley, LCA 141
M. Irwin, LWLC 97
G. Oliver, UKPP 75
S. Scott-Fawcett, Ref. 57
L. Hodges, DSSP 48
G. Valente, NLP 35
L. Lovebucket, PNDTP 26
J. Davies, Ind. ESCC 24
P. May, EPP 24
A. Hope, Loony 20
T. Samuelson, Stop 15
C. majority, 6706

Kingston and Surbiton
E.73,879 T.75.35%
E. Davey, LD 20,411
R. Tracey, C. 20,355
Ms S. Griffin, Lab. 12,811
Mrs G. Tchiprout, Ref. 1,470
Ms P. Burns, UK Ind. 418
C. Port, Dream 100
M. Leighton, NLP 100
LD majority 56
(Boundary change: notional C.)

Lewisham Deptford
E.58,141 T.57.87%
Mrs J. Ruddock, Lab. 23,827
Mrs I. Kimm, C. 4,949
K. Appiah, LD 3,004
J. Mulrenan, Soc. Lab. 996
Ms S. Shepherd, Ref. 868
Lab. majority 18,878
(Boundary change: notional Lab.)

Lewisham East
E.56,333 T.66.41%
Ms B. Prentice, Lab. 21,821
P. Hollobone, C. 9,694
D. Buxton, LD 4,178
S. Drury, Ref. 910
R. Croucher, NF 431
P. White, Lib. 277
Capt. Rizz, Dream 97
Lab. majority 12,127
(Boundary change: notional Lab.)

Lewisham West
E.58,659 T.64.00%
J. Dowd, Lab. 23,273
Mrs C. Whelan, C. 8,936
Miss K. McGrath, LD 3,672
A. Leese, Ref. 1,098
N. Long, Soc. Lab. 398
Ms E. Oram, Lib. 167
Lab. majority 14,337
(April 1992, Lab. maj. 1,809)

Leyton and Wanstead
E.62,176 T.63.24%
H. Cohen, Lab. 23,922
R. Vaudry, C. 8,736
C. Anglin, LD 5,920
S. Duffy, ProLife 488
A. Mian, Ind. 256
Lab. majority 15,186
(Boundary change: notional Lab.)

Mitcham and Morden
E.65,385 T.73.33%
Ms S. McDonagh, Lab. 27,984
Rt. Hon. Dame A. Rumbold, C. 14,243
N. Harris, LD 3,632
P. Isaacs, Ref. 810
Ms L. Miller, BNP 521
T. Walsh, Green 415
K. Vasan, Ind. 144
J. Barrett, UK Ind. 117
N. Dixon, ACC 80
Lab. majority 13,741
(April 1992, C. maj. 1,734)

Old Bexley and Sidcup
E.68,044 T.75.53%
Rt. Hon. Sir E. Heath, C. 21,608
R. Justham, Lab. 18,039
I. King, LD 8,284
B. Reading, Ref. 2,457
C. Bullen, UK Ind. 489
Ms V. Tyndall, BNP 415
R. Stephens, NLP 99
C. majority 3,569
(Boundary change: notional C.)

Orpington
E.78,749 T.76.40%
J. Horam, C. 24,417
C. Maines, LD 21,465
Ms S. Polydorou, Lab. 10,753
D. Clark, Ref. 2,316
J. Carver, UK Ind. 526
R. Almond, Lib. 494
N. Wilton, ProLife 191
C. majority 2,952
(Boundary change: notional C.)

Poplar and Canning Town
E.67,172 T.58.46%
J. Fitzpatrick, Lab. 24,807
B. Steinberg, C. 5,892
Ms J. Ludlow, LD 4,072
J. Tyndall, BNP 2,849
I. Hare, Ref. 1,091
Ms J. Joseph, Soc. Lab. 557
Lab. majority 18,915
(Boundary change: notional Lab.)

Putney
E.60,176 T.73.11%
A. Colman, Lab. 20,084
Rt. Hon. D. Mellor, C. 17,108
R. Pyne, LD 4,739
Sir J. Goldsmith, Ref. 1,518
W. Jamieson, UK Ind. 233

L. Beige, Stan 101
M. Yardley, Spts All. 90
J. Small, NLP 66
Ms A. Poole, Beaut. 49
D. Vanbraam, Ren. Dem. 7
Lab. majority 2,976
(April 1992, C. maj. 7,526)

Regent's Park and Kensington North
E.73,752 T.64.19%
Ms K. Buck, Lab. 28,367
P. McGuinness, C. 13,710
Miss E. Gasson, LD 4,041
Ms S. Dangoor, Ref. 867
J. Hinde, NLP 192
Ms D. Sadowitz, Dream 167
Lab. majority 14,657
(Boundary change: notional Lab.)

Richmond Park
E.71,572 T.79.43%
Dr J. Tonge, LD 25,393
Rt. Hon. J. Hanley, C. 22,442
Ms S. Jenkins, Lab. 7,172
J. Pugh, Ref. 1,467
D. Beaupre, Loony 204
B. D'Arcy, NLP 102
P. Davies, Dream 73
LD majority 2,951
(Boundary change: notional C.)

Romford
E.59,611 T.70.66%
Mrs E. Gordon, Lab. 18,187
Sir M. Neubert, C. 17,538
N. Meyer, LD 3,341
S. Ward, Ref. 1,431
T. Hurlstone, Lib. 1,100
M. Carey, BNP 522
Lab. majority 649
(Boundary change: notional C.)

Ruislip-Northwood
E.60,393 T.74.24%
J. Wilkinson, C. 22,526
P. Barker, Lab. 14,732
C. Edwards, LD 7,279
Ms C. Griffin, NLP 296
C. majority 7,794
(Boundary change: notional C.)

Southwark North and Bermondsey
E.65,598 T.62.19%
S. Hughes, LD 19,831
J. Fraser, Lab. 16,444
G. Shapps, C. 2,835
M. Davidson, BNP 713
W. Newton, Ref. 545
I. Grant, Comm L. 175
J. Munday, Lib. 157
Ms I. Yngvison, Nat. Dem. 95
LD majority 3,387
(Boundary change: notional LD)

Streatham
E.74,509 T.60.24%
K. Hill, Lab. 28,181

E. Noad, C. 9,758
R. O'Brien, LD 6,082
J. Wall, Ref. 864
Lab. majority 18,423
(Boundary change: notional Lab.)

Sutton and Cheam
E.62,785 T.75.01%
P. Burstow, LD 19,919
Lady O. Maitland, C. 17,822
M. Allison, Lab. 7,280
P. Atkinson, Ref. 1,784
S. McKie, UK Ind. 191
Ms D. Wright, NLP 96
LD majority 2,097
(April 1992, C. maj. 10,756)

Tooting
E.66,653 T.69.17%
T. Cox, Lab. 27,516
J. Hutchings, C. 12,505
S. James, LD 4,320
Mrs A. Husband, Ref. 829
J. Rattray, Green 527
P. Boddington, BFAIR 161
J. Koene, Rights 94
D. Bailey-Bond, Dream 83
P. Miller, NLP 70
Lab. majority 15,011
(April 1992, Lab. maj. 4,107)

Tottenham
E.66,173 T.56.98%
B. Grant, Lab. 26,121
A. Scantlebury, C. 5,921
N. Hughes, LD 4,064
P. Budge, Green 1,059
Ms E. Tay, ProLife 210
C. Anglin, WRP 181
Ms T. Kent, SEP 148
Lab. majority 20,200
(April 1992, Lab. maj. 11,968)

*(by-election 22 June 2000)
E. 64,554 T. 25.4%
David Lammy, Lab. 8,875
Duncan Hames, LD 3,139
Jane Ellison, C. 2,634
Weyman Bennett, London Soc. All. 885
Peter Budge, Green 606
Erol Barsarik, Reform 2000 177
Ashwin Tanna, UK Ind. 136
Derek Dorian de Braan, Ind. Lab., 55
Lab. majority 5,646

Twickenham
E.73,281 T.79.34%
Dr V. Cable, LD 26,237
T. Jessel, C. 21,956
Ms E. Tutchell, Lab. 9,065
Miss J. Harrison, Ind. ECR 589
T. Haggar, Dream 155
A. Hardy, NLP 142
LD majority 4,281
(Boundary change: notional C.)

Upminster
E.57,149 T.72.30%
K. Darvill, Lab. 19,085
Sir N. Bonsor, C. 16,315
Mrs P. Peskett, LD 3,919
T. Murray, Ref. 2,000
Lab. majority 2,770
(Boundary change: notional C.)

Uxbridge
E.57,497 T.72.26%
Sir M. Shersby, C. 18,095
D. Williams, Lab. 17,371
Dr A. Malyan, LD 4,528
G. Aird, Ref. 1,153
Ms J. Leonard, Soc. 398
C. majority 724
(Boundary change: notional C.)

*(by-election 31 July 1997)
E. 57,733 T.55.2%
J. Randall, C. 16,288
A. Slaughter, Lab. 12,522
K. Kerr, LD 1,792
Lord Sutch, Loony 396
Ms J. Leonard, Soc 259
Ms F. Taylor, BNP 205
I. Anderson, Nat. Dem. 157
J. Macauley, NF 110
H. Middleton, Original Lib. Party 69
J. Feisenberger, UK Ind. 39
R. Carroll, Emerald Rainbow Islands Dream Ticket 30
C. majority 3,766

Vauxhall
E.70,402 T.55.49%
Ms K. Hoey, Lab. 24,920
K. Kerr, LD 6,260
R. Bacon, C. 5,942
I. Driver, Soc. Lab. 983
S. Collins, Green 864
R. Headicar, SPGB 97
Lab. majority 18,660
(Boundary change: notional Lab.)

Walthamstow
E.63,818 T.62.76%
N. Gerrard, Lab. 25,287
Mrs J. Andrew, C. 8,138
Dr J. Jackson, LD 5,491
Revd G. Hargreaves, Ref. 1,139
Lab. majority 17,149
(Boundary change: notional Lab.)

West Ham
E.57,058 T.58.99%
A. Banks, Lab. 24,531
M. MacGregor, C. 5,037
Ms S. McDonough, LD 2,479
K. Francis, BNP 1,198
T. Jug, Loony 300
J. Rainbow, Dream 116
Lab. majority 19,494
(Boundary change: notional Lab.)

Wimbledon
E.64,070 T.75.47%
R. Casale, Lab. 20,674
Dr C. Goodson-Wickes, C. 17,694
Ms A. Willott, LD 8,014
H. Abid, Ref. 993
R. Thacker, Green 474
Ms S. Davies, ProLife 346
M. Kirby, Mongolian 112
G. Stacey, Dream 47
Lab. majority 2,980
(April 1992, C. maj. 14,761)

Party Abbreviations

ANP - All Night Party
Barts - Independent Save Barts Candidate
Beaut. - Independently Beautiful Party
BFAIR - British Freedom and Individual Rights
BNP - British National Party
C. – Conservative
Care - Care in the Community
Choice - People's Choice
Ch. P. - Christian Party
Comm. - Communist League
Comm. - Communist Party of Britain
Constit. - Constitutionalist
Dream - Rainbow Dream Ticket Party
DSSP - Daily and Sunday Sport Party
EPP - Equal Parenting Party
EUP - European Unity Party
Fellowship - Fellowship Party for Peace and Justice
Glow - Glow Bowling Party
Green – Green Party
Heart - Heart 106.2 Alien Party
Hemp - Hemp Coalition
Ind. ECR - Independent English Conservative and Referendum
JP - Justice Party
Lab. – Labour Party
LCA – Legalise Cannabis Alliance
LD – Liberal Democrat Party
Lib. - Liberal
Loony - Monster Raving Loony Party
LWLC - Living Will Legislation Campaign
Nat. Dem. - National Democrat
New Labour – New Labour Party
NF - National Front
NLP - Natural Law Party
PNDTP - People's Net Dream Ticket Party
ProECP - Pro Euro Conservative Party
ProLife - ProLife Alliance
Rain. - Rainbow Referendum
Real Lab. – Real Labour Party
Ref. - Referendum Party
Ren. Dem. - Renaissance Democrat
Rizz – Rizz Party
SEP - Socialist Equality Party
Soc. - Socialist Party
Soc. Dem - Social Democrat
Soc. F. – Social Foundation
Soc. Lab. - Socialist Labour Party
Spts All - Sportsman's Alliance: Anything but Mellor
Stan - Happiness Stan's Freedom to Party Party
Stop - Stop Tobacco Companies Farming our Children
Teddy - Teddy Bear Alliance Party
Third – Third Way Party
UK Ind. - UK Independence Party
UKPP - UK Pensioners Party
WRP - Workers' Revolutionary Party

EUROPEAN PARLIAMENT

European Parliament elections take place at five-yearly intervals; the first direct elections to the Parliament were held in 1979. In mainland Britain MEPs were elected in all constituencies on a first-past-the-post basis until the elections of June 1999; in Northern Ireland three MEPs have been elected by the single transferable vote system of proportional representation since 1979. From 1979 to 1994 the number of seats held by the UK in the European Parliament was 81. At the June 1994 election the number of seats increased to 87 (England 71, Wales 5, Scotland, 8, Northern Ireland 3). At the European Parliament elections held on 10 June 1999, all British MEPs were elected under a 'closed-list' regional system of proportional representation, with England being divided into nine regions (London being one region) and Scotland and Wales each constituting a region. Parties submitted a list of candidates for each region in their own order of preference. Voters voted for a party or an independent candidate, and the first seat in each region was allocated to the party or candidate with the highest number of votes. The rest of the seats in each region were then allocated broadly in proportion to each party's share of the vote. Each region returned the following number of members: East Midlands, 6; Eastern, 8; London, 10; North East, 4; North West, 10; South East, 11; South West, 7; West Midlands, 8; Yorkshire and the Humber, 7; Wales, 5; Scotland, 8.

If a vacancy occurs due to the resignation or death of and MEP, the vacancy is filled by the next available person on that party's list. If an independent MEP resigns or dies, a by-election is held. Where an MEP leaves the party on whose list he/she was elected, there is no requirement to resign and he/she can remain in office until the next general election.

British subjects and citizens of the Irish Republic are eligible for election to the European Parliament provided they are 21 or over and not subject to disqualification. Since 1994, nationals of member states of the European Union have had the right to vote in elections to the European Parliament in the UK as long as they are entered on the electoral register.

MEPs currently receive a salary from the parliaments or governments of their respective member states, set at the level of the national parliamentary salary and subject to national taxation rules. A proposal that all MEPs should be paid the same rate of salary out of the EU budget, and subject to the EC tax rate, was under negotiation between the European Parliament and the Council of Ministers at the time of going to press.

Press Office: 2 Queen Anne's Gate, London SW1H 9AA (Tel: 020-7227 4300; Fax: 020-7227 4302; Email: eplondon@europarl.eu.int; Web: http://www.europarl.org.uk)

LONDON REGION
E.4,940,493 T.23.10%

Lab.	399,466 (35.00%)
C.	372,989 (32.68%)
LD	133,058 (11.66%)
Green	87,545 (7.67%)
UK Ind.	61,741 (5.41%)
Soc. Lab.	19,632 (1.72%)
BNP	17,960 (1.57%)
Lib.	16,951 (1.49%)
Pro Euro C.	16,383 (1.44%)
AHRPE	4,851 (0.43%)
Anti VAT	2,596 (0.23%)
Hum.	2,586 (0.23%)
Hemp	2,358 (0.21%)
NLP	2,263 (0.20%)
WW	846 (0.07%)
Lab. majority	26,477

(June 1994, Lab. maj. 346,850)

LONDON MEMBERS

Balfe, Richard A. (b. 1944), Lab., London
Bethell, The Lord (b. 1938), C., London
Bowis, John C., OBE (b. 1945), C., London
Evans, Robert J. E. (b. 1956), Lab., London
Honeyball, Mrs Mary (b. 1952) Lab. London
Lambert, Ms Jean D. (b. 1950), Green, London
Ludford, The Baroness (b. 1951), LD, London
Moraes, Claude (b. 1965), Lab., London
Tannock, Dr Charles (b. 1957), C., London
Villiers, Ms Theresa (b. 1968), C., London

GOVERNMENT DEPARTMENTS AND PUBLIC OFFICES

In this section you will find information on the Cabinet, Central Government departments and their Executive Agencies. Although these departments and agencies have remits extending further than London we feel that they merit inclusion in order to comprehensively convey the structure of governance in London on a local and national level. Immediately following the government departments and executive agencies is a list comprising regulatory bodies, other statutory independent organisations, and bodies which are government-financed or whose head is appointed by a government minister.

The Civil Service
Under the Next Steps programme, launched in 1988, many semi-autonomous executive agencies have been established to carry out much of the work of the Civil Service. Executive agencies operate within a framework set by the responsible minister which specifies policies, objectives and available resources. All executive agencies are set annual performance targets by their minister. Each agency has a chief executive, who is responsible for the day-to-day operations of the agency and who is accountable to the minister for the use of resources and for meeting the agency's targets. The minister accounts to Parliament for the work of the agency. Nearly 60 per cent of civil servants now work in executive agencies. Customs and Excise, the Inland Revenue, the Crown Prosecution Service and the Serious Fraud Office, which employ a further 17 per cent of civil servants, also operate on 'Next Steps' lines. In January 1999 there were about 463,700 permanent civil servants.

The Senior Civil Service was created in 1996 and comprises about 3,000 staff from Permanent Secretary to the former Grade 5 level, including all agency chief executives. All government departments and executive agencies are now responsible for their own pay and grading systems for civil servants outside the Senior Civil Service.

CABINET
Prime Minister, First Lord of the Treasury and Minister for the Civil Service: Tony Blair
Deputy Prime Minister and Secretary of State for the Environment, Transport and the Regions: John Prescott
Chancellor of the Exchequer: Gordon Brown
Secretary of State for Foreign and Commonwealth Affairs (Foreign Secretary): Robin Cook
Lord Chancellor: Lord Irvine of Lairg
Secretary of State for Education and Employment: David Blunkett
President of the Council and Leader of the House of Commons: Margaret Beckett
Minister for the Cabinet Office and Chancellor of the Duchy of Lancaster: Mo Mowlam
Secretary of State for Scotland: John Reid
Secretary of State for Defence: Geoff Hoon
Secretary of State for Health: Alan Milburn
Chief Whip (Commons): Ann Taylor
Secretary of State for Culture, Media and Sport: Chris Smith
Secretary of State for Northern Ireland: Peter Mandelson
Secretary of State for Wales: Paul Murphy
Secretary of State for International Development: Clare Short
Secretary of State for Social Security: Alistair Darling
Minister of Agriculture, Fisheries and Food: Nick Brown
Lord Privy Seal and Leader of the House of Lords: Baroness Jay of Paddington
Secretary of State for Trade and Industry: Stephen Byers
Chief Secretary to the Treasury: Andrew Smith

DEPARTMENT MINISTERS

Ministry of Agriculture, Fisheries and Food
Minister: Nick Brown
Ministers of State: Joyce Quin; Baroness Hayman
Parliamentary Secretary: Elliot Morley

Cabinet Office
Minister for the Cabinet Office and Chancellor of the Duchy of Lancaster: Mo Mowlam
Lord Privy Seal, Leader of the House of Lords and Minister for Women: Baroness Jay
Ministers of State: Lord Falconer; Ian McCartney

Department for Culture, Media and Sport
Secretary of State: Chris Smith
Parliamentary Under Secretaries
  Sport: Kate Hoey
  Arts: Alan Howarth
  Tourism, Film, Broadcasting: Janet Anderson

Ministry of Defence
Secretary of State: Geoff Hoon
Ministers of State: Baroness Symons of Vernham Dean
  Armed Forces: John Spellar
Parliamentary Under Secretary: Peter Kilfoyle

Department for Education and Employment
Secretary of State: David Blunkett
Ministers of State
  Employment, Welfare to Work and Equal Opportunities: Tessa Jowell
  School Standards: Estelle Morris; Baroness Blackstone
Parliamentary Under Secretaries
  Employment and Equal Opportunities: Margaret Hodge; Michael Wills; Malcolm Wicks; Jacqui Smith

Department of the Environment, Transport and the Regions
Deputy Prime Minister and Secretary of State: John Prescott
Ministers of State
  Environment: Michael Meacher
  Local Government and Housing: Nick Raynsford
  Transport: Lord Macdonald of Tradeston
  Regions, Regeneration and Planning: Richard Caborn
Parliamentary Under Secretaries
  Roads: Lord Whitty; Chris Mullin; Beverley Hughes
  London: Keith Hill

Government Departments

Foreign and Commonwealth Office
Secretary of State: Robin Cook
Ministers of State: Keith Vaz; John Battle; Peter Hain
Parliamentary Under Secretary: Baroness Scotland of Asthal

Department of Health
Secretary of State: Alan Milburn
Ministers of State: John Denham; John Hutton
Parliamentary Under Secretaries: Gisela Stuart; Yvette Cooper; Lord Hunt of King's Heath

Home Office
Secretary of State: Jack Straw
Ministers of State: Paul Boateng; Charles Clarke; Barbara Roche
Parliamentary Under Secretaries: Mike O'Brien; Lord Bassam of Brighton

Department for International Development
Secretary of State: Clare Short
Parliamentary Under Secretary: George Foulkes

Law Officers' Department
Attorney General: Lord Williams of Mostyn
Solicitor General: Ross Cranston

Lord Chancellor's Department
Lord Chancellor: Lord Irvine of Lairg
Parliamentary Under Secretaries: Jane Kennedy; David Lock

Northern Ireland Office
Secretary of State: Peter Mandelson
Minister of State: Adam Ingram
Parliamentary Under Secretaries: John McFall; Lord Dubs; George Howarth

Privy Council Office
President of the Council and Leader of the House of Commons: Margaret Beckett
Parliamentary Secretary: Paddy Tipping

Scotland Office
Secretary of State: Dr John Reid
Advocate General: Dr Lynda Clark
Minister of State: Brian Wilson

Department of Social Security
Secretary of State: Alistair Darling
Minister of State: Jeff Rooker
Parliamentary Under Secretaries: Angela Eagle; Hugh Bayley; Baroness Hollis of Heigham

Department of Trade and Industry
Secretary of State: Stephen Byers
Ministers of State: Helen Liddell; Patricia Hewitt; Richard Caborn
Parliamentary Under Secretaries
  Competition and Consumer Affairs: Dr Kim Howells
  Science: Lord Sainsbury of Turville; Alan Johnson

HM Treasury
Chancellor of the Exchequer: Gordon Brown
Chief Secretary: Andrew Smith

Paymaster General: Dawn Primarolo
Financial Secretary: Stephen Timms
Economic Secretary: Melanie Johnson

Office of the Secretary of State for Wales
Secretary of State: Paul Murphy

Government Whips – Commons
Chief Whip: Ann Taylor
Deputy Chief Whip: Keith Bradley
No 3 Whip: Thomas MvAvoy
No 3 Whip: Graham Allen
Senior Whips: Robert Ainsworth; James Dowd; Clive Betts; David Jamieson
Assistant Whips: Anne McGuire; David Clelland; Michael Hall; Kevin Hughes; Greg Popwe; Gerry Sutcliffe

Government Whips – Lords
Chief Whip: Lord Carter
Deputy Chief Whip: Lord McIntosh of Haringey
Whips: Baroness Farrington of Ribbleton; Baroness Ramsay of Cartvale; Baroness Amos

MINISTRY OF AGRICULTURE, FISHERIES AND FOOD

Nobel House, 17 Smith Square, London SW1P 3PR (Tel: 020-7238 3000; Fax: 020-7238 6591; Email: helpline@inf.maff.gov.uk; Web: http://www.maff.gov.uk/maffhome.htm)

The Ministry of Agriculture, Fisheries and Food is responsible for government policies on agriculture, horticulture and fisheries in England and for policies relating to the safety and quality of food in the UK as a whole, including composition, labelling, additives, contaminants and new production processes. In association with the agriculture departments of the Scottish Executive, the National Assembly for Wales and the Northern Ireland Office and with the Intervention Board, the Ministry is responsible for negotiations in the EU on the common agricultural and fisheries policies, and for single European market questions relating to its responsibilities. Its remit also includes international agricultural and food trade policy.

The Ministry exercises responsibilities for the protection and enhancement of the countryside and the marine environment, for flood defence and for other rural issues. It is the licensing authority for veterinary medicines and the registration authority for pesticides. It administers policies relating to the control of animal, plant and fish diseases. It provides scientific, technical and professional services and advice to farmers, growers and ancillary industries, and it commissions research to assist in the formulation and assessment of policy and to underpin applied research and development work done by industry. Responsibility for food safety and standards was transferred to the new Food Standards Agency in April 2000.

GROUPS/UNITS/DIRECTORATES/DIVISIONS

Establishments Group; Establishments and Office Services Division; Information Technology Directorate; Communications Directorate; Agency Ownership Unit;

82 Governed London

Finance Department; Financial Policy Division; Procurement and Contracts Division; Audit, Consultancy and Management Services; Resource Management Division; Resource Management Strategy Unit; Business Planning Unit; Legal Department; Investigation Unit; Economics and Statistics; Statistics Division; Chief Scientist's Group; Fisheries Department; Agricultural Crops and Commodities Directorate; European Union and International Policy; Agriculture Group; Food Industry, Competitiveness and Consumers; Regional Services and Defence Group; Plant Variety Rights Office and Seeds Division; Food Safety and Environment Group; Environment Group; Food Safety and Standards Group; Animal Health Group; Chief Veterinary Officer's Group; Veterinary Field Service.

EXECUTIVE AGENCIES

Central Science Laboratory
Sand Hutton, York YO41 1LZ (Tel: 01904-462000; Fax: 01904-462111)
The Agency provides MAFF with technical support and policy advice on the protection and quality of the food supply and on related environmental issues.

Centre for Environment, Fisheries and Aquaculture Science
Pakefield Road, Lowestoft, Suffolk NR33 0HT (Tel: 01502-562244; Fax: 01502-513865)
The Agency, established in April 1997, provides research and consultancy services in fisheries science and management, aquaculture, fish health and hygiene, environmental impact assessment, and environmental quality assessment.

Farming and Rural Conservation Agency
Nobel House, 17 Smith Square, London SW1P 3JR (Tel: 020-7238 5432; Fax: 020-7238 5588)
The Agency, established in April 1997, is responsible jointly to MAFF and the National Assembly for Wales. It assists the Government in the design, development and implementation of policies on the integration of farming and conservation, environmental protection, rural land use and the diversification of the rural economy. This includes agri-environment schemes such as Environmentally Sensitive Areas, Countryside Stewardship and access, rural development, milk hygiene inspections and wildlife management.

Pesticides Safety Directorate
Mallard House, Kings Pool, 3 Peasholme Green, York YO1 7PX (Tel: 01904-640500; Fax: 01904-455733)
The Pesticides Safety Directorate is responsible for the evaluation and approval of pesticides and the development of policies relating to them, in order to protect consumers, users and the environment.

Veterinary Laboratories Agency
Woodham Lane, New Haw, Addlestone, Surrey KT15 3NB (Tel: 01932-341111; Fax: 01932-347046)
The Veterinary Laboratories Agency provides scientific and technical expertise in animal and public health.

Veterinary Medicines Directorate
Woodham Lane, New Haw, Addlestone, Surrey KT15 3LS (Tel: 01932-336911; Fax: 01932-336618)
The Veterinary Medicines Directorate is responsible for all aspects of the authorisation and control of veterinary medicines, including post-authorisation surveillance of residues in meat and animal products, and the provision of policy advice to ministers.

THE CABINET OFFICE

70 Whitehall, London SW1A 2AS (Tel: 020-7270 3000)
Horse Guards Road, London SW1P 3AL (Tel: 020-7270 1234; Web: http://www.cabinet-office.gov.uk)

The Cabinet Office comprises the Secretariat, who support Ministers collectively in the conduct of Cabinet business; and units responsible for modernising government and helping to improve the quality, coherence and responsiveness of public services. It is also responsible for Senior Civil Service and public appointments, market testing and efficiency in the Civil Service, and Civil Service recruitment. The Cabinet Office supports the Prime Minister in his capacity as Minister for the Civil Service, with responsibility for day-to-day supervision delegated to the Minister for the Cabinet Office, who is also responsible for the Central Office of Information.

PRIME MINISTER'S OFFICE

10 Downing Street, London SW1A 2AA (Tel: 020-7270 3000; Fax: 020-7925 0918;
Web: http://www.number-10.gov.uk)

Secretariat: Economic and Domestic Secretariat; Defence and Overseas Affairs Secretariat; Intelligence Co-ordination Group; European Secretariat; Constitution Secretariat; Central Secretariat; Ceremonial Branch; Public Service Delivery; Central IT Unit; Regulatory Impact Unit; Modernising Government.

EXECUTIVE AGENCIES

Civil Service College
11 Belgrave Road, London SW1V 1RB (Tel: 020-7834 6644; Fax: 01344-634451)
The College provides training in management and professional skills for the public and private sectors.

Government Car and Despatch Agency
46 Ponton Road, London SW8 5AX (Tel: 020-7217 3839; Fax: 020-7217 3840)
The Agency provides secure transport and document transfers between government departments.

Property Advisers to the Civil Estate
Trevelyan House, Great Peter Street, London SW1P 2BY (Tel: 020-7271 2833; Fax: 020-7271 2622; Web: http://www.property.gov.uk)
The Agency promotes co-operation between government departments to enable them to obtain best value for money in the management of their property assets. It also provides them with property guidance and other property-related services. From April 2000 it became part of the new Office of Government Commerce reporting to the Chief Secretary to the Treasury.

Government Departments 83

CENTRAL OFFICE OF INFORMATION
Hercules Road, London SE1 7DU (Tel: 020-7928 2345; Fax: 020-7928 5037)

The Central Office of Information (COI) is a government department which offers consultancy, procurement and project management services to central government for publicity. Though the majority of the COI's work is for government departments in the UK, it also procures a range of publicity materials for overseas consumption. Administrative responsibility for the COI rests with the Minister for the Cabinet Office.

DEPARTMENT FOR CULTURE, MEDIA AND SPORT
2-4 Cockspur Street, London SW1Y 5DH (Tel: 020-7211 6200; Fax: 020-7211 6032; Email: enquiries@culture.gov.uk; Web: http://www.culture.gov.uk)

The Department for Culture, Media and Sport was established in April 1992 as the department of national heritage and is responsible for government policy relating to the arts, broadcasting, the media, museums and galleries, libraries, sport and recreation, historic buildings and ancient monuments, tourism, and the creative industries. It is also responsible for policy on the National Lottery and the Millennium.

GROUPS/UNITS/DIRECTORIES/ DIVISIONS
Museums, Galleries, Libraries and Heritage Group; Strategy and Communication Group; Corporate Services Group; Creative Industries, Media and Broadcasting Group; Regions, Tourism, Millennium and International Group; Education, Training, Arts and Sport

EXECUTIVE AGENCY

Royal Parks Agency
The Old Police House, Hyde Park, London W2 2UH (Tel: 020-7298 2000; Fax: 020-7298 2005)
The Royal Parks Agency is responsible for maintaining and developing the Royal Parks.

MINISTRY OF DEFENCE
Main Building, Whitehall, London SW1A 2HB (Tel 020-7218 9000; Public Enquiry Office: Tel 020 -7218 6645; Web: http://www.mod.uk)

DEPARTMENT FOR EDUCATION AND EMPLOYMENT
Sanctuary Buildings, Great Smith Street, London SW1P 3BT (Tel: 0870-001 2345; Fax: 020-7925 6000; Email: info@dfee.gov.uk; Web: http://www.dfee.gov.uk) Caxton House, Tothill Street, London SW1H 9NF (Tel: 020-7273 3000; Fax: 020-7273 5124)

The Department for Education and Employment was formed in July 1995, bringing together the functions of the former Department for Education with the training and labour market functions of the former Employment Department Group. It includes an executive agency, the Employment Service. The Department aims to support economic growth and improve the nation's competitiveness and quality of life by raising standards of educational achievement and skill and by promoting an efficient and flexible labour market.

GROUPS/UNITS/DIRECTORIES/ DIVISIONS
Employment, Lifelong Learning and International Directorate; Further and Higher Education and Youth Training Directorate; Legal Adviser's Office; Operations Directorate; Personnel and Support Services Directorate; Schools Directorate; Strategy and Communications

EXECUTIVE AGENCY

The Employment Service
Caxton House, Tothill Street, London SW1H 9NA (Tel: 020-7273 6060; Fax: 020-7273 6099)
The aim of the Employment Service is to help people without jobs to find work and employers to fill their vacancies.

DEPARTMENT OF THE ENVIRONMENT, TRANSPORT AND THE REGIONS
Eland House, Bressenden Place, London SW1E 5DU
Great Minster House, 76 Marsham Street, London SW1P 4DR
Ashdown House, 123 Victoria Street, London SW1E 6DE (Tel: 020-7944 3000;
Web: http://www.detr.gov.uk)

The Department of the Environment, Transport and the Regions (DETR) was formed in June 1997 by the merger of the Department of the Environment and the Department of Transport. It is responsible for policies relating to the environment, housing, transport services, rural affairs, planning, local government, regional development, regeneration, the construction industry and health and safety.

The Department's ministers are based at Eland House.

EXECUTIVE AGENCIES

Driver and Vehicle Licensing Agency
Longview Road, Morriston, Swansea SA6 7JL (Tel: 01792-772151 (drivers); 01792-772134 (vehicles))
The Agency issues driving licences, registers and licenses vehicles, and collects excise duty.

Driving Standards Agency
Stanley House, Talbot Street, Nottingham NG1 5GU (Tel: 0870 240 0010 (Vehicles Customer Services); Tel: 0870 240 0009 (Drivers Customer Services).
The Agency's responsibilities are the issuing of driving licences, the registration and licensing of vehicles in Great Britain, and the collection and enforcement of vehicle excise duty in the UK. The Agency also offers for sale attractive registration marks through the Sale of Marks scheme.

Highways Agency
St Christopher House, Southwark Street, London SE1 0TE (Tel: 0645-556575; Fax: 020-7921 4899; Email: ha_info@highways.gov.uk;

84 Governed London

Web: www.highways.gov.uk)
The Agency is responsible for the operation, management and maintenance of the motorway and trunk road network and for road construction and improvement.

Maritime and Coastguard Agency
Spring Place, 105 Commercial Road, Southampton SO15 1EG (Tel: 023-8032 9100; Fax: 023-8032 9105; Email: mcamic@mcga.gov.uk;
Web: http://www.mcagency.org.uk)
The Agency was formed in April 1998 by the merger of the Coastguard Agency and the Marine Safety Agency. Its role is to develop, promote and enforce high standards of marine safety; to minimise loss of life amongst seafarers and coastal users; and to minimise pollution from ships of the sea and coastline.

Planning Inspectorate
Tollgate House, Houlton Street, Bristol BS2 9DJ (Tel: 0117-987 8000; 0117-987 8408;
Email: enquiries.pins@gtnet.gov.uk;
Web: http://www.open.gov.uk/pi/pihome.htm)
The Inspectorate is responsible for casework involving planning, housing, roads, environmental and related legislation. It is a joint executive agency of the Department of the Environment, Transport and the Regions and the National Assembly for Wales.

Queen Elizabeth II Conference Centre
Broad Sanctuary, London SW1P 3EE (Tel: 020-7222 5000; Fax: 020-7798 4200)
The Centre provides conference and banqueting facilities for both private sector and government use.

Vehicle Certification Agency
1 Eastgate Office Centre, Eastgate Road, Bristol BS5 6XX (Tel: 0117-951 5151; Fax: 0117-952 4103)
The Agency tests and certificates vehicles to UK and international standards.

Vehicle Inspectorate
Berkeley House, Croydon Street, Bristol BS5 0DA (Tel: 0117-954 3200; Fax: 0117-954 3212)
The Agency carries out annual testing and inspection of heavy goods and other vehicles and administers the MOT testing scheme.

GOVERNMENT OFFICES FOR THE REGIONS
The Government Offices for the Regions were established in 1994. The regional directors are accountable to the Secretary of State for the Environment, Transport and the Regions, the Secretary of State for Trade and Industry, and the Secretary of State for Education and Employment. The offices' role is to promote a coherent approach to competitiveness, sustainable economic development and regeneration using public and private resources.

Central Unit
1st Floor, Eland House, Bressenden Place, London SW1E 5DU (Tel: 020-7944 5157; Fax: 020-7944 5019)
There are a number of area offices: East Midlands; East of England; London; North-East; North-West; South-East; South-West; West Midlands; Yorkshire and the Humber.

London
Riverwalk House, 157-161 Millbank, London SW1P 4RR (Tel: 020-7217 3456; Fax: 020-7217 3450)
Director of Office: Miss E. C. Turton, CB
Directors: J. A. Owen (Skills, Education and Regeneration); S. Lord (Transport and Corporate); R. Allan (New London Governance); (G5), A. Sargent (Skills and Education); Mrs J. Bridges (Planning); Ms A. Munro (Transport Division); K. Timmins (Enterprise and North-West); Ms M. Winckler (London East and European Programmes); S. Gooding (London Transport Division); P. Sanders (Transport for London Bill Division); A. Melville (Greater London Authority Implementation); Ms E. Meek (GLA Division); A. Weedon (Transport Task Force); Ms C. Lyons (Corporate); J. Sienkiewicz (London Development Unit); R. Wragg (Operations and Business Management); N. Robinson (Exports and Trade, and Business Development); P. Fiddeman (Regeneration London South); B. Mann (Home Office Liaison); Z. Kowalczyk (London Readiness 2000/Millennium Access); I. Jordan (Transport for London Project Division)

FOREIGN AND COMMONWEALTH OFFICE
Downing Street, London SW1A 2AL (Tel: 020-7270 3000; Web: http://www.fco.gov.uk)

The Foreign and Commonwealth Office provides, mainly through diplomatic missions, the means of communication between the British Government and other governments and international governmental organisations for the discussion and negotiation of all matters falling within the field of international relations. It is responsible for alerting the Government to the implications of developments overseas; for protecting British interests overseas; for protecting British citizens abroad; for explaining British policies to, and cultivating friendly relations with, governments overseas; and for the discharge of British responsibilities to the UK overseas territories.

EXECUTIVE AGENCY

Wilton Park Conference Centre
Wiston House, Steyning, W. Sussex BN44 3DZ (Tel: 01903-815020; Fax: 01903-816373)
The Centre organises international affairs conferences and is hired out to government departments and commercial users.

DEPARTMENT OF HEALTH
Richmond House, 79 Whitehall, London SW1A 2NL (Tel: 020-7210 3000;
Web: http://www.open.gov.uk/doh/dhhome.htm)

The Department of Health is responsible for the provision of the National Health Service in England and for social care, including oversight of personal social services run by local authorities in England for children (except day care, which is now the responsibility of the DfEE), the elderly, the infirm, the handicapped and other persons in need. It is responsible for health promotion and has functions relating to public and environmental health, food safety and nutrition. The Department is also responsible for the ambulance and

Government Departments

emergency first aid services, under the Civil Defence Act 1948. The Department represents the UK at the European Union and other international organisations including the World Health Organisation. It also supports UK-based healthcare and pharmaceutical industries.

Responsibility for food safety was transferred to the new Food Standards Agency in operation by April 2000.

EXECUTIVE AGENCIES

Medicines Control Agency
Market Towers, 1 Nine Elms Lane, London SW8 5NQ (Tel: 020-7273 0000; Fax: 020-7273 0353; Email: info@mca.gov.uk; Web: http://www.open.gov.uk/mca/mcahome.htm)
The MCA safeguards public health by ensuring that all medicines on the UK market meet appropriate standards of safety, quality and efficiency. This is achieved by a system of licensing, inspection, enforcement and monitoring of medicines after they have been licensed.

Medical Devices Agency
Hannibal House, Elephant and Castle, London SE1 6TQ (Tel: 020-7972 8000; Fax: 020-7972 8108)
The Agency safeguards the performance, quality and safety of medical devices and ensures that they comply with relevant EU directives.

NHS Estates
1 Trevelyan Square, Boar Lane, Leeds LS1 6AE (Tel: 0113-254 7000; Fax: 0113-254 7299)
NHS Estates provides advice and support in the area of healthcare estate and facilities management to the NHS and the healthcare industry.

NHS Pensions
Hesketh House, 200-220 Broadway, Fleetwood, Lancs FY7 8LG (Tel: 01253 774774; Fax: 01253 774860; Web: http://www.nhspa.gov.uk)
NHS Pensions administers the NHS occupational pension scheme.

HOME OFFICE

50 Queen Anne's Gate, London SW1H 9AT (Tel: 020-7273 4000; Fax: 020-7273 2190; Email: gen.ho@gtnet.gov.uk; Web: http://www.homeoffice.gov.uk)

The Home Office deals with those internal affairs in England and Wales which have not been assigned to other government departments. The Home Secretary is particularly concerned with the administration of justice; criminal law; the treatment of offenders, including probation and the prison service; the police; immigration and nationality; passport policy matters; community relations; certain public safety matters; and fire and civil emergencies. The Home Secretary personally is the link between The Queen and the public, and exercises certain powers on her behalf, including that of the royal pardon.

Other subjects dealt with include electoral arrangements; ceremonial and formal business connected with honours; scrutiny of local authority by-laws; granting of licences for scientific procedures involving animals; cremations, burials and exhumations; firearms; dangerous drugs and poisons; general policy on laws relating to shops, liquor licensing, gaming and marriage; theatre and cinema licensing; and race relations policy.

The Home Secretary is also the link between the UK government and the governments of the Channel Islands and the Isle of Man.

EXECUTIVE AGENCIES

Fire Service College
Moreton-in-Marsh, Glos GL56 0RH (Tel: 01608-650831)

UK Passport Agency
Clive House, Petty France, London SW1H 9HQ (National Enquiry Line: 0870 521 0410; Web: http://www.ukpa.gov.uk).
Application forms for British passports are available from main Post Offices, large travel agents and Passport Offices. There are seven regional passport offices based in London, Durham, Liverpool, Newport, Peterborough, Glasgow and Belfast. The Passport Agency is only able to issue and service passports to British nationals who are resident in the UK at the time of application. If a new passport is needed whilst outside the UK, the nearest British Consulate or Embassy should be contacted.

DEPARTMENT FOR INTERNATIONAL DEVELOPMENT

94 Victoria Street, London SW1E 5JL (Tel: 020-7917 7000; Fax: 020-7917 0019; Web: http://www.dfid.gov.uk)

The Department for International Development (DFID) was established in May 1997 from the former Overseas Development Administration of the Foreign and Commonwealth Office. It takes the lead on British policy towards developing countries. It also manages the development assistance budget, including financial aid and technical assistance (specialist staff abroad and training facilities in the UK), whether provided directly to developing countries or through the various multilateral aid organisations, including the EU, the World Bank and the UN agencies.

LAW OFFICERS' DEPARTMENTS

Legal Secretariat to the Law Officers, Attorney-General's Chambers, 9 Buckingham Gate, London SW1E 6JP (Tel: 020-7271 2400; Fax: 020-7271 2430; Email: lslo@gtnet.gov.uk; Web: http://www.lslo.gov.uk)

The Law Officers of the Crown for England and Wales are the Attorney-General and the Solicitor-General. The Attorney-General, assisted by the Solicitor-General, is the chief legal adviser to the Government and is also ultimately responsible for all Crown litigation. He has overall responsibility for the work of the Law Officers' Departments (the Treasury Solicitor's Department, the Crown Prosecution Service, the Serious Fraud Office and the Legal Secretariat to the Law Officers). He has a specific statutory duty to superintend the discharge of their duties by the Director of Public Prosecutions (who heads the Crown Prosecution Service) and the Director of the Serious Fraud Office.

86 Governed London

The Director of Public Prosecutions for Northern Ireland is also responsible to the Attorney-General for the performance of his functions. The Attorney-General has additional responsibilities in relation to aspects of the civil and criminal law.

LORD CHANCELLOR'S DEPARTMENT

Selborne House, 54-60 Victoria Street, London SW1E 6QW (Tel: 020-7210 8500; Email: enquiries.lcdhq@gtnet.gov.uk; Web: http://www.open.gov.uk/lcd)

The Lord Chancellor appoints Justices of the Peace (except in the Duchy of Lancaster) and advises the Crown on the appointment of most members of the higher judiciary. He is responsible for promoting general reforms in the civil law, for the procedure of the civil courts and for legal aid. Since April 2000, civil legal aid is the Community Legal Service. The Lord Chancellor is a member of the Cabinet. He also has ministerial responsibility for magistrates' courts, which are administered locally. Administration of the Supreme Court and county courts in England and Wales was taken over by the Court Service, an executive agency of the department, in 1995.

The Lord Chancellor is also responsible for ensuring that letters patent and other formal documents are passed in the proper form under the Great Seal of the Realm, of which he is the custodian. The work in connection with this is carried out under his direction in the Office of the Clerk of the Crown in Chancery.

The Lord Chancellor is also the senior Lord of Appeal in Ordinary and speaker of the House of Lords.

EXECUTIVE AGENCIES

The Court Service
Southside, 105 Victoria Street, London SW1E 6QT (Tel: 020-7210 2266; Fax: 020-7210 1797; Email: cust.ser.cs@gtnet.gov.uk; Web: http://www.courtservice.gov.uk)
The Court Service provides administrative support to the Supreme Court, the Crown Court, County Courts and a number of tribunals in England and Wales.

HM Land Registry
Lincoln's Inn Fields, London WC2A 3PH (Tel: 020-7917 8888; Fax: 020-7955 0110)
The registration of title to land was first introduced in England and Wales by the Land Registry Act 1862; HM Land Registry operates today under the Land Registration Acts 1925 to 1988. The object of registering title to land is to create and maintain a register of landowners whose title is guaranteed by the state and so to simplify the transfer, mortgage and other dealings with real property. Registration on sale is now compulsory throughout England and Wales. The register has been open to inspection by the public since 1990.

Public Trust Office
Stewart House, 24 Kingsway, London WC2B 6JX (Tel: 020-7664 7000; Fax: 020-7664 7702) Court Funds Office, 22 Kingsway, London WC2B 6LE (Tel: 020-7936 6000; Fax: 020-7936 6882)
The Public Trust Office became an executive agency of the Lord Chancellor's Department in 1994.

The current Acting Chief Exective holds the statutory title of Accountant General of the Supreme Court. Jill Martin, as the Acting Public Trustee, discharges the statutory responsibilities vested in the Public Trustee. The Public Trustee, through the Public Trust Office, is a trust corporation created to undertake the business of executorships and trusteeship, acting as executor or administrator of the estate of a deceased person, or as trustee of a will or settlement.

The Public Trustee is also responsible for the performance of all the administrative, but not the judicial, tasks required of the Court of Protection under Part VII of the Mental Health Act 1983, relating to the management and administration of the property and affairs of persons suffering from mental disorder. The Public Trustee also acts as receiver when so directed by the Court, usually where there is no other person willing or able to act. The Office also deals with the registration of Enduring Powers of Attorney. The Accountant General of the Supreme Court, through the Court Funds Ofice, is responsible for the investment and accounting of funds in court for persons under a disability, monies in court subject to litigation and statutory deposits. The Office is currently undergoing a process of restructuring and it is possible that the functions described above will be re-allocated to other organisations during 2000/1.

OFFICE OF FAIR TRADING

Fleetbank House, 2-6 Salisbury Square, London EC4Y 8JX (Tel: 020-7211 8000; Fax: 020-7211 8800; Email: enquiries@oft.gov.uk; Web: http://www.oft.gov.uk)

The Office of Fair Trading is a non-ministerial government department headed by the Director-General of Fair Trading. It keeps commercial activities in the UK under review and seeks to protect consumers against unfair trading practices. The Director-General's consumer protection duties under the Fair Trading Act 1973, together with his responsibilities under the Consumer Credit Act 1974, the Estate Agents Act 1979, the Control of Misleading Advertisements Regulations 1988, and the Unfair Terms in Consumer Contracts Regulations 1999, are administered by the Office's Consumer Affairs Division. The Competition Policy Division is concerned with monopolies and mergers (under the Fair Trading Act 1973) and the Director-General's other responsibilities for competition matters, including those under the Competition Act 1998, the Financial Services Act 1986 and the Broadcasting Act 1990. The Office is the UK competent authority on the application of the European Commission's competition rules, and also liaises with the Commission on consumer protection initiatives.
Director-General: J. Bridgeman

SCOTLAND OFFICE

Dover House, Whitehall, London SW1A 2AU (Tel: 020-7270 6754; Fax: 020-7270 6812; Web: http://www.scottishsecretary.gov.uk)

The Scotland Office is the Office of the Secretary of State for Scotland, who represents Scottish interests in the Cabinet on matters reserved to the UK Parliament, i.e. national financial and economic matters, social security, defence and international relations, and employment.

Government Departments

DEPARTMENT OF SOCIAL SECURITY
Richmond House, 79 Whitehall, London SW1A 2NS (Tel: 020-7238 0800)

The Department of Social Security (DSS) is responsible for the payment of benefits including child benefit, one-parent benefit, income support and family credit. It administers the Social Fund, and is responsible for assessing the means of applicants for legal aid. It is also responsible for the payment of war pensions and the operation of the child maintenance system. Responsibility for the operation of the national insurance contributions scheme was transferred from the DSS to the Inland Revenue in April 1999.

EXECUTIVE AGENCIES

Benefits Agency
Quarry House, Quarry Hill, Leeds LS2 7UA (Tel: 0113-232 4000; Fax: 0113-232 4085;
Email: baadmin@baadmin.demon.co.uk;
Web: http://www.dss.gov.uk/ba)
The Agency administers claims for and payments of social security benefits.

Child Support Agency (CSA)
DSS Long Benton, Benton Park Road, Newcastle upon Tyne NE98 1YX (Helpline: 0845 713 3133)
The Agency was set up in April 1993. It is responsible for the administration of the Child Support Act and for the assessment, collection and enforcement of maintenance payments for all new cases.

Information Technology Services Group
Control Centre, Peel park, Brunel Way, Blackpool, Lancashire FY4 5ES (Tel 01253 714114)
The Agency maintains and oversees policies on information technology strategy, procurement, technical standards and security.

War Pensions Agency
Norcross, Blackpool, Lancs FY5 3WP (Tel: 01253-856123; Email: warpensions@gtnet.gov.uk;
Web: http://dss.gov.uk/wpa/index.htm)
The Agency administers the payment of war disablement and war widows' pensions and provides welfare services and support to war disablement pensioners, war widows and their dependants and carers.

DEPARTMENT OF TRADE AND INDUSTRY
1 Victoria Street, London SW1H 0ET (Tel: 020-7215 5000; Fax: 020-7222 2629; Web: http://www.dti.gov.uk)

The Department is responsible for international trade policy, including the development of UK trade interests in the European Union, GATT, OECD, UNCTAD and other international organisations; the policy in relation to industry and commerce, including industrial relations policy; policy towards small firms; regional industrial assistance; legislation and policy in relation to the Post Office; competition policy and consumer protection; the development of national policies in relation to all forms of energy and the development of new sources of energy, including international aspects of energy policy; policy on science and technology research and development; space policy; standards, quality and design; and company legislation.

EXECUTIVE AGENCIES

Patent Office
Concept House, Cardiff Road, Newport NP9 1RH (Tel: 0645-500505; Fax: 01633-814444)
The duties of the Patent Office are to administer the Patent Acts, the Registered Designs Act and the Trade Marks Act, and to deal with questions relating to the Copyright, Designs and Patents Act 1988. The Search and Advisory Service carries out commercial searches through patent information.

HM TREASURY
Parliament Street, London SW1P 3AG (Tel: 020-7270 5000; Web: http://www.hm-treasury.gov.uk)

The Office of the Lord High Treasurer has been continuously in commission for well over 200 years. The Lord High Commissioners of HM Treasury are the First Lord of the Treasury (who is also the Prime Minister), the Chancellor of the Exchequer and five junior Lords (who are government whips in the House of Commons). This Board of Commissioners is assisted at present by the Chief Secretary, the Parliamentary Secretary who is also the government Chief Whip, the Paymaster-General, the Financial Secretary, the Economic Secretary, the Minister of State and the Permanent Secretary.

The Prime Minister is not primarily concerned in the day-to-day aspects of Treasury business; the management of the Treasury devolves upon the Chancellor of the Exchequer and the other Treasury ministers.

The Chief Secretary is responsible for public expenditure planning and control; public sector pay; value for money in the public services; public/private partnerships and procurement policy; strategic oversight of banking, financial services and insurance; departmental investment strategies; welfare reform; devolution; and resource accounting and budgeting. From April 2000 is be responsible for a new Office of Government Commerce which will centralise government procurement activities.

The Paymaster-General is responsible for the Inland Revenue, Customs and Excise and the Treasury, with overall responsibility for the Finance Bill. She leads on personal and business taxation, VAT and European/international tax issues. The Paymaster-General's Office is part of the National Investment and Loans Office.

The Financial Secretary is responsible for growth and productivity; small firms and venture capital; science, research and development; competition and deregulation policy; environmental issues; export credit; most Customs and Excise taxes; vehicle excise duty; and parliamentary financial business.

The Economic Secretary is responsible for National Savings, the Debt Management Office, the National Investment and Loans Office, the Office for National Statistics, the Royal Mint, and the Government Actuary's Department; banking, financial services and insurance; foreign exchange reserves; debt management policy; women's issues; and charity taxation.

EXECUTIVE AGENCIES

The Buying Agency
Royal Liver Building, Pier Head, Liverpool L3 1PE (Tel: 0151-227 4262; Fax: 0151-227 3315)
The Agency provides a professional purchasing service to government departments and other public bodies. From April 2000 it became part of the new Office of Government Commerce reporting to the Chief Secretary to the Treasury.

CCTA (Central Computer and Telecommunications Agency)
Rosebery Court, St Andrew's Business Park, Norwich NR7 0HS (Tel: 01603-704567; Fax: 01603-704817)
Steel House, 11 Tothill Street, London SW1H 9NF (Tel: 020-7273 6565; Fax: 020-7273 6555)
CCTA's objective is to develop, maintain and make available expertise about information technology which public sector organisations can draw on in order to operate more effectively and efficiently. From April 2000 it became part of the new Office of Government Commerce reporting to the Chief Secretary to the Treasury.

National Savings
Charles House, 375 Kensington High Street, London W14 8SD (Tel: 020-7605 9300;
Web: http://www.nationalsavings.co.uk)
National Savings was established as a government department in 1969. It became an executive agency of the Treasury in 1996 and is responsible for the design, marketing and administration of savings and investment products for personal savers and investors. In April 1999 Siemens Business Services took over all the back office functions at National Savings.

Office for National Statistics
1 Drummond Gate, London SW1V 2QQ (Tel: 020-7533 6363; Fax: 020-7533 5719)
The Office for National Statistics was created in 1996 by the merger of the Central Statistical Office and the Office of Population, Censuses and Surveys. It is responsible for preparing and interpreting key economic statistics for government policy; collecting and publishing business statistics; publishing annual and monthly statistical digests; providing researchers, analysts and other customers with a statistical service; administration of the marriage laws and local registration of births, marriages and deaths in England and Wales; provision of population estimates and projections and statistics on health and other demographic matters in England and Wales; population censuses in England and Wales; surveys for government departments and public bodies; and promoting these functions within the UK, the European Union and internationally to provide a statistical service to meet European Union and international requirements.
The Office for National Statistics is also responsible for establishing and maintaining a central database of key economic and social statistics produced to common classifications, definitions and standards.

Family Records Centre, 1 Myddelton Street, London EC1R 1UW (Tel: 020-8392 5300)

Office of Government Commerce (OGC)
Fleetbank House, 2-6 Salisbury Square, London EC4Y 8JX (Tel 020-7211 1300; Web http://www.ogc.gov.uk)
The Office of Government Commerce was set up on the 1st April 2000. It is a unique body within government, overseen by a supervisory board of ministers and officials from across the departments of government. Its aim is to achieve the best value for money for the Government's commercial relationships and coherence of purchasing activity across 200 Government departments, non-governmental bodies and agencies. The OGC is an office of HM Treasury.

Royal Mint
Llantrisant, Pontyclun CF72 8YT (Tel: 01443-623060; Fax: 01443-623185; Web: http://www.royalmint.com)
The prime responsibility of the Royal Mint is the provision of United Kingdom coinage, but it actively competes in world markets for a share of the available circulating coin business and about two-thirds of the 20,000 tonnes of coins it produces annually are exported. The Mint also manufactures special proof and uncirculated quality coins in gold, silver and other metals; military and civil decorations and medals; commemorative and prize medals; and royal and official seals.
The Royal Mint became an executive agency of the Treasury in 1990. The Government announced in July 1999 that the Royal Mint would be given greater commercial freedom to expand its business into new areas and develop partnerships with the private sector.

United Kingdom Debt Management Office
Cheapside House, 138 Cheapside, London EC2V 6BB (Tel: 020-7862 6500; Fax: 020-7862 6509)
The UK Debt Management Office was launched as an executive agency of the Treasury in April 1998 after the transfer from the Bank of England to the Treasury of responsibility for debt management, the sale of gilts and oversight of the gilts market. It assumed responsibility for the management of the Exchequer's daily cash flows on 3 April 2000.

TREASURY SOLICITOR

Queen Anne's Chambers, 28 Broadway, London SW1H 9JS (Tel: 020-7210 3000; Fax: 020-7210 3004)

The Treasury Solicitor's Department provides legal services for many government departments. Those without their own lawyers are provided with legal advice, and both they and other departments are provided with litigation services. The Treasury Solicitor is also the Queen's Proctor, and is responsible for collecting Bona Vacantia on behalf of the Crown. The Department became an executive agency in 1996.

WALES OFFICE

Gwydyr House, Whitehall, London SW1A 2ER (Tel: 020-7270 3000; Fax: 020-7270 0577;
Web: http://www.ossw.wales.gov.uk)
The Wales Office is the Office of the Secretary of State for Wales, who represents Welsh interests in the Cabinet.

PUBLIC SERVICES
LONDON

EDUCATION
EMERGENCY SERVICES
  AMBULANCE
  FIRE
  POLICE
HEALTH
HOUSING
LIBRARIES
TRANSPORT
UTILITIES

PUBLIC SERVICES LONDON

EDUCATION

STRUCTURE
In these first years of the new millennium, educational provision in London is experiencing a period of far-reaching, turbulent change. For the moment, however, the basic structure of the educational system remains unchanged. Children begin formal education in nursery schools from the age of three and the primary sector is responsible for education between five and eleven years old, covering Key Stages 1 and 2 of the prescribed National Curriculum, recently revised and now in its thirteenth year. The secondary sector covers Key Stages 3 and 4 and takes students up to the age of sixteen, the last year of compulsory education for children in the UK. These same schools may accommodate a student's choice of courses post-16. In some London boroughs the small number of post-16 students in individual schools make courses not viable, so provision is concentrated in specialist sixth form colleges.

Further Education Colleges provide a range of academic, vocational and recreational courses for those beyond the compulsory age of schooling. Universities (including the new sector that transferred from polytechnic status in the past decade) allow the student to proceed along the higher education route towards the award of academic degrees and post-graduate research.

LEA RESPONSIBILITIES
Education continues to be administered by LEAs (Local Education Authorities) which coincide with the 33 London boroughs. In fact, education accounts for the highest proportion of local government spending. The main responsibilities of LEAs include:
- Determining their education budget within the constraints imposed by central government.
- Deciding the structure of education in its area - whether to have infant and junior schools; first and middle schools; comprehensives or grammar schools; single sex or co-educational schools.
- Supervising the education service, focusing more on monitoring and evaluating the curriculum and general management of schools.
- Overseeing admissions policies and providing appeals procedures.
- Providing educational psychology and welfare services; free school transport, free school meals, board and lodgings, clothing to pupils who qualify. The Department lays down complex regulations for education and employment for many of these services.
- Providing a wide range of central support services from in-service training for teachers and governors, to personnel and financial services.
- Adult Education, Youth Service and the provision of education of the under fives.

LONDON EDUCATION STATISTICS
In London, this infrastructure needs to meet the needs of a rising school population. Latest statistics show that in the five-year period leading up to 1999, the numbers of nursery children rose from 59,235 to 71,696. This is mainly because of the policies of successive governments to provide more places for children in this age group. The numbers of primary and secondary pupils in London's schools have also shown a sharp rise. Primary school pupils increased by more than 50,000 (nine per cent), and secondary pupils by more than 48,000 (14 per cent). The number of teachers in all sectors also increased.

The number of school pupils eligible for free school meals, a frequently used proxy for deprivation and poverty, has fallen in the primary sector but risen in the secondary sector over the five year period – 27.5 per cent of primary school pupils are now eligible for free school meals. Almost a third (31 per cent) of all secondary pupils are also eligible for free school meals. In Inner London 46.3 per cent of secondary pupils in London LEA schools are eligible for free school meals.

The cosmopolitan nature of London is reflected in its school population. In London as a whole, 40 per cent of pupils came from ethnic minority backgrounds with 300 languages finding representation. Over a half (53 per cent) of inner London pupils and 35 per cent of outer London were from ethnic minority backgrounds.

EDUCATION AND GOVERNMENT POLICY
There are a number of educational policy themes that will influence London education (along with the rest of the country) in the year ahead. The consistent line out of government is that the main item on the education agenda is raising standards. Secretary of State for Education David Blunkett has even threatened to resign if national targets for literacy (80 per cent of 11year-olds meet the expected standard) and numeracy (75 per cent) are not met by 2002. Government requires schools to set themselves "challenging but realistic" targets for performance in the KS2 tests and GCSE examinations. The announcement has already been made that this requirement will soon be extended to the KS3 tests. Another source of pressure for schools to raise standards comes from the fact that the outcomes of these examinations are now in the public domain. The Secretary of State remains committed to the publication of measures of value added by schools and colleges, based on the progress made by individual pupils and students from one stage of their education to another.

UK EDUCATION POLICY PRIORITIES
In September 2000, the Government's framework for performance management comes into force. Schools will be asked to review existing arrangements for monitoring and for appraisal in the light of the new proposals and agree new performance management policies. The most controversial element of the policy lies with the Government's insistence that an element of teacher appraisal will feature a link with pupil examination performance.

The reforms to 16-19 qualifications which the Government announced in March 1999, following the 1997 Qualifying for Success consultation, are designed to encourage schools and colleges to offer, and young people to take up, programmes of study which reflect the importance of additional breadth without compromising on rigour. From September 2000 students will have the opportunity to take advantage of a more flexible range of qualifications which will enable them to take on additional subjects over the course of two years, and to combine vocational and academic learning more easily. They will also be able to gain recognition for competence in communication, application of number and information technology via the new Key Skills qualification.

PRIORITIES FOR URBAN EDUCATION

Whereas the above policies relate to all UK schools, cities have particular characteristics that require a specific response from policy-makers. As the largest city in the UK, London has a particular need to address issues that include the cosmopolitan nature of its population; pockets of urban deprivation poverty and the transient nature of some of its communities. In a major policy initiative that recognises the phenomenon of social exclusion, the Labour government identifies an underclass with multiple (and interconnected) difficulties in the areas of health, education and employment. Two particular programmes, *Education Action Zones* and *Excellence In Cities*, target social exclusion from the education perspective and seem set to be influential upon London education in the first decade of the new millennium.

EDUCATION ACTION ZONES

Education Action Zones (EAZs) are based on a cluster of about 20 primary, secondary and special schools in a local area. Their task is to stimulate innovation and new approaches and so further lever up standards in schools in deprived areas. The zone is run by a forum of businesses, parents, schools, the local authority and community organisations.

In July 1998, 25 EAZs were created with Newham, Lambeth and Croydon the successful London bids in this first round. Shell International led the bid in Lambeth with Tate and Lyle playing a similar role in Newham. Innovations that are being promoted as good practice in the Newham EAZ include:
- the development of a competency based staff development model to stimulate the recruitment and retention of quality teaching staff.
- new recruitment materials being produced for all zone schools, which has resulted in the number of teachers leaving EAZ schools this summer down 28 per cent on a year ago, compared with a 1 per cent fall for the whole of Newham
- support for the Urban Learning Foundation (a provider of teacher training) in their successful bid for part time PGCE places and by providing hostel accommodation in the EAZ area for students on teaching practice.

Bids from Lewisham, Hackney and Islington were accepted in the second round.

EXCELLENCE IN CITIES

The Prime Minister and David Blunkett launched *Excellence in Cities* in March 1999. It aims to concentrate efforts to raise standards in six of the largest city areas around the country, which obviously includes inner London. The *Excellence in Cities* LEAs included in the London scheme are: Camden, City of London, Greenwich, Hackney, Hammersmith & Fulham, Haringey, Islington, Kensington & Chelsea, Lambeth, Lewisham, Newham, Southwark, Tower Hamlets, Wandsworth, Waltham Forest and Westminster. The project bundles up a number of smaller policy initiatives which neatly demonstrates the current administration's philosophy of providing both "pressure and support" in equal measure.

Support comes in the form of:
- A radical expansion of the specialist and beacon schools programmes, giving them a particular focus on inner cities. Specialist schools are existing secondary schools which are designed to provide enrichment programmes in either languages, sports, arts or technology in addition to the National Curriculum. Beacon schools are schools which have been identified as amongst the best performing in the country and represent examples of successful practice which are to be brought to the attention of the rest of the education service with a view to sharing that practice with others. They work in partnership with other schools to pass on their particular areas of expertise. By 2002/3 it is expected that there will be at least 800 specialist schools and over 1000 beacon schools;
- Introducing smaller Education Action Zones for rapid improvement of small clusters of schools;
- Expanding the summer school and after school programmes to continue to build literacy and numeracy standards and so help with the transition from primary to secondary school.

Government talks about "strengthening school leadership with new measures to recruit and train teachers and headteachers and to appoint school governors with skills and vision" and this is, in part, an admission that there is a very real recruitment crisis in this area. Potential London headteachers will not be encouraged by the insistence that there will be a determination to "tackle poor performance, ensuring that every failing school is improved, closed or given a fresh start, six monthly monitoring checks are made on the 5 per cent of schools with the lowest exam performance." There is a policy tension here between the standards agenda and that of social inclusion. High expectations must be maintained but not at the expense of an underclass of inner city failing schools that is already beginning to emerge, some of which are led by gifted headteachers. LEAs do not escape scrutiny either. Government policy speaks of "modernising local education authorities - accelerating the inspection of inner city LEAs and intervening where authorities are seen to be failing - by using contractors if necessary." This has already happened in the Hackney, where contractors Nord-Anglia were brought in to replace the east London borough's failing school improvement service. The directly elected Greater London Assembly became a reality in May 2000, although as yet it has no responsibilities for education. The Mayor will, however, be a powerful commentator on the success or failure of London schools and as such is likely to have a considerable impact upon policy.

The government has raised the stakes when it comes to urban education and there is a great deal riding on the success (or otherwise) of the EAZs and the "Excellence in Cities" package of initiatives. Whereas the outer London boroughs lack the financial and political support given to their inner London neighbours, they also lack the pressure to deliver that accompanies life under the spotlight. Besides, given Curriculum 2000 and

Local Education Authorities 93

performance management to contend with, they can argue that they have quite enough to be getting on with in the year ahead.

LOCAL EDUCATION AUTHORITIES

Barking and Dagenham
Town Hall, Barking, Essex, IG11 7LU (Tel: 020-8227 3181/2; Fax: 020-8227 3471;
Web: http://www.bardaglea.org.uk)
Director: A. Larbalestier

Barnet
The Old Town Hall, Friern Barnet Lane, London N11 3DL (Tel: 020-8359 3048; Fax: 020-8359 3013;
Email: lyndsey.stone@barnet.gov.uk;
Web: http://www.barnet.gov.uk)
Head of Education and Chief Education Officer: Ms L. Stone

Bexley
Hill View, Hill View Drive, Welling, Kent, DA16 3RY (Tel: 020-8303 7777; Fax: 020-8319 4302;
Web: http://www.bexley.gov.uk)
Director: P. McGee

Brent
Chesterfield House, 9 Park Lane, Wembley, Middx, HA9 7RW (Tel: 020-8937 3190)
Director: vacant

Bromley
Civic Centre, Stockwell Close, Bromley, Kent, BR1 3UH
(Tel: 020-8464 3333; Fax: 020-8313 4049;
Web: http://www.bromley.gov.uk)
Director: K. Davis

Camden
Crowndale Centre, 218-220 Eversholt Street, London, NW1 1BD (Tel: 020-7974 1505; Fax: 020-7974 1536;
Email: r.litchfield@camden.gov.uk)
Director: R. Litchfield

Corporation of London
Corporation of London, PO Box 270, Guildhall, London, EC2P 2EJ (Tel: 020-7332 1750; Fax: 020-7331 1621;
Email: dep.education@corpoflondon.gov.uk)
City Education Officer: D. Smith

City of Westminster
City Hall, 64 Victoria Street, London, SW1E 6QP (Tel: 020-7641 1947; Fax: 020-7641 3406)
Director: J. Harris

Croydon
Taberner House, Park Lane, Croydon, CR9 1TP (Tel: 020-8760 5452; Fax: 020-8760 5603;
Email: education-information@croydon.gov.uk;
Web: http://www.croydon.gov.uk)
Director: D. Sands

Ealing
Perceval House, 14-16 Uxbridge Road, London, W5 2HL (Tel: 020-8579 2424; Fax: 020-8280 1291;
Email: education@ealing.gov.uk)
Director of Education: A. Parker

Enfield
PO Box 56, Civic Centre, Silver Street, Enfield, Middx, EN1 3XQ (Tel: 020-8379 3201; Fax: 020-8379 3243)
Director: Ms E. Graham

Greenwich
Riverside House, Woolwich High Street, London, SE18 6DF (Tel: 020-8921 8038; Fax: 020-8921 8228;
Web: http://www.greenwich.gov.uk)
Director: G. Gyte

Hackney
Edith Cavell Building, Enfield Road, London, N1 5BA (Tel: 020-8356 5000; Fax: 020-8356 7235;
Email: tmahoney@hackney.gov.uk;
Web: http://www.learninglive.co.uk)
Director: Mrs E. Reid

Hammersmith and Fulham
Cambridge House, Cambridge Grove, London, W6 0LE (Tel: 020-8576 5536; Fax: 020-8576 5501;
Email: publicity@hafed.org.uk;
Web: http://www.lbhf.gov.uk)
Director: Ms C. Whatford

Haringey
48 Station Road, Wood Green, London, N22 7TY (Tel: 020-8489 0000; Fax: 020-8489 3864;
Email: deborah.bolt@haringey.gov.uk)
Director: Ms F. Magee

Harrow
PO Box 22, Civic Centre, Station Road, Harrow, Middx, HA1 2UW (Tel: 020-8424 1304)
Director: P. Osburn

Havering
The Broxhill Centre, Broxhill Road, Harold Hill, Romford, Essex, RM14 1XN (Tel: 01708-773839)
Executive Director Children and Lifelong Learning: S. Evans

Hillingdon
Civic Centre, High Street, Uxbridge, Middx, UB8 1UW (Tel: 01895-250528; Fax: 01895-250831)
Corporate Director: P. O'Hear

Hounslow
Civic Centre, Lampton Road, Hounslow, Middx, TW3 4DN (Tel: 020-8583 2901; Fax: 020-8583 2907; Email: lesley.crossley@education.hounslow.gov.uk)
Director: D. Trickett

Islington
Laycock Street, Islington, London, N1 1TH (Tel: 020-7527 5753)
Director: A. Roberts

Kensington and Chelsea
Town Hall, Hornton Street, London, W8 7NX (Tel: 020-7361 3303; Fax: 020-7361 3481;
Email: edurw@rbkc.gov.uk)
Executive Director Education and Libraries: R. Wood

94 Public Services London

Kingston upon Thames
Guildhall 2, Kingston upon Thames, KT1 1EU (Tel: 020-8547 5220; Fax: 020-8547 5296; Email: john.braithwaite@rbk.kingston.gov.uk)
Director of Education and Leisure: J. Braithwaite

Lambeth
International House, Canterbury Crescent, London, SW9 7QE (Tel: 020-7926 9768; Fax: 020-7926 9778; Email: jbringons@lambeth.gov.uk)
Acting Executive Director of Education: A. Wood

Lewisham
3rd Floor, Laurence House, 1 Catford Road, London, SE6 4RU (Tel: 020-8314 6200; Fax: 020-8314 3039; Web: http://www.lewisham.gov.uk)
Executive Director for Education and Culture: Ms A. Efunshile

Merton
Civic Centre, London, Morden, Surrey, SM4 5DX (Tel: 020-8545 3251; Fax: 020-8545 3443; Email: jenny.cairns@merton.gov.uk)
Director of Education, Leisure and Libraries: Ms J. Cairns

Newham
Broadway House, 322 High Street, Stratford, London E15 1AJ (Tel: 020-8555 5552; Fax: 020-8503 0014; Email: ian.harrison@newham.gov.uk)
Director: I. Harrison

Redbridge
Lynton House, 255-259 High Road, Ilford, Essex, IG1 1NY (Tel: 020-8478 3020; Fax: 020-8708 3972)
Acting Chief Education Officer: J. Pallet

Richmond upon Thames
1st Floor, Regal House, London Road, Twickenham, Middx, TW1 3SQ (Tel: 020-8891 7500; Fax: 020-8891 7714; Email: education@richmond.gov.uk; Web: http://www.richmond.gov.uk)
Acting Chief Education Officer: P. J. Lomax

Southwark
1 Bradenham Close, London, SE17 2QA (Tel: 020-7525 5050)
Director Education and Leisure Services: G. Mott

Sutton
The Grove, Carshalton, Surrey, SM5 3AL (Tel: 020-8770 6568; Fax: 020-8770 6545; Web: http://www.sutton.gov.uk)
Strategic Director: Dr I. Birnbaum

Tower Hamlets
Town Hall, Mulberry Place, 5 Clove Crescent, London, E14 2BG (Tel: 020-7364 5000; Fax: 020-7364 4976; Email: burgessp@dial.pipex.com; Web: http://www.towerhamlets.gov.uk)
Corporate Director Education: Ms C. Gilbert

Waltham Forest
Leyton Municipal Offices, High Road, Leyton, London, E10 5QJ (Tel: 020-8527 5544 ext. 5001)
Chief Education Officer: K. J. Evans

Wandsworth
Town Hall, Wandsworth High Street, London, SW18 2PU (Tel: 020-8871 8013)
Director: P. Robinson

UNIVERSITIES

The list below includes contact information for universities in London and their attached colleges.

BRUNEL UNIVERSITY
Uxbridge, Middx UB8 3PH
(Tel: 01895-274000; Fax: 01895-232806; Web: http://www.brunel.ac.uk/information/html)

300 St Margarets Road, Twickenham, TW1 1DT

Borough Road, Isleworth, TW7 5DU

Englefield Green, Egham, Surrey, TW20 0JZ

CITY UNIVERSITY
Northampton Square, London EC1V 0HB
(Tel: 020-7477 8000; Email: registry@city.ac.uk; Web: http://www.city.ac.uk)

KINGSTON UNIVERSITY
Kingston upon Thames, Surrey KT1 1LQ
(Tel: 020-8547 2000; Fax: 020-8547 7080; Email: admissions-info@kingston.ac.uk; Web: http://www.kingston.ac.uk)

LONDON GUILDHALL UNIVERSITY
31 Jewry Street, London EC3N 2EY
(Tel: 020-7320 1000; Web: http://www.lgu.ac.uk)

MIDDLESEX UNIVERSITY
White Hart Lane, London N17 8HR
(Tel: 020-8362 5000; Fax: 020-8362 6878; Email: admissions@mdx.ac.uk; Web: http://www.mdx.ac.uk)

UNIVERSITY OF SURREY ROEHAMPTON
Roehampton Lane, London SW15 5PH
(Tel: 020-8392 3000; Fax: 020-8392 3029; Web: http://www.roehampton.ac.uk)

Royal College of Art
Kensington Gore, London SW7 2EU
(Tel: 020-7590 4444; Fax: 020-7590 4500; Email: info@rca.ac.uk; Web: http://www.rca.ac.uk)

Royal College of Music
London SW7 2BS
(Tel: 020-7589 3643; Fax: 020-7589 7740; Email: info@rcm.ac.uk; Web: http://www.rcm.ac.uk)

Southlands College
80 Roehampton Lane, SW15 5SL (Tel: 020-8392 3400; Fax: 020-8392 3431;
E-mail: southlands@roehampton.ac.uk;
Web: http://www.roehampton.ac.uk)
Principal: M. Leigh

Universities

SOUTH BANK UNIVERSITY
103 Borough Road, London SE1 0AA (Tel: 020-7928 8989; Fax: 020-7815 8273; Email: registry@sbu.ac.uk; Web: http://www.sbu.ac.uk)

THAMES VALLEY UNIVERSITY
St Mary's Road, Ealing, London W5 5RF (Tel: 020-8579 5000; Fax: 020-8566 1353; Email: learning.advice@tvu.ac.uk; Web: http://www.tvu.ac.uk)

UNIVERSITY OF EAST LONDON
Longbridge Road, Dagenham, Essex RM8 2AS (Tel: 020-8223 3000)

UNIVERSITY OF GREENWICH
Bexley Road, Eltham, London SE9 2PQ (Tel: 020-8331 8000; Email: courseinfo@gre.ac.uk; Web: http://www.gre.ac.uk)

Avery Hill
Avery Hill Road, Eltham, London SE9 2PQ

Dartford
Oakfield Lane, Dartford, Kent DA1 2SZ

Maritime
30 Park Row, Greenwich, London SE10 9LS

Medway
Central Avenue, Chatham Maritime, Kent ME4 4TB

Woolwich
Island Site, Beresford Street, London SE18 6BU

UNIVERSITY OF LONDON
Senate House, Malet Street, London WC1E 7HU (Tel: 020-7862 8000; Fax: 020-7862 8358; Email: webmaster@admin.lon.ac.uk; Web: http://www.lon.ac.uk)

Birkbeck College
Malet Street, London WC1E 7HX (Tel: 020-7631 6000; Email: admissions@bbk.ac.uk; Web: http://www.bbk.ac.uk)

British Institute in Paris
9-11 rue de Constantine, 75340 Paris Cedex 07, France (Tel: 00-331-4411 7373; Email: c.buchanan@admin.lon.ac.uk; Web: http://www.bip.lon.ac.uk)

Centre for Defence Studies
King's College London, Strand, London WC2R 2LS (Tel: 020-7848 2338; Email: cds@ckl.ac.uk; Web: http://www.kcl.ac.uk/kis/schools/hums/war/index)

Courtauld Institute of Art
North Block, Somerset House, Strand, London WC2R 0RN (Tel: 020-7848 2777; Email: website@courtauld.ac.uk; Web: http://www.courtauld.ac.uk)

Goldsmiths College
Lewisham Way, New Cross, London SE14 6NW (Tel: 020-7919 7171; Email: ext-comm@gold.ac.uk; Web: http://www.gold.ac.uk)

Heythrop College
Kensington Square, London W8 5HQ (Tel: 020-7795 6600; Email: a.clarkson@heythrop.ac.uk; Web: http://www.heythrop.ac.uk)

Imperial College of Science, Technology and Medicine
South Kensington, London SW7 2AZ (Tel: 020-7589 5111; Email: info@ic.ac.uk; Web: http://www.ic.ac.uk)

Institute of Advanced Legal Studies
Charles Clore House, 17 Russell Square, London WC1B 5DR (Tel: 020-7637 1731; Email: ials@sas.ac.uk; Web: http://www.sas.ac.uk)

Institute of Cancer Research
Royal Cancer Hospital, Chester Beatty Laboratories, 17A Onslow Gardens, London SW7 3AL (Tel: 020-7352 8133; Email: j.kipling@icr.ac.uk; Web: http://www.icr.ac.uk)

Institute of Classical Studies
Senate House, Malet Street, London WC1E 7HU (Tel: 020-7862 8700; Email: mpacker@sas.ac.uk; Web: http://www.sas.ac.uk)

Institute of Commonwealth Studies
27-28 Russell Square, London WC1B 5DS (Tel: 020-7862 8844; Email: ics@sas.ac.uk; Web: http://www.ihr.sas.ac.uk/ics)

Institute of Education
20 Bedford Way, London WC1H 0AL (Tel: 020-7580 1122; Email: l.loughran@ioe.ac.uk; Web: http://www.ioe.ac.uk)

Institute of English Studies
Senate House, Malet Street, London WC1E 7HU (Tel: 020-7862 8000; Email: ies@sas.ac.uk; Web: http://www.sas.ac.uk)

Institute of Germanic Studies
29 Russell Square, London WC1B 5DP (Tel: 020-7862 8965/6; Email: igs@sas.ac.uk; Web: http://www.sas.ac.uk)

Institute of Historical Research
Senate House, Malet Street, London WC1E 7HU (Tel: 020-7862 8740; Email: ihr@sas.ac.uk; Web: http://www.ihr.info.ac.uk)

Institute of Latin American Studies
31 Tavistock Square, London WC1H 9HA (Tel: 020-7862 8870; Email: ilas@sas.ac.uk; Web: http://www.sas.ac.uk/ilas)

Institute of Psychiatry
De Crespigny Park, Denmark Hill, London SE5 8AF (Tel: 020-7836 5454; Email: d.heavey@iop.kcl.ac.uk; Web: http://www.iop.kcl.ac.uk/main)

Institute of Romance Studies
Senate House, Malet Street, London WC1E 7HU (Tel: 020-7862 8675; Email: irs@sas.ac.uk; Web: http://www.sas.ac.uk)

96 Public Services London

Institute of United States Studies
Senate House, Malet Street, London WC1E 7HU (Tel: 020-7862 8693; Email: iuss@sas.ac.uk; Web: http://www.sas.ac.uk)

King's College London
Strand, London WC2R 2LS (Tel: 020-7836 5454; Email: enquiries@kcl.ac.uk; Web: http://www.kcl.ac.uk)

London Business School
Sussex Place, Regent's Park, London NW1 4SA (Tel: 020-7262 5050; Email: jdefries@lbs.ac.uk; Web: http://www.lbs.ac.uk)

London School of Economics and Political Science
Houghton Street, London WC2A 2AE (Tel: 020-7405 7686; Email: general-course@lse.ac.uk; Web: http://www.lse.ac.uk)

London School of Hygiene and Tropical Medicine
Keppel Street, London WC1E 7HT (Tel: 020-7636 8636; Email: registry@lshtm.ac.uk; Web: http://www.lshtm.ac.uk)

London School of Jewish Studies
44A Albert Road, London NW4 2SJ (Tel: 020-8203 6427; Email: lsj@mailbox:ulcc.ac.uk; Web: http://www.brijnet.org/isjs)

Queen Mary and Westfield College
Mile End Road, London E1 4NS (Tel: 020-7975 5555; Email: admissions@qmn.ac.uk; Web: http://www.qmn.ac.uk)

Royal Academy of Music
Marylebone Road, London NW1 2BS (Tel: 020-7873 7373; Email: registry@ram.ac.uk; Web: http://www.ram.ac.uk)

Royal Holloway
Egham Hill, Egham, Surrey TW20 0EX (Tel: 01784-434455; Email: a.price@rhbnc.ac.uk; Web: http://www.rhbnc.ac.uk)

Royal Veterinary College
Royal College Street, London NW1 0TU (Tel: 020-7468 5000; Email: registry@rvc.ac.uk; Web: http://www.rvc.ac.uk)

School of Advanced Study
Senate House, Malet Street, London WC1E 7HU (Tel: 020-7862 8000; Email: school@sas.ac.uk; Web: http://www.sas.ac.uk)

School of Oriental and African Studies
Thornhaugh Street, Russell Square, London WC1H 0XG (Tel: 020-7637 2388; Email: study@soas.ac.uk; Web: http://www.soas.ac.uk)

School of Pharmacy
29-39 Brunswick Square, London WC1N 1AX (Tel: 020-7753 5800; Email: mistone@ulsop.ac.uk; Web: http://www.ulsop.ac.uk)

St George's Hospital Medical School
Cranmer Terrace, London SW17 0RE (Tel: 020-8672 9944; Email: g.jones@sghms.ac.uk; Web: http://www.sghms.ac.uk)

University College London
Gower Street, London WC1E 6BT (Tel: 020-7679 2000; Email: degree-info@ucl.ac.uk; Web: http://www.ucl.ac.uk)

University Marine Biological Station Millport
Isle of Cumbrae, Scotland KA28 0EG (Tel: 01475-530581; Email: milport@gla.ac.uk; Web: http://www.gla.ac.uk/acad/marine)

Warburg Institute
Woburn Square, London WC1H 0AB (Tel: 020-7862 8949; Email: apollard@sas.ac.uk; Web: http://www.sas.ac.uk)

Wye College
Wye, near Ashford, Kent TN25 5AH (Tel: 01233-812401; Email: webmaster@wye.ac.uk; Web: http://www.wye.ac.uk)

UNIVERSITY OF NORTH LONDON
166-220 Holloway Road, London N7 8DB (Tel: 020-7607 2789; Email: admissions@unl.ac.uk; Web: http://www.unl.ac.uk)

UNIVERSITY OF SURREY
Guildford, Surrey GU2 5XH (Tel: 01483-300800; Fax: 01483-300803; Email: information@surrey.ac.uk; Web: http://www.surrey.ac.uk)

UNIVERSITY OF WESTMINSTER
309 Regent Street, London W1R 8AL (Tel: 020-7911 5000; Email: admissions@wmin.ac.uk; Web: http://www.wmin.ac.uk)

COLLEGES

The list below includes a selection of colleges in London. Where possible we have included information on what type of college they are, e.g. Further or Higher Education

Babel Technical College
David Game House, 69 Notting Hill Gate, London, W11 3JS (Tel: 020-7221 1483; Fax: 020-7243 1730; E-mail: babel@babeltech.ac.uk; Web: http://www.babeltech.ac.uk)
Principal: Ms J. Kubba
Type of college: Computer and information technology

Barnet College
Wood Street, Barnet, Herts, EN5 4AZ (Tel: 020-8440 6321; Fax: 020-8441 5236; E-mail: info@barnet.ac.uk; Web: http://www.barnet.ac.uk)
Principal: J. Skitt
Type of college: Further education

Borough College London Ltd
210 Borough High Street, London, SE1 1JX (Tel: 020-7407 2863; Fax: 020-7407 2869; E-mail: jmc@ukinc.com; Web: http://www.ukinc.com/jmc)
Principal: J. Ogunleye

Colleges 97

Bromley College
Rookery Lane, Bromley, Kent, BR2 8HE (Tel: 020-8295 7000; Fax: 020-8295 7099;
E-mail: info@bromley.ac.uk;
Web: http://www.bromley.ac.uk)
Principal and Chief Executive: R. Pritchard

Building Crafts College
153 Great Titchfield Street, London, W1P 7FR (Tel: 020-7636 0480; Fax: 020-7323 4532;
Web: http://www.thecarpenterscompany.co.uk)
Director: J. C. M. Taylor
Type of college: Traditional building crafts, conservation and restoration, fine woodwork, stone masonry

Carshalton College
Nightingale Road, Carshalton, Surrey, SM5 2EJ (Tel: 020-8770 6800; Fax: 020-8770 6899;
Web: http://www.carshalton.ac.uk)
Principal: Dr D. Watkins
Type of college: Further and higher education

City and Islington College
Sixth Form Centre, Annette Road, London, N7 6EX (Tel: 020-7609 8401; Fax: 020-7700 4416;
E-mail: tjupp@candi.ac.uk;
Web: http://www.candi.ac.uk)
Principal: T. Jupp

Marlborough Building, 383 Holloway Road, London, N7 0RN (Tel: 020-7700 9333; Fax: 020-7700 9222)
Willen House, 8-26 Bath Street, EC1V 9PL (Tel: 020-7250 4026)
Benwell Road, N7 7BW (Tel: 020-7700 7585)
Bunhill Row, EC1Y 8LQ (Tel: 020-7588 9024)
Shepperton Arts Centre, Shepperton Road, N1 3DH (Tel: 020-7226 6001; Fax: 020-7354 1477)
444 Camden Road, N7 0SP (Tel: 020-7700 1008)
Montem 3D Arts Centre, 179 Hornsey Road, N7 6RA (Tel: 020-7263 8309; Fax: 020-7272 8446)
Finsbury Park Centre, Prah Road, N4 2RA (Tel: 020-7226 9190; Fax: 020-7359 8769)

City of London College
71 Whitechapel High Street, London, E1 7PL (Tel: 020-7247 2166; Fax: 020-7247 1226;
E-mail: registry@clc-london.ac.uk;
Web: http://www.clc-london.ac.uk)
Principal: R. A. Wright

College of Central London
60 Great Ormond Street, London, WC1N 3HR (Tel: 020-7833 0987; Fax: 020-7837 2959;
E-mail: ccl@btinternet.com;
Web: http://www.central-college.com)
Principal: N. Kailidis
Type of college: Private

Croydon College
Fairfield, College Road, Croydon, CR9 1DX (Tel: 020-8686 5700; Fax: 020-8760 5880;
E-mail: info@croydon.ac.uk;
Web: http://www.croydon.ac.uk)
Principal: V. Seddon

Ealing Tertiary College
Southall Centre, Beaconsfield Road, Southall, Middx, UB1 1DP (Tel: 020-8231 6000; Fax: 020-8574 5354;
Web: http://www.etc.ac.uk)
Chief Executive: M. Griffin
Type of college: Further Education

Enfield College
173 Hertford Road, Enfield, EN3 5HA (Tel: 020-8443 3434; Fax: 020-8804 7028)
Principal: J. Carter

European College
Neil House, 7 Whitechapel Road, London, E1 1DU (Tel: 020-7247 2316/7377 8962; Fax: 020-7247 5907;
E-mail: registrar@europeancollege2000.com;
Web: http://www.europeancollege2000.com)
Principal: S. Ahmad
Type of college: English and European languages, computer training

Greenwich School of Management
Meridian House, Royal Hill, London, SE10 8RD (Tel: 020-8516 7800; Fax: 020-8516 7801;
E-mail: enquiries@greenwich-college.ac.uk;
Web: http://www.greenwich-college.ac.uk)
Principal: W. Hunt
Type of college: University business education

Hammersmith and West London College
Barons Court, Gliddon Road, London, W14 9BL (Tel: 020-8741 1688; Fax: 020-8741 2491;
E-mail: cic@hwlc.ac.uk; Web: http://www.hwlc.ac.uk)
Principal: J. Stone

Hendon College
Grahame Park Way, London, NW9 5RA (Tel: 020-8200 8300; Fax: 020-8205 7177;
E-mail: info@hendon.ac.uk;
Web: http://www.hendon.ac.uk)
Acting Principal: A. Whitaker

Imperial College of Science, Technology and Medicine
Exhibition Road, London, SW7 2AZ (Tel: 020-7589 5111; Web: http://www.ic.ac.uk)
Rector: Lord Oxburgh
Type of college: Science, technology and medicine

Lewisham College
Lewisham Way, London, SE4 1UT (Tel: 020-8692 0353; Fax: 020-8691 1842;
E-mail: rsi@statt.lewisham.ac.uk;
Web: http://www.lewisham.ac.uk
Principal: Ms R. Silver

London College of Business and Computer Studies
159-163 Clapham High Street, London, SW4 7SS (Tel: 020-7720 4414; Fax: 020-7720 2010;
E-mail: lcbcs@telinco.co.uk;
Web: http://www.lcbcs.ndo.co.uk)
Principal: T. Hastings
Type of college: Higher and further education

London College of Traditional Acupuncture and Oriental Medicines
HR House, 447 High Road, London, N12 0AZ (Tel: 020-8371 0820; Fax: 020-8371 0830;
E-mail: enquiries@lcta.com;
Web: http://www.lcta.com)

98 Public Services London

Principal: Ms S. Dowie
Type of college: Acupunture and Oriental herbal medicine

London International College of Homeopathy
Bushmaster House, 204 Uxbridge Road, London, W12 7JD (Tel: 020-8749 0093; E-mail: lich@btinternet.com; Web: http://www.homeopathycharity.com)
Director and Principal: P. Chappell
Type of college: Homeopathy

London Tower College
89A Kingsland High Street, London, E8 2PB (Tel: 020-7690 7324; Fax: 020-7503 536)
Proprietor and Registrar: L. Adeoye
Type of college: Computing, business and law

Marymount College
22 Brownlow Mews, London, WC1N 2LA (Tel: 020-7242 7004; Fax: 020-7831 7185; E-mail: marymount.london@mailbox.ulcc.ac.uk; Web: http://www.marymt.edu)
Director: P. M. Pelan

University of London
327 Mile End Road, London, E1 4NS (Tel: 020-7882 5555; Fax: 020-7882 5500; Web http://www.qmw.ac.uk)
Principal: Prof. A. Smith
Type of college: Higher education college of London University

Redbridge College
Little Heath, Romford, Essex, RM6 4XT (Tel: 020-8548 7400; Fax: 020-8599 8224; E-mail: info@redbridge.essex.sch.uk)
Principal: Dr J. A. McGrath
Type of college: Further education; special needs

Sir George Monoux College
Chingford Road, Walthamstow, London, E17 5AA (Tel: 020-8523 3544; Fax: 020-8498 2443; E-mail: info@george-monoux.ac.uk; Web: http://www.george-monoux.ac.uk)
Principal: R. Chambers
Type of college: Sixth form

Southgate College
High Street, London, N14 6BS (Tel: 020-8886 6521; Fax: 020-8982 5053; E-mail: admiss@southgate.ac.uk; Web: http://www.southgate.ac.uk
Principal and Chief Executive: M. Blagden

South Thames College
Wandsworth High Street, London, SW18 2PP (Tel: 020-8918 7000; E-mail: student-services@south-thames.ac.uk; Web: http://www.south-thames.ac.uk)
Principal: Ms J. Scribbins
Type of college: Further education and adult community
Roehampton Centre, 166 Roehampton Lane, SW15 4HR (Tel: 020-8918 7676; Fax: 020-8918 7618)

Southwark College
Surrey Docks Centre, Drummond Road, London, SE16 4EE (Tel: 020-7815 1500; Fax: 020-7261 1301; Web: http://www.southwark.ac.uk)
Principal and Chief Executive: Ms D. Jones

Tower Hamlets College
Poplar Centre, Poplar High Street, London, E14 0AF (Tel: 020-7510 7510; Fax: 020-7538 9153; E-mail: thc@tower.ac.uk; Web: http://www.tower.ac.uk)
Principal: Ms A. Zera

Transatlantic College
138 Kingsland Road, London, E2 8DY (Tel: 020-7729 2525; Fax: 020-7729 1010)
Principal: Dr P. Efere
Type of college: Housing, welfare, law, social care

West Thames College
London Road, Isleworth, TW7 4HS (Tel: 020-8326 2000; Fax: 020-8569 7787; Web: http://www.west-thames.ac.uk)
Principal: T. Marriott

Westminster College
Castle Lane, London, SW1E 6DR (Tel: 020-7828 3771; Fax: 020-7233 8509; E-mail: admissions@westminster-cfe.ac.uk; Web: http://www.westminster-cfe.ac.uk)
Head: Ms L. Roberts
Type of college: Languages

Woodhouse College
Woodhouse Road, London, N12 9EY (Tel: 020-8445 1210; Fax: 020-8445 5210; E-mail: ggeorge@woodhouse.ndirect.co.uk; Web: http://www.woodhouse.org.uk)
Principal: Ms A. Robinson
Type of college: Sixth form

Woolwich College
Plumstead Centre, Villas Road, London, SE18 7PN (Tel: 020-8488 4800; Fax: 020-8488 4899; E-mail: info@woolwich.ac.uk; Web: http://www.woolwich.ac.uk
Principal: G. Pine
Type of college: Further education

EDUCATIONAL BODIES

Assessment and Qualifications Alliance
Stag Hill House, Guildford, Surrey, GU2 5XJ (Tel: 01483-506506; Fax: 01483-300152; Web: http://www.aqa.org.uk)
Director-General: Ms K. Tattersall

City and Guilds of London Institute
1 Giltspur Street, London, EC1A 9DD (Tel: 020-7294 2468; Fax: 020-7294 2400; Email: enquiry@city-and-guilds.co.uk; Web: http://www.city-and-guilds.co.uk)
Director-General: N. Carey, Ph.D.

Further Education Development Agency (FEDA)
Citadel Place, Tinworth Street, London, SE11 5EH (Tel: 020-7840 5400; Fax: 020-7840 5401; Web: http://www.feda.ac.uk)
Chief Executive: C. Hughes
Chair: Dr T. Melia, CBE

Qualifications and Curriculum Authority
29 Bolton Street, London, W1Y 7PD (Tel: 020-7509

Professional Education

5555; Fax: 020-7509 6975; Email: stubbsw@qca.org.uk; Web: http://www.open.gov.uk/qca/)
Chairman: Sir William Stubbs

HIGHER EDUCATION
Association of Commonwealth Universities
John Foster House, 36 Gordon Square, London, WC1H 0PF (Tel: 020-7387 8572; Fax: 020-7387 2655; Email: info@acu.ac.uk; Web: http://www.acu.ac.uk)
Secretary-General: Prof. M. G. Gibbons

Committee of Vice-Chancellors and Principals of the Universities of the United Kingdom
Woburn House, 20 Tavistock Square, London, WC1H 9HQ (Tel: 020-7419 4111; Email: info@cvcp.ac.uk; Web: http://www.cvcp.ac.uk)
President: H. Newby
Chief Executive: Baroness Warwick

Teacher Training Agency
Portland House, Stag Place, London, SW1E 5TT (Tel: 020-7925 3700; Fax: 020-7925 3792; Email: boothc@teach-tta.gov.uk; Web: http://www.teach-tta.gov.uk)
Chief Executive: R. Tubberer
Chairman: Prof. C. Booth

INDEPENDENT SCHOOLS
Independent Schools Council
Grosvenor Gardens House, 35-37 Grosvenor Gardens, London, SW1W 0BS (Tel: 020-7798 1500; Fax: 020-7798 1501; Email: national@isis.org.uk; Web: http://www.isis.org.uk)
General Secretary: Dr A. B. Cooke
National Director: D. J. Woodhead

Independent Schools Information Service/ISC
Grosvenor Gardens House, 35-37 Grosvenor Gardens, London, SW1W 0BS (Tel: 020-7798 1500; Fax: 020-7798 1501; Email: national@isis.org.uk; Web: http://wwwoisis.org.uk)
National Director: D. Woodhead
Joint Director: D. Davison

SCHOOLS
Education Otherwise
PO Box 7420, London, N9 9SG (Tel: Helpline 0870-730 0074; Email: webmaster@education-otherwise.org; Web: http://www.education-otherwise.org)
General Secretary: Ms J. Wilkinson

Special Education Needs Tribunal
7th Floor, Windsor House, 50 Victoria Street, London, SW1H 0NW (Tel: 020-7925 6925; Fax: 020-7925 6926; Email: sen.tribunal@gtnet.gov)
President: T. Aldridge
Secretary: P. Craggs

UNITARY AWARDING BODIES
Edexcel Foundation
Stewart House, 32 Russell Square, London, WC1B 5DN (Tel: 020-7393 4444; Fax: 020-7393 4445)

PROFESSIONAL EDUCATION

There are a number of professional bodies in the London area offering courses in and information and advice on professional and vocational qualifications. The list below provides, by subject area in alphabetical order, a list of those bodies which, by providing specialist training or conducting examinations, control entry into a profession, or are responsible for maintaining a register of those with professional qualifications in their sector.

ACCOUNTANCY

Chartered Institute of Management Accountants
63 Portland Place, London, W1N 4AB (Tel: 020-7637 2311)

Chartered Institute of Public Finance and Accountancy (CIPFA)
3 Robert Street, London, WC2N 6BH (Tel: 020-7543 5600; Fax: 020-7543 5700; Email: webco-ordinator@cipfa.org)

Institute of Chartered Accountants in England and Wales
Chartered Accountants' Hall, PO Box 433, Moorgate Place, London, EC2P 2BJ (Tel: 020-7920 8100; Fax: 020-7920 0547; Web: http://www.icaew.co.uk)

ACTURIAL SCIENCE

Institute of Actuaries
Staple Inn Hall, High Holborn, London, WC1V 7QJ (Tel: 020-7632 2100; Fax: 020-7632 2111; Email: institute@actuaries.org.uk; Web: http://www.actuaries.org.uk)

ARCHITECTURE

Architectural Association
34-36 Bedford Square, London, WC1B 3ES (Tel: 020-7887 4000)

Architects Registration Board
8 Weymouth Street, London, W1N 3FB (Tel: 020-7580 5861; Fax: 020-7436 5269; Email: info@arb.org.uk; Web: http://www.arb.org.uk)

Royal Institute of British Architects
66 Portland Place, London, W1N 4AD (Tel: 020-7580 5533; Fax: 020-7255 1541; Email: bal@inst.riba.org; Web: http://www.riba.net)

School of Architecture and the Building Arts
19-22 Charlotte Road, London, EC2A 3SG (Tel: 020-7613 8500; Fax: 020-7613 8599)

ACCOUNTANCY

Association of Chartered Certified Accountants (ACCA)
29 Lincoln's Inn Fields, London, WC2A 3EE (Tel: 020-7242 6855)

100 Public Services London

BANKING

Chartered Institute of Bankers
90 Bishopsgate, London, EC2N 4AS (Tel: 020-7444 7111)

BUILDING

Institute of Clerks of Works of Great Britain
41 The Mall, London, W5 3TJ (Tel: 020-8579 2917/8; Fax: 020-8579 0554; Email: gensec@icwgb.sagehost.co.uk; Web: http://www.icwgb.sagehost.co.uk)

BUSINESS, MANAGEMENT AND ADMINISTRATION

Association of MBAs
15 Duncan Terrace, London, N1 8BZ (Tel: 020-7837 3375)

CAM Foundation (Communications, Advertising and Marketing Education Foundation)
Abford House, 15 Wilton Road, London, SW1V 1NJ (Tel: 020-7828 7506)

Chartered Institute of Transport
80 Portland Place, London, W1N 4DP (Tel: 020-7467 9400)

Institute of Chartered Secretaries and Administrators
16 Park Crescent, London, W1N 4AH (Tel: 020-7580 4741; Email: icsa@dial.pipex.com; Web: http://www.icsa.org.uk/icsa)

Institute of Chartered Shipbrokers
3 St Helen's Place, London, EC3A 6EJ (Tel: 020-7628 5559; Fax: 020-7628 5445; Email: icslon@dial.pipex.com; Web: http://www.ics.org.uk)

Institute of Export
Export House, 64 Clifton Street, London, EC2A 4HB (Tel: 020-7247 9812; Fax: 020-7377 5343; Email: institute@export.org.uk; Web: http://www.export.org.uk)

Institute of Healthcare Management
7-10 Chandos Street, London, W1M 9DE (Tel: 020-7460 7654)

Institute of Practitioners in Advertising
44 Belgrave Square, London, SW1X 8QS (Tel: 020-7235 7020)

Institute of Quality Assurance
12 Grosvenor Crescent, London, SW1X 7EE (Tel: 020-7245 6722; Fax: 020-7245 6788; Email: iqa@iqa.org; Web: http://www.iqa.org)

Chartered Institute of Personnel and Development
IPD House, Camp Road, London, SW19 4UX (Tel: 020-8971 9000; Fax: 020-8263 3333; Email: cipd@cipd.co.uk; Web: http://www.cipd.co.uk)

CHIROPRACTIC

General Chiropractic Council
344-354 Gray's Inn Road, London, WC1X 8BP (Tel: 020-7713 5155; Fax: 020-7713 5844; Email: enquiries@gcc-uk.org; Web: http://www.gcc-uk.org)

COMPLEMENTARY MEDICINE

Institute for Complementary Medicine
PO Box 194, London, SE16 7QZ (Tel: 020-7237 5165; Fax: 020-7237 5175; Email: info@icmedicine.co.uk; Web: http://www.icmedicine.co.uk)

DANCE

Council for Dance Education and Training (UK)
Studio 8, The Glasshouse, 49A Goldhawk Road, London, W12 8QP (Tel: 020-8746 0076; Fax: 020-8746 1937; Email: cdet@btconnect.com; Web: http://www.cdet.org.uk)

Imperial Society of Teachers of Dancing
Imperial House, 22-26 Paul Street, London, EC2A 4QE (Tel: 020-7377 1577; Fax: 020-7247 8979; Email: admin@istd.org; Web: http://www.istd.org)

Royal Academy of Dancing
36 Battersea Square, London, SW11 3RA (Tel: 020-7223 0091)

Royal Ballet School
155 Talgarth Road, London, W14 9DE (Tel: 020-8748 6335; Fax: 020-8563 0649; Email: info@royalballetschool.co.uk; Web: http://www.royal-ballet-school.org.uk)

DEFENCE

Royal College of Defence Studies
Seaford House, 37 Belgrave Square, London, SW1X 8NS (Tel: 020-7915 4800; Fax: 020-7915 4999; Email: rcdsone@demon.co.uk; Web: http://www.mod.uk/rcds)

DENTISTRY

General Dental Council
37 Wimpole Street, London, W1M 8DQ (Tel: 020-7887 3800; Fax: 020-7224 3294; Email: information@gdc-uk.org; Web: http://www.gdc-uk.org)

DRAMA

National Council for Drama Training
5 Tavistock Place, London, WC1H 9SS (Tel: 020-7387 6350; Fax: 020-7387 1310; Email: ncdt@lineone.net; Web: http://www.ncdt.co.uk)

ENGINEERING

Chartered Institution of Building Services Engineers
222 Balham High Road, London, SW12 9BS (Tel: 020-8675 5211)

Professional Education 101

Institute of Energy
18 Devonshire Street, London, W1N 2AU (Tel: 020-7580 7124)

Institute of Marine Engineers
80 Coleman Street, London, EC2R 5BJ (Tel: 020-7382 2600; Fax: 020-7382 2670; Email: imare@imare.org.uk; Web: http://www.imare.org.uk)

Institute of Materials
1 Carlton House Terrace, London, SW1Y 5DB (Tel: 020-7451 7300)

Institute of Measurement and Control
87 Gower Street, London, WC1E 6AA (Tel: 020-7387 4949; Fax: 020-7388 8431; Email: education@instmc.org.uk; Web: http://www.instme.org.uk)

Institute of Physics
76 Portland Place, London, W1N 3DH (Tel: 020-7470 4800)

Institute of Quality Assurance
12 Grosvenor Crescent, London, SW1X 7EE (Tel: 020-7245 6722; Fax: 020-7245 6788; Email: iqa@iqa.org; Web: http://www.iqa.org)

Institution of Civil Engineers
One Great George Street, London, SW1P 3AA (Tel: 020-7222 7722; Fax: 020-7222 7500; Web: http://www.ice.org.uk)

Institution of Electrical Engineers
Savoy Place, London, WC2R 0BL (Tel: 020-7240 1871; Fax: 020-7240 7735; Email: postmaster@iee.org.uk; Web: http://www.iee.org.uk/)

Institution of Gas Engineers
21 Portland Place, London, W1N 3AF (Tel: 020-7636 6603; Fax: 020-7636 6602; Email: general@igaseng.demon.co.uk; Web: http://www.igaseng.com)

Institution of Incorporated Engineers
Savoy Hill House, Savoy Hill, London, WC2R 0BS (Tel: 020-7836 3357)

Institution of Mechanical Engineers
1 Birdcage Walk, London, SW1H 9JJ (Tel: 020-7222 7899; Fax: 020-7222 4557; Email: enquiries@imeche.org.uk; Web: http://www.imeche.org.uk)

Institution of Nuclear Engineers
1 Penerley Road, London, SE6 2LQ (Tel: 020-8698 1500; Fax: 020-8695 6409; Email: inuce@lineone.net; Web: http://www.inuce.co.uk)

Institution of Plant Engineers
77 Great Peter Street, London, SW1P 2EZ (Tel: 020-7233 2855; Fax: 020-7233 2604; Email: mail@iplante.org.uk; Web: http://www.iplante.org.uk)

Institution of Structural Engineers
11 Upper Belgrave Street, London SW1X 8BH (Tel: 020-7235 4535; Fax: 020-7235 4294; Email: mail@istructe.org.uk; Web: http://www.istructe.org.uk)

Royal Aeronautical Society
4 Hamilton Place, London, W1V 0BQ (Tel: 020-7499 3515; Fax: 020-7499 6230; Email: keith.mans@raes.org.uk)

Royal Institution of Naval Architects
10 Upper Belgrave Street, London, SW1X 8BQ (Tel: 020-7235 4622)

FOOD AND NUTRITION SCIENCE

Institute of Food Science and Technology
5 Cambridge Court, 210 Shepherd's Bush Road, London, W6 7NJ (Tel: 020-7603 6316; Email: info@ifst.org; Web: http://www.ifst.org)

FUEL AND ENERGY SCIENCE

Institute of Energy
18 Devonshire Street, London, W1N 2AU (Tel: 020-7580 7124; Fax: 020-7580 4420; Email: info@instenergy.org.uk; Web: http://www.instenergy.org.uk)

Institute of Petroleum
61 New Cavendish Street, London, W1M 8AR (Tel: 020-7467 7100)

Institution of Gas Engineers
21 Portland Place, London, W1N 3AF (Tel: 020-7636 6603; Fax: 020-7636 6602; Email: general@igaseng.demon.co.uk; Web: http://www.igaseng.com)

HOTELKEEPING, CATERING AND INSTITUTIONAL MANAGEMENT

Hotel and Catering International Management Association
191 Trinity Road, London, SW17 7HN (Tel: 020-8672 4251; Fax: 020-8682 1707; Email: general@hcima.co.uk; Web: http://www.hcima.org.uk)

INSURANCE

Association of Average Adjusters
200 Aldersgate Street, London, EC1A 4JJ (Tel: 020-7956 0099; Email: secretariat@average-adjusters.com; Web: http://www.average-adjusters.com)

Chartered Institute of Loss Adjusters
Peninsular House, 36 Monument Street, London, EC2R 8LJ (Tel: 020-7337 9960; Fax: 020-7929 3082; Email: info@cila.co.uk; Web: http://www.cila.co.uk)

Chartered Insurance Institute
20 Aldermanbury, London, EC2V 7HY (Tel: 020-7417 4425)

102 Public Services London

JOURNALISM

Periodicals Training Council
Queen's House, 55-56 Lincoln's Inn Fields, London, WC2A 3LJ (Tel: 020-7404 4168; Fax: 020-7404 4167; Email: training@ppa.co.uk; Web: http://www.ppa.co.uk/ptc)

LAW

CACH, Education and Training Department
2-3 Cursitor Street, London, EC4A 1NE (Tel: 020-7440 4000; Fax: 020-7440 4002; Email: cach@barcouncil.org.uk; Web: http://www.barcouncil.org.uk/et)

General Council of the Bar
3 Bedford Row, London, WC1R 4DB (Tel: 020-7242 0082; Fax: 020-7831 9217; Email: chairman@barcouncil.org.uk; Web: http://www.barcouncil.org.uk)

Gray's Inn
8 South Square, London, WC1R 5EU (Tel: 020-7458 7900; Web: http://www.graysinn.org.uk)

Honourable Society of the Inner Temple
Treasury Office, London, EC4Y 7HL (Tel: 020-7797 8250; Fax: 020-7797 8178)

Inns of Court School of Law
4 Gray's Inn Place, Gray's Inn, London, WC1R 5DX (Tel: 020-7404 5787; Fax: 020-7831 4188; Email: brc@icsl.ac.uk; Web: http://www.icsl.ac.uk)

Law Society of England and Wales
113 Chancery Lane, London, WC2A 1PL (Tel: 020-7242 1222)

Lincoln's Inn
London, WC2A 3TL (Tel: 020-7405 1393; Fax: 020-7831 1839; Email: mail@lincolnsinn.org.uk; Web: http://www.lincolnsinn.org.uk)

Middle Temple
London, EC4Y 9AT (Tel: 020-7427 4800)

LIBRARIANSHIP AND INFORMATION SCIENCE/MANAGEMENT

Library Association
7 Ridgmount Street, London, WC1E 7AE (Tel: 020-7255 0500; Fax: 020-7255 0501; Email: info@la-hq.org.uk; Web: http://www.la-hq.org.uk)

MATERIALS STUDIES

Institute of Materials
1 Carlton House Terrace, London, SW1Y 5DB (Tel: 020-7451 7300)

MEDICINE

Faculty of Accident and Emergency Medicine
Royal College of Surgeons of England, 35-43 Lincoln's Inn Fields, London, WC2A 3PN (Tel: 020-7405 7071; Fax: 020-7405 0318; Email: faem@compuserve.com)

Faculty of Occupational Medicine
6 St Andrew's Place, London, NW1 4LB (Tel: 020-7317 5890; Fax: 020-7317 5899; Email: fom@facoccmed.ac.uk; Web: http://www.facoccmed.ac.uk)

Faculty of Pharmaceutical Medicine
1 St Andrew's Place, London, NW1 4LB (Tel: 020-7224 0343; Fax: 020-7224 5381; Email: fpm@f-pharm-med.org.uk; Web: http://www.f-pharm-med.org.uk)

Faculty of Public Health Medicine
4 St Andrew's Place, London, NW1 4LB (Tel: 020-7935 0243; Fax: 020-7224 6973; Email: enquiries@fphm.org.uk; Web: http://www.fphm.org.uk)

General Medical Council
178 Great Portland Street, London, W1N 6JE (Tel: 020-7580 7642; Fax: 020-7915 3641; Email: gmc@gmc-uk.org; Web: http://www.gmc-uk.org)

Royal College of Anaesthetists
48-49 Russell Square, London, WC1B 4JY (Tel: 020-7813 1900; Fax: 020-7813 1876; Email: info@rcoa.ac.uk; Web: http://www.rcoa.ac.uk)

Royal College of General Practitioners
14 Princes Gate, London, SW7 1PU (Tel: 020-7581 3232; Fax: 020-7225 3047; Email: info@rcgp.org.uk; Web: http://www.rcgp.org.uk)

Royal College of Obstetricians and Gynaecologists
27 Sussex Place, London, NW1 4RG (Tel: 020-7772 6200)

Royal College of Paediatrics and Child Health
50 Hallam Street, London, W1N 6DE (Tel: 020-7307 5600; Fax: 020-7307 5601; Email: enquiries@rcpch.ac.uk; Web: http://www.rcpch.ac.uk)

Royal College of Pathologists
2 Carlton House Terrace, London, SW1Y 5AF (Tel: 020-7930 5861; Fax: 020-7451 6701; Email: info@rcpath.org; Web: http://www.rcpath.org)

Royal College of Physicians
11 St Andrew's Place, Regent's Park, London, NW1 4LE (Tel: 020-7935 1174; Fax: 020-7487 5218; Web: http://www.rcplondon.ac.uk)

Royal College of Psychiatrists
17 Belgrave Square, London, SW1X 8PG (Tel: 020-7235 2351; Fax: 020-7245 2351; Email: rcpsych@rcpsych.ac.uk; Web: http://www.rcpsych.ac.uk)

Royal College of Radiologists
38 Portland Place, London, W1N 4QJ (Tel: 020-7636 4432)

Professional Education

Royal College of Surgeons of England
35-43 Lincoln's Inn Fields, London, WC2A 3PN (Tel: 020-7405 3474)

Society of Apothecaries of London
14 Blackfriars Lane, London, EC4V 6EJ (Tel: 020-7236 1189; Fax: 020-7329 3177)

MUSIC

Associated Board of the Royal Schools of Music
14 Bedford Square, London, WC1B 3JG (Tel: 020-7636 5400; Fax: 020-7367 0234; Email: abrsm@abrsm.ac.uk; Web: http://www.abrsm.ac.uk)

Guildhall School of Music and Drama
Silk Street, London, EC2Y 8DT (Tel: 020-7628 2571; Fax: 020-7256 9438; Web: http://www.qsmd.ac.uk)

London College of Music and Media
Thames Valley University, St Mary's Road, London, W5 5RF (Tel: 020-8231 2304; Fax: 020-8231 2546; Email: clare.beckett@tvu.ac.uk; Web: http://www.elgar.tvu.ac.uk)

Royal Academy of Music
Marylebone Road, London, NW1 5HT (Tel: 020-7873 7373)

Royal College of Organists
7 St Andrew Street, London, EC4A 3LQ (Tel: 020-7936 3606)

Trinity College of Music
11-13 Mandeville Place, London, W1M 6AQ (Tel: 020-7935 5773; Fax: 020-7224 6278; Email: info@tcm.ac.uk; Web: http://www.tcm.ac.uk)

NURSING

English National Board for Nursing, Midwifery and Health Visiting
Victory House, 170 Tottenham Court Road, London, W1P 0HA (Tel: 020-7391 6229; Fax: 020-7383 3525; Web: http://www.enb.org.uk)

Royal College of Nursing of the United Kingdom
20 Cavendish Square, London, W1M 0AB (Tel: 020-7409 3333)

UK Central Council for Nursing, Midwifery and Health Visiting
23 Portland Place, London, W1N 4JT (Tel: 020-7637 7181; Fax: 020-7436 2924; Email: communications@ukcc.org.uk; Web: http://www.ukcc.org.uk)

OPHTHALMIC AND DISPENSING OPTICS

Association of British Dispensing Opticians
6 Hurlingham Business Park, Sulivan Road, London, SW6 3DU (Tel: 020-7736 0088; Fax: 020-7731 5531; Email: general@abdo.org.uk; Web: http://www.abdo.org.uk)

College of Optometrists
42 Craven Street, London, WC2N 5NG (Tel: 020-7839 6000; Fax: 020-7839 6800; Email: optometry@college-optometrists.org; Web: http://www.college-optometrists.org)

OSTEOPATHY

General Osteopathic Council
Osteopathy House, 176 Tower Bridge Road, London, SE1 3LU (Tel: 020-7357 6655; Fax: 020-7357 0011; Email: info@osteopathy.org.uk; Web: http://www.osteopathy.org.uk)

PHARMACY

Royal Pharmaceutical Society of Great Britain
1 Lambeth High Street, London, SE1 7JN (Tel: 020-7735 9141)

PRINTING

British Printing Industries Federation
11 Bedford Row, London, WC1R 4DX (Tel: 020-7915 8300; Fax: 020-7405 7784; Email: info@bpif.org.uk; Web: http://www.bpif.org.uk)

PROFESSIONS SUPPLEMENTARY TO MEDICINE

British Association of Art Therapists
Mary Ward House, 5 Tavistock Place, London, WC1H 9SN (Tel: 020-7383 3774)

British Association of Dramatherapists
41 Broomhouse Lane, London, SW6 3DP (Tel: 020-7731 0160)

British Orthoptic Society
Tavistock House North, Tavistock Square, London, WC1H 9HX (Tel: 020-7387 7992)

Chartered Society of Physiotherapy
14 Bedford Row, London, WC1R 4ED (Tel: 020-7306 6666)

College of Occupational Therapists
106-114 Borough High Street, London, SE1 1LB (Tel: 020-7357 6480)

College of Radiographers
207 Providence Square, London, SE1 2EW (Tel: 020-7740 7200; Email: info@sol.org; Web: http://www.sol.org)

Council for Professions Supplementary to Medicine
Park House, 184 Kennington Park Road, London, SE11 4BU (Tel: 020-7582 0866)

Institute of Biomedical Science
12 Coldbath Square, London, EC1R 5HL (Tel: 020-7713 0214; Fax: 020-7436 4946; Email: mail@ibms.org; Web: http://www.ibms.org)

104 Public Services London

Society of Chiropodists and Podiatrists
53 Welbeck Street, London, W1M 7HE (Tel: 020-7486 3381; Fax: 020-7935 6359; Email: eng@scpod.org; Web: http://www.feetforlife.org)

SCIENCE

Geological Society of London
Burlington House, Piccadilly, London, W1V 0JU (Tel: 020-7434 9944; Fax: 020-7439 8975; Email: enquiries@geolsoc.org.uk)

Institute of Biology
20-22 Queensberry Place, London, SW7 2DZ (Tel: 020-7581 8333; Fax: 020-7823 9409; Email: info@iob.org; Web: http://www.iob.org)

Institute of Physics
76 Portland Place, London, W1N 3DH (Tel: 020-7470 4800)

Royal Society of Chemistry
Burlington House, Piccadilly, London, W1V 0BN (Tel: 020-7437 8656; Fax: 020-7437 8883; Email: rsc1@rsc.org; Web: http://www.rsc.org)

SOCIAL WORK

Central Council for Education and Training in Social Work
Derbyshire House, St Chad's Street, London, WC1H 8AD (Tel: 020-7278 2455; Fax: 020-7278 2934; Web: http://www.ccetsw.org.uk)

SPEECH AND LANGUAGE THERAPY

Royal College of Speech and Language Therapists
7 Bath Place, Rivington Street, London, EC2A 3SU (Tel: 020-7613 3855)

SURVEYING

Incorporated Society of Valuers and Auctioneers
3 Cadogan Gate, London, SW1X 0AS (Tel: 020-7235 2282)

Institute of Revenues, Rating and Valuation
41 Doughty Street, London, WC1N 2LF (Tel: 020-7831 3505)

Royal Institution of Chartered Surveyors
12 Great George Street, London, SW1P 3AD (Tel: 020-7222 7000; Fax: 020-7222 9430; Email: info@rics.org.uk; Web: http://www.rics.org)

THEOLOGICAL COLLEGES

Allen Hall
28 Beaufort Street, London, SW3 5AA (Tel: 020-7351 1296; Fax: 020-7349 5601; Email: secretary@allenhall.co.uk)

Campion House College
112 Thornbury Road, Isleworth, Middx, TW7 4NN (Tel: 020-8560 1924; Fax: 020-8569 9645; Email: campionhouse.asterley@compuserve.com; Web: http://www.campionhouse.org.uk)

Jew's College
Schaller House, Albert Road, London, NW4 2SJ (Tel: 020-8203 6427)

Leo Baeck College
Sternberg Centre for Judaism, 80 East End Road, London, N3 2SY (Tel: 020-8349 5600; Fax: 020-8343 2558; Email: info@lbc.ac.uk; Web: http://www.lbc.ac.uk)

London Theological Seminary
104 Hendon Lane, London, N3 3SQ (Tel: 020-8346 7587; Email: principal@lts.u-net.com; Web: http:/www.lts.u-net.com)

Oak Hill College
Chase Side, London, N14 4PS (Tel: 020-8449 0467; Fax: 020-8441 5996; Email: mailbox@oakhill.ac.uk; Web: http://www.oakhill.ac.uk)

Spurgeon's College
South Norwood Hill, London, SE25 6DJ (Tel: 020-8653 0850; Fax: 020-8771 0959; Email: enquiries@spurgeons.ac.uk; Web: http://www.spurgeons.ac.uk)

St Edwards College
46 Totteridge Common, London, N20 8ND (Tel: 020-8959 2553; Fax: 020-8201 1850)

TOWN AND COUNTRY PLANNING

Royal Town Planning Institute
26 Portland Place, London, W1N 4BE (Tel: 020-7636 9107; Fax: 020-7323 1582; Email: online@rtpi.org.uk; Web: http://www.rtpi.org.uk)

TRANSPORT

Institute of Logistics and Transport
80 Portland Place, London, W1N 4DP (Tel: 020-7467 9400)

VETERINARY MEDICINE

British Veterinary Association
7 Mansfield Street, London, W1M 0AT (Tel: 020-7636 6541; Fax: 020-7436 2970; Email: bvahq@bva.co.uk; Web: http://www.bva.co.uk)

Royal College of Veterinary Surgeons
Belgravia House, 62-64 Horseferry Road, London, SW1P 2AF (Tel: 020-7222 2001; Fax: 020-7222 2004; Email: admin@rcvs.org.uk; Web: http://www.rcvs.org.uk)

EMERGENCY SERVICES

AMBULANCE SERVICE

LONDON AMBULANCE SERVICE (LAS) NHS TRUST

220 Waterloo Road, London SE1 8SD (Tel: 020 7921 5100)

The London Ambulance Service in one of the largest Ambulance Services in the World. On average, London Ambulance Service Crews take 1.6 million patients to hospital each year. There are seventy ambulance stations spanning the 620 square miles of greater London. They are divided into seven sectors. A Chief Executive and a board of directors manage the LAS as a whole. They report to the LAS Trust board.

LAS Trust Board
Trust Board Executive Directors: Mr. Peter Bradley (*Acting Chief Executive*); Mr. Owen Disley (*Acting Director of Operations*); Mr. Mark Jones (*Director of Finance and Business Planning*); Mrs Wendy Foers (*Director of Human Resources*); Mr. Ian Tighe (*Director of Technology and Trust Secretary*)
Trust Board Non-Executive Directors: Mr. Sigurd Reinton (*Chairman*); Mr. Colin Douglas (*Vice-Chairman*); Lord Toby Harris; Mr. Barry MacDonald; Mr. Gareth Spier; Mrs Suzanne Burn

FIRE SERVICE

LONDON FIRE AND EMERGENCY PLANNING AUTHORITY

The London Fire and Civil Defence Authority was responsible for the capital's fire service and Emergency planning provision. The LFCDA ceased to exist when the Greater London Authority assumed responsibilities in July 2000. The new body, the London Fire and Emergency Planning Authority, comprises of three command areas as did the LFCDA, with an Assistant Chief Fire officer in charge of each one. There will be 17 members of the LFEPA, 9 will be drawn from the London Assembly and 8 will be nominated by the London boroughs. For further information of the LFEPA as part of the Greater London Authority; see the Governed London section.
The London Fire Brigades cover the 620 square miles of Greater London. There are 113 fire stations and one river station divided amongst the three command areas, Eastern, Western and Southern Commands. London has one River Station at Lambeth. It was built in 1900 with a pontoon on two floors, opposite the Brigade Headquarters at 8 Albert Embankment. It covers the River Thames from Dartford to East Molesey with two fireboats called Fireflash and Firedart.

LONDON FIRE BRIGADE EASTERN COMMAND

Headquarters, 2 Ferns Road, Stratford, London E15 4LX (Tel: 020-7587 2411; Fax: 020-7587 2437)

Assistant Chief Fire Officer: Roy Bishop

Fire Stations: Barking, Bethnal Green, Bow, Chingford, Clerkenwell, Dagenham, Dowgate, East Ham, Edmonton, Enfield, Hainault, Holloway, Homerton, Hornchurch, Hornsey, Ilford, Islington, Kingsland, Leyton, Leytonstone, Millwall, Plaistow, Poplar, Romford, Shadwell, Shoreditch, Silvertown, Southgate, Stoke Newington, Stratford, Tottenham, Walthamstow, Wennington, Whitechapel, Woodford

Boroughs served: Barking and Dagenham, City of London, Enfield, Hackney, Haringey, Islington, Newham, Redbridge, Tower Hamlets, Waltham Forest.

FIRE SAFETY OFFICES SOUTHERN COMMAND

Headquarters, 249/259 Lewisham High Street, London SE13 6NH (Tel: 020-7587 2561)

Assistant Chief Fire Officer: Mr. L. Gill

Fire Stations: Addington, Battersea, Beckenham, Bexley, Biggin Hill, Brixton, Bromley, Clapham, Croydon, Deptford, Dockhead, Downham, East Greenwich, Eltham, Erith, Forest Hill, Greenwich, Kingston, Lambeth, Lambeth (River), Lee Green, Lewisham, Mitcham, New Cross, New Malden, Norbury, Old Kent Road, Orpington, Peckham, Plumstead, Purley, Sidcup, Southwark, Surbiton, Sutton, Tooting, Wallington, Wandsworth, West Norwood, Wimbledon, Woodside, Woolwich.

Boroughs served: Bexley, Bromley, Croydon, Greenwich, Kingston-upon-Thames, Lambeth, Lewisham, Merton, Southwark, Sutton, Wandsworth

LONDON FIRE BRIGADE WESTERN COMMAND

Headquarters, 591A, Harrow Road, Wembley, Middlesex HA0 2EG (Tel: 020-7587 2731)

Assistant Chief Fire Officer: Mr M. Kelly

Fire Stations: Acton, Barnet, Belsize, Chelsea, Chiswick, Ealing, Euston, Feltham, Finchley, Fulham, Hammersmith, Harrow, Hayes, Heathrow, Hendon, Heston, Hillingdon, Kensington, Kentish Town, Knightsbridge, Manchester Square, Mill Hill, North Kensington, Northolt, Paddington, Park Royal, Richmond, Ruislip, Soho, Southall, Stanmore, Twickenham, Wembley, West Hampstead, Westminster, Willesden.

Boroughs served: Barnet, Brent, Camden, Ealing, Harrow, Hillingdon, Hammersmith and Fulham, Hounslow, Kensington and Chelsea, Richmond upon Thames, Westminster

POLICE SERVICE

Policing in London is carried out by the Metropolitan Police and the City of London Police. The authority for the Metropolitan Police is the Home Secretary, advised by the Metropolitan Police Committee and for the City of London Police the authority is a committee of the Corporation of London and includes councillors and magistrates. Police authorities are financed by central and local government grants and a precept on the council tax.

Public Services London

The Home Secretary is responsible for the organisation, administration and operation of the police service in London. He makes regulations covering matters such as police ranks, discipline, hours of duty, and pay and allowances.
In April 1999 the Home Secretary set targets for recruitment of officers from ethnic minorities for each force in England and Wales to achieve within ten years. From 2000 targets for promotion and retention of these officers will also be set.

COMPLAINTS

The investigation and resolution of a serious complaint against a police officer is subject to the scrutiny of the Police Complaints Authority. An officer who is dismissed, required to resign or reduced in rank, whether as a result of a complaint or not, may appeal to a police appeals tribunal established by the relevant police authority.

METROPOLITAN POLICE SERVICE

New Scotland Yard, Broadway, London SW1H 0BG (Tel: 020-7230 1212; Web: http://www.met.police.uk)
The Metropolitan Police Force came into existence on 30 September 1829 following Sir Robert Peel's committee recommending the setting up of an organised police force. The Metropolitan Police is one of the largest services in the United Kingdom, serving an area of 787 square miles within a radius of approximately 15 miles of Trafalgar Square. The Metropolitan Police serves a population of over seven million and is divided into five areas, comprising 62 Operational Command Units.

Commissioner: J. Stevens, QPM

METROPOLITAN POLICE, SPECIAL CONSTABULARY

The Special Constabulary was originally formed in 1831 to cope with times of emergency. At this time people did not volunteer – they were called up and fines were imposed on people who did not respond. The modern idea of special constables was used extensively during the world wars on a volunteer basis and over 11,000 special constables served during WW2. The Metropolitan Special Constabulary currently employs approximately 1,400 officers.

METROPOLITAN POLICE, RIVER DIVISION

Erith: Tel: 01322 352212
Shepperton: Tel: 01932 229281
Waterloo: Tel: 020-7321 7278
Wapping: Tel: 020-7488 5291

CITY OF LONDON POLICE

26 Old Jewry, London EC2R 8DJ (Tel: 020-7601 2222; Email: postmaster@city-of-london.police.uk; Web: http://www.city-of-london.police.uk)

Community Safety (Crime Prevention): Tel: 020-7601 2323
Force Recruitment: Tel: 020-7601 2251
Special Constabulary: Tel: 020-7601 2713
Fraud Department: Tel: 020-7601 2999
Crimestoppers: Tel: 0800 555111

The City of London Police Force was formally established by the City of London Police Act 1839. The first commissioner, Daniel Whittle-Harvey, was responsible for about 500 men. In 1842 the Force moved its headquarters from the Corporation's Guildhall to 26 Old Jewry, where it has since remained.
The City of London Police Force is responsible for the safety of everyone who lives and works in or visits London's square mile. There are approximately 6,000 residents in the City of London although this number is swelled daily by an influx of some 350,000 commuters and tourists. The only significant difference between the City of London Police Force and other police forces in the UK is that the Force has retained the link with the local authority for the area – the Corporation of London. Around 1,200 people work for the City of London Police, with approximately one third of these undertaking civilian support duties.
The Operational Support Department co-ordinates the Force's activities to prevent terrorist crime, as well as providing a range of support and specialist uniformed services including the Communications Centre, planning for major operations, traffic patrol, horse and dog sections and firearms experts. The Specialist Crime Department is responsible for co-ordinating crime prevention strategies, providing scientific supports and for investigating major crimes including fraud and money laundering. The City of London Police serves a unique community. Today, the City is host to 565 foreign banks, branches and subsidiaries and contains more corporate headquarters than any other city in Europe.
In January 1999 the Force established a new branch called the Community Safety Branch whose aim is to protect City communities through partnership, support and prevention. The Scientific Support Unit has the remit of examining crime scenes for forensic and fingerprint evidence and to undertake all aspects of photography for the force. Blood, shoeprints, toolmarks, fibres, tyremarks and other trace material may yield valuable intelligence or evidence for investigating officers.

Commissioner: P. Nove

POLICE COMPLAINTS AUTHORITY

10 Great George Street, London SW1P 3AE (Tel: 020-7273 6450; Fax: 020-7273 6401; Email: info@pca.gov.uk; Web: http://www.pca.gov.uk)

The Police Complaints Authority was established under the Police and Criminal Evidence Act 1984 to provide an independent system for dealing with complaints by members of the public against police officers in England and Wales. It is funded by the Home Office. The authority has powers to supervise the investigation of certain categories of serious complaints. It does not deal with police operational matters; these are usually dealt with by the Chief Constable of the relevant force.

NATIONAL POLICE FUNCTIONS

BRITISH TRANSPORT POLICE

15 Tavistock Place, London WC1H 9SJ (Tel: 020-7388 7541; Web: http://www.btp.police.uk)

British Transport Police is the national police force for the railways in England, Wales and Scotland, including the London Underground system, Docklands Light Railway, the Midland Metrotram and Croydon Tramlink systems. The Chief Constable reports to the British Transport Police Committee. The members of the Committee are appointed by the British Railways Board and include representatives of Railtrack and London Underground Ltd as well as independent members. Officers are paid the same as other police forces. There are approximately 2,100 officers.

Chief Constable: D. J. Williams, QPM
Deputy Chief Constable: J. A. Lake

FORENSIC SCIENCE SERVICE

Headquarters: Priory House, Gooch Street North, Birmingham B5 6QQ (Tel: 0121-607 6800)

The Forensic Science Service (FSS) provides forensic science support to the police forces in England and Wales for the investigation of scenes of crime, scientific analysis of material, and interpretation of scientific results. The FSS is organised into serious crime, volume crime, drugs and specialist services, supported by intelligence and consultancy services. Laboratories are located at London, Birmingham, Chepstow, Chorley, Huntingdon, and Wetherby.

Chief Executive: Dr J. Thompson

MINISTRY OF DEFENCE POLICE

Wethersfield, Braintree, Essex CM7 4AZ (Tel: 01371-854000; Fax: 01371 854060)

The primary role of the Ministry of Defence Police is the prevention, detection and investigation of crime within the Ministry of Defence and Crown Estate and other locations policed under repayment arrangements. In addition to its policing role, the Ministry of Defence Police also provides a security and guarding service, armed when required, at a number of key defence and other installations. The Chief Constable is also responsible for the professional management and training of the Ministry of Defence Guard Service.

Chief Constable/Chief Executive: Walter Boreham, OBE
Deputy Chief Constable: Anthony Comben
Head of Secretariat: P. A. Crowther

NCS SERVICE AUTHORITY

Headquarters: PO Box 2600, London SW1V 2WG (Tel: 020-7238 2600; Fax: 020-7328 2602)

The Service Authority is responsible for ensuring the effective operation of the National Crime Squad. It fulfills a similar role to a police authority. It works alongside the National Criminal Intelligence Service Service Authority. There are 26 members, of whom the chairman and nine others serve as 'core members' on both authorities.

Chairman: Rt. Hon. Sir John Wheeler, JP, DL
Clerk: T. Simmons
Treasurer: P. Derrick

NATIONAL CRIME SQUAD

PO Box 2500, London, SW1V 2WF (Tel: 020-7238 2500; Fax: 020-7238 2520)

The National Crime Squad (NCS) was established on 1 April 1998, replacing the six regional crime squads in England and Wales. It investigates national and international organised and serious crime. It also supports police forces investigating serious crime. The squad is accountable to the National Crime Squad Service Authority.

Director General: Roy Penrose, OBE, QPM

POLICE INFORMATION TECHNOLOGY ORGANISATION

New Kings Beam House, 22 Upper Ground, London SE1 9QY (Tel: 020-8358 5678; Fax: 020-8358 5534; Email: anna.richards@pito.org.uk; Web: http://www.pito.org.uk)

The Police Information Technology Organisation (PITO) became a non-departmental public body on 1 April 1998. It develops and manages the delivery of national police information technology services, such as the Police National Computer, co-ordinates the development of local information technology systems where common standards and systems are needed, and provides a procurement service.

Chairman: Sir Trefor Morris
Chief Executive: Vivienne Dews

POLICE NATIONAL MISSING PERSONS BUREAU

Headquarters: New Scotland Yard, Broadway, London, SW1H 0BG (Tel: 020-7230 1212)

The Police National Missing Persons Bureau (PNMPB) acts as a central clearing house of information, receiving reports about vulnerable missing persons that are still outstanding after 14 days and details of unidentified persons or remains within 48 hours of being found from all forces in England and Wales. Reports are also received from Scottish police forces, the RUC, and foreign police forces via Interpol.

Director: C. J. Coombes

ROYAL PARKS CONSTABULARY

The Old Police House, Hyde Park, London W2 2UH (Tel: 020-7298 2000)

The Royal Parks Constabulary is maintained by the Royal Parks Agency, an executive agency of the Department for Culture, Media and Sport, and is responsible for the policing of eight royal parks in and around London. These comprise an area in excess of 6,300 acres. There are approximately 150 officers who are appointed under the Parks Regulations Act 1872 as amended and are paid around 85 per cent of the Metropolitan Police rate.

Chief Officer: W. Ross, OBE
Deputy Chief Officer: A. McLean

108 Public Services London

POLICE STATIONS

Acton
250 High Street, London, W3 9BH

Addington
Addington Village Road, Croydon, Surrey, CR0 5AO

Albany Street
60 Albany Street, London, NW1 4EE

Arbour Square
East Arbour Street, London, E1 0PU

Barking
6 Ripple Road, Barking, Essex, IG11 7NF

Barkingside
1 High Street, Ilford, Essex, IG6 1QB

Barnes
371 Lonsdale Road, London, SW13

Battersea
112-118 Battersea Bridge Road, London, SW11 3AP

Beckenham
45 High Street, Beckenham, Kent, BR3 1AW

Belgravia
202-206 Buckingham Palace Road, London, SW1V 6SX

Belvedere
2 Nuxley Road, Belvedere, Kent, DA17 5JF

Bethnal Green
12 Victoria Park Square, London, E2 9NZ

Bexleyheath
2 Arnsbery Way, Bexleyheath, Kent, DA7 4QS

Bow
111 Bow Road, London, E3 2AN

Brentford
The Half Acre, Brentford, Middx, TW3 8BH

Brick Lane
25 Brick Lane, London, E1 6PU

Brixton
267 Brixton Road, London, SW9 7DD

Brockley
4 Howson Road, London, SE4 2AS

Bromley & Orpington
48 Widmore Road, Bromley, Kent, BR1 3BG

Brompton - Chelsea
2 Lucan Place, London, SW3 3PB

Brompton - Kensington
72-74 Earls Court Road, London, W8 6EQ

Caledonian Road
470 Caledonian Road, London, N7

Camberwell
22a Camberwell Church Street, London, SE5 8QU

Canning Town
23 Tarling Road, London, E16 1HN

Carey Way
Unit 5-8, Towers Business Park, Carey Way, Wembley, Middx, HA9 0LQ

Catford
Bromley Road, Southend Village, London, SE6 2RJ

Chadwell Heath
14 Wangey Road, Chadwell Heath, Essex, RM6 4AJ

Chalkhill
Golbeters Walk, Wembley, Middx, HA9 9BA

Charing Cross
Agar Street, London, WC2N 4JP

Chelsea
2 Lucan Place, London, SW3

Cheshunt
101 Turner's Hill, Cheshunt, Herts, EN8 9BD

Chingford
King's Head Hill, London, E4 7EA

Chislehurst
47 High Street, Chislehurst, Kent, BR7 5AF

Chiswick
205-211 Chiswick High Road, London, W4 2DR

Clapham
51 Union Grove, London, SW8

Colindale
Grahame Park Way, London, NW9 5TW

Collier Row
22 Collier Row Lane, Romford, Essex, RM5 3BP

Cray
43-45 High Street, St Mary Cray, Kent, BR5 3NH

Croydon
71 Park Lane, Croydon, Surrey, CR9 1BP

Dagenham
561 Rainham Road South, Dagenham, Essex, RM10 7TU

Deptford
116 Amersham Vale, London, SE14 6LG

Ealing
67-69 Uxbridge Road, London, W5 5SJ

Police Stations

Earlsfield
522 Garratt Lane, London, SW17 0NZ

East Dulwich
173-183 Lordship Lane, London, SE22 8HA

East Ham
4 High Street South, London, E6 4ES

Edgware
Whitchurch Lane, Edgware, Middx, HA8 6LA

Edmonton
462 Fore Street, London, N9 0PW

Eltham
20 Well Hall Road, London, SE9 6SF

Enfield
41 Baker Street, Enfield, Middx, EN1 3EU

Erith
22 High Street, Erith, Kent, DA8 1QY

Feltham
34 Hanworth Road, Feltham, Middx, TW13 5BD

Finchley
193 Ballards Lane, London, N3 1LZ

Forest Gate
370 Romford Road, London, E7 8BS

Fulham
Heekfield Place, London, SW6 5NL

Gipsy Hill
66 Central Hill, London, SE19 1DT

Golders Green
1069 Finchley Road, London, NW11 0QE

Greenford
21 Oldfield Lane, Greenford, Middx, UB6 9LQ

Greenwich
31 Royal Hill, London, SE10 8RR

Hackney
2 Lower Clapton Road, London, E5 0PA

Haggerston
228 Haggerston Road, London, E8

Ham
18 Ashburnham Road, Ham, Richmond, Surrey, TW10

Hammersmith
226 Shepherds Bush Road, London, W6 7NX

Hampstead
26 Rosslyn Hill, London, NW3 1PD

Harefield
24 Rickmansworth Road, Harefield, Middx, UB9 6JX

Harlesden
76 Craven Park, London, NW10 8RJ

Harold Hill
Gooshays Drive, Romford, Essex, RM3 8AE

Harrow
74 Northolt Road, South Harrow, Middx, HA2 0DN

Harrow Road
325 Harrow Road, London, W9

Havering
19 Main Road, Romford, Essex, RM1 3BJ

Hayes
755 Uxbridge Road, Hayes, Middx, UB4 8HU

Heathrow Airport
Heathrow Airport, Hounslow, Middx, TW6 1JH

Highbury Vale
211 Blckstock Road, London, N5 2LZ

Highgate
407-409 Archway Road, London, N6 4NW

Hillingdon
1 Warwick Place, Uxbridge, Middx, UB8 1PG

Holborn
70 Theobalds Road, London, WC1X 8SD

Holloway
284 Hornsey Road, London, N7 7QY

Hornchurch
74 Station Lane, Hornchurch, Essex, RM12 6NA

Hornsey
98 Tottenham Lane, London, N8 7EJ

Hounslow
5 Montague Road, Hounslow, Middx, TW3 1LB

Ilford
270-294 High Road, Ilford, Essex, IG1 1GT

Isle of Dogs
160-174 Manchester Road, London, E14 9HW

Islington
2 Tolpuddle Street, London, N1 0YY

Kenley
94-96 Godstone Road, Kenley, Surrey, CR8 5AB

Kennington
49 Kennington Road, London, SE1

Kentish Town
12a Holmes Road, London, NW5 3AE

Kilburn
38 Salusbury Road, London, NW6 6NN

110 Public Services London

Kingsbury
5 The Mall, Harrow, Middx, HA3 9TF

King's Cross Road
76 King's Cross Road, London, WC1X 8QH

Kingston
5-7 High Street, Kingston-upon-Thames, Surrey, KT1 1LB

Lavender Hill
176 Lavender Hill, London, SW11 1JX

Lee Road
418 Lee High Road, London, SE12 8RW

Leman Street
74 Leman Street, London, E1

Lewisham
2 Ladywell Road, London, SE13 7UR

Leyton
215 Francis Road, London, E10 6NJ

Leytonstone
470 High Road, London, E11 3HN

Limehouse
29 West India Dock Road, London, E14 8EZ

Marks Gate
78 Rose Lane, Romford, Essex, RM6 5JU

Marylebone
1-9 Seymour Street, London, W1H 5AA

Mitcham
58 Cricket Green, Mitcham, Surrey, CR4 4LA

Morden
4 Crown Parade, Crown Lane, Morden, Surrey, SM4 5DA

Muswell Hill
115 Fortis Green, London, N2 9HW

New Malden
184 High Street, New Malden, Surrey, KT3 4ES

Norbury
1516 London, Road, London, SW16 4ES

Northwood
2 Murray Road, Northwood, Middx, HA6 2YW

North Woolwich
Albert Road, London, E16 2JJ

Norwood Green
190 Norwood Road, Southall, Middx, UB2 4JT

Notting Hill
101 Ladbroke Road, London, W11 3PL

Orpington
The Walnuts, Orpington, Kent, BR6 0TW

Paddington
4 Harrow Road, London, W2 1XJ

Paddington Green
2-4 Harrow Road, London, W2 1XJ

Peckham
177 Peckham High Street, London, SE15 5SL

Penge
175 High Street, London, SE20 7DS

Pinner
Bridge Street, Pinner, Middx, HA4 3LA

Plaistow
444 Barking Road, London, E13 8HJ

Plumstead
200 Plumstead High Street, London, SE18 1JY

Ponders End
204-214 High Street, Ponders End, Middx, EN3 4EZ

Poplar
2 Market Way, London, E14 8ET

Putney
215 Upper Richmond Road, London, SW15 6SH

Rainham
3 New Road, Rainham, Essex, RM13 9PW

Richmond
8 Red Lion Street, Richmond, Surrey, TW9 1RW

Roehampton
117 Danebury Avenue, London, SW15 4DH

Rotherhithe
99 Lower Road, London, SE16 2XQ

Ruislip
The Oaks, Manor Road, Ruislip, Middx, HA4 7LE

St Ann's Road
289 St Ann's Road, London, N15 5RD

St John's Wood
20 Newcourt Street, London, NW8 7AA

Shepherds Bush
252-258 Uxbridge Road, London, W12 7JB

Shooters Hill
Shooters Hill, London, SE18 4RF

Shoreditch
4-6 Shepherdess Walk, London, N1 7LF

Sidcup
87 Main Road, Sidcup, Kent, DA14 6ND

Southall
67 High Street, Southall, Middx, UB1 3HG

Police Stations

Southgate
25 Chase Side, London, N14 5BW

South Norwood
11 Oliver Grove, London, SE25 6ED

Southwark
323 Borough High Street, London, SE1 1JL

Stoke Newington
33 High Street, London, N16 8DS

Stratford
18 West Ham Lane, London, E15 4SG

Streatham
101 Streatham High Road, London, SW16 1HT

Surbiton
299 Ewell Road, Surbiton, Surrey, KT6 6RD

Sutton
6 Carshalton Road West, Sutton, Surrey, SM1 4RF

Sydenham
179 Dartmouth Road, London, SE26 4RN

Teddington
18 Park Road, Teddington, Middx, TW11 0AQ

Thamesmead
Titmuss Avenue, London, SE28 8BJ

Tooting
251 Mitcham Road, London, SW17 9JQ

Tottenham
398 High Road, London, N17 9JA

Tower Bridge
209 Tooley Street, London, SE1 2JX

Trinity Road
76 Trinity Road, London, SW17 7RJ

Twickenham
41 London, Road, Twickenham, Middx, TW1 3SY

Upminster
223 St Mary's Lane, Upminster, Essex, RM14 3BX

Uxbridge
1 Warwick Place, Uxbridge, Middx, UB8 1PG

Vauxhall
49-51 Kennington Road, London, SE1 7QA

Vauxhall – Cavendish Road
47 Cavendish Road, London, SW12 0BL

Wallington
84 Stafford Road, Wallington, Surrey, SM6 9AY

Walthamstow
360 Forest Road, London, E17 5JQ

Walworth
12-18 Manor Place, London, SE17 3RL

Wandsworth
146 High Street, London, SW18 4JJ

Wanstead
Spratt Hall Road, London, E11 2RQ

Wapping
98 Wapping High Street, London, E1 9NE

Waterloo Pier
Waterloo Pier, Victoria Embankment, London, WC2R 0DB

Wealdstone
78 High Street, Wealdstone, Middx, HA3 7AG

Wembley
603 Harrow Road, Wembley, Middx, HA0 2HH

Westcombe Park
11-13 Combedale Road, London, SE10 0LQ

West Drayton
Station Road, West Drayton, Middx, UB7 7JQ

West End Central
27 Savile Row, London, W1X 2DU

West Hampstead
21 Fortune Green Road, London, NW6 1DX

West Hendon
The Broadway, London, NW9 7AL

West Wickham
9 High Street, West Wickham, Kent, BR4 0LP

Whetstone
1170 High Road, London, N20 0LW

Willesden Green
96 High Road, London, NW10 2PP

Wimbledon
15 Queen's Road London, SW19 8NN

Winchmore Hill
687 Green Lanes, London, N21 3RT

Woodford
509 High Road, Woodford Green, Essex, IG8 0SR

Wood Green
347 High Road, London, N22 4HZ

Woolwich
29 Market Street, London, SE18 6QS

Worcester Park
154 Central Road, Worcester Park, Surrey, KT4 8HH

CRIME STATISTICS
Notifiable Offences* in London Recorded by the Police and percentage Cleared Up (Rates and percentages)

	Offences Recorded by 100,000 population			Percentage Cleared up		
	1992	1996	1997	1992	1996	1997
Violence against the person	514	664	695	61	62	70
Sexual offences	08	98	100	58	54	61
Burglary	2,614	2,206	1,869	11	21	23
Robbery	320	439	362	13	22	24
Theft & handling stolen goods	6,377	5,179	4,903	13	19	19
Fraud & Forgery	545	526	571	44	45	41
Criminal damage†	1,632	1,835	1,737	8	13	18
Other	92	149	167	91	87	87
All notifiable offences	12,174	11,094	10,404	16	23	26

* *Excluding offences of criminal damage valued at £20 or less*
† *Metropolitan Police and City of London Police areas*
Source: Focus on London '99, Office for National Statistics © Crown Copyright 1999

HEALTH CARE

NATIONAL HEALTH SERVICE

The National Health Service (NHS) came into being on 5 July 1948 under the National Health Service Act 1946, covering England and Wales, and under separate legislation for Scotland and Northern Ireland. The NHS is now administered by the Secretary of State for Health (in England), the National Assembly for Wales, the Scottish Executive and the Secretary of State for Northern Ireland.

The function of the NHS is to provide a comprehensive health service designed to secure improvement in the physical and mental health of the people and to prevent, diagnose and treat illness. It was founded on the principle that treatment should be provided according to clinical need rather than ability to pay, and should be free at the point of delivery. However, prescription charges were provided for by legislation in 1949 and implemented in 1952, and charges for some dental and ophthalmic treatment have also been introduced.

The NHS covers a comprehensive range of hospital, specialist, family practitioner (medical, dental, ophthalmic and pharmaceutical), artificial limb and appliance, ambulance, and community health services. Everyone normally resident in the UK is entitled to use any of these services.

Structure

The National Health Service and Community Care Act 1990 provided for more streamlined Regional Health Authorities and District Health Authorities, and for the establishment of Family Health Services Authorities (FHSAs) and NHS Trusts. The concept of the 'internal market' was introduced into health care, whereby care was provided through NHS contracts where health authorities or boards and GP fundholders (the purchasers) were responsible for buying health care from hospitals, non-fundholding GPs, community services and ambulance services (the providers).

NHS Trusts operate as self-governing health care providers independent of health authority control and responsible to the Secretary of State. Until 1999 they derived their income principally from contracts to provide services to health authorities and fund-holding GPs.

The eight Regional Health Authorities in England were abolished in April 1996 and replaced by eight regional offices which, together with the headquarters in Leeds, form the NHS Executive. The regional offices are part of the Department of Health, and their functions include financial and performance monitoring of local purchasers and providers, public health, regional research and development, and education programmes. London is co-ordinated by the two regions of North Thames and South Thames. Listings of the Health Authorities and Trusts, which fall under the jurisdiction of these two Regional Offices, are given below.

In April 1996 the District Health Authorities and Family Health Service Authorities were merged to form Health Authorities (HAs) which are responsible for health and health services in their areas. They are also responsible for assessing the health care needs of the local population and developing integrated strategies for meeting these needs in partnership with GPs and in consultation with the public, hospitals and others. HAs' resources are allocated by the NHS Executive headquarters, to which they are also accountable for their performance. HA chairmen are appointed by the Health Secretary and non-executive members by the regional offices of the NHS Executive.

There are also Community Health Councils throughout the UK; their role is to represent the interests of the public to health authorities and boards. The Government announced in March 1998 that public consultation and patient representation in the NHS would be increased.

Under the Health Act 1999 the NHS internal market in England was replaced by teams of GPs and community nurses working together in primary care groups from 1 April 1999. Long-term service agreements are beginning to replace annual contracts between primary care groups, health authorities, and NHS Trusts. A National Institute for Clinical Excellence has been established to produce new national guidelines and National Service Frameworks are being prepared to guarantee consistency in access to services. The first of these, to be published in late 1999, will address mental health and coronary heart disease services.

The NHS is still funded mainly through general taxation, although in recent years more reliance has been placed on the NHS element of National Insurance contributions, patient charges and other sources of income.

REGIONAL OFFICE OF THE NHS EXECUTIVE

LONDON REGION

40 Eastbourne Terrace, London W2 3QR (Tel: 020-7725 5300; Fax: 020-7258 0530)

Regional Chairman: Mr I. Mills
Regional Director: Mr N. Crisp
Communications: Mr J. Street; Ms K. Talbot

HEALTH AUTHORITIES AND TRUSTS

BARKING AND HAVERING
The Clock House, East Street, Barking, Essex, IG11 8EY (Tel: 020-8591 9595; Fax: Fax: 020-8532 6201)

Barking, Havering and Brentwood Community Health Care
The Willows, 117 Sutton Lane, Hornchurch, RM12 6RS (Tel: 01402-452577; Fax: 01402-441049)

Havering Hospitals Trust
Harold Wood Hospital, Gubbins Lane, Romford, RM3 0BE (Tel: 01708-345533; Fax: 01708-384730)

Redbridge Health Care
King George Hospital, Barley Lane, Goodmayes, Essex, IG5 8YB (Tel: 020-8983 8000; Fax: 020-8970 8001)

BARNET
Hyde House, The Hyde, Edgware Road, London, NW9 6QQ (Tel: 020-8201 4700; Fax: 020-8201 4701)

Barnet and Chase Farm Hospitals NHS Trust
Trent House, Barnet General Hospital, Barnet, EN5 3DJ (Tel: 020-8366 6600 ext. 5028; Fax: 020-8366 1361)

Barnet Healthcare NHS Trust
Colindale Hospital, Colindale Avenue, London, NW9 5HG (Tel: 020-8200 1555; Fax: 020-8200 9499)

114 Public Services London

BEXLEY AND GREENWICH
221 Erith Road, Bexleyheath, DA7 6HZ (Tel: 020-8928 6000; Fax: 020-8298 6010)

Bexley Primary Care Group
1st Floor, Marlowe House, 109 Station Road, Sidcup, Kent, DA15 7EU (Tel: 020-8298 6242; Fax: 020-8298 6241)

Greenwich Healthcare NHS Trust
Greenwich District Hospital, Vanbrugh Hill, London, SE10 9HE (Tel: 020-8312 5160; Fax: 020-8312 6159)

Greenwich Primary Care Group
1 Hyde Vale, London, SE10 8QG (Tel: 020-8694 7322; Fax: 020-8694 0631)

Oxleas NHS Trust
Pinewood House, Old Bexley Lane, Bexley, DA5 2BW (Tel: 01322-526 282; Fax: 01322-555491)

Queen Mary's Sidcup NHS Trust
Queen Mary's Hospital, Sidcup, DA14 6LT (Tel: 020-8302 2678; Fax: 020-8308 3052)

BROMLEY AND HARROW
Grace House, Harrovian Business Village, Bessborough Road, Harrow, HA1 3EX (Tel: 020-8422 6644; Fax: 020-8426 8646)

Central Middlesex Hospital
Acton Lane, Park Royal, London, NW10 7NS (Tel: 020-8965 5733; Fax: 020-8961 0012)

Harrow and Hillingdon Healthcare NHS Trust
Malt House, 285 Field End Road, Ruislip, HA4 9NJ (Tel: 020-8956 3200; Fax: 020-8830 1373)

North West London Hospital NHS Trust
Northwick Park Hospital, Watford Road, Harrow, Middx, HA1 3UJ

Northwick Park and St Mark's Hospitals
Watford Road, Harrow, HA1 3UJ (Tel: 020-8864 3232; Fax: 020-8869 2009)

Parkside Health NHS Trust
Courtfield House, St Charles Hospital, London, W10 6DZ (Tel: 020-8962 4557; Fax: 020-8962 4545)

Royal National Orthopaedic Hospital NHS Trust
Brockley Hill, Stanmore, Middx, HA7 4LP (Tel: 020-8954 2300; Fax: 020-8954 7249)

BROMLEY
Global House, 10 Station Approach, Bromley, Kent, BR2 7EH (Tel: 020-8315 8315; Fax: 020-8462 6767)

Bromley Hospital NHS Trust
Farnborough Common, Orpington, Kent, BR6 8ND (Tel: 01689-814100; Fax: 01689-862423)

Oxleas NHS Trust
Pinewood House, Old Bexley Lane, Bexley, Kent, DA5 2BF (Tel: 01322-526282; Fax: 01322-555491)

Ravensbourne NHS Trust
Bassetts House, Broadwater Gardens, Farnborough, Kent, BR6 7UA (Tel: 01689-853339; Fax: 01689-855662)

CROYDON
Knollys House, 17 Addiscombe Road, Croydon, CR0 6SR (Tel: 020-8401 3900; Fax: 020-8680 2418)

Croydon and Surrey Downs Community NHS Trust
12-18 Lennard Road, Croydon, CR9 4RS (Tel: 020-8680 2008; Fax: 020-8666 0495)

Mayday Healthcare NHS Trust
Mayday University Hospital, London Road, Croydon, Surrey, CR7 7YE (Tel: 020-8401 3000; Fax: 020-8665 1974)

South London and Maudsley NHS Trust
The Bethlam Royal Hospital, Monks Ordand Road, Beckenham, Kent, BR3 3BX (Tel: 020-8777 6611; Fax: 020-8777 1668)

Surrey Oaklands NHS Trust
Oaklands House, Coulsdon Road, Cateham, CR3 5YA (Tel: 01883-383838; Fax: 01883-383522)

EALING, HAMMERSMITH AND HOUNSLOW
1 Armstrong Way, Southall, UB2 4SA (Tel: 020-8893 0303; Fax: 020-8893 0398)

Ealing Hospital NHS Trust
Uxbridge Road, Southall, UB1 3HW (Tel: 020-8574 2444; Fax: 0920-8967 5630)

Ealing, Hammersmith and Fulham Mental Health NHS Trust
Uxbridge Road, Southall, UB1 3EU (Tel: 020-8574 2444; Fax: 020-8967 5002)

Hammersmith Hospitals NHS Trust
Du Cane Road, London, W12 0HS (Tel: 020-8383 1000; Fax: 020-8470 3169)

Hounslow and Spelthorne Community and Mental Health NHS Trust
Phoenix Court, 531 Staines Road, Hounslow, TW4 5DP (Tel: 020-8321 2211; Fax: 020-8321 2490)

Riverside Community Healthcare NHS Trust
5-7 Parsons Green, London, SW6 4UL (Tel: 020-8846 6767; Fax: 020-8846 7654)

West Middlesex University Hospital NHS Trust
Twickenham Road, Isleworth, Middx, TW7 6AF (Tel: 020-8560 2121; Fax: 020-8565 5982)

EAST LONDON AND THE CITY
81-91 Commercial Road, London, E1 1RD (Tel: 020-7655 6600; Fax: 020-7655 6666)

Barts and The Royal London NHS Trust
Whitechapel Road, London, E1 1BB (Tel: 020-7377 7000; Fax: 020-7377 7361)

Health 115

City and Hackney Community Services NHS Trust
St Leonard's Primary Care Centre, Nuttall Street, London, N1 5LZ (Tel: 020-7601 7740; Fax: 020-7739 8455)

Homerton Hospital NHS Trust
Homerton Row, London, E9 6SR (Tel: 020-8919 5555; Fax: 020-8986 8241)

Newham General Hospital NHS Trust
Glen Road, London, E13 8SL (Tel: 020-7476 4000)

Tower Hamlets Healthcare NHS Trust
Elizabeth Fry House, Mile End Hospital, London, E1 4DG (Tel: 020-7377 7920; Fax: 020-7377 7931)

ENFIELD AND HARINGEY
Holbrook House, Cockfosters Road, Barnet, EN4 0DR (Tel: 020-8272 5500; Fax: 020-8272 5700)

Chase Farm Hospitals NHS Trust
Chase Farm Hospital, The Ridgeway, Enfield, EN2 8JL (Tel: 020-8366 6600; Fax: 020-8366 1361)

Enfield Community Care NHS Trust
Avon Villa, Chase Farm Hospital, Enfield, EN2 8JL (Tel: 020-8366 6600; Fax: 020-8366 9166)

Haringey Healthcare NHS Trust
St Ann's Hospital, St Ann's Road, London, N15 3TH (Tel: 020-8442 6000; Fax: 020-8442 6567)

North Middlesex Hospital NHS Trust
Sterling Way, London, N18 1QX (Tel: 020-8887 2000; Fax: 020-8887 4219)

KENSINGTON, CHELSEA AND WESTMINSTER
50 Eastbourne Terrace, London, W2 6LX (Tel: 020-7725 3333; Fax: 020-7725 3398)

Brent, Kensington, Chelsea and Westminster Mental Health NHS Trust
30 Eastbourne Terrace, London, W2 6LA (Tel: 020-8237 2000; Fax: 020-8746 8978)

Chelsea and Westminster Healthcare NHS Trust
369 Fulham Road, London, SW10 9NH (Tel: 020-8746 8000; Fax: 020-8846 6539)

Parkside Health NHS Trust
Courtfield House, St Charles Hospital, Exmoor Street, London, W10 6DZ (Tel: 020-8962 2488; Fax: 020-8962 4652)

Riverside Community Healthcare NHS Trust
Parsons Green Centre, 5-7 Parsons Green, London, SW6 4UL (Tel: 020-8846 6767; Fax: 020-8846 7654)

Royal Brompton Hospital NHS Trust
Sydney Street, London, SW3 6NP (Tel: 020-7352 8121; Fax: 020-7351 8473)

Royal Marsden NHS Trust
Fulham Road, London, SW3 6JJ (Tel: 020-7352 8171; Fax: 020-7351 3785)

KINGSTON AND DISTRICT
Woodroofe House, Tolworth Hospital, Surbiton, KT6 7QU (Tel: 020-8390 0102; Fax: 020-8390 1236)

Kingston Hospital NHS Trust
Galsworthy Road, Kingston upon Thames, KT2 7QB (Tel: 020-8546 7711; Fax: 020-8547 2182)

South West London Community NHS Trust
Roehampton House, Roehampton Lane, London, SW15 5PN (Tel: 020-8789 6611; Fax: 020-8780 1089)

Teddington Memorial Hospital NHS Trust
Hampton Road, Teddington, Middx, TW11 0JL (Tel: 020-8977 2212; Fax: 020-8977 1914)

LAMBETH, SOUTHWARK AND LEWISHAM
1 Lower Marsh, London, SE1 7NT (Tel: 020-7716 7000; Fax: 020-7716 7039)

Community Health South London NHS Trust
Elizabeth Blackwell House, Wardalls Grove, London, SE14 5ER (Tel: 020-7635 5555; Fax: 020-7771 5115)

Guy's and St Thomas' Hopsital Trust
St Thomas's Street, London, SE1 9RT (Tel: 020-7928 9292; Fax: 020-7633 0347)

King's Healthcare NHS Trust
Denmark Hill, London, SE5 9RS (Tel: 020-7737 4000; Fax: 020-7346 3445)

South London and Maudsley NHS Trust
Leegate House, Burnt Ash Road, London, SE12 8RG (Tel: 020-8297 0707; Fax: 020-8297 0377)

MERTON, SUTTON AND WANDSWORTH
The Wilson, Cranmer Road, Mitcham, CR4 4TP (Tel: 020-8468 3021; Fax: 020-8646 6240)

Epsom and St Helier NHS Trust
St Helier Hospital, Wrythe Lane, Carshalton, Surrey, SM5 1AA (Tel: 020-8296 2000; Fax: 020-8641 4546)

South West London and St George's Mental Health NHS Trust
Springfield University Hospital, 61 Glenburnie Road, London, SW17 7DL (Tel: 020-8672 9911; Fax: 020-8682 6703)

South West London Community NHS Trust
Clare House, St George's Hospital, Blackshaw Road, London, SW17 0QT (Tel: 020-8700 0550; Fax: 020-8700 0593)

St George's Healthcare NHS Trust
St George's Hospital, Blackshaw Road, London, SW17 0QT (Tel: 020-8672 1255; Fax: 020-8672 5304)

The Royal Marsden NHS Trust
Fulham Road, London, SW3 6JJ (Tel: 020-7352 8171; Fax: 020-7351 3785)

REDBRIDGE AND WALTHAM FOREST
Becketts House, 2-14 Ilford Hill, Ilford, Essex, IG1 2QX (Tel: 020-8478 5151; Fax: 020-8926 5001)

116 Public Services London

Forest Healthcare Trust
Whipps Cross Hospital, London, E11 1NR

Redbridge Community Healthcare
201-205 Cranbrook Road, Ilford, Essex, IG1 5TD

Redbridge Health Care Trust
King George Hospital, Barley Lane, Goodmayes, Essex IG3 8YB

Waltham Forest Community Healthcare
722 High Road, London, E11 3AJ

COMMUNITY HEALTH COUNCILS (CHC)

Community Health Councils are statutory bodies, which are independent. They represent the interests of local people to the NHS. They aim to perform the following tasks:
- to provide information about the services available from local health care providers and to review plans for new services
- to make recommendations to healthcare providers about improvements which are in the local community's interest
- to help patients where necessary make official complaints
- to forge links with the local community

ASSOCIATION OF COMMUNITY HEALTH COUNCILS FOR ENGLAND AND WALES

30 Drayton Park, London N5 1PB (Tel: 020-7609 8405; Fax: 020-7700 1152)

The Association was established in 1977. The objectives of the Association are to provide a forum for the exchange of views and for the discussion of matters of common concern to member Community Health Councils. Where appropriate the Association will express views on national health matters to ministers, government departments and other relevant bodies and the Association provides advice and support to CHCs to assist them in the performance of their functions and the meeting of their objectives.

COMMUNITY HEALTH COUNCILS

Barking, Dagenham and Havering
The Victoria Centre, Pettits Lane, Romford Essex RM1 4HP (Tel: 01708 766412; Fax: 01708 738010)

Barnet
159 Ballards Lane. Finchley London N3 1LJ (Tel: 020-8349 4364; Fax: 020-8343 3502)

Bexley
11a Upton Road, Bexleyheath, Kent DA6 8LQ (Tel 020-8301 0920; Fax: 020-8303 1102)

Brent
22-24 High Road, London NW10 2QD (Tel: 020-8451 4697; Fax: 020-8451 4533)

Bromley
Babbacombe House, 2 Babbacombe Road, Bromley BR1 3LW (Tel: 020-464 0249; Fax: 020-8313 98990)

Camden
197 Kentish Town Road, London NW5 2JU (Tel: 020-7530 5266/5155; Fax: 020-7530 5325)

City and Hackney
210 Kingsland Road, London E2 8EB (Tel : 020-7739 6308; Fax: 020-7729 5943)

Croydon
90 London Road, Croydon, Surrey CR0 2TB (Tel: 020-8680 1503; Fax: 020-8401 3919)

Ealing
119 Uxbridge Road, London W7 3ST (Tel: 020-8579 2211; Fax: 020-7579 4257)

Enfield
51-53 Lancaster Road, Enfield Middlesex EN2 0BU (Tel: 020-8366 6665; Fax: 020-8366 6650)

Greenwich
23 Anglesea Road, London SE18 6EG (Tel: 020-8317 9994; Fax: 020-8317 3444)

Hammersmith and Fulham
42 Fulham Palace Road, London W6 9PH (Tel: 020-8748 0639; Fax: 020-8741 1865)

Haringey
332 High Road, London N15 4BN (Tel: 020-8808 1694; Fax 020-8801 9590)

Harrow
2 Junction Road, Harrow Middlesex HA1 1NL (Tel: 020-8863 6432; Fax 020-8424 9780)

Hillingdon
65 Belmont Road, Uxbridge Middlesex UB8 1QT (Tel: 01895 257858; Fax: 01895 813300)

Hounslow
7-9 Spur Road, Isleworth Middlesex TW7 5BD (020-8568 8558; Fax 020-8568 8418)

Islington
164 Holloway Road, London N7 8DD (Tel: 020-7609 6096; Fax 020-7609 4015)

Kensington & Chelsea and Westminster
45-47 Praed Street, London W2 1NR 9 (Tel: 020-7706 7100; Fax: 020-7402 1271)

Kingston
UMI House, 9-13 St James Road, Surbiton Surrey KT6 4QH (Tel: 020-8399 8467; Fax: 020-8399 8415)

Lambeth
2 Cleaver Street, Kennington, London SE11 4DP (Tel: 020-7582 3288; Fax: 020-7735 9071)

Lewisham
246 Lewisham High Street, London SE13 6JU (Tel: 020-8318 3435; Fax: 020-8318 3655)

Merton and Sutton
29 West Street, Sutton Surrey SM1 1SJ (Tel: 020-8642 6405; Fax: 020-8770 9618)

Newham
128 The Grove, Stratford E15 1NS (Tel: 020-8534 4217/8; Fax: 020-8536 0091)

Health 117

Redbridge
201 Cranbrook Road, Iford Essex IGL 4TD (Tel: 020-8518 5736; Fax: 020-8518 5738)

Richmond and Twickenham
55 Heath Road, Twickenham TW1 4AW (Tel: 020-8744 1144; Fax: 020-8744 0682)

Southwark
75 Denmark Hill, London SE5 8RS (Tel: 020-7703 9498; Fax: 020-7277 1805)

Tower Hamlets
Unit 1 and 2 Albion Yard, Whitechapel Road, London E1 1BW (Tel: 020-7375 1555; Fax: 020-7375 0700)

Waltham Forest
772 High Road, Leytonstone, London E11 3AJ (Tel: 020-8539 7180; Fax: 020-8539 0949)

Wandsworth
1 Balham Station Road, London SW12 9SG (Tel: 020-8675 8820/29; Fax: 020-8675 8863)

NATIONAL BLOOD SERVICE

North London Centre, Colindale Avenue, Colindale, London NW9 5BG (Tel: 0345 711711)
South Thames Centre, 75 Cranmer Terrace, London SW17 0RB (Tel: 020-8258 8300)

NATIONAL MISSING PERSONS HELPLINE

Roebuck House, 284-286 Upper Richmond Road West, London SW14 7JE (Tel: 020-8392 4545; Fax: 020-8878 7752)

This is the national helpline for people who are trying to trace missing friends and relatives. The National Missing Persons Helpline also run another helpline, Message Home, which is a helpline for people who have runaway or left home to send messages to their families or carers, or to seek confidential help and advice. Message Home: Tel: 020-8392 4550; Helpline: 0800 700740; Fax: 020-8878 7752)

HOUSING

HOUSING STOCK BY TENURE* 1981-1997 (PERCENTAGES AND 000s)

	1981	1991	1994	1995	1996	1997
LONDON						
Owner-occupied	50	57	57	57	57	56
Rented from local authority	32	24	22	22	22	20
Rented from private owners or with job/business	13	12	14	15	15	17
Rented from registered social landlord	5	5	7	7	7	7
Total dwellings (000s)	2,682	2,928	2,980	2,997	3,011	3,025
GREAT BRITAIN						
Owner-occupied	57	66	67	67	67	67
Rented from from local authority or New Town**	30	21	19	19	19	17
Rented from private owners or with job/business	11	10	10	10	10	11
Rented from registered social landlord	2	3	4	4	5	5
Total dwellings (000s)	21,085	23,138	23,652	23,832	23,998	24,216

* At December each year
** Including Scottish Homes, formerly the Scottish Special Housing Association
Source: Focus on London '99, Office for National Statistics © Crown Copyright 1999

GREATER LONDON – ALL LENDERS SIMPLE AVERAGE HOUSE PRICE SERIES

	New Dwellings		2nd Hand Dwellings		All Dwellings		1st Time Purchasers	
	Price (£)	1yr % Change	Price (£)	1yr % Change	Price (£)	1yr % Change	Price (£)	1yr % Change
1993	78,084		80,707		81,332		65,554	
1994	75,200	-3.7	87,563	8.5	87,631	7.7	62,214	-5.1
1995	83.933	11.6	88,277	0.8	89,528	2.2	65,912	5.9
1996	99,292	18.3	93,321	5.7	94,065	5.1	67,153	1.9
1997	116,242	17.1	104,827	12.3	105,819	12.5	73,962	10.1
1998	125,079	7.6	114,116	8.9	114,783	8.5	90,160	21.9
1999	178,274	42.5	140,347	22.9	142,321	24.0	115,002	27.6

Source: DETR 5% Survey of Mortgage lenders, All Lenders, first mortgages
Average of all property prices.
© Crown Copyright

Housing

Housing in London is monitored, regulated and provided by many different bodies and organisations. The Department of the Environment Transport and the Regions is primarily responsible for Housing policy in the UK. The Housing Directorate of the DETR works in conjunction with local authorities and numerous housing bodies to provide good quality housing for all members of society, including initiatives to provide housing for the homeless and for people with special needs. This involves interaction with the rented and the privately owned sectors. Housing is also a key aspect of the role of the Greater London Authority and the London Mayor. Issues highlighted by the London Mayor to be tackled are the lack of affordable housing to buy for Londoners; the high number of households on waiting lists for council housing and the disproportionately high amounts charged in rent for properties in London compared to other cities in the UK. Also playing a major role in the provision of housing are Registered Social Landlords or Housing Associations. These are non-profit making organisations which form the voluntary housing movement. The common aim of housing associations is to provide housing and related services for people on low incomes and in housing need. The term "voluntary" derives from the nature of housing association provision which is not undertaken through statutory duty but by virtue of the work of people who combine to form an association to meet particular housing needs.

BRITISH PROPERTY FEDERATION

1 Warwick Row, London SW1E 5ER (Tel: 020-7828 0111; Fax: 020-7834 3442; Email: info@bpf.org.uk)

EMPTY HOMES AGENCY

195-197 Victoria Street, London, SW1E 5NE (Tel: 020-7828 6288; Fax: 020-7828 7006;
E-mail: info@emptyhomes.com;
Web: http://www.emptyhomes.com)

The Empty Homes Agency is an independent housing charity established in 1992. Its objective is to devise solutions and disseminate good practice on how to tackle the problem of empty homes.
There is a London Empty Homes Hotline which aims to bring London's 100,000 empty homes back into use, the telephone number for which is 0870 901 6303. The Empty Homes Agency estimates that there are 114,000 vacant dwellings in London and 26,729 homeless households. The agency is funded by The Housing Corporation and other bodies and has the backing of the government and local authorities.

HOUSING CORPORATION

149 Tottenham Court Road, London W1P 0BN (Tel: 020-7393 2000; Fax: 020-7393 2111)

Established by Parliament in 1964, the Housing Corporation regulates, funds and promotes the proper performance of registered social landlords, which are non-profit making bodies run by voluntary committees.
There are over 2,200 registered social landlords, most of which are housing associations, and they now provide homes for more than 1.5 million people. Under the Housing Act 1996, the Corporation's regulatory role was widened to embrace new types of landlords, in particular local housing companies. The Corporation is funded by the Department of the Environment, Transport and the Regions.

Chairman: The Rt. Hon Baroness Dean of Thornton-le-Fylde
Deputy Chairman: E. Armitage

London Regional Office
Waverley House, 7-12 Noel Street, London W1V 4BA
Tel: 020-7292 4400; Fax 020-7292 4401)

HOUSING ORGANISATIONS MOBILITY AND EXCHANGE SERVICES (HOMES)

242 Vauxhall Bridge Road, London SW1V 1AU (Tel: 020-7963 0200; Fax: 020-7963 0249;
Email: pcd@homes.demon.co.uk;
Web: http://www.homes.org.uk)

HOMES works with local authorities and housing associations to help thousands of people move home each year.

Director: Sheila Button

INDEPENDENT HOUSING OMBUDSMAN

Norman House, 105-109 Strand, London WC2R 0AA (Tel: 020-7836 3630; 0345-125973; Fax: 020-7836 3900; Email: ombudsman@ihos.org.uk)

The Independent Housing Ombudsman was established in 1997 under the Housing Act 1996. The Ombudsman deals with complaints against registered social landlords (not including local authorities) and some private landlords.

Ombudsman: R. Jefferies
Chair of Board: Ms P. Brown
General Manager: L. Greenberg

LEASEHOLD ADVISORY SERVICE

8 Maddox Street, London, W1R 9PN (Tel: 020-7493 3116 Fax: 020-7493 4318;
E-mail info@lease-advice.org;
Web: http://www.lease-advice.org)

The Leasehold Advisory Service is an independent body giving legal advice about residential leaseholding. The service is free of charge and is used by landlords, leaseholders and anyone else concerned with leaseholding.

LONDON HOUSING UNIT

2nd Floor, Bedford House, 125-133 Camden High Street, London NW1 7JR (Tel: 020-7428 4910; Fax: 020-7267 9334; Email: lhu@btinternet.com)

The London Housing Unit provides policy, research and information services on social housing within London Borough Councils. The work of the London Housing Unit includes monitoring the delivery of housing services, assessing the future of housing provision and related issues and encompassing the wider aspects of regeneration, welfare and social policy. On 1 April 2000 the

120 Public Services London

London Housing Unit merged with the Association of London Government.

LONDON RENT ASSOCIATION PANEL/LEASEHOLD VALUATION TRIBUNAL

Whittington House, 19-30 Alfred Place, London WC1E 7LR (Tel: 020-7446 7700; Fax: 020-7637 1250)

RENT SERVICE

London Region: Chesham House, 4th Floor, 150 Regent Street, London W1R 5FA (Tel: 020-7728 3403; Fax: 020-7728 2949)

The Rent Service is an Executive Agency of the Department for the Environment, Transport and the Regions. It is a specialist valuation agency, assessing rents charged to private tenants and has taken over responsibility for the former rent officer service. Its operations cover two areas: establishing 'fair rents' for regulated tenancies, and assessing rents for private sector tenancies where Housing Benefit is to be paid. In London, the Service is divided into six administrative regions as shown below:

Central: 6th Floor, 17 Old Court Place, London W8 4PL (Tel: 020-7938 4266; Fax: 020-7937 0182)
North: Nicholas House, River Front, Enfield, Middx., EN1 3TF (Tel: 020-8367 1521; Fax: 020-8366 7564)
North East: 7th Floor, Forest House, 16-20 Clements Road, Ilford, Essex, IG1 1BA (Tel: 020-8478 1693; Fax: 020-8478 9779)
South East: Stane House, 225A Streatham High Road, London, SW16 6EN (Tel: 020-7926 6640; Fax: 020-7926 6704)
South West: 1st Floor, Suffolk House, George Street, Croydon, CR0 0YN (Tel: 020-8686 2201/2; Fax: 020-8649 7977)
West: 4th Floor, Dawley House, 91-5 Uxbridge Road, London, W5 5TH (Tel: 020-8579 6881; Fax: 020-8840 8170)

SHELTER

88 Old Street, London EC1V 9HU (Tel: 020-7505 2000; Fax: 020-7505 2167; Email: info@shelter.org.uk; Web: http://www.shelter.org.uk) Freephone 24 hour helpline: 0808 800 444

VALUATION OFFICE

New Court, Carey Street, London WC2A 2JE (Tel: 020-7234 1156; Fax: 020-7324 1073)

There are also Valuation Offices in Barking, Bromley, Camden, City, Enfield, Harow, Lambeth, Tower Hamlets, Westminster, Wimbledon

VALUATION TRIBUNALS

The Valuation Tribunals hear appeals concerning the council tax, non-domestic rating and land drainage rates in England and Wales, and have the residual jurisdiction to hear appeals concerning the community charge, the pre-1900 rating list, disabled rating and mixed hereditaments.

Central London Valuation Tribunal: Floor 2, Black Lion House, 45 Whitechapel Road, London E1 (020-7497 1757; Fax 020-7497 0752).
London North East Valuation Tribunal: Floor 2 Black Lion House, 45 Whitechapel Road, London E1 (020-8554 4004; Fax 020-8518 3342).
London North West Valuation Tribunal: 34 Greenhill Way, Harrow HA1 1LE (020-8863 6382; Fax 020-8427 9436).
London South East Valuation Tribunal: 4th Floor, AMP House, Dingwall Road, Croydon CR0 9XA (020-8681 8843; Fax 020-8681 3892).
London South West Valuation Tribunal: 4th Floor, AMP House, Dingwall Road, Croydon CR0 9XA (020-8680 2445; Fax 020-8686 7444).

LIBRARIES

Local authorities are responsible for maintaining and funding libraries within their area. Many libraries now offer not just the traditional services of booklending but also audio-visual and multimedia services. The list below provides contact details of libraries within each London Borough.

BARKING AND DAGENHAM

Head of Library Services: T. Brown

Central Library
Barking, Essex, IG11 7NB (Tel: 020-8517 8666; Fax: 020-8594 1156; Email: tbrown@barking-dagenham.gov.uk;
Web: http://www.earl.org.uk/partners/barking/)

Fanshawe Library
Barnmead Road, Dagenham, Essex, RM9 5DX (Tel: 020-8592 1513)

Marks Gate Library
Rose Lane, Chadwell Heath, Romford, Essex, RM6 5NJ (Tel: 020-8599 9953)

Markyate Library
Markyate Road, Dagenham, Essex, RM8 3HT (Tel: 020-8592 1309)

Rectory Library
Rectory Road, Dagenham, Essex, RM10 9SA (Tel: 020-8592 4757)

Rush Green Library
Dagenham Road, Rush Green, Romford, Essex, (Tel: 01708-744795)

Thames View Library
2A Farr Avenue, Barking, Essex, IG11 0NZ (Tel: 020-8594 3408)

Valence Library
Becontree Avenue, Dagenham, Essex, RM8 3HT (Tel: 020-8592 6537)

Wantz Library
Rainham Road North, Dagenham, Essex, RM10 7DX (Tel: 020-8592 2903)

Whalebone Library
High Road, Chadwell Heath, Romford, Essex, RM6 6AS (Tel: 020-8590 4636)

Woodward Library
Woodward Road, Dagenham, Essex, RM9 4SP (Tel: 020-8592 5235)

BARNET

Head of Cultural Services: Mrs P. Usher

Barnet Library
General Enquiries, Cultural Services, The Old Town Hall, Friern Barnet Lane, London, N11 3DL (Tel: 020-8359 3164; Fax: 020-8359 3171;
Web: http://www.barnet.gov.uk/profile/librarires/)

Burnt Oak Library
Watling Avenue, Edgware, Middx, HA8 0UB (Tel: 020-8959 3112)

Childs Hill Library
320 Cricklewood Lane, London, NW2 2QE (Tel: 020-8455 5390)

Chipping Barnet Library
3 Stapylton Road, Barnet, Herts, EN5 4QT (Tel: 020-8359 4040)

Church End Library
24 Hendon Lane, Finchley, London, N3 1TR (Tel: 020-8346 5711)

East Barnet Library
85 Brookhill Road, East Barnet, Herts, EN4 8SG (Tel: 020-8440 4376)

East Finchley Library
226 High Road, London, N2 9BB (Tel: 020-8883 2664)

Edgware Library
Hale Lane, Edgware, Middx, HA8 8NN (Tel: 020-8359 2626)

Friern Barnet Library
Friern Barnet Road, London, N11 3DS (Tel: 020-8368 2680)

Golders Green Library
156 Golders Green Road, London, NW11 8HE (Tel: 020-8359 2060)

Grahame Park Library
The Concourse, London, NW9 5XL (Tel: 020-8200 0470)

Hampstead Garden Suburb Library
15 Market Place, London, NW11 6LB (Tel: 020-8455 1235)

Hendon Library
The Burroughs, London, NW4 4BQ (Tel: 020-8359 2628)

Local Studies and Archives
Chapel Walk, Egerton Gardens, London, NW4 (Tel: 020-8359 2876)

Mill Hill Library
Hartley Avenue, London, NW7 2HX (Tel: 020-8959 5066)

North Finchley Library
Ravensdale Avenue, London, N12 9HP (Tel: 020-8445 4081)

Osidge Library
Brunswick Park Road, London, N11 1EY (Tel: 020-8368 0532)

South Friern Library
Colney Hatch Lane, London, N10 1HD (Tel: 020-8883 6513)

Totteridge Library
109 Totteridge Lane, London, N20 8DZ (Tel: 020-8445 5288)

BEXLEY
Head of Libraries and Cultural Services: F. V. Johnson

Barnehurst Library
168 Mayplace Road East, Barnehurst, Kent, DA7 6EJ (Tel: 01322-521663; Email: info@bexley.gov.uk; Web: http://www.bexley.gov.uk/service/library.html)

Bexley Village Library
Bourne Road, Bexley, Kent, DA1 1LU (Tel: 01322-522168)

Blackfen Library
Cedar Avenue, Sidcup, Kent, DA15 8NJ (Tel: 020-8300 3010)

Bostall Library
King Harold's Way, Bexleyheath, Kent, DA7 5RE (Tel: 020-8310 1779)

Central Library
Townley Road, Bexleyheath, Kent, DA6 7HJ (Tel: 020-8301 5151; Fax: 020-8303 7872; Web: http://www.bexley.gov.uk/service/lib-central.html)
Head Librarian: G. H. Boulton

Crayford Library
Crayford Road, Crayford, Kent, DA1 4ER (Tel: 01322-526050)

Erith Library
Walnut Tree Road, Erith, Kent, DA8 1RS (Tel: 01322-336582)

Local Studies Centre
Hall Place, Bourne Road, Bexley, Kent, DA5 1PQ (Tel: 01322-526574)

North Heath Library
200 Bexley Road, Erith, Kent, (Tel: 01322-333663)

Sidcup Library
Hadlow Road, Sidcup, Kent, DA14 4AQ (Tel: 020-8300 2958)

Slade Green Library
Bridge Road, Slade Green, Erith, Kent, DA8 2HS (Tel: 01322-335027)

Thamesmead Library
Binsey Walk, Thamesmead, London, SE2 9TS (Tel: 020-8310 9944)

Upper Belvedere Library
Woolwich Road, Upper Belvedere, Kent, DA17 5EQ (Tel: 01322-439760)

Welling Library
Bellegrove Road, Welling, Kent, DA16 3PA (Tel: 020-8303 2788)

BRENT
Head of Library Service: Ms K. Tyerman

Brent Library
4th Floor, Chesterfield House, 9 Park Lane, Wembley, Middx, HA9 7RJ (Tel: 020-8937 3144; Fax: 020-8937 3023; Email: karen.tyerman@brent.gov.uk; Web: http://www.brent.gov.uk/services/lib/indxlibs.htm)

Cricklewood Library and Archive
152 Olive Road, London, NW2 6UY (Tel: 020-8937 3540; Fax: 020-8450 5211)
Customer Services Officer: D. Vara

Grange Road Mobile Library
2-12 Grange Road, London, NW10 2QY (Tel: 020-8937 3460)
Customer Services Officer: S. Palmer

Harlesden Library
Craven Park Road, London, NW10 8SE (Tel: 020-8965 7132/8937 3570; Fax: 020-8838 2199; Web: lth@brent.gov.uk)
Principal Librarian: M. Perry

Neasden Library
277 Neasden Lane, London, NW10 1QJ (Tel: 020-8937 3580; Fax: 020-8208 3909)

Town Hall Library
Brent Town Hall, Forty Lane, Wembley, Middx, HA9 9HU (Tel: 020-8937 3500; Fax: 020-8937 3504; Web: th.library@brent.gov.uk)
Principal Librarian: K. Batchelor

Willesden Green Library
95 High Road, London, NW10 2SF (Tel: 020-8937 3400; Fax: 020-8937 3401)
Principal Librarian: J. Verstraete

BROMLEY

Anerley Library
Anerley Town Hall, Anerley Road, London, SE20 8BD (Tel: 020-8778 7457; Web: http://www.bromley.gov.uk/)

Beckenham Library
Beckenham Road, Beckenham, BR3 4PE (Tel: 020-8650 7292)

Biggin Hill Library
Church Road, Biggin Hill, TN16 3LB (Tel: 01959-574468)

Bromley Central Library
High Street, Bromley, Kent, BR1 1EX (Tel: 020-8460 9955; Fax: 020-8313 9975)

Burnt Ash Library
Burnt Ash Lane, Bromley, BR1 5AF (Tel: 020-8460 3405)

Chislehurst Library
Red Hill, Chislehurst, BR7 6DA (Tel: 020-8467 1318)

Libraries

Hayes Library
Hayes Street, Hayes, Middx, BR2 7LH (Tel: 020-8462 2445)

Mottingham Library
31 Mottingham Road, London, SE9 4QZ (Tel: 020-8857 5406)

Orpington Library
The Priory, Church Hill, Orpington, Kent, BR6 0HH (Tel: 01689-831551)

Penge Library
186 Maple Road, London, SE20 8HT (Tel: 020-8778 8772)

Petts Wood Library
Frankswood Avenue, Petts Wood, BR5 1BP (Tel: 01689-821607)

Shortlands Library
110 Shortlands Road, Bromley, BR2 0JP (Tel: 020-8460 9692)

Southborough Library
Southborough Lane, Bromley, BR2 8HP (Tel: 020-8467 0355)

St Paul's Cray Library
Mickleham Road, St Paul's, Cray, BR5 2RW (Tel: 020-8800 5454)

West Wickham Library
Glebe Way, West Wickham, BR4 0SH (Tel: 020-8777 4139)

CAMDEN

Belsize Library
Antrim Road, London, NW3 4XN (Tel: 020-7974 6518; Email: camdeninformationservices@camden.gov.uk; Web: http://www.camden.gov.uk)

Camden Libraries and Information Services
Crowndale Centre, 218 Eversholt Street, London, NW1 1BD (Tel. 020-7974 1656; Fax: 010 7974 1566)

Chalk Farm Library
Sharpleshall Street, London, NW1 8YN (Tel: 020-7974 6526)

Heath Library
Keats Grove, London, NW3 2RR (Tel: 020-7974 6520)

Highgate Library
Chester Road, London, N19 5DH (Tel: 020-7974 5752)

Holborn Library
32-38 Theobald's Road, London, WC1X 8PA (Tel: 020-7974 6345/6)

Kentish Town Library
Kentish Town Road, London, NW5 2AA (Tel: 020-7974 6253)

Kilburn Library
Cotleigh Road, London, NW6 2NP (Tel: 020-7974 1965)

Local Studies and Archives Centre
32-38 Theobald's Road, London, WC1X 8PA (Tel: 020-7974 6342)

Queens Crescent Library
165 Queens Crescent, London, NW5 4HH (Tel: 020-7974 6243)

Regent's Park Library
Compton Close, Robert Street, London, NW1 3QT (Tel: 020-7974 1530)

St Pancras Library
Camden Town Hall, Argyle Street, London, WC1H 8NL (Tel: 020-7974 5833)

Swiss Cottage Central Library
88 Avenue Road, London, NW3 3HA (Tel: 020-7974 6522)

West Hampstead Library
Dennington Park Road, London, NW6 1AU (Tel: 020-7974 6610)

CITY OF LONDON

Barbican Library
Barbican Centre, London, EC2Y 8DS (Tel: 020-7638 0569;
Web: http://www.earl.org.uk/partners/corp_of_london/)

Camomile Street Library
12-20 Camomile Street, London, EC3A 7EX (Tel: 020-7247 8895)

City Business Library
Brewers Hall Garden, London, EC2V 5BX (Tel: 020-7332 1812)

Guildhall Library
Aldermanbury Lane, London, EC2P 2EG (Tel: 020-7332 1868)

Shoe Lane Library
Little New Street, London, EC4A 3GR (Tel: 020-7583 7178)

St Bride Printing Library
Bride Lane, London, EC4Y 8EE (Tel: 020-7353 4660)

CROYDON

Head of Libraries: Ms A. Scott

Ashburton Library
Lower Addiscombe Road, Croydon, CR0 6RX (Tel: 020-8656 4148; Email: ascott@library.croydon.gov.uk; Web: http://www.croydon.gov.uk/index-library.htm) ashburton@library.croydon.gov.uk

Bradmore Green Library
Bradmore Way, Coulsdon, CR5 1PE (Tel: 01737-

553267;
E-mail: bradmoregreen@library.croydon.gov.uk)

Broad Green Library
89 Canterbury Road, Croydon, CR0 3HH (Tel: 020-8684 4829; E-mail: broadgreen@library.croydon.gov.uk)

Coulsdon Library
Brighton Road, Coulsdon, CR5 2NH (Tel: 020-8660 1548; E-mail: coulsdon@library.croydon.gov.uk)

Croydon Central Library
Katharine Street, Croydon, CR9 1ET (Tel: 020-8760 5400; Fax: 020-8253 1004; Web: http://www.croydon.gov.uk)/index-library.htm)

Mobile Library
c/o Selsdon Library, Addington Road, Selsdon, CR2 8LA (Tel: 020-8657 7210: E-mail: selsdon@library.croydon.gov.uk)

New Addington Library
Central Parade, New Addington, CR0 0JB (Tel: 01689-841248; E-mail: newaddington@library.croydon.gov.uk)

Norbury Library
Beatrice Avenue, Norbury, London, SW16 4UW (Tel: 020-8679 1597; E-mail: norbury@library.croydon.gov.uk)

Purley Library
Banstead Road, Purley, CR8 3YH (Tel: 020-8660 1171; E-mail: purley@library.croydon.gov.uk)

Sanderstead Library
Farm Fields, South Croydon, CR2 0HL (Tel: 020-8657 2882; E-mail: Sanderstead@library.croydon.gov.uk)

Selsdon Library
Addington Road, Selsdon, CR2 8LA (Tel: 020-8657 7210; E-mail: selsdon@library.croydon.gov.uk)

Shirley Library
Wickham Road/Hartland Way, Shirley, CR0 8BH (Tel: 020-8777 7650; E-mail: shirley@library.croydon.gov.uk)

South Norwood Library
Selhurst Road/Lawrence Road, South Norwood, London, SE25 5AA (Tel: 020-8653 4545; E-mail: southnorwood@library.croydon.gov.uk)

Thornton Heath Library
Brigstock Road, Thornton Heath, CR7 7JB (Tel: 020-8684 4432; E-mail: thorntonheath@library.croydon.gov.uk)

EALING

Acton Library
High Street, London, W3 6NA (Tel: 020-8752 0999; Fax: 020-8992 6086; Web: http://www.ealing.gov.uk)

Central Library
103 Ealing Broadway Centre, London, W5 5JY (Tel: Lending 020-8567 3670; Reference 020-8567 3656; Fax: 020-8840 2351)

Greenford Library
Oldfield Lane South, Greenford, Middx, UB6 9LG (Tel: 020-8578 1466; Fax: 020-8575 7800)

Hanwell Library
Cherington Road, London, W7 3HL (Tel: 020-8567 5041)

Jubilee Gardens library
Jubilee Gardens, Southall, Middx, UB1 2TJ (Tel: 020-8578 1067)

Northfields Library
Northfields Avenue, London, W5 4UA (Tel: 020-8567 5700; Fax: 020-8567 5572)

Northolt Library
Church Road, Northolt, Middx, UB5 5AS (Tel: 020-8845 3380)

Perivale Library
Harsenden Lane South, Perivale, Middx, UB6 7NT (Tel: 020-8997 2830)

Pitshanger Library
143-145 Pitshanger Lane, London, E5 1RH (Tel: 020-8997 0230)

Southall Library
Osterley Park Road, Southall, Middx, UB2 4BL (Tel: 020-8574 3412; Fax: 020-8571 7629)

West Ealing Library
Melbourne Avenue, Ealing, W13 9BT (Tel: 020-8567 2812; Fax: 020-8567 1736)

Wood End Library
Whitton Avenue West, Greenford, Middx, UB6 0EE (Tel: 020-8422 3965)

ENFIELD

Assistant Director - Libraries and Culture: Ms C. Lewis

Bowes Road Library
Bowes Road, London, N11 1BD (Tel: 020-8379 1707; Fax: 020-8368 6025; Web: http://www.enfield.gov.uk/libs.htm)

Bullsmoor Library
Kempe Road, Enfield, Middx, EN1 1QS (Tel: 020-8379 1723; Fax: 01992-788761)

Bush Hill Park Library
Agricola Place, Enfield, Middx, EN1 1DW (Tel: 020-8379 1709; Fax: 020-8367 2213)

Edmonton Green Library
36-44 South Mall, Edmonton, London, N9 0TN (Tel: 020-8379 2600; Fax: 020-8379 2615; E-mail: edmonton.library@dial.pipex.com)

Enfield Business Library
Enfield Business Centre, 201 Hertford Road, Enfield, Middx, EN3 5JH (Tel: 020-8443 1701; Fax: 020-8443 2193; E-mail: ebl@dial.pipex.com)

Libraries

Enfield Central Library
Cecil Road, Enfield, Middx, EN2 6TW (Tel: 020-8379 8366; Fax: 020-8379 8401;
E-mail: enfield.library@dial.pipex.com
Library Network Manager: M. Allen

Enfield Highway Library
258 Hertford Road, Enfield, Middx, EN3 5BN (Tel: 020-8379 1710; Fax: 020-8443 5034)

Enfield Libraries
PO Box 58, Civic Centre, Silver Street, Enfield, EN1 3XJ (Tel: 020-8379 3710; Fax: 020-8379 3777; Web: http://www.enfield.gov.uk/libs.htm)

Library Resources Unit, Bibliographical Services
Town Hall, Green Lane, London, N13 4XD (Tel: 020-8379 2760; Fax: 020-8379 2761)
Bibliographic Services Manager: Ms R. Hellen

Merryhills Library
Enfield Road, Enfield, Middx, EN2 7HL (Tel: 020-8379 1711)

Ordnance Road Library
645 Hertford Road, Enfield, Middx, EN3 6ND (Tel: 020-8379 1725; Fax: 01992-788763;
E-mail: ordnance@enfieldlibrary.demon.co.uk)

Palmers Green Library
Broomfield Lane, Palmers Green, London, N13 4EY (Tel: 020-8379 2711; Fax: 020-8379 2712;
E-mail: palme@dial.pipex.com)

Ponders End Library
College Court, High Street, Ponders End, Middx, EN3 4EY (Tel: 020-8379 1712; Fax: 020-8443 5035)

Ridge Avenue Library
Ridge Avenue, Winchmore Hill, London, N21 2RH (Tel: 020-8379 1714; Fax: 020-8364 1352)

Southgate Circus Library
High Street, Southgate, London, N14 6BP (Tel: 020-8350 1124)

Weir Hall Library
Millfield Arts Complex, Silver Street, Edmonton, London, N18 1PJ (Tel: 020-8379 1717; Fax: 020-8807 3193)

Winchmore Hill Library
Green Lanes, Winchmore Hill, London, N21 3AP (Tel: 020-8379 1718; Fax: 020-8364 1060)

GREENWICH

Abbey Wood Library
Eynsham Drive, London, SE2 9PT (Tel: 020-8310 4185; Web: http://www.greenwich.gov.uk/)

Blackheath Library
Old Dover Road, London, SE3 7BT (Tel: 020-8858 1131)

Charlton Library
Charlton House, Charlton Road, London, SE7 8RE (Tel: 020-8319 2525)

Claude Ramsey Library
Thamesmere Leisure Centre, London, SE28 8DT (Tel: 020-8310 4246)

Coldharbour Library
William Barefoot Drive, London, SE9 3AY (Tel: 020-8857 7346)

East Greenwich Library
Woolwich Road, London, SE10 0RL (Tel: Closed for repairs)

Eltham Library
Eltham High Street, London, SE9 1TS (Tel: 020-8850 2268)

Ferrier Library
Telemann Square, London, SE3 9YR (Tel: 020-8856 5149)

Greenwich Ethnic Library Service
c/o Plumstead Library, Plumstead High Street, London, SE18 1JL (Tel: 020-8317 1544)

Local History Library
Woodlands, Mycenae Road, London, SE3 7SE (Tel: 020-8858 4631)

Mobile and Home Service
(Mobile Libraries/Hospitals/Housebound/Homes), c/o Plumstead Library, Plumstead High Street, London, SE18 1JL (Tel: 020-8317 4466)

New Eltham Library
Southwood Road, London, SE9 3QT (Tel: 020-8850 2322)

Plumstead Library
Plumstead High Street, London, SE18 1JL (Tel: 020-8854 1728)

Project Loans (School Library Service)
c/o West Greenwich Library, Greenwich High Road, London, SE10 8NN (Tel: 020-8853 1691)

Slade Library
Erindale, London, SE18 2QQ (Tel: 020-8854 7900)

West Greenwich Library
Greenwich High Road, London, SE10 8NN (Tel: 020-8858 4289)

Woolwich Library and Reference Library
Calderwood Street, London, SE18 6QZ (Tel: 020-8921 5750; Reference: 020-8316 6663)

HACKNEY

Hackney Central Library, Mare Street, London, E8 1HG (Tel: 020-8525 2560; Fax: 020-8533 3712;
Web: http://www.hackney.gov.uk/library/library1.html)

126 Public Services London

Principal Library: Hackney Central Library, Mare Street, London, E8 1HG (Tel: 020-8525 2542)

Stoke Newington Library
Stoke Newington Church Street, London, N16 0JS (Tel: 020-8356 5230)

Shoreditch Library
80 Hoxton Street, London, N1 6LP (Tel: 020-8356 4350)

Mare Street Library
Mare Street, London, E8 (Tel: 020-8356 2542)

Stamford Hill Library
Portland Avenue, London, N16 6SB (Tel: 020-8356 2573)
Collection enquiries: Hackney Central Library, Mare Street, London, E8 1HG (Tel: 020-8525 2542)

Clapton Library
Northwold Road, London, E5 8RA (Tel: 020-8356 2570)

Homerton Library
Homerton High Street, London, E9 6AS (Tel: 020-8356 2572)

CLR James Library
24-30 Dalston Lane, London, E8 3AZ (Tel: 020-8356 2571)

HAMMERSMITH AND FULHAM

Head of Libraries and Archives: N. Bouttell

Fulham Library
598 Fulham Road, London, SW6 5NX (Tel: 020-8576 5252; Fax: Reference library: 020-7736 3741)
Senior Librarian: H. Cosker

Hammersmith Library
Shepherds Bush Road, London, W6 7AT (Tel: 020-8576 5050; Fax: 020-8576 5022)
Senior Librarian: Ms J. Samuels

Libraries Administration
Hammersmith Library, Shepherds Bush Road, London, W6 7AT (Tel: 020-8576 5055; Fax: 020-8576 5022)

HARINGEY

Alexandra Park Library
Alexandra Park Road, London, N22 4LU (Tel: 020-8883 8553; Web: http://www.haringey.gov.uk/)

Coombes Croft Library
Tottenham High Road, London, N17 8AG (Tel: 020-8808 0022)

Highgate Library
Shepherd's Hill, London, N6 5QT (Tel: 020-8348 3443)

Hornsey Library
Haringey Park, London, N8 9JA (Tel: 020-8489 1427)

Marcus Garvey Library
Tottenham Green Centre, 1 Philip Lane, London, N15 (Tel: 020-8489 5332)

Muswell Hill Library
Queens Avenue, London, N10 3PE (Tel: 020-8883 6734)

St Ann's Library
Cissbury Road, London, N15 5PU (Tel: 020-8800 4390)

Stroud Green Library
Quernmore Road, London, N4 4QR (Tel: 020-8348 4363)

Wood Green Central Library
High Road, London, N22 6XD (Tel: 020-8489 2782)

HARROW

Bob Lawrence Library
6-8 Northy Parade, Mollison Way, Edgware, HA8 5QH (Tel: 020-8952 4140;
Web: http://www.viscount.org.uk/metrolib/harrow.htm)

Central Reference Library
Station Road, Harrow, Middx, HA1 2UU (Tel: 020-8424 1055/6)

Gayton Central Lending Library
Gayton Road, Harrow, Middx, HA1 2HL (Tel: 020-8427 6012/8986)

Hatch End Library
Uxbridge Road, Hatch End, Middx, HA5 4EA (Tel: 020-8428 2636)

Kenton Library
Kenton Lane, Kenton, Middx, HA3 8UJ (Tel: 020-8907 2463)

Pinner Library
Marsh Road, Pinner, Middx, HA5 5NQ (Tel: 020-866 7827)

Rayners Lane Library
Imperial Drive, Rayners Lane, Middx, HA2 7HJ (Tel: 020-8866 9185)

Roxeth Library
Northolt Road, South Harrow, Middx, HA2 8EQ (Tel: 020-8422 0809)

Stanmore Library
8 Stanmore Hill, Stanmore, Middx, HA7 3BQ (Tel: 020-8954 9955)

Wealdstone Library
Grant Road, Wealdstone, Middx, HA3 7SD (Tel: 020-8427 8670)

HAVERING

Central Library
St Edward's Way, Romford, Essex, RM1 3AR (Tel:

Libraries

Lending 01708-772389; Reference 01708-772394; Web: http://www.earl.org.uk/partners/havering/)

Collier Row Library
45 Collier Row Road, Collier Row, Romford, Essex, RM5 3NR (Tel: 01708-451270)

Elm Park Library
Balgores Lane, Gidea Park, Romford, Essex RM2 6BS (Tel: 01708-441856)

Harold Hill Library
Hilldene Avenue, Harold Hill, Romford, Essex, RM3 8DJ (Tel: 01708-342749)

Harold Wood Library
Arundel Road, Harold Wood, Romford, Essex, RM3 0RX (Tel: 01708-342071)

Hornchurch Library
44 North Street, Hornchurch, Essex, RM11 1LW (Tel: 01708-452248)

Rainham Library
7-11 The Broadway, Rainham, Essex, RM13 9YW (Tel: 01708-551905)

South Hornchurch Library
Rainham Road, Rainham, Essex, RM13 7RD (Tel: 01708-554126)

Upminster Library
26 Corbets Tey Road, Upminster, Essex, RM14 2BB (Tel: 01708-222864/221578)

HILLINGDON

Head of Libraries: Ms T. Grimshaw

Central Library
14-15 High Street, Uxbridge, Middx, UB8 1HD (Tel: 01895-250700; Reference 01895-250600; Fax: 01895-239794; Web: http://www.hillingdon.gov.uk)
Central Library Manager: Ms S. Lake

Eastcote Library
Field End Road, Eastcote, Middx, HA5 1RL (Tel: 020-8866 3688)

Harefield Library
Park Lane, Harefield, UB9 6BJ (Tel: 01895-822171)

Harlington Library
Pinkwell Lane, Hayes, Middx, UB3 1PD (Tel: 020-8569 1612; Fax: 020-8569 1625)

Hayes End Library
Uxbridge Road, Hayes, Middx, UB4 8JQ (Tel: 020-8573 4209)

Hayes Library
Golden Crescent, Hayes, Middx, UB3 1AQ (Tel: 020-8573 2855; Fax: 020-8848 0269)

Hillingdon Libraries Art and Information
Central Library, 14-15 High Street, Uxbridge, Middx, UB8 1HD (Tel: 01895-250700; Fax: 01895-811164)

Ickenham Library
Long Lane, Ickenham, Middx, UB10 8RE (Tel: 01895-635945)

Kingshill Library
Bury Avenue, Hayes, Middx, UB4 8LF (Tel: 020-8845 3773)

Northwood Hills Library
Potter Street, Northwood, Middx, HA6 1QQ (Tel: 01923-826690)

Oak Farm Library
Sutton Court Road, Hillingdon, Middx, UB10 9PB (Tel: 01895-234690)

Oaklands Gate Library
Green Lane, Northwood, Middx, HA6 3AB (Tel: 01923-826690)

Ruislip (Manor Farm) Library
Bury Street, Ruislip, Middx, HA4 7SU (Tel: 01895-633651; Fax: 01895-677555)

Ruislip Manor Library
Victoria Road, Ruislip Manor, Middx, HA4 9BW (Tel: 01895-633668)

South Ruislip Library
Victoria Road, South Ruislip, Middx, HA4 0JE (Tel: 020-8845 0188)

West Drayton Library
Station Road, West Drayton, Middx UB7 7JS (Tel: 01895-443238)

Yeading Library
Yeading Lane, Hayes, Middx, UB4 4EW (Tel: 020-8573 0261)

Yiewsley Library
High Street, Yiewsley, Middx, UB7 0BE (Tel: 01895-442539)

HOUNSLOW

Borough Librarian: Ms L. Simpson

Chiswick Library
Dukes Avenue, London, W4 2AB (Tel: 020-8994 1008; Web: http://www.cip.org.uk/)

Hounslow Library
24 Treaty Centre, High Street, Hounslow, TW3 1ES (Tel: 020-8583 4545)

Hounslow Library, Bibliographical Services
24 Treaty Centre, High Street, Hounslow, TW3 1ES (Tel: 020-8583 4716)

ISLINGTON

Archway Library
Hamlyn House, Highgate Hill, London, N19 5PH (Tel: 020-7527 7820;
Web: http://www.islington.gov.uk/libraries)

128 Public Services London

Arthur Simpson Library
Hanley Road, London, N4 3DL (Tel: 020-7527 7800)

Central Library
2 Fieldway Crescent, London, N5 1PF

Finsbury Library
245 St John Street, London, EC1V 4NB (Tel: 020-7527 7960)

John Barnes Library
275 Camden Road, London, N7 0JN (Tel: 020-7527 7900)

Lewis Carroll Children's Library
180 Copenhagen Street, London, N1 0ST (Tel: 020-7527 7936)

Mildmay Library
21-23 Mildmay Park, London, N1 4NA (Tel: 020-7527 7880)

North Library
Manor Gardens, London, (Tel: 020-7527 7840)

South Library
115-117 Essex Road, London, N1 2SL (Tel: 020-7527 7860)

West Library
Bridgeman Road, London, N1 1BD (Tel: 020-7527 7920)

KENSINGTON AND CHELSEA

Head of Libraries and Arts: J. McEachen

Central Library
Phillimore Walk, London, W8 7RX (Tel: 020-7937 2542; Fax: 020-7937 0515;
Email: information.services@rbkc.gov.uk;
Web: http://www.rbkc.gov.uk/kcservices/libraries/default.htm)

KINGSTON-UPON-THAMES

Head of Library Services: Ms B. Lee

Home and Mobile Library Service
Surbiton Library, Ewell Road, Surbiton, KT6 6AG (Tel: 020-8399 7900; Web: http://www.kingston.gov.uk/libs)
Library Manager: Ms I. Abrahams

Hook and Chessington Library
Hook Road, Chessington, Surrey, KT9 1EJ (Tel: 020-8397 4931; Fax: 020-8391 4416)
Library Manager: R. Fryer

Kingston Library
Bibliographical Services, Fairfield Road, Kingston, Surrey, KT1 2PS (Tel: 020-8547 6420)
ICT Development Manager: S. Cooper

Kingston Library
Fairfield Road, Kingston, Surrey, KT1 2PS (Tel: 020-8547 6413; Fax: 020-8547 6426)
Library Manager: Ms S. Hurlock

New Malden Library
Glaster Road, New Malden, Surrey (Tel: 020-8547 6540; Fax: 020-8547 6545)
Library Manager: Ms C. Roberts

Old Malden Library
Church Road, Worcester Park, KT4 7RD (Tel: 020-8337 6344; Fax: 020-8330 3118)
Library Manager: Ms M. Vine

Schools Library Service
The Fairfield Centre; Fairfield East; Kingston upon Thames; KT1 2PT (Tel: 020-8408 9100)
Senior Team Librarian: M. Treacy

Surbiton Library
Ewell Road, Surbiton, Surrey, KT6 6AG (Tel: 020-8399 2331; Fax: 020-8339 9805)
Senior Library Manager: C. Dale

Tolworth Community Library and IT Learning Centre
37-39 The Broadway, Tolworth, Surbiton, Surrey, KT6 7DJ (Tel: 020-8339 6950; Fax: 020-8339 6955; E-mail: tolworth.library@rbk.kingston.gov.uk)
Library Manager: Ms V. Gower

Tudor Drive Library
Tudor Drive, Kingston upon Thames, KT2 5QH (Tel: 020-8546 1198; Fax: 020-8547 2295)
Library Manager: Ms S. Montague

LAMBETH

Lambeth Libraries
Courtney House, New Park Road, London, SW2 4DU (Tel: 020-7926 7142; Fax: 020-7926 9467;
Web: http://www.viscount.org.uk/metrolib/lambeth.htm)

Collection enquiries: Bibliographic Services, Herne Hill Library, 188 Herne Hill Road, London, SE24 0AG (Tel: 020-7926 6062)

Principal Library: Tate Library, Brixton Oval, London, SW2 1JQ (Tel: 020-7926 1067)

LEWISHAM

Head of Libraries and Information Service: Ms J. Newton

Blackheath Village Library
3-4 Blackheath Grove; London, SE3 0DD (Tel: 020-8852 5309; Web: http://www.lewisham.gov.uk/)

Catford Library
Laurence House, Catford, London, SE6 4RU (Tel: 020-8314 6399; Fax: 020-8314 1110)

Central Library
199-201 Lewisham High Street, London, SE13 6LG (Tel: 020-8297 9677; Fax: 020-8297 1169)
Operations Manager: J. Simmons

Crofton Park Library
Brockley Road, London, SE4 2AF (Tel: 020-8692 1683)

Downham Library
Moorside Road, Downham, BR1 5EP (Tel: 020-8698 1475)

Forest Hill Library
Dartmouth Road, London, SE23 3HZ (Tel: 020-8699 2065; Fax: 020-8699 8296)

Grove Park Library
Somertrees Avenue, London, SE12 0BX (Tel: 020-8857 5794)

Lewisham Libraries, Management Services Group
3rd Floor, Laurence House, Catford, London SE6 4RU (Tel: 020-8314 8024; Fax: 020-8314 3039)

Lewisham Reference Library
199-201 Lewisham High Street, London, SE13 6LG (Tel: 020-8297 9430; Fax: 020-8297 1169)

Local Studies Centre
199-201 Lewisham High Street, London, SE13 6LG (Tel: 020-8297 0682; Fax: 020-8297 1169)

Manor House Library
Old Road, Lee, London, SE13 5SY (Tel: 020-8852 0357)

New Cross Library
283-285 New Cross Road, London, SE14 6AS (Tel: 020-8694 2534)

Sydenham Library
Sydenham Road, London, SE26 5SE (Tel: 020-8778 7563)

Torridon Road Library
Torridon Road, Catford, London, SE6 1RQ (Tel: 020-8698 1590)

Wavelengths Library
Giffin Street, Deptford, London, SE8 4RJ (Tel: 020-8694 2535; Fax: 020-8694 9652)

MERTON

Head of Library and Heritage Services: J. Pateman

Donald Hope Library
Cavendish House, High Street, London, SW19 2HR (Tel: 020-8542 1975; Fax: 020-8543 9767;
Email: mertonlibs@compuserve.com;
Web: http://www.merton.gov.uk)

Merton Heritage Centre
The Canons, Madeira Road, Mitcham, CR4 4HD (Tel: 020-8640 9387; Fax: 020-8640 7266)

Merton Library and Heritage Services
Civic Centre, London Road, Morden, SM4 5DX (Tel: 020-8545 3783; Fax: 020-8545 3629)

Mitcham Library
London Road, Mitcham, CR4 2YR (Tel: 020-8648 4070; Fax: 020-8646 6260)

Libraries 129

Morden Library
Merton Civic Centre, London Road, Morden, SM4 5DX (Tel: 020-8545 4040; Fax: 020-8545 4037)

Pollards Hill Library
South Lodge Avenue, Mitcham, CR4 1LT (Tel: 020-8764 5877; Fax: 020-8765 0925)

Raynes Park Library
Approach Road, London, SW20 8BA (Tel: 020-8542 1893; Fax: 020-8543 6132)

West Barnes Library
Station Road, New Malden, KT3 6JF (Tel: 020-8942 2635; Fax: 020-8336 0554)

Wimbledon Library
35 Wimbledon Hill Road, London, SW19 7NB (Tel: 020-8946 7432; Fax: 020-8944 6804;
E-mail: wimref@merlib.dialnet.com)

NEWHAM

Head Librarian: R. McMaster

Beckton Library
1 Kingsford Way, London, E6 4JQ (Tel: 020-8557 6060; Fax: 020-8557 6061;
Web: http://www.newham.gov.uk/)
Site Manager: A. de Heer

Canning Town Library
Barking Road, Canning Town, London, E16 4HQ (Tel: 020-7476 2696; Fax: 020-7511 8693)
Site Manager: Ms J. Udell

Collection enquiries: Technical Services Department, Canning Town Library, Barking Road, London, E16 4HQ (Tel: 020-7511 1332; Fax: 020-7511 8693)
Bibliographical and Financial Services Librarian: Ms N. Parker

Custom House Library
Prince Regent Lane, Custom House, London, E16 3JJ (Tel: 020-7476 1565)
Site Manager: Ms C. Garvey

East Ham Library
High Street South, London, E6 6EL (Tel: 020-8557 8882)
Site Manager: D. Hemmings

Forest Gate Library
38 Woodgrange Road, Forest Gate, London, E7 0QH (Tel: 020-8534 6952)
Site Manager: Ms M. Newman

Green Street Library
337-341 Green Street, Upton Park, London, E13 9AR (Tel: 020-8472 4101; Fax: 020-8472 0927)
Site Manager: G. Ahadi

Local Studies Library
Stratford Library, Water Lane, London, E15 4NJ (Tel: 020-8557 8856; Fax: 020-8503 1525)
Archivist: R. Durack

130 Public Services London

Manor Park Library
Romford Road, Manor Park, London, E12 5JY (Tel: 020-8478 1177; Fax: 020-8514 8221)
Site Manager: M. Blair

Newham Libraries
292 Barking Road, East Ham, London, E6 3BA (Tel: 020-8472 1430; Fax: 020-8557 8845)

North Woolwich Library
St Johns Centre, Albert Road, London, E16 2JD (Tel: 020-7511 2387)
Site Manager: L. Pickard

Plaistow Library
North Street, Plaistow, London, E13 9HL (Tel: 020-8472 0420; Fax: 020-8471 3148)
Site Manager: Ms E. Norris

Schools Library Service
c/o Canning Town Library, Barking Road, London, E16 4HQ (Tel: 020-7476 2696; Fax: 020-7511 8693)
Schools Library Manager: Ms J. Stannard

Stratford Library
Water Lane, London, E15 4NJ (Tel: 020-8557 8968; Fax: Reference library: 020-8503 1525)
Site Manager: Ms H. Allsop

REDBRIDGE

Head Librarian: M. Timms

Aldersbrook Library
2A Park Road, London, E12 5HQ (Tel: 020-8989 9319; Email: martin.timms@redbridge.gov.uk; Web: http://www.redbridge.gov.uk/)

Central Library
Clements Road, Ilford, Essex IG1 1EA (Tel: 020-8478 7145; Fax: 020-8553 3299)

Fullwell Cross Library
140 High Street, Barkingside, Ilford, Essex, IG6 2EA (Tel: 020-8550 4457)

Gants Hill Library
490 Cranbrook Road, Gants Hill, Ilford, IG2 6LA (Tel: 020-8554 5211)

Goodmayes Library
76 Goodmayes Lane, Goodmayes, Ilford, Essex, IG3 9QB (Tel: 020-8590 8362)

Hainault Library
100 Manford Way, Chigwell, Essex, IG7 4DD (Tel: 020-8500 1204)

Mobile Libraries
Central Library, Clements Road, Ilford, Essex, IG1 1EA (Tel: 020-8478 7145)

South Woodford Library
116 High Road, London, E18 2QS (Tel: 020-8504 1407)

Wanstead Library
Spratt Hall Road, London, E11 2RQ (Tel: 020-8989 9462)

Woodford Green Library
Snakes Lane, Woodford Green, Essex, IG8 0DX (Tel: 020-8504 4642)

RICHMOND-UPON-THAMES

Castelnau Library
75 Castelnau, London, SW13 9RT (Tel: 020-8748 3837; Web: http://www.richmond.gov.uk/leisure/librarires/library.html)

East Sheen Library
Sheen Lane, London, SW14 8LP (Tel: 020-8876 6801)

Ham Library
Ham Street, Richmond, TW10 7HR (Tel: 020-8940 8703)

Hampton Hill Library
Windmill Road, Richmond, TW12 1RF (Tel: 020-8979 3705)

Hampton Library
Rosehill, Richmond, TW12 2AB (Tel: 020-8979 5110)

Hampton Wick Library
Bennet Close, Kingston, KT1 4AT (Tel: 020-8977 1559)

Heathfield Library
Percy Road, Richmond, TW2 6JL (Tel: 020-8894 1017)

Kew Library
106 North Road, Richmond, TW9 4HJ (Tel: 020-8876 8654)

Reference Library
Old Town Hall, Whittaker Avenue, Richmond, TW9 1TP (Tel: 020-8940 5529; Fax: 020-8940 6899)

Richmond Lending Library
Little Green, Richmond, TW9 1QL (Tel: 020-8940 0981; Fax: 020-8940 6857)

Richmond-upon-Thames Library and Information Services
Langholm Lodge, 146 Petersham Road, Richmond, TW10 6UX (Tel: 020-8940 0031; Fax: 020-8940 7568)

Teddington Library
Waldegrave Road, Teddington, TW11 8LG (Tel: 020-8977 1284; Fax: 020-8977 8264)

Twickenham Library
Garfield Road, Twickenham, TW1 3JT (Tel: 020-8892 8091)

Whitton Library
141 Nelson Road, Richmond, TW2 7BB (Tel: 020-8894 9828)

Libraries

SOUTHWARK

Arts, Libraries and Museums Service Manager: A. Olsen

Arts, Libraries and Museums Services
15 Spa Road, Bermondsey, London, SE16 3QW (Tel: 020-7525 1993; Fax: 020-7525 1505; Email: adrian.olsen@southwark.gov.uk; Web: http://www.southwark.gov.uk)

Blue Anchor Library
Market Place, Southwark Park Road, London, SE16 3UQ
(Tel: 020-7231 0475; Fax: 020-7232 1842)

Brandon Library
Maddock Way, Cooks Road, London, SE17 3NH (Tel: 020-7735 3430; Fax: 020-7735 3430)

Camberwell Library
17-21 Camberwell Church Street, London, SE5 8TR (Tel: 020-7703 3763; Fax: 020-7708 4597)

Collection enquiries; Bibliographical Services: 15 Spa Road, London, SE16 3QW (Tel: 020-7525 1536; Fax: 020-7525 1505)

Dulwich Library
368 Lordship Lane, London, SE22 8NB (Tel: 020-8693 5171; Fax: 020-8693 5135)

Education Library Service
Southwark Education Resource Centre, Cator Street, London, SE15 6AA (Tel: 020-7525 2830; Fax: 020-7525 2837)

John Harvard Library
211 Borough High Street, London, SE1 1JA (Tel: 020-7407 0807; Fax: 020-7407 0807)

Kingswood Library
Seeley Drive, London, SE21 8QR (Tel: 020-8670 4803; Fax: 020-8761 5125)

Local Studies Library
211 Borough High Street, London, SE1 1JA (Tel: 020-7403 3507; Fax: 020-7403 8633)

Newington Library
155-157 Walworth Road, London, SE17 1RS (Tel: 020-7703 3324; Fax: 020-7252 6115)

Newington Reference Library
155-157 Walworth Road, London, SE17 1RS (Tel: 020-7708 0516; Fax: 020-7252 6115)

Nunhead Library
Gordon Road, London, SE15 3RW (Tel: 020-7639 0264; Fax: 020-7277 5721)

Peckham Library
122 Peckham Hill Street, London, SE15 5JR (Tel: 020-7525 0200; Fax: 020-7525 0201)

Rotherhithe Library
Albion Street, London, SE16 1JA (Tel: 020-7237 2010; Fax: 020-7394 0672)

Special Library Services
Rotherhithe Library, Albion Street, London, SE16 1JA (Tel: 020-7237 1487; Fax: 020-7394 0672)

SUTTON

Library Manager: Ms J. Selby

Beddington Library
18 The Broadway, Plough Lane, Beddington, Croydon, CR0 4QR (Tel: 020-8688 5093; Email: sutton.information@sutton.gov.uk; Web: http://www.earl.org.uk)/partners/sutton/)

Carshalton Library
The Square, Carshalton, Surrey, SM5 3BN (Tel: 020-8647 1151)

Cheam Library
Church Road, Cheam, Sutton, Surrey, SM3 8QH (Tel: 020-8644 9377)

Middleton Circle Library
Green Wrythe Lane, Carshalton, Surrey, SM5 1JJ (Tel: 020-8648 6608)

Ridge Road Library
Ridge Road, Sutton, Surrey, SM3 9LY (Tel: 020-8644 9696)

Roundshaw Library
Mollison Drive, Roundshaw, Wallington, Surrey, SM6 9HG (Tel: 020-8770 4901)

Sutton Central Library
St Nicholas Way, Sutton, Surrey, SM1 1EA (Tel: 020-8770 4700; Fax: 020-8770 4777)

Wallington Library
Shotfield, Wallington, Surrey, SM6 0HY (Tel: 020-8770 4900)

Worcester Park Library
Windsor Road, Worcester Park, Surrey, KT4 8ES (Tel: 020-8337 1609)

TOWER HAMLETS

Bancroft and Local History Library
277 Bancroft Road, London, E1 4DQ (Tel: 020-8980 4366; Web: http://www.earl.org.uk/partners/tower_hamlets/)

Bethnal Green and Reference Library
Cambridge Heath Road, London, E2 0HL (Tel: 020-8980 6274)

Bow Library
William Place, London, E3 5ET (Tel: 020-8980 2282)

Cubitt Town Library
Strattondale Street, London, E14 3HG (Tel: 020-7987 3152)

132 Public Services London

Dorset Library
Ravenscroft Street, London, E2 7QX (Tel: 020-7739 9489)

Fairfoot Library
102 Campbell Road, London, E3 4EA (Tel: 020-7987 3338)

Lansbury Library
23-27 Market Way, London, E14 6AH (Tel: 020-7987 3573)

Limehouse Library
638 Commercial Road, London, E14 7HS (Tel: 020-7364 2527/2552)

Stepney Library
Lindly Street, London, E1 3AX (Tel: 020-7790 5616)

Wapping Library
St Peter's Centre, Reardon Street, London, E1 9QN (Tel: 020-7488 3535)

Watney Market Library
30-32 Watney Market, London, E1 2PR (Tel: 020-7790 4039)

Whitechapel and Arts Library
77 Whitechapel High Street, London, E1 7QX (Tel: 020-7247 5272)

WALTHAM FOREST

Central Library
Information Services, High Street, Walthamstow, London, E17 7JN (Tel: 020-8520 3031; Fax: 020-8509 9539; Web: http://www.earl.org.uk/partners/waltham/)

Hale End Library
Castle Avenue, London, E4 9QD (Tel: 020-8531 6423; Fax: 020-8527 6995)

Harrow Green Library
Cathall Road, London, E11 4LF (Tel: 020-8539 5997)

Higham Hill Library
North Countess Road, London, E17 5HF (Tel: 020-8531 6424)

Lea Bridge Library
Lea Bridge Road, London, E10 7HU (Tel: 020-8539 5652)

Leyton Library
High Road, London, E10 5QH (Tel: 020-8539 1223)

Leytonstone Library
Church Lane, London, E11 1HG (Tel: 020-8539 2730; Fax: 020-8556 1026)

North Chingford Library
The Green, London, E4 7EN (Tel: 020-8529 2993)

South Chingford Library
Hall Lane, London, E4 8EU (Tel: 020-8529 2332)

St James Street Library
Coppermill Lane, London, E17 7HA (Tel: 020-8520 1292)

Wood Street Library
Forest Road, London, E17 4AA (Tel: 020-8521 1070)

WANDSWORTH

Head of Libraries, Museums and Arts: Ms J. Allen

Balham Library
Ramsden Road, London, SW12 8QY (Tel: 020-8871 7195; Fax: 020-8675 4015; Web: http://www.wandsworth.gov.uk)
Head Librarian: Mrs P. Kirwan

Battersea Library
265 Lavender Hill, London, SW11 1JB (Tel: 020-8871 7466; Fax: 020-7978 4376)
Head Librarian: Mrs U. Morgan

Interloans/Special Collections
Library Technical Services West Hill Library, West Hill, London, SW18 1RZ (Tel: 020-8870 3100)
Head Librarian: G. Hedges

Libraries, Museums and Arts
Room 223, Wandsworth Town Hall, High Street, London, SW18 2PU (Tel: 020-8871 6364; Fax: 020-8871 7630)

Putney Library
Disraeli Road, London, SW15 2DR (Tel: 020-8871 7090; Fax: 020-8789 6175)
Head Librarian: C. Lally

WESTMINSTER

Libraries Manager: A. Stevens

Charing Cross Library
4 Charing Cross Road, London, WC2H 0HG (Tel: 020-7641 4628; Fax: 020-7641 4629; Web: http://www.westminster.gov.uk/el/libarch/index.html)
Site Manager: Ms C. Mack

Church Street Library
Church Street, London, NW8 8EU (Tel: 020-7641 5479; Fax: 020-7641 5482)
Site Manager: Ms M. Finn

City of Westminster Archives Centre
10 St Ann's Street, London, SW1P 2DE (Tel: 020-7641 5180; Fax: 020-7641 5179)
City Archivist: vacant

Home Library Service
Moberly Centre, Kilburn Lane, London, W10 4AH (Tel: 020-7641 4806; Fax: 020-7641 4854)
Library Service Manager: Ms P. A'Bear

Maida Vale Library
Sutherland Avenue, London, W9 2QT (Tel: 020-7641 3659; Fax: 020-7641 3660)
Site Manager: M. Knowles

Libraries 133

Marylebone Library
109-117 Marylebone Road, London, NW1 5PS (Tel: 020-7641 1037; Fax: 020-7641 1044)
Site Manager: Ms L. Tobey

Mayfair Library
25 South Audley Street, London, W1Y 5DJ (Tel: 020-7641 4903; Fax: 020-7641 4901)
Site Manager: V. Stewart

Paddington Library
Porchester Road, London, W2 5DU (Tel: 020-7641 4475; Fax: 020-7641 4471)
Site Manager: Ms S. Barnes

Pimlico Library
Rampayne Street, London, SW1V 2PU (Tel: 020-7641 2983; Fax: 020-7641 2980)
Site Manager: Ms M. Hoolihan

Queen's Park Library
666 Harrow Road, London, W10 4NE (Tel: 020-7641 4575; Fax: 020-7641 4576)
Site Manager: Ms S. Moran

Schools Library Service
62 Shirland Road, London, W9 2EH (Tel: 020-7641 4321; Fax: 020-7641 4322)
Library Service Manager: N. Fuller

St James's Library
62 Victoria Street, London, SW1E 6QP (Tel: 020-7641 2989; Fax: 020-7641 2986)
Site Manager: Ms A. Farrell

St John's Wood Library
20 Circus Road, London, NW8 6PD (Tel: 020-7641 5087; Fax: 020-7641 5089)
Site Manager: D. Waller; Ms A. Lopez

Victoria Library
160 Buckingham Palace Road, London, SW1W 9UD (Tel: 020-7641 4287; Fax: 020-7641 4281)
Site Manager: C. Jones

Westminster Libraries
Charing Cross Library, 4 Charing Cross Road, London, WC2H 0HG (Tel: 020-7641 4632; Fax: 020-7641 6551)

Westminster Reference Library
35 St Martin's Street, London, WC2H 7HP (Tel: 020-7641 4636; Fax: 020-7641 4606)
Library Manager: Ms T. Arathoon

COUNCIL FOR MUSEUMS, ARCHIVES AND LIBRARIES

16 Queen Anne's Gate, London SW1H 9AA (Tel: 020-7233 4200; Fax: 020-7233 3686)

The Council for Museums, Archives and Libraries is a new strategic agency which will work with museums, archives and libraries throughout the UK.
Chairman: Lord Evans
Chief Executive: Nevill Mackay

TRANSPORT

Ways to get about in London and beyond are many and varied. Within this section you will find statistical data, contact details on the major transport service providers and useful information about how to get in, out and around the capital. The management of London's transport networks has in the past been under the jurisdiction of a number of different bodies. The formation of the Greater London Authority, and within this Transport for London (TfL), has consolidated the co-ordination of transport policy. At the time of going to press, it is anticipated that the London Borough Councils will maintain the role of highway and traffic authorities for 95 per cent of London's roads. TfL will take over all the responsibilities of London Transport except London Underground. London Transport will be responsible solely for the London Underground until the completion of Public Private Partnership. London Transport will then be wound up and the Underground transferred to the Mayor.

People who live in, work in or visit London on a regular basis will be all too familiar with the concept of 'rush hour'. The table below indicates the numbers of people travelling in London and the modes of transport that they use.

For ease of use, this section has been split up into the following transport modes: Rail, Underground, Road (including Bus, Coach, Taxi, Car), River and Air. As the main service provider of transport services in London, London Transport, covers Bus, Underground and River Thames services, details of London Transport appear here out of the context of specific transport modes.

LONDON TRANSPORT

55 Broadway, London SW1H 0BD (Tel: 020-7222 5600)

Subject to the financial objectives and principles approved by the Secretary of State for the Environment, Transport and the Regions, London Transport has a general duty to provide or secure the provision of public transport services for Greater London.

London Transport provides a wide range of underground, bus and riverboat services throughout Greater London.

For up-to-the-minute fare and journey information and map or timetable requests, contact: LT Travel Information Service (Tel: 020-7222 1234 (24 hours); 020-7222 1200 (regularly updated recorded travel news); Email travinfo@londontransport.co.uk; Web: http://www.londontransport.co.uk).

For general enquiries, comments or complaints, contact: Customer Service Centre, London Transport, 55 Broadway, London SW1H 0BD (Tel: 020-7918 4040 (Underground); 020-7918 4300 (Bus); Fax: 020-7918 4093; Email: enquire@londontransport.co.uk).

For posters, souvenirs, books and educational services, licensing of maps and logos, contact: London Transport Museum, Covent Garden, London WC2E 7BB (Tel: 020-7379 6344; Web: http://www.ltmuseum.co.uk).

For travel information and advice for disabled passengers, contact: Unit for Disabled Passengers, 55 Broadway, London SW1H 0BD (Tel: 020-7918 3312; Email: lt.udp@ltbuses.co.uk).

For lost property, contact: LT Lost Property Office Manager, 200 Baker Street, London NW1 5RZ (Tel: 020-7486 2496 (recorded information); Fax: 020-7918 1028. The office is open to personal callers between 09.30 and 14.00, Monday to Friday).

For information on corporate visits and events and public affairs, contact: London Transport Public Affairs, 55 Broadway, London SW1H 0BD (Tel: 020-7918 3209).

For information on advertising opportunities on London's buses and the Underground network, contact: TDI (Tel: 020-7482 3000; Email: tdisales@tdimedia.com; Web: http://www.tdimedia.com)

For useful travel information on all modes of transport in and around the capital, visit: http://www.pti.org.uk/london/london.htm

COMMISSION FOR INTEGRATED TRANSPORT

5th Floor, Romney House, Tufton Street, London SW1P 3RA (Tel: 020-7944 4101/4813; Fax: 020-7944 2919)

The Commission for Integrated Transport was proposed in the 1998 Transport White Paper and was set up in June 1999. Its role is to provide independent expert advice to the Government in order to achieve a transport system that supports sustainable development. Members of the Commission are appointed by the Secretary of State for the Environment, Transport and the Regions.

PEOPLE ENTERING LONDON* DURING MORNING PEAK 7–10AM, 1981–1997 (000s)

	Surface Rail Total	Of which transfers to LUL/DLR†	LUL and DLR only†	LT bus†	Coach/ Minibus	Private Car	Motor/ Pedal cycle	All modes
1981	394	127	336	105	16	173	26	1,050
1986	421	166	381	91	25	166	21	1,105
1988	468	188	411	80	21	160	17	1,157
1991	426	169	347	74	20	155	21	1,042
1996	399	176	361	68	20	143	21	1,011
1997	435	195	373	68	20	142	22	1,059

* Excludes passengers in taxis
† LUL = London Underground Ltd; DLR = Docklands Light Railway; LT = London Transport
Source: Focus on London '99, Office for National Statistics © Crown Copyright 1999

RAIL

Greater London is served by an extensive network of rail services which connect London to the rest of the UK, and with the advent of Eurostar services, to Europe. Since 1 April 1994 ownership of operational track and land has been vested in Railtrack, which was floated on the Stock Exchange in 1996. Railtrack is responsible for management of the track and charging train operating companies for access to it. It is also responsible for signalling and timetabling. It does not operate train services.

The independent Rail Regulator is responsible for the licensing of new railway operators, approving access agreements, promoting the use and development of the network, preventing anti-competitive practices and protecting the interests of rail users.

Following privatisation of the rail system, domestic passenger services were divided into 25 train-operating units throughout the UK, which (with the exception of Eurostar) have been franchised to private sector companies via a compulsory competitive tendering process overseen by the Director General of the Office of Passenger Rail Franchising (OPRAF).

Rail Users' Consultative Committees monitor the policies and performance of train and station operators in their area. They are statutory bodies and have a legal right to make recommendations for changes. The London Regional Passengers Committee has a similar role representing users of buses, the Underground, Docklands Light Railway and rail services in the London area.

London Regional Passengers Committee
Clements House, 14-18 Gresham Street, London, EC2V 7PR
Tel: 020-7505 9000
Fax: 020-7505 9003

TRAIN OPERATING COMPANIES SERVING LONDON

The list below provides a general contact point for the head offices of train operating companies serving London. If you have an enquiry relating to train services and timetabling contact National Rail Enquiries on 08457 484950.

Anglia Railways
Press Office, Anglia Railways Train Services Limited, 15-25 Artillery Lane, London E1 7HA (Tel: 020-7465 9009; Fax: 020-7465 9053)
Operates services between London and Colchester, Ipswich, Norwich and Harwich and a variety of local services.

Chiltern Railways
The Chiltern Railway Company Limited, 2nd Floor, Western House, 14 Rickfords Hill, Aylesbury HP20 2RX (Tel: 01296 332113; Fax: 01296 332100; Web: http://www.chilternrailways.co.uk)
Operates rail passenger services from London Marylebone through High Wycombe and Banbury to Birmingham Snow Hill, and via the London Underground Metropolitan line to Aylesbury.

Connex Rail (South Central)
Connex Communications, Connex Rail, Friars Bridge Court, 41-45 Blackfriars Road, London SE1 8PG (Tel: 020-7620 5505; Fax: 020-7620 5522)
Customer Services, 3 Priory Road, Tunbridge TN9 2AF (Tel: 0870 603 0405; Fax 0870 603 0505).
Operates services from London through West Sussex and along the South Coast to Brighton, Ashford and Bournemouth. Services through West London to Guildford. Through services from Rugby to Gatwick Airport.

Connex Rail (South Eastern)
Connex Communications, Connex Rail, Friars Bridge Court, 41-45 Blackfriars Road, London SE1 8PG (Tel: 020-7620 5505; Fax: 020-7620 5522)
Customer Services, 3 Priory Road, Tunbridge TN9 2AF (Tel: 0870 603 0405; Fax: 0870 603 0505).
Operates services between South East London, Kent and parts of East Sussex and Surrey.

Eurostar
Eurostar Group, Eurostar House, Waterloo Station, London SE1 8SE (Tel: 020-7922 4486; Fax: 020-7922 4499)
Operates high speed services between London, Kent and mainland Europe.

First Great Eastern
First Great Eastern, 35 Artillery Lane, London E1 7LP (Tel: 08459 505000;
Email: customer.services@ger.firstgroup.com)
Operates services in East London, Essex and parts of Suffolk. Two of First Great Eastern's three main routes operate to and from London – the "Metro" service between Liverpool Street and Shenfield and the Southend Line service between Southend and London.

First Great Western Trains
Corporate Affairs Manager, First Great Western Trains, Milford House, Milford Street, Swindon SN1 1HL (Tel: 01793 499499/499406; Fax: 01793 499453; Web: http://www.great-western-trains.co.uk)
Operates services between London, South Wales, the Cotswolds and the South West.

First North Western
Corporate Affairs, First Floor, Bridgewater House, 58 Whitworth Street, Manchester M1 6LT (0161-228 2141; Fax. 0161 228 5909;
Email: customer-relations.nwt@ems.rail.co.uk;
Web: http://www.nwt.rail.co.uk)
Operates services between London Euston and the North West of England and North Wales, serving the major centres of Manchester and Liverpool.

Gatwick Express
Marketing and Media Relations, Gatwick Express Limited, 52 Grosvenor Gardens, London SW1W 0AU (Tel: 020-7973 5000; Fax: 020-7973 5048;
Web: http://www.gatwickexpress.co.uk)
Operates a dedicated rail/air link between London Victoria Station and London Gatwick Airport.

Great North Eastern Railway
Press Office, Great North Eastern Railway Limited, Headquarters, Station Road, York YO1 6HT (Tel: 01904 653022; Fax: 01904 523022; Customer Enquiry Line: 08457 225225; Email: customer.care@gner.co.uk; Web: http://www.gner.co.uk)

136 Public Services London

Operates inter-city services on the East Coast mainline between London King's Cross and Scotland.

LTS Rail
LTS Rail Limited, Central House, Clifftown Road, Southend-on-Sea, Essex SS1 1AB (Tel: 01702 357810; Fax: 01702 357819)
Operates services between a variety of busy Essex suburban locations, including Barking, Basildon, Benfleet, Grays, Southend and Upminster.

Midland Mainline
Midland Mainline Limited, Midland House, Nelson Street, Derby DE1 2SA (Tel: 01332 262010; Email: feedback.mml@ems.rail.co.uk; Web: http://www.mml.rail.co.uk)
Operates services between London St. Pancras through Nottingham and Derby to Sheffield and Leeds.

Silverlink
Communications Department, Silverlink Train Services Limited, Melton House, 65-67 Clarendon Road, Watford WD1 1DP (Tel: 01923 207777; Press Office: 01923 246480; Fax: 01293 246480)
Silverlink County Services operates services between London Euston, Milton Keynes and Birmingham New Street via Northampton. Silverlink Metro services operate between North Woolwich and Richmond, Willesden Junction and Clapham Junction, Barking and Gospel Oak, with a branch to St. Albans Abbey and a link between Watford and Croxley Green.

South West Trains
South West Trains Limited, Friars Bridge Court, 41-45 Blackfriars Road, London SE1 8NZ (Tel: 020-7928 5151 (Switchboard); 020-7620 5229 (Press Office))
Operates services between London Waterloo and 204 stations throughout south London, Berkshire, Devon, Dorset, East and West Sussex, Hampshire, Somerset and Wiltshire.

Thames Trains
Public Affairs, Thames Trains Limited, Venture House, 37 Blagrave Street, Reading RG1 1PZ (Tel: 0118-908 3637; Fax: 0118-957 9648;
Email: tatelthames@ems.rail.co.uk;
Web: http://www.thamestrains.co.uk)
Operates services between London Paddington and Oxford via Maidenhead and Reading, with certain services extending to Stratford-upon-Avon and via Worcester to Hereford. There is also a service operating between London Paddington and Bedwyn via Reading and Newbury. Thames Trains also run between Reading and London Gatwick Airport via Guildford and Reading and Basingstoke.

Thameslink
Marketing and Communications Manager, Thameslink Rail Limited, Friars Bridge Court, 41-45 Blackfriars Road, London SE1 8NZ (Tel: 020-7620 5002; Fax: 020-7620 5099)
Operates services between Bedford, through five London stations, to Brighton. London stops include King's Cross Thameslink, Farringdon, City Thameslink, Blackfriars and London Bridge.

Virgin Trains
Corporate Affairs, West Wing Offices, Euston Station, London NW1 2HS (Tel: 0870 789 1111; Web: http://www.virgintrains.co.uk)
Operates more than 1,600 services a week calling at over 130 stations throughout Great Britain, including London Euston and London Paddington.

WAGN Railway
External Relations Manager, West Anglia Great Northern Railway, Hertford House, 1 Cranwood Street, London EC1V 9QS (Tel: 020-7713 2121; Fax: 020-7713 2116)
Operates services between London King's Cross, Moorgate and Liverpool Street and North East London, Cambridgeshire, Hertfordshire and West Norfolk.

Wales and West
Wales and West Passenger Trains Limited, Brunel House, 2 Fitzalan Road, Cardiff CF2 1SU (Tel: 01222 430400; Fax: 01222 430528)
Operates services between London Paddington and Waterloo and many parts of Great Britain including Manchester, Birmingham, Cardiff, Swansea, Brighton, Exeter, Bath, Liverpool and Penzance.

OTHER TRANSPORT ORGANISATIONS

Association of Train Operating Companies (ATOC)
40 Bernard Street, London WC1N 1BY (Tel: 020-7904 3010; Fax 020-7904 3081)

British Railways Board and Shadow Strategic Rail Authority
26 Old Queen Street, London SW1H 9HP (Tel: 020-7960 1500; Fax: 020-7960 1501)

National Rail Enquiries (Tel: 08457 484950)

Office of Passenger Rail Franchising (OPRAF)
Golding's House, 2 Hay's Lane, London SE1 2HB (Tel: 020-7654 6000)

Office of the Rail Regulator
1 Waterhouse Square, 138-142 Holborn, London EC1N 2TQ (Tel: 020-7282 2000; Fax: 020-7282 2040; Email: orr@dial.pipex.com;
Web: http://www.rail-reg.gov.uk)
Chief Executive: Tom Winsor

Railtrack plc
Railtrack House, Euston Square, London NW1 2EE (Tel: 020-7557 8000; Fax 020-7557 9000;
Web: http://www.railtrack.co.uk)

Shadow Strategic Rail Authority (SSRA)
The Secretariat, SSRA, Golding's House, 2 Hay's Lane, London SE1 2HB Tel: 020-7940 4200;
Web: http://www.ssra.gov.uk)

Transport

UNDERGROUND

THE LONDON UNDERGROUND

There are approximately 2.5 million passenger journeys on the London Underground each day, with over 500 trains serving over 260 stations. The majority of people probably use the underground without giving it a second thought – below are some facts and figures for you to contemplate on your next journey.
- the average train speed is 33kph
- the maximum tunnel depth below ground level is 221ft
- there are 303 escalators in the underground system
- during the Second World War, tube platforms were used as air raid shelters
- penalty fares were introduced in 1994
- the opening of the "Twopenny Tube" from Shepherd's Bush to Bank took place in 1900 and now forms part of the Central line
- the first escalators in service were at Earl's Court in 1911
- work started on the Jubilee line extension in 1993. The Jubilee line originally opened in 1979
- in 1987 a fire at King's Cross station resulted in 31 deaths
- 41 fatalities occurred in an accident at Moorgate station in 1975
- the Circle line was completed in 1884
- the first underground railway took passengers between Paddington and Farringdon in 1863

For further information about the history and development of the London underground, visit http://www.londontransport.co.uk

DOCKLANDS LIGHT RAILWAY

Docklands Railway Management, Castor Lane, London, E14 0DS (Tel: 020-7363 9500)
The Docklands Light Railway opened in 1987. It is owned by DLR Ltd, a public body. Following the completion of new lines in 2000, the DLR covers 27 kilometres and 33 stations in and around the Docklands area of east London. Operation of the system was privatised in 1997, when it was franchised to Docklands Railway Management Ltd for seven years. With the establishment of the GLA, DLR Ltd has become part of Transport for London.

ROAD

ROAD DISTANCES FROM LONDON

Town/City	Distance from London (miles)
Aberdeen	547
Aberystwyth	238
Birmingham	120
Bristol	120
Cardiff	155
Colchester	61
Dover	79
Edinburgh	413
Exeter	200
Glasgow	412
Inverness	573
Leeds	198
Liverpool	216
Manchester	204
Newcastle	286
Norwich	115

UNDERGROUND RAIL TRAFFIC IN LONDON, 1981–1998

	London Underground passenger journeys (millions)	London Underground passenger kilometres	Average passenger journey length (km)	Train kilometres (millions)	Occupancy-passengers per train
1981	541	4,088	7.6	50	81.8
1987-88	798	6,257	7.8	51	122.7
1988-89	815	6,293	7.7	51	123.4
1991-92	751	5,895	7.8	53	111.2
1997-98	832	6,179	7.8	62	104.3
% change 1987-88 to 1997-98	4.3	3.5	−0.7	21.8	−15.0

Source: Focus on London '99, Office for National Statistics © Crown Copyright 1999

BUS TRAFFIC IN LONDON, 1981–1998

	Bus passenger journeys (millions)	Bus passenger kilometres (millions)	Average passenger journey length (km)	Bus kilometres (millions)	Occupancy-passengers per bus
1981	1,080	4,039	3.7	280	14.4
1987-88	1,211	4,258	3.5	262	16.3
1991-92	1,149	3,996	3.5	301	13.3
1996-97	1,234	4,159	3.4	332	12.5
1997-98	1,277	4,350	3.4	342	12.7
% change 1987-88 to 1997-98	5.5	2.2	−3.1	30.5	−21.7

Source: Focus on London '99, Office for National Statistics © Crown Copyright 1999

138 Public Services London

Nottingham	131
Oxford	57
Plymouth	241
Sheffield	169
Southampton	80
York	212

BUS SERVICES

There are many bus routes operating within the London area. London Transport Buses was established in April 1994 and its responsibilities include management of the tendering of bus routes, management of bus stops, stations and shelters and planning the entire bus route network for London.

In London there are 5,400 buses running on 700 routes, with 10,000 bus shelters and 140 bus stations and stands. On a typical weekday there are 4 million bus journeys in the capital, compared with 2.5 million on the London Underground. Flat bus fares are making bus travel simpler and potentially cheaper. The new fares comprise of £1 per single journey in central London and 70p in outer zones.

For bus services linking the main London railway stations, Stationlink provides a daily service to all travellers needing to make cross-London connections. Stationlink currently links Paddington, Marylebone, Euston, King's Cross St. Pancras, Liverpool Street, Fenchurch Street, London Bridge, Waterloo, Victoria and Victoria Coach stations and routes operate clockwise and anticlockwise, starting and finishing at Paddington. The service is free to people with elderly or disabled travel permits, holders of British Rail Disabled Persons and Senior Railcards Travelcards, LT cards and Bus Passes which include Zone 1 are also valid.

For further information contact London Travel Information (Tel: 020-7222 1234)

LONDON BUS COMPANIES

First Capital
Chequers Lane, Dagenham, Essex RM9 6QD (Tel: 020-8517 9924; Fax: 020-8595 3369)

London Central
London General House, 25 Raleigh Gardens, Mitcham, Surrey CR4 3NS (Tel: 020-8646 1747; Fax: 020-8640 2317)

Metrobus
Farnborough Hill, Orpington, Kent BR6 6DA (Tel: 01689 861432; Fax: 01689 857324;
Email: info@metrobus.co.uk;
Web: http://www.metrobus.co.uk)
Managing Director: Peter Larking

Metroline
118-122 College Road, Harrow, Middx HA1 1DB (Tel: 020-8218 8888; Fax: 020-8218 8899;
Email: dofarrell@metroline.co.uk;
Web: http://www.metroline.co.uk)
Chief Executive: Declan O'Farrell

Stagecoach East London
2-4 Clements Road, Ilford, Essex IG1 1BA (Tel: 020-8553 3420; Fax: 020-8477 7200)

Stagecoach Selkent
180 Bromley Road, Catford, London SE6 2XA (Tel: 020-8695 0707; Fax: 020-8695 9232)

COACH

Many coaches providing travel from London depart from Victoria Coach station and in addition, there are a number of commuter routes providing frequent services between London and the surrounding counties. The list below gives details of a selection of companies providing leisure and/or commuter coach travel to and from London.

Airlinks
Heathrow Coach Centre, Sipson Road, West Drayton, Middlesex UB 7 0HN (Tel: 0990 747777; Email: info@airlinks.co.uk; Web: http://www.airlinks.co.uk)
Operates services to and from London airports and other other major UK airports.

Berry's Coach Services
New Wellington Road, Taunton, Somerset TA1 5NA (Tel: 01823 331356; Fax: 01823 322347;
Email: info@berryscoaches.co.uk;
Web: http://www.berryscoaches.co.uk)
Operates an express coach service between London and the West country.

Buzzlines
Unit G1, Lympne Industrial Park, Nr Hythe, Kent CT21 4LR (Tel: 01303 261870;
Email: kathryn@buzzlines.co.uk;
Web: http://www.buzzlines.co.uk)
Operates a commuter service between London and Kent.

Chenery Travel
20a Castle Meadow, Norwich (Tel: 01603 630676; Fax: 01603 76523;
Web: http://www.chenerytravel.com/london.html)
Operates services between East Anglia and London Liverpool Street, Temple, Whitehall and Victoria.

Greenline
Greenline Travel Limited, 21 Croydon Road, Reigate, Surrey RH2 0LY (Tel: 0870 608 7261; Fax: 01737 224379; Email: enquire@greenline.co.uk;
Web: http://www.greenline.co.uk)
Operates a variety of scheduled services between London and the home counties.

London Coaches Kent
Lower Road, Northfleet, Kent DA11 9BB (Tel: 01474 356961; Fax: 01474 335176; Email: grahamwykes@londoncoaches.demon.co.uk; Web: http://www.london-coaches.com)
Operates a number of services between London and Kent.

Marshall's Coaches
Firbank Way, Leighton Buzzard, Bedfordshire LU7 8YP (Tel: 020-7837 6663 or 01525 376077; Fax: 01525 850967; Email: bookings@marshalls-coaches.co.uk;
Web: http://www.marshalls-coaches.co.uk)
For all types of private hire, UK and continental.

Transport

National Express
(Tel: 08705 808080;
Web: http://www.nationalexpress.co.uk)
Operates a wide range of national services.

Oxford Express
395 Cowley Road, Oxford OX4 2DJ (Tel: 01865 785410; Fax: 01865 711745;
Email: info@oxfordbus.co.uk;
Web: http://www.oxfordbus.co.uk)
Operates express services 24 hours every day between London and Oxford and Gatwick and Heathrow airports.

Reading Buses
Reading Transport Limited, Great Knollys Street, Reading RG1 7HH (Tel: 0118 959 4000)
Operates services between London and Reading.

London United Busways
Busways House, Wellington Road, Twickenham TW2 5NX (Tel: 020-8400 6665; Fax: 020-8943 2688)
Local bus routes in Central and Greater London.

TAXI
Licensed black taxis are found all over London but operate mostly within the central London area. They are strictly regulated by the Metropolitan Police Public Carriage Office. A white numbered license plate is displayed inside and on the rear of every licensed Taxi. Every taxi driver has to pass a series of examinations known as "The Knowledge", which tests their knowledge of the streets of central and suburban London. They are also required to pass a medical and driving test.

Drivers are under no duty to accept a hiring of six miles or more, or over 20 miles for a journey from London Heathrow Airport, however, if they do accept such a hiring and the journey is wholly within the London area, the fare indicated by the meter is payable. Alternatively, if the driver accepts a hiring to a destination outside of Greater London, the fare is negotiable. Taxis are most commonly hailed in the street, however, they can be booked in advance: **Computer Cab:** 020-7286 0286; **Dial-a Cab:** 020-7253 5000; **Radio Taxis:** 020-7272 0272.

Metropolitan Police Public Carriage Office
15 Penton Street, London N1 9PU (Tel: 020-7833 0996; Fax: 020-7230 1662;
Email: pco.mps@gtnet.gov.uk;
Web: http://www.mps@gtnet.gov.uk)

There are also many mini cab services operating within the London area, some offering specialist services such as women only drivers and services to and from airports.

PARKING

PARKING COMMITTEE FOR LONDON
New Zealand House, 80 Haymarket, London SW1Y 4TE (Tel: 020-7747 4700; Fax: 020-7747 4848)

The Parking Committee for London was established by virtue of the Road Traffic Act 1991 which transferred responsibility for parking enforcement in London from the Metropolitan Police and traffic wardens to the 33 London Borough Councils. The Parking Committee for London is made up of one councillor from each of these London Boroughs who meet twice per year.

Under the Road Traffic Act local authorities can apply to the Secretary of State for Transport to be given the power to create Special Parking Areas (SPAs). Within these areas the local authorities are responsible for almost all parking enforcement, with the exception of 'red routes" which can be found on major roads and are regulated by the police. London Borough Councils exercise control over "permitted" parking which includes parking meters, residents' bays and pay and display.

Enforcement of the Road Traffic Act within local authority areas is carried out by Parking Attendants who issue Penalty Charge Notices to offenders. Other aspects of parking enforcement such as wheel clamping, car-pound operation and vehicle removal, as well as the employment of Parking Attendants, can be subject to compulsory competitive tendering (CCT) meaning that they are run, not by the local authority, but by private companies.

Motorists who feel that they have been unfairly ticketed, clamped or towed away can appeal against the decision. In the first instance they should contact the local authority that issued the ticket and if this does not bring about a satisfactory conclusion, matters should be referred to the Parking Appeals Service.

Under the Road Traffic Act, the Parking Committee for London has several statutory duties, including setting the level of Penalty Charge Notices, setting a discount rate for early settlements of Penalty Charge Notices in full and operating the Parking Appeals service. Non-statutory duties include operating a single telephone number that motorists can call in the event of their car going missing (020-7747 4747) and providing information on vehicles which have been removed by the police; maintaining a training standard for all Parking Attendants; maintaining a database of persistent offenders and motorists with outstanding penalties and maintaining data links with bodies such as the Driver and Vehicle Licensing Agency (DVLA) and the County Court.

CAR PARKING

NCP operate a number of car parks throughout London. For information on pricing and opening times, please contact car parks direct or visit the NCP website at http://www.ncp.co.uk. Readers should note that some car parks operate on a contract basis only. The list below contains NCP car parks by area of London, according to the categories on the NCP website.

Area	Car Park	Telephone
Bayswater	Arthur Court	020-7221 2906
	Bayswater Road	020-7229 9381
	Collonades	020-7221 8020
Bloomsbury	Brunswick Square	020-7278 9792
	Russell Court	020-7837 6101
Clerkenwell	Bowling Green Lane	020-7278 1745
	Skinner Street	020-7837 4645
Central	Drury Lane	020-7242 8611
	Holborn	020-7836 2039

140 Public Services London

	Judd Street	020-7713 7936
	Upper St Martin's Lane	020-7836 7451
	YMCA	020-7637 0967
City	Aldersgate	020-7600 2895
	Barbican	020-7382 7071
	Cardinal House	020-7490 5782
	Caxton House	020-7253 6518
	Hillgate House	020-7248 5467
	International Press Centre	020-7353 7322
	Saffron Hill	020-7405 5871
	Smithfield (Rotunda)	020-7236 4549
	Snowhill	020-7489 0406
	Vintry	020-7248 6089
Docklands	City Harbour	020-7537 3079
Ealing	Sandringham Mews	020-8840 0657
Edgware Rd	Bilton Towers	020-7723 8840
	Crawford Street	020-7706 2273
	Kendal Street	020-7262 2011
	Park West Garage	020-7723 8941
	Sherwood Court	—
	Water Gardens	020-7723 2920
Eltham	Allders, High Street	020-8859 8051
Finsbury	Bishopsgate	020-7247 2595
	Clere Street	020-7490 2574
	Drill Hall	020-7251 3617
	Finsbury Square	020-7588 5545
	Great Eastern Street	020-7739 2508
	Holywell Lane	020-7739 4786
	Oakden Works	—
	Paul Street	020-7613 3639
	Tabernacle Street	020-7638 0670
Hammersmith	Hammersmith Grove	020-8563 7847
Islington	Britannia Walk	020-7608 2362
	Macclesfield Road	020-7608 2362
	Westland Place	020-7336 8392
Kensington	Royal Garden Hotel	020-7376 1493
	Young Street	020-7937 7420
Knightsbridge	Cadogan Place	020-7235 5106
	Knightsbridge Green	020-7584 1144
	Park Towers Hotel	020-7235 0733
	Pavillion Road	020-7584 5667
Lewisham	Myron Place	020-8318 3571
Marylebone	Bryanston Street	020-7499 8313
	Chiltern Street	020-7935 4271
	Cranmer Street	020-7935 5966
	Marylebone Road	020-7935 6078
	Montague Mews South	020-7499 7050
	Portland Place	020-7636 6313
	Portman Square	020-7935 5310
	Welbeck Street	020-7486 2296
Mayfair	Arlington House	020-7499 3312
	Britannia Hotel	020-7493 1400
	Carrington Street	020-7629 9806
	Chesterfield House	020-7629 6702
	Grosvenor Hill	020-7499 4331
	London Marriott Hotel	020-7491 8038
Olympia	Broadwood Terrace	020-7940 3448
	Olympia Hilton Hotel	020-7603 0492
Soho	Berners Street	020-7637 9333
	Brewer Street	020-7734 9497
	Cleveland Street	020-7580 6254
	Collingwood House	020-7307 4846
	Denman Street	020-7734 5760
	Regent Crest Hotel	020-7387 7587
	Swiss Centre	020-7734 5760
	Wardour Street	020-7437 5383
Southwark	Coin Street	020-7620 1293
	Doon Street	020-7401 3884
	Elephant and Castle Shopping Centre	020-7703 9095
	Library Street	020-7633 9445
	Snowsfield	020-7407 1053
West/North West London	Lanark Road	020-7289 7729
	Park Road	020-7723 0353
Victoria	Semley Place	020-7730 7905
Westminster	Abingdon Street	020-7222 8621
Whitechapel	Rodwell House	020-7247 7923
	Houndsditch	020-7623 4739

RIVER

The Port of London Authority has statutory responsibility for the conservancy and safe navigation of 95 miles (150km) of the River Thames from Teddington, Middlesex, to the sea.

PORT OF LONDON AUTHORITY

Devon House, 58-60 St. Katharine's Way, London E1W 1JZ (Tel: 020-7265 2656; Fax: 020-7265 2699; Web: http://www.portoflondon.co.uk)
Chief Executive: S. Cuthbert
Secretary: G. E. Ennals
Chief Harbour Master: Tel: 01474 562200
Central Enquiries: Tel: 0171-265 2656
PLA Public Piers: Tel: 0171-265 2666

Denton Wharf, Mark Lane, Gravesend, Kent (Tel: 01474 562444; Fax: 01474 562403)
London River House, Royal Pier Head, Gravesend, Kent DA12 2BG (Tel: 01474 562200; Fax: 01474 562281)
Thames Barrier Navigation, Control Centre, Unit 28 Bowater Road, London SE18 5TF (Tel: 020-8855 0315; Fax: 020-8854 7422).

In recent years the River Thames has been more frequently used for leisure and commuter transport. London River Services Limited, a subsidiary of London

Transport, aims to develop long term river passenger transport in London and develop new piers and boat services. London River Services Limited is currently responsible for the management of Westminster, Waterloo Festival, Embankment, Blackfriars Bankside, Tower and Greenwich piers.

LONDON RIVER SERVICES LIMITED

1st Floor, 172 Buckingham Palace Road, London SW1W 9TN (Tel: 020-7918 4753; Fax: 020-7918 3804; Web: http://www.londontransport.co.uk/river)

The major services operating on the River Thames are:
Westminster to Greenwich
Westminster to Tower
Westminster – St. Katharine's – Westminster
Westminster to St. Katharine's and Thames Barrier
Wesminster to Kew, Richmond and Hampton Court
Waterloo and Blackfriars to The Millennium Dome
Embankment to Tower and Greenwich
Central London Fast Ferry
Greenwich to Thames Barrier
Gravesend and Tilbury to Greenwich
Greenwich to The Millennium Dome
Circular, Luncheon and Evening Cruises
Woolwich Ferry

For travel information, fares and timetabling, call London Travel Information on 020-7222 1234 or visit http://www.londontransport.co.uk

AIR

There are five major airports serving London: London Gatwick, London Heathrow and London Stansted (regulated and operated by BAA plc/Civil Aviation Authority) and London Luton and London City Airports.

The London Airports are amongst the busiest in the world and below you will see a range of statistical data on the subject of air travel to and from the capital.

Sources: BAA plc/Civil Aviation Authority. The Editor would like to acknowledge BAA plc for allowing us to reproduce statistics from their website: http://www.baa.co.uk

TERMINAL PASSENGERS IN 1998

UK Airport	Terminal Passengers (000's)
London Heathrow	60,336.6
London Gatwick	29,034.3
London Stansted	6,831.5
London City	1,360.2

TOP 5 BUSIEST ROUTES AT BAA AIRPORTS IN 1998

London Heathrow	Terminal Passengers (000's)
New York (JFK)	2,499.4
Amsterdam	2,101.4
Dublin	1,894.2
Paris (Charles de Gaulle)	1,847.0
Edinburgh	1,591.0
Other routes	50,404.0
TOTAL	60,337.0

London Gatwick	Terminal Passengers (000's)
Malaga	897.6
Palma	703.3
Orlando	702.3
Tenerife	700.7
Faro	608.7
Other routes	25,421.7
TOTAL	29,034.3

London Stansted	Terminal Passengers (000's)
Dublin	1,103.6
Amsterdam	373.1
Milan	290.5
Edinburgh	265.1
Cork	253.8
Other routes	4,545.4
TOTAL	6,831.5

ORIGIN AND DESTINATION OF TERMINAL PASSENGERS IN 1998

Airport	Domestic Passengers (000's)	Europe Passengers (000's)	North Atlantic Passengers (000's)	Other Long Haul Passengers (000's)	Total Passengers (000's)
London Heathrow	7,190.1	29,016.1	12,014.3	12,116.3	60,336.8
London Gatwick	2,734.4	14,954.3	5,509.1	5,836.5	29,034.3
London Stansted	1,226.2	5,239.5	75.3	290.5	6,831.5
Total	11,150.7	49,209.9	17,598.7	18,243.3	96,202.6

ORIGIN AND DESTINATION OF CARGO IN 1998

Airport	Domestic Tonnes	Europe Tonnes	North Atlantic Tonnes	Other Long Haul Tonnes	Total Tonnes
London Heathrow	7,832	233,362	458,389	509,604	1,209,817
London Gatwick	2,962	18,775	172,000	81,348	275,085
London Stansted	8,231	58,459	50,182	63,851	180,723
Total	19,025	310,596	680,571	654,803	1,664,995

TOP 5 LEADING AIRLINES AT BAA AIRPORTS IN 1998

London Heathrow

Airline	Passengers (000's)
British Airways	26,748.6
British Midland	5,231.7
Virgin Atlantic	2,234.8
Lufthansa	1,985.6
United Airlines	1,866.3
Other	22,269.8
TOTAL	60,333.6

London Gatwick

Airline	Passengers (000's)
British Airways	11,688.1
Monarch Airlines	2,021.6
Britannia Airways	1,810.4
Air 2000	1,555.9
Caledonian Airways	1,524.4
Other	10,752.5
TOTAL	29,332.9

London Stansted

Airline	Passengers (000's)
Ryanair	2,143.7
KLM UK	1,608.5
Go	380.5
Aer Lingus	312.9
Britannia Airways	304.4
Other	2,081.5
TOTAL	6,831.5

BAA PLC

130 Wilton Road, London SW1V 1LQ (Tel: 020-7834 9449; Fax: 020-7932 6699; Web: http://www.baa.co.uk)

CIVIL AVIATION AUTHORITY

CAA House, 45-59 Kingsway, London WC2B 6TE (Tel: 020-7379 7311; Fax: 020-7240 1153; Web: http://www.caa.co.uk)

The CAA is responsible for the economic regulation of UK airlines and for the safety regulation of UK civil aviation by the certification of airlines and aircraft and by licensing aerodromes, flight crew and aircraft engineers. Through its subsidiary company, National Air Traffic Services Ltd (NATS), it is also responsible for the provision of air traffic control and telecommunications services. The Government announced in July 1999 that it planned to separate safety regulation from service provision and sell 49 per cent of NATS to the private sector.

The CAA advises the Government on aviation issues, represents consumer interests, conducts economic and scientific research, produces statistical data, and provides specialist services and other training and consultancy services to clients world-wide.

LONDON CITY AIRPORT

London City Airport Limited, Royal Docks, London E16 2PX (Tel: 020-7646 0088; Email: info@londoncityairport.com; Web: http://www.londoncityairport.com)

London City Airport operates services to: Amsterdam, Antwerp, Basel, Belfast, Berne, Brussels, Dublin, Dundee, Dusseldorf, Edinburgh, Frankfurt, Geneva, Glasgow, Isle of Man, Jersey, Le Havre, Luxembourg, Malmo, Milan, Munster, Paris, Rennes, Rotterdam, Sheffield, Zurich.

Airlines serving London City Airport include: Aer Lingus, Air France, Braathens Malmo Aviation, British Airways, Crossair, Jersey European, KLM Alps, KLM UK, Lufthansa, Luxair, Sabena, Scot Airways, VLM.

Getting there...

...by Train

Travellers can take the Jubilee line on the London Underground to Canary Wharf to connect with the Airport Shuttlebus services. The Silverlink Metro operates every 30 minutes from Richmond via Canning Town, and Docklands Light Railway (DLR) links Bank and Tower Gateway stations to Canary Wharf and Canning Town where passengers can again connect with the Airport Shuttlebus.

...by Road

Car parking is available adjacent to the terminal building and is available on a long or short stay basis. There is no need to pre-book.

There are two airport shuttlebuses. One runs between the airport and Canning Town on the Jubilee line every 5 minutes and takes only 5 minutes. The second operates every 10 minutes between Liverpool Street Station and London City Airport with the route going via Canary Wharf. Other bus services include routes 69, 473 and 474

LONDON GATWICK AIRPORT

Gatwick Airport Limited, West Sussex RH6 0NP (Tel: 01293 535353; Web: http://www.baa.co.uk)

London Gatwick Airport welcomes over 30 million passengers each year and is the busiest single runway airport in the world. It is the second largest airport in the UK and the seventh busiest airport in the world. There are over 102 airlines flying to over 280 destinations and the airport's scheduled network includes direct services to more US cities than any other european airport, including London Heathrow.

Airlines serving London Gatwick include: (North Terminal) Air 2000, Air France/Britair, British Airways, Brymon Airways, Deutsche BA, TAT European, Delta Airlines, Emirates, Finnair, LOT, Malev, Royal Nepal (South Terminal) Aeroflot, Air Alfa, Air Algerie, Air Europa, Air Gabon, Air Malawi, Air Malta, Air Moldova, Air Nostrum, Air Seychelles, Air Transat, Air Via, Air Zimbabwe, Airtours International, Alitalia, American Airlines, American Transair, Arkia, Armenian Airlines, Azerbaijan Airlines, Balkan Bulgarian, Base Business, BCM Airlines, Belavia, Britannia, British Midland, British World, Caledonian, Canada 3000, City Flyer Express, Cameroon Airlines, Continental, Croatia Airlines, Cubana, Cyprus Airways, Debonair Airlines, El Al, Estonian Air, Eurocypria, European Aviation Air Charter, European Regional Airlines, Futura International, Garuda Indonesia, Iberia, Istanbul Airlines, Jersey European, Lauda Air, Maersk Air, Meridiana, Monarch, Nouvelair Tunisie, Novair, Onur Air, Peach Air, Pegasus, Riaair Riga Airlines, Royal Airlines, Royal

Jordanian, Ryanair, Sabena, Sabre Airways, Sata-Air Acores, Spanair, TWA, Top Air, Transaero, Transavia, TransBrasil, US Airways, Ukraine International, Virgin Express, Virgin Sun, Viva Air, Yemenia

Getting there….

…by Road

London Gatwick Airport is situated 28 miles south of London, linked to the M23 at junction 9 and to the A23 London to Brighton road. For passengers travelling to London Gatwick by road, there are petrol stations at both the North and South terminals which are open 24 hours a day. Parking is available on a Short Stay (up to 5 hours) or Long Stay (enabling people to park their car for the duration of their holiday/trip) basis. Short Stay car parking is available at both North and South terminals and are operated by TFM Parking Services who can be contacted on 01293 569671. Long Stay parking is operated by Parking Express (APCOA) and Flightpath (NCP) and spaces can be pre-booked by calling the BAA Holiday Parking Line on 0345 405000.

All coach services stop at the coach station which is situated on the ground floor of London Gatwick's South terminal. Some coach services also call at the North terminal. Speedlink Airport Services Ltd operates coach and bus information desks in both terminals and in the South terminal coach station.

There are several companies providing direct express coaches to London Gatwick. They can be contacted at:

Bus and Coach Travel Line (0800-2200h daily Tel: 0990 747777 (Speedlink, Jetlink, Flightline, Flightlink)
National Express Airport Services (Tel: 0990 808080)

…by Train

The Gatwick Express, based at London's Victoria Station, takes 30 minutes to reach London Gatwick and trains depart every 15 minutes during the day and every 30 minutes during the night. Passengers travelling from the city can be at London Gatwick within 40 minutes using Thameslink services. Connex operates regular services to London Gatwick direct from Milton Keynes, Northampton, Rugby, Tonbridge, Tunbridge Wells and Watford Junction.

To find out about ticket prices and train services to and from London Gatwick contact:

Gatwick Express	0990 301530
Thameslink	0171-620 6333
Connex	0870 6303405
National Rail Enquiries	08457 484950

LONDON HEATHROW AIRPORT

Heathrow Airport Limited, 234 Bath Road, Harlington, Hayes, Middlesex UB3 5AP (Tel: 0870 000 0123; Fax: 020-8745 4290; Web: http://www.heathrowairport.co.uk)

Getting there…

…by Road

The M4 (junction 4), M25 (junction 15) and A4 motorways serve terminals 1, 2 and 3 while terminal 4 can be accessed by M4 (junction 3), M25 (junction 15) and A30. For people travelling to London Heathrow by road the Department of Environment, Transport and the Regions has set up a journey-planner information line on 01234 276376. There are two petrol stations at London Heathrow, both open 24 hours a day and car parking is available on a Short Stay (up to 5 hours) or Long Stay/Holiday Parking basis. Short Stay car parking is operated by NCP at terminals 2 and 3 (020-8745 7260 – terminal 2; 020-8745 5394 – terminal 3) and Central Parking System at terminals 1 and 4 (020-8745 6520 – terminal 1; 020-8745 7906 – terminal 4). Long Stay/Holiday car parking is operated by Parking Express (APCOA) and spaces can be pre-booked by calling the BAA Holiday Parking Line on 0345 405000.

There are many bus and coach services connecting London Heathrow with more than 500 destinations across the UK. Most of the coach services operate from the central bus station which can be accessed by the subways that link terminals 1, 2 and 3. For information on coach services and to book tickets call the Travelline on 0990 747777.

…by Train

The Heathrow Express is a non-stop train service operating every 15 minutes between Paddington and London Heathrow. Trains travel at up to 100 miles per hour and journey times are 15 to and from terminals 1, 2 and 3 and 20 minutes to and from terminal 4. For details of timetabling and ticket prices call 0845 600 1515. Train services to and from London Heathrow are also operated by Railair who provide links from Feltham, Reading and Woking. National Rail Enquiries (0345 484950) provides information on all Railair services.

The London Heathrow terminals can also be accessed by two stations on the Piccadilly line of the London Underground, one serving terminals 1, 2 and 3, the other serving terminal 4. The average tube journey time from central London is approximately 50-60 minutes. For full details of tube train frequency and fares, call London Transport Travel Information on 020-7222 1234 (24 hours)

LONDON LUTON AIRPORT

Percival House, Percival Way, Luton, Bedfordshire LU2 9LY (Tel: 01582 405100;
Email: info@london-luton.co.uk;
Web: http://www.london-luton.com)

London Luton operates scheduled services to the following destinations: Aberdeen, Alicante, Amsterdam, Athens, Barcelona, Belfast, Dublin, Dusseldorf, Edinburgh, Finland, Geneva, Gibraltar, Glasgow, Inverness, Isle of Man, Jersey, Liverpool, Madrid, Malaga, Mahon, Munich, Nice, Palma, Paris, Tenerife and Zurich.

Airlines serving London Luton Airport include: Britannia Airlines, easyjet, European Air Express, Jersey European, Manx Airlines, Monarch Airlines, Monarch Crown Service, Ryanair, ScotAirways.

Getting there…

…by Road

London Luton Airport is situated 30 minutes from north London, 15 minutes from the M25 and 5 minutes from the M1. The airport is conveniently situated for access to and from north and north-east London, Essex, Kent, Surrey and Sussex.

Parking at London Luton Airport can be on a long, short or executive stay basis. Long term car-parking may be booked in advance.

...by Train
There is a frequent Thameslink service operating between London and Bedford. Luton Parkway Station is approximately 2km from the airport terminal building. The approximate journey time from London King's Cross is 30 minutes.

...by Coach
There are a number of coach services serving London Luton Airport including:
Express Coach 757 which runs between London Luton Airport and central London, calling at Brent Cross, Finchley Road, Baker Street, Marble Arch and Victoria. For further information telephone 0345 788788.
Speedlink Airport Services Jetlink 747 which connects London Luton with London Gatwick and London Heathrow Airports. For further information telephone 0990 747777.
National Express operates various services to London Luton Aiport. For further information telephone 0990 808080.

LONDON STANSTED AIRPORT
Stansted Airport Limited, Enterprise House, Bassingbourne Road, Stansted CM24 1QW (Tel: 01279 680500; Fax: 01279 662066;
Web: http://www.stansted.co.uk)

Getting there...
...by Road
London Stansted can be accessed via Junction 8 of the M11 and is 20 minutes from Junction 27 of the M25. London Stansted links to Bedfordshire and Hertfordshire via the A505 and A414; to East Anglia via the A11, A12 and A120 and to the North and Midlands by the A1 and A14. Parking is available on a short or long stay basis and car parks are operated by Meteor Parking. Tel: 01279 681192.

Jetlink 777 connects London Stansted with London Victoria Coach Station and various other coach services are available serving Bedfordshire, Cambridgeshire, Essex, Norfolk, Oxford and Suffolk. For further information, call 0990 808080.

...by Train
The Stansted Express offers frequent services, seven days per week between London Stansted and Liverpool Street station, the journey taking approximately 40 minutes. The service also serves Tottenham Hale station where travellers can link to London Underground services. There is also an hourly local train service operating between London Stansted and Liverpool Street station. For details, call National Rail Enquiries on 08457 484950.

UTILITIES

WATER

In England, the Secretary of State for the Environment, Transport and the Regions has overall responsibility for water policy and sets the environmental and health and safety standards for the water industry. The Director-General of Water Services, as the independent economic regulator, is responsible for ensuring that the private water companies are able to fulfil their statutory obligation to provide water supply and sewerage services, and for protecting the interests of consumers.

The Minister of Agriculture, Fisheries and Food is responsible for policy relating to land drainage, flood protection, sea defences and the protection and development of fisheries.

The Environment Agency is responsible for water quality and the control of pollution, the management of water resources and nature conservation. The Drinking Water Inspectorate and local authorities are responsible for the quality of drinking water.

The Water Act 1989 provided for the creation of a privatised water industry under public regulation, and the functions of the regional water authorities were taken over by ten holding companies and the regulatory bodies.

Most of these have public limited company (PLC) status and many are now in foreign ownership or are part of larger multi-utility companies. They are represented by Water UK, which also represents the ten water service companies responsible for sewerage and sewage disposal in England and Wales, and the state-owned water authorities of Scotland and Northern Ireland.

Water UK is the trade association for all the water service companies except Mid Kent Water.

THAMES WATER UTILITIES PLC

14 Cavendish Place, London W1M ONU
Chairman: Roger Carr
Chief Executive: Bill Alexander
For further information contact the 24 hour Customer Centre on: 0845 9200 800 (UK Or write to Thames Water Customer Centre, PO Box 436, Swindon. SN38 1TU

WATER UK

1 Queen Anne's Gate, London, SW1H 9BT (Tel: 020-7344 1844)
Chief Executive: Ms P. Taylor

OFFICE OF WATER SERVICE

Centre City Tower, 7 Hill Street, Birmingham B5 4UA (Tel: 0121-625 1300; Fax: 0121-625 1400;
Email: enquiries@ofwat.gtnet.gov.uk;
Web: http://www.open.gov.uk/ofwat)

The Office of Water Services (Ofwat) was set up under the Water Act 1989 and is a non-ministerial government department headed by the Director-General of Water Services. It is the independent economic regulator of the water and sewerage companies in England and Wales. Ofwat's main duties are to ensure that the companies can finance and carry out the functions specified in the Water Industry Act 1991 and to protect the interests of water customers. There are ten regional customer service committees which are concerned solely with the interests of water customers. Representation of customer interests at national level is the responsibility of the Ofwat National Customer Council (ONCC).

GAS AND ELECTRICITY

The Office of Gas and Electricity Markets is the regulator for the gas industry. It was formed in 1999 by the merger of the Office of Gas Supply and the Office of Electricity Regulation. Under the Competition Act 1998, from 1 March 2000 the Competition Commission has heard appeals against the regulator's decisions regarding anti-competitive agreements and abuse of a dominant position in the marketplace.

The gas industry in Britain was nationalised in 1949 and operated as the Gas Council. The Gas Council was replaced by the British Gas Corporation in 1972 and the industry became more centralised. The British Gas Corporation was privatised in 1986 as British Gas PLC.

In 1993 the Monopolies and Mergers Commission found that British Gas's integrated business in Great Britain as a gas trader and the owner of the gas transportation system could be expected to operate against the public interest. In February 1997 British Gas demerged its trading arm and now operates as two separate companies: BG PLC, which runs the Transco pipeline business in Britain and oil and gas exploration and production in the UK and abroad; and Centrica PLC, which runs the trading, service and retail operations under the British Gas brand name in Great Britain.

Supply of gas to the domestic market was opened to companies other than British Gas, starting in April 1996. With the electricity market also open, many suppliers now offer their customers both gas and electricity.

Under the Electricity Act 1989, 12 regional electricity companies (RECs), which are responsible for the distribution of electricity from the national grid to consumers, were formed from the former area electricity boards in England and Wales. Four companies were formed from the Central Electricity Generating Board: three generating companies (National Power PLC, Nuclear Electric PLC and PowerGen PLC) and the National Grid Company PLC, which owns and operates the transmission system. National Power and PowerGen were floated on the stock market in 1991. Nuclear Electric was split into two parts in 1995, the part comprising the more modern nuclear stations was incorporated into a new company, British Energy, which was floated on the stock market in 1996. Magnox Electric, which owns the magnox nuclear reactors, remained in the public sector and was integrated into British Nuclear Fuels (BNFL) in 1999. Ownership of the National Grid Company was transferred to the RECs and it was subsequently floated in 1995.

Generators sell the electricity they produce into an open commodity market (the Pool) from which buyers purchase. The introduction of competition into the domestic electricity market was completed in May 1999. With the gas market also open, many suppliers now offer their customers both gas and electricity.

The Office of Gas and Electricity Markets is the regulator for the electricity industry. It was formed in 1999 by the merger of the Office of Electricity Regulation and the Office of Gas Supply. Under the Competition Act 1998, from 1 March 2000 the Competition Commission will hear appeals against the regulator's decisions regard-

146 Public Services London

ing anti-competitive agreements and abuse of a dominant position in the marketplace.

The Electricity Association is the electricity industry's main trade association, providing representational and professional services for the electricity companies. EA Technology Ltd provides distribution and utilisation research, development and technology transfer.

ELECTRICITY ASSOCIATION

30 Millbank, London, SW1P 4RD (Tel: 020-7963 5700; Fax: 020-7963 5959)

OFFICE OF GAS AND ELECTRICITY MARKETS

Stockley House, 130 Wilton Road, London SW1V 1LQ (Tel: 020-7828 0898; Fax: 020-7932 1600)

The Office of Gas and Electricity Markets (Ofgem) was formed in 1999 by the merger of the separate regulators for electricity and gas set up under the Electricity Act 1989 and the Gas Act 1986 respectively. It is headed by the Director-General for Electricity and Gas Supply and is the independent regulatory body for the electricity and gas supply industries in England, Scotland and Wales. Its functions are to promote competition and to protect customers' interests in relation to prices, security of supply and quality of services.

Director-General for Electricity and Gas Supply: C. McCarthy
Deputy Directors-General: A. J. Boorman (*Customers*); Dr Eileen Marshall, CBE (*Supply Chain*); R. Morse (*Electricity and Gas Transportation Regulation*)

BUSINESS
LONDON

BANKING
FINANCIAL SERVICES REGULATION
INSURANCE
LONDON STOCK EXCHANGE
OMBUDSMEN
BUSINESS AND THE WORKFORCE
TRADE UNIONS AND EMPLOYERS' ASSOCIATIONS
TRAINING AND ENTERPRISE
CHARITY AND THE VOLUNTARY SECTOR
CONFERENCE AND EXHIBITION VENUES

BUSINESS LONDON

History

London has long been the world's leading financial centre, building on its historic sea-faring routes, sharing the universal language of business, English, and straddling the time-zones between East and West. But while it remains dominant, the London of the new millennium is entirely different to that of 30 years ago, with its bowler-hatted City gents and clubbish ways of doing business. The modern London is infinitely more cosmopolitan and indeed fragmented, with the historic centre of finance, the square mile, ceding some of its power to the increasingly dominant Canary Wharf in London's Docklands.

Age-old institutions such as the London Stock Exchange have been increasingly marginalised with the advent of computerised trading and e-commerce. Londoners today are more cosmopolitan, with American, Asian and European nationals working in banking, accountancy and law. Ranked as among the world's most expensive cities, with Paris, Tokyo and Moscow, London nevertheless remains a vibrant and pulsating metropolis, setting the pace with its coffee bars and cybercafes.

It is hard to picture London as it once was: a tiny Roman settlement, squatting on the north side of the Thames in the area where the City of London lies today. Access to the sea and the rise of Empire gave Britain, through London, the means to consolidate its place as a global seat of power. It was this that gave rise to the merchant banker: literally bankers who would finance trade expeditions. Today's merchant banker is more likely to advise on multi-billion pound deals in global telecoms or media, but with London continuing to set the tone.

The Economy and Employment

London has long been the generator driving Britain's economy. It accounts for more than 15 per cent of the UK's Gross Domestic Product (the measure of total productive activity in the economy). The size of the London economy, at more than £100 billion, is similar in size to Austria and Sweden and larger than Saudi Arabia. Greater London has a labour pool of more than 3.5 million people, supplemented by a further 4 million in the surrounding region. This is the largest regional pool of labour anywhere in Europe.

What do Londoners do for a living? Not surprisingly, finance is a huge employer, both in deal-making and in all the panoply of support services that goes with it, but this is an eclectic mix. Manufacturing, for instance, traditionally associated with regions such as the West Midlands, speaks for over 275,000 jobs in London. Manufacturing accounts for more than 10 per cent of London's GDP. London has the largest slice of professionals trained in digital media and related skills at 32 per cent of the UK total. Almost 11,000 businesses operate in the media industries. Advertising and design agencies employ more than 40,000 people in London, earning the UK more than £1.7 billion annually in overseas income. London has the largest concentration of software and services companies in the UK and some 80,000 people are employed in computer and related services. Pharmaceuticals is a big employer and more than 12,000 people work in research and development.

But it is of course finance that powers London's economy. Financial services accounts for 6.4 per cent of UK GDP and employs more than 1 million people, more than the population of Frankfurt. Many work in high street banks and insurance companies, with 210,000 working specifically in central London. Some 13 per cent of all those who work in financial services in the UK are based in the City, contributing to a sector that generates net overseas earnings for Britain of more than £32 billion a year. By the mid-1990s, the City had overtaken UK manufacturing to become Britain's single biggest wealth creator, contributing about a quarter of Britain's economic wealth and generating overseas earnings of more than £17.5 billion a year. Output of financial services doubled between 1986 and 1992. London has 2,900 accountancy firms, led by Big Five firms like Arthur Andersen and KPMG, and dozens of big-league law firms, with over 23,000 practising solicitors. City law firms like Clifford Chance generate overseas earnings for Britain in excess of £644 million a year. Demand for professional and support staff is satisfied through over 500 recruitment consultancies, from millionaire headhunters to clerical outplacement agencies.

Employment in the City has shifted since the 1970s, when rising staff and property costs forced employers to relocate to regional cities like Bristol, Swindon and Peterborough. Tens of thousands of jobs in printing, telecommunications and manufacturing went elsewhere. Routine clerical work in banking and insurance has given way to jobs in corporate finance and fund management. This change has heralded a striking increase in City incomes. In the 1970s, City incomes were typically 10–20 per cent higher than the national average. By the late 1990s, they were as much as 80 per cent higher. This has resulted in more value seeping into London's economy – typically in the housing market, where the annual payment of City bonuses has the effect of spurring house prices to ever-greater heights.

Banking and Finance

The City's continuing dominance of world banking and finance is truly remarkable. London has 537 foreign banks, more than any other centre worldwide. London is the world's largest fund management centre, with $2,170 billion of institutional equity holdings in 1998. It is also the world's largest foreign exchange market with a daily turnover of more than $600 billion, more than New York and Tokyo combined. London is the world's largest centre for international bank lending (with a 20 per cent global market share), international bonds (with 60 per cent of primary markets) and international trade in equities (65 per cent).

Even today, the gold mines of South Africa and Australia continue to dance to London's tune. Gold and silver prices are fixed daily in London through the *London Bullion Market Association*. The *London Metal Exchange* is the biggest exchange of its kind in the world and handles over 90 per cent of trading in non-ferrous base metals. The price of crude oil, too, is influenced from London, where two thirds of worldwide business at the *International Petroleum Exchange* trades consists of trading in Brent Crude. This is used as the price marker for internationally traded crude oil. The London Stock Exchange is the largest such exchange in Europe and the Bank of England is still looked upon as a bedrock of international banking.

Lloyd's of London

One of London's historic roles lives on in shipbroking, which generates net overseas earnings for the UK of up to £2 billion annually. London offers the most comprehensive range of specialist maritime services in the world, covering shipbroking, legal services, finance, insurance, ship classification, arbitration and publishing. Most of the world's fleet these days might be Greek-owned and flying flags of convenience from places like Liberia and Panama, but still looks to London as its historic home port. The Baltic Exchange is the world's premier and oldest shipping market.

Shipbroking is intimately bound up with *Lloyd's of London*, housed in its controversial Richard Rogers-designed metal and glass building at One Lime Street. Lloyd's dates to the 1680s, when ships' captains and merchants were inclined to meet in coffee houses run by Edward Lloyd with a view to negotiating insurance for ships and cargoes. Wealthy individuals in the coffee houses would each take a share of the risk, signing their names one beneath the other on the policy together with the amount they agreed to cover. These 'underwriters' live on in the Lloyd's of today which, despite having changed almost beyond recognition since the early 1990s, continues to dominate in world insurance, providing valuable earnings for London and hence the UK. Lloyd's has 13 per cent of the world's marine market and nearly a quarter of the aviation market, insuring aircraft and airlines against everything from lost baggage to the ultimate in worst case scenarios.

Lloyd's, ironically, became a victim of its own success. A series of unparalleled disasters in the late 1980s, including the *Exxon Valdez* tanker spill off Alaska and the *Piper Alpha* oil rig explosion in the North Sea left Lloyd's swamped with crippling losses running to £8 billion or more. Health claims from American workers who had inhaled asbestos dust threatened to spiral out of control. The modern-day equivalent of those wealthy coffee house patrons – private investors known as 'Names' – were swamped by ruinous cash-calls as Lloyd's sought to restore its finances. Faced with the real possibility of collapse, insurance claims for 1992 and earlier were spun-off into a reinsurance company, Equitas, leaving the 'new' Lloyd's to go forward, but in a very different shape. The Names have largely been replaced by corporate investors, giving Lloyd's more the feel of a *General Accident* or *Zurich Re*. It faces increasing competition from offshore centres like Bermuda, but remains powerful and continues to be a major driver of London's economy, both in sustaining an entire sub-industry of brokers and underwriters around Lime Street and as an earner of overseas revenues.

Infrastructure

While bankers in Tokyo and New York still routinely refer to the 'City', they will increasingly be thinking of a concentrated patch of land some miles to the east. In the early 1990s, Canary Wharf in London's Docklands looked a dead loss. The site looked hopelessly impractical, with no direct rail links and a poor supporting infrastructure. Britain was in recession and the location looked doomed. But slowly, the place came right. The transport links came in, led by the Docklands Light Railway and the much-delayed Jubilee Line extension. Having been mired in receivership, Canary Wharf at last began to give the square mile a run for its money, increasingly luring away big name institutions. *Credit Suisse First Boston, Morgan Stanley Dean Witter* and *Barclays Capital* were among those to decamp to Docklands. London's new super-regulator, the *Financial Services Authority*, made Canary Wharf its home. It became a microcosm of Fleet Street, housing newspapers including the *Daily Mirror*, the *Independent* and the *Daily Telegraph*. Future tenants were set to include *Citibank* (encompassing Salomon Smith Barney, situated for years over Victoria railway station) and *HSBC*, which commissioned a 41-storey skyscraper, almost as tall as Canary Wharf's landmark tower. The number of people working at Canary Wharf was set to triple from 27,000 in 1999 to about 100,000 by 2006.

An important but generally overlooked side of London is its role as a transport hub. London's three main airports, Heathrow, Gatwick and Stansted, handle more than 96 million passengers a year, making London the number one city in the world for international air travel. Heathrow is the most important gateway airport to Europe, with a majority of travellers from America, Africa and the East making Heathrow their preferred transit point. This has a huge economic spin-off. The connecting passenger market is worth more than £1 billion a year to the UK economy, with more than 90 airlines flying direct from Heathrow to more than 200 destinations. This helps Britain strengthen business links, promotes inward investment and eases access for the overseas visitors who annually pump £53 billion into the UK economy, much of it in London. Tourism accounts for 4–5 per cent of UK GDP.

Airports play an important role in job creation, just as the Channel Tunnel rail links brought benefits in first construction and later in services. According to a study by DTZ Pieda Consulting commissioned by BAA, the UK airport operator, Heathrow alone generates more than 217,000 jobs for the UK economy. Of these, about 70,000 are directly linked to the airport. For every 1,000 direct airport jobs, a further 400 spin-off posts are typically created in the regional economy. The importance of airports to Greater London will increase with plans for a fifth terminal at Heathrow and a second runway at Gatwick, lifting capacity at London's second airport from 29 million to 40 million passengers.

While the world might take its lead from London in banking and finance, the threat of competition is always there. Up until the mid-1980s, City workers were used to doing business face to face on the floor of the Stock Exchange. The so-called 'Big Bang' of 1986 shifted trading onto computers, taking with it a gentlemanly, face-to-face way of doing business. The tradition lived on – without the manners – at the *London International Financial Futures and Options Exchange (Liffe)* where, at its peak in the early 1990s, literally thousands of traders in colourful striped jackets struck deals using an arcane system of hand signals. *Liffe* at the time was a big employer and an important contributor to London's economy. However, its influence was steadily whittled away in the face of competition from rival exchanges, notably in Chicago and Frankfurt, and by

2000, *Liffe's* jacketed traders were down to perhaps 400 people. Liffe remains an important trading force – but driven by computers, not people.

A Cosmopolitan Capital

Just as London's finance is primarily international, so has its workforce become increasingly cosmopolitan. Some 40 per cent of people working in the City and Canary Wharf work for foreign employers. Business in London has become Americanised, with executives in New York and Chicago driving mergers in accountancy, industry and banking. Accountancy firms like *KPMG* and *PricewaterhouseCoopers* are dominated by US-led management boards. Europe, too, exerts its influence, with old British names like *Barings*, *Warburgs* and *Morgan Grenfell* now in Dutch, Swiss and German hands. London is home to 47,000 Americans, more than 36,000 Germans, more than 30,000 French nationals, 35,000 Italians, 25,000 Japanese, 24,000 Spaniards and 12,000 Koreans. Many of them work for banks, stockbrokers, legal firms and insurance companies.

London has been unable to escape the Internet, with its anarchic effect of cutting out the middleman, whether in stockbroking or in buying cars and groceries. It has not been untouched by the rise of e-commerce. Yet such is London's dominance on the world stage, led by its strategic position straddling the world's time-zones, that it is hard to imagine a day when it will have been completely marginalised. Budding rivals – notably Frankfurt and Paris – will continue to claw business away from London, but will never replace it. Businessmen around the world find a common language in English; Heathrow is their preferred destination. The London markets, regulated without being stifled by red tape, are admired for their integrity. In the old days, City gents used to do business on a handshake and the motto: 'My word is my bond'. Even in the increasingly global electronic world, that remains true of London today.

The Five big accountancy firms	London Employees
PricewaterhouseCoopers	12,000
KPMG	5,500
Ernst & Young	4,423
Deloitte & Touche	3,500
Arthur Andersen	1,500

The Top 10 UK Law firms	Number of Solicitors
1. Eversheds	975
2. Clifford Chance	932
3. Linklaters	721
4. Allen & Overy	614
5. Dibb Lupton Alsop	586
6. Freshfields	577
7. Lovell White Durrant	473
8. CMS Cameron McKenna	459
9. Herbert Smith	456
10. Simmons & Simmons	404

Source: Chambers Guide to the Legal Profession 1999-2000

The top 10 UK insurance companies	Net Premium Income
1. Prudential	£7.7bn
2. GCU*	£6.3bn
3. Barclays Life	£6bn
4. AXA Group (inc. Guardian and PPP)	£5.9bn
5. Royal & Sun Alliance	£5bn
6. Norwich Union*	£4.8bn
7. ZFS Group (inc. Eagle Star, Allied Dunbar, Zurich)	£4.5bn
8. Standard Life	£4bn
9. Equitable Group	£3.6bn
10. National Westminster Life	£3.4bn

Source: ABI Annual Returns, ranked by 1998 net premium income, long term business and general business combined. Rankings as of March 2000. * Pending merger of NU and GCU will make GCNU the biggest UK insurer.

The top financial advisors	Value of deals	Number of deals
1. Goldman Sachs	$398bn	120
2. Morgan Stanley Dean Witter	$349bn	155
3. Merrill Lynch	$226bn	129
4. JP Morgan	$187bn	104
5. Credit Suisse First Boston	$149bn	136
6. Lazards	$145bn	108
7. Warburg Dillon Read	$125bn	139
8. Rothchild	$115bn	160
9. Lehman Brothers	$107bn	70
10. Dresdner Kleinwort Benson	$95bn	81

Source: Thomson Financial Securities Data. Firms advising on mergers and acquisitions involving European companies in 1999.

GROSS DOMESTIC PRODUCT AT CURRENT PRICES, BY LOCAL AREA

	£ m				£ per head			
	1993	1994	1995	1996	1993	1994	1995	1996
UK*	540,139	570,944	597,741	629,839	9,282	9,777	10,199	10,711
London	93,128	97,043	100,762	106,658	13,433	13,928	14,380	15,077
Inner London	56,759	59,390	61,979	65,255	21,440	22,315	23,152	24,099
Inner London – West	37,394	39,380	41,385	43,928	39,595	41,367	43,089	44,811
Inner London – East	19,365	20,010	20,594	21,327	11,371	11,706	11,997	12,346
Outer London	36,369	37,653	38,783	41,402	8,486	8,744	8,957	9,482
Outer London – E&NW	9,787	10,198	10,553	11,241	6,410	6,682	6,910	7,350
Outer London – South	8,967	9,414	9,811	10,268	8,140	8,489	8,775	9,095
Outer London – W&NW	17,615	18,041	18,419	19,893	10,629	10,796	10,932	11,647

*Excluding Extra-Regio and the statistical discrepancy of the income-based measure
Source: Focus on London '99, Office for National Statistics © Crown Copyright 1999

152 Business London

SHARE OF GROSS DOMESTIC PRODUCT*, BY INDUSTRY GROUP**, 1996	
Industry Group	%
Financial & Business Services	38.6
Education, Social Work, Health & Other services	16.3
Distribution, Hotel and Catering etc	14.2
Manufacturing	10.4
Transport, Storage & Communication	10.3
Public Administration & Defence	4.8
Other Industries†	5.5

* At factor cost before adjustment for financial services
** Industry breakdown based on SIC 1992
† Agriculture, mining, energy, construction etc.

Source: *Focus on London '99, Office for National Statistics* © Crown Copyright 1999

BANKING

Deposit-taking institutions may be broadly divided into two sectors: the monetary sector, which is predominantly banks, and those institutions outside the monetary sector, of which the most important are the building societies and National Savings. Both sectors are supervised by the Financial Services Authority. As a result of the conversion of several building societies into banks in recent years, the size of the banking sector, which was already substantially greater than the non-bank deposit-taking sector, has increased further.

The main institutions within the British banking system are the Bank of England (the central bank), the retail banks, the merchant banks and the overseas banks. In its role as the central bank, the Bank of England acts as banker to the Government and as a note-issuing authority; it also oversees the efficient functioning of payment and settlement systems.

Since May 1997, the Bank of England has had operational responsibility for monetary policy. At monthly meetings of its monetary policy committee the Bank sets the interest rate at which it will lend to the money markets.

Official Interest Rates 1999-2000
10 June 1999	5.00%
8 September 1999	5.25%
4 November 1999	5.50%
13 January 2000	5.75%
10 February 2000	6.00%

BANK OF ENGLAND

Threadneedle Street, London EC2R 8AH (Tel: 020-7601 4444; Fax: 020-7601 4771)

The Bank of England was incorporated in 1694 under royal charter. It is the banker of the Government and manages the note issue. Since May 1997 it has been operationally independent and its Monetary Policy Committee has had responsibility for setting short-term interest rates to meet the Government's inflation target. As the central reserve bank of the country, the Bank keeps the accounts of British banks, who maintain with it a proportion of their cash resources, and of most overseas central banks. The Bank has three main areas of activity: Monetary Stability, Market Operations and Financial Stability. Its responsibility for banking supervision has been transferred to the Financial Services Authority.

Governor: The Rt. Hon. E. A. J. George
Deputy Governors: D. Clementi; M. A. King
Non-Executive Directors: C. J. Allsopp; R. Bailie, OBE; A. R. F. Buxton; Sir David Cooksey; H. J. Davies; Sir Ian Gibson; G. Hawker; Mrs F.A. Heaton; Sir Chips Keswick; Dame Sheila Masters, dbe; Ms S. McKechnie, OBE; W. Morris; J. Neill, CBE, PhD.; N. I. Simms; J. Stretton; Ms K. A. O'Donovan
Monetary Policy Committee: The Governor; the Deputy Governors; I. Plenderleith; Prof. C. Goodhart; Dr D. Julius; J. Vickers; Dr S. Wadhwani; Prof. Stephen Nickell
Advisers to the Governor: Sir Peter Petrie; L. Berkowitz; D. Brealey
Chief Cashier and Deputy Director, Banking and Market Services: Ms M. V. Lowther
Chief Registrar: G. P. Sparkes
General Manager, Printing Works: A. W. Jarvis
Secretary: P. D. Rodgers
The Auditor: K. Butler

Merchant Banks
Broadly, a merchant bank is an institution that is involved in investment banking and the negotiation of mergers and acquisitions.

Retail Banks
Retail banks offer a wide variety of financial services to companies and individuals, including current and deposit accounts, loan and overdraft facilities, cash dispenser machines (ATMs), mortgages, cheque guarantee cards, credit cards and debit cards. Several banks also now offer telephone and Internet banking facilities.

Payment Clearings
The Association for Payment Clearing Services (APACS) is an umbrella organisation for payment clearings in the UK. It operates three clearing companies:
–BACS Ltd is the UK's automated clearing house for bulk clearing of electronic debits and credits (e.g. direct debits and salary credits)
–the Cheque and Credit Clearing Company Ltd operates bulk clearing systems for inter-bank cheques and paper credit items in Great Britain
–CHAPS Clearing Company Ltd provides same-day clearing for high-value electronic funds transfers throughout the UK in sterling and globally in euros
Membership of APACS and the clearing companies is open to any appropriately regulated financial institution providing payment services and meeting the relevant membership criteria.

ASSOCIATION FOR PAYMENT CLEARING SERVICES (APACS)

Mercury House, Triton Court, 14 Finsbury Square, London EC2A 1LQ (Tel: 020-7711 6200; Fax: 020-7256 5527; Email: mailto:publicaffairs@apacs.org.uk; Web: http://www.apacs.org.uk)

Head of Public Affairs: R. Tyson-Davies

BACS Ltd
De Havilland Road, Edgware, Middx HA8 5QA (Tel: 0870 1650019; Fax: 020-8951 7489;
Web: http://www.apacs.org.uk/bacs.htm)

Chief Executive: G. Younger

CHEQUE AND CREDIT CLEARING COMPANY LTD

Mercury House, Triton Court, 14 Finsbury Square, London EC2A 1LQ
(Web: http:// www.apacs.org.uk/redchequered.htm)

CHAPS CLEARING COMPANY LTD

Mercury House, Triton Court, 14 Finsbury Square, London EC2A 1LQ (Tel: 020-7711 6200; Fax: 020-7256 5527; Email: mailto:publicaffairs@apacs.org.uk; Web: http://www.apacs.org.uk www.apacs.org.uk)

Company Manager: Michael Lewis

Authorised Institutions

Banking in the UK is regulated by the Banking Act 1987 as amended by the European Community's Second Banking Co-ordination Directive, which came into effect on 1 January 1993. The Banking Act 1987 established a single category of banks eligible to carry out banking business; these are known as authorised institutions. Authorisation under the Act is granted by the Bank of England; it is an offence for anyone not on its list of authorised institutions to conduct deposit-taking business, unless they are exempted from the requirements of the Act (e.g. building societies). The Government has announced that it will transfer responsibility for banking supervision to the Financial Services Authority. Once the necessary legislation has been passed the FSA will be responsible for the authorisation and supervision of banks and the supervision of clearing and settlement systems.

The implementation of the Second Banking Co-ordination Directive permits banks incorporated in one EU member state to carry on certain banking activities in another member state without the need for authorisation by that state. Consequently, the Bank of England no longer authorises banks incorporated in other EU states with branches in the UK; the authorisation of their home state supervisor is sufficient provided that certain notification requirements are met.

Financial Services Regulation 153

FINANCIAL SERVICES REGULATION

In May 1997 the Government announced plans to establish a new statutory single financial regulator responsible for the supervision of banks, building societies, insurance companies, investment firms and markets and to replace the current supervisory framework, established under a number of different statutes. The new regulator is the Financial Services Authority (FSA), which in corporate and legal terms is the Securities and Investments Board (SIB) renamed.

The FSA is acquiring its full range of responsibilities in two stages. The first stage was completed on 1 June 1998 when the FSA acquired responsibility, under the Bank of England Act 1998, for supervising banks, listed money market institutions and related clearing houses; the Bank of England had previously exercised this responsibility. The majority of functions previously carried out by the Insurance Directorate of HM Treasury (including Lloyd's of London), has now been taken over by the FSA. The second stage will follow the enactment of the Financial Services and Markets Bill, introduced into Parliament in June 1999 and given Royal Assent on 14 June 2000. When this bill is implemented, a date commonly referred to as N2, the FSA will acquire its full range of powers and will take on responsibility for the regulation and registration functions of the following regulators and supervisors:

Self-Regulating Organisations
Investment Management Regulatory Organisation (IMRO)
Personal Investment Authority (PIA)
Securities and Futures Authority Ltd (SFA)

Others
Building Societies Commission
Friendly Societies Commission
Registry of Friendly Societies
Recognised professional Bodies (RPBs)

All the above organisations are based at the FSA's offices in Canary Wharf.

The FSA also supervises the recognised investment exchanges and recognised clearing houses, ensuring that they continue to fulfil their regulatory responsibilities. On 1 May 2000, the FSA also took over from the London Stock Exchange the role of the UK's listing authority.

Until N2, the above organisations will continue to have legal responsibility for regulating their firms under the existing statutory or contractual arrangements. However, in order to facilitate speedy operational integration, the staff of the SROs have transferred contracts of employment to the FSA and now operate under a single management structure. Detailed contracts have been put in place providing the services of the FSA staff to these bodies to enable them to carry out their work.

Under the new legislation the FSA will have statutory objectives in four main areas:
- maintaining confidence in the UK financial system
- promoting public understanding of the financial system, including awareness of the benefits and risks associated with different kinds of investment or other financial dealing
- securing the appropriate degree of protection for consumers, having regard to the differing degrees of risk

involved in different kinds of investment or other transaction, the differing degrees of experience and expertise which different consumers may have, and the general principle that consumers should take responsibility for their decisions
- the reduction of financial crime

It is the Government's intention that the FSA should pursue its objectives in a way that is efficient and economic; facilitates innovation in financial services; balances restrictions on firms with the benefits of regulation; and takes account of the international nature of financial services business and the value of competition between firms. The FSA is currently preparing its policy, regulatory approach and rules. It is issuing consultation papers and feedback and policy statements. It has also established a Practitioner Panel and Consumer Panel and set up various advisory groups to look at specific topics. It is also the intention that there will be one compensation scheme and one Ombudsman scheme to deal with complaints.

Central Register/Public Enquiries

The FSA maintains the Central Register of all firms which are, or were, authorised to carry on investment business and authorised deposit takers. The entry for each firm gives its name, address and telephone number; a reference number; its authorisation status; and states which organisation regulates it; and whether it can handle client money. The Consumer Helpline is available to members of the public seeking information about firms listed on the Register as well as booklets or other information and assistance on financial services issues.
Consumer Helpline: 0845-606 1234;
E-mail: consumerhelp@fsa.gov.uk

FINANCIAL SERVICES COMPENSATION SCHEME

The Financial Services and Markets Bill will simplify the current arrangements for compensating investors where a firm authorised to carry on regulated activity is unable to meet claims against it. The six existing schemes covering depositors, policyholders and investors will be replaced by a single scheme. A new company, the Financial Services Compensation Scheme Ltd, has been set up to manage the scheme from N2. The new scheme will take over from the following existing organisations: The Deposit Protection Board, The Building Societies Investor Protection Scheme, The Investors Compensation Scheme, The S43 Scheme, The Policyholders Protection Board, The Friendly Societies Investor Protection Scheme. These schemes will continue to operate until N2 and will respectively deal with claims in respect of deposits held by insolvent banks, claims against persons authorised under the Financial Services Act 1986 to carry on investment business and claims on protected policies of insurance where the insurer is insolvent.

FINANCIAL SERVICES AUTHORITY

25 The North Colonnade, Canary Wharf, London E14 5HS (Tel: 020-7676 1000);
Email: publicenquiries@fsa.gov.uk;
Web: http://www.fsa.gov.uk)

Chairman: H. Davies

ASSOCIATION OF CHARTERED CERTIFIED ACCOUNTANTS

29 Lincoln's Inn Fields, London WC2A 3EE (Tel: 020-7242 6855; Web: http://www.acca.org.uk)

INSTITUTE OF ACTUARIES

Staple Inn Hall, High Holborn, London WC1V 7QJ (Tel: 020-7242 0106)

INSTITUTE OF CHARTERED ACCOUNTANTS IN ENGLAND AND WALES

Chartered Accountants' Hall, PO Box 433, Moorgate Place, London EC2P 2BJ (Tel: 020-7920 8100; Web: http://www.icaew.co.uk)

Recognised Investment Exchanges

Investment exchanges are exempt from needing authorisation under the Financial Services Act. A recognised investment exchange (RIE) is recognised by legislation as providing facilities for trading investment products (e.g. stocks and shares or futures). To be a recognised investment exchange, it must fulfil the following requirements: adequate financial resources; proper conduct of business rules; a proper market in its products; procedures for recording transactions; effective monitoring and enforcement of rules; proper arrangements for the clearing and performance of contracts.

INTERNATIONAL PETROLEUM EXCHANGE (IPE)

International House, 1 St Katharine's Way, London E1 9UN (Tel: 020-7481 0643; Web: http://www.ipe.uk.com)

LONDON INTERNATIONAL FINANCIAL FUTURES AND OPTIONS EXCHANGE (LIFFE)

Cannon Bridge, London EC4R 3XX (Tel: 020-7623 0444; Web: http://www.liffe.com)

LONDON METAL EXCHANGE (LME)

56 Leadenhall Street, London EC3A 2BJ (Tel: 020-7264 5555; Web: http:// www.lme.co.uk)

LONDON STOCK EXCHANGE (LSE)

Old Broad Street, London EC2N 1HP (Tel: 020-7797 1000; Web: http://www.londonstockexchange.co.uk)

LONDON SECURITIES AND DERIVATIVES EXCHANGE LTD (OM LONDON EXCHANGE LTD)

107 Cannon Street, London EC4N 5AF (Tel: 020-7283 0678)

TRADEPOINT STOCK EXCHANGE

35 King Street, London WC2E 8JD (Tel: 020-7240 8000)

INVESTOR PROTECTION

Following the implementation of the EC Investment Services Directive, recognition by the UK authorities is no longer required for exchanges within the European Economic Area (with certain exceptions).

RECOGNISED CLEARING HOUSES

A recognised clearing house (RCH) is recognised by legislation as providing a service enabling companies trading financial products on a RIE to settle transactions quickly and efficiently. A RCH must satisfy similar criteria to those which apply to be an RIE. There are two RCHs which act as clearing houses for some of the above RIEs. In addition, Crest also operates a system for dematerialised settlement of share transactions.

CRESTCO LTD

33 Cannon Street, London EC4M 5SB (Tel: 020-7849 0000; Web: http://www.crestco.co.uk)

LONDON CLEARING HOUSE LTD (LCH)

Roman Wall House, 1-2 Crutched Friars, London EC3N 2AN (Tel: 020-7265 2000; Web: http://www.lch.co.uk)

DESIGNATED INVESTMENT EXCHANGES

The FSA has drawn up a list of designated overseas investment exchanges. These are deemed to provide protection for investors of an equivalent standard to that provided by RIEs.

OTHER FINANCIAL BODIES

ADJUDICATOR'S OFFICE

Haymarket House, 28 Haymarket, London SW1Y 4SP (Tel: 020-7930 2292; Fax: 020-7930 2298; Email: adjudicators@gtnet.gov.uk; Web: http://www.open.gov.uk)
The Adjudicator's Office opened in 1993 and investigates complaints about the way the Inland Revenue (including the Valuation Office Agency) and Customs and Excise have handled an individual's affairs.

The Adjudicator: Dame Barbara Mills, dbe, QC
Head of Office: Charlie Gordon

INLAND REVENUE LONDON

New Court, 48 Carey Street, London WC2A 2JE
Chief Executive: C. R. Massingale

INSURANCE

In addition to the many insurers who operate from branch and head offices in London and the famous Lloyd's market based in Lime Street, there is also a distinct separate part of the UK insurance and reinsurance industry called the London Insurance Market. While there is no strict definition for this market it is widely accepted that it is the world's leading market for internationally traded insurance and reinsurance business. This is mainly international, high exposure, non-life (general) risks.

The market is made up of insurance companies, reinsurance companies, syndicates at Lloyd's and Marine Protection and Indemnity Clubs and is physically centred on a small area in the City of London near to the main Lloyd's building. This allows brokers wishing to place risks to have face-to-face contact with underwriters. Usually, the risks are very large and need to be covered by several insurers who each take a proportion of the total amount at risk. It is quite common for UK insurance companies, underwriters at Lloyd's and overseas insurance companies to all share in covering one large piece of business.

Because a number of insurers and underwriters may be involved in the administration work in collecting premiums and handling claims these are processed electronically through two market bureaux, The Lloyd's Policy Signing Office and The London Processing Centre. It is estimated that around 40,000 people are employed in the market with up to 10,000 more based outside London or involved in ancillary services like accountancy, law and loss adjustment

The total written gross premium income of the London Insurance Market in 1998 was £14.4 billion. This represents over one-third of the total non-life insurance and reinsurance business written in Britain by the UK insurance industry. Despite its name, participants in the market do not need to be London or UK owned. In fact, the reverse is true. For example, virtually all of the world's top twenty reinsurers are represented in the London Market, and over three-quarters of the companies are foreign-owned. Almost all the companies operating in the market are members of the International Underwriting Association of London (IUA) which was formed in 1999 from a merger of the London International Insurance and Reinsurance Market Association (LIRMA) with the Institute of London Underwriters.

LONDON INSURANCE MARKET GROSS WRITTEN PREMIUMS, 1998

	MAT & MAT Reinsurance £m	Home Foreign £m	Non-MAT Treaty Reinsurance £m	Total Business £m
Insurance Companies	1,681	1,891	3,948	7,520
Marine Protection and Indemnity Clubs	1,381	5	–	1,386
Lloyd's	1,937	2,185	1,454	5,576
Total	4,999	4,081	5,402	14,482

INSURANCE EMPLOYMENT IN THE LONDON INSURANCE MARKET

	1987	1989	1991	1993	1995	1997
City of London[1]	40,400	32,300	31,500	28,800	26,100	31,700
Camden and Tower Hamlets	10,200	12,900	11,400	8,700	7,800	8,1000
Total	50,600	45,100	42,900	37,500	33,900	39,800

[1] Including the areas of EC1, EC2, EC3 and EC4

Business London

The challenges for the London Insurance Market are largely the same as those faced by the UK and international insurance industry as a whole. In the UK the Financial Services Authority has responsibility for the authorisation and regulation of insurance where this is required by law. London Market companies have, therefore, been involved in the consultation processes, where appropriate.

The increasingly global nature of insurance also means that there is increasing competition which brings with in greater demands for efficiency and profitability. As a result, the London Market has undergone substantial restructuring in the past few years. Further changes are likely as the London Market moves further towards greater use of e-commerce.

Although the UK has chosen not to join the first wave of countries participating in economic and monetary union, the London Market is fully prepared and has been able to trade in the euro since 1 October 1998. Other challenges facing the market include the problems of climate change and global warming, increasing levels of compensation payments and losses arising from environmental damage and pollution both in Europe and North America.

INTERNATIONAL UNDERWRITING ASSOCIATION OF LONDON (IUA)

London Underwriting Centre, 3 Minster Court, Mincing Lane, London EC3R 7DD (Email: info@iua.co.uk; Web: http://www.iua.co.uk)

LONDON INSURANCE MARKET ACTIVE PARTICIPANTS IN 1999

ILU member companies	107
Lloyd's syndicates	139
Marine Protection and Indemnity Clubs	39
Lloyd's Brokers	145

INSURANCE COMPANIES

Aachen and Munich Insurance Company
14 Fernchurch Avenue, London, EC3M 5BS

ACE Insurance Company of Europe
Mincing Lane, London, EC3R 7XA

AGF Insurance Limited
41 Botolph Lane, London, EC3R 8DL

Albion Insurance Company Ltd
5 Greenwich View Place, London, E14 9NN

American Re-Insurance Company
77 Gracechurch Street, London, EC3V 0AS

Arig Insurance Company Limited
50 Mark Lane, London, EC3R 7RB

Avon Insurance plc
130 Fenchurch Street, London, EC3M 5JB

AXA Insurance plc
Royal Exchange, London, EC3V 3LS

AXA Nordstern Art Insurance Limited
78 Leadenhall Street, London, EC3A 3DH

AXA Sun Life Assurance Society plc
107 Cheapside, London, EC2V 6DU

Baptist Insurance Co plc
19-21 Billiter Street, London, EC3M 2RY

Barclays Life Assurance Co Ltd
25 Farringdon Street, London, EC4A 4JA

Beaufort Insurance Co Ltd
65-68 Leadenhall Street, London, EC3A 2AD

Bishopsgate Insurance Limited
Warnford Court, London, EC2N 2AT

Britannia Steam Ship Insurance Assurance Ltd
20 St Thomas Street, London, SE1 9RR

British Aviation Insurance Group
10 St Mary Axe, London, EC3A 8EQ

CAN Maritime Insurance Company Limited
77 Gracechurch Street, London, EC3V 0DL

CGU Insurance plc
St Helen's, 1 Undershaft, London, EC3P 3DQ

CGU Linked Life Assurance Limited
25-31 Moorgate, London, EC2R 6BA

China Insurance Co (UK) Ltd
48 Leicester Square, London, WC2H 7LT

Chubb Insurance Company of Europe
106 Fenchurch Street, London, EC3M 5JB

CIGNA Life Insurance Co of Europe S A - N V
38 Trinity Square, London, EC3N 4DJ

City Fire Insurance Company Limited
24B Lime Street, London, EC3M 7HR

Colonia-Baltica Insurance Management Ltd
69-70 Mark Lane, London, EC3R 7HJ

Cologne Reinsurance Co Ltd
13 Haydon Street, London, EC3N 1DB

Cornhill Insurance plc
32 Cornhill, London, EC3V 3LJ

Dai-Tokyo Insurance Co (UK) Ltd
66 Mark Lane, London, EC3R 7HS

DAS Legal Expenses Insurance Co Limited
16 St Helens Place, London, EC3A 6DF

Domestic & General Insurance Co Ltd
Mansel Road, London, SW19 4AA

Dowa Insurance Company (Europe) Ltd
9-13 Fenchurch Buildings, London, EC3M 5HR

Eagle Star Insurance Co Ltd
60 St Mary Axe, London, EC3A 8JQ

Insurance Companies 157

Eagle Star Insurance Company (Ireland) Limited
Cornwall House, London, EC3N 2BQ

Ecclesiastical Insurance plc
19-21 Billiter Street, London, EC3M 2RY

Equitable Life Assurance Society
Crown House, London, WC2B 4AX

Friend's Provident Life Office Ltd
15 Old Bailey, London, EC4M 7AP

GAN Insurance Company Limited
Arthur Street, London, EC4R 9BJ

General and Cologne Life Reinsurance UK Ltd
55 Mark Lane, London, EC3R 7NE

Gerling Global Life Reinsurance Company Ltd
50 Fenchurch Street, London, EC3M 3JY

Hibernian Insurance UK Limited
Portsoken House, London, EC3N 1EE

Hiscox Insurance Company Ltd
1 Great St Helen's, London, EC3A 6HX

Independent Insurance Company Limited
Mincing Lane, London, EC3R 7DD

International Insurance Company of Hanover
130 Fenchurch Street, London, EC3M 5DG

Iron Trades Insurance Company Ltd
21-24 Grosvenor Place, London, SW1X 7JA

J Rothschild Assurance plc
27 St James's Street, London, SW1A 1NR

JP Morgan Life Assurance Limited
28 King Street, London, SW1Y 6XA

Koa Insurance Co (Europe) Ltd
8 Devonshire Square, London, EC2M 4PL

Legal & General Assurance Society Ltd
Temple Court, London, EC4N 4TP

Liberty Mutual Insurance Company (UK) Ltd
1 Minster Court, London, EC3R 7YE

Lloyds TSB General Insurance Limited
71 Lombard Street, London, EC3P 3BS

Lombard General Insurance Company Ltd
GAN House, London, EC4R 9BJ

London, General Insurance Company Limited
1st Floor, 16 St Helen's Place, London, EC3A 6DF

Ludgate Insurance Co Ltd
40 Duke's Place, London, EC3A 7LP

M & G Assurance Group Ltd
3 Minster Court, London, EC3R 7XH

Mitsui Marine and Fire Insurance Co Europe Ltd
New London, House, London, EC3R 7LP

Munich Reinsurance Company Ltd
154 Fenchurch Street, London, EC3M 6JJ

NCM Credit Insurance Limited
63 Queen Victoria Street, London, EC4N 4UA

New Hampshire Insurance Co
120 Fenchurch Street, London, EC3M 5BP

New India Insurance Co Ltd
14 Fenchurch Avenue, London, EC3M 5BS

Nippon Insurance Company of Europe
50 Mark Lane, London, EC3R 7QH

Norwich Union Insurance Group
34-36 Lime Street, London, EC3M 7JE

Prudential Assurance plc
Laurence Pountney Hill, London, EC4R 0EU

QBE International Insurance Limited
Mark Lane, London, EC3R 7NE

Reliance National Insurance Company (Europe) Ltd
80 Leadenhall Street, London, EC3A 3DH

Royal & SunAlliance Insurance plc
30 Berkeley Square, London, W1X 5HA

ST Paul International Insurance Company
27 Camperdown Street, London, E1 8DS

Save & Prosper Insurance Ltd
20 Finsbury Street, London, EC2Y 9AY

Sirius International Insurance Corporation
Marlon House, 71-74 Mark Lane, London, EC3R 7RH

Skandia P&C Insurance Company Limited
23 College Hill, London, EC4R 2SE

Sun Life Assurance Co of Canada (UK) Ltd
75 King William Street, London, EC4N 7HA

Swiss Reinsurance Company UK Ltd
71-77 Leadenhall Street, London, EC3A 2PQ

Terra Nova Insurance Co Ltd
41-43 Mincing Lane, London, EC3R 7SP

TIG Reinsurance Company
Suite 4/12, 3 Minster Court, London, EC3R 7DD

Tobacca Insurance Co Ltd
4 Temple Place, London, WC2R 2PG

Tokio Marine and Fire Insurance Co (UK) Ltd
150 Leadenhall Street, London, EC3V 4TE

Tradex Insurance Company Ltd
Glengall Bridge, London, E14 9QY

Travel & General Insurance Co plc
86 Jermyn Street, London, SW1Y 6JD

Westminster Motor Insurance Associates Ltd
21 Buckingham Palace Road, London, SW1W 0PN

Winterthur International Insurance Co Ltd
34 Leadenhall Street, London, EC3A 1AT

Yasuda Kasai Insurance Company Ltd
Moorgate Hall, 155 Moorgate, London, EC2M 6UB

Zurich Insurance Company
90 Fenchurch Street, London, EC3M 4JX

LONDON STOCK EXCHANGE

London Stock Exchange Ltd, Old Broad Street, London EC2N 1HP (Tel: 020-7797 1000; Web: http://www.londonstockexchange.co.uk)

The London Stock Exchange Ltd serves the needs of government, industry and investors by providing facilities for raising capital and a central market-place for securities trading. This market-place covers government stocks (called gilts), UK and overseas company shares (called equities and fixed interest stocks), and traditional options.

Primary Markets

The Exchange enables companies to raise capital for development and growth through the issue of securities. For a company entering the market for the first time there is a choice of Exchange markets, depending upon the size, history and requirements of the company. The first is the Official List, the main market, which exists for well-established companies; these must comply with stringent criteria relating to all aspects of their operations. At present, companies coming to this market require a minimum market capitalisation of £700,000 and a three-year trading record with a minimum of 25 per cent of the shares held in public hands. The Alternative Investment Market (AIM) began trading in June 1995. It enables small, young and growing companies to raise capital, widen their investor base and have their shares traded on a regulated market without the expense of a full Exchange listing.

Once admitted to the Exchange, all companies are obliged to keep their shareholders informed of their progress, making announcements of a price-sensitive nature through the Exchange's company announcements department.

Big Bang

During 1986 the London Stock Exchange went through the greatest period of change in its 200-year history. In March 1986 it opened its doors for the first time to overseas and corporate membership of the Exchange, allowing banks, insurance companies and overseas securities houses to become members of the Exchange and to buy existing member firms. On 27 October 1986, three major reforms took place, changes which became known as 'Big Bang':

- the abolition of scales of minimum commissions, allowing clients to negotiate freely with their brokers about the charge for their services
- the abolition of the separation of member firms into brokers and jobbers: firms are now broker/dealers, able to act as agents on behalf of clients; to act as principals buying and selling shares for their own account; and to become registered market makers, making continuous buying and selling prices in specific securities
- the introduction of the Stock Exchange automated quotations (SEAQ) system

Since the introduction of SEAQ, dealing in stocks and shares takes place via the telephone in the firms' own dealing rooms, rather than face to face on the floor of the Exchange, or can be done through the Stock Exchange Electronic Trading Service (SETS), launched in 1997. The new systems also provide increased investor protection. All deals taking place via the Exchange's SEAQ system are recorded on a database which can be used to resolve disputes or to carry out investigations.

Members of the London Stock Exchange buy and sell shares on behalf of the public, as well as institutions such as pension funds or insurance companies. In return for transacting the deal, the broker will charge a commission, which is usually based upon the value of the transaction. The market makers, or wholesalers, in each security do not charge a commission for their services, but will quote the broker two prices, a price at which they will buy and a price at which they will sell. It is the middle of these two prices which is published in lists of Stock Exchange prices in newspapers.

Regulatory Bodies
The London Stock Exchange Ltd and the Securities and Futures Authority are the two regulatory bodies. They were formed under the provisions of the Financial Services Act 1986, which requires investment businesses to be authorised and regulated by a self-regulating organisation (SRO), of which the Securities and Futures Authority is one. The Act also requires business to be conducted through a recognised investment exchange (RIE). The London Stock Exchange is an RIE, regulating three main markets: UK equities, international equities and gilts. The changes to the financial regulatory system which are to be introduced in the next few years will affect the Stock Exchange's role as a regulatory body.

The Governing Board
The London Stock Exchange has its headquarters in London, and representative offices around the UK. At present there are about 264 member firms.

The governing board is responsible for overall policy and the strategic direction of the Exchange. The board consists of representatives drawn from listed companies, investors and other major users, elected at the annual general meeting, and the Government Broker, the Chief Executive and up to five senior executives of the Stock Exchange.

Chairman: Sir John Kemp-Welch
Chief Executive: G. Casey
Government Broker: I. Plenderleith (Deputy Chairman)
Other Board members: G. Allen, CBE; G. Allen; J. Bond; J. Howell; M. Marks; P. Meinertzhagen; S. Robertson; I. Salter; H. Sants; N. Sherlock; M. Wheatley

OMBUDSMEN

Independent ombudsman schemes have been set up for banks, building societies, insurance companies, financial institutions and independent financial advisers. They provide an independent and impartial method of resolving disputes that arise between a company and a customer. In most ombudsman schemes there is a council which appoints and supervises the Ombudsman. The Ombudsman Council is composed of people representing public and consumer interests and member companies. The schemes are funded in various ways: annual subscription from member companies, a levy on member companies according to the size of their assets, a charge for each complaint handled against a particular company, or a combination of these.

The Investment Ombudsman is responsible for resolving disputes that arise between a customer and a company regulated by IMRO. The Personal Investment Authority (PIA) Ombudsman is primarily responsible for resolving complaints against PIA members about personal investments.

The Pensions Ombudsman is appointed and operates under the Pension Schemes Act 1993 as amended by the Pensions Act 1995; he is responsible to Parliament. He investigates and decides complaints and disputes concerning occupational pension schemes, primarily alleged maladministration by the persons responsible for managing an occupational pension scheme. Personal pension complaints are normally dealt with only if outside the jurisdiction of the Personal Investment Authority.

FINANCIAL OMBUDSMEN SERVICE

South Quay Plaza, 183 Marsh Wall, London E14 9SR (Tel: 020-7964 1000; Fax: 020-7964 1001; Web: http://www.financial-ombudsman.org.uk)

The Financial Services and Markets Act will simplify the current arrangements by providing one Ombudsman to handle consumers' disputes, the Financial Ombudsman Service (FOS). The FOS has now been established but the following existing Ombudsman schemes continue to operate until N2 when the FOS will take over as the single Ombudsman: Office of the Investment Ombudsman; Personal Investment Authority Ombudsman Bureau; Securities and Futures Authority Complaints Bureau; Financial Services Authority Complaints Unit/Independent Investigator; Insurance Ombudsman Bureau; Office of the Banking Ombudsman; Office of the Building Societies Ombudsman Bureau and the Personal Insurance Arbitration Service.

INSURANCE OMBUDSMAN BUREAU

City Gate One, 135 Park Street, London SE1 9EA (Tel: 020-7928 4488; Web: http:// www.theiob.org.uk)

Insurance Ombudsman: W. Merricks

OFFICE OF THE BANKING OMBUDSMAN

70 Gray's Inn Road, London WC1X 8NB (Tel: 020-7404 9944; Web: http://www.obo.org.uk)

Banking Ombudsman: D. Thomas

OFFICE OF THE BUILDING SOCIETY OMBUDSMAN

South Quay Plaza, 183 Marsh Wall, London E14 9SR (Tel: 020-7931 0044; Fax: 020-7964 1001; Email: bldgsocombudsman@easynet.co.uk)
Building Societies Ombudsman: J. Thompson

OFFICE OF THE INVESTMENT OMBUDSMAN

South Quay Plaza, 183 Marsh Wall, London E14 9SR (Tel: 020-7796 3065; Fax: 020-7726 0574)

Investment Ombudsman: P. Dean, CBE

PENSION OMBUDSMAN

6th Floor, 11 Belgrave Road, London SW1V 1RB (Tel: 020-7834 9144)

Pensions Ombudsman: Dr J. T. Farrand

160 Business London

PIA OMBUDSMAN BUREAU

Hertsmere House, Hertsmere Road, London E14 4AB (Tel: 020-7216 0016)

Principal Ombudsman: A. J. Holland; **Ombudsmen:** R. Prior; M. Thomas

TAKEOVER PANEL

PO Box 226, The Stock Exchange Building, London, EC2P 2JX (Tel: 020-7242 6855)

The Takeover Panel was set up in 1968 in response to concern about practices unfair to shareholders in takeover bids for public and certain private companies. Its principal objective is to ensure equality of treatment, and fair opportunity for all shareholders to consider on its merits an offer that would result in the change of control of a company. It is a non-statutory body that operates the City code on take-overs and mergers.

The chairman, deputy chairmen and three lay members of the panel are appointed by the Bank of England. The remainder are representatives of the banking, insurance, investment, pension fund and accountancy professional bodies, the CBI, IMRO and the Stock Exchange.

BUSINESS AND THE WORKFORCE

BRITISH TRADE INTERNATIONAL

Kingsgate House, 66-74 Victoria Street, London SW1E 6SW (Tel: 020-7215 5000; Web: http://www.brittrade.com)

British Trade International has lead responsibility within government for international trade development and promotion. The Chief Executive reports to the Secretary of State for Trade and Industry and the Foreign and Commonwealth Secretary, and to the Board of British Trade International, chaired jointly by DTI and FCO Ministers. The department co-ordinates all trade support provided nationally in the UK, the commercial work of more than 200 diplomatic posts worldwide and trade development and promotion organised by the Business Link network in the English regions. A wide range of information, advice and assistance is available to exporters of goods and services and to British firms investing abroad. Support is provided for firms to take part in small and medium sized businesses that are new to exporting. The website provides detailed information and is linked to the TradeUK export sales leads service and national exporters database.

Chairmen: Brian Wilson, MP; Geoffrey Hoon, MP
Chief Executive: Sir David Wright

COMPANIES HOUSE LONDON

PO Box 29019, 21 Bloomsbury Street, London WC1B 3XD (Tel: 029-2038 0801; Fax: 029-2038 0900; Email: enquiries@companieshouse.gov.uk; Web: http://www.companies-house.gov.uk)

The key role of companies house is to provide company information to the public and to maintain the register of companies in the UK by adding, re-registering and striking off companies. There is an information pack available for those wishing to start up their own business and many further guidance booklets are available. The companies house website offers free access to searchable databases of disqualified directors and a companies name and address index. The head office of Companies House is in Cardiff and there are also regional offices in Birmingham, Edinburgh, Glasgow, Leeds and Manchester.

London Information Centre Manager: Lorraine Connelly

COMPETITION COMMISSION

New Court, 48 Carey Street, London WC2A 2JT (Tel: 020-7271 0100; Fax: 020-7271 0367; Email: info@competition-commission.gov.uk; Web: www.competition-commission.gov.uk)

The Commission was established in 1948 as the Monopolies and Restrictive Practices Commission (later the Monopolies and Mergers Commission); it became the Competition Commission in April 1999 under the Competition Act 1998. Its role is to investigate and report on matters which are referred to it by the Secretary of State for Trade and Industry or the Director-General of Fair Trading or, in the case of regulated utilities, by the appropriate regulator. It has no power to initiate its own investigations.

The Appeal Tribunals of the Competition Commission hears appeals against decisions by the Director-General of Fair Trading and the utility regulators in respect of the prohibitions on anti-competitive agreements and abuse of a dominant position to be introduced in March 2000 under the Competition Act 1998.

The Commission has a full-time chairman, two part-time deputy chairmen and about 35 reporting panel members to carry out investigations. All are appointed by the Secretary of State for Trade and Industry.

Chairman: Dr D. Morris, PhD.
Deputy Chairmen: P. G. Corbett, CBE; Ms D. Kingsmill,CBE
President, Appeal Tribunals: His Hon. Sir Christopher Bellamy, QC
Secretary: Miss P. Boys
Appeal Panel Registrar: Mr C. Dhanowa

CONFEDERATION OF BRITISH INDUSTRY (CBI)

London Region, Centre Point, 103 New Oxford Street, London WC1A 1DU (Tel: 020-7395 8195; Fax: 020-7379 0945; Web: http://www.cbi.org.uk).

The Confederation of British Industry is an independent non-party political body financed by industry and commerce. It exists primarily to ensure that the Government understands the intentions needs and problems of British Business. The Governing body of the CBI is the 200-strong Council, which meets four times a year in London under the Chairmanship of the President. There are also 13 regional councils and offices one of which concentrates purely on London. Currently, CBI London is focusing on the following issues: promoting the City of London internationally to enhance its position in the face of mounting competition; promoting the interest of its members in Brussels; helping businesses to attain the highest possible environmental

BUSINESS REGISTRATIONS AND DEREGISTRATIONS* (000s)

	London			UK		
	1995	1996	1997	1995	1996	1997
Registrations	32.7	34.1	37.2	164.0	168.2	182.6
Deregistration	29.1	29.3	28.3	173.2	165.1	164.5
Net change	3.6	4.7	8.9	−9.3	−3.1	18.1

* Enterprises registered for VAT
Source: Focus on London '99, Office for National Statistics © Crown Copyright 1999

performance without cost rising unduly; encouraging a positive approach to London's manufacturing industries to ensure its continued growth.

President: Sir Iain Vallance
Director-General: Digby Jones
Secretary: Peter Forder

CBI London Staff
Director: Jane Calvet-Lee
Assistant Directors: Howard Dolan, Wendy Simpson, David Tinkler, John Walter

LONDON FIRST/LONDON FIRST CENTRE

1 Hobhouse Court, Suffolk Street, SW1Y 4HH (Tel: 020-7665 1500; Fax: 020-7665 1501;
Email: mail@london-first.co.uk;
Web: http://www.london-first.co.uk).

London First was set up on the early 1990s as a vehicle to mobilise business leaders to improve and promote London. Funded entirely by 300 private sector organisations and most of the capital's high and further education institutions, London First aims to engage business leaders in decision-making about London's future. Its core activities include campaigning for improved transport and environment, promoting London as the Millennium City and increasing employability of Londoners. London First works in partnership with Business, local government, voluntary organisations and other decision-makers to ensure London's position as the leading world class city. Its sister organisation is the London First Centre, the inward investment agency for the capital. In over five years of operation, London First Centre has helped over 350 companies from 28 countries around the world locate or expand in the capital. London First's principal sponsors are Argent Group, BAA, British Airways, BT, Canary Wharf plc, Clifford Chance, Ernst and Young, ExCel, KPMG, Land Securities, Nelson Bakewell, Paddington Basin Developments, Regalian Properties, Resolution Property and Thames Water.

Chief Executive: Stephen O'Brien
Membership: Ian Handley
Director of Communications: Patrick Kerr
Sub-regions and Skilling: Jo Valentine
Transport & Environment: Irving Yass
Inward Investment: Michael Charlton

LABOUR FORCE

COMPONENTS OF THE LABOUR FORCE*

	Employees	Self-employed	Others in Employment†	ILO Unemployed‡	Total Labour Force (000s)
Males					
London					
1988	74.0	16.7	1.0	8.3	1,992
1998	73.6	17.1	0.6	8.7	1,934
UK					
1988	73.9	15.0	2.1	9.0	16,299
1998	77.3	15.0	0.9	6.8	15,997
Females					
London					
1988	85.3	6.1	1.0	7.6	1,500
1998	83.2	8.6	0.9	7.3	1,555
UK					
1988	88.3	6.6	1.7	8.4	12,046
1998	86.8	6.8	1.1	5.3	12,716

*At Spring each year
†Covers people on government-supported employment and training schemes, unpaid family workers (1998 only) and those who did not state their employment status (1998 only).
‡ILO Unemployed = An International Labour Organisation recommended measure, used in household surveys such as the Labour Force Survey, which counts as unemployed those aged 16 or over who are without a job, are available to start work within the next two weeks and who have been seeking a job in the last four weeks, or who are waiting to start a job already obtained.
Source: Focus on London '99, Office for National Statistics © Crown Copyright 1999

EMPLOYEES WORKING PART-TIME †‡° (PERCENTAGES)

	Inner London	Outer London	Total London	UK
Males				
1988	5.9	4.9	5.3	4.7
1998	10.9	9.2	9.8	8.1
Females				
1988	29.5	33.3	32.0	42.8
1998	27.6	37.1	33.7	44.1

†Based on respondents' own definition of part-time
‡At Spring each year
°Basis for calculation of percentages excludes people who do not state whether they worked full or part-time.
Source: Focus on London '99, Office for National Statistics © Crown Copyright 1999

OCCUPATIONS OF EMPLOYEES, SPRING 1998 (PERCENTAGES AND 000s)

	Males		Females	
	London†	UK	London†	UK
Managers & Administrators	21.8	19.0	14.8	10.5
Professional, Associate Professional & Technical	26.4	19.8	25.1	19.9
Clerical & Secretarial	10.5	8.0	28.8	26.0
Craft & related	11.5	17.3	1.1	2.3
Personal & Protective Services	8.9	7.6	13.8	16.7
Sales	5.6	5.4	8.5	11.7
Plant & other Machine Operatives	7.6	15.0	1.5	4.2
Other	7.6	7.9	6.4	8.7
All Employees (000s)‡	1,424	12,368	1,294	11,040

†Resident in London
‡Includes those who did not state their occupation, but percentages are based on totals that exclude this group.
Source: Focus on London '99, Office for National Statistics © Crown Copyright 1999

GROSS WEEKLY EARNINGS*, APRIL 1998

		Average Gross Weekly Earnings	% Earning Under £200	£250	£350	£460
London						
Males	Manual	366.7	9.2	21.1	53.1	78.0
	Non-manual	645.9	3.5	8.6	23.2	41.2
Females	Manual	242.1	38.5	62.3	88.6	96.6
	Non-manual	420.1	5.6	15.4	44.0	69.2
Great Britain						
Males	Manual	328.5	12.4	29.3	64.4	86.4
	Non-manual	506.1	6.3	13.9	33.2	55.3
Females	Manual	210.8	53.3	75.4	94.3	98.6
	Non-manual	330.1	17.3	36.7	65.0	84.3

* Data relates to earnings of full-time employees on adult rates whose pay for the survey period was not affected by absence
Source: Focus on London '99, Office for National Statistics © Crown Copyright 1999

EARNINGS OF LONDONERS BY BOROUGH*

London Boroughs	Average gross annual earnings (£)	Average hourly earnings excl. overtime (£)	Increase in total average weekly pay April 98–April 99 (%)
London Average	28,812	13.38	3.1
City of London	43,288	19.01	−0.8
Barking and Dagenham	23,626	10.41	–
Barnet	22,041	10.81	2.9
Bexley	21,089	10.29	−1.3
Brent	21,933	11.12	0.7
Bromley	20,707	11.04	11.1
Camden	29,732	14.35	6.6
Croydon	21,832	10.70	5.7
Ealing	23,339	11.27	5.4
Enfield	20,545	9.95	−0.1
Greenwich	22,006	10.52	−1.3
Hackney	–	14.83	2.2
Hammersmith and Fulham	27,095	13.86	1.8
Haringey	21,260	10.31	3.9
Harrow	22,682	11.55	4.8
Havering	18,498	8.57	1.2
Hillingdon	28,830	12.34	2.6
Hounslow	23,908	12.08	5.0
Islington	26,155	12.68	−2.2
Kensington and Chelsea	–	13.22	4.4
Kingston upon Thames	22,356	10.96	−4.9
Lambeth	27,257	13.11	1.1
Lewisham	22,655	11.58	11.3
Merton	20,698	9.86	−8.0
Newham	20,362	10.07	−0.6
Redbridge	–	10.18	7.3
Richmond Upon Thames	–	–	6.4
Southwark	26,282	12.82	3.0
Sutton	–	11.52	10.0
Tower Hamlets	36,511	16.01	6.6
Waltham Forest	19,859	10.00	1.3
Wandsworth	24,525	11.65	4.7
City of Westminster	35,080	15.53	5.9

* Data relates to earnings of full-time employees on adult rates whose pay for the survey period was not affected by absence
Source: New Earning Survey 1999, Office for National Statistics © Crown Copyright 1999

TRADE UNIONS AND EMPLOYER'S ASSOCIATIONS

There are over 20 million people in paid employment in the UK and almost 7 million workers belong to unions affiliated to the Trades Union Congress. Trade Unions fulfil a number of different functions including: giving advice to members with work-related problems, negotiating with employers in regard to pay and conditions, helping members take cases to employment tribunals or courts and fight discrimination and help promote equal opportunities. Unions are funded by the contributions of their members.

The following list comprises trade unions based in London which are affiliated to the Trades Union Congress. Unions marked * are non-TUC affiliated.

TRADE UNIONS

*British Dental Association
64 Wimpole Street, London, W1M 8AL (Tel: 020-7935 0875; Email: enquiries@bda-dentistry.org.uk)
Chief Executive: J. M. G. Hunt

*Chartered Institute of Journalists
2 Dock Offices, Surrey Quays Road, London, SE16 2XU (Tel: 020-7252 1187; Fax: 020-7252 2302; Email: memberservices@ioj.co.uk; Web: http://www.ioj.co.uk)
General Secretary: C. Underwood

*Prison Governors Association
Room 718, Horseferry House, Dean Ryle Street, London, SW1P 2AW (Tel: 020-7217 8591; Fax: 020-7217 8923)
General Secretary: D. Roddan

*Royal College of Midwives
15 Mansfield Street, London, W1M 0BE (Tel: 020-7312 3535)
General Secretary: Mrs K. Davis

*Society of Authors
84 Drayton Gardens, London, SW10 9SB (Tel: 020-7373 6642; Fax: 020-7373 5768; Email: authorsoc@writers.org.uk;
Web: http://www.writers.org.uk/society)
General Secretary: M. Le Fanu, OBE

Amalgamated Engineering and Electrical Union (AEEU)
Hayes Court, West Common Road, Bromley, Kent, BR2 7AU (Tel: 020-8462 7755; Fax: 020-8315 8234; Web: http://www.aeeu.org.uk)
General Secretary: Sir Ken Jackson

Association of First Division Civil Servants (FDA)
2 Caxton Street, London, SW1H 0QH (Tel: 020-7343 1111; Fax: 020-7343 1105;
Email: head-office@fda.org.uk;
Web: http://www.fda.org.uk)
General Secretary: J. Baume

Association of Flight Attendants
United Airlines Cargo Centre, Shoreham Road East, Heathrow Airport, Hounslow, Middx, TW6 3RD (Tel: 020-8276 9723)
President: K. Creighan

Association of Magisterial Officers
231 Vauxhall Bridge Road, London, SW1V 1EG (Tel: 020-7630 5455)

Association Society of Locomotive Engineers and Firemen (ASLEF)
9 Arkwright Road, London, NW3 6AB (Tel: 020-7317 8600)
General Secretary: M. D. Rix

Association of Teachers and Lecturers
7 Northumberland Street, London, WC2N 5DA (Tel: 020-7930 6441; Fax: 020-7930 1359;
Email: info@atl.org.uk)
General Secretary: P. Smith

Association of University Teachers
Egmont House, 25-31 Tavistock Place, London, WC1H 9UT (Tel: 020-7670 9700; Fax: 020-7670 9799; Email: hq@aut.org.uk;
Web: http://www.aut.org.uk)
General Secretary: D. Triesman

British Actors' Equity Association
Guild House, Upper St Martin's Lane, London, WC2H 9EG (Tel: 020-7379 6000)
General Secretary: I. McGarry

British Air Line Pilots Association (BALPA)
81 New Road, Harlington, Hayes, Middx, UB3 5BG (Tel: 020-8476 4000; Fax: 020-8476 4077;
Email: balpa@balpa.org.uk;
Web: http://www.balpa.org.uk)
General Secretary: C. Darke

British Orthoptic Society
Tavistock House North, Tavistock Square, London, WC1H 9HX (Tel: 020-7387 7992)
Executive Secretary: Mrs A. Armour

Broadcasting, Entertainment, Cinematograph and Theatre Union (BECTU)
111 Wardour Street, London, W1V 4AY (Tel: 020-7437 8506; Fax: 020-7437 8268)
General Secretary: R. Bolton

Chartered Society of Physiotherapy
14 Bedford Row, London, WC1R 4ED (Tel: 020-7306 6666)
Chief Executive: P. Gray

Communication Workers Union
150 The Broadway, Wimbledon, London, SW19 1RX (Tel: 020-8971 7200; Fax: 020-8971 7300;
Email: cproctor@cwu.org;
Web: http://www.cwu.org.uk)
General Secretary: D. Hodgson

Community and District Nursing Association
Thames Valley University, 8 University House, Ealing Green, London, W5 5ED (Tel: 020-8231 2776)
Hon. General Secretary: Ms A. Keen

Connect
30 St George's Road, London, SW19 4BD (Tel: 020-8971 6000; Fax: 020-8971 6002;
Email: eunion@connectuk.org;

Trade Unions

Web: http://www.connect.org)
General Secretary: S. Petch

Fire Brigades Union
Bradley House, 68 Coombe Road, Kingston upon Thames, Surrey, KT2 7AE (Tel: 020-8541 1765; Fax: 020-8546 5187)
General Secretary: A. Gilchrist

GMB
22-24 Worple Road, London, SW19 4DD (Tel: 020-8947 3131)
General Secretary: J. Edmonds

Guinness Staff Association
Sun Works Cottage, Park Royal Brewery, London, NW10 7RR (Tel: 020-8963 5249; Fax: 020-8963 5184)
Acting Chair: W. Wardell

Institution of Professionals, Managers and Specialists
75-79 York Road, London, SE1 7AQ (Tel: 020-7902 6600; Fax: 020-7902 6667; Email: ipmshq@ipms.org.uk; Web: http://www.ipms.org.uk)
General Secretary: P. Noon

Iron and Steel Trades Confederation
Swinton House, 324 Gray's Inn Road, London, WC1X 8DD (Tel: 020-7387 6691)
General Secretary: M. J. Leahy

Manufacturing, Science and Finance (MSF)
MSF Centre, 33-37 Moreland Street, London, EC1V 8HA (Tel: 020-7505 3000; Fax: 020-7505 3030; Web: http://www.msf.org.uk)
General Secretary: R. Lyons

Musicians' Union
60-62 Clapham Road, London, SW9 0JJ (Tel: 020-7582 5566; Fax: 020-7582 9805; Email: info@musiciansunion.org.uk; Web: http://www.musiciansunion.org.uk)
General Secretary: D. Scard

NASUWT (National Association of Schoolmasters/Union of Women Teachers)
5 King Street, London, WC2E 8HN (Tel: 020-7420 9670; Email: nigel.degruchy@nasuwt.org.uk; Web: http://www.teachersunion.org.uk)
General Secretary: N. de Gruchy

NATFHE (University and College Lecturers Union)
27 Britannia Street, London, WC1X 9JP (Tel: 020-7837 3636; Fax: 020-7837 4403; Web: http://www.natfhe.org.uk)
General Secretary: P. Mackney

National Association of Probation Officers
4 Chivalry Road, London, SW11 1HT (Tel: 020-7223 4887)
General Secretary: Ms J. McKnight

National League of the Blind and Disabled
2 Tenterden Road, London, N17 8BE (Tel: 020-8808 6030)
General Secretary: J. Mann

National Union of Insurance Workers
27 Old Gloucester Street, London, WC1N 3AF (Tel: 020-7405 6798)
Secretary General: K. Perry

National Union of Journalists (NUJ)
Acorn House, 314-320 Gray's Inn Road, London, WC1X 8DP (Tel: 020-7278 7916; Fax: 020-7837 8143; Email: acorn.house@nuj.org.uk)
General Secretary: J. Foster

National Union of Marine, Aviation and Shipping Transport Officers
Oceanair House, 750-760 High Road, London, E11 3BB (Tel: 020-8989 6677)
General Secretary: B. D. Orrell

National Union of Rail, Maritime and Transport Workers (RMT)
Unity House, 205 Euston Road, London, NW1 2BL (Tel: 020-7387 4771)
General Secretary: J. Knapp

National Union of Teachers (NUT)
Hamilton House, Mabledon Place, London, WC1H 9BD (Tel: 020-7388 6191; Fax: 020-7387 8458; Web: http://www.teachers.org.uk)
General Secretary: D. McAvoy

Prison Officers' Association
Cronin House, 245 Church Street, London, N9 9HW (Tel: 020-8803 0255; Fax: 020-8803 1761)
General Secretary: B. Caton

Public and Commercial Services Union (PCS)
160 Falcon Road, London, SW11 2LN (Tel: 020-7924 2727; Fax: 020-7924 1847; Web: http://www.pcs.org.uk)
Joint General Secretaries: B. Reamsbotton; J. Sheldon

Society of Chiropodists and Podiatrists
53 Welbeck Street, London, W1M 7HE (Tel: 020-7486 3381)
Chief Executive: Ms H. B. De Lyon

Society of Radiographers
2 Carriage Row, 183 Eversholt Street, London, NW1 1BU (Tel: 020-7391 4533)
General Secretary: S. Evans

Transport and General Workers' Union (TGWU)
Transport House, 16 Palace Street, London, SW1E 5JD (Tel: 020-7828 7788)
General Secretary: W. Morris

Transport Salaried Staffs' Association
Walkden House, 10 Melton Street, London, NW1 2EJ (Tel: 020-7387 2101)
General Secretary: R. A. Rosser

UNiFI
1B Amity Grove, London, SW20 0LG (Tel: 020-8946 9151)
Joint General Secretaries: E. Sweeney; R. Murphy

Union of Construction, Allied Trades and Technicians (UCATT)
UCATT House, 177 Abbeville Road, London, SW4 9RL (Tel: 020-7622 2442)
General Secretary: G. Brumwell

UNISON
1 Mabledon Place, London, WC1H 9AJ (Tel: 020-7388 2366; Fax: 020-7387 6692;
Web: http://www.unison.org.uk)
General Secretary: R. Bickerstaffe

Writers' Guild of Great Britain
430 Edgware Road, London, W2 1EH (Tel: 020-7723 8074; Fax: 020-7706 2413;
Email: postie@wggb.demon.co.uk;
Web: http://www.writers.org.uk/guild)
Acting General Secretary: J. Ecclestone

EMPLOYERS' ASSOCIATIONS

The following list comprises employers' and trade associations which are based in London.

Advertising Association
Abford House, 15 Wilton Road, London, SW1V 1NJ (Tel: 020-7828 2771; Fax: 020-7931 0376; E-mail: aa@adassoc.org.uk; Web: http://www.adassoc.org.uk)
Director-General: A. Brown

Association of British Insurers
51 Gresham Street, London, EC2V 7HQ (Tel: 020-7600 3333)
Director-General: M. Francisbrew

Brewers and Licensed Retailers Association
42 Portman Square, London, W1H 0BB (Tel: 020-7486 4831)
Chief Executive Officer: R. Hayward, OBE

BRF (British Road Federation)
Pillar House, 194-202 Old Kent Road, London, SE1 5TG (Tel: 020-7703 9769; Fax: 020-7701 0029; E-mail: brf@brf.uk.com; Web: http://www.brf.co.uk)
Director: R. Diment

British Apparel and Textile Confederation Ltd
5 Portland Place, London, W1N 3AA (Tel: 020-7636 7788)
Director-General: J. R. Wilson

British Bankers' Association
Pinners Hall, 105-108 Old Broad Street, London, EC2N 1EX (Tel: 020-7216 8800; Fax: 020-7216 881; Web: http://www.bba.org.uk)
Director-General: T. P. Sweeney

British Clothing Industry Association Ltd
5 Portland Place, London, W1N 3AA (Tel: 020-7636 7788)
Director: J. R. Wilson

British Office Systems and Stationery Federation
6 Wimpole Street, London, W1M 8AS (Tel: 020-7637 7692)
Chief Executive: K. Davies

British Plastics Federation
6 Bath Place, Rivington Street, London, EC2A 3JE (Tel: 020-7457 5000)
Director-General: P. Davis, OBE

British Ports Association
Africa House, 64-78 Kingsway, London, WC2B 6AH (Tel: 020-7242 1200; Fax: 020-7405 1069; E-mail: info@britishports.org.uk)
Director: D. Whitehead

British Printing Industries Federation
11 Bedford Row, London, WC1R 4DX (Tel: 020-7915 8300; Fax: 020-7405 7784; E-mail: info@bpif.org.uk; Web: http://www.bpif.org.uk)
Chief Executive: T. P. E. Machin

British Property Federation
7th Floor, 1 Warwick Row, London, SW1E 5ER (Tel: 020-7828 0111; Fax: 020-7834 3442; E-mail: info@bpf.org.uk; Web: http://www.bpf.org.uk)
Director-General: W. A. McKee

British Retailers Consortium
5 Grafton Street, London, W1X 3LB (Tel: 020-7647 1500)
Director-General: Ms A. Robinson

British Rubber Manufacturers' Association Ltd
6 Bath Place, Rivington Strteet, London, EC2A 3JE (Tel: 020-7457 5040; Fax: 020-7972 9008)
Director: A. J. Dorken

Chamber of Shipping Ltd
Carthusian Court, 12 Carthusian Street, London, EC1M 6EZ (Tel: 020-7417 8400)
Director-General: Vice-Adm. Sir Christopher Morgan, KBE

Chemical Industries Association Ltd
Kings Buildings, Smith Square, London, SW1P 3JJ (Tel: 020-7834 3399; Fax: 020-7834 4469)
Director-General: Dr E. G. Finer

Commercial Radio Companies Association
77 Shaftesbury Avenue, London, W1V 7AD (Tel: 020-7306 2603)
Chief Executive: P. Brown

Confederation of Passenger Transport UK
Imperial House, 15-19 Kingsway, London, WC2B 6UN (Tel: 020-7240 3131; Fax: 020-7240 6565; E-mail: cpt@cpt-uk.org;
Web: http://www.cpt-uk.org/cpt)
Director-General: Mrs V. Palmer, OBE

Construction Confederation
Construction House, 56-64 Leonard Street, London, EC2A 4JX (Tel: 020-7608 5000)
Chief Executive: I. A. Deslandes

Construction Products Association
26 Store Street, London, WC1E 7BT (Tel: 020-7323 3770; Fax: 020-7323 0307; E-mail: enquiries@const-prod.org.uk; Web: http://www.constprod.org.uk)
Chief Executive Officer: M. G. Ankers, FRSA

Employers' Associations 167

Dairy Industry Federation
19 Cornwall Terrace, London, NW1 4QP (Tel: 020-7486 7244)
Director-General: J. Begg

Engineering Employers' Federation
Broadway House, Tothill Street, London, SW1H 9NQ (Tel: 020-7222 7777; Fax: 020-7222 2782; E-mail: enquiries@eef-fed.org.uk; Web: http://www.eef.org.uk)
Director-General: M. J. Temple

Federation of Bakers
6 Catherine Street, London, WC2B 5JW (Tel: 020-7420 7190)
Executive Director: Mrs A. Linehan

Federation of British Electrotechnical and Allied Manufacturers' Associations (BEAMA)
Westminster Tower, 3 Albert Embankment, London, SE1 7SL (Tel: 020-7793 3000; Fax: 020-7793 3003; E-mail: info@beama.org.uk; Web: http://www.beama.org.uk)
Director-General: A. A. Bullen

Federation of Master Builders
Gordon Fisher House, 14-15 Great James Street, London, WC1N 3DP (Tel: 020-7242 7583; Fax: 020-7405 0854; E-mail: ian.davis@fmb.org.uk; Web: http://www.fmb.org.uk)
Director-General: I. Davis

Finance and Leasing Association
15-19 Imperial House, Kingway, London, (Tel: 020-7836 6511)
Director-General: M. A. Hall, MVO

Food and Drink Federation
Catherine Street, London, WC2B 5JJ (Tel: 020-7836 2460; Fax: 020-7836 0580)
Director-General: M. P. Mackenzie

Management Consultancies Association
11 West Halkin Street, London, SW1X 8JL (Tel: 020-7235 3897)
Executive Director: B. Petter

National Farmers' Union (NFU)
164 Shaftesbury Avenue, London, WC2H 8HL (Tel: 020-7331 7200)
Director-General: R. Macdonald

National Federation of Retail Newsagents
Yeoman House, Sekforde Street, London, EC1R 0HD (Tel: 020-7253 4225; Fax: 020-7250 0927; E-mail: info@nfrn.org.uk; Web: http://www.nfrn.org.uk)
Chief Executive: R. Clarke

Newspaper Publishers Association Ltd
34 Southwark Bridge Road, London, SE1 9EU (Tel: 020-7207 2200)
Director: S. Oram

Newspaper Society
Bloomsbury House, 74-77 Great Russell Street, London, WC1B 3DA (Tel:020-7636 7014; Fax: 020-7631 5119; Web: http://www.newspapersoc.org.uk)
Director: D. Newell

Publishers Association
1 Kingsway, London, WC2B 6XF (Tel: 020-7565 7474)
Chief Executive: R. Williams, OBE

Society of British Aerospace Companies Ltd
Duxbury House, 60 Petty France, London, SW1H 9EU (Tel: 020-7227 1000)
Director-General: D. Marshall

Society of Motor Manufacturers and Traders Ltd
Forbes House, Halkin Street, London, SW1X 7DS (Tel: 020-7235 7000)
Chief Executive: C. McGowan

Timber Trade Federation
Clareville House, 26-27 Oxendon Street, London, SW1Y 4EL (Tel: 020-7839 1891; Fax: 020-7930 0094; E-mail: ttf@ttf.co.uk; Web: http://www.ttf.co.uk)
Acting Director-General: P. C. Martin

UK Offshore Operators Association Ltd
1st Floor, 30 Buckingham Gate, London, SW1E 6NN (Tel: 020-7802 2400)
Director-General: J. May

UK Petroleum Industry Association Ltd
9 Kingsway, London (Tel: 020-7240 0289; Fax: 020-7379 3102; E-mail: ukpia@aol.com; Web: http://www.ukpia.co)
Director-General: Dr M. A. Frend

ADVISORY, CONCILIATION AND ARBITRATION SERVICE

Brandon House, 180 Borough High Street, London SE1 1LW (Tel: 020-7210 3613; Fax: 020-7210 3708) Regional Office - London and the South East, Clifton House, 83-117 Euston Road, London NW1 2RB (Tel: 020-7396 5100)

The Advisory, Conciliation and Arbitration Service (ACAS) was set up under the Employment Protection Act 1975 (the provisions now being found in the Trade Union and Labour Relations (Consolidation) Act 1992). ACAS is directed by a Council consisting of a full-time chairman and part-time employer, trade union and independent members, all appointed by the Secretary of State for Trade and Industry. The functions of the Service are to promote the improvement of industrial relations in general, to provide facilities for conciliation, mediation and arbitration as means of avoiding and resolving industrial disputes, and to provide advisory and information services on industrial relations matters to employers, employees and their representatives.

Chairman: J. Hougham, CBE
Chief Conciliator: D. Evans

TRADES UNION CONGRESS

Congress House, 23-28 Great Russell Street, London WC1B 3LS (Tel: 020-7636 4030; Email: info@tuc.org.uk; Web: http://www.tuc.org.uk)

The Trades Union Congress was founded in 1868 and is an independent association of trade unions. The TUC promotes the rights and welfare of those in work and helps the unemployed; helps its member unions promote membership in new areas and industries; campaigns for rights at work for all employees; carries out research on employment-related issues and brings unions together with a view to drawing up common policies.

TRAINING AND ENTERPRISE

BRITISH CHAMBERS OF COMMERCE

Manning House, 22 Carlisle Street, London SW1P 1JA (Tel: 020-7565 2000; E-mail: administrator@chambers.org.uk; Web: http://www.britishchambers.org.uk) British Chambers of Commerce are the accreditation and regulation service for Chambers of Commerce in the UK, ensuring that they provide high standards of support to businesses.

London Chamber of Commerce and Industry
33 Queen Street, London EC4R 1AP (Tel: 020-7248 4444; Fax 020-7489 0391; E-mail: lc@londonchamber.co.uk; Web: http://www.londonchamber.co.uk) London Chamber of Commerce and Industry states its mission is 'to help London businesses succeed by promoting their interests and expanding their opportunities as members of a world-wide business network'. It is independent of government and has a wide membership of London businesses.

Barnet Chamber of Commerce
23-35 Hendon Lane, Finchley, London N3 1RT (Tel: 020-8343 3833; Fax: 020-8343 3455; Email: barnet@nlcc.co.uk)

Bexley and Greenwich Chamber of Commerce
1 Morden Wharf Road, Tunnel Avenue, Greenwich, London SE10 0NU (Tel: 020-8293 3456)

Croydon and South London Chamber of Commerce and Industry
1 Wandle Road, Croydon CR9 (Tel: 020-8680 2165; Fax: 020-8688 4587; Email: info@croydonchamber.freeserve.co.uk)

Ealing Chamber of Commerce
Rove Mews, 42 The Grove, Ealing, London W5 5LH (Tel: 020-8840 6332)

East London Chamber of Commerce
Boardman House, 64 Broadway, London E15 1NT (Tel: 020-8432 0551)

Enfield Chamber of Commerce
201 Hertford Road, Enfield, Middx. EN3 5JH (Tel: 020-8443 4464; Fax: 020-8443 3822; Email: enfield@nlcc.co.uk)

Hackney Chamber of Commerce
3rd Floor, Netil House, 1-7 Westgate Street, London E8 3RL (Tel: 020-8356 4092; Fax: 020-8356 4089; Email: enquiries@hackney chamber.co.uk)

Haringey Chamber of Commerce
Lee Valley Technopark, Ashley Road, Tottenham, London N17 9LN (Tel: 020-8880 4235; Fax: 020-888-4237; Email: haringey@nlcc.co.uk)

Islington Chamber of Commerce
64 Essex Road, London N1 8LR (Tel: 020-7226 1593; Fax: 020-7226 8437; Email: admin@islchamber.org.uk)

Kensington and Chelsea Chamber of Commerce
Lodge House, 69 Beaufort Street, London SW3 5AH (Tel: 020-7795 0304; Fax: 020-7795 0306)

Kingston Chamber of Commerce
1st Floor, Cheltenham House, 22 Eden Street, Kingston upon Thames, Surrey KT1 1EP (Tel: 020-8296 9595; Fax: 020-8974 8770)

Merton Chamber of Commerce
5th Floor, Tuition House, 27-37 St George's Road, Wimbledon, London SW19 4EU (Tel: 020-8944 5501; Fax: 020-8286 2552)

Newham Chamber of Commerce
(Tel: 020-8534 0363; Fax: 020-8257 2552)

North London Chamber of Commerce
Dumayne House, 1 Fox Lane, Palmers Green, London N13 4AB (Tel: 020-8882 0180)

Waltham Forest Chamber of Commerce
113 George Lane, London E18 1AB (Tel: 020-8989 5164)

Wandsworth Chamber of Commerce
125 Upper Richmond Road, Putney, London SW15 2TL (Tel: 020-7780 6541; Fax: 020-7780 6501; Email: wcc@bllsw.co.uk)

West London Chamber of Commerce
West London Centre, 15/21 Staines Road, Hounslow, Middx. TW3 3HA (Tel: 020-8577 1010; Fax: 020-8570 9969)

Worcester Park and District Chamber of Commerce
105 Central Road, Worcester Park, Surrey KT4 8DY (Tel: 020-8296 0444)

BUSINESS LINK

Business Link offers support services to businesses through a network of local advice centres. They offer information and advice on the following: developing of business; selling and marketing, conducting business abroad, Information Communications Technology and E-commerce; money and financial management, legal issues and regulation and starting up a business. A list of the Business Link advice centres in the London area is given below.

Brent Business Venture
38-40 High Street, Harlesden, London, NW10 4LS (Tel: 020-8901 5030; Fax: 020-8961 7347; E-mail@bbv.co.uk; Web: http://www.bbv.co.uk)
Executive Director: J. Stoll

Haringey
Unit 141, Haringey Technopark, Ashley Road, London, N17 9LN (Tel: 020-8880 4475; Fax: 020-8880 4476; E-mail: info@londoneast.businesslink.co.uk; Web: http://www.londoneast.businesslink.co.uk)

London Central
3rd Floor, Centre Point, 103 New Oxford Street, London, WC1A 1DP (Tel: 020-7316 1000; Fax: 020-7316 1001; E-mail: hotline@bllc.co.uk;

Training and Enterprise   169

Web: http://www.bllc.co.uk)
Chief Executive: Ms V. Thompson

London City Partners
78 Great Eastern Street, London, EC2A 3RF (Tel: 020-7324 2700; Fax: 020-7739 2989;
E-mail: info@city-partners.co.uk;
Web: http://www.city-partners.co.uk)
Chief Executive: Miss E. Evans

London East
Boardman House, 64 Broadway, Stratford, London, E15 1NT (Tel: 07000-40 50 60;
E-mail: info@londoneast.businesslink.co.uk;
Web: http://www.londoneast.businesslink.co.uk)

London North
Dumayne House, 1 Fox Lane, Palmers Green, London, N13 4AB (Tel: 020-8447 9422; Fax: 020-8882 6978;
E-mail: post@nltec.co.uk; Web: http://www.nltec.co.uk)
Executive Director: D. Croxson

London North West
Kirkfield House, 118-120 Station Road, Harrow, Middx, HA1 2RL (Tel: 020-8901 5000; Fax: 020-8901 5007; E-mail: enquiry@bllnw.co.uk;
Web: http://www.bllnw.co.uk)

London South
Lancaster House, 7 Elmfield Road, Bromley, Kent, BR1 1LT (Tel: 020-8315 6666; Fax: 020-8315 6686;
E-mail: info@solotec.co.uk;
Web: http://www.blls.co.uk)
Chief Executive: J. Saunders

London South West
125 Upper Richmond Road, Putney, London, SW15 2TL (Tel: 020-8780 6500; Fax: 020-8780 6501;
E-mail: info@bllsw.co.uk;
Web: http://www.londonsw-businesslink.co.uk)
Chief Executive: D. Whiddett

London West
West London Centre, 15-21 Staines Road, Hounslow, TW3 3HA (Tel: 020-8577 9119; Fax: 020-8814 3431;
E-mail: info@westlondon.com;
Web: http://www.londonwest.businesslink.co.uk)
Chief Executive: J. Olaofe

GREATER LONDON ENTERPRISE (GLE)

28 Park Street, London SE1 9EQ (Tel: 020-7403 0300; Fax: 020-7403 1742; E-mail: contact@gle.org.uk)
Founded in 1983, GLE is a profitable, commercially run Company, jointly owned by all 33 London Borough Councils. GLE provides services to aid the economic development and regeneration of industries. Services are provided to public, private and voluntary sector clients in London and internationally. The GLE Group includes a number of subsidiaries. They are: GLE Development Capital; GLE Invoice Finance; GLE Properties; GLE Strategies; GLE International and the Joint Venture Unit; GLE Small Business Services.

LONDON ENTERPRISE AGENCY (LEntA)

4 Snow Hill, EC1A 2BS (Tel: 020-7236 3000; Fax: 020-7329 0226; Email: info@lenta.co.uk;
Web: http://www.lenta.co.uk)

The key function of LEntA is to assist large companies to work together on issues of job creation and to anticipate social and economic change. This is achieved by providing a business planning service and by establishing projects that examine and provide strategies to tackle various social and economic issues, such as homelessness, racial equality, and unemployment. LEntA provides support and guidance to new small businesses and offers many services including training and assistance to secure the support of private investors.

Chair: Sarah Anderson
Vice Chair: Trevor Evans, Marks & Spencer
Board: Stephen Serpell, BT; David Springer, Lloyds/TSB Bank; Neil Makin, Cadbury Schweppes; Dominic Fry, J Sainsbury; Mark Peters, Diageo; Cliff Grantham, Unilever; David Shelley, HSBC; Alan Coates, United Biscuits; Michael Hamilton, J. Laing; Simon Ward, Whitbread.
Chief Executive: Brian Wright

TRAINING AND ENTERPRISE COUNCILS (TECs)

Some of the most prominent of local institutions in England and Wales have been the Training and Enterprise Councils (TECs). TECs are independent companies comprised of a board of directors, two-thirds of which must come from senior management or executive positions within other private companies. The priorities of TECs include: establishing a world-class labour force and creating a society which fosters learning and the skills necessary to create successful businesses and people; supporting competition in business via investment in innovation and the supervision and development of people; increasing the use of business support services via Business Links and creating and maintaining effective local economies with strategic partners, e.g., local authorities. TECs are involved in co-ordinating youth and adult programmes directed at training and work placements. In 2001, the Government is planning to introduce the Learning Skills Council and a network of local councils to replace the training and workplace development functions of TECs. The enterprise role of TECs will be taken up by the Department of Trade and Industries new Small Business Service network.

AZTEC

Manorgate House, 2 Manorgate Road, Kingston KT2 7AL (Tel: 020-8547 3934; Fax: 020-8547 3884;
Email: info@aztec-iip.co.uk;
Web: http://www.aztec-iip.co.uk)
Chair: Lister Fielding
Chief Executive: Ian Parkes
Area: Kingston, Merton, Wandsworth.

FOCUS CENTRAL LONDON

Centrepoint, 103 New Oxford Street, London WC1A 1DR (Tel: 020-7896 8484; Fax 020-7896 8686;
Web: http://www.focusnet.uk.com)

Chair: Clive Strowger
Chief Executive: Alan Calder
Area: Camden, City, Hackney, Hammersmith and Fulham, Islington, Kensington and Chelsea, Lambeth, Southwark, Westminster

LETEC

Boardman House, 64 Broadway E15 1NT (Tel: 020-8432 0000; Fax 020-8432 0399; Email: info@letec.co.uk; Web: http://www.letec.co.uk)
Chair: Peter Lynes
Chief Executive: Susan Fey
Area: Barking and Dagenham, Havering, Newham, Redbridge, Tower Hamlets, Waltham Forest

LONDON TEC

9th Floor Westminster Tower, 3 Albert Embankment, London SE1 7SP (Tel: 020-7735 6000; Fax: 020-7735 6600; Email: francine@london-tec-council.com; Web: http://www.skills-unit.com)
Director: Ms J. Rutherford

NORTH LONDON TEC

Dumayne House, 1 Fox Lane N13 4AB (Tel: 020-8447 9422; Fax: 020-8882 5931; Email: post@nltec.co.uk)
Chair: Derek Wheeler
Chief Executive: Mike Nixon
Press Officer: Anne Crago
Area: Barnet, Enfield, Haringey

NORTH WEST LONDON TEC

118-120 Station Road, Harrow HA1 2RL (Tel: 020-8901 5000; Fax 020-8882 5931)
Chair: Gordon Younger
Chief Executive: Brendon Walsh
Area: Brent, Harrow

SOLOTEC

Lancaster House, 7 Elmfield Road, Bromley BR1 1BR (Tel: 0800 800 0222 Web: http://www.solotec.co.uk)
Chair: Mr. R. Ellis
Chief Executive: John Howell
Area: Bexley, Bromley, Croydon, Lewisham, Greenwich, Sutton

WEST LONDON TEC

West London Centre, 15-21 Staines Road TW3 3HA (Tel: 020-8577 1010; Fax: 020-8570 9969; Web: http://www.wltec.co.uk)
Chair: Michael Frye
Chief Executive: Dr. Phil Blackburn

CHARITY AND THE VOLUNTARY SECTOR

Charities and voluntary organisations form a significant part of modern society and are increasingly active in all aspects of human life. Their contribution to society is immense. To acquire legal charitable status a charity must be registered. In England and Wales there are some 187,000 registered charities, over 10,000 of which operate in greater London.

The Charity Commission for England and Wales is the Government department whose aim is to give the public confidence in the integrity of charity. It is accountable for its decisions to the courts and for its efficiency to the Home Secretary. There are five commissioners, each appointed by the Home Office for a fixed term, and the Commission has offices in London, Liverpool and Taunton, employing more than 500 staff.

The Commission carries out a wide range of functions, including the registration, monitoring and support of charities and the investigation of alleged wrong-doing. The operation of the Charity Register is one of its most high-profile activities. The computerised Register of some 187,000 charities can be viewed on the Commission's website or at any of its offices and shows details of each charity's registration number, objectives, governing instruments and the contact details of its named correspondent. It is possible to see the accounts and annual report of every charity with an income or expenditure of more than £10,000 per annum in the public Central Registry at each office.

An appointment is necessary, and the records contained in these public files can be copied for a small fee. The Commission decides which organisations merit charitable status. If the Commission finds that a charity is no longer active, it may be wound up and removed from the Register. Charity trustees are encouraged to seek the Commission's advice on matters concerning the governance of their charities. Staff attend hundreds of workshops, surgeries, presentations and conferences each year in order to deal with queries from both the sector and the general public. The Commission has powers to alter the administrative machinery of charities in order to help them operate efficiently and effectively.

A wide range of publications and guidance is made available to educate trustees in some of the legal and practical issues arising as they carry out their responsibilities. However, the Commission cannot intervene in the management of a charity: all such decisions are for the trustees. The Commission also has powers to look into the affairs of any charity at the centre of suspected wrong-doing. Its aim is always to protect funds or assets for the beneficiaries of a charity and the Commission will intervene in cases where there is evidence of maladministration, fraud or where the property of a charity is at risk. As well as the range of administrative powers it can use to help trustees, the Commission has regulatory powers which include the ability to freeze charities' bank accounts, appoint a Receiver and Manager and suspend and remove trustees under certain circumstances.

Charity and the Voluntary Sector 171

CHARITY COMMISSION

(London Office) Harmsworth House, 13-15 Bouverie Street, London EC4Y 8DP (Tel: 0870-333 0123; Fax: 020-7674 2310;
Web: http://www.charity-commission.gov.uk)

Chief Commissioner: J. Stoker
Legal Commissioner: M. Carpenter
Commissioners (part-time): J. Bonds; Ms J. Warburton; Ms J. Unwin
Heads of Legal Sections: J. A. Dutton; G. S. Goodchild; K. M. Dibble; S. Slack
Executive Director: Ms L. Berry
Head of Policy Division: R. Carter
Establishment Officer: Ms C. Stewart
Information Systems Controller: Ms G. Cruickshank

LONDON BOROUGHS GRANTS (LBG)

Regal House, London Road, Twickenham TW1 3QS (Tel: 020-8891 5021; Fax: 020-8831 6903; Email: info@lbgrants.org)

London Boroughs Grants, which is part of the Association of London Government, is run by a committee comprising of a representative from all of the thirty three London Borough Councils. It is governed by four key principles which are: to help voluntary organisations tackle poverty in London; to respond to the changing needs of the people of London; to support the voluntary sector in providing high quality services in tackling equality; to support voluntary services provided in more than one London borough.

LONDON VOLUNTARY SERVICE COUNCIL (LVSC)

356 Holloway Road, London, N7 6PA (Tel: 020-7700 8107; Fax: 020-7700 8108)

LONDON VOLUNTARY SECTOR TRAINING CONSORTIUM (LVSTC)

The Print House, 18 Ashwin Street, London, E8 3DL (Tel: 020-7249 4441; Fax: 020-7923 4280)

NATIONAL ASSOCIATION FOR COUNCILS FOR VOLUNTARY SERVICE

3rd Floor, Arundel, 177 Arundel, Sheffield S1 2NU (Tel: 0114-278 6636; Fax: 0114-278 7004)

NACVS supports a network of over 260 councils for Vountary Service throughout England. A Council for Voluntary Service is formed and run by local voluntary and community groups.

NATIONAL ASSOCIATION OF VOLUNTEER BUREAUX (NAVB)

London Development Project, 356 Holloway Road, London N7 6PA (Tel: 020-7700 8128;
Email: navb@ukf.net)

NAVB is the membership organisation which supports and represents the network of over 400 local Volunteer Bureaux. The head office of the NAVB can be found at New Oxford House, 16 Waterloo Street, Birmingham B2 5UG (Tel: 0121-633 4555; Fax: 0121-633 4043)

NATIONAL CENTRE FOR VOLUNTEERING

Regent's Wharf, 8 All Saints Street, London N1 9RL Information Line: 020-7520 8900 Mondays to Fridays 2-4pm; Email: information@thecentre.org.uk;
Web: http://www.volunteering.org.uk)

The National Centre for Volunteering aims to support the voluntary sector through a number of channels including the promotion of best practice, offering training, information, publications and mounting awareness campaigns.

NATIONAL COUNCIL FOR VOLUNTARY ORGANISATIONS (NCVO)

Regent's Wharf, 8 All Saints Street, London, N1 9RL (Tel: 020-7713 6161; Fax: 020-77136300;
Email: ncvo@ncvo-vol.org.uk;
Web: http://www.ncvo-vol.org.uk)

The National Council for Voluntary Organisations is an umbrella body for the voluntary sector in England. NCVO has a growing membership of over 1,400 voluntary organisations.

Chief Executive: Stuart Etherington
Press Officer: Lindsay Wright

NATIONAL COUNCIL FOR VOLUNTARY YOUTH SERVICES

2 Plough Yard, Shoreditch High Street, London EC2A 3LP (Tel: 020-7422 8630; Fax: 020-7422 8631;
E-mail: mail@ncvys.org.uk;
Web: http://www.ncvys.org.uk)

NCVYS represents, supports and informs its members from across the voluntary youth sector. It acts as an umbrella body for over 140 national, regional and county-wide members.

Chief Executive: Susanne Rauprich
Press Officer: Nick Dearden

NATIONAL LOTTERY CHARITIES BOARD

St Vincent House, 16 Suffolk Street, London SW1Y 4NL (Tel: 020-7747 5299; Fax: 020-7747 5214;
Web: http://www.nlcb.org.uk)

The Board was set up under the National Lottery Act 1993 to distribute funds from the Lottery to support charitable, benevolent and philanthropic organisations. The Chair and members are appointed by the Secretary of State for Culture, Media and Sport. The Board's main aim is to help meet the needs of those at greatest disadvantage in society and to improve the quality of life in the community through grants programmes in the UK and an international grants programme for UK-based agencies working abroad.

Chair: Lady Brittan, CBE
Deputy Chairman: Sir Adam Ridley
Members: Mrs T. Baring, CBE; A. Bhatia, OBE; S. Burkeman; J. Carroll; Mrs A. Clark; Ms K. Hampton; T. Jones, OBE; Ms A. Jordan; Mrs B. Lowndes, MBE; R. Martineau; W. Osborne; R. Partington; J. Simpson, OBE; N. Stewart, OBE; Mrs E. Watkins
Chief Executive: T. Hornsby

NEW OPPORTUNITIES FUND

Heron House, 322 High Holborn, London WC1V 7PW (Tel: 020-7211 1800; Fax: 020-7211 1750; E-mail: general.enquiries@nof.org.uk; Web: http://www.nof.org.uk)

The New Opportunities Fund was established under the National Lottery Act 1998 and is responsible for distributing funds allocated from the proceeds of the National Lottery to health, education and environment projects under initiatives determined by the Government.

Chair of the Board: The Baroness Pitkeathley
Members of the Board: Ms J. Barrow; Prof. E. Bolton; Ms N. Clarke; Prof. A. Patmore; D. Mackie; D. Campbell; Prof. S. Griffiths; Ms R. McDonough
Chief Executive: S. Dunmore

REACH

89 Albert Embankment, London SE1 7TP (Tel: 020-7582 6543; Fax: 020-7582 2423; E-mail: volwork@btinternet.com; Web: http://www.volwork.org.uk)

REACH aims to recruit managerial or professional people with time available and place them as volunteers with voluntary organisations needing their experience.

Chief Executive: Sue Evans
Press Oficer: Keith Galpin

VOLUNTARY SERVICE OVERSEAS (VSO LONDON)

317 Putney Bridge Road, London SW15 2PN (Tel: 020-8780 7200; Fax: 020 8780 7300; Web: http://www.vso.org.uk)

Founded in 1958, VSO is a charity which sends aid to developing countries in the form of skilled volunteers. It currently has 1800 qualified and experienced volunteers around the world.

COUNCILS FOR VOLUNTARY SERVICE

Barking & Dagenham
Faircross Community Complex, Hulse Avenue, Barking, Essex, IG11 9UP (Tel: 020-8591 5275; Fax: 020-8591 0363; E-mail: cvsbd@netscapeonline)
Director: Ms S. Scott

Barnet
1st Floor, The Annexe, Hertford Lodge, East End Road, London, N3 3QE (Tel: 020-8346 9723; Fax: 020-8343 3698; E-mail: ce@barnetvsc.org.uk; Web: http://www.barnetvsc.org.uk)
Chief Executive: Ms J. Hawkins

Bexley
8 Brampton Road, Bexleyheath, DA7 4EY (Tel: 020-8304 0911; Fax: 020-8298 9583; E-mail: information@bvsc.org.uk)
Chief Executive: Ms J. Smithbrom

Bromley
28A Beckenham Road, Beckenham, BR3 4LS (Tel: 020-8663 3773; Fax: 020-8658 8697; E-mail: admin@bromleycvs.demon.co.uk)
Director: L. Gillians

Camden
1st Floor, Instrument House, 207-215 King's Cross Road, London, WC1X 9DB (Tel: 020-7837 5544; Fax: 020-7837 5731)
Director: Ms S. Hensby

Croydon
97 High Street, Thornton Heath, CR7 8RY (Tel: 020-8684 3862; Fax: 020-8665 1334; E-mail: francis-cva@library.croydon.gov.uk; Web: http://www.cvaline.co.uk)
General Manager: S. Phaure

Ealing
24 Uxbridge Road, London, W5 2BP (Tel: 020-8579 6273; Fax: 020-8567 4683; E-mail: evsc@evsc.demon.co.uk)
Executive Director: Ms D. Moore

Enfield
Community House, 311 Fore Street, London, N9 0PZ (Tel: 020-8373 6268; Fax:020-8373 6267)
Director: Ms P. Jeffery

Greenwich
St Mary's Church, Greenlaw Street, London, SE18 5AR (Tel: 020-8316 4774; Fax: 020-8316 4755)
Chief Officer (acting): D. Hannay

Hammersmith & Fulham
Aspen House, 1 Gayford Road, London, W12 9BY (Tel: 020-8762 0862; Fax: 020-8749 3874; E-mail: vsral@yahoo.co.uk)
Director: Ms P. Harrison

Haringey
Resource Centre, 2 Factory Lane, London, N17 9FL (Tel: 020-8365 1873; Fax: 020-8801 8957)
Director: T. Modu

Harrow
The Lodge, 64 Pinner Road, Middx, HA1 4HZ (Tel: 020-8863 6707; Fax: 020-8863 8401; E-mail: havs1@aol.com)
Organising Secretary: Ms M. Nunn

Hounslow
Unit 9, Hounslow Business Park, Alice Way, Hanworth Road, TW3 3UD (Tel: 020-8572 5929; Fax: 020-8572 9027; E-mail: hvsf@yahoo.co.uk)
Director: M. Tuohy

Islington
322 Upper Street, London, N1 2XQ (Tel: 020-7226 4862; Fax: 020-7359 7442; E-mail: info@ivac.demon.co.uk)
Director: D. Abse

Kensington & Chelsea
St Luke's Crypt, Sydney Street, London, SW3 6NH (Tel: 020-7351 3210; Fax: 020-7352 3405;

Charity and the Voluntary Sector 173

E-mail: csc@chelseasc.demon.co.uk)
Director: Ms S. Copland

Kingston upon Thames
Siddeley House, 50 Canbury Park Road, KT2 6LX (Tel: 020-8255 3335; Fax: 020-8255 8804; E-mail: info@kva.org.uk; Web: http://www.kingstonlondon.gov.uk)
General Secretary: H. Garner

Lambeth
95 Acre Lane, London, SW2 5TU (Tel: 020-7737 1419; Fax: 020-7737 4328; E-mail: lvac@dial.pipex.com; Web: http://www.lambethvac.org.uk)
Director: Ms E. Ladimeji

Lewisham
120 Rushey Green, London, SE6 4HQ (Tel: 020-8314 9411; Fax: 020-8314 1315; E-mail: lewcvs@dircon.co.uk; Web: http://www.lewcvs.dircon.co.uk)
Director: Ms L. Garner

London
Voluntary Sector Resource Centre, 356 Holloway Road, London, N7 6PA (Tel: 020-7700 8107; Fax: 020-7700 8108; E-mail: lvsc@lvsc.org.uk; Web: http://www.lvsc.org.uk)
Director: Ms C. Holloway

Merton
The Vestry Hall, London Road, Mitcham, CR4 3UD (Tel: 020-8685 1771; Fax: 020-8685 0249; E-mail: info@mvsc.co.uk)
Director: C. Frost

Newham
53 The Broadway, London, E15 4BQ

Redbridge
1st Floor, North Broadway Chambers, 1 Cranbrook Road, Ilford, IG1 4DU (Tel: 020-8554 5049; Fax: 020-8478 9640; E-mail: redbridge-cvs@hotmail.com)
Director: N. Boston

Richmond
The Centre for Voluntary Services, 1 Princes Street, TW9 1ED (Tel: 020-8255 8500; Fax: 020-8401 1967; E-mail: richmondcvs@dial.pipex.com)
Chief Executive: C. Whelan

Southwark
64 Camberwell Road, London, SE5 0EN (Tel: 020-7703 8733; E-mail: 020-7703 9393; E-mail: mail@savo.org.uk; Web: http://www.savo.org.uk)
Director: P. Tulloch

Sutton
Unilink House, 21 Lewis Road, Surrey, SM1 4BR (Tel: 020-8643 3277; Fax: 020-8643 4178; E-mail: enquiries@suttoncvs.org)
Director: I. Beever

Tower Hamlets
Davenant Centre, 179-181 Whitechapel Road, London, E1 1DN (Tel: 020-7426 9970; Fax: 020-7377 0956; E-mail: jill@towerhamlets.org.uk)
Director: Ms J. Walsh

Waltham Forest
Unit 37, Alpha Business Centre, South Grove Road, E17 7NX (Tel: 020-8521 0377; Fax: 020-8521 1672; E-mail: vawf@dial.pipex.com)
Director: M. Wenham

Westminster
37 Chapel Street, NW1 5DP (Tel: 020-7723 1216; Fax: 020-7723 8929; E-mail: general@vawestminster.demon.co.uk; Web: http://www.vawestminster.demon.co.uk)
Director: M. Loughan

174 Business London

CITIZENS' ADVICE BUREAUX

Anyone can obtain advice from a Citizens' Advice Bureau. The service is free. Bureaux offer advice on many legal and financial matters, for example benefit entitlement and debt. The list below provides contact details for CABs in the Greater London area.

Addington
1a Overbury Crescent, New Addington, Croydon, Surrey, CR0 0LR (Tel: 01689-846890; Fax: 01689-845105)

Barking
55 Ripple Road, Essex, IG11 7NT (Tel: 020-8594 6715; Fax: 020-8591 0440)

Battersea
14 York Road, London, SW11 3QA (Tel: 020-7228 9462; Fax: 020-7978 5348)

Beckenham & Penge
20 Snowdown Close, Avenue Road, London, SE20 7RU (Tel: 020-8778 0921; Fax: 020-8776 6056)

Beddington & Wallington
16 Stanley Park Road, Wallington, SM6 0EU (Tel: 020-8669 3435; Fax: 020-8770 4928)

Bermondsey
8 Market Place, Southwark Park Road, London, SE16 3UQ (Tel: 020-7231 1118; Fax: 020-7231 4410)

Bethnal Green
Tower Hamlets Office, 62 Roman Road, London, E2 0QJ (Tel: 020-7364 2266)

Bexleyheath
8 Brampton Road, Kent, DA7 4EY (Tel: 020-8303 5100; Fax: 020-8303 9524)

Brentford & Chiswick
Town Hall, Heathfield Terrace, London, W4 4JN (Tel: 020-8994 4846; Fax: 020-8995 4674)

Bromley Town
The Old Library, 83 Tweedy Road, Bromley, BR1 1RG (Tel: 020-8464 6023; Fax: 020-8466 0581)

Camden
94 Avenue Road, London, NW3 3EX (Tel: 020-7586 2694; Fax: 020-7483 1858)

City of London
32 Ludgate Hill, London, EC4M 7DR (Tel: 020-7236 1156; Fax: 020-7329 4547)

Dagenham
339 Heathway, RM9 5AF (Tel: 020-8592 1084; Fax: 020-8593 2511)

Dalston
491-493 Kingsland Road, London, E8 4AU (Tel: 0870-126 4013; E-mail: manager@dalston-cab.demon.co.uk)

Edmonton
Edmonton Methodist Church, Lower Fore Street, London, N9 0PN (Tel: 020-8807 4253; Fax: 020-8807 1730; E-mail: edmonton.cab@dial.pipex.com)

Eltham
Eltham Library, High Street, SE9 1TS (Tel: 020-8850 6044; Fax: 020-8850 7774)

Enfield
10 Little Park Gardens, Middx, EN2 6PQ (Tel: 020-8363 0928; Fax: 020-8364 5644;
E-mail: enfield.cab@dial.pipex.comfelt)

Feltham
Peoples Centre, TW13 4AH (Tel: 020-8707 0078; Fax: 020-8707 0077)

Finchley
Hertford Lodge Annexe, East End Road, London, N3 3QE (Tel: 0870-126 4018; Fax: 020-8349 9840)

Fulham
The Pavilion, 1 Mund Street, London, W14 9LY (Tel: 020-7385 1322)

Ham
Ham Health Clinic, Ashburnham Road, Richmond, TW10 7NS

Hampton
White House Community Centre, 45 The Avenue, TW12 3RN (Tel: 020-8941 8330; Fax: 020-8979 3827)

Harrow
Civic Centre, Station Road, HA1 2XH (Tel: 020-8427 9443; Fax: 020-8863 3267)

Hayes
49-51 Station Road, UB3 4BE (Tel: 0870-126 4021; Fax: 020-8606 2939)

Hendon
40-42 Church End, London, NW4 4JT (Tel: 020-8203 5801; Fax: 020-8203 3202)

Holborn
3rd Floor, Holborn Library, 32-38 Theobalds Road, London, WC1X 8PA (Tel: 020-7404 1497; Fax: 020-7404 1507)

Holloway
Caxton House, 129 St Johns Way, London, N19 3RQ (Tel: 020-7272 5577)

Hornchurch
59A Billet Lane, RM11 1AX (Tel: 01708-445983)

Hornsey
7 Hatherley Gardens, London, N8 9JJ (Tel: 020-8374 3704; Fax: 020-8374 2646)

Hounslow
45 Treaty Centre, TW3 1ES (Tel: 020-8570 2983)

Kentish Town
242 Kentish Town Road, London, NW5 2AB (Tel: 020-7485 7034; Fax: 020-7485 5150)

Citizen's Advice Bureaux 175

Kilburn
200 Kilburn High Road, London, NW6 4JD (Tel: 020-7372 6888)

Kingston & Surbiton
Neville House, 55 Eden Street, Kingston-upon-Thames, KT1 1BW (Tel: 0870-126 4019; Fax: 020-8255 6053

Lambeth
Ilex House, 1 Barrhill Road, London, SW2 4RJ (Tel: 020-8674 8993; Fax: 020-8678 6593)

Leytonstone
Greater London House, 547-551 High Road, London, E11 4PB (Tel: 020-8988 9620)

Mitcham
326 London Road, CR4 3ND (Tel: 020-8288 0450; Fax: 020-8685 9483)

Morden
7 Crown Parade, Crown Lane, SM4 5DA (Tel: 020-8715 0707; Fax: 020-8715 0550)

New Barnet
30 Station Road, Barnet, Herts, EN5 1PL (Tel: 020-8449 0975; Fax: 020-8441 2384)

Newham Docklands
The Advice Arcade, 107-109 The Grove, London, E15 1HP (Tel: 020-8536 1620; Fax: 020-8536 1622)

North Cheam
320 Malden Road, SM3 8EP (Tel: 020-8770 4851; Fax: 020-8770 4917)

Orpington
Wallis House, 1 Church Hill, BR6 0HE (Tel: 01689-827732)

Paddington
441 Harrow Road, London, W10 4RE (Tel: 020-8960 4481; Fax: 020-8960 4244)

Palmers Green
Green Lanes, London, N13 4XD (Tel: 020 8350 2963; Fax: 020-8447 9343)

Peckham
97 Peckham High Street, London, SE15 5RS (Tel: 020-7639 4471; Fax: 020-7732 2497;
E-mail: peckcab@aol.com)

Pimlico
140 Tachbrook Street, London, SW1V 2NE (Tel: 020-7834 5727)

Putney & Roehampton
228 Upper Richmond Road, London, SW15 6TG (Tel: 020-8479 0046; Fax: 020-8479 0049;
E-mail: roehampton.cab@btinternet.com)

Redbridge
2nd Floor South, Broadway Chambers, 1 Cranbrook Road, Ilford, IG1 4DU (Tel: 020-8514 1878; Fax: 020-8514 5700)

Richmond
Linfield House, 26 Kew Road, TW9 2NA (Tel: 020-8940 0617; Fax: 020-8332 0708;
E-mail: richmond.cab@btinternet.com)

Romford
7-9 Victoria Road, RM1 2JT (Tel: 0870-120 4200; Fax: 01708-739319)

Ruislip
9 Eastcote Road, HA4 8BD (Tel: 01895-622818)

St Helier
5-6 Rose Hill Court Parade, St Helier Avenue, SM4 6JS (Tel: 020-8640 4170; Fax: 020-8648 9128)

Sutton
Central Library, St Nicholas Way, SM1 1EA (Tel: 020-8643 5291; Fax: 020-8770 4929)

Sydenham
299 Kirkdale, London, SE26 4QD (Tel: 0870-126 4037; Fax: 020-8776 7499;
Web: http://www.adviceguide.org.uk)

Thornton Heath
Strand House, Zion Road, CR7 8RG (Tel: 020-8684 2236; Fax: 020-8683 4790)

Tooting & Balham
4th Floor, Bedford House, 215 Balham High Road, London, SW17 7BQ (Tel: 020-8333 6960; Fax: 020-8378 5892; Web: http://www.careline.org.uk/cab)

Tottenham
Town Hall Approach, London, N15 4RY (Tel: 020-8376 3700; Fax: 020-8376 0909)

Tower Hamlets East
86 Bow Road, London, E3 4DL (Tel: 0870-126 4014; Fax: 020-8981 8761)

Twickenham
The Advice Centre, 61 Heath Road, TW1 4AW (Tel: 020-8892 5917; Fax: 20-8744 1167;
E-mail: twickenham.cab@btinternet.com)

Uxbridge
Link 1A, Civic Centre, UB8 1UX (Tel: 01895-277306)

Walthamstow
167 Hoe Street, London, E17 3AL

Whitechapel
Unit 32, Greatorex Street, London, E1 5NP (Tel: 020-7247 4172; Fax: 020-7375 2256;
E-mail: whitechapel@cabx.demon.co.uk)

Woodford
112 High Road, London, E18 2QS (Tel: 020-8502 9194)

Woolwich
Old Town Hall, Polytechnic Street, London, SE18 6NP (Tel: 020-8854 9607; Fax: 020-8317 7571;
Web: http://www.nacab.org.uk)

Yiewsley
106 High Street, UB7 7QJ (Tel: 01895-430421)

176 Business London

CONFERENCE AND EXHIBITION VENUES

The business community increasingly makes use of the many conference and exhibition venues situated in London. The list below provides contact and facilities information on a range of venues which cater for all manner of conference and exhibition requirements, whether for individuals, small groups or large international organisations. Please use the key below to see which specialised facilities each venue has to offer.

Key:
1 = Auditorium
2 = Sound Equipment
3 = Theatre Lighting
4 = Computer Linkup
5 = Audio/Video Equipment
6 = Disabled Facilities
7 = Catering
8 = Accommodation Discounts
Capacity relates to maximum capacity of the venue

CONFERENCE VENUES

Basil Street Hotel
Knightsbridge, London, SW3 1AH (Tel: 020-7581 3311; Fax: 020-7581 3693; Email: thebasil@aol.com; Web: http://www.thebasil.com)
Banqueting Co-ordinator: Miss C. McCarthy
Capacity: 140 – 4, 5, 6, 7, 8

Bateaux London, Catamaran
Charing Cross Pier, Victoria Embankment, London, WC2N 6NU (Tel: 020-7925 2215; Fax: 020-7839 1034; E-mail: bateauxldn@aol.com; Web: http://www.bateauxlondon.com)
Corporate Account Manager: Ms C. Scarr
Capacity: 300 – 2, 7

Battersea Park Events Office
Battersea Park, London, SW11 4NJ (Tel: 020-7223 6241; Fax: 020-7223 7919;
Email: asmith@wandsworth.gov.uk;
Web: http://www.wandsworth.gov.uk)
Events Manager: J. Adam

The Berkeley
Wilton Place, Knightsbridge, London, SW1X 7RL (Tel: 020-7235 6000; Fax: 020-7235 4330; Email: info@the-berkeley.co.uk;
Web: http://www.savoy-group.co.uk)
Senior Banqueting Account Manager: Ms K. Garland
Capacity: 200 – 4, 5, 6, 7, 8

The Berkshire
350 Oxford Street, London, W1N 0BY (Tel: 020-7629 7474; Fax: 020-7629 8156;
Web: http://www.radissonedwardian.com)
Conference and Banqueting Sales Manager: N. Jaffer
Capacity: 16 – 2, 4, 5, 6, 7, 8

Berners Hotel
10 Berners Street, London, W1A 3BE (Tel: 020-7666 2000; Fax: 020-7666 2001;
Email: berners@berners.co.uk;
Web: http://www.thebernershotel.co.uk)
Conference Co-ordinators: Ms G. Dwyer; Ms M. Glover
Capacity: 160 – 4, 6, 7, 8

Bloomsbury Square Training Centre
2-3 Bloomsbury Square, London, WC1A 2RL (Tel: 020-7212 7510; Fax: 020-7212 7550)
Training Centre Manager: Ms S. van Leeuwen Brown
Capacity: 110 – 1, 2, 3, 4, 5, 7

The Bonnington in Bloomsbury
Southampton Row, London, WC1B 4BH (Tel: 020-7242 2828; Fax: 020-7831 9170)
Conference Co-ordinator: Ms J. Proud
Capacity: 120 – 2, 5, 6, 7, 8

The Brewery
Chiswell Street, London, EC1Y 4SD (Tel: 020-7638 8811; Fax: 020-7638 5713;
Email: thebrewery@chiswellstreet.com;
Web: http://www.thebrewery.chiswellstreet.com)
Conference and Events Manager: R. Paton
Capacity: 900 – 2, 3, 4, 5, 6, 7

The Britannia
Grosvenor Square, Mayfair, London, W1A 3AN (Tel: 020-7629 9400; Fax: 020-7408 0699;
Email: sarah.cox@mill-cop.com;
Web: http://www.britanniahotel.com)
Meetings and Events Manager: Ms S. Cox
Capacity: 460 – 2, 3, 4, 5, 6, 7, 8

Brown's Hotel
Albemarle Street, London, W1X 4BP (Tel: 020-7493 6020; Fax: 020-7493 9381;
Email: brownshotel@brownshotel.com;
Web: http://www.brownshotel.com)
Banqueting Co-ordinator: T. Harvey
Capacity: 70 – 5, 7, 8

Cabinet War Rooms
Clive Steps, King Charles Street, London, SW1A 2AQ (Tel: 020-7930 6961; Fax: 020-7839 5897;
Email: cwr@iwm.org.uk; Web: http://www.iwm.org.uk)
Marketing Officer: Ms V. Rayner
Capacity: 50 – 4, 5, 6

Café Royal
68 Regent Street, London, W1R 6EL (Tel: 020-7437 9090; Fax: 020-7439 7672;
Email: banqueting@caferoyal.demon.co.uk;
Web: http://www.lemeridien-hotels.com)
Conference and Banqueting Director: G. Bush
Capacity: 700 – 2, 3, 4, 5, 6, 7, 8

Cannizaro House
West Side, Wimbledon Common, London, SW19 4UE (Tel: 020-8879 1464; Fax: 020-8879 1464;
Email: cannizaro.house@thistle.co.uk)
Event Sales Manager: Miss K. Whitby
Capacity: 120 – 5, 6, 7, 8

Cavendish St James's
81 Jermyn Street, London, SW1Y 6JF (Tel: 020-7930 2111; Fax: 020-7839 4551)

Conference and Exhibition Venues 177

Conference and Banqueting Administrations Manager: Ms T. Grehan
Capacity: 100 – 2, 4, 5, 6, 7, 8

Central Hall Westminster
Storey's Gate, London, SW1H 9NH (Tel: 020-7222 8010; Fax: 020-7222 6883; Email: events@wch.co.uk; Web: http://www.wch.co.uk)
Senior Events Manager: Ms C. Williamson
Capacity: 2500 – 1, 2, 3, 4, 5, 6, 7, 8

The Chelsea Green Hotel
35 Ixworth Place, Chelsea, London, SW3 3QX (Tel: 020-7225 7500; Fax: 020-7225 7555; Email: cghotel@dircon.co.uk; Web: http://www.welcome2london.com)
Food and Beverage Manager: B. Wilkinson
Capacity: 60 – 1, 2, 3, 4, 5, 6, 7, 8

The Chesterfield, Mayfair
35 Charles Street, Mayfair, London, W1X 8LX (Email: meetings@chesterfield.redcarnationhotels.com)
Deputy General Manager: R. Dixon
Capacity: 100 – 2, 4, 5, 7, 8

Chiswick House
Burlington Lane, Chiswick, London, W4 2RP (Tel: 020-8742 1978; Fax: 020-8742 3104; Email: marion.doherty@english-heritage.org.uk)
Hospitality Manager: Ms M. Doherty
Capacity: 50

Churchill Inter-Continental London,
30 Portman Square, London, W1A 4ZX (Tel: 020-7486 5800; Fax: 020-7486 1255; Email: churchill@interconti.com; Web: http://www.interconti.com)
Senior Events Manager: Ms A. Stokes
Capacity: 250 – 4, 5, 6, 7, 8

City of London Club
19 Old Broad Street, London, EC2N 1DS (Tel: 020-7588 7991; Fax: 020-7374 2020; Email: cityclub@dial.pipex.com)
Functions Administrator: Ms L. Hasler
Capacity: 350 – 2, 3, 4, 5, 7

Claridge's
Brook Street, Mayfair, London, W1A 2JQ (Tel: 020-7629 8860; Fax: 020-7872 8092)
Deputy Banqueting Manager: R. Marek
Capacity: 240 – 2, 4, 5, 6, 7, 8

Commonwealth Conference and Events Centre
Kensington High Street, London, W8 6NQ (Tel: 020-7603 3412; Fax: 020-7603 9634; Email: conference@commonwealth.org.uk; Web: http://www.commonwealth.org.uk)
Conference Centre Managers: C. Fielder; B. Thorp
Capacity: 460 – 1, 2, 3, 4, 5, 6, 7, 8

Congress Centre
23-28 Great Russell Street, London, WC1B 3LS (Tel: 020-7580 5664; Fax: 020-7580 8227; Email: congress.centre@tuc.org.uk)
Conference and Sales Co-ordinator: Ms R. Lyall
Capacity: 500 – 1, 2, 3, 4, 5, 6, 7

Copthorne Tara
Scarsdale Place, Wrights Lane, Kensington, London, W8 5SR (Tel: 020-7937 7211; Fax: 020-7872 2965; Email: cathal.leonard@mill.com)
Meetings and Events Manager: C. Leonard
Capacity: 250 – 1, 4, 5, 6, 7, 8

Dolphin Square Hotel
Chichester Street, London, SW1V 3LX (Tel: 020-7798 6701; Fax: 020-7798 6782; Email: events@dolphinsquarehotel.co.uk; Web: http://www.dolphinsquarehotel.co.uk)
Business and Events Co-ordinator: Ms J. Connolly
Capacity: 100 – 2, 4, 5, 6, 7, 8

The Dorchester
Park Lane, London, W1A 2HJ (Tel: 020-7629 8888; Fax: 020-7317 6363; Email: banqueting@dorchesterhotel.com; Web: http://www.dorchesterhotel.com)
Senior Conference Co-ordinator: Ms D. Hubbard
Capacity: 550 – 4, 5, 6, 7, 8

Duke of York's Headquarters
Kings Road, Chelsea, London, SW3 4RY (Tel: 020-7414 5513; Fax: 020-7414 5513; Email: secretary@reserve-forces-london.org.uk)
Marketing and Events Manager: Ms S. Stuart
Capacity: 240 – 4, 6, 7

Ealing Conference and Banqueting Centre
Halls and Events, Perceval House, 14-16 Uxbridge Road, London, W5 2HL (Tel: 020-8280 1185; Fax: 020-8566 5088; Email: rabinek@ealing.gov.uk; Web: http://www.ealing.gov.uk/he&m)
Marketing Manager: K. Rabine
Capacity: 500 – 1, 2, 3, 5, 6, 7, 8

Earl's Court Exhibition Centre
Warwick Road, London, SW5 9TA (Tel: 020-7385 1200; Web: http://www.ecc/co.uk)

Eltham Palace
Court Yard, Court Road, Eltham, London, SE9 5QE (Tel: 020-8294 2577; Fax: 020-8294 2621)
Hospitality Manager: Ms A. Dadd
Capacity: 250 – 6, 7

Euston Plaza Hotel
17-18 Upper Woburn Place, Euston, London, WC2H 0HT (Tel: 020-7383 4105; Fax: 020-7383 4106; Email: cb@euston-plaza-hotel.com; Web: http://www.euston-plaza-hotel.com)
Conference and Banqueting Co-ordinator: J. Oya Demirci
Capacity: 150 – 2, 5, 6, 7, 8

ExCel
London, E16 1XL (Tel: 020-7476 0101; Email: leighjagger@excel-London,.co.uk)
Director of Conference and Special Events: Leigh Jagger
Capacity: 1200 – 2, 3, 4, 5, 6, 7

Forte Posthouse Bloomsbury
Coram Street, London, WC1 (Tel: 0870-400 9222; Fax: 020-7278 0989)

178 Business London

Conference Office Manager: Ms T. Arthur
Capacity: 180 – 4, 5, 6, 7

The Forum
97-109 Cromwell Road London, SW7 4DN (Tel: 020-7341 3208; Fax: 020-7244 9909;
Email: forumlondon@interconti.com;
Web: http://www.interconti.com)
Conference and Events Executive: Ms S. Fusi
Capacity: 380 – 2, 4, 5, 6, 7, 8

Glaziers Hall
9 Montague Close, London Bridge, London, SE1 9DD (Tel: 020-7403 3300; Fax: 020-7407 6036;
Email: sales@glaziershall.co.uk;
Web: http://www.glaziershall.co.uk)
Sales and Marketing Executive: Ms D. Dawson
Capacity: 500 – 1, 2, 4, 5, 6, 7, 8

The Grafton
Tottenham Court Road, London, W1P 9HP (Tel: 020-7388 4131; Fax: 020-7753 0334;
Email: graftcb@radisson.com)
Conference and Banqueting Manager: D. Lord
Capacity: 110 – 2, 3, 4, 5, 7, 8

The Hatton
51-53 Hatton Garden, London, EC1N 8HN (Tel: 020-7242 4123; Fax: 020-7242 1818;
Email: hatton@etclimited.co.uk)
Conference and Sales Manager: Ms L. Henderson
Capacity: 150 – 2, 4, 5, 6, 7

The Henry VIII Hotel
19 Leinster Gardens, London, W2 3AN (Tel: 020-7262 0117; Fax: 020-7706 0472;
Email: admin@henryviii.co.uk;
Web: http://www.henry-viii.net)
Food and Beverage Manager: J. Edwards
Capacity: 80 – 4, 5, 7, 8

Hilton Hyde Park
129 Bayswater Road, London, W2 4RJ (Tel: 020-7221 2217; Fax: 020-7229 0557;
Web: http://www.hilton.com)
Revenue Co-ordinator: Ms T. Brown
Capacity: 100 – 4, 5, 7, 8

HMS Belfast
Morgan's Lane, Tooley Street, London, SE1 2JH (Tel: 020-7403 6246; Fax: 020-7407 0708;
Email: natasha.malcolm@sodexho.co.uk;
Web: http://www.iwm.co.uk)
Sales Manager: Ms N. Malcolm
Capacity: 400 – 1, 2, 5, 6, 7, 8

Hotel Antoinette
26 Beaufort Road, Kingston upon Thames, Surrey, KT1 2TQ (Tel: 020-8546 1044; Fax: 020-8547 2595;
Email: hotelantoinette@btinternet.com;
Web: http://www.hotelantoinette.co.uk)
Food and Beverages Manager: P. Hartnell
Capacity: 150 – 1, 2, 4, 5, 6, 7, 8,

Hotel Inter-Continental
One Hamilton Place, Hyde Park Corner, London, W1V 0QY (Tel: 020-7409 3131; Fax: 020-7491 0926;
Web: http://www.interconti.com)
Conference and Banqueting Sales Manager: T. Widdowson
Capacity: 1000 – 2, 3, 4, 5, 6, 7, 8

Hyde Park Ryan Hotel
66 Lancaster Gate, London, W2 3NZ (Tel: 020-7262 5090; Fax: 020-7723 1244;
Email: hotel@hydepark-ryan.com;
Web: http://www.ryan-hotels.com)
General Manager: Ms A. Frigieri
Capacity: 30 – 2, 4, 5, 7, 8

Imagination Gallery
South Crescent, 25 Store Street, London, WC1E 7BL (Tel: 020-7323 3300; Fax: 020-7323 5801;
Email: christopher.bridge@imagination.co.uk;
Web: http://www.imagination.co.uk)
Gallery Director: C. Bridge
Capacity: 350 – 1, 4, 5, 7

Imperial College
Conference Office, Prince's Gardens, London, SW7 1LU (Tel: 020-7594 9494; Fax: 020-7594 9504/5;
Email: conference@ic.ac.uk;
Web: http://www.ad.ic.ac.uk/conferences)
Conference Sales Manager: Ms S. Brace
Capacity: 200 – 1, 2, 3, 4, 5, 6, 7

Imperial War Museum
Lambeth Road, London, SE1 6HZ (Tel: 020-7416 5394; Fax: 020-7416 5396;
Email: swilliams@iwm.org.uk;
Web: http://www.iwm.org.uk)
Corporate Hospitality Officer: Ms S. Williams
Capacity: 1000 – 1, 2, 3, 4, 5, 6, 7, 8

Institute of Contemporary Arts (ICA)
Nash House, The Mall, London, SW1Y 5AH (Tel: 020-7930 0493; Fax: 020-7306 0122; Email: hires@ica.org.uk; Web: http://www.ica.org.uk)
Hires Manager: Ms D. Hay
Capacity: 350 – 1, 2, 3, 4, 5, 6, 7

Insurance Hall
20 Aldermanbury, London, EC2V 7HY (Tel: 020-7417 4417; Fax: 020-7600 4838;
Email: insurance.hall@cii.co.uk;
Web: http://www.cii.co.uk)
Sales and Functions Co-ordinator: Ms M. Backhurst
Capacity: 300 – 1, 3, 4, 5, 6, 7, 8

International Coffee Organisation
22 Berners Street, London, W1P 4DD (Tel: 020-7580 8591; Fax: 020-7580 6129; Email: maqueda@ico.org; Web: http://www.icoffee.com)
Conference Organiser: Ms C. Maqueda
Capacity: 284 – 1, 2, 4, 5, 7, 8

International Students House
229 Great Portland Street, London, W1N 5HD (Tel: 020-7631 8300/8306; Fax: 020-7631 8315/8307; Email: cont@ish.org.uk; Web: http://www.ish.org.uk)
Senior Conference Co-ordinator: Å. Axelsdotter
Capacity: 300 – 1, 5, 7

Conference and Exhibition Venues   179

Islington Business Design Centre
52 Upper Street, London, N1 0QH (Tel: 020-7359 3535; Fax: 020-7266 0590;
Web: http://www.business-design-centre.com)

Jarvis International Hotel
Ealing Common, London, W5 3HN (Tel: 020-8896 8400; Fax: 020-8992 7082)
Conference and Events Co-ordinator: Ms K. Olivier
Capacity: 200 – 1, 2, 3, 4, 5, 6, 7, 8

K & K Hotel George
1-5 Templeton Place, Earl's Court, London, SW5 9NB (Tel: 020-7598 8700; Fax: 020-7370 2285;
Email: hotelgeorge@kkhotels.co.uk;
Web: http://www.kkhotels.com)
Reservations Manager: Ms D. Glaser
Capacity: 30 – 4, 5, 7, 8

The Kenilworth
97 Great Russell Street, London, WC1B 3LB (Tel: 020-7637 3477)
Conference and Banqueting Sales Manager: Ms A. Barnett
Capacity: 130 – 2, 4, 5, 7, 8

Le Meridien Grosvenor House
Park Lane, London, W1A 3AA (Tel: 020-7499 6363; Fax: 020-7495 5618; Email: gros.house@virgin.net;
Web: http://www.grosvenorhouse.co.uk)
Diary Manager: Ms V. Rooke
Capacity: 1500 – 2, 3, 4, 5, 6, 7, 8

Lee Valley Leisure Centre
Picketts Lock Lane, Edmonton, London, N9 0AS (Tel: 020-8884 1197; Fax: 020-8884 4975)
Events Manager: R. Garvey
Capacity: 2000 – 2, 3, 5, 6, 7

Le Meridien Piccadilly
21 Piccadilly, London, W1V 0BH (Tel: 020-7734 8000)
Conference and Banqueting Sales Manager: C. Cubria
Capacity: 250 – 2, 3, 4, 5, 6, 7, 8

Le Meridien Waldorf
Aldwych, London, WC2B 4DD (Tel: 020-7836 2400; Fax: 020-7240 9277)
Senior Conference and Events Co-ordinator: Ms S. J. Hanshaw
Capacity: 400 – 4, 5, 7, 8

Limelight
136 Shaftesbury Avenue, London, W1V 7DN (Tel: 020-7287 1426; Fax: 020-7434 3780;
Email: info@thelimelightclub.com;
Web: http://www.thelimelightclub.com)
Functions Manager: Ms J. Vernol
Capacity: 860 – 1, 2, 3, 7

London Bridge Hotel
8-18 London Bridge Street, London, SE1 9SG (Tel: 020-7855 2200;
Email: sales@london-bridge-hotel.co.uk;
Web: http://www.london-bridge-hotel.co.uk)
Conference Co-ordinator: Ms A. Lodato
5, 6, 7, 8

London Hilton on Park Lane
22 Park Lane, London, W1Y 4BE (Tel: 020-7493 8000; Fax: 020-7208 4145; Web: http://www.hilton.com)
Senior Conference and Banqueting Co-ordinator: C. Chapman
Capacity: 1000 – 1, 2, 4, 5, 6, 7, 8

London Kensington Hilton
179-199 Holland Park Avenue, Holland Park, London, W11 4UL (Tel: 020-7603 3355; Fax: 020-7602 9397;
Email: cb-kensington@hilton.com; Web: http://www.kensington-hilton.com)
Events Manager: H. Cakan
Capacity: 300 – 2, 3, 4, 5, 6, 7, 8

London Marriott Hotel - Marble Arch
134 George Street, London, W1H 6DN (Tel: 020-7723 1277)
Senior Executive Meetings Manager: Ms U. Schmoock
Capacity: 130 – 2, 4, 6, 7, 8

London Ryan Hotel
Gwynne Place, King's Cross Road, London, WC1X 9QN (Tel: 020-7278 2480)
Events Sales Manager: R. Wall
Capacity: 100 – 2, 3, 4, 5, 6, 8

London Transport Museum
The Piazza, Covent Garden, London, WC2E 7BB (Tel: 020-7379 6344; Fax: 020-7565 7253;
Email: rodw@ltmuseum.co.uk;
Web: http://www.ltmuseum.co.uk)
Events Co-ordinator: R. Wilson
Capacity: 400 – 1, 2, 3, 4, 5, 6, 7

London Zoo
Outer Circle, Regent's Park, London, NW1 4RY (Tel: 020-7722 3333)
Conference Executive: T. Lester
Capacity: 250 – 1, 2, 4, 5, 7

The Lowndes Hyatt Hotel
21 Lowndes Street, London, SW1X 9ES (Tel: 020-7823 1234; Fax: 020-7235 1154;
Email: lowndes@hyattintl.com;
Web: http://www.london.hyatt.com/lownd/)
Sales Co-ordinator: M. Compagnon
Capacity: 18 – 2, 3, 4, 5, 7, 8

The Marlborough
9-13 Bloomsbury Street, London, WC1B 3QD (Tel: 020-7636 5601)
Conference and Banqueting Sales Manager: Ms A. Barnett
Capacity: 270 – 2, 4, 5, 6, 7, 8

May Fair Inter-Continental
Stratton Street, London, W1A 2AW (Tel: 020-7629 7777; Fax: 020-7409 7016)
Group Sales and Catering Manager: Ms S. Segoura
Capacity: 250 – 1, 2, 3, 4, 5, 6, 7, 8

Millennium Bailey's
140 Gloucester Road, London, SW7 4QH (Tel: 020-7373 6000; Fax: 020-7370 3760;
Email: baileys@mill-cop.com;

Web: http://www.mill-cop.com)
Group Sales Executive: A. Dupas
Capacity: 20 – 4, 5, 7, 8

Millennium Knightsbridge
17 Sloane Street, London, SW1X 9NU (Tel: 020-7235 4377; Fax: 020-7235 3705;
Email: reservations.chelsea@mill-cop.com;
Web: http://www.mill-cop.com)
Meetings and Events Co-ordinator: Ms A. Laurence Chapalan
Capacity: 120 – 2, 4, 5, 7, 8

Motcombs Restaurant and Bar
26 Motcomb Street, Belgravia, London, SW1X 8JT (Tel: 020-7235 5532; Fax: 020-7245 6351;
Email: motcombs@dial.pipex.com;
Web: http://www.motocombs.co.uk)
Sales and Marketing Executive: Ms S. Ealey
Capacity: 50 – 4, 5, 7

The Mountbatten
20 Monmouth Street, Seven Dials, London, WC2H 9HD (Tel: 020-7836 4300; Fax: 020-7240 3540;
Email: mountc&b@radisson.com;
Web: http://www.radissonedwardian.com)
Conference and Banqueting Sales Manager: N. Jaffer
Capacity: 100 – 2, 4, 5, 6, 7, 8

National Army Museum
Royal Hospital Road, Chelsea, London, SW3 4HT (Tel: 020-7730 0717; Fax: 020-7823 6573;
Email: info@national-army-museum.ac.uk;
Web: http://www.national-army-museum.ac.uk)
Head of the Department of Commercial Activities: M. J. Millo
Capacity: 300 – 6, 7, 8

National Maritime Museum
Royal Observatory, Queen's House, Romney Road, Greenwich, London, SE10 9NF (Tel: 020-8312 6693/6674; Fax: 020-8312 6722;
Email: jcpres@nmm.ac.uk;
Web: http://www.mnn.ac.uk)
Events Manager: Ms L. Cooke
Capacity: 100 – 1, 2, 4, 5, 6, 7, 8

New Connaught Rooms
61-65 Great Queen Street, Holborn, London, WC2B 5DA (Tel: 020-7405 7811; Fax: 020-7831 1851;
Email: admin@connaught.u-net.com;
Web: http://www.cityscan.co.uk/newconnaught)
Events and Conference Co-ordinator: Ms N. Dunderdale
Capacity: 1000 – 2, 5, 6, 7, 8

Old Town Hall, Stratford
29 Broadway, Stratford, London, E15 4BQ (Tel: 020-8534 7835; Fax: 020-8534 8411; Email: maurice.hill@newham.gov.uk)
Assistant Centre Manager: Ms S. Lowe
Capacity: 500 – 1, 2, 3, 4, 5, 6, 7

Olympia
Kensington, London, W14 8UX (Tel: 020-7385 1200;
Web: http://www.eco.co.uk)

The Park Lane Hotel
Piccadilly, London, W1Y 8BX (Tel: 020-7499 6321; Fax: 020-7290 7566;
Email: carolina-magdelena@sheraton.com;
Web: http://www.starwood.com)
Events Co-ordinator: S. Baird
Capacity: 550 – 2, 3, 4, 5, 6, 7, 8

Planet Hollywood
13 Coventry Street, London, W1V 7FE (Tel: 020-7478 1543; Fax: 020-7478 1501/3)
Corporate Sales and Events Co-ordinator: Ms E. Richards
Capacity: 500 – 1, 2, 4, 5, 6, 7

Quality Eccleston Hotel
Eccleston Square, London, SW1V 1PS (Tel: 020-7834 8042; Fax: 020-7630 8942;
Email: admin@gb614.u-net.com;
Web: http://www.choicehotelseuorpe.com)
Conference and Banqueting Co-ordinator: Ms L. Beckett
Capacity: 150 – 1, 5, 7, 8

Queen Elizabeth II Conference Centre
Broad Sanctuary, London, SW1P 3EE (Tel: 020-7222 5000; Fax: 020-7798 4200)

The Radisson SAS Portman Hotel
22 Portman Square, London, W1H 9FL (Tel: 020-7208 6000; Fax: 020-7224 4928;
Email: sales@lonza.rdsas.com;
Web: http://www.radissonsas.com)
Conference and Banqueting Co-ordinator: Ms F. Nigri; Ms L. Luoma
Capacity: 550 – 2, 4, 5, 6, 8

Really Useful Theatres
Manor House, 21 Soho Square, London, W1V 5FD (Tel: 020-7494 5200; Fax: 020-7434 1217;
Email: production@stoll-moss.com;
Web: http://www.stoll-moss.com)
Concerts and Hirings Manager: D. Kinsey
1, 2, 3, 6, 7

Regent's College Conference Centre
Regent's Park, Inner Circle, London, NW1 4NS (Tel: 020-7487 7540/1; Fax: 020-7487 7567;
Email: conferences@regents.ac.uk;
Web: http://www.regents.ac.uk/conferences)
Conference Manager: Ms C. Arouche
Capacity: 400 – 1, 2, 4, 5, 6, 7

The Ritz
150 Piccadilly, London, W1V 9DG (Tel: 020-7493 8181/7300 2246; Fax: 020-7300 2245;
Email: enquire@theritzhotel.co.uk;
Web: http://www.theritzhotel)
Group Sales Co-ordinator: S. Parry
Capacity: 50 – 4, 5, 7, 8

Roof Gardens
99 High Street, Kensington, London, W8 5ED (Tel: 020-7937 7994; Fax: 020-7938 2774)
Events Co-ordinator: Ms V. Loake
Capacity: 120 – 2, 4, 5, 7

Conference and Exhibition Venues   181

Royal Aeronautical Society
4 Hamilton Place, London, W1V 0BQ (Tel: 020-7670 4316; Fax: 020-7670 4319;
Email: roomhire@raes.org.uk)
Sales and Facilities Manager: J. Morris
Capacity: 280 – 1, 2, 3, 4, 5, 7, 8

Royal Air Force Museum
Grahame Park Way, London, NW9 5LL (Tel: 020-8205 2266; Fax: 020-8205 8044)
Conference and Events: Ms F. McGuinness
Capacity: 1000 – 3, 4, 5, 6, 7

Royal College of Physicians
11 St Andrew's Place, Regent's Park, London, NW1 4LE (Tel: 020-7935 1174; Fax: 020-7224 0900;
Email: events@rcplondon.ac.uk;
Web: http://www.rcplondon.ac.uk)
Events Co-ordinator: Miss A. Bachtler
Capacity: 300 – 1, 2, 3, 4, 5, 6, 7, 8

Royal Festival Hall
Commercial Department, SBC Royal Festival Hall, Belvedere Road, London, SE1 8XX (Tel: 020-7921 0680; Fax: 020-7921 0892;
Web: http://www.sbc.org.uk)
Conference Manager:
Capacity: 2600 – 1, 2, 3, 4, 5, 6, 7

Royal Horticultural Halls and Conference Centre
80 Vincent Square, London, SW1P 2PE (Tel: 020-7828 4125; Fax: 020-7834 2072; Email: horthalls@rhs.org.uk;
Web: http://www.horticultural-halls.co.uk)
Sales and Marketing Assistant: Ms H. Jones
Capacity: 1800 – 2, 3, 5, 7, 8

Royal Lancaster
Lancaster Terrace, London, W2 2TY (Tel: 020-7262 6737)
Assistant Administration Manager: Ms F. Barella
Capacity: 1000 – 2, 3, 4, 5, 6, 7

Royal National Theatre
South Bank, London, SE1 9PX (Tel: 020-7452 3560)
Event Hospitality Manager: Ms P. Klein
Capacity: 500 – 1, 2, 3, 4, 5, 6, 7

Royal Overseas League
Park Place, St James's Street, London, SW1A 1LR (Tel: 020-7408 0214; Fax: 020-7499 6738; Email: info@rosl.org.uk; Web: http://www.rosl.org.uk)
Conference and Banqueting Co-ordinators: Ms L. Medcalf; T. Hanmer
Capacity: 200 – 5, 6, 7

RSA
8 John Adam Street, London, WC2N 6EZ (Tel: 020-7839 5049; Fax: 020-7321 0271;
Email: conference@rsa-uk.demon.co.uk;
Web: http://www.rsa.org.uk)
Conference Administrator: Ms N. Kyle
Capacity: 200 – 1, 2, 3, 4, 5, 6, 7

School of Oriental and African Studies
Brunei Gallery, 10 Thornhaugh Street, Russell Square, London, WC1H 0XG (Tel: 020-7898 4917; Fax: 020-7323 6010; Email: sj10@soas.ac.uk)
Conference Manager: Ms S. Jones
Capacity: 290 – 1, 2, 3, 4, 5, 6, 7

Shakespeare's Globe
21 New Globe Walk, Bankside, London, SE1 9DT (Tel: 020-7902 1500; Fax: 020-7902 1515)
Exhibition Resources Manager: Ms C. Abbott
Capacity: 300 – 2, 3, 5, 6, 7

Sherlock Holmes Hotel
Baker Street, London, W1M 2LJ (Tel: 020-7486 6161; Fax: 020-7486 0884; Email: lonshafrm@hilton.com;
Web: http://www.hilton.com)
Conference and Banqueting Co-ordinator: Ms K. Leifels
4, 5, 6, 7, 8

Southwark Cathedral
Montague Close, London, SE1 9DA (Tel: 020-7367 6722; Fax: 020-7367 6725;
Email: cathedral@dswark.org.uk;
Web: http://www.dswark.org)
Events Co-ordinator: Ms R. Harding
Capacity: 120 – 2, 4, 5, 6, 7

Stakis Islington Hotel
53 Upper Street, Islington, London, N1 0UY (Tel: 020-7354 7700; Fax: 020-7354 7711;
Email: cb.office@islington.stakis.co.uk)
Conference Co-ordinator: Ms M. Holgren
Capacity: 24 – 4, 5, 6, 7, 8

The Strand Palace Hotel
372 The Strand, London, WC2R 0JJ (Tel: 020-7836 8080; Fax: 020-7257 9025;
Email: sophia.thomas@forte-hotels.com;
Web: http://www.forte-hotels.com)
Conference Manager: Ms S. Thomas
Capacity: 170 – 2, 4, 5, 6, 7, 8

Swallow Regent's Plaza Hotel
Plaza Parade, Maida Vale, London, NW6 5RP (Tel: 020-7543 6000; Fax: 020-7543 2495;
Email: regentsplaza@btinternet.com;
Web: http://www.regentsplazal.co.uk)
Business Development Manager: Miss M. Elyahou
Capacity: 200 – 4, 5, 6, 7, 8

The Thistle Bloomsbury
Bloomsbury Way, London, WC1A 2SD (Tel: 020-7242 5881; Fax: 020-7831 0225;
Email: bloomsbury@thistle.co.uk;
Web: http://www.thistlehotels.com)
Events Services Co-ordinator: Ms L. Bartlett
Capacity: 100 – 6, 7, 8

Thistle Euston Hotel
Cardington Street, London, NW1 2LP (Tel: 020-7387 4400; Fax: 020-7387 5413; Email: euston@thistle.co.uk;
Web: http://www.thistlehotels.com)
Conference Manager: A. McLean
Capacity: 90

Thistle Hyde Park
Lancaster Gate, London, W2 3NR (Tel: 020-7262 2711; Fax: 020-7262 2147;
Email: hyde.park@thistle.co.uk)
Revenue Manager: Ms T. Spillane
Capacity: 22 – 5, 6, 7, 8

Thistle Kings Cross
100 King's Cross Road, London, WC1X 9DT (Tel: 020-7278 2434; Fax: 020-7833 0798)
Conference Sales Manager: Ms K. Gilbert
Capacity: 160 – 2, 4, 5, 6, 7, 8

Thistle Lancaster Gate
75-89 Lancaster Gate, London, W2 3NN (Tel: 020-7402 4272; Fax: 020-7298 0208)
Events Manager: Louise Bennett
Capacity: 100 – 5, 6, 7, 8

Thistle Westminster
49 Buckingham Palace Road, London, SW1W 0QT (Tel: 020-7834 1821; Fax: 020-7931 7542;
Email: royalwestminster@thistle.co.uk;
Web: http://www.thistlehotels.com.uk)
Conference, Banqueting and Sales Co-ordinators: Ms M. Moltd
Capacity: 150 – 3, 4, 5, 7, 8

Tower Bridge Experience
Tower Bridge, London, SE1 2UP (Tel: 020-7407 9222; Fax: 020-7357 7935;
Email: enquiries@towerbridge.org.uk;
Web: http://www.towerbridge.org.uk)
Capacity: 250 – 6, 7

Tower Thistle Hotel
St Katharine's Way, London, E1 9LD (Tel: 020-7481 2575; Fax: 020-7488 1667)
Event Services Manager: Ms G. Belcher
Capacity: 550 – 2, 4, 5, 6, 7, 8

Twickenham Conference Centre
Rugby Road, Twickenham, Middx, TW1 1DZ (Tel: 020-8891 4565; Fax: 020-8744 2104;
Web: http://www.rfu.com)
Conference Co-ordinator: Ms P. Cheetham
Capacity: 350 – 2, 4, 5, 6, 7

University of Westminster
Commercial Services, Luxborough Suite, 35 Marylebone Road, London, NW1 5LS (Tel: 020-7911 5796/5799/5807; Fax: 020-7911 5141;
Email: comserv@westminster.ac.uk)
Reservation and Sales Executive: Ms M. Di Palmo
Capacity: 350 – 1, 2, 5, 6, 7, 8

Westminster Hotel
16 Leinster Square, Bayswater, London, W2 4PR (Tel: 020-7221 9131; Fax: 020-7221 4073)
Food and Beverage Manager: Ms L. Hankins
Capacity: 120 – 2, 5, 6, 7, 8

LEGAL LONDON

LEGAL SYSTEM
CIRCUIT JUDGES
CROWN COURTS
COUNTY COURTS
MAGISTRATES' COURTS
CORONERS' COURTS
TRIBUNALS
CROWN PROSECUTION SERVICE
PRISON SERVICE
PROBATION SERVICE
LEGAL BODIES

LEGAL LONDON

Introduction

Throughout its history, London has been the centre and focus of the legal system of the United Kingdom. The reasons are manifold but political and economic centralisation as well as London's position as a centre for trade and finance are among the main historical determinants. As the capital, London lies at the heart of the political system of the UK and despite the separate Scottish legal system and the recent devolution of power to the Scottish Parliament and Welsh Assembly, the highest courts in the UK remain in London. A disproportionate amount of legal activity is still conducted in the capital for this reason. London's pre-eminence as an international financial centre can be added as another factor in this equation. Over the years international trade and finance, concentrated in the square mile of the City of London has led to a specialised industry of commercial lawyers unrivalled in size and scope in other parts of the country. The London legal community has always embraced this trend and has actively promoted London as a centre for commercial law and dispute resolution.

There are approximately one hundred and fifty courts in London, ranging from magistrates courts and county courts, to the various divisions of the High Courts, the Court of Appeal (unique outside Scotland which has its own Court of Appeal) and the judicial division of the House of Lords (uniquely based in London and the UK's highest judicial authority). This inevitably means that the highest levels of the judiciary in the United Kingdom remain concentrated in London. In addition to this there are a number of specialist tribunals and courts based in London, for example, the Commercial Court, the Technology and Construction Court, the Employment Appeal Tribunal and the Immigration Appeal Tribunal.

Equally important to the London legal market is the fact that many bodies which control and regulate the legal professions remain based in London, namely the Law Society, the Inns of Court and the General Council of the Bar. Further, many industries which may be of interest to lawyers are controlled and/or regulated by bodies based in London. These include the Financial Services Authority, the Stock Exchange (recently merged with the Exchange in Frankfurt), Lloyd's of London, the Competition Commission and government departments such as the Lord Chancellor's Department and the Department of Trade and Industry.

Solicitors

The number of solicitors registered in England and Wales is around 95,000 (1998 Law Society figures), with 75,000 of those holding practising certificates. Of those holding such certificates, some 60,000 work in private practice and the remaining 15,000 practice 'in-house'. The remaining 20,000 registered solicitors are mainly in employment performing a number of tasks but not formally in practice. The number of solicitors' firms in England and Wales is around 8,200.

According to Law Society research, about one-third of all solicitors holding practising certificates are employed by organisations based in London, with almost half of all solicitors' firms being based either in London or the south east of England. As one looks at firms which are larger in size, the concentration increases, with 60 per cent of 'large firms' (defined as having 26 partners or more) being based in London. The greater number of these large firms are concentrated in the City of London, specialising in corporate or commercial law, often of an international flavour.

In London the largest firms are concentrated in the City of London, and elite group often organised internationally, with offices abroad specialising in both English and local law. According to some surveys, the bulk of solicitors' overseas earnings (estimated at some £600 million by the Law Society in 1997) is earned by these firms alone. City firms are often in a position to dictate the price to the client as a result of their concentration of expertise and consequent abililty to deal with a range of transactions for large clients, for example, corporate transactions, corporate finance and associated litigation. Competition amongst these firms is often intense, the largest ten of which are known informally as the 'magic circle' of firms.

Barristers

There are about 9,000 barristers in independent practice in England and Wales, about 6,000 of whom practice in London. The concentration in London of courts and of legal activity generally goes some way to explain these figures. There are currently around 250 sets of barristers chambers in London handling work of all kinds. Despite the many recent changes in the regulation of the legal professions it is still true to say that barristers specialise as independent advocates in whichever area of law they chose to practice and that barristers continue to dominate as advocates in the higher courts, both criminal and civil. The recent development of rights of audience for solicitors in the higher courts and the reforms both of the legal aid system and the civil litigation procedure have, however, led to widespread changes for the bar in London as they have elsewhere, and it is common ground among commentators that the bar as an industry is in the process of restructuring, although only the beginnings of this process are currently being witnessed. It is evident that many barristers in London are changing the way they work, whether this takes the form of joining chambers which specialise in one area of law, undertaking more advisory, non-litigious work, or trying to develop completely new areas of work in, for example, e-commerce or Alternative Dispute Resolution.

THE LEGAL SYSTEM

The Judicature of England and Wales

The supreme judicial authority for England and Wales is the House of Lords, which is the ultimate Court of Appeal from all courts in Great Britain and Northern Ireland (except criminal courts in Scotland) for all cases except those concerning the interpretation and application of European Community law, including preliminary rulings requested by British courts and tribunals, which are decided by the European Court of Justice. Under the Human Rights Act 1998, which is due to come into force on 2 October 2000, the European Convention on Human Rights will be incorporated into British law; unresolved cases will still be referred to the European Court of Human Rights. As a Court of Appeal the House of Lords consists of the Lord Chancellor and the Lords of Appeal in Ordinary (law lords).

Supreme Court of Judicature

The Supreme Court of Judicature comprises the Court of Appeal, the High Court of Justice and the Crown Court. The High Court of Justice is the superior civil court and is divided into three divisions. The Chancery Division is concerned mainly with equity, bankruptcy and contentious probate business. The Queen's Bench Division deals with commercial and maritime law, serious personal injury and medical negligence cases, cases involving a breach of contract and professional negligence actions. The Family Division deals with matters relating to family law. Sittings are held at the Royal Courts of Justice in London. High Court judges sit alone to hear cases at first instance. Appeals from lower courts are heard by two or three judges, or by single judges of the appropriate division. Appeals from the High Court are heard in the Court of Appeal (Civil Division), presided over by the Master of the Rolls, and may go on to the House of Lords.

Criminal Cases

In criminal matters the decision to prosecute in the majority of cases rests with the Crown Prosecution Service, the independent prosecuting body in England and Wales. The Service is headed by the Director of Public Prosecutions, who works under the superintendence of the Attorney-General. Certain categories of offence continue to require the Attorney-General's consent for prosecution.

The Crown Court sits in about 90 centres throughout England and Wales, divided into six circuits, and is presided over by High Court judges, full-time circuit judges, and part-time recorders and assistant recorders, sitting with a jury in all trials which are contested. The Crown Court deals with trials of the more serious criminal offences, the sentencing of offenders committed for sentence by magistrates' courts (when the magistrates consider their own power of sentence inadequate), and appeals from magistrates' courts. Magistrates usually sit with a circuit judge or recorder to deal with appeals and committals for sentence. Appeals from the Crown Court, either against sentence or conviction, are made to the Court of Appeal (Criminal Division), presided over by the Lord Chief Justice. A further appeal from the Court of Appeal to the House of Lords can be brought if a point of law of general public importance is considered to be involved.

Minor criminal offences (summary offences) are dealt with in magistrates' courts, which usually consist of three unpaid lay magistrates (justices of the peace) sitting without a jury, who are advised on points of law and procedure by a legally-qualified clerk to the justices. In busier courts a full-time, salaried and legally-qualified stipendiary magistrate presides alone. Cases involving people under 18 are heard in youth courts, specially constituted magistrates' courts which sit apart from other courts. Preliminary proceedings in a serious case to decide whether there is evidence to justify committal for trial in the Crown Court are also dealt with in the magistrates' courts. Appeals from magistrates' courts against sentence or conviction are made to the Crown Court. Appeals upon a point of law are made to the High Court, and may go on to the House of Lords.

Civil Cases

Most minor civil cases are dealt with by the county courts. Cases are heard by circuit judges or district judges. For cases involving small claims there are special simplified procedures. Where there are financial limits on county court jurisdiction, claims which exceed those limits may be tried in the county courts with the consent of the parties, or in certain circumstances on transfer from the High Court. Outside London, bankruptcy proceedings can be heard in designated county courts. Magistrates' courts can deal with certain classes of civil case and committees of magistrates license public houses, clubs and betting shops. For the implementation of the Children Act 1989, a new structure of hearing centres was set up in 1991 for family proceedings cases, involving magistrates' courts (family proceedings courts), divorce county courts, family hearing centres and care centres. Appeals in family matters heard in the family proceedings courts go to the Family Division of the High Court; affiliation appeals and appeals from decisions of the licensing committees of magistrates go to the Crown Court. Appeals from county courts are heard in the Court of Appeal (Civil Division), and may go on to the House of Lords.

Coroners' Courts

Coroners' courts investigate violent and unnatural deaths or sudden deaths where the cause is unknown. Cases may be brought before a local coroner (a senior lawyer or doctor) by doctors, the police, various public authorities or members of the public. Where a death is sudden and the cause is unknown, the coroner may order a post-mortem examination to determine the cause of death rather than hold an inquest in court.

Appointments to the Judiciary

Judicial appointments are made by The Queen; the most senior appointments are made on the advice of the Prime Minister and other appointments on the advice of the Lord Chancellor.

Under the provisions of the Criminal Appeal Act 1995, a Commission was set up to direct and supervise investigations into possible miscarriages of justice and to refer cases to the courts on the grounds of conviction and sentence; these functions were formerly the responsibility of the Home Secretary.

Circuit Judges 187

High Court and Crown Court Centres
The London area is served by the south-eastern circuit. First-tier centres deal with both civil and criminal cases and are served by High Court and circuit judges. Second-tier centres deal with criminal cases only and are served by High Court and circuit judges. Third-tier centres deal with criminal cases only and are served only by circuit judges. The High Court in Greater London sits at the Royal Courts of Justice.

South-Eastern Circuit
First-tier – Chelmsford, **Croydon**, Lewes, Norwich
Second-tier – Chichester, Ipswich, **London (Central Criminal Court)**, Luton, Maidstone, Reading, St Albans
Third-tier – Aylesbury, Basildon, Bury St Edmunds, Cambridge, Canterbury, Guildford, Hove, King's Lynn, **London (Blackfriars, Harrow, Inner London Sessions House, Isleworth, Kingston, Knightsbridge, Middlesex Guildhall, Snaresbrook, Southend, Southwark, Wood Green, Woolwich)**

South-Eastern Circuit Administrator's Office
R. J. Clark, New Cavendish House, 18 Maltravers Street, London WC2R 3EU (Tel: 020-7936 7234; Fax: 020-7936 7230)

Provincial Administrator
J. Powell, 1st Floor, Steeple House, Church Lane, Chelmsford CM1 1NH (Tel: 01245-257425)

Group Managers
London Group (Civil): D. Marsh; London Group (Crime): K. Budgen

CIRCUIT JUDGES

*Senior Circuit Judges
South-Eastern Circuit

Presiding Judges: The Hon. Mr Justice Gage; The Hon. Mr Justice Moses
Circuit Judges: J. D. R. Adams; M. F. Addison; P. C. Ader; Mrs S. C. Andrew; A. R. L. Ansell; M. G. Anthony; S. A. Anwyl, QC; M. F. Baker, QC; A. F. Balston; G. S. Barham; C. J. A. Barnett, QC; W. E. Barnett, QC; R. A. Barratt, QC; K. Bassingthwaighte; *G. A. Bathurst Norman; P. J. L. Beaumont, QC; N. E. Beddard; Mrs C. V. Bevington; M. G. Binning; J. E. Bishop; B. M. B. Black; H. O. Blacksell, QC; J. G. Boal, QC; A. V. Bradbury; P. N. Brandt; R. G. Brown; J. M. Bull, QC; *N. M. Butter, QC; The Hon. C. W. Byers; C. V. Callman; J. Q. Campbell; M. J. Carroll; B. E. F. Catlin; *B. L. Charles, QC; P. C. L. Clark; P. C. Clegg; Miss S. Coates; N. J. Coleman; S. H. Colgan; P. H. Collins; C. C. Colston, QC; S. S. Coltart; J. S. Colyer, QC; C. D. Compston; T. A. C. Coningsby, QC; J. G. Connor; R. D. Connor; M. J. Cook; R. A. Cooke; M. R. Coombe; P. E. Copley; Dr E. Cotran; P. R. Cowell; R. C. Cox; M. L. S. Cripps; J. F. Crocker; D. L. Croft, QC; H. M. Crush; D. M. Cryan; P. Curl; *D. M. T. Dangor; M. Dean, QC; *P. G. Dedman; *W. N. Denison, QC (Common Serjeant); J. E. Devaux; M. N. Devonshire, TD; P. H. Downes; W. H. Dunn, QC; C. M. Edwards; D. F. Elfer, QC; D. R. Ellis; R. C. Elly; C. Elwen; F. P. E. Evans; J. D. Farnworth; P. Fingret; P. E. J. Focke, QC; P. Ford; G. C. F. Forrester; Ms D. A. Freedman; L. Gerber; C. A. H. Gibson; Miss A. F. Goddard, QC; A. Goldstein; C. G. M. Gordon; J. B. Gosschalk; *A. A. Goymer; *M. Graham, QC; B. S. Green, QC; D. J. Griffiths; G. D. Grigson; R. B. Groves, td, vrd; N. T. Hague, QC; A. B. R. Hallgarten, QC; Miss G. Hallon; J. Hamilton; Miss S. Hamilton, QC; C. R. H. Hardy; B. Hargrove, OBE, QC; M. F. Harris; *W. G. Hawkesworth; R. G. Hawkins, QC; J. M. Haworth; R. J. Haworth; R. M. Hayward; A. N. Hitching; H. E. G. Hodge, OBE; *D. Holden; J. F. Holt; A. C. W. Hordern, QC; K. A. D. Hornby; M. Hucker; J. G. Hull, QC; M. J. Hyam (Recorder of London); D. A. Inman; A. B. Issard-Davies; Dr P. J. E. Jackson; T. J. C. Joseph; I. G. F. Karsten, QC; S. S. Katkhuda; C. J. B. Kemp; M. Kennedy, QC; A. M. Kenny; T. R. King; B. J. Knight, QC; L. G. Krikler; L. H. C. Lait; P. St J. H. Langan, QC; Capt. J. B. R. Langdon, RN; P. H. Latham; R. Laurie; T. Lawrence; D. M. Levy, QC; C. C. D. Lindsay, QC; S. H. Lloyd; F. R. Lockhart; Mrs C. M. Ludlow; Capt. S. Lyons; A. G. McDowall; R. J. McGregor-Johnson; K. M. McHale; K. A. Machin, QC; R. G. McKinnon; W. N. McKinnon; K. C. Macrae; T. Maher; F. J. M. Marr-Johnson; D. N. N. Martineau; N. A. Medawar, QC; D. B. Meier; D. J. Mellor; G. D. Mercer; D. Q. Miller; Miss A. E. Mitchell; F. I. Mitchell; H. M. Morgan; D. Morton Jack; R. T. Moss; Miss M. J. S. Mowat; T. M. E. Nash; M. H. D. Neligan; Mrs M. F. Norrie; Brig. A. P. Norris, obe; P. W. O'Brien; M. A. Oppenheimer; D. C. J. Paget, QC; D. J. Parry; A. Patience, QC; *Mrs N. Pearce; Prof. D. S. Pearl; Miss V. A. Pearlman; B. P. Pearson; J. R. Peppitt, QC; N. A. J. Philpot; T. D. Pillay; D. C. Pitman; J. R. Platt; J. S. Playford, QC; B. P. Pollock; T. G. Pontius; W. D. C. Poulton; S. Pratt; R. J. C. V. Prendergast; J. E. Previté, QC; B. H. Pryor, QC; J. E. Pullinger; D. W. Radford; J. W. Rant, CB, QC; E. V. P. Reece; J. R. Reid, QC; M. P. Reynolds; G. K. Rice; M. S. Rich, QC; N. P. Riddell; G. Rivlin, QC; S. D. Robbins; J. M. Roberts; *D. A. H. Rodwell, QC; G. H. Rooke, td, QC; W. M. Rose; P. C. R. Rountree; J. H. Rucker; T. R. G. Ryland; J. E. A. Samuels, QC; R. B. Sanders; A. R. G. Scott-Gall; J. S. Sennitt; D. Serota, QC; J. L. Sessions; D. R. A. Sich; A. G. Simmons; K. T. Simpson; P. R. Simpson; M. Singh, QC; S. P. Sleeman; C. M. Smith, QC; S. A. R. Smith; R. J. Southan; S. B. Spence; S. M. Stephens, QC; N. A. Stewart; D. M. A. Stokes, QC; *W. F. C. Thomas; P. J. Thompson; A. G. Y. Thorpe; C. H. Tilling; C. J. M. Tyrer; Mrs A. P. Uziell-Hamilton; J. E. van der Werff; A. O. R. Vick, QC; T. L. Viljoen; Miss A. P. Wakefield; R. Wakefield; R. Walker; S. P. Waller; D. B. Watling, QC; A. R. Webb; C. S. Welchman; A. F. Wilkie, QC; S. R. Wilkinson; R. J. Winstanley; D. Worsley; M. P. Yelton; K. H. Zucker, QC

188 Legal London

CROWN COURTS

Blackfriars
Pocock Street, London, SE1 0BJ (Tel: 020-7922 5800; Fax: 020-7922 5815; DX: 400800 LAMBETH 3)
Court Manager: Ms C. Read

Central Criminal
Old Bailey, London, EC4M 7EH (Tel: 020-7248 3277; Fax: 020-7248 5735; DX: 46700 OLD BAILEY)
Court Manager: J. Owen

Croydon Combined
The Law Courts, Altyre Road, Croydon, CR9 5AB (Tel: 020-8410 4700; Fax: 020-8781 1007; DX: 97473 CROYDON 6)

Harrow
Hailsham Drive, Harrow, Middx, HA1 4TU (Tel: 020-8424 2294; Fax: 020-8424 2209; DX: 97335 HARROW 5)

Inner London
Sessions House, Newington Causeway, London, SE1 6AZ (Tel: 020-7234 3100; Fax: 020-7234 3222; DX: 97345 SOUTHWARK 3)
Court Manager: Ms P. Hochfelder

Isleworth
36 Ridgeway Road, Isleworth, Middx, TW7 5LP (Tel: 020-8568 8811; Fax: 020-8568 5368; DX: 97420 ISLEWORTH 1)
Court Manager: Ms J. Coles

Kingston-upon-Thames
6-8 Penrhyn Road, Kingston-upon-Thames, KT1 2BB (Tel: 020-8240 2500; Fax: 020-8240 2675; DX: 97430 KINGSTON-UPON-THAMES 2)
Court Manager: R. Foster

Middlesex Guildhall
Little George Street, London, SW1P 3BB (Tel: 020-7799 2131; Fax: 020-7233 1612; DX: 122920 PARLIAMENT SQUARE)
Court Manager: S. Courtney

Snaresbrook
75 Hollybush Hill, Snaresbrook, London, E11 1QW (Tel: 020-8982 5500; Fax: 020-8989 1371; DX: 9824 WANSTEAD 2)

Southwark
1 English Grounds, off Battlebridge Lane, Southwark, London, SE1 2HU (Tel: 020-7522 7200; Fax: 020-7522 7300; DX: 39913 LONDON BRIDGE SOUTH)
Court Manager: C. A. Harper

Wood Green
Woodall Lane, Lordship Lane, Wood Green, London, N22 5LF (Tel: 020-8881 1400; Fax: 020-8881 4802; DX: 130346 WOOD GREEN 3)

Woolwich
2 Belmarsh Road, London, SE28 0EY (Tel: 020-8312 7000; Fax: 020-8312 7078; DX: 117650 WOOLWICH 7)
Court Manager: J. Crampsey

COUNTY COURTS

Barnet
St Mary's Court, Regents Park Road, Finchley Central, London, N3 1BQ (Tel: 020-8343 4272; Fax: 020-8343 1324; DX: 122570 FINCHLEY (CHURCH END)
Court Manager: Mrs S. Mosley
District Judges: M. Trent; S. Gerlis; J. Karet

Bow
96 Romford Road, Stratford, E15 4EG (Tel: 020-8536 5200; Fax: 020-8503 1152; DX: 97490 STRATFORD (LONDON; DX: 2)
Court Manager: Ms J. Holland
District Judges: R. W. Mullis; D. L. Millard; F. J. Wilkinson; R. H. Naqui-Gregory

Brentford
Alexandra Road, High Street, Brentford, Middx, TW8 0JJ (Tel: 020-8560 3424; Fax: 020-8568 2401; Web: http://www.courtservice.gov.uk; DX: 97840 BRENTFORD 2)
Court Manager: J. Bones
District Judges: C. Edwards; S. Plaskow; J. Allen; T. Jenkins

Central London
13-14 Park Crescent, London, W1N 4HT (Tel: 020-7917 5000; Fax: 020-7917 5014; DX: 97325 REGENTS PARK 2)
Court Manager: Mrs J. Lewis
District Judges: C. P. Wigfield; Mrs S. Hasan; Mrs M. Langley; M. J. Haselgrove; M. Gilchrist

Clerkenwell
33 Duncan Terrace, Islington, London, N1 8AN (Tel: 020-7359 7347; Fax: 020-7354 1166; DX: 58284 ISLINGTON)
Court Manager: I. Anderson
District Judges: A. Armon-Jones; R. Southcombe

Edmonton
Court House, 59 Fore Street, Upper Edmonton, London, N18 2TN (Tel: 020-8807 1666; Fax: 020-8803 0564; DX: 36206 EDMONTON 1)
Court Manager: P. Joseph
District Judges: G. Silverman; S. Morley; L. Cohen
Circuit Judge: N. Riddell

Ilford
Buckingham Road, Ilford, Essex, IG1 1BR (Tel: 020-8478 1132; Fax: 020-8553 2824; DX: 97510 ILFORD 3)
Court Manager: Miss K. Langan
District Judges: I. V. Sheratte; A. Thomas

Lambeth
Court House, Cleaver Street, Kennington Road, London, SE11 4DZ (Tel: 020-7735 4425; Fax: 020-7735 8147; DX: 33254 KENNINGTON)
Court Manager: M. Burke
District Judges: R. M. Jacey; M. Zimmels

The Mayor's and City of London
Guildhall Buildings, Basinghall Street, London, EC2V 5AR (Tel: 020-7796 5400; Fax: 020-7796 5424; Web: http://www.courtservice.gov.uk;

County Courts 189

DX: 97520 MOORGATE EC2)
Court Manager: Ms Collins
District Judges: S. M. Samuels; J. S. Lipton

Romford
2A Oaklands Avenue, Romford, Essex, RM1 4DP (Tel: 01708-750677; Fax: 01708-756653; DX: 97530 ROMFORD 2)
Court Manager: J. Ward
District Judges: N. E. Jackson: J. H. G. Chrispin; A. D. Thomas

Shoreditch
19 Leonard Street, London, EC2A 4AL (Tel: 020-7253 0956; Fax: 020-7490 5613;
DX: 121000 SHOREDITCH 2)
Court Manager: Ms A. Latham
District Judge: J. Wright; J. Beattie

Wandsworth
76-78 Upper Richmond Road, Putney, London, SW15 2SU (Tel: 020-8333 4351; Fax: 020-8877 9854;
Email: wandsworth.cty.cm@courtservice.gsi.gov.uk;
Web: http://www.courtservice.gov.uk;
DX: 97540 PUTNEY 2)
Court Manager: Mrs T. Wildash
District Judges: I. G. Tilbury; J. Gittens; M. Walker

West London
43 North End Road, West Kensington, London, W14 8SZ (Tel: 020-7602 8444; Fax: 020-7602 1820;
DX: 97550 WEST KENSINGTON 2)
Court Manager: P. M. Skidmore
District Judges: N. Madge; T. Jenkins

Willesden
9 Acton Lane, Harlesden, London, NW10 8SB (Tel: 020-8963 8200; Fax: 020-8453 0946;
DX: 97560 HARLESDEN 2)
Court Manager: P. Downer
District Judges: A. J. Morris; D. V. Steel; E. Cohen; C. Dabezies

Woolwich
The Court House, Powis Street, London, SE18 6JW (Tel: 020-8854 2127; Fax: 020-8316 4842;
DX: 12345 WOOLWICH 8)
Court Manager: Mrs J. Collins
District Judges: M. Lee

MAGISTRATES' COURTS

City of London
The Justice Rooms, 1 Queen Victoria Street, London, EC4N 4XY (Tel: 020-7332 1830; Fax: 020-7332 1493; DX: 98943 CHEAPSIDE 2)
Justices' Chief Executive and Clerk to the Justices: J. D. Wignall

Inner London
65 Romney Street, London, SW1P 3RD (Tel: 0845-600 8889; Fax: 020-7805 1099; DX: 120550 VICTORIA 6)
Justices' Chief Executive: Miss C. Glenn

Acton
The Court House, Winchester Street, Acton, London, W3 8PB (Tel: 020-8992 9014; Fax: 020-8993 9647; DX: 82606 WEST EALING)
Justices' Clerk: H. J. Dingwall

Barking
The Court House, East Street, Barking, Essex, IG11 8EW (Tel: 020-8594 5311; Fax: 020-8594 4297; DX: 8518 BARKING 1)
Justices' Clerk: R. Wright

Barnet
Justices' Clerk's Office, 7C High Street, Barnet, Herts, EN5 5UE (Tel: 020-8441 9042; Fax: 020-8441 6753; DX: 8626 BARNET)
Justices' Clerk: J. Clark

Bexley
Norwich Place, Bexleyheath, Kent, DA6 7NB (Tel: 020-8304 5211; Fax: 020-8303 6849;
DX: 100150 BEXLEYHEATH 3)
Justices' Clerk: Mrs C. A. Pilmore-Bedford

Bow Street
28 Bow Street, London, WC2E 7AS (Tel: 020-7379 4713; Fax: 020-7379 5634;
DX: 40041 COVENT GARDEN 2)

Brent
Church End, 448 High Road, Brent, London, NW10 2DZ (Tel: 020-8955 0555; Fax: 020-8955 0543;
DX: 110850 WILLESDEN 2)
Justices' Clerk: P. W. H. Lydiate

Brentford
Market Place, Brentford, Middx, TW8 8EN (Tel: 020-8568 9811; Fax: 020-8560 3578;
DX: 133823 FELTHAM 3)
Justices' Clerk: A. J. M. Baldwin

Bromley
The Court House, 1 London Road, Bromley, Kent, BR1 1RA (Tel: 020-8325 4000; Fax: 020-8325 4006;
Email: admin@bromley.olmcs-law.co.uk;
Web: http://www.bromleymagscourt.demon.co.uk;
DX: 119601 BROMLEY 8)
Justices' Clerk: R J Haynes

Camberwell Green
15 D'Eynsford Road, Camberwell Green, London, SE5 7UP (Tel: 0845-600 8889; Fax: 020-7805 9897;
DX: 35305 CAMBERWELL GREEN)
Justices' Clerk: Miss B. A. Morse

Croydon
Barclay Road, Croydon, CR9 3NG (Tel: 020-8686 8680; Fax: 020-8680 9801)
Justices' Clerk: Mrs C. J. Bridges

Ealing
The Court House, Green Man Lane, Ealing, London, W13 0SD (Tel: 020-8579 9833; Fax: 020-8579 2985; DX: 82606 WEST EALING)
Justices' Clerk: H. J. Dingwall

Enfield
The Court House, Lordship Lane, Tottenham, London, N17 6RT (Tel: 020-8808 5411; Fax: 020-8885 4343;

190 Legal London

DX: 134490 TOTTENHAM 3)
Justices' Clerk: A. P. G. S. Shepstone

Feltham
Hanworth Road, Feltham, Middx, TW13 5AF (Tel: 020-8890 4811; Fax: 020-8844 1779; DX: 133821 FELTHAM 3)
Justices' Clerk: A. J. M. Baldwin

Greenwich
9 Blackheath Road, Greenwich, London, SE10 8PG (Tel: 020-8276 1356; Fax: 020-8692 3910; DX: 35203 GREENWICH WEST)
Justices' Clerk: Miss B. L. Barnes

Haringey
The Court House, Bishops Road, off Archway Road, Highgate, London, N6 4HS (Tel: 020-8340 3472; Fax: 020-7348 3343; DX: 1235501/1/2 HIGHGATE 3)
Justices' Clerk: G. Fillingham

Harrow
PO Box 164, Rosslyn Crescent, Wealdstone, Harrow, Middx, HA1 2JY (Tel: 020-8427 5146; Fax: 020-8863 9518; DX: 30451 HARROW 3)
Justices' Clerk: G. Cropper

Havering
Main Road, Romford, Essex, RM1 3BH (Tel: 01708-771771; Fax: 01708-771777;
Email: general.office@havering.olmcs-law.co.uk;
DX: 131527 ROMFORD 8)
Justices' Clerk: T. J. Ring

Hendon
Court House, The Hyde, Hendon, London, NW9 7BY (Tel: 020-8441 9042; Fax: 020-8205 4595;
DX: 8626 BARNET)
Justices' Clerk: J. Clark

Highbury Corner
51 Holloway Road, London, N7 8JA (Tel: 0845-600 8889; Fax: 020-7506 3191; DX: 51855 HIGHBURY)
Justices' Clerk: Mrs J. Woolley

Horseferry Road
70 Horseferry Road, London, SW1P 2AX (Tel: 020-7233 2000; Fax: 020-7233 0174;
DX: 120551 VICTORIA 6)
Justices' Clerk: Mrs G. Houghton Jones

Kingston-upon-Thames
19 High Street, Kingston-upon-Thames, Surrey, KT1 1JW (Tel: 020-8546 5603; Fax: 020-8481 4848;
Email: general@kingston.olmcs-law.co.uk;
DX: 119975 KINGSTON-UPON-THAMES 6)
Justices' Clerk: A. R. Vickers

Marylebone
181 Marylebone Road, London, NW1 5QJ (Tel: 020-7706 1261; Fax: 020-7724 9884;
DX: 41740 MARYLEBONE 2)
Justices' Clerk: E. Houghton

Richmond-upon-Thames
Parkshot, Richmond, Surrey, TW9 2RF (Tel: 020-8948 2101; Fax: 020-8332 0698;

DX: 100257 RICHMOND 2)
Justices' Clerk: D. K. Lowdell

Stratford
389-397 High Street, London, E15 4SB (Tel: 020-8522 5000; Fax: 020-8519 9214; DX: 5417 STRATFORD)
Justices' Clerk: G. K. Norris

Sutton
The Court House, Shotfield, Wallington, Surrey, SM6 0JA (Tel: 020-8770 5950; Fax: 020-8770 5977;
DX: 59957 WALLINGTON)
Justices' Clerk: J. C. Sunderland

Thames
58 Bow Road, London, E3 4DJ (Tel: 020-8980 1000; Fax: 020-8980 0670; DX: 55654 BOW)
Justices' Clerk: K. T. Griffiths

Tower Bridge
211 Tooley Street, London, SE1 2JY (Tel: 020-7407 4232; Fax: 020-7378 0712;
DX: 39921 LONDON BRIDGE SOUTH)

Uxbridge
The Court House, Harefield Road, Uxbridge, Middx, UB8 1PQ (Tel: 01895-814646; Fax: 01895-274280;
DX: 98053 UXBRIDGE 2)
Justices' Clerk: P. J. M. Hamilton

Waltham Forest
The Court House, 1 Farnan Avenue, Walthamstow, London, E17 4NX (Tel: 020-7527 8000; Fax: 020-7527 9063; DX: 124542)
Justices' Clerk: P. F. Cozens

West London
181 Talgarth Road, London, W6 8DN (Tel: 020-8741 1234; Fax: 020-8700 9344;
DX: 124800 HAMMERSMITH 8)
Justices' Clerk: Miss M. H. Parry

Wimbledon
The Law Courts, Alexandra Road, Wimbledon, London, SW19 7JP (Tel: 020-8946 8622; Fax: 020-8946 7030; DX: 116610 WIMBLEDON 4)
Justices' Clerk: E. Packer

Woolwich
Market Street, Woolwich, London, SE18 6QY (Tel: 020-8855 8518; Fax: 020-8316 5190)

FAMILY PROCEEDINGS COURT

Inner London and City Family Proceedings
59-65 Wells Street, London, W1A 3AE (Tel: 020-7805 3400; Fax: 020-7805 3490;
Email: familycourt@ilmcl.freeserve.co.uk;
DX: 89268 SOHO SQUARE)
Justices' Clerk: Miss A. F. Damazer

GREATER LONDON MAGISTRATES' COURTS AUTHORITY

Londoners are set to benefit from a better justice system due to the launch of the Greater London Magistrates' Courts Authority under the Access to Justice Act 1999. Throughout 2000 the new authority will prepare to

Tribunals 191

replace the existing network of 22 London Magistrates' Courts Committees (MCCs), assuming full responsibility for the efficient and effective running of Greater London magistrates' courts in April 2001. The 22 MCCs that will be replaced by the Greater London Magistrates' Courts Authority are: City of London, Inner London, Barking, Barnet, Bexley, Brent, Bromley, Croydon, Ealing, Enfield, Haringey, Harrow, Havering, Hillingdon, Hounslow, Kingston-upon-Thames, Merton, Newham, Redbridge, Richmond-upon-Thames, Sutton and Waltham Forest. The new authority will be more accountable to the people of London as it will have two elected members from local authorities and two nominated by the Mayor of London.

The aims behind amalgamating the MCCs into a single authority are to:
* reduce delay in the processing and hearing of cases
* improve the efficiency of the courts through economies of scale, greater flexibility to allocate cases to courts and central administration
* make better use of public money by reducing bureaucracy
* improve co-ordination and communication with other criminal justice agencies such as the police and the Crown Prosecution Service by greater alignment of boundaries

Members: (*Local Authority*) Narinder Singh Matharoo, JP, Derek Sawyer; (*District Judge Magistrates' Court*) Stephen Dawson, DJMC; (*Magistrates*) Prof. Brian Gomes da Costa, Chris Lowe, Dr. Patrick Davies, Mrs Elizabeth Hurst, Brian Ward, Dr Malcolm Cohen, Mrs Yvonne Constance, Dr Zaka Khan, Mrs Lesley White

MAGISTRATES' COURTS COMMITTEE FOR THE INNER LONDON AREA

65 Romney Street, London SW1P 3RD (Tel: 0845 600 8889)
Justices' Chief Executive and Clerk to the Committee: Miss C. Glenn
Justices' Clerk (Training): Miss J. Whitby
Chief Metropolitan Stipendiary Magistrate and Chairman of Magistrates' Courts Committee for Inner London Area: G. E. Parkinson (Bow Street)

CORONERS' COURTS

City of London
Milton Court, Moor Lane, London, EC2Y 9BL (Tel: 020-7332 1598; Fax: 020-7601 2714)
Coroner: D. R. Chambers

Eastern
Queens Road, Walthamstow, E17 8QP (Tel: 020-8520 7245/6/7; Fax: 020-8521 0896)
Coroner: Dr E. J. Stearns

Inner North
Poplar Coroners' Court, Camley Street, NW1 0PP (Tel: 020-7387 4882; Fax: 020-7383 2485)
Coroner: Dr S. M. T. Chan

Inner South
Southwark Coroners' Court, Municipal Offices, 151 Walworth Road, SE17 1RY (Tel: 020-7525 2051; Fax: 020-7378 8401)
Coroner: Mrs Selena Lynch

Inner West
65 Horseferry Road, SW1P 2ED (Tel: 020-7834 6515; Fax: 020-7828 2837)
Coroner: Dr P. Knapman

North
Myddleton Road, Hornsey, N8 7PY (Tel: 020-8348 4411; Fax: 020-8347 5229)
Coroner: W. F. G. Dolman

South
The Law Courts, Barclay Road, Croydon, CR9 3NE (Tel: 020-8681 5019; Fax: 020-8686 3491)
Coroner: P. B. Rose

West
Hammersmith Coroners' Court, 25 Bagley's Lane, London, SW6 2QA (Tel: 020-7371 9935; Fax: 020-7384 2762)

TRIBUNALS

Agricultural Land Tribunals
c/o Rural and Marine Environment Division, Ministry of Agriculture, Fisheries and Food, Nobel House, 17 Smith Square, London, SW1P 3JR (Tel: 020-7238 6991; Fax: 020-7238 5671;
E-mail: g.homs@env.maff.gsi.gov.uk)

Appeals Service
4th Floor, Whittington House, 19-30 Alfred Place, WC1E 7LW (Tel: 020-7712 2600; Fax: 020-7712 2650)
Chief Executive: N. Ward

Copyright Tribunal
Harmsworth House, 13-15 Bouverie Street, EC4Y 8DP (Tel: 020-7596 6510; Fax: 020-7596 6526;
E-mail: copyright.tribunal@patent.gov.uk;
Web: http://www.patent.gov.uk)
Secretary: Ms J. Durdin

Data Protection Tribunal
c/o The Home Office, Queen Anne's Court, SW1H 9AT (Tel: 020-7273 3755; Fax: 020-7273 3205)
Chairman: J. A. C. Spokes

Employment Tribunals
Central Office (England and Wales), 19-29 Woburn Place, WC1H 0LU (Tel: 020-7273 8666)

Employment Appeal Tribunal
Audit House, 58 Victoria Embankment, EC4Y 0DS (Tel: 020-7273 1041; Fax: 020-7273 1045; E-mail: http://www.employmentappeals.gov.uk)
Registrar: Miss V. J. Selio

Immigration Appellate Authorities
Taylor House, 88 Rosebery Avenue, EC1R 4QU (Tel: 020-7862 4200)
Tribunal Manager: S. Hill

Land Tribunal
48-49 Chancery Lane, WC2A 1JR (Tel: 020-7936 7200; Fax: 020-7936 7215)

Mental Health Review Tribunals
Health Service Directorate, Room 302A, Wellington

192 Legal London

House, 133-155 Waterloo Road, SE1 8UG (Tel: 020-7972 4503)

Office of the Social Security and Child Support Commissioners
5th Floor, Newspaper House, 8-16 Great New Street, EC4A 3BN (Tel: 020-7353 5145; Fax: 020-7936 2171)
Secretary: L. Pereira

Pensions Appeal Tribunals
Central Office (England and Wales), 48-49 Chancery Lane, WC2A 1JR (Tel: 020-7936 7032/3/4)

Solicitors' Disciplinary Tribunal
3rd Floor, Gate House, 1 Farringdon Street, EC4M 7NS (Tel: 020-7329 4808; Fax: 020-7329 4833; E-mail: enquiries@solicitorsdt.com)
Clerk: Ms S. Elson

Special Commissioners of Income Tax
15-19 Bedford Avenue, WC1B 3AS (Tel: 020-7631 4242; Fax: 020-7436 4150/1;
E-mail: http://www.courtservice.gov.uk/tribunals/comtax/index.htm)
Clerk: R. P. Lester

Special Immigration Appeals Commission
Taylor House, 88 Rosebery Avenue, EC1R 4QU (Tel: 020-7862 4200
Tribunal Manager: S. Hill

Transport Tribunal
48-49 Chancery Lane, WC2A 1JR (Tel: 020-7936 7493; Fax: 020-7036 7215;
E-mail: http://www.courservice.gov.uk/tribunals/comtax/index.htm
Register: R. P. Lester

VAT and Duties Tribunals
15-19 Bedford Avenue, WC1B 3AS (Tel: 020-7631 4242; Fax: 020-7436 4150/1)

CROWN PROSECUTION SERVICE

50 Ludgate Hill, London EC4M 7EX (Tel: 020-7796 8000; Email: enquiries@cps.gov.uk;
Web: http://www.cps.gov.uk)
The Crown Prosecution Service (CPS) is responsible for the independent review and conduct of criminal proceedings instituted by police forces in England and Wales, with the exception of cases conducted by the Serious Fraud Office and certain minor offences.
The Service is headed by the Director of Public Prosecutions (DPP), who works under the superintendence of the Attorney-General, and a chief executive. The Service comprises a headquarters and 42 Areas, each Area corresponding to a police area in England and Wales. Each Area is headed by a Chief Crown Prosecutor, supported by an Area Business Manager.

Director of Public Prosecutions: D. Calvert-Smith, QC
Chief Executive: M. E. Addison
Directors: C. Newell (Casework); G. Patten (Policy); J. Graham (Finance); L. Carey (Business Information Systems); I. Seehra (Human Resources)
Head of Communications: Ms L. Salisbury
Head of Management Audit Services: Ms R. Read

CPS AREAS

In the list below you will find details of Crown Prosecution Areas in London, along with the Crown and Magistrates' Courts that operate within the area.

CPS London
Area HQ, 50 Ludgate Hill, London, EC4M 7EX (Tel: 020-7796 8000); DX: 300850 LUDGATE EC4)
Chief Crown Prosecutor: Peter Boeuf
Assistant Chief Crown Prosecutors: Howard Cohen; Ms Melanie Werrett; Mrs Alison Saunders
Area Business Manager: Alex Machray

Barking and Stratford
Solar House, 1-9 Romford Road, Stratford, London, E15 4LJ (Tel: 020-8221 3500; Fax: 020-8221 3501; DX: 5449 STRATFORD (LONDON))
Crown Courts: Central Criminal Court; Snaresbrook
Magistrates Courts: Barking; Stratford

Barnet and Haringey
6th and 8th Floors, River Park House, 225 High Road, Wood Green, London, N22 8HQ (Tel: 020-8826 4600; Fax: 020-8826 4601; DX: 35699 WOOD GREEN 1))
Branch Crown Prosecutor: Ms C. Ward
Crown Courts: Central Criminal Court; Harrow; Wood Green
Magistrates Courts: Enfield; Haringey; Hendon

Thames
50 Ludgate Hill, London, EC4M 7EX (Tel: 020-7796 8000; Fax: 020-7796 8268/9; DX: 300850 LUDGATE EC4)
Branch Crown Prosecutor: D. Atkins
Crown Courts: Central Criminal Court; Southwark; Hackney and Tower Hamlets
Magistrates Courts: Thames

Brent, Harrow and Uxbridge
2nd Floor, Kings House, Kymberley Road, Harrow, Middx, HA1 1YH (Tel: 020-8901 5700; Fax: 020-8901 5739; DX: 4204 HARROW 1)
Crown Courts: Central Criminal Court; Harrow; Isleworth
Magistrates Courts: Harrow; Uxbridge

Camberwell
8 Gainsford Street, London, SE1 2NE (Tel: 020-7378 4100; Fax: 020-7378 4301; DX: 80712 BERMONDSEY)
Crown Courts: Central Criminal Court; Inner London
Magistrtates Courts: Camberwell Green

Croydon
8th Floor, Prospect West, 81 Station Road, Croydon, CR0 2RD (Tel: 020-8662 2800; Fax: 020-8662 2828; DX: 2698 CROYDON)
Branch Crown Prosecutor: P. Ragnauth
Crown Courts: Central Criminal Court; Croydon
Magistrates Courts: Bromley; Croydon; Bexley

Ealing and Hounslow
2nd Floor, Kings House, Kymberley Road, Harrow, Middx, HA1 1YH (Tel: 020-8901 5700; Fax: 020-8901 5919; DX: 4204 HARROW 1)

CPS Areas

Crown Courts: Central Criminal Court; Isleworth
Magistrates Courts: Acton; Brentford; Ealing; Feltham

Greenwich and Bexley
8 Gainsford Street, London, SE1 2NE (Tel: 020-7378 4000; Fax: 020-7378 4248;
DX: 80712 BERMONDSEY)
Crown Courts: Central Criminal Court; Woolwich
Magistrates Courts: Bexley; Greenwich; Woolwich

Havering and Redbridge
Solar House, 1-9 Romford Road, Stratford, London E15 4LJ (Tel: 020-8221 3500; Fax: 020-8221 3504/5; DX: 5449 STRATFORD (LONDON))
Crown Courts: Central Criminal Court; Snaresbrook
Magistrates Courts: Havering; Redbridge

Highbury
Solar House, 1-9 Romford Road, Stratford, London, E15 4LJ (Tel: 020-8221 3623; Fax: 020-8221 3506; DX: 5449 STRATFORD (LONDON))
Principal Team Leader: F. O'Toole
Crown Courts: Central Criminal Court; Snaresbrook
Magistrates Court: Highbury Corner

Kingston
17th Floor, Tolworth Tower, Surbiton, Surrey, KT6 7DS (Tel: 020-7335 1500; Fax: 020-7335 1601/2/3; DX: 57549 TOLWORTH)
Branch Crown Prosecutor: M. Haddon
Crown Courts: Central Criminal Court; Kingston
Magistrates Courts: Kingston-upon-Thames; Richmond-upon-Thames; South Western; Wimbledon; Sutton

Tower Bridge and City
8 Gainsford Street, London, SE1 2NE (Tel: 020-7378 4100; Fax: 020-7378 4201/2;
DX: 80712 BERMONDSEY)
Crown Courts: Central Criminal Court; Inner London
Magistrates Court: City of London; Tower Bridge

Waltham Forest and Enfield
5th Floor, River Park House, 225 High Road, Wood Green, London, N22 8HQ (Tel: 020-8826 4600; Fax: 020-8826 4700; DX: 35699 WOOD GREEN 1)
Branch Crown Prosecutor: Ms C. Ward
Crown Courts: Central Criminal Court; Snaresbrook; Wood Green
Magistrates Courts: Enfield; Waltham Forest

West London
50 Ludgate Hill, London, EC4M 7EX (Tel: 020-7796 8000; Fax: 020-7796 8028; DX: 300850 LUDGATE EC4)
Branch Crown Prosecutor: R. Barclay
Crown Courts: Central Criminal Court;Blackfriars
Magistrates Court: West London

London Westminster
50 Ludgate Hill, London, EC4M 7EX (Tel: 020-7796 8000; Fax: 020-7796 8560/8580; DX: 300850 LUDGATE EC4))
Branch Crown Prosecutor: B. Butler
Crown Courts: Central Criminal Court; Middlesex; Southwark
Magistrates Courts: Horseferry Road; Bow Street

Youth and City
1st Floor, 8 Gainsford Street, London, SE1 2NE (Tel: 020-7378 4100; Fax: 020-7378 4101; DX: 80712 BERMONDSEY)
Branch Crown Prosecutor: Miss H. Bradfield
Crown Courts: Inner London; Southwark; Central Criminal Court
Magistrates Courts: Youth Courts (Inner London and City of London Magistrates Court)

194 Legal London

THE PRISON SERVICE

The Prison Service in England is the responsibility of the Home Secretary. The chief executive officers of the Prison Service are responsible for the day-to-day running of the system.

Convicted prisoners are classified according to their assessed security risk and are housed in establishments appropriate to that level of security. Female prisoners are housed in women's establishments or in separate wings of mixed prisons. Remand prisoners are, where possible, housed separately from convicted prisoners. Offenders under the age of 21 are usually detained in a young offenders' institution, which may be a separate establishment or part of a prison.

Every prison establishment also has an independent board of visitors or visiting committee made up of local volunteers. Any prisoner whose complaint is not satisfied by the internal complaints procedures may complain to the Prisons Ombudsman for England and Wales.

HM PRISON SERVICE

Cleland House, Page Street, London SW1P 4LN (Tel: 020-7217 6000; Fax: 020-7217 6403)

The Prison Service Strategy Board
Chairman: The Rt. Hon. Paul Boateng, MP (Home Office minister for prisons and probation)
Director-General: M. Narey
Staff Officer: W. Payne
Deputy Director-General: P. Wheatley
Director of High Security Prisons: P. Atherton
Director of Security: B. Clark
Director of Personnel: G. Hadley
Director of Finance: J. Le Vay
Director of Corporate Affairs: Ms C. Pelham
Director of Regimes: K. D. Sutton
Area Manager, London: Adrian Smith

PAROLE BOARD FOR ENGLAND AND WALES

Abell House, John Islip Street, London SW1P 4LH (Tel: 020-7217 5314; Fax: 020-7217 5793; Email: info@paroleboard.gov.uk; Web: http://www.paroleboard.gov.uk)

The Board was constituted under the Criminal Justice Act 1967 and continued under the Criminal Justice Act 1991. It is an executive non-departmental public body and its duty is to advise the Home Secretary with respect to matters referred to it by him which are connected with the early release or recall of prisoners. Its functions include giving directions concerning the release on licence of prisoners serving discretionary life sentences and of certain prisoners serving long-term determinate sentences.

PRISONS OMBUDSMAN

Ashley House, 2 Monck Street, London SW1P 2BQ (Tel: 020-7276 2876; Fax: 020-7276 2860)

The post of Prisons Ombudsman was instituted in 1994. The Ombudsman is appointed by the Home Secretary and is an independent point of appeal for prisoners' grievances about their lives in prison, including disciplinary issues. The Ombudsman cannot investigate grievances relating to issues which are the subject of litigation or criminal proceedings, the merits of decisions taken by ministers or the actions of bodies outside the Prison Service.

Ombudsman: Stephen Short

PRISONS

Belmarsh
Western Way, Thamesmead, London, SE28 0EB (Tel: 020-8317 2436; Fax: 020-8317 2421)
Governor: H. Banks

Brixton
P.O. Box 369, Jebb Avenue, London, SW2 5XF (Tel: 020-8674 9811; Fax: 020-8671 7946)
Governor: R. Chapman

Chelmsford
200 Springfield Road, Essex, CM2 6LQ
Governor: Ms A. Gomme

Downview
Sutton Lane, Sutton, Surrey, SM2 5PD (Tel: 020-8770 7500; Fax: 020-8770 7673)
Governor: C. Lambert

Feltham
Bedfont Road, Middx, TW13 4ND (Tel: 020-8890 0061; Fax: 020-8893 7496)
Governor: N. D. Clifford

High Down
Sutton Lane, Sutton, SM2 5PJ (Tel: 020-8643 0063; Fax: 020-8643 2035)
Governor: D. Wilson

Holloway
Parkhurst Road, London, N7 0NU (Tel: 020-7607 6747; Fax: 020-7700 0269)
Governor: D. Lancaster

Latchmere House
Church Road, Ham Common, Richmond, TW10 5HH (Tel: 020-8948 0215; Fax: 020-8332 1359)
Governor: T. Hinchliffe

Pentonville
Caledonian Road, London, N7 8TT (Tel: 020-7607 5353; Fax: 020-7700 0244)
Governor: R. Duncan

Wandsworth
P.O. Box 757, Heathfield Road, London, SW18 3HS (Tel: 020-8874 7292; Fax: 020-8877 0358)
Governor: S. Rimmer

Wormwood Scrubs
P.O. Box 757, Du Cane Road, London, W12 0AE (Tel: 020-8743 0311; Fax: 020-8749 5655)
Governor: S. Moore

National Probation Service   195

NATIONAL PROBATION SERVICE OF ENGLAND AND WALES

The National Probation Service of England and Wales consists of probation officers and supporting staff who are employed by probation committees. There are composed of magistrates and members co-opted from the local community. It contributes to crime reduction through its work with offenders and liaison with the courts and the community.

The National Probation Service of England and Wales strives to develop strong and effective partnerships with organisations in the statutory and independent sector. The aims of the service are to: protect society from crime; to rehabilitate offenders; to supervise offenders effectively; to safeguard the interests of children.

In London there are five probation service areas covering inner, south east, south west and north east London and Middlesex.

Inner London
71/73 Great Peter Street, London SW1P 2BN (Tel: 020-7222 5656; Fax: 020-7222 0473)
North East London
4th Floor, Olympic House, 28/42 Clements Road, Ilford IG1 1BA (Tel: 020-8514 5353)
South East London
Crosby House, 9-13 Elmfield Road, Bromley BR1 1LT (Tel: 020-8464 3430)
South West London
45 High Street, Kingston upon Thames KT1 1LQ (Tel: 020-8546 0018; Fax: 020-8549 8990)
Middlesex
Glen House, 4th Floor, 200 Tottenham Court Road, London W1P 9LA (Tel: 020-7436 7121)

OTHER LEGAL BODIES

GENERAL COUNCIL OF THE BAR

3 Bedford Row, London WC1R 4DB (Tel: 020-7242 0082; Fax: 020-7831 9217;
Web: http://www.barcouncil.org.uk)
The General Council of the Bar is the professional body for barristers.
Chief Executive: Niall Morison

LAW CENTRES FEDERATION

Duchess House, 18-19 Warren Street, London W1P 5DB (Tel: 020-7387 8570; Fax: 020-7387 8368)

LAW CENTRES

Brent Community Law Centre: 389 High Road, Willesden, London NW10 2JR (Tel: 020-8451 1122; Fax: 020-8830 2462)

Camden Community Law Centre: 2a Prince of Wales Road, London NW5 3LG (Tel: 020-7485 6672; Fax: 020-7267 6218)

Central London Law Centre: 19 Whitcomb Street, London WC2H 7HA (Tel: 020-7839 2998; Fax: 020-7839 6158)

Greenwich Law Centre: 187 Trafalgar Road, London SE10 9EQ (Tel: 020-8853 2250; Fax: 020-8858 2018)

Hackney Law Centre: 236/8 Mare Street, London E8 1HE (Tel: 020-8985 8364; Fax: 020-8986 9891)

Hammersmith and Fulham Law Centre: 142/4 King Street, London W6 0QU (Tel: 020-8741 4021; Fax: 020-8741 1450)

Hillingdon Legal Resource Centre: 12 Harold Avenue, Hayes UB8 4QW (Tel: 020-8561 9400; Fax: 020-8756 0837)

Hounslow Law Centre: 51 Lampton Road, Hounslow TW3 1JG (Tel: 020-8570 9505; Fax: 020-8572 0730)
North Islington Law Centre: 161 Hornsey Road, London N7 6DU (Tel: 020-7607 2461; Fax: 020-7700 0072)

North Kensington Law Centre: 74 Golbourne Road, London W10 5PS (Tel: 020-8969 7473; Fax: 020-8968 0934)

North Lambeth Law Centre: 14 Bowden Street, London SE11 5DS (Tel: 020-7582 4373; Fax: 020-7582 2148)

North Lewisham Law Centre: 28 Deptford High Street, London SE8 3NU (Tel: 020-8692 5355; Fax: 020-8694 2516)

Newham Rights Centre: 285 Romford Road, Newham, London E7 9HJ (Tel: 020-8968 0417; Fax: 020-8519 7348)

Paddington Law Centre: 439 Harrow Road, London W10 4RE (Tel: 020-8960 3155; Fax: 020-8968 0417)

Plumstead Law Centre: 105 Plumstead High Street, London SE18 1SB (Tel: 020-8855 9817; Fax: 020-8316 7903)

Southwark Law Centre: Hanover Park House, 14-16 Hanover Park, London SE15 5HS (Tel: 020-7732 2008; Fax: 020-7732 2034)

Springfield Law Centre: Springfield Hospital, Glenburnie Road, London SW17 7DJ (Tel: 020-8767 6884; Fax: 020-8767 6996)

Stockwell and Clapham Law Centre: 57-59 Old Town, Clapham, London SW4 0JQ (Tel: 020-7720 6231; Fax: 020-7498 6760)

Tottenham Law Centre: 415 Green Lanes, Haringey, London N4 1EZ (Tel: 020-8347 9710; Fax: 020-8347 9613)

Tower Hamlets Law Centre: 341 Commercial Road, London E1 2PS (Tel: 020-7791 0741; Fax: 020-7702 7302)

Wandsworth and Merton Law Centre: 101a Tooting High Street, London SW17 0SU (Tel: 020-8767 2777; Fax: 020-8767 2711)

196 Legal London

ASSOCIATE MEMBERS OF THE LAW CENTRES FEDERATION IN LONDON

AIRE (Advice on Individual Rights in Europe): 74 Euro Link Business Centre, Effra Road, London SW2 1BZ (Tel: 020-7924 0927; Fax: 020-7733 6786)

Cambridge House Legal Centre: 137 Camberwell Road, London SE5 0HF (Tel: 020-7701 9499; Fax: 020-7703 3051)

Disability Law Service: Room 241, 49/51 Bedford Row, London WC1R 4LR (Tel: 020-7831 8031; Fax: 020-7831 5582)

Mary Ward Legal Advice Centre: 26-27 Boswell Street, London WC1N 3JZ (Tel: 020-7831 7079)

LAW COMMISSION

Conquest House, 37-38 John Street, London WC1N 2BQ (Tel: 020-7453 1220; Fax: 020-7453 1297; Email: secretary.lawcomm@gtnet.gov.uk; Web: http://www.lawcom.gov.uk)

The Law Commission was set up in 1965, under the Law Commissions Act 1965, to make proposals to the Government for the examination of the law in England and Wales and for its revision where it is unsuited for modern requirements, obscure, or otherwise unsatisfactory. It recommends to the Lord Chancellor programmes for the examination of different branches of the law and suggests whether the examination should be carried out by the Commission itself or by some other body. The Commission is also responsible for the preparation of Consolidation and Statute Law (Repeals) Bills.

Chairman: The Hon. Mr Justice Carnwath
Commissioners: C. Harpum; Prof. H. Beale; Miss D. Faber; Mr A. Wilkie, QC
Secretary: M. W. Sayers

LAW SOCIETY

113 Chancery Lane, London WC2A 1PL (Tel: 020-7242 1222; Fax: 020-7831 0344; Web: http://www.lawsociety.org.uk)
Greater London Regional Office: Newspaper House, 8-16 Great New Street, London EC4A 3EU (Tel: 020-7316 5556; Fax: 020-7320 5971)

The Law Society is the professional body for solicitors.

Secretary-General: Jane Betts.

LAW SOCIETY GOVENMENT GROUP

113 Chancery Lane, London WC2A 1PL (Tel: 020-7242 1222)

The Law Society Government Group is a part of the Law Society whose aim is to represent the interests of local authority solicitors and to provide support to local government solicitors. All solicitors working in local government automatically become part of this group.

Chairman 2000-2001: Roger Bowden, Wyre Borough Council, Civic Centre, Breck Road, Poulton-le-Fylde FY6 7PU.

LCIA (LONDON COURT OF INTERNATIONAL ARBITRATION

The International Dispute Resolution Centre, 8 Breams Buildings, Chancery Lane, London EC4A 1HP (Tel: 020 7405 8008; Fax: 020 7405 8009; Email: lcia@lcia-arbitration.com; Web: http://www.lcia-arbitration.com/lcia/)

The LCIA is probably the longest-established of all the major international institutions for dispute resolution, but also one of the most modern and forward looking. Its organisation, operation and outlook and the services which it provides are worldwide. Although based in London it is an international institution, offering efficiency, flexibility and neutrality to all parties involved in dispute resolution under its auspices. The LCIA provides cost-effective administration of arbitration, mediation and other methods of ADR in any venue and under any system of law.

Executive Director: Madeleine May, CBE
Registrar: Adrian Winstanley

LEGAL SERVICES COMMISSION

85 Gray's Inn Road, London WC1X 8AA (Tel: 020-7759; Fax: 020-7759 0546; Web: http://www.legalservices.gov.uk)

The Access to Justice Act 1999 replaced the legal aid system with two new schemes: the Community Legal Service and the Criminal Defence System. It established a Legal Services Commission to run the two schemes and replace the Legal Aid Board. The Commission assumed this role on 1 April 2000. The Community Legal Service fund will replace the legal aid fund in a way that reflects priorities set by the Lord Chancellor and its duty to secure the best possible value for money, to procure or provide a range of legal services. The Commission will plan what can be done towards meeting the need for legal services, and liaise with other funders of legal services to facilitate the development of co-ordinated plans for making the best use of all available resources. The intention is to develop comprehensive referral networks of legal service providers or assured quality, offering the widest possible access to information and advice about the law and help with legal problems. The Criminal Defence Service will replace the legal aid system in criminal cases. The new scheme will ensure that people suspected or accused of crime are properly represented, while securing better value for money than is possible under the legal aid scheme. The Criminal Defence Service will be launched in October 2000.

Chairman: Peter G. Birch, CBE
Members: Michael Barnes, CBE; Richard Buxton; Anthony Edwards; Philip Ely; Brian Harvey; Juliet Herzog; Sheila Hewitt; Yvonne Mosquito; Steve Orchard, CBE; Richard Penn; Jim Shearer

VALUATION

Valuation Office Agency
New Court, 48 Carey Street, London WC2A 2JE (Tel: 020-7506 1700; Fax: 020-7506 1998; Email: customer.voa@gtnet.gov.uk; Web: http://www.voa.gov.uk)
Chief Executive: Michael A. Jouns

Valuation Tribunals

VALUATION TRIBUNALS

Central London Valuation Tribunal
2nd Floor, Black Lion House, 45 Whitechapel Road, London E1 1DU (Tel: 020-7247 3898; Fax: 020-7247 6598)
Clerk of the Tribunal: W. R. Shaw

London North East Valuation Tribunal
2nd Floor, Black Lion House, 45 Whitechapel Road, London E1 1DU (Tel: 020-7247 3898; Fax: 020-7247 6898; Email: amas165@aol.com)
Clerk of the Tribunal: A. Masella

London South West Valuation Tribunal
4th Floor, AMP House, Dingwall Road, Croydon CR0 9XA (Tel: 020-8681 8843; Fax: 020-8686 7444
Clerk of the Tribunal: Peter L. Kain

Public Records
Public Records Office: Kew, Richmond, Surrey TW9 4DU (Tel: 020-8876 3444;
Web: http://www.pro.gov.uk)

Births Deaths and Marriage Certificates: Family Record Centre, 1 Myddleton Street, London EC1R 1UW (General enquiries) Tel: 020-8392 5300; (Certificate Enquiries) Tel: 0151-471 4200. For your local Registrar of Births, Deaths and Marriages see the Governed London section and your Local Council's entry.

Divorce and Adoption: Family Proceedings Department, First Avenue House, 42-49 High Holborn, London WC1V 6NP Tel: 020-936 6000.

Wills before 1858: Family Record Centre, 1 Myddleton Street, London EC1R 1UW General enquiries tel: 020-8392 5300.

Wills after 1858: The Probate Department of the Principal Registry of the Family Division, First Division, First avenue House, 42-49 High Holborn, London WC1V 6NP Tel: 020-936 7000.

LEGAL NOTES

These notes outline certain aspects of the law as they might affect the average person. They are intended only as a broad guideline and are by no means definitive. The law is constantly changing so expert advice should always be taken. In some cases, sources of further information are given in these notes.

It is always advisable to consult a solicitor without delay; timely advice will set your mind at rest but sitting on your rights can mean that you lose them. Anyone who does not have a solicitor already can contact the Citizens' Advice Bureau, the Law Society of England and Wales (113 Chancery Lane, London WC2A 1PL).

The legal aid and assistance schemes exist to make the help of a lawyer available to those who would not otherwise be able to afford one. Entitlement depends on an individual's means but a solicitor or Citizens' Advice Bureau will be able to advise about entitlement.

Adoption of Children
In England and Wales the adoption of children is mainly governed by the Adoption Act 1976 and the Children Act 1989.

Anyone over 21 can legally adopt a child. Married couples must adopt 'jointly', unless one partner cannot be found, is incapable of making an application, or if a separation is likely to be permanent. Unmarried couples may not adopt 'jointly' although one partner in that couple may adopt. The only organisations allowed to arrange adoptions are the social services departments of local authorities or voluntary agencies which are registered with the local authorities.

Once an adoption has been arranged, a court order is necessary to make it legal. These are obtained from the High Court (Family Division) or from a county or family proceedings court. The child's natural parents (or guardians) must consent to the adoption, unless the court dispenses with the consent, e.g. where the natural parent has neglected the child or is incapable of giving consent. Once adopted, the child has the same status as a child born to the adoptive parents and the natural parents cease to have any rights or responsibilities where the child is concerned. The adopted child will be treated as the natural child of the adoptive parents for the purposes of intestate succession, national insurance, family allowances, etc. The adopted child ceases to have any rights to the estates of his/her natural parents.

Registration and Certificates
All adoptions in England and Wales are registered in the Adopted Children Register kept by the Office of National Statistics. Certificates from the registers can be obtained in a similar way to birth certificates

Tracing Natural Parents or Children Who Have Been Adopted
An adult adopted person may apply to the Registrar-General for information to enable him/her to obtain a full birth certificate. For those adopted before 12 November 1975 it is obligatory to receive counselling services before this information is given; for those adopted after that date counselling services are optional. There is also an Adoption Contact Register (created after the 1989 Act) in which details of adult adopted people and of their relatives may be recorded. The BAAF (see below) can provide addresses of organisations which offer advice, information and counselling to adopted people, adoptive parents and people who have had their children adopted.

Further information can be obtained from:
British Agencies for Adoption and Fostering (BAAF), Skyline House, 200 Union Street, London SE1 0LX Tel: 020-7593 2000

Births (Registration)
The birth of a child must be registered within 42 days of birth at the register office of the district in which the baby was born. In England and Wales it is possible to give the particulars to be registered at any other register office. Responsibility for registering the birth rests with the parents, except in the case of an illegitimate child, when the mother is responsible for registration. Responsibility rests firstly with the parents but if they fail, particulars may be given to the registrar by:
- the occupier of the house in which the baby was born
- a person present at the birth
- the person having charge of the child

Failure to register the birth within 42 days without reasonable cause may leave the parents liable to a penalty in England and Wales.

If the parents were married at the time of the birth, either parent may register the birth and details about both parents will be entered on the register. If the parents were unmarried at the time of the birth, the father's details are entered only if both parents attend or if the parents have made a statutory declaration confirming the identity of the father. Copies of the forms necessary to make such a declaration are available at the register offices. A short birth certificate is issued free when the birth is registered.

Still Births
If a baby is stillborn, i.e. born dead after the 24th week of pregnancy, the birth must be registered. The doctor or midwife who attends the birth or afterwards examines the body of the child will issue a Medical Certificate of Stillbirth and this must be presented at the register office.

Re-registration
In certain circumstances it may be necessary to re-register a birth, e.g. where the birth of an illegitimate child is legitimated by the subsequent marriage of the parents. It is also possible to re-register the birth of an illegitimate child so that the father's name is entered on the register.

Birth Abroad
Births of British subjects occurring abroad are registered with consular officers and certificates of birth are subsequently available from the Registrar-General. The registration of births among members of the armed forces that occur abroad or on military ships or aircraft is governed by the Registration of Births, Deaths and Marriages (Special Provisions) Act 1957.

Certificates of Births, Deaths and Marriages
Certificates of births, deaths or marriages that have taken place in England and Wales since 1837 can be obtained from the Office of National Statistics (General Register Office). Applications can be made:
- by a personal visit to the Family Records Centre, London

– by postal application to the General Register Office, Southport

Certificates are also available from the Superintendent Registrar for the district in which the event took place or, in the case of marriage certificates, from the minister of the church in which the marriage took place. Any register office can advise about the best way to obtain certificates.

Indexes prepared from the registers are available for searching by the public at the Family Records Centre in London or at a Superintendent Registrar's Office; indexes at the latter relate only to births, deaths and marriages which occurred in that registration district. There is no charge for searching the indexes in the Public Search Room at the Family Records Centre but a general search fee is charged for searches at a Superintendent Registrar's Office. A fee is charged for verifying index references against the records.

The Society of Genealogists has many records of baptisms, marriages and deaths prior to 1837.

Further information can be obtained from:

The General Register Office
Office for National Statistics, Smedley Hydro, Trafalgar Road, Birkdale, Southport, Merseyside PR8 2HH (Tel: 01704-569824)

Family Records Centre
1 Myddelton Street, London EC1R 1UW

Society of Genealogists
14 Charterhouse Buildings, Goswell Road, London EC1M 7BA (Tel: 020-7251 8799)

British Citizenship
The British Nationality Act 1981 which came into force on 1 January 1983 established three types of citizenship to replace the single form of Citizenship of the UK and Colonies created by the British Nationality Act 1948. The three forms of citizenship are: British Citizenship; British Dependent Territories Citizenship; and British Overseas Citizenship. Three residual categories were created: British Subjects; British Protected Persons; and British Nationals (Overseas).

British Citizenship
Almost everyone who was a citizen of the UK and colonies and had a right of abode in the UK prior to the 1981 Act became British citizens when the Act came into force. British citizens have the right to live permanently in the UK and are free to leave and re-enter the UK at any time.

A person born on or after 1 January 1983 in the UK (including, for this purpose, the Channel Islands and the Isle of Man) is entitled to British citizenship if he/she falls into one of the following categories:
– he/she has a parent who is a British citizen
– he/she has a parent who is settled in the UK
– he/she is a newborn infant found abandoned in the UK
– his/her parents subsequently settle in the UK
– he/she lives in the UK for the first ten years of his/her life and is not absent for more than 90 days in each of those years
– he/she is adopted in the UK and one of the adopters is a British Citizen

A person born outside the UK may acquire British citizenship if he/she falls into one of the following categories:
– he/she has a parent who is a British citizen otherwise than by descent, e.g. a parent who was born in the UK
– he/she has a parent who is a British citizen serving the Crown overseas
– the Home Secretary consents to his/her registration while he/she is a minor
– he/she is a British Dependent Territories citizen, a British Overseas citizen, a British subject or a British protected person and has been lawfully resident in the UK for five years
– he/she is a British Dependent Territories citizen who acquired that citizenship from a connection with Gibraltar
– he/she is adopted (see above) or naturalised (see below)

Where parents are married, the status of either may confer citizenship on their child. If a child is illegitimate, the status of the mother determines the child's citizenship.

Under the 1981 Act, Commonwealth citizens and citizens of the Republic of Ireland were entitled to registration as British citizens before 1 January 1988. In 1985 citizens of the Falkland Islands were granted British citizenship.

Renunciation of British citizenship must be registered with the Home Secretary and will be revoked if no new citizenship or nationality is acquired within six months. If the renunciation was required in order to retain or acquire another citizenship or nationality, the citizenship may be reacquired once.

British Dependent Territories Citizenship
Under the 1981 Act, this type of citizenship was conferred on citizens of the UK and colonies by birth, naturalisation or registration in British Dependent Territories. British Dependent Territories citizens may be entitled to registration as British citizens on completion of five years' legal residence in the UK.

On 1 July 1997 citizens of Hong Kong who did not qualify to register as British citizens under the British Nationality (Hong Kong) Act 1990 lost their British Dependent Territories citizenship on the handover of sovereignty to China; they may, however, have applied to register as British Nationals (Overseas).

Eligibility for British Dependent Territories citizenship is determined by similar rules to those for acquiring British citizenship, except that the connection is with the dependent territory rather than with the UK.

British Overseas Citizenship
Under the 1981 Act, this type of citizenship was conferred on any UK and colonies citizens who did not qualify for British citizenship or citizenship of the British Dependent Territories. British Overseas citizenship may be acquired by the wife and minor children of a British Overseas citizen in certain circumstances. British Overseas citizens may be entitled to registration as British citizens on completion of five years' legal residence in the UK.

Residual Categories

British subjects, British protected persons and British Nationals (Overseas) may be entitled to registration as British citizens on completion of five years' legal residence in the UK.

Citizens of the Republic of Ireland who were also British subjects before 1 January 1949 can retain that status if they fulfil certain conditions.

European Union Citizenship

British citizens (including Gibraltarians who are registered as such) are also EU citizens and are entitled to travel freely to other EU countries to work, study, reside and set up a business. EU citizens have the same rights with respect to the United Kingdom.

Naturalisation

Naturalisation is granted at the discretion of the Home Secretary. The basic requirements are five years' residence (three years if the applicant is married to a British citizen), good character, adequate knowledge of the English, Welsh or Scottish Gaelic language, and an intention to reside permanently in the UK.

Status of Aliens

Aliens may not hold public office or vote in Britain and they may not own a British ship or aircraft. Citizens of the Republic of Ireland are not deemed to be aliens. Certain provisions of the Immigration and Asylum Act 1999 came into force on the 11 November 1999. This act makes provision about immigration and asylum and about procedures in connection with marriage on superintendent registrar's certificate.

CONSUMER LAW

Sale of Goods

A sale of goods contract is the most common type of contract. It is governed by the Sale of Goods Act 1979 (as amended by the Sale and Supply of Goods Act 1994). The Act provides protection for buyers by implying terms into every sale of goods contract. These terms are:
- a condition that the seller will pass good title to the buyer (unless the seller agrees to transfer only such title as he has)
- where the seller sells goods by reference to a description, a condition that the goods will match that description and, where the sale is by sample and description, a condition that the bulk of the goods will correspond with such sample and description
- where goods are sold by a business seller, a condition that the goods will be of satisfactory quality if they meet the standard that a reasonable person would regard as satisfactory taking into account any description of the goods, the price, and all other relevant circumstances. The quality of the goods includes their state and condition, relevant aspects being whether they are suitable for their common purpose, their appearance and finish, freedom from minor defects and their safety and durability. This term will not be implied, however, if a buyer has examined the goods and should have noticed the defect or if the seller specifically drew the buyer's attention to the defect
- where goods are sold by a business seller, a condition that the goods are reasonably fit for any purpose made known to the seller by the buyer, unless the buyer does not rely on the seller's judgement, or it is not reasonable for him/her to do so
- where goods are sold by sample, conditions that the bulk of the sample will correspond with the sample in quality, that the buyer will have a reasonable opportunity of comparing the two and that the goods are free from any defect rendering them unsatisfactory which would not be obvious from the sample

Some of the above terms can be excluded from contracts by the seller. The seller's right to do this is, however, restricted by the Unfair Contract Terms Act 1977. The Act offers more protection to a buyer who 'deals as a consumer', that is where the sale is a business sale, the goods are of a type ordinarily bought for private use and the goods are bought by a buyer who is not a business buyer. In a sale by auction or competitive tender, a buyer never deals as consumer. Also, a seller can never exclude the implied term as to title mentioned above.

Hire-purchase Agreements

Terms similar to those implied in contracts of sales of goods are implied into contracts of hire-purchase, under the Supply of Goods (Implied Terms) Act 1973. The 1977 Act limits the exclusion of these implied terms as before.

Supply of Goods and Services

Under the Supply of Goods and Services Act 1982, similar terms are also implied in other types of contract under which ownership of goods passes, e.g. a contract for 'work and materials' such as supplying new parts while servicing a car, and contracts for the hire of goods. These types of contracts have additional implied terms:
- that the supplier will use reasonable care and skill
- that the supplier will carry out the service in a reasonable time (unless the time has been agreed)
- that the supplier will make a reasonable charge (unless the charge has already been agreed)

The 1977 Act limits the exclusion of these implied terms in a similar manner as before.

Unfair Terms

The Unfair Terms in Consumer Contracts Regulations 1994 apply to contracts between business sellers (or suppliers of goods and services) and consumers, where the terms have not been individually negotiated, i.e where the terms were drafted in advance so that the consumer was unable to influence those terms. An unfair term is one which operates to the detriment of the consumer. An unfair term does not bind the consumer but the contract will continue to bind the parties if it is capable of existing without the unfair term. The regulations contain a non-exhaustive list of terms which are regarded as unfair. Whether a term is regarded as fair or not will depend on many factors, including the nature of the goods or services, the surrounding circumstances (such as the bargaining strength of both parties) and the other terms in the contract.

The 1994 Regulations have been replaced by The Unfair Terms in Consumer Contracts Regulations 1999 from October 1999. These new Regulations give the same protection as the 1994 Regulations and stress the importance of plain English in contractual documents.

Trade Descriptions

It is a criminal offence under the Trade Descriptions Act 1968 for a business seller to apply a false trade description of goods or to supply or offer to supply any goods to which a false description has been applied. A 'trade description' includes descriptions of quality, size, composition, fitness for purpose and method, and place and date of manufacture of the goods. It is also an offence to give a false indication of the price of goods.

Fair Trading

The Fair Trading Act 1973 is designed to protect the consumer. It provides for the appointment of a Director-General of Fair Trading, one of whose duties is to review commercial activities in the UK relating to the supply of goods and services to consumers. An example of a practice which has been prohibited by a reference made under this Act is that of business sellers posing in advertisements as private sellers.

Consumer Protection

Under the Consumer Protection Act 1987, producers of goods are liable for any injury or for any damage exceeding £275 caused by a defect in their product (subject to certain defences).

The Consumer Protection (Cancellation of Contracts Concluded Away from Business Premises) Regulations 1987 allow consumers a seven-day period in which to cancel contracts for the supply of goods and services, where the contracts were made during an unsolicited visit to the consumer's home or workplace. This only applies to contracts where the cost exceeds £35.

Consumer Credit

In matters relating to the provision of credit (or the supply of goods on hire or hire-purchase), consumers are also protected by the Consumer Credit Act 1974. Under this Act a licence, issued by the Director-General of Fair Trading, is required to conduct a consumer credit or consumer hire business or to deal in credit brokerage, debt adjusting, counselling or collecting. Any 'fit' person may apply to the Director-General of Fair Trading for a licence, which is normally renewable after ten years. A licence is not necessary if such types of business are only transacted occasionally, or if only exempt agreements are involved. The provisions of the Act only apply to 'regulated' agreements, i.e. those that are with individuals or partnerships, those that are not exempt (such as certain local authority and building society loans), and those where the total credit does not exceed £25,000. Provisions include:

- the terms of the regulated agreement can be altered by the creditor provided the agreement gives him/her the right to do so; in such cases the debtor must be given proper notice of this
- in order for a creditor to enforce a regulated agreement, the agreement must comply with certain formalities and must be properly executed. The debtor must also be given specified information by the creditor or his/her broker or agent during the negotiations which take place before the signing of the agreement. The agreement must state certain information such as the amount of credit, the annual interest rate, the amount and timing of repayments
- if an agreement is signed other than at the creditor's (or credit broker's or negotiator's) place of business and oral representations were made in the debtor's presence during discussions pre-agreement, the debtor has a right to cancel the agreement. Time for cancellation expires five clear days after the debtor receives a second copy of the agreement. The agreement must inform the debtor of his right to cancel and how to cancel
- if the debtor is in arrears (or otherwise in breach of the agreement), the creditor must serve a default notice before taking any action such as repossessing the goods
- if the agreement is a hire-purchase or conditional sale agreement, the creditor cannot repossess the goods without a court order if the debtor has paid one-third of the total price of the goods
- in agreements where the debtor is required to make grossly exorbitant payments or where the agreement grossly contravenes the ordinary principles of fair trading, the debtor may request that the court alter or set aside some of the terms of the agreement. The agreement can also be reopened during enforcement proceedings by the court itself

Where a credit reference agency has been used to check the debtor's financial standing, the creditor must give the agency's name to the debtor, who is entitled to see the agency's file on him. A fee of £1 is payable to the agency.

Proceedings Against the Crown

Until 1947, proceedings against the Crown were generally possible only by a procedure known as a petition of right, which put the litigant at a considerable disadvantage. The Crown Proceedings Act 1947 placed the Crown (not the Sovereign in his/her private capacity, but as the embodiment of the State) largely in the same position as a private individual. The Act did not, however, extinguish or limit the Crown's prerogative or statutory powers, and it granted immunity to HM ships and aircraft. It also left certain Crown privileges unaffected. The Act largely abolished the special procedures which previously applied to civil proceedings by and against the Crown. Civil proceedings may be instituted against the appropriate government department or against the Attorney-General.

DEATHS

When a Death Occurs

If the death was expected, the doctor who attended the deceased during their final illness should be contacted. If the death was sudden or unexpected, the family doctor (if known) and police should be contacted. If the cause of death is quite clear the doctor will provide:

- a medical certificate that shows the cause of death (this will be in a sealed envelope, addressed to the registrar)
- a formal notice that states that the doctor has signed the medical certificate and that explains how to get the death registered

If the death was known to be caused by a natural illness but the doctor wishes to know more about the cause of death, he/she may ask the relatives for permission to carry out a post-mortem examination. This should not delay the funeral.

In England and Wales a coroner is responsible for investigating deaths occurring in the following circumstances:

- when no doctor has treated the deceased during his or her last illness or when the doctor attending the patient did not see him or her within 14 days before death, or after death; or
- when the death occurred during an operation or before recovery from the effect of an anaesthetic; or
- when the death was sudden and unexplained or attended by suspicious circumstances; or
- when the death might be due to an industrial injury or disease, or to accident, violence, neglect or abortion, or to any kind of poisoning; or
- the death occurred in prison or in police custody

The doctor will write on the formal notice that the death has been referred to the coroner; if the post mortem shows that death was due to natural causes, the coroner may issue a notification which gives the cause of death so that the death can be registered. If the cause of death was violent or unnatural, the coroner is obliged to hold an inquest.

Registering a Death
In England and Wales the death must be registered by the registrar of births and deaths for the district in which it occurred. From April 1997, information concerning a death can be given before any registrar of births and deaths in England and Wales. The registrar will pass the relevant details to the registrar for the district where the death occurred, who will then register the death or, if different in the registration district in which the death took place. In England and Wales the death must normally be registered within five days. If the death has been referred to the coroner/local procurator fiscal it cannot be registered until the registrar has received authority from the coroner/local procurator fiscal to do so. Failure to register a death involves a penalty in England and Wales.

If the death occurred at a house, the death may be registered by:
- any relative of the deceased present at the death or in attendance during the last illness
- any relative of the deceased residing or being in the sub-district where the death occurred
- any person present at the death
- the occupier or any inmate of the house if he/she knew of the occurrence of the death
- any person causing the disposal of the body

The person registering the death should take the medical certificate of the cause of death with them; it is also useful, though not essential, to take the deceased's birth and marriage certificates, medical card (if possible), pension documents and life assurance details. The registrar will issue a certificate for burial or cremation and a certificate of registration of death; both are free of charge. A death certificate is a certified copy of the entry in the death register; these can be provided on payment of a fee and may be required for the following purposes:
- the will
- bank and building society accounts
- savings bank certificates and premium bonds
- insurance policies
- pension claims

If the death occurred abroad or on a foreign ship or aircraft, the death should be registered according to the local regulations of the relevant country and a death certificate should be obtained. The death can also be registered with the British Consul in that country and a record will be kept at the General Register Office. This avoids the expense of bringing the body back.

After 12 months of death or the finding of a dead body, no death can be registered without the consent of the Registrar-General.

Burial and Cremation
In most circumstances in England and Wales a certificate for burial or cremation must be obtained from the registrar before the burial or cremation can take place. If the death has been referred to the coroner, an order for burial or a certificate for cremation must be obtained.

Funeral costs can normally be repaid out of the deceased's estate and will be given priority over any other claims. If the deceased has left a will it may contain directions concerning the funeral; however, these directions need not be followed by the executor.

The deceased's papers should also indicate whether a grave space had already been arranged. Most town churchyards and many suburban churchyards are no longer open for burial because they are full. Most cemeteries are non-denominational and may be owned by local authorities or private companies; fees vary.

If the body is to be cremated, an application form, two cremation certificates (for which there is a charge) or a certificate for cremation if the death was referred to the coroner, and a certificate signed by the medical referee must be completed in addition to the certificate for burial or cremation (the form is not required if the coroner has issued a certificate for cremation). All the forms are available from the funeral director or crematorium. Most crematoria are run by local authorities; the fees usually include the medical referee's fee and the use of the chapel. Ashes may be scattered, buried in a churchyard or cemetery, or kept.

The registrar must be notified of the date, place and means of disposal of the body within 96 hours. If the death occurred abroad or on a foreign ship or aircraft, a local burial or cremation may be arranged. If the body is to be brought back to England or Wales, a death certificate from the relevant country or an authorisation for the removal of the body from the country of death from the coroner or relevant authority will be required. To arrange a funeral in England or Wales an authenticated translation of a foreign death certificate or a death certificate issued in Scotland or Northern Ireland which must show the cause of death, is needed, together with a certificate of no liability to register from the registrar in England and Wales in whose sub-district it is intended to bury or cremate the body. If it is intended to cremate the body a cremation order will be required from the Home Office or a certificate for cremation.

Further information can be obtained from:
The General Register Office
Office for National Statistics, Smedley Hydro, Trafalgar Road, Birkdale, Southport, Merseyside PR8 2HH (Tel: 01704-569824)

DIVORCE AND RELATED MATTERS
There are two types of matrimonial suit: those seeking the annulment of a marriage, and those seeking a judicial separation or divorce. To obtain an annulment, judicial separation or divorce in England and Wales, one or both of the parties must have their permanent home in

England and Wales when the petition is started, or have been living in England and Wales for at least a year on the day the petition is started. All cases are commenced in divorce county courts or in the Divorce Registry in London. If a suit is defended it may be transferred to the High Court.

Nullity of Marriage
Various circumstances will render a marriage invalid from the beginning including if: the parties were within the prohibited degrees of consanguinity, affinity or adoption; the parties were not respectively male and female; either of the parties was already married; either of the parties was under the age of 16; the formalities of the marriage were defective, e.g. the marriage did not take place in an authorised building, and both parties knew of the defect. Declarations of nullity are sought in very few cases.

Separation
A couple may enter into an agreement to separate by consent but for the agreement to be valid it must be followed by an immediate separation; a solicitor should be contacted.

Judicial separation does not dissolve a marriage and it is not necessary to prove that the marriage has irretrievably broken down. Either party can petition for a judicial separation at any time; the grounds listed below as grounds for divorce are also grounds for judicial separation.

Divorce
Neither party can petition for divorce until at least one year after the date of the marriage. The sole ground for divorce is the irretrievable breakdown of the marriage; this must be proved on one or more of the following grounds:
- the respondent has committed adultery and the petitioner finds it intolerable to live with him/her; however the petitioner cannot rely on an act of adultery by the other party if they have lived together for more than six months after the discovery that adultery had been committed
- the respondent has behaved in such a way that the petitioner cannot reasonably be expected to continue living with him/her
- the respondent deserted the petitioner for two years immediately before the petition. Desertion may be defined as a voluntary withdrawal from cohabitation by the respondent without just cause and against the wishes of the petitioner; where one party is guilty of serious misconduct which forces the other party to leave, the party at fault is said to be guilty of constructive desertion
- the respondent and the petitioner have lived separately for two years immediately before the petition and the respondent consents to the decree
- the respondent and the petitioner have lived separately for five years immediately before the petition

A total period of less than six months during which the parties have resumed living together is disregarded in determining whether the prescribed period of separation or desertion has been continuous (but cannot be included as part of the period of separation).

The Matrimonial Causes Act 1973 requires the solicitor for the petitioner in certain cases to certify whether the possibility of a reconciliation has been discussed with the petitioner.

(The Family Law Act 1996 provides that irretrievable breakdown would be the sole ground for divorce; the partner initiating the divorce would be required to attend an information session about the nature of divorce and the options available; and divorce would be granted after one year, or 18 months if the couple have children, during which time the couple would have the chance to take part in mediation sessions. These changes may not be implemented at all as the pilot schemes have not been very successful).

The Decree Nisi
A decree nisi does not dissolve or annul the marriage but must be obtained before a divorce or annulment can take place. Where the suit is undefended, the evidence normally takes the form of a sworn written statement made by the petitioner which is considered by a district judge. If the judge is satisfied that the petitioner has proved the contents of the petition, he/she will set a date for the pronouncement of the decree nisi in open court; neither party need attend.

If the judge is not satisfied that the petitioner has proved the contents of the petition, or if the suit is defended, the petition will be heard in open court with the parties giving oral evidence.

The Decree Absolute
The decree nisi is usually made absolute after six weeks and on the application of the petitioner. If the judge thinks it may be necessary to exercise any of his/her powers under the Children Act 1989, he/she can in exceptional circumstances delay the granting of the decree absolute. The decree absolute dissolves or annuls the marriage.

Children
Neither parent is now awarded 'custody' of any children of the marriage in England and Wales. Both parents, if married, have 'parental responsibility'. Either parent can exercise this, independently of the other. Any dispute between the parents can be resolved by the courts. In all court cases concerning children, whether connected to a matrimonial suit or not, the welfare of the child is the paramount consideration.

Maintenance, etc.
Either party may be liable to pay maintenance to their former spouse. If there were any children of the marriage, both parents have a legal responsibility to support them financially if they can afford to do so. These so-called ancillary matters, including any property settlements, may be settled before the divorce goes through but currently can go on long after the marriage is dissolved.

The courts are responsible for assessing maintenance for the former spouse, taking into account each party's income and essential outgoings and other aspects of the case. The court also deals with any maintenance for a child which has been treated by the spouses as a 'child of the family', e.g. a stepchild, and any property settlements.

The Child Support Agency (CSA) was set up under the Child Support Act 1991 and is now responsible for assessing the maintenance that absent parents should pay for their natural or adopted children (whether or not a marriage has taken place). The CSA accepts applications only when all the people involved are habitually resident in the UK; the courts will continue to deal with cases where one of the people involved lives abroad. The CSA deals with all new cases, and is gradually taking on cases where the parent with care (or his/her new partner) was already receiving income support, family credit or disability working allowance before 5 April 1993. People with existing court orders or written maintenance agreements made before 5 April 1993 should continue to use the courts. Where it is already collecting child maintenance, the CSA has the power to offer a collection and enforcement service for certain other payments of maintenance.

A formula is used to work out how much child maintenance is payable. The formula ensures that after the payment of child maintenance the absent parent's income, and that of any second family he/she may now have, remains significantly above basic income support rates. Also, no absent parent will normally be assessed to pay more than 30 per cent of his/her net income in current child maintenance, or more than 33 per cent if he/she is also liable for any arrears. Absent parents are normally expected to pay at least a minimum amount of child maintenance.

A scheme has begun to be introduced since the end of 1996 which allows departures from the formula in certain tightly defined circumstances, e.g. the high costs of travel to maintain contact with a child, or to have a property and capital transfer ('clean break' settlement) entered into before April 1993 taken into account; there will also be some additional grounds which may result in liability being increased.

Some cases involving unusual circumstances are treated as special cases and the assessment is modified. Where there is financial need (e.g. because of disability or continuing education), maintenance may be ordered by the court for children even beyond the age of 18.

The level of maintenance is reviewed automatically every two years. Either parent can report a change of circumstances and request a review at any time. An independent complaints examiner for the CSA was appointed in early 1997.

If the absent parent does not pay the child maintenance, the CSA may make an order for payments to be deducted directly from his/her salary or wages; if all other methods fail, the CSA may take court action to enforce the payment.

Court Orders

Magistrates' courts used for domestic proceedings are now called family proceedings courts. A spouse can apply to the family proceedings court for a court order on the ground that the other spouse:
- has failed to pay reasonable maintenance for the applicant
- has failed to make a proper contribution towards the reasonable maintenance of a 'child of the family'
- has deserted the applicant
- has behaved in such a way that the applicant cannot reasonably be expected to live with the respondent

If the case is proved, the court can order:
- periodical payments for the applicant and/or a 'child of the family'
- a lump sum payment (not exceeding £1,000) to the applicant and/or a 'child of the family'

In deciding what orders (if any) to make, the court must consider guidelines which are similar to those governing financial orders in divorce cases. There are also special provisions relating to consent orders and separation by agreement. An order may be enforceable even if the parties are living together, but in some cases it will cease to have effect if they continue to do so for six months.

Domestic Violence

If one spouse has been subjected to violence at the hands of the other, it is now possible to obtain a court order very quickly to restrain further violence and if necessary to have the other spouse excluded from the home. Such orders may also relate to unmarried couples and to a range of other relationships.

Further information can be obtained from any divorce county court, solicitor or Citizens' Advice Bureau, the Lord Chancellor's Department, or the following:
The Principal Registry
First Avenue House, 42-49 High Holborn, London WC1V 6NP (Tel: 020-7936 6000)
The Child Support Agency
Longbenton, Newcastle upon Tyne NE98 1YX (Tel: 0191-213 5000)

EMPLOYMENT LAW

Pay and Conditions

The Employment Rights Act 1996 consolidates the statutory provisions relating to employees' rights. Employers must give each employee based in Great Britain and employed for more than one month a written statement containing the following information:
- names of employer and employee
- date when employment began
- remuneration and intervals at which it will be paid
- job title or description of job
- hours and place(s) of work
- holiday entitlement and holiday pay
- entitlement to sick leave and sick pay
- details of pension scheme(s)
- length of notice period that employer and employee need to give to terminate employment, or the end date for a fixed-term contract
- details of any collective agreement which affects the terms of employment
- details of disciplinary and grievance procedures
- if the employee is to work outside the UK for more than one month, the period of such work and the currency in which payment is made

This must be given to the employee within two months of the start of their employment. The Working Time Regulation 1998 and the National Minimum Wage Act now supplement the 1996 Act.

Sick Pay

Employees absent from work through illness or injury are entitled to receive Statutory Sick Pay (SSP) from the employer for a maximum period of 28 weeks in any three-year period. This applies to all employees, both men and women, up to the age of 65.

Deductions From Pay

Employers may not make deductions from an employee's wages without the employee's prior written consent or unless authorised by statute (e.g. deductions for national insurance or tax).

Legal Notes 205

Sunday Trading
The Sunday Trading Act 1994 gave new rights to shop workers. They have the right not to be dismissed, selected for redundancy or to suffer any detriment (such as the denial of overtime, promotion or training) if they refuse to work on Sundays. This does not apply to those who, under their contracts, are employed to work on Sundays.

Trade Union Membership
Under employment legislation, employees or potential employees may not be penalised because they are or are not a member of a trade union.

Disputes
Where it has not been possible to settle a dispute in the workplace, it may be possible for employees to make a complaint to an industrial tribunal. ACAS (the Advisory, Conciliation and Arbitration Service; for entry, see Index) offers advice and conciliation in employment disputes.

Termination of Employment
An employee may be dismissed without notice if guilty of gross misconduct but in other cases a period of notice must be given by the employer. The minimum periods of notice specified in the Employment Rights Act 1996 are:
- at least one week if the employee has been continuously employed for one month or more but for less than two years
- at least two weeks if the employee has been continuously employed for two years or more. A week is added for every complete year of continuous employment up to 12 years
- at least 12 weeks for those who have been continuously employed for 12 years or more
- longer periods apply if these are specified in the contract of employment

If an employee is dismissed with less notice than he/she is entitled to, the employer is generally liable to pay wages for the period of proper notice (or for the period of the contract for those on fixed-term contracts). Generally, no notice needs to be given of the expiry of a fixed-term contract.

Redundancy
An employee dismissed because of redundancy may be entitled to a lump sum. This applies if:
- the employee has at least two years' continuous service
- the employee is actually dismissed by the employer (even in cases of voluntary redundancy)
- dismissal is due to a reduction in the work force

An employee may not be entitled to a redundancy payment if offered a new job by the same employer. The amount of payment depends on the length of service, the salary and the age of the employee.

Unfair Dismissal
Complaints about unfair dismissal are dealt with by an employment tribunal. Since 1 June 1999 any employee, with one years' continuous service subject to exceptions, regardless of their hours of work, can make a complaint to the tribunal. For dismissals prior to that date, it is necessary for the employee to have two years' continuous service in order to bring a complaint (although this requirement has been referred by the House of Lords to the European Court of Justice). At the tribunal the employer must prove that the dismissal was due to one or more of the following reasons:
- the employee's capability for the job
- the employee's conduct
- redundancy
- a legal restriction preventing the continuation of the employee's contract
- some other substantial reason

If so, the tribunal must decide whether the employer acted reasonably in dismissing the employee for that reason. If the employee is found to have been unfairly dismissed, the tribunal can order that he/she be reinstated or compensated.

Discrimination
Discrimination in employment on the grounds of sex, race or (subject to wide exceptions) disability is unlawful. The following legislation applies to those employed in Great Britain but not to employees in Northern Ireland or (subject to EC exceptions) to those who work mainly abroad:
- The Equal Pay Act 1970 (as amended) entitles men and women to equality in matters related to their contracts of employment. Those doing like work for the same employer are entitled to the same pay and conditions regardless of their sex
- The Sex Discrimination Act 1975 (as amended by the Sex Discrimination Act 1986) makes it unlawful to discriminate on grounds of sex or marital status. This covers all aspects of employment, including advertising for recruits, terms offered, opportunities for promotion and training, and dismissal procedures
- The Race Relations Act 1976 gives individuals the right not to be discriminated against in employment matters on the grounds of race, colour, nationality, or ethnic or national origins. It applies to all aspects of employment
- The Disability Discrimination Act 1995 makes discrimination against a disabled person in all aspects of employment unlawful. Unlike sex and race discrimination, an employer may show that the treatment is justified and that the employer acted reasonably. Employers with fewer than 15 employees are exempt

The Equal Opportunities Commission, the Commission for Racial Equality and the Disablility Rights Commission (for entries, see Index) have the function of eliminating such discriminations in the workplace and can provide further information and assistance.

In Northern Ireland like provisions exist but are constituted in separate legislation. The Fair Employment (Northern Ireland) Act 1989 adds specific provisions aimed at preventing religious discrimination.

Recent Legislation
The Employment Relations Act 1999 has made a number of important changes to the existing law. The main changes are :-
- a right of accompaniment. A worker attending a serious disciplinary or grievance hearing will have a right to be accompanied by a trade union representative or co-worker of their choice
- a new scheme of compulsory trade union recognition following a workplace ballot
- greater protection from dismissal for striking employees

- more 'family friendly' measures, including greater rights to maternity leave and parental leave
- the maximum compensatory award in unfair dismissal cases is to be increased from £12,000 to £50,000.

ILLEGITIMACY AND LEGITIMATION

The Children Act 1989 gives the mother parental responsibility for the child when she is not married to the father. The father can acquire parental responsibility either by agreement with her (in prescribed form) or by applying to the court. If an illegitimate child is to be adopted, the father's consent is required only where he has been awarded parental rights by the court.

Every child born to a married woman during marriage is presumed to be legitimate, unless the couple are separated under court order when the child is conceived, in which case the child is presumed not to be the husband's child. It is possible to challenge the presumption of legitimacy or illegitimacy through civil proceedings.

Legitimation

Under the Legitimacy Act 1976, an illegitimate person automatically becomes legitimate when his/her parents marry. This applies even where one of the parents was married to a third person at the time of the birth. In such cases it is necessary to re-register the birth of the child.

Rights of Illegitimate People

For the purposes of most legislation, illegitimate and legitimate people have the same rights and responsibilities. In particular, under the Family Law Reform Acts 1969 and 1987, legitimate and illegitimate children have broadly the same rights on an intestacy. Furthermore, in any will made after 31 December 1969, it is assumed that any reference to children or relatives will include those who are illegitimate and those related through another person who is illegitimate.

JURY SERVICE

In England and Wales a person charged with any but the most minor offences is entitled to be tried by jury. There are 12 members of a jury in a criminal case and eight members in a civil case. Jurors are normally asked to serve for ten working days, although jurors selected for longer cases are expected to sit for the duration of the trial.

Every parliamentary or local government elector between the ages of 18 and 70 who has lived in the UK (including, for this purpose, the Channel Islands and the Isle of Man) for any period of at least five years since reaching the age of 13 is qualified to serve on a jury unless he/she is ineligible or disqualified.

England and Wales

Those ineligible for jury service include:
- those who have at any time been judges, magistrates or senior court officials

those who have within the previous ten years been concerned with the administration of justice
- priests of any religion and vowed members of religious communities
- certain sufferers from mental illness

Those disqualified from jury service include:
- those who have at any time been sentenced by a court in the UK (including, for this purpose, the Channel Islands and the Isle of Man) to a term of imprisonment or custody of five years or more
- those who have within the previous ten years served any part of a sentence of imprisonment, youth custody or detention, been detained in a young offenders' institution, received a suspended sentence of imprisonment or order for detention, or received a community service order
- those who have within the previous five years been placed on probation
- those who are on bail in criminal proceedings

Those who may be excused as of right from jury service include:
- persons over the age of 65
- members and officers of the Houses of Parliament
- members of the National Assembly for Wales
- representatives to the European Parliament
- full-time serving members of the armed forces
- registered and practising members of the medical, dental, nursing, veterinary and pharmaceutical professions
- those who have served on a jury in the previous two years

The court has the discretion to excuse a juror from service, or defer the date of service, if the service would be a hardship to the juror. If a person serves on a jury knowing himself/herself to be ineligible or disqualified, he/she is liable to be fined up to £5,000 if disqualified and up to £1,000 for all other offences. The defendant can object to any juror if he/she can show cause.

A juror may claim travelling expenses, a subsistence allowance and an allowance for other financial loss (e.g. loss of earnings or benefits, fees paid to carers or childminders) up to a stated limit.

It is an offence for a juror to disclose what happened in the jury room even after the trial is over. A jury's verdict must normally be unanimous, but if no verdict has been reached after two hours' consideration (or such longer period as the court deems to be reasonable) a majority verdict is acceptable if ten jurors agree to it.

Further information can obtained from:
The Court Service
105 Victoria Street, London SW1E 6QT (Tel: 020-7210 2266)

LANDLORD AND TENANT

When a property is rented to a tenant, the rights and responsibilities of the landlord and the tenant are determined largely by the tenancy agreement but also by statutory provisions. Some of the main provisions are outlined below but it is advisable to contact the Citizens' Advice Bureau or the local authority housing department for further information.

Residential Lettings

The provisions outlined here apply only where the tenant lives in a separate dwelling from the landlord and where the dwelling is the tenant's only or main home. It does not apply to licensees such as lodgers, guests or service occupiers.

The 1996 Housing Act radically changes certain aspects of the legislation referred to below, in particular the grant of assured and assured shorthold tenancies under the Housing Act 1988. It is advisable to check

Legal Notes

whether the new legislation has come into force before relying on the provisions set out below.

Assured Shorthold Tenancies
If a tenancy was granted on or after 15 January 1989 and before 28 February 1997, the tenant may have an assured tenancy giving that tenant greater rights. The tenant could, for example, stay in possession of the dwelling for as long as the tenant observed the terms of the tenancy. The landlord cannot obtain possession from such a tenant unless the landlord can establish a specific ground for possession (set out in the Housing Act 1988) and obtains a court order. The rent payable is that agreed with the landlord unless the rent has been fixed by the rent assessment committee of the local authority. The tenant or the landlord may request that the committee set the rent in line with open market rents for that type of property. Any rent increases that are to take place should be written into the agreement but failing that, the landlord must give advance notice of the increase.

Under the Housing Act 1996, most new lettings entered into on or after 28 February 1997 will be assured shorthold tenancies. This means that tenants are given limited rights. The landlord must obtain a court order, however, to obtain possession if the tenant refuses to vacate at the end of the tenancy.

Regulated Tenancies
Before the Housing Act 1988 came into force (15 January 1989) there were regulated tenancies; some are still in existence and are protected by the Rent Act 1977. Under this Act it is possible for the landlord or the tenant to apply to the local rent officer to have a 'fair' rent registered. The fair rent is then the maximum rent payable.

Secure Tenancies
Secure tenancies are generally given to tenants of local authorities, housing associations and certain other bodies. This gives the tenant lifelong tenure unless the terms of the agreement are broken by the tenant. In certain circumstances those with secure tenancies may have the right to buy their property. In practice this right is generally only available to council tenants.

Agricultural Property
Tenancies in agricultural properties are governed by the Agricultural Holdings Act 1986 and the Rent (Agricultural) Act 1976, which give similar protections to those described above, e.g. security of tenure, right to compensation for disturbance, etc.

Eviction
Under the Protection from Eviction Act 1977 (as amended by the Housing Act 1988), a landlord must give reasonable notice that he/she is to evict the tenant, and in most cases a possession order, granted in court, is necessary. Notice is generally to be at least four weeks and in prescribed statutory form (notices are available from law stationers). It is illegal for a landlord to evict a person by putting their belongings onto the street, by changing the locks and so on. It is also illegal for a landlord to harass a tenant in any way in order to persuade him/her to give up the tenancy.

Landlord Responsibilities
Under the Landlord and Tenant Act 1985, where the term of the lease is less than seven years the landlord is responsible for maintaining the structure and exterior of the property and all installations for the supply of water, gas and electricity, for sanitation, and for heating and hot water.

Leaseholders
Legally leaseholders have bought a long lease rather than a property and in certain limited circumstances the landlord can end the tenancy. Under the Leasehold Reform Act 1967 (as amended by the Housing Acts 1969, 1974 and 1980), leaseholders of houses may have the right to buy the freehold or to take an extended lease for a term of 50 years. This applies to leases where the term of the lease is over 21 years and where the leaseholder has occupied the house as his/her main residence for the last three years, or for a total of three years over the last ten.

The Leasehold Reform, Housing and Urban Development Act came into force in 1993 and allows the leaseholders of flats in certain circumstances to buy the freehold of the building in which they live.

Responsibility for maintenance of the structure, exterior and interior of the building should be set out in the lease. Usually the upkeep of the interior of his/her part of the property is the responsibility of the leaseholder, and responsibility for the structure, exterior and common interior areas is shared between the freeholder and the leaseholder(s).

Leasehold Advisory Service, 8 Maddox Street, London, W1R 9PN, Tel: 020-7493 3116, Fax: 020-7493 4318, Web: http://www.lease-advice.org

Business Lettings
The Landlord and Tenant Acts 1927 and 1954 (as amended) give security of tenure to the tenants of most business premises. The landlord can only evict the tenant on one of the grounds laid down in the 1954 Act, and in some cases where the landlord repossesses the property the tenant may be entitled to compensation.

LEGAL AID
Under the Legal Aid Act 1988 (as amended) and subsequent Regulations, people on low or moderate incomes may qualify for help with the costs of legal advice or representation. The scheme is administered in England and Wales by the Legal Aid Board (for entries, see Index). There are three types of legal aid: civil legal aid, legal advice and assistance, and criminal legal aid.

Civil Legal Aid
Applications for legal aid are made through a solicitor; the Citizens' Advice Bureau will have addresses for local solicitors. Franchised solicitors are those approved by the Legal Aid Boards, which can provide details.

Civil legal aid is available for proceedings in the following:
– the House of Lords
– the High Court
– the Court of Appeal
– county courts
– lands tribunals
– the Employment Appeal Tribunal
– the Restrictive Practices Court
– the Commons Commissioners
– civil proceedings in magistrates' courts
– family proceedings courts

It is not available for the following:
- tribunals other than those mentioned above
- defamation proceedings
- obtaining the decree in undefended divorce and judicial separation
- court cases outside England and Wales

Eligibility
The Legal Aid Board will only grant a civil legal aid certificate where:
- the applicant qualifies financially, and
- the applicant has reasonable grounds for taking or defending the action, and
- it is reasonable to grant legal aid in the circumstances of the case. For example, civil legal aid will not be granted where it appears that the applicant will gain only trivial advantage from the proceedings

In order to qualify for civil legal aid, a person's disposable income must be £7,940 a year or less and his or her disposable capital must be £6,750 or less. (The financial limits are different for pensioners and in personal injury claims). Disposable income is the total income, less outgoings such as tax and national insurance contributions, rent, council tax, mortgage payments, etc., with allowances made for dependants. The income of a spouse or cohabitee is taken into account unless they are living apart or have a contrary interest in the proceedings. Disposable capital includes savings, insurances, any personal possessions of substantial value and property owned. For applications from 1 June 1996, the applicant's dwelling house is treated as follows:
- the capital value of the property (i.e. market value, less amount outstanding on any mortgage) will be taken into account in so far as it exceeds £100,000
- the capital amount allowed in respect of mortgage debt or charge over the property cannot exceed £100,000
- if the mortgage debt exceeds £100,000, the amount allowed against income for mortgage payments will be reduced in proportion
- the total amount of mortgage debt allowed for all properties (including second and subsequent dwellings) cannot exceed £100,000

Contributions
Some of those who qualify for legal aid will have to contribute towards their legal costs:
- if in receipt of income support, no contributions are due
- if annual disposable income is between £2,680 and £7,940, a contribution must be made from disposable income
- if disposable capital is over £3,000, all disposable capital in excess of £3,000 must be paid as a contribution

Contributions from disposable income are paid monthly for as long as the person has legal aid. The amount of the contribution depends on the amount of disposable income in excess of £2,680; the greater the excess income, the greater the contribution. Contributions from capital are payable immediately.

Statutory Charges
A statutory charge is made if a person receives money or property in a case for which they have received legal aid. This means that the amount paid by the Legal Aid Fund on their behalf is deducted from the amount that the person receives. This does not apply if the court has ordered that the costs be paid by the other party or if the payments are for maintenance. In family proceedings cases, the first £2,500 is exempt and the statutory charge is taken from anything in excess of that.

In urgent cases, e.g. domestic violence, legal aid may be granted without the means test. This will be carried out later and the person will have to reimburse the Legal Aid Fund for any aid that they received which exceeded their entitlement.

Legal Advice and Assistance
The legal advice and assistance scheme (commonly referred to as the green form scheme) covers the costs of getting advice and help from a solicitor, and, in some cases, representation in court under the 'assistance by way of representation' scheme (see below).

A person is eligible for legal advice and assistance if:
- he or she has a disposable income of £83 a week or less and disposable capital of £1,000 or less (£1,335 if the person has one dependant, £1,535 if two dependants)
- he or she is eligible for income support, family credit, income-based jobseeker's allowance or disability working allowance (unless they have disposable capital of more than £1,000)

There are no contributions under this scheme.

If a person is eligible, the Legal Aid Board will pay for up to two hours' work by a solicitor on behalf of the person (three hours where drafting a petition for divorce). The solicitor must seek the approval of the Legal Aid Board to claim for longer periods of time. The work the solicitor does may include giving advice, writing letters, making an application for civil/criminal legal aid, seeking the advice of a barrister, etc. The scheme does not cover any form of proceedings before a court or tribunal. Any money or property recovered with the help of legal advice and assistance will be subject to a 'solicitor's charge', which is similar to a statutory charge in civil legal aid but with some differences.

Contingency or Conditional Fees
This system was introduced by the Courts and Legal Services Act 1990. It offers legal representation on a 'no win, no fee' basis. It provides an alternative form of assistance, especially to those who are ineligible for the Legal Aid schemes. The main area for such work is in the field of personal injuries.

Not all solicitors offer such a scheme and different solicitors may well have different terms.

The effect of the agreement is that solicitors will not make any charges until the case is concluded successfully. The charges are usually linked to a percentage of the amount recovered. The merits of a case are usually assessed before the scheme is offered to potential litigants. Should the case be accepted, then the percentage charges will be linked to the risks involved: the higher the risks, the higher the percentage. Any agreement should be in writing and set out the exact terms of the agreement and the effects of success and failure.

Assistance by Way of Representation
This type of assistance is available for most cases in a family proceedings court and to patients before a mental health review tribunal. It covers the cost of preparing a case and of legal representation in the court.

Under this scheme the two-hour limit does not apply and the approval of the Legal Aid Board is needed in all cases. The income and capital limits are different to legal advice and assistance. In order to qualify, a person's disposable income must be £178 a week or less and their savings must not exceed £3,000. There is no means test for patients due before a mental health review tribunal. Contributions may have to be made and a solicitor's charge will apply to money or property recovered.

Duty Solicitors

The Legal Aid Act 1988 also provides free advice and assistance to anyone questioned by the police (whether under arrest or helping the police with their enquiries). No means test or contributions are required for this. The advice or assistance can be from the duty solicitor at the police station, from a person's own solicitor or from any local solicitor (a list is available at police stations).

Duty solicitors are usually available at the magistrates' court, in criminal cases, for advice and/or representation on first appearances. This assistance is not means-tested. The Legal Aid Fund also covers the costs of a solicitor present in the buildings of family proceedings or county courts who may be requested by the court to advise or represent someone in need of help.

Criminal Legal Aid

The courts will grant criminal legal aid if it is desirable in the interests of justice (e.g. if there are important questions of law to be argued or the case is so serious that if found guilty the person may go to prison) and the person needs help to pay their legal costs.

Criminal legal aid covers the cost of preparing a case and legal representation (including the cost of a barrister) in criminal proceedings. It is also available for appeals against verdicts or sentences in magistrates' courts, the Crown Court or the Court of Appeal. It is not available for bringing a private prosecution in a criminal court.

If granted criminal legal aid, either the person may choose their own solicitor or the court will assign one. Contributions to the legal costs must be paid by anyone who has a disposable income of over £51 a week or disposable capital of over £3,000. These contributions are payable each month and will probably be returned to the person if they are acquitted. If the payments are not made, the legal aid order may be revoked.

Marriage

Any two persons may marry provided that:
- they are at least 16 years old on the day of the marriage (in England and Wales persons under the age of 18 must generally obtain the consent of their parents; if consent is refused an appeal may be made to the High Court, the county court or a court of summary jurisdiction)
- they are not related to one another in a way which would prevent their marrying (see below)
- they are unmarried (a person who has already been married must produce documentary evidence that the previous marriage has been ended by death, divorce or annulment)
- they are not of the same sex
- they are capable of understanding the nature of a marriage ceremony and of consenting to marriage
- the marriage would be regarded as valid in any foreign country of which either party is a citizen

Degrees of Relationship

A marriage between persons within the prohibited degrees of consanguinity, affinity or adoption is void.

A man may not marry his mother, daughter, grandmother, granddaughter, sister, aunt, niece, great-grandmother, great-granddaughter, adoptive mother, former adoptive mother, adopted daughter or former adopted daughter. In some circumstances he may now be allowed to marry his former wife's daughter, former wife's granddaughter, father's former wife or grandfather's former wife. A woman may not marry her father, son, grandfather, grandson, brother, uncle, nephew, great-grandfather, great-grandson, adoptive father, former adoptive father, adopted son or former adopted son. In some circumstances she may now be allowed to marry her former husband's son, former husband's grandson, mother's former husband or grandmother's former husband.

Types of Marriage Ceremony

It is possible to marry by either religious or civil ceremony. A religious ceremony can take place at a church or chapel of the Church of England or the Church in Wales, or at any other place of worship which has been formally registered by the Registrar-General.

A civil ceremony can take place at a register office, a registered building or any other premises approved by the local authority.

An application for an approved premises licence must be made by the owners or trustees of the building concerned; it cannot be made by the prospective marriage couple. Approved premises must be regularly open to the public so that the marriage can be witnessed; the venue must be deemed to be a permanent and immovable structure. Open-air ceremonies are prohibited.

Non-Anglican marriages may also be solemnised following the issue of a Registrar-General's licence in unregistered premises where one of the parties is seriously ill, is not expected to recover, and cannot be moved to registered premises. Detained and housebound persons may be married at their place of residence.

MARRIAGE IN THE CHURCH OF ENGLAND OR THE CHURCH IN WALES

Marriage by banns

The marriage must take place in a parish in which one of the parties lives, or in a church in another parish if it is the usual place of worship of either or both of the parties. The banns must be called in the parish in which the marriage is to take place on three Sundays before the day of the ceremony; if either or both of the parties lives in a different parish the banns must also be called there. After three months the banns are no longer valid.

Marriage by common licence

The vicar who is to conduct the marriage will arrange for a common licence to be issued by the diocesan bishop; this dispenses with the necessity for banns. One of the parties must have lived in the parish for 15 days immediately before the issuing of the licence or must usually worship at the church. Affidavits are prepared from the personal instructions of one of the parties and the licence will be given to the applicant in person.

Marriage by special licence

A special licence is granted by the Archbishop of Canterbury in special circumstances for the marriage to take place at any place, with or without previous residence in the parish, or at any time. Application must be made to the Faculty Office of the Archbishop of Canterbury, 1 The Sanctuary, London SW1P 3JT. Tel: 020-7222 5381.

Marriage by certificate
The marriage can be conducted on the authority of the superintendent registrar's certificate, provided that the vicar's consent is obtained. One of the parties must live in the parish or must usually worship at the church.

Marriage by Other Religious Ceremony
One of the parties must normally live in the registration district where the marriage is to take place. In addition to giving notice to the superintendent registrar, it may also be necessary to book a registrar to be present at the ceremony.

Civil Marriage
A marriage may be solemnised at any register office, registered building or approved premises in England and Wales. The superintendent registrar of the district should be contacted, and, if the marriage is to take place at approved premises, the necessary arrangements at the venue must also be made.

Notice of Marriage
Unless it is to take place by banns or under common or special licence in the Church of England or the Church in Wales, a notice of the marriage must be given in person to the superintendent registrar. Notice of marriage may be given in the following ways:
- by certificate. Both parties must have lived in a registration district in England or Wales for at least seven days immediately before giving notice at the local register office. If they live in different registration districts, notice must be given in both districts. The marriage can take place in any register office in England and Wales 21 days after notice has been given
- by licence (often known as 'special licence'). One of the parties must have lived in a registration district in England or Wales for at least 15 days before giving notice at the register office; the other party need only be a resident of, or be physically in, England and Wales on the day notice is given. The marriage can take place one clear day (other than a Sunday, Christmas Day or Good Friday) after notice has been given

A notice of marriage is valid for 12 months. It is not therefore possible to give formal notice of a marriage more than three months before it is to take place, but it should be possible to make an advance (provisional) booking 12 months before the ceremony. In this case it is still necessary to give formal notice three months before the marriage. When giving notice of the marriage it is necessary to produce official proof, if relevant, that any previous marriage has ended in divorce or death by producing a decree absolute or death certificate; it is also useful, but not necessary, to take birth certificates or passports as proof of age and identity.

Solemnisation of the Marriage
On the day of the wedding there must be at least two other people present who are prepared to act as witnesses and sign the marriage register. A registrar of marriages must be present at a marriage in a register office or at approved premises, but an authorised person may act in the capacity of registrar in a registered building.

If the marriage takes place at approved premises, the room must be separate from any other activity on the premises at the time of the ceremony, and no food or drink can be sold or consumed in the room during the ceremony or for one hour beforehand.

The marriage must be solemnised between 8 a.m. and 6 p.m., with open doors. At some time during the ceremony the parties must make a declaration that they know of no legal impediment to the marriage and they must also say the contracting words; the declaratory and contracting words may vary according to the form of service in use but the most basic forms are:
- (declaratory words) 'I declare that I know of no legal reason why I, A. B., may not be joined in marriage to C. D.' Alternatively, the couple may answer 'I am' to the question 'Are you, A. B., free lawfully to marry C. D.?'
- (contracting words) 'I, A. B., take you, C. D., to be my wedded wife [or husband]'

A civil marriage cannot contain any religious aspects, but it may be possible for non-religious music and/or poetry readings to be included. It may also be possible to embellish the marriage vows taken by the couple.

If both parties are Jewish, they may be married in a synagogue, in a private house or elsewhere. The wedding may take place at any time of day and must be registered by the secretary of the synagogue of which the man is a member. The presence of a registrar of marriages is not necessary.

If both parties are members of the Society of Friends (Quakers), they may be married in a Friends' meeting-house. The marriage must be registered by the registering officer of the Society appointed to act for the district in which the meeting-house is situated. The presence of a registrar of marriages is not necessary.

Further information can be obtained from:
The General Register Office
Office for National Statistics, Smedley Hydro, Trafalgar Road, Birkdale, Southport, Merseyside PR8 2HH (Tel: 01704-569824)

TOWN AND COUNTRY PLANNING
The principal legislation governing the development of land and buildings in England and Wales is the Town and Country Planning Act 1990 (as amended by the Planning and Compensation Act 1991). The uses of buildings are classified by the Town and Country Planning (Use Classes) Order 1987 (as amended) in England and Wales. It is advisable in all cases to contact the planning department of the local authority to check whether planning or other permission is needed.

Planning Permission
Planning permission is needed if the work involves:
- making a material change in use, such as dividing off part of the house so that it can be used as a separate home or dividing off part of the house for commercial use, e.g. for a workshop
- going against the terms of the original planning permission, e.g. there may be a restriction on fences in front gardens on an open-plan estate
- building, engineering for mining, except for the permissions below

Legal Notes 211

- new or wider access to a main road
- additions or extensions to flats or maisonettes

Planning permission is not needed to carry out internal alterations or work which does not affect the external appearance of the building.

There are certain types of development for which the Secretary of State for the Environment has granted general permissions. These include:
- house extensions and additions (including conservatories, loft conversions, garages and dormer windows). Up to 10 per cent or up to 50 cubic metres (whichever is the greater) can be added to the original house for terraced houses. Up to 15 per cent or 70 cubic metres (whichever is the greater) to other kinds of houses. The maximum that can be added to any house is 115 cubic metres
- buildings such as garden sheds and greenhouses so long as they are no more than 3 metres high (or 4 metres if the roof is ridged), are no nearer to a highway than the house, and at least half the ground around the house remains uncovered by buildings
- adding a porch with a ground area of less than 3 square metres and that is less than 3 metres in height
- putting up fences, walls and gates of under 1 metre in height if next to a road and under 2 metres elsewhere
- laying patios, paths or driveways for domestic use

Other Restrictions

It may be necessary to obtain other types of permissions before carrying out any development. These permissions are separate from planning permission and apply regardless of whether or not planning permission is needed, e.g.:
- building regulations will probably apply if a new building is to be erected, if an existing one is to be altered or extended, or if the work involves building over a drain or sewer The building control department of the local authority will advise on this
- any alterations to a listed building or the grounds of a listed building must be approved by the local authority
- local authority approval is necessary if a building (or, in some circumstances, gates, walls, fences or railings) in a conservation area is to be demolished; each local authority keeps a register of all local buildings that are in conservation areas
- many trees are protected by tree preservation orders and must not be pruned or taken down without local authority consent
- bats and other species are protected and English Nature or the Countryside Council for Wales must be notified before any work is carried out that will affect the habitat of protected species, e.g. timber treatment, renovation or extensions of lofts
- any development in areas designated as a National Park, an Area of Outstanding Natural Beauty, a National Scenic Area or in the Norfolk or Suffolk Broads is subject to greater restrictions. The local planning authority will advise or refer enquirers to the relevant authority

VOTERS' QUALIFICATIONS

Those entitled to vote at parliamentary, European Union (EU) and local government elections are those who are:
- resident in the constituency or ward on the qualifying date i.e. 10 October in the year before the electoral register (see below) comes into effect; in Northern Ireland the qualifying date is 15 September and voters must have been resident in Northern Ireland for the three months leading up to that date
- over 18 years old
- Commonwealth (which includes British) citizens or citizens of the Republic of Ireland

British citizens resident abroad are entitled to vote, for 20 years after leaving Britain, as overseas electors in parliamentary and EU elections in the constituency in which they were last resident. Members of the armed forces, Crown servants and employees of the British Council who are overseas and their spouses are entitled to vote regardless of how long they have been abroad.

European Union citizens resident in the UK may vote in EU and local government elections.

The following people are not entitled to vote:
- peers, and peeresses in their own right, who are members of the House of Lords (except that they may vote in EU and local government elections)
- patients detained under mental health legislation
- voluntary mental patients (unless they make a prescribed declaration)
- those serving prison sentences
- those convicted within the previous five years of corrupt or illegal election practices

Registering to Vote

Voters must be entered on an electoral register, which runs from 16 February in one year to 15 February in the following year. The registration officer for each constituency is responsible for preparing and publishing the register. A registration form is sent to all households in the autumn of each year and the householder is required to provide details of all occupants who are eligible to vote, including ones who will reach their 18th birthday in the year covered by the register. Those who fail to give the required information or who give false information are liable to be fined. A draft register is usually published at the end of November. Any person whose name has been omitted may ask to be registered and should contact the registration officer. Anyone on the register may object to the inclusion of another person's name, in which case he/she should notify the registration officer, who will investigate that person's eligibility. Supplementary electors lists are published throughout the duration of the register.

Voting

Voting is not compulsory in the UK. Those who wish to vote must generally vote in person at the allotted polling station. Those who will be away at the time of the election, those who will not be able to attend in person due to physical incapacity or the nature of their occupation, and those who have changed address during the period for which the register is valid, may apply for a postal vote or nominate a proxy to vote for them. Overseas electors who wish to vote must do so by proxy.

Further information can be obtained from the local authority's electoral registration officer in England and Wales.

WILLS AND INTESTACY

In a will a person leaves instructions as to the disposal of their property after they die. A will is also used to appoint

executors (who will administer the estate), give directions as to the disposal of the body, appoint guardians for children and, for larger estates, can operate to reduce the level of inheritance tax. It is best to have a will drawn up by a solicitor but if a solicitor is not employed, the following points must be taken into account:
- if possible the will must not be prepared on behalf of another person by someone who is to benefit from it or who is a close relative of a major beneficiary
- the language used must be clear and unambiguous and it is better to avoid the use of legal terms where the same thing can be expressed in plain language
- it is better to rewrite the whole document if a mistake is made. If necessary, alterations can be made by striking through the words with a pen, and the signature or initials of the testator and the witnesses must be put in the margin opposite the alteration. No alteration of any kind should be made after the will has been executed
- if the person later wishes to change the will or part of it, it is better to write a new will revoking the old. The use of codicils (documents written as supplements or containing modifications to the will) should be left to a solicitor
- the will should be typed or printed, or if handwritten be legible and preferably in ink. Commercial will forms can be obtained from some stationers

The form of a will varies to suit different cases; the following is an example of how a will might be written. The notes after this example explain the terms used and procedures that need to be followed in drawing up a will.

This is the last will and testament of me [Thomas Smith] of [Heather Cottage, Prospero Road, Manchester M1 4DK] which I make this [seventeenth] day of [May 1999] and I revoke all previous wills and testamentary dispositions.

1. I appoint as my executors and trustees [Ann Green of _____ and Richard Brown of _____]. In my will the expression 'my Trustees' means any executors and trustees for the time being of my will and of any trust arising under it.

2. I give all my property to [such of my children as shall survive me by 28 days and if more than one in equal shares or as the case may be].

or

2. I give to [Pamela Henderson of _____] the sum of [£___] and to [Michael Broadbent of _____] the sum of [£___] and to [Ruth Walker of _____] all of my [jewellery, books or as the case may be]

and

3. I give everything not otherwise disposed of to [Richard Black of _____]

Signed by the testator in our joint presence and then by us in his.

Thomas Smith
[Signature of the person making the will]
Elizabeth Wall
[Signature of witness] of 67 Beatrice Lane, Manchester M1 4DK, journalist
William Jones
[Signature of witness] of 17 Paris Road, Manchester M1 4EN, tailor

Specific Gifts and Legacies

Gifts of specific items usually fail if the property is not owned by the person making the will on their death. This problem can be avoided by making a gift of any property fulfilling a particular description, e.g. a car, which is owned at the date of death. It is better in all cases where such gifts are made, to insert a clause which reads 'I give everything not otherwise disposed of to [Richard Black of _____], even if it seems that all property has already been disposed of in the will.

Lapsed Legatees

If a person who has been left property in a will dies before the person who made the will, the gift fails and will pass to the person entitled to everything not otherwise disposed of (the residuary estate).

If the person left the residuary estate dies before the person who made the will, their share will generally pass to the closest relative(s) of the person who made the will (as in intestacy) unless the will names a beneficiary such as a charity who will take as a 'long stop' if this gift is unable to take effect for any reason.

It is always better to draw up a new will if a beneficiary predeceases the person who made the will.

Executors

It is usual to appoint two executors, although one is sufficient. No more than four persons can deal with the estate of the person who has died. The name and address of each executor should be given in full (the addresses are not essential but including them adds clarity to the document).

Executors should be 18 years of age or over. An executor may be a beneficiary of the will.

Witnesses

A person who is a beneficiary of a will, or the spouse of a beneficiary at the time the will is signed, must not act as a witness or else he/she will be unable to take his/her gift. Husband and wife can both act as witnesses provided neither benefits from the will. It is better that a person does not act as an executor and as a witness, as he/she can take no benefit under a will to which he/she is witness. The identity of the witnesses should be made as explicit as possible.

Execution of a Will

The person making the will should sign his/her name at the foot of the document, in the presence of the two witnesses. The witnesses must then sign their names while the person making the will looks on. If this procedure is not adhered to, the will will be considered invalid. There are certain exceptional circumstances where these rules are relaxed, e.g. where the person may be too ill to sign, and in these cases the attestation clause which normally reads 'signed by the testator in our joint presence and then by us in his/hers' should be reworded as follows:

'The will was read over to Thomas Smith in our presence when he stated that he understood it. It was then signed on his behalf by Thomas Brown in the presence of the testator and by his direction in our joint presence and then by us in his'.

Capacity to Make a Will

Anyone aged 18 or over can make a will. However, if there is any suspicion that the person making the will is

Legal Notes

not, through reasons of infirmity or age, fully in command of his/her faculties, it is advisable to arrange for a medical practitioner to examine the person making the will at the time it is to be executed to verify his/her mental capacity and to record that medical opinion in writing, and to ask the examining practitioner to act as a witness. If a person is not mentally able to make a will, the Court may do this for him/her by virtue of the Mental Health Act 1983.

Revocation
A will may be revoked or cancelled in a number of ways:
- a later will revokes an earlier one if it says so; otherwise the earlier will is impliedly revoked by the later one to the extent that it contradicts or repeats the earlier one
- a will is also revoked if the physical document on which it is written is destroyed by the person whose will it is. There must be an intention to revoke the will. It may not be sufficient to obliterate the will with a pen
- a will is revoked when the person marries, unless it is clear from the will that the person intended the will to stand after the marriage
- where a marriage ends in divorce or is annulled or declared void, gifts to the spouse and the appointment of the spouse as executor fail unless the will says that this is not to happen. A former spouse is treated as having predeceased the testator. A separation does not change the effect of a married person's will.

Probate and Letters of Administration
Probate is granted to the executors named in a will and once granted, the executors are obliged to carry out the instructions of the will. Letters of administration are granted where no executor is named in a will or is willing or able to act or where there is no will or no valid will; this gives a person, often the next of kin, similar powers and duties to those of an executor.

Applications for probate or for letters of administration can be made to the Principal Registry of the Family Division, to a district probate registry or to a probate sub-registry. Applicants will need the following documents: the original will (if any); a certificate of death; oath for executors or administrators; particulars of all property and assets left by the deceased; a list of debts and funeral expenses. Certain property, up to the value of £5,000, may be disposed of without a grant of probate or letters of administration.

Where to Find A Proved Will
Since 1858 wills which have been proved, that is wills on which probate or letters of administration have been granted, must have been proved at the Principal Registry of the Family Division or at a district probate registry. The Lord Chancellor has power to direct where the original documents are kept but most are filed where they were proved and may be inspected there and a copy obtained. The Principal Registry also holds copies of all wills proved at district probate registries and these may be inspected at Somerset House. An index of all grants, both of probate and of letters of administration, is compiled by the Principal Registry and may be seen either at the Principal Registry or at a district probate registry.

It is also possible to discover when a grant of probate or letters of administration is issued by requesting a standing search. In response to a request and for a small fee, a district probate registry will supply the names and addresses of executors or administrators and the registry in which the grant was made, of any grant in the estate of a specified person made in the previous 12 months or following six months. This is useful for applicants under the Inheritance (Provision for Family and Dependants) Act 1975 (see Intestacy, page 669) and for creditors of the deceased.

Principal Registry (Family Division)
First Avenue House, 42-49 High Holborn, London, WC1V 6NP (Tel: 020-7936 6000)

INTESTACY
Intestacy occurs when someone dies without leaving a will or leaves a will which is invalid or which does not take effect for some reason. In such cases the person's estate (property, possessions, other assets following the payment of debts) passes to certain members of the family. The relevant legislation is the Administration of Estates Act 1925, as amended by various legislation including the Intestates Estates Act 1952, the Law Reform (Succession) Act 1995, and the Trusts of Land and Appointment of Trustees Act 1996 and Orders made there under. Some of the provisions of this legislation are described below. If a will has been written that disposes of only part of a person's property, these rules apply to the part which is undisposed of.

If the person (intestate) leaves a spouse who survives for 28 days and children (legitimate, illegitimate and adopted children and other descendants), the estate is divided as follows:
- the spouse takes the 'personal chattels' (household articles, including cars, but nothing used for business purposes), £125,000 free of tax (with interest payable at 6 per cent from the time of the death until payment) and a life interest in half of the rest of the estate (which can be capitalised by the spouse if he/she wishes)
- the rest of the estate goes to the children*

If the person leaves a spouse who survives for 28 days but no children:
- the spouse takes the personal chattels, £200,000 free of tax (interest payable as before) and full ownership of half of the rest of the estate
- the other half of the rest of the estate goes to the parents (equally, if both alive) or, if none, to the brothers and sisters of the whole blood*
- if there are no parents or brothers or sisters of the whole blood or their children, the spouse takes the whole estate

If there are no surviving spouse, the estate is distributed among those who survive the intestate as follows:
- to surviving children*, but if none to
- parents (equally, if both alive), but if none to
- brothers and sisters of the whole blood*, but if none to
- brothers and sisters of the half blood*, but if none to
- grandparents (equally, if more than one), but if none to
- aunts and uncles of the whole blood*, but if none to
- aunts and uncles of the half blood*, but if none to
- the Crown, Duchy of Lancaster or the Duke of Cornwall (bona vacantia)

* To inherit, a member of these groups must survive the intestate and attain 18, or marry under that age. If they

die under 18 (unless married under that age), their share goes to others, if any, in the same group. If any member of these groups predeceases the intestate leaving children, their share is divided equally among their children.

In England and Wales the provisions of the Inheritance (Provision for Family and Dependants) Act 1975 may allow other people to claim provision from the deceased's assets. This Act also applies to cases where a will has been made and allows a person to apply to the Court if they feel that the will or rules of intestacy or both do not make adequate provision for them. The Court can order payment from the deceased's assets or the transfer of property from them if the applicant's claim is accepted. The application must be made within six months of the grant of probate or letters of administration and the following people can make an application:

– the spouse
– a former spouse who has not remarried
– a child of the deceased
– someone treated as a child of the deceased's family
– someone maintained by the deceased
– someone who has cohabited for two years before the death in the same household as the deceased and as the husband or wife of the deceased

MEDIA LONDON

TELEVISION
RADIO
PRESS
ADVERTISING
PUBLIC RELATIONS
COMMUNICATIONS
POSTAL SERVICES

MEDIA LONDON

London has a very high concentration of media activity and in this section you will find numerous contacts from television, radio, press, advertising and public relations.

CROSS-MEDIA OWNERSHIP

There are rules on cross-media ownership to prevent undue concentration of ownership. These were amended by the Broadcasting Act 1996. Radio companies are now permitted to own one AM, one FM and one other (AM or FM) service; ownership of the third licence is subject to a public interest test. Local newspapers with a circulation under 20 per cent in an area are also allowed to own one AM, one FM and one other service, and may control a regional Channel 3 television service subject to a public interest test. Local newspapers with a circulation between 20 and 50 per cent in an area may own one AM and one FM service, subject to a public interest test, but may not control a regional Channel 3 service. Those with a circulation over 50 per cent may own one radio service in the area (provided that more than one independent local radio service serves the area) subject to a public interest test.

Ownership controls on the number of television or radio licences have been removed; holdings are now restricted to 15 per cent of the total television audience or 15 per cent of the total points available in the radio points scheme. Ownership controls on cable operators have also been removed. National newspapers with less than 20 per cent of national circulation may apply to control any broadcasting licences, subject to a public interest test. National newspapers with more than 20 per cent of national circulation may not have more than a 20 per cent interest in a licence to provide a Channel 3 service, Channel 5 or national and local analogue radio services.

BROADCASTING

The British Broadcasting Corporation is responsible for public service broadcasting in London and throughout the UK. Its constitution and finances are governed by royal charter and agreement. On 1 May 1996 a new royal charter came into force, establishing the framework for the BBC's activities until 2006.

The Independent Television Commission and the Radio Authority were set up under the terms of the Broadcasting Act 1990. The ITC is the regulator and licensing authority for all commercially funded television services, including cable and satellite services. The Radio Authority is the regulator and licensing authority for all independent radio services.

BROADCASTING STANDARDS COMMISSION

7 The Sanctuary, London SW1P 3JS (Tel: 020-7233 0544)

The Broadcasting Standards Commission was set up in April 1997 under the Broadcasting Act 1996 and was formed from the merger of the Broadcasting Complaints Commission and the Broadcasting Standards Council. The Commission considers and adjudicates upon complaints of unfair treatment or unwarranted infringement of privacy in all broadcast programmes and advertisements on television, radio, cable, satellite and digital services. It also monitors the portrayal of violence and sex, and matters of taste and decency. Its new code of practice came into force on 1 January 1998.

Chairman: Lord Holme
Deputy Chairmen: Ms J. Leighton; Lady Warner
Director: S. Whittle

TELEVISION

All channels are broadcast in colour on 625 lines UHF from a network of transmitting stations. The BBC's transmission network was sold to the Castle Tower Consortium in February 1997; ITV transmission services are owned and operated by National Transcommunications Ltd. Transmissions are available to more than 99 per cent of the population.

DIGITAL TELEVISION

Digital broadcasting will increase the number and quality of television channels. It uses digital modulation to improve reception and digital compression to make more effective use of the frequency channels available than PAL, the analogue system currently used.

The Broadcasting Act 1996 provided for the licensing of 20 or more digital terrestrial television channels (on six frequency channels or 'multiplexes'). Analogue broadcasting will eventually be discontinued, with the frequencies being sold to mobile telephone companies.

In June 1997 the licences to run the remaining digital multiplexes were awarded by the ITC to British Digital Broadcasting (now called ONdigital), a consortium led by Carlton Communications and Granada. The first digital services went on air in autumn 1998. A set-top digital decoder or an integrated digital television set is required to convert the digital signals into analogue sound and picture waves in order to watch the digital channels. Digital television services are also offered by cable and satellite companies.

BRITISH BROADCASTING CORPORATION

Broadcasting House, Portland Place, London W1A 1AA (Tel: 020-7580 4468)
Television Centre, Wood Lane, London W12 7RJ (Tel: 020-8743 8000)
BBC Information – 0870 010 0222;
Web: http://www.bbc.co.uk

The BBC was incorporated under royal charter in 1926 as successor to the British Broadcasting Company Ltd. The BBC's current charter came into force on 1 May 1996 and extends to 31 December 2006. The chairman, vice-chairman and other governors are appointed by The Queen-in-Council. The BBC is financed by revenue from receiving licences for the home services and by grant-in-aid from Parliament for the World Service (radio).

Chairman: Sir Christopher Bland
Director-General and Editor-in-Chief: G. Dyke

218 Media London

INDEPENDENT TELEVISION

INDEPENDENT TELEVISION COMMISSION

33 Foley Street, London W1P 7LB (Tel: 020-7255 3000; Fax: 020-7306 7800; Email: publicaffairs@itc.org.uk; Web: http://www.itc.org.uk)

The Independent Television Commission replaced the Independent Broadcasting Authority in 1991. The Commission is responsible for licensing and regulating all commercially funded television services broadcast from the UK. Members are appointed by the Secretary of State for Culture, Media and Sport.

Chairman: Sir Robin Biggam
Chief Executive: P. Rogers
Secretary and Director of Administration: M. Redley

ITV NETWORK CENTRE/ITV ASSOCIATION

200 Gray's Inn Road, London WC1X 8HF (Tel: 020-7843 8000)

The ITV Network Centre is wholly owned by the ITV companies and undertakes the commissioning and scheduling of those television programmes which are shown across the ITV network. Through its sister organisation, the ITV Association, it also provides a range of services to the ITV companies where a common approach is required.

Chairman: R. Eyre

INDEPENDENT TELEVISION NETWORK COMPANIES IN LONDON

Carlton Television Ltd
101 St Martin's Lane, London WC2N 4AZ (Tel: 020-7240 4000; Fax: 020-7240 4171; Web: http://www.carlton.com)

Chief Executive: Clive Jones

GMTV Ltd
The London Television Centre, Upper Ground, London SE1 9LT (Tel: 020-7827 7000)

London Weekend Television Ltd
The London Television Centre, Upper Ground, London SE1 9LT (Tel: 020-7620 1620)

OTHER INDEPENDENT TELEVISION COMPANIES IN LONDON

Channel 5 Broadcasting Ltd
22 Long Acre, London WC2E 9LY (Tel: 020-7550 5555)

Channel Four Television Corporation
124 Horseferry Road, London SW1P 2TX (Tel: 020-7396 4444)

Independent Television News Ltd
200 Gray's Inn Road, London WC1X 8XZ (Tel: 020-7833 3000)

Teletext Ltd
Unit 24, 101 Farm Lane, London SW6 1QJ (Tel: 020-7386 5000) Provides teletext services for the ITV companies and Channel 4.

DIRECT BROADCASTING BY SATELLITE TELEVISION

BRITISH SKY BROADCASTING LTD

Grant Way, Isleworth, Middx TW7 5QD (Tel: 020-7705 3000; Web: http://www.sky.com)

Broadcasts 13 channels which are wholly owned by Sky. In addition, Sky Ventures consists of 9 joint venture partnerships which between them broadcast fourteen television channels and forty four audio channels.

Chief Executive and Managing Director: Tony Ball

RADIO

UK domestic radio services are broadcast across three wavebands: FM (or VHF), medium wave (also referred to as AM) and long wave. In the UK the FM waveband extends in frequency from 87.5 MHz to 108 MHz and the medium wave band extends from 531 kHz to 1602 kHz.

DIGITAL RADIO

Digital radio allows more services to be broadcast to a higher technical quality and provides the data facility for text or pictures associated with sound programmes. It improves the robustness of high fidelity radio services, especially compared with current FM and AM radio transmissions.

The Broadcasting Act 1996 provided for the licensing of digital radio services (on seven frequency channels or 'multiplexes'). The BBC has been allocated a multiplex capable of broadcasting six to eight national stereo services; BBC digital broadcasts began in the London area in September 1995.

The Radio Authority is responsible for awarding licences for capacity on the non-BBC multiplexes The first national independent radio digital licence was awarded in October 1998 to Digital One, a company owned by GWR Digital Radio, NTL Digital Radio and Talk Radio UK.

THE RADIO AUTHORITY

Holbrook House, 14 Great Queen Street, London WC2B 5DG (Tel: 020-7430 2724; Fax: 020-7405 7062)

The Radio Authority was established in 1991 under the Broadcasting Act 1990. It is the regulator and licensing authority for all independent radio services. Members of the Authority are appointed by the Secretary of State for Culture, Media and Sport; senior executive staff are appointed by the Authority.

Chairman: Sir Peter Gibbings
Chief Executive: A. Stoller
Secretary to the Authority and Head of Legal Affairs: Ms E. Salomon

Independent Radio

BBC NETWORK RADIO SERVICES
Radio 1 – Frequencies: 97.6–99.8 FM
Radio 2 – Frequencies: 88–90.2 FM
Radio 3 – Frequencies: 90.2–92.4 FM
Radio 4 – Frequencies: 94.6–96.1 FM and 103.5–105 FM; 1449 AM, plus eight local fillers on AM
Radio 5 – Frequencies: 693 AM and 909 AM, plus one local filler.

BBC LOCAL RADIO STATIONS IN LONDON

BBC LONDON LIVE
PO Box 94.9, The Strand, London WC2B 4QH (Tel: 020-7224 2424; Fax: 020-7208 9209;
Email: londonlive@bbc.co.uk;
Web: http://www.bbc.co.uk/londonlive)
Frequency: 94.9 FM.
Editor: David Robey

INDEPENDENT RADIO

The Radio Authority began advertising new licences for the development of commercial radio in January 1991. Since then it has awarded three national licences, 101 new local radio licences (including ten regional licences) and one additional service licence (to use the spare capacity in an existing channel which is not used by the programme service). The Authority has also issued about 2,000 restricted service licences (for temporary low-powered radio services). In 1999-2000 the Authority advertised one new analogue licence a month. It also advertised one digital multiplex licence a month and re-advertised existing analogue licences.

Commercial Radio Companies Association
77 Shaftesbury Avenue, London W1V 7AD (Tel: 020-7306 2603; Fax: 020-7470 0062;
Email: info@crca.co.uk; Web: http://www.crca.co.uk)
Chief Executive: P. Brown

INDEPENDENT NATIONAL RADIO STATIONS BASED IN LONDON

Classic FM, Academic House, 24-28 Oval Road, London NW1 7DQ (Tel: 020-7343 9000) 24 hours a day. Frequencies: 99.9 101.9 FM

Talk Radio, 76 Oxford Street, London W1N 0TR (Tel: 020-7636 1089) 24 hours a day. Frequencies: 1053/1089 AM

Virgin Radio, 1 Golden Square, London W1R 4DJ. (Tel: 020-7434 1215) 24 hours a day. Frequencies: 1215/1197/1233/1242/1260 AM

INDEPENDENT LOCAL RADIO STATIONS

Liberty Radio, 7th Floor, Trevor House, 100 Brompton Road, London SW3 1ER. (Tel: 020-7893 8966) Frequency: 963/972 AM

Capital FM and Gold, 30 Leicester Square, London WC2H 7LA. (Tel: 020-7766 6000) Frequencies: 1548 AM (Gold), 95.8 FM

Choice FM, 291-299 Borough High Street, London SE1 1JG. (Tel: 020-7378 3969) Frequency: 96.9 FM

FLR 107.3, Astra House, Arklow Road, London SE14 6EB. (Tel: 020-8691 9202) Frequency: 107.3 FM

Heart 106.2 The Chrysalis Building, Bramley Road, London W10 6SP. (Tel: 020-7468 1062) Frequency: 106.2 FM

Jazz FM 102.2, 26-27 Castlereagh Street, London W1H 6DJ. (Tel: 020-7706 4100) Frequency: 102.2 FM

Kiss 100 FM, Kiss House, 80 Holloway Road, London N7 8JG. (Tel: 020-7700 6100) Frequency: 100.0 FM

LBC 1152 AM, 200 Gray's Inn Road, London WC1X 8XZ. (Tel: 020-7973 1152) Frequency: 1152 AM

London Greek Radio, Florentia Village, Vale Road, London N4 1TD. (Tel: 020-8800 8001) Frequency: 103.3 FM

London Turkish Radio LTR, 185b High Road, Wood Green, London N22 6BA. (Tel: 020-8881 0606) Frequency: 1584 AM

Magic 105.4 FM, The Network Building, 97 Tottenham Court Road, London W1P 9HF. (Tel: 020-7504 6000) Frequency: 105.4 FM

Millennium Radio, Harrow Manor Way, Thamesmead, London SE2 9XH. (Tel: 020-8311 3112) Frequency: 106.8 FM

News Direct 97.3 FM, 200 Gray's Inn Road, London WC1X 8XZ. (Tel: 020-7973 1152) Frequency: 97.3 FM

Premier Christian Radio, Glen House, Stag Place, London SW1E 5AG. (Tel: 020-7316 1300) Frequencies: 1305/1332/1413 AM

Ritz 1035 AM, 33-35 Wembley Hill Road, London HA9 8RT. (Tel: 020-8733 1300) Frequency: 1035 AM

Sunrise Radio, Sunrise House, Sunrise Road, Southall, Middx UB2 4AU. (Tel: 020-8574 6666) Frequency: 1458 AM

Virgin 105.8, 1 Golden Square, London W1R 4DJ. (Tel: 030-7434 1215) Frequency: 105.8 FM

XFM, 30 Leicester Square, London WC2H 7LA. (Tel: 020-7766 6600) Frequency: 104.9 FM

220 Media London

THE PRESS

The press is subject to laws on publication and the Press Complaints Commission was set up by the industry as a means of self-regulation. It is not state-subsidised and receives few tax concessions. The income of most newspapers and periodicals is derived largely from sales and advertising.

PRESS COMPLAINTS COMMISSION

1 Salisbury Square, London EC4Y 8JB (Tel: 020-7353 1248; Fax: 020-7353 8355; Email: pcc@pcc.org.uk; Web: http://www.pcc.org.uk)

The Press Complaints Commission was founded by the newspaper and magazine industry in 1991 to replace the Press Council. It is a voluntary, non-statutory body set up to operate the press's self-regulation system following the Calcutt report in 1990 on privacy and related matters when the industry feared that a failure to regulate itself might lead to statutory regulation of the press. The Commission's objects are to consider, adjudicate, conciliate and resolve complaints of unfair treatment by the press and to ensure that the press maintains the highest professional standards with respect for generally recognised freedoms, including freedom of expression, the public's right to know and the right of the press to operate free from improper pressure. The Commission judges newspaper and magazine conduct by a code of practice drafted by editors, agreed by the industry and ratified by the Commission.

Chairman: Lord Wakeham
Director: G. Black

NEWSPAPERS

Newspapers are largely financially independent of any political party, though most adopt a political stance in their editorial comments, usually reflecting proprietorial influence. Ownership of the national and regional daily newspapers is concentrated in the hands of large corporations whose interests cover publishing and communications. The rules on cross-media ownership as amended by the Broadcasting Act 1996, limit the extent to which newspaper organisations may become involved in broadcasting.

London has a number of local daily and weekly newspapers in addition to the daily and weekly national newspapers that are published there.

NATIONAL NEWSPAPERS

The list below details all national newspapers which are published in London.

Daily Mail
Northcliffe House, 2 Derry Street, London, W8 5TT (Tel: 020-7938 6000)
Editor: P. Dacre

Daily Star
Ludgate House, 245 Blackfriars Road, London, SE1 9UX (Tel: 020-7928 8000; Fax: 020-7633 0244; Web: http://www.megastar.co.uk)
Editor: Peter Hill

Daily Telegraph
1 Canada Square, Canary Wharf, London, E14 5DT (Tel: 020-7538 5000)
Editor: Charles Moore

The Express
Ludgate House, 245 Blackfriars Road, London, SE1 9UX (Tel: 020-7928 8000)
Editor: Rosie Boycott

Financial Times
1 Southwark Bridge, London, SE1 9HL (Tel: 020-7873 3000)
Editor: Richard Lambert

The Guardian
119 Farringdon Road, London, EC1R 3ER (Tel: 020-7278 2332)
Editor: Alan Rusbridger

The Independent
1 Canada Square, Canary Wharf, London, E14 5DL (Tel: 020-7293 2000; Fax: 020-7293 2053; Email: letters@independent.co.uk; Web: http://www.independent.co.uk)
Editor-in-Chief: Simon Kelner

The Mirror
1 Canada Square, Canary Wharf, London, E14 5AP (Tel: 020-7293 3000)
Editor: Piers Morgan

Morning Star
1st Floor, Cape House, 787 Commercial Road, London, E14 7HG (Tel: 020-7517 9722; Fax: 020-7538 5125; Email: morsta@geo2.poptel.org.uk; Web: http://www.poptel.org.uk/morning-star/)
Editor: J. Haylett

Racing Post
1 Canada Square, Canary Wharf, London, E14 5AP (Tel: 020-7293 3000; Fax: 020-7293 3758; Email: editor@racingpost.co.uk; Web: http://www.racingpost.co.uk)
Editor: A. Byrne

The Sun
1 Virginia Street, London, E1 9XR (Tel: 020-7782 4000)
Editor: David Yelland

The Times
1 Pennington Street, London, E1 9XN (Tel: 020-7782 5000)
Editor: Peter Stothard

Evening Standard
Northcliffe House, 2 Derry Street, London, W8 5TT (Tel: 020-7938 6000;
Web: http://www.thisislondon.com)
Editor: M. Hastings

Express on Sunday
Ludgate House, 245 Blackfriars Road, London, SE1 9UX (Tel: 020-7928 8000)

Regional Newspapers 221

Independent on Sunday
1 Canada Square, Canary Wharf, London, E14 5DL (Tel: 020-7293 2000)

Mail on Sunday
Northcliffe House, 2 Derry Street, London, W8 5TS (Tel: 020-7938 6000)

News of the World
1 Virginia Street, London, E1 9XR (Tel: 020-7782 4000)

The Observer
119 Farringdon Road, London, EC1R 3ER (Tel: 020-7278 2332; Fax: 020-7713 4250; Web: http://www.observer.co.uk)
Editor: R. Alton

Sunday Business
The Isis Building, 193 Marsh Wall, London, E14 5DT (Tel: 020-7418 9600)

Sunday Mirror
1 Canada Square, Canary Wharf, London, E14 5AP (Tel: 020-7293 3000)

Sunday People
1 Canada Square, Canary Wharf, London, E14 5AP (Tel: 020-7293 3000)

Sunday Telegraph
1 Canada Square, Canary Wharf, London, E14 5DT (Tel: 020-7538 5000; Fax: 020-7538 7872; Email: stnews@telegraph.co.uk)
Editor: D. Lawson

Sunday Times
1 Pennington Street, London, E1 9XN (Tel: 020-7782 5000)

REGIONAL NEWSPAPERS

The list below details all regional newspapers which are based in London and whose audience is the London community.

Barking & Dagenham Express
Newspaper House, 2 Whalebone Lane South, Dagenham, Essex, RM8 1HB (Tel: 020-8517 5577; Fax: 020-8592 7407)
Editor: Dave Russell

Barking & Dagenham Post
Newspaper House, 2 Whalebone Lane South, Dagenham, Essex, RM8 1HB (Tel: 020-8517 5577; Fax: 020-8592 7407)
Editor: Dave Russell

Barking & Dagenham Recorder
539 High Road, Ilford, Essex, IG1 1UD (Tel: 020-8478 4444; Fax: 020-8478 6606)
Editor: C. Carter

Barnet Borough Times
124 Rickmansworth Road, Watford, Herts, WD1 7JW (Tel: 01923-242211; Fax: 01923-235201)

Bexley Borough Mercury
2-4 Leigham Court Road, Streatham, London, SW16 2PD (Tel: 020-8769 4444; Fax: 020-8664 7247)

Bexley & Eltham Leader
38-46 Harmer Street, Gravesend, Kent, DA12 2AY (Tel: 01474-363363; Fax: 01474-353758)
Editor: Pip Clarkson

Bexley Times Group
38-46 Harmer Street, Gravesend, Kent, DA12 2AY (Tel: 01474-363363; Fax: 01474-363363)
Editor: Pip Clarkson

Bexleyheath & Welling News Shopper
Mega House, Crest View Drive, Petts Wood, Orpington, Kent, BR5 1BT (Tel: 01689-836211; Fax: 01689-890253; Email: ngs@newsquest.media.co.uk; Web: http://www.newsquestmedia.co.uk)
Editor: Ivan MacQuisten

Bexleyheath & Welling Times
38-46 Harmer Street, Gravesend, Kent, DA12 2AY (Tel: 01474-363363; Fax: 01474-320316)
Editor: Pip Clarkson

Biggin Hill News
Winterton House, High Street, Westerham, Kent, TN16 1AL (Tel: 01959-564766; Fax: 01959-562760; Email: kbi55@dial.pipex.com)
Editor: Gillie Bowen

Brent Leader
3rd Floor, Refuge House, 9-10 River Front, Enfield, Middx, EN1 3SZ (Tel: 020-8367 2345; Fax: 020-8366 9376)

Brentwood Recorder
3 River Chambers, High Street, Romford, Essex, RM1 1JD (Tel: 01708-766044; Fax: 01708-733423)
Editor: Mark Sweetingham

Bromley & Beckenham Leader
38-46 Harmer Street, Gravesend, Kent, DA12 2AY (Tel: 01474-363363; Fax: 01474-320316)
Editor: Pip Clarkson

Bromley & Beckenham Times
38-46 Harmer Street, Gravesend, Kent, DA12 2AY (Tel: 01474-363363; Fax: 01474-320316)
Editor: Pip Clarkson

Bromley & Hayes News Shopper
Mega House, Crest View Drive, Petts Wood, Orpington, Kent, BR5 1BT (Tel: 01689-885700; Fax: 01689-875367; Email: ngs@newsquestmedia.co.uk; Web: http://www.newsquestmedia.co.uk)
Editor: A. Parkes

Bromley News
Winterton House, High Street, Westerham, Kent, TN16 1AL (Tel: 01959-564766; Fax: 01959-562760; Email: kbi55@dial.pipex.com)
Editor: Gillie Bowen

222 Media London

Bromley Times Group
38-46 Harmer Street, Gravesend, Kent, DA12 2AY (Tel: 01474-363363; Fax: 01474-320316)
Editor: Pip Clarkson

Camden New Journal
40 Camden Road, London, NW1 9DR (Tel: 020-7419 9000; Fax: 020-7482 7317; Email: letters.cnj@cablenet.co.uk)
Editor: E. Gordon

Camden & St Pancras Chronicle
161 Tottenham Lane, Hornsey, London, N8 9BU (Tel: 020-8340 6868; Fax: 020-8340 2444)
Editor: Tony Allcock

Chelsea News
Newspaper House, Winslow Road, Hammersmith, London, W6 9SF (Tel: 020-8741 1622; Fax: 020-8741 1973)
Editor: Paul Mosley

Chingford Guardian
News Centre, Fulbourne Road, Walthamstow, London, E17 4EW (Tel: 020-8531 4141; Fax: 020-8527 3696)
Editor: Peter Dyke

Circuit Newsletter
45 Beaufort Court, Admirals Way, South Quay, London, E14 9XL (Tel: 020-7515 1166; Fax: 020-7515 1188; Email: bhaken@pcif.org.uk)

City of London Recorder
539 High Road, Ilford, Essex, IG1 1UD (Tel: 020-8478 4444; Fax: 020-8478 6606)
Editor: T. Duncan

City Post
Newspaper House, Winslow Road, Hammersmith, London, W6 9SF (Tel: 020-8741 1622; Fax: 020-8741 1973)
Editor: Paul Mosley

City of Westminster Post
Newspaper House, Winslow Road, Hammersmith, London, W6 9SF (Tel: 020-8741 1622; Fax: 020-8741 1973)
Editor: Paul Mosley

Coulsdon & Purley Advertiser
Advertiser House, 19 Bartlett Street, South Croydon, Surrey, CR2 6TB (Tel: 020-8763 6666; Fax: 020-8763 6633; Email: croydonad@compuserve.com)
Editor: M. Starbrook

Croydon Advertiser
Advertiser House, 19 Bartlett Street, South Croydon, Surrey, CR2 6TB (Tel: 020-8763 6666; Fax: 020-8763 6633; Email: croydonad@compuserve.com)
Editor: M. Starbrook

Croydon Guardian
Newspaper House, 34-44 London Road, Morden, Surrey, SM4 5BR (Tel: 020-8646 6336; Fax: 020-8687 4403; Email: slg@newsquestmedia.co.uk; Web: http://www.newsquestmedia.co.uk)
Editor: Margaret Strayton

Croydon Post
Advertiser House, 19 Bartlett Street, South Croydon, Surrey, CR2 6TB (Tel: 020-8763 6666; Fax: 020-8763 6633; Email: croydonad@compuserve.com)
Editor: M. Starbrook

Docklands Express
138 Cambridge Heath Road, London, E1 5QJ (Tel: 020-7790 8822; Fax: 020-7790 0646)
Editor: Pat O'Conner

Docklands Recorder
184 High Street North, London, E6 2JD (Tel: 020-8472 1421; Fax: 020-8471 7908)
Editor: Tom Duncan

Dulwich Guardian
Newspaper House, 34-44 London Road, Morden, Surrey, SM4 5BR (Tel: 020-8646 6336; Fax: 020-8687 4403)

Ealing Leader
3rd Floor, Refuge House, 9-10 River Front, Enfield, Middx, EN1 3SZ (Tel: 020-8367 2345; Fax: 020-8366 9376)
Editor: John Moore

Ealing & Southall Informer
9-11 High Street, Egham, Surrey, TW20 9EA (Tel: 01784-433773; Fax: 01784-472608)
Editor: Steve Bennet

East London Advertiser
138 Cambridge Heath Road, London, E1 5QJ (Tel: 020-7790 8822; Fax: 020-7790 0646)
Editor: Richard Tidiman

Edgware & Mill Hill Times
124 Rickmansworth Road, Watford, Herts, WD1 7JW (Tel: 01923-242211; Fax: 01923-235201)

Eltham & Greenwich Times
38-46 Harmer Street, Gravesend, Kent, DA12 2AY (Tel: 01474-363363; Fax: 01474-320316)
Editor: Pip Clarkson

Eltham News Shopper
Mega House, Crest View Drive, Petts Wood, Orpington, Kent, BR5 1BT (Tel: 01689-836211; Fax: 01689-890253; Email: nsg@newsquestmedia.co.uk; Web: http://www.newsquestmedia.co.uk)
Editor: Ivan MacQuisten

Enfield Advertiser
3rd Floor, Refuge House, 9-10 River Front, Enfield, Middx, EN1 3SZ (Tel: 020-8367 2345; Fax: 020-8366 9376)
Editor: Ms J. Woods

Enfield Gazette
3rd Floor, Refuge House, 9-10 River Front, Enfield, Middx, EN1 3SZ (Tel: 020-8367 2345; Fax: 020-8366 9376; Email: news@enfieldgazette.demon.co.uk)
Editor: Ms J. Woods

Regional Newspapers 223

Enfield Independent
News Centre, Fulbourne Road, Walthamstow, London, E17 4EW (Tel: 020-8531 4141; Fax: 020-8527 3696)
Editor: Wendy McClemont

Epping Forest & Redbridge Independent
Guardian House, 480-500 Larkshall Road, London, E4 9GD (Tel: 020-8498 3400; Fax: 020-8531 2017; Email: djackman@london.newsevent.co.uk; Web: http://www.thisiseppingforest.co.uk)
Editor: M. Oldaker

Epsom & Banstead Informer
Informer House, 2 High Street, Teddington, Middx, TW11 8EW (Tel: 020-8943 5171; Fax: 020-8943 1555)
Editor: Andy O'Hara

Erith & Crayford Times
38-46 Harmer Street, London, DA12 2AY (Tel: 01474-363363; Fax: 01474-320316)
Editor: Pip Clarkson

Esher & Elmbridge Guardian
News Centre, Fulbourne Road, Walthamstow, London, E17 4EW (Tel: 020-8531 4141; Fax: 020-8527 3696)

Fulham Chronicle
Newspaper House, Winslow Road, Hammersmith, London, W6 9SF (Tel: 020-8741 1622; Fax: 020-8741 1973)
Editor: Paul Mosley

Fulham and Hammersmith Chronicle
Newspaper House, Winslow Road, Hammersmith, London, W6 9SF (Tel: 020-8741 1622; Fax: 020-8741 1973)
Editor: Ian Patel

Greenwich Borough Mercury
2-4 Leigham Court Road, Streatham, London, SW16 2PD (Tel: 020-8769 4444; Fax: 020-8664 7247)

Greenwich & Charlton News Shopper
Mega House, Crest View Drive, Petts Wood, Orpington, Kent, BR5 1BT (Tel: 01689-836211; Fax: 01689-890253)
Editor: Ivan MacQuisten

Hackney Gazette and North London Advertiser
138 Cambridge Heath Road, London, E1 5QJ (Tel: 020-7790 8822; Fax: 020-7791 0401)
Editor: N. O'Flynn

Hammersmith Chronicle
Newspaper House, Winslow Road, Hammersmith, London, W6 9SF (Tel: 020-8741 1622; Fax: 020-8741 1973)
Editor: Paul Mosley

Hammersmith & Fulham Independent
Unit 8, Concord Business Centre, Concord Road, London, W3 0TR (Tel: 020-8752 0052; Fax: 020-8896 3654)
Editor: David Hetherington

Hampstead & Highgate Express
100A Avenue Road, Hampstead, London, NW3 3HF (Tel: 020-7433 5566; Fax: 020-7483 5566; Email: editorial@hamhigh.co.uk; Web: http://www.hamhigh.co.uk)
Editor: M. Lewin

Haringey Advertiser
3rd Floor, Refuge House, 9-10 River Front, Enfield, Middx, EN1 3SZ (Tel: 020-8367 2345; Fax: 020-8366 9376)
Editor: Aaron Gransby

Haringey Independent
News Centre, Fulbourne Road, Walthamstow, London, E17 4EW (Tel: 020-8531 4141; Fax: 020-8527 3696)
Editor: Wendy McClemont

Haringey Weekly Herald
161 Tottenham Lane, Hornsey, London, N8 9BU (Tel: 020-8340 6868; Fax: 020-8340 6577)
Editor: Tony Allcock

Harrow Informer
9-11 High Street, Egham, Surrey, TW20 9EA (Tel: 01784-433773; Fax: 01784-472608)
Editor: Steve Bennet

Harrow Leader
3rd Floor, Refuge House, 9-10 River Front, Enfield, Middx, EN1 3SZ (Tel: 020-8367 2345; Fax: 020-8366 9376)
Editor: Mrs S. Crawley

Harrow Observer
3rd Floor, Refuge House, 9-10 River Front, Enfield, Middx, EN1 3SZ (Tel: 020-8367 2345; Fax: 020-8366 9376)
Editor: Mrs S. Crawley

Heathrow Villager
260 Kingston Road, Staines, Middx, TW18 1PG (Tel: 01784-453196; Fax: 01784-453196)
Editor: I. West

Hendon & Finchley Times
124 Rickmansworth Road, Watford, Herts, WD1 7JW (Tel: 01923-242211; Fax: 01923-235201)

Highbury & Islington Express
1 Aztec Row, Berners Road, Islington, London, N1 0PW (Tel: 020-7359 4886; Fax: 020-7288 1065; Web: http://www.islingtonexpress.co.uk)
Editor: R. Lydall

Hornsey, Wood Green & Tottenham Journal
161 Tottenham Lane, Hornsey, London, N8 9BU (Tel: 020-8340 6868; Fax: 020-8340 6577)
Editor: Tony Allcock

Hounslow & Chiswick Informer
Informer House, 2 High Street, Teddington, Middx, TW11 8EW (Tel: 020-8943 5171; Fax: 020-8943 1555)
Editor: Andy O'Hara

Media London

Hounslow Leader
134-136 Broadway, London, W13 0TL (Tel: 020-7381 6262; Fax: 020-8566 1201)
Editor: Anthony Longden

Ilford Recorder
539 High Road, Ilford, Essex, IG1 1UD (Tel: 020-8478 4444; Fax: 020-8478 6606)
Editor: C. Carter

Ilford & Redbridge Post
Newspaper House, 2 Whalebone Lane South, Dagenham, Essex, RM8 1HB (Tel: 020-8517 5577; Fax: 020-8592 7407)
Editor: Dave Russell

India Times
Global House, 90 Ascot Gardens, Southall, Middx, UB1 2SB (Tel: 020-8575 0151; Fax: 020-8575 5661)
Editor: Ram Kumar Virka

Islington Chronicle
161 Tottenham Lane, Hornsey, London, N8 9BU (Tel: 020-8340 6868; Fax: 020-8340 6577)
Editor: Tony Allcock

Islington Gazette
161 Tottenham Lane, Hornsey, London, N8 9BU (Tel: 020-8340 6868; Fax: 020-8340 6577)
Editor: J. Isherwood

Jobs & Careers
Mega House, Crest View Drive, Petts Wood, Orpington, Kent, BR5 1BT (Tel: 01689-836211; Fax: 01689-890253; Email: slg@newsquestmedia.co.uk)
Editor: Roger Mills

Kensington & Chelsea Independent
Unit 8, Concord Business Centre, Concord Road, London, W3 0TR (Tel: 020-8572 0052; Fax: 020-8896 3654)
Editor: David Hetherington

Kensington & Chelsea Post
Newspaper House, Winslow Road, Hammersmith, London, W6 9SF (Tel: 020-8741 1622; Fax: 020-8741 1973)
Editor: Paul Mosley

Kensington News
Newspaper House, Winslow Road, Hammersmith, London, W6 9SF (Tel: 020-8741 1622; Fax: 020-8741 1973)
Editor: Paul Mosley

Kentish Times Series & Leader Series
38-46 Harmer Street, Gravesend, Kent, DA12 2AY (Tel: 01474-363363; Fax: 01474-320316)
Editor: Pip Clarkson

Kingston Borough Guardian
Newspaper House, 34-44 London Road, Morden, Surrey, SM4 5BR (Tel: 020-8646 6336; Fax: 020-8687 4403; Email: slg@newsquestmedia.co.uk; Web: http://www.newsquestmedia.co.uk)

Kingston Informer
Informer House, 2 High Street, Teddington, Middx, TW11 8EW (Tel: 020-8943 5171; Fax: 020-8943 1555)
Editor: Andy O'Hara

Lewisham Borough Mercury
2-4 Leigham Court Road, Streatham, London, SW16 2PD (Tel: 020-8769 4444; Fax: 020-8664 7247)

Lewisham & Catford News Shopper
Mega House, Crest View Drive, Petts Wood, Orpington, Kent, BR5 1BT (Tel: 01689-836211; Fax: 01689-890253)

Leytonstone Guardian
News Centre, Fulbourne Road, Walthamstow, London, E17 4EW (Tel: 020-8531 4141; Fax: 020-8527 3696)
Editor: Peter Dyke

London Gazette
The Stationery Office, PO Box 7923, London, SE1 5ZH (Tel: 020-7394 4580; Fax: 020-7394 4581; Web: http://www.london-gazette.co.uk)
Managing Editor: D. Mabbutt

Loot
Lynwood House, 24-32 Kilburn High Road, London, NW6 5TF (Tel: 020-7625 0266; Fax: 020-7625 7921; Email: freeads.london@loot.com; Web: http://www.loot.com)
Editor: Susannah Hughes

Marylebone Mercury
Newspaper House, Winslow Road, Hammersmith, London, W6 9SF (Tel: 020-8741 1622; Fax: 020-8741 1973)
Editor: Paul Mosley

New Addington Advertiser
Advertiser House, Brighton Road, South Croydon, Surrey CR2 6UB (Tel: 020-8668 4111)

Notting Hill & Bayswater Independent
Unit 8, Concord Business Centre, Concord Road, London, W3 0TR (Tel: 020-8752 0052; Fax: 020-8896 3654)
Editor: David Hetherington

Orpington, Chislehurst & Beckenham News Shopper
Mega House, Crest View Drive, Petts Wood, Orpington, Kent, BR5 1BT (Tel: 01689-836211; Fax: 01689-890253; Email: nsg@newsquestmedia.co.uk; Web: http://www.newsquestmedia.co.uk)
Editor: Ivan MacQuisten

Orpington & Chislehurst Leader
38-46 Harmer Street, Gravesend, Kent, DA12 2AY (Tel: 01474-363363; Fax: 01474-320316)
Editor: Pip Clarkson

Orpington & Petts Wood Times
38-46 Harmer Street, Gravesend, Kent, DA12 2AY (Tel: 01474-363363; Fax: 01474-320316)
Editor: Pip Clarkson

Regional Newspapers 225

Paddington Mercury
Newspaper House, Winslow Road, Hammersmith, London, W6 9SF (Tel: 020-8741 1622; Fax: 020-8741 1973)
Editor: Paul Mosley

Penge & Sydenham News Shopper
Mega House, Crest View Drive, Petts Wood, Orpington, Kent, BR5 1BT (Tel: 01689-836211; Fax: 01689-890253; Email: ngs@newsquestmedia.co.uk; Web: http://www.newsquestmedia.co.uk)
Editor: Ivan MacQuisten

Putney Chronicle
Newspaper House, Winslow Road, Hammersmith, London, W6 9SF (Tel: 020-8741 1622; Fax: 020-8741 1973)
Editor: Paul Mosley

Putney & Wimbledon Times
14 King Street, Richmond, Surrey, TW9 1NF (Tel: 020-8940 6030; Fax: 020-8332 1899; Email: ed@dimbleby.co.uk; Web: http://www.dimbleby.co.uk)
Editor: M. Richards

Richmond & Twickenham Informer
Informer House, 2 High Street, Teddington, Middx, TW11 8EW (Tel: 020-8943 5171; Fax: 020-8943 1555)
Editor: Andy O'Hara

Richmond & Twickenham Times
14 King Street, Richmond, Surrey, TW9 1NF (Tel: 020-8940 6030; Fax: 020-8332 1899; Email: ed@dimbleby.co.uk; Web: http://www.dimbleby.co.uk)
Editor: Malcolm Richards

Romford & Havering Post
Newspaper House, 2 Whalebone Lane South, Dagenham, Essex, RM8 1HB (Tel: 020-8517 5577; Fax: 020-8592 7407)
Editor: Dave Russell

Romford & Hornchurch Recorder
3 River Chambers, High Street, Romford, Essex, RM1 1JD (Tel: 01708-771500; Fax: 01708-771520)
Editor: M. Sweetingham

Ruislip Informer
9-11 High Street, Egham, Surrey, TW20 9EA (Tel: 01784-433773; Fax: 01784-472608)
Editor: Steve Bennet

Sidcup & Blackfen Times
38-46 Harmer Street, Gravesend, Kent, DA12 2AY (Tel: 01474-363363; Fax: 01747-320316)
Editor: Pip Clarkson

South London Press
2-4 Leigham Court Road, Streatham, London, SW16 2PD (Tel: 020-8769 4444; Fax: 020-8664 7247)

Southwark News
Unit J104, Tower Bridge Business Complex, Clement's Road, London, SE16 4DG (Tel: 020-7231 5258)
Editor: David Clark

Stratford & Newham Express
138 Cambridge Heath Road, London, E1 5QJ (Tel: 020-7790 8822; Fax: 020-7790 0646)
Editor: Pat O'Conner

Streatham & Clapham Guardian
Newspaper House, 34-44 London Road, Morden, Surrey, SM4 5BR (Tel: 020-8646 6336; Fax: 020-8687 4403)

Streatham, Tooting, Brixton & Clapham Mercury
2-4 Leigham Court Road, London, SW16 2PD (Tel: 020-8769 4444; Fax: 020-8664 7247)

Surrey Comet
Newspaper House, 34-44 London Road, Morden, Surrey, SM4 5BR (Tel: 020-8646 6336; Fax: 020-8687 4403)
Editor: Margaret Strayton

Sutton Borough Guardian
Newspaper House, 34-44 London Road, Morden, Surrey, SM4 5BR (Tel: 020-8646 6336; Fax: 020-8687 4403; Email: slg@newsquestmedia.co.uk; Web: http://www.newsquestmedia.co.uk)
Editor: Margaret Strayton

Sutton Herald
Trinity House, 51 London Road, Reigate, Surrey, RH2 9PR (Tel: 01737-732000; Fax: 01737-732001)
Editor: Adrian Seal

Tottenham & Wood Green Journal
161 Tottenham Lane, Hornsey, London, N8 9BU (Tel: 020-8340 6868; Fax: 020-8340 6577)
Editor: Tony Allcock

Uxbridge & Hillingdon Leader
3rd Floor, Refuge House, 9-10 River Front, Enfield, Middx, EN1 3SZ (Tel: 020-8567 2345; Fax: 020-8366 9376)
Editor: Richard Parsons

Uxbridge Informer
9-11 High Street, Egham, Surrey, TW20 9EA (Tel: 01784-433773; Fax: 01784-472608)
Editor: Steve Bennet

Waltham Forest Guardian
News Centre, Fulbourne Road, Walthamstow, London, E17 4EW (Tel: 020-8531 4141; Fax: 020-8527 3696)
Editor: Peter Dyke

Waltham Forest Independent
News Centre, Fulbourne Road, Walthamstow, London, E17 4EW (Tel: 020-8531 4141; Fax: 020-8527 3696)
Editor: Peter Dyke

Walthamstow Guardian
News Centre, Fulbourne Road, Walthamstow, London, E17 4EW (Tel: 020-8531 4141; Fax: 020-8527 3696)
Editor: Peter Dyke

Walton & Weybridge Informer
Informer House, 2 High Street, Teddington, Middx, TW11 8EW (Tel: 020-8943 5171; Fax: 020-8943 1555)
Editor: Andy O'Hara

226 Media London

Wandsworth Borough Guardian
Unecol House, 819 London Road, Cheam, Surrey, SM5 9BN (Tel: 020-8646 6336; Fax: 020-8329 9364)
Editor: Ms G. Gray

Wandsworth Borough News
14 King Street, Richmond, Surrey, TW9 1NF (Tel: 020-8940 6030; Fax: 020-8332 1899; Email: ed@dimbleby.co.uk; Web: http://www.dimbleby.co.uk)
Editor: M. Richards

Wanstead & Woodford Guardian
News Centre, Fulbourne Road, Walthamstow, London, E17 4EW (Tel: 020-8531 4141; Fax: 020-8527 3696)
Editor: David Jackman

West Essex Gazette
News Centre, Fulbourne Road, Walthamstow, London, E17 4EW (Tel: 020-8531 4141; Fax: 020-8527 3696)
Editor: David Jackman

Westminster Independent Series
Unit 8, Concord Business Centre, Concord Road, London, W3 0TR (Tel: 020-8752 0052; Fax: 020-8896 3654)
Editor: David Hetherington

Westminster & Pimlico News
Newspaper House, Winslow Road, Hammersmith, London, W6 9SF (Tel: 020-8741 1622; Fax: 020-8741 1973)
Editor: Paul Mosley

Wimbledon - Mitcham - Morden Guardian
Unecol House, 819 London Road, Cheam, Surrey, SM5 9BN (Tel: 020-8646 6336; Fax: 020-8329 9364)
Editor: Ms G. Gray

Woolwich & Plumstead News Shopper
Mega House, Crest View Drive, Petts Wood, Orpington, Kent, BR5 1BT (Tel: 01689-836211; Fax: 01689-890253)
Editor: Ivan MacQuisten

Yellow Advertiser East End Series
137 George Lane, South Woodford, London, E18 1AJ (Tel: 020-8989 6688; Fax: 020-8530 4217)
Editor: Hannah Walker

Yellow Advertiser - Havering Services (Romford & Hornchurch Edition)
137 George Lane, South Woodford, London, E18 1AJ (Tel: 020-8989 6688; Fax: 020-8530 4217)
Editor: Hannah Walker

Yellow Advertiser Redbridge Series (Ilford, Redbridge)
137 George Lane, South Woodford, London, E18 1AJ (Tel: 020-8989 6688; Fax: 020-8530 4217)
Editor: Hannah Walker

Yellow Advertiser Waltham Forest Series (Walthamstow, Epping Forest, Chingford)
137 George Lane, South Woodford, London, E18 1AJ (Tel: 020-8989 6688; Fax: 020-8530 4217)
Editor: Hannah Walker

TRADE PERIODICALS
The list below details popular trade periodicals which are published in London.

Accountancy
Institute of Chartered Accountants, 40 Bernard Street, London, WC1N 1LD (Tel: 020-7833 3291; Fax: 020-7833 2085; Email: postmaster@theabg.demon.co.uk; Web: http://www.accountancymagazine.com)
Editor: B. Singleton-Green

Accountancy Age
VNU House, 32-34 Broadwick Street, London, W1A 2HG (Tel: 020-7316 9000)

Antique Dealer and Collectors Guide
PO Box 805, London, SE10 8TD (Tel: 020-8691 4820; Fax: 020-8691 2489;
Email: antiquedealercollectorsguide@ukbusiness.com; Web: http://www.antiquecollectorsguide.co.uk)
Editor: P. Bartlam

Antiques Trade Gazette
17 Whitcomb Street, London, WC2H 7PL (Tel: 020-7930 7192)

The Architects' Journal
151 Rosebery Avenue, London, EC1R 4QW (Tel: 020-7505 6740)

The Architectural Review
151 Rosebery Avenue, London, EC1R 4GB (Tel: 020-7505 6725; Fax: 020-7505 6701; Email: peterd@construct.emap.co.uk; Web: http://www.arplus.com)
Editor: P. Davey

The Author
Society of Authors, 84 Drayton Gardens, London, SW10 9SB (Tel: 020-7373 6642; Fax: 020-7373 5768; Email: authorsoc@writers.org.uk;
Web: http://www.writers.org.uk/society)
Editor: D. Parker

The Biochemist
The Biochemical Society, 59 Portland Place, London, W1M 3AJ (Tel: 020-7580 5530; Fax: 020-7323 1136; Email: editorial@portlandpress.com;
Web: http://www.biochemistry.org)
Editor: Dr F. Burnet

Biologist
Institute of Biology, 20-22 Queensberry Place, London, SW7 2DZ (Tel: 020-7581 8333; Fax: 020-7823 9409; Email: biologist@iob.org; Web: http://www.iob.org)
Editor: Ms A. Bailey

The Bookseller
12 Dyott Street, London, WC1A 1DF (Tel: 020-7420 6000; Fax: 020-7420 6177;
Web: http://www.thebookseller.com)
Editor: N. Clee

British Dental Journal
BMA House, Tavistock Square, London, WC1H 9JR (Tel: 0800-056 1424)

Trade Periodicals 227

British Journal of Photography
39 Earlham Street, London, WC2H 9LD (Tel: 020-7306 7000)

British Journal of Psychiatry
Royal College of Psychiatrists, 17 Belgrave Square, London, SW1X 8PG (Tel: 020-7235 2351; Fax: 020-7259 6507; Web: http://www.rcpsych.ac.uk)
Editor: Prof. G. Wilkinson

British Medical Journal
British Medical Association, BMA House, Tavistock Square, London, WC1H 9JR (Tel: 020-7387 4499; Fax: 020-7383 6418; Email: bmj@bmj.com; Web: http://www.bmj.com)
Editor: Dr R. Smith

British Tax Review
100 Avenue Road, London, NW3 3PF (Tel: 020-7393 7000)

Building
Exchange Tower, 2 Harbour Exchange Square, London, E14 9GE (Tel: 020-7560 4000)

Business Education Today
Pitman Publishing, 128 Long Acre, London, WC2E 9AN (Tel: 020-7447 2000)

Campaign
174 Hammersmith Road, London, W6 7JP (Tel: 020-8943 5000)

Chemistry and Industry
15 Belgrave Square, London, SW1X 8PS (Tel: 020-7235 3681; Fax: 020-7235 9410; Email: enquiries@chemind.demon.co.uk; Web: http://www.cc.mond.org)
Editor: A. Crawford

Chemistry in Britain
Royal Society of Chemistry, Burlington House, Piccadilly, London, W1V 0BN (Tel: 020-7440 3360; Fax: 020 7494 1134; Email: editorial@chembrit.co.uk; Web: http://www.chemsoc.org)
Editor: R. Stevenson

Classical Music
241 Shaftesbury Avenue, London, WC2H 8EH (Tel: 020-7333 1742; Fax: 020-7333 1769; Email: classical.music@rhinegold.co.uk; Web: http://www.rhinegold.co.uk)
Editor: K. Clarke

Community Care
Quadrant House, The Quadrant, Sutton, Surrey, SM2 5AS
Editor: Ms P. Neate

Computer Weekly
Quadrant House, The Quadrant, Sutton, Surrey, SM2 5AS

Computing
VNU House, 32-34 Broadwick Street, London, W1A 2HG (Tel: 020-7316 9000)

Construction News
151 Rosebery Avenue, London, EC1R 4QW (Tel: 020-7505 6888)

Container Management
4th Floor, Regal House, 70 London Road, Twickenham, Middx, TW1 3QS (Tel: 020-8891 1199; Fax: 020-8892 2292; Email: cm.editor@ukgateway.net)
Editor: Ms J. Nunan

Contract Journal
Quadrant House, The Quadrant, Sutton, Surrey, SM2 5AS

Control and Instrumentation
St Giles House, 50 Poland Street, London, W1V 4AY (Tel: 020-7970 4119; Fax: 020-7970 4191; Email: pgay@centaur.co.uk)
Editor: P. Gay

Crafts Magazine
Crafts Council, 44A Pentonville Road, London, N1 9BY (Tel: 020-278 7700; Fax: 020-7837 6891; Web: http://www.craftscouncil.org.uk)
Editor: G. Rudge

The Criminologist
Tolley House, 2 Addiscombe Road, Croydon, CR9 5AF

The Dentist
Unit 2, Riverview Business Park, Walnut Tree Close, Guildford, Surrey, GU1 4QT (Tel: 01483-304944; Fax: 01483-303191; Email: geowarman@aol.com)
Editor: Ms J. Dyer

Design Week
St Giles House, 49-50 Poland Street, London, W1V 4AX (Tel: 020-7439 4222)

The Director
(Journal of the Institute of Directors), 116 Pall Mall, London, SW1Y 5ED (Tel: 020-7766 8950; Fax: 020-7766 8840; Email: director-ed@iod.co.uk; Web: http://www.iod.co.uk)
Editor: Ms J. Higgins

Drapers Record
67 Clerkenwell Road, London, EC1R 5BH (Tel: 020-7417 2831)

Electrical Review
Quadrant House, The Quadrant, Sutton, Surrey, SM2 5AS

Electrical Times
Quadrant House, The Quadrant, Sutton, Surrey, SM2 5AS

Electronic Engineering
City Reach, 5 Greenwich View Place, Millharbour, London, E14 9NN (Tel: 020-7861 6346)

The Engineer
St Giles House, 50 Poland Street, London, W1V 4AX (Tel: 020-7970 4100; Fax: 020-7970 4189; Web: http://www.e4engineering.com)
Editor: P. Carslake

Equity Journal
Guild House, Upper St Martin's Lane, London, WC2H 9EG (Tel: 020-7379 6000;
Email: mbrown@equity.org.uk;
Web: http://www.equity.org.uk)
Editor: M. Brown

Estates Gazette
151 Wardour Street, London, W1V 4BN (Tel: 020-7437 0141)

Farmers Weekly
Quadrant House, The Quadrant, Sutton, Surrey, SM2 5AS (Tel: 020-8652 4911; Fax: 020-8652 4005;
Email: farmers.weekly@rbi.co.uk;
Web: http://www.fwi.co.uk)
Editor: S. D. Howe

Fishing News International
Meed House, 21 John Street, London, WC1N 2BP (Tel: 020-7470 6200)

Flight International
Quadrant House, The Quadrant, Sutton, Surrey, SM2 5AS (Tel: 020-8652 3307; Fax: 020-8652 8923;
Email: vaughan.gordon@rbi.co.uk;
Web: http://www.flightinternational.com)
Editor: Ms C. Reed

Gas Engineering and Management
Institution of Gas Engineers, 21 Portland Place, London, W1N 3AF (Tel: 020-7636 6603; Fax: 020-7636 6602; Email: julie@igaseng.demon.co.uk;
Web: http://www.igaseng.com)
Editor: P. Marsden

Hairdressers' Journal International
Quadrant House, The Quadrant, Sutton, Surrey, SM2 5AS

The Health Service Journal
Porters South, 4-6 Crinan Street, London, N1 9XW (Tel: 020-843 4526)

Heating, Ventilating and Plumbing
Hereford House, Bridle Path, Croydon, Surrey, CR9 4NL

Index on Censorship
Writers and Scholars International Ltd, 33 Islington High Street, London, N1 9LH (Tel: 020-7278 2313)

The Journalist
National Union of Journalists, Acorn House, 314-320 Gray's Inn Road, London, WC2X 8DP (Tel: 020-7278 7916)

Journal of Alternative and Complementary Medicine
9 Rickett Street, London, SW6 1RU (Tel: 020-7385 0012)

Journal of the British Astronomical Association
Burlington House, Piccadilly, London, W1V 9AG (Tel: 020-7734 4145; Web: http://www.star.ucl.ac.uk/~htm)
Editor: Mrs H. McGee

Justice of the Peace Reports
Tolley House, 2 Addiscombe Road, Croydon, CR9 5AF (Tel: 020-8722 3400; Fax: 020-8722 3403; Email: jpn@tolley.co.uk)
Editor: Dr R. Munday

The Lancet
42 Bedford Square, London, WC1B 3SL (Tel: 020-7436 4981)

Law Quarterly Review
100 Avenue Road, London, NW3 3PF (Tel: 020-7393 7000; Fax: 020-7393 7020;
Web: http://www.sweetandmaxwell.co.uk)
Editor: Prof. F. Reynolds

The Law Reports
Megarry House, 119 Chancery Lane, London, WC2A 1PP (Tel: 020-7242 6741; Fax: 020-7831 5247;
Email: postmaster@iclr.co.uk;
Web: http://www.lawreports.co.uk)
Editor: R. Williams

Law Society Gazette
6th Floor, Newspaper House, 8-16 Great New Street, London, EC4A 3BN (Tel: 020-7320 5820; Fax: 020-7831 0869; Email: gazette-editorial@lawsociety.org.uk;
Web: http://www.lawgazette.co.uk)
Editor: Ms E. Gilvarry

Leisure Week
St Giles House, 49-50 Poland Street, London, W1V 4AX (Tel: 020-7970 4588; Fax: 020-7970 4891;
Email: leisure-week@centaur.co.uk;
Web: http://www.leisureweek.co.uk)
Editor: Ms M. Swift

Library Association Record
7 Ridgmount Street, London, WC1E 7AE (Tel: 020-7636 7543)

Local Government Chronicle
33-39 Bowling Green Lane, London, EC1R 0DA (Tel: 020-7833 7311; Fax: 020-7837 2725)
Editor: J. Arnold-Forster

Machinery Market
6 Blyth Road, Bromley, Kent, BR1 3RX

Management Accounting
Chartered Institute of Management Accountants, 63 Portland Place, London, W1N 4AB (Tel: 020-7637 2311)

Management Today
174 Hammersmith Road, London, W6 7JP (Tel: 020-8267 4956; Fax: 020-8267 4966;
Email: management.today@haynet.com;
Web: http://www.managementtoday.co.uk)
Editor: V. Smart

Managing Information
ASLIB, Staple Hall, Stone House Court, London, EC3A 7PB (Tel: 020-7903 0000)

Trade Periodicals 229

Manufacturing Chemist
City Reach, 5 Greenwich View Place, London, E14 9NN (Tel: 020-7861 6061)

Marketing
174 Hammersmith Road, London, W6 7JP (Tel: 020-7413 4162)

Marketing Week
St Giles House, 49-50 Poland Street, London, W1V 4AX (Tel: 020-7970 4000)

Materials Recycling Week
19th Floor, Leon House, 233 High Street, Croydon, Surrey, CR0 9XT (Tel: 020-8277 5540; Fax: 020-8277 5560; Email: recycling@maclaren.emap.co.uk)
Editor: S. Eminton

Materials World
Institute of Materials, 1 Carlton House Terrace, London, SW1Y 5DB (Tel: 020-7451 7300; Fax: 020-7451 7319; Email: materials_world@materials.org.uk; Web: http://www.materials.org.uk)
Editor: Dr S. Hill

Meat Trades Journal
Quantum House, 19 Scarbrook Road, Croydon, Surrey, CR9 1QH (Tel: 020-8565 4200; Fax: 020-8565 4250; Email: freda@qpp.co.uk)
Editor: F. A'Court

Media Week
Quantum House, 19 Scarbrook Road, Croydon, Surrey, CR9 1LX (Tel: 020-8565 4200; Fax: 020-8565 4394; Email: mweeked@qpp.co.uk; Web: http://www.mediaweek.co.uk)
Editor: P. Barrett

Mining Journal
60 Worship Street, London, EC2A 2HD (Tel: 020-7216 6060)

Motor Transport
Quadrant House, The Quadrant, Sutton, Surrey, SM2 5AS

Municipal Journal
32 Vauxhall Bridge Road, London, SW1V 2SS (Tel: 020-7973 6400)

Musician
241 Shaftesbury Avenue, London, WC2H 8EH (Tel: 020-7333 1733; Fax: 020-7333 1736; Web: http://www.musiciansunion.org.uk)
Editor: B. Blain

Music Journal
Incorporated Society of Musicians, 10 Stratford Place, London, W1N 9AE (Tel: 020-7629 4413; Fax: 020-7408 1538; Email: membership@ism.org; Web: http://www.ism.org)
Editor: N. Hoyle

Music Week
8 Montague Close, London Bridge, London, SE1 9UR (Tel: 020-7940 8500)

Nursing Times
Porters South, Crinan Street, London, N1 9XW (Tel: 020-7843 4526)

Optician
Quadrant House, The Quadrant, Sutton, Surrey, SM2 5AS

Patent World
Informa Professional Publishing, 69-77 Paul Street, London, EC2A 4LQ (Tel: 020-7553 1000; Fax: 020-7553 1107; Email: kelly.wemmers@informa.com; Web: http://www.ipworldonline.com)
Editor: K. Wemmers

People Management
Institute of Personnel and Development, 17 Britton Street, London, EC1M 9NQ (Tel: 020-7880 6200; Fax: 020-7336 7635;
Email: editorial@peoplemanagement.co.uk;
Web: http://www.peoplemanagement.co.uk)
Editor: S. Crabb

Personal Computer World
VNU House, 32-34 Broadwick Street, London, W1A 2HG (Tel: 020-7316 9000)

Pharmaceutical Journal
Royal Pharmaceutical Society of Great Britain, 1 Lambeth High Street, London, SE1 7JN (Tel: 020-7735 9141)

Police Review
5th Floor, Celcon House, 289-293 High Holborn, London, WC1V 7HZ (Tel: 020-7440 4700)

The Practitioner
City Reach, 5 Greenwich View Place, Millharbour, London, E14 9NN (Tel: 020-7861 6479)

Probation Journal
217A Balham High Road, London, SW17 7BP (Tel: 020-8671 0640; Fax: 020-8671 0640;
Email: prbjournal@aol.com)
Editor: H. Singh Bhui

Railway Gazette International
Quadrant House, The Quadrant, Sutton, Surrey, SM2 5AS (Tel: 020-8652 8608; Fax: 020-8652 3738; Web: http://www.railwaygazette.com)
Editor: M. Hughes

Rating and Valuation Reporter
4 Breams Buildings, London, EC4A 1AQ

Retail Newsagent
11 Angel Gate, City Road, London, EC1V 2PT (Tel: 020-7689 0600; Fax: 020-7689 0500;
Email: rn@newtrade.co.uk;
Web: http://www.worldofmagazines.co.uk)
Editor: A. Desforges

Retail Week
Maclaren House, PO Box 109, Croydon, CR9 1QH

230 Media London

RUSI Journal
Royal United Services Institute for Defence Studies, Whitehall, London, SW1A 2ET (Tel: 020-7930 5854; Fax: 020-7321 0943; Web: http://www.rusi.org)
Editorial Manager: Ms I. Bleken

Screen International
33-39 Bowling Green Lane, London, EC1R 0DA (Tel: 020-7505 8080)

Solicitors Journal
100 Avenue Road, London, NW3 3PF (Tel: 020-7393 7000; Fax: 020-7393 7880; Email: solicitors.journal@sweetandmaxwell.co.uk; Web: http://www.sweetandmaxwell.co.uk)
Editor: Ms S. Hart

The Stage
47 Bermondsey Street, London, SE1 3XT (Tel: 020-7403 1818; Fax: 020-7357 9287; Email: editor@thestage.co.uk; Web: http://www.thestage.co.uk)
Editor: B. Attwood

Structural Engineer
(Institution of Structural Engineers), 11 Upper Belgrave Street, London, SW1X 8BH (Tel: 020-7235 4535; Email: stansfield@istructe.org.uk; Web: http://www.istructe.org.uk)
Editor: Ms K. Stansfield

Surveyor
32 Vauxhall Bridge Road, London, SW1V 2SS (Tel: 020-7973 6402; Fax: 020-7973 6677; Email: editorial.surveyor@hemming-group.co.uk; Web: http://www.hemming-group.co.uk)
Editor: P. Hughes

Taxation Practitioner
(Chartered Institute of Taxation), 12 Upper Belgrave Street, London, SW1X 8BB (Tel: 020-7235 9381)

Taxi
Taxi House, 7-11 Woodfield Road, London, W9 2BA (Tel: 020-7432 1429; Fax: 020-7266 2297; Email: spessok@comcab.co.uk)
Editor: S. Pessok

The Teacher
National Union of Teachers, Hamilton House, Mabledon Place, London, WC1H 9BD (Tel: 020-7380 4708)
Editor: M. Howard

Teaching History
The Historical Association, 59A Kennington Park Road, London, SE11 4JH (Tel: 020-7735 3901)

Television
Royal Television Society, Holborn Hall, 100 Gray's Inn Road, London, WC1X 8AL (Tel: 020-7691 2465; Fax: 020-7430 0924; Email: publications@rts.org.uk; Web: http://www.rts.org.uk)
Editor: P. Fiddick

Town and Country Planning
Town and Country Planning Association, 17 Carlton House Terrace, London, SW1Y 5AS (Tel: 020-7930 8903)

Travel Trade Gazette (UK and Ireland)
1st Floor, City Reach, 5 Greenwich View Place, Millharbour, London, E14 9NN (Tel: 020-7861 6096; Fax: 020-7861 6227; Email: phil.davies@unmf.com)
Editor: P. Davies

Veterinary Record
British Veterinary Association, 24-28 Oval Road, London, NW1 7DX (Tel: 020-7240 2032)

Weekly Law Reports
Megarry House, 119 Chancery Lane, London, WC2A 1PP (Tel: 020-7242 6471; Fax: 020-7831 5247; Email: postmaster@iclr.co.uk; Web: http://www.lawreports.co.uk)
Editor: R. Williams

CONSUMER PERIODICALS
The list below details popular consumer periodicals which are published in London.

19
King's Reach Tower, Stamford Street, London, SE1 9LS

Al Majalla
Arab Press House, 184 High Holborn, London, WC1V 7AP (Tel: 020-7831 8181; Fax: 020-7831 4051)
Editor: A. Alkhamis

Amateur Photographer
King's Reach Tower, Stamford Street, London, SE1 9LS

Apollo
1 Castle Lane, London, SW1E 6DR (Tel: 020-7233 6640; Fax: 020-7630 7791)
Editor: D. Ekserdjian

Arena
3rd Floor, Block A, Exmouth House, Pine Street, London, EC1R 0JL

Art Monthly
Suite 17, 26 Charing Cross Road, London, WC2H 0DG (Tel: 020-7240 0389; Fax: 020-7497 0726)
Editor: Ms P. Bickers

Autocar
38-42 Hampton Road, Teddington, Middx, TW11 0JE

BBC Gardener's World
Woodlands, 80 Wood Lane, London, W12 0TT

BBC Good Food Magazine
Woodlands, 80 Wood Lane, London, W12 0TT

BBC Homes and Antiques
Woodlands, 80 Wood Lane, London, W12 0TT

BBC Top Gear
Woodlands, 80 Wood Lane, London, W12 0TT

Consumer Periodicals 231

BBC Vegetarian Good Food
Woodlands, 80 Wood Lane, London, W12 0TT

BBC Wildlife Magazine
Woodlands, 80 Wood Lane, London, W12 0TT

Bella
2nd Floor, Shirley House, 25-27 Camden Road, London, NW1 9LL

The Big Issue
236-240 Pentonville Road, London, N1 9JY (Tel: 020-7526 3320; Fax: 020-7526 3301; Email: london@bigissue.com; Web: http://www.bigissue.com)
Editor: M. Collin

Boxing Monthly
40 Morpeth Road, London, E9 7LD

Brides and Setting up Home
Vogue House, Hanover Square, London, W1R 0AD (Tel: 020-7499 9080; Fax: 020-7460 6369; Web: http://www.bridesuk.net)
Editor: Ms S. Boler

Chat
King's Reach Tower, Stamford Street, London, SE1 9LS (Tel: 020-7261 6565; Fax: 020-7261 6534; Web: http://www.ipc.co.uk)
Editor: K. Kendrick

Classic and Sports Car
38-42 Hampton Road, Teddington, Middx, TW11 0JE

Company
National Magazine House, 72 Broadwick Street, London, W1V 2BP

Computer and Video Games
Priory Court, 30-32 Farringdon Lane, London, EC1R 3AU

Computer Shopper
19 Bolsover Street, London, W1P 7HJ

Cosmopolitan
National Magazine House, 72 Broadwick Street, London, W1V 2BP

Country Homes and Interiors
King's Reach Tower, Stamford Street, London, SE1 9LS (Tel: 020-7261 6451; Fax: 020-7261 6895)
Editor: Ms K. Hadley

Country Life
King's Reach Tower, Stamford Street, London, SE1 9LS (Tel: 020-7261 7058; Fax: 020-7261 5139; Web: http://www.countrylife.co.uk)

Country Living Magazine
National Magazine House, 72 Broadwick Street, London, W1V 2BP (Tel: 020-7439 5000; Fax: 020-7439 5093; Web: http://www.natmags.co.uk)
Editor: Ms S. Smith

The Countryman
King's Reach Tower, Stamford Street, London, SE1 9LS (Tel: 020-7261 7262; Fax: 020-7261 7273)
Editor: T. Quinn

Cycling Weekly
Link House, Dingwall Avenue, Croydon, CR2 0PH (Tel: 020-8774 0811; Fax: 020-8686 0947; Email: cycling@ipc.co.uk)
Editor: R. Garbutt

Daltons Weekly
Ci Tower, St George's Square, New Malden, Surrey, KT3 4JA

Dance Theatre Journal
Laban Centre London, Laurie Grove, London, SE14 6NH (Tel: 020-8692 4070; Fax: 020-8694 8749; Email: dtj@laban.co.uk; Web: http://www.laban.co.uk)
Editor: I. Bramley

Dancing Times
Clerkenwell House, 45-47 Clerkenwell Green, London, EC1R 0EB (Tel: 020-7250 3006; Fax: 020-7253 6679; Email: dt@dancing-times.co.uk; Web: http://www.dt-itd.dircon.co.uk)
Editor: Ms M. Clarke

The Ecologist
Unit 18, Chelsea Wharf, 15 Lots Road, London, SW10 0QJ

The Economist
25 St James's Street, London, SW1A 1HG (Tel: 020-7830 7000; Fax: 020-7839 2968; Web: http://www.economist.com)
Editor: B. Emmott

Elle
Endeavour House, 189 Shaftesbury Avenue, London, WC2H 8JG (Tel: 020-7437 9011; Fax: 020-7208 3599)
Editor: Ms F. McIntosh

Empire
Mappin House, 4 Winsley Street, London, W1N 7AR (Tel: 020-7436 1515; Fax: 020-7312 8249; Email: empire@ecm.emap.com; Web: http://www.empireonline.co.uk)
Editor: Ms E. Cochrane

Esquire
National Magazine House, 72 Broadwick Street, London, W1V 2BP

Essentials
King's Reach Tower, Stamford Street, London, SE1 9LS

The Face
3rd Floor, Block A, Exmouth House, Pine Street, London, EC1R 0JL

Family Circle
King's Reach Tower, Stamford Street, London, SE1 9LS (Tel: 020-7261 6195; Fax: 020-7261 5929; Email: familycircle@ipc.co.uk; Web: http://www.ipc.co.uk)
Editor: Ms G. Carter

232 Media London

FHM
Mappin House, 4 Winsley Street, London, W1N 7AR (Tel: 020-7312 8707; Fax: 020-7312 8191; Web: http://www.fhm.com)
Editor: A. Noguera

The Field
King's Reach Tower, Stamford Street, London, SE1 9LS (Tel: 020-7261 5198; Fax: 020-7261 5358; Email: marcella_bingley@ipc.co.uk; Web: http://www.thefield.co.uk)
Editor: J. Young

Film Review
9 Blades Court, Deodar Road, London, SW15 2NU (Tel: 020-8875 1520; Fax: 020-8875 1588; Email: filmreview@visimag.com; Web: http://www.visimag.com/filmreview)
Editor: N. Corry

Gay Times
Ground Floor, Worldwide House, 116-134 Bayham Street, London, NW1 0BA (Tel: 020-7482 2576; Fax: 020-7284 0329; Email: edit@gaytimes.co.uk; Web: http://www.gaytimes.co.uk)
Editor: C. Richardson

Geographical Journal
Royal Geographical Society/IBG, 1 Kensington Gore, London, SW7 2AR (Tel: 020-7591 3026; Fax: 020-7591 3001; Email: g.lowman@rgs.org; Web: http://www.rgs.org)
Hon. Editor: Prof. A. Millington

Good Holiday Magazine
3A High Street, Esher, Surrey, KT10 9RP

Good Housekeeping
National Magazine House, 72 Broadwick Street, London, W1V 2BP

The Good Ski Guide
3A High Street, Esher, Surrey, KT10 9RP

GQ
Vogue House, Hanover Square, London, W1R 0AD
Editor: D. Jones

Gramophone
135 Greenford Road, Sudbury Hill, Harrow, Middx, HA1 3YD

Granta
2-3 Hanover Yard, Noel Road, London, N1 8BE

The Guardian Weekly
119 Farringdon Road, London, EC1R 3ER

Guiding
17-19 Buckingham Palace Road, London, SW1W 0PT (Tel: 020-7592 1821; Fax: 020-7828 5791; Email: guiding@guides.org.uk; Web: http://www.guides.org.uk)
Editor: Ms J. Clampett

Harpers and Queen
National Magazine House, 72 Broadwick Street, London, W1V 2BP

Having a Baby
National Magazine House, 72 Broadwick Street, London, W1V 2BP (Tel: 020-7439 5000; Fax: 020-7439 5337; Email: hab@natmags.co.uk; Web: http://www.natmags.co.uk)
Editor: Ms L. Murphy

Hello!
69-71 Upper Ground, London, SE1 9PQ (Tel: 020-7667 8700; Fax: 020-7667 8716)
Editor: Ms M. Koumi

History Today
20 Old Compton Street, London, W1V 5PE (Tel: 020-7534 8000; Email: p.furtado@historytoday.com; Web: http://www.historytoday.com)
Editor: P. Furtado

Homes and Gardens
King's Reach Tower, Stamford Street, London, SE1 9LS (Tel: 020-7261 5678; Fax: 020-7261 6247)
Editor: M. Line

Horse & Hound
King's Reach Tower, Stamford Street, London, SE1 9LS (Tel: 020-7261 5306; Fax: 020-7261 5429; Web: http://www.ipc.co.uk)
Editor: A. Garvey

House and Garden
Vogue House, Hanover Square, London, W1R 0AD

House Beautiful
National Magazine House, 72 Broadwick Street, London, W1V 2BP (Tel: 020-7439 5000; Fax: 020-7439 5595; Web: http://www.natmags.co.uk)
Editor: Ms L. Norman

Ideal Home
King's Reach Tower, Stamford Street, London, SE1 9LS

i-d Magazine
Universal House, 251 Tottenham Court Road, London, W1P 0AB

Illustrated London News
20 Upper Ground, London, SE1 9PF

In Britain
Haymarket House, 1 Oxendon Street, London, SW1Y 4EE

Irish Post
Cambridge House, Cambridge Grove, London, W6 0LE (Tel: 020-8741 0649; Fax: 020-8741 3382; Email: irishpost@irishpost.co.uk; Web: http://www.irishpost.co.uk)
Editor: Ms N. Casey

J17
Endeavour House, 189 Shaftesbury Avenue, London, WC2H 8JG (Tel: 020-7208 3408; Fax: 020-7208 3590)
Editor: Ms S. Wilson

Jazz Journal International
3 and 3A Forest Road, Loughton, Essex, IG10 1DR (Tel: 020-8532 0456; Fax: 020-8532 0440)
Editor: E. Cook

Labour Research
78 Blackfriars Road, London, SE1 8HF

The Lady
39-40 Bedford Street, London, WC2E 9ER (Tel: 020-7379 4717; Fax: 020-7836 4620)
Editor: Ms A. Usden

Land and Liberty
Suite 427, London Fruit Exchange, Brushfield Street, London, E1 6EL (Tel: 020-7377 8885; Fax: 020-7377 8686; Email: henrygeorge@charity.vfree.com; Web: http://www.henrygeorgeuk.cjb.net)
Editor: F. Harrison

Literary Review
44 Lexington Street, London, W1R 3LH (Tel: 020-7437 9392; Fax: 020-7734 1844; Email: litrev@dircon.co.uk)
Editor-in-Chief: A. Waugh

Loaded
King's Reach Tower, Stamford Street, London, SE1 9LS

London Review of Books
28-30 Little Russell Street, London, WC1A 2HN

M
National Magazine House, 72 Broadwick Street, London, W1V 2BP

Majesty
26-28 Hallam Street, London, W1N 6BP

Marie Claire
King's Reach Tower, Stamford Street, London, SE1 9LS

Melody Maker (MM)
King's Reach Tower, Stamford Street, London, SE1 9LS (Tel: 020-7261 6229; Fax: 020-7261 6706; Email: your-shout@ipc.co.uk; Web: http://www.melodymaker.co.uk)
Editor: M. Sutherland

Meteorological Magazine
The Stationery Office, P.O. Box 276, London, SW8 5DT

Mizz
King's Reach Tower, Stamford Street, London, SE1 9LS

Model Boats
Nexus House, Azalea Drive, Swanley, Kent, BR8 8HU

Moneywise
11 Westferry Circus, Canary Wharf, London, E14 4HE (Tel: 020-7715 8465; Fax: 020-7715 8725; Email: matthew_vincent@readersdigest.co.uk; Web: http://www.moneywise.co.uk)
Editor: M. Vincent

More!
Victory House, 14 Leicester Place, London, WC2H 7BP

Mother and Baby
Victory House, 14 Leicester Place, London, WC2H 7BP

Nature
Porters South, Crinan Street, London, N1 9SQ

New Musical Express (NME)
King's Reach Tower, Stamford Street, London, SE1 9LS

New Scientist
151 Wardour Street, London, W1V 4BN

New Statesman
7th Floor, Victoria Station House, 191 Victoria Street, London, SW1E 5NE (Tel: 020-7828 1232; Fax: 020-7828 1881; Email: info@newstatesman.co.uk; Web: http://www.newstatesman.co.uk)
Editor: P. Wilby

Newsweek
18 Park Street, London, W1Y 4HH (Tel: 020-7629 8361; Fax: 020-7408 1403; Web: http://www.newsweek.com)

New Woman
Endeavour House, 189 Shaftesbury Avenue, London, WC2H 8JG (Tel: 020-7208 3456; Fax: 020-7208 3585)
Editor: Ms J. Elvin

OK!
Northern and Shell Tower, City Harbour, London, E14 9GL

The Oldie
45-46 Poland Street, London, W1V 4AU (Tel: 020-7734 2225; Fax: 020-7734 2226; Email: theoldie@theoldie.co.uk; Web: http://www.theoldie.co.uk)
Editor: R. Ingrams

Opera
1A Mountgrove Road, London, N5 2LU

Opera Now
241 Shaftesbury Avenue, London, WC2H 8EH

Parents
Victory House, 14 Leicester Place, London, WC2H 7BP

Parliamentary Debates (Commons) (Hansard)
The Stationery Office, P.O. Box 276, London, SW8 5DT

Parliamentary Debates (Lords) (Hansard)
The Stationery Office, P.O. Box 276, London, SW8 5DT

Poetry Review
22 Betterton Street, London, WC2H 9BU (Tel: 020-7420 9883; Fax: 020-7240 4818;

234 Media London

Email: poetrysoc@dial.pipex.com;
Web: http://www.poetrysoc.com)
Editor: P. Forbes

Practical Caravan
60 Waldegrave Road, Teddington, Middx, TW11 8LG

Practical Householder
Nexus House, Azalea Drive, Swanley, Kent, BR8 8HU

Practical Parenting
King's Reach Tower, Stamford Street, London, SE1 9LS

Private Eye
6 Carlisle Street, London, W1V 5RG (Tel: 020-7437 4017; Fax: 020-7437 0705;
Web: http://www.private-eye.co.uk)
Editor: I. Hislop

Prospect
4 Bedford Square, London, WC1B 3RA (Tel: 020-7255 1281; Fax: 020-7255 1279;
Email: editorial@prospect-magazine.co.uk;
Web: http://www.prospect-magazine.co.uk)
Editor: D. Goodhart

The Puzzler
Glenthorne House, Hammersmith Grove, London, W6 0LG

Q
Mappin House, 4 Winsley Street, London, W1M 7AR

Radio Times
Woodlands, 80 Wood Lane, London, W12 0TT

The Railway Magazine
King's Reach Tower, Stamford Street, London, SE1 9LS (Tel: 020-7261 5821; Fax: 020-7261 5269;
Email: railway@ipc.co.uk)
Editor: N. Pigott

Reader's Digest
11 Westferry Circus, Canary Wharf, London, E14 4HE (Tel: 020-7715 8000; Fax: 020-7715 8716; Web: http://www.readersdigest.co.uk)
Editor: R. Twisk

Rugby World
King's Reach Tower, Stamford Street, London, SE1 9LS

Scouting
Baden-Powell House, Queen's Gate, London, SW7 5JS

She
National Magazine House, 72 Broadwick Street, London, W1V 2BP (Tel: 020-7439 5000; Fax: 020-7312 3981; Web: http://www.natmags.co.uk)
Editor: Ms A. Pylkkanen

Shoot
King's Reach Tower, Stamford Street, London, SE1 9LS

Shooting Times and Country Magazine
King's Reach Tower, Stamford Street, London, SE1 9LS

Sky Magazine
1st Floor, Mappin House, 4 Winsley Street, London, W1N 7AR (Tel: 020-7312 8253; Fax: 020-7312 8248;
Email: sky@ecm.emap.com;
Web: http://www.skymagazine.co.uk)
Editor: M. Hogan

Slimming Magazine
Endeavour House, 189 Shaftesbury Avenue, London, WC2H 8JG (Tel: 020-7208 3214; Fax: 020-7208 3302)
Editor: Ms J. Kellow

Smash Hits
Mappin House, 4 Winsley Street, London, W1M 7AR

The Spectator
56 Doughty Street, London, WC1N 2LL (Tel: 020-7405 1706; Fax: 020-7242 0603;
Email: editor@spectator.co.uk;
Web: http://www.spectator.co.uk)
Editor: B. Johnson

Tatler
Vogue House, Hanover Square, London, W1R 0AD
(Tel: 020-7499 9080)
Editor: G. Greig

Time Magazine
Brettenham House, Lancaster Place, London, WC2E 7TL (Tel: 020-7499 4080; Fax: 020-7322 1230;
Web: http://www.time.com)
Editor: C. Redman

Time Out
Universal House, 251 Tottenham Court Road, London, W1P 0AB (Tel: 020-7813 3000; Fax: 020-7813 6001;
Web: http://www.timeout.com)
Editor: Ms L. Lee Davies

The Times Educational Supplement
Admiral House, 66-68 East Smithfield, London, E1W 1BX (Tel: 020-7782 3000; Fax: 020-7782 3202;
Email: editor@tes.co.uk; Web: http://www.tes.co.uk)
Editor: Ms C. St John-Brooks

The Times Higher Education Supplement
Admiral House, 66-68 East Smithfield, London, E1W 1BX (Tel: 020-7782 3375; Fax: 020-7782 3300;
Email: editor@thes.co.uk;
Web: http://www.thesis.co.uk)

The Times Literary Supplement
Admiral House, 66-68 East Smithfield, London, E1W 1BX (Tel: 020-7782 3000; Fax: 020-7782 3100;
Email: letters@the-tls.co.uk;
Web: http://www.the-tls.co.uk)
Editor: F. Mount

Tribune
308 Gray's Inn Road, London, WC1X 8DY (Tel: 020-7278 0911;
Web: http://www.rost2000.abel.co.uk/tribune)
Editor: M. Seddon

TV Times
King's Reach Tower, Stamford Street, London, SE1 9LS

Publishers

Vanity Fair
Vogue House, Hanover Square, London, W1R 0AD

Viz Magazine
The New Boathouse, 136-142 Bramley Road, London, W10 6SR (Tel: 020-7565 3000; Fax: 020-7565 3055; Email: viz.comic@virgin.net)
Editors: S. Donald; G. Dury; S. Thorp

Vogue
Vogue House, Hanover Square, London, W1R 0AD

The Voice
370 Coldharbour Lane, London, SW9 8PL

The Weekly Telegraph
1 Canada Square, Canary Wharf, London, E14 5DT (Tel: 020-7538 6000; Fax: 020-7513 2509; Email: weeklyt@telegraph.co.uk; Web: http://www.globalnetwork.co.uk)
Editor: K. Jenkins

What Car?
60 Waldegrave Road, Teddington, Middx, TW11 8LG (Tel: 020-8267 5688; Fax: 020-8267 5750; Email: whatcar@haynet.com; Web: http://www.whatcar.co.uk)
Editor: S. Fowler

Which?
2 Marylebone Road, London, NW1 4DF

Woman
King's Reach Tower, Stamford Street, London, SE1 9LS (Tel: 020-7261 7023; Fax: 020-7261 5997; Email: woman@ipc.co.uk; Web: http://www.ipc.co.uk)
Editor: Ms C. Russell

Woman and Home
King's Reach Tower, Stamford Street, London, SE1 9LS

Woman's Journal
King's Reach Tower, Stamford Street, London, SE1 9LS

Woman's Own
King's Reach Tower, Stamford Street, London, SE1 9LS (Tel: 020-7261 5500; Fax: 020-7261 5346)
Editor: Ms T. Tayner

Woman's Realm
King's Reach Tower, Stamford Street, London, SE1 9LS

Woman's Weekly
King's Reach Tower, Stamford Street, London, SE1 9LS

The World of Interiors
Vogue House, Hanover Square, London, W1R 0AD

Yachting Monthly
King's Reach Tower, Stamford Street, London, SE1 9LS (Tel: 020-7261 6040; Fax: 020-7261 7555; Email: yachting-monthly@ipc.co.uk; Web: http://www.yachtingmonthly.com)
Editor: Ms S. Norbury

Zest
National Magazine House, 72 Broadwick Street, London, W1V 2BP

ZM
National Magazine House, 72 Broadwick Street, London, W1V 2BP

NEWS AGENCIES
News agencies provide general, business, sport and television news to a variety of subscribers including the press, other media, and industrial, commercial, financial and business users.

Associated Press
12 Norwich Street, London EC4A 4BP (Tel: 020-7353 1515; Fax: 020-7353 8118)

Hayters
146-148 Clerkenwell Road, London EC1R 5DP (Tel: 020-7837 7171; Fax: 020-7837 2420)

Parliamentary Monitoring Services
19 Douglas Street, London SW1P 4PA (Tel: 020-7233 8283)

Press Association Ltd
292 Vauxhall Bridge Road, London SW1V 1AE (Tel: 020-7963 7000; Fax: 020-7963 7192)

Reuters Ltd
85 Fleet Street, London EC4P 4AJ (Tel: 020-7250 1122; Fax: 020-7542 7921)

Two-Ten Communications Ltd
Communications House, 210 Old Street, London EC1V 9UN (Tel: 020-7490 8111; Fax: 020-7490 1255)

PUBLISHERS
Publishers based in London and details of the types of book they publish.

Allen & Unwin
Osborne House, 111 Bartholomew Road, London, NW5 2BJ (Tel: 020-7482 3546; Fax: 020-7482 2723; Email: allanunwin@compuserve.com)
Type of books: Adult non-fiction; academic. Children's - fiction; non-fiction; picture books

Allison & Busby
114 New Cavendish Street, London, W1M 7FD (Tel: 020-7636 2942; Fax: 020-7323 2023; Email: all@allisonbusby.co.uk; Web: http://www.allisonandbusby.ltd.uk)
Type of books: Contemporary fiction; crime fiction; non-fiction

Arnold
338 Euston Road, London, NW1 3BH (Tel: 020-7873 6000; Fax: 020-7873 6325; Email: arnold@hodder.co.uk; Web: http://www.arnoldpublishers.com)
Type of books: Academic and professional

Arrow Books
20 Vauxhall Bridge Road, London, SW1V 2SA (Tel: 020-7840 8400; Fax: 020-7233 6127;

Web: http://www.randomhouse.co.uk)
Type of books: Fiction; non-fiction; general

Athlone Press
1 Park Drive, London, NW11 7SG (Tel: 020-8458 0888; Fax: 020-8201 8115;
Email: athlonepress@btinternet.com)
Type of books: Academic; university student textbooks

Aurum Press
25 Bedford Avenue, London, WC1B 3AT (Tel: 020-7637 3225; Fax: 020-7580 2469;
Email: aurum@attglobal.net;
Web: http://www.aurumpress.co.uk)
Type of books: General non-fiction

Bantam Books
61-63 Uxbridge Road, London, W5 5SA (Tel: 020-8579 2652; Fax: 020-8231 6612; Email: info@transworld-publishers.co.uk)
Type of books: General fiction; non-fiction

Barrie & Jenkins
20 Vauxhall Bridge Road, London, SW1V 2SA (Tel: 020-7840 8400; Fax: 020-7840 8406; Web: http://www.randomhouse.co.uk)
Type of books: Art; collecting

B. T. Batsford
9 Blenheim Court, Brewery Road, London, N7 9NT (Tel: 020-7700 7611; Fax: 020-7700 4552;
Email: batsford@chrysalisbooks.co.uk;
Web: http://www.batsford.com)
Type of books: General non-fiction

A. & C. Black
35 Bedford Row, London, WC1R 4JH (Tel: 020-7242 0946; Fax: 020-7831 8478;
Email: enquiries@acblack.co.uk)
Type of books: Reference; nautical; music; travel; sport; ceramics; theatre; children's - fiction; non-fiction

Bloomsbury Publishing
38 Soho Square, London, W1V 5DF (Tel: 020-7494 2111; Fax: 020-7434 0151;
Web: http://www.bloomsbury.com)
Type of books: Fiction; biography/ illustrated; reference; travel and children's

Boxtree
25 Eccleston Place, London, SW1W 9NF (Tel: 020-7881 8000; Fax: 020-7881 8280;
Web: http://www.macmillan.com)
Type of books: Media, tie-ins

Marion Boyars
24 Lacy Road, London, SW15 1NL (Tel: 020-8788 9522; Fax: 020-8789 8122;
Email: marion.boyars@talk21.com)
Web: http://www.marionboyars.co.uk)
Type of books: Fiction; drama; cultural studies; film; drama; music

Butterworths Tolley
Halsbury House, 35 Chancery Lane, London, WC2A 1EL (Tel: 020-7400 2500; Fax: 020-7400 2842;

Web: http://www.butterworths.co.uk)
Type of books: Legal, tax; reference

Cadogan Guides
Morris Publications, West End House, 11 Hills Place, London, W1R 1AG (Tel: 020-7287 6555; Fax: 020-7734 1733; Email: guides@morrispub.co.uk)
Type of books: Travel guides

Cavendish Publishing
The Glass House, Wharton Street, London, WC1X 9PX (Tel: 020-7278 8000; Fax: 020-7278 8080;
Email: info@cavendishpublishing.com)
Web: http://www.cavendishpublishing.com)
Type of books: Law; medical

Century Publishing Co.
20 Vauxhall Bridge Road, London, SW1V 2SA (Tel: 020-7840 8400; Fax: 020-7233 6127;
Web: http://www.randomhouse.co.uk)
Type of books: Novels; health; celebrity biography and autobiography; popular science; history; archaeology

Chambers Harrap
New Penderel House, 283-288 High Holborn, London, WC1V 7HZ (Tel: 020-7903 9999; Fax: 020-7242 5009;
Web: http://www.chambersharrap.com)
Type of books: English language; bi-lingual dictionaries; reference; ELT; scrabble books

Church House Publishing
Church House, Great Smith Street, London, SW1P 3NZ (Tel: 020-7898 1451; Fax: 020-7898 1449;
Email: publishing@c-of-e.org.uk;
Web: http://www.chpublishing.co.uk)
Type of books: Religious; reference

Constable & Robinson Ltd
3 The Lanchesters, 162 Fulham Palace Road, London, W6 9ER (Tel: 020-8741 3663; Fax: 020-8748 7562;
Email: enquiries@constablerobinson.com)
Web: http://www.constablerobinson.com)
Type of books: Novels; history; military history; health; reference; children's

Corgi Books
61-63 Uxbridge Road, London, W5 5SA (Tel: 020-8579 2652; Fax: 020-8231 6612;
Email: info@transworld-publishers.co.uk)
Type of books: General fiction; non-fiction

Darton, Longman & Todd
1 Spencer Court, 140-142 Wandsworth High Street, London, SW18 4JJ (Tel: 020-8875 0155; Fax: 020-8875 0133; Email: mail@darton-longman-todd.co.uk)
Type of books: Religious

Andre Deutsch
76 Dean Street, London, W1V 5HA (Tel: 020-7316 4450; Fax: 020-7316 4499;
Email: dnicholson@andredeutsch.co.uk)
Type of books: Non-fiction

Doubleday
61-63 Uxbridge Road, London, W5 5SA (Tel: 020-8579 2652; Fax: 020-8579 5479;

Email: info@transworld-publishers.co.uk
Type of books: Fiction; non-fiction

Duckworth & Co.
61 Frith Street, London, W1V 5TA (Tel: 020-7434 4242; Fax: 020-7287 8092;
Web: http://www.duckw.com)
Type of books: Fiction; non-fiction; academic

Egmont Children's Books United
239 Kensington High Street, London, W8 6SA (Tel: 020-7761 3500; Fax: 020-7761 3510)
Type of books: Children's

Epworth Press
SCM Press, 9-17 St Albans Place, London, N1 0NX (Tel: 020-7359 8033; Fax: 020-7359 0049;
Email: scmpress@btinternet.com)
Type of books: Religious; theology

Everyman's Library
4th Floor, Gloucester Mansions, 140a Shaftesbury Avenue, London, WC2H 8HD (Tel: 020-7539 7600; Fax: 020-7379 4060; Email: books@everyman.uk.com)
Web: http://www.everyman.uk.com)
Type of books: Classics; pocket poets; travel guides; children's classics, chess books

Fourth Estate
6 Salem Road, London, W2 4BU (Tel: 020-7727 8993; Fax: 020-7792 3176)
Type of books: Fiction; popular science; cookery; history; biography

Samuel French
52 Fitzroy Street, London, W1P 6JR (Tel: 020-7387 9373; Fax: 020-7387 2161;
Email: theatre@samuelfrench-london.co.uk;
Web: http://www.samuelfrench-london.co.uk)
Type of books: Theatre

Robert Hale
45 Clerkenwell Green, London, EC1R 0HT (Tel: 020-7251 2661; Fax: 020-7490 4958)
Type of books: Fiction; general non-fiction

Hamish Hamilton
27 Wrights Lane, London, W8 5TZ (Tel: 020-7416 3000; Fax: 020-7416 3099;
Web: http://www.penguin.co.uk)
Type of books: Fiction; non-fiction

Herbert Press
35 Bedford Row, London, WC1R 4JH (Tel: 020-7242 0946; Fax: 020-7831 7489)
Type of books: Design; architecture; art

Kegan Paul International
PO Box 256, London, WC1B 3SW (Tel: 020-7580 5511; Fax: 020-7436 0899;
Email: books@keganpaul.demon.co.uk;
Web: http://www.demon.co.uk/keganpaul/)
Type of books: Reference; scholarly

Kingfisher
New Penderel House, 283-288 High Holborn, London, WC1V 7HZ (Tel: 020-7903 9999; Fax: 020-7242 5009)
Type of books: Children's fiction; non-fiction

Kogan Page
120 Pentonville Road, London, N1 9JN (Tel: 020-7278 0433; Fax: 020-7837 6348;
Email: kpinfo@kogan-page.co.uk;
Web: http://www.kogan-page.co.uk)
Type of books: Professional business; education

Letts Educational
Aldine House, 9-15 Aldine Street, London, W12 8AW (Tel: 020-8740 2266; Fax: 020-8743 8451;
Email: mail@lettsed.co.uk;
Web: http://www.letts-education.com)
Type of books: Educational

Frances Lincoln Limited
4 Torriano Mews, Torriano Avenue, London, NW5 2RZ (Tel: 020-7284 4009; Fax: 020-7485 0490; Email: francesl@frances-lincoln.com)
Type of books: Illustrated gardening; interiors; travel; mind, body and spirit; children's

Little, Brown & Co.
Brettenham House, Lancaster Place, London, WC2E 7EN (Tel: 020-7911 8000; Fax: 020-7911 8100; Email: email.uk@littlebrown.com)
Type of books: General fiction; non-fiction

Macmillan Publishers
25 Eccleston Place, London, SW1W 9NF (Tel: 020-7881 8000; Fax: 020-7881 8001;
Web: http://www.macmillan.com)
Type of books: All types

Methuen Publishing Limited
215 Vauxhall Bridge Road, London, SW1V 1EJ (Tel: 020-7798 1600; Fax: 020-7828 2098;
Web: http://www.methuen.co.uk)
Type of books: Literary fiction; non-fiction; travel; biography; autobiography; history; drama; humour; film; performing arts; plays

Minerva Press
6th Floor, Canberra House, 315-317 Regent Street, London, W1R 7YB (Tel: 020-7580 4114; Fax: 020-7580 9256;
Email: publicity&promotions@minerva-press.co.uk;
Web: http://www.minerva-press.co.uk)
Type of books: General

John Murray
50 Albemarle Street, London, W1X 4BD (Tel: 020-7493 4361; Fax: 020-7499 1792;
Email: johnmurray@dial.pipex.com)
Type of books: Educational; biography; travel; general history

W. W. Norton & Company
10 Coptic Street, London, WC1A 1PU (Tel: 020-7323 1579; Fax: 020-7436 4553;
Email: office@wwnorton.co.uk)
Type of books: Art and architecture; biography; business; classical studies; computer studies; current affairs; economics; history; language; literature; medicine;

238 Media London

music; nautical; philsophy; photography; politics; psychology; science; sport; leisure; travel

Michael O'Mara Books
9 Lion Yard, Tremadoc Road, London, SW4 7NQ (Tel: 020-7720 8643; Fax: 020-7627 8953; Web: http://www.michaelomarabooks.com)
Type of books: General non-fiction; history; biography; humour; children's

Orion Publishing Group
5 Upper St Martin's Lane, London, WC2H 9EA (Tel: 020-7240 3444; Fax: 020-7240 4822)
Type of books: All types

Phaidon Press Limited
Regent's Wharf, All Saints Street, London, N1 9PA (Tel: 020-7843 1000; Fax: 020-7843 1010)
Type of books: Visual arts

George Philip
2-4 Heron Quay, London, E14 4JB (Tel: 020-7531 8400; Fax: 020-7531 8464; Email: george.philip@philips-maps.co.uk; Web: http://www.philips-maps.co.uk)
Type of books: maps; atlases; astronomy guides; reference books

Piatkus Books
5 Windmill Street, London, W1P 1HF (Tel: 020-7631 0710; Fax: 020-7436 7137; Email: info@piatkus.co.uk; Web: http://www.piatkus.co.uk)
Type of books: Fiction; non-fiction

Quiller Press
46 Lillie Road, London, SW6 1TN (Tel: 020-7499 6529; Fax: 020-7381 8941; Email: greenwood@quiller.conx.uk)
Type of books: Non-fiction; sponsored

Random House Group Ltd
20 Vauxhall Bridge Road, London, SW1V 2SA (Tel: 020-840 8400; Web: http://www.randomhouse.co.uk)
Type of books: General fiction; non-fiction

Rough Guides
62-70 Shorts Gardens, London, WC2H 9AB (Tel: 020-7556 5000; Fax: 020-7556 5050; Email: mail@roughguides.co.uk; Web: http://www.roughguides.com)
Type of books: Reference; travel; music; internet

Sage Publications
6 Bonhill Street, London, EC2A 4PU (Tel: 020-7374 0645; Fax: 020-7374 8741; Email: info@sagepub.co.uk; Web: http://www.sagepub.co.uk)
Type of books: Academic; educational

Scholastic Children's Books
Commonwealth House, 1-19 New Oxford Street, London, WC1A 1NU (Tel: 020-7421 9000; Web: http://www.scholastic.co.uk)
Type of books: Children's fiction; non-fiction; picture; baby and young adult

Serpent's Tail
4 Blackstock Mews, London, N4 2BT (Tel: 020-7354 1949; Fax: 020-7704 6467; Email: info@serpentstail.com)
Type of books: Fiction; non-fiction

Severn House Publishers Ltd
9-15 Sutton High Street, Sutton, Surrey, SM1 1DF (Tel: 020-8770 3930; Fax: 020-8770 3850; Email: info@severnhouse.com) Web: http://www.severnhouse.com)
Type of books: Adult fiction

Sidgwick & Jackson
25 Eccleston Place, London, SW1W 9NF (Tel: 020-7881 8000; Fax: 020-7881 8001; Web: http://www.panmacmillan.com)
Type of books: Popular non-fiction; biography; autobiography; popular culture; history; military

Souvenir Press
43 Great Russell Street, London, WC1B 3PA (Tel: 020-7580 9307; Fax: 020-7580 5064)
Type of books: Non-fiction; fiction

SPCK - The Society for Promoting Christian Knowledge
Holy Trinity Church, Marylebone Road, London, NW1 4DU (Tel: 020-7387 5282; Fax: 020-7388 2352; Email: spck@spck.org.uk; Web: http://www.spck.org.uk)
Type of books: Religious; medica; psychological self-help

The Stationery Office Ltd
51 Nine Elms Lane, London SW8 5DR (Tel: 0870-600 5522; Fax: 0870-600 5533; Email: customer.services@theso.co.uk; Web: http://www.ukstate.com)
Type of books: Official; business; professional

Sweet & Maxwell
100 Avenue Road, London, NW3 3PF (Tel: 020-7393 7000; Web: http://sweetandmaxwell.co.uk)
Type of books: Legal

Taylor & Francis Books Ltd
11 New Fetter Lane, London, EC4P 4EE (Tel: 020-7583 0490; Fax: 020-7842 2307; Email: info@tandf.co.uk; Web: http://www.tandf.co.uk)
Type of books: Academic; professional

Thames & Hudson Ltd
181A High Holborn, London, WC1V 7QX (Tel: 020-7845 5000; Fax: 020-7845 5050; Email: mail@thameshudson.co.uk; Web: http://www.thameshudson.co.uk)
Type of books: Arts; illustrated

Transworld Publishers
61-63 Uxbridge Road, London, W5 5SA (Tel: 020-8579 2652; Fax: 020-8579 5479; Email: info@transworld-publishers.co.uk)
Type of books: General fiction; non-fiction; children's books; sports; leisure

Usborne Publishing
Usborne House, 83-85 Saffron Hill, London, EC1N 8RT (Tel: 020-7430 2800; Fax: 020-7430 1562; Email: mail@usborne.co.uk; Web: http://www.usborne.com)
Type of books: Children's

Virago Press
Brettenham House, Lancaster Place, London, WC2E 7EN (Tel: 020-7911 8000; Fax: 020-7911 8100; Email: email.uk@littlebrown.com)
Type of books: Women's issues; non-fiction; novels

Virgin Publishing
Thames Wharf Studios, Rainville Road, London, W6 9HA (Tel: 020-7386 3300; Fax: 020-7386 3360; Web: http://www.virgin-books.com)
Type of books: City guides; reference; music reference; music biography; film; TV; radio; popular culture; motoring; sports; humour; novelty

Watts Publishing Group Ltd
96 Leonard Street, London, EC2A 4XD (Tel: 020-7739 2929; Fax: 020-7739 2318; Web: http://www.wattspub.co.uk)
Type of books: Children's fiction and non-fiction

Yale University Press
23 Pond Street, London, NW3 2PN (Tel: 020-7431 4422; Fax: 020-7431 3755)
Type of books: Academic

ADVERTISING

ADVERTISING STANDARDS AUTHORITY

Brook House, 2 Torrington Place, London WC1E 7HW (Tel: 020-7580 5555)
Director-General: Christopher Graham

ADVERTISING AGENCIES

The following list comprises a selection of Advertising Agencies/Media Consultancies based in London. Due to the extremely high number of agencies we have not been able to include all of those located in London. Those listed have not been chosen under any specific criteria but are those that responded to our enquiries.

Acumen Partnership
186 Drury Lane, London, WC2B 5QD (Tel: 020-7440 4301; Fax: 020-7440 4310; E-mail: k.hurdwell@acumenpartners.co.uk; Web: http://www.acumenpartners.co.uk)
Partners: K. Hurdwell; Ms J. Lunnon; Ms G. Evans; A. King; P. Robinson; P. Stewart; S. Kelleher

The Brand Development Company Ltd
50 Long Acre, WC2E 9JR (Tel: 020-7497 9727; Fax: 020-7497 3581; E-mail: brandevo@aol.com)
Managing Director: P. Morgan

Carat International Ltd
Parker Tower, 4-49 Parker Street, WC2B 5PS (Tel: 020-7405 1050; Fax: 020-7405 1058; Web: http://www.carat.com)
Chief Operating Officer: J. Bohlman

C.G.T.
1 Fitzroy Mews, W1P 5DQ (Tel: 020-7874 5100; Fax: 020-7874 5101; E-mail: colours@c-g-t.co.uk; Web: http://www.c-g-t.co.uk)
Managing Director: J. Coleman

Citigate Albert Frank
26 Finsbury Square, EC2A 1SH (Tel: 020-7282 8000; Fax: 020-7282 8080; Web: http://www.citigate.com)
Managing Director: P. Gregory

Clarity IBD Ltd
1 Long Lane, Barbican, WC1A 9HA (Tel: 020-7397 2900; Fax: 020-7397 2939; Web: http://www.marketing.co.uk)
Managing Director: A. Skates

Clark McKay and Walpole
42-46 Weymouth Street, Marylebone, W1N 3LQ (Tel: 020-7487 9750; Fax: 020-7224 4604; E-mail: j-clark@cmw-uk.com; Web: http://www.clarkmckayandwalpole.com
Chairman: J. Clark

Craik Jones Watson Mitchell Voelkel Ltd
120 Regent Street, W1R 5FE (Tel: 020-7734 1650; Fax: 020-7734 1649; Web: www.craikjones.co.uk)
Managing Director: D. Watson

Datamail Direct Advertising Ltd (DDA Ltd)
St Johns House, 366 North End Road, Fulham, SW6 1LY (Tel: 020-7381 0222; Fax: 020-7610 1639; Web: http://www.dda.uk.com)
Managing Director: P. Jewiss

epb.communications
10 Berners Mews, W1P 3LF (Tel: 020-7462 0400; Fax: 020-7462 0401; E-mail: ken.buckfield@epbuk.com; Web: http://www.epb.com)
Managing Director: K. Buckfield

First Financial Advertising Ltd
1 Red Lion Court, EC4A 3EB (Tel: 020-7353 3444; Fax: 020-7353 6777)
Managing Director: J. Wood

Frontline Media Ltd
26 Nassau Street, W1N 7RF (Tel: 020-7436 4080; Fax: 020-7637 7022; E-mail: frontlinemedia@frontlinemedia.com)
Joint Managing Directors: P. Prince; J. Nichols

Interfocus Network Ltd
Lancer Square, Kensington, W8 4ES (Tel: 020-7376 9000; Fax: 020-7376 9090; E-mail: matthew.hooper@interfocus.co.uk; Web: http://www.interfocus.co.uk)
Managing Director: M. Hooper

Just Media Ltd
Brighton House, 9 Brighton Terrace, SW9 8DJ (Tel: 020-7737 8000; Fax: 020-7737 8080; Web: http://www.justmedia.co.uk)
Managing Director: D. Gibson

240 Media London

Lowe Lintas
Bowater House, 6-114 Knightsbridge, SW1X 7LT (Tel: 020-7584 5033; Fax: 020-7584 9557; Web: http://www.lowelintas.co.uk)
Managing Director: C. Thomas

Maher Bird Associates Ltd
Academy House, 61-167 Oxford Street, W1R 1TA (Tel: 020-7287 1718; Fax: 20-7287 0917; E-mail: stephen.maher@mba.co.uk)
Chief Executive: S. Maher

Mansfield Lang Direct Media Ltd
Heron House, 10 Dean Farrer Street, SW1H 0DX (Tel: 020-7799 9888; Fax: 020-7799 9898; Web: http://www.mldm.co.uk)
Managing Director: S. Cannaford

MBO Ltd
Jubilee House, 2 Jubilee Place, SW3 3TQ (Tel: 020-7352 1900; Fax: 020-7352 4700; E-mail: solutions@mbo.co.uk; Web: http://www.mbo.co.uk)
Managing Director: J. Taylor

Media Campaign Services Limited
20 Orange Street, WC2H 7ED (Tel: 020-7389 0800; Fax: 020-7839 6997)
Managing Director: A. Sullivan

Media Insight Limited
40 The Strand, WC2N 5HZ (Tel: 020-7969 4141; Fax: 020-7316 0241)
Managing Director: T. Jenner

Media Moguls
65-67 Wembley Hill Road, Wembley, Middx, HA9 8DP (Tel: 020-8902 5575; Fax: 020-8902 5585; E-mail: info@mediamoguls.com; Web: http://www.mediamoguls.com)
Managing Director: A. Raheja

Mediacom Direct
95 New Cavendish Street, W1M 7FR (Tel: 020-7526 1150; Fax: 020-7526 1169)
Managing Director: Ms D. Rhodes

MediaVest UK
123 Buckingham Palace Road, SW1W 9DZ (Tel: 020-7233 5678; Fax: 020-7233 5677; E-mail: robert.ray@mediavest.co.uk)
Joint Managing Directors: C. Locke; R. Ray

The Mediawise Partnership Ltd
Fairgate House, 78 New Oxford Street, WC1A 1HB (Tel: 020-7419 8800; Fax: 020-7419 8801; E-mail: mail@mediawise.co.uk; Web: http://www.mediawise.co.uk)
Managing Partners: M. Gill; M. Anderson; K Jamie

Mediacom TMB
180 North Gower Street, NW1 2NB (Tel: 020-7874 5500; Fax: 020-7874 5999; Web: http://www.mediacomtmb.com)
Joint Managing Directors: J. Ratcliffe; N. Lawson

Mustoe Merriman Herring Levy
133 Long Acre, Covent Garden, WC2E 9AG (Tel: 020-7379 9999; Fax: 020-7379 8487; Web: http://www.mmhl.co.uk)
Chief Executive: N. Mustoe

Ogilvy & Mather Ltd
10 Cabot Square, Canary Wharf, E14 4QB (Tel: 020-7345 3000; Fax: 020-7345 9030)
Chairman & CEO: P. Simons

Optimedia UK
12 Dorset Street, W1H 4DN (Tel: 020-7935 0040; Fax: 020-7486 1985; E-mail: simon.mathews@optimedia.co.uk)
Managing Director/Partner: S. Mathews

Perspectives
Swan Court, Swan Street, Old Isleworth, TW7 6RJ (Tel: 020-8568 4422; Fax: 020-8847 5482; Web: http://www.perspectives.co.uk)
Chairman and Chief Executive: J. Williams

Publicis Technology Ltd
82 Baker Street, WC1M 2AG (Tel: 020-7486 5555; Fax: 020-7486 9955; E-mail: ptadmin@ptglobal.com; Web: http://www.ptglobal.com)
Chief Executive Officer: M. Tod

Rapier Ltd
The Network Building, 97 Tottenham Court Road, W1P 9HF (Tel: 020-7369 8000; Fax: 020-7369 8010; E-mail: mblake@rapier.ltd.uk)
Chief Executive: J. Stead

Squires Robertson Gill plc
9 Cavendish Place, W1M 0BL (Tel: 020-7323 0343; Fax: 020-7580 0586; E-mail: enquiries@srgplc.co.uk)
Managing Director: N. Rive

Starcom Motive Partnership
24-27 Great Pulteney Street, W1R 3DB (Tel: 020-7453 4444; Fax: 020-7437 2401; E-mail: starcom.motive@uk.starcomworldwide.com)
Managing Director: M. Cranmer

Strattons Ltd
21-23 Ives Street, SW3 2ND (Tel: 020-7838 5000; Fax: 020-7838 5001; Web: http://www.strattons.com)
Managing Director: R. Stratton

TEAM LGM Ltd
1 Dorset Street, W1H 4BB (Tel: 020-7535 9800; Fax: 020-7535 9900; E-mail: debbie.holt@teamlgm.co.uk; Web: http://www.teamlgm.co.uk)
Managing Director: Ms D. Holt

Tequila Payne Stracey Ltd
82 Charing Cross Road, WC2H 0BA (Tel: 020-7557 6100; Fax: 020-7557 6111; Web: http://www.tequila-uk.com)
Managing Director: A. Wylie

Tullo Marshall Warren Ltd
81 Kings Road, Chelsea, SW3 4NX (Tel: 020-7349 4000; Fax: 020-7349 4001; E-mail: direct@tmw.co.uk;

Web: http://www.tmw.co.uk)
Managing Director: C. Warren

Universal McCann
McCann Erickson Hosue, 36 Howland Street, W1A 1AT (Tel: 020-7436 7711; Fax: 020-7915 8101)
Joint Managing Directors: Ms F. Smedley; C. Shaw

Walsh Trott Chick Smith
Holden House, 57 Rathbone Place, W1P 1AW (Tel: 020-7734 0050; Fax: 020-7734 1172;
E-mail: keirc@wtcs.co.uk)
Managing Director: K. Cooper

Warman and Bannister
40 Marsh Wall, E14 9TP (Tel: 020-7512 1000; Fax: 020-7512 1999; E-mail: w&b@warban.co.uk;
Web: http://www.warban.com
Joint Chief Executives: R. Warman; T. Bannister

PUBLIC RELATIONS/MEDIA CONSULTANCIES

The following list comprises a selection of Public Relations Agencies/Media Consultancies based in London. Due to the extremely high number of agencies we have not been able to include all of those located in London. Those listed have not been chosen under any specific criteria but are those that responded to our enquiries.

33 R P M
Unit 226, 28 Old Brompton Road, London, SW7 3SS (Tel: 020-7584 6622; Fax: 020-7584 1960; E-mail: pr33rpm@aol.com)
Director: R. Marshall

9 PR
65-69 White Lion Street, London, N1 9PP (Tel: 020-7833 9303; Fax: 020-7833 9322; E-mail: joe@nine-pr.demon.co.uk)
Directors: Ms J. Bland; J. Kessler

A Kevorkian Public Relations
44 Baker Street, London, W1M 1DH (Tel: 020-7935 0309; Fax: 020-7486 1416; E-mail: akprouk@aol.com)
Principal: A. Kevorkianabel

Abel Hadden & Co Ltd
15 Berkeley Street, London, W1X 5AE (Tel: 020-7629 8771; Fax: 020-7629 8772;
E-mail: central@ahadden.com;
Web: http://www.ahadden.com)
Managing Director: A. Hadden

ANA Communications Ltd
16 Berkeley Street, London, W1X 5AE (Tel: 020-7629 8118; Fax: 020-7629 8119;
E-mail: sara.rama@ana-communications.com)
Managing Director: Ms A. Nicholas

Anderson Associates (Publicity) Ltd
33 Gordon Road, Beckenham, Kent, BR3 3QF (Tel: 020-8325 1762; Fax: 020-8249 0823;
E-mail: andpub@aol.com)
Managing Director: K. Tearle

Andrea Marks Public Relations
146 Edgwarebury Lane, Edgware, Middx, HA8 8NE (Tel: 020-8958 4398; Fax: 020-8905 3727;
E-mail: andrea-marks@compuserve.com)
Managing Director: Ms A. Marks

ASAP Communications Ltd
2 Tunstall Road, London, SW9 8DA (Tel: 020-7978 9488; Fax: 020-7940 9490)
Managing Director: Ms Y. Thompson

Athena Medical PR Ltd
500 Chiswick High Road, London, W4 5RG (Tel: 020-8956 2299; Fax: 020-8956 2295;
E-mail: ampr@athenamedicalpr.co.uk;
Web: http://www.athenamedicalpr.co.uk)
Managing Director: Ms C. Slater

242 Media London

Avenue Communications
26 Ives Street, London, SE3 2ND (Tel: 020-7589 7463; Fax: 020-7584 0825; E-mail: avenue@compuserve.com)
Managing Director: Ms E. Aves

B Jane Dickson
70 Royal Hill, London, SE10 8RF (Tel: 020-8694 9056; Fax: 020-8694 9368; E-mail: bjda@compuserve.com)
Principal: Ms B. J. Dickson

Bacchus PR Ltd
13 St Barnabas Road, London, E17 8JZ (Tel: 020-8521 2010; Fax: 020-8521 2010;
E-mail: info@bacchuspr.fsbusiness.co.uk;
Web: http://www.bacchuspr.fsbusiness.co.uk)
Director: C. Deane

BCPR/Beverley Cable PR
11 St Christopher's Place, London, W1M 5HB (Tel: 020-7935 1314; Fax: 020-7935 8314;
E-mail: bcpr@dial.pipex.com)
Managing Director: Ms B. Cable

Beaumark Ltd
14 Great College Street, London, SW1P 3RX (Tel: 020-7222 1371; Fax: 020-7222 1440;
Web: http://www.beaumark.com)
Managing Director: D. Bennett

The Benchmark Agency Limited
2-4 Lambton Place, London, W11 2SH (Tel: 020-7221 9264; Fax: 020-7221 9265;
E-mail: info@benchmarkagency.com;
Web: http://www.benchmarkagency.com)
Managing Director: H. Madsen

Biddick Associates Ltd
31-35 Sun Street, London, EC2M 2PY (Tel: 020-7377 6677; Fax: 020-7377 1177;
E-mail: zoe.biddick@biddick.co.uk)
Director: Ms K. Tzouliadis

Bloomfield Turner Associates
42-44 Carter Lane, London, EC4V 5EA (Tel: 020-7248 1225; Fax: 020-7248 1228;
E-mail: info@bloomfieldturner.com;
Web: http://www.bloomfieldturner.com)
Partner: Ms C. Turner

Braben Company
18B Pindock Mews, London, W9 2PY (Tel: 020-7289 1616; Fax: 020-7289 1166;
E-mail: alison@braben.co.uk;
Web: http://www.braben.co.uk)
Managing Director: Ms S. Braben

British Design Initiative
2-4 Peterborough Mews, Parsons Green, London, SW6 3BL (Tel: 020-7384 3435; Fax: 020-7371 5343;
E-mail: initiative@britishdesign.co.uk;
Web: http://www.britishdesign.com)
Chief Executive Officer: Ms M. Horn

Brook Wilkinson Ltd
87 Notting Hill Gate, London, W11 3JZ (Tel: 020-7229 9907; Fax: 020-7229 8809;
E-mail: rbrook@brook-wilkinson.co.uk)
Chairman: Ms R. Brook

Brown Lloyd James
25 Lower Belgrave Street, London, SW1W 0NR (Tel: 020-7591 9610; Fax: 020-7591 9611;
E-mail: pr@blj.co.uk)
Chairman: Sir Nicholas Lloyd

Cairns & Associates Ltd
28-30 Ives Street, London, SW3 2ND (Tel: 020-7584 2776; Fax: 020-7584 2998;
E-masil: inforequest@cairnsassociates.co.uk)
Managing Director: Ms C. Schram

Cardew & Co
12 Suffolk Street, London, SW1Y 4HQ (Tel: 020-7930 0777; Fax: 020-7925 0647/8;
E-mail: cardew@cardew.co.uk)
Chairman: A. Cardew

Cawdell Douglas
10-11 Lower John Street, London, W1R 3PE (Tel: 020-7439 2822; Fax: 020-7287 5488;
E-mail: press@cawdelldouglas.com)
Managing Partner: Ms D. Cawdell

Charles Barker BSMG Worldwide
110 St Martin's Lane, London, WC2N 4DY (Tel: 020-7841 5555; Fax: 020-7847 5777;
E-mail: nwilliam@cbarker.bsmg.com;
Web: http://www.bsmg.com)
Chief Executive: Ms N. Williams

Coalition Group Ltd
Devonshire House, 12 Barley Mow Passage, London, W4 4PH (Tel: 020-8987 0723; Fax: 020-8987 0345;
E-mail: pr@coalitiongroup.co.uk)
Joint Managing Directors: Ms R. Fitzgerald; T. Linkin; Ms J. Acton

Colette Hill Associates Ltd
18-20 Bromells Road, London, SW4 0BG (Tel: 020-7622 8252; Fax: 020-7622 8253;
E-mail: cha@chapr.co.uk;
Web: http://www.chapr.co.uk)
Managing Director: Ms C. S. Hill

Command Communications Ltd
2-6 Curtain Road, London, EC2A 3NQ (Tel: 020-7247 4457; Fax: 020-7247 4035;
E-mail: info@command-group.ltd.uk;
Web: http://www.command-group.ltd.uk)
Managing Director: J. Nicholson

Context Communications
63 Honeybrook Road, London, SW12 0DL (Tel: 020-8675 6114; Fax: 020-8675 2516;
E-mail: carole@contextcomms.demon.co.uk)
Chief Executive Officer: Ms C. North

Cothelstone Consulting
40 Grosvenor Gardens, London, SW1W 0EB (Tel: 020-7823 5024; Fax: 020-7823 4335)
Senior Consultant: D. Hughes

Public Relations 243

Cypher Press & Promotions
Queens Studios, 117-121 Salusbury Road, London, NW6 6RG (Tel: 020-7372 4474; Fax: 020-7372 4484; E-mail: cypher@newstate.co.uk; Web: http://www.newstate.co.uk)
General Manager: S. Ward

Definite Article
Grove House, 320 Kensal Road, London, W10 5BZ (Tel: 020-8968 1331; Fax: 020-8960 1428; E-mail: info@definite.co.uk; Web: http://www.definite.co.uk)
Director: Ms B. Webb

Denmead Marketing Europe Ltd
23 Pembridge Square, London, W2 4DR (Tel: 020-7243 1040; Fax: 020-7221 1936; E-mail: pr@denmeaduk.com)
Director: Ms C. Stott

The Direct Communications Co
Rosedale House, Rosedale Road, Richmond, Surrey, TW9 2SZ (Tel: 020-8939 9040; Fax: 020-8940 9504; E-mail: dccpr@aol.com)
Managing Director: M. Kamlish

DWRC Associates Ltd
3 Catherine Place, London, SW1E 6DX (Tel: 020-7630 5122; Fax: 0870-130 8892; E-mail: dwrc@livepr.net; Web: http://www.dwrclivepr.com)
Director: R. Clarke

Eligo International Ltd
186-188 Queen's Gate, London, SW7 5HL (Tel: 020-7591 0619; Fax: 020-7225 5279; E-mail: info@eligo.net; Web: http://www.eligo.net)
Managing Director: A. J. Bailey

Ellis Kopel
16 Duncan Terrace, London, N1 8BZ (Tel: 020-7278 3633; Fax: 020-7278 3699; E-mail: e.kopel@btinternet.com)
Principal: E. Kopel

Emma Chapman Publicity
2nd Floor, 18 Great Portland Street, London, W1N 5AB (Tel: 020-7637 0990; Fax: 020-7637 0660; E-mail: emmachapmanpublicity@btinternet.com)
Company Director: Ms E. Chapman

Englender Ltd
43 South Parade, Mollison Way, HA8 5QL (Tel: 020-8952 5808; Fax: 020-8951 0190)
PR Director: G. Englender

Entrepreneur Public Relations
11A Pratt Mews, London, NW1 0AD (Tel: 020-7380 1108; Fax: 020-7388 1190; E-mail: entrepreneur@dc-inter.net)
Director: Ms K. Fardell

Euro Strategies Ltd
120 Wilton Road, London, SW1V 1JZ (Tel: 020-7828 7029; Fax: 020-7630 9198; E-mail: info@eurostrategies.co.uk; Web: http://www.eurostrategies.co.uk)
Managing Director: G. Kelly

Europhase Communications
62 Courtfield Gardens, London, SW5 0NQ (Tel: 020-7565 2584; Fax: 020-7565 2887)
Director: H. McKenna

Faust Talbot
87 Palewell Park, London, SW14 8JJ (Tel: 020-8392 1085; Fax: 020-8878 5262; E-mail: faustpr@aol.com)
Proprietor: Ms J. Faust

Financial Dynamics Ltd
Holborn Gate, 26 Southampton Buildings, London, WC2A 1PB (Tel: 020-7831 3113; Fax: 020-7831 7961; E-mail: buscom@fd.com; Web: http://www.fd.com)
Chief Executive: N. Miles

Firefly Communications Ltd
Suite 4, Unit 25, The Coda Centre, 189 Munster Road, London, SW6 6AW (Tel: 020-7386 1400; Fax: 020-7385 4768; E-mail: claire.walker@firefly.co.uk; Web: http://www.firefly.co.uk)
Managing Director: Ms C. Walker

Fisher Marketing Limited
Kingfisher House, 54 Banstead Road, Carshalton, SM5 3NW (Tel: 020-8643 0240; Fax: 020-8770 9511; E-mail: fmpr@fishermarketing.co.uk; Web: http://www.fishermarketing.co.uk)
Managing Director: J. Fisher

Flagship Consulting
140 Great Portland Street, London, W1N 5TA (Tel: 020-7299 1500; Fax: 020-7299 1550; E-mail: susanna.c@flagconsult.co.uk; Web: http://www.flagshipgroup.co.uk)
Chief Executive: Ms D. Soltmann

Food & Other Matters
58 Blythe Road, London, W14 0HA (Tel: 020-7371 6466; Fax: 020-7371 4717; E-mail: carolyn@foodmatters.co.uk)
Managing Director: Ms C. J. Cavele

G & O Public Relations
Equity House, 79 George Street, Croydon, CR0 1LD (Tel: 020-8681 1147; Fax: 020-8681 1181; E-mail: paulineyounggopr@compuserve.com)
Director: Ms P. Young

Garland International
178 Battersea Park Road, London, SW11 4ND (Tel: 020-7738 8008; Fax: 020-7498 6153; E-mail: team@garlandintl.co.uk)
Partner: D. Hewett

Gledhill-Gwyer Enterprises
Nightingale Centre, 8 Balham Hill, London, SW12 9EA (Tel: 020-8675 5343; Fax: 020-8675 8457; E-mail: barbara_gledhill@gwyer.demon.co.uk)
Chief Executive: Dr B. Gledhill

Grand Field Ltd
69 Wilson Street, London, EC2A 2BB (Tel: 020-7417 4170; Fax: 020-7417 9180; E-mail: enquiries@grand-field.com; Web: http://www.grandfield.com)
Chief Executive: C. Cook

Grant Butler Coomber
Westminster House, Kew Road, TW9 2ND (Tel: 020-8322 1922; Fax: 020-8322 1923;
E-mail: info@gbc.co.uk;
Web: http://www.grantbutlercoomber.com)
Partner: Ms J. Coomber

Hammond & Deacon Ltd
64 Linden Gardens, London, W4 2EW (Tel: 020-8994 4010; Fax: 020-8994 7808;
E-mail: mail@hammond-pr.co.uk)
Managing Director: J. Hammond

Harcourt Public Affairs Ltd
49 Whitehall, London, SW1A 2BX (Tel: 020-7839 8422; Fax: 020-7930 0037;
E-mail: harcourt.publicaffairs@virgin.net)
Managing Director: Ms C. Cawston

Hards PR
Meridian House, Royal Hill, London, SE10 8RD (Tel: 020-8293 7150; Fax: 020-8293 7050;
E-mail: general@hardspr.co.uk;
Web: http://www.hardspr.co.uk)
Managing Director: R. Hards

Harvard Centro
100 Dean Street, London, W1V 5RA (Tel: 020-7494 6100; Fax: 020-7494 6111;
E-mail: michellet@harvard.co.uk;
Web: http://www.harvard.co.uk)
Director: F. Butters

Hayes Anderson Ltd
18 Winton Avenue, London, N11 2AT (Tel: 020-8245 1010; Fax: 020-8245 2557;
E-mail: hayes@webmaker.co.uk)
Managing Director: J. Hayes

Headley Public Relations Ltd
22 Mount View Road, London, N4 4HX (Tel: 020-8348 1234; E-mail: whitakers@heritage.co.uk;
Web: http://www.heritage.co.uk/hpr
Chief Executive Officer: G. Headley

Heady Public Relations Ltd
4 Melina Road, London, W12 9HZ (Tel: 020-8743 7797; Fax: 020-8749 2498; E-mail: headypr@aol.com)
Managing Director: Ms H. Heady

Henry's House
10 Acklam Road, London, W10 5QZ (Tel: 020-8960 1462; Fax: 020-8968 9308;
E-mail: jhenry337@aol.com)
Director: J. Henry

Hillgate Public Relations
Studio E, 2 Woodstock Studios, Woodstock Grove, London, W12 8LE (Tel: 020-8749 6905; Fax: 020-8746 0562; E-mail: info@hillgatepr.co.uk)
Managing Director: Ms K. Paine

IBIKS Public Relations Ltd
Suite 13, St Lukes Enterprise Centre, 85 Tarling Road, London, E16 1HN (Tel: 020-7366 6302; Fax: 020-7366 6301; E-mail: info@ibikspr.com;
Web: http://www.ibikspr.com)
Managing Consultant: K. Thomas

Impact Publishing & Public Relations
21 Perry Vale, London, SE23 2NE (Tel: 020-8291 5724)
Chief Executive: R. Morris

Indigo Public Relations Ltd
PO Box 22530, London, W8 4GS (Tel: 020-7229 3214; Fax: 020-7727 6983; E-mail: info@indigopr.co.uk;
Web: http://www.indigopr.co.uk)
Managing Director: Ms M. Cutcliffe

Jackie Cooper Public Relations
54 Poland Street, London, W1V 3DF (Tel: 020-7287 7799; Fax: 020-7436 4527; E-mail: info@jcpr.com;
Web: http://www.jcpr.com)
Founding Partners: Ms J. Cooper; R. Phillips

Jervis Read
28-31 High Street, London, SW19 5BY (Tel: 020-8971 3355; Fax: 020-8971 3770;
E-mail: diana.r@jervisread.co.uk)
Managing Director: Ms D. Read

John D. Wood & Co Marketing Department
48 Elizabeth Street, London, SW1W 9PA (Tel: 020-7824 7909; Fax: 020-7824 7910;
E-mail: marketing@johndwood.co.uk;
Web: http://www.johndwood.co.uk)
Marketing Director: R. Page

John Kendall Associates
132 Ebury Street, London, SW1W 9QQ (Tel: 020-7824 8681; Fax: 020-7730 1390;
E-mail: mail@kendallspr.co.uk)
Managing Director: A. Kendall

Keene Public Affairs Consultants Ltd
Victory House, 99-101 Regent Street, London, W1R 7HB (Tel: 020-7287 0652; Fax: 020-7494 0493)
Managing Director: A. G. Richard

Kelso Consulting
89 Great Eastern Street, London, EC2A 3HY (Tel: 020-7729 7595; Fax: 020-7729 9409;
E-mail: jamess@kelsopr.com;
Web: http://www.kelsopr.com)
Director: T. Prizeman

Key Communications Ltd
Kings Court, 2-16 Goodge Street, London, W1P 1FF (Tel: 020-7580 0222; Fax: 020-7580 0333;
E-mail: davidw@keycommunications.co.uk;
Web: http://www.keycommunications.co.uk)
Managing Director: D. Watson

Kingfisher Public Relations Consultants Ltd
23 Rectory Grove, London, CR0 4JA (Tel: 020-8686 5602; Fax: 020-8680 3861;
E-mail: mailus@kingfisherpr.co.uk;
Web: http://www.kingfisherpr.co.uk)
Director: J. Fisher

Public Relations 245

Kinross & Render Ltd
192-198 Vauxhall Bridge Road, London, SW1V 1DX (Tel: 020-7592 3100; Fax: 020-7931 9640; E-mail: sara@kinross-and-render.co.uk; Web:http://www.kinross-and-render.co.uk)
Chief Executive Officer: Ms S. Render

Kirwin Media
21 Buckingham Street, London, WC2N 6EF (Tel: 020-7930 7003; Fax: 020-7930 4226; E-mail: office@kirwinmedia.co.uk)
Proprietor: Ms L. Kirwin

Landmark PR Ltd
23 Earls Court Square, London, SW5 9BY (Tel: 020-7835 1833; Fax: 020-7835 0192; E-mail: info@lmpr.co.uk)
Managing Director: S. Taylor

Lansons Communications
42 St John Street, London, EC1M 4DL (Tel: 020-7490 8828; Fax: 020-7490 5460; E-mail: pr@lansons.com; Web: http://www.lansons.com)
Joint Managing Directors: T. Langham; Ms C. Parsons

Launch Communications
258 Belsize Business Centre, Belsize Road, London, NW6 4BT (Tel: 020-7316 1837; Fax: 020-7316 6337; E-mail: launch@zoom.co.uk)
Managing Director: Ms K. Williams

Link Public Relations Ltd
20 Mortlake High Street, London, SW14 8JN (Tel: 020-8392 6629; Fax: 020-8392 6651; E-mail: mail@linkpr.co.uk; Web: http://www.linkpr.co.uk)
Executive Director: S. Anson

Ludgate Communications Ltd
111 Charterhouse Street, London, EC1M 6AW (Tel: 020-7253 2252; Fax: 020-7253 4717; E-mail: ali@ludgate.co.uk; Web: http://www.ludgate.co.uk)
Chief Executive: R. Hepburn

M Public Relations Ltd
Suite 13, Haybridge House, Mount Pleasant Hill, London, E5 9NB (Tel: 020-8880 0838; Fax: 020-8806 4324)
Chief Executive: Mrs K. Zanes

Macbeth Media Relations
Mountfort House, 15-16 Barnsbury Square, London, N1 1JL (Tel: 020-7700 5959; Fax: 020-7700 1329; E-mail: macbethg@btinternet.com)
Proprietor: Ms G. Macbeth

MacLaurin Group Ltd
Berghem Mews, Blythe Road, London, W14 0HN (Tel: 020-7371 3333; Fax: 020-7610 5219; E-mail: group@maclaurin.com; Web: http://www.maclaurin.com)
Chairman and Managing Director: B. MacLaurin

Marketeer PLC
2 Dolphin Square, Edensor Road, London, W4 2ST (Tel: 020-8742 3388; Fax: 020-8995 2374; E-mail: e-desk@marketeer.com.uk)
Chief Executive Officer: K. Searsby

Mason Williams
4 Kingly Street, London, W1R 5LF (Tel: 020-7439 4164; Fax: 020-7439 4165; E-mail: lesley@mason-williams.com; Web: http://www.mason-williams.co.uk)
Joint Managing Directors: Ms R. Rowe; J. Williams

Mathews & Mann Ltd
129 Portland Road, London, W11 4LW (Tel: 020-7727 7198; E-mail: marrenske@aol.com)
Managing Director: R. Mann

Max Clifford Associates Ltd
109 New Bond Street, London, W1Y 9AA (Tel: 020-7408 2350; Fax: 020-7409 2294; E-mail: max@mcapr.demon.co.uk)
Managing Director: M. Clifford

McQueen Rose Ltd
2 Fox Hill Gardens, London, SE19 2XB (Tel: 020-8653 0066; Fax: 020-8653 3524; E-mail: croserose@aol.com.uk)
Managing Director: E. M. Rose

Mega Bullet Promotions
Arch 74, Ranelagh Gardens, London, SW6 3UR (Tel: 020-7384 3222; Fax: 020-7384 3223; E-mail: soul2000@megabullet.com)
Diector: Ms M. Resen

Mercury PR
21-22 Great Castle Street, London, W1N 7AA (Tel: 020-7499 1191; Fax: 020-7629 2975; E-mail: sharong@mercurypr.co.uk)
Joint Managing Directors: Ms S. Good; Ms L. Laderman

Midas Public Relations Ltd
7-8 Kendrick Mews, London, SW7 3HG (Tel: 020-7584 7474; Fax: 020-7584 7123; E-mail: steven@midaspr.co.uk; Web: http://www.midaspr.co.uk)
Joint Managing Directors: S. Williams; T. Mulliken

Millham Communications
4 City Road, London, EC1Y 2AA (Tel: 020-7256 5756; Fax: 020-7638 7370; E-mail: millcoms@dircon.co.uk; Web: http://www.millham.co.uk)
Chairman: D. Millham

Morgan Allen Moore
104-110 Goswell Road, London, EC1V 7DH (Tel: 020-7253 0802; Fax: 020-7253 0803; Web: http://www.morganallenmoore.com)
Managing Director: S. Morgan

Mulberry Marketing Communications Ltd
1 Waterloo Court, Theed Street, London, SE1 8ST (Tel: 020-7528 7676; Fax: 020-7928 7979; E-mail: info@mulberrymc.com; Web: http://www.mulberrymc.com)
Chief Executive Officer: C. Klopper

246 Media London

Panic (Publicity) Ltd
2 Mortimer House, Furmage Street, London, SW18 4DF (Tel: 020-8871 9980; Fax: 020-8871 9949)
Managing Director: Ms G. Pascal

Patcom Media Relations
Flat 101, Globe Wharf, 205 Rotherhithe Street, London, SE16 1XX (Tel: 020-7231 9300; Fax: 020-7231 2990; E-mail: hughp@patcom-media.com; Web: http://www.patcom-media.com)
Chief Executive: H. Paterson

Peter Hope Lumley
32 Cromwell Grove, London, W6 7RG (Tel: 020-7603 5541; Fax: 020-7603 6669)
PR Consultant: P. Hope Lumley

Peter Thompson
134 Great Portland Street, London, W1N 5PH (Tel: 020-7436 5991; Fax: 020-7436 0509)
Director: P. Thompson

Phenomenon Communications Ltd
112A Sevenoaks Road, Orpington, BR6 9JZ (Tel: 01689-855073; Fax: 01689-607944; E-mail: info@phenomenon.co.uk; Web: http://www.phenomenon.co.uk)
Director: D. Owens

Philippa Perry Associates
91 Brick Lane, London, E1 6QL (Tel: 020-7247 9695; Fax: 020-7247 6069; E-mail: pnlp@dircon.co.uk)
Director: Ms P. Perry

Phoenix Public Relations
Farringdon House, 105-107 Farringdon Road, London, EC1R 3BT (Tel: 020-7833 8487; Fax: 020-7833 5726; E-mail: phoenix@legend.co.uk; Web: http://www.phoenixpr.com)
Partner: P. Leppard

Pielle Public Relations
Museum House, 25 Museum Street, London, WC1A 1PL (Tel: 020-7323 1587; Fax: 020-7631 0029; E-mail: teampielle@compuserve.com)
Executive Chairman: P. L. Walker

PIMS UK Ltd
PIMS House, Mildmay Avenue, London, N1 4RS (Tel: 020-7354 7000; Fax: 020-7354 7053; E-mail: marketing@pims.co.uk; Web: http://www.pims.co.uk)
Executive Chairman: J. Henchley

Policy Partnership Ltd
51 Causton Street, London, SW1P 4AT (Tel: 020-7976 5555; Fax: 020-7976 5353; E-mail: tpp@policypartnership.co.uk; Web: http://www.policypartnership.co.uk)
Managing Director: A. M. Smith

Polo Public Relations
30 Shrewsbury Avenue, London, SW14 8JZ (Tel: 020-8876 4242; Fax: 020-8876 8900; E-mail: info@polopr.co.uk)
Managing Director: Ms P. Lotery

Powerhouse PR Ltd
12 Berghem Mews, Blythe Road, London, W14 0HN (Tel: 020-7371 333; Fax: 020-7371 4099; E-mail: pow@maclaurinpowerhouse.com; Web: http://www.powerhousepr.com)
Managing Director: Ms V. Stace

PPS Group
69 Grosvenor Street, London, W1X 9DB (Tel: 020-7629 7377; Fax: 020-7629 7514; E-mail: sk6@ppsgroup.co.uk; Web: http://www.ppsgroup.co.uk)
Joint Managing Director: S. Byfield

PR Direct Ltd
PO Box 53, Twickenham, TW10 5EZ (Tel: 020-8878 8550; Fax: 020-8878 8559; E-mail: info@prdirect.net; Web: http://www.prdirect.net)
Director: Ms E. Boden-Lee

Presswatch Analysis Ltd
1st Floor, Chaucer House, White Hart Yard, London, SE1 1NX (Tel: 020-7403 4674; Fax: 020-7403 4673; E-mail: info@presswatch.com; Web: http://www.presswatch.com)
General Manager: R. Saunders

Republic Communications Ltd
Dudley House, 36-38 Southampton Street, London, WC2E 7HE (Tel: 020-7379 5000; Fax: 020-7379 5122; Web:http://www.republic-communications.co.uk)
Director: Ms J. Howard

Richard Franklin Associates
Redlow House, 2 Michael Road, London, SW6 2AD (Tel: 020-7736 3393; Fax: 020-7736 3775; E-mail: richard.franklinassociates@virgin.net)
Managing Director: R. Franklin

Richman & Associates (Public Relations) Ltd
2 Bloomsbury Place, London, WC1A 2QE (Tel: 020-7636 7975; Fax: 020-7436 5169; E-mail: randapr@itl.net)
Managing Director: J. K. Richman

Roche Communications
London House, 53-54 Haymarket, London, SW1Y 4RP (Tel: 020-7930 3191; Fax: 020-7930 3192)
Managing Director: R. Cohen

The Rowland Company
67-69 Whitfield Street, London, W1P 5RL (Tel: 020-7436 4060; Fax: 020-7255 2131; E-mail: richard.moss@rowland-pr.com; Web: http://www.rowland.com)
Chief Executive Officer: Ms B. Kaye

Rostron Parry Ltd
Clerkenwell House, 45-47 Clerkenwell Green, London, EC1R 0HT (Tel: 020-7490 8062; Fax: 020-7490 8063; E-mail: rpint@aol.com)
Managing Directors: S. Rostron; J. Parry

Rough House
19 First Cross Road, Twickenham, London, TW2 5QA (Tel: 020-8287 2008; Fax: 020-8287 2035;

E-mail: inquiries@roughhouse.co.uk)
Managing Director: G. Fitzgerald

Ruder Finn UK Ltd
Isis House, 74 New Oxford Street, London, WC1A 1BL (Tel: 020-7462 8900; Fax: 020-7462 8999; E-mail: mail@ruderfinn.co.uk; Web: http://www.ruderfinn.co.uk)
Managing Director: Ms A. Miles

S W C Media Services Ltd
Seedbed Business Centre, Langston Road, Loughton, Essex, IG10 3TQ (Tel: 020-8504 3389; Fax: 020-8506 1011; E-mail: contact@swcmedia.co.uk; Web: http://www.swcmedia.co.uk)
Managing Director: S. Webb

The Saltmarsh Partnership
25 Copperfield Street, London, SE1 0EN (Tel: 020-7928 1600; Fax: 020-7928 1700; E-mail: geoff@saltmarshpr.co.uk; Web: http://www.saltmarshpr.dircon.co.uk)
Managing Partner: G. Saltmarsh

Sam Weller Associates
155 Upper Street, London, N1 1RA (Tel: 020-7288 2522; Fax: 020-7288 2533; E-mail: samweller@swa-pr.co.uk)
Chief Executive: S. Weller

Shandwick Welbeck plc
43 King Street, London, WC2E 8RJ (Tel: 020-7836 6677; Fax: 020-7836 5820)
Chief Executive Officer: Ms C. Davidson

Shilland & Co
55-56 Poland Street, London, (Tel: 020-7439 2559; Fax: 020-7734 6388; E-mail: mail@shilland.co.uk)
Chief Executive: P. Shilland

Shine Communications Ltd
101 Goswell Road, London, EC1V 7ER (Tel: 020-7553 3333; Fax: 020-7553 3330; E-mail: brilliance@shinecom.com; Web: http://www.shineon-line.com)
Managing Director: Ms R. Bell

Sister Public Relations Ltd
27 Lexington Street, London, W1R 3HQ (Tel: 020-7287 9601; Fax: 020-7287 9602; E-mail: sisterpr@virgin.net)
Managing Director: Ms S. Millar

Sky Communications Ltd
The 1927 Building, London, SW6 2ER (Tel: 020-7731 6999; Fax: 020-7731 4999; E-mail: skycoms@dircon.co.uk)
Director: Ms J. Arnold

Spear Communications
36 Bruton Street, London, W1X 7DD (Tel: 020-7409 0494; Fax: 020-7409 1018; E-mail: pr@spear.uk.com)
Managing Director: Ms S. Glasgow

Starfish Communications
Oxford House, 76 Oxford Street, London, W1N 0HP (Tel: 020-7323 2121; Fax: 020-7323 0234; E-mail: speed@star-fish.net; Web: http://www.star-fish.net)
Managing Partner: J. Speed

Stratton & Reekie Public Relations Consultancy
46 Broadwick Street, London, W1V 1FF (Tel: 020-7287 8456; Fax: 020-7287 8455; E-mail: streek@dircon.co.uk)
Partner: Ms D. Stratton

The Susan Babchick Agency (Public Relations and Creatives)
34 Lexington Street, London, W1R 3HR (Tel: 020-7287 1497; Fax: 020-7439 4083; E-mail: susan@babchick.freeserve.co.uk)
Director: Ms S. Babchick

Synapse Communication Ltd
101 The Foundry Annexe, 65 Glasshill Street, London, SE1 0QR (Tel: 020-7721 8575; Fax: 020-7721 8574; E-mail: tim.lewis7@virgin.net)
Director: T. Lewis

Tavistock Communications Ltd
1 Angel Court, London, EC2R 7HX (Tel: 020-7600 2288; Fax: 020-7600 5084; Web: http://www.tavistock.co.uk)
Chairman: J. Carey

Tideway Communications
Tapestry Court, Mortlake High Street, London, SW14 8HJ (Tel: 020-8878 0787; Fax: 020-8876 2145; E-mail: tidewaycom@aol.com)
Chief Executive Officer: K. Clark

Vanbrugh Financial Communications Ltd
118 Piccadilly, London, W1V 9FJ (Tel: 020-7569 6720; Fax: 020-7569 6721; E-mail: sophie@vanbrughfinancial.com)
Managing Director: Ms S. Hull

Warrior Communications Ltd
25 Tite Street, London, SW3 4JR (Tel: 020-7352 7671; Fax: 020-7351 3217; E-mail: warriorcom@prlondon.com; Web: http://www.prlondon.com
Chief Executive: Mrs C. Hughes

WAT Public Relations
91 Brick Lane, London, E1 6QL (Tel: 07000-723 999; Fax: 07000-782 982; E-mail: info@watpr.com; Web: http://www.watpr.com
Managing Director: Ms J. Weisbasm

The Waterfront Partnership
9 Grosvenor Gardens, London, SW1W 0BD (Tel: 020-7233 7500; Fax: 020-7233 7511; E-mail: partnership@thewaterfront.co.uk)
Managing Director: N. Finney

Woodhead & Associates
39 Lilyville Road, London, SW6 5DP (Tel: 020-7610 6109; Fax: 020-7371 5450; E-mail: stategems@wpr.co.uk)
Senior Managing Partner: C. Woodhead

The Wriglesworth Consultancy
Friars House, 157-168 Blackfriars Road, London, SE1 8EZ (Tel: 020-7620 2228; Fax: 020-7620 2229; E-mail: enquiries@wriglesworth.com; Web: http://www.wriglesworth.com)
Managing Director: J. Wriglesworth

COMMUNICATIONS

TELECOMMUNICATIONS INDUSTRY

London has historically been an attractive market for many industries due to its strategic location and importance as a global player. The communications industry is no exception and although the industry is by no means London-centric, communications and technological innovation in the area have an increasing effect on Londoners, be they consumer or business users.

Compared with other world markets the UK's communications industry is relatively mature; liberalisation of service provision was introduced early and as a result an advanced range of services is available through a choice of competitive suppliers. The appeal of the industry is also reflected in the amount of inward investment attracted to each of the communications sectors.

The communications industry now encompasses fixed line telephony services, mobile telephony services, multi-channel TV, Digital TV and the Internet and where these previously operated as separate sectors; the definition between them is becoming increasingly blurred.

There are two ways in which this convergence can be tracked
- convergence between telecommunications services e.g. fixed mobile offerings
- convergence between telecommunications and other communications industries – the convergence between telecommunications and the Internet is the most notable

REGULATION

The regulation of the telecommunications industry falls under the jurisdiction of Oftel. The Radiocommunications Agency, which is part of the Department of Trade and Industry (DTI), is responsible for radio frequency allocation.

Oftel was created by the 1984 Telecommunications Act and was empowered to ensure that the UK communications industry became as competitive as possible. In order to achieve this Oftel has authority over licensing procedures, tariffing, interconnection as well as acting as an arbitrator between operators.

The policies adopted and enforced by Oftel have been largely driven by the European Commission (with the support of the Parliament and Council of Ministers) since the European Court of Justice allowed the European Commission to apply the competition rules of the Treaty of Rome to telecommunications (in 1985) and the formation of DGXIII (Telecommunications, Information Industries and Innovation) in 1986.

In general, policy has been aimed at providing access to networks and public services and guaranteeing harmonised, objective, transparent and non-discriminatory conditions based on the so called 'Open Network Provision' (ONP) principles which aim to ensure fair competition and access for new entrants. To date the Commission has addressed:

- Interconnection
New operators often construct their own long distance networks but it does not make economic sense to run a second line to every home so this last part of the network (referred to either as the 'last mile' or the 'Local Loop') is owned by the incumbent and accessed by the new entrant for a fee. Calls to fixed telephones from mobile telephone must also be routed over the Local Loop.
- Universal Service
This is the stipulation by which services must be provided to all customers irrespective of their location.
- Number Portability
This allows the customer to keep his or her telephone number even if they change service provider so the telephone number is seen to belong to the customer not the service provider. Number portability was introduced to the UK's fixed line communications industry in June 1997 and to the mobile industry in January 1999.
- Licensing
The provision of and requirements of the licensing process.
- Incumbent's Tariffs
This provision is to stop incumbent operators abusing their positions as providers of both local, national and long distance services by cross-subsidising one with another
- Cable Television Networks
Many incumbents also own Cable TV networks but EU legislation requires that cable TV networks be operated as separate legal entities

The two major pieces of legislation that have shaped the communications industry are the 1981 and the 1984 Telecommunications Acts. The former divided the General Post office (which prior to this had provided telecommunications services) into British Telecommunications and the Post Office and made provision for the introduction of competition. The latter established BT as a public limited company and created Oftel as the industry watchdog.

Since its creation, Oftel has licensed many companies to compete in the various sectors of the communications industry. These licenses are divided into the following four categories:
- PTO or Public Telecommunications Operator
- IFS or International Facilities Based Service Provider
- ISVR or International Simple Voice Reseller
- Satellite Services Provider

PTOs can provide either fixed or mobile services and will own their network (the physical infrastructure over which the call is routed). IFS providers also own infrastructure although this is limited by the nature of the services they offer i.e. international calls only. ISR providers do not own any infrastructure but buy capacity from other operators. Finally, as the name suggests, Satellite Services Providers offer satellite-based services.

Since much of the early regulation of the UK telecommunications industry was concerned with the promotion of competition, and since this has by and large been achieved in most of the sectors covered by Oftel, the regulator has announced that it intends to take a much "softer" approach to regulation in the future. In light of this Oftel's activities can broadly be divided into
- Continuing to review its current customer protection policies
- Policing the regulation of licenses
- Conducting separate twice yearly reviews of each sector - fixed, mobile, Internet access and interactive

Communications

broadcasting – to monitor for anti-competitive behaviour, excessive profits and market share

One aspect of the industry the regulator will continue to monitor closely is the development of mobile Internet access. Oftel is currently allowing operators to develop mobile Internet access services unhindered but may look again at mobile Internet access if or when it becomes a vital way of accessing information and services.

FIXED COMMUNICATIONS

The fixed line communications sector is still dominated by the ex-incumbent BT despite facing competition since 1984 when Cable & Wireless subsidiary Mercury was licensed as the UK's second fixed line operator. This duopoly existed until 1991 when further entrants were allowed.

BT now competes with new entrants in all of its core telephony areas; local, national and international calls. Since no operator can hope to take on BT in all its markets at once, competitors have tended to focus on one area in particular. The UK has witnessed the entrance of cable TV operators (e.g. TeleWest, NTL and Cable & Wireless Communications), Utilities companies who previously operated their own private networks (e.g. Energis) and broadcasting companies (e.g. BskyB) to the fixed telephony provision sector.

The emergence of strong competition in all areas of operation has meant that fixed line operators are no longer content and indeed can no longer make a strong business case in providing basic telephony connection and services. The trend is now towards the development of value added services and the convergence with other communications related industries – in particular the Internet. Fixed line operators are positioning themselves to capitalise on the growth of the Internet not just in the increase of usage through connection charges but in becoming Internet service providers themselves. Customers are looking for higher speed services at a reasonable cost and in the short to medium term operators are achieving this through the deployment of digital ISDN lines.

Oftel figures show that in 1998 there were a total of 142,897 million calls made over the UK's fixed line networks. Overall BT still retains a 74.5 per cent market share although in some sectors - most notably international business calls – its share is much weaker (39 per cent).

The strongest competitor is Cable & Wireless Communications (C&WC) who began operations in 1984, in the form of Mercury Communications. C&WC as the company stands today is the result of the merger of Cable & Wireless' UK fixed line subsidiary, Mercury, and its three cable operators Videotron, Bell Cablemedia and NYNEX. C&WC now operates in local, national and international telephony provision as well as in the cable TV sector. Despite this the operator only has an estimated 11.8 per cent share of the entire fixed line telephony market.

The various cable TV operators, who offer fixed line services account for 5 per cent and the remaining 8.7 per cent is distributed among other, mainly niche operators.

The largest market segment is the residential user group but the most profitable is the business user group whose calling pattern is during peak times i.e. during working hours, and involves more international calls.

BT still retains 82 per cent of all residential calls made but in recent years this grip in the market is weakening due to the attractive packages offered by the cable operators and other alternative operators and BT in continuing to lose ground. Residential calling patterns increasingly include Internet access calls and all of the major operators are addressing this burgeoning market either by launching ISP (Internet Service Provider) activities themselves or by partnering with existing ISPs. BT itself is taking a two-pronged approach to tackling this area by promoting its BT Highway transmission service and in offering BT Click Internet access.

The business segment is also fiercely contended. Operators here have a much larger scope for offering innovative value added services such as high speed transmission facilities, Virtual Private Networks, Internet access and so on. In this area BT is facing competition from highly specialised niche operators such as ACC Telecom, Telstra UK and COLT – even the traditionally residential focused cable operators are attracting an increasing proportion of business customers. These operators are focusing on a specific market (ACC is now the UK's leading supplier to universities) a region (COLT's business is built around its London network and offers services to the multinational corporates sited there) or simply in offering cheaper international calls to lucrative business customers (Telstra).

The result is that the provision of international calls (particularly for business users but also for residential customers) has become the most competitive segment. The barrier to entry this market is much lower as no infrastructure is required. Here BT is estimated to have an overall 64.8 per cent market share but its share for international business calls has dropped to 39.5 per cent from 57 per cent the previous year. BT hopes that its alliance with the US based AT&T which specialises in developing solutions for corporate customers will help address this area.

CABLE TV OPERATORS

Both the Telecommunications Act of 1984 and the Broadcasting Act of 1990 cover Cable TV operators. The former covers cable infrastructure while the latter covers the content of the services. The 1984 Cable and Broadcasting act established the Cable Communications Association and empowered it to grant franchises for the installation and operation cable networks. These franchises could further be licensed to provide telephony services by applying for a license from the DTI. However, the cable operators' licenses stipulate that they may provide local calls only within their franchised areas and that all national and international calls must be routed through BT or C&WC. Of the 132 franchises in the UK 129 of them offer telephony. In 1998 the cable operators passed 11 million households.

The cable industry is coming out of a period of consolidation which has left just three cable operators; C&WC, Telewest and NTL. All three have reported that the ability to offer a bundled telephony and cable TV package has improved the take up of cable services in the UK. Indeed the cable operators now have more cable telephony customers than multi-channel customers. 1998 figures released showed that there were 2.7 million multi-channel subscribers and 3.5 million cable telephony customers. They are an increasing threat to BT's dominance over the local telephony sector.

PAGING

Paging in the UK, as in many European countries, has been declining in popularity since mobile telephony has decreased in price and particularly since the uptake of pre paid mobile services and the development of Short Message Service (SMS) based applications where mobile subscribers can send text messages to one another. Many industry observers view SMS as the death knell for paging.

Currently paging services are provided by four operators; BT Mobile, Vodapage, Page One Communications and Hutchison. BT Mobile is by far the largest operator and still has over 1 million customers. It operates two brands, BT Advanced Messaging for business users and Easy Reach for private users. Vodapage is part of the Vodafone AirTouch group of operations and is the next largest with around half the number of subscribers of BT Mobile. It operates the Business Paging service and Vodazap for residential customers. Neither Page One nor Hutchison make their subscriber figures available.

SATELLITE MARKET

The Satellite Services sector offers another method of transmission of communications content, whether it is voice, TV or data. Satellite telephony itself, as promoted by the failed Iridium venture, has no future in the UK. Everything about the UK communications market is against the introduction of satellite based telephony; existing telephony services, both fixed and mobile, offer near total coverage of the UK and the pricing of satellite telephony would not be competitive in terms of airtime charges or handset cost.

Once again BT is the dominant player in the market sector. BT has two main satellite Services
- The Global Satellite Services Division which provides satellite solutions to large corporate customers and Very Small Aperture Terminal (VSAT) capability supply to BT joint ventures in Europe
- Broadcast Services which is responsible for TV uplinks for satellite news gathering services

Satellite Information Services (SIS) is the UK largest business services player in the UK. SIS core activity is in news gathering but the company has also acquired a license to interconnect with the telephone infrastructure (PSTN) which gives he possibility of simultaneous voice and broadcast signal transmission.

Other players in the satellite services sector are Kingston Satellite Services, a subsidiary of Kingston Communications and joint venture with British Aerospace and Alphameric.

Satellite broadcasting is also beginning to play its part in the communications industry. BskyB, which operates the Sky and Sky Digital brands, has a subscriber base of around 6.8 million although some of the subscribers take the service as part of a cable offering. In keeping with the general trend to convergence of communications services in the UK, BskyB announced that it would be offering international telecommunications services in November 1997 in partnership with another international reseller. While they are not expected to become a major player in the telecommunications industry as such it was a slight blow to the cable TV operators whose competitive advantage over BskyB had been the ability to offer telecommunications services in a bundled packed with multi-channel TV.

MOBILE COMMUNICATIONS

Mobile telephony services are currently provided by four operators. However a further operator is due to enter the scene in 2001 following the licensing for so called third Generation or UMTS services.

UNIVERSAL MOBILE TELECOMMUNICATIONS SYSTEM (UMTS)

The UK was the third European country to license 3G operators after Finland and Spain but was the first to auction its licenses. Auctions are not new to the European communications industry, many of the second and third entrants had to bid for their license, what is spectacular about the UK's 3G auction is the height of the bids. While industry observers has speculated that the auction might reach £4 billion, in the event a total of £22 billion was raised.

As in the fixed line communications, mobile operators are no longer content to offer connection, voice telephony and standard applications i.e. voicemail, SMS, bundled airtime and so on. Competition has driven down price and therefore revenue from the basic services and operators are now seeking to differentiate themselves by offering innovative value added services. The most important of these to date is the development of WAP applications.

CURRENT MOBILE MARKET

Operator	Ownership	Technology	Launch Date
BT Cellnet	100% BT	Tacs-900	January 1985
		GSM	January 1994
Vodafone	100% Vodafone Air-Touch	Tacs-900	January 1985
		GSM	July 1992
One2One	100% Deutsche Telekom	GSM 1800	September 1993
Orange	100% France Telekom	GSM 1800	April 1994
TIW	100% TIW	UMTS	To begin operations 2001

MARKET SHARE

	BT Cellnet	Vodafone	One2One	Orange
Total Market Share	27.6%	32%	18.4%	22%

SUBSCRIBER GROWTH

Jan 1996	Jan 1997	Jan 1998	Jan 1999	Jan 2000	April 2000
9.4%	11.7%	14.3%	22.3%	41%	46.3%

Telecommunications Companies 251

WAP, or Wireless Application Protocol is a language that allows data from the Internet to be viewed from the mobile phone. To date applications have been uninspiring, news and weather reports, sports information, horoscopes etc. but its important for the development of 3G services that subscribers accept the idea of Internet based services.

UMTS will offer subscribers much faster transfer rates (up to 2mbps is commonly quoted) which will expand the facility of the network to include full Internet browsing and streamed video content.

PUBLIC MOBILE RADIO (PMR)

There is a fifth operational national mobile network which must be mentioned in a discussion of the communications industry in the UK. Dolphin Telecom operates a national mobile network based on the TETRA standard. PMR (Public Mobile Radio) or PAMR (Public Access Mobile Radio) as it is also referred to differs from other mobile networks in its ability to allow group communication, a single user has the ability to push a button which allows him to broadcast to members of a pre-selected group. Most often PMR is used by the emergency services but the Dolphin network interconnects with the fixed network and is offered primarily to business users as the UK's fifth mobile network. However, the take up of services has been much slower than anticipated.

OFTEL

50 Ludgate Hill, London, EC4M 7JJ (Tel: 020-7634 8700; Fax: 020-7634 8943;
Web: http://www.oftel.gov.uk)

DEPARTMENT OF TRADE AND INDUSTRY (DTI)

Telecommunications Division, 151 Buckingham Palace Road, London SW1W 9SS (Tel: 020-7215 5000; Fax: 020-7215 2909)

BT

81 Newgate Street, London, EC1A 7AJ
(Tel: 020-7356 5000; Fax: 020-7356 5520; Web: http://www.bt.com)

CABLE & WIRELESS COMMUNICATIONS

26 Red Lion Square, London WC1R 4HQ (Tel: 020-7528 2000; Fax: 020-7528 2181;
Web: http://www.cwc.com)

BT CELLNET

260 Bath Road, Slough, Berkshire SL1 4DX (Tel: 01753 565 000; Fax: 01753 565 010;
Web: http://www.cellnet.co.uk)

COLT TELECOMMUNICATIONS

Bishopsgate Court, 4 Norton Folgate, London E1 6DQ (Tel: 020-7390 3900; Fax: 020-7390 3901;
Web: http://www.colt.co.uk)

ORANGE PLC

The Economist Building, 25 St James Street, London SW1A 1HA (Tel: 020-7766 1766; Fax: 020-7766 1767;
Web: http://www.orange.co.uk)

ONE2ONE

Imperial Place, Maxwell Road, Borehamwood WD6 1EA (Tel: 020-8214 2121; Fax: 020-8214 3601;
Web: http://www.one2one.co.uk)

VODAFONE GROUP

The Courtyard, 2 – 4 London Road, Newbury, Berkshire RG14 1JX (Tel: 01635 33251; Fax: 01635 45713; Web: http://www.vodafone.co.uk)

POSTAL SERVICES

THE POST OFFICE
148 Old Street, London, EC1V 9HQ (Tel: 020-7490 2888)
Responsibility for running postal services rests in the UK with the Post Office. The Post Office is comprised of three components – Parcelforce, Post Office Counters Ltd and Royal Mail. For further information on the products and services of the Post Office, contact your nearest post office. Alternatively, the main Post Office website provides information on all products and services, along with links to other useful websites.

ROYAL MAIL
Established over 350 years ago, the Royal Mail is the letters 'arm' of the Post Office and provides a number of products and services for both business and residential customers.

PARCELFORCE
Parcelforce Worldwide is the UK's leading carrier of time critical packages, parcels and freight. Parcelforce Worldwide Enquiry Centre (Tel: 0800 224466 – lines open 08.30 – 17.30 Monday – Friday); Parcelforce Worldwide Collections Centre (Tel: 0800 884422 – lines open 08.30 – 17.30 Monday to Friday). Parcelforce can also be contacted via email at parcelforce@parcelforce.co.uk

CULTURAL LONDON

HISTORY TIMELINE
ENGLISH KINGS AND QUEENS
ORDER OF SUCCESSION
ORDER OF PRECEDENCE
SCENES AND SIGHTS OF LONDON
BLUE PLAQUES
CLUBS
MUSEUMS AND GALLERIES
THEATRES
TOURISM
SPORT
CULTURAL, HISTORICAL AND RECREATIONAL ORGANISATIONS

CULTURAL LONDON

This section contains a variety of information ranging from London's history, its historic buildings, monuments, scenes and sights to leisure, sport and tourism. London has a rich and vibrant history and a wealth of places to visit and the information listed in this section provides a snapshot of London's cultural, artistic and recreational assets.

HISTORY AND HERITAGE

HISTORY TIMELINE

BC 54 – Julius Caesar lands his invasion force of five legions and 2,000 cavalry on the South Eastern Coast of England near Deal. The Celts use the Thames as their main line of defence and it is at this time that it is thought that a small Roman settlement on the Thames may have sprung up.

AD 43 – 97 years after Caesar left, the Romans mount their second invasion. During the reign of Claudius, 40,000 roman troops land in Kent and approach the Thames, which is again utilised as the main line of defence.

50 – A bridge is built across the Thames at this time and this is generally recognised as the founding of London. The first recorded name, Londinium, is Roman but is thought to be based on the earlier Celtic name Londinion. Within ten years of the Roman invasion, Londinium is a flourishing town built on two hills, seperated by the river Walbrook.

60 – Tacticus refers to London as 'filled with traders and a celebrated centre of commerce'.

61 – British tribes in the West and North oppose the roman occupation. In a revenge attack for the death of her husband the King of Iceni (a Norfolk Territory), Queen Boudicca (popularly Boadecia), marches on London. The inhabitants of London are massacred and London itself is sacked and burned before Boudicca is finally defeated and commits suicide. London survives the attack due to its established status as a port and commercial centre. The city is rebuilt in the next half century.

200 – a defensive wall is built around the whole city. It consists of a 'v' shaped ditch with 21 bastions around its perimeter. Six main fortified gateways lead out to the Roman roads. By this time London has taken over from Colchester as the capital of the region. The Basilica is built and serves as the Town Hall, Law Courts and Exchange and is larger than the Basilica in Rome.

286 – The Roman Empire is moving in to its decline. Marcus Carausius, commander of the channel fleet, mutinies and assumes the title of Emperor of Britain. His reign lasts six years when he is deposed by his lieutenant Allectus, who names himself emperor.

290 – The London mint is established

296 – Constantius Chlorus is sent by Rome to restore order and Allectus is killed.

410 – Emperor Honorius sends a warning to the people of Britain that they must make preparations to protect themselves in the future. Soon after, the Romans progressively withdraw from Britain to defend Italy. During the 6th Century the Saxons control most of England and London becomes known as Lundenwic. London continues to expand outside the city walls.

604 – St Paul's Cathedral is founded by King Aethelbert. The Christian church is revived and elements of Roman culture such as literacy and learning become important again.

834-1014 – The Danish Vikings are a constant threat to the peace and security of Saxon London and mount numerous attacks during this period which leave London in ruins. By 871 The Danes have established London as their winter settlement. They are ousted by King Alfred the Great in 886 and he re-establishes Lundenberg, within the city walls. In 980 the Vikings invade once again but London is recaptured by King Ethelred in 1014.

1016 – Ethelred is succeeded briefly by Edmund II and then by the Danish King Canute (Cnut) who is crowned King of All England. During this reign, London replaces Winchester as the capital of England.

1042 – Edward the confessor becomes king of England. Royal governance is based at Westminster during his reign and the city of London remains the commercial centre.

1065 – Westminster Abbey, rebuilt by Edward the Confessor, is consecrated.

1066 – Edward the Confessor dies. Harold II is crowned his successor but is defeated and killed at the battle of Hastings by Duke William of Normandy. William claims his right to the throne and is crowned at Westminster Abbey on the 25 December 1066 whilst standing on the grave of Edward the Confessor. William grants the city of London a charter guaranteeing to preserve the privileges it enjoyed under Edward the Confessor. Neither the Normans nor their successors the Plantagenets succeed in diluting London's autonomy.

1078 – The Building of the Tower of London is started by Gandulf, Bishop of Rochester, for William the Conqueror. Baynard's Castle is built on the river a mile west of the Tower, as is Montfichet Castle, a moated keep near Ludgate.

1077–1136 – London is destroyed by fire and requires rebuilding four times. One great fire in 1087 destroys St. Paul's Cathedral which is later rebuilt. The successor of William the Conqueror, William Rufus, is responsible for the building of the great hall at Westminster, the reinforcement of the Tower of London and the rebuilding of the Thames Bridge which was destroyed by flood.

1189 – Henry Fitz Ailwyn becomes the first Mayor of London. His term of office lasts until his death in 1212.

1195 – In the absence of Richard I (popularly 'the Lionheart'), his brother John is recognised as regent and the City of London wins the right to be recognised as an 'independent commune'.

1215 – On the 9 May, King John grants a charter to the City confirming its right to choose a Mayor by annual election. This is the foundation of the City's municipal autonomy. Twenty four aldermen begin to advise the Mayor. In later years they represent specific wards.

1348 – The Black Death, believed to have started in Dorchester takes a heavy toll on the population of London. By the end of 1349 it is thought that half of London's population had died as a result of the plague, totalling around 30,000 people.

1381 – The Peasants Revolt takes place when the city gates of London are opened to Wat Tyler's Kentish rebels. The ensuing riots culminate in the lynching of the Archbishop of London and numerous merchants and clerics. Tyler was subsequently lured to Smithfield and murdered by Mayor Walworth.

1397 – The first of Richard Whittington's four terms as Mayor begins.

1400 – London has become one of the greatest ports in Western Europe. Trading guilds such as the Merchant Adventurers promote trade abroad. In order to improve their industries, trades and craftsmen organise themselves into guilds, the successors of which remain today as the City Livery Companies.

1411 – the first Guildhall is built.

1450 – Jack Cade launches his unsuccessful rebellion against the government of Henry VI.

1515 – Major building of Dockyards and shipbuilding at Deptford and Woolwich begins.

1536 – Tudor London – Henry VIII implements the Dissolution of the Monasteries. Vast numbers of the religious buildings and treasures of London are destroyed as Londoner's enthusiastically embrace Protestantism. Also during Henry's reign the Palace of Sheen, St. James's Palace and Hampton Court Palace are constructed, creating a suburban dimension to the increasingly cramped confines of the 'Walled City'.

1558 – The reign of Elizabeth I begins, bringing a new period of growth and prosperity for London. The works of Christopher Marlowe, Ben Johnson and William Shakespeare fuel a literary renaissance.

1561 – The spire of St. Paul's Cathedral is lost when its is struck by lightning.

1574 – James Burbage designs the first purpose-built playhouse in London. Eventually built south of the River Thames at Southwark; the Globe theatre premieres many of Shakespeare's works.

1603 – King James VI of Scotland becomes James I of England and London experiences an influx of Scots. The New River Scheme introduced at this time brings a more reliable water supply to Londoners.

1605 – Guy Fawkes' plot to blow up Parliament is discovered. It is in fact an attempt to assassinate James I, who has caused discontent due to his anti-Catholic laws.

1605 – The Great Frost Fair is held on the Thames.

1664-5 – The Great Plague claims an estimated 100,000 lives at a rate of 12,000 a week. The City's cat and dog population is thought to be the source of the epidemic and is exterminated.

1666 – The Great Fire of London. Almost the entire City of London within the walls is consumed with only the Aldgate and Tower areas escaping destruction. 87 Churches, 44 Livery Company Halls and 13,200 houses are destroyed. Among the losses are St. Paul's Cathedral and the Royal Exchange.

1671 – 9,000 houses are rebuilt using bricks and mortar (timber housing is now banned). The opportunity is taken to improve the building laws and infrastructure of London's streets making it one of the safest cities in the world in structural terms.

1675-1711 – Sir Christopher Wren rebuilds St. Paul's Cathedral.

1694 – The Bank of England is founded to raise funds to conduct war against France.

1715 – The Riot Act is passed to suppress increasing numbers of disturbances in London and England generally. Its impact is limited and fails to prevent the 1743 Gin riots.

1720-1751 – Gin drinking is rife in the slum areas of London and at its height it is estimated that the amount being drunk is equivalent to 2 pints per week for every man, woman and child. This leads to increases in crime, prostitution, poverty and child mortality amongst the poor. Parliament responds to this crisis by significantly increasing the duties on Gin, successfully reducing its consumption.

1721-42 – Robert Walpole is the first politician to live at 10 Downing Street and is commonly regarded at Britain's first Prime Minister.

1760-66 – the last gates to the city and the remaining portions of the walls are demolished.

1780 – In his opposition to proposals for Catholic Emancipation, Lord George Gordon leads a crowd of 50,000 people to the House of Commons. The 'Gordon Riots' which ensue are reported to have caused the deaths of 285 rioters and the destruction of numerous Catholic Chapels and private houses.

Kings and Queens 257

1829 – Sir Robert Peel creates the Metropolitan Police Service.

1833 – 10,000 Londoners die in a cholera epidemic that leads to a law banning burials within the city boundaries.

1833 – The Horse Omnibus is sanctioned stimulating the spread of the population of London.

1837 – Queen Victoria accedes the throne.

1839 – Admiral Nelson's triumph at the Battle of Trafalgar is celebrated with the construction of Nelson's Column in Trafalgar Square.

1851 – The Great Exhibition is held in the Crystal Palace erected in Hyde Park.

1855 – The Metropolitan Board of Works is established with a remit of duties including slum clearance, building regulations, road improvements and main drainage maintenance.

1863 – The Metropolitan Railway opens the first Underground line. It runs between Paddington and Farringdon Street and consists of carriages pulled by steam engines.

1888 – London County Council (LCC) is established in the place of the Board of Works. This is the first directly elected London-wide Government body. At the turn of the century it concentrates its efforts on re-housing by building the first suburban housing estates complemented by an ever growing network of suburban railway lines.

1894 – Tower Bridge opens.

1899 – London Government Act – London is divided into 28 Boroughs. Under the LCC a two tier system of local government is sustained until 1965.

1915-18 – German Zeppelins bomb London. The first Zeppelin raid on London takes place on 31st May 1915. The raid kills 28 people and injures 60 more.

1940 – Sept 7 witnesses the first bombing campaign on London by the German Airforce (Luftwaffe). The Blitz has devastating effects with an estimated 30,000 civilians losing their lives, a further 50,000 injured and 130,000 houses destroyed.

1951 – The Festival of Britain takes place on the South Bank of the Thames, a site which will eventually become the South Bank Centre.

1956 – The Clean Air Act makes London's infamous 'pea-soupers' a thing of the past. The burning of any fuel which is not smokeless is banned.

1965 – The LCC is replaced by the Greater London Council (GLC) and larger London Boroughs are created.

1982 – The Thames Barrier is completed. It is the world's largest movable flood barrier, spanning 520 metres across the Thames at Woolwich Reach, South East London.

1986 – The GLC is abolished.

1990 – Poll Tax riots take place on the streets on London.

1994 – The Eurostar terminal is completed at Waterloo Station. It is now possible, via the Channel Tunnel, to travel by train from London to Brussels, Paris and Lille.

1997 – 6 September – Following a procession of her coffin through the streets of London, the Funeral of Diana Princess of Wales is held at Westminster Abbey.

1998 – The Government publishes a White Paper 'A Mayor and Assembly for London' on 25 March, setting out the Government's proposals for the future governance of London. In the Referendum on 7 May, 72 per cent of those who voted said 'yes' to the proposals. Every borough and the City of London voted in favour. On 3 December the Greater London Authority Bill is published.

1999 – On 11 November the Bill receives Royal Assent to become the Greater London Authority Act.

1999 – On the night of the 31 December, to celebrate the coming of the year 2000, an elaborate show is held at the newly completed Millennium Dome at Greenwich and the immense 'River of Fire' firework display is held on the Thames.

2000 – The Greater London Authority comes into power. On 4 May, Independent candidate Ken Livingstone is elected as its first Mayor.

ENGLISH KINGS AND QUEENS 927 TO 1603

HOUSES OF CERDIC AND DENMARK

Reign	
927–939	Æthelstan Son of Edward the Elder, by Ecgwynn, and grandson of Alfred Acceded to Wessex and Mercia c.924, established direct rule over Northumbria 927, effectively creating the Kingdom of England Reigned 15 years
939—946	Edmund I Born 921, son of Edward the Elder, by Eadgifu Married (1) Ælfgifu (2) Æthelflæd Killed aged 25, reigned 6 years
946–955	Eadred Son of Edward the Elder, by Eadgifu Reigned 9 years
955–959	Eadwig Born before 943, son of Edmund and Ælfgifu Married Ælfgifu Reigned 3 years

258 Cultural London

959–975	**Edgar I** Born 943, son of Edmund and Ælfgifu Married (1) Æthelflæd (2) Wulfthryth (3) Ælfthryth Died aged 32, reigned 15 years		Married Matilda, daughter of Baldwin, count of Flanders Died aged c.60, reigned 20 years
975–978	**Edward I (the Martyr)** Born c.962, son of Edgar and Æthelflæd Assassinated aged c.16, reigned 2 years	1087–1100	**William II (Rufus)** Born between 1056 and 1060, third son of William I; succeeded his father in England only Killed aged c.40, reigned 12 years
978–1016	**Æthelred (the Unready)** Born c.968/969, son of Edgar and Ælfthryth Married (1) Ælfgifu (2) Emma, daughter of Richard I, count of Normandy 1013–14 dispossessed of kingdom by Swegn Forkbeard (king of Denmark 987–1014) Died aged c.47, reigned 38 years	1100–1135	**Henry I (Beauclerk)** Born 1068, fourth son of William I Married (1) Edith or Matilda, daughter of Malcolm III of Scotland (2) Adela, daughter of Godfrey, count of Louvain Died aged 67, reigned 35 years
1016	**Edmund II (Ironside)** Born before 993, son of Æthelred and Ælfgifu Married Ealdgyth Died aged over 23, reigned 7 months (April–November)	1135–1154	**Stephen** Born not later than 1100, third son of Adela, daughter of William I, and Stephen, count of Blois Married Matilda, daughter of Eustace, count of Boulogne 1141 (February–November) held captive by adherents of Matilda, daughter of Henry I, who contested the crown until 1153 Died aged over 53, reigned 18 years
1016–1035	**Cnut (Canute)** Born c.995, son of Swegn Forkbeard, king of Denmark, and Gunhild Married (1) Ælfgifu (2) Emma, widow of Æthelred the Unready Gained submission of West Saxons 1015, Northumbrians 1016, Mercia 1016, king of all England after Edmund's death King of Denmark 1019–35, king of Norway 1028–35 Died aged c.40, reigned 19 years		**THE HOUSE OF ANJOU (PLANTAGENETS)**
		1154–1189	**Henry II (Curtmantle)** Born 1133, son of Matilda, daughter of Henry I, and Geoffrey, count of Anjou Married Eleanor, daughter of William, duke of Aquitaine, and divorced queen of Louis VII of France Died aged 56, reigned 34 years
1035–1040	**Harold I (Harefoot)** Born c.1016/17, son of Cnut and Ælfgifu Married Ælfgifu 1035 recognised as regent for himself and his brother Harthacnut; 1037 recognised as king Died aged c.23, reigned 4 years	1189–1199	**Richard I (Coeur de Lion)** Born 1157, third son of Henry II Married Berengaria, daughter of Sancho VI, king of Navarre Died aged 42, reigned 9 years
1040–1042	**Harthacnut** Born c.1018, son of Cnut and Emma Titular king of Denmark from 1028 Acknowledged king of England 1035–7 with Harold I as regent; effective king after Harold's death Died aged c.24, reigned 2 years	1199–1216	**John (Lackland)** Born 1167, fifth son of Henry II Married (1) Isabella or Avisa, daughter of William, earl of Gloucester (divorced) (2) Isabella, daughter of Aymer, count of Angoulême Died aged 48, reigned 17 years
1042–1066	**Edward II (the Confessor)** Born between 1002 and 1005, son of Æthelred the Unready and Emma Married Eadgyth, daughter of Godwine, earl of Wessex Died aged over 60, reigned 23 years	1216–1272	**Henry III** Born 1207, son of John and Isabella of Angoulême Married Eleanor, daughter of Raymond, count of Provence Died aged 65, reigned 56 years
1066	**Harold II (Godwinesson)** Born c.1020, son of Godwine, earl of Wessex, and Gytha Married (1) Eadgyth (2) Ealdgyth Killed in battle aged c.46, reigned 10 months (January–October)	1272–1307	**Edward I (Longshanks)** Born 1239, eldest son of Henry III Married (1) Eleanor, daughter of Ferdinand III, king of Castile (2) Margaret, daughter of Philip III of France Died aged 68, reigned 34 years
	THE HOUSE OF NORMANDY	1307–1327	**Edward II** Born 1284, eldest surviving son of Edward I and Eleanor Married Isabella, daughter of Philip IV of France Deposed January 1327, killed September 1327 aged 43, reigned 19 years
1066–1087	**William I (the Conqueror)** Born 1027/8, son of Robert I, duke of Normandy; obtained the Crown by conquest		

Kings and Queens

1327–1377 Edward III
Born 1312, eldest son of Edward II
Married Philippa, daughter of William, count of Hainault
Died aged 64, reigned 50 years

1377–1399 Richard II
Born 1367, son of Edward (the Black Prince), eldest son of Edward III
Married (1) Anne, daughter of Emperor Charles IV (2) Isabelle, daughter of Charles VI of France
Deposed September 1399, killed February 1400 aged 33, reigned 22 years

THE HOUSE OF LANCASTER

1399–1413 Henry IV
Born 1366, son of John of Gaunt, fourth son of Edward III, and Blanche, daughter of Henry, duke of Lancaster
Married (1) Mary, daughter of Humphrey, earl of Hereford (2) Joan, daughter of Charles, king of Navarre, and widow of John, duke of Brittany
Died aged c. 47, reigned 13 years

1413–1422 Henry V
Born 1387, eldest surviving son of Henry IV and Mary
Married Catherine, daughter of Charles VI of France
Died aged 34, reigned 9 years

1422–1471 Henry VI
Born 1421, son of Henry V
Married Margaret, daughter of René, duke of Anjou and count of Provence
Deposed March 1461, restored October 1470
Deposed April 1471, killed May 1471 aged 49, reigned 39 years

THE HOUSE OF YORK

1461–1483 Edward IV
Born 1442, eldest son of Richard of York (grandson of Edmund, fifth son of Edward III, and son of Anne, great-granddaughter of Lionel, third son of Edward III)
Married Elizabeth Woodville, daughter of Richard, Lord Rivers, and widow of Sir John Grey
Acceded March 1461, deposed October 1470, restored April 1471
Died aged 40, reigned 21 years

1483 Edward V
Born 1470, eldest son of Edward IV
Deposed June 1483, died probably July–September 1483, aged 12, reigned 2 months (April–June)

1483–1485 Richard III
Born 1452, fourth son of Richard of York
Married Anne Neville, daughter of Richard, earl of Warwick, and widow of Edward, Prince of Wales, son of Henry VI
Killed in battle aged 32, reigned 2 years

THE HOUSE OF TUDOR

1485–1509 Henry VII
Born 1457, son of Margaret Beaufort (great-granddaughter of John of Gaunt, fourth son of Edward III) and Edmund Tudor, earl of Richmond
Married Elizabeth, daughter of Edward IV
Died aged 52, reigned 23 years

1509–1547 Henry VIII
Born 1491, second son of Henry VII
Married (1) Catherine, daughter of Ferdinand II, king of Aragon, and widow of his elder brother Arthur (divorced) (2) Anne, daughter of Sir Thomas Boleyn (executed) (3) Jane, daughter of Sir John Seymour (died in childbirth) (4) Anne, daughter of John, duke of Cleves (divorced) (5) Catherine Howard, niece of the Duke of Norfolk (executed) (6) Catherine, daughter of Sir Thomas Parr and widow of Lord Latimer
Died aged 55, reigned 37 years

1547–1553 Edward VI
Born 1537, son of Henry VIII and Jane Seymour
Died aged 15, reigned 6 years

1553 Jane
Born 1537, daughter of Frances (daughter of Mary Tudor, the younger daughter of Henry VII) and Henry Grey, duke of Suffolk
Married Lord Guildford Dudley, son of the Duke of Northumberland
Deposed July 1553, executed February 1554 aged 16, reigned 14 days

1553–1558 Mary I
Born 1516, daughter of Henry VIII and Catherine of Aragon
Married Philip II of Spain
Died aged 42, reigned 5 years

1558–1603 Elizabeth I
Born 1533, daughter of Henry VIII and Anne Boleyn
Died aged 69, reigned 44 years

BRITISH KINGS AND QUEENS SINCE 1603

THE HOUSE OF STUART

1603–1625 James I (VI of Scotland)
Born 1566, son of Mary, queen of Scots (granddaughter of Margaret Tudor, elder daughter of Henry VII), and Henry Stewart, Lord Darnley
Married Anne, daughter of Frederick II of Denmark
Died aged 58, reigned 22 years

1625–1649 Charles I
Born 1600, second son of James I
Married Henrietta Maria, daughter of Henry IV of France
Executed 1649 aged 48, reigned 23 years

Commonwealth Declared 19 May 1649
1649–53 Government by a council of state

260 Cultural London

	1653–8 Oliver Cromwell, Lord Protector
	1658–9 Richard Cromwell, Lord Protector
1660–1685	**Charles II**
	Born 1630, eldest son of Charles I
	Married Catherine, daughter of John IV of Portugal
	Died aged 54, reigned 24 years
1685–1688	**James II (VII of Scotland)**
	Born 1633, second son of Charles I
	Married (1) Lady Anne Hyde, daughter of Edward, earl of Clarendon (2) Mary, daughter of Alphonso, duke of Modena
	Reign ended with flight from kingdom December 1688
	Died 1701 aged 67, reigned 3 years
	Interregnum 11 December 1688 to 12 February 1689
1689–1702	**William III**
	Born 1650, son of William II, prince of Orange, and Mary Stuart, daughter of Charles I
	Married Mary, elder daughter of James II
	Died aged 51, reigned 13 years
1689–1694	**Mary II**
	Born 1662, elder daughter of James II and Anne
	Died aged 32, reigned 5 years
1702–1714	**Anne**
	Born 1665, younger daughter of James II and Anne
	Married Prince George of Denmark, son of Frederick III of Denmark
	Died aged 49, reigned 12 years

THE HOUSE OF HANOVER

1714–1727	**George I (Elector of Hanover)**
	Born 1660, son of Sophia (daughter of Frederick, elector palatine, and Elizabeth Stuart, daughter of James I) and Ernest Augustus, elector of Hanover
	Married Sophia Dorothea, daughter of George William, duke of Lüneburg-Celle
	Died aged 67, reigned 12 years
1727–1760	**George II**
	Born 1683, son of George I
	Married Caroline, daughter of John Frederick, margrave of Brandenburg-Anspach
	Died aged 76, reigned 33 years
1760–1820	**George III**
	Born 1738, son of Frederick, eldest son of George II
	Married Charlotte, daughter of Charles Louis, duke of Mecklenburg-Strelitz
	Died aged 81, reigned 59 years
	Regency 1811–20
	Prince of Wales regent owing to the insanity of George III
1820–1830	**George IV**
	Born 1762, eldest son of George III
	Married Caroline, daughter of Charles, duke of Brunswick-Wolfenbüttel
	Died aged 67, reigned 10 years
1830–1837	**William IV**
	Born 1765, third son of George III
	Married Adelaide, daughter of George, duke of Saxe-Meiningen
	Died aged 71, reigned 7 years
1837–1901	**Victoria**
	Born 1819, daughter of Edward, fourth son of George III
	Married Prince Albert of Saxe-Coburg and Gotha
	Died aged 81, reigned 63 years

THE HOUSE OF SAXE-COBURG AND GOTHA

1901–1910	**Edward VII**
	Born 1841, eldest son of Victoria and Albert
	Married Alexandra, daughter of Christian IX of Denmark
	Died aged 68, reigned 9 years

THE HOUSE OF WINDSOR

1910–1936	**George V**
	Born 1865, second son of Edward VII
	Married Victoria Mary, daughter of Francis, duke of Teck
	Died aged 70, reigned 25 years
1936	**Edward VIII**
	Born 1894, eldest son of George V
	Married (1937) Mrs Wallis Simpson
	Abdicated 1936, died 1972 aged 77, reigned 10 months (20 January to 11 December)
1936–1952	**George VI**
	Born 1895, second son of George V
	Married Lady Elizabeth Bowes-Lyon, daughter of 14th Earl of Strathmore and Kinghorne
	Died aged 56, reigned 15 years
1952–	**Elizabeth II**
	Born 1926, elder daughter of George VI
	Married Philip, son of Prince Andrew of Greece

ORDER OF SUCCESSION

1 HRH The Prince of Wales
2 HRH Prince William of Wales
3 HRH Prince Henry of Wales
4 HRH The Duke of York
5 HRH Princess Beatrice of York
6 HRH Princess Eugenie of York
7 HRH The Earl of Wessex
8 HRH The Princess Royal
9 Peter Phillips
10 Zara Phillips
11 HRH The Princess Margaret, Countess of Snowdon
12 Viscount Linley
13 Charles Armstrong-Jones
14 Lady Sarah Chatto
15 Samuel Chatto
16 Arthur Chatto
17 HRH The Duke of Gloucester
18 Earl of Ulster
19 Lady Davina Windsor
20 Lady Rose Windsor

21 HRH The Duke of Kent
22 Baron Downpatrick
23 Lady Marina Charlotte Windsor
24 Lady Amelia Windsor
25 Lord Nicholas Windsor
26 Lady Helen Taylor
27 Columbus Taylor
28 Cassius Taylor
29 Lord Frederick Windsor
30 Lady Gabriella Windsor
31 HRH Princess Alexandra, the Hon. Lady Ogilvy
32 James Ogilvy
33 Alexander Ogilvy
34 Flora Ogilvy
35 Marina, Mrs Paul Mowatt
36 Christian Mowatt
37 Zenouska Mowatt
38 The Earl of Harewood

ORDER OF PRECEDENCE IN ENGLAND AND WALES

The Sovereign
The Prince Philip, Duke of Edinburgh
The Prince of Wales
The Sovereign's younger sons
The Sovereign's grandsons
The Sovereign's cousins
Archbishop of Canterbury
Lord High Chancellor
Archbishop of York
The Prime Minister
Lord President of the Council
Speaker of the House of Commons
Lord Privy Seal
Ambassadors and High Commissioners
Lord Great Chamberlain
Earl Marshal
Lord Steward of the Household
Lord Chamberlain of the Household
Master of the Horse
Dukes, according to their patent of creation:
(1) of England
(2) of Scotland
(3) of Great Britain
(4) of Ireland
(5) those created since the Union
Ministers and Envoys
Eldest sons of Dukes of Blood Royal
Marquesses, according to their patent of creation:
(1) of England
(2) of Scotland
(3) of Great Britain
(4) of Ireland
(5) those created since the Union
Dukes' eldest sons
Earls, according to their patent of creation:
(1) of England
(2) of Scotland
(3) of Great Britain
(4) of Ireland
(5) those created since the Union
Younger sons of Dukes of Blood Royal
Marquesses' eldest sons
Dukes' younger sons
Viscounts, according to their patent of creation:
(1) of England
(2) of Scotland
(3) of Great Britain
(4) of Ireland
(5) those created since the Union
Earls' eldest sons
Marquesses' younger sons
Bishops of London, Durham and Winchester
Other English Diocesan Bishops, according to seniority of consecration
Suffragan Bishops, according to seniority of consecration
Secretaries of State, if of the degree of a Baron
Barons, according to their patent of creation:
(1) of England
(2) of Scotland
(3) of Great Britain
(4) of Ireland
(5) those created since the Union
Treasurer of the Household
Comptroller of the Household
Vice-Chamberlain of the Household
Secretaries of State under the degree of Baron
Viscounts' eldest sons
Earls' younger sons
Barons' eldest sons
Knights of the Garter
Privy Counsellors
Chancellor of the Exchequer
Chancellor of the Duchy of Lancaster
Lord Chief Justice of England
Master of the Rolls
President of the Family Division
Vice-Chancellor
Lords Justices of Appeal
Judges of the High Court
Viscounts' younger sons
Barons' younger sons
Sons of Life Peers
Baronets, according to date of patent
Knights of the Thistle
Knights Grand Cross of the Bath
Members of the Order of Merit
Knights Grand Cross of St Michael and St George
Knights Grand Commanders of the Indian Empire
Knights Grand Cross of the Royal Victorian Order
Knights Grand Cross of the British Empire
Companions of Honour
Knights Commanders of the Bath
Knights Commanders of St Michael and St George
Knights Commanders of the Indian Empire
Knights Commanders of the Royal Victorian Order
Knights Commanders of the British Empire
Knights Bachelor
Vice-Chancellor of the County Palatine of Lancaster
Official Referees of the Supreme Court
Circuit judges and judges of the Mayor's and City of London Court
Companions of the Bath
Companions of the Star of India
Companions of St Michael and St George
Companions of the Indian Empire
Commanders of the Royal Victorian Order
Commanders of the British Empire
Companions of the Distinguished Service Order
Lieutenants of the Royal Victorian Order
Officers of the British Empire
Companions of the Imperial Service Order

262 Cultural London

Eldest sons of younger sons of Peers
Baronets' eldest sons
Eldest sons of Knights, in the same order as their fathers
Members of the Royal Victorian Order
Members of the British Empire
Younger sons of the younger sons of Peers
Baronets' younger sons
Younger sons of Knights, in the same order as their fathers
Naval, Military, Air, and other Esquires by office

Women

Women take the same rank as their husbands or as their brothers; but the daughter of a peer marrying a commoner retains her title as Lady or Honourable. Daughters of peers rank next immediately after the wives of their elder brothers, and before their younger brothers' wives. Daughters of peers marrying peers of lower degree take the same order of precedence as that of their husbands; thus the daughter of a Duke marrying a Baron becomes of the rank of Baroness only, while her sisters married to commoners retain their rank and take precedence of the Baroness. Merely official rank on the husband's part does not give any similar precedence to the wife. Peeresses in their own right take the same precedence as peers of the same rank, i.e. from their date of creation.

SCENES AND SIGHTS OF LONDON

There are quite literally thousands of things to see and do in and around London and listed below is a selection of interesting buildings, monuments and attractions.

ALEXANDRA PALACE

Alexandra Palace Way, Wood Green, London N22 7AY (Tel: 020-8365 2121; Email: alexandrapalace@dial.pipex.com; Web: http://www.alexandrapalace.com)

The Victorian Palace was severely damaged by fire in 1980 but was restored, and reopened in 1988. Alexandra Palace now provides modern facilities for exhibitions, conferences, banquets and leisure activities. There is an ice rink, open daily, a boating lake, the Phoenix Bar and a conservation area.

BARBICAN CENTRE

Silk Street, London EC2Y 8DS (Tel: 020-7638 4141; Fax: 020-7382 7270; Web: http://www.barbican.org.uk)

Owned, funded and managed by the Corporation of London, the Barbican Centre opened in 1982 and houses the 1,156-seat Barbican Theatre, a 200-seat studio theatre (The Pit), and the 1,989-seat Barbican Hall. There are also three cinemas, two art galleries, a sculpture court, a lending library, conference, trade and banqueting facilities, conservatory, shops, restaurants, cafés and bars.

BLUE PLAQUES

The Royal Society of Arts was the first organisation to erect commemorative plaques at the homes of famous people who had lived in London. The purpose of the scheme has been to draw attention to buildings of interest because of their associations with notable people. The first plaque was erected in 1867 at the birthplace of the poet Byron and 36 plaques had been erected by 1901. In 1901 the London County Council took over the blue plaques scheme. In 1965, when the scheme was taken over by the Greater London Council, there were 298 plaques in existence. By virtue of the Local Government Act 1985, responsibility for the erection and maintenance fell to English Partnerships.

The earliest surviving plaques are those for Napoleon III in King Street, St James's and John Dryden in Gerrard Street. These were erected by the Royal Society of Arts in 1875. English Heritage has a number of selection criteria when assessing the erection of a blue plaque. The criteria include that there shall be reasonable grounds for believing that the subjects are regarded as eminent by a majority of members of their profession or calling; they shall have made some important positive contribution to human welfare or happiness; they shall have had such exceptional and outstanding personalities that the well-informed passer-by immediately recognises their names; or that they deserve recognition. Proposals for the commemoration of famous people shall not be considered until they have been dead for 20 years or until the centenary of their birth, whichever is the earlier.

The list below contains details of blue plaques in London, by Borough.
Key:
B = Born at the address given
L = Lived at the address given
D = Died at the address given
W = Worked at the address given
S = Stayed at the address given

BARNET

Blake, William (1757-1827)
Old Wyldes, North End, London, NW3
S

Donat, Robert (1905-58)
8 Meadway, Hampstead Garden Suburb, London, NW11
L

Hess, Dame Myra (1890-1964)
48 Wildwood Road, London, NW11
L

Johnson, Amy (1903-41)
Vernon Court, Hendon Way, London, NW2
L

Linnell, John (1792-1882)
Old Wyldes, North End, London, NW3
L

Pick, Frank (1878-1941)
15 Wildwood Road, London, NW11
L

Relph, Harry (1851-1928)
93 Shirehall Park, London, NW4
L, D

Waugh, Evelyn (1903-66)
145 North End Road, London, NW11
L

BEXLEY

Viscount Castlereagh (1769-1822)
Loring Hall, Water Lane, North Cray, London
L, D

Morris, William (1834-96)
Red House Lane, Bexleyheath, London
L (1860-65)

BRENT

Lucan, Arthur (Arthur Towle) (1887-1954)
11 Forty Lane, Wembley, London
L

BROMLEY

Grace, W. G. (1848-1915)
Fairmount, Mottingham Lane, London, SE9
L

Kropotkin, Prince Peter (1842-1921)
6 Crescent Road, London
L

Muirhead, Alexander (1848-1920)
20 Church Road, Shortlands, London
L

CAMDEN

Baillie, Joanna (1762-1851)
Bolton House, Windmill Hill, London, NW3
L

Barnett, Dame Henrietta (1851-1936)
Heath End House, Spaniards Road, London, NW3
L

Barnett, Canon Samuel (1844-1913)
Heath End House, Spaniards Road, London, NW3
L

Bello, Andres (1781-1865)
58 Grafton Way, London, W1
L (1810)

Bergman Österberg, Martina (1849-1915)
1 Broadhurst Gardens, London, NW6
L, W

Besant, Sir Walter (1836-1901)
Frognal End, Frognal Gardens, London, NW3
L, D

Bliss, Sir Authur (1891-1975)
East Heath Lodge, 1 East Heath Road, London, NW3
L (1929-39)

Bomberg, David (1900-1957)
10 Fordwych Road, London, NW2
L, W (1928-34)

Boult, Sir Adrian (1889-1983)
78 Marlborough Mansions, Cannon Hill, London, NW6
L (1966-77)

Brailsford, Henry Noel (1873-1958)
37 Belsize Park Gardens, London, NW3
L

Brain, Dennis (1921-57)
37 Frognal, London, NW3
L

Brittain, Vera (1893-1970)
58 Doughty Street, London, WC1
L

Burne-Jones, Sir Edward C. (Coley) (1833-98)
17 Red Lion Square, London, WC1
L

Butt, Dame Clara (1873-1937)
7 Harley Road, London, NW3
L (1901-29)

Butterfield, William (1814-1900)
42 Bedford Square, London, WC1
L

Caldecott, Randolph (1846-86)
46 Great Russell Street, London, WC2
L

Carlyle, Thomas (1795-1881)
33 Ampton Street, London, WC1
L

Cavendish, Honble Henry (1731-1810)
11 Bedford Square, London, WC1
L

Cockerell, C. R. (Charles Robert) (1788-1863)
13 Chester Terrace, London, NW1
L, D

Constable, John (1776-1837)
40 Well Walk, London, NW3
L

Cruikshank, George (1792-1878)
263 Hampstead Road, London, NW1
L (1850-78)

Dale, Sir Henry (1875-1968)
Mount Vernon House, Mount Vernon, London, NW3
L

Dance, George (the younger) (1741-1825)
91 Gower Street, London, WC1
L, D

Daniell, William (1769-1837)
135 St Pancras Way, London, NW1
L, D

Darwin, Charles (1809-82)
Biological Sciences Building, University College, Gower Street, London, WC1
L (1838-42)

Delius, Frederick (1862-1934)
44 Belsize Park Gardens, London, NW3
L (1918-19)

De Miranda, Francisco (1750-1816)
58 Grafton Way, London, W1
L (1802-10)

Dickens, Charles (1812-70)
48 Doughty Street, London, WC1
L

Disraeli, Benjamin - Earl of Beaconsfield (1804-81)
22 Theobalds Road, London, WC1
B

Du Maurier, George Louis Palmella Busson (1834-96)
New Grove House, 28 Hampstead Grove, London, NW3
L (1874-95)

Du Maurier, Sir Gerald (1873-1934)
Cannon Hall, 14 Cannon Place, London, NW3
L

Du Maurier, George Louis Palmella Busson (1834-96)
91 Great Russell Street, London, WC1
L (1863-68)

Earnshaw, Thomas (1749-1829)
119 High Holborn, London, WC1
W

Eastlake, Charles (1793-1865)
7 Fitzroy Square, London, W1
L

Edwards, John Passmore (1823-1911)
51 Netherhall Gardens, London, NW3
L

Lord Eldon, John Scott (1751-1838)
6 Bedford Square, London, WC1
L

Engels, Friedrich (1820-95)
121 Regent's Park Road, London, NW1
L (1870-94)

Fabian Society
The White House, Osnaburgh Street, London, NW1

Fawcett, Dame Millicent Garrett (1847-1929)
2 Gower Street, London, WC1
L, D

Fenton, Roger (1819-69)
2 Albert Terrace, London, NW1
L

Ferrier, Kathleen (1912-53)
97 Frognal, London, NW3
L

Flinders RN, Captain Matthew (1774-1814)
56 Fitzroy Street, London, W1
L

Freud, Sigmund (1856-1939)
20 Maresfield Gardens, London, NW3
L (1938-39)

Gaitskell, Hugh (1906-63)
18 Frognal Gardens, London, NW3
L

Galsworthy, John (1867-1933)
Grove Lodge, Admiral's Walk, London, NW3
L (1918-33)

Gillies, Sir Harold (1882-1960)
71 Frognal, London, NW3
L

Greenaway, Kate (1846-1901)
39 Frognal, London, NW3
L, D

Gresley, Sir Nigel (1876-1941)
West Offices, King's Cross Station, Euston Road, London, N1
W (1923-41)

Hammond, J. L. and Barbara
Hollycot, Vale of Health, NW3
L (1906-13)

Harmsworth, Alfred - Viscount Northcliffe (1865-1922)
31 Pandora Road, London, NW6
L

Harrison, John (1693-1776)
Summit House, Red Lion Square, London, WC1
L, D

Hawkins, Sir Anthony Hope (1863-1933)
41 Bedford Square, London, WC1
L (1903-17)

Herford, Robert Travers (1860-1950)
Dr Williams's Library, 14 Gordon Square, London, WC1
L, W

Hill, KCB, Sir Rowland (1795-1879)
Royal Free Hospital, Pond Street, London, NW3
L (1849-79)

Hodgkin, Thomas (1798-1866)
35 Bedford Square, London, WC1
L

Hofmann, A. W. (1818-92)
9 Fitzroy Square, London, W1
L

Holtby, Winifred (1898-1935)
58 Doughty Street, London, WC1
L

Howard, John (176?-90)
23 Great Ormond Street, London, WC1
L

Hughes, Hugh Price (1847-1902)
8 Taviton Street, London, WC1
L, D

Huxley, Aldous (1894-1963)
16 Bracknell Gardens, London, NW3
L

Huxley, Julian (1887-1975)
16 Bracknell Gardens, London, NW3
L

Huxley, Leonard (1860-1933)
16 Bracknell Gardens, London, NW3
L

Hyndman, Henry Mayers (1842-1921)
13 Well Walk, London, NW3
L, D

Jacobs, W. W. (1863-1943)
15 Gloucester Gate, London, NW1
L

Karsavina, Tamara (1885-1978)
108 Frognal, London, NW3
L

Keats, John (1795-1821)
Keats House (Wentworth Place), Keats Grove,
London, NW3
L

Keynes, John Maynard (1883-1946)
46 Gordon Square, London, WC1
L, 1916-46

Khan, Sir Syed Ahmed (1817-98)
21 Mecklenburgh Square, London, WC1
L (1869-70)

Lambert, Constant (1905-51)
197 Albany Street, London, NW1
L (1947-51)

Laughton, Charles (1899-1962)
15 Percy Street, London, W1
L (1928-31)

Lawrence, David Herbert (1885-1930)
1 Byron Villas, Vale of Heath, London, NW3
L (1915)

Lethaby, William Richard (1857-1931)
Central School of Arts and Crafts, Southampton Row,
London, WC1

Lethaby, William Richard (1857-1931)
20 Calthorpe Street, London, WC1
L (1880-91)

Macdonald, Ramsay (1866-1937)
9 Howitt Road, London, NW3
L (1916-25)

Madox Brown, Ford (1821-93)
56 Fortess Road, London, NW5
L

Mansfield, Katherine (1888-1923)
17 East Heath Road, London, NW3
L

Marsden, William (1796-1867)
65 Lincoln's Inn Fields, London, WC2
L

Matthay, Tobias (1858-1945)
21 Arkwright Road, London, NW3
L

Maxim, Sir Hiram (1840-96)
57D Hatton Garden, London, EC1
W

Mayhew, Henry (1812-87)
55 Albany Street, London, NW1
L

Mazzini, Giuseppe (1805-72)
183 Gower Street, London, NW1
L

Mondrian, Piet Cornelis (1872-1944)
60 Parkhill Road, London, NW3
L

Morris, William (1834-96)
17 Red Lion Square, London, WC1
L (1856-96)

Murry, John Middleton (1889-1957)
17 East Heath Road, London, NW3
L

Nash, Paul (1889-1946)
Queen Alexandra Mansions, Bidborough Street,
London, WC1
L (1914-36)

Orwell, George (1903-50)
50 Lawford Road, London, NW5
L

Patmore, Coventry (1823-96)
14 Percy Street, London, W1
L (1863-64)

Pearson, Karl (1857-1936)
7 Well Road, London, NW3
L

Perceval, The Hon. Spencer (1762-1812)
59-60 Lincoln's Inn Fields, London, WC2
L

Petrie, Sir William Matthew Flinders (1853-1942)
5 Cannon Place, London, NW3
L

Polhill Bevan, Robert (1865-1925)
14 Adamson Road, London, NW3
L (1900-25)

266 Cultural London

The Pre-Raphaelite Brotherhood (1848)
7 Gower Street, London, WC1

Priestley, J. B. (1894-1984)
3 The Grove, London, N6
L

Rackham, Arthur (1867-1939)
16 Chalcot Gardens, London, NW3
L

Rizal, Dr José (1861-96)
37 Chalcot Crescent, London, NW1
L

Robinson, James (1813-62)
14 Gower Street, London, WC1
L, W

Romilly, Samuel (1757-1818)
21 Russell Square, London, WC1
L

Romney, George (1734-1802)
Holly Bush Hill, London, NW3
L

Rosetti, Christina Georgina (1830-94)
30 Torrington Square, London, WC1
L, D

Rossetti, Dante Gabriel (1828-82)
17 Red Lion Square, London, WC1
L (1851)

Roy, Ram Mohun (1772-1833)
49 Bedford Square, London, WC1
L

Salisbury, Robert Gascoyne Cecil, 3rd Marquess of (1830-1903)
21 Fitzroy Square, London, W1
L

Scott, Sir George Gilbert (1811-78)
Admiral's House, Admiral's Walk, London, NW3
L

Sharp, Cecil (1859-1924)
4 Maresfield Gardens, London, NW3
L

Shaw, George Bernard
29 Fitzroy Square, London, W1
L (1887-98)

Sickert, Walter (1860-1942)
6 Mornington Crescent, London, NW1
L, W

Sitwell, Dame Edith (1887-1964)
Greenhill, Hampstead High Street, London, NW3
L

Sloane, Sir Hans (1660-1753)
4 Bloomsbury Place, London, WC1
L (1695-1742)

Smirke, Sir Robert (1781-1867)
81 Charlotte Street, London, W1
L

Smith, Sydney (1771-1846)
14 Doughty Street, London, WC1
L

Stephen, Virginia (Virginia Woolf) (1882-1941)
29 Fitzroy Square, London, W1
L, (1907-11)

Stevens, Alfred (1817-75)
9 Eton Villas, London, NW3
L

Strachey, Lytton (1880-1932)
51 Gordon Square, London, WC1
L

Tagore, Rabindranath (1861-1941)
3 Villas on the Heath, Vale of Health, London, NW3
S (1912)

Tawney, Richard Henry (1880-1962)
21 Mecklenburgh Square, London, WC1
L

Thomas, Dylan (1914-53)
54 Delancey Street, London, NW1
L

Turner, Charles (1774-1857)
56 Warren Street, London, W1
L

Vane, Sir Harry (the younger) (1612-62)
Vane House, Rosslyn Hill, London, NW3
L

Ventris, Michael (1922-56)
19 North End, London, NW3
L

Von Hugel, Baron Friedrich (1852-1925)
4 Holford Road, London, NW3
L (1882-1903)

Wakley, Thomas (1795-1862)
35 Bedford Square, London, WC1
L

Webb, Beatrice (1858-1943)
10 Netherhall Gardens, London, NW3
L

Webb, Sidney (1859-1947)
10 Netherall Gardens, London, NW3
L

Wellcome, Sir Henry (1853-1936)
6 Gloucester Gate, London, NW1
L

Willan, Dr Robert (1757-1812)
10 Bloomsbury Square, London, WC1
L

Willis, 'Father' Henry (1812-1901)
9 Rochester Terrace, London, NW1
L

Wood, Sir Henry (1869-1944)
4 Elsworth Road, London, NW3
L

Wyatt, Thomas Henry (1807-80)
77 Great Russell Street, London, WC1
L, D

Yeats, William Butler (1865-1939)
23 Fitzroy Road, London, NW1
L

CITY

Labour Party
Caroone House, Farringdon Street, London, EC4

CROYDON

Coleridge-Taylor, Samuel (1875-1912)
30 Dagnall Park, London, SE25
L

Conan Doyle, Sir Arthur (1859-1930)
12 Tennison Road, London, SE25
L (1891-4)

Creed, Frederick George (1871-1957)
20 Outram Road, Addiscombe, London
L, D

Horniman, Frederick John (1835-1906)
Coombe Cliff Centre, Coombe Road, Croydon, London
L

Horniman, John (1803-93)
Coombe Cliff Centre, Coombe Road, Croydon, London
L

Stanley, W. F. R. (1829-1909)
Stanley Halls, 12 South Norwood Hill, London, SE25

Wallace, Alfred Russel (1823-1913)
44 St Peter's Road, London
L

Zola, Emile (1840-1902)
Queen's Hotel, 122 Church Road, London, SE19
L (1898-99)

EALING

Blumlein, Alan Dower (1903-42)
37 The Ridings, London, W5
L

ENFIELD

Lamb, Charles (1775-1834)
Lamb's Cottage, Church Street, London, N9
L

Lamb, Mary (1764-1847)
Lamb's Cottage, Church Street, London, N9
L

Whitaker, Joseph (1820-95)
White Lodge, Silver Street, Enfield, London
L, D

GREENWICH

Barlow, William Henry (1812-1902)
Highcombe, 145 Charlton Road, London, SE7
L, D

Chesterfield, Philip - 4th Earl of (1694-1773)
Rangers House, Chesterfield Walk, London, SE10
L

Day-Lewis, C. (1904-72)
6 Crooms Hill, London, SE10
L (1957-72)

Dyson, Sir Frank (1868-1939)
6 Vanbrugh Hill, London, SE3
L (1894-1906)

Eddington OM, Sir Arthur (1882-1944)
4 Bennett Park, London, SE3
L

Gounod, Charles (1818-93)
15 Morden Road, London, SE3
S (1870)

Hawthorne, Nathaniel (1804-64)
4 Pond Road, London, SE3
S (1856)

Jefferies, Richard (1848-87)
59 Footscray Road, London, SE29
L

McGill, Donald (1875-1962)
5 Bennett Park, London, SE3
L

The Rachel McMillan College
Creek Road, London, SE8
L

Morrison, Herbert - Lord Morrison of Lambeth (1888-1965)
55 Archery Road, London, SE9
L (1929-60)

Svevo, Italo (1861-1928)
67 Charlton Church Lane, London, SE7
L (1903-13)

Waugh, Benejamin (1839-1908)
26 Croom's Hill, London, SE10
L

Wolfe, General James (1727-59)
Macartney House, Greenwich Park, London, SE10
L

268 Cultural London

Wolseley, Garnet, 1st Viscount (1833-1913)
Rangers House, Chesterfield Walk, London, SE10
L

HACKNEY

Defoe, Daniel (1661-1731)
95 Stoke Newington Church Street, London, N16
L

Gosse, Sir Edmund (1849-1928)
56 Mortimer Road, London, N1

Gosse, Philip Henry (1810-88)
56 Mortimer Road, London, N1
L

Howard, Ebenezer (1850-1928)
50 Durley Road, London, N16
L

Lloyd, Marie (1870-1922)
55 Graham Road, London, E8
L

Priestley, Joseph (1733-1804)
Ram Place, London, E9

Priory of St John the Baptist, Holywell
86-88 Curtain Road, London, EC2

HAMMERSMITH & FULHAM

Brangwyn, Sir Frank (1867-1956)
Temple Lodge, 51 Queen Caroline Street, London, W6
L

Cobden-Sanderson, Thomas James (1840-1922)
15 Upper Mall, London, W6
L, D

Coleridge, Samuel Taylor (1772-1834)
7 Addison Bridge Place, London, W14
L

Devine, George (1910-66)
9 Lower Mall, London, W6
L

Elgar, Sir Edward (1857-1934)
51 Avonmore Road, London, W14
L (1890-91)

Gandhi, Mahatma (1869-1948)
20 Baron's Court Road, London, W14
L

Gaudier-Brzeska, Henri (1891-1915)
454 Fulham Road, London, SW6
L

The Goossens Family
70 Edith Road, London, W14

Haggard, Sir Henry Rider (1856-1925)
69 Gunterstone Road, London, W14
L (1885-88)

Herbert, Sir Alan (1890-1971)
12 Hammersmith Terrace, London, W6
L, D

Johnston, Edward (1872-1944)
3 Hammersmith Terrace, London, W6
L (1905-12)

Laski, Harold (1893-1950)
5 Addison Bridge Place, London, W14
L (1926-50)

Ouida (Maria Louisa de la Ramée) (1839-1908)
11 Ravenscourt Square, London, W6
L

Pissarro, Lucien (1863-1944)
27 Stamford Brook Road, London, W6
L

Ravilious, Eric (1903-42)
48 Upper Mall, London, W6
L (1931-35)

Short, Sir Frank (1857-1945)
56 Brook Green, London, W6
L

The Silver Studio
84 Brook Green Road, London, W6

Silver, Arthur (1853-86)
84 Brook Green Road, London, W6
L

Silver, Harry (1881-1971)
84 Brook Green Road, London, W6
L

Silver, Rex (1879-1965)
84 Brook Green Road, London, W6
L

Walker, Sir Emery (1851-1933)
7 Hammersmith Terrace, London, W6
L (1903-33)

Whall, Christopher Whitworth (1849-1924)
19 Ravenscourt Road, London, W6
L

HARINGEY

Housman, A. E. (1859-1936)
17 North Road, London, N6
L

Kingsley, Mary (1862-1900)
22 Southwood Lane, London, N6
L

Savarkar, Vinayak Damodar (1883-1966)
65 Cromwell Avenue, London, N6
L

Waley, Arthur (1889-1966)
50 Southwood Lane, London, N6
L, D

HARROW

Ballantyne, R. M. (1825-94)
Duneaves, Mount Park Road, London
L

Heath Robinson, W. (1872-1944)
75 Moss Lane, Pinner, London
L

Shaw, R. Norman
Grims Dyke, Old Redding, Harrow Weald, London

HOUNSLOW

Forster, E. M. (1879-1970)
Arlington Park Mansions, Sutton Lane, Turnham Green, London, W4
L

Pope, Alexander (1688-1744)
Mawson Arms PH, 110 Chiswick Lane South, London, W4
L (1716-19)

Zoffany, Johann (1733-1810)
65 Strand-on-the-Green, London, W4
L (1790-1810)

ISLINGTON

Caslon, William (1692-1766)
21-23 Chiswell Street, London, EC1

Chamberlain, Joseph (1836-1914)
25 Highbury Place, London, N5
L

Chisholm, Caroline (1808-77)
32 Charlton Place, London, N1
L

Collins Music Hall
10-11 Islington Green, London, N1

Grimaldi, Joseph (1778-1837)
56 Exmouth Market, London, EC1
L (1818-28)

Groom, John (1845-1919)
8 Sekforde Street, London, EC1
L

Irving, Edward (1792-1834)
4 Claremont Square, London, N1
L

Lamb, Charles 'Elia' (1775-1834)
64 Duncan Terrace, London, N1
L

Leybourne, George (1824-1884)
136 Englefield Road, London, N1
L, D

Macneice, Louis (1907-63)
52 Canonbury Park South, London, N1
L (1947-52)

Phelps, Samuel (1804-78)
8 Canonbury Square, London, N1
L

Shepherd, Thomas Hosmer (1793-1864)
26 Batchelor Street, London, N1
L

Wesley, John (1703-91)
47 City Road, London, EC1
L

KENSINGTON & CHELSEA

Alexander, Sir George (1858-1918)
57 Pont Street, London, SW1
L

Allenby, Field Marshal Viscount Edmund Henry Hynman (1861-1936)
24 Wetherby Gardens, London, SW5
L

Arnold, Sir Edwin (1832-1904)
31 Bolton Gardens, London, SW5
L, D

Astafieva, Princess Seraphine (1876-1934)
152 King's Road, London, SW3
L, W

Baden-Powell, Robert (1857-1941)
9 Hyde Park Gate, London, SW7
L

Bagnold, Enid (1889-1981)
29 Hyde Park Gate, London, SW7
L

Bartók, Béla (1881-1945)
7 Sydney Place, London, SW7
S

Beerbohm, Sir Max (1872-1956)
57 Palace Gardens Terrace, London, W8
B

Belloc, Hilaire (1870-1953)
104 Cheyne Walk, London, SW10
L (1900-05)

Bennett, Arnold (1867-1931)
75 Cadogan Square, London, SW1
L

Benson, E. F. (1867-1940)
25 Brompton Square, London, SW3
L

Bonar Law, Andrew (1858-1923)
24 Onslow Gardens, London, SW7
L

Booth, Charles (1840-1916)
6 Grenville Place, London, SW7
L

270 Cultural London

Borrow, George (1803-81)
22 Hereford Square, London, SW7
L

Bridge, Frank (1879-1941)
4 Bedford Gardens, London, W8
L

Brunel, Isambard Kingdom (1806-59)
98 Cheyne Walk, London, SW10
L

Brunel, Sir Marc Isambard (1769-1849)
98 Cheyne Walk, London, SW10
L

Burne-Jones, Sir Edward (1833-98)
41 Kensington Square, London, W8
L (1865-79)

Carlile, Prebendary Wilson (1847-1942)
34 Sheffield Terrace, London, W8
L

Carter, Howard (1874-1939)
19 Collingham Gardens, London, SW5
L

Chelsea China (1745-1784)
16 Lawrence Street, London, SW3

Chesterton, Gilbert Keith (1874-1936)
11 Warwick Gardens, London, W14
L

Chevalier, Albert (1861-1923)
17 St Ann's Villas, London, W11
B

Churchill KG, Sir Winston (1874-1965)
28 Hyde Park Gate, Kensington Gore, London, SW7
L, D

Clementi, Muzio (1752-1832)
128 Kensington Church Street, London, W8
L

Cole, Sir Henry (1808-82)
33 Thurloe Square, London, SW7
L

Compton-Burnett, Dame Ivy (1884-1969)
5 Braemar Mansions, Cornwall Gardens, London, SW7
L (1934-69)

Crane, Walter (1845-1915)
13 Holland Street, London, W8
L

Cripps, Sir Stafford (1899-1952)
32 Elm Park Gardens, London, SW10
B

Crookes, Sir William (1832-1919)
7 Kensington Park Gardens, London, W11
L

Daniell, Thomas (1749-1840)
14 Earls Terrace, London, W8
L

De Morgan, Evelyn (1855-1919)
127 Old Church Street, London, SW3
L, D

De Morgan, William (1839-1917)
127 Old Church Street, London, SW3
L, D

Dickinson, Goldsworth Lowes (1862-1932)
11 Edwardes Square, London, W8

Dilke, Sir Charles Wentworth (1843-1911)
76 Sloane Street, London, SW1
L

Dobson, Frank (1886-1963)
14 Harley Gardens, London, SW10
L

Dobson, Henry Austin (1840-1921)
10 Redcliffe Street, London, SW10
L

Eliot, George (Mary Ann Cross née Evans) (1819-80)
4 Cheyne Walk, London, SW3
D

Eliot, OM, T. S. (1888-1965)
3 Kensington Court Gardens, London, W8
L, D

Fildes, Sir Samuel Luke (1844-1927)
31 Melbury Road, London, W14
L (1878-1927)

Fitzroy, Admiral Robert (1805-65)
38 Onslow Square, London, SW7
L

Fleming, Sir Alexander (1881-1955)
20A Danvers Street, London, SW3
L

Forbes, Vivian (1891-1937)
Lansdowne House, 80 Lansdowne Road, London, W11
L, W

Ford, Ford Madox (1873-1939)
80 Campden Hill Road, London, W8
L

Fortune, Robert (1812-80)
9 Gilston Road, London, SW10
L (1857-80)

Foscolo, Ugo (1778-1827)
19 Edwardes Square, London, W8
L (1817-8)

Franklin, Rosalind (1920-58)
Donovan Court, Drayton Gardens, London, SW10
L (1951-58)

Freake, Sir Charles James (1814-84)
21 Cromwell Road, London, SW7
L

Froude, James Anthony (1818-94)
5 Onslow Gardens, London, SW7
L

Gaskell, Mrs Elizabeth Cleghorn (1810-65)
93 Cheyne Walk, London, SW10
B

Gilbert, Sir W. S. (William Schwenck) (1836-1911)
39 Harrington Gardens, London, SW7
L

Gissing, George (1857-1903)
33 Oakley Gardens, London, SW3
L (1882-84)

Godwin, George (1813-88)
24 Alexander Square, London, SW3
L

Grahame, Kenneth (1859-1932)
16 Phillimore Place, London, W8
L (1901-08)

Grainger, Percy (1882-1961)
31 King's Road, London, SW3
L

Greaves, Walter (1846-1930)
104 Cheyne Walk, London, SW10
L, (1855-97)

Hall, Radclyffe (1880-1943)
37 Holland Street, London, W8
L (1924-29)

Hansom, Joseph Aloysius (1803-1882)
27 Sumner Place, London, SW7
L

Hitchcock, Sir Alfred (1899-1980)
153 Cromwell Road, London, SW5
L, (1926-39)

Holman-Hunt OM, William (1827-1910)
18 Melbury Road, London, W14
L, D

Hudson, W. H. (William Henry) (1841-1922)
40 St Luke's Road, London, W11
L, D

Hunt, James Henry Leigh (1784-1859)
22 Upper Cheyne Row, London, SW3
L

Ireland, John (1879-1962)
14 Gunter Grove, London, SW10
L

James, Henry (1843-1916)
34 De Vere Gardens, London, W8
L (1886-1902)

Earl Jellicoe OM, Admiral of the Fleet (1859-1935)
25 Draycott Place, London, SW3
L

Jinnah, Mohammed Ali (Quaid i Azam) (1876-1948)
35 Russell Road, London, W14
S (1895)

John, Augustus (1878-1961)
28 Mallord Street, London, SW3

Jordan, Mrs Dorothy (née Bland) (1762-1816)
30 Cadogan Place, London, SW1
L

Joyce, James (1882-1941)
28 Campden Grove, London, W8
L (1931)

Kingsley, Charles (1819-75)
56 Old Church Street, London, SW3
L

Kossuth, Louis (1802-94)
39 Chepstow Villas, London, W11
S

Lang, Andrew (1844-1912)
1 Marloes Road, London, W8
L (1876-1912)

Langtry, Lillie (1852-1929)
Cadogan Hotel, 21 Pont Street, London, SW1
L

Lavery, Sir John (1856-1941)
5 Cromwell Place, London, SW7
L (1899-1940)

Lecky, W. E. H. (William Edward Hartpole) (1838-1903)
38 Onslow Gardens, London, SW7
L, D

Lord Leighton, Frederick (1830-96)
Leighton House, 12 Holland Park Road, London, W14
L, D

Lewis, Percy Wyndham (1882-1957)
61 Palace Gardens Terrace, London, W8
L

Lind, Jenny (Madame Goldschmidt) (1820-87)
189 Old Brompton Road, London, SW7
L

Low, Sir David (1891-1963)
Melbury Court, Kensington High Street, London, W8
L

Lord Macaulay, Thomas Babington (1800-59)
Holly Lodge (now Atkins Buildings, Queen Elizabeth College), Campden Hill, London, W8
L

Mallarme, Stephane (1842-98)
6 Brompton Square, London, SW3
S (1863)

Maxwell, James Clerk (1831-79)
16 Palace Gardens Terrace, London, W8
L

May, Phil (1864-1903)
20 Holland Park Road, London, W14
L, W

Meredith OM, George (1828-1909)
7 Hobury Street, London, SW10
L

Mill, John Stuart (1806-73)
18 Kensington Square, London, W8
L

Millais, Bt., PRA, Sir John Everett (1829-96)
2 Palace Gate, London, W8
L, D

Milne, A. A. (1882-1956)
13 Mallord Street, London, SW3
L

Monckton Copeman, Sydney (1862-1947)
57 Redcliffe Gardens, London, SW10
L

Morgan, Charles (1894-1958)
16 Campden Hill Square, London, W8
L, D

Nehru, Jawaharlal (1889-1964)
60 Elgin Crescent, London, W11
L (1910-12)

Newbolt, Sir Henry (1862-1938)
29 Campden Hill Road, London, W8
L

Orpen, Sir William (1878-1931)
8 South Bolton Gardens, London, SW5
L

Palmer, Samuel (1805-81)
6 Douro Place, London, W8
L, 1851-61

Pankhurst, Sylvia (1882-1960)
120 Cheyne Walk, London, SW10
L

Parry, Sir Charles Hubert (1848-1918)
17 Kensington Square, London, W8
L

Peake, Mervyn (1911-68)
1 Drayton Gardens, London, SW10
L, 1960-68

Philpot, Glyn (1863-1937)
Lansdowne House, Lansdowne Road, W11
L, W

Place, Francis (1771-1854)
21 Brompton Square, London, SW3
L (1833-51)

Playfair, Sir Nigel (1874-1934)
26 Pelham Crescent, London, SW7
L

Pryde, James (1866-1941)
Lansdowne House, 80 Lansdowne Road, London, W11
L, W

Rambert, Dame Marie (1888-1982)
19 Campden Hill Gardens, London, W8
L

Ricketts, Charles (1866-1931)
Lansdowne House, 80 Lansdowne Road, London, W11
L, W

Marquess of Ripon, George Frederick Samuel Robinson (1827-1909)
9 Chelsea Embankment, London, SW3
L

Robinson, F. Cayley (1862-1927)
Lansdowne House, 80 Lansdowne Road, London, W11
L, W

Rossetti, Dante Gabriel (1828-82)
16 Cheyne Walk, London, SW3
L

Sargent, Sir Malcolm (1895-1967)
Albert Hall Mansions, Kensington Gore, London, SW7
L, D

Sartorius, John F. (c. 1775-c.1830)
155 Old Church Street, London, SW3
L (1807-12)

Sassoon, Siegfried (1886-1967)
23 Campden Hill Square, London, W8
L (1925-32)

Scott, Captain Robert Falcon (1868-1912)
56 Oakley Street, London, SW3
L

Shannon, Charles (1863-1937)
Lansdowne House, Lansdowne Road, London, W11
L, W

Sibelius, Jean (1865-1957)
15 Gloucester Walk, London, W8
L (1909)

Simon, Sir John (1816-1904)
40 Kensington Square, London, W8
L

Sloane, Sir Hans (1660-1753)
Kings Mead, King's Road, London, SW3

Smollett, Tobias (1721-71)
16 Lawrence Street, London, SW3
L (1750-62)

Stanford, Sir Charles (1852-1924)
56 Hornton Street, London, W8
L (1894-1916)

Staunton, Howard (1810-74)
117 Lansdowne Road, London, W11
L (1871-74)

Steer, Philip Wilson (1860-1942)
109 Cheyne Walk, London, SW10
L, D

Stephen, Sir Leslie (1832-1904)
22 Hyde Park Gate, London, SW7
L

Stoker, Bram (1847-1912)
18 St Leonard's Terrace, London, SW3
L

Stone, Marcus (1840-1921)
8 Melbury Road, London, W14
L (1877-1921)

Stuart, John McDouall (1815-66)
9 Campden Hill Square, London, W8
L, D

Swinburne, Algernon Charles (1837-1909)
16 Cheyne Walk, London, SW3
L

Terry, Dame Ellen (1847-1928)
22 Barkston Gardens, London, SW5
L

Thackeray, William Makepeace (1811-63)
2 Palace Green, London, W8
L

Thackeray, William Makepeace (1811-63)
16 Young Street, London, W8
L

Thackeray, William Makepeace (1811-63)
36 Onslow Square, London, SW7
L (1854-62)

Thompson, Sir Benjamin - Count Rumford (1753-1814)
168 Brompton Road, London, SW3
L

Thorndike, Dame Sybil (1882-1976)
6 Carlyle Square, London, SW3
L (1921-32)

Thornycroft, Sir Hamo (1850-1925)
2A Melbury Road, London, W14
L

Tree, Sir Herbert Beerbohm (1853-1917)
31 Rosary Gardens, London, SW7
L

Twain, Mark (Samuel Langhorne Clemens) (1835-1910)
23 Tedworth Square, London, SW3
L (1896-97)

Tweed, John (1863-1933)
108 Cheyne Walk, London, SW10
L

Underhill, Evelyn (1875-1941)
50 Campden Hill Square, London, W8
L (1907-39)

Warlock, Peter, Philip Arnold Hesseltine (1894-1930)
30 Tite Street, London, SW3
L

Weizmann, Chaim (1874-1952)
67 Addison Road, London, W14
L

Whistler, James Abbot McNeil (1834-1903)
96 Cheyne Walk, London, SW10
L

Wilberforce, William (1759-1833)
44 Cadogan Place, London, SW1
D

Wilde, Oscar O'Flahertie Wills (1854-1900)
34 Tite Strteet, London, SW3
L

KINGSTON UPON THAMES

Blyton, Enid (1897-1968)
207 Hook Road, Chessington, London
L (1920-24)

LAMBETH

Barry, Sir Charles (1795-1860)
The Elms, Clapham Common North Side, London, SW4
L, D

Bax, Sir Arnold (1883-1953)
13 Pendennis Road, London, SW16
B

Baylis, Lilian (1874-1937)
27 Stockwell Park Road, London, SW9
L, D

Bentley, John Francis (1839-1902)
43 Old Town, London, SW4
L

Bligh, William (1754-1817)
100 Lambeth Road, London, SE1
L

The County Hall
Main Entrance, County Hall, London, SE1

Cox, David (1783-59)
34 Foxley Road, London, London, SW9
L

274 Cultural London

Ellis, Henry Havelock (1859-1939)
14 Dover Mansions, Canterbury Crescent, London, SW9
L

Greet, Sir Philip Ben (1857-1936)
160 Lambeth Road, London, SE1
L (1920-36)

Henderson, Arthur (1863-1935)
13 Rodenhurst Road, London, SW4
L

Hobbs, Jack (1882-1963)
17 Englewood Road, London, SW12
L

Leno, Dan (1860-1904)
56 Akerman Road, London, SW9
L (1898-1901)

Macaulay, Thomas Babington (later Lord Macaulay) (1800-59)
5 The Pavement, London, SW4
L

Macaulay, Zachary (1768-1838)
5 The Pavement, London, SW4
L

Mee, Arthur (1875-1943)
27 Lanercost Road, London, SW2
L

Montgomery, Field Marshal - Vicount of Alamein (1887-1976)
Oval House, 52-54 Kennington Oval, London, SE11
B

Ruskin, John (1819-1900)
26 Herne Hill, London, SE24
L

Szabo GC, Violette (1921-45)
18 Burnley Road, London, SW9
L

Van Gogh, Vincent (1834-90)
87 Hackford Road, London, SW9
L (1873-74)

Wilberforce, William
Holy Trinity Church, Clapham Common, London, SW4

LEWISHAM

Baird, John Logie (1888-1946)
3 Crescent Wood Road, London, SE26
L

Flecker, James Elroy (1884-1915)
9 Gilmore Road, London, SE13
B

Glaisher, James (1809-1903)
20 Dartmouth Hill, London, SE10
L

The Horniman Museum and Gardens
London Road, London, SE23

Ross, Sir James Clark (1800-62)
2 Eliot Place, London, SE3
L

Shackleton, Sir Ernest Henry (1874-1922)
12 Westwood Hill, London, SE26
L

Smiles, Samuel (1812-1904)
11 Granville Park, London, SE13
L

Tallis, John (1816-76)
233 New Cross Road, London, SE14
L

Unwin, Sir Stanley (1884-1968)
13 Handen Road, London, SE12
B

Wallace, Edgar (1875-1932)
6 Tressillian Crescent, London, SE4
L

MERTON

Graves, Robert (1895-1985)
1 Lauriston Road, London, SW19
B

Innes, John (1829-1904)
Manor House, Watery Lane, London, SW20
L

NEWHAM

Thorne, Will (1857-1946)
1 Lawrence Road, London, E13
L

REDBRIDGE

Attlee, Richard Clement (1883-1976)
17 Monkhams Avenue, Woodford Green, London
L

Mansbridge, Albert (1876-1952)
198 Windsor Road, Ilford. London
L

RICHMOND

Fielding, Henry (1707-54)
Milbourne House, Barnes Green, London, SW13
L

Newman, John Henry (1801-90)
Grey Court, Ham Street, Ham. London

Schwitters, Kurt (1887-1948)
39 Westmoreland Road, London, SW13
L

Turner RA, J. M. W. (1775-1851)
40 Sandycombe Road, Twickenham, London
L

Woolf, Leonard and Virginia
Hogarth House, Paradise Road, London
L

RICHMOND UPON THAMES

Beard, John (c.1717-91)
Hampton Branch Library, Rose Hill, Hampton, London
L

Chadwick, Sir Edwin (1801-90)
5 Montague Road, Richmond, London
L

Coward, Sir Noël (1899-1973)
131 Waldegrave Road, Teddington, London

de la Mare, Walter (1873-1956)
South End House, Montpelier Row, Twickenham, London
L (1940-56)

Ewart, William (1798-1869)
Hampton Branch Library, Rose Hill, Hampton, London
L

Garrick, David (1717-79)
Garrick's Villa, Hampton Court Road, London
L

Hughes, Arthur (1832-1915)
Eastside House, 22 Kew Green, Richmond, London
L, D

O'Higgins, Bernardo (1778-1842)
Clarence House, 2 The Vineyard, Richmond, London
L

Wren, Sir Christopher (1632-1723)
The Old Court House, Hampton Court Green, East Molesey, London
L

SOUTHWARK

Besant, Annie (1847-1933)
39 Colby Road, London, SE19
L (1874)

Chamberlain, Joseph (1836-1914)
188 Camberwell Grove, London, SE5
L

Drysdale, Dr Charles Vickery (1874-1961)
153A East Street, London, SE17

Forester, C. S. (1899-1966)
50 Underhill Road, London, SE22
L

Karloff, Boris (1887-1969)
36 Forest Hill Road, London, SE22
B

Moody, Dr Harold (1882-1947)
164 Queen's Road, London, SE15
L, W

Myers, George (1803-75)
131 St George's Road, London, SE1
L (1842-53)

Oliver, Percy Lane (1878-1944)
5 Colyton Road, London, SE22
L, W

Rohmer, Sax, Arthur Henry Ward (1883-1959)
51 Herne Hill, London, SE24
L

SUTTON

White, William Hale (Mark Rutherford) (1831-1913)
19 Park Hill, Carshalton, London
L

TOWER HAMLETS

Barnardo, Dr Thomas John (1845-1905)
58 Solent House, Ben Jonson Road, London, E1

Borough, Stephen (1525-85)
King Edward Memorial Park, Shadwell, London, E1

Borough, William (1536-99)
King Edward Memorial Park, Shadwell, London, E1

Bradlaugh, Charles (1833-91)
29 Turner Street, London, E1
L (1870-77)

Cavell, Edith (1865-1915)
London Hospital, London, E1
W (1896-1901)

Clayton, Revd. P. T. B. 'Tubby' (1885-1972)
43 Trinity Square, London, EC3
L

Cook, Captain James (1728-79)
88 Mile End Road, London, E1
L

Flanagan, Bud (1896-1968)
12 Hanbury Street, London, E1
B

Flying Bomb
Railway Bridge, Grove Road, London, E3

Frobisher, Sir Martin (1535-94)
King Edward Memorial Park, Shadwell, London, E1

Gandhi, Mahatma (1869-1948)
Kingsley Hall, Powis Road, London, E3
S (1931)

Garthwaite, Anna Maria (1690-1763)
2 Princelet Street, London, E1
L, W

276 Cultural London

Gertler, Mark (1891-1939)
32 Elder Street, London, E1
L

The Great Eastern (Launched 1858)
Burrells Wharf, 262 West Ferry Road, London, E14

Green, John Richard (1837-83)
St Philip's Vicarage, Newark Street, London, E1
L (1866-69)

Groser, Revd St John (1890-1966)
Royal Foundation of St Katharine, 2 Butcher Row, London, E14
L

Hughes, Mary (1860-1941)
71 Vallance Road, London, E2
L, W (1926-41)

Mallon CH, Dr Jimmy (1874-1961)
Toynbee Hall, Commercial Street, London, E1
L

Rosenberg, Isaac (1890-1918)
Whitechapel Library, 77 High Street, London, E1

Strype Street
10 Leyden Street, London, E1

Wainwright, Lincoln Stanhope (1847-1929)
Clergy House, Wapping Lane, London, E1
L (1884-1929)

Willoughby, Sir Hugh (d. 1554)
King Edward Memorial Park, Shadwell, London, E1

Zangwill, Israel (1864-1926)
288 Old Ford Road, London, E2
L

WALTHAM FOREST

Hilton, James (1900-54)
42 Oakhill Gardens, London
L

Plaatje, Sol (1876-1932)
25 Carnarvon Road, London, E10
L

Roe, Alliott Verdon
Railway arches at Walthamstow Marsh Railway Viaduct, Walthamstow Marshes, London, E17

WANDSWORTH

Bateman, H. M. (1887-1970)
40 Nightingale Lane, London, SW12
L (1910-14)

Benes, Dr Edward (1884-1948)
26 Gwendolen Avenue, London, SW15
L

Burns, John (1858-1943)
110 North Side, Clapham Common, London, SW4
L

Douglas, Norman (1868-1952)
63 Albany Mansions, Albert Bridge Road, London, SW11
L

Elen, Gus (1862-1940)
3 Thurleigh Avenue, London, SW12
L

Eliot, George (Mary Ann Cross) (1819-80)
Holly Lodge, 31 Wimbledon Park Road, London, SW18
L

Hardy, Thomas (1840-1928)
172 Trinity Road, London, SW17
L (1878-81)

Henty, G. A. (George Alfred) (1832-1902)
33 Lavender Gardens, London, SW11
L

Hopkins, Gerard Manley (1844-89)
Gatepost at Manresa House, Holybourne Avenue, London, SW15
L

Knee, Fred (1868-1914)
24 Sugden Road, London, SW11
L

Lauder, Sir Harry (1870-1950)
46 Longley Road, London, SW17
L (1903-11)

Lloyd George, David (1865-1945)
3 Routh Road, London, SW18
L

Oates, Captain Lawrence (1880-1912)
309 Upper Richmond Road, London, SW15
L

O'Casey, Sean (1880-1964)
49 Overstrand Mansions, Prince of Wales Drive, London, SW11
L

Sargeant Jagger, Charles (1885-1934)
67 Albert Bridge Road, London, SW11
L, D

Saunders, Sir Edwin (1814-1901)
Fairlawns, 89 Wimbledon Parkside, London, SW19
L, D

Spurgeon, Charles Haddon (1834-92)
99 Nightingale Lane, London, SW12
L

Swinburne, Algernon Charles (1837-1909)
11 Putney Hill, London, SW15
L, D

Tate, Harry (Ronald MacDonald Hutchison) (1872-1940)
72 Longley Road, London, SW17
L

Thomas, Edward (1878-1917)
61 Shelgate Road, London, SW11
L

Walter, John (1739-1812)
113 Clapham Common North Side, London, SW4
L

Watts-Dunton, Theodore (1832-1914)
11 Putney Hill, London, SW15
L, D

Wilberforce, William (1759-1833)
111 Broomwood Road, London, SW11
L

Wilson, Edward Adrian (1872-1912)
Battersea Vicarage, 42 Vicarage Crescent, London, SW11
L

WESTMINISTER

Asquith, Herbert Henry - 1st Earl of Oxford and Asquith (1852-1928)
20 Cavendish Square, London, W1
L

Roberts, Earl Fredrick Sleigh (1832-1914)
47 Portland Place, London, W1
L

Ada, Countess of Lovelace (1815-52)
12 St James's Square, London, SW1
L

Adam, Robert (1728-82)
1-3 Robert Street, London, WC2
L

Adelphi Terrace
The Adelphi, London, WC2

Alma-Tadema OM, Sir Laurence (1886-1912)
44 Grove End Road, London, NW8
L (1886-1912)

Arkwright, Sir Richard (1732-92)
8 Adam Street, London, WC2
L

Arne, Thomas (1710-78)
31 King Street, London, WC2
L

Arnold, Matthew (1822-88)
2 Chester Square, London, SW1
L

Lord Ashfield, Albert Henry Stanley (1874-1948)
43 South Street, London, W1
L

Astor, Nancy (1879-1964)
4 St James's Square, London, SW1
L

Baron Avebury, Sir John Lubbock (1834-1913)
29 Eaton Place, London, SW1
B

Bagehot, Walter (1826-77)
12 Upper Belgrave Street, London, SW1
L

Baird, John Logie (1888-1946)
22 Frith Street, London, W1

Bairnsfather, Bruce (1888-1959)
1 Sterling Street, off Montpelier Square, London, SW7
L

Balfe, Michael William (1808-70)
12 Seymour Street, London, W1
L

Banks, Sir Joseph (1743-1820)
32 Soho Square, London, W1
L

Baring, Evelyn - 1st Earl of Cromer (1841-1917)
36 Wimpole Street, London, W1
L, D

Barrie, Sir James (1860-1937)
1-3 Robert Street, London, WC2

Barrie, Sir James (1860-1937)
100 Bayswater Road, London, W2
L

Basevi, George (1794-1845)
17 Savile Row, London, W1

Bazalgette, Sir Joseph William (1819-91)
17 Hamilton Terrace, London, NW8
L

Beardsley, Aubrey (1872-98)
114 Cambridge Street, London, SW1
L

Beatty OM, Earl David (1871-1936)
Hanover Lodge, Outer Circle, London, NW1
L

Beaufort, Sir Francis (1774-1857)
51 Manchester Street, London, W1

Beecham CH, Sir Thomas (1879-1961)
31 Grove End Road, London, NW8
L

Benedict, Sir Julius (1804-85)
2 Manchester Square, London, W1
L

Ben-Gurion, David (1886-1973)
75 Warrington Crescent, London, W9
L

Bentham, George (1800-84)
25 Wilton Place, London, SW1
L

Berlioz, Hector (1803-69)
58 Queen Anne Street, London, W1
S (1851)

Lady Bonham Carter, Violet - Baroness Asquith of Yarnbury (1887-1969)
43 Gloucester Square, London, W2

Boswell, James (1740-95)
122 Great Portland Street, London, W1
L, D

Bridgeman, Charles
54 Broadwick Street, London, W1
L (1723-38)

Bridgeman, Sir Orlando (c.1606-74)
Essex Hall, Essex Street, London, WC2
L

Bright, Richard (1789-1858)
11 Savile Row, London, W1
L

Brooke, Sir Charles Vyner (1874-1963)
13 Albion Street, London, W2
L

Browning, Elizabeth Barrett (1806-61)
99 Gloucester Place, London, W1
L

Browning, Elizabeth Barrett (1806-61)
50 Wimpole Street, London, W1
L (1838-46)

Brown, Robert (1773-1858)
32 Soho Square, London, W1
L

Brummell, Beau (1778-1840)
4 Chesterfield Street, London, W1
L

Burgoyne, General John (1722-92)
10 Hertford Street, London, W1
L, D

Burke, Edmund (1729-97)
37 Gerrard Street, London, W1
L

Burnett, Frances Hodgson (1849-1924)
63 Portland Place, London, W1
L

Burney, Fanny (Madam D'Arblay) (1752-1840)
11 Bolton Street, London, W1
L

Campbell, Colen (1676-1729)
76 Brook Street, London, W1
L, D

Campbell-Bannerman, Sir Henry (1836-1908)
6 Grosvenor Place, London, SW1
L

Canal, Antonio (Canaletto) (1697-1768)
41 Beak Street, London, W1
L

Canning, George (1770-1827)
50 Berkeley Square, London, W1
L

Cato Street Conspiracy
1A Cato Street, London, W1

Cayley, Sir George (1773-1857)
20 Hertford Street, London, W1
L

Cecil, Viscount of Chelwood (1864-1958)
16 South Eaton Place, London, SW1
L

Chamberlain, Neville (1869-1940)
37 Eaton Square, London, SW1
L (1923-35)

Chippendale, Thomas
61 St Martin's Lane, London, WC2
W (1753-1813)

Chopin, Frederic (1810-49)
4 St James's Place, London, SW1

Churchill, Lord Randolph (1849-95)
2 Connaught Place, London, W2
L (1883-92)

Clarkson, Willy (1861-1934)
41-43 Wardour Street, London, W1
L, D

Lord Clive of India (1725-74)
45 Berkeley Square, London, W1
L

Cobden, Richard (1804-65)
23 Suffolk Street, London, SW1
D

Cochrane, Thomas - Earl of Dundonald (1775-1860)
Hanover Lodge, Outer Circle, London, NW1
L

Coleridge, Samuel Taylor (1772-1834)
71 Berners Street, London, W1
B

Collins, William Wilkie (1824-89)
65 Gloucester Place, London, W1
L

Blue Plaques 279

Conrad, Joseph (1857-1924)
17 Gillingham Street, London, SW1
L

Cons, Emma (1837-1912
136 Seymour Place, London, W1
L

Crosby, Brass (1725-93)
Essex Hall, Essex Street, London, WC2
L

Cubitt, Thomas (1788-1855)
3 Lyall Street, London, SW1
L

Curzon, George Nathaniel - Marquess Curzon of Kedleston (1859-1925)
1 Carlton House Terrace, London, SW1
L

Dadd, Richard (1817-86)
15 Suffolk Street, London, SW1
L

Davies, Emily (1830-1921)
17 Cunningham Place, London, NW8
L

De Gaulle, General Charles
4 Carlton Gardens, London, SW1

De Quincey, Thomas (1785-1859)
36 Tavistock Street, London, WC2

Disraeli, Benjamin - Earl of Beaconsfield (1804-81)
19 Curzon Street, London, W1
D

Don, David (1800-41)
32 Soho Square, London, W1
L

Dryden, John (1631-1700)
43 Gerrard Street, London, W1
L

Etty, William (1787-1849)
14 Buckingham Street, London, WC2
L

Evans, Dame Edith (1888-1976)
109 Ebury Street, London, SW1
L

Ewart, William (1798-1869)
16 Eaton Place, London, SW1
L

Faraday, Michael (1791-1867)
48 Blandford Street, London, W1
W

Fielding, Henry (1707-54)
Essex Hall, Essex Street, London, WC2
L

Fielding, Henry (1707-54)
19-20 Bow Street, London, WC2
L

Fielding, Sir John (d.1780)
19-20 Bow Street, London, WC2
L

Lord Fisher OM, Admiral of the Fleet (1841-1920)
16 Queen Anne's Gate, London, SW1
L (1905-10)

Flaxman, John (1755-1826)
7 Greenwell Street, London, W1
L, D

Fleming, Ian (1908-64)
22 Ebury Street, London, SW1
L

Fleming, Sir Ambrose (1849-1945)
9 Clifton Gardens, London, W9
L

Fox, Charles James (1749-1806)
46 Clarges Street, London, W1
L

Frampton, George (1860-1928)
32 Queen's Grove, London, NW8
L, W (1894-1908)

Franklin, Benjamin (1706-90)
36 Craven Street, London, WC2
L

Friese-Greene, William Edward (1855-1921)
136 Maida Vale, London, W9
L

Frith, W. P. (1819-1909)
114 Clifton Hill, London, NW8
L, D

Fuseli, Henry (1741-1825)
37 Foley Street, London, W1
L (1788-1803)

Gage, Thomas (1721-87)
41 Portland Place, London, W1
L

Gainsborough, Thomas (1727-88)
82 Pall Mall, London, SW1
L

Galsworthy, John (1867-1933)
1-3 Robert Street, London, WC2
L

Galton, Sir Francis (1822-1911)
42 Rutland Gate, London, SW7
L

Garrett Anderson, Elizabeth (1836-1917)
20 Upper Berkeley Street, London, W1
L

Gibbon, Edward (1737-92)
7 Bentinck Street, London, W1
L (1773-83)

Gibbons, Grinling (1648-1721)
19-20 Bow Street, London, WC2
L

Gladstone, William Ewart (1809-98)
11 Carlton House Terrace, London, SW1
L

Gladstone, W. E. (William Ewart) (1809-98)
73 Harley Street, London, W1
L (1876-82)

Gladstone, William Ewart (1809-98)
10 St James's Square, London, SW1
L

Godley, John Robert (1814-61)
48 Gloucester Place, London, W1
L, D

Gordon Fenwick, Ethel (1857-1947)
20 Upper Wimpole Street, London, W1
L (1887-1924)

Gray, Henry (1827-61)
8 Wilton Street, London, SW1
L

Green, John Richard (1837-83)
4 Beaumont Street, London, W1
L

Grey, Sir Edward - Viscount Grey of Falloden (1862-1933)
3 Queen Anne's Gate, London, SW1
L

Grossmith Sr, George (1847-1912)
28 Dorset Square, London, NW1
L

Grossmith Jr, George (1874-1935)
3 Spanish Place, London, W1
L

Grote, George (1794-1871)
12 Savile Row, London, W1
D

Lord Haldane (1856-1928)
28 Queen Anne's Gate, London, SW1
L

Hallam, Henry (1777-1859)
67 Wimpole Street, London, W1
L

Handel, George Frederick (1685-1759)
25 Brook Street, London, W1
L, D

Handley Page, Sir Frederick (1885-1962)
18 Grosvenor Square, London, W1
L

Handley, Tommy (1892-1949)
34 Craven Road, Paddington, London, W2
L

Harley, Robert - Earl of Oxford (1661-1724)
14 Buckingham Street, London, WC2
L

Harte, Francis Bret (1836-1902)
74 Lancaster Gate, London, W2
L

Haydon, Benjamin Robert (1786-1846)
116 Lisson Grove, London, NW1
L

Hazlitt, William (1778-1830)
6 Frith Street, London, W1
D

Heine, Heinrich (1799-1856)
32 Craven Street, London, WC2
L (1827)

Hendrix, Jimi (1942-70)
23 Brook Street, London, W1
L (1968-69)

Herzen, Alexander (1812-70)
1 Orsett Terrace, London, W2
L (1860-63)

Hill, Sir Rowland (1795-1879)
1 Orme Square, London, W2
L

Hill, Octavia (1838-1912)
2 Garbutt Place, London, W1

Hogg, Quintin (1845-1903)
5 Cavendish Square, London, W1
L (1885-98)

Hood, Thomas (1799-1845)
1-3 Robert Street, London, WC2
L

Hood, Thomas (1799-1845)
Devonshire Lodge, 28 Finchley Road, London, NW8
D

Lord Hore-Belisha (1893-1957)
16 Stafford Place, London, SW1
L

Hughes, David Edward (1831-1900)
94 Great Portland Street, London, W1
L, W

Hunter, John (1728-93)
31 Golden Square, London, W1
L

Blue Plaques 281

Hunter, William (1718-83)
Lyric Theatre (rear portion), Great Windmill Street, London, W1

Huskisson, William (1770-1830)
28 St James's Place, London, SW1
L

Hutchinson, Sir Jonathan (1828-1913)
15 Cavendish Square, London, W1
L

Huxley, Thomas (1825-95)
38 Marlborough Place, London, NW8
L

Irving, Sir Henry (1838-1905)
15A Grafton Street, London, W1
L (1872-99)

Irving, Washington (1783-1859)
8 Argyll Street, London, W1
L

Isaacs, Rufus - 1st Marquess of Reading (1860-1935)
32 Curzon Street, London, W1
L, D

Jackson, John Hughlings (1835-1911)
3 Manchester Square, London, W1
L

Jerome, Jerome K (1859-1927)
91-104 Chelsea Gardens, Chelsea Bridge Road, London, SW1
L

Johnson, Dr Samuel
Essex Hall, Essex Street, London, WC2
L

Johnson, Samuel (1709-84)
8 Russell Street, London, WC2
L

Jones, Dr Ernest (1879-1958)
19 York Terrace East, London, NW1
L

Kalvos, Andreas (1792-1869)
182 Sutherland Avenue, London, W9
L

Kelly, Sir Gerald (1879-1972)
117 Gloucester Place, London, W1
L (1916-72)

Lord Kelvin (1824-1907)
15 Eaton Place, London, SW1
L

Kempe, Charles Eamer (1837-1907)
37 Nottingham Place, London, W1
L, W

Kipling, Rudyard (1865-1936)
43 Villiers Street, London, WC2
L (1889-91)

Kitchener of Khartoum KG, Field Marshal, Earl (1850-1916)
2 Carlton Gardens, London, SW1
L (1914-15)

Klein, Melanie (1882-1960)
42 Clifton Hill, London, NW8
L

Knight, Harold (1874-1961)
16 Langford Place, London, NW8
L

Knight, Dame Laura (1877-1970)
16 Langford Place, London, NW8
L

Kokoschka, Oskar (1886-1980)
Eyre Court, Finchley Road, London, NW8
L

Lawrence, Susan (1871-1947)
44 Westbourne Terrace, London, W2
L

Lawrence, T. E. (1888-1935)
14 Barton Street, London, SW1
L

Lear, Edward (1812-88)
30 Seymour Street, London, W1
L

Leigh, Vivien (1913-67)
54 Eaton Square, London, SW1
L

Lindsey, Revd Theophilus (1723-1808)
Essex Hall, Essex Street, London, WC2
L

Lord Lister, Joseph (1827-1912)
12 Park Crescent, London, W1
L

Loudon, Jane (1807-58)
3 Porchester Terrace, London, W2
L

Loudon, John Claudius (1783-1843)
3 Porchester Terrace, London, W2
L

Lord Lugard (1858-1945)
51 Rutland Gate, London, SW7
L, 1912-19

Lutyens, Sir Edwin Landseer (1869-1944)
13 Mansfield Street, London, W1
L, D

Lyell, Sir Charles (1797-1875)
73 Harley Street, London, W1
L (1854-75)

282 Cultural London

Macaulay, Rose (1881-1958)
Hinde House, 11-14 Hinde Street, London, W1
L, D

Macklin, Charles (1697?-1797)
19-20 Bow Street, London, WC2
L

Macmillan, Douglas (1884-1969)
15 Ranelagh Road, London, SW1
L

Malone, Edmond (1741-1812)
40 Langham Street, London, W1
L (1779-1812)

Manby, Charles (1804-84)
60 Westbourne Terrace, London, W2
L

Manning, Cardinal Henry Edward (1808-92)
22 Carlisle Place, London, SW1
L

Manson, Sir Patrick (1844-1922)
50 Welbeck Street, London, W1
L

Marconi, Guglielmo (1874-1937)
71 Hereford Road, London, W2
L (1896-97)

Marryat, Captain Frederick (1792-1848)
3 Spanish Place, London, W1
L

Marx, Karl (1818-83)
28 Dean Street, London, W1
L (1851-56)

Maugham, William Somerset (1874-1965)
6 Chesterfield Street, London, W1
L (1911-19)

Maurice, Frederick Denison (1805-72)
2 Upper Harley Street, London, NW1
L (1862-66)

Mayer, Sir Robert (1879-1985)
2 Mansfield Street, London, W1
L

Metternich, Prince (1773-1859)
44 Eaton Square, London, SW1
L (1848)

Meynell, Alice (1847-1922)
47 Palace Court, London, W2
L

Millbank Prison
Millbank, London, SW1

Lord Milner, Alfred (1854-1925)
14 Manchester Square, London, W1
L

Mitford, Nancy (1904-73)
Heywood Hill's Bookshop, 10 Curzon Street, London, W1
W (1942-45)

Montefiore, Sir Moses (1784-1885)
99 Park Lane, London, W1
L

Moore, George (1852-1933)
121 Ebury Street, London, SW1
L, D

Moore, Tom (1779-1852)
85 George Street, London, W1
L

Morrell, Lady Ottoline (1873-1938)
10 Gower Street, London, WC1
L

Morse, Samuel (1791-1872)
141 Cleveland Street, London, W1
L (1812-15)

Mozart, Wolfgang Amadeus (1756-91)
180 Ebury Street, London, W1

Napoleon III (1808-73)
1C King Street, London, SW1
L (1848)

Lord Nelson, Horatio (1758-1805)
147 New Bond Street, London, W1
L (1797)

Lord Nelson, Horatio (1758-1805)
103 New Bond Street, London, W1
L (1798)

Newton, Sir Isaac (1642-1727)
87 Jermyn Street, London, SW1
L

Nicolson, Harold (1886-1968)
182 Ebury Street, London, SW1
L

Nightingale, Florence (1820-1910)
10 South Street, London, W1
L, D

Noel-Baker, Philip (1889-1982)
16 South Eaton Place, London, SW1
L

Nollekens, Joseph (1737-1823)
44 Mortimer Street, London, W1
L, D

Novello, Ivor (1893-1951)
11 Aldwych, London, WC2
L, D

Oldfield, Ann (1683-1730)
60 Grosvenor Street, London, W1
W (1725-30)

Blue Plaques 283

Onslow, Arthur (1691-1768)
20 Soho Square, London, W1
L

Palgrave, Francis Turner (1824-97)
5 York Gate, London, NW1
L (1862-75)

Palmerston, Henry John Temple, 3rd Viscount (1784-1865)
4 Carlton Gardens, London, SW1
L

Palmerston, Henry John Temple, 3rd Viscount (1784-1865)
20 Queen Anne's Gate, London, SW1
B

Lord Palmerston (1784-1865)
Naval and Military Club, 94 Piccadilly, London, W1
L

Patel, Sardar (1875-1950)
23 Aldridge Road Villas, London, W11
L

Peabody, George (1795-1869)
80 Eaton Square, London, SW1
D

Pearson, John Loughborough (1817-97)
13 Mansfield Street, London, W1
L, D

Peel, Sir Robert (1750-1830)
16 Upper Grosvenor Street, London, W1
L

Pelham, Henry (c.1695-1754)
22 Arlington Street, London, SW1
L

Pepys, Samuel (1633-1703)
12 Buckingham Street, London, WC2
L (1679-88)

Pepys, Samuel (1633-1703)
14 Buckingham Street, London, WC2
L

Pinero, Sir Arthur (1855-1934)
115A Harley Street, London, W1
L (1909-34)

Pitt, William - Earl of Chatham (1708-78)
10 St James's Square, London, SW1
L

Pitt-Rivers, Lt. Gen. Augustus Henry Lane Fox (1827-1900)
4 Grosvenor Gardens, London, SW1
L

Pitt, William (the younger) (1759-1806)
120 Baker Street, London, W1
L (1803-04)

Portuguese Embassy
23-24 Golden Square, London, W1

Radcliffe, John (1650-1714)
19-20 Bow Street, London, WC2
L

Raglan, Lord Fitzroy Somerset, 1st Baron (1788-1855)
5 Stanhope Gate, London, W1
L

Rathbone, Eleanor (1782-1946)
Tufton Court, Tufton Street, London, SW1
L

Lord Reith (1889-1971)
6 Barton Street, London, SW1
L (1924-30)

Reschid, Mustapha Pasha (1800-58)
1 Bryanston Square, London, W1
L (1839)

Reynolds, Sir Joshua (1723-92)
Fanum House, Leicester Square, London, WC2
L, D

Richmond, George (1809-96)
20 York Street, London, W1
L (1843-96)

Rogers, Dr Joseph (1821-89)
33 Dean Street, London, W1
L

Rosebery, 5th Earl (1847-1929)
20 Charles Street, London, W1
B

Rossetti, Dante Gabriel (1828-82)
110 Hallam Street, London, W1
B

Rossi, John Charles Felix (1762-1839)
116 Lisson Grove, London, NW1
L

Ross, Sir Ronald (1857-1932)
18 Cavendish Square, London, W1

Rowlandson, Thomas (1757-1827)
16 John Adam Street, London, WC2
L

Roy, Major-General William (1726-90)
10 Argyll Street, London, W1
L

Russell, Lord John, 1st Earl (1792-1878)
37 Chesham Place, London, SW1
L

Sackville, Charles - Earl of Dorset (1638-1706)
19-20 Bow Street, London, WC2
L

284 Cultural London

Sackville-West, Vita (1892-1962)
182 Ebury Street, London, SW1
L

Salvin, Anthony (1799-1881)
11 Hanover Terrace, London, NW1
L

San Martin, José de (The Liberator) (1778-1850)
23 Park Road, London, NW1
S

Santley, Sir Charles (1834-1922)
13 Blenheim Road, London, NW8
L, D

Savage, James (1779-1852)
Essex Hall, Essex Street, London, WC2
W

Scawen-Blunt, Wilfrid (1840-1922)
15 Buckingham Gate, London, SW1
L

Schreiner, Olive (1855-1920)
16 Portsea Place, London, W2
L

Site of Scotland Yard
Ministry of Agriculture Building, Whitehall Place, London, SW1

Scott, Sir Giles Gilbert (1880-1960)
Chester House, Clarendon Place, London, W2
L (1926-60)

Seacole, Mary (1805-81)
157 George Street, London, W1
L

Shelley, Percy Bysshe (1792-1822)
15 Poland Street, London, W1
L

Shepard, E. H. (1879-1976)
10 Kent Terrace, London, NW1
L

Sheraton, Thomas (1751-1806)
163 Wardour Street, London, W1
L

Sheridan, Richard Brinsley (1751-1816)
14 Savile Row, London, W1
L

Sheridan, Richard Brinsley (1751-1816)
10 Hertford Street, London, W1
L (1795-1802)

Smith, F. E. - Earl of Birkenhead (1872-1930)
32 Grosvenor Gardens, London, SW1
L

Smith, W. H. (1825-91)
12 Hyde Park Street, London, W2
L

Smith MP, William (1756-1835)
16 Queen Anne's Gate, London, SW1
L

Sopwith, Sir Thomas (1888-1989)
46 Green Street, London, W1
L (1934-40)

Stanfield, Clarkson (1793-1867)
14 Buckingham Street, London, WC2
L

Stanhope, Charles, 3rd Earl (1753-1816)
20 Mansfield Street, London, W1
L

Stanley, Edward Geoffrey - Earl of Derby (1799-1869)
10 St James's Square, London, SW1
L

Stanley, Sir Henry Morton (1814-1904)
2 Richmond Terrace, London, SW1
L, D

Stephenson, Robert (1803-59)
35 Gloucester Square, London, W2
D

Sterndale Bennett, Sir William (1816-75)
38 Queensborough Terrace, London, W2
L

Still, Sir George Frederic (1868-1941)
28 Queen Anne Street, London, W1
L

Stothard, Thomas (1755-1834)
28 Newman Street, London, W1
L

Strang, William (1859-1921)
20 Hamilton Terrace, London, NW8
L (1900-21)

Street, George Edmund (1824-81)
14 Cavendish Place, London, W1
L

Stuart, Prince Charles Edward
Essex Hall, Essex Street, London, WC2
S

Taglioni, Marie (1809-84)
14 Connaught Square, London, W2
L (1875-76)

Talleyrand, Prince (1754-1838)
21 Hanover Square, London, W1
L

Tauber, Richard (1891-1948)
Park West, Edgware Road, London, W2
L, (1947-8)

Tempest, Dame Marie (1864-1942)
24 Park Crescent, London, W1
L (1899-1902)

Lord Tennyson, Alfred (1809-92)
9 Upper Belgrave Street, London, SW1
L (1880-81)

Tilak, Lokamanya (1856-1920)
10 Howley Place, London, W2
L (1918-19)

Townley, Charles (1737-1805)
14 Queen Anne's Gate, London, SW1
L

Trollope, Anthony (1815-82)
39 Montague Square, London, W1
L

Turing, Alan (1912-54)
2 Warrington Crescent, London, W9
B

Van Buren, Martin (1782-1862)
7 Stratford Place, London, W1
L

Vaughan Williams, Ralph (1872-1958)
10 Hanover Terrace, London, NW1
L (1953-58)

Voysey, C. F. A. (1857-1941)
6 Carlton Hill, London, NW8
L

Walpole, Horace (1717-97)
5 Arlington Street, London, SW1
L

Walpole, Sir Robert (1676-1745)
5 Arlington Street, London, SW1
L

Waterhouse, Alfred (1830-1905)
61 New Cavendish Street, London, W1
L

Weisz, Victor 'Vicky' (1913-66)
Welbeck Mansions, 35 Welbeck Street, London, W1
L

Wells, H. G. (1866-1946)
13 Hanover Terrace, London, NW1
L, D

Wesley, Charles (1707-88)
1 Wheatley Street, London, W1
L, D

Wesley, Charles (1757-1834)
1 Wheatley Street, London, W1
L

Wesley, Samuel (1766-1837)
1 Wheatley Street, London, W1
L

Westmacott, Sir Richard (1775-1856)
14 South Audley Street, London, W1
L, D

Wheatstone, Sir Charles (1802-75)
19 Park Crescent, London, W1
L

Wheeler, Sir Mortimer (1890-1976)
27 Whitcomb Street, London, WC2
L

Winant, John Gilbert (1889-1947)
7 Aldford Street, London, W1
L

Wingfield, Major Walter Clopton (1833-1912)
33 St George's Square, London, SW1
L

Wodehouse, P. G. (1881-1975)
17 Dunraven Street, London, W1
L

Wood, Edward - 1st Earl of Halifax (1881-1959)
86 Eaton Square, London, SW1
L

Wyatville, Sir Jeffry (1766-1840)
39 Brook Street, London, W1
L, D

Wycherley, William (1640?-1716)
19-20 Bow Street, London, WC2
L

Wyndham, Sir Charles (1837-1919)
20 York Terrace East, London, NW1
L, D

Young, Thomas (1773-1829)
48 Welbeck Street, London
L

BRITISH LIBRARY

96 Euston Road, London NW1 2DB (Tel: 020-7412 7332; Fax: 020-7412 7340; Web: http://www.bl.uk)

The British Library was established in 1973. It is the UK's national library and occupies a key position in the library and information network. The Library aims to serve scholarship, research, industry, commerce and all other major users of information. Its services are based on collections which include over 16 million volumes, 1 million discs, and 55,000 hours of tape recordings. The Library is now based at two sites: London (St Pancras and Colindale) and Boston Spa, W. Yorks. The Library's sponsoring department is the Department for Culture, Media and Sport.

Access to the reading rooms at St Pancras is limited to holders of a British Library Reader's Pass; information about eligibility is available from the Reader Admissions Office. The exhibition galleries and public areas are open to all, free of charge.

Opening hours of services vary; some services may close for one week each year. Specific information should be checked by telephone.

Reader Admissions (Tel: 020-7412 7677); Reader Services (Tel: 020-7412 7676); West European Collections, Slavonic and East European Collections, English Language Collections (Tel: 020-7412 7676); Newspaper Library, Colindale Avenue, London NW9 5HE. (Tel: 020-7412 7353); National Preservation Office (Tel: 020-7412 7612); Special Collections (Tel: 020-7412 7513); Oriental and India Office Collections (Tel: 020-7412 7873); Western Manuscripts (Tel: 020-7412 7513); Map Library (Tel: 020-7412 7702); Music Collections (Tel: 020-7412 7772); Philatelic Collections (Tel: 020-7412 7635); National Sound Archive (Tel: 020-7412 7440); Science and Technology (Tel: 020-7412/7288/7494/7496); British and EPO Patents (Tel: 020-7412 7919); Foreign Patents (Tel: 020-7412 7902); Business (Tel: 020-7412 7454/7977); Social Policy Information Service (Tel: 020-7412 7536).

CEMETERIES

Abney Park, Stamford Hill, N16 (35 acres), tomb of General Booth, founder of the Salvation Army, and memorials to many non-conformist divines.
Brompton, Old Brompton Road, SW10 (40 acres), graves of Sir Henry Cole, Emmeline Pankhurst, John Wisden.
City of London Cemetery and Crematorium, Aldersbrook Road, E12 (200 acres); Golders Green Crematorium, Hoop Lane, NW11 (12 acres), with Garden of Rest and memorials to many famous men and women.
Hampstead, Fortune Green Road, NW6 (36 acres), graves of Kate Greenaway, Lord Lister, Marie Lloyd.
Highgate, Swains Lane, N6 (38 acres), tombs of George Eliot, Faraday and Marx; guided tours only, west side, £3.00.
Kensal Green, Harrow Road, W10 (70 acres), tombs of Thackeray, Trollope, Sydney Smith, Wilkie Collins, Tom Hood, George Cruikshank, Leigh Hunt, Isambard Kingdom Brunel and Charles Kemble.
Churchyard of the former Marylebone Chapel, Marylebone High Street, W1, Charles Wesley and his son Samuel Wesley buried; chapel demolished in 1949, now Garden of Rest.
Nunhead, Linden Grove, SE15 (26 acres), closed in 1969, recently restored and opened for burials.
St Marylebone Cemetery and Crematorium, East End Road, N2 (47 acres).
West Norwood Cemetery and Crematorium, Norwood High Street, SE27 (42 acres), tombs of Sir Henry Bessemer, Mrs Beeton, Sir Henry Tate and Joseph Whitaker (Whitaker's Almanack).

CENOTAPH, WHITEHALL, LONDON SW1

The word 'cenotaph' means 'empty tomb'. The monument, erected 'To the Glorious Dead', is a memorial to all ranks of the sea, land and air forces who gave their lives in the service of the Empire during the First World War. Designed by Sir Edwin Lutyens and erected as a temporary memorial in 1919, it was replaced by a permanent structure unveiled by George V on Armistice Day 1920. An additional inscription was made after the Second World War to commemorate those who gave their lives in that conflict.

CHARTERHOUSE

Charterhouse Square, London EC1M 6AN (Tel: 020-7253 9503; Fax: 020-7251 3929)

A Carthusian monastery from 1371 to 1537, purchased in 1611 by Thomas Sutton, who endowed it as a residence for aged men 'of gentle birth' and a school for poor scholars (removed to Godalming in 1872).
Registrar and Clerk to the Governors, R. B. Heaton-Watson, BA, FRGS

CHELSEA PHYSIC GARDEN

66 Royal Hospital Road, London SW3 4HS (Tel: 020-7352 5646).

A garden of general botanical research and education, maintaining a wide range of rare and unusual plants. The garden was established in 1673 by the Society of Apothecaries.

CINEMA

There is a vast number of cinemas in the capital, both independent and those forming part of a national or international chain. Performance and ticket information can be found in the local press, on Teletext and on the Internet. Constraints of space preclude listings of film-houses in London, however, details on the BFI's recently opened IMAX Cinema have been included as this cinema is of technological significance and boasts a building that has already, in its short life, become a unique London landmark.

BFI London Imax Cinema
1 Charlie Chaplin Walk, South Bank, London SE1 8XR (Tel: 020-7902 1234; Web: http://www.bfi.org.uk/imax/)

The BFI London Imax Cinema was opened on 1 May 1999. It cost approximately £20m to build and received

£15m from the Arts Council of England's Lottery Fund. Situated on the roundabout adjacent to Waterloo mainline and tube stations, it is the largest and most significant motion picture cinema in the world. The distinctive building was designed by Bryan Avery and the mural featured on the exterior wall is the work of artist Howard Hodgkin. The cinema houses 482 seats and boasts the largest cinema screen in the UK. The cinema shows a range of large format films of an educational nature and many showings are on natural history topics.

CLUBS

Alpine Club
55 Charlotte Road, London, EC2A 3QF (Tel: 020-7613 0755; E-mail: sec@alpine-club.org.uk; Web: http://www.alpine-club.org.uk)
Hon. Secretary: G. D. Hughes

Arts Club
40 Dover Street, London, W1X 3RB (Tel: 020-7499 8581; Fax: 020-7409 0913;
E-mail: secretary@artsclub.fsnet.co.uk)
Secretary: I. Campbell

The Athenéum
107 Pall Mall, London, SW1Y 5ER (Tel: 020-7930 4843)
Secretary: J. G. F. Stoy

Authors' Club
40 Dover Street, London, W1X 3RB (Tel: 020-7499 8581; Fax: 020-7409 0913)
Secretary: Mrs A. de la Grange

Beefsteak Club
9 Irving Street, London, WC2H 7AT (Tel: 020-7930 5722; Fax: 020-7925 2325)
Secretary: Sir John Lucas-Toath, Bt.

Brooks's
St James's Street, London, SW1A 1LN (Tel: 020-7493 4411; Fax: 020-7499 3736;
E-mail: secretary@brooksclub.org)
Secretary: G. Snell

Buck's Club
18 Clifford Street, London, W1X 1RG (Tel: 020-7734 6896; Fax: 020-7287 2097;
E-mail: secretary@bucksclub.co.uk)
Secretary: Capt. P. G. J. Murison, RN

Caledonian Club
9 Halkin Street, London, SW1X 7DR (Tel: 020-7235 5162; Fax: 020-7235 4635;
E-mail: secy@caledonian-club.org.uk;
Web: http://www.caledonian-club.org.uk)
Secretary: P. J. Varney

Canning Club
4 St James's Square, London, SW1Y 4JU (Tel: 020-7827 5757; Fax: 020-7827 5724;
E-mail: canningclub@compuserve.com)
Secretary: T. M. Harrington

Carlton Club
69 St James's Street, London, SW1A 1PJ (Tel: 020-7493 1164; Fax: 020-7495 4090;
E-mail: secretary@carltonclub.co.uk;
Web: http://www.carltonclub.co.uk)
Secretary: A. E. Telfer

The Cavalry and Guards Club
127 Piccadilly, London, W1V 0PX (Tel: 020-7499 1261; Fax: 020-7495 5956)
Secretary: Cdr. I. R. Wellesley-Harding, RN

City Livery Club
20 Aldermanbury, London, EC2V 7HP (Tel: 020-7814 0200; Fax: 020-7814 0201)
Hon. Secretary: W. C. Hammond, MBE

City of London Club
19 Old Broad Street, London, EC2N 1DS (Tel: 020-7588 7991; Fax: 020-7374 2020;
E-mail: cityclub@dial.pipex.com)
Secretary: G. Jones

East India Club
16 St James's Square, London, SW1Y 4LH (Tel: 020-7930 1000; Fax: 020-7315 2701;
E-mail: eastindie@globalnet.co.uk)
Secretary: M. Howell

Farmers Club
3 Whitehall Court, London, SW1A 2EL (Tel: 020-7930 3751; Fax: 020-7839 7864)
Secretary: Gp Capt. G. P. Carson

Flyfishers' Club
69 Brook Street, London, W1Y 2ER (Tel: 020-7629 5958)
Secretary: Cdr. T. H. Boycott, OBE, RN

Garrick Club
15 Garrick Street, London, WC2E 9AY (Tel: 020-7379 6478; Fax: 020-7379 5966)
Secretary: M. J. Harvey

Green Room Club
9 Adam Street, London, WC2N 6AA (Tel: 020-7836 7453; Fax: 020-7836 8073)
Secretary: D. Lamden

Groucho Club
45 Dean Street, London, W1V 5AP (Tel: 020-7439 4685; Fax: 020-7437 0373)
Chairman: A. Mackintosh

The Kennel Club
1-5 Clarges Street, London, W1Y 8AB (Tel: 0870-606 6750; Fax: 020-7518 1050;
E-mail: e-mail-info@the-kennel-club.org.uk;
Web: http://www.the-kennel-club.org.uk)
Chief Executive: R. French

London Rowing Club
Embankment, Putney, London, SW15 1LB (Tel: 020-8788 1400; Fax: 020-8874 9056;
E-mail: metregatta@compuserve.com;
Web: http://www.londonrc.org.uk)
Hon. Secretary: N. A. Smith

288 Cultural London

MCC (Marylebone Cricket Club)
Lord's Cricket Ground, London, NW8 8QN (Tel: 020-7289 1611; Fax: 020-7289 9100; Web: http://www.lords.org)
Secretary: R. D. V. Knight

National Liberal Club
Whitehall Place, London, SW1A 2HE (Tel: 020-7930 9871; Fax: 020-7839 4768; Web: http://www.nlc.org.uk)
Secretary: S. J. Roberts

Naval and Military Club
4 St James's Square, London, SW1Y 4JU (Tel: 020-7827 5757; Fax: 020-7827 5758)
Secretary: M. G. G. Ebbitt

Naval Club
38 Hill Street, London, W1X 8DP (Tel: 020-7493 7672; Fax: 020-7629 7995; E-mail: thenavalclub@btinternet.com)
Chief Executive: Cdr. J. L. L. Pritchard

New Cavendish Club
44 Great Cumberland Place, London, W1H 8BS (Tel: 020-7723 0391; Fax: 020-7262 8411)
General Manager: J. P. Dauvergne

Oriental Club
Stratford House, Stratford Place, London, W1N 0ES (Tel: 020-7629 5126; Fax: 020-7629 0494; E-mail: sec@orientalclub.org.uk)
Secretary: S. C. Doble

Portland Club
69 Brook Street, London, W1Y 2ER (Tel: 020-7499 1523)
Secretary: J. Burns, CBE

Railway Club
Room 208, 25 Marylebone Road, London, NW1 5JS
Hon. Secretary: A. G. Wells

Reform Club
104-105 Pall Mall, London, SW1Y 5EW (Tel: 020-7930 9374; Fax: 020-7930 1857; E-mail: reform.club@msn.com)
Secretary: R. A. M. Forrest

Roehampton Club
Roehampton Lane, London, SW15 5LR (Tel: 020-8480 4205; Fax: 020-8480 4265)
Chief Executive: M. Yates

Royal Air Force Club
128 Piccadilly, London, W1V 0PY (Tel: 020-7399 1000; Fax: 020-7355 1516; E-mail: admin@rafclub.org.uk; Web: http://www.rafclub.org.uk)
Chairman: Air Vice-Marshal P. W. Roser

Royal Ocean Racing Club
20 St James's Place, London, SW1A 1NN (Tel: 020-7493 2248; Fax: 020-7493 5252; E-mail: rorc@saintjames.demon.co.uk; Web: http://www.rorc.org)
General Manager: D. J. Minords, OBE

Royal Over-Seas League
Over-Seas House, Park Place, London, SW1A 1LR (Tel: 020-7408 0214; Fax: 020-7499 6738; E-mail: info@rosl.org.uk; Web: http://www.rosl.org.uk)
Director-General: R. F. Newell

Royal Thames Yacht Club
60 Knightsbridge, London, SW1X 7LF (Tel: 020-7235 2121; Fax: 020-7245 9470; E-mail: club@rtyc.org.uk)
Secretary: Capt. D. Goldson

St Stephen's Constitutional Club
34 Queen Anne's Gate, London, SW1H 9AB (Tel: 020-7222 1382; Fax: 020-7222 8740)
Secretary: L. D. Mawby

Savile Club
69 Brook Street, London, W1Y 2ER (Tel: 020-7629 5462; Fax: 020-7499 7087; E-mail: adminstration@savileclub.co.uk; Web: http://www.savileclub.co.uk)
Secretary: N. Storey

Travellers Club
106 Pall Mall, London, SW1Y 5EP (Tel: 020-7930 8688; Fax: 020-7930 2019; E-mail: secretary@thetravellersclub.org.uk; Web: http://www.csma.org.uk)
Secretary: M. S. Allcock

Turf Club
5 Carlton House Terrace, London, SW1Y 5AQ (Tel: 020-7930 8555; Fax: 020-7930 7206; E-mail: mail@turfclub.co.uk)
Secretary: Lt.-Col. O. R. St J. Breakwell

United Oxford and Cambridge University Club
71 Pall Mall, London, SW1Y 5HD (Tel: 020-7930 5151; Fax: 020-7930 9490; E-mail: uocuc@uocuc.demon.co.uk; Web: http://www.uocuc.org.uk)
Secretary: G. R. Buchanan

The University Women's Club
2 Audley Square, South Audley Street, London, W1Y 6DB (Tel: 020-7499 2268; Fax: 020-7499 7046; E-mail: uwc@globalnet.co.uk; Web: http://www.the-university-womens-club.co.uk)
Acting Secretary: Ms S. McCue

White's
37-38 St James's Street, London, SW1A 1JG (Tel: 020-7493 6671; Fax: 020-7493 6671)
Secretary: D. A. Anderson

DOWNING STREET

10 Downing Street, London SW1A 2AA (Tel: 020-7270 3000; Fax: 020-7925 8918; Web: http://www.number-10.gov.uk)

Number 10 Downing Street is the official town residence of the Prime Minister, No. 11 of the Chancellor of the Exchequer and No. 12 is the office of the Government Whips. The street was named after Sir George Downing, Bt., soldier and diplomatist, who was MP for Morpeth from 1660 to 1684. Chequers, a Tudor mansion in the Chilterns near Princes Risborough, was presented by Lord and Lady Lee of Fareham in 1917 to serve, from 1921, as a country residence for the Prime Minister of the day.

GEORGE INN

Borough High Street, London SE1.

The last galleried inn in London, built in 1677. Now run as an ordinary public house.

GREENWICH

Royal Observatory, Greenwich, London SE10 9NF (Tel: 020-8858 6575; Fax: 020-8312 6734; Web: http://www.rog.nmm.ac.uk. National Maritime Museum, same address as above Tel: 020-8858 4422; Fax: 020-8312 6632; Web: http://www.nmm.ac.uk).

The Royal Naval College was until 1873 the Greenwich Hospital. It was built by Charles II, largely from designs by John Webb, and by Queen Anne and William III, from designs by Wren. It stands on the site of an ancient royal palace and of the more recent Palace of Placentia constructed by Humphrey, Duke of Gloucester (1391-1447), son of Henry IV. Henry VIII, Mary I and Elizabeth I were born in the royal palace (which reverted to the Crown in 1447) and Edward VI died there. Greenwich Park was enclosed by Humphrey, Duke of Gloucester, and laid out by Charles II from the designs of Le Nôtre. On a hill in Greenwich Park is the former Royal Observatory (founded 1675). Its buildings are now managed by the National Maritime Museum and the earliest observatory is named Flamsteed House, after John Flamsteed (1646-1719), the first Astronomer Royal. The Cutty Sark, the last of the famous tea clippers, has been preserved next to Greenwich Pier as a memorial to ships and men of a past era. Sir Francis Chichester's round-the-world yacht, Gipsy Moth IV, can also be seen.

HISTORIC BUILDINGS

DR JOHNSON'S HOUSE

17 Gough Square, London EC4A 3DE (Tel: 020-7353 3745; Email: curator@drjh.dircon.co.uk; Web: http://www.drjh.dircon.co.uk)

Home of Samuel Johnson, poet, essayist, novelist and compiler of a 'Dictionary of the English Language'. Lived at Gough Square for ten years and is buried in Westminster Abbey.

ELTHAM PALACE

Court Yard, Eltham, London SE9 5QE (Tel: 020-8294 2548; Fax: 020-8294 2621; Web: http://www.english-heritage.org.uk)

Eltham Palace combines a 1930s country house and remains of a medieval palace set in moated gardens. It was used as a royal residence until the 16th century. It was eventually bought and rebuilt by the Courtauld family in 1935.

THE QUEEN'S HOUSE

Park Row, Greenwich SE10 9NF (Tel: 020-8858 4422)

The Queen's House was designed for Queen Anne (the wife of James I) by Inigo Jones as part of the Tudor Royal Palace of Placentia. This is now an exhibition venue run by the National Maritime Museum.

THE GUILDHALL

PO Box 270, London EC2P 2EJ (Tel: 020-7332 1460; Web: http://www.cityoflondon.gov.uk)

The Guildhall is the centre of civic government of the City. It was built between 1411-1429 and the facade built 1788-9. It is the only secular stone structure dating from before 1666 still standing in the city. The Great Hall is the third largest civic hall in England and was the site of the trial of Lady Jane Grey in 1553. The Guildhall is still used as a venue for the meetings of the Corporation of London elected assembly, the Court of Common Council and for the Honorary Freedom of the City ceremony as well as for state banquets in honour of royalty and state visits.

KENSINGTON PALACE

State Apartments, Kensington, London W8 4PX (Tel: 020-7937 9561; Fax: 020-7376 0198; Web: http://www.hrp.org.uk)

Kensington Palace was built in 1605 and bought by William and Mary in 1689. It was adapted for royal residents by Chrisopher Wren at this time. Kensington Palace is also the birthplace of Queen Victoria. The Orangery was built for Queen Anne in 1704-5 and the formal 'Sunken Garden' opened in 1909. The Royal Ceremonial Dress Collection is housed here and the state apartments are open to the public.

LAMBETH PALACE

Lambeth Palace Road, London SE1 7JU (Tel: 020-7898 1200)

Lambeth Palace has been the official residence of the Archbishop of Canterbury since 1200. It consists of a 19th-century house with parts dating from the 12th century a mixture of Tudor, Gothic and Neo-gothic architecture. There is also a library and gardens, which are occasionally open to the public. Visits by written application.

HM TOWER OF LONDON

London EC3N 4AB (Tel: 020-7709 0765; Fax: 020-7680 0687; Web: http://www.hrp.org.uk)

The construction of what we now call 'the Tower of London' was begun by William the Conqueror in 1080 with the building of the White Tower. Over the next two centuries, this was encircled with two curtain walls containing a further twenty one towers and a moat. During the middle ages, the Tower was a royal palace and a place of refuge for the monarch, as well as a mint, armoury, zoo, treasury and prison. Under the Tudors, may religious and political prisoners were held in the tower, including Sir Thomas More, Lady Jane Grey and two of Henry VIII's

Queens. This period also saw many executions, both inside the castle or outside on Tower Hill. While the appearance of many parts has changed over the centuries, the survival of so many medieval and later buildings is exceptional. The Tower of London now houses parts of the Royal Armouries collection of arms and armour, and is world-famous as the home of the Crown Jewels.

HORSE GUARDS

Whitehall, London SW1

Archway and offices built about 1753. The mounting of the guard takes place at 11 a.m. (10 a.m. on Sundays) and the dismounted inspection at 4 p.m. Only those with the Queen's permission may drive through the gates and archway into Horse Guards' Parade (230,000 sq. ft), where the Colour is 'trooped' on The Queen's official birthday.

HOUSES OF PARLIAMENT

House of Commons Information Office, House of Commons, London SW1A 2TT (Tel: 020-7219 4272; Fax: 020-7219 5839 Email: hcinfo@parliament.uk; Web: http//www.parliament.uk; House of Lords Information Office, House of Lords, London SW1A 0PW Tel: 020-7219 3107; Fax 020-7219 0620; E-mail hlinfo@parliament.uk)

The royal palace of Westminster, originally built by Edward the Confessor, was the normal meeting place of Parliament from about 1340. St Stephen's Chapel was used from about 1550 for the meetings of the House of Commons, which had previously been held in the Chapter House or Refectory of Westminster Abbey. The House of Lords met in an apartment of the royal palace. The fire of 1834 destroyed much of the palace and the present Houses of Parliament were erected on the site from the designs of Sir Charles Barry and Augustus Welby Pugin between 1840 and 1867. The chamber of the House of Commons was destroyed by bombing in 1941 and a new Chamber designed by Sir Giles Gilbert Scott was used for the first time in 1950. Westminster Hall was the only part of the old palace of Westminster to survive the fire of 1834. It was built by William Rufus (1097-9) and altered by Richard II (1394-9). The hammerbeam roof of carved oak dates from 1396-8. The Hall was the scene of the trial of Charles I.

The Victoria Tower of the House of Lords is about 330 ft high, and when Parliament is sitting the Union flag flies by day from its flagstaff. The Clock Tower of the House of Commons is about 320 ft high and contains 'Big Ben', the hour bell said to be named after Sir Benjamin Hall, First Commissioner of Works when the original bell was cast in 1856. This bell, which weighed 16 tons 11 cwt, was found to be cracked in 1857. The present bell (13.5 tons) is a recasting of the original and was first brought into use in 1859. The dials of the clock are 23 ft in diameter, the hands being 9 ft and 14 ft long (including balance piece). A light is displayed from the Clock Tower at night when Parliament is sitting.

For security reasons tours of the Houses of Parliament are available only to those who have made advance arrangements through an MP or peer.

Admission to the Strangers' Gallery of the House of Lords is arranged by a peer or by queue via St Stephen's Entrance. Admission to the Strangers' Gallery of the House of Commons is by Members' order (Members' orders should be sought several weeks in advance), or by queue via St Stephen's Entrance. Queues are usually shorter after 6 p.m. Monday to Wednesday, on Wednesday mornings and on Thursdays after 2 p.m. The House does not always sit on Fridays. Overseas visitors may write to the Parliamentary Education Unit to obtain a permit to tour the Houses of Parliament, or obtain cards of introduction from their Embassy or High Commission to attend the public gallery.

LORD CHANCELLOR'S RESIDENCE

Lord Chancellor's Office, House of Lords, London, SW1A 0PW. Tel: 020-7219 2394. Postal requests in advance to 'Residence visit', Lord Chancellor's Office.

LLOYD'S

1 Lime Street, London EC3M 7HA (Tel: 020-7327 1000; Fax: 020-7327 6233; Email: lloyds-external-enquiries@lloyds.com; Web: http://www.lloyds.com)

The International insurance market which evolved during the 17th century from Lloyd's Coffee House. The present building was opened for business in May 1986, and houses the Lutine Bell. Underwriting is on three floors with a total area of 114,000 sq. feet.

LONDON ATTRACTIONS

LONDON ARENA

Limeharbour, London, E14 9TH (Tel: 020-7538 1212; Credit Card Hotline 0990 121212; Web: http://www.londonarena.co.uk)

London Arena is now firmly established as a modern and exciting sporting and entertainment venue in the UK. Following major investment in 1998, London Arena now meets a world-class benchmark of excellence in arena entertainment. Events staged at London Arena are diverse ranging from pop concerts to sporting tournaments and key features of the venue include: Olympic-size ice floor, hospitality boxes, luxury seating and videoboard. London Arena is also home to the London Knights ice hockey club, London's only Super League ice hockey team.

LONDON DUNGEON

24-28 Tooley Street, London, SE1 (Tel: 020-7403 7221)

The London Dungeon is a museum housing gruesome exhibits depicting European history.

LONDON EYE

Web: http://www.british-airways.com/londoneye For further information and advance bookings, call 0870 5000 600.

The London Eye is a 443 ft high wheel situated on the South Bank of the River Thames, along from County Hall. The wheel provides a 30 minute ride offering spectacular panoramic views of the capital.

The wheel is 90 ft taller than the previous tallest

Scenes and Sights of London

wheel in Japan's Yokohama Bay, and has 32 pods attached, each with a 25 person capacity – a maximum of 800 passengers at a time (15,000 passengers per day). The wheel has planning permission in its current situation for five years, however, if the ride proves popular it may be able to have a longer life on the South Bank. Following safety concerns, the opening of the London Eye was postponed from January until March 2000.

LONDON PLANETARIUM

Marylebone Road, London NW1 5LR (Tel: 0870 400 3000; Fax: 020-7465 0862;
Web: http://www.madame-tussauds.com)

Open daily, star show and interactive exhibits.

LONDON ZOO

Regent's Park, London NW1 4RY (Tel: 020-7722 3333; Web: http://www.zsl.org/londonzoo)

London Zoo is one of the world's great zoos, committed to the conservation of wildlife and threatened habitats, and successfully breeding species facing extinction. There are daily events and activities at the zoo for people of all ages. The new web of life (http://www.weboflife.co.uk) exhibit explains biodiversity and the astonishing variety of life on earth.

MADAME TUSSAUD'S

Marylebone Road, London NW1 5LR (Tel: 0870 400 3000; Web: http://www.madame-tussauds.com)

Waxwork exhibition. Open daily.

MARKETS

The London markets are mostly administered by the Corporation of London.

Billingsgate (fish), Thames Street site dating from 1875, a market site for over 1,000 years, moved to the Isle of Dogs in 1982.
Borough, SE1 (vegetables, fruit, flowers), established on present site 1756, privately owned and run.
Covent Garden (vegetables, fruit, flowers), established in 1661 under a charter of Charles II, moved in 1973 to Nine Elms Lane.
Leadenhall, EC3 (meat, poultry, fish), built 1881, part recently demolished. London Fruit Exchange, **Brushfield Street**, built by Corporation of London 1928-9 as buildings for Spitalfields market; not connected with the market since it moved in 1991.
Petticoat Lane, Middlesex Street, E1, a market has existed on the site for over 500 years, now a Sunday morning market selling almost anything.
Portobello Road, W11, originally for herbs and horse-trading from 1870; became famous for antiques after the closure of the Caledonian Market in 1948; Saturdays. Smithfield, Central Meat, Fish, Fruit, Vegetable and Poultry Markets, built 1851-66, the site of St Bartholomew's Fair from 12th to 19th century, new hall built 1963, market refurbished 1993-4.
Spitalfields, E1 (vegetables, fruit), established 1682, modernised 1928, moved to Leyton in 1991.

There are a number of other markets in London selling a wide range of goods including: Camden Market, Greenwich Market, Charing Cross Collector's Fair, Merton Abbey Mills Market, East Street Market and Roman Road Market.

MARLBOROUGH HOUSE

Pall Mall, London SW1A 5HX (Tel: 020-7839 3411; Fax: 020-7930 0827; Email: info@commonwealth.int; Web: http://www.thecommonwealth.org)

Built by Wren for the first Duke of Marlborough and completed in 1711, the house reverted to the Crown in 1835. In 1863 it became the London house of the Prince of Wales and was the London home of Queen Mary until her death in 1953. In 1959 Marlborough House was given by The Queen as the headquarters for the Commonwealth Secretariat and it was opened as such in 1965. The Queen's Chapel, Marlborough Gate, begun in 1623 from the designs of Inigo Jones for the Infanta Maria of Spain, and completed for Queen Henrietta Maria.

MILLENNIUM DOME

Greenwich, London SE10 (Tel: 020-8293 8600; Fax: 020-293 8700; Email: info@newmill.co.uk; Web: http://www.dome2000.co.uk

The Millennium Dome opened to the public on 1 January 2000. Its circumference is over one km, it is over 80,000 m^2 and the roof is 50m high. It is divided into fourteen zones – Body, Faith, Home Planet, Journey, Learning, Living Island, Mind, Money, Play, Self Portrait, Shared Ground, Rest, Talk and Work. Visitors can also enjoy the latest Blackadder episode in the entertainment venue Skyscape, see over 200 performances by local communities on the Our Town Stage and experience a spectacular millennium show in the Dome's Central Arena.

MONUMENTS

LONDON MONUMENT

(commonly 'The Monument'), Monument Street, London EC3.

The London Monument was built from designs of Wren, 1671-7, to commemorate the Great Fire of London, which broke out in Pudding Lane on 2 September 1666. The fluted Doric column is 120 ft high; the moulded cylinder above the balcony supporting a flaming vase of gilt bronze is an additional 42 ft; and the column is based on a square plinth 40 ft high (with fine carvings on the west face) making a total height of 202 ft. There are splendid views of London from the gallery at top of the column (311 steps).

MONUMENTS (Sculptor's name in brackets)

Albert Memorial (*Durham*), Kensington Gore; Royal Air Force (*Blomfield*), Victoria Embankment; Viscount Alanbrooke, Whitehall; Beaconsfield, Parliament Square; Beatty (*Macmillan*), Trafalgar Square; Belgian Gratitude (*setting by Blomfield, statue by Rousseau*), Victoria Embankment; Boadicea (or Boudicca), Queen of the

Iceni (*Thornycroft*), Westminster Bridge; Brunel (*Marochetti*), Victoria Embankment; Burghers of Calais (*Rodin*), Victoria Tower Gardens, Westminster; Burns (*Steel*), Embankment Gardens; Canada Memorial (*Granche*), Green Park; Carlyle (*Boehm*), Chelsea Embankment; Cavalry (Jones), Hyde Park; Edith Cavell (*Frampton*), St Martin's Place; Cenotaph (*Lutyens*), Whitehall; Charles I (*Le Sueur*), Trafalgar Square; Charles II (*Gibbons*), South Court, Chelsea Hospital; Churchill (*Roberts-Jones*), Parliament Square; Cleopatra's Needle (68.5ft high, c.1500 bc, erected on the Thames Embankment in 1877-8; the sphinxes are Victorian); Clive (*Tweed*), King Charles Street; Captain Cook (*Brock*), The Mall; Crimean, Broad Sanctuary; Oliver Cromwell (*Thornycroft*), outside Westminster Hall; Cunningham (*Belsky*), Trafalgar Square; Gen. Charles de Gaulle, Carlton Gardens; Lord Dowding (*Faith Winter*) Strand; Duke of Cambridge (*Jones*), Whitehall; Duke of York (124 ft), Carlton House Terrace; Edward VII (*Mackennal*), Waterloo Place; Elizabeth I (1586, oldest outdoor statue in London; from Ludgate), Fleet Street; Eros (Shaftesbury Memorial) (*Gilbert*), Piccadilly Circus; Marechal Foch (Mallisard, copy of one in Cassel, France), Grosvenor Gardens; Charles James Fox (*Westmacott*), Bloomsbury Square; George III (*Cotes Wyatt*), Cockspur Street; George IV (*Chantrey*), riding without stirrups, Trafalgar Square; George V (*Reid Dick*), Old Palace Yard; George VI (*Macmillan*), Carlton Gardens; Gladstone (*Thornycroft*), Strand; Guards' (Crimea) (*Bell*), Waterloo Place; (Great War) (*Ledward, figures, Bradshaw, cenotaph*), Horse Guards' Parade; Haig (*Hardiman*), Whitehall; Sir Arthur (Bomber) Harris (*Faith Winter*), Strand; Irving (*Brock*), north side of National Portrait Gallery; James II (*Gibbons and/or pupils*), Trafalgar Square; Jellicoe (*Wheeler*), Trafalgar Square; Samuel Johnson (*Fitzgerald*), opposite St Clement Danes; Kitchener (*Tweed*), Horse Guards' Parade; Abraham Lincoln (*Saint-Gaudens, copy of one in Chicago*), Parliament Square; Milton (*Montford*), St Giles, Cripplegate; The Monument (see above); Mountbatten, Foreign Office Green; Nelson (170 ft 2 in), Trafalgar Square, with Landseer's lions (cast from guns recovered from the wreck of the Royal George); Florence Nightingale (*Walker*), Waterloo Place; Palmerston (*Woolner*), Parliament Square; Peel (*Noble*), Parliament Square; Pitt (*Chantrey*), Hanover Square; Portal (*Nemon*), Embankment Gardens; Prince Consort (*Bacon*), Holborn Circus; Queen Elizabeth Gate, Hyde Park Corner; Raleigh (*Macmillan*), Whitehall; Richard I (Coeur de Lion) (*Marochetti*), Old Palace Yard; Roberts (Bates), Horse Guards' Parade; Franklin D. Roosevelt (*Reid Dick*), Grosvenor Square; Royal Artillery (South Africa) (*Colton*), The Mall; (Great War), Hyde Park Corner; Captain Scott (*Lady Scott*), Waterloo Place; Shackleton (*Sarjeant Jagger*), Kensington Gore; Shakespeare (*Fontana, copy of one by Scheemakers in Westminster Abbey*), Leicester Square; Smuts (Epstein), Parliament Square; Sullivan (*Goscombe John*), Victoria Embankment; Trenchard (*Macmillan*), Victoria Embankment; Victoria Memorial, in front of Buckingham Palace; Raoul Wallenberg (*Phillip Jackson*), Great Cumberland Place; George Washington (*Houdon copy*), Trafalgar Square; Wellington (*Boehm*), Hyde Park Corner, (*Chantrey*) riding without stirrups, outside Royal Exchange; John Wesley (*Adams Acton*), City Road; William III (*Bacon*), St James's Square; Wolseley (*Goscombe John*), Horse Guards' Parade.

MUSEUMS AND GALLERIES

BARNET

Barnet Museum
31 Wood Street, Barnet, Herts, EN5 4BE (Tel: 020-8440 8066)
Hon. Secretary: Dr G. Gear

Church Farmhouse Museum
Greyhound Hill, London, NW4 4JR (Tel: 020-8203 0130; Fax: 020-8359 2666;
Web: http://www.earl.org.uk/partners/barnet/churchf.htm)
Curator: G. Roots

Jewish Museum
The Sternberg Centre, 80 East End Road, London, N3 2SY (Tel: 020-8349 1143; Fax: 020-8343 2162;
Email: jmc.finchley@lineone.net;
Web: http://www.jewmus.ort.org)
Director: Ms R. Burman

Museum of Advertising
45 Lyndale Avenue, London, NW2 2QB (Tel: 020-7435 6540; Fax: 020-7794 6584;
Email: library@advertisingarchives.co.uk;
Web: http://www.advertisingarchives.co.uk)
Managing Director: Ms S. Viner

Royal Air Force Museum
Grahame Park Way, London, NW9 5LL (Tel: 020-8205 2266; Fax: 020-8200 1751;
Email: info@rafmuseum.org.uk;
Web: http://www.rafmuseum.org.uk)
Director: Dr M. A. Fopp

BECKENHAM

Bethlem Royal Hospital Archives and Museum
Monks Orchard Road, Beckenham, Kent, BR3 3BX (Tel: 020-8776 4307)
Chief Executive: S. Bell

BRENT

Grange Museum
Neasden Roundabout, Neasden Lane, London, NW10 1QB (Tel: 020-8452 8311; Fax: 020-8208 4233;
Email: stephen@grangemus.freeserve.co.uk)
Principal Curator: S. Allen

BROMLEY

Bromley Museum
The Priory, Church Hill, Orpington, BR6 0HH (Tel: 01689-873826;
Email: bromley.museum@bromley.gov.uk;
Web: http://www.bromley.gov.uk)
Curator: Dr A. Tyler

Crystal Palace Museum
Anerley Hill, London, SE19 2BA (Tel: 020-8676 0700; Fax: 020-8676 0700)
Trustee Chairman: B. McKay

Museums and Galleries

CAMDEN

British Museum
Great Russell Street, London, WC1B 3DG (Tel: 020-7636 1555; Fax: 020-7323 8616;
Email: info@british-museum.ac.uk;
Web: http://www.british-museum.ac.uk)
Director: Dr Anderson

Dickens House Museum
48 Doughty Street, London, WC1N 2LF (Tel: 020-7405 2127; Fax: 020-7831 5175;
Email: dhmuseum@rmplc.co.uk;
Web: http://www.dickensmuseum.com)
Curator: A. Xavier

Jewish Museum
129-131 Albert Street, London, NW1 7NB (Tel: 020-7284 1997; Fax: 020-7267 9008;
Email: admin@jmus.org.uk;
Web: http://www.jewmusm.ort.org)
Director: Ms R. Burman

Keats House
Keats Grove, London, NW3 2RR (Tel: 020-7435 2062;
Email: keatshouse@corpoflondon.gov.uk;
Web: http://www.cityoflondon.gov.uk)
Head Archivist: Ms D. Jenkins

Percival David Foundation of Chinese Art
53 Gordon Square, London, WC1H 0DD (Tel: 020-7387 3909; Fax: 020-7383 5163)
Curator: Ms S. Pierson

Petrie Museum of Egyptian Archaeology
London, WC1E 6BT (Tel: 020-7679 2884; Fax: 020-7679 2886; Email: petrie.museum@ucl.ac.uk)
Manager: Ms S. MacDonald

Pollock's Toy Museum
1 Scala Street, London, W1P 1LT (Tel: 020-7636 3452;
Email: toymuseum@hotmail.com;
Web: http://www.pollocks.wc.net)
Curator: Ms V. Sheppard

Sir John Soane's Museum
13 Lincolns Inn Fields, London, WC2A 3BP (Tel: 020-7405 2107; Fax: 020-7831 3957;
Web: http://www.soane.org)
Curator: Mrs M. Richardson

CITY OF LONDON

Bank of England Museum
Threadneedle Street, London, EC2 (Tel: 020-7601 5545; Email: museum@bankofengland.co.uk;
Web: http://www.bankofengland.co.uk)
Curator: J. Keyworth

Barbican Gallery
Silk Street, Barbican, London, EC2Y 8DS (Tel: 020-7382 7105; Fax: 020-7628 0364;
Web: http://www.barbican.org.uk)
Director: J. Hoole

HMS Belfast
Morgans Lane, Tooley Street, London, SE1 2JH (Tel: 020-7940 6300; Fax: 020-7403 0719;
Web: http://www.hmsbelfast.org.uk)
Director: J. Wenzel

St Brides Church Museum
Fleet Street, London, EC4Y 8AU (Tel: 020-7353 1301/7583 0239; Fax: 020-7583 4867;
Email: info@stbrides.com)
Rector: Canon J. Oates

EALING

Pitshanger Manor & Gallery
Walpole Park, Mattock Lane, London, W5 5EQ (Tel: 020-8567 1227; Fax: 020-8567 0595;
Email: pitshanger@ealing.gov.uk)
Head of Arts and Cultural Services: Ms N. Somal

ENFIELD

Forty Hall Museum
Forty Hill, Enfield, Middx, EN2 9HA (Tel: 020-8363 8196; Fax: 020-8367 9098)

GREENWICH

Fan Museum
12 Crooms Hill, London, SE10 8ER (Tel: 020-8305 1441; Fax: 020-8293 1889;
Email: admin@fan-museum.org;
Web: http://www.fan-museum.org)
Administrator: J. Allen

Museum of Artillery in the Rotunda
Rotunda, Greenhill, London, SE18 4BN (Tel: 020-8781 3127; Fax: 020-8316 5402;
Email: raht@btinternet.com;
Web: http://www.firepower.uk.org)
Director: Col. J. M. Phillips

HACKNEY

Geffrye Museum
Kingsland Road, London, E2 8EA (Tel: 020-7739 9893; Fax: 020-7729 5647,
Email: info@geffrye-museum.org.uk;
Web: http://www.geffrye-museum.org.uk)
Director: D. Dewing

HAMMERSMITH AND FULHAM

CCA Galleries
517-523 Fulham Road, London, SW6 1HD (Tel: 020-7386 4900; Fax: 020-7386 4919;
Email: gallery@ccagalleries.com;
Web: http://www.ccagalleries.com)
Managing Director: L. Trevellyan

Museum of Fulham Palace
Bishops Avenue, London, SW6 6EA (Tel: 020-7736 3233; Fax: 020-7736 3233;
Email: curator.fulhampalace@excite.co.uk)
Curator: Ms M. Poliakoff

294 Cultural London

HOUNSLOW

Kew Bridge Steam Museum
Green Dragon Lane, Brentford, Middx, TW8 0EN (Tel: 020-8568 4757; Fax: 020-8569 9978; Web: http://www.kbsm.org.uk)
General Manager: A. A. Cundick

ISLINGTON

London Canal Museum
12-13 New Wharf Road, London, N1 9RT (Tel: 020-7713 0836; Email: martins@dircon.co.uk; Web: http://www.canalmuseum.org.uk)
Trust Secretary: M. Sach

Museum of the Order of St John
St John's Gate, St John's Lane, London, EC1M 4DA (Tel: 020-7253 6644; Fax: 020-7336 0587; Web: http://www.sja.org.uk/history)
Curator: Ms P. Willis

KENSINGTON AND CHELSEA

National Army Museum
Royal Hospital Road, London, SW3 4HT (Tel: 020-7730 0717; Fax: 020-7823 6573; Email: info@national-army-museum.ac.uk; Web: http://www.national-army-museum.ac.uk)
Director: I. G. Robertson

Natural History Museum
Cromwell Road, London, SW7 5BD (Tel: 020-7942 5000; Web: http://www.nhm.ac.uk)
Director: Dr N. Chalmers

Victoria and Albert Museum
Cromwell Road, South Kensington, London, SW7 2RL (Tel: 020-7942 2000; Fax: 020-7942 2266; Web: http://www.vam.ac.uk)
Director: Dr A. Borge CBE, FSA

LAMBETH

Florence Nightingale Museum
Gassiot House, 2 Lambeth Palace Road, London, SE1 7EW (Tel: 020-7620 0374; Fax: 020-7928 1760; Email: curator@florence-nightingale.co.uk; Web: http://www.florence-nightingale.co.uk)
Director: A. Attewell

Hayward Gallery
Belvedere Road, London, SE1 8XX (Tel: 020-7928 3144; Email: visual_arts@hayward.org.uk; Web: http://www.hayward-gallery.org.uk)
Director: Ms S. Ferleger Brades

LEWISHAM

Horniman Museum and Gardens
100 London Road, London, SE23 3PQ (Tel: 020-8699 1872; Fax: 020-8291 5506; Email: enquiry@horniman.demon.co.uk; Web: http://www.horniman.demon.co.uk)
Director: Ms J. Vitmayer

Museum of Installation
175 Deptford High Street, London, SE8 3NU (Tel: 020-8692 8778; Fax: 020-8692 8122; Email: moi@dircon.co.uk; Web: http://www.moi.dircon.co.uk)
Directors: Ms N. Oxley; N. De Oliveira; M. Petry

MERTON

Wimbledon Lawn Tennis Museum
Church Road, London, SW19 5AE (Tel: 020-8946 6131)
Curator: Ms H. Godfrey

Wimbledon Society Museum of Local History
22 Ridgway, London, SW19 4QN (Tel: 020-8296 9914)
Chairman of Curators: C. Maidment

RICHMOND

Museum of Richmond
Old Town Hall, Whittaker Avenue, Richmond, Surrey, TW9 1TP (Tel: 020-8332 1141; Fax: 020-8948 7570; Email: musrich@globalnet.co.uk)
Curator: S. Lace

Orleans House Gallery
Riverside, Twickenham, Middx, TW1 3DJ (Tel: 020-8892 0221; Fax: 020-8744 0501)
Curator: Ms R. Tranter

SOUTHWARK

Bramah Tea and Coffee Museum
Clove Building, Macguire Street, London, SE1 (Tel: 020-7378 0222)

Cuming Museum
155-157 Walworth Road, London, SE17 (Tel: 020-7701 1342)

Clink Museum
1 Clink Street, London, SE1 (Tel: 020-7378 1558)

Imperial War Museum
Lambeth Road, London, SE1 6HZ (Tel: 020-7416 5000; Fax: 020-7416 5374; Email: mail@iwm.org.uk; Web: http://www.iwm.org.uk)
Director-General: R. Crawford

Jerwood Gallery
171 Union Street, London, SE1 0LN (Tel: 020-7654 0173; Fax: 020-7654 0172; Email: curator@jerwoodspace.co.uk; Web: http://www.jerwoodspace.co.uk)
Curator: S. Hepworth

Livesey Museum
682 Old Kent Road, London, SE1 (Tel: 020-7739 5604)

London Fire Brigade Museum
Winchester House, Southwark Bridge Road, London, SE1 0EG (Tel: 020-7587 2894; Fax: 020-7587 2878;
Chief Officer: B. Robinson

Museums and Galleries 295

Old Operating Theatre Museum
9A St Thomas Street, London, SE1 9RY (Tel: 020-7955 4791; Fax: 020-7378 8383;
Email: oldopmus@aol.com;
Web: http://www.users.aol.com/nwleumweb/oot.htm)
Director: K. Flude

Pumphouse Educational Museum
Lavender Pond, Nature Park, Lavender Road, off Rotherhithe Street, London, SE16 5DZ (Tel: 020-7231 2976)
Head of Centre: Ms C. Marais

Shakespeare Globe Exhibition
Bankside, London, SE1 9DT (Tel: 020-7902 1500; Fax: 020-7902 1515; Email: clare@shakespeareglobe.com;
Web: http://www.shakespeare-globe.org)
General Director: P. Kyle

Tate Modern
Bankside, London, SE1 (Tel: 020-7887 8000)

TOWER HAMLETS

Bethnal Green Museum of Childhood
Cambridge Heath Road, London, E2 9PA (Tel: 020-8983 5200; Fax: 020-8983 5225;
Email: suel@vam.ac.uk)
Acting Head: Ms S. Laurence

Chisenhale Gallery
64-84 Chisenhale Road, London, E3 5QZ (Tel: 020-8981 4518; Fax: 020-8980 7169;
Email: mail@chisenhale.org.uk;
Web: http://www.chisenhale.org.uk)
Director: Ms S. Jones

Ragged School Museum
46-50 Copperfield Road, London, E3 4PR (Tel: 020-8980 6405; Fax: 020-8983 3481;
Email: museum@raggedschool.freeserve.co.uk;
Web: http://www.ics-london.co.uk/rsm)
Manager: Ms M. A. Edwards

Spitz Gallery
109 Commercial Street, London, E1 6BG (Tel: 020-7392 9032; Fax: 020-7377 8915;
Email: mail@spitz.co.uk;
Web: http://www.spitz.co.uk)
Manager: T. Dickin

WALTHAM FOREST

Vestry House Museum
Vestry Road, London, E17 9NH (Tel: 020-8509 1917;
Email: vestry.house@al.lbwf.gov.uk)

William Morris Gallery
Lloyd Park, Forest Road, London, E17 4PP (Tel: 020-8527 3782; Fax: 020-8527 7070;
Web: http://www.lbwf.gov.uk/wmg)
Keeper: Ms N. C. Gillow

WESTMINSTER

Aspley House, The Wellington Museum
149 Piccadilly, Hyde Park Corner, London, W1V 9FA (Tel: 020-7499 5676; Fax: 020-7493 6576)
Head: Ms A. Robinson

Cabinet War Rooms
King Charles Street, London, SW1A 2AQ (Tel: 020-7930 6961; Fax: 020-7839 5897;
Email: cwr@iwm.org.uk;
Web: http://www.iwm.org.uk)
Director: P. Reed

Courtauld Institute Galleries
Courtauld Institute of Art, Somerset House, Strand, London, WC2R 0RN (Tel: 020-7848 2526; Fax: 020-7848 2589; Web: http://www.courtauld.ac.uk)
Director: J. Murdoch

London Transport Museum
The Piazza, Covent Garden, London, WC2E 7BB (Tel: 020-7379 6344; Fax: 020-7565 7254;
Email: contact@ltmuseum.co.uk;
Web: http://www.ltmuseum.co.uk)
Director: S. Mullins

MCC Museum
Lord's Cricket Ground, London, NW8 8QN (Tel: 020-7289 1611; Fax: 020-7432 1062)
Curator: S. Green

National Gallery
Trafalgar Square, London, WC2N 5DN (Tel: 020-7747 2885; Fax: 020-7747 2423;
Email: information@ng-london.org.uk;
Web: http://www.nationalgallery.org.uk)
Director: N. MacGregor

National Portrait Gallery
2 St Martins Place, London, WC2H 0HE (Tel: 020-7306 0055; Fax: 020-7306 0056;
Web: http://www.npg.org.uk)
Director: C. Saumarez Smith

The Photographers' Gallery
5-8 Great Newport Street, London, WC2H 7HY (Tel: 020-7831 1772; Fax: 020-7836 9704;
Email: info@photonet.org.uk;
Web: http://www.photonet.org.uk)
Director: P. Wombell

Polish Institute & Sikorski Museum
20 Princes Gate, London, SW7 1PT (Tel: 020-7589 9249)
Curator: K. Barbarski

Royal Academy of Arts
Burlington House, Piccadilly, London, W1V 0DS (Tel: 020-7300 8000; Fax: 020-7300 8001;
Web: http://www.royalacademy.org.uk)
Secretary: D. Gordon

Royal Mews
Buckingham Palace, London, SW1A 1AA (Tel: 020-7839 1377; Web: http://www.royal.gov.uk)
Chief Executive: H. Roberts

296 Cultural London

Sherlock Holmes Museum
221B Baker Street, London, NW1 6XE (Tel: 020-7935 8866; Fax: 020-7738 1269;
Email: sherlock@easynet.co.uk;
Web: http://www.sherlock-holmes.co.uk)
Director: Ms G. Riley

Tate Gallery
Millbank, London, SW1P 4RG (Tel: 020-7887 8000; Fax: 020-7887 8007; Web: http://www.tate.org.uk)
Director: N. Serata

Theatre Museum
1E Tavistock Street, London, WC2E 7PA (Tel: 020-7943 4700; Fax: 020-7943 4777;
Web: http://www.vam.ac.uk)
Director: Ms M. Benton

Wallace Collection
Hertford House, Manchester Square, London, W1N 6BN (Tel: 020-7563 9500; Fax: 020-7224 2155;
Web: http://www.the-wallace-collection.org.uk)
Director: Ms R. Savill

The Weiss Gallery
1B Albemarle Street, London, W1X 3HF (Tel: 020-7409 0035; Fax: 020-7491 9604;
Email: mark@weissgallery.com;
Web: http://www.weissgallery.com)
Owner: M. A. F. Weiss

OPEN AIR THEATRE

Inner Circle, Regent's Park, London NW1 4NP (Booking Line: 020-7486 2431/1933; Fax: 020-7487 4562; Web: http://www.open-air-theatre.org.uk)

Situated in Regent's Park, the Open Air Theatre is one of the largest theatres in London with seating for 1,187 people. The Theatre was founded in 1932 by Sydney Carroll and Robert Atkins. The existing auditorium was built in 1975 and is famous for its summer seasons of classical theatre including two plays by William Shakespeare, a Broadway musical and a play for children. Audiences may bring picnics or take advantage of the bar, buffet and barbecue facilities.

PARKS

Ashtead Common (500 acres), Surrey
Burnham Beeches and Fleet Wood (540 acres), Bucks. Purchased by the Corporation for the benefit of the public in 1880, Fleet Wood (65 acres) being presented in 1921
Coulsdon Common (133 acres), Surrey
Epping Forest (6,000 acres), Essex. Purchased by the Corporation and opened to the public in 1882. The present forest is 12 miles long by 1 to 2 miles wide, about one-tenth of its original area
Farthing Downs (121 acres), Surrey
Hampstead Heath (789 acres), London NW3. Including Golders Hill (36 acres) and Parliament Hill (271 acres)
Highgate Wood (70 acres), London N6/N10
Kenley Common (138 acres), Surrey
Queen's Park (30 acres), London NW6
Riddlesdown (90 acres), Surrey

Spring Park (51 acres), Kent
West Ham Park (77 acres), London E15
West Wickham Common (25 acres), Kent
Woodredon and Warlies Park Estate (740 acres), Waltham Abbey
Also smaller open spaces within the City of London, including Finsbury Circus Gardens
Maintained by Historic Royal Palaces
Hampton Court Gardens (54 acres), Surrey
Hampton Court Green (17 acres), Surrey
Hampton Court Park (622 acres), Surrey

ROMAN REMAINS

The city wall of Roman Londinium was largely rebuilt during the medieval period but sections may be seen near the White Tower in the Tower of London; at Tower Hill; at Coopers' Row; at All Hallows, London Wall, its vestry being built on the remains of a semi-circular Roman bastion; at St Alphage, London Wall, showing a succession of building repairs from the Roman until the late medieval period; and at St Giles, Cripplegate. Sections of the great forum and basilica, more than 165 metres square, have been encountered during excavations in the area of Leadenhall, Gracechurch Street and Lombard Street. Traces of Roman activity along the river include a massive riverside wall built in the late Roman period, and a succession of Roman timber quays along Lower and Upper Thames Street. Finds from these sites can be seen at the Museum of London. Other major buildings are the amphitheatre at Guildhall; remains of bath-buildings in Upper and Lower Thames Street; and the temple of Mithras in Walbrook.

ROYAL ALBERT HALL

Kensington Gore, London SW7 2AP (Tel: 020-7589 3203; Fax: 020-7823 7725;
Email: admin@royalalberthall.com;
Web: http://www.royalalberthall.com)

The elliptical hall, one of the largest in the world, was completed in 1871. It was constructed in memory of Prince Albert, Consort of Queen Victoria. Designed by British Army Engineer Major General H. Y. D. Scott, the hall seats around 8,266 people. The brick exterior is decorated with a terracotta relief depicting the development of the arts and sciences through history. Since 1941 it has been the venue each summer for the Promenade Concerts, founded in 1895 by Sir Henry Wood. Other events include pop and classical music concerts, dance, opera, sporting events, conferences and banquets.

ROYAL HOSPITAL, CHELSEA

Royal Hospital Road, London SW3 4SR (Tel: 020-7730 0161)

Founded by Charles II in 1682, and built by Wren; The Royal Hospital, Chelsea opened in 1692 for old and disabled soldiers. The extensive grounds include the former Ranelagh Gardens and are the venue for the Chelsea Flower Show each May.

ROYAL OPERA HOUSE

Covent Garden, London, WC2E 9DD Box Office, 48 Floral Street, London WC2E 7QA (Tel: 020-7304 4000; Fax: 020-7497 1256; Web: http://www.royaloperahouse.org.uk)

Home of The Royal Ballet (1931) and The Royal Opera (1946), The Royal Opera House is the third theatre to be built on the Covent Garden site. The first, the Theatre Royal at Covent Garden was opened in 1732 and was primarily a playhouse. This theatre was destroyed by fire in 1808 and replaced by the second Theatre Royal which opened in 1809. This Theatre was also destroyed by fire and replaced by the third and present theatre in 1858. The Theatre became the Royal Opera House in 1892. After extensive redevelopment and restoration the Theatre reopened in December 1999.

ROYAL PARKS

The Royal Parks of London are maintained and managed by The Royal Parks Agency. The Royal Parks, The Old Police House, Hyde Park, London W2 (Tel: 020-7298 2000; Royal Parks Police Tel: 020-7298 2076) There are seven Royal Parks in London. They are Hyde Park; Kensington Gardens; St. James's Park and The Green Park; Regent's Park and Primrose Hill; Greenwich Park; Richmond Park; Bushy Park. The Royal Parks Agency also manages Brompton Cemetery and a number of other public open spaces, including Parliament Square and Victoria Tower Gardens. The aims of the Agency are threefold:
- to offer peaceful enjoyment, recreation, entertainment and delight to those that use them
- to enhance, protect and preserve the parks for this and future generations.
- to manage the parks with levels of efficiency and effectiveness in accordance with the key principals of public service as dictated by the Citizen's Charter.

Bushy Park
Covering an area of 1,100 acres, Bushy Park comprises of woodland areas and many ponds and streams which are fed by the Longford River. The park was created as three separate parks by Henry VIII and Cardinal Wolsey between 1500 and 1537 and is famous for its tree-lined avenues such as Chestnut Avenue leading to the Diana Fountain. Other facilities offered by the park are horse riding, fishing (by permit only), cycling tracks, cricket, hockey and rugby pitches, and a model boat pool.
Stockyard Education Centre, Bushy Park, Hampton Court Road, Hampton Hill, Middlesex TW12 2EJ (Tel: 020-8979 1586).

Greenwich Park
Greenwich Park was created in 1433 and is around 185 acres in size. As well as the Royal Observatory at its centre, the park also contains a deer enclosure and areas of formal gardens. Other facilities include tennis courts, rugby, cricket and hockey pitches, a children's playground and a children's boating pool.
Park Manager, Blackheath Gate, Greenwich Park, London SE10 8QY (Tel: 020-8858 2608).

Hyde Park
Hyde Park was originally formed in 1536 when the land was acquired for hunting purposes. Its most famous features include the Serpentine, a lake of approximately 11.34 hectares which has been used for swimming, boating and fishing; and 'Rotten Row', a riding track. Other facilities include bowling and putting greens, tennis courts, a playground, band concerts, a restaurant, cycle routes and an outdoor riding arena.
Park Manager, Rangers Lodge, Hyde Park, London W2 2UH (Tel: 020-7298 2100).

Kensington Gardens
The Gardens were originally formed in 1689 from land taken from Hyde Park, when William and Mary moved into Nottingham House, now Kensington Palace. The gardens were redesigned and extended by Charles Bridgeman in the Early 18th Century and have received only minor additions and alterations since. These include the Albert Memorial and the Italian Gardens. Other facilities include the Serpentine Gallery, playgrounds and sailing for model boats on Round Pond.
Park Manager, Magazine Storeyard, Magazine Gate, Kensington Gardens, London W2 2UH (Tel: 020-7298 2117).

Regent's Park and Primrose Hill
The original planning of Regent's park was the responsibility of John Nash, Crown Architect and friend of the Prince Regent in 1811. The site includes the summit of Primrose Hill and boasts views of Westminster and the City. Originally the park was private, but it is now open to the public and incorporates numerous attractions and facilities. These include London Zoo, an open air theatre, bandstands, tennis and netball courts, tennis and golf schools, an athletics track, cricket, softball pitches, rounders pitches, football, rugby, hockey, playgrounds, boating on the main lake and the Waterbus on the Regent's Canal.
Park Manager, The Store Yard, Inner Circle, Regent's Park, London NW1 4NR (Tel: 020-7486 7905).

Richmond Park
Richmond Park was enclosed as a hunting ground by Charles I in 1637 and still contains many of the characteristics of a deer park today. The park comprises of a mixture of Wetland, Woodland and numerous herds of Red and Fallow deer. In 1992 the park was given the status of a Site of Special Scientific Interest by English Nature. Other facilities offered by the park are two public golf courses, horse riding, fishing on Pen Ponds and cycling tracks.
Superintendent's Office, Holly Lodge, Richmond Park, Surrey TW10 5HS (Tel: 020-8948 3209).

St James's Park and The Green Park
Lying to the east of Buckingham Palace and The Mall, these parks were acquired by Henry VIII in the early 16th Century. Many minor alterations and improvements have taken place through the years but the park as it is today is markedly loyal to the original designs of Crown Architect John Nash from 1827.
Other facilities that the park has to offer are deck chairs, band concerts and a children's playground.
Park Manager, The Storeyard, St. James's Park, Horse Guards Approach, London SW1A 2BJ (Tel: 020-7930 1793).

ST JAMES'S PALACE

Pall Mall, London SW1 (Tel: 020-7930 4832; Web: http://www.royal.gov.uk)

St James's Palace was built by Henry VIII. The Gatehouse and Presence Chamber remain; later alterations were made by Wren and Kent. The Chapel Royal is open for services on Sundays at 8.30 a.m. and 11.15 a.m. between the beginning of October and Good Friday (see Marlborough House for summer services in The Queen's Chapel). Representatives of foreign powers are still accredited 'to the Court of St James's'. Clarence House (1825) in the palace precinct is the home of The Queen Mother.

ST PAUL'S CATHEDRAL

The Chapter House, St Paul's Churchyard, London EC4M 8AD (Tel: 020-7246 8348; Fax: 020-7248 3104; Email: chapterhouse@stpaulscathedral.org.uk; Web: http://stpauls.london.anglican.org)

St Paul's Cathedral was built in 1675-1710 at a cost of £747,660. The cross on the dome is 365 ft above the ground level, the inner cupola 218 ft above the floor. 'Great Paul' in the south-west tower weighs nearly 17 tons. The organ by Father Smith (enlarged by Willis and rebuilt by Mander) is in a case carved by Grinling Gibbons, who also carved the choir stalls.

SOMERSET HOUSE

Strand and Victoria Embankment, London WC2 (Web: http://www.somerset-house.org.uk)

Somerset House was the property of Lord Protector Somerset, at whose attainder in 1552 the palace passed to the Crown. It was a royal residence until 1692.

The river façade (600 ft long) was built in 1776-86 from the designs of Sir William Chambers. The eastern extension, which houses part of King's College, was built by Smirke in 1829. Somerset House has had many purposes including housing the Royal Academy (1771-1836), the Society of Antiquities and the Register of Births, Deaths and Marriages. After considerable refurbishment, Somerset House is now open to the public offering access to museums, galleries, cafes, shops and restaurants. The South Building houses the Gilbert Collection of decorative arts and the Courtauld Institute Gallery. Concerts are also to be held in the famous courtyard of Somerset House, one of London's newest open-air venues.

SOUTH BANK CENTRE

Box Office, Level 1, Royal Festival Hall, Belvedere Road, London SE1 8XX (Tel: 020-7960 4242; Fax: 020-7921 0821/0063; Email: boxoffice@rfh.org.uk; Web: http://www.main.sbc.org.uk)

The Royal Festival Hall and Hayward Gallery stand on the south bank of the River Thames on a site covering 27 acres of land dedicated to the arts. The South Bank Board directly manages the Royal Festival Hall (2,931 seats, opened in 1951 as part of the Festival of Britain), the Queen Elizabeth Hall (913 seats), the Purcell Room (367 seats), the Voice Box (77 seats), the Saison Poetry Library (housing the Arts Council Collection) and the Hayward Gallery (opened in 1968).

The Royal Festival Hall and Hayward Gallery host a range of concerts and events from jazz, classical, rock, world and folk music, the visual arts, poetry and literature to outdoor events and contemporary dance.

The National Touring Exhibition programme is also based on the South Bank and administered by the Board on behalf of the Arts Council of England, along with the Arts Council Collection of post-war art. The South Bank Centre shares the site with the independently managed Royal National Theatre and the National Film Theatre.

The National Film Theatre (opened 1952), administered by the British Film Institute, has three auditoria showing over 2,000 films a year. The London Film Festival is held there every November.

The Royal National Theatre (opened 1976) and stages classical, modern, new and neglected plays in its auditoria: the 1,160-seat Olivier theatre, the 890-seat Lyttleton theatre and the Cottesloe theatre which seats up to 400.

SOUTHWARK CATHEDRAL

London SE1 9DA (Tel: 020-7367 6700; Fax: 020-7367 6725; Email: cathedral@dswark.org.uk; Web: http://www.dswark.org)

Southwark Cathedral is mainly 13th century, but the nave is largely rebuilt. The tomb of John Gower (1330-1408) is between the Bunyan and Chaucer memorial windows in the north aisle; Shakespeare's effigy, backed by a view of Southwark and the Globe Theatre, is in the south aisle; the tomb of Bishop Andrewes (died 1626) is near the screen. The lady chapel was the scene of the consistory courts of the reign of Mary (Gardiner and Bonner) and is still used as a consistory court. John Harvard, after whom Harvard University is named, was baptised here in 1607, and the chapel by the north choir aisle is his memorial chapel.

RIVER THAMES

The River Thames stretches from the sea as far inland as Teddington in Middlesex. The Port of London Authority is the governing body for the Thames.

There are numerous companies organising trips on the River Thames from sightseeing tours through to dinner cruises and corporate charters. The list below details a selection of companies offering such services.

Bateau London (Tel: 020-7925 2215)
Campion Launches (Tel: 020-8305 0300)
Catamaran Cruisers Ltd (Tel: 020-7987 1185; Fax: 020-7839 1034)
City Cruises (Tel: 020-7237 5734)
London Launches Ltd (Tel: 020-7930 3373)
Westminster Passenger Services Association (Tel: 020-7930 4097)
Woods River Cruises. Tel: 020-7481 2711; Fax: 020-7481 8300

River Trip Line 0839 123432 (24 hour information on river trips)

BRIDGES

The bridges over the Thames from east to west. (Architect's name in parenthesis).
The Queen Elizabeth II Bridge – opened 1991, from Dartford to Thurrock
Tower Bridge – opened 1894
London Bridge – opened after rebuilding by Rennie, 1831; the new London Bridge opened 1973
Alexandra Bridge – built 1863-6
Southwark Bridge (Rennie) – built 1814-19; rebuilt 1912-21
Blackfriars Railway Bridge – completed 1864
Blackfriars Bridge – built 1760-9; rebuilt 1860-9; widened 1907-10
Waterloo Bridge (Rennie) – opened 1817; rebuilt 1937-42
Hungerford Railway Bridge (Brunel) – suspension bridge built 1841-5; replaced by present railway and footbridge 1863
Westminster Bridge – opened 1750; rebuilt 1854-62
Lambeth Bridge – built 1862; rebuilt 1929-32
Vauxhall Bridge – built 1811-16; rebuilt 1895-1906
Grosvenor Bridge – built 1859-60; rebuilt 1963-7
Chelsea Bridge – built 1851-8; replaced by suspension bridge 1934; widened 1937
Albert Bridge – opened 1873; restructured (Bazalgette) 1884; strengthened 1971-3
Battersea Bridge (Holland) – opened 1772; rebuilt (Bazalgette) 1890
Battersea Railway Bridge – opened 1863
Wandsworth Bridge – opened 1873; rebuilt 1940
Putney Railway Bridge – opened 1889
Putney Bridge – built 1727-9; rebuilt (Bazalgette) 1882-6; starting point of Oxford and Cambridge Boat Race
Hammersmith Bridge – built 1824-7; rebuilt (Bazalgette) 1883-7
Barnes Railway Bridge – built 1846-9; restructured 1893
Chiswick Bridge – opened 1933
Kew Railway Bridge – opened 1869
Kew Bridge – built 1758-9; rebuilt and renamed King Edward VII Bridge 1903
Richmond Lock – lock, weir and footbridge opened 1894
Twickenham Bridge – opened 1933
Richmond Railway Bridge – opened 1848; restructured 1906-8
Richmond Bridge – built 1774-7; widened 1937
Teddington Lock – footbridge opened 1889; marks the end of the tidal reach of the Thames
Kingston Bridge – built 1825-8; widened 1914
Hampton Court Bridge – built 1753; replaced by iron bridge 1865; present bridge built 1933
Two new footbridges are under construction; the Millennium Bridge will link the City and the new Tate Gallery of Modern Art; and a second bridge is being constructed alongside the railway on Hungerford Bridge.

THAMES EMBANKMENTS

The Victoria Embankment, on the north side from Westminster to Blackfriars, was constructed by Sir Joseph Bazalgette (1819-91) for the Metropolitan Board of Works, 1864-70; the seats, of which the supports of some are a kneeling camel, laden with spicery, and of others a winged sphinx, were presented by the Grocers' Company and by W. H. Smith, MP, in 1874; the Albert Embankment, on the south side from Westminster Bridge to Vauxhall, 1866-9; the Chelsea Embankment, 1871-4. The total cost exceeded £2,000,000. Bazalgette also inaugurated the London main drainage system, 1858-65. A medallion (Flumini vincula posuit) has been placed on a pier of the Victoria Embankment to commemorate the engineer.

THAMES FLOOD BARRIER

Officially opened in May 1984, though first used in February 1983, the barrier consists of ten rising sector gates, spanning 570 yards from bank to bank of the Thames at Woolwich Reach. When not in use the gates lie horizontally, allowing shipping to navigate the river normally; when the barrier is closed, the gates turn through 90 degrees to stand vertically more than 50 feet above the river bed. The barrier took eight years to complete and can be raised within about 30 minutes.

THAMES TUNNELS

The Rotherhithe Tunnel, opened 1908, connects Commercial Road, London E14, with Lower Road, Rotherhithe; it is 1 mile 332 yards long, of which 525 yards are under the river. The first Blackwall Tunnel (northbound vehicles only), opened 1897, connects East India Dock Road, Poplar, with Blackwall Lane, East Greenwich. The height restriction on the northbound tunnel is 13ft 4in. A second tunnel (for southbound vehicles only) opened 1967. The lengths of the tunnels measured from East India Dock Road to the Gate House on the south side are 6,215 ft (old tunnel) and 6,152 ft. Greenwich Tunnel (pedestrians only), opened 1902, connects the Isle of Dogs, Poplar, with Greenwich; it is 406 yards long. The Woolwich Tunnel (pedestrians only), opened 1912, connects North and South Woolwich below the passenger and vehicular ferry from North Woolwich Station, London E16, to High Street, Woolwich, London SE18; it is 552 yards long.

THEATRES

BRENT

Tricycle
269 Kilburn High Road, London, NW6 7JR (Tel: 020-7372 6611; Fax: 020-7328 0795)
Hotline number: 020-7328 1000
Seating Capacity: 225

BROMLEY

Wickham
Corkscrew Hill, West Wickham, Kent, BR4 9BA (Tel: 020-8777 9989)
Hotline number: 020-8777 3037
Seating Capacity: 80-100

CAMDEN

Ambassadors Theatre
West Street, London, WC2H 9ND (Tel: 020-7836 4105; Fax: 020-7836 8012)
Hotline number: 020-7836 6111
Seating Capacity: 418

300 Cultural London

Bloomsbury
15 Gordon Street, London, WC1H 0AH (Tel: 020-7679 2777; Fax: 020-7383 4080)
Hotline number: 020-7388 8822
Seating Capacity: 550

Dominion
268-269 Tottenham Court Road, London W1P 0AQ (Tel: 020-7580 1889; Fax: 020-7580 0246;
Web: http://www.london-dominion.co.uk)
Hotline number: 020-7656 1888
Seating Capacity: 2182

Donmar Warehouse
41 Earlham Street, London, WC2H 9LD (Tel: 020-7240 4882; Fax: 020-7240 4878;
Web: http://www.donmar-warehouse.com)
Hotline number: 020-7369 1732
Seating Capacity: 251

Hampstead
98 Avenue Road, London, NW3 3EX (Tel: 020-7722 9224; Fax: 020-7722 3860;
Web: http://www.hampstead-theatre.co.uk)
Seating Capacity: 174

Lion & Unicorn
42-44 Gaisford Street, London, NW5 2ED (Tel: 020-7482 0850; Fax: 020-7388 7329)
Hotline number: 020-7482 0850
Seating Capacity: 50

Roundhouse
Chalk Farm Road, London, NW1 8EH (Tel: 020-7424 9991; Fax: 020-7424 9992;
Web: http://www.roundhouse.org.uk)
Hotline number: 020-7424 9800
Seating Capacity: 1400

CITY OF LONDON

Bridewell
14 Bride Lane, London, EC4Y 8EQ (Tel: 020-7353 0259; Fax: 020-7583 5289)
Hotline number: 020-7936 3456
Seating Capacity: 120-177

ENFIELD

Theatre at the Fox
413 Green Lanes, Palmers Green, London, N13 4JD (Tel: 020-8882 4488; Fax: 020-8882 4488)
Hotline number: 020-8882 4488
Seating Capacity: 56

GREENWICH

Bob Hope
Wythfield Road, Eltham, London, SE9 5TG (Tel: 020-8850 3702; Fax: 020-8850 8763;
Web: http://www.bobhopetheatre.co.uk)
Seating Capacity: 201

Greenwich
Crooms Hill, London, SE10 8ES (Tel: 020-8858 4447; Fax: 020-8858 8042;
Web: http://www.greenwichtheatre.org.uk)
Hotline number: 020-8858 7755
Seating Capacity: 423

HACKNEY

Brick Lane Music Hall
134—146 Curtain Road, London, EC2A 3AR (Tel: 020-7739 9996; Fax: 020-7739 9998;
Web: http://www.brick-lane-music-hall.co.uk)
Hotline number: 020-7739 9997
Seating Capacity: 200

Hackney Empire
291 Mare Street, London, E8 1EJ (Tel: 020-8510 4500; Fax: 020-8510 4530;
Web: http://www.hackneyempire.co.uk)
Hotline number: 020-8985 2424
Seating Capacity: 1200

HAMMERSMITH AND FULHAM

Bush
Shepherd's Bush Green, London, W12 8QD (Tel: 020-7602 3703; Fax: 020-7602 7614;
Web: http://www.bushtheatre.co.uk)
Hotline number: 020-8743 3388
Seating Capacity: 105

Lyric – Hammersmith
King Street, London, W6 0QL (Tel: 020-8741 0824; Fax: 020-8741 5965; Web: http://www.lyric.co.uk)
Hotline number: 020-8741 2311
Seating Capacity: 555

HOUNSLOW

Tabard
2 Bath Road, London, W4 1LW (Tel: 020-8994 5985)
Hotline number: 020-8995 6035
Seating Capacity: 49

ISLINGTON

Almeida
Almeida Street, London, N1 1TA (Tel: 020-7226 7432; Fax: 020-7704 9581; Web: http://www.almeida.co.uk)
Hotline number: 020-7359 4404
Seating Capacity: 300

Courtyard
The Courtyard, 10 York Way, Kings Cross, London, N1 9AA (Tel: 020-7833 0870; Fax: 020-7833 0870)
Hotline number: 020-7833 0876
Seating Capacity: 70

Kings Head
115 Upper Street, London, N1 1QN (Tel: 020-7226 8561; Fax: 020-7226 8507)
Hotline number: 020-7226 1916
Seating Capacity: 120

Little Angel
14 Dagmar Pass, London, N1 2DN (Tel: 020-7226 1787; Fax: 020-7359 7565)
Seating Capacity: 100

Theatres

Rosemary Branch
Shepperton Road, London, N1 3DT (Tel: 020-7704 6665; Fax: 020-7249 4786;
Web: http://www.rosemarybranch.co.uk)
Hotline number: 020-7704 6665
Seating Capacity: 50

Sadler's Wells
Rosebery Avenue, London, EC1R 4TN (Tel: 020-7863 8198; Fax: 020-7863 8199;
Web: http://www.sadlers-wells.com)
Hotline number: 020-7863 8000
Seating Capacity: 1500

Tower
Canonbury Place, London, N1 2NQ (Tel: 020-7226 3633; Fax: 020-7226 5111;
Web: http://www.tower-theatre.org.uk)
Seating Capacity: 150

Union Chapel Project
Union Chapel, Compton Avenue, London, N1 2XD (Tel: 020-7226 3750; Fax: 020-7354 8343)
Hotline number: 020-7226 1686
Seating Capacity: 50-1000

KENSINGTON AND CHELSEA

Chelsea Centre
Worlds End Place, Kings Road, London, SW10 0DR (Tel: 020-7352 1967; Fax: 020-7352 2024;
Web: http://www.btinternet.com/~chelseacentre/)
Hotline number: 020-7351 1967
Seating Capacity: 100

Finborough
118 Finborough Road, London, SW10 9ED (Tel: 020-7244 7439; Fax: 020-7835 1853)
Hotline number: 020-7373 3842
Seating Capacity: 50

Gate
11 Pembridge Road, London, W11 3HQ (Tel: 020-7299 5387; Fax: 020-7221 6055)
Hotline number: 020-7229 0706
Seating Capacity: 100

Man in the Moon
392 Kings Road, London, SW3 5UZ (Tel: 020-7351 5701; Fax: 020-7351 1873)
Hotline number: 020-7351 2876
Seating Capacity: 68

LAMBETH

Landor
70 Landor Road, London, SW9 9PH (Tel: 020-7737 7276; Fax: 020-7737 2728;
Web: http://www.fringetheatre.org.uk)
Hotline number: 020-7737 7276
Seating Capacity: 55

Old Vic
103 The Cut, London, SE1 8BN (Tel: 020-7928 2651; Fax: 020-7261 9161;
Web: http://www.oldvictheatre.com)
Seating Capacity: 1077

Oval House
52-54 Kennington Oval, London, SE11 5SW (Tel: 020-7582 0080; Fax: 020-7820 0990;
Web: http://www.ovalhouse.dircon.co.uk)
Hotline number: 020-7582 7680
Seating Capacity: 150

Royal National
Upper Ground, London, SE1 9PX (Tel: 020-7452 3333; Fax: 020-7452 3344;
Web: http://www.nt-online.org)
Hotline number: 020-7452 3000
Seating Capacity: 1160, 890 and 350

Young Vic
66 The Cut, London, SE1 8LZ (Tel: 020-7633 0133; Fax: 020-7928 1585)
Hotline number: 020-7928 6363
Seating Capacity: 40-450

LEWISHAM

Blackheath Halls
23 Lee Road, London, SE3 9RQ (Tel: 020-8463 0100; Fax: 020-8852 5154;
Web: http://www.blackheathhalls.com)
Seating Capacity: 650 and 250

Deptford Albany
Douglas Way, London, SE8 4AG (Tel: 020-8692 0231; Fax: 020-8469 2253;
Web: http://www.deptfordnet.org.uk/albany)
Seating Capacity: 239

NEWHAM

Theatre Royal Stratford East
Gerry Raffles Square, London, E15 1BN (Tel: 020-8534 7374; Fax: 020-8534 8381;
Web: http://www.stratfordeast.org.uk)
Hotline number: 020-8534 0310
Seating Capacity: 460

REDBRIDGE

Kenneth More
Oakfield Road, Ilford, Essex, IG1 1BT (Tel: 020-8553 4466; Fax: 020-8553 5476;
Web: http://www.kenneth-more-theatre.co.uk)
Seating Capacity: 365

RICHMOND

Landmark Arts Centre
Ferry Road, Teddington, Middx, TW11 9NN (Tel: 020-8977 7558; Fax: 020-8977 4830)
Hotline number: 020-8977 7558
Seating Capacity: 342

Richmond
The Little Green, Richmond, Surrey, TW9 1QJ (Tel: 020-8940 0220; Fax: 020-8948 3601)
Hotline number: 020-8940 0088
Seating Capacity: 820

302 Cultural London

SOUTHWARK

Blue Elephant
59A Bethwin Road, London, SE5 0XT (Tel: 020-7701 0100; Fax: 020-7701 7870)
Hotline number: 020-7701 0100
Seating Capacity: 76

SUTTON

Charles Cryer Studio
39 High Street, Carshalton, Surrey, SM5 3BB (Tel: 020-8770 4950; Fax: 020-8770 4969; Web: http://www.charlescryer.org.uk)
Seating Capacity: 180

TOWER HAMLETS

Broomhill Opera
Wilton's Music Hall, 1 Graces Alley, Wellclose Square, London, E1 8HY (Tel: 020-7702 9555; Fax: 020-7702 9555; Web: http://www.broomhill.co.uk)
Seating Capacity: 300

Space
269 Westferry Road, London, E14 3RS (Tel: 020-7515 2453; Fax: 020-7987 0444; Web: http://www.space.org.uk)
Hotline number: 020-7515 7799
Seating Capacity: 100-140

WANDSWORTH

Bridge Lane
Bridge Lane, off Battersea Bridge Road, London, SW11 3AD (Tel: 020-7228 5185; Fax: 020-7228 8828)
Hotline number: 020-7228 8828
Seating Capacity: 500

Grace
Latchmere Pub, 503 Battersea Park Road, London, SW11 3BW (Tel: 020-7924 1517; Web: http://www.fringetheatre.org.uk)
Hotline number: 020-7794 0022
Seating Capacity: 80

WESTMINSTER

Adelphi
Strand, London, WC2N 5HZ (Tel: 020-7836 1166; Fax: 020-7379 5709)
Hotline number: 020-7344 0055
Seating Capacity: 1500

Apollo Victoria
17 Wilton Road, London, SW1V 1LG (Tel: 020-7834 6318; Fax: 020-7630 7716; Web: http://www.tickets-direct.co.uk)
Hotline number: 020-7416 6059
Seating Capacity: 1524

Canal Café
Bridge House, Delamere Terrace, London W2 6ND (Tel: 020-7289 6056; Fax: 020-7266 1717)
Hotline number: 020-7289 6054
Seating Capacity: 60

Comedy
7-10 Panton Street, London, SW1Y 4DN (Tel: 020-7321 5300; Fax: 020-7321 5311; Web: http://www.act-arts.co.uk)
Hotline number: 020-7369 1731
Seating Capacity: 780

Gielgud
Shaftesbury Avenue, London, W1V 8AR (Tel: 020-7437 6003; Fax: 020-7437 0784)
Hotline number: 020-7494 5065
Seating Capacity: 882

Her Majesty's
Haymarket, London, SW1Y 4QR (Fax: 020-7930 8467; Web: http://www.stoll-moss.com)
Hotline number: 020-7494 5400
Seating Capacity: 1161

Open Air
Inner Circle, Regent's Park, London, NW1 4NP (Tel: 020-7935 5756; Fax: 020-7487 4562; Web: http://www.open-air-theatre.org.uk)
Hotline number: 020-7486 2431
Seating Capacity: 1200

Palace
Shaftesbury Avenue, London, W1V 8AY (Tel: 020-7434 0088; Fax: 020-7734 6157)
Hotline number: 020-7434 0909
Seating Capacity: 1400

Palladium
8 Argyll Street, London, W1A 3AB (Tel: 020-7437 6678; Fax: 020-7437 4010; Web: http://www.stoll-moss.com)
Hotline number: 020-7494 5020
Seating Capacity: 2291

Peacock
Portugal Street, London, WC2A 2HT (Tel: 020-7863 8268; Fax: 020-7314 9004; Web: http://www.sadlers-well.com)
Hotline number: 020-7863 8222/8000
Seating Capacity: 1000

Players
The Arches, Villiers Street, London, WC2N 6NG (Tel: 020-7976 1307; Fax: 020-7839 8067; Web: http://www.playerstheatre.co.uk)
Hotline number: 020-7839 1134
Seating Capacity: 250

Playhouse
Northumberland Avenue, London, WC2N 5DE (Tel: 020-7839 4292; Fax: 020-7839 1195)
Hotline number: 020-7839 4401
Seating Capacity: 786

Prince Edward
Old Compton Street, London, W1V 6HS (Tel: 020-7437 2024; Fax: 020-7734 1454)
Hotline number: 020-7447 5400
Seating Capacity: 1600

Scenes and Sights of London 303

Royal Opera House
Covent Garden, London, WC2E 9DD (Tel: 020-7240 1200; Fax: 020-7240 0141;
Web: http://www.royaloperahouse.org)
Hotline number: 020-7304 4000
Seating Capacity: 2000

St John's Smith Square
Smith Square, London, SW1P 3HA (Tel: 020-7222 2168; Fax: 020-7233 1618;
Web: http://www.sjss.org.uk)
Hotline number: 020-7222 1061
Seating Capacity: 780

Strand
5 Aldwych, London, WC2B 4LD (Tel: 020-7836 4144;
Web: http://www.trh.co.uk)
Hotline number: 020-7930 8800
Seating Capacity: 1050

Sunset Strip
30A Dean Street, London, W1V 5AN (Tel: 020-7437 7229; Fax: 020-7404 7282;
Web: http://www.sunsetstrip.co.uk)
Hotline number: 020-7437 7229
Seating Capacity: 60

Wigmore Hall
36 Wigmore Street, London, W1H 0BP (Tel: 020-7486 1907; Fax: 020-7224 3800)
Hotline number: 020-7935 2141
Seating Capacity: 539

TOWER BRIDGE EXPERIENCE

Tower Bridge, London, SE1

The Tower Bridge Experience gives an insight into the history and construction of this famous landmark.

WALKING

London is a magnificent place to explore on foot and a number of companies offer guided tours to key sights and places of interest. Below are the details of two such companies with some information about the walks they lead in the capital.

DISCOVERY WALKS

Chancery Lane, London, WC2A 1AF (Tel: 020-8530 844)

Walks take place every day, regardless of weather conditions and last approximately two hours. These include the *London Ghost Walk* and the *Jack the Ripper Walk*.

LONDON WALKS

P.O. Box 1708, London, NW6 4LW (Tel: 020-7624 5978; Fax: 020-7625 1932;
Web: http://www.walks.co.uk)

London Walks is the oldest established walking tour company in London and offers a wide selection of trips, walks and explorer days in and around the capital. For a full timetable please contact London Walks at the address above. Walks and tours offered include:

Shakespeare's London, Old Mayfair, The British Museum Walk, The Old Jewish Quarter, Legal London, Diana, Princess of Wales, Along the Thames Pub Walk, The Victoria and Albert Museum Walk, Ghosts of the West End, Jack the Ripper Haunts, The London of Oscar Wilde, Old Westminster, Charles Dickens London, The Beatles, Sherlock Holmes.

WESTMINSTER ABBEY

The Chapter Office, Dean's Yard, Westminster Abbey, London SW1P 3PA (Tel: 020-7222 5152; Fax: 020-7233 2072; E-mail: press@westminster-abbey.org;
Web: http://www.westminster-abbey.org)

The original abbey was a Benedictine monastery begun by Edward the Confessor in 1050, however, the present building was built by Henry III in 1245. The abbey contains the chapel of Henry VII, chapter house and cloisters, Edward the Confessor's shrine, tombs of kings and queens and many other monuments, including the grave of 'The Unknown Warrior' and Poets' Corner. The Coronation Chair formerly enclosed the Stone of Scone, removed from Scotland by Edward I in 1296 and returned to Scotland in 1996.

WESTMINSTER CATHEDRAL

Cathedral Clergy House, 42 Francis Street, London SW1P 1QW (Tel: 020-7798 9055/6; for service times: 020-7798 9097; Fax: 020-7798 9090;
Web: http://www.westminstercathedral.org.uk)

Westminster Roman Catholic cathedral was built from 1895-1903 in the early Christian Byzantine style, by the architect J F. Bentley. The campanile is 283 feet high.

WETLANDS CENTRE

Queen Elizabeth's Walk, Barnes, London, SW13 (Tel: 020-8409 4400; E-mail: info@wetlandscentre.org.uk;
Web: http://www.wetlandscentre.org.uk)

The Wetlands Centre was opened on 26 May 2000 by the Wildfowl and Wetlands Trust (WWT), the ninth such centre to be opened in the UK. Situated 25 minutes away from Westminster, the Wetland Centre is the first created wetland habitat on such a large scale to have been developed in any capital city. It is a designated Site of Special Scientific Interest (SSSI) and is built on the former Barn Elms reservoirs and waterworks. It is open seven days a week until 6pm in summer and 5pm in winter and facilities include three outdoor exhibition areas, a shop and activities for children. The Wildfowl and Wetlands Trust promotes the conservation of wetlands, focusing on the protection of rare wetland birds. WWT is the largest international wetland conservation charity in the UK, founded by Sir Peter Scott in 1946. It aims to promote wetland conservation by bringing people closer to wildlife, saving threatened waterbirds, promoting a safe haven for birds, protecting wetlands for life and developing wetlands.

WORLD SQUARES FOR ALL

(Trafalgar Square and Parliament Square)
For further information contact the Greater London Authority at Romney House, Marsham Street, London SW1P 3PY.

World Squares for All is an initiative which aims to improve pedestrian access to the historic area around Parliament Square and Trafalgar Square and to redesign, improve and enhance the setting of the listed buildings. The World Squares for All plan, prepared by a team of multi-disciplinary consultants led by Lord Norman Foster, was presented to the Deputy Prime Minister in August 1998. Key features are: no traffic in front of the National Gallery; to improve access to Trafalgar Square; Parliament Square to be transformed; to establish a new gateway between Trafalgar Square and the West End; Whitehall to be transformed and the purpose of the Cenotaph to be respected; Old Palace Yard to be reinforced as a public space. It is thought that work on this project will commence in spring 2001 and will be completed in 2004 at an estimated cost of £70 million.

SPORT

An abundance of sports have developed in London over the centuries, ranging from the barbaric events of yesteryear to the sports that are enjoyed today.

ARCHERY

From its early development in ancient times until the 1500s, the bow was a popular accoutrement and history shows it as being the most used of all weapons. The bow first appears in Egyptian artwork and folklore.

In 1252 Henry III (1207-1272) decreed that all men between the ages of 15 and 60 shall keep a bow and arrow. By 1388 Richard II (1367-1399) stipulated that all men must practice the sport on Sundays and holidays. Henry VIII (1491-1547) introduced rules for the regulation of archery, its practice and made such alternative pastimes as football and handball unlawful.

Queen Victoria (1819-1901) participated in archery and Henry VIII was a renowned bowman, a patron of the sport and organised competitions during his reign. The first archery club, The Fraternity of St George, was co-founded by Henry VIII in 1537. In 1787, as the Prince of Wales (later George IV (1762-1830)) established the 'prince's-length' with target distances of 60, 80 and 100 yards and the 'prince's reckoning' of various target rings of 9, 7, 5, 3 and 1 point. He was also patron of the *Royal Toxophilite Society, Kentish Bowmen* and the *Royal British Bowmen* and with royal commendation came an increase in the sport's popularity.

Archery was commonly practised at public schools including Harrow and Eton. A Harrow custom called shooting for the 'Silver Arrow' lasted until 1771, when it was abolished because undesirable characters were drawn to the school.

The citizens of London and surrounding areas used the fields around the capital from a very early date to practice the sport. This caused problems with the landowners who had enclosed their properties with hedges. Citizens pulled down these hedges which resulted in laws being passed allowing people direct access to the fields.

In 1661 in Hyde Park, 400 archers took part in a grand display under the command of Sir E. Hungerford, Knight of the Bath. The Finsbury Archers marched to Hampton court in 1681 to shoot before the King at 160 yards for prizes. The King was so pleased with what he saw, he asked for the marshal to be presented and kissed his hand.

The father of modern archery is Sir Ashton Lever, a Lancashire baronet and antiquary, who also was the instigator of the Royal Toxophilite Society, founded in 1781. The formation of this society, started many other associations throughout England, Scotland and Wales (thought at first to be chiefly around London), with members amongst the gentry and aristocracy.

Between 1789 and 1793 a series of Annual General Meetings (AGM) for the archers of Great Britain were held in Blackheath, with the AGMs in 1794-5 taking place in Dulwich. The Blackheath meetings were dominated by participants from the capital and surrounding areas. On 29 May 1792, there were a total of 13 societies, competing against London, Kent and Surrey's 10 best clubs. The York round for men consisted of six dozen arrows at 100 yards, four dozen at 80 yards and two dozen at 60 yards for a total of 144 arrows. The Double York round used 288 arrows and had competitors shooting 144 arrows on each of the two days.

Revd Octavius Luard, writer of the archers' register, was convinced that meetings would not be a total success unless women competed. A number of women appeared at the meeting on 25-26 July 1851 at Wisden's Cricket Ground in Leamington, where the women's national round was established. It consisted of four dozen arrows at 60 yards and two dozen at 50 yards for a total of 72 arrows, making a two-day competition a total of 144 arrows being shot. In 1947 came the Double Hereford for women, with two rounds of six dozen arrows at 80 yards, four dozen at 60 yards and two dozen at 50 yards for a total of 144, with a two-day competition having 288 arrows shot.

A meeting held at York in April 1845 saw women compete in public for the first time. However, in the following year (1846) they were absent once again. Female presence was established at the Grand National Archery Meeting (GNAM) in 1847 and continued from then on.

In 1864 a meeting was held at Alexandra Park, where construction of the Palace was just beginning. There were special trains from Kings Cross to take both the archers and spectators to Wood Green. The Grand National Archery Society received £400 from the Alexandra Park company directors, who considered the contest a major public attraction.

The year 1875 saw the meeting return to the south east. This time the venue was a cricket ground at Richmond near Kew Gardens. The following year the chosen site was Sandown racecourse, which had just been completed.

Queen Victoria (1819-1901) was patron of the *Royal British Bowmen* and each year gave £25 to each winner. In 1834, the Queen and her mother HRH the Duchess of Kent became patrons of the St Leonards Archers at Hastings. By doing so, the club was entitled to the Royal prefix. Prince Albert became a patron in 1840 and a series of prizes were give by the royal couple.

Today there are many archery clubs around the country, with meetings being contested annually.

BEAR AND BULL BAITING

Bear baiting was introduced into England during the reign of King John (1167-1216) by a group of Italians and was displayed for the monarch in Ashby-de-la-Zouch. It is said that both King John and his court were highly delighted with the spectacle.

Elizabeth I (1533-1603) was such a fan of the sport that orders were issued via the Privy Council forbidding theatrical plays being held on Thursdays – the chosen day for bear baiting contests at Bankside.

Hockley in the Hole existed as a sporting arena from the time of Elizabeth I to that of William III (1650-1702) and events held at this venue were bear and bull baiting, dog fights and gladitorial contests. There were other sporting arenas located around the capital at Tothill Fields, Westminster, Saffron Hill, Clerkenwell and Marylebone.

Bears used for sport were the property of great nobles and peasants were given free admission to watch the baiting contests.

Both bears and bulls were chained to a stake in an arena or pit by a 15-foot chain which allowed for the movement within a 30-foot circle. The dog chosen to attack the bear would be held by the ears until it was filled with range and would then be released.

For nearly seven centuries this sport was part of English life.

BILLIARDS/SNOOKER

The game of billiards has been attributed to several different countries including France, Spain, Italy and England. Originally the game was played on a table that did not have any pockets and each player had only two balls to use.

There is evidence that a form of billiards was played on a lawn with a stick called a mace and became a feature of table billiards. This version grew in popularity among not only English nobility, but also the French.

In London near the end of the 18th century there were a large number of inns, taverns and coffeehouses. These venues were used by famous men associated with the arts and sciences as clubs, to debate matters of interest. A company called the *Mail and Stage Coaches* travelled to well-known taverns up and down the country. John Thurston travelled on these coaches setting up billiard tables, putting on the cloth and carrying out any necessary repairs. Up until 1840, there were hundreds of billiard tables in principal inns, taverns and clubs throughout London and the rest of the country, which had been made by Thurston.

Thurston had his first factory in Newcastle Street in the Strand in 1799 and then moved to Catherine Street in 1814. He was the sole appointment granted the Royal Warrant of HM King William IV (1765-1837) in 1833 and again was the sole appointment granted the Royal Warrant of HM Queen Victoria (1819-1901) in 1837. Once again the Royal Warrant was give to Thurston in 1907, this time for HM King Edward VII (1841-1910) followed by another Royal Warrant in 1911 for HM King George V (1865-1936).

His continued improvements to billiards tables saw him earn the Prize Medal at the Great Exhibition in 1851 and 19 years later he moved his factory to 33 Cheyne Walk in Chelsea. In 1892 he designed and made the original 'standard' billiard table that was officially adopted by the Billiards' Association.

J. Thurston's Company, now part of E. A. Clare and Son Ltd based in Liverpool, have the only billiard museum in the world and viewing is by appointment only. (Tel: 0151-207 1336).

The game of snooker apparently began in 1875 in Jubbulpore, India. Days would be spent by British officers of the Devonshire regiment around the billiard tables devising new versions of the game.

Sir Neville Chamberlain started adding various coloured balls to the table and from this the basic form of snooker was started. It began with 15 red balls, a yellow, green, pink and black and years later the blue and brown were added. Word of this new game made its way back to England during the 1880s thanks to John Roberts, who was introduced to Sir Neville while in India.

The sport's popularity grew and in 1927 Joe Davis won his first World Championship taking home a mere £6 10s 0d. By the time Stephen Hendry took the Embassy World Championship trophy in 1994 the top prize was £180,000.

BOXING

Starting in 1867, amateur boxing championships were held in three weights – light, middle and heavy. These contests followed the Marquis of Queensberry rules even though these rules were primitive and vague. Due to the way the champions were held there was much dissatisfaction as absurd decisions were handed down. A group of leading London clubs decided to form an authoritative body and revised the rules.

This meeting was held in 1880 to revise the rules and to form an association. At a second meeting a set of rules was drafted and the Amateur Boxing Association (ABA) was formed.

From the 16 agreed upon rules, the decision to have judges award points was so successful that it was quickly used not only by the professional side of the sport, but also throughout the world.

The first championships were held on 18 April 1881 and there were four weight categories – feather (9 stone), light (ten stone), middle (11 stone 4lbs) and heavy (no limit). All entrants paid five shillings and winners received a silver cup. The venue for the contests was St James's Hall on Piccadilly, which could hold 2000 spectators and cost 35 guineas to hire.

Boxing rules were revised in 1898 with points being awarded for each round. There were two rounds of three minutes and one round of four minutes with five points being awarded in the first two rounds and seven points in the final round.

At the 1901 championships there were entrants from Ireland, Scotland and Wales, but English boxers won all titles.

In 1902, a boxing tournament was held at the Royal Albert Hall to commemorate the coronation of King Edward VII (1841-1910).

In 1906 it was decided that boxers would be required to take a medical examination before competing in the championships. This decision was due to the death of a boxer (though not affiliated to the ABA) at a Battersea Boxing Club novice competition.

Boxing was first included in the Olympic Games at London in 1908, however the number of entrants was not large.

In 1920, a meeting was held in Paris at which the ABA proposed to form a world federation. A proposed constitution was accepted and the new body was called Fédèration Internationale de Boxe Amateur (FIBA). The headquarters for the FIBA are based in Atlanta, Georgia USA.

After creating a world association, the ABA also brought in three new championship weight categories – fly (8 stone), welter (10 stone 7lbs) and light-heavy (12 stone 7lbs).

The ABA decided in 1928 that all rounds would be three minutes and two years later it was decided that referees no longer had the power to order an extra round (if judges could not decide on a winner) and both referees and judges were told that a winner must be nominated.

The ABA enjoyed royal patronage for many years when the Prince of Wales granted the privilege by attending the championships in 1929 at the Royal Albert Hall and in 1936 King George VI became a patron. Following the death of George VI there was no royal patronage until 1953 when HRH the Duke of Edinburgh consented to become patron of the association.

The ABA prepared to re-create an International Association in 1945 and in London the following year more than 20 nations were present for a meeting. A new constitution was approved and it was agreed the new title would be Association Internationale de Box Amateur (AIBA).

In 1947 rule changes saw the officials judging each bout and the referee would be inside the ring. Having a referee in the ring did not come into full effect until five years later.

Two new weights were added for the 1951 championships, these being – light-welter (10 stone) and light-middle (11 stone 2lbs).

LONDON PRIZE-RING

The popular sporting venue of 'Great Booth at Tottenham Court' was the site for many bareknuckle fights along with Barnet and Finchley Common.

The Prince of Wales (later George IV) was the person responsible for a fight at Barnet on 17 April 1787 between Daniel Mendoza and Sam 'Bath Butcher' Martin. These two fighters were originally scheduled to do battle at Shepherd's Bush but on the order of a magistrate it was stopped. The prince rearranged the fight to take place at a secret venue on the 16th so that it could proceed without interference from the magistrates. The location turned out to be a specially built stage at the Barnet Racecourse with 5000 spectators on hand including the prince's brother the Duke of York. Following the Prince of Wales' enthusiasm, the sport saw an increase in interest as he frequented several matches between 1786 and 1788. However, after witnessing the death of a fighter at Brighton he said he would never watch another match.

Shortly before his coronation in 1820, the prince hired a man named John Jackson to get together 18 leading prize-fighters who would see that order was kept at Westminster Abbey during the ceremony.

This sport was undoubtedly one of London's most dramatic sporting pastimes, but over time its popularity decreased.

COCKFIGHTING

The sport of cockfighting became an annual event for schoolboys on Shrove Tuesday when the boys would bring their gamecock to their schoolmasters. This event would take place in the school itself with desks being moved to make available the necessary space. The schoolmaster who supervised the fights would receive all cocks that were killed in combat and occasionally be given money from all pupils participating.

Henry VIII (1491-1547) had a cockpit built in the palace at Whitehall called the 'Royal Cockpit' thus popularising the sport. Although there is no evidence he attended many fights, the fact that he acknowledged it was reason enough for society to follow it. Popularity in the sport quickly grew and when Elizabeth I (1533-1603) took the throne it had been firmly established. James I (1566-1625) recognised cockfighting as a national sport and went as far as appointing a 'cockmaster'. It was the cockmasters responsibility to supervise the breeding, rearing and training of all birds that would appear in the royal arena. Other members of the monarchy who were patrons of the sport included Charles II (1630-1685), William III (1650-1702) and George IV (1762-1837).

The 12th Earl of Derby was perhaps the most noted aristocratic figure who ever owned his own birds. After his death on 21 October 1834 an obituary was printed stating that he was the most celebrated cocker of either ancient or modern days.

Cockfights and horseracing began to be held simultaneously with its popularity increasing with each contest. Towards the end of the 18th century and the beginning of the 19th century cockfighting was an added attraction of race-weeks. During its heyday it attracted far more attention than horseracing.

From time to time authorities took steps to regulate the sport rather than stop it all together. There was a short-lived prohibitory measure in 1654 followed by a restrictive act in 1835, but the sport continued until the passing of the Cruelty to Animals Act in 1849.

CRICKET – LORD'S

The first reference to the game of cricket dates from around 1550. In Eltham, south-east London, church-wardens and overseers fined seven of their parishioners 2 shillings each for playing cricket on the Lord's Day.

The earliest description of a cricket match was written in 1706 by the old Etonian, William Goldwin, who published a collection of poems in Latin. The poem '*In Certamen Pilae*' describes a cricket match.

London society enjoyed cricket, but had yet to form any clubs. In 1719, Kent played London in the first county match. However, there are some that consider the matches in 1728 as the first real county matches.

Cricket first earned the patronage of royalty in 1723 when Frederick, Prince of Wales played his first match at Kensington Gardens in September 1735.

The formation in 1787 and the rise of Marylebone Cricket Club (MCC) were two of the most significant events in the game. Other events of major importance are listed below under the heading 'Milestones'.

Cricket owes a great deal to Thomas Lord, a Yorkshireman, who migrated first to Norfolk with his family and then travelled to London to seek his fortune. He found employment at the White Conduit Club, which was formed at Islington in 1782, as a bowler and handyman. Prompted by the Earl of Winchilsea and Charles Lennox, later the Duke of Richmond, a guarantee against loss was made to Thomas Lord if he would establish a new private cricket ground.

In May 1787, Lord opened his first ground on what is now Dorset Square. The last match played on these grounds was in 1810. In 1808 he developed two fields on the St John's Wood Estate. These new grounds were ready in 1809, and for two years Lord had two grounds. As London spread outwards, Parliament forced Lord to move again as a decree was passed for the Regent Canal to be cut through the centre of the grounds. Lord found a new site, which is where Lord's now resides. The ground opened in 1814 and was immediately popular with both players and the public.

Thomas Lord sold his share of the ground for £5000 to William Ward (a director of the Bank of England and later an MP for the City of London). His contract with the famous ground ceased in 1825 and he died in Hampshire in 1832, aged 76.

A wooden pavilion was built in 1814 and later enlarged. In 1825, it was destroyed by fire and all the clubs original possessions; records, score-books and trophies were lost. A new pavilion was built in 1826 and enlarged again in 1865.

In 1816, E. H. Budd hit the first century at Lord's. The bat used for this milestone is located in the museum (Tel: 020-7289 1611). Both the Ashes urn (the trophy which England and Australia have competed for since England's 1882-3 tour of Australia) and the Widen trophy (awarded to the winners of the England and West Indies Test Series) are permanently housed at Lord's. Also of note, between the 1840s and 1850s Lord's was used for pony races once the cricket season ended.

Lord's was purchased in 1866. In 1868 the famous Tavern was built and in 1967 it was torn down and replaced with a public house and banqueting site.

In 1877, international matches between England and Australia started in Melbourne, with early test matches in England being played at The Oval and Old Trafford.

308 Cultural London

Many famous test and county matches have been played at Lord's over the years. The last major event to he held was the Cricket World Cup. The final on 20 June 1999 saw Australia beat Pakistan by eight wickets.

Cricket events in 2000

The Cornhill Insurance Test Series was staged at Lord's with the 1st test match between England and Zimbabwe from 18–22 May, and the 2nd test series matching England's against the West Indies from 29 June to 3 July.

The NatWest Series saw England play the West Indies on 9 July and the final being held on 22 July.

Secretaries at Lord's

B. Aislabie 1822–42; R. Kyndston 1842–58; A. Baillie 1858–63; R. A. FitzGerald (1863-1876); Henry Perkins (1876-1898); Sir Francis Lacey (1898); William Findlay (1936); R. S. Rait Kerr (1936-1952); Ronald Aird (1952-1962); S. C. (Billy) Griffith (1962-1974); Jack Bailey (1974-1987); Lt. Col. John Stevenson (1987-1994); R. D. V. Knight (1994-present)

Milestones

1805 first Eton and Harrow match; 1806 first Gentleman v Players match; 1827 first Oxford v Cambridge match; 1837 jubilee of MCC celebrated with a match between North v South; 1846 first telegraph scoreboard installed; 1848 first printing tent erected on the ground and match cards sold; 1864 first groundsman hired; 1866-7 first Grandstand built; 1877 Middlesex County Cricket Club first played; 1884 first test match; 1898 first Board of Control for Test Matches met; 1906 press box built; 1937 MCC 150th anniversary; 1953 HRH The Duke of Edinburgh opened the Memorial Gallery in memory of all cricketers worldwide who lost their lives in the two World Wars; 1962 last Gentleman v Players match; 1963 first Gillette Cup final; 1972 first Benson & Hedges Cup final; 1975 first Prudential World Cup final; 1980 centenary Test match between England and Australia; 1997 cricket's governing bodies form the England and Wales Cricket Board; 1999 the Cricket World Cup.

Lord's Cricket Ground

London NW8 8QN (Tel: 020-7432 1200; Web: http://www.lords.org/mcc
Ticket information: Tel: 0870-533 8833;
Email: ticketing@mcc.org.uk. For information regarding tours and entrance to the museum Tel: 020-7432 1033 or fax 020-7266 3825. Email: Tours@mcc.org.uk).

THE OVAL

For over 150 years, The Oval has been the home of Surrey County Cricket Club and has witnessed some of the most significant moments in English sporting history.

In 1845, at the Horns Tavern in Kennington a meeting was held at which a proposal transpired to form a cricket club for the county of Surrey and to find and bring together the playing strength of the county. A resolution was passed and a Surrey Club was born, but the formal inauguration was delayed until later that year.

The Duchy of Cornwall, who owned property in Kennington, was willing to let it for the purpose of a cricket ground. A lease was granted for 31 years at £120 per annum, with an additional charge of £20 for taxes.

The contract for turfing Kennington Oval was awarded to Mr M. Tuttle of Clapham Road for £300, with 10,000 turfs coming from Tooting Common and the first being laid in March 1845.

With a lack of spectator seating and no pavilion changes were necessary. By 1880, a stand, pavilion, tavern and scorebox had been erected.

There is a difference of opinion as to when the first match was played at The Oval. The first match officially connected with the Surrey Club was between the Gentlemen of Surrey and the Players of Surrey on 21-22 August 1845. Surrey's first County Championship match occurred on 5 June 1873 against Sussex, and was lost by 29 runs.

The year 1872 saw the first ever F. A. Cup final between The Wanderers and The Royal Engineers which was played at the ground. The Cup finals continued until 1892, along with international football matches against Scotland and Wales. Rugby Union's first match in England versus Scotland (1872) and the first match between Oxford and Cambridge was played in 1873.

A remarkable run of County Championships were won by Surrey between 1890 and 1899. For over half a century, Surrey were not outright champions. Between 1952 and 1958 under the captaincy of Stuart Surridge, they achieved glory again. After rebuilding the amazing team of the 1950s, Surrey were not champions again until 1971.

Their first one-day championship came in 1974 when they won the Benson & Hedges Cup, followed by winning the NatWest Bank Trophy in 1982. Surrey CCC were Sunday League Champions in 1996, Benson & Hedges Cup winners again in 1997 and County Championship victors in 1999.

From the association with the Duchy of Cornwall comes the club's badge – the Prince of Wales feathers. The Prince granted permission for its use in 1905, due to the initiative of Lord Dalmeny (later Lord Rosebery).

In 1988, The Oval was re-named The Foster's Oval, as a result of a sponsorship agreement with the Australian brewery.

The President for 2000 is one of cricket's biggest fans – the Rt. Hon. John Major, CH. MP. Key events which too place during 2000: one-day international England v. Zimbabwe on 8 July in the NatWest Series and the 5th test match England v West Indies from 31 August to 4 September.

Past Presidents of Surrey CCC

1844 W. Strahan; 1856 H. Marshall; 1867 Col. F. Marshall (later General Sir F. Marshall); 1895 Sir Richard Webster (later Lord Alverstone); 1916 Sir Jeremiah Colman; 1923 The Earl of Midleton; 1926 G. H. Longman; 1929 H. D. G. Leveson-Gower; 1940 B. A. Glanvill; 1947 The Earl of Rosebery; 1950 Sir Walter Monkton; 1953 Lord Tedder; 1959 Viscount Monkton; 1965 Lord Nugent; 1969 C. Thain; 1960 M. J. C. Allom; 1978 W. E. Gerrish; 1979 Sir George Edwards, OM, CBE, FRSDL; 1980 A. R. Gover; 1981 W. S. Surridge; 1982 Brig. G. A. Rimbault, CBE, DSO, MC, DL; 1983 M. R. Barton; 1984 Sir Alexander Durie, CBE; 1985 The Rt. Hon. The Lord Carr of Hadley, PC; 1986 M. F. Turner; 1987 A. V. Bedser, CBE; 1988 Sir Michael Sandberg, CBE; 1989 C. G. Howard; 1990 E. A. Bedser; 1991 B. Coleman, OBE; 1992 W. D. Wickson / D. F. Cox; 1993 Sir John Stocker, MC, TD; 1994 J. M. Poland; 1995 P. B. H. Moy, CBE; 1996 J. Paul Getty, KBE; 1997 Mrs Betty Surridge; 1998-9 M. J. Steward, OBE

Sport

The Foster's Oval
Kennington, London SE11 5SS (Tel: 020-7582 6660; Fax: 020-7735 7769; Email: enquiries@surreyccc.co.uk; Web: http://www.surreyccc.co.uk; Ticket information: Tel: 020-7582 7764 (9.30am – 4pm Monday to Friday) Fax: 020-7793 7520)

CRYSTAL PALACE

Crystal Palace was originally built in Hyde Park to host the Great Exhibition of 1851 and a year later moved to its current location in south east London. In 1914 King George V watched Burnley play Liverpool and by doing so became the first reigning monarch to attend a Cup Final. Fire completely destroyed the venue in 1936 and it remained derelict until 1951 when an Act of Parliament was passed to develop the site.

The building of a National Sports Centre was proposed by Sir Gerald Barry. Work started in 1960 and was completed in 1964.

Crystal Palace has also played host to many athletic meetings over the years featuring the best athletes from around the world including the world record holders Maurice Greene and Michael Johnson of the United States of America.

There are various outdoor and indoor training facilities including: an athletics stadium (consisting of a 400m – 8 lane track, floodlights, a grassed central area, seating capacity of 16,500) four swimming pools (racing, diving, and two for training), an indoor track, indoor arena, four badminton courts, five squash courts, two training halls, boxing hall, two weight rooms, fitness centre, dance studio and climbing wall.

It also houses one of the leading sports injury clinics in the country with consultants and expert specialists.

Crystal Palace
National Sports Centre, Ledrington Road, London SE19 2BB (Tel: 020-8778 0131; Fax: 020-8676 8754; Email: janinec@crystalpalace.co.uk; Web: http://www.crystalpalace.co.uk).

FOOTBALL

Around 200 BC in ancient China, a game called Tsu Chu was played using two 30-foot high bamboo poles as goal posts. This was followed with the Greek game Pheninda around the fourth century BC and involved kicking, running and handling a ball. The Romans called their game Haipastum, which was played on rectangular field between two teams, who defended the ends of the field. The ball was thrown amongst players who moved forward at all times in an effort to throw it over the opponents' goal line. Defenders were allowed to tackle and kick. Japan played a game around the fifth century AD called Kemari. It was played on a ground 14 metres square and involved eight players kicking the ball between themselves.

It was during the 15th and 16th centuries that the Italians started a game called calcio (meaning to kick) in which two sides played in the town square at Florence, on the feast day of St John the Baptist.

There is written confirmation in the 12th century that a ball game was played on Shrove Tuesday at Ashbourne, Derbyshire. The idea was to gain ball possession and deliver it back to the town or parish. Edward II, Edward III, Richard II, Henry V and Elizabeth I had, through the centuries, tried to ban the game, but were unsuccessful in stopping people's interest in the sport.

Modern football came into its own with the expansion of public schools in the mid-19th century. Schools including Harrow, Eton, Charterhouse and Westminster organised games that were a vital part of the curriculum, with emphasis on order, discipline and team spirit.

Ebenezer Cobb Morley was the first Secretary of the Football Association. The main aims of the Football Association were to draw up a set of rules that would be acceptable to its founding members. Captains and representatives from several London teams met on 26 October 1863 in the Freemason's Tavern at Lincoln's Inn Fields to arrange the rules 'for the regulation of the game of football'. However, the first attempt to draw up a set of rules was by Cambridge University in 1848.

The Secretary of The F. A. between 1870 and 1895 was Charles Alcock and in 1871 he decided to start a knock-out competition, similar to the one being played at Harrow. On 20 July 1871 at the office of *The Sportsman*, off Ludgate Hill in London a meeting was held. Alcock suggested that a Challenge Cup should be started, in which all the clubs belonging to The Association should be invited to attend. The motion was passed and three months later the F. A. Challenge Cup was born.

The first F. A. Cup final was splayed at Kennington Oval on 16 March 1872, before 2000 spectators. The match was between The Wanderers and The Royal Engineers with the aforementioned team winning by a score of 1-0.

On 30 November 1872 the first international match between England and Scotland was played at Partick, near Glasgow.

July 1885 saw professional football legalised by The F. A., as a result of the increasing number of working class players. The formation of the Football League in 1888 and a second division in 1892 followed this.

Once again it was Charles Alcock who was the driving force behind the induction of an England team. It was 1908 before a full England squad went overseas to Austria, Hungary and Bohemia (now part of the Czech Republic) winning all their games. In 1923, Belgium were the first team from the continent to play an international match in England.

England's crowning glory on the international football stage came on 30 July, 1966 at Wembley when they beat West Germany 4-2 in extra-time to win the World Cup. England also competes in the European Football Championship.

LONDON BASED PROFESSIONAL FOOTBALL TEAMS

Dates shown in brackets indicate when the club was founded.

Arsenal Football Club (1886)
Arsenal Stadium, Highbury, London N5 1BU (Tel: 020-7704 4000; Fax: 020-7704 4001; Ticket Office: 020-7704 4242; Email: info@arsenal.co.uk; Web: http://www.arsenal.co.uk)
Manager: Arsène Wenger; **Shirt sponsor:** Sega (Dreamcast)

Barnet Football Club (1888)
Underhill Stadium, Barnet Lane, Barnet, Herts EN5 2BE (Tel: 020-8441 6932; Fax: 020-8447 0655; Ticket Office: 020-8449 6325)
Manager: John Still; **Shirt sponsor:** Loaded

310 Cultural London

Brentford Football Club (1889)
Griffin Park, Braemar Road, Brentford, Middx TW8 0NT (Tel: 020-8847 2511; Fax: 020-8568 9940; Email: enquiries@brentfordfc.co.uk; Web: http://www.brentfordfc.co.uk)
Manager: Ron Noades; **Shirt sponsor:** Patrick

Charlton Athletic Football Club (1905)
The Valley, Floyd Road, London SE7 8BL (Tel: 020-8333 4000; Fax: 020-8333 4001; Ticket Office: 020-8333 4010; Web: http://www.cafa.co.uk)
Manager: Alan Curbishley; **Shirt sponsor:** Red Bus

Chelsea Football Club (1905)
Stamford Bridge, Fulham Road, London SW6 1HS (Tel: 020-7385 5545; Fax: 020-7381 4831; Ticket Office: 020-7386 7799; Web: http://www.chelseafc.co.uk)
Manager: Gianluca Vialli; **Shirt sponsor:** Autoglass

Crystal Palace Football Club (1905)
Selhurst Park, London SE25 6PU (Tel: 020-8768 6000; Fax: 020-8771 5311; Ticket Office: 020-8771 8841; Web: http://www.cpfc.co.uk
Manager: Steve Coppell

Fulham Football Club (1879)
Craven Cottage, Stevenage Road, London SW6 6HH (Tel: 020-7893 8383; Fax: 020-7384 4707; Ticket Office: 020-7384 4710; Email: enquiries@fulham-fc.demon.co.uk; Web: http://www.fulhamfc.co.uk)
Manager: Jean Tigana; **Shirt sponsor:** Demon Internet

Leyton Orient Football Club (1881)
Matchroom Stadium, Brisbane Road, London E10 5NE (Tel: 020-8926 1111; Fax: 020-8926 1110; Ticket Office: 020-8926 1008)
Manager: Tommy Taylor; **Shirt sponsor:** Bravo

Queens Park Rangers Football Club (1882)
Loftus Road Stadium, South Africa Road, London W12 7PA (Tel: 020-8743 0262; Fax: 020-8740 4171; Ticket Office: 020-8540 6655)
Manager: Gerry Francis; **Shirt sponsor:** Ericsson

Tottenham Hotspur Football Club (1882),
Bill Nicholson Way, 748 High Road, London N17 0AP (Tel: 020-8365 5000; Fax: 020-8365 5005; Ticket Office: 020-8365 5100; Email: hotspur@globalnet.co.uk; Web: http://www.spurs.co.uk)
Manager: George Graham; **Shirt sponsor:** Holsten

Watford Football Club (1881)
Vicarage Road Stadium, Watford, Herts WD1 8ER (Tel: 01923-496000; Fax: 01923-496001; Ticket Office: 01923-496010; Email: yourvoice@watfordfc.com; Web: http://www.watfordfc.com)
Manager: Graham Taylor; **Shirt sponsor:** Phones 4u

West Ham United Football Club (1895)
Boleyn Ground, Green Street, Upton Park, London E13 9AZ (Tel: 020-8548 2748; Fax: 020-8548 2758; Ticket Office: 020-8548 2700; Email: pkelly@westhamunited.co.uk;
Web: http://www.westhamunited.co.uk)
Manager: Harry Redknapp; **Shirt sponsor:** Dr Marten's

Wimbledon Football Club (1888)
Selhurst Park Stadium, South Norwood, London SE25 6PY (Tel: 020-8771 2233; Fax: 020-8768 0640; Ticket Office: 020-8771 8841;
Web: http://www.wimbledon-fc.co.uk)
Manager: Terry Burton; **Shirt sponsor:** Tiny Computers

GREYHOUND RACING

Greyhounds can be traced back over 7000 years, with links to the ancient Egyptians and Mesopotamians and were also popular during the Roman Empire. These dogs can reach speeds of up to 61 km/h.

The first attempt to introduce the sport of greyhound racing happened in 1876, in Hendon, north London, over a straight course of 400 yards. Even though an enthusiastic article appeared in The Times on 11 September, the novelty of the sport died out.

Attempts were made to entice the dogs onto an oval circuit, but after consent failure the idea of greyhound racing was abandoned for almost a quarter of a century.

Racing made its British debut at Belle Vue stadium in Manchester on 24 July 1926. Spectator turnout was low and organisers were faced with a financial loss. A week later, 16,000 people arrived at the stadium and the sport was formally established. In 1927, the focus of racing moved to London with an event at White City stadium in west London that attracted a crowd of approximately 100,000. Business increased and 30 dog tracks opened by the end of the year. There are currently four dog tracks located in the capital.

The National Greyhound Racing Club was formed in 1928 and rules governing the sport were introduced. Track-side betting is a distinguished part of racing and each course must possess a betting license.

There are over 70,000 races run a year throughout Great Britain with 3.8 million spectators. Track-side bets are in excess of £320 million with £1.7 billion being spent at various betting shops.

London Racecourses
Catford Stadium, Catford Bridge, London SE6 4RJ (Tel: 020-8690 8000/2240; Fax: 020-8314 0223)
Romford Stadium, London Road, Romford, Essex RM7 9DU (Tel: 01708-762345; Fax: 01708-744899)
Walthamstow Stadium, Chingford Road, London E4 8SJ (Tel: 020-8531 4255; Fax: 020-8523 2747)
Wimbledon Stadium, Plough Lane, London SW17 0BL (Tel: 020-8946 8000; Fax: 020-8947 0821)

HORSERACING

It is suggested that horses have been domesticated since 2000BC and therefore could have possibly been raced as early as the bronze age.

Royalty in Britain has had a long association with the sport. King Richard I (1157-1199) imported breeding stock that he had seen in the East and racing was a natural result of this. Evidence shows regular racehorse sales and races were held at Smithfield in London.

As a result of horse losses during the War of the Roses, Henry VIII (1491-1547) set up royal studs at Hampton Court in Surrey, Eltham in south-east London, Tutbury in Staffordshire and Malmesbury in Wiltshire. There was also a racing stable in Greenwich.

Elizabeth I (1533-1603) raced at Croydon in 1574 and Salisbury in 1585. Charles II (1630-1685) not only participated in races, but set rules and served as a judge in disputes. William III (1650-1702) was also keen on the sport and more racecourses sprang up across the country. He restarted the Royal Stud at Hampton Court and hired William Tregonwell Frampton (1641-1727) as 'Keeper of the Running Horses' – a racing manager. The Royal Stud enjoyed success until it was dissolved in 1894.

While still the Prince of Wales, George IV (1762-1830) was the first royal to own a winning horse. At The Derby in 1788, he won with *Sir Thomas*. He was elected to the Jockey Club in 1921, but until his accession in 1936 took little part in racing.

The Princess Royal has won two races – the Diamond Stakes at Ascot in 1987 on *Ten No Trumps* and the Queen Mother's Cup at York on *Insular* in 1988. Prince Charles has also ridden in races, but without the success of his sister.

Racing at the beginning of the 18th century was in the form of matches. Records were kept in private match books, diaries and local records. Racing was transformed by the end of the century with shorter races and younger horses being utilised.

The number of entrants increased for two reasons. Handicapped races were introduced whereby horses would be assessed as to how much weight they should carry which was determined from past performances. The second was the number of sweepstakes that increased quickly from around 1770, as each owner contributed to the prize money. With more entrants running over shorter distances it was more exciting for the spectators and offered greater betting opportunities.

The Jockey Club that began as a London Gentlemen's Club had significant influence on the transformation of racing. It was over a century before the Club centralised the regulatory and administrative aspects of the sport. Starting in 1879 the Club ensured that jockeys were licensed and they could no longer own or partly own horses. Starting machines were introduced in 1896. In 1966 the Club began licensing women trainers, but women jockeys were not licensed until 1972 (amateur) and 1975 (professional). It was not until 1977 that the Jockey Club elected its first women members.

The British Horseracing Board was founded in 1993 to take over the leadership and strategy of the racing industry. The day-to-day running of the sport is the responsibility of Weatherby's, a family firm going back to 1770, under contract to the British Horseracing Board.

There are five racecourses (Ascot, Epsom, Sandown, Windsor and Kempton) around the London area and the two classics held annually near the capital are both at Epsom Downs, Surrey and run over a distance of 1 mile 4 furlongs. The Derby was first run in 1780 and The Oaks first took place in 1779.

British Horseracing Board
42 Portman Square, London W1H 0EN (Tel: 020-7396 0011; Fax: 020-7935 3626; Email: info@bhb.co.uk; Web: http://www.bhb.co.uk)

LONDON MARATHON

Early in 1980 Chris Brasher (who ran in the 1979 New York marathon and later wrote a major article in The Observer) and Donald Trelford (then editor of The Observer) met with the Greater London Council, the police and athletics' governing bodies and as a result of this meeting the London Marathon was born.

The budget for the first marathon was prepared by Brasher showing an expected expenditure of £75,000. Gillette became the first sponsors and offered £50,000 towards costs.

Brasher and John Disley established charitable status and devised six aims for the marathon:
- to improve the overall standard and status of British marathon running by providing a fast course and strong international competition.
- to show to mankind that, on occasions, the Family of Man can be united.
- to raise money for the provision of recreational facilities in London.
- to help London tourism.
- to prove that when it comes to organising major events, 'Britain is best'.
- to promote fun and provide some happiness and sense of achievement in a troubled world.

On 29 March 1981 the first marathon was run. Around 20,000 people had applied to run, but only 7,747 were accepted. A total of 6,255 runners finished with Dick Beardsley of the United States and Inge Simonsen of Norway becoming the joint men's champions, while Joy Smith became the women's champion and in the process broke the British marathon record.

After a successful first year the 1982 race had more than 90,000 applicants with 18,059 being accepted.

Since 1981, 413,481 runners have completed the 26.2 mile course and in 1999 30,809 people succeeded in completing the run through London's streets.

More than £110 million has been raised for charity by entrants and The London Marathon has produced a surplus of £7,422,685 for The London Marathon Charitable Trust, which funds recreational projects throughout the capital.

From 1982–93 the race finished on Westminster Bridge, but repair work the following year forced organisers to move the finish line to The Mall, in front of Buckingham Palace.

The following companies have sponsored the marathon. Gillette 1981–3; Mars 1984–8; ADT 1989–92; NutraSweet 1994–5 and Flora 1996–2002.

Twenty of the world's top male marathon runners took to the streets of London on 16 April 2000, including last years champion Abdelkader El Mouaziz of Morocco, Olympic champion Josia Thugwane of South Africa, European champion Stefano Baldini of Italy and Britain's Jon Brown, who was forced to pull out before the race due to injury.

Twelve of the world's best women were also competing. These included last years winner Joyce Chepchumba of Kenya, Tegla Loroupe also of Kenya, who has run the fastest marathon ever for women and Lidia Simon the Romanian bronze medallist in the 1999 World Athletics Championship marathon.

Included in the marathon are wheelchair races covering a 26.2 mile course, the Times mini-marathon (2.8 miles) for boys and girls aged 11–17 and the Times mini-wheelchair marathon for under 18's.

A total of 32,620 people were registered in the 2000 marathon with approximately 31,542 crossing the finishing line. An estimated £20 million was raised for various charities.

Winners of the 2000 race were Antonio Pinto of Portugal whose winning time of 2hr 6min 36sec set both a European and course record and Tegla Loroupe of Kenya in 2hr 24min 33sec. Both runners received $55,000 for winning, with Pinto receiving an additional $50,000 for his record breaking time and $25,000 for breaking the course record. Loroupe was awarded $10,000 for a time bonus.

The London Marathon 2000 was broadcast live to 178 countries and between 8.45 a.m. and 11.50 a.m., four million viewers watched the race on BBC. This figure represents 52.4 per cent of the viewing audience during that time slot.

OLYMPICS

The modern Olympic Games were first contested in 1896 in Athens, Greece and Great Britain is one of only five countries to have competed in every version of the Games (Summer and Winter).

London hosted its first Games in 1908 from 27 April to 31 October with 22 countries participating. The site chosen as the main venue was the newly constructed complex that became known as White City in West London. Derived during the Games was what would become the standard marathon distance of 26 miles, 385 yards.

In 1948 the Games made a return to London. They were originally awarded to Rome, Italy, but in 1945 the Italian government informed the International Olympic Committee that they would be unable to host the Games because of financial problems.

The main events took place at Wembley from 29 July to 14 August, with 59 countries taking part. Live television broadcasts of the Games were transmitted to some 80,000 homes within range of the stadium.

RACKETS

The game of rackets originated in the 18th century in the Fleet and King's Bench debtor's prisons, where balls were hit against the high prison walls. Both closed and open courts were built, often in association with taverns and the game's popularity increased rapidly when some leading public schools adopted it.

The first world champion was Robert Mackay in 1820 and the longest reigning champion is Geoffrey Atkins (1954-72).

Rackets has close links with real tennis and is governed by the Tennis and Rackets Association, which was founded in 1907. It's headquarters are based in West London at the Queen's Club.

REAL TENNIS

Real tennis is the oldest of all racquet games and unlike other racquet games, it is a product of evolution rather than pure invention.

The forerunner of this game was first played in the 11th century. It started as hand ball played by monks around the cloister of monasteries in Italy and France. As the monks travelled to other monasteries, new rules were adopted and others abandoned.

The game was originally played with bare hands. Later a glove was used and then someone thought of attaching cord to the fingers to form a net, which could be tightened by stretching the hand. The next evolution was attaching the cord to a frame a adding a handle, hence the racket.

The first formal rules came into force in 1599 and bear a remarkable resemblance to those still used today. The court that Charles I (1600-1649) had built at Hampton Court is still used for championship play.

In the 16th and 17th centuries real tennis was the fashionable game of the court in England and France, but prohibited the ordinary citizens from taking part. Henry VIII (1509-1547) was an accomplished player.

The 18th century saw a decline in the game of tennis. In England there was a revival of sorts in the mid-19th century with the construction of many courts. There has been a resurgence in the game within the UK over the last decade with new courts being built around the country.

London area real tennis courts
The Burroughs Club (Middlesex University), Hendon Campus, 2 Campus Way, London NW4 4JF (Tel: 020-8362 6343)

The Harbour Club, Watermeadow Lane, London SW6 2RR (Tel: 020-7371 7700; Fax: 020-7371 7770)

MCC, The Tennis Court, Lord's Ground, St John's Wood, London NW8 8QN (Tel: 020-7432 1013; Fax: 020-7289 9100)

The Queen's Club, Palliser Road, West Kensington, London W14 9EQ (Tel: 020-7385 3421; Fax: 020-7386 8295)

The Royal Tennis Court, Hampton Court Palace, East Molesey, Surrey KT8 9AU (Tel: 020-8977 3015; Fax: 020-8943 5382; Email: rtchcp@aol.com)

ROWING

Rowing began on the River Thames centuries ago with the wherry being used as the Londoner's water taxi. The wherry had a sharply-angled prow so it could nudge its way through a cluster of boats to reach the landing steps or take itself up the beach at low tide. The men who operated the boats were called 'wherrymen' and their combined skills with oars and with their knowledge of the river knew the best routes to take. These boats were operated by licensed men and ferried passengers from Gravesend to Richmond, between Southwark, London and Westminster. The other types of boats that also worked the Thames were the shallop and the livery company barge. The shallop was rowed by six or eight liveried watermen and were owned by wealthy families, including the monarchy. Today the Queen still has royal watermen and a bargemaster. The livery company barges were large vessels that were owned by city livery companies and used for entertaining and displaying wealth on occasions like the Lord Mayor's River Pageant.

Racing competitions started with professional boatmen (those who earned their living transporting people and goods) in the 1700s, with victors receiving substantial prizes. During the 1800s racing became both a popular gambling and spectator sport on the Thames.

Thomas Doggett, an actor and manager at the Drury Lane Theatre at London, offered a coat and badge to the winning waterman over a five-mile course from London Bridge to Chelsea in 1715. The entrants were those who had one year's experience – after their five years of apprenticeship, with the race being held during an incoming tide on the busy river. This was a test of not only watermanship, but also sculling.

Doggett's reason for holding the race was to commemorate the accession of the Hanovarians to the throne and his legacy to the Fishmongers Company was that the race would run for ever.

The Watermen's Company was established by Acts of Parliament in 1514 and 1555 and it was the company's responsibility to regulate the watermen and bring them to court for offences such as over-charging and drunkenness.

The first year of the Boat Race between Oxford and Cambridge Universities was in 1829 at Henley. The s-bend course from Putney to Mortlake over 4.25 miles (6.48km) took place in 1845 and was a test for both oarsmen and coxes. The dark blue of Oxford and the light blue of Cambridge came into effect the same year (1845) that the 'Blues' trophy was introduced.

The Henley Royal Regatta first took place in 1839 and was organised by the town. It has been repeated every year since, apart from during the two world wars (1914-18 and 1939-45). It is Britain's most prestigious regatta and received royal patronage in 1851.

The development of clubs happened in 1818 with the establishment of the Leander club, whose origins began in Lambeth and are now based in Henley. Leander was basically a club of old Oxford and Cambridge students. The London Rowing Club established in 1856 saw the most significant development along the Thames, bringing with it the best oarsmen from smaller clubs.

The Amateur Rowing Association (ARA) was formed in 1882 from the Metropolitan Rowing Association established in 1879. Most of the founding members were from the London area and included Oxford, Cambridge and Dublin universities boat clubs. Their goals were to govern the sport and form crews that could beat competitors from other countries at the Henley Royal Regatta. The ARA failed at the latter, but this was rectified years later. There were problems over the definition of an amateur, causing a schism that lasted for 60 years.

In 1890, the National Amateur Rowing Association was formed as an alternative to the ARA, who excluded menial and manual workers from amateur clubs and regattas. Its size grew considerably and it organised eight autonomous regions, each with its own regatta.

The two associations had words over who would represent Great Britain at the Olympic Games and in the late 1930s set out to settle their differences. Finally in 1953 they decided to merge, but this did not come into effect until 1 January 1956.

British women's rowing began with the colleges of London, Oxford and Cambridge universities, along with clubs like Furnivall Sculling Club (1896) and Weybridge Ladies Amateur Rowing Club (1926).

Today the ARA's membership has approximately 500 clubs with 15,000 members and holds 300 regattas and river races.

SWIMMING

It is not clear how or where the activity of swimming originated. It is known, however, that the Romans taught their soldiers to swim in the River Tiber.

By a decree of 1571, the University of Cambridge did not allow its members to swim anywhere in the county. There is no specific explanation for this apart from stating it was because of serious and grave reasons.

Swimming began in England in the 18th century, but took place in baths rather than in the sea, rivers or lakes. The Pearless Pool was located at Finsbury in London and was established by a jeweller named William Kemp in 1743 from a natural pond caused by an overflowing spring. Twice a week boys from the nearby Christs Hospital School would come to swim, but by 1850 the pool had been closed.

In 1836, Mr J. Strachan of Westminster established the National Swimming Society (NSA). Its aim was the promotion of health and cleanliness by encouraging swimming and offering free instruction.

The earliest of public schools to engage in the art of swimming was Eton College. A fatal accident of a boy whilst boating in 1839 led George Selwyn and William Evans (masters at the school) to prevail upon the headmaster to adopt the teaching of swimming. After that, all the boys had to pass a 250 yard swim before they were allowed to go on a boat on the River Thames. The Baths and Wash-houses Act of 1846 resulted in many towns building public baths.

The Turnhalle at Kings Cross was originally opened in 1866 as a purpose built gymnasium established by Ernest Ravenstein for Germans living in London. A meeting at this venue on 7 January 1869 between Mr Ravenstein and a group of leaders from London swimming clubs saw what may have been the beginning of the Amateur Swimming Association. Another meeting was held in February and it was decided to take the name of the Associated Metropolitan Swimming Clubs. They had established a group to formulate a constitution and on 24 June it was adopted along with a name change to the London Swimming Association (LSA).

The founding members of the LSA were the following swimming clubs: the Alliance, North London, Serpentine, National, West London and St Pancras. The amateur English Men's Mile Championships became their annual event with the first one taking place on the Thames from Putney Aqueduct to Hammersmith Bridge. The venue changed in 1873 to the Serpentine because of river currents and pollution. The second championship to be instituted was the Long distance in 1877 and was known as the Lords and Commons race as the first cup was presented by Members of Parliament. This event was swum until 1939. Today there is a 5km event with winners receiving the House of Commons trophies.

Near the beginning of 1870 the LSA changed its name again to the Metropolitan Swimming Association (MSA). Their main goal was to promote and encourage the art of swimming with the highest values associated with the 'amateur'.

The MSA comprised only of London clubs, but at a meeting in 1873 it was decided the name should change to the Swimming Association of Great Britain (SAGB) to encourage clubs around the country to join.

On 7 April 1884 the Otter Swimming club of London withdrew their membership from the SAGB and along with some smaller clubs formed the Amateur Swimming Union (ASU). On 3 March the SAGB and the ASU decided to establish the Amateur Swimming Association (ASA). This new association set up 135 laws covering procedures for dealing with suspensions and appeals, the conduct of meetings for both council and races, along with organising championship competitions. The ASA as it is known today came into being on 12 April 1886.

Lord Charles Beresford was elected president of the ASA between 1887 and 1889. He obtained royal patronage for the ASA in 1887.

By 1902 there were 595 clubs around the country. Within two years the numbers of clubs increased to 675. During the last full year of peace before the start of World War I, there were an amazing 1,409 clubs based throughout the country.

In 1891 the London School Board accepted a free offer by the ASA for the services of members who were competent to teach swimming.

The ASA started in 1899 its Professional Certificate and by the 31 December 1900 it had been awarded to 26 male and female candidates from all over England. Minimum age restrictions for this certificate were imposed in 1909 with men being 21 and women at 18. In 1910 the Professional Certificate was thoroughly revised whereby applicants had to pass both a theoretical (instructing the breast stroke, back stroke and breathing) and a practical exam.

The ASA's first formal recognition to women competitors was established in 1901 when they had a 100 yard national competition. By 1912 there was also a race of 200 yards.

On 19 July 1908, the Olympic Games held at White City in west London saw the formation of Fédération Internationale de Natation (FINA), who are the world governing body of swimming based in Lausanne, Switzerland.

Over the years the ASA has improved the sport in this country with unprecedented success. So much so that many British swimmers are now among an elite group of athletes from around the world and will be striving not only for personal and world-record times at Sydney 2000, but also for Olympic glory in the form of a gold medal.

TWICKENHAM

For 40 years (1871-1910) the Rugby Football Union (RFU) used various grounds around the country for international matches. The cost of using these different locations was expensive, so the RFU decided to purchase land and build it's own stadium.

William Williams, an RFU committee member was given the task of finding a suitable location. A piece of land (10 acres) was found near the small town of Twickenham in 1907 and subsequently purchased for £5,572.12s.6d. Construction began on this site in 1908 and by October 1909 the 30,000 capacity stadium was ready.

The first international match was played between England and Wales in January 1910 with over 20,000 spectators.

After England's Grand Slam successes in 1921, 1923 and 1924, work was started again on the stadium with various sections being enlarged. In 1979 the first major work in almost 50 years began with the replacement of the crumbling south terrace and erection of a new south stand. Following the disaster at Hillsborough in 1989, the RFU decided that the stadium would be all-seating only.

Twickenham Stadium is the largest arena in world rugby (a capacity of 74,000).

Rugby Football Union
Rugby House, Rugby Road, Twickenham, Middx TW1 1DS (Tel: 020-8892 2000; Fax: 020-8892 9816; Web: http://www.rfu.com; Museum of Rugby and Twickenham Experience Tour Tel: 020-8892 8877)

GREATER LONDON BASED RUGBY TEAMS

Esher RFC (1923), The Rugby Ground, 369 Molesey Road, Hersham, Surrey KT12 3PF (Tel: 01932-220295; Fax: 01932-254627; Ticket Office: 01932-220295; Email: webmaster@esherrfc.org; Web: http://www.esherrfc.org.uk)
Coach: Hugh McHardy; **Shirt sponsor:** Virgin Radio

Harlequin FC (1866)
Stoop Memorial Ground, Langhorn Drive, Twickenham TW2 7SX (Tel: 020-8410 6000; Fax: 020-8410 6001; Ticket Office: 0870-887 0230; Email: postmaster@quins.co.uk; Web: http://www.quins.co.uk)
Coaches: Z. Brook and R. Hill; **Shirt sponsor:** NEC

London Irish RFC (1898)
Stoop Memorial Ground, Langhorn Drive, Twickenham TW2 7SX (Tel: 01932-783034; Fax: 01932-784462; Ticket Office: 0870-887 0232; Email: londonirishrfc@aol.com; Web: http://www.london-irish-rugby.com)
Coach: Dick Best; **Shirt sponsor:** Aer Lingus

London Wasps
Loftus Road Stadium, South Africa Road, London W12 7PA (Tel: 020-8743 0262; Fax: 020-8740 2525; Ticket Office: 020-8740 2545; Email: wasps@loftusroadplc.co.uk; Web: http://www.waspsrfc.co.uk)
Director of Rugby: Nigel Melville; **Shirt sponsor:** Ericsson

London Welsh RFC (1885)
Old Deer Park, Kew Road, Richmond, Surrey TW9 2AZ (Tel: 020-8940 2368; Fax: 020-8940 1106; Ticket Office: 020-8940 2368; Email: ron.holleylondon-welsh.co.uk; Web: http://www.london-welsh.co.uk)
Coach: Clive Griffiths; **Shirt sponsor:** Basildon Chemicals

Metropolitan Police RFC (1924)
Metropolitan Police (Imben Court) Sports Club, Ember Lane, East Molesey, Surrey KT8 0BT (Tel: 020-8398 1267; Fax: 020-8398 9755; Ticket Office: 020-8398 1267)
Coach: David Thrower

Saracens FC (1876)
Vicarage Road Stadium, Vicarage Road, Watford, Herts WD1 8ER (Tel: 01923-496200; Fax: 01923-496201; Ticket Office: 01923-496200; Email: comment@saracens.net; Web: http://www.saracens.com)
Director of Rugby: Alan Zondagh; **Shirt sponsor:** Kenwood

OTHER LONDON BASED RUGBY TEAMS – ALPHABETICAL ORDER

(Note: Space limitation has caused this list to be downsized and we regret we are unable to print all the London based clubs)

Bank of England RFC (Eastern Counties 1); Barclays Bank RFC (Eastern Counties 1); Barnes RFC (Eastern Counties 1); Chiswick RFC (Herts & Middx 1); Civil Service FC (RU) (Herts & Middx 1); Ealing (Herts & Middx 1); East London RUFC (Herts & Middx 1); Economicals RUFC (Herts & Middx 1); Enfield Ignatians RFC (Herts & Middx 1); Eton Manor RFC (Herts & Middx 1); Feltham RFC (Herts & Middx 1); Finchley RFC (Herts & Middx 1); Footscray RUFC (Herts & Middx 1); London Nigerian RFC (Kent 1); Loughton RFC (Kent 1); May and Baker (Kent 1); Merton RFC (Kent 1); Millwall Albion (London 2 North); Old Abbotstonians RFC (London 2 North); Old Actonians RFC (London 2 North); Old Alleynian FC (London 2 South); Old Ashmoleans RFC (London 2 South); Old Bevonians RFC (London 2 South); Old Cofeians RFC (Division 1); Old Cooperians RUFC (London 3 North East); Old Edwardians RFC (London 3 North East); Old Elthamians RFC (London 3 North West); Old Emanuel RFC (London 3 North West); Old Gaytonians RFC (London 3 North West); Old Grammarians RFC (London 3 North West); Old Haileyburians (London 3 North West) Old Hamptonians RFC (London 3 North West); Old Isleworthians RFC (London 3 North West); Old Johnian RFC (London 3 North West); Old Millhillians RFC (London 3 North West); Old Pauline FC (London 3 North West); Old Rutlishians RFC (London 3 North West); Old Shootershillians RFC (London 3 South East); Old Suttonians RFC (London 3 South East); Old Tiffinian RFC (London 3 South West); Old Tottonians RFC (London 3 South West); Old Wellingtonian RFC (London 3 South West); Old Whitgiftian RFC (London 3 South West); Old Wimbledonians RFC (Surrey 1); Orleans F.P. RFC (Surrey 1); Osterley RFC (Surrey 1); Park House RFC (Surrey 1); Pinner and Grammarians RFC (Surrey 1); Quintin RFC (Surrey 1); Ravens RFC (Surrey 1); Ruislip RFC (Division 1); Staines RFC (Division 1); Sutton and Epsom RFC (Division 1); Wimbledon (Division 1)

WEMBLEY STADIUM

Wembley Stadium cost £750,000 to build and took only 300 working days to complete. The twin towers are 38.4m (126ft) high. In 1955 floodlights were used when London played Frankfurt in the Inter-Cities Fairs Cup.

In 1963, an electronic scoreboard was first used and it was suspended from the new roof. Computerised display boards were first used in 1988 for the England v Brazil Schools International Match. They measure 25m (82ft) wide by 4.5m (15ft) high and have adjoining advertising panels that are 6m (20ft).

Behind Wembley's famous twin towers on the 28 April 1923, The Football Association's (F. A.) Challenge Cup was played between Bolton Wanderers and West Ham United. This became the permanent home for future F. A. contests. The F. A. final on 20 May between Chelsea and Aston Villa was the last one to be played before demolition of the stadium. The result of the match was Chelsea, 1 – Aston Villa, 0. On Saturday, 7 October 2000 England will play Germany in a World Cup 2000 qualifier match with an estimated 75,000 in attendance.

The architects for the new stadium are Sir Norman Foster of Fosters and Partners and HOK Lobb, who have built 50 stadiums throughout the USA. There will be seating for 90,000 and is scheduled for completion in time for the F.A. Cup Final in 2003. An further £200–£355 million will be spent turning Wembley into one of the finest sports arenas in the world. The National Lottery has given £120 million towards the cost of the new stadium.

Wembley has been the site of many great sporting and non-sporting events over the years. The Rugby League Cup Final was first played in 1929; the first World Speedway Championships were held here in 1936; the XIV Olympic Games in 1948; the European Cup final between AC Milan and Benfica was held in 1963; the World Cup in 1966, which saw England defeat West Germany 4-2; the Royal International Horse show in 1969; the first pop music event in 1972; an exhibition game of American Football between the Minnesota Vikings and St Louis Rams in 1983; Bob Geldof's Live Aid concert in 1985 raising money for African famine victims; the Freddie Mercury Tribute concert in 1992; The WBC Heavyweight Boxing in 1995 which saw Frank Bruno defeat the American Oliver McCall and in 1996 it was the venue for football's Euro '96.

Wembley National Stadium
Wembley, Middx HA9 0WS (Web: http://www.wembleynationalstadium.co.uk)

WIMBLEDON

The All England Lawn Tennis and Croquet Club is a private club, founded in 1868 as the All England Croquet Club, with its first grounds off Worple Road in Wimbledon. In the spring of 1877, the Club was renamed the All England Croquet and Lawn Tennis Club and the first lawn tennis Championships were held.

These Championships began with a garden party atmosphere evident at the first meeting in 1877 of the Gentlemen's Singles (won by Spencer Gore). They have grown to a highly professional tournament that now attracts over 450,000 spectators. The game of lawn tennis was introduced by Major Walter Clopton Wingfield in 1874.

The word 'croquet' was dropped from the name of the Club, as activity in 1882 was confined mostly to lawn tennis. For sentimental reasons in 1899, the word 'croquet' was reinstated to the title and it has remained 'The All England Lawn Tennis and Croquet Club'.

Ladies' Singles play started in 1884 with Maud Watson becoming the champion. Also in that year was the start of the Gentlemen's Doubles. In 1905 an American, May Sutton became the first overseas champion. The Australian, Norman Brookes was the first overseas Gentlemen's champion in 1907.

In 1922 the Club moved to its present location at Church Road and was opened by King George V. The new stadium held 14,000 people and because of this, the popularity of the game grew enormously. A total of 20 courts, including the centre court are now used throughout The Championships.

316 Cultural London

1934 to 1937 was the golden era for British tennis when 11 titles were won. Fred Perry won three singles Championships and Dorothy Round won two. During World War II, the premises of Wimbledon were used for a variety of civil defence and military functions. In October 1940, a bomb hit the Centre Court, which resulted in the loss of 1200 seats.

With the War over, The Championships started again in 1946. The person in charge of making sure the tournament went ahead was Lt. Col. Duncan Macaulay, the newly appointed Secretary.

In 1973, 81 members of the Association of Tennis Professionals (ATP) stayed away from The Championships as a result of the Yugoslavian Lawn Tennis Association suspending Nikki Pilic earlier in the year. Despite this over 300,000 spectators (throughout the two-week tournament) watched as Jan Kodes of Czechoslovakia and American's Billie Jean King (for the sixth time) became champions.

The Championships celebrated their Centenary in 1977 with 41 of the 52 surviving champions parading on Centre Court and being presented with a commemorative medal by H.R.H. The Duke of Kent (the club's President) to mark this milestone.

Each year The Championships are bettered as the world's top players continue to strive for what is undoubtedly the top honour in the sport – being Wimbledon Champion.

Wimbledon Lawn Tennis Museum – hours of opening 10.30am to 5.00pm (extended hours during the tournament). (Tel: 020-8946 6131).

The All England Lawn Tennis and Croquet Club
Church Road, London SW19 5AE (Tel: 020-8944 1066; Fax: 020-8947 8752;
Web: http://www.wimbledon.org)

SPORTS BODIES

CENTRAL COUNCIL OF PHYSICAL RECREATION
Francis House, Francis Street, London, SW1P 1DE (Tel: 020-7828 3163; Fax: 020-7630 7046;
E-mail: admin@ccpr.org.uk)
Chief Executive: M. Denton

SPORT ENGLAND
16 Upper Woburn Place, London, WC1H 0QP (Tel: 020-7273 1500; Fax: 020-7383 5740;
E-mail: info@english.sports.gov.uk;
Web: http://www.english.sports.gov.uk)
Chief Executive Officer: D. Casey

UK SPORTS COUNCIL
40 Bernard Street, London, NW1N 1BR (Tel: 020-7841 9500; Web: http://www.uksport.gov.uk)
Chief Executive: R. Callicott

ENGLISH SPORT COUNCIL LONDON AND SOUTH EAST REGIONS
PO Box 480, London, SE19 2BQ (Tel: 020-8778 8600; Fax: 020-8676 9812)
Chief Executive: D. Casey

AMATEUR BOXING ASSOCIATION OF ENGLAND LTD
Crystal Palace National Sports Centre, London, SE19 2BB (Tel: 020-8778 0251; Fax: 020-8778 9324;
E-mail: hq@abae.org.uk;
Web: http://www.amateurboxing.freeserve.co.uk)
General Secretary: T. Collier

AMATEUR MARTIAL ARTS ASSOCIATION
120 Cromer Street, London, WC1H 8BS (Tel: 020-7837 4406; Fax: 020-7278 7738)
Chief Executive: T. Hibbert

AMATEUR ROWING ASSOCIATION
The Priory, 6 Lower Mall, London, W6 9DJ (Tel: 020-8748 3632; Fax: 020-8741 4658;
Web: http://www.ara-rowing.org)
National Manager: Mrs R. Napp

AMATEUR ROWING ASSOCIATION
6 Lower Mall, London, W6 9DJ (Tel: 020-8748 3632; Fax: 020-8741 4658)
Chief Executive: Mrs D. M. Ellis

AMATEUR SWIMMING ASSOCIATION
Harold Fern House, Derby Square, Loughborough, Leics LE11 5AL (Tel: 01509-618700; Fax: 01509-618701; Email: cserv@asagb.org.uk)

BRITISH BOXING BOARD OF CONTROL
Petersen House, 52A Borough High Street, SE1 1XW (Tel: 020-7403 5879; Fax: 020-7378 6670;
E-mail: bbbc@dial.pipex.co;
Web: http://www.dspace.dial.pipex.com/bbbc/)
General Secretary: S. J. Block

Sports Bodies 317

BRITISH DARTS ORGANISATION

2 Pages Lane, Muswell Hill, London, N10 1PS (Tel: 020-8883 5544; Fax: 020-8883 0109; E-mail: 101776.666@compuserve.com; Web: http://www.bdodarts.com)
General Secretary/Director: O. A. Croft

BRITISH FENCING ASSOCIATION

1 Baron's Gate, 33-35 Rothschild Road, London, W4 5HT (Tel: 020-8742 3032; Fax: 020-8742 3033; E-mail: britishfencing@compuserve.com; Web: http://www.britishfencing.com)
General Secretary: Miss G. Kenneally

BRITISH HORSERACING BOARD

42 Portman Square, London, W1H 0EN (Tel: 020-7396 0011; Fax: 020-7935 3626; E-mail: info@bhb.co.uk; Web: http://www.bhb.co.uk)
Chief Executive: R. T. Ricketts

BRITISH OLYMPIC ASSOCIATION

1 Wandsworth Plain, London, SW18 1EH (Tel: 020-8871 2677; Fax: 020-8871 9104; E-mail: boa@boa.org.uk; Web: http://www.olympics.org.uk)
Chief Executive: S. Clegg

BRITISH TENNIS FOUNDATION

Queens Club, Palliser Road, London, W14 9EG (Tel: 020-7381 7140; Fax: 020-7381 6507; Web: http://www.lta.org.uk)
Director: Ms S. Wolstenholme

BRITISH TENPIN BOWLING ASSOCIATION

114 Balfour Road, Ilford, Essex, London, IG1 4JD (Tel: 020-8478 1745; Fax: 020-8514 3665)
Chairman: Mrs P. White

BRITISH UNIVERSITIES SPORTS ASSOCIATION

8 Union Street, London, SE1 1SZ (Tel: 020-7357 8555; Fax: 020-7403 0127)
Chief Executive: G. Gregory-Jones

COMMONWEALTH GAMES COUNCIL FOR ENGLAND

Tavistock House South, Tavistock Square, London, WC1H 9JZ (Tel: 020-7388 6643; Fax: 020-7388 6744; E-mail: info@cgce.co.uk; Web: http://www.cgce.co.uk)
Chief Executive: Miss A. Hogbin

COMMONWEALTH GAMES FEDERATION

Walkden House, 3-10 Melton Street, London, NW1 2EB (Tel: 020-7383 5596; Fax: 020-7383 5506; E-mail: commonwealthgamesfederation@btinternet.com; Web: http://www.commonwealthgames-fed.org)
Hon. Secretary: L. Martin

COUNTRYSIDE ALLIANCE

The Old Town Hall, 367 Kennington Road, London, SE11 4PT (Tel: 020-7840 9200; Fax: 020-7793 8484; E-mail: info@countryside-alliance.org; Web: http://www.countryside-alliance.org)
Chief Executive: R. Burge

CROQUET ASSOCIATION

c/o The Hurlingham Club, Ranelagh Gardens, SW6 3PR (Tel: 020-7736 3148; Fax: 020-7736 3148 E-mail: caoffice@croquet.org.uk; Web: http://www.croquet.org.uk)
Secretary: N. R. Graves

FOOTBALL ASSOCIATION

16 Lancaster Gate, London, W2 3LW (Tel: 20-7262 4542; Fax: 020-7402 0486)
Executive Director: D. Davies

GRAND NATIONAL ARCHERY SOCIETY

Lilleshall, National Sport Centre, Nr. Newport, Shropshire, TF10 9AT (Tel: 01952 677888; Fax: 01952 606019; Web: http://www.guas.u-net.com)

INTERNATIONAL TENNIS FEDERATION

Bank Lane, Roehampton, London, SW15 5XZ (Tel: 020-8878 6464; Fax: 020-8878 7799)
Chief Executive: J. Garnham

JOCKEY CLUB

42 Portman Square, W1H 0EN (Tel: 020-7486 4921; Fax: 020-7486 8689; E-mail: info@thejockeyclub.co.uk; Web: http://www.thejockeyclub.co.uk)
Senior Steward: C. Spence

KEEP FIT ASSOCIATION

Francis House, Francis Street, London, SW1P 1DE (Tel: 020-7233 8898; Fax: 020-7630 7936; E-mail: kfa@keepfit.org.uk; Web: http://www.keepfit.org.uk)
Chair: Ms A. Bayley

LAWN TENNIS ASSOCIATION

The Queen's Club, London, W14 9EG (Tel: 020-7381 7000; Fax: 020-7381 5965; Web: http://www.lta.org.uk)
Chief Executive: J. A. Crowther

LONDON AMATEUR BOXING ASSOCIATION

58 Comber Grove, London, SE5 0LD (Tel: 020-7252 7008; Fax: 020-7708 0904)
Hon. Secretary: K. Walters

LONDON MARATHON

PO Box 1234, London, SE1 8RZ (Tel: 020-7620 4117; Fax: 020-7620 4208; Web: http://www.london-marathon.co.uk)
Chief Executive: N. Bitel

318 Cultural London

MCC
Lord's Cricket Ground, London, NW8 8QN (Tel: 020-7289 1611; Fax: 020-7289 9700; Web: http://www.lords.org/mcc)
Secretary: R. D. V. Knight

NATIONAL GREYHOUND RACING CLUB
Twyman House, 16 Bonny Street, London, NW1 9QD (Tel: 020-7267 9256; Fax: 020-7482 1023; E-mail: ngrc@clara.net)
Chief Executive: F. Melville

NATIONAL ICE SKATING ASSOCIATION OF THE UK
1st Floor, 114-116 Curtain Road, London, EC2A 3AH (Tel: 020-7613 1188; Fax: 020-7739 2445; E-mail: nisa@iceskating.org.uk; Web: http://www.iceskating.org.uk)
Chief Executive: R. Gordon

NFL EUROPE LEAGUE
97-99 Kings Road, London, SW3 4PA (Tel: 020-7225 3070; Fax: 020-7376 5070)
Chief Executive Officer: K. Saunders

PROFESSIONAL WINDSURFING ASSOCIATION
The Green Room, 1 Burston Road, London, SW15 6AR (Tel: 020-8785 9190; Fax: 020-8785 9195; E-mail: pwa@ssm-freesports.com; Web: http://www.world-windsurfing.com)
Chairman: P. McGain

RICHMOND GYMNASTICS ASSOCIATION
RGA Centre, Townmead Road, Richmond, Surrey, London, TW9 4EL (Tel: 020-8878 8682)
Chairman: Mrs L. Gray

RUGBY FOOTBALL UNION
Rugby House, Rugby Road, Twickenham, Middx, London, TW1 1DS (Tel: 020-8892 2000; Fax: 020-8892 9816)
Chief Executive: F. Baron

SANEX WTA TOUR
Bank Lane, London, SW15 5XZ (Tel: 020-8392 4760 020-8392 4765; Web: http://www.sanexwta.com)
Director of European Operations: Ms G. Clark

SOUTH OF ENGLAND ATHLETICS ASSOCIATION
106 London Fruit Exchange, Brushfield Street, London, E1 6EX (Tel: 020-7247 2963; Fax: 020-7247 3439; E-mail: south@sseaa.freeserve.co.uk)
Chief Execcutive: Ms L. Whitehead

TENNIS AND RACKETS ASSOCIATION
c/o The Queen's Club, London, W14 9EQ (Tel: 020-7386 3447/8; Fax: 020-7385 7424; E-mail: ceo@tennis-rackets.net)
Chief Executive: Brig. A. D. Myrtle CB, CBE

WORLD PROFESSIONAL BILLIARDS AND SNOOKER ASSOCIATION
27 Oakfield Road, Clifton, Bristol BS8 2AT (Tel: 0117-974 4491; Fax: 0117-974 4931; Email: wsa@wpbsa.com; Web: http://www.wpbsa.com)

CULTURAL, HERITAGE AND LEISURE ORGANISATIONS

ARTS COUNCIL OF ENGLAND
14 Great Peter Street, London SW1P 3NQ (Tel: 020-7333 0100; Fax: 020-7973 6590; Email: enquiries@artscouncil.org.uk; Web: http://www.artscouncil.org.uk)

The Arts Council is the national body for the arts in England. It distributes public money from government and the lottery to artists and arts organisations, both directly and through the ten Regional Arts Boards. The Government grant for 2000/1 is £237.3 million. The Arts Council uses this to provide regular funding to arts organisations and one-off development funds. The Council also commissions new work; conducts research; provides advice and information and develops awareness and support for the arts in England. The Arts Council is an independent, non-political body.
Chief Executive: Peter Hewitt
Head of Press and Public Relations: David McNeil

London Arts Board
Elme House, 133 Long Acre, London WC2E 9AF (Tel: 020-7240 1313)
Chair: vacant

BRITISH FILM COMMISSION
70 Baker Street, London W1M 1DJ (Tel: 020-7224 5000; Fax: 020-7224 1013

The British Film Commission was set up in 1991 and is funded by the Department for Culture, Media and Sport. The Commission promotes the UK as an international production centre, encourages the use of locations, facilities, services and personnel, and provides, at no charge to the film makers, comprehensive advice and information relating to the practical aspects of filming in the UK.
Commissioner and Chief Executive: S. Norris

BRITISH FILM INSTITUTE
21 Stephen Street, London W1P 2LN (Tel: 020-7255 1444; Fax: 020-7436 7950; Email: firstname.lastname@bfi.org.uk; Web: http://www.bfi.org.uk)

Founded in 1933 the British Film Institute offers opportunities to experience, enjoy and discover more about the world of film and television. Its three main departments are: bfi Education, comprising the bfi National Library, bfi Publishing and Sight and Sound magazine, as well as bfi Education Projects which encourages life-long learning about the moving image; bfi Exhibition, which runs the National Film Theatre on London's South Bank and the annual London Film Festival and supports local cinemas and film festivals UK-wide; and bfi Collections,

which preserves the UK's moving image heritage and promotes access to it through a variety of means including film, video and DVD releases and touring exhibitions. The bfi also runs the bfi London IMAX Cinema at Waterloo, featuring the UK's largest screen.
Patron: HRH The Prince of Wales, KG, KT, GCB
Chair: Joan Bakewell, CBE
Director: Jon Teckman

COMMISSION FOR ARCHITECTURE AND THE BUILT ENVIRONMENT

7 St James's Square, London SW1Y 4JU (Tel: 020-7839 6537; Fax: 020-7839 8475;
Email: enquiries@cabe.org.uk;
Web: http://www.cabe.org.uk)

The Commission for Architecture and the Built Environment (CABE) replaced the Royal Fine Art Commission (RFAC) in August 1999. It has taken over the RFAC's design review function, and is also responsible for promoting the importance of high quality architecture and urban design and encouraging the understanding of architecture through educational and regional initiatives.
Chairman: Stuart Lipton
Chief Executive: Jon Rouse (from 1 October 2000)

CORPORATION OF LONDON RECORDS OFFICE

Guildhall, London EC2P 2EJ (Tel: 020-7332 1251; Fax: 020-7710 8682; Email: clro@corpoflondon.gov.uk; Web: http://www.cityoflondon.gov.uk/archives/clro)

The Corporation of London Records Office contains the municipal archives of the City of London which are regarded as the most complete collection of ancient municipal records in existence. The collection includes charters of William the Conqueror, Henry II, and later kings and queens to 1957; ancient custumals: Liber Horn, Dunthorne, Custumarum, Ordinacionum, Memorandorum and Albus, Liber de Antiquis Legibus, and collections of statutes; a continuous series of judicial rolls and books from 1252 and Council minutes from 1275; records of the Old Bailey and Guildhall sessions from 1603; financial records from the 16th century; the records of London Bridge from the 12th century; and numerous subsidiary series and miscellanea of historical interest. The Readers' Room is open Monday–Friday, 9.30 a.m.-4.45 a.m.
Keeper of the City Records: The Town Clerk
City Archivist: J. R. Sewell
Deputy City Archivist: Mrs J. M. Bankes

COUNCIL FOR MUSEUMS, ARCHIVES AND LIBRARIES

16 Queen Anne's Gate, London SW1H 9AA (Tel: 020-7233 4200; Fax: 020-7233 3686)

The Council for Museums, Archives and Libraries is a new strategic agency which will work with museums, archives and libraries throughout the UK.
Chairman: Matthew Evans
Chief Executive: Nevill Mackay

Cultural Organisations 319

COVENT GARDEN MARKET AUTHORITY

Covent House, New Covent Garden Market, London SW8 5NX (Tel: 020-7720 2211; Fax: 020-7622 5307; Email: info@cgma.gov.uk; Web: http://cgma.gov.uk)

The Covent Garden Market Authority is constituted under the Covent Garden Market Acts 1961 to 1977, the members being appointed by the Minister of Agriculture, Fisheries and Food. The Authority owns and operates the 56-acre New Covent Garden Markets (fruit, vegetables, flowers) which have been trading since 1974.
Chairman (part-time): L. Mills, OBE
General Manager: Dr P. M. Liggins
Secretary: C. Farey

CROWN ESTATE

16 Carlton House Terrace, London SW1Y 5AH (Tel: 020-7210 4377; Fax: 020-7930 8187)

The Crown Estate includes substantial blocks of urban property, primarily in London, almost 120,000 hectares of agricultural land and extensive marine holdings throughout the United Kingdom. Its origins go back to the reign of King Edward the Confessor and, until the accession of King George III, the Sovereign received its rents and profits. However, since 1760 the annual surplus, after deducting management expenses, has been surrendered by the Sovereign to Parliament to help meet the cost of civil government. In return, the Sovereign receives the Civil List and the Government meets other official expenditure incurred in support of the Sovereign.
First Commissioner and Chairman (part-time): Sir Denys Henderson
Second Commissioner and Chief Executive: Sir Christopher Howes, KCVO, CB
Commissioners (part-time), Mrs H. M. R. Chapman, CBE, FRICS; The Lord De Ramsey; I. D. Grant, CBE; D. E. G. Griffiths, CBE; J. H. M. Norris, CBE; R. R. Spinney, FRICS
Director of Finance and Administration: R. Bright, MA
Director of Urban Estates: D. A. Bickmore, FRICS

ENGLISH HERITAGE

23 Savile Row, London W1X 1AB (Tel: 020-7973 3000; Fax: 020-7973 3001;
Web: http://www.english-heritage.org.uk)

National Monuments Record Centre, Kemble Drive, Swindon SN2 2GZ (Tel: 01793-414600; Fax: 01793-414606) London Search Room: 55 Blandford Street, London W1H 3AF (Tel: 020-7208 8200; Fax: 020-7224 5333)

English Heritage was established under the National Heritage Act 1983, and its duties are to offer expert advice and skills and give grants to secure the preservation of listed buildings, cathedrals, churches, archaeological sites, ancient monuments and historic houses in England; to encourage the imaginative re-use of historic buildings to aid regeneration of the centres of cities, towns and villages; to manage the historic houses and monuments in its care; and to promote access to and enjoyment of ancient monuments and historic buildings in England. It is funded by the Department for Culture, Media and Sport.

On 1 April 1999 English Heritage merged with the Royal Commission on the Historical Monuments of England (RCHME). It is therefore now responsible for the National Monuments Record, which includes all the material gathered since the formation of the RCHME in 1908 and now contains over 12 million photographs, maps and drawings.
Chairman: N. Cossons
Chief Executive: Ms P. Alexander

FILM COUNCIL

Queen's Yard, 179 Tottenham Court Road, London W1P 2LN (Tel 020-7580 9120; Fax 020-7580 9130)

The Council was created in April 2000 by the Department for Culture, Media and Sport to develop a coherent strategy for the development and leadership of film culture and the film industry. It will be responsible for the majority of the Department for Culture, Media and Sport funding for film as well as lottery and grant-in-aid (with the exception of the National Film and Television School).
Chairman: A. Parker
Deputy Chairman: S. Till

HERITAGE OF LONDON TRUST

23 Savile Row, London W1X 1AB (Tel: 020-7973 3809; Fax: 020-7973 3792)

Director: J. Spicer

HISTORIC ROYAL PALACES

Hampton Court Palace, East Molesey, Surrey KT8 9AU (Tel: 020-8781 9500; Fax: 020-8781 9754; Web: http://hrp.org.uk)

Historic Royal Palaces was formerly an executive agency of the Department for Culture, Media and Sport; it is now a non-departmental public body with charitable trust status. The Secretary of State for Culture, Media and Sport is still accountable to Parliament for the care and presentation of the palaces, which are owned by the Sovereign in right of the Crown. The chairman of the trustees is appointed by The Queen on the advice of the Secretary of State.

Historic Royal Palaces is responsible for the Tower of London, Hampton Court Palace, Kensington Palace State Apartments and the Royal Ceremonial Dress Collection, Kew Palace with Queen Charlotte's Cottage, and the Banqueting House, Whitehall.
Chairman: The Earl of Airlie, KT, GCVO
Appointed by The Queen: The Lord Camoys, GCVO, DL; Sir Michael Peat, KCVO; H. Roberts, CVO
Appointed by the Secretary of State: M. Herbert, CBE; Ms A. Heylin, OBE; S. Jones, LVO; Ms J. Sharman
Ex officio: Field Marshal the Lord Inge, GCB (Constable of the Tower of London)
Chief Executive: A. Coppin
Director of Finance: Ms A. McLeish
Director of Human Resources: G. Josephs
Surveyor of the Fabric: R. Davidson
Curator, Historic Royal Palaces: Dr E. Impey
Director, Palaces Group: D. McGuinnes

Resident Governor: HM Tower of London, Maj.-Gen. G. Field, CB, OBE

LORD GREAT CHAMBERLAIN'S OFFICE

House of Lords, London SW1A 0PW (Tel: 020-7219 3100; Fax: 020-7219 2500)

The Lord Great Chamberlain is a Great Officer of State, the office being hereditary since the grant of Henry I to the family of De Vere, Earls of Oxford. It is now a joint hereditary office between the Cholmondeley and Carington families. The Lord Great Chamberlain is responsible for the royal apartments of the Palace of Westminster, i.e. The Queen's Robing Room, the Royal Gallery and, in conjunction with the Lord Chancellor and the Speaker, Westminster Hall. The Lord Great Chamberlain has particular responsibility for the internal administrative arrangements within the House of Lords for State Openings of Parliament.
Lord Great Chamberlain: The Marquess of Cholmondeley
Secretary to the Lord Great Chamberlain: Gen. Sir Edward Jones, KCB, CBE
Clerks to the Lord Great Chamberlain: Miss C. J. Bostock; Miss R. M. Wilkinson

MILLENNIUM COMMISSION

Portland House, Stag Place, London SW1E 5EZ (Tel: 020-7880 2001; Fax: 020-7880 2000)

The Millennium Commission was established in February 1994 and is accountable to the Department for Culture, Media and Sport. It is an independent body which distributes money from National Lottery proceeds to projects to mark the millennium.
Chairman: The Rt. Hon. Chris Smith, MP
Members: The Rt. Hon. Dr Jack Cunningham, MP; Prof. Heather Couper, FRAS; Earl of Dalkeith; The Lord Glentoran, CBE; Sir John Hall; The Rt. Hon. M. Heseltine, MP; S. Jenkins; The Baroness Scotland of Asthal, QC
Director: M. O'Connor

ROYAL COMMISSION ON HISTORICAL MANUSCRIPTS

Quality House, Quality Court, Chancery Lane, London WC2A 1HP (Tel: 020-7242 1198; Fax: 020-7831 3550; Email: nra@hmc.gov.uk; http://www.hmc.gov.uk)

The Commission was set up by royal warrant in 1869 to enquire and report on collections of papers of value for the study of history which were in private hands. In 1959 a new warrant enlarged these terms of reference to include all historical records, wherever situated, outside the Public Records and gave it added responsibilities as a central co-ordinating body to promote, assist and advise on their proper preservation and storage. The Commission is sponsored by the Department for Culture, Media and Sport.

The Commission also maintains the National Register of Archives (NRA), which contains over 42,000 unpublished lists and catalogues of manuscript collections describing the holdings of local record offices, national and university libraries, specialist repositories and others in the UK and overseas. The

NRA can be searched using computerised indices which are available in the Commission's search room and on its website.

The Commission also administers the Manorial and Tithe Documents Rules on behalf of the Master of the Rolls.

Chairman: The Lord Bingham of Cornhill, PC
Commissioners: Sir Patrick Cormack, FSA, MP; The Lord Egremont and Leconfield; Sir Matthew Farrer, GCVO; Sir John Sainty, KCB, FSA; Very Revd H. E. C. Stapleton, FSA; Sir Keith Thomas, FBA; The Earl of Scarbrough; Mrs A. Dundas-Bekker; G. E. Aylmer, D.PHILl, FBA; Mrs S. J. Davies, PHD.; Mrs A. Prochaska, PHD; Miss R. Dunhill, FSA; Dr Caroline Barron, FSA; Prof. T. C. Smout, CBE, PHD., FBA, FRSE, FSAScot.
Secretary: C. J. Kitching, PHD., FSA

ROYAL NATIONAL THEATRE BOARD

South Bank, London, SE1 9PX (Tel: 020-7452 3333; Fax: 020-7452 3344)

The chairman and members of the Board of the Royal National Theatre are appointed by the Secretary of State for Culture, Media and Sport.

Chairman: Sir Christopher Hogg
Members: Ms J. Bakewell, CBE; The Hon. P. Benson; Sir David Hancock, KCB; G. Hutchings; Ms K. Jones; Ms S. MacGregor, OBE; Ben Okri; M. Oliver; Sir Tom Stoppard, CBE; P. Wiegand
Company Secretary: Mrs M. McGregor; Prof. Lola Young
Director: T. Nunn, CBE
Executive Director: The Baroness McIntosh of Hudnall

TOURISM

LONDON TOURIST INFORMATION SERVICE

(Tel: 0839 337799 or 020-7244 9999; Fax: 020-7341 9999)

LONDON TOURIST BOARD AND CONVENTION BUREAU

Glen House, Stag Place, London, SW1E 5LT. (Tourist information: 0839 123456)

BRITISH TOURIST AUTHORITY

Thames Tower, Black's Road, London W6 9EL (Tel: 020-8846 9000; Fax: 020-8563 0302)
Chief Executive: J. Hamblin

ENGLISH TOURISM COUNCIL

Thames Tower, Black's Road, London W6 9EL (Tel: 020-8563 3000; Fax: 020-8563 3254; Web: http://www.englishtourism.org.uk)
Chief Executive: Mary Lynch

REASONS FOR VISITING* LONDON (PERCENTAGES AND MILLIONS)

	Overseas visits		Domestic visits	
	1991	1997	1991	1997
Holiday	49	52	41	21
Visiting Friends/Relatives	16	16	21	62
Business/Conference	23	21	21	12
Other	12	11	6	5
Total visits** (millions)	9.2	13.5	6.6	14.6

* Staying one night or more
** Ranked according to percentage of visits to London in 1997.
Excludes visits made by residents of the Irish Republic
Source: Focus on London '99, Office for National Statistics © Crown Copyright 1999

TOP TOURIST ATTRACTIONS, BY NUMBER OF VISITS, 000s, 1997*

Ranking	Attraction	Total visits	Ranking	Attraction	Total visits
1	British Museum	6,057	11	London Zoo	1,098
2	National Gallery	4,809	12	Victoria and Albert Museum	1,041
3	Madame Tussaud's	2,799	13	Royal Botanical Gardens	937
4	Tower of London	2,615	14	National Portrait Gallery	888
5	Westminster Abbey†	2,500	15	Royal Academy of Arts	859
6	St. Paul's Cathedral†	2,000	16	Hampton Court Palace	643
7	Natural History Museum	1,793	17	Rock Circus	613
8	Tate Gallery	1,758	18	Imperial War Museum	519
9	World of Adventures†	1,750	19	National Maritime Museum	476
10	Science Museum	1,537	20	Photographer's Gallery†	450

* The number of visitors to the London Dungeon in 1997 is not available. In 1995 there were 610,000 admissions
† Estimate

ENVIRONMENTAL
LONDON

NATURE RESERVES
SIGHTS OF SPECIAL SCIENTIFIC INTEREST
RIVER THAMES
ENVIRONMENTAL GROUPS
WASTE MINIMISATION AND RECYCLING

ENVIRONMENTAL LONDON

The establishment of the Greater London Authority (GLA) will change the way the environment is managed in London. The authority comprises the Mayor, who is responsible for developing sustainable strategies across all of the GLAs functions, including the environment, and the Assembly, which is there to scrutinise the Mayor's policies and act as a check to his powers.

The Mayor's environmental duties cover a wide remit and a number of bodies that carry out environmental work will be absorbed into the GLA including, the London Research Centre and the London Ecology Unit.

In addition to the Assembly's role in scrutinising the Mayor's strategies and reports on the environment, it has the power to conduct its own investigations into environmental issues. This can either be as an input into policy development or for other reasons.

Mayor's responsibilities
The first of the Mayor's four-yearly reports on the state of London's environment is due within three years. The report will include information on air quality, energy use and progress towards climate change targets, groundwater levels, traffic levels and emissions. It will be drawn up in consultation with the Environment Agency, which currently produces a state of the environment report for England and Wales, and local authorities.

Air
Much of London's air quality problems are the result of traffic emissions. The Mayor is tasked with developing an integrated transport policy that will deliver air quality improvements.

He will also be responsible for working with the London boroughs and developing an air quality strategy for London. This must tie in with the government's National Air Quality Strategy. The aim of this is to map the future ambient air quality in the UK. The strategy is designed to be evolutionary and is regularly monitored and reviewed. Under the strategy, all district and unitary authorities have a duty to review air quality, including likely future air quality, in their areas. This is accompanied by an assessment of whether air quality objectives (set in the strategy) are being, or are likely to be, achieved.

If authorities find that any part of their area breaches the objectives, an air quality management area must be declared and an action plan drawn up for improvements.

Local councils will continue with the process and will deal with all local pollution episodes, although the Mayor will have the power to ensure they also comply with the London-wide action plan.

Climate change
The government has set a target of reducing greenhouse gases by 21.5 per cent by 2010. This is almost double the UK's 12.5 per cent target agreed in the Kyoto Protocol. The Mayor will have a responsibility to report on London's contribution to meeting this target.

Waste
The Mayor must also publish an integrated municipal waste management strategy for London, the first of which must be drawn up within two years. It will then be reviewed every four years. The strategy will cover recovery, recycling, treatment and disposal and will be developed in consultation with waste disposal and collection authorities and the private sector. The aim is to develop and encourage new ideas.

The London plan will have to be in line with the government's national waste strategy – *A Way with Waste*. This strategy sets a target to reduce the amount of industrial and commercial waste that is landfilled by 85 per cent by 2005 and raises the target recovery rate of met its commitments under the Agenda 21 agreement that was signed at the 1992 Conference on Environment and Development in Rio (the Earth Summit). Although not a statutory obligation, the government wants all local councils to have adopted Local Agenda 21 by the end of 2000. Currently some 70 per cent have adopted it, with a further 20 per cent planning to do so by the end of the year. Work is under way to bring the remaining 40 or so on board.

The government's Beacon Council scheme also addresses encouraging environmental improvement at a local level. Two London councils are Beacon Councils for 2000/01 for their waste management initiatives - the London Borough of Bexley and the London Borough of Hounslow. Beacon status demonstrates that these councils are providing high quality services. They spread their best practice to others through open days and other activities.

The environment will continue to play an important role in the second year of Beacon Councils, with local environmental quality as one of the themes.

LONDON'S LOCAL NATURE RESERVES

Barnet
Coppetts Wood & Glebelands
Oak Hill Wood
Rowley Green Common
Scratchwood and Moat Mount Open
Big Wood & Little Wood

Brent
Fryent Country Park

Bromley
Jubilee Country Park
Scadbury Park

Camden
Camley Street Nature Park

Croydon
Bramley Park
Selsdon Wood
South Norwood Country Park

Ealing
Fox Wood
Islip Manor
Litten Nature Reserve
Long Wood
Northolt Manor
Perivale Wood

326 Environmental London

Enfield
Covert Way

Greenwich
Oxleas Wood

Hackney
Abney Park Cemetery
Springfield Park

Haringey
Parkland Walk
Queen's Wood
Railway Fields

Harrow
Bentley Priory
Stanmore Common
Stanmore Country Park

Hillingdon
Denham Country Park
Yeading Brook Meadows
Yeading Woods

Hounslow
Chiswick Eyot
Duke's Hollow
Gunnersbury Triangle
Hounslow Heath
Pevensey Road

Islington
Barnsbury Wood
Gillespie Park

Kingston upon Thames
Bonesgate Open Space
Castle Hill
Coombe Wood
Edith Gardens Nature Reserve
Hogsmill River Park
Jubilee Wood
Raeburn Open Space
The Wood and Richard Jefferies Bird Sanctuary

Merton
Bennett's Hole
Cannon Hill Common
Fishpond Wood and Beverley Meads
Myrna Close
Sir Joseph Hood Memorial Wood
Wandle Meadow Nature Park

Redbridge
Hainault Lodge

Richmond upon Thames
Barnes Common
Crane Park Island
Ham Lands
Leg of Mutton Reservoir
Oak Avenue Hampton

Southwark
Sydenham Hill Wood and Fern Bank

Sutton
Roundshaw Downs
Ruffet and Bid Woods
Spencer Road Wetlands
Sutton Ecology Centre
The Spinney, Carshalton
Wilderness Island

Waltham Forest
Ainslie Wood

Wandsworth
Battersea Park Nature Areas

Westminster
St John's Wood Church Grounds Wildlife Garden

SSSI SITES IN GREATER LONDON

Abbey Wood, Bexley
Barn Elms Reservoir, Richmond
Bentley Priory, Harrow
Brent Reservoir (Welsh Harp), Barnet, Brent
Chingford Reservoir, Enfield, Epping Forest, Waltham Forest
Crofton Woods, Bromley
Croham Hurst, Croydon
Denham Lock Wood, Hillingdon
Downe Bank and High Elms, Bromley
Elmstead Pit, Bromley
Epping Forest, Epping Forest, Waltham Forest
Farthing Downs and Happy Valley, Croydon
Fray's Farm Meadows, Hillingdon
Gilbert's Pit, Greenwich
Hainault Forest, Epping Forest, Redbridge
Hampstead Heath Woods, Barnet, Camden, Haringey
Harefield Pit, Hillingdon
Harrow Weald, Harrow
Hornchurch Cutting, Havering
Ingrebourne Marshes, Havering
Inner Thames Marshes, Havering, Thurrock
Keston and Hayes Commons, Bromley
Mid Colne Valley, Hillingdon, South Bucks
Old Park Woods, Hillingdon
Oxleas Woodlands, Greenwich
Perivale Wood, Ealing
Richmond Park, Richmond
Riddlesdown, Croydon
Ruislip Woods, Hillingdon
Ruxley Gravel Pits, Bromley
Saltbox Hill, Bromley
Syon Park, Hounslow
Wansunt Pit, Bexley, Dartford
Walthamstow Marshes, Waltham Forest
Walthamstow Reservoirs, Hackney, Haringey, Waltham Forest
Wimbledon Common, Merton, Wandsworth

LONDON LAND COVER*, 1988-1991 (THOUSAND HECTARES AND PERCENTAGES)

	Thousands of hectares†	Percentages
Suburban	66	38
Continuous urban	36	20
Semi-natural grass	29	17
Mown grass	13	8
Tilled land	12	7
Deciduous woodland	8	4
Other vegetation	5	3
Inland water	2	1
Estuary	1	1
Other land	3	2
Total	174	100

* Data taken from the Land Cover Map of Great Britain
† The satellite classification may involve a degree of imprecision and misallocation and the results should be used with caution.
Source: Focus on London '99, Office for National Statistics © Crown Copyright 1999

ENVIRONMENT AGENCY

25th Floor, Millbank Tower, 21-24 Millbank, London SW1P 4XL (Tel: 020-7863 8600; Fax 020-7863 8650)
Rio House, Waterside Drive, Aztec West, Almondsbury, Bristol BS32 4UD (Tel: 01454 624400; Fax 01454 624409)

The Environment Agency was established in 1996 under the Environment Act 1995 and is a non-departmental public body sponsored by the Department of the Environment, Transport and the Regions, Ministry of Agriculture Fisheries and Food and the National Assembly for Wales. The Agency is responsible for pollution prevention and control in England and Wales, and for the management and use of water resources, including flood defences, fisheries and navigation. It has head offices in London and Bristol and eight regional offices.
Chairman: Sir John Harman
Director of Finance: N. Reader
Director of Personnel: G. Duncan
Director of Environmental Protection: Dr P. Leinster
Director of Water Management: G. Mance
Director of Operations: A. Robertson
Director of Corporate Affairs: Vacant
Director of Legal Services: R. Navarro
Chief Scientist: Dr. John Murlis

THE RIVER THAMES

The River Thames is the basis on which the city of London was built. Its freshwater stretches and tributaries provide water supplies for millions of people and the river serves as the main recipient of London's treated waste water. Substantial investment over the last thirty years has greatly improved water quality in the Thames, creating one of the cleanest metropolitan estuaries in the world. There have been 116 species of fish recorded in the tideway, including salmon which had been absent from the river for 140 years.

Historically, the nerve centre of London was the river – as a port, a market and as a source of fish. The foreshores and drawdocks were a hive of activity, and thus formed an important economic centre. Over the years, this role has changed and much of the riverside industry has disappeared. The river remains an important transport route: over 50 million tonnes of freight were shipped in and out of the Port of London in 1997. The Thames Path and other riverside walks encourage people to visit the Thames, but there are still many opportunities for recreation and economic benefit which are being neglected.

Thames21
Thames21 is a joint initiative between Tidy Britain Group, the Port of London Authority (PLA), the Environment Agency, Thames Water and the Corporation of London, to address poor local environmental quality on the Thames and its tributaries throughout London. It was launched officially by Michael Meacher MP in 1998. It continues the work of ThamesClean (established in 1994) and the PLA's Debris Clearance Operation (collecting up to 1,000 tonnes of litter each year from the Thames).

The Thames is blighted by thousands of tonnes of litter which is blown, thrown and washed into it. It also exports litter to the marine environment where it pollutes beaches around the UK and the rest of the world. Thames21 aims to prevent and remedy this problem through a range of programmes, including its pioneering Adopt-a-River scheme, work with offenders on community service and improving the condition of the Thames Path National Trail. In 1999, 1,600 volunteers were involved across London.

THAMES21

c/o Corporation of London, Walbrook Wharf, Upper Thames Street, London EC4R 3TD (Tel: 020-7236 1281; Fax: 020-7236 1289;
Email: thames21.tbg@virgin.net;
Web: http://www.thames21.org.uk)

Project Manager: Mark Lloyd (Tel: 020-7248 2916)
Project Officer (Adopt-a-River): Lynsey Butterfield (Tel: 020-7248 2916)
Project Officer (Community Service): Alistair Maltby (Tel: 020-7329 4255)
Project Officer (Thames Path National Trail): Deanne Jones (Tel: 020-7236 5657)

Environmental London

OTHER LONDON ENVIRONMENTAL BODIES

BRITISH TRUST FOR CONSERVATION VOLUNTEERS

London Region: 80 York Way, London N1 9AG (Tel: 020-7278 4294; Fax: 020-7278 5095; Email: london@btcv.org..uk; Web: http://www.btcv.org)

The British Trust for Conservation Volunteers in the London region aims to support and encourage Londoners in taking action to protect and improve their environment through programmes of practical conservation and community environmental improvement.
Marketing Officer: Patrick Wilson

CHARTERED INSTITUTION OF WATER AND ENVIRONMENTAL MANAGEMENT

15 John Street, London WC1N 2EB (Tel: 020-7831 3110; Fax: 020-7405 4967; Email: jtaberham@ciwem.org.uk; Web: http://www.ciwem.org.uk)

The aims and objectives of the Chartered Institution of Water and Environmental Management are to develop and promote the better and integrated management of the environment, to foster a better understanding of water and environmental issues and to enhance the quality of people's lives.
Policy and Technical Manager: Justin Taberham

FRIENDS OF THE EARTH LONDON

26-28 Underwood Street, London N1 7JQ (Tel: 020-7490 1555; Fax: 020-7490 0881; Email: pauldz@foe.co.uk; Web: http://www.foe.co.uk)

Friends of the Earth works to protect and improve conditions for life on earth, now and in the future. In London, work is on a local and regional level on a diverse range of social, economic and environmental issues, using campaigning, lobbying, public information and collaborative working to ensure that London shows the way as a sustainable city.
London Campaigns Co-ordinator: Paul De Zylva

GOING FOR GREEN LONDON

Premier House, 12-13 Hatton Garden, London EC1N 8HG (Tel: 020-7831 4484; Fax: 020-7430 2859; Email: tbg.london@virgin.net; Web: http://www.tidybritain.org.uk)

Going for Green aims to raise environmental awareness for people in London both in the workplace and at home.
National Director for London: Christopher Harris

LONDON 21 SUSTAINABILITY NETWORK

7 Chamberlain Street, London NW1 8XB (Tel: 020-7722 3710; Fax: 020-7722 3959; Email: admin@london21.org; Web: http://www.lonfon 21.org)

LONDON ENVIRONMENTAL EDUCATION FORUM

c/o Strategy Directorate, Greater London Authority, 4th Floor, Romney House, 43 Marsham Street, London SW1P 3TY (Tel: 020-7983 4311; Fax: 020-7983 4706; Email: julie.brownbridge@london-research.gov.uk)

The London Environmental Education Forum develops, promotes and facilitates the delivery of environmental education throughout London.
Contact: Julie Brownbridge

LONDON RIVERS ASSOCIATION

24-31 Greenwich Market, London SE10 9HZ (Tel: 020-8293 9275; Fax: 020-8293 9277; E-mail: londonriversassociation@btinternet.com)

The London Rivers Association aims to promote the development of the River Thames and ensure that the environment and character of the Thames is conserved and enhanced.
Contact: Rose Jaijee

LONDON TREE OFFICERS ASSOCIATION

Dartmouth Lodge, Dartmouth Park Hill, Waterlow Park, London N19 5JF(Tel: 020-7272 9890; Fax: 020-7272 9890; Email: ltoa@dial.pipex.com)

The London Tree Officers Association is involved in improving the management of London's trees and woodlands.
Contact: Becky Hesch

LONDON WILDLIFE TRUST

Central Office, Harling House, 47-51 Great Suffolk Street, London SE1 0BS (Tel: 020-7261 0447; Fax: 020-7261 0538; Email: enquiries@londonwt.cix.co.uk; Web: http://www.wildlifetrust.org.uk/london/)

The prinicipal objective of the London Wildlife Trust is to sustain and enhance London's wildlife habitats in order to create a city richer in wildlife. This is achieved through community initiatives, land management, education, campaigning and influencing decision makers in the capital.

PORT OF LONDON AUTHORITY

Devon House, 58-60 St Katharine's Way, London E1 9LB (Tel: 020-7265 2656; Fax: 020-7265 2699)

The Port of London Authority is a public trust constituted under the Port of London Act 1908 and subsequent legislation. It is the governing body for the Port of London, covering the tidal portion of the River Thames from Teddington to the seaward limit. The Board comprises a chairman and up to seven but not less than four non-executive members appointed by the Secretary of State for the Environment, Transport and the Regions, and up to four but not less than one executive members appointed by the Board.
Chief Executive: S. Cuthbert
Secretary: G. E. Ennals

Environmental Bodies 329

SUSTAINABLE LONDON TRUST

7 Chamberlain Street, London NW1 8XB (Tel: 020-7722 3710; Fax: 020-7722 3959; Email: slt@gm.apc.org; Web: http://www.greenchannel.com-slt-index.htm

THAMES ESTUARY PARTNERSHIP

School of Public Policy, University College London, 29-30 Tavistock Square, London WC1H 9EZ (Tel: 020-7679 4920; Fax: 020-7916 8546; Email: tep@thamesweb.com; Web: http://www.thamesweb.com)

The Thames Estuary Partnership is involved in the sustainable use of the Thames Estuary by seeking to achieve a balance between the competing demands being placed on the Thames Estuary. It seeks to do this via information sharing, action plans and a wide range of projects involving government agencies, local communities, local authorities and the voluntary and commercial sector.

Partnership Co-ordinator: Caroline Davis

URBAN POLLUTION RESEARCH CENTRE

Middlesex University, Bounds Green Road. London N11 2NQ (Tel: 020-8362 5229; Fax: 020-8362 6580; Email: n.priest@mdx.ac.uk; Web: http://www.mdx.ac.uk)

The main activity of the Urban Pollution Research Centre is research into all aspects of air and water pollution with special reference to air quality, urban run-off and environmental radionuclides.

Contact: Prof. Nick Priest

WASTE MINIMISATION AND RECYCLING IN LONDON

As households, businesses and industry create increasingly large amounts of waste, London's local authorities are making greater provision for waste minimisation and recycling. In addition to the bottle and can banks that can be seen on most street corners, the recycling concept has grown to encompass composting, door-to-door collection of bulky household items (such as old fridge-freezers which can be used for CFC recycling) and Christmas tree recycling.

Following the 1992 Rio Earth Summit Conference, where world leaders met to discuss ways to prevent future irreversible harm to the planet, Agenda 21 was born, laying down targets for the minimisation of waste and environmental damage. At a local level, these targets broadly include: reducing the amount of waste produced and sent for disposal; increasing the use of recycling, composting and recovery of waste materials; encouraging the repair and re-use of goods and materials and encouraging households and businesses to buy products with less packaging.

The Environmental Protection Act 1990 places a duty on all local authorities to issue a Waste Recycling Plan (WRP) and stipulates that each WRP should include data on the authorities arrangements regarding waste collection and recycling. The Department of the Environment, Transport and the Regions has issued guidance notes to a local authorities preparing WRPs.

WASTE MANAGEMENT IN LONDON, 1995-96 (MILLION TONNES)

Waste Generated	
Household waste from:-	
Refuse collection vehicles	2.3
Other household collections	0.3
Civic amenity sites	0.4
Materials separately collected for recycling	0.1
Total household waste	3.1
Municipally collected non-household waste	0.7
Non-household waste collected for recycling	–
Total municipal waste	3.9
Treatment/disposal method	
Landfill	2.9
Incineration with Energy from Waste	0.7
Recycled/composted	0.1
Total waste treated/disposed of	3.7

Source: *Focus on London '99*, Office for National Statistics © Crown Copyright 1999

The list above provides details of the waste and recycling facilities that are available within London's 33 local authority areas along with address and contract information for civic amenity sites where available. For further information on local government in London please see the Governed London section.

BARNET LBC

Barnet House, 1255 High Road, Whetstone, London N20 0EJ (Tel: 020-8359 2000; Fax: 020-8359 4154; Email: dens.lib@barnet.gov.uk; Web: http://www.barnet.gov.uk)

Barnet LBC encourages residents and local businesses to consider the amount of waste they produce for disposal with the aim of reducing as much of it as possible. The council offers a range of home composting units to residents and schools at competitive prices to help achieve this aim.

In the borough of Barnet there are 80 recycling sites where recyclable items include glass bottles and jars, newspapers and magazines, cans, textiles and shoes, soft toys, metal, vehicle oil and vehicle batteries. There is a Civic Amenity Site at Brent Terrace, off Tilling Road, London NW2 where there are facilities for recycling paper, glass, cans, textiles, batteries, oil, gas cylinders and refridgeration units. The council collects paper for recycling from households with road frontages on a fortnightly basis. Cans and tins are currently collected from a limited number of trial roads. In addition, the council organises Waste Minimisation Clubs, details of which can be acquired from the Recycling Officer (Tel: 020-8359 4669)

BEXLEY LBC

Works and Contracts Department, Crayford Town Hall, 112 Crayford Road, Crayford DA1 4ER (Tel: 020-8303 7777; Fax: 020-8319 9607; Web http://www.bexley.gov.uk)

There are 57 mini-recycling facilities in the borough of Bexley where materials such as cans, paper and cardboard, glass, metal, oil, textiles, batteries, hardcore, green waste, timber waste, books and shoes can be recycled. There are two municipal dumps/civic amenity sites:

Foots Cray Civic Amenity Site, Maidstone Road, Sidcup, Kent DA14 5HS

Thames Road Civic Amenity Site, Thames Road, Crayford, Kent DA1 5QJ

For further information about recycling and waste minimisation in the area, call the 'Green Line' on 020-8319 9619.

BRENT LBC

Brent has approximately 140 recycling sites throughout the borough where a range of materials can be recycled including newspapers, magazines, textiles, glass bottles and jars, food and drinks cans (steel and aluminium), shoes and books.

Full details of all the recycling sites are available on the Brent's web site at www.brent.gov.uk/recycling

Brent has a Civic Amenity Site which is located at First Way, Wembley, Middx, where the full range of materials above can be recycled. In addition engine oil and scrap metal are accepted. There are also facilities for degassing fridges containing CFCs. It is estimated that during 1999/2000, 6,200 tonnes of household waste will be recycled.

There is a 'Green Box Service' in operation which covers 48,000 households and by the end of March 2000 there were approximately 70,000 households covered. Each household receives a weekly collection of textiles, newspapers and magazines, shoes, food tins and cans, glass bottles and jars, engine oil (in a sealed can) and aluminium foil.

The Waste Management and Recycling section is part of StreetCare which in turn is part of Environmental Services (Tel: 020 8937 5050; Fax: 020 8937 5090; Email: street.services@brent.gov.uk)

BROMLEY LBC

Environmental Service Department, Civic Centre, Stockwell Close, Bromley BR1 3UH

There are two Civic Amenity Sites in the borough, Waldo Road in Bromley and Churchfields Road in Beckenham. Household and garden waste can be deposited there free of charge, however, to dispose of soil, brick, rubble and construction waste, charges will be applied. At each Civic Amenity Site there are a number of recycling facilities where paper, card, bottles, cans, books, car batteries, wellington boots, fridge freezers, metals and textiles can be recycled. In addition, there are also 50 mini-recycling sites for the recycling of glass, paper, cans and textiles.

CAMDEN LBC

Regis Road Recycling Centre, Regis Road, Kentish Town, London NW5 3EW (Tel: 020-7485 1553; Fax: 020-7267 0763)

Camden LBC provides almost 100 mini-recycling sites throughout the borough where residents can recycle glass and paper, and in most sites, cans, textiles and books. There is a fortnightly door-to-door paper and multi-material collection and on special request we collect garden waste, fridge-freezers and cookers. All services are free of charge.

CORPORATION OF LONDON

Whalbrook Wharf, Upper Thames Street, London EC4R 3TD (Tel: 020-7236 9541; Fax: 020-7236 6560)

The City's residential population is very small and thus, waste recycling schemes are largely deemed to be non cost-effective. Further, security considerations prevent the siting of bottle banks and similar containers in public spaces. However, the City attracts private sector waste recyclers whenever waste materials can be collected for recycling at a profit. Cleansing Services aim to provide waste recycling services if there is strong local need and the necessary service is not available through private sector service providers.

Due to the City being a large commercial centre, glass and good quality waste paper are the two commodities most commonly recycled. The financial and business sector of the City has an immense concentration of IT equipment which is continuously updated and the Corporation promotes better policies for the recycling or environmentally responsible disposal of such goods through its active membership of the Industry Council of Electronic Equipment Recycling (ICER) Ltd. Cleansing Services are able to provide trade waste customers with a free waste analysis to determine the composition of the waste they wish to recycle.

CROYDON LBC

Environmental and Recycling Unit, Public Services and Works, Taberner House, Park Lane, Croydon CR9 3RN (Tel: 020-8760 5524; Fax: 020-8407 1306)

Croydon has approximately 38 recycling banks where paper, glass, textiles, cans, books can be recycled and there are three main recycling centres where additional materials can be recycled such as cardboard, metal, car batteries, engine oil, wood and garden waste:

Factory Lane Amenity and Recycling Centre, Factory Lane, West Croydon (Tel: 020-8828 8700); Purley Oaks Civic Amenity and Recycling Centre, Brighton Road, South Croydon (Tel: 020-8668 2086); Fishers Farm Civic Amenity and Recycling Centre, North Downs Crescent, New Addington (Tel: 01689 848092)

EALING LBC

Environmental Services, Perceval House, 14-16 Uxbridge Road, London W5 2HL (Tel: 020-8758 5957; Fax: 020-8840 5575)

The following commodities can be recycled in the borough: glass, cans, paper, clothes and shoes, textiles, scrap metal, VFVs, engine oil, garden waste, paint, car batteries and cardboard. Household refuse which cannot be collected as part of the normal household refuse collection service can be disposed of at the borough recycling centres, free of charge.

Acton Waste and Recycling Centre, Stirling Road, London W3 (Tel: 020-8832 3402)
Greenford Waste and Recycling Centre, Greenford Depot, Greenford Road (Tel: 020-8832 3402)
Southall Waste and Recycling Centre, Gordon Road, Southall (Tel: 020-8832 3402)

ENFIELD LBC

Waste Reduction Officer, Montagu Road Depot, Edmonton, London N9 0ET (Tel: 020-8379 1789; Fax: 020-8379 1769)

There are numerous recycling facilities throughout the borough recycling such materials as glass bottles and jars, drinks cans, newspapers and magazines and clothes.

For information about composting activity in the borough contact the Waste Reduction Officer (Tel: 020 8379 1788)

GREENWICH LBC

Waste Services, Directorate of Public Services, Birchmere Business Site, Eastern Way, London SE28 8BF (Tel: 020-8921 4663)

In the borough of Greenwich there are 82 recycling banks for the recycling of textiles, cans, paper, glass and other materials.

Civic amenity facilities can be found at: Nathan Way Civic Amenity Site, Nathan Way, Thamesmead, London SE28 0AN (Tel: 020-8311 5229). Papers, glass, textiles, oil, scrap metal, green wastes, domestic appliances, cardboard and car batteries can be recycled here.

HACKNEY LBC

Waste Management and Technical Unit, The Portacabin, c/o Maurice Bishop House, Reading Lane, London E8 1HH (Tel: 020-8356 3617; Fax 020-8356 3507)

The borough of Hackney currently has a pilot kerbside-recycling scheme in operation, providing a service to approximately 13,000 residents, with plans to introduce the service to all residents in the future. There are approximately 59 bring-sites/mini-recycling centres located around the borough at which residents can recycle glass, paper, magazines, cans and textiles. The borough also provides a bulk waste removal service, which provides collection of up to five items free of charge to all residents.

HAMMERSMITH AND FULHAM LBC

Town Hall, King Street, London W6 9JU (Tel: 020-8748 3020)

The borough of Hammersmith and Fulham runs two types of service; kerbside collections and public recycling banks. There is a free weekend amenity skip service available and there are special recycling services for disabled residents of the borough. Bulky items such as fridge freezers can be collected for recycling.

A Civic Amenity Site is based at: Smugglers Way, Wandsworth, London SW18 (Tel: 020-8871 2788)

HARINGEY LBC

The Civic Amenity Centre, Park View Road, London N17; Recycling Centre, Western Road, Wood Green, London N22 9JJ (Tel: 020-8801 5556 (Customer Care Team))

The borough has 2 major recycling centres and 27 recycling banks. All of the banks collect glass, paper and cans.

HARROW LBC

Harrow Council Information Office, Station Road, Harrow HA1 2XF (Tel: 020-8424 1778)

For information on recycling facilities in the borough contact: Forward Drive, Wealdstone HA3 8NT (Tel: 020-8424 1778)

HILLINGDON LBC

Civic Centre, High Street, Uxbridge UB8 1UW (Tel: 01895 250111; Fax: 01895 273636)

There are nearly 100 recycling sites in the borough and there is also a kerbside recycling initiative which involves the fortnightly collection of recyclables from 16,000 households. Recyclable materials include glass, cans, paper, textiles and metal.

HOUNSLOW LBC

Environmental Services, Civic Centre, Lampton Road, Hounslow TW3 4DN (Tel: 020-8583 5060)

In the borough of Houslow there are 50 mini-recycling sites where items such as paper, glass, cans, textiles, oil and cardboard may be recycled. In addition, approximately 71,450 households are covered by a kerbside recycling service via which the following items can be recycled: glass, newspapers and magazines, tin foil, engine oil, tins and cans, textiles, shoes, flattened cardboard boxes.

Space Waye Civic Amenity Site is based at: Pier Road, North Feltham Trading Estate, Feltham, Middlesex TW14 0TH (Tel: 020 8890 0917). Glass, shoes, books, scrap metal, cardboard, tins/cans, timber, engine oil, car batteries, paper and clothing can be recycled at this site. Green waste is also collected, removed for composting and resold to the public on site.

ISLINGTON LBC

Environment and Leisure Services, Albany Place, Benwell Road, London N7 7DH (Tel: 020 7527 4667; Fax: 020 7527 0261)

The borough provides a number of bottle banks and banks for paper and textiles. These containers are serviced by private contractors on a regular basis. There is a Recycling Centre based at Queensland Place, London N7 7DH (Tel: 020-7527 4679; Fax: 020-7527 0261). The centre accepts metal, glass, motor oil and old clothing for recycling.

For any queries relating to waste and recycling in Islington call Wasteline on 0870 234 0136.

KENSINGTON AND CHELSEA LBC

Environmental Services, Council Offices, Pembroke Road, London W8 6PW (Tel: 020-7937 5464; Fax: 020-7341 5200; Email: ehejkg@rbkc.gov.uk)

There are 24 mini-recycling centres throughout the borough and there are doorstep collections for cans and tins, newspapers and magazines, cardboard, junk mail and telephone directories, rags, plastic bottles and juice and milk cartons.

There are civic amenity skips for the disposal of bulky household waste and green waste sited at Cremorne Wharf, 27 Lots Road, London SW10 (Tel: 020-7376 4527); Western Riverside Waste Authority, Smugglers Way, Wandsworth, London SW18 1JS (Tel: 020-8871 2788);

Waste and Recycling 333

Cringle Dock, Cringle Street, Battersea, London SW8 5BA. A Materials Recycling Facility is located at the Cremorne Wharf site where the following items can be recycled: green garden waste, scrap metal, furniture, fridges, oil and household electricals.

KINGSTON UPON THAMES LBC

Guildhall, High Street, Kingston upon Thames, KT1 1EU

For any queries on waste and recycling within the borough, contact the Recycling Officer (Tel: 020-8547 5567)

LAMBETH LBC

1-9 Acre Lane, London SW2 5SD (Tel: 020-7926 2640; Fax: 020-7926 2486)

Recycling services are offered to 67,000 households in the borough by Lambeth Community Recycling Ltd. There is a network of 43 sites on streets and at major public facilities such as supermarkets.

MERTON LBC

Waste Service Review, 13th Floor, London Road, Morden, Surrey SM4 5DX (Tel: 020-8543 2222; Fax: 020-8545 3942)

There are 37 recycling sites in the borough of Merton where materials such as glass, paper, textiles, cans and oil can be recycled. For general information telephone the Environmental Control Line on 020-8545 4157. There is a civic amenity site at Amenity Way, Garth Road, Lower Morden, Surrey SM4 4NJ which is the main facility for tipping large items of waste and recyclables.

NEWHAM LBC

Public Works, Central Depot, Folkestone Road, London E6 6BX (Tel: 020-8430 2000; Fax: 020-8557 8989)

There are 100 recycling sites where people can take a range of materials to be recycled. Items such as bottles, cans, textiles, paper, batteries, shoes, oils and metals. There is a civic amenity site at Jenkins Lane, E6, where refuse from household and commercial collections is put in containers for transport to landfill or incineration sites. Recyclable materials are taken for sorting and bundling prior to transport and recycling plants.

REDBRIDGE LBC

Town Hall, PO Box 2, Ilford IG1 1DD (Tel: 020-8478 3020)

In Redbridge over 92,000 domestic properties receive a weekly refuse collection and approximately 2000 businesses use the Council's Commercial Waste Service. Bulky household waste collections are made and there is also a skip service. There are over 70 recycling sites in the borough and kerbside collections are available to 50 per cent of the borough's residents. Recycling targets include: to reduce the total amount of waste produced; to increase the percentage of residents with access to recycling facilities; to establish home composting in 40 per cent of all properties with gardens; to involve 100 per cent of schools in recycling and anti-litter activities and to respond to 100 per cent of community groups who want to get involved in recycling initiatives.

Ilford Recycling Centre is based at 409 High Road, Ilford (Tel: 020-8478 3020 Extn. 2600)

SUTTON LBC

Environment and Leisure, 24 Denmark Road, Carshalton SM5 2JG (Tel: 020-8770 6400; Fax: 020-8770 6410)

There are 67 recycling sites within the borough of Sutton where the following materials can be recycled: glass, cardboard, aluminium, textiles, shoes, batteries, books, cans, plastic, foil, oil, cooking oil and wood.

TOWER HAMLETS LBC

Waste Disposal and Recycling, Council Offices, Southern Grove, London E3 4PN (Tel: 020-7364 6689; Fax: 020-7364 6922)

Within Tower Hamlets there is a network of over 50 bring-sites where clear/green/brown glass, newspapers, magazines, junk mail, textiles, cardboard and cans can be recycled. A kerbside recycling service is offered to 10,800 houses collecting glass, cans, textiles, paper and cardboard.

The main Civic amenity site is located at: Northumberland Wharf, Yabsley Street, London E14 9RG. At this site glass, newspapers, magazines, junk mail, food and drink containers, textiles, cardboard, waste engine oils and car batteries can be recycled.

For information on recycling and waste matters within Tower Hamlets, contact Streetline (Tel: 020 8364 3364)

WALTHAM FOREST LBC

Recycling Centre, Kings Road, Chingford, London E4 7LH (Tel: 0181 527 4040)
South Access Road Household Waste Centre, Walthamstow, London E17.

The borough of Waltham Forest has a variety of recycling schemes including: a large recycling centre in Chingford; a green garden waste composting scheme; a network of mini-recycling centres; support for community based projects such as 'Community Re-paint Waltham Forest', the 'Foiled Again' aluminium foil collection scheme, the 'Tools for Self Reliance' scheme and the 'Renov8' furniture re-use project and a 'Sorted' multi-material recycling collection service involving 22,000 homes in the borough.

Recyclable materials at the Kings Road Recycling Centre include: cans, glass, textiles, paper, cardboard, garden waste, scrap metal, paint, wood, tools, aluminium foil, engine oil and car batteries.

At the South Access Road Household Waste Centre the above materials can be recycled plus furniture, beds,

334 Environmental London

concrete, bricks, ceramic tiles, plaster, rubble and other material used in the construction of a building.

WANDSWORTH LBC

Leisure and Amenity Services Department, The Town Hall, Wandsworth High Street, London SW18 2PU (Tel: 020-8871 6000; Fax: 020-8871 6383)

Special collection services are offered and items such as unwanted fridges and freezers are collected free of charge. Other bulky items are collected at a small charge and this can be arranged through the Amenity Services Department. Civic Amenity Sites can be found at:

Smugglers Way, Wandsworth, London SW18 (Tel: 020-8871 2788)
Cringle Street, London SW8 (Te: 020-7622 6233)

At these sites there are facilities for recycling garden waste, wood, scrap metal, fridges and freezers, car batteries, oil, paper and card, glass, textiles, cans and books.

Each week there is also a collection of glass, paper and cans for recycling from properties where ordinary rubbish is collected in sacks or dustbins.

There are 39 recycling sites in the borough where glass, paper, cans, textiles and books can be recycled.

WESTMINSTER CITY LBC

Environmental Services, Contracts Group, Westminster City Hall, 64 Victoria Street, London SW1E 6QP (Tel: 020-7641 7956; Fax: 020-7641 7964)

In the borough of Westminster there are 65 mini-recycling centres where paper, glass, cans and textiles can be recycled. To increase the convenience of recycling the borough is currently in the process of expanding its door-to-door recycling services which collects paper, cardboard, glass bottles and drinks cans on a weekly basis. There is also a comprehensive range of waste minimisation and recycling services for schools and businesses in the area.

LONDON AND
THE WORLD

TOURIST BOARDS
EMBASSIES
INTERNATIONAL ORGANISATIONS
EUROPEAN UNION
TIME ZONES
AIR DISTANCES FROM LONDON TO WORLD
  CAPITAL CITIES
INTERNATIONAL DIRECT DIALLING CODES

LONDON AND THE WORLD

London is well established as a 'world class' city. It cannot be summed up in any one context as its diversity is so great. It is a business centre, a tourist centre, a cultural centre, a historical centre, a religious centre, an environmental centre, but is also an International centre.

None of these facets takes precedence over the others and it is this which gives London its diversity and quality as a world capital city.

Many international organisations base themselves in London or choose to locate premises in London. There are also people of many nationalities who live, work or travel in London. This section offers information of the institutions and bodies which have an international focus and are based in the London area. It also provides full listings of international time zones and international dialling codes.

TOURIST BOARDS

The list below details the London offices of foreign tourist boards.

Anguilla Tourist Office
3 Epirus Road, London, SW6 (Tel: 020-7937 7725)

Antigua and Barbuda Tourist Office
15 Thayer Street, London, W1M 5LD (Tel: 020-7486 7073; Fax: 020-7486 1466; Email: antbar@msn.com; Web: http://www.antigua-barbuda.com)

Austrian National Tourist Office
PO Box 2363, London, W1A 2QB (Tel: 020-7629 0461; Fax: 020-7499 6038; Email: info@anto.co.uk; Web: http://www.austria-tourism.at/)

Barbados Tourism Authority
263 Tottenham Court Road, London, W1P (Tel: 020-7636 9448)

British Virgin Islands Tourist Board
54 Baker Street, London, W1M 1DJ (Tel: 020-7240 4259; Fax: 020-7240 4270; Email: bvi@bho.fcb.com; Web: http://www.bviwelcome.com)

Caribbean Tourism Organisation
42 Westminster Palace Gardens, Artillery Row, London, SW1P (Tel: 020-7222 4335; Fax: 020-7222 4325; Email: cto@carib-tourism.com; Web: http://www.caribtourism.com)

Catalan Tourist Board
17 Fleet Street, London, EC4Y (Tel: 020-7583 8855; Fax: 020-7583 8877; Email: catalonia@catalantouristboard.co.uk; Web: http://www.gencat.es/turisme)

Cayman Islands Department of Tourism
6 Arlington Street, London, SW1A (Tel: 020-7491 7771)

Cuba Tourist Board
154 Shaftesbury Avenue, London, WC2H 8JT (Tel: 020-7240 6655; Fax: 020-7836 9265; Email: cubatouristboard.london@virgin.net)

Cyprus Government Tourist Office
17 Hanover Street, London, W1R 0AA (Tel: 020-7569 8800; Fax: 020-7499 4935; Email: ctolon@ctolon.demon.co.uk)

Danish Tourist Board
55 Sloane Street, London, SW1X 9SY (Tel: 020-7259 5958; Fax: 020-7259 5955; Email: dtb.london@dt.dk; Web: http://www.visitdenmark.com)

Dominica Tourist Office
1 Collingham Gardens, London, SW5 (Tel: 020-7835 1937)

Dubai Commerce & Tourism Promotion
125 Pall Mall, London, SW1Y (Tel: 020-7839 0580)

Egyptian State Tourism Office
Egyptian House, 170 Piccadilly, London, W1V (Tel: 020-7493 5283; Fax: 020-7408 0295; Email: egypt@freenetname.co.uk; Web: http://www.interoz.com/egypt)

Finnish Tourist Board
30-35 Pall Mall, London, SW1Y 5LP (Tel: 020-7839 4048; Fax: 020-7321 0696; Email: mek.lon@mek.fi; Web: http://www.finland-tourism.com)

French Tourist Office
178 Piccadilly, London, W1V 0AL (Tel: 09068 244123; Fax: 020-7493 6594; Email: info@mdlf.co.uk; Web: http://www.franceguide.com)

Gambia National Tourist Office
57 Kensington Court, London, W8 5DG, (Tel: 020-7376 0093; Fax: 020-7938 3644; Email: info@thegambia-touristoff.co.uk; Web: http://www.itsnet.co.uk)

German National Tourist Office
PO Box 2695, London, W1A 3TN (Tel: 09001-600 100; Fax: 020-7495 6129; Email: gntolon@d-z-t.com; Web: http://www.germany-tourism.de)

Government of Gibraltar
179 The Strand, London, WC2R (Tel: 020-7836 0777; Fax: 020-7420 6612; Email: giblondon@aol.com; Web: http://www.gilbraltar.gi)

Greece: Hellenic Tourism Organisation
4 Conduit Street, London, W1R (Tel: 020-7734 5997; Fax: 020-7287 1369; Email: got-greektouristoffice@btinternet.com; Web: http://www.gnto.gr)

Grenada National Tourist Office
1 Collingham Gardens, London, SW5 (Tel: 020-7370 5164)

Hong Kong Tourist Association
6 Grafton Street, London, W1X (Tel: 020-7533 7100)

338 London and the World

Hungarian National Tourist Office
46 Eaton Place, London, SW1X 8AL (Tel: 020-7823 1032; Fax: 020-7823 1459;
Web: http://www.tourist-offices.org.uk)

Iceland Tourist Information Bureau
172 Tottenham Court Road, London, W1P (Tel: 020-8286 8008; Fax: 020-7387 5711;
Email: london@icelandair.is;
Web: http://www.goiceland.org)

India Tourist Office
7 Cork Street, London, W1X 2LN (Tel: 020-7437 3677; Fax: 020-7494 1048)

Irish Tourist Board
150 New Bond Street, London, W1Y 0AQ (Tel: 020-7493 3201/7518 0800; Fax: 020-7493 9065;
Email: info@irishtouristboard.co.uk;
Web: http://www.ireland.travel.uk)

Israel Government Tourist Office
UK House, 180 Oxford Street, London, W1N 9DJ (Tel: 020-7299 1111; Fax: 020-7299 1112;
Email: information@igto.co.uk;
Web: http://www.infotour.co.il)

Italian State Tourist Office
1 Princes Street, London, W1R (Tel: 020-7408 1254)

Jamaica Tourist Board
1-2 Prince Consort Road, London, SW7 2BZ (Tel: 020-7224 0505; Fax: 020-7224 0551)

Japan National Tourist Organisation
Heathcoat House, 20 Savile Row, London, W1X (Tel: 020-7734 9638; Fax: 020-7734 4290;
Email: jntolon@dircon.co.uk)

Jersey Tourism & Information Office
7 Lower Grosvenor Place, London, SW1W 0EN (Tel: 020-7630 8787; Fax: 020-7630 0747;
Email: london@jtourism.com;
Web: http://www.jtourism.com)

Kenya Tourist Office
25 Brook's Mews, London, W1Y (Tel: 020-7355 3144; Fax: 020-7495 8656;
Web: http://www.kenya.tourism.org)

Korea National Tourist Organisation
8th Floor, New Zealand House, Haymarket, London, SW1Y 4TE (Tel: 020-7321 2535; Fax: 020-7321 0876;
Email: koreatb@dircon.co.uk;
Web: http://www.knto.org.ky)

Lebanon Tourist & Information Office
90 Piccadilly, London, W1V (Tel: 020-7409 2031)

Luxembourg Tourist Office
122 Regent Street, London, W1R (Tel: 020-7434 2800; Fax: 020-7734 1205;
Email: tourism@luxembourg.co.uk;
Web: http://www.luxembourg.co.uk)

Malaysian Tourism Promotion Board
Malaysian House, 57 Trafalgar Square, London, WC2N 5DU (Tel: 020-7930 7932; Fax: 020-7930 9015;
Email: mtpb.london@tourism.gov.my;
Web: http://www.tourism.gov.my)

Malta Tourist Office
Malta House, 36-38 Piccadilly, London, W1V 0PP (Tel: 020-7292 4900; Fax: 020-7734 1880;
Email: maltauk@aol.com;
Web: http://www.visitmalta.com)

Mauritius Tourism Promotion Authority
32 Elvaston Place, London, SW7 (Tel: 020-7584 3666)

Mexican Ministry of Tourism
Wakefield House, 41 Trinity Square, London, EC3N 4DJ (Tel: 020-7488 9392; Fax: 020-7265 0704;
Email: info@mexicotravel.co.uk;
Web: http://www.mexicotravel.co.uk)

Monaco Government Tourist & Convention Office
The Chambers Chelsea Harbour, London, SW10 0XF (Tel: 020-7352 9962; Fax: 020-7352 2103;
Email: monaco@monaco.co.uk;
Web: http://www.monaco-congres.com)

Moroccan National Tourist Office
205 Regent Street, London, W1R 7DE (Tel: 020-7437 0073; Fax: 020-7734 8172;
Email: mnto@btconnect.com;
Web: http://www.tourism-in-morocco.com)

Namibia Tourism
6 Chandos Street, London, W1M (Tel: 020-7636 2924)

Tourism New Zealand
New Zealand House, Haymarket, London SW1Y 4TQ (Tel: 020-7930 1662; Fax: 020-7839 8929;
Web: http://www.purenz.com)

North Cyprus Tourism Centre
29 Bedford Square, London, WC1B 8EG (Tel: 020-7631 1930; Fax: 020-7631 1873)

Northern Ireland Tourist Board
24 Haymarket, London, SW1Y (Tel: 08701-555 250; Fax: 020-7766 9929; Web: http://www.ni-tourism.com)

Norwegian Tourist Board
Charles House, 5-11 Lower Regent Street, London, SW1Y (Tel: 020-7839 6255; Fax: 020-7839 6014;
Email: infouk@ntr.no;
Web: http://www.visitnorway.com)

Philippine Cultural and Tourism Office
146 Cromwell Road, London, SW7 4EF (Tel: 020-7835 1100; Fax: 020-7835 1926; Email: tourism@pdot.co.uk;
Web: http://www.tourism.gov.ph)

Polish National Tourist Office
Remo House, 310-312 Regent Street, London, W1R (Tel: 020-7580 8811; Fax: 020-7580 8866;
Email: pnto@dial.pipex.com;
Web: http://www.pnto.dial.pipex.com)

Tourist Boards 339

Portuguese National Tourist Office
22-25A Sackville Street, London, W1X 2LY (Tel: 020-7494 1441; Fax: 020-7494 1868;
Email: iceplondt@aol.com;
Web: http://www.portugalinsite.pt)

Romanian National Tourist Office
22 New Cavendish Street, London, W1M 7LH (Tel: 020-7224 3692; Fax: 020-7935 6435;
Email: uktouroff@romania.freeserve.co.uk)

Russian Federation, Sport & Tourism
Orchard House, 167-169 Kensington High Street, London, W8 6SH (Tel: 020-7937 7217; Fax: 020-7938 2912; Email: rusoffice@imtcltd.force9.co.uk;
Web: http://www.russia-travel.com)

St Kitts & Nevis Tourism Office
10 Kensington Court, London, W8 (Tel: 020-7376 0881)

St Vincent & The Grenadines Tourist Office
10 Kensington Court, London, W8 5DL (Tel: 020-7937 6570; Fax: 020-7937 3611;
Email: svgtourismeurope@aol.com;
Web: http://www.svgtourism.com)

Scottish Tourist Board
19 Cockspur Street, London, SW1Y (Tel: 020-7930 8661)

Seychelles Tourist Office
2nd Floor, Eros House, 111 Baker Street, London, W1M 1FE (Tel: 020-7224 1670; Fax: 020-7486 1352;
Email: sto@seychelles.uk.com;
Web: http://www.seychelles.uk.com)

Singapore Tourist Board
Carrington House, 126-130 Regent Street, London, W1R (Tel: 020-7437 0033)

Slovenia Tourist Board
49 Conduit Street, London, W1R 9FB (Tel: 020-7287 7133; Fax: 020-7287 5476;
Web: http://www.slovenia-tourism.si)

Spanish Tourist Office
22-23 Manchester Square, London, W1M 5AP (Tel: 020-7486 8077; Fax: 020-7486 8034;
Email: info.londres@tourspain.es;
Web: http://tourspain.co.uk)

Sri Lanka Tourist Board
The Sri Lanka Centre, 22 Regent Street, London, SW1Y (Tel: 020-7930 2627; Fax: 020-7930 9070;
Email: srilanka@carbernet.co.uk;
Web: http://www.lanka.net/ctb)

Swedish Travel & Tourism Council
11 Montagu Place, London, W1H 2AL (Tel: 020-7870 5600; Fax: 020-7724 5872;
Email: info@swetourism.org.uk;
Web: http://www.visit-sweden.com)

Switzerland Travel Centre
Swiss Court, London, W1V 8EE (Tel: 020-7734 1921)

Thailand Tourism Authority
49 Albermarle Street, London, W1X (Tel: 0870-900 2007; Fax: 020-7629 5519;
Email: info@tat-uk.demon.co.uk;
Web: http://www.tourismthailand.org)

Tunisian National Tourist Office
77A Wigmore Street, London, W1H (Tel: 020-7224 5561; Fax: 020-7224 4053; Email: tntolondon@aol.com;
Web: http://www.tourismtunisia.com)

Turkish Tourist Office
1st Floor, Egyptian House, 170-173 Piccadilly, London, W1V (Tel: 020-7629 7771)

Venezuela Tourist Office
56 Grafton Way, London, W1P 5LB (Tel: 020-7387 6727)

Zambia National Tourist Board
2 Palace Gate, Kensington, London, W8 (Tel: 020-7589 6343; Fax: 020-7225 3221; Email: zntb@aol.com;
Web: http://www.africa-insites.com/zambia)

Zimbabwe Tourist Information
429 The Strand, London, WC2R (Tel: 020-7240 6169)

340 London and the World

EMBASSIES

The list below details the London-based embassies of foreign countries.

Embassy of the Islamic State of Afghanistan
31 Princes Gate, London, SW7 1QQ (Tel: 020-7589 8891; Fax: 020-7581 3452;
Email: embassyofafghanistan@compuserve.com;
Web: http://www.afghan.gov.af)
Ambassador Extraordinary and Plenipotentiary: vacant

Embassy of the Republic of Albania
2nd Floor, 24 Buckingham Gate, London, SW1E 6LB (Tel: 020-7828 8897; Fax: 020-7828 8869)
Ambassador Extraordinary and Plenipotentiary: His Excellency Mr Agim Besim Fagu

Embassy of Algeria
54 Holland Park, London, W11 3RS (Tel: 020-7221 7800; Fax: 020-7221 0448)
Ambassador Extraordinary and Plenipotentiary: His Excellency Mr Ahmed Benyamina

American Embassy
24 Grosvenor Square, London, W1A 1AE (Tel: 020-7499 9000; Fax: 020-7493 3425)
Ambassador Extraordinary and Plenipotentiary: His Excellency Mr Philip Lader

Embassy of the Republic of Angola
98 Park Lane, London, W1Y 3TA (Tel: 020-7495 1752; Fax: 020-7495 1635)
Ambassador Extraordinary and Plenipotentiary: His Excellency Senhor Añtonio Da Costa Fernandes

High Commission for Antigua and Barbuda
15 Thayer Street, London, W1M 5LD (Tel: 020-7486 7073; Fax: 020-7486 9970;
Web: http://www.antigua-barbuda.com)
High Commissioner: His Excellency Mr Ronald M. Sanders CMG

Embassy of the Argentine Republic
65 Brook Street, London, W1Y 1YE (Tel: 020-7318 1300; Fax: 020-7318 1301)
Ambassador Extraordinary and Plenipotentiary: His Excellency Señor Vicent Berasategui

Embassy of the Republic of Armenia
25A Cheniston Gardens, London, W8 6TG (Tel: 020-7938 5435; Fax: 020-7938 2595;
Email: armembuk@dircon.co.uk)
Ambassador Extraordinary and Plenipotentiary: His Excellency Dr Armen Sarkkissian

Australian High Commision
Australia House, Strand, London, WC2B 4LA (Tel: 020-7379 4334; Fax: 020-7240 5333)
High Commissioner: His Excellency Mr Philip Flood

Austrian Embassy
18 Belgrave Mews West, London, SW1X 8HU (Tel: 020-7235 3731; Fax: 020-7344 0292;
Email: embassy@austria.org.uk;
Web: http://www.austria.org.uk)
Ambassador Extraordinary and Plenipotentiary: Dr Alexander Christiani

Embassy of the Azerbaijan Republic
4 Kensington Court, London, W8 5DL (Tel: 020-7938 5482/3412; Fax: 020-77937 1783; Email: sefir@btinternet.com)
Ambassador Extraordinary and Plenipotentiary: His Excellency Mr Mahmud Mamed-Kuliyev

High Commission for the Commonwealth of the Bahamas
10 Chesterfield Street, London, W1X 8AH (Tel: 020-7408 4488; Fax: 020-7499 9937)
High Commissioner: His Excellency Mr Basil G. O'Brien, CMG

Embassy of the State of Bahrain
98 Gloucester Road, London, SW7 4AU (Tel: 020-7370 5132/3; Fax: 020-7370 7773)
Ambassador Extraordinary and Plenipotentiary: His Excellency Shaikh Abdul Aziz Bin Murbarak Al Khalfia

High Commission for the People's Republic of Bangladesh
28 Queen's Gate, London, SW7 5JA (Tel: 020-7584 0081; Fax: 020-7225 2130)
High Commissioner: His Excellency Mr A. H. Mahmood Ali

Barbados High Commission
1 Great Russell Street, London, WC1B 3JY (Tel: 020-7631 4975; Fax: 020-7323 6872)
High Commissioner: His Excellency Mr Peter Patrick Simmons

Embassy of the Republic of Belarus
6 Kensington Court, London, W8 5DL (Tel: 020-7937/3288; Fax: 020-7361 0005;
Web: http://www.belemb.freeserve.co.uk)
Counsellor, Charge d'Affairs: Mr Valery Kurdyukov

Belgian Embassy
103 Eaton Square, London, SW1W 9AB (Tel: 020-7470 3700; Fax: 020-7259 6213;
Web: http://www.belgium-embassy.co.uk)
Ambassador Extraordinary and Plenipotentiary: His Excellency Mr Lode Willems

Belize High Commission
22 Harcourt House, 19 Cavendish Square, London, W1M 9AD (Tel: 020-7499 9728; Fax: 020-7491 4139)
High Commissioner: His Excellency Mr Assad Shoman

Embassy of Bolivia
106 Eaton Square, London, SW1W 9AD (Tel: 020-7235 4248/2257; Fax: 020-7235 1286)
Ambassador Extraordinary and Plenipotentiary: His Excellency Señor Jaime Quiroga Matos

Embassy of Bosnia and Herzegovina
4th Floor, Morley House, 320 Regent Street, London, W1R 5AB (Tel: 020-7255 3758; Fax: 020-7255 3760)
Ambassador Extraordinary and Plenipotentiary: His Excellency Mr Osman Topcagic

Botswana High Commission
6 Stratford Place, London, W1N 9AE (Tel: 020-7499 0031; Fax: 020-7495 8595)
High Commissioner: His Excellency Mr Roy Blackbeard

Embassies 341

Brazilian Embassy
32 Green Street, Mayfair, London, W1Y 4AT (Tel: 020-7499 0877; Fax: 020-7399 9100)
Ambassador Extraordinary and Plenipotentiary: His Excellency Senhor Sergio Silva Do Amaral, KBE

Brunei Darussalam High Commission
19-20 Belgrave Square, London, SW1X 9PG (Tel: 020-7581 0521; Fax: 020-7235 9717)
High Commissioner: His Excellency Dato Haji Yusof Hamid

Embassy of the Republic of Bulgaria
186-188 Queen's Gate, London, SW7 5HL (Tel: 020-7584 9400/9433; Fax: 020-7584 4948)
Ambassador Extraordinary and Plenipotentiary: His Excellency Mr Valentin Dobrev

Embassy of the Republic of Burundi
26 Armitage Road, London, NW11 8RD (Tel: 020-8381 4092; Fax: 020-8458 8596)
Ambassador Extraordinary and Plenipotentiary: His Excellency Monsieur Jonathas Niyungeko

High Commission for the Republic of Cameroon
84 Holland Park, London, W11 3SB (Tel: 020-7727 0771; Fax: 020-7792 9353)
High Commissioner: His Excellency Mr Samuel Libock Mbel

Canadian High Commission
Macdonald House, 1 Grosvenor Square, London, W1X 0AB (Tel: 020-7258 6600; Fax: 020-7258 6333; Web: http://www.dfait-maeci.gc.ca/london)
High Commissioner: His Excellency The Hon. Roy MacLaren, PC

Embassy of Chile
12 Devonshire Street, London, W1N 2DS (Tel: 020-7580 6392; Fax: 020-7436 5204; Web: http://www.echileuk.demon.co.uk)
Ambassador Extraordinary and Plenipotentiary: His Excellency Señor Pablo Cabrera

Embassy of the People's Republic of China
49-51 Portland Place, London, W1N 4JL (Tel: 020-7636 5197; Fax: 020-7637 0399; Web: http://www.chinese-embassy.org.uk)
Ambassador Extraordinary and Plenipotentiary: His Excellency Mr Ma Zhengang

Colombian Embassy
Flat 3A, 3 Hans Crescent, London, SW1X 0LN (Tel: 020-7589 9177/5037; Fax: 020-7581 1829; Web: http://www.colombia.demon.co.uk)
Ambassador Extraordinary and Plenipotentiary: His Excellency Mr Humberto De La Calle-Lombana

Embassy of the Democratic Republic of the Congo
38 Holne Chase, London, N2 0QQ (Tel: 020-8458 0254)
Ambassador Extraordinary and Plenipotentiary: Henri Nswana

Costa Rican Embassy
Flat 1, 14 Lancaster Gate, London, W2 3LH (Tel: 020-7706 8844; Fax: 020-7706 8655; Web: http://www.emberlon.demon.co.uk)
Ambassador Extraordinary and Plenipotentiary: His Excellency Señor Rodolfo Gutiérrez

Embassy of the Republic of Côte d'Ivoire
2 Upper Belgrave Street, London, SW1X 8BJ (Tel: 020-7235 6991; Fax: 020-7259 5320)
Ambassador Extraordinary and Plenipotentiary: His Excellency Mr Kouadio Adjoumani

Embassy of the Republic of Croatia
21 Conway Street, London, W1P 5HL (Tel: 020-7387 2022; Fax: 020-7387 0310)
Ambassador Extraordinary and Plenipotentiary: His Excellency Mr Andrija Kojakovic

Embassy of the Republic of Cuba
167 High Holborn, London, WC1V 6PA (Tel: 020-7240 2488; Fax: 020-7836 2602)
Ambassador Extraordinary and Plenipotentiary: His Excellency Señor Rodney Alejandro Lopez Clemente

Cyprus High Commission
93 Park Street, London, W1Y 4ET (Tel: 020-4799 8272; Fax: 020-4791 0691)
High Commissioner: His Excellency Mr Michalis Attalides

Embassy of the Czech Republic
26 Kensington Palace Gardens, London, W8 4QY (Tel: 020-7243 1115; Fax: 020-7727 9654)
Ambassador Extraordinary and Plenipotentiary: His Excellency Mr Pavel Siefter

Royal Danish Embassy
55 Sloane Street, London, SW1X 9SR (Tel: 020-7333 0200; Fax: 020-7333 0270)
Ambassador Extraordinary and Plenipotentiary: His Excellency Mr Ole Lønsmann Poulsen

Office of the High Commissioner for the Commonwealth of Dominica
1 Collingham Gardens, South Kensington, London, SW5 0HW (Tel: 020-7370 5194/5; Fax: 020-7373 8743; Web: http://www.dominica.com)
High Commissioner: His Excellency Mr George E. Williams

Embassy of the Dominican Republic
139 Inverness Terrace, Bayswater, London, W2 6JF (Tel: 020-7727 6285; Consular: 020-7727 6214; Fax: 020-7727 3693)
Ambassador Extraordinary and Plenipotentiary: His Excellency Dr Pedro L Padilla Tonos

Embassy of Ecuador
Flat 3B, 3 Hans Crescent, Knightsbridge, London, SW1X 0LS (Tel: 020-7584 2648/1367/8084; Fax: 020-7823 9701)
Ambassador Extraordinary and Plenipotentiary: His Excellency Señor Oswaldo Ramírez-Landázuri

Embassy of the Arab Republic of Egypt
26 South Street, London, W1Y 6DD (Tel: 020-7499 3304; Fax: 020-7491 1542)
Ambassador Extraordinary and Plenipotentiary: His Excellency Mr Adel El-Gazzar

342 London and the World

Embassy of El Salvador
Tennyson House, 159 Great Portland Street, London, W1N 5FD (Tel: 020-7436 8282; Fax: 020-7436 8181)
Ambassador Extraordinary and Plenipotentiary: His Excellency Mr Mauricio Castro-Aragon

Embassy of the Republic of Estonia
16 Hyde Park Gate, London, SW7 5DG (Tel: 020-7589 7690; Fax: 020-7589 3430;
Web: http://www.estonia.gov.uk)
Ambassador Extraordinary and Plenipotentiary: His Excellency Mr Raul Mälk

High Commission of the Republic of Fiji
34 Hyde Park Gate, London, SW7 5DN (Tel: 020-7584 3661; Fax: 020-7584 2838)
High Commissioner: His Excellency Mr Filimone Jitoko

Embassy of Finland
38 Chesham Place, London, SW1X 8HW (Tel: 020-7838 6200; Fax: 020-7235 3680;
Web: http://www.finemb.org.uk)
Ambassador Extraordinary and Plenipotentiary: His Excellency Mr Pertti Salolainen

French Embassy
58 Knightsbridge, London, SW1X 7JT (Tel: 020-7201 1000; Fax: 020-7201 1004;
Web: http://www.embafrance.org.uk)
Ambassador Extraordinary and Plenipotentiary: His Excellency Monsieur Daniel Bernard, CMG, CBE

Embassy of the Republic of Gabon
27 Elvaston Place, London, SW7 5NL (Tel: 020-7823 9986; Fax: 020-7584 0047)
Ambassador Extraordinary and Plenipotentiary: Her Excellency Madame Honorne Dossou-Naki

Gambia High Commission
57 Kensington Court, Kensington, London, W8 5DG (Tel: 020-7937 6316/7/8; Fax: 020-7937 9095)
Acting High Commissioner: His Excellency Mr Bala Garba-Jahumpa

Embassy of Georgia
3 Hornton Place, London, W8 4LZ (Tel: 020-7937 8233; Fax: 020-7938 4108)
Ambassador Extraordinary and Plenipotentiary: His Excellency Mr Teimuraz Mamatsashvili

Embassy of the Federal Republic of Germany
23 Belgrave Square, Chesham Place, London, SW1X 8PZ (Tel: 020-7824 1300; Fax: 020-7824 1435;
Web: http://www.german-embassy.org.uk)
Ambassador Extraordinary and Plenipotentiary: His Excellency Dr Hans-Friedrich von Ploetz

High Commission for Ghana
Main Chancery, 13 Belgrave Square, London, SW1X 8PN (Tel: 020-7235 4142; Fax: 020-7245 9552)
High Commissioner: His Excellency Mr James E. K. Aggrey-Orleans

Embassy of Greece
1A Holland Park, London, W11 3TP (Tel: 020-7229 3850; Fax: 020-7229 7221)
Ambassador Extraordinary and Plenipotentiary: vacant

High Commission for Grenada
1 Collingham Gardens, Earl's Court, London, SW5 0HW (Tel: 020-7373 7809; Fax: 020-7370 7040)
High Commissioner: Her Excellency Ms Ruth Elizabeth Rouse

Embassy of Guatemala
13 Fawcett Street, London, SW10 9HN (Tel: 020-7351 3042; Fax: 020-7376 5708;
Web: http://www.guatemala.travel.com.gt)
Ambassador Extraordinary and Plenipotentiary: His Excellency Señor Fernando Andrade Diaz-Duran

High Commission for Guyana
3 Palace Court, Bayswater Road, London, W2 4LP (Tel: 020-7229 7684/8; Fax: 020-7727 9809)
High Commissioner: His Excellency Mr Laleshwar K. N. Singh, CCH

Embassy of Honduras
115 Gloucester Place, London, W1H 3PJ (Tel: 020-7486 4880; Fax: 020-7486 4550)
Ambassador Extraordinary and Plenipotentiary: His Excellency Señor Hernan Antonio Bermudez-Aguilar

Embassy of the Republic of Hungary
35 Eaton Place, London, SW1X 8BY (Tel: 020-7235 5218; Fax: 020-7823 1348;
Web: http://www.huemblon.org.uk)
Ambassador Extraordinary and Plenipotentiary: His Excellency Mr Gábor Szentiványi, GCVO

Embassy of Iceland
1 Eaton Terrace, London, SW1W 8EY (Tel: 020-7590 1100; Fax: 020-7730 1683;
Web: http://www.iceland.org.uk)
Ambassador Extraordinary and Plenipotentiary: His Excellency Mr Thorsteinn Pálsson

High Commission for India
India House, Aldwych, London, WC2B 4NA (Tel: 020-7836 8484; Fax: 020-7836 4331;
Web: http://www.hcilondon.org)
High Commissioner: Mr Nareshwar Dayal

Embassy of the Republic of Indonesia
38 Grosvenor Square, London, W1X 9AD (Tel: 020-7499 7661; Fax: 020-7491 4993)
Ambassador Extraordinary and Plenipotentiary: His Excellency Mr Nana S. Sutresna

Embassy of the Islamic Republic of Iran
16 Prince's Gate, London, SW7 1PT (Tel: 020-7225 3000; Fax: 020-7589 4440;
Web: http://www.iran-embassy.org.uk)
Ambassador Extraordinary and Plenipotentiary: His Excellency Mr Gholamreza Ansari

Iraqi Interests Section
21 Queen's Gate, London, SW7 5JG (Tel: 020-7584 7141; Fax: 020-7584 7716)
Minister/Head of Interests Section: Dr Mudhafar Amin

Embassy of Ireland
17 Grosvenor Place, London, SW1X 7HR (Tel: 020-7235 2171; Fax: 020-7245 6961)
Ambassador Extraordinary and Plenipotentiary: His Excellency Mr Edward Barrington

Embassies 343

Embassy of Israel
2 Palace Green, Kensington, London, W8 4QB (Tel: 020-7957 9500; Fax: 020-7957 9555)
Ambassador Extraordinary and Plenipotentiary: His Excellency Mr Dror Zeigerman

Italian Embassy
14 Three Kings Yard, Davies Street, London, W1Y 2EH (Tel: 020-7312 2200; Fax: 020-7312 2230; Web: http://www.embitaly.org.uk)
Ambassador Extraordinary and Plenipotentiary: His Excellency Signor Luigi Amaduzzi

Jamaican High Commission
1-2 Prince Consort Road, London, SW7 2BZ (Tel: 020-7823 9911; Fax: 020-7589 5154)
High Commissioner: His Excellency The Hon. David Muirhead, QC, OJ

Embassy of Japan
101-104 Piccadilly, London, W1V 9FN (Tel: 020-7465 6500; Fax: 020-7491 9348)
Ambassador Extraordinary and Plenipotentiary: His Excellency Mr Sadayuki Hayashi

Embassy of the Hashemite Kingdom of Jordan
6 Upper Phillimore Gardens, Kensington, London, W8 7HA (Tel: 020-7937 3685; Fax: 020-7937 8795)
Ambassador Extraordinary and Plenipotentiary: His Excellency Mr Timoor Daghistani

Embassy of the Republic of Kazakhstan
33 Thurlowe Square, London, SW7 2DS (Tel: 020-7581 4646; Fax: 020-7584 8481)
Ambassador Extraordinary and Plenipotentiary: His Excellency Dr Adil Akhmentov

Kenya High Commission
45 Portland Place, London, W1N 4AS (Tel: 020-7636 2371/5; Fax: 020-7323 6717)
Acting High Commissioner: His Excellency Leonard Ngaithe

Embassy of the Republic of Korea
60 Buckingham Gate, London, SW1E 6AJ (Tel: 020-7227 5500/2; Fax: 020-7227 5503)
Ambassador Extraordinary and Plenipotentiary: His Excellency Mr Choi Sung-Hong

Embassy of the State of Kuwait
2 Albert Gate, Knightsbridge, London, SW1X 7JU (Tel: 020-7590 3400; Fax: 020-7823 1712)
Ambassador Extraordinary and Plenipotentiary: His Excellency Mr Khaled Al-Duwaisan GCVO

Embassy of the Kyrgyz Republic
Ascot House, 119 Crawford Street, London, W1H 1AE (Tel: 020-7935 1462; Fax: 020-7935 7449; Web: http://www.kyrgyz-embassy.org.uk)
Ambassador Extraordinary and Plenipotentiary: Her Excellency Mrs Roza Otunbayeva

Embassy of the Republic of Latvia
45 Nottingham Place, London, W1M 3FE (Tel: 020-7312 0040. Visa info: 020-7312 0125; Fax: 020-7312 0042)
Ambassador Extraordinary and Plenipotentiary: His Excellency Mr Normans Penke

Lebanese Embassy
21 Kensington Palace Gardens, London, W8 4QM (Tel: Consulate: 020-7229 7265. Embassy: 020-7276 6696; Fax: 020-7243 1699)
Ambassador Extraordinary and Plenipotentiary: His Excellency Mr Jihad Mortada

High Commission of the Kingdom of Lesotho
7 Chesham Place, Belgravia, London, SW1 8HN (Tel: 020-7235 5686; Fax: 020-7235 5023)
High Commissioner: His Excellency Mr Benjamin M. Masilo

Embassy of the Republic of Liberia
2 Pembridge Place, London, W2 4XB (Tel: 020-7221 1036; Fax: 020-7727 2914)
Ambassador Extraordinary and Plenipotentiary: His Excellency Mr William V. S. Bull

The Libyan People's Bureau
61-62 Ennismore Gardens, London, SW7 1NH (Tel: 020-7589 6120; Fax: 020-7589 6087)
Chargé d'Affaires: Mr Isa Baruni Edaeki

Embassy of the Republic of Lithuania
84 Gloucester Place, London, W1H 3HN (Tel: 020-7486 6401/2; Fax: 020-7486 6403; Web: http://www.users.globalnet.co.uk/~iralon)
Ambassador Extraordinary and Plenipotentiary: His Excellency Mr Justas V. Paleckis

Embassy of Luxembourg
27 Wilton Crescent, London, SW1X 8SD (Tel: 020-7235 6961; Fax: 020-7235 9734)
Ambassador Extraordinary and Plenipotentiary: His Excellency Monsieur Joseph Weyland

Embassy of the Republic of Macedonia
10 Harcourt House, 19A Cavendish Square, London, W1M 9AD (Tel: 020-7499 5152/1854; Fax: 020-7499 2864)
Ambassador Extraordinary and Plenipotentiary: His Excellency Mr Stevo Crvenkovski

High Commission for the Republic of Malawi
33 Grosvenor Street, London, W1X 0DE (Tel: 020-7491 4172/7; Fax: 020-7491 9916)
High Commissioner: His Excellency Mr Bright McBin Msaka

Malaysian High Commission
45 Belgrave Square, London, SW1X 8QT (Tel: 020-7235 8033; Fax: 020-7235 5161)
High Commissioner: His Excellency Dato' Mohamad Amir Jaafar

High Commission of the Republic of Maldives
22 Nottingham Place, London, W1M 3FB (Tel: 020-7224 2135; Fax: 020-7224 2157; Web: http://www.visitmaldives.com)
High Commissioner: vacant

344 London and the World

Malta High Commission
Malta House, 36-38 Piccadilly, London, W1V 0PQ (Tel: 020-7292 4800; Fax: 020-7734 1831)
High Commissioner: His Excellency Dr George Bonello Du Puis

Embassy of the Islamic Republic of Mauritania
140 Bow Common Lane, London, E3 4BH (Tel: 020-8980 4382; Fax: 020-8980 2232)
Ambassador Extraordinary and Plenipotentiary: vacant

Mauritius High Commission
32/33 Elvaston Place, London, SW7 5NW (Tel: 020-7581 0294/5; Fax: 020-7823 8437)
High Commissioner: His Excellency Sir Satcam Boolell QC

Embassy of Mexico
42 Hertford Street, Mayfair, London, W1Y 7TF (Tel: 020-7499 8586; Fax: 020-7495 4035;
Web: http://www.demon.co.uk/mexuk)
Ambassador Extraordinary and Plenipotentiary: His Excellency Señor Santiago Oñate

Embassy of Mongolia
7 Kensington Court, London, W8 5DL (Tel: 020-7937 0150; Fax: 020-7937 1117)
Ambassador Extraordinary and Plenipotentiary: His Excellency Mr Tsedenjavyn Suhbaatar

Embassy of the Kingdom of Morocco
49 Queen's Gate Gardens, London, SW7 5NE (Tel: 020-7581 5001/4; Fax: 020-7225 3862)
Ambassador Extraordinary and Plenipotentiary: His Excellency Mr Mohammed Belmahi

High Commission of the Republic of Mozambique
21 Fitzroy Square, London, W1P 5HJ (Tel: 020-7383 3800; Fax: 020-7383 3801)
High Commissioner: His Excellency Dr Eduardo Jose Bagiao Koloma

Embassy of the Union of Myanmar
19A Charles Street, Berkeley Square, London, W1X 8ER (Tel: 020-7499 8841; Fax: 020-7629 4169;
Web: http://www.myanmar.com)
Ambassador Extraordinary and Plenipotentiary: His Excellency Dr Kyaw Win

High Commission for the Republic of Namibia
6 Chandos Street, London, W1M 0LQ (Tel: 020-7636 6244; Fax: 020-7637 5694)
High Commissioner: Her Excellency Ms Monica Ndiliawike Nashandi

Royal Nepalese Embassy
12A Kenginston Palace Gardens, London, W8 4QU (Tel: 020-7229 1594/6231/5352; Fax: 020-7792 9861)
Ambassador Extraordinary and Plenipotentiary: His Excellency Dr Singha B. Basnyat

Royal Netherlands Embassy
38 Hyde Park Gate, London, SW7 5DP (Tel: 020-7590 3200; Fax: 020-7225 0947)
Ambassador Extraordinary and Plenipotentiary: His Excellency Baron Willem Oswald Bentinck Van Schoonheten

New Zealand High Commission
New Zealand House, Haymarket, London, SW1Y 4TQ (Tel: 020-7930 8422; Fax: 020-7839 4580;
Web: http://www.newzealandhc.org.uk)
High Commissioner: His Excellency Rt. Hon. Paul Clayton East, QC

Embassy of Nicaragua
Suite 31, Vicarage House, 58-60 Kensington Church Street, London, W8 4DP (Tel: 020-7938 2373; Fax: 020-7937 0952;
Web: http://www.freespace.virgin.net/emb.ofnicaragua)
Ambassador Extraordinary and Plenipotentiary: Her Excellency Señora Nora Campos De Lankes

High Commission for the Federal Republic of Nigeria
Nigeria House, 9 Northumberland Avenue, London, WC2N 5BX (Tel: 020-7839 1244; Fax: 020-7839 8746;
Web: http://www.nigeriahouseuk.com)
High Commissioner: His Excellency Prince Bola Adesombo Ajibola, KEB

Royal Norwegian Embassy
25 Belgrave Square, London, SW1X 8QD (Tel: 020-7591 5500; Fax: 020-7245 6993;
Web: http://www.norway.org.uk)
Ambassador Extraordinary and Plenipotentiary: His Excellency Mr Tarald O. Brautaset

Embassy of the Sultanate of Oman
167 Queen's Gate, London, SW7 5HE (Tel: 020-7225 0001; Fax: 020-7589 2505)
Ambassador Extraordinary and Plenipotentiary: His Excellency Mr Hussain Ali Abdullatif

High Commission for the Islamic Republic of Pakistan
35-36 Lowndes Square, London, SW1X 9JN (Tel: 020-7664 9200; Fax: 020-7664 9224)
High Commissioner: His Excellency Dr Akbar S. Ahmed

Embassy of the Republic of Panama
Ground Floor and Basement, 40 Hertford Street, London, W1Y 7TG (Tel: 020-7493 4646; Fax: 020-7493 4333)
Ambassador Extraordinary and Plenipotentiary: Her Excellency Señora Ariadne Singares Robinson

Papua New Guinea High Commission
3rd Floor, 14 Waterloo Place, London, SW1Y 4AR (Tel: 020-7930 0922/7; Fax: 020-7930 0828)
High Commissioner: His Excellency Sir Kina Bona, KBE

Embassy of Paraguay
Braemar Lodge, Cornwall Gardens, London, SW7 4AQ (Tel: 020-7937 1253/6629; Fax: 020-7937 5687)
Ambassador Extraordinary and Plenipotentiary: His Excellency Señor Raul Dos Santos

Embassy of Peru
52 Sloane Street, London, SW1X 9SP (Tel: 020-7235 1917/2545/3802; Fax: 020-7235 4463)
Ambassador Extraordinary and Plenipotentiary: Señor Gilbert Chauny de Porturas Hoyle

Embassies 345

Embassy of the Republic of the Philippines
9A Palace Green, London, W8 4QE (Tel: 020-7937 1600; Fax: 020-7937 2925;
Web: http://www.philemb.demon.co.uk)
Ambassador Extraordinary and Plenipotentiary: His Excellency Mr Cesar B. Bautista

Embassy of the Republic of Poland
47 Portland Place, London, W1N 4JH (Tel: 020-7580 4324; Fax: 020-7323 4018;
Web: http://www.poland-embassy.org.uk)
Ambassador Extraordinary and Plenipotentiary: His Excellency Dr Stanislaw Komorowski

Portuguese Embassy
11 Belgrave Square, London, SW1X 8PP (Tel: 020-7235 5331; Fax: 020-7245 1287;
Web: http://www.portembassy.gla.ac.uk)
Ambassador Extraordinary and Plenipotentiary: His Excellency Senhor José Gregório Faria

Embassy of the State of Qatar
1 South Audley Street, London, W1Y 5DQ (Tel: 020-7493 2200; Fax: 020-7493 2661)
Ambassador Extraordinary and Plenipotentiary: His Excellency Mr Ali M. Jaidah

Embassy of Romania
Arundel House, 4 Palace Green, London, W8 4QD (Tel: 020-7937 9666; Fax: 020-7937 8069)
Ambassador Extraordinary and Plenipotentiary: His Excellency Mr Radu Onofrei

Embassy of the Russian Federation
13 Kensington Palace Gardens, London, W8 4QX (Tel: 020-7727 8625; Fax: 020-7229 8027)
Ambassador Extraordinary and Plenipotentiary: His Excellency Mr Yuri E. Fokine

Embassy of the Republic of Rwanda
Uganda House, 58-59 Trafalgar Square, London, WC2N 5DX (Tel: 020-7930 2570; Fax: 020-7930 2572)
Ambassador Extraordinary and Plenipotentiary: His Excellency Dr Zag Nsenga

High Commission for St Christopher and Nevis
2nd Floor, 10 Kensington Court, London, W8 5DL (Tel: 020-7937 9522; Fax: 020-7937 5514)
High Commissioner: His Excellency Mr Aubrey E. Hart

High Commission for St Lucia
10 Kensington Court, London, W8 5DL (Tel: 020-7937 9522; Fax: 020-7937 8704)
High Commissioner: His Excellency Mr Emmanuel H. Cotter, MBE

High Commission for St Vincent and the Grenadines
10 Kensington Court, London, W8 5DL (Tel: 020-7565 2874; Fax: 020-7937 6040)
High Commissioner: His Excellency Mr Caryle Dennis Dougan, QC

Royal Embassy of Saudi Arabia
30 Charles Street, Mayfair, London, W1X 8LP (Tel: 020-7917 3000)
Ambassador Extraordinary and Plenipotentiary: His Excellency Dr Ghazi A. Algosaibi

Embassy of the Republic of Senegal
39 Marloes Road, London, W8 6LA (Tel: 020-7937 7237/938 4048; Fax: 020-7938 2546)
Ambassador Extraordinary and Plenipotentiary: His Excellency Mr Gabriel Alexandre Sar

High Commission for Seychelles
PO Box 4PE, 2nd Floor, Eros House, 111 Baker Street, London, W1M 1FE (Tel: 020-7224 1660; Fax: 020-7487 5756)
High Commissioner: His Excellency Mr Bertrand Rassool

Sierra Leone High Commission
Oxford Circus House, 245 Oxford Street, London, W1R 1LF (Tel: 020-7287 9884; Fax: 020-7734 3822)
High Commissioner: His Excellency Prof. Cyril Patrick Foray

High Commission for the Republic of Singapore
9 Wilton Crescent, London, SW1X 8SP (Tel: 020-7235 8315; Fax: 020-7245 6583)
High Commissioner: His Excellency Prof. Pang Eng Fong

Embassy of the Slovak Republic
25 Kensington Palace Gardens, London, W8 4QY (Tel: 020-7243 0803; Fax: 020-7727 5824;
Web: http://www.slovakembassy.co.uk)
Ambassador Extraordinary and Plenipotentiary: His Excellency Mr Igor Slobodník

Embassy of the Republic of Slovenia
Suite 1, Cavendish Court, 11-15 Wigmore Street, London, W1H 9LA (Tel: 020-7495 7775; Fax: 020-7495 7776; Web: www.embassy-slovenia.org.uk)
Ambassador Extraordinary and Plenipotentiary: His Excellency Mr Marjan Setinc

High Commission for the Republic of South Africa
South Africa House, Trafalgar Square, London, WC2N 5DP (Tel: 020-7451 7299; Fax: 020-7451 7284;
Web: http://www.southafricahouse.com)
High Commissioner: Her Excellency Ms Cheryl Ann Carolus

Spanish Embassy
39 Chesham Place, London, SW1X 8SB (Tel: 020-7235 5555; Fax: 020-7235 9905)
Ambassador Extraordinary and Plenipotentiary: His Excellency The Marqués de Tamarón

High Commission for the Democratic Socialist Republic of Sri Lanka
13 Hyde Park Gardens, London, W2 2LU (Tel: 020-7262 1841/7; Fax: 020-7262 7970;
Web: http://www.users.globalnet.co.uk/~slhc)
High Commissioner: His Excellency Dr Lal Jayawardena

Embassy of the Republic of the Sudan
3 Cleveland Row, St James's, London, SW1A 1DD (Tel: 020-7839 8080; Fax: 020-7839 7560)
Ambassador Extraordinary and Plenipotentiary: His Excellency Dr Hasan Abdeen

346 London and the World

Kingdom of Swaziland High Commission
20 Buckingham Gate, London, SW1E 6LB (Tel: 020-7630 6611; Fax: 020-7630 6564)
High Commissioner: His Excellency Revd Percy S. Mngomezulu

Embassy of Sweden
11 Montagu Place, London, W1H 2AL (Tel: 020-7917 6400; Fax: 020-7724 4174;
Web: http://www.swednet.org.uk)
Ambassador Extraordinary and Plenipotentiary: His Excellency Mr Mats Bergquist, CMG

Embassy of Switzerland
16-18 Montagu Place, London, W1H 2BQ (Tel: 020-7616 6000; Fax: 020-7724 7001;
Web: http://www.swissembassy.org.uk)
Ambassador Extraordinary and Plenipotentiary: His Excellency Mr Bruno Spinner

Embassy of the Syrian Arab Republic
8 Belgrave Square, London, SW1X 8PH (Tel: 020-7245 9012; Fax: 020-7235 4621)
Ambassador Extraordinary and Plenipotentiary: vacant

High Commission for the United Republic of Tanzania
43 Hertford Street, London, W1Y 8DB (Tel: 020-7499 8951/4; Fax: 020-7491 9321)
High Commissioner: His Excellency Dr Abdul-kader A. Shareef

Royal Thai Embassy
29-30 Queen's Gate, London, SW7 5JB (Tel: 020-7589 2944; Fax: 020-7823 9695)
Ambassador Extraordinary and Plenipotentiary: His Excellency Mr Vidhya Rayananonda, KCVO

Tonga High Commission
36 Molyneux Street, London, W1H 6AB (Tel: 020-7724 5828; Fax: 020-7723 9074)
High Commissioner: Her Excellency Mr Fetu'utolu Tupou

Office of the High Commissioner for the Republic of Trinidad and Tobago
42 Belgrave Square, London, SW1X 8NT (Tel: 020-7245 9351; Fax: 020-7823 1065)
High Commissioner: Her Excellency Mrs Sheelagh M. De Osuna

Tunisian Embassy
29 Prince's Gate, London, SW7 1QG (Tel: 020-7584 8117; Fax: 020-7225 2884)
Ambassador Extraordinary and Plenipotentiary: His Excellency Mr Khemaies Jhinaoui

Turkish Embassy
43 Belgrave Square, London, SW1X 8PA (Tel: 020-7393 0202; Fax: 020-7393 0066;
Web: http://www.turkishembassy/london.com)
Ambassador Extraordinary and Plenipotentiary: His Excellency Mr Korkmaz Haktanir

Embassy of Turkmenistan
2nd Floor South, St George's House, 14-17 Wells Street, London, W1P 3FP (Tel: 020-7255 1071; Fax: 020-7323 9184)
Ambassador Extraordinary and Plenipotentiary: His Excellency Mr Chary Babaev

Uganda High Commission
Uganda House, 58-59 Trafalgar Square, London, WC2N 5DX (Tel: 020-7839 5783; Fax: 020-7839 8925)
High Commissioner: His Excellency Prof. George Kirya

Embassy of Ukraine
60 Holland Park, London, W11 3SJ (Tel: 020-7727 6312; Fax: 020-7792 1708)
Ambassador Extraordinary and Plenipotentiary: His Excellency Prof. Volodymyr Vassylenko

Embassy of the United Arab Emirates
30 Prince's Gate, London, SW7 1PT (Tel: 020-7581 1281; Fax: 020-7581 9616)
Ambassador Extraordinary and Plenipotentiary: His Excellency Mr Easa Saleh Al-Gurg, CBE

Embassy of the Oriental Republic of Uruguay
2nd Floor, 140 Brompton Road, London, SW3 1HY (Tel: 020-7589 8835; Fax: 020-7581 9585)
Ambassador Extraordinary and Plenipotentiary: His Excellency Dr Agustín Espinosa-Lloveras

Embassy of the Republic of Uzbekistan
41 Holland Park, London, W11 2RP (Tel: 020-7229 7679; Fax: 020-7229 7029)
Ambassador Extraordinary and Plenipotentiary: His Excellency Mr Alisher Faizullaev

Venezuelan Embassy
1 Cromwell Road, London, SW7 2HR (Tel: 020-7584 4206/7; Fax: 020-7589 8887)
Ambassador Extraordinary and Plenipotentiary: His Excellency Señor Roy Chaderton-Matos

Embassy of the Socialist Republic of Vietnam
12-14 Victoria Road, London, W8 5RD (Tel: 020-7937 1912; Fax: 020-7937 6108/7565 3853)
Ambassador Extraordinary and Plenipotentiary: His Excellency Mr Vuong Thua Phong

Embassy of the Republic of Yemen
57 Cromwell Road, London, SW7 2ED (Tel: 020-7584 6607; Fax: 020-7589 3350)
Ambassador Extraordinary and Plenipotentiary: His Excellency Dr Hussein Abdullah Al-Amri

High Commission for the Republic of Zambia
2 Palace Gate, London, W8 5NG (Tel: 020-7589 6655; Fax: 020-7581 1353)
High Commissioner: His Excellency Prof. Moses Musonda

High Commission for the Republic of Zimbabwe
Zimbabwe House, 429 Strand, London, WC2R 0QE (Tel: 020-7836 7755; Fax: 020-7379 1167;
Web: http://www.zimbabwelink.com)
High Commissioner: His Excellency Mr Simbarashe Simbanenduku Mumbengegwi

International Organisations

INTERNATIONAL ORGANISATIONS

The list below details London-based international organisations and the London offices of international organisations.

Association of South East Asian Nations
ASEAN Committee in the UK, Indonesian Embassy, 38 Grosvenor Square, London W1X 9AD

Bank for International Settlements
London Agent, Bank of England, Threadneedle Street, London EC2R 8AH (Tel: 020-7601 4444; Fax: 020-7601 4771)

Commonwealth Secretariat
Marlborough House, Pall Mall, London SW1Y 5HX (Tel: 020-7839 3411; Fax: 020-7839 9081; Web: http://www.thecommonwealth.org)
Secretary-General: Chief Emeka Anyaoku (Nigeria)

Commonwealth Foundation
Marlborough House, Pall Mall, London SW1Y 5HY (Tel: 020-7930 3783)
Director: Dr Humayun Khan (Pakistan)

Commonwealth Institute
Kensington High Street, London W8 6NQ (Tel: 020-7603 4535)
Director-General: David French

European Bank for Reconstruction and Development
One Exchange Square, London EC2A 2EH (Tel: 020-7338 6000; Fax: 020-7338 6100; Web: http://www.ebrd.com)

INMARSAT
99 City Road, London EC1Y 1AX (Tel: 020-7728 1000; Fax: 020-7728 1044; Email: information@inmarsat.org; Web: http://www.inmarsat.org)

International Criminal Organisation
UK Office, NCIS Interpol, PO Box 8000, London SE11 5EN (Tel: 020-7238 8000)
UK Representative: J. M. Abbott, QPM

International Labour Organisation
UK Office, Millbank Tower, 21-24 Millbank, London SW1P 4QP (Tel: 020-7828 6401; Fax: 020-7233-5925; Email: london@ilo-london.org.uk)

International Maritime Organisation
4 Albert Embankment, London SE1 7SR (Tel: 020-7735 7611; Fax: 020-7587 3210; Email: info@imo.org; Web: http://www.imo.org)

International Red Cross and Red Crescent Movement
British Red Cross, 9 Grosvenor Crescent, London SW1X 7EJ (Tel: 020-7235 5454; Fax: 020-7245 6315; Email: information@redcross.org.uk; Web: http://www.redcross.org.uk/vauxhall.thm)

League of Arab States
UK Office, 52 Green Street, London W1Y 3YH (Tel: 020-7629 0044; Fax: 020-7493 7943)

United Nations
The United Nations High Commissioner for Refugees (UNHCR)
UK Office, 76 Westminster Palace Gardens, London SW1P 1RL (Tel: 020-7828 9191)

UN Office and Information Centre
Millbank Tower, 21-24 Millbank, London SW1 4QH (Tel: 020-7630 1981; Fax: 020-7976 6478)

World Bank
UK Office, New Zealand House, Haymarket, London SW1Y 4TQ (Tel: 020-7930 8511; Fax: 020-7930 8515)

EUROPEAN UNION

European Commission Representative Officer
8 Storey's Gate, London SW1P 3AT (Tel: 020-7973 1992)

UK European Parliament Information Office
2 Queen Anne's Gate, London SW1H 9AA (Tel: 020-7227 4300)

European Agency for the Evaluation of Medicinal Products (EMEA)
7 Westferry Circus, Canary Wharf, London E14 4HB (Tel: 020-7418 8400; Fax: 020-7418 8416; Email: mail@emea.eudra.org; Web: http://www.eudra.org/emea.html)
Chairman: Strachan Heppell

EUROPEAN INFORMATION CENTRES (INFORMATION ADVICE TO SMALL BUSINESSES)

London (City) European Information Centre
London Chamber of Commerce, 33 Queen Street, London EC4R 1AP (Tel: 020-7489 1992; Fax: 020-7489 0391; Email: tony@naslem.win_uk.net)

London (Westminster) European Information Centre
London Chamber of Commerce and Industry, 25 Maddox Street, London W1R 3AW (Tel: 020-7629 2151; Fax: 020-7629 2057; Email: tony@naslem.win_uk.net)

TIME ZONES

Standard time differences from the Greenwich meridian
+ hours ahead of GMT
- hours behind GMT
* may vary from standard time at some part of the year
(Summer Time or Daylight Saving Time)

Country	Hours +/- GMT
Afghanistan	+ 4.5
*Albania	+ 1
Algeria	+ 1
*Andorra	+ 1
Angola	+ 1
Anguilla	- 4
Antigua and Barbuda	- 4
Argentina	- 3
*Armenia	+ 4
Aruba	- 4
Ascension Island	0
*Australia	+10
ACT, NSW (except Broken Hill area)	
Qld, Tas, Vic, Whit Sunday Islands	+10
*Broken Hill area (NSW)	+ 9.5
*Lord Howe Island	+10.5
Northern Territory	+ 9.5
*South Australia	+ 9.5
Western Australia	+ 8
*Austria	+ 1
*Azerbaijan	+ 4
*Bahamas	- 5
Bahrain	+ 3
Bangladesh	+ 6
Barbados	- 4
*Belarus	+ 2
*Belgium	+ 1
Belize	- 6
Benin	+ 1
*Bermuda	- 4
Bhutan	+ 6
Bolivia	- 4
*Bosnia-Hercegovina	+ 1
Botswana	+ 2
Brazil	
Acre	- 5
central states	-4
N. and NE coastal states	-3
*S. and E. coastal states, including Brasilia	- 3
Fernando de Noronha Island	- 2
western states	- 5
British Antarctic Territory	- 3
British Indian Ocean Territory	+ 5
Diego Garcia	+ 6
British Virgin Islands	- 4
Brunei	+ 8
*Bulgaria	+ 2
Burkina Faso	0
Burundi	+ 2
Cambodia	+ 7
Cameroon	+ 1
Canada	
*Alberta	- 7
*British Columbia	- 8
*Labrador	- 4
*Manitoba	- 6
*New Brunswick	- 4
*Newfoundland	- 3.5
*Northwest Territories	
east of 85° W.	- 5
85° W.-102° W.	- 6
*Nunavut	- 7
*Nova Scotia	- 4
*Ontario	
east of 90° W.	- 5
west of 90° W.	- 6
*Prince Edward Island Quebec	- 4
east of 63° W.	- 4
*west of 63° W.	- 5
Saskatchewan	- 6
*Yukon	- 8
*Canary Islands	0
Cape Verde	- 1
Cayman Islands	- 5
Central African Republic	+ 1
Chad	+ 1
*Chatham Islands	+12.75
*Chile	- 4
China (inc. Hong Kong and Macao)	+ 8
Christmas Island (Indian Ocean)	+ 7
Cocos (Keeling) Islands	+ 6.5
Colombia	- 5
Comoros	+ 3
Congo (Dem. Rep.)	
east	+ 2
west	+ 1
Congo (Rep. of)	+ 1
Cook Islands	- 10
Costa Rica	- 6
Côte d'Ivoire	0
*Croatia	+ 1
*Cuba	- 5
*Cyprus	+ 2
*Czech Republic	+ 1
*Denmark	+ 1
Faroe Islands	0
Greenland	- 3
Danmarkshavn	0
Mesters Vig	0
*Scoresby Sound	- 1
*Thule area	- 4
Djibouti	+ 3
Dominica	- 4
Dominican Republic	- 4
East Timor	+ 8
Ecuador	- 5
Galápagos Islands	- 6
*Egypt	+ 2
El Salvador	-6
Equatorial Guinea	+ 1
Eritrea	+ 3
*Estonia	+ 2
Ethiopia	+ 3
*Falkland Islands	- 4
Fiji	+12
*Finland	+ 2
*France	+ 1
French Guiana	- 3
French Polynesia	-10
Guadeloupe	- 4
Martinique	- 4
Réunion	+ 4
Marquesas Islands	- 9.5

Time Zones

Gabon	+ 1	Maldives	+ 5
The Gambia	0	Mali	0
Georgia	+ 3	*Malta	+ 1
*Germany	+ 1	Marshall Islands	+12
Ghana	0	Ebon Atoll	-12
*Gibraltar	+ 1	Mauritania	0
*Greece	+ 2	Mauritius	+ 4
Grenada	- 4	*Mexico	- 6
Guam	+10	Nayarit, Sinaloa, Sonora, S. Baja California	- 7
Guatemala	- 6	N. Baja California	- 8
Guinea	0	Micronesia	
Guinea-Bissau	0	Caroline Islands	+10
Guyana	- 4	Kosrae	+11
*Haiti	- 5	Pingelap	+11
Honduras	- 6	Pohnpei	+11
*Hungary	+ 1	*Moldova	+ 2
Iceland	0	*Monaco	+ 1
India	+ 5.5	*Mongolia	+ 8
Indonesia		Montserrat	- 4
Bali	+ 8	Morocco	0
Flores	+ 8	Mozambique	+ 2
Irian Jaya	+ 9	Myanmar	+ 6.5
Java	+ 7	*Namibia	+ 1
Kalimantan (south and east)	+ 8	Nauru	+12
Kalimantan (west and central)	+ 7	Nepal	+ 5.75
Moluku Islands	+ 9	*Netherlands	+ 1
Sulawesi	+ 8	Netherlands Antilles	- 4
Sumatra	+ 7	New Caledonia	+11
Sumbawa	+ 8	*New Zealand	+12
Tanimbar	+ 9	Nicaragua	- 6
West Timor	+ 8	Niger	+ 1
*Iran	+ 3.5	Nigeria	+ 1
*Iraq	+ 3	Niue	-11
*Ireland, Republic of	0	Norfolk Island	+11.5
*Israel	+ 2	Northern Mariana Islands	+10
*Italy	+ 1	*Norway	+ 1
Jamaica	- 5	Oman	+ 4
Japan	+ 9	Pakistan	+ 5
*Jordan	+ 2	Palau	+ 9
*Kazakhstan		Panama	- 5
western (Aktau)	+ 4	Papua New Guinea	+10
central (Atyrau)	+ 5	*Paraguay	- 4
eastern	+ 6	Peru	- 5
Kenya	+ 3	Philippines	+ 8
Kiribati	+12	*Poland	+ 1
Line Islands	+14	*Portugal	0
Phoenix Islands	+13	Azores	- 1
Korea, North	+ 9	Puerto Rico	- 4
Korea, South	+ 9	Qatar	+ 3
Kuwait	+ 3	*Romania	+ 2
*Kyrgyzstan	+ 5	*Russia	
Laos	+ 7	Zone 1	+ 2
*Latvia	+ 2	Zone 2	+ 3
*Lebanon	+ 2	Zone 3	+ 4
Lesotho	+ 2	Zone 4	+ 5
Liberia	0	Zone 5	+ 6
*Libya	+ 2	Zone 6	+ 7
*Liechtenstein	+ 1	Zone 7	+ 8
Line Islands not part of Kiribati	-10	Zone 8	+ 9
*Lithuania	+ 1	Zone 9	+10
*Luxembourg	+ 1	Zone 10	+11
*Macedonia	+ 1	Zone 11	+12
Madagascar	+ 3	Rwanda	+ 2
*Madeira	0	St Helena	0
Malawi	+ 2	St Christopher and Nevis	- 4
Malaysia	+ 8	St Lucia	- 4

350 London and the World

*St Pierre and Miquelon	- 3
St Vincent and the Grenadines	- 4
Samoa	-11
Samoa, American	-11
*San Marino	+ 1
São Tomé and Princípe	0
Saudi Arabia	+ 3
Senegal	0
Seychelles	+ 4
Sierra Leone	0
Singapore	+ 8
*Slovakia	+ 1
*Slovenia	+ 1
Solomon Islands	+11
Somalia	+ 3
South Africa	+ 2
South Georgia	- 2
*Spain	+ 1
*Canary Islands	
Sri Lanka	+ 6
Sudan	+ 2
Suriname	- 3
Swaziland	+ 2
*Sweden	+ 1
*Switzerland	+ 1
*Syria	+ 2
Taiwan	+ 8
Tajikistan	+ 5
Tanzania	+ 3
Thailand	+ 7
Togo	0
Tonga	+13
Trinidad and Tobago	- 4
Tristan da Cunha	0
Tunisia	+ 1
*Turkey	+ 2
Turkmenistan	+ 5
*Turks and Caicos Islands	- 5
Tuvalu	+12
Uganda	+ 3
*Ukraine	+ 2
United Arab Emirates	+ 4
*United Kingdom	0
*United States of America	
Alaska	- 9
Aleutian Islands, east of 169° 30 W.	- 9
Aleutian Islands, west of 169° 30 W.	-10
eastern time	- 5
central time	- 6
Hawaii	-10
mountain time	- 7
Pacific time	- 8
Uruguay	- 3
Uzbekistan	+ 5
Vanuatu	+11
*Vatican City State	+ 1
Venezuela	- 4
Vietnam	+ 7
Virgin Islands (US)	- 4
Yemen	+ 3
*Yugoslavia (Fed. Rep. of)	+ 1
Zambia	+ 2
Zimbabwe	+ 2

Source: reproduced with permission from data produced by HM Nautical Almanac Office

AIR DISTANCES FROM LONDON TO WORLD CAPITAL CITIES (MILES)

Abu Dhabi (United Arab Emirates)	3409
Abuja (Nigeria)	3115
Accra (Ghana)	3177
Addis Ababa (Ethiopia)	3673
Algiers (Algeria)	1035
Amman (Jordan)	2280
Amsterdam (Netherlands)	231
Ankara (Turkey)	1765
Asuncion (Paraguay)	7100
Athens (Greece)	1500
Baghdad (Iraq)	2550
Bangkok (Thailand)	5929
Banjul (The Gambia)	2798
Beijing (China)	5053
Beirut (Lebanon)	2162
Berlin (Germany)	593
Berne (Switzerland)	472
Bogota (Colombia)	5295
Brasilia (Brazil)	6342
Bratislave (Slovakia)	990
Bridgetown (Barbados)	4192
Brussels (Belgium)	217
Bucharest (Romania)	1298
Budapest (Hungary)	923
Buenos Aires (Argentina)	6926
Cairo (Egypt)	2192
Canberra (Australia)	10700
Caracas (Venezuela)	4657
Copenhagen (Denmark)	608
Czech Republic	649
Dakar (Senegal)	3035
Dhaka (Bangladesh)	4969
Dhoa (Qatar)	3253
Dodoma (Tanzania)	4663
Dublin (Republic of Ireland)	279
Freetown (Sierra Leone)	3147
Gaborone (Botswana)	5592
Georgetown (Guyana)	6003
Guatemala City (Guatemala)	6542
Havana (Cuba)	4664
Hanoi (Vietnam)	6345
Harare (Zimbabwe)	5160
Helsinki (Finland)	1147
Islamabad (Pakistan)	3755
Jakarta (Indonesia)	7287
Jerusalem (Israel)	2242
Kabul (Afghanistan)	3643
Kampala (Uganda)	4566
Kathmandu (Nepal)	4675
Khartoum (Sudan)	3071
Kingston (Jamaica)	4668
Kinshasa (Zaire)	3983
Kuala Lumpur (Malaysia)	6557
Kuwait City (Kuwait)	2903
La Paz (Bolivia)	2356
Libreville (Gabon)	1953
Lilongwe (Malawi)	5007
Lima (Peru)	6951
Lisbon (Portugal)	971
Lome (Togo)	3172
Lusaks (Zambia)	4985
Luxembourg Ville (Luxembourg)	310

Madrid (Spain)	774	Riyadh (Saudi Arabia)	3073
Managua (Nicaragua)	5453	Rome (Italy)	896
Manama (Bahrain)	3163	Sana'a (Yemen)	4343
Manil (Philippines)	6681	San Jose (Costa Rica)	6078
Maseru (Lesotho)	5864	San Salvador (El Salvador)	5564
Mbabane (Swaziland)	5790	Santiago (Chile)	7509
Mexico City (Mexico)	5544	Santo Domingo (Dominican Republic)	4943
Mogadishu (Somalia)	4873	Seoul (Korea, Republic of South)	7247
Monrovia (Liberia)	3547	Singapore City (Singapore)	6754
Montevideo (Uruguay)	7030	Sofia (Bulgaria)	1258
Moscow (Russia)	1557	Sri Jayawardenapura (Sri Lanka)	5413
Muscat (Oman)	3622	St. George's (Grenada)	4355
Nairobi (Kenya)	4247	Stockholm (Sweden)	906
Nassau (Bahamas)	4332	Suva (Fiji)	11246
New Delhi (India)	5177	Tegucigalpa (Honduras)	5291
Nicosia (Cyprus)	2008	Tehran (Iran)	2741
Nuku'alofa (Tonga)	12912	Teipei (Taiwan)	9245
Oslo (Norway)	723	Tokyo (Japan)	5955
Ottawa (Canada)	3322	Tripoli (Libya	1170
Ouagadougou (Burkina Faso)	3663	Tunis (Tunisia)	1137
Panama City (Panama)	4664	Ulaan Bator (Mongolia)	6481
Paris (France)	215	Valetta (Malta)	1305
Port Louis (Mauritius)	6075	Victoria (Seychelles)	5547
Port Moresby (Papua New Guinea)	9815	Vienna (Austria)	790
Port of Spain (Trinidad and Tobago)	4405	Warsaw (Poland)	912
Porto Novo (Benin)	3381	Washington DC (United States of America)	3672
Pretoria (South Africa)	5640	Wellington (New Zealand)	11965
Quito (Ecuador)	8779	Yamoussoukro (Cote d'Ivoire)	3209
Rabat (Morocco)	1258	Yangon (Myanmar)	5582
Reykjavik (Iceland)	1167	Yaounde (Cameroon)	3475

INTERNATIONAL DIRECT DIALLING

International dialling codes are composed of four elements which are dialled in sequence:

(i)   the international code
(ii) the country code (*see* below)
(iii) the area code
(iv) the customer's telephone number

Calls to some countries must be made via the international operator. (*Source:* BT)

† Connection is currently unavailable
‡ Calls must be made via the international operator
p A pause in dialling is necessary whilst waiting for a second tone
*Varies in some areas
**Varies depending on carrier

Country	IDD from UK	IDD to UK
Afghanistan	†	†
Albania	00 355	00 44
Algeria	00 213	00*p*44
Andorra	00 376	00 44
Angola	00 244	00 44
Anguilla	00 1 264	011 44
Antigua and Barbuda	00 1 268	011 44
Argentina	00 54	00 44
Armenia	00 374	810 44
Aruba	00 297	00 44
Ascension Island	00 247	00 44
Australia	00 61	00 11 44
Austria	00 43	00 44
Azerbaijan	00 994	810 44
Azores	00 351	00 44
Bahamas	00 1 242	011 44
Bahrain	00 973	0 44
Bangladesh	00 880	00 44
Barbados	00 1 246	011 44
Belarus	00 375	810 44
Belgium	00 32	00 44
Belize	00 501	00 44
Benin	00 229	00*p*44
Bermuda	00 1 441	011 44
Bhutan	00 975	00 44
Bolivia	00 591	00 44
Bosnia-Hercegovina	00 387	00 44
Botswana	00 267	00 44
Brazil	00 55	00 44
British Virgin Islands	00 1 284	011 44
Brunei	00 673	00 44
Bulgaria	00 359	00 44
Burkina Faso	00 226	00 44
Burundi	00 257	90 44
Cambodia	00 855	00 44
Cameroon	00 237	00 44
Canada	00 1	011 44
Canary Islands	00 34	00 44
Cape Verde	00 238	0 44
Cayman Islands	00 1 345	011 44
Central African Republic	00 236	19 44
Chad	00 235	15 44
Chile	00 56	00 44
China	00 86	00 44
Hong Kong	00 852	001 44
Colombia	00 57	009 44
Comoros	00 269	00 44
Congo, Dem. Rep. of	00 243	00 44
Congo, Republic of	00 242	00 44
Cook Islands	00 682	00 44
Costa Rica	00 506	00 44
Coˆte d'Ivoire	00 225	00 44
Croatia	00 385	00 44
Cuba	00 53	119 44
Cyprus	00 357	00 44
Czech Republic	00 420	00 44
Denmark	00 45	00 44
Djibouti	00 253	00 44
Dominica	00 1 767	011 44
Dominican Republic	00 1 809	011 44
Ecuador	00 593	00 44
Egypt	00 20	00 44
Equatorial Guinea	00 240	00 44
Eritrea	00 291	00 44
Estonia	00 372	800 44
Ethiopia	00 251	00 44
Falkland Islands	00 500	0 44
Faroe Islands	00 298	009 44
Fiji	00 679	05 44
Finland	00 358	00 44**
France	00 33	00 44
French Guiana	00 594	00 44
French Polynesia	00 689	00 44
Gabon	00 241	00 44
The Gambia	00 220	00 44
Georgia	00 995	810 44
Germany	00 49	00 44
Ghana	00 233	00 44
Gibraltar	00 350	00 44
Greece	00 30	00 44
Greenland	00 299	009 44
Grenada	00 1 473	011 44
Guadeloupe	00 590	00 44
Guam	00 1 671	001 44
Guatemala	00 502	00 44
Guinea	00 224	00 44
Guinea-Bissau	00 245	099 44
Guyana	00 592	001 44
Haiti	00 509	00 44
Honduras	00 504	00 44
Hungary	00 36	00 44
Iceland	00 354	00 44
India	00 91	00 44
Indonesia	00 62	001 44** 00844**
Iran	00 98	00 44
Iraq	00 964	00 44
Ireland, Republic of	00 353	00 44
Israel	00 972	00 44**
Italy	00 39	00 44
Jamaica	00 1 876	011 44
Japan	00 81	00144** 004144** 006144**
Jordan	00 962	00 44*
Kazakhstan	00 7	810 44
Kenya	00 254	00 44
Kiribati	00 686	00 44
Korea, North	00 850	00 44
Korea, South	00 82	001 44** 00244**

International Direct Dialling

Kuwait	00 965	00 44
Kyrgystan	00 996	00 44
Laos	00 856	00 44
Latvia	00 371	00 44
Lebanon	00 961	00 44
Lesotho	00 266	00 44
Liberia	00 231	00 44
Libya	00 218	00 44
Liechtenstein	00 423	00 44
Lithuania	00 370	810 44
Luxembourg	00 352	00 44
Macao	00 853	00 44
Macedonia	00 389	99 44
Madagascar	00 261	00 44
Madeira	00 351 91	00 44*
Malawi	00 265	101 44
Malaysia	00 60	00 44
Maldives	00 960	00 44
Mali	00 223	00 44
Malta	00 356	00 44
Mariana Islands, Northern	00 1 670	011 44
Marshall Islands	00 692	011 44
Martinique	00 596	00 44
Mauritania	00 222	00 44
Mauritius	00 230	00 44
Mayotte	00 269	10 44
Mexico	00 52	98 44
Micronesia, Federated States of	00 691	011 44
Moldova	00 373	810 44
Monaco	00 377	00 44
Mongolia	00 976	00 44
Montenegro	00 381	99 44
Montserrat	00 1 664	011 44
Morocco	00 212	00*p*44
Mozambique	00 258	00 44
Myanmar	00 95	00 44
Namibia	00 264	00 44
Nauru	00 674	00 44
Nepal	00 977	00 44
Netherlands	00 31	00 44
Netherlands Antilles	00 599	00 44
New Caledonia	00 687	00 44
New Zealand	00 64	00 44
Nicaragua	00 505	00 44
Niger	00 227	00 44
Nigeria	00 234	009 44
Niue	00 683	00 44
Norfolk Island	00 672	0101 44
Norway	00 47	00 44
Oman	00 968	00 44
Pakistan	00 92	00 44
Palau	00 680	011 44
Panama	00 507	00 44
Papua New Guinea	00 675	05 44
Paraguay	00 595	00 44**
		003 44**
Peru	00 51	00 44
Philippines	00 63	00 44
Poland	00 48	00 44
Portugal	00 351	00 44
Puerto Rico	00 1 787	011 44
Qatar	00 974	00 44
Réunion	00 262	00 44
Romania	00 40	00 44
Russia	00 7	810 44
Rwanda	00 250	00 44
St Christopher and Nevis	00 1 869	011 44
St Helena	00 290	0 44
St Lucia	00 1 758	011 44
St Pierre and Miquelon	00 508	00 44
St Vincent and the Grenadines	00 1 784	001 44
El Salvador	00 503	0 44
Samoa	00 685	0 44
Samoa, American	00 684	00 44
San Marino	00 378	00 44
Sao Tomé and Principe	00 239	00 44
Saudi Arabia	00 966	00 44
Senegal	00 221	00*p*44
Serbia	00 381	99 44
Seychelles	00 248	00 44
Sierra Leone	00 232	00 44
Singapore	00 65	001 44
Slovak Republic	00 421	00 44
Slovenia	00 386	00 44
Solomon Islands	00 677	00 44
Somalia	00 252	16 44
South Africa	00 27	09 44
Spain	00 34	00 44
Sri Lanka	00 94	00 44
Sudan	00 249	00 44
Suriname	00 597	00 44
Swaziland	00 268	00 44
Sweden	00 46	007 44**
		00944**
		008744**
Switzerland	00 41	00 44
Syria	00 963	00 44
Taiwan	00 886	002 44
Tajikistan	00 7	810 44
Tanzania	00 255	00 44
Thailand	00 66	001 44
Tibet	00 86	00 44
Togo	00 228	00 44
Tonga	00 676	00 44
Trinidad and Tobago	00 1 868	011 44
Tristan da Cunha	00 2 897	‡
Tunisia	00 216	00 44
Turkey	00 90	00 44
Turkmenistan	00 993	810 44
Turks and Caicos Islands	00 1 649	0 44
Tuvalu	00 688	00 44
Uganda	00 256	00 44
Ukraine	00 380	810 44
United Arab Emirates	00 971	00 44
Uruguay	00 598	00 44
USA	00 1	011 44
Alaska	00 1 907	011 44
Hawaii	00 1 808	011 44
Uzbekistan	00 998	810 44
Vanuatu	00 678	00 44
Vatican City State	00 390 66982	00 44
Venezuela	00 58	00 44
Vietnam	00 84	00 44

Virgin Islands (US)	00 1 340	011 44
Yemen	00 967	00 44
Yugoslav Fed. Rep.	00 381	99 44
Zambia	00 260	00 44
Zimbabwe	00 263	00 44

RELIGIOUS
LONDON

CHRISTIANITY
BAHA'I FAITH
BUDDHISM
HINDUISM
ISLAM
JAINISM
JUDAISM
SIKHISM
ZOROASTRIANISM
CHURCHES

RELIGIOUS LONDON

The national church of England (but not of the rest of the United Kingdom) is the Church of England.
About 64 per cent of the population of the UK would call itself broadly Christian (in the Trinitarian sense), with 25.1 million people identifying with Anglican churches, 5.8 million with the Roman Catholic Church, 2.6 million with Presbyterian Churches, 1.3 million with the Methodist Churches and 1.96 million with other Christian churches. About 1.3 million people are affiliated to non-Trinitarian churches, e.g. Jehovah's Witnesses, the Church of Jesus Christ of Latter-Day Saints (Mormons), the Church of Christ, Scientist and the Unitarian churches.

A further 7 per cent of the population (4.5 million people) are adherents of other faiths, including Hinduism, Islam, Judaism and Sikhism.

About 29 per cent of the population is non-religious.

AVERAGE CHURCH ATTENDANCE IN LONDON BY DENOMINATION (000s)

Denomination	Attendance
Anglican	101.1
Roman Catholic	237.2
Baptist	45.8
Methodist	23.7
Orthodox	16.4
Pentecostal	93.7
United Reformed	16.6
Independent Churches	19.7
New Churches	39.6
Others	24.1
Total	617.9

Adherents of non-Christian faiths and of non-indigenous forms of Christianity form a higher proportion of the population in London than in the UK as a whole, although separate statistics are not available.

Source: *Christian Research/Harper Collins Religious - UK Christian Handbook Religious Trends 2000-1; figures in text are for 1998*

Inter-Church and Inter-Faith Co-operation

The main umbrella body for the Christian churches in the UK is the Churches Together in Britain and Ireland (formerly the Council of Churches for Britain and Ireland). There is also an ecumenical body for England, Churches Together in England. The Free Churches' Council comprises most of the Free Churches in England and Wales, and the Evangelical Alliance represents evangelical Christians.

The Inter Faith Network for the United Kingdom promotes co-operation between faiths, and the Council of Christians and Jews works to improve relations between the two religions. Churches Together in Britain and Ireland also has a Commission on Inter Faith Relations.

Churches Together in Britain and Ireland

Inter-Church House, 35-41 Lower Marsh, London SE1 7SA (Tel: 020-7523 2121; Fax: 020-7928 0010; Email: gensec@ctbi.org.uk;
Web: http://www.ctbi.org.uk)
General Secretary: Dr D. Goodbourn

Churches Together in England

101 Queen Victoria Street, London EC4V 4EN (Tel: 020-7332 8230; Fax: 020-7332 8234;
Web: http://www.cte-one.clara.net)
General Secretary: The Revd Bill Snelson

Council of Christians and Jews

5th Floor, Camelford House, 87-89 Albert Embankment, London SE1 7TP (Tel: 020-7829 0090; Fax: 020-7820 0504;
Email: ccjuk@aol.com;
Web: http://www.ccj.org.uk)
Director: Sr M. Shepherd, NDS

Evangelical Alliance

Whitefield House, 186 Kennington Park Road, London SE11 4BT (Tel: 020-7207 2100; Fax: 020-7207 2150; Email: london@eauk.org; Web: http://www.eauk.org)
General Director: Revd J. Edwards

Free Churches' Council

27 Tavistock Square, London WC1H 9HH (Tel: 020-7387 8413) **General Secretary:** Revd G. H. Roper
Inter Faith Network for the United Kingdom
5-7 Tavistock Place, London WC1H 9SN (Tel: 020-7388 0008; Fax: 020-7387 7968; Email: ifnet@interfaith.org.uk; Web: http://www.interfaith.org.uk)
Director: B. Pearce, OBE

CHRISTIANITY

Christianity is a monotheistic faith based on the person and teachings of Jesus Christ and all Christian denominations claim his authority. Central to its teaching is the concept of God and his son Jesus Christ, who was crucified and resurrected in order to enable mankind to attain salvation.

Jesus' birth, teachings, crucifixion and subsequent resurrection are recorded in the Gospels, which, together with other scriptures that summarise Christian belief, form the New Testament. This, together with the Hebrew scriptures, entitled the Old Testament by Christians, makes up the Bible, the sacred texts of Christianity.

Christians believe that sin distanced mankind from God, and that Jesus was the Son of God, sent to redeem mankind from that sin by his death. The Gospels assure Christians that those who believe in Jesus and obey his teachings will be forgiven their sins and will be resurrected from the dead.

Christian practices vary widely between different Christian churches, but prayer is universal to all, as is charity, giving for the maintenance of the church buildings, for the work of the church, and to the poor and needy. Baptism and the Eucharist are practised by most Christians. Baptism, symbolising repentance and faith in Jesus is an act marking entry into the Christian community; the Eucharist, the ritual re-enactment of the Last Supper, Jesus' final meal with his disciples, is also practised by most denominations.

Most Christians believe that God actively guides the Church.

Christianity in London

Christianity was introduced to England by the Romans and the first Bishop of London, Restitutus, was installed in AD 314. Following the invasion of the pagan Angles, Saxons and Jutes, Pope Gregory sent Augustine to evangelise the English in AD 596 and in AD 604, the first St. Paul's Cathedral was built in by Bishop Mellitus. Conflicts between Church and State during the Middle Ages culminated in the Act of Supremacy in 1534, which repudiated papal supremacy and declared King Henry VIII to be the supreme head of the Church in England. Since 1559 the English monarch has been termed the Supreme Governor of the Church of England.

Non-Christian Religions

London is a multi-faith society comprised of many non-Christian religions. Below we have provided some information about a selection of faiths, along with key governing bodies or associations based in London.

BAHÁ'Í FAITH

The Bahá'í faith was founded by Mirza Husayn-`Ali, known as Bahá'u'lláh (Glory of God), who was born in Iran in 1817.

The Bahá'í faith recognises the unity and relativity of religious truth and teaches that there is only one God, whose will has been revealed to mankind by a series of messengers, such as Zoroaster, Abraham, Moses, Buddha, Krishna, Christ, Muhammad, the Báb and Bahá'u'lláh, whose common purpose was to bring God's message to mankind. It teaches that all races and both sexes are equal and deserving of equal opportunities and treatment, that education is a fundamental right and encourages a fair distribution of wealth.

Bahá'í Community of the United Kingdom
27 Rutland Gate, London SW7 1PD (Tel: 020-7584 2566; Fax: 020-7584 9402;
Email: nsa.bahai.org.uk; Web: http://www.bahai.org.uk)

BUDDHISM

Buddhism originated in northern India in the teachings of Siddhartha Gautama, known to his followers as the Buddha ('the one who knows'). It is most generally accepted that he lived in the sixth/fifth centuries BC.

Although Buddhism died out in its country of origin, it spread widely through Asia developing into a number of forms which are superficially very different. This diversity makes it difficult to summarise Buddhist doctrines in a form which would be accepted by all Buddhists, but the following points would likely be accepted by the majority: Budhists do not believe in one kind of supreme deity central to religions more familiar in the West.

Instead, the course of the universe is determined by the law of karma, a form of moral causation. According to this, the good and bad volitions of beings tend to produce pleasant or painful consequences in present and future lives. Karma generally operates to maintain beings in the familiar cycle of rebirth and death (samsara) which is inevitably a state of suffering (dukkha) in the long run notwithstanding the possibility of interludes of happiness and fulfilment. Buddhism teaches that escape from this cycle requires the threefold development of morality (including the practice of qualities such as generosity and patience), concentration (development of the powers of the mind, including loving-kindness and compassion for all beings) and wisdom (insight into the real nature of things, including out own mind and body).

The methods of achieving this development vary from one school of Buddhism to another. The Buddhist Society seeks to raise awareness of Buddhist teachings and practice without favouring one school above another. It runs courses, gives lectures and publishes books about Buddhism.

Britain Burma Buddhist Trust
1 Old Church Lane, London NW9 8TG (Tel: 020-8567 7858)

British Buddhist Association
11 Biddulph Road, London, W9 1JA (Tel: 020-7286 5575; Fax: 020-7289 5545)
Director: A. Haviland-Nye

Buddhapadipa Temple
14 Calonne Road, Wimbledon, London SW19 5HJ (Tel: 020-8879 7542; Fax: 020-8894 5788)
Abbot: Phra Bhavanakitkoson

Buddhist Society
58 Eccleston Square, London SW1V 1PH (Tel: 020-7834 5858; Fax: 020-7976 5238;
Web: http://www.buddsoc.org.uk)
Librarian: R. B. Parsons
General Secretary: R. C. Maddox

Croydon Buddhist Centre
96-98 High Street, Croydon, Surrey CR0 1ND (Tel: 020-8688 8624; Fax: 020-8688 8624;
Email: croydonbc@lineone.net;
Web: http://www.croydonbuddhistcentre.com)
Chairman: Dharmacarini Vijayasri

London Buddhist Centre
51 Roman Road, Bethnal Green, London E2 0HU (Tel: 020-8981 1225; Fax: 020-8980 1960;
Email: info@lbc.org.uk; Web: http://www.lbc.org.uk)
Centre Director: Prasannavira

London Buddhist Vihara
The Avenue, Chiswick, London W4 1UD (Tel: 020-8995 9493; Fax: 020-8994 8130;
Email: london.vihara@virgin.net;
Web: http://www.freespace.virgin.net/london.vihara)
Head of Vihara: Most Ven Dr M. Vajiragnana

London Zendo
10 Belmont Street, Chalk Farm, London NW1 8HH (Tel: 020-7485 9576)

Soka Gakkai UK
1 The Green, Richmond, Surrey TW9 1PL (Tel: 020-8992 1120)

Thames Buddhist Vihara
Dulverton Road, Selsdon, Surrey CR2 8PJ (Tel: 020-8657 7120)
Head of Vihara: Ven. P. Somaratana Thera

Vietnamese Buddhist Society
Linh Son Temple, 89 Bromley Road, Catford, London, SE6 2UF (Tel: 020-8461 1887)

West London Buddhist Centre
7 Coleville House, Talbot Road, London W11 1JB (Tel: 020-7727 9382)

HINDUISM

Hinduism has no historical founder but had become highly developed in India by about 1200 bc. Most Hindus hold that satya (truthfulness), ahimsa (non-violence), honesty, physical labour and tolerance of other faiths are essential for good living. They believe in one supreme spirit (Brahman), and in the transmigration of atman (the soul). Most Hindus accept the doctrine of karma (consequences of actions), the concept of samsara (successive lives) and the possibility of all atmans achieving moksha (liberation from samsara) through jnana (knowledge), yoga (meditation), karma (work or action) and bhakti (devotion).

Most Hindus recognise the authority of the Vedas, the oldest holy books, and accept the philosophical teachings of the Upanishads, the Vedanta Sutras and the Bhagavad-Gita.

Brahman is formless, limitless and all-pervading, and is represented in worship by murtis (images or statues). Brahma, Vishnu and Shiva are the most important gods worshipped by Hindus; their respective consorts are Saraswati, Lakshmi and Durga or Parvati, also known as Shakti. There are believed to have been ten avatars (incarnations) of Vishnu, of whom the most important are Rama and Krishna. Other popular gods are Ganesha, Hanuman and Subrahmanyam. All gods are seen as aspects of the supreme God, not as competing deities. The commonest form of worship is a puja, in which offerings of red and yellow powders, rice grains, water, flowers, food, fruit, incense and light are made to the murti (image) of a deity.

Arya Pratinidhi Sabha (UK) and Arya Samaj London
69a Argyle Road, London W13 0LY (Tel: 020-8991 1732)
President: Prof. S. N. Bharadwaj

Bharatiya Vidya Bhavan
Institute of Indian Art and Culture, 4a Castletown Road, London W14 9HQ (Tel: 020-7381 4608;
Web: http://www.bhavan.co.uk)
Executive Director: Dr M. N. Nandakumara

International Society for Krishna Consciousness (ISKCon)
Bhaktivedanta Manor, Dharam Marg, Hilfield Lane, Aldenham, Watford, Herts WD2 8EZ (Tel: 01923-859578)
Governing Body Commissioner: P. Latai

Swaminarayan Hindu Mission
105-119 Brentfield Road, Neasden, London NW10 8JP (Tel: 020-8965 2651; Fax: 020-8965 6313;
Email: shm@swaminarayan-baps.org.uk;
Web: http://www.swaminarayan-baps.org.uk)
Mahant: Sadhu Atmaswarupdas

Vishwa Hindu Parishad (UK)
48 Wharfedale Gardens, Thornton Heath, Surrey CR7 6LB (Tel: 020-8684 9716; Fax: 020-8684 9716)
General Secretary: K. Ruparelia

Vivekananda Centre London
6 Lea Gardens, Wembley, Middlesex, HA9 7SE (Tel: 020-8902 0840; Fax: 020-8903 0763;
Email: hindy@btinternet.com;
Web: http://www.btinternet.com/~vivekananda)

ISLAM

Islam (which means 'peace arising from submission to the will of Allah' in Arabic) is a monotheistic religion which was taught by the Prophet Muhammad, who was born in Mecca (Makkah) in ad 570.

For Muslims (adherents of Islam), there is one God (Allah), who holds absolute power. His commands were revealed to mankind through the prophets, who include Abraham, Moses and Jesus, but his message was gradually corrupted until revealed finally and in perfect form to Muhammad through the angel Jibril (Gabriel) over a period of 23 years. This last, incorruptible message has been recorded in the Qur'an (Koran), and is held to be the essence of all previous scriptures. The Ahadith are the records of the Prophet Muhammad's deeds and sayings (the Sunnah) as recounted by his immediate followers. The Shari'ah is the sacred law of Islam based upon prescriptions derived from the Qur'an and the Sunnah of the Prophet.

There is no central organisation, but the Islamic Cultural Centre, which is the London Central Mosque, and the Imams and Mosques Council are influential bodies; there are many other Muslim organisations in Britain.

East London Mosque Trust
82 Whitechapel Road, London E1 1JQ (Tel: 020-7247 1357; Fax: 020-7377 9879;
Email: admin@eastlondon-mosque.org.uk;
Web: http://www.eastlondon-mosque.org.uk)
Chairman: Akbor Ali

Imams and Mosques Council
20-22 Creffield Road, London W5 3RP (Tel: 020-8992 6636) Director of the Council and Principal of the Muslim College: Dr M. A. Z. Badawi

Islamic Cultural Centre and London Central Mosque
146 Park Road, London NW8 7RG (Tel: 020-7724 3363; Fax: 020-7211 0493)
Director: Dr. H. Al-Majed

Muslim Council of Britain
P.O. Box 52, Wembley, Middx HA9 7AL (Tel: 020-8903 9024; Fax: 020-8903 9026;
Email: admin@mcb.org.uk;
Web: http://www.mcb.org.uk)
Secretary-General: Iqbal Sacranie

Muslim World League
46 Goodge Street, London W1P 1FJ (Tel: 020-7636 7568; Fax: 020-7637 5034; Email: mwl@webstar.co.uk)
Deputy Director: G. Rahman

Union of Muslim Organisations of the UK and Eire
109 Campden Hill Road, London W8 7TL (Tel: 020-7229 0538; Fax: 020-7221 6608)
General Secretary: Dr S. A. Pasha

JAINISM

Jainism was founded in the sixth century BC by Vardhamana Jnatiputra, known as Mahavira (The Great Hero), but it traces its roots to a succession of 24 Jinas (those who overcome), of which Mahavira is considered the last.

Jains believe that the universe is eternal and exists as a series of layers, including heaven, the earth and hell. Karma, the fruit of past actions, determines the place of every person and creature within the universe. Moksha (liberation from an endless succession of reincarnations) is achieved by enlightenment, which can be attained only through asceticism.

Institute of Jainology
31 Lancaster Gate, London, W2 3LP

JUDAISM

The primary authority of Judaism is the Hebrew Bible or Tanakh. The first section (Torah) records how the descendants of Abraham were led by Moses out of their slavery in Egypt to Mount Sinai where God's law was revealed to them as the chosen people. The often two sections are Nevi'im (Prophets) and Ketuvim (Sacred Writings). The Talmud, which consists of commentaries on the Mishnah (the first text of rabbinical Judaism), is also held to be authoritative. Orthodox Jews regard Jewish law as derived from God and therefore unalterable; Reform and Liberal Jews seek to interpret it in the light of contemporary considerations; and Conservative Jews aim to maintain most of the traditional rituals but to allow changes in accordance with tradition.

The Chief Rabbi of the United Hebrew Congregations of the Commonwealth is the rabbinical authority of the Orthodox sector of the Ashkenazi Jewish community. His authority is not recognised by the Reform Synagogues of Great Britain (the largest progressive group), the Union of Liberal and Progressive Synagogues, the Union of Orthodox Hebrew Congregations, the Federation of Synagogues, the Sephardi community or the Assembly of Masorti Synagogues. He is, however, generally recognised outside the Jewish community as the public religious representative of the totality of British Jewry. The Chief Rabbi is President of the Beth Din (Court of Judgment) of the United Synagogue. The Board of Deputies of British Jews is the representative body of British Jewry.

Chief Rabbinate
735 High Road, London N12 0US (Tel: 020-8343 6301)
Chief Rabbi: Prof. Jonathan Sacks
Executive Director: Mrs S. Weinberg

London Beth Din (Court of the Chief Rabbi)
735 High Road, London N12 0US (Tel: 020-8343 6280; Fax: 020-8343 6257)
Registrar: David Frei
Dayanim: Rabbi C. Ehrentreu; Rabbi I. Binstock; Rabbi C. D. Kaplin; Rabbi M. Gelley

Board of Deputies of British Jews
Commonwealth House, 1-19 New Oxford Street, London WC1A 1NF (Tel: 020-7543 5400; Email: info@bod.org.uk; Web: http://www.bod.org.uk)
President: E. Tabachnik, QC
Director-General: N. A. Nagler

Assembly of Masorti Synagogues
1097 Finchley Road, London NW11 0PU (Tel: 020-8201 8772; Fax: 020-8201 8917;
Email: office@masorti.org.uk;
Web: http://www.masorti.org)
Director: Dr. H. Freedman

Federation of Synagogues
65 Watford Way, London NW4 3AQ (Tel: 020-8202 2263)
Head of Administration: G. D. Coleman

Beth Din of the Federation of Synagogues
65 Watford Way, London NW4 3AQ (Tel: 020-8202 2263)
Registrar: Rabbi S. Zaiden
Dayanim: Dayan Y. Y. Lichtenstein, Dayan B. Berkovits, Dayan M. D. Elzas

Reform Synagogues of Great Britain
The Sternberg Centre for Judaism, 80 East End Road, London N3 2SY (Tel: 020-8349 5640; Fax: 020-8343 0901; Email: admin@reformjudaism.org.uk;
Web: http://www.refsyn.org.uk)
Chief Executive: Rabbi T. Bayfield

Spanish and Portuguese Jews' Congregation
2 Ashworth Road, London W9 1JY (Tel: 020-7289 2573; Fax: 020-7289 2709)
Chief Administrator: H. Miller

Union of Liberal and Progressive Synagogues
The Montagu Centre, 21 Maple Street, London W1P 6DS (Tel: 020-7580 1663; Fax: 020-7436 4184; Email: c.middleburgh@ulps.org;
Web: http://www.ulps.org)
Executive Director: Rabbi Dr C. H. Middleburgh

Union of Orthodox Hebrew Congregations
140 Stamford Hill, London N16 6QT (Tel: 020-8802 6226; Fax: 020-8809 7092)
Principal Rabbinical Authority: H. B. Padwa

United Synagogue Head Office
735 High Road, London N12 0US (Tel: 020-8343 8989)
Chief Executive: George Willman

SIKHISM

The Sikh religion dates from the birth of Guru Nanak in the Punjab in 1469, who taught that there is one God and that different religions are like different roads leading to the same destination. He condemned religious conflict, ritualism and caste prejudices. 'Guru' means teacher but in Sikh tradition has come to represent the divine presence of God giving inner spiritual guidance. Nanak's role as the human vessel of the divine guru was passed on to nine successors, the last of whom (Guru Gobind Singh) died in 1708. The immortal guru is now

held to reside in the sacred scripture, Guru Granth Sahib, and so to be present in all Sikh gatherings.
Every gurdwara (temple) manages its own affairs and there is no central body in the UK. The Sikh Missionary Society provides an information service.

Sikh Divine Fellowship
46 Sudbury Court Drive, Harrow, Middx HA1 3TD (Tel: 020-8904 9244)
Secretary: Prof. H. Singh

Sikh Missionary Society UK
10 Featherstone Road, Southall, Middx UB2 5AA (Tel: 020-8574 1902)
Hon. General Secretary: M. Singh

World Sikh Foundation
33 Wargrave Road, South Harrow, Middx HA2 8LL (Tel: 020-8864 9228)
Managing Editor: Amar Singh Chhatwal

ZOROASTRIANISM

Zoroastrianism was founded by Zarathushtra in Persia around 1500 BC. Zarathushtra's words are recorded in five poems called the Gathas, which, together with other scriptures, forms the Avesta.

Zoroastrianism teaches that there is one God, Ahura Mazda (the Wise Lord), and that all creation stems ultimately from God; the Gathas teach that human beings have free will, are responsible for their own actions and can choose between good and evil: Zoroastrians believe that after death, the immortal soul is judged by God, and is then sent to paradise or hell.

In Zoroastrian places of worship, an urn containing fire is the central feature; the fire symbolises the presence of Ahura Mazda in every human being.

World Zoroastrian Organization
135 Tennison Road, London SE25
(Email: chairman@w-z-o.org)
Chairman: S. F. Captain

THE CHURCHES

THE CHURCH OF ENGLAND

The Church of England is the established (i.e. state) church in England and the mother church of the Anglican Communion. The Thirty-Nine Articles, a set of doctrinal statements which, together with the Book of Common Prayer of 1662 and the Ordinal, define the position of the Church of England, were adopted in their final form in 1571 and include the emphasis on personal faith and the authority of the scriptures common to the Protestant Reformation throughout Europe.

Structure
The Church of England is divided into the two provinces of Canterbury and York, each under an archbishop. The two provinces are subdivided into 44 dioceses, of which six, all within the province of Canterbury, include parts of Greater London.

Decisions on matters concerning the Church of England are made by the General Synod, established in 1970. It also discusses and expresses opinion on any other matter of religious or public interest.

The Archbishops' Council was established in January 1999. The Council undertakes strategic planning, co-ordinates the work of all the central institutions and oversees the internal and external affairs of the Church of England. It reports frequently to the General Synod and seeks Synodical approval of its decisions.

General Synod of the Church of England
Church House, Great Smith Street, London SW1P 3NZ (Tel: 020-7222 9011)
Secretary-General: P. Mawer

Archbishop and Primate of All England
Most Revd and Rt. Hon. George L. Carey, PhD, Lambeth Palace, London SE1 7JU

Church Commissioners
1 Millbank, London SW1P 3JZ (Tel: 020-7222 7010; Fax: 020-7233 0171)

The Church Commissioners were established in 1948 by the amalgamation of Queen Anne's Bounty (established 1704) and the Ecclesiastical Commissioners (established 1836). They are responsible for the management of most of the Church of England's assets, the income from which is predominantly used to pay, house and pension the clergy. The Commissioners own a number of residential estates in central London.

Dioceses which lie within or partly within Greater London

Chelmsford
8th Bishop
Rt. Revd John F. Perry, Bishopscourt, Margaretting, Ingatestone CM4 0HD (Tel: 01277-352001)

Guildford
8th Bishop
Rt. Revd John W. Gladwin, Willow Grange, Woking Road, Guildford GU4 7QS (Tel: 01483 598878; Fax: 01483 598401).

362 Religious London

London
132nd Bishop
Rt. Revd and Rt. Hon Richard J. C. Chartres, The Old Deanery, Dean's Court, London EC4V 5AA.

Rochester
106th Bishop
Rt. Revd Dr Michael Nazir-Ali, Bishopscourt, Rochester ME1 1TS (Tel: 01634-830333)

St Albans
9th Bishop
Rt. Revd Christopher W. Herbert, Abbey Gate House, St Albans AL3 4HD (Tel: 01727-853305; Fax: 01727 846715)

Southwark
9th Bishop
Rt. Revd Thomas F. Butler, PhD, LLD, Bishop's House, 38 Tooting Bec Gardens, London SW16 1QZ (Tel: 020-7403 8686)

THE ROMAN CATHOLIC CHURCH

The Roman Catholic Church is one world-wide Christian Church acknowledging as its head the Bishop of Rome, known as the Pope (Father). The Pope is held to be the successor of St Peter and thus invested with the power which was entrusted to St Peter by Jesus Christ. A direct line of succession is therefore claimed from the earliest Christian communities.

The Pope exercises spiritual authority over the Church with the advice and assistance of the Sacred College of Cardinals, the supreme council of the Church. He is also advised about the concerns of the Church locally by his ambassadors, who liaise with the Bishops' Conference in each country.

Sovereign Pontiff
His Holiness Pope John Paul II (Karol Wojtyta), born Wadowice, Poland, 18 May 1920; ordained priest 1946; appointed Archbishop of Kraków 1964; created Cardinal 1967; elected Pope 16 October 1978

Secretariat of State
Secretary of State, HE Cardinal Angelo Sodano
First Section (General Affairs), Mgr G. B. Re (Titular Archbishop of Vescovio)
Second Section (Relations with other states), Mgr J.-L. Tauran (Titular Archbishop of Telepte)

Bishops' Conference
The Roman Catholic Church in England and Wales is governed by the Bishops' Conference, membership of which includes all the Diocesan Bishops, the Apostolic Exarch of the Ukrainians, the Bishop of the Forces and the Auxiliary Bishops.

The Bishops' Standing Committee has general responsibility for continuity and policy between the plenary sessions of the Conference.

Bishops' Conference of England and Wales
39 Eccleston Square, London SW1V 1BX (Tel: 020-7630 8220)
General Secretary: Manager Arthur Roche

Apostolic Nuncio to Great Britain
H. E. Archbishop Pablo Puente, 54 Parkside, London SW19 5NE (Tel: 020-8946 1410; Fax: 020-8974 2494)

The Most Revd Archbishops and Bishops in dioceses which lie within or partly within in Greater London (The dioceses of Westminister and Southwark are led by their respective archbishops; the diocese of Brentwood is led by its bishop)

Westminster, Cormac Murphy O'Connor, Archbishop's House, Ambrosden Avenue, London SW1P 1QJ (Tel: 020-7798 9033; Fax: 020-7798 9077; Web: http://www.westminsterdiocese.org.uk)

Southwark, Michael G. Bowen, Archbishop's House, 150 St George's Road, London SE1 6HX (Tel: 020-7928 2495; Web: http://www.rcsouthwark.co.uk)

Brentwood, Thomas McMahon, Bishop's Office, Cathedral House, Ingrave Road, Brentwood, Essex CM15 8AT (Tel: 01277-232266)

ROMAN CATHOLIC CHURCHES SERVING OTHER NATIONALITIES IN LONDON

Croatian Roman Catholic Church
17 Boutflower Road, London SW11 1RE (Tel: 020-7223 3530)
Priest: Revd. Fr. Drago Beriöiæ

German Roman Catholic Church
St. Boniface, 47 Adler Street, London E1 1EE (Tel: 020-7247 9529; Fax: 020-7247 3879)
Parish Priest: Heinz Medoch

Hungarian Roman Catholic Chaplaincy
Dunstan House, 141 Gunnersbury Avenue, London W3 8LE (Tel: 020-8992 2054; Fax: 020-8992 2054)
Snr. Chaplain: Rt. Revd. Mgr. George Tutto

Lithuanian Roman Catholic Church
21 The Oval, London E2 9DT (Tel: 020-7739 8735; Email: london@ptverijonas.freeserve.co.uk)
Rector: Revd Petras Tverijonas

Slovenian Catholic Mission
62 Offley Road, London SW9 0LS (Tel: 020-7735 6655)
Chaplain: Revd. Stanislav Cikanek

OTHER CHURCHES WITH HEADQUARTERS OR REGIONAL OFFICES IN LONDON

AFRICAN AND AFRO-CARIBBEAN CHURCHES

There are more than 160 Christian churches or groups of African or Afro-Caribbean origin in the UK. These include the Apostolic Faith Church, the Cherubim and Seraphim Church, the New Testament Assembly, the New Testament Church of God, the Wesleyan Holiness Church and the Aladura Churches.

The Afro-West Indian United Council of Churches and the Council of African and Afro-Caribbean Churches UK (which was initiated as the Council of African and Allied Churches in 1979 to give one voice

Churches

to the various Christian churches of African origin in the UK) are the media through which the member churches can work jointly to provide services they cannot easily provide individually.

Afro-West Indian United Council of Churches
c/o New Testament Church of God, Arcadian Gardens, High Road, London N22 5AA (Tel: 020-8888 9427)
Secretary: Bishop E. Brown

Council of African and Afro-Caribbean Churches UK
31 Norton House, Sidney Road, London SW9 0UJ (Tel: 020-7274 5589; Fax: 020-7771 8302)
Chairman: His Grace The Most Revd Father Olu A. Abiola

THE BAPTIST CHURCH

Baptists trace their origins to John Smyth, who in 1609 in Amsterdam reinstituted the baptism of conscious believers as the basis of the fellowship of a gathered church. Members of Smyth's church established the first Baptist church in England in 1612. They came to be known as 'General' Baptists and their theology was Arminian, whereas a later group of Calvinists who adopted the baptism of believers came to be known as 'Particular' Baptists. The two sections of the Baptists were united into one body, the Baptist Union of Great Britain and Ireland, in 1891. In 1988 the title was changed to the Baptist Union of Great Britain.

Baptists emphasise the complete autonomy of the local church, although individual churches are linked in various kinds of associations. There are international bodies (such as the Baptist World Alliance) and national bodies, but some Baptist churches belong to neither. However, in Great Britain the majority of churches and associations belong to the Baptist Union of Great Britain.

Baptist Union of Great Britain
Baptist House, PO Box 44, 129 Broadway, Didcot, Oxfordshire OX11 8RT.
The General Secretary: The Revd D. R. Coffey

THE LUTHERAN CHURCH

Lutheranism is based on the teachings of Martin Luther, the German leader of the Protestant Reformation. The key doctrine is that of justification by faith alone. Lutheranism is one of the largest Protestant denominations and it is particularly strong in northern Europe and the USA. Many Lutheran churches are episcopal, while others have a different form of organisation; unity is based on doctrine rather than structure. Lutheran services in Britain are held in 17 languages, including English, to serve different nationalities. Most Lutheran churches in Britain are members of the Lutheran Council of Great Britain.

Evangelical Lutheran Church of England
110 Warwick Way, London SW1V 1SD (Tel: 020-7834 3033)
Chairman: Revd. Marvin Brammeir

Latvian Lutheran Church
17 Ivanhoe House, Balham, London SW12 8PS (Tel: 020-8673 3537)

Lutheran Council of Great Britain
30 Thanet Street, London WC1H 9QH (Tel: 020-7554 2900; Fax: 020-7383 3081;
Web: http://www.lutheran.co.uk)
General Secretary: Revd T. Bruch
Spiritual Head and Dean: Ringolds Muziks

Swedish Church (Lutheran)
6 Harcourt Street, London W1H 2BD (Tel: 020-7723 5681)
Chief Officer: Revd. Lennart Sjöström

THE METHODIST CHURCH

The Methodist movement started in England in 1729 when the Revd John Wesley, an Anglican priest, and his brother Charles met with others in Oxford and resolved to conduct their lives and study by 'rule and method'. In 1739 the Wesleys began evangelistic preaching and the first Methodist chapel was founded in Bristol in the same year. In 1744 the first annual conference was held, at which the Articles of Religion were drawn up. Doctrinal emphases included repentance, faith, the assurance of salvation, social concern and the priesthood of all believers. After John Wesley's death in 1791 the Methodists withdrew from the established Church. In 1932 the Wesleyan Methodist Church, the United Methodist Church and the Primitive Methodist Church united to form the Methodist Church in Britain as it now exists.

The governing body and supreme authority of the Methodist Church is the Conference.

President of the Conference in Great Britain (1999-2000): The Revd S. J. Burgess
Vice-President of the Conference (1999-2000): Mr. B. Thornton
Secretary of the Conference: The Revd Dr N. T. Collinson

Methodist Church, Conference Office
25 Marylebone Road, London NW1 5JR (Tel: 020-7486 5502; Fax: 020-7935 1507;
Web: http://www.methodist.org.uk)

THE (EASTERN) ORTHODOX CHURCH

The Eastern (or Byzantine) Orthodox Church is a communion of self-governing Christian churches recognising the honorary primacy of the Oecumenical Patriarch of Constantinople.

The position of Orthodox Christians is that the faith was fully defined during the period of the Oecumenical Councils. In doctrine it is strongly trinitarian, and stresses the mystery and importance of the sacraments. It is episcopal in government. The structure of the Orthodox Christian year differs from that of western Churches.

EASTERN ORTHODOX CHURCHES IN LONDON

The Patriarchate of Antioch
There are ten parishes served by 13 clergy. In London the Patriarchate is represented by the Revd Fr Samir Gholam, 1a Redhill Street, London NW1 4BG (Tel: 020-7383 0403)

364 Religious London

The Greek Orthodox Church (Patriarchate of Constantinople)

The presence of Greek Orthodox Christians in Britain dates back at least to 1677 when Archbishop Joseph Geogirenes of Samos fled from Turkish persecution and came to London. The present Greek cathedral in Moscow Road, Bayswater, was opened for public worship in 1879 and the Diocese of Thyateira and Great Britain was established in 1922. There are now 110 parishes and other communities (including monasteries) in Great Britain, served by six bishops, 95 clergy and about 100 churches.

In London the Patriarchate of Constantinople is represented by Archbishop Gregorios of Thyateira and Great Britain, 5 Craven Hill, London W2 3EN (Tel: 020-7723 4787; Fax: 020-7224 9301)

The Russian Orthodox Church (Patriarchate of Moscow) and The Russian Orthodox Church Outside Russia

The records of Russian Orthodox Church activities in Britain date from the visit to England of Tsar Peter I in the early 18th century. Clergy were sent from Russia to serve the chapel established to minister to the staff of the Imperial Russian Embassy in London.

In London the Patriarchate of Moscow is represented by Metropolitan Anthony of Sourozh, 67 Ennismore Gardens, London SW7 1NH (Fax: 020-7584 9864) He is assisted by one archbishop, one vicar bishop and 26 clergy. There are 27 parishes and smaller communities. The Russian Orthodox Church Outside Russia is represented by Archbishop Mark of Berlin, Germany and Great Britain, c/o 57 Harvard Road, London W4 4ED (Tel: 020-8742 3493). There are eight communities, including two monasteries, served by eight clergy.

Other Nationalities
Most of the Ukrainian parishes in Britain have joined the Patriarchate of Constantinople, leaving a small number of Ukrainian parishes in Britain under the care of other patriarchates (not all of which are recognised by the other Orthodox churches). The Latvian, Polish and some Belorussian parishes are also under the care of the Patriarchate of Constantinople. The Patriarchate of Romania has one parish served by two clergy. The Patriarchate of Bulgaria has one parish served by one priest. The Belorussian Autocephalous Orthodox Church has five parishes served by two priests.

British Orthodox Church
10 Heathwood Gardens, Charlton, London SE7 8EP (Tel: 020-8854 3090; Fax: 020-8854 3090;
Email: boc@cwcom.net;
Web: http://www.uk-christian.net/boc)
Metropolitan of Glastonbury: H.E. Abba Seraphim

Latvian Orthodox Church Abroad
53 Shakespeare Road, London NW7 4BA (Tel: 020-7959 1413)

Romanian Orthodox Church in London
St. Dunstan's in the West, 184A Fleet Street, London EC4A 2AE (Tel: 020-7242 6027; Fax: 020-7735 9515;
Email: ppufulete@compuserve.com)
Priest-in-Charge: Revd. S. P. Pufulete

THE ORIENTAL ORTHODOX CHURCHES
The term 'Oriental Orthodox Churches' is now generally used to describe a group of six ancient eastern churches which reject the Christological definition of the Council of Chalcedon (AD 451) and use Christological terms in different ways from the Eastern Orthodox Church.

ORIENTAL ORTHODOX CHURCHES IN THE UK

Council of Oriental Orthodox Churches
Armenian Vicarage, Iverna Gardens, London W8 6TP (Tel: 020-7937 0152)
Secretary: Deacon Aziz M. A. Nour (Tel: 020-8368 8447)

Armenian Orthodox Church (Patriarchate of Etchmiadzin)
The Armenian Orthodox Church is the longest-established Oriental Orthodox community in Great Britain. It is represented by Archbishop Yeghishe Gizirian, Armenian Primate of Great Britain, Armenian Vicarage, Iverna Gardens, London W8 6TP (Tel: 020-7937 0152)

Coptic Orthodox Church
The Coptic Orthodox Church is the largest Oriental Orthodox community in Great Britain. It has four dioceses (Birmingham; Scotland, Ireland and North-East England; the British Orthodox Church; and churches directly under Pope Shenouda III). The senior bishop in Great Britain is Metropolitan Seraphim, 10 Heathwood Gardens, London SE7 8EP (Tel: 020-8854 3090)
London Coptic Orthodox Church
Allen Street, London W8 6UX (Tel: 020-7937 5782; Fax: 020-7798 8335) Hon. Sec. Dr. F. Megally

Eritrean Orthodox Church
78 Edmund Street, Camberwell London SE5 7NR (Tel: 020-7703 5147; Fax: 020-7703 5147)
Priest in Charge: Father Yohannes Sibhatu

Ethiopian Orthodox Church
The acting head of the Ethiopian Orthodox Church in Europe is Revd Berhanu Beserat, 33 Jupiter Crescent, London NW1 8HA (Tel: 0956-513700)

London Ethiopian Orthodox Church
253b Ladbroke Grove, London W10 6HF (Tel: 020-8960 3848)
Head Priest: Very Revd. Aragawi Wolde Gabriel

Malankara Orthodox Syrian (Indian) Church
The Malankara Orthodox Syrian Church is part of the Diocese of Europe under Metropolitan Thomas Mar Makarios. His representative in Great Britain is Fr M. S. Skariah, Paramula House, 44 Newbury Road, Newbury Park, Ilford, Essex IG2 7HD (Tel: 020-8599 3836; Fax: 020-8599 3836;
Web: http://www.indian-orthodox.co.uk)
Place of worship: St Andrew by the Wardrobe Church, Queen Victoria Street, London EC4.

Syrian Orthodox Church
St. Jacob Baradaeus Parish in London and Environs, 5 Canning Road, Croydon CR0 6QA (Tel: 020-8654

7531; Fax: 020-8654 7531) Patriarch of Antioch and all the East: H. H. Mar Ignatius Zakka I. Iwas.

The Indian congregation under the Syrian Patriarch of Antioch is represented by Fr Eldhose Koungampillil, 1 Roslyn Court, Roslyn Avenue, East Barnet, Herts EN4 8DJ (Tel: 020-8368 2794)

St Matthews Westminster
20 Great Peter Street, Westminster, London SW1 2BU (Tel: 020-7222 3704; Fax: 020-7233 0255)
Priest: Revd Philip Chester

THE RELIGIOUS SOCIETY OF FRIENDS (QUAKERS)

Quakerism is a movement which was founded in the 17th century by George Fox and others in an attempt to revive what they saw as 'primitive Christianity'. The movement was based originally in the Midlands, Yorkshire and north-west England, but there are now Quakers in 36 countries around the world. The colony of Pennsylvania, founded by William Penn, was originally Quaker.

Emphasis is placed on the experience of God in daily life rather than on sacraments or religious occasions. There is no church calendar. Worship is largely silent and there are no appointed ministers, however, worshippers may speak if inspired to do so; the responsibility for conducting a meeting is shared equally among those present. Social reform and religious tolerance have always been important to Quakers, together with a commitment to non-violence in resolving disputes.

Central Office
Friends House, 173 Euston Road, London NW1 2BJ (Tel: 020-7663 1000; Fax: 020-7663 1001; Email: qhs@quaker.org.uk;
Web: http://www.quaker.org.uk)

THE SALVATION ARMY

The Salvation Army was founded by a Methodist minister, William Booth, in the east end of London in 1865, and has since become established in 104 countries world-wide. It was first known as the Christian Mission, and took its present name in 1878 when it adopted a quasi-military command structure intended to inspire and regulate its endeavours and to reflect its view that the Church was engaged in spiritual warfare. Salvationists emphasise evangelism, social work and the relief of poverty.

The world leader, known as the General, is elected by a High Council composed of the Chief of the Staff and senior ranking officers known as commissioners.

There are about 1.5 million members, 17,362 active officers (full-time ordained ministers) and 15,669 worship centres and outposts world-wide.
General: J. Gowans

Territorial HQ
101 Newington Causeway, London SE1 6BN (Tel: 020-7367 4500)
UK Territorial Commander: A. Hughes

London Central Division
First Floor, 25/27 Kings Exchange, Tileyard Road, London N7 9AH (Tel: 020-7619 6100; Fax: 020-7619 6111; Email: john.wainwright@salvationarmy.org.uk)
Divisional Commander: Major John Wainwright

London South-East
1 East Court, Enterprise Road, Maidstone, Kent ME15 6JF (Tel: 01622 775000)
Divisional Commander: Major David Jones

London North East
Maldon Road, Hatfield Peverel, Essex CM3 2HL (Tel: 01245 383000)
Divisional Commander: Lt. Col David Phillips

THE SEVENTH-DAY ADVENTIST CHURCH

The Seventh-day Adventist Church was founded in 1863 in the USA. Its members look forward to the second coming of Christ and observe the Sabbath (the seventh day) as a day of rest, worship and ministry. The Church bases its faith and practice wholly on the Bible and has developed 27 fundamental beliefs.

In the British Isles the administrative organisation of the church is arranged in three tiers: the local churches; the regional conferences for south England, north England, Wales, Scotland and Ireland; and the national 'union' conference.

There are about 9 million Adventists and 42,321 churches in 204 countries world-wide. In the UK and Ireland there are 19,702 members, 152 ministers and 238 churches.

President of the British Union Conference: Pastor C. R. Perry
South England Conference Office: Stanborough Park, Watford WD2 6JP (Tel: 01923-672251)

THE UNITED REFORMED CHURCH

The United Reformed Church was formed by the union of most of the Congregational churches in England and Wales with the Presbyterian Church of England in 1972.

Congregationalism dates from the mid 16th century. It is Calvinistic in doctrine, and its followers form independent self-governing congregations bound under God by covenant, a principle laid down in the writings of Robert Browne (1550-1633).

The Presbyterian Church in England also dates from the mid 16th century, and was Calvinistic and evangelical in its doctrine. It was governed by a hierarchy of courts.

In 1981 a further unification took place, with the Reformed Association of Churches of Christ becoming part of the URC. In 2000 the United Reformed Church and the Congregational Union of Scotland United under the name of the United Reformed Church.

The General Assembly is the central body, and is made up of equal numbers of ministers and lay members.

General Secretary: Revd A. G. Burnham, 86 Tavistock Place, London WC1H 9RT (Tel: 020-7916 2020; Fax: 020-7916 1928; Email: agburnam@urc.org.uk; Web: http://www.urc.org.uk)

NON-TRINITARIAN CHURCHES

THE CHURCH OF CHRIST, SCIENTIST

The Church of Christ, Scientist was founded by Mary Baker Eddy in the USA in 1879 to 'reinstate primitive Christianity and its lost element of healing'. Christian Science teaches the need for spiritual regeneration and salvation from sin, but is best known for its reliance on prayer alone in the healing of sickness. Adherents believe that such healing is a law, or Science, and is in direct line with that practised by Jesus Christ (revered, not as God, but as the Son of God) and by the early Christian Church.

The denomination consists of The First Church of Christ, Scientist, in Boston, Massachusetts, USA (the Mother Church) and its branch churches in over 60 countries world-wide. Branch churches are democratically governed by their members, while a five-member Board of Directors, based in Boston, is authorised to transact the business of the Mother Church. The Bible and Mary Baker Eddy's book, Science and Health with Key to the Scriptures, are used at services; there are no clergy. Those engaged in full-time healing are called practitioners.

Christian Science Committee on Publication
9 Elysium Gate, 126 New Kings Road, London SW6 4LZ (Tel: 020-7384 0600; Fax: 020-731 8600; Email: joynesh@compub.org;
Web: http://www.tfccs.com)
District Manager: H. Joynes

THE CHURCH OF JESUS CHRIST OF LATTER-DAY SAINTS

The Church (often referred to as 'the Mormons') was founded in New York State, USA, in 1830, and came to Britain in 1837. Mormons are Christians who claim to belong to the 'Restored Church' of Jesus Christ. They believe that true Christianity died when the last original apostle died, but that it was given back to the world by God and Christ through Joseph Smith, the Church's founder and first president. They accept and use the Bible as scripture, but believe in continuing revelation from God and use additional scriptures, including The Book of Mormon: Another Testament of Jesus Christ. The importance of the family is central to the Church's beliefs and practices.

The Church has no paid ministry; local congregations are headed by a leader chosen from amongst their number.

President of the England London Mission: Steven C. Wheelwright; Elder S. J. Condie

London Mission, 64 Exhibition Road, London SW7 2PA (Tel: 020-7584 7553; Fax: 020-7581 5199)

JEHOVAH'S WITNESSES

The movement now known as Jehovah's Witnesses grew from a Bible study group formed by Charles Taze Russell in 1872 in Pennsylvania, USA. In 1896 it adopted the name of the Watch Tower Bible and Tract Society, and in 1931 its members became known as Jehovah's Witnesses. Jehovah's (God's) Witnesses believe in the Bible as the word of God, and consider it to be inspired and historically accurate. They take the scriptures literally, except where there are obvious indications that they are figurative or symbolic, and reject the doctrine of the Trinity. Witnesses also believe that the earth will remain for ever and that all those approved of by Jehovah will have eternal life on a cleansed and beautified earth; only 144,000 will go to heaven to rule with Christ. They believe that the second coming of Christ began in 1914 and his thousand-year reign on earth is imminent, and that Armageddon (a final battle in which evil will be defeated) will precede Christ's rule of peace. They refuse to take part in military service, and do not accept blood transfusions. They publish two magazines, The Watchtower and Awake!

There is no paid ministry, but each congregation has elders assigned to look after various duties and every Witness is assigned homes to visit in their congregation. British Isles Headquarters, Watch Tower House, The Ridgeway, London NW7 1RN (Tel: 020-8906 2211; 020-8371 0051; Email: pr@wtbts.org.uk;
Web: http://www.watchtower.org)

UNITARIAN AND FREE CHRISTIAN CHURCHES

Unitarianism has its historical roots in the Judaeo-Christian tradition but rejects the deity of Christ and the doctrine of the trinity. It allows the individual to embrace insights from all the world's faiths and philosophies, as there is no fixed creed. It is accepted that beliefs may evolve in the light of personal experience.

The first avowedly Unitarian place of worship in the British Isles opened in London in 1774.

General Assembly of Unitarian and Free Christian Churches
Essex Hall, 1-6 Essex Street, London WC2R 3HY (Tel: 020-7240 2384; Fax: 020-7240 3089;
Email: ga@unitarian.org.uk;
Web: http://www.unitarian.org.uk)
General Secretary: J. J. Teagle

SOCIETIES AND INSTITUTIONS

… Societies and Institutions 369

SOCIETIES AND INSTITUTIONS

The list below contains a selection, in alphabetical order, of societies, institutions, charities and professional associations based in London. Where an organisation is very relevant to a particular section of the book, for example, Environmental London, an entry will appear in that section and not in the list below.

Action for Blind People
14-16 Verney Road, London, SE16 3DZ (Tel: 020-7732 8771; Email: central@afbp.org)
Chief Executive: S. Remington

Actors' Charitable Trust
255-256 Africa House, 67-78 Kingsway, London, WC2B 6BD (Tel: 020-7242 0111; Fax: 020-7242 0234; Email: tact.actors@virgin.net)
General Secretary: B. Batchelor

Actors' Church Union
St Paul's Church, Bedford Street, London, WC2E 9ED (Tel: 020-7836 5221)
Senior Chaplain: Canon W. Hall

Advertising Standards Authority
2 Torrington Place, London, WC1E 7HW (Tel: 020-7580 5555; Fax: 020-7631 3051;
Web: http://www.asa.org.uk)
Director-General: C. Graham

African Medical and Research Foundation
4 Grosvenor Place, London, SW1X 7HJ (Tel: 020-7201 6070; Fax: 020-7201 6170; Email: amref.uk@amref.org; Web: http://www.amref.org)
Executive Director: A. Héroys

Air League
Broadway House, Tothill Street, London, SW1H 9NS (Tel: 020-7222 8463; Fax: 020-7222 8462; Email: exec@airleague.co.uk;
Web: http://www.airleague.co.uk)
Director: E. Cox

Alzheimer's Society
Gordon House, 10 Greencoat Place, London, SW1P 1PH (Tel: 020-7306 0606; Fax: 020-7306 0808; Email: info@alzheimers.org.uk;
Web: http://www.alzheimers.org.uk)
Chief Executive: H. Cayton

Amnesty International United Kingdom
99-119 Rosebery Avenue, London, EC1R 4RE (Tel: 020-7814 6200; Fax: 020-7833 1510;
Web: http://www.amnesty.org.uk/)
Director: Ms K. Allen

Ancient Monuments Society
St Ann's Vestry Hall, 2 Church Entry, London, EC4V 5HB (Tel: 020-7236 3934; Fax: 020-7329 3677)
Secretary: J. J. Saunders, MBE

Anglo-Arab Association
The Arab British Centre, 21 Collingham Road, London, SW5 0NU (Tel: 020-7373 8414; Fax: 020-7835 2088)
Executive Director: A. C. W. Lee

Anglo-Belgian Society
5 Hartley Close, Bickley, Kent, BR1 2TP (Tel: 020-8467 8442)
Hon. Secretary: P. R. Bresnan

Anglo-Brazilian Society
32 Green Street, London, W1Y 3FD (Tel: 020-7493 8493; Email: anglo@brazeliansociety.freeserve.co.uk)
Secretary: J. Wright

Anglo-Danish Society
25 New Street Square, London, EC4A 3LN
Chairman: H. Castenskiold, OBE

Anglo-Norse Society
25 Belgrave Square, London, SW1X 8QD (Tel: 020-7591 5500; Fax: 020-7245 6993)
Chairman: Sir John Robson KCMG

Anthroposophical Society in Great Britain
Rudolf Steiner House, 35 Park Road, London, NW1 6XT (Tel: 020-7723 4400; Fax: 020-7724 4364; Email: rsh@cix.compulink.co.uk;
Web: http://www.anth.org.uk)
General Secretary: N. C. Thomas

Anti-Slavery International
Thomas Clarkson House, The Stableyard, Broomgrove Road, London, SW9 9TL (Tel: 020-7501 8920; Fax: 020-7738 4110; Email: antislavery@antislavery.org; Web: http://www.antislavery.org)
Director: M. Dottridge

Architectural Heritage Fund
Clareville House, 26-27 Oxendon Street, London, SW1Y 4EL (Tel: 020-7925 0199; Fax: 020-7930 0295; Email: ahf@ahfund.org.uk;
Web: http://www.ahfund.org.uk)
Secretary: J. Thompson

Army Benevolent Fund
41 Queen's Gate, London, SW7 5HR (Tel: 020-7591 2000; Fax: 020-7584 0889)
Controller: Maj.-Gen. M. D. Regan CB, OBE

Arthritis Care
18 Stephenson Way, London, NW1 2HD (Tel: 020-7916 1500; Fax: 020-7916 1505;
Web: http://www.arthritiscare.org.uk)
Chief Executive: R. Gutch

Asian Family Counselling Service
76 Church Road, Hanwell, London, W7 1LB (Tel: 020-8567 5616; Fax: 020-8567 5616;
Email: afcs99@hotmail.com)
Director: R. Atma

Societies and Institutions

ASLIB (Association for Information Management)
Staple Hall, Stone House Court, London, EC3A 7PB (Tel: 020-7903 0000; Fax: 020-7903 0011; Email: aslib@aslib.com; Web: http://www.aslib.com)
Chief Executive: R. Bowes

Association of Accounting Technicians
154 Clerkenwell Road, London, EC1R 5AD (Tel: 020-7837 8600; Fax: 020-7837 6970; Email: aatuk@dial.pipex.com; Web: http://www.aat.co.uk)
Chief Executive: Ms J. Scott Paul

Association of Anaesthetists of Great Britain and Ireland
9 Bedford Square, London, WC1B 3RA (Tel: 020-7631 1650; Fax: 020-7631 4352; Email: info@aagbi.org; Web: http://www.aagbi.org)
Hon. Secretary: Dr P. G. M. Wallace

Association of British Correspondence Colleges
PO Box 17926, London, SW19 3WB (Tel: 020-8544 9559; Fax: 020-8540 7657; Email: abcc@msn.com; Web: http://www.homestudy.org.uk)
Secretary: Mrs H. Owen

Association of British Insurers
51 Gresham Street, London, EC2V 7HQ (Tel: 020-7600 3333)
Director-General: Ms M. Francis

Association of British Travel Agents (ABTA)
68-71 Newman Street, London, W1P 4AH (Tel: 020-7637 2444; Fax: 020-7637 0713; Email: abta@abta.co.uk; Web: http://www.abtanet.com)
Chief Executive: I. Reynolds

Association of Consulting Engineers
Alliance House, 12 Caxton Street, London, SW1H 0QL (Tel: 020-7222 6557; Fax: 020-7222 0750; Email: consult@acenet.co.uk; Web: http://www.acenet.co.uk)
Chief Executive: N. Bennett

Association of Corporate Treasurers
Ocean House, 10-12 Little Trinity Lane, London, EC4V 2DJ (Tel: 020-7213 9728; Fax: 020-7248 2591; Email: enquiries@treasurers.co.uk; Web: http://www.corporate-treasurers.co.uk)
Director-General: Dr D. Creed

Association of Friendly Societies
10-13 Lovat Lane, London, EC3R 8DT (Tel: 020-7397 9550; Fax: 020-7397 9551; Email: info@afs.org.uk)
General Secretary: Miss M. Poole

Association of London Borough Planning Officers
Civic Centre, Stockwell Close, Bromley, Kent, BR1 3UH (Tel: 020-8313 4441; Fax: 020-8313 4460; Email: stuartmacmillan@bromley.gov.uk)
Secretary/Treasurer: S. Macmillan

Association of Royal Navy Officers
70 Porchester Terrace, London, W2 3TP (Tel: 020-7402 5231; Fax: 020-7402 5533; Email: arno@eurosurf.com; Web: http://www.eurosurf.com/ARNO)
Secretary: Lt.-Cdr. I. M. P. Coombes

Association of Sports Historians
Ground Floor Offices, 13-16 Faro Close, Coates Hill Road, Bromley, Kent, BR1 2RR (Tel: 020-8467 1951)
Chief Executive: C. Harte

Baltic Air Charter Association
The Baltic Exchange, St Mary Axe, London, EC3A 8BH (Tel: 020-7623 5501; Fax: 020-7623 1623)
Chairman: Capt. N. J. Harris

BackCare
16 Elmtree Road, Teddington, Middx, TW11 8ST (Tel: 020-8977 5474; Fax: 020-8943 5318; Email: back-pain@compuserve.com; Web: http://www.backpain.org)
Executive Director: Ms E. Tait

Baltic Exchange
St Mary Axe, London, EC3A 8BH (Tel: 020-7623 5501; Fax: 020-7369 1622; Email: enquiries@balticexchange.co.uk; Web: http://www.balticexchange.com)
Chief Executive: J. Buckley

Baltic Exchange Charitable Society
38 St Mary Axe, London, EC3A 8BH (Tel: 020-7369 1643)
Secretary: D. A. Painter

Barnardo's
Tanners Lane, Barkingside, Ilford, Essex, IG6 1QG (Tel: 020-8550 8822; Fax: 020-8551 6870)
Chief Executive: R. Singleton

Barristers' Benevolent Association
14 Gray's Inn Road, London, WC1R 5JP (Tel: 020-7242 4761; Fax: 020-7831 5366; Email: linda@thebba.swinternet.co.uk)
Secretary: Mrs L. C. Carlier

Battersea Arts Centre
Lavender Hill, London, SW11 5TN (Tel: 020-7223 6557; Fax: 020-7978 5207; Email: mailbox@bac.org.uk; Web: http://www.bac.org.uk)
Director: T. Morris

BI - British Invisibles
Windsor House, 39 King Street, London, EC2V 8DQ (Tel: 020-7600 1198; Fax: 020-7606 4248; Email: enquiries@bi.org.uk; Web: http://www.bi.org.uk)
Chief Executive: E. J. Seddon

Bibliographical Society
c/o The Wellcome Library, 183 Euston Road, London, NW1 2BE (Tel: 020-7611 7244; Fax: 020-7611 8703; Email: jm93@dial.pipex.com; Web: http://www.bibsoc.org.uk)
Hon. Secretary: D. Pearson

Societies and Institutions 371

Biochemical Society
59 Portland Place, London, W1N 3AJ (Tel: 020-7580 5530; Fax: 020-7637 3626;
Email: genadmin@biochemistry.org;
Web: http://www.biochemistry.org)
Executive Secretary: G. D. Jones

Book Aid International
39-41 Coldharbour Lane, London, SE5 9NR (Tel: 020-7733 3577; Fax: 020-7978 8006;
Email: info@bookaid.org;
Web: http://www.bookaid.org)
Director: Mrs S. Harrity, MBE

Book Trust
Book House, 45 East Hill, London, SW18 2QZ (Tel: 020-8516 2977; Fax: 020-8516 2978;
Web: http://www.booktrust.org.uk)
Executive Director: C. Meade

Booksellers Association of the UK and Ireland Ltd
Minster House, 272 Vauxhall Bridge Road, London, SW1V 1BA (Tel: 020-7834 5477; Fax: 020-7834 8812;
Email: mail@booksellers.org.uk;
Web: http://www.booksellers.org.uk)
Chief Executive: T. E. Godfray

Botanical Society of the British Isles
c/o Department of Botany, The Natural History Museum, Cromwell Road, London, SW7 5BD (Tel: 020-7938 8701; Email: bsbihgs@aol.com;
Web: http://www.members.aol.com/bsbihgs)
Hon. General Secretary: R. Gwynn Ellis

British Association for Early Childhood Education
136 Lavell Street, London, E1 2JA (Tel: 020-7539 5400; Fax: 020-7539 5409;
Email: office@early-education.org.uk;
Web: http:/www.early-education.org.uk)
Chief Executive: Ms W. Scott

Britain-Nepal Society
3C Gunnersbury Avenue, London, W5 3NH (Tel: 020-8992 0173)
Hon. Secretary: Mrs P. Mellor

British-Russia Centre and British East West Centre
1 Nine Elms Lane, London, SW8 5NQ (Tel: 020-7498 6640, Fax: 020-7498 4660,
Email: mail@briteastwest.org.uk;
Web: http://www.briteastwest.org.uk)
Interim Director: Ms F. Cave, MBE

British Association of Composers and Songwriters
British Music House, 25-27 Berners Street, London, W1P 3DB (Tel: 020-7629 0992; Fax: 020-7636 2929;
Email: info@britishacademy.com;
Web: http://www.britishacademy.com)
Chief Executive: C. Green

British Academy of Forensic Sciences
Anaesthetic Unit, The Royal London Hospital, Whitechapel, London, E1 1BB (Tel: 020-7377 9201)
Secretary-General: Dr P. J. Flynn

British Antique Dealers' Association
20 Rutland Gate, London, SW7 1BD (Tel: 020-7589 4128; Fax: 020-7581 9083; Web: http://www.bada.org)
Secretary-General: Mrs E. J. Dean

British Association for the Advancement of Science
23 Savile Row, London, W1X 2NB (Tel: 020-7973 3500; Fax: 020-7973 3065;
Web: http://www.britassoc.org.uk)
Chief Executive: Dr P. Briggs

British Association of Communicators in Business
42 Borough High Street, London, SE1 1XW (Tel: 020-7378 7139; Fax: 020-7378 7140;
Email: bacb@globalnet.co.uk;
Web: http://www.bacb.org)
Secretary-General: Mrs K. Jones

British Astronomical Association
Burlington House, Piccadilly, London, W1V 9AG (Web: http://www.ast.cam.ac.uk/~baa)
Assistant Secretary: Miss P. M. Barber

British Board of Film Classification
3 Soho Square, London, W1V 6HD (Tel: 020-7439 7961; Fax: 020-7287 0141;
Email: Webmaster@bbfc.co.uk;
Web: http://www.bbfc.co.uk)
Director: R. Duval

British Chambers of Commerce
Manning House, 22 Carlisle Place, London, SW1P 1JA (Tel: 020-7565 2000; Fax: 020-7565 2049;
Email: info@britishchambers.org.uk;
Web: http://www.britishchambers.org.uk)
Director-General: C. Humphries, CBE

British Commonwealth Ex-Services League
48 Pall Mall, London, SW1Y 5JG (Tel: 020-7973 7263; Fax: 020-7973 7308)
Secretary-General: Lt.-Col. S. Pope, OBE, RM

British Copyright Council
29-33 Berners Street, London, W1P 4AA (Tel: 01986-788122; Fax: 01906-788847;
Email: copyright@bcc2.demon.co.uk)
Secretary: Ms J. Ibbotson

British Dental Association
64 Wimpole Street, London, W1M 8AL (Tel: 020-7935 0875; Fax: 020-7487 5232;
Email: enquiries@bda-dentistry.org.uk;
Web: http://www.bda-dentistry.org.uk)
Chief Executive: J. M. G. Hunt

British Diabetic Association
10 Queen Anne Street, London, W1M 0BD (Tel: 020-7323 1531; Fax: 020-7637 3644;
Email: bda@diabetes.org.uk;
Web: http://www.diabetes.org.uk)
Chief Executive: P. Streets

British Executive Service Overseas
164 Vauxhall Bridge Road, London, SW1V 4RB (Tel: 020-7630 0644; Fax: 020-7630 0624;
Email: team@beso.org; Web: http://www.beso.org)
Chief Executive: G. Ramsey, CBE

372 Societies and Institutions

British Foundation of Women Graduates
4 Mandeville Courtyard, 142 Battersea Park Road, London, SW11 4NB (Tel: 020-7498 8037; Fax: 020-7498 8037; Email: bfwg@bfwg.demon.co.uk; Web: http://homepages.wyenet.co.uk/bfwg)
Secretary: Mrs A. B. Stein

British Heart Foundation
14 Fitzhardinge Street, London, W1H 4DH (Tel: 020-7935 0185; Fax: 020-7486 5820; Web: http://www.bhf.org.uk)
Director-General: Maj.-Gen. L. F. H. Busk, CB

British Homoeopathic Association
27A Devonshire Street, London, W1N 1RJ
General Secretary: Mrs E. Segall

British Hospitality Association
Queens House, 55-56 Lincoln's Inn Fields, London, WC2A 3BH (Tel: 020-7404 7744; Fax: 020-7404 7799; Email: bha@bha.org.uk; Web: http://www.bha-online.org.uk)
Chief Executive: B. Cotton

British Humanist Association
47 Theobald's Road, London, WC1X 8SP (Tel: 020-7430 0908; Email: info@humanism.org.uk; Web: http://www.humanism.org.uk)
Executive Director: R. Ashby

British Institute in Eastern Africa
10 Carlton House Terrace, London, SW1Y 5AH (Tel: 020-7969 5201; Fax: 020-7969 5401; Email: biea@britac.ac.uk)
London Secretary: Mrs J. Moyo

British Institute of Archaeology at Ankara
10 Carlton House Terrace, London, SW1Y 5AH (Tel: 020-7969 5204; Fax: 020-7969 5401; Email: biaa@britac.ac.uk; Web: http://www.britac.ac.uk/institutes/ankara)
Director: Dr R. J. Matthews

British Institute of Human Rights
8th Floor, King's College London, 75-79 York Road, London, SE1 7AW (Tel: 020-7401 2712)
Director: Ms S. Cooke

British Institute of Persian Studies
c/o The British Academy, 10 Carlton House Terrace, London, SW1Y 5AH (Tel: 020-7969 5203; Fax: 020-7969 5401; Email: bips@britac.ac.uk; Web: http://www.britac.ac.uk/institutes/bips)
Hon. Secretary: Dr R. Gleave

British Institute of Radiology
36 Portland Place, London, W1N 4AT (Tel: 020-7307 1400; Fax: 020-7307 1414; Email: admin@bir.org.uk; Web: http://www.bir.org.uk)
General Secretary: T. Hudson

British Interplanetary Society
27-29 South Lambeth Road, London, SW8 1SZ (Tel: 020-7735 3160; Fax: 020-7820 1504; Email: bis.bis@virgin.net)
Executive Secretary: Ms S. A. Jones

British Israel World Federation
8 Blades Court, Deodar Road, London, SW15 2NU (Tel: 020-8877 9010; Fax: 020-8871 4770; Email: admin@britishisrael.co.uk; Web: http://www.britishisrael.co.uk)
Secretary: A. E. Gibb

British Lung Foundation
78 Hatton Garden, London, EC1N 8LD (Tel: 020-7831 5831; Fax: 020-7831 5832; Email: blf_users@gpiag-asthma.org; Web: http://www.lunguk.org)
Chief Executive: B. Walden

British Medical Association
BMA House, Tavistock Square, London, WC1H 9JP (Tel: 020-7387 4499; Fax: 020-7383 6400; Web: http://www.bma.org.uk)
Secretary: Dr E. M. Armstrong

British Music Hall Society
82 Fernlea Road, London, SW12 9RW (Tel: 020-8673 2175)
Hon. Secretary: Mrs D. Masterton

British Music Information Centre
10 Stratford Place, London, W1N 9AE (Tel: 020-7499 8567; Fax: 020-7499 4795; Email: info@bmic.co.uk; Web: http://www.bmic.co.uk)
Director: M. Greenall

British Naturalists' Association
1 Bracken Mews, London, E4 7UT
(Web: http://www.bna-naturalists.org)
Hon. Membership Secretary: Mrs Y. H. Griffiths

British Nuclear Energy Society
1-7 Great George Street, London, SW1P 3AA (Tel: 020-7665 2241; Fax: 020-7799 1325; Email: tillbrook_a@ice.org.uk; Web: http://www.bnes.com)
Executive Officer: A. Tillbrook

British Nutrition Foundation
High Holborn House, 52-54 High Holborn, London, WC1V 6RQ (Tel: 020-7404 6504; Fax: 020-7404 6747; Email: postbox@nutrition.org.uk; Web: http://www.nutrition.org.uk)
Director-General: Prof. R. S. Pickard, Ph.D, CBiol, FIBiol

British Orthopaedic Association
c/o The Royal College of Surgeons of England, 35-43 Lincoln's Inn Fields, London, WC2A 3PN (Tel: 020-7405 6507; Fax: 020-7831 2676; Email: secretary@boa.ac.uk; Web: http://www.boa.ac.uk)
Chief Executive: D. C. Adams

British Pharmacological Society
16 Angel Gate, City Road, London, EC1V 2SG (Fax: 020-7417 0114; Email: admin@bphs.org.uk; Web: http://www.bphs.org.uk)
President: Prof. N. G. Bowery

Societies and Institutions 373

British Records Association
40 Northampton Road, London, EC1R 0HB (Tel: 020-7833 0428; Fax: 020-7833 0416; Email: britishrecordsassn@charity.vfree.com)
Hon. Secretary: Mrs E. Hughes

British Red Cross
9 Grosvenor Crescent, London, SW1X 7EJ (Tel: 020-7235 5454; Fax: 020-7245 6315; Email: information@redcross.org.uk; Web: http://www.redcross.org.uk)
Director-General: S. Younger

British Refugee Council
Bondway House, 3-9 Bondway, London, SW8 1SJ (Tel: 020-7820 3000; Fax: 020-7820 3004; Email: info@refugeecouncil.demon.co.uk; Web: http://www.refugeecouncil.org)
Chief Executive: N. Hardwick

British Standards Institution (BSI)
389 Chiswick High Road, London, W4 4AL (Tel: 020-8996 9000; Fax: 020-8996 7344)
Chairman: V. E. Thomas, CBE

British Union for the Abolition of Vivisection
16A Crane Grove, London, N7 8NN (Tel: 020-7700 4888; Fax: 020-7700 0252; Email: info@buav.org; Web: http://www.buav.org)
Chief Executive: Ms M. Thew

British Veterinary Association
7 Mansfield Street, London, W1M 0AT (Tel: 020-7636 6541; Fax: 020-7436 2970; Email: bvahq@bva.co.uk; Web: http://www.bva.co.uk)
Chief Executive: J. H. Baird

British Wood Preserving and Damp-Proofing Association
6 The Office Village, 4 Romford Road, London, E15 4EA (Tel: 020-8519 2588; Fax: 020-8519 3444; Email: info@bwpda.co.uk; Web: http://www.bwpda.co.uk)
Director: Dr C. R. Coggins

Building Societies Association
3 Savile Row, London, W1X 1AF (Tel: 020-7437 0655; Fax: 020-7734 6416; Email: info@bsa.org.uk; Web: http://www.bsa.org.uk)
Director-General: A. Coles

Business Archives Council
3rd and 4th Floors, 101 Whitechapel High Street, London, E1 7RE (Tel: 020-7247 0024; Fax: 020-7422 0026)
Secretary-General: Ms W. S. Quinn-Robinson

Cameron Fund
Tavistock House North, Tavistock Square, London, WC1H 9HR (Tel: 020-7388 0796)
Secretary: Mrs J. Martin

Campaign for an Independent Britain
81 Ashmole Street, London, SW8 1NF (Tel: 020-8340 0314; Fax: 020-7582 7021; Email: 106342.2657@compuserve.com; Web: http://www.ourworld.compuserve.com/homepages/cibhq/cibhp.htm)
Hon. Secretary: Sir Robin Williams, Bt.

Campaign for Nuclear Disarmament (CND)
162 Holloway Road, London, N7 8DQ (Tel: 020-7700 2393; Fax: 020-7700 2357; Email: enquiries@cnduk.org; Web: http://www.cnduk.org)
Chair: D. Knight

Canada-United Kingdom Chamber of Commerce
38 Grosvenor Street, London, W1X 0DP (Tel: 020-7258 6572; Fax: 020-7258 6594; Email: info@canada-uk.org; Web: http://www.canada-uk.org)
Executive Director: M. Hall

Cancer Research Campaign
10 Cambridge Terrace, London, NW1 4JL (Tel: 020-7224 1333; Fax: 020-7487 4310; Web: http://www.crc.org.uk)
Director-General: Prof. J. G. McVie

Capital Housing
318-320 St Paul's Road, London, N1 2LF (Tel: 020-7354 2909; Fax: 020-7359 9690)
Chief Executive: B. Symons

Carers National Association
Ruth Pitter House, 20-25 Glasshouse Yard, London, EC1A 4JT (Tel: 020-7490 8818; Fax: 020-7490 8824; Email: internet@ukcarers.org; Web: http://www.carersuk.demon.co.uk)
Chief Executive: Ms D. Whitworth

Cathedrals Fabric Commission for England
Fielden House, 13 Little College Street, London, SW1P 3SH (Tel: 020-7898 1863; Fax: 020-7898 1881; Email: enquiries@cfce.c-of-e.org.uk)
Secretary: Dr R. Gem

Catholic Housing Aid Society
209 Old Marylebone Road, London, NW1 5QT (Tel: 020-7723 7273; Fax: 020-7723 5943; Email: info@chasnat.demon.co.uk; Web: http://www.chasnat.demon.co.uk)
Director: Ms R. Rafferty

Catholic Truth Society
40-46 Harleyford Road, London, SE11 5AY (Tel: 020-7640 0042; Fax: 020-7640 0046; Email: ctspublisher@mcmail.com)
General Secretary: F. Martin

Catholic Union of Great Britain
St Maximilian Kolbe House, 63 Jeddo Road, London, W12 9EE (Tel: 020-8749 1321 or 01474-702439; Fax: 020-8735 0816)
Secretary: P. H. Higgs

Societies and Institutions

Central Bureau for International Education and Training
10 Spring Gardens, London, SW1A 2BA (Tel: 020-7389 4487)
Director: P. Upton

Central Council of Physical Recreation
Francis House, Francis Street, London, SW1P 1DE (Tel: 020-7828 3163; Fax: 020-7630 7046; Email: admin@ccpr.org.uk)
Chief Executive: M. Denton

Centre for Metropolitan History
Institute of Historical Research, Senate House, Malet Street, London, WC1E 7HU (Tel: 020-7862 8790; Fax: 020-7862 8793; Email: o-myhill@sas.ac.uk; Web: http://ihr.sas.ac.uk/ihr/associnstits)
Director: Dr D. J. Keene

Central London Dial-a-Ride
Hathaway House, 7D Woodfield Road, London, W9 2BA (Tel: 020-7266 6100; Fax: 020-7266 5079)
Company Manager: Ms J. Cobhill

Central and Cecil Housing Trust
2 Priory Road, Kew, Richmond, Surrey, TW9 3DG (Tel: 020-8940 9828; Fax: 020-8332 1044)
Chief Executive: G. Brighton

Centre for Economic Policy Research
90-98 Goswell Road, London, EC1V 7RR (Tel: 020-7878 2900; Fax: 020-7878 2999; Web: http://www.cepr.org)
Chief Executive Officer: S. Yeo

Centre for Independent Transport Research in London (CILT)
3rd Floor, Universal House, 88-94 Wentworth Street, London, E1 7SA (Tel: 020-7247 1302; Fax: 020-7247 4725; Email: cilt@dial.pipex.com; Web: http://www.cilt.dial.pipex.com/)
Chair: R. Higman

Centre for Policy on Ageing
25-31 Ironmonger Row, London, EC1V 3QP (Tel: 020-7253 1787; Fax: 020-7490 4206; Email: cpa@cpa.org.uk; Web: http://www.cpa.org.uk)
Director: Dr G. Dalley

Centrepoint
Neil House, 7 Whitechapel Road, London, E1 1DU (Tel: 020-7426 5300; Fax: 020-7426 5301; Web: http://www.centrepoint.org.uk)
Chief Executive: V. O. Adebowale

Chadwick Trust
Department of Civil and Environmental Engineering, University College London, Gower Street, London, WC1E 6BT (Tel: 020-7380 7327/7766; Fax: 020-7679 7920; Email: t.jastrzebska@ucl.ac.uk)
Secretary to the Trustees: Ms T. Jastrzebska

Chartered Institute of Arbitrators
24 Angel Gate, City Road, London, EC1V 2RS (Tel: 020-7837 4483; Fax: 020-7837 4185; Email: info@arbitrators.org; Web: http://www.arbitrators.org)
Secretary-General: D. Farrar-Hockley, MC

Chartered Institute of Bankers
90 Bishopsgate, London, EC2N 4DQ (Tel: 020-7444 7111; Fax: 020-7444 7115; Email: customerservices@cib.org.uk; Web: http://www.cib.org.uk)
Chief Executive: G. Shreeve

Chartered Institute of Logistics and Transport
80 Portland Place, London, W1N 4DP (Tel: 020-7467 9400; Fax: 020-7467 9440; Email: enquiry@iolt.org.uk; Web: http://www.iolt.org.uk)
Chief Executive: G. A. Ewer, CB, CBE

Chartered Institute of Patent Agents
Staple Inn Buildings, High Holborn, London, WC1V 7PZ (Tel: 020-7405 9450; Fax: 020-7430 0471; Email: mail@cipa.org.uk; Web: http://www.cipa.org.uk)
Secretary: M. C. Ralph

Chartered Institute of Taxation
12 Upper Belgrave Street, London, SW1X 8BB (Tel: 020-7235 9381; Fax: 020-7235 2562; Email: post@ciot.org.uk)
Secretary-General: R. A. Dommett

Chartered Institution of Water and Environmental Management
15 John Street, London, WC1N 2EB (Tel: 020-7831 3110; Fax: 020-7405 4967; Email: admin@ciwem.org.uk; Web: http://www.ciwem.org.uk)
Executive Director: N. Reeves

Chartered Insurance Institute
20 Aldermanbury, London, EC2V 7HY (Tel: 020-8989 8464; Fax: 020-8530 3052; Email: customer.serv@cii.co.uk; Web: http://www.cii.co.uk)
Director-General: D. E. Bland, OBE, Ph.D

The Children's Society
Edward Rudolf House, Margery Street, London, WC1X 0JL (Tel: 020-7841 4000; Fax: 020-7837 0211; Email: info@childsoc.org.uk; Web: http://www.the-childrens-society.org.uk)
Chief Executive: I. Sparks

China Association
Swire House, 59 Buckingham Gate, London, SW1E 6AJ (Tel: 020-7821 3220; Fax: 020-7630 0353)
Executive Director: D. F. L. Turner

Church Mission Society
Partnership House, 157 Waterloo Road, London, SE1 8UU (Tel: 020-7928 8681; Fax: 020-7401 3215; Email: info@cms-uk.org; Web: http://www.cms-uk.org)
General Secretary: Revd T. J. Dakin

Societies and Institutions 375

Church Monuments Society
c/o Society of Antiquaries, Burlington House, Piccadilly, London, W1V 0HS (Tel: 020-7734 0193)
Hon. Secretary: C. J. Easter

Church Union
Faith House, 7 Tufton Street, London, SW1P 3QN (Tel: 020-7222 6952; Fax: 020-7976 7180;
Email: jmiller@thechurchunion.demon.co.uk;
Web: http://www.churchunion.care4free.net)
House Manager: Mrs J. Miller

Churches Main Committee
Fielden House, 13 Little College Street, London, SW1P 3SH (Tel: 020-7222 4984; Fax: 020-7898 1899; Email: cmc@c-of-e.org.uk)
Secretary: D. Taylor Thompson, CB

City Business Library
Brewers Hall Garden, London, EC2V 5BX (Tel: 020-7332 1812; Fax: 020-7332 1847)

City Parochial Foundation
6 Middle Street, London, EC1A 7PH (Tel: 020-7606 6145; Fax: 020-7600 1866;
Email: info@cityparochial.org.uk;
Web: http://www.cityparochial.org.uk)
Clerk: B. Mehta

Civic Trust
17 Carlton House Terrace, London, SW1Y 5AW (Tel: 020-7930 0914; Fax: 020-7321 0180;
Email: pride@civictrust.org.uk;
Web: http://www.civictrust.org.uk)
Director: M. Gwilliam

Clergy Orphan Corporation
1 Dean Trench Street, London, SW1P 3HB (Tel: 020-7799 3696; Fax: 020-7233 1913)
Registrar: R. A. M. Welsford

Commonwealth Society for the Deaf (Sound Seekers)
34 Buckingham Palace Road, London, SW1W 0RE (Tel: 020-7233 5700; Fax: 020-7233 5800;
Email: sound.seekers@btinternet.com)
Chief Executive: Brig. J. A. Davies

Contemporary Applied Arts
2 Percy Street, London, W1P 9FA (Tel: 020-7436 2344; Fax: 020-7436 2446; Web: http://www.caa.org.uk)
Director: Ms M. La Trobe-Bateman

Co-operative Party
77 Weston Street, London, SE1 3SD (Tel: 020-7357 0230; Fax: 020-7407 4476;
Email: d.jones@co-op-party.org.uk;
Web: http://www.co-op-party.org.uk)
Secretary: P. Hunt

Coroner's Society of England and Wales
44 Ormond Avenue, Hampton, Middx, TW12 2RX
Hon. Secretary: M. J. C. Burgess

Corporation of Church House
Church House, Dean's Yard, London, SW1P 3NZ (Tel: 020-7898 1310; Fax: 020-7898 1321)
Secretary: C. D. L. Menzies

Corps of Commissionaires
Market House, 85 Cowcross Street, London, EC1M 6PF (Tel: 020-7490 1125; Fax: 020-7251 2398;
Email: information@the-corps.co.uk;
Web: http://www.the-corps.co.uk)
Group Managing Director: F. J. Peck

Council for the Care of Churches
Fielden House, 13 Little College Street, London, SW1P 3SH (Tel: 020-7898 1866; Fax: 020-7898 1881; Email: enquiries@ccc.c-of-e.org.uk)
Secretary: Dr T. Cocke

Council for World Mission
IPALO House, 32-34 Great Peter Street, London, SW1P 2DB (Tel: 020-7222 4214; Fax: 020-7233 1747; Email: council@cwmission.org.uk;
Web: http://www.cwmission.org.uk)
General Secretary: D. P. Niles, Ph.D

Council of Christians and Jews
5th Floor, Camelford House, 87-89 Albert Embankment, London, SE1 7TP (Tel: 020-7820 0090; Fax: 020-7820 0504; Email: ccjuk@aol.com;
Web: http://www.ccj.org.uk)
Director: Sr M. Shepherd

Council of Mortgage Lenders
3 Savile Row, London, W1X 1AF (Tel: 020-7437 0655; Fax: 020-7734 6416; Email: info@cml.org.uk;
Web: http://www.cml.org.uk)
Director-General: M. Coogan

Countryside Alliance
The Old Town Hall, 367 Kennington Road, London, SE11 4PT (Tel: 020-7840 9200; Fax: 020-7793 8484; Email: info@countryside-alliance.org;
Web: http://www.countryside-alliance.org)
Chief Executive: R. Burge

CPRE (Council for the Protection of Rural England)
Warwick House, 25 Buckingham Palace Road, London, SW1W 0PP (Tel: 020-7976 6433; Fax: 020-7976 6373; Email: info@cpre.org.uk;
Web: http://www.greenchannel.com/cpre)
Director: Ms K. Parminter

Crafts Council
44A Pentonville Road, London, N1 9BY (Tel: 020-7278 7700; Fax: 020-7837 6891;
Email: admin@craftscouncil.org.uk;
Web: http://www.craftscouncil.org.uk)
Director: Ms J. Barnes

Crimestoppers Trust
100 West Hill, London, SW15 2UT (Tel: 020-8877 0337; Fax: 020-8877 3799;
Email: cst@crimestoppers-uk.org;
Web: http://www.crimestoppers-uk.org)
Director of Marketing and Fundraising: R. Greaves

Crosslinks
251 Lewisham Way, London, SE4 1XF (Tel: 020-8691 6111; Fax: 020-8694 8023; Email: info@crosslinks.org; Web: http://www.crosslinks.org)
General Secretary: (until October 2000) Revd R. Bowen; (from October 2000) Revd A. Lines

Societies and Institutions

Croydon Almshouse Charities
74 High Street, Croydon, CR9 2UU (Tel: 020-8680 2638)
Clerk to the Trustees: W. B. Rymer

Cruse Bereavement Care
126 Sheen Road, Richmond, Surrey, TW9 1UR (Tel: 020-8940 4818. Helpline: 020-88332 7227; Fax: 020-8940 7638; Email: info@crusebereavementcare.org.uk)
Executive Director: Dr C. Easton

Design and Industries Association
11 St Gabriel's Manor, Cormont Road, Lambeth, London, SE5 9RH (Tel: 020-7735 8661)
Chairman: E. Pond

Development Trusts Association
20 Conduit Place, London, W2 1HS (Tel: 020-7706 4951; Fax: 020-7706 8447; Email: info@dta.org.uk; Web: http://www.dta.org.uk)
Director: Ms A. Monaghan

Diana, Princess of Wales Memorial Fund
County Hall, Westminster Bridge Road, London, SE1 7PB (Tel: 020-7902 5500; Fax: 020-7902 5511; Email: memfund@memfund.org; Web: http://www.theworkcontinues.org)
Chief Executive: Dr A. Purkis

Dickens Fellowship
Dickens House, 48 Doughty Street, London, WC1N 2LF (Tel: 020-7405 2127; Fax: 020-7831 5175; Email: arwilliams33@compuserve.com; Web: http://www.dickens.fellowship.btinternet.co.uk)
Joint Hon. General Secretaries: Mrs T. Grove, Dr T. Williams

Directory & Database Publishers Association
PO Box 23034, London, W6 0RJ (Tel: 020-8846 9707; Email: rosemarypettit@msn.com; Web: http://www.directory-publisher.co.uk)
Secretary: Ms R. Pettit

Downs Syndrome Association
155 Mitcham Road, London, SW17 9PG (Tel: 020-8682 4001; Fax: 020-8682 4012; Web: http://www.downs-syndrome.org.uk)
Chief Executive: Ms C. Boys

Dulwich Picture Gallery
Gallery Road, London, SE21 7AD (Tel: 020-8693 5254; Fax: 020-8299 8700; Web: http://www.dulwichpicturegallery.org.uk)
Director: D. Shawe-Taylor

Dyslexia Institute
133 Gresham Road, Staines, Middx, TW18 2AJ (Tel: 01784-463851; Fax: 01784-460747; Email: info@dyslexia-inst.org.uk; Web: http://www.dyslexia-inst.org.uk)
Executive Director: Mrs E. J. Brooks

Edexcel
Stewart House, 32 Russell Square, London, WC1B 5DN (Tel: 020-7393 4444; Fax: 020-7393 4445; Web: http://www.edexcel.org.uk)
Chief Executive: Dr C. Townsend

Egypt Exploration Society
3 Doughty Mews, London, WC1N 2PG (Tel: 020-7242 1880; Fax: 020-7404 6118; Email: eeslondon@talk21.com; Web: http://www.ees.ac.uk)
Secretary: Dr P. A. Spencer

Electoral Reform Society
6 Chancel Street, London, SE1 0UU (Tel: 020-7928 1622; Fax: 020-7401 7789; Email: ers@reform.demon.co.uk; Web: http://www.electoral-reform.org.uk)
Chief Executive: Dr K. Ritchie

Emergency Planning Society
Northumberland House, 11 The Pavement, Popes Lane, London, W5 4NG (Tel: 020-8579 7971; Fax: 020-8579 7972; Email: headquarters@emergplansoc.org.uk; Web: http://www.emergplansoc.org.uk)
Hon. Secretary: I. Hoult

Empty Homes Agency
195-197 Victoria Street, London, SW1E 5NE (Tel: 020-7828 6288; Hotline: 0870-901 6303; Fax: 020-7828 7006; Email: eha@globalnet.co.uk; Web: http://www.emptyhomes.com)
Chief Executive: A. Horsey

Engineering Industries Association
Broadway House, Tothill Street, London, SW1H 9NS (Tel: 020-7222 2367; Fax: 020-7799 2206; Email: quary@eia.co.uk; Web: http://www.eia.co.uk)
Director of Operations: R. A. Stubbs

English National Board for Nursing, Midwifery and Health Visiting
Victory House, 170 Tottenham Court Road, London, W1P 0HA (Tel: 020-7391 6229; Fax: 020-7383 3525; Web: http://www.enb.org.uk)
Chief Executive Officer: A. P. Smith, CBE

English Partnerships
16-18 Old Queen Street, London, SW1H 9HP (Tel: 020-7976 3235; Fax: 020-7976 8016; Web: http://www.englishpartnerships.co.uk)
Chief Executive: Mrs P. M. Hay-Plumb

English-Speaking Union of the Commonwealth
Dartmouth House, 37 Charles Street, London, W1X 8AB (Tel: 020-7493 3328; Fax: 020-7495 6108; Email: esu@esu.org; Web: http://www.esu.org)
Director-General: Mrs V. Mitchell

Evangelical Library
78A Chiltern Street, London, W1M 2HB (Tel: 020-7935 6997; Email: stlibrary@aol.com)
Librarian: S. J. Taylor

Fabian Society
11 Dartmouth Street, London, SW1H 9BN (Tel: 020-7227 4900; Fax: 020-7976 7153; Email: info@fabian-society.org.uk; Web: http://www.fabian-society.org.uk)
General Secretary: M. Jacobs

Societies and Institutions 377

Faculty of Royal Designers for Industry
RSA, 8 John Adam Street, London, WC2N 6EZ (Tel: 020-7451 6801; Fax: 020-7839 5805; Email: general@rsa-uk.demon.co.uk)
Administrator: Ms J. Thackray

F.A.N.Y. (Princess Royal's Volunteer Corps)
Right Wing, The Duke of York's HQ, London, SW3 4RX (Tel: 020-7730 2058; Fax: 020-7414 5399; Email: fanyhq@cwcom.net)
Corps Commander: Mrs L. Rose

Federation of British Artists
17 Carlton House Terrace, London, SW1Y 5BD (Tel: 020-7930 6844; Fax: 020-7839 7830; Email: vnewlandsmallgalleries@dial.pipex.com; Web: http://www.mallgalleries.org.uk)
Chairman: T. Muir

Federation of Small Businesses
2 Catherine Place, London, SW1E 6HF (Tel: 020-7592 8100; Fax: 020-7233 7899; Email: london@fsb.org.uk; Web: http://www.fsb.org.uk)

FELORS (Further Education London Region Services)
c/o Corporation of London: Education Department, Guildhall, London, EC2P 2EJ (Tel: 020-7332 1537; Fax: 020-7332 3702; Email: john.wise@corpoflondon.gov.uk)
Executive Officer: Dr J. Wise

FIAC Federation of Independent Advice Centres
4 Deans Court, St Paul's Churchyard, London, EC4V 5AA (Tel: 020-7489 1800; Fax: 020-7489 1804; Email: national@fiac.org.uk; Web: http://www.fiac.org.uk)
Chief Executive: S. Johnson

Fire Protection Association
Bastille Court, 2 Paris Garden, London, SE1 8ND (Tel: 020-7902 5300; Fax: 020-7902 5301; Email: fpa@thefpa.co.uk; Web: http://www.thefpa.co.uk)
Managing Director: J. O'Neill

Fleet Air Arm Officers' Association
4 St James's Square, London, SW1Y 4JU (Tel: 020 7930 7722; Fax: 020-7930 7728; Email: faaoa@fleetairarmoa.org; Web: http://www.fleetairarmoa.org)
Administration Director: Cdr. J. D. O. Macdonald

Folklore Society
c/o University College London, Gower Street, London, WC1E 6BT (Tel: 020-7387 5894)
Hon. Secretary: Dr J. Simpson

Foreign Press Association in London
11 Carlton House Terrace, London, SW1Y 5AJ (Tel: 020-7930 0445; Fax: 020-7925 0469; Email: secretariat@foreign-press.org.uk; Web: http://www.foreign-press.org.uk)
Secretary: Ms D. Crole

Foundation for the Study of Infant Deaths
Artillery House, 11-19 Artillery Row, London, SW1P 1RT (Tel: 020-7222 8001. Helpline: 020-7233 2090; Fax: 020-7222 8002; Email: fsid@sids.org.uk; Web: http://www.sids.org.uk/fsid/)
Secretary-General: Mrs J. Epstein

fpa
2-12 Pentonville Road, London, N1 9FP (Tel: 020-7837 5432; Fax: 020-7837 3034; Web: http://www.fpa.org.uk)
Chief Executive: Ms A. Weyman

Freedom Association
Room 222, Southbank House, Black Prince Road, London, SE1 7SJ (Tel: 020-7793 4228; Fax: 020-7463 2054; Email: mail@tfa.net; Web: http://www.tfa.net)
Administrator: Mrs P. North

Friends of the Friendless Churches
St Ann's Vestry Hall, 2 Church Entry, London, EC4V 5HB (Tel: 020-7236 3634; Fax: 020-7329 3677)
Hon. Director: M. Saunders, MBE

Friends of the Elderly
40-42 Ebury Street, London, SW1W 0LZ (Tel: 020-7730 8263; Fax: 020-7259 0154)
Chief Executive: Mrs S. Levett

Friends of the National Libraries
c/o Department of Manuscripts, The British Library, 96 Euston Road, London, NW1 2DB (Tel: 020-7412 7559)
Hon. Secretary: M. Borrie, OBE, FSA

Galton Institute
19 Northfields Prospect, London, SW18 1PE (Tel: 020-8874 7257)
General Secretary: Mrs B. Nixon

Garden History Society
70 Cowcross Street, London, EC1M 6EJ (Tel: 020-7608 2409; Fax: 020-7490 2974; Email: gardenhistorysociety@compuserve.com; Web: http://www.gardenhistorysociety.org)
Director: A. Plumridge

Gemmological Association and Gem Testing Laboratory of Great Britain
27 Greville Street, (Saffron Hill entrance), London, EC1N 8TN (Tel: 020-7404 3334; Fax: 020-7404 8843; Email: gagtl@btinternet.com; Web: http://www.gagtl.ac.uk/gagtl)
Director: Dr R. R. Harding

General Dental Council
37 Wimpole Street, London, W1M 8DQ (Tel: 020-7887 3800; Fax: 020-7224 3294; Email: information@gdc-uk.org; Web: http://www.gdc-uk.org)
Chief Executive: Mrs R. M. Hepplewhite

378 Societies and Institutions

General Medical Council
178 Great Portland Street, London, W1N 6JE (Tel: 020-7580 7642; Fax: 020-7915 3641; Email: gmc@gmc-uk.org; Web: http://www.gmc-uk.org)
Chief Executive and Registrar: F. M. Scott, TD

General Optical Council
41 Harley Street, London, W1N 2DJ (Tel: 020-7580 3898; Fax: 020-7436 3525; Email: goc@optical.org; Web: http://www.optical.org)
Registrar: R. Wilshin

General Osteopathic Council
Osteopathy House, 176 Tower Bridge Road, London, SE1 3LU (Tel: 020-7357 6655; Fax: 020-7357 0011; Email: info@osteopathy.org.uk; Web: http://www.osteopathy.org.uk)
Registrar: Miss M. J. Craggs

Geologists' Association
Burlington House, Piccadilly, London, W1V 9AG (Tel: 020-7434 9298)
Executive Secretary: Mrs S. Stafford

Georgian Group
6 Fitzroy Square, London, W1P 6DX (Tel: 020-7387 1720; Fax: 020-7387 1721; Email: office@georgian-group.org.uk)
Secretary: N. Burton

Gingerbread
16-17 Clerkenwell Close, London, EC1R 0AN (Tel: 020-7336 8183)
Chief Executive: Ms L. Sewell

Girls' Friendly Society in England and Wales
126 Queens Gate, London, SW7 5LQ (Tel: 020-7589 9628; Fax: 020-7225 1458; Email: platform@gfs.u-net.com; Web: http://www.tabor.co.uk/gfs/)
Chief Executive: Mrs H. Crompton

Grand Lodge of Mark Master Masons
Mark Masons' Hall, 86 St James's Street, London, SW1A 1PL (Tel: 020-7839 5274; Fax: 020-7930 9750; Email: grandsecretary@markmasonshall.org.uk)
Grand Secretary: T. J. Lewis

Greater London Enterprise
28 Park Street, London, SE1 9EQ (Tel: 020-7403 0300; Fax: 020-7403 1742; Email: mail@gle.co.uk)
Chief Executive: D. Walburn

Guild of Glass Engravers
35 Ossulton Way, London, N2 0JY (Tel: 020-8731 9352; Fax: 020-8731 9352; Email: admin.gge@talk21.com)
Secretary: Mrs C. Weatherhead

Guild of Pastoral Psychology
PO Box 1107, London, W3 6ZP (Tel: 020-8993 8366)
Administrator: Mrs N. Stanley

Haemophilia Society
Chesterfield House, 385 Euston Road, London, NW1 3AU (Tel: 020-7380 0600; Fax: 020-7387 8220; Email: info@haemophilia.org.uk; Web: http://www.haemophilia.org.uk)
Chief Executive: Ms K. Pappenheim

Haig Homes
Alban Dobson House, Green Lane, Morden, Surrey, SM4 5NS (Tel: 020-8685 5777; Fax: 020-8685 5778; Email: haig@haighomes.org.uk; Web: http://www.haighomes.org.uk)
Director: A. N. Carlier

Hakluyt Society
c/o Map Library, The British Library, 96 Euston Road, London, NW1 2DB (Tel: 01986-788359; Fax: 01986-788181; Email: office@hakluyt.com; Web: http://www.hakluyt.com)
Hon. Secretary: Dr A. Cook

Hampstead Garden Suburb Institute
Central Square, London, NW11 7BN (Tel: 020-8455 9951; Fax: 020-8201 8063; Web: http://www.hgsi.ac.uk)
Principal and Chief Executive: Mrs F. Naylor

Hearing Concern (British Association of the Hard of Hearing)
7-11 Armstrong Road, London, W3 7JL (Tel: 020-8743 1110. Helpline: 01245-344600; Fax: 020-8742 9043)
Director: F. W. de Bere

Heathrow Airport Consultative Committee
234 Bath Road, Hayes, Middx, UB3 5AP (Tel: 020-8745 7589; Fax: 020-8745 0580)
Chairman: S. Jones, CBE

Help the Aged
St James's Walk, Clerkenwell Green, London, EC1R 0BE (Tel: 020-7253 0253; Fax: 020-7251 0747; Email: info@helptheaged.org.uk; Web: http://www.helptheaged.org.uk)
Director-General: C. M. Lake, CBE

Hong Kong Association
Swire House, 59 Buckingham Gate, London, SW1E 6AJ (Tel: 020-7821 3220; Fax: 020-7630 0353)
Executive Director: D. F. L. Turner

Hospital Saturday Fund
24 Upper Ground, London, SE1 9PD (Tel: 020-7928 6662; Fax: 020-7928 0446; Email: sales@hsf.co.uk; Web: http://www.hsf.co.uk)
Chief Executive: K. R. Bradley

Howard League for Penal Reform
1 Ardleigh Road, London, N1 4HS (Tel: 020-7249 7373; Fax: 020-7249 7788; Email: howardleague@ukonline.co.uk; Web: http://www.howardleague.org)
Director: Ms F. Crook

Societies and Institutions

Huguenot Society of Great Britain and Ireland
The Huguenot Library, University College London, Gower Street, London, WC1E 6BT (Tel: 020-7380 7094; Email: s.massil@ucl.ac.uk; Web: http://www.ucl.ac.uk/ucl-info/divisions/library/huguenot.htm)
Hon. Secretary: Mrs M. A. Bayliss

Hydrographic Society
c/o University of East London, Longbridge Road, Dagenham, Essex, RM8 2AS (Tel: 020-8597 1946; Fax: 020-8590 9730)
Hon. Secretary: P. J. H. Warden

ICAN (National Educational Charity for Children with Speech and Language Difficulties)
4 Dyers Buildings, Holborn, London, EC1N 2QP (Tel: 0870-010 4066; Fax: 0870-010 4067)
Chief Executive: Ms G. Edelman

Imperial Cancer Research Fund
PO Box 123, Lincoln's Inn Fields, London, WC2A 3PX (Tel: 020-7242 0200; Web: http://www.icnet.uk)
Director-General: Sir Paul Nurse, FRS

Incorporated Church Building Society
Fulham Palace, London, SW6 6EA (Tel: 020-7736 3054; Fax: 020-7736 3880)
Secretary: M. W. Tippen

Incorporated Council of Law Reporting for England and Wales
Megarry House, 119 Chancery Lane, London, WC2A 1PP (Tel: 020-7242 6471; Fax: 020-7831 5247; Email: postmaster@iclr.co.uk; Web: http://www.lawreports.co.uk)
Secretary: J. Cobbett

Incorporated Society of Musicians
10 Stratford Place, London, W1N 9AE (Tel: 020-7629 4413; Fax: 020-7408 1538; Email: membership@ism.org; Web: http://www.ism.org)
Chief Executive: N. Hoyle

Independent Schools Council
Grosvenor Gardens House, 35-37 Grosvenor Gardens, London, SW1W 0BS (Tel: 020-7798 1590, Fax: 020-7798 1591; Email: abc@isis.org.uk; Web: http://www.isis.org.uk)
General Secretary: Dr A. B. Cooke, OBE

Independent Schools Information Service
35-37 Grosvenor Gardens, London, SW1W 0BS (Tel: 020-7798 1500; Fax: 020-7798 1501; Email: national@isis.org.uk; Web: http://www.isis.org.uk)
Director: D. J. Woodhead

Industrial Christian Fellowship
c/o St Matthews House, 100 George Street, Croydon, CR0 1PE (Tel: 020-8656 1644; Fax: 020-8656 1644; Email: yrq86@dial.pipex.com)
Chairman: Revd Canon G. Brown

Industrial Society
Robert Hyde House, 48 Bryanston Square, London, W1H 7LN (Tel: 020-7479 2000; Fax: 020-7706 1240)
Chief Executive: W. Hutton

Institute of Administrative Management
40 Chatsworth Parade, Petts Wood, Orpington, Kent, BR5 1RW (Tel: 01689-875555; Fax: 01689-870891; Email: enquiries@instam.org; Web: http://www.instam.org)
Chief Executive: Prof. G. Robinson

Institute of Cancer Research: Royal Cancer Hospital
123 Old Brompton Road, London, SW7 3RP (Tel: 020-7352 8133; Fax: 020-7370 5261; Web: http://www.icr.ac.uk)
Chief Executive: Dr P. W. J. Rigby

Institute of Chartered Accountants in England and Wales
Chartered Accountants' Hall, PO Box 433, Moorgate Place, London, EC2P 2BJ (Tel: 020-7920 8100; Fax: 020-7920 0547; Web: http://www.icaew.co.uk)
Secretary-General: J. Collier

Institute of Directors
116 Pall Mall, London, SW1Y 5ED (Tel: 020-7839 1233; Fax: 020-7930 1949; Email: join-iod@iod.co.uk; Web: http://www.iod.co.uk)
Director-General: G. Cox

Institute of Economic Affairs
2 Lord North Street, London, SW1P 3LB (Tel: 020-7799 3745; Fax: 020-7799 2137; Email: iea@iea.org.uk; Web: http://www.iea.org.uk)
General Director: J. Blundell

Institute of Food Science and Technology
5 Cambridge Court, 210 Shepherd's Bush Road, London, W6 7NJ (Tel: 020-7603 6316; Fax: 020-7602 9936; Email: info@ifst.org; Web: http://www.ifst.org)
Chief Executive: Ms H. G. Wild

Institute of Information Scientists
39-41 North Road, London, N7 9DP (Tel: 020-7619 0624/5; Fax: 020-7619 0627; Email: iis@dial.pipex.com; Web: http://www.iis.org.uk)
Director: E. Hyams

Institute of Linguists
Saxon House, 48 Southwark Street, London, SE1 1UN (Tel: 020-7940 3100; Fax: 020-7940 3101; Email: info@iol.org.uk; Web: http://www.iol.org.uk)
Director: H. Pavlovich

Institute of Marine Engineers
80 Coleman Street, London, EC2R 5BJ (Tel: 020-7382 2600; Fax: 020-7382 2670; Email: imare@imare.org.uk; Web: http://www.imare.org.uk)
Director-General: K. F. Read

Institute of Measurement and Control
87 Gower Street, London, WC1E 6AA (Tel: 020-7387 4949; Fax: 020-7388 8431; Email: secretary@instmc.org.uk; Web: http://www.instmc.org.uk)
Secretary: M. J. Yates

380 Societies and Institutions

Institution of Patentees and Inventors
Suite 505A, Triumph House, 189 Regent Street, London, W1R 7WF (Tel: 020-7434 1818; Fax: 020-7434 1727; Email: ipi@invent.org.uk; Web: http://www.invent.org.uk/)
Secretary: R. Magnus

Institute of Petroleum
61 New Cavendish Street, London, W1M 8AR (Tel: 020-7467 7100; Fax: 020-7255 1472; Email: ip@petroleum.co.uk; Web: http://www.petroleum.co.uk)
Director-General: J. Pym

Institute of Public Relations
The Old Trading House, 15 Northburgh Street, London, EC1V 0PR (Tel: 020-7253 5151; Web: http://www.ipr.org.uk)
Executive Director: C. Farrington

Institute of Quality Assurance
12 Grosvenor Crescent, London, SW1X 7EE (Tel: 020-7245 6722; Fax: 020-7245 6788; Email: iqa@iqa.org; Web: http://www.iqa.org)
Secretary-General: D. G. Campbell

Institute of Sports Medicine
c/o Department of Surgery, University College London, 67 Riding House Street, London, W1P 7LD (Tel: 020-7813 2832; Fax: 020-7813 2832; Email: m.hobsley@ucl.ac.uk)
Hon. Secretary: Dr W. T. Orton

Institute of Trade Mark Attorneys
Canterbury House, 2-6 Sydenham Road, Croydon, CR0 9XE (Tel: 020-8686 2052; Fax: 020-8680 5723; Email: tm@itma.uk; Web: http://www.itma.org.uk)
Secretary: Mrs M. J. Tyler

Institute of Translation and Interpreting
377 City Road, London, EC1V 1ND (Tel: 020-7713 7600; Fax: 020-7713 7650; Email: info@iti.org.uk; Web: http://www.iti.org.uk)
Chairman: G. Cross

Institution of Civil Engineers
One Great George Street, London, SW1P 3AA (Tel: 020-7222 7722; Fax: 020-7222 7500; Web: http://www.ice.org.uk)
Chief Executive: M. Casebourne

Institution of Electrical Engineers
Savoy Place, London, WC2R 0BL (Tel: 020-7240 1871; Fax: 020-7240 7735; Email: postmaster@iee.org.uk; Web: http://www.iee.org.uk)
Chief Executive: Dr A. Roberts

Institution of Gas Engineers
21 Portland Place, London, W1N 3AF (Tel: 020-7636 6603; Fax: 020-7636 6602; Email: general@igaseng.demon.co.uk; Web: http://www.igaseng.com)
Chief Executive: C. Bleach

Institution of Structural Engineers
11 Upper Belgrave Street, London, SW1X 8BH (Tel: 020-7235 4535; Fax: 020-7235 4294; Email: mail@istructe.org.uk; Web: http://www.istructe.org.uk)
Chief Executive: Dr K. J. Eaton

International African Institute
SOAS, Thornhaugh Street, Russell Square, London, WC1H 0XG (Tel: 020-7898 4420; Fax: 020-7898 4419; Email: iai@soas.ac.uk; Web: http://www.oneworld.org/iai/)
Hon. Director: Prof. P. Spencer

International Friendship League
3 Creswick Road, London, W3 9HE (Web: http://www.ifl-world.org)
Chairman: M. J. A. Prowse

International Hospital Federation
46 Grosvenor Gardens, London, SW1W 0EP (Tel: 020-7881 9222; Fax: 020-7881 9223; Email: 101662.1262@compuserve.com; Web: http://www.ihf.co.uk)
Director-General: Prof. P. G. Svensson

International Institute for Conservation of Historic and Artistic Works
6 Buckingham Street, London, WC2N 6BA (Tel: 020-7839 5975; Fax: 020-7976 1564; Email: iicon@compuserve.com; Web: http://www.iiconservation.org)
Secretary-General: D. Bomford

International PEN
9-10 Charterhouse Buildings, Goswell Road, London, EC1M 7AT (Tel: 020-7253 4308; Fax: 020-7253 5711; Email: intpen@dircon.co.uk; Web: http://www.oneworld.org/internatpen)
International Secretary: T. Carlbom

International Underwriting Association
London Underwriting Centre, 3 Minster Court, Minster Lane, London, EC3R 7DD (Tel: 020-7617 4444; Fax: 020-7617 4440; Email: info@iua.co.uk; Web: http://www.iua.co.uk)
Chief Executive: Ms M. L. Rossi

International Union for Land-Value Taxation and Free Trade
Room 427, London Fruit Exchange, Brushfield Street, London, E1 6EL (Tel: 020-7377 8885; Fax: 020-7377 8686; Email: iu@interunion.org.uk)
Hon. Secretary: Mrs B. P. Sobrielo

INTERSERVE
325 Kennington Road, London, SE11 4QH (Tel: 020-7735 8227; Fax: 020-7587 5362; Email: enquiries@isewi.org; Web: http://www.interserve.org/ew)
National Director: R. Clark

Invalids-at-Home
17 Lapstone Gardens, Kenton, Harrow, Middx, HA3 0EB (Tel: 020-8907 1706)
Executive Officer: Mrs S. Lomas

Societies and Institutions 381

Iran Society
2 Belgrave Square, London, SW1X 8PJ (Tel: 020-7235 5122)
Chairman: M. Noël-Clarke

Irish Genealogical Research Society
The Irish Club, 82 Eaton Square, London, SW1W 9AJ (Tel: 020-7235 4164)
Hon. Librarian: T. G. Chartres

ITRI Ltd
Kingston Lane, Uxbridge, Middx, UB8 3PJ (Tel: 01895-272406; Fax: 01895-251841;
Email: postmaster@itri.co.uk;
Web: http://www.itri.co.uk)
Managing Director: D. Bishop

Japan Association
Swire House, 59 Buckingham Gate, London, SW1E 6AJ (Tel: 020-7821 3221; Fax: 020-7630 0353)
Executive Director: D. F. L. Turner

Jewish Historical Society of England
33 Seymour Place, London, W1H 5AP (Tel: 020-7723 5852; Fax: 020-7723 5852; Email: jhse@dircon.co.uk; Web: http://www.jhse.dircon.co.uk)
Hon. Secretary: C. M. Drukker

Justice (British Section of the International Commission of Jurists)
59 Carter Lane, London, EC4V 5AQ (Tel: 020-7329 5100; Fax: 020-7329 5055;
Email: admin@justice.org.uk)
Director: Ms A. Owers

King George's Fund for Sailors
8 Hatherley Street, London, SW1P 2YY (Tel: 020-7932 0000; Fax: 020-7932 0095; Email: dg@kgfs.org.uk; Web: http://www.kgfs.org.co.uk)
Director-General: Capt. M. J. Appleton RN

King's Fund
11-13 Cavendish Square, London, W1M 0AN (Tel: 020-7307 2400; Fax: 020-7307 2801;
Web: http://www.kingsfund.org.uk)
Chief Executive: Rabbi J. Neuberger

Landscape Institute
6-8 Barnard Mews, London, SW11 1QU (Tel: 020-7350 5200; Fax: 020-7350 5201;
Email: mail@l-i.org.uk; Web: http://www.l-i.org.uk)
Director-General: S. Royston

League Against Cruel Sports
83-87 Union Street, London, SE1 1SG (Tel: 020-7403 6155; Fax: 020-7403 4532;
Email: league@compuserve.com;
Web: http://www.league.uk.com)
Chief Executive: D. Batchelor

League of the Helping Hand
Petersham Hollow, 226 Petersham Road, Petersham, Richmond, Surrey, TW10 7AL (Tel: 020-8940 7303)
Secretary: Mrs I. Goodlad

Lee Valley Partnership
6-8 Great Eastern Street, London, EC2A 3NT (Tel: 020-7247 5556; Fax: 020-7247 8544;
Email: bill@llvp.com; Web: http://www.llvp.com)
Chief Executive: B. McQuillan

Lee Valley Regional Park Authority
Myddleton House, Bulls Cross, Enfield, EN2 9HG (Tel: 01992-717711; Fax: 01992-719937;
Email: info@leevalleypark.org.uk;
Web: http://www.leevalleypark.org.uk)
Chief Executive: S. Dawson

Leukaemia Research Fund
43 Great Ormond Street, London, WC1N 3JJ (Tel: 020-7405 0101; Fax: 020-7405 3139;
Email: info@leukaemia-research.org.uk;
Web: http://www.leukaemia-research.org.uk)
Executive Director: D. L. Osborne

Liberty (National Council for Civil Liberties)
21 Tabard Street, London, SE1 4LA (Tel: 020-7403 3888; Fax: 020-7407 5354;
Email: info@liberty-human-rights.org.uk;
Web: http://www.liberty-human-rights.org.uk)
Director: J. Wadham

Library Association
7 Ridgmount Street, London, WC1E 7AE (Tel: 020-7255 0500; Fax: 020-7255 0501;
Email: info@la-hq.org.uk;
Web: http://www.la-hq.org.uk)
Chief Executive: B. McKee, Ph.D., FRSA

Linnean Society of London
Burlington House, Piccadilly, London, W1V 0LQ (Tel: 020-7434 4479; Fax: 020-7287 9364;
Email: john@linnean.org)
President: Sir David Smith, FRS, FRSE

Lloyd's Register of Shipping
71 Fenchurch Street, London, EC3M 4BS (Tel: 020-7709 9166; Fax: 020-7488 4796;
Email: lloydsreg@lr.org; Web: http://www.lr.org)
Chairman and Chief Executive Officer: D. G. Moorhouse

Lloyd's of London Tercentenary Foundation
Lloyd's of London, Lime Street, London, EC3M 7HA (Tel: 020-7327 5925; Fax: 020-7327 6368;
Email: linda.harper@lloyds.com)
Assistant Secretary: Ms L. Harper

Local Economy Policy Unit (LEPU)
South Bank University, Wandsworth Road, London, SW8 2JZ (Tel: 020-7815 7798; Fax: 020-7815 7799;
Email: lepu@sbu.ac.uk;
Web: http://www.sbu.ac.uk/lepu)
Co-Directors: Prof. M. Gibson; Prof. I. Bruegel

Local Government International Bureau
Local Government House, Smith Square, London, SW1P 3HZ (Tel: 020-7664 3100; Fax: 020-7664 3128;
Email: Webmaster@lgib.gov.uk;
Web: http://www.lgib.gov.uk)
Director: J. Smith

Societies and Institutions

London 21 Sustainability Network
7 Chamberlain Street, London, NW1 8XB (Tel: 020-7722 3710; Fax: 020-7722 3959; Email: admin@london21.org; Web: http://www.london21.org)

London and South East Library Region
4th Floor, Gun Court, 70 Wapping Lane, London, E1 9RL (Tel: 020-7702 2020; Fax: 020-7702 2019; Web: http://www.viscount.org.uk/laser)
Director: G. F. Hendrix

London Appreciation Society
7-20 Hampden Gurney Street, London, W1H 5AL (Tel: 020-7724 0221)
Chairman: Miss V. C. Colin-Russ

London Bullion Market Association
6 Frederick's Place, London, EC2R 8BT (Tel: 020-7796 3067; Fax: 020-7796 4345; Email: mail@lbma.org.uk; Web: http://www.lbma.org.uk)
Chief Executive: S. Murray

London Chest Hospital Appeal
London Chest Hospital, Bonner Road, London, E2 9JX (Tel: 020-8983 2345; Fax: 020-8983 2307)
Senior Manager, Appeals: Mrs P. Gray

London City Mission
175 Tower Bridge Road, London, SE1 2AH (Tel: 020-7407 7585; Fax: 020-7403 6711; Email: lcm.uk@btinternet.com; Web: http://www.lcm.org.uk)
General Secretary: Revd J. McAllen

London Connection
12 Adelaide Street, London, WC2N 4HW (Tel: 020-7766 5544; Fax: 020-7839 6277; Email: info@london-connection.org.uk)
Director: C. Glover

London Film Commission
20 Euston Centre, Regent's Place, London, NW1 3JH (Tel: 020-7387 8787; Fax: 020-7387 8788; Email: ifc@lonfon-film.co.uk)
Chief Executive: D. Reid

London Flotilla
40 Endlesham Road, London, SW12 8JL (Tel: 020-8673 1879; Fax: 020-8673 1879; Email: richardupton@freenet.co.uk)
Hon. Membership Secretary: Lt.-Cdr. H. C. R. Upton, RD, RNR

London Forum of Amenity and Civic Societies
70 Cowcross Street, London, EC1M 6EJ (Tel: 020-7250 0606; Fax: 020-7747 3281; Email: lonfor@wayahead.demon.co.uk; Web: http://www.community Web.org/thelondonforum)
Chairman: Ms M. Harvey, MBE

London Hostels Association
54 Eccleston Square, London, SW1V 1PG (Tel: 020-7834 1545; Fax: 020-7834 7146; Email: rgray@london-hostels.co.uk)
General Manager: R. C. Gray

London Investment Banking Association
6 Frederick's Place, London, EC2R 8BT (Tel: 020-7796 3606; Fax: 020-7796 4345; Email: liba@liba.org.uk; Web: http://www.liba.org.uk)
Director-General: Sir Adam Ridley

London Library
14 St James's Square, London, SW1Y 4LG (Tel: 020-7930 7705; Fax: 020-7766 4766; Email: membership@londonlibrary.co.uk; Web: http://www.londonlibrary.co.uk)
Librarian: A. S. Bell

London Mathematical Society
D. E. Morgan House, 57-58 Russell Square, London, WC1B 4HP (Tel: 020-7637 3686; Fax: 020-7323 3655; Email: lms@lms.ac.uk; Web: http://www.lms.ac.uk)

London Money Market Association
c/o Investec Bank (UK) Limited, 2 Gresham Street, London, EC2V 7QP (Tel: 020-7597 4485; Fax: 020-7597 4491)
Secretary: R. Vardy

London Playing Fields Society
Fraser House, 29 Albemarle Street, London, W1X 3FA (Tel: 020-7493 3211; Fax: 020-7409 3405; Email: lonplayingfields@aol.com)
Chief Executive: Dr C. Goodson-Wickes

London Principal Youth Officers Group
Perceval House, 14-16 Uxbridge Road, London, W5 2HL (Tel: 020-8758 8735; Fax: 020-8758 8727; Email: rfogg@ealing.gov.uk)
Head of Youth and Community Service: Ms R. Fogg

London Record Society
c/o Institute for Historical Research, Senate House, Malet Street, London, WC1E 7HU (Tel: 020-7862 8798; Fax: 020-7862 8793; Email: creaton@sas.ac.uk Web: http://www.ihr.sas.ac.uk/ihr/associnstits/lrsmnu.html)
Chairman: H. S. Cobb

London Regeneration Network
356 Holloway Road, London, N7 6PA (Tel: 020-7700 8119; Fax: 020-7700 8108; Email: lrn@lvsc.org.uk; Web: http://www.lvsc.org.uk)
Co-ordinator: G. Tarifa

London Society
4th Floor, Senate House, Malet Street, London, WC1E 7HU (Tel: 020-7580 5537)
Hon. Secretary: Mrs B. Jones

London Sports Board
c/o ALG, 36 Old Queen Street, London, SW1H 9JF (Tel: 020-7222 7799; Fax: 020-7799 2339)
Chairman: P. Turner

London Subterranean Survey Association
98 Cambridge Gardens, London, W10 6HS (Tel: 020-8968 1360)
Hon. Secretary: R. J. Morgan

Societies and Institutions 383

London Swing Dance Society
31 Rashleigh House, Thanet Street, London, WC1H 9ER (Tel: 020-7387 1011;
Email: swinguk@zetnet.co.uk;
Web: http://www.swingdanceuk.com)

London Symphony Orchestra
Barbican Centre, London, EC2Y 8DS (Tel: 020-7588 1116; Fax: 020-7374 0127; Web: http://www.lso.co.uk)
Managing Director: C. Gillinson

London Topographical Society
36 Old Deer Park Gardens, Richmond, Surrey, TW9 2TL (Tel: 020-8940 5419; Web: http://www.topsoc.org)
Hon. Secretary: P. Frazer

London Underground Railway Society
54 Brinkley Road, Worcester Park, KT4 8JF (Tel: 020-8330 1855; Web: http://www.lurs.demon.co.uk)
Secretary: E. Felton

London Youth Matters
Pastures Youth Centre, Davies Lane, London, E11 3DR (Tel: 020-8558 1233; Fax: 020-8558 7878;
Email: londonyouth@compuserve.com)
Co-ordinator: vacant

Macmillan Cancer Relief
Anchor House, 15-19 Britten Street, London, SW3 3TZ (Tel: 020-7351 7811; Fax: 020-7376 8098;
Email: information-line@macmillan.org.uk;
Web: http://www.macmillan.org.uk)
Chief Executive: N. Young

Magistrates' Association
28 Fitzroy Square, London, W1P 6DD (Tel: 020-7387 2353; Fax: 020-7383 4020;
Web: http://www.magistrates-association.org.uk/magistrates)
Secretary: Ms S. Dickinson

Marie Curie Cancer Care
28 Belgrave Square, London, SW1X 8QG (Tel: 020-7235 3325; Fax: 020-7823 2380;
Email: info@mariecurie.org.uk;
Web: http://www.mariecurie.org.uk)
Chief Executive: Sir Nicholas Fenn, GCMG

Marine Society
202 Lambeth Road, London, SE1 7JW (Tel: 020-7261 9535; Fax: 020-7401 2537;
Email: enq@marine-society.org;
Web: http://www.marine-society.org)
Director: Capt. J. J. Howard

Marriage Care
Clitherow House, 1 Blythe Mews, Blythe Road, London, W14 0NW (Tel: 020-7371 1341; Fax: 020-7371 4921; Email: marriagecare@btinternet.com;
Web: http://www.marriagecare.org.uk)
Chief Executive: vacant

Maternity Alliance
45 Beech Street, London, EC2P 2LX (Tel: 020-7588 8583; Fax: 020-7588 8584;
Email: info@maternityalliance.org.uk)
Director: Ms C. Gowdridge

Medical Society for the Study of Venereal Diseases
1 Wimpole Street, London, W1M 8AE (Tel: 020-7290 2968; Fax: 020-7290 2989;
Web: http://www.mssvd.org.uk)
Hon. Secretary: Dr A. J. Robinson

Medical Women's Federation
Tavistock House North, Tavistock Square, London, WC1H 9HX (Tel: 020-7387 7765; Fax: 020-7387 7765;
Email: lyn@m-w-f.demon.co.uk;
Web: http://www.m-w-f.demon.co.uk)
President: Dr F. Subotsky

Mental Health Foundation
20-21 Cornwall Terrace, London, NW1 4QL (Tel: 020-7535 7400; Fax: 020-7535 7474;
Email: mhf@mentalhealth.org.uk;
Web: http://www.mhf.org.uk)
Director: Ms R. Lesirge

Merchant Navy Welfare Board
19-21 Lancaster Gate, London, W2 3LN (Tel: 020-7723 3642; Fax: 020-7723 3643;
Email: enquiries@mnwb.org.uk;
Web: http://www.msn.co.uk)
General Secretary: Capt. D. A. Parsons

Metropolitan Hospital-Sunday Fund
45 Westminster Bridge Road, London, SE1 7JB (Tel: 020-7922 0200; Fax: 020-7401 3641;
Email: mhsf@peabody.org.uk;
Web: http://www.mhsf.org.uk)
Secretary: H. F. Doe

Military Historical Society
National Army Museum, Royal Hospital Road, London, SW3 4HT (Tel: 01980-615689/01380-723371; Fax: 01980-618746)
Secretary: Lt.-Col. R. E. L. Hodges

Mineralogical Society
41 Queen's Gate, London, SW7 5HR (Tel: 020-7584 7516; Fax: 020-7823 8021;
Email: adrian@minersoc.demon.co.uk;
Web: http://www.minersoc.org)
General Secretary: Ms F. Wall

Mission to Seafarers
St Michael Paternoster Royal, College Hill, London, EC4R 2RL (Tel: 020-7248 5202; Fax: 020-7248 4761;
Email: general@missiontoseafarers.org;
Web: http://www.missiontoseafarers.org)
Secretary-General: Revd Canon G. Jones

Modern Churchpeople's Union
MCU Office, 25 Birch Grove, London, W3 9SP (Tel: 020-8932 4379; Fax: 020-8993 5812;
Web: http://www.mcm.co.uk/modchurunion)
General Secretary: Revd N. P. Henderson

Monumental Brass Society
Lowe Hill House, Stratford St Mary, Colchester, Essex, CO7 6JX (Tel: 020-8520 5249; Fax: 020-8521 8387;
Email: martin.stuchfield@intercitygroup.co.uk)
Hon. Secretary: H. M. Stuchfield

384 Societies and Institutions

Mothers' Union
Mary Sumner House, 24 Tufton Street, London, SW1P 3RB (Tel: 020-7222 5533; Fax: 020-7222 1591; Email: mu@themothersunion.org; Web: http://www.themothersunion.org)
Chief Executive: R. Bailey

Multiple Sclerosis Society
25 Effie Road, London, SW6 1EE (Tel: 020-7610 7171; Fax: 020-7736 9861; Web: http://www.mssociety.org.uk)
Chief Executive: P. Cardy

Museum Association
42 Clerkenwell Close, London, EC1R 0PA (Tel: 020-7608 2933; Fax: 020-7250 1929; Email: info@museumassociation.org; Web: http://www.museumassociation.org)
Director: M. Taylor

Musicians Benevolent Fund
16 Ogle Street, London, W1P 8JB (Tel: 020-7636 4481; Fax: 020-7637 4307; Email: info@mbf.org.uk; Web: http://www.mbf.org.uk)
Secretary: Ms H. Faulkner

NABS
32 Wigmore Street, London, W1H 9DF (Tel: 020-7299 2888; Fax: 020-7299 2887; Email: nabs@nabs.org.uk; Web: http://www.nabs.org.uk)
Director: Ms H. Tridgell

NACRO (National Association for the Care and Resettlement of Offenders)
169 Clapham Road, London, SW9 0PU (Tel: 020-7582 6500; Fax: 020-7735 4666)
Chief Executive: Ms H. Edwards

National Art Collections Fund
Millais House, 7 Cromwell Place, London, SW7 2JN (Tel: 020-7225 4800; Fax: 020-7225 4848; Email: info@nacf.org; Web: http://www.nacf.org)
Director: D. Barrie

National Association of Citizen's Advice Bureaux
Myddelton House, 115-123 Pentonville Road, London, N1 9LZ (Tel: 020-7833 2181; Fax: 020-7833 4371; Web: http://www.nacab.org.uk)
Chief Executive: D. Harker

National Association of Clubs for Young People
371 Kennington Lane, London, SE11 5QY (Tel: 020-7793 0787; Fax: 020-7820 9815; Email: office@nacyp.org.uk; Web: http://www.nacyp.org.uk)
National Director: C. Groves, FIPD, FIMgt

National Association of Local Councils
109 Great Russell Street, London, WC1B 3LD (Tel: 020-7637 1865; Fax: 020-7436 7451; Email: nalc@nalc.gov.uk; Web: http://www.nalc.gov.uk)
Chief Executive: J. Findlay

National Asthma Campaign
Providence House, Providence Place, London, N1 0NT (Tel: 020-7226 2260; Fax: 020-7704 0740; Web: http://www.asthma.org.uk)
Chief Executive: Ms A. Bradley

National Benevolent Institution
61 Bayswater Road, London, W2 3PG (Tel: 020-7723 0021)
Secretary: Gp Capt. D. St J. Homer, MVO

National Blood Authority
Oak House, Reeds Crescent, Watford, Herts, WD1 1QH (Tel: 01923-486800; Fax: 01923-486801; Web: http://www.bloodnet.nbs.nhs.uk)
Chairman: M. Fogden, CB

National Campaign for the Arts
Pegasus House, 37-42 Sackville Street, London, W1X 1DB (Tel: 020-7333 0375; Fax: 020-7333 0660)
Director: Ms V. Todd

National Childbirth Trust
Alexandra House, Oldham Terrace, London, W3 6NH (Tel: 020-8992 2616. Enquiries: 020-8992 8637; Fax: 020-8992 5926; Web: http://www.nct-online.org)
Chief Executive: Ms B. Phipps

National Consumer Council
20 Grosvenor Gardens, London, SW1W 0DH (Tel: 020-7730 3469; Fax: 020-7730 0191; Email: info@ncc.org.uk; Web: http://www.ncc.org.uk)
Director: Ms A. Bradley

National Council for One-Parent Families
255 Kentish Town Road, London, NW5 2LX (Tel: 020-7428 5400; Fax: 020-7482 4851; Email: info@oneparentfamilies.org.uk; Web: http://www.oneparentfamilies.org.uk)
Director: Ms M. Sherlock, OBE

National Council for Voluntary Organisations
Regents Wharf, 8 All Saints Street, London, N1 9RL (Tel: 020-7713 6161; Fax: 020-7713 6300)
Chief Executive: S. Etherington

National Council of Women of Great Britain
36 Danbury Street, London, N1 8JU (Tel: 020-7354 2395; Fax: 020-7354 2395; Email: ncwgb@danburystreet.freeserve.org.uk; Web: http://www.ncwgb.org)
President: (until October 2000) Dr D. Glick; (from October 2000) Ms M. Birkenhead

National Federation of Women's Institutes
104 New Kings Road, London, SW6 4LY (Tel: 020-7371 9300; Fax: 020-7736 3652; Email: hq@nfwi.org.uk; Web: http://www.nfwi.org.uk)
General Secretary: Mrs J. Osborne

National Operatic and Dramatic Association
NODA House, 1 Crestfield Street, London, WC1H 8AU (Tel: 020-7837 5655; Fax: 020-7833 0609; Email: everyone@noda-hq.org; Web: http://www.noda-hq.org)
Chief Executive: M. Pemberton

Societies and Institutions 385

National Peace Council
162 Holloway Road, London, N7 8DD (Tel: 020-7609 9666; Fax: 020-7609 9777; Email: npc@gn.apc.org; Web: http://www.peacecouncil.org.uk)
Chief Executive: T. Milne-Wallis

National Playing Fields Association
25 Ovington Square, London, SW3 1LQ (Tel: 020-7584 6445; Fax: 020-7581 2402; Email: npfa@npfa.co.uk; Web: http://www.npfa.co.uk)
Director: Mrs E. Davies

National Secular Society Ltd
25 Red Lion Square, London, WC1R 4RL (Tel: 020-7404 3126; Fax: 020-7404 3126; Email: secretariat@secularism.org.uk; Web: http://www.secularism.org.uk)
General Secretary: K. P. Wood

The National Society
Church House, Great Smith Street, London, SW1P 3NZ (Tel: 020-7898 1518; Fax: 020-7898 1493; Email: info@natsoc.c-of-e.org.uk; Web: http://www.natsoc.org.uk)
General Secretary: Canon J. Hall

National Society for the Prevention of Cruelty to Children (NSPCC)
42 Curtain Road, London, EC2A 3NH (Tel: 020-7825 2500; Fax: 020-7825 2525; Email: infounit@nspcc.org.uk; Web: http://www.nspcc.org.uk)
Director: J. Harding

The National Trust for Places of Historic Interest and Natural Beauty
36 Queen Anne's Gate, London, SW1H 9AS (Tel: 020-7222 9251; Fax: 020-7222 5097; Web: http://www.nationaltrust.org.uk)
Director-General: M. D. Drury

Naval, Military & Air Force Bible Society
Radstock House, 3 Eccleston Street, London, SW1W 9LZ (Tel: 020-7463 1468; Fax: 020-7730 0240; Email: nma@sgm.org)
General Secretary: J. M. Hines

Navy Records Society
c/o Department of War Studies, King's College, The Strand, London, WC2R 2LS
Hon. Secretary: Prof. A. D. Lambert

New Times Network
6 Cynthia Street, London, N1 9JF (Tel: 020-7278 4443; Fax: 020-7278 4425; Email: info@newtimes.org.uk)
Director: A. Pakes

Newcomen Society
The Science Museum, London, SW7 2DD (Tel: 020-7371 4445; Fax: 020-7371 4445; Email: thomas@newcomen.com; Web: http://www.nmsi.ac.uk/research/newchome.htm)
Executive Secretary: C. Armstrong

North London Dial-a-Ride
Units C/D, Regents Avenue Industrial Estate, Regents Avenue, London, N13 5UR (Tel: 020-8829 1200; Fax: 020-8829 1221; Email: nldar1@yahoo.com; Web: http://www.nldar.co.uk)
General Manager: J. Awuni

Norwood Ravenswood
Broadway House, 80-82 The Broadway, Stanmore, Middx, HA7 4HB (Tel: 020-8954 4555; Fax: 020-8420 6800; Email: norwoodravenswood@nwrw.org; Web: http://www.nwrw.org)
Chief Executive: Ms N. Brier

The Nuffield Trust
59 New Cavendish Street, London, W1M 7RD (Tel: 020-7631 8450; Fax: 020-7631 8451; Email: mail@nuffieldtrust.org.uk; Web: http://www.nuffieldtrust.org.uk)
Secretary: J. Wyn Owen, CB

Nutrition Society
10 Cambridge Court, 210 Shepherds Bush Road, London, W6 7NJ (Tel: 020-7602 0228; Fax: 020-7602 1756; Email: mail@nutsoc.org.uk; Web: http://www.nutsoc.org.uk)
Hon. Secretary: Dr J. Buttriss

Open-Air Mission
19 John Street, London, WC1N 2DL (Tel: 020-7405 6135; Fax: 020-7405 6135; Email: oamission@btinternet.com; Web: http://www.btinternet.com/~oamission)
Secretary: A. J. Greenbank

Orders and Medals Research Society
123 Turnpike Link, Croydon, CR0 5NU (Tel: 020-8680 2701; Web: http://www.omrs.org.uk)
General Secretary: N. G. Gooding

Oriental Ceramic Society
30B Torrington Square, London, WC1E 7LJ (Tel: 020-7636 7985; Fax: 020-7580 6749)
Hon. Secretary: Dr F. Wood

Osteopathic Association Clinic
8-10 Boston Place, London, NW1 6QH (Tel: 020-7262 1128; Fax: 020-7723 7492)
Clinic Manager: Mrs A. Dalby

Outward Bound Trust
207 Waterloo Road, London, SE1 8XD (Tel: 020-7928 1991; Fax: 020-7928 3733; Email: enquiries@outwardbound-uk.org; Web: http://www.outwardbound-uk.org)
Director: Sir Michael Hobbs, KCVO, CBE

Park Royal Partnership
Elliot House, Victoria Road, London, NW10 6NY (Tel: 020-8961 9696; Fax: 020-8961 6298; Email: info@parkroyallondon.co.uk)
Chief Executive: D. Little

Parkinson's Disease Society of the United Kingdom
215 Vauxhall Bridge Road, London, SW1V 1EJ (Tel: 020-7931 8080; Helpline: 020-7233 5373)
Chief Executive: Ms M. G. Baker MBE

Societies and Institutions

Parliamentary and Scientific Committee
48 Westminster Palace Gardens, 1-7 Artillery Row, London, SW1P 1RR (Tel: 020-7222 7085; Fax: 020-7222 5355)
Administrative Secretary: Dr A. Whitehouse

Patients Association
PO Box 935, Harrow, Middx, HA1 3YJ (Tel: 020-8423 9111. Helpline: 020-8423 8999; Fax: 020-8423 9119; Email: mailbox@patients-association.com; Web: http://www.patients-association.com)
Director: M. Stone

Pedestrians Association
31-33 Bondway, London, SW8 1SJ (Tel: 020-7820 1010; Fax: 020-7820 8208; Email: info@pedestrians.org.uk; Web: http://www.pedestrians.org.uk)
Director: B. Plowden

Philological Society
School of Oriental and African Studies, University of London, Thornhaugh Street, London, WC1H 0XG
Hon. Secretary: Prof. N. Sims-Williams

Pilgrim Trust
Fielden House, Little College Street, London, SW1P 3SH (Tel: 020-7222 4723; Fax: 020-7976 0461)
Director: Miss G. Nayler

Poetry Society
22 Betterton Street, London, WC2H 9BU (Tel: 020-7420 9880; Fax: 020-7240 4818; Email: poetrysoc@dial.pipex.com; Web: http://www.poetrysoc.com)
Director: C. Patterson

Post Office Users' National Council
6 Hercules Road, London, SE1 7DN (Tel: 020-7928 9458; Fax: 020-7928 9076; Email: enquiry@pounc.org.uk; Web: http://www.pounc.org.uk)
Chief Executive: J. Dodds

The Prince's Trust, King George's Jubilee Trust and The Queen's Silver Jubilee Trust
18 Park Square East, London, NW1 4LH (Tel: 020-7543 1234; Fax: 020-7543 1200; Web: http://www.princes-trust.org.uk)
Director: T. Shebbeare, CVO

Princess Royal Trust for Carers
142 Minories, London, EC3N 1LB (Tel: 020-7480 7788; Fax: 020-7481 4729; Email: info@carers.org; Web: http://www.carers.org)
Chief Executive: Ms A. Ryan

Prisoners Abroad
89-93 Fonthill Road, London, N4 3JH (Tel: 020-7561 6820; Fax: 020-7561 6821; Email: info@prisonersabroad.org.uk; Web: http://www.prisonersabroad.org.uk)
Director: C. Laurenzi

Private Libraries Association
Ravelston, South View Road, Pinner, Middx, HA5 3YD (Web: http://www.praxis.co.uk/ppuk/pla.htm)
Hon. Secretary: F. Broomhead

Queen's English Society
20 Jessica Road, London, SW18 2QN (Tel: 020-8874 2200; Web: http://www.queens-english-society.co.uk)
Hon. Secretary: Miss P. Raper

Queen Victoria Clergy Fund
Church House, Dean's Yard, London, SW1P 3NZ (Tel: 020-7898 1310; Fax: 020-7898 1321)
Secretary: C. D. L. Menzies

QUIT (National Society of Non-Smokers)
Victory House, 170 Tottenham Court Road, London, W1P 0HA (Tel: 020-7388 5775; Fax: 020-7388 5995; Email: quit@clara.net; Web: http://www.quit.org.uk)
Chief Executive: P. McCabe

RADAR (Royal Association for Disability and Rehabilitation)
12 City Forum, 250 City Road, London, EC1V 8AF (Tel: 020-7250 3222; Fax: 020-7250 0212; Email: radar@radar.org.uk; Web: http://www.radar.org.uk)
Chief Executive Officer: P. Mansell

Ramblers' Association
2nd Floor, Camelford House, 87-90 Embankment, London, SE1 7TW (Tel: 020-7339 8500; Fax: 020-7339 8501; Email: ramblers@london.ramblers.org.uk; Web: http://www.ramblers.org.uk)
Director: A. Mattingly

Regular Forces Employment Association Ltd
49 Pall Mall, London, SW1Y 5JG (Tel: 020-7321 2011; Fax: 020-7839 0970; Email: rfea@primex.co.uk; Web: http://www.interreach.com/rfea)
Chief Executive: Maj.-Gen. M. F. L. Shellard CBE

Research Defence Society
58 Great Marlborough Street, London, W1V 1DD (Tel: 020-7287 2818; Fax: 020-7287 2627; Email: admin@rds-online.org.uk; Web: http://www.rds-online.org.uk)
Executive Director: Dr M. Matfield

Reserve Forces Association
The Duke of York's HQ, London, SW3 4SG (Tel: 020-7730 6122; Fax: 020-7414 5589; Email: rfa.council@btinternet.com)
Secretary-General: Maj.-Gen. W. A. Evans, CB

Richard III Society
4 Oakley Street, London, SW3 5NN (Fax: 01745-550176; Email: info@rimms.co.uk; Web: http://www.richardiii.net)
Secretary: Miss E. M. Nokes

ROOM: The National Council for Housing and Planning
14-18 Old Street, London, EC1V 9BH (Tel: 020-7251 2363; Fax: 020-7680 2830)
Director: K. MacDonald

Societies and Institutions 387

Royal Air Force Benevolent Fund
67 Portland Place, London, W1N 4AR (Tel: 020-7580 8343)
Controller: Air Chief Marshal Sir David Cousins, KCB, AFC

Royal Agricultural Society of the Commonwealth
2 Grosvenor Gardens, London, SW1W 0DH (Tel: 020-7259 9678; Fax: 020-7259 9675;
Email: rasc@commagshow.demon.co.uk;
Web: http://www.commagshow.org)
Hon. Secretary: J. Anderson, FRICS

Royal Anthropological Institute
50 Fitzroy Street, London, W1P 5HS (Tel: 020-7387 0455; Fax: 020-7383 4235;
Email: rai@cix.compulink.co.uk;
Web: http://www.rai.anthropology.org.uk)
Director: J. C. M. Benthall

Royal Archaeological Institute
c/o Society of Antiquaries of London, Burlington House, Piccadilly, London, W1V 0HS (Tel: 020-7479 7092)
Secretary: J. G. Coad, FSA

Royal Artillery Association
Artillery House, Front Parade, Royal Artillery Barracks, London, SE18 4BH (Tel: 020-8781 3003; Fax: 020-8854 3617)
General Secretary: Lt.-Col. M. G. Felton

Royal Asiatic Society
60 Queen's Gardens, London, W2 3AF (Tel: 020-7724 4742; Fax: 020-7706 4008)
Publications Officer: A. P. A. Belloli

Royal British Legion
48 Pall Mall, London, SW1Y 5JY (Tel: 08457-725725; Fax: 020-7973 7399; Email: info@britishlegion.org.uk; Web: http://www.britishlegion.org.uk)
Secretary-General: Brig. I. G. Townsend

Royal Caledonian Schools Trust
80A High Street, Bushey, Watford, Herts, WD2 3DE (Tel: 020-8421 8845; Fax: 020-8421 8845;
Email: rcst@calcybushey.demon.co.uk)
Chief Executive: J. Horsfield

Royal College of General Practitioners
14 Princes Gate, London, SW7 1PU (Tel: 020-7581 3232; Fax: 020-7225 3047; Email: info@rcgp.org.uk; Web: http://www.rcgp.org.uk)
Hon. Secretary: Ms M. Baker

Royal College of Nursing
20 Cavendish Square, London, W1M 0AB (Tel: 020-7409 3333; Fax: 020-7647 3435;
Web: http://www.rcn.org.uk)
General Secretary: Miss C. Hancock

Royal College of Obstetricians and Gynaecologists
27 Sussex Place, London, NW1 4RG (Tel: 020-7772 6200; Fax: 020-7723 0575; Email: coll.sec@rcog.org.uk; Web: http://www.rcog.org.uk)
Secretary: P. A. Barnett

Royal College of Paediatrics and Child Health
50 Hallam Street, London, W1N 6DE (Tel: 020-7307 5600; Fax: 020-7307 5601;
Email: enquiries@rcpch.ac.uk)
Hon. Secretary: Dr P. Hamilton

Royal College of Pathologists
2 Carlton House Terrace, London, SW1Y 5AF (Tel: 020-7451 6700; Fax: 020-7451 6701;
Email: info@rcpath.org; Web: http://www.rcpath.org)
Secretary: D. Ross

Royal College of Radiologists
38 Portland Place, London, W1N 4JQ (Tel: 020-7636 4432; Fax: 020-7323 3100; Email: enquiries@rcr.ac.uk; Web: http://www.rcr.ac.uk)
General Secretary: A. J. Cowles

Royal College of Surgeons of England
35-43 Lincoln's Inn Fields, London, WC2A 3PN (Tel: 020-7405 3474)
Secretary: C. Duncan

Royal College of Veterinary Surgeons
Belgravia House, 62-64 Horseferry Road, London, SW1P 2AF (Tel: 020-7222 2001; Fax: 020-7222 2004;
Email: admin@rcvs.org.uk;
Web: http://www.rcvs.org.uk)
Registrar: Miss J. C. Hern

Royal Geographical Society (with The Institute of British Geographers)
1 Kensington Gore, London, SW7 2AR (Tel: 020-7591 3000; Fax: 020-7591 3001; Email: info@rgs.org; Web: http://www.rgs.org)
Director: Dr R. Gardner

Royal Historical Society
University College London, Gower Street, London, WC1E 6BT (Tel: 020-7387 7532; Fax: 020-7387 7532; Email: royalhistsoc@ucl.ac.uk;
Web: http://www.rhs.ac.uk)
Executive Secretary: Mrs J. N. McCarthy

Royal Horticultural Society
80 Vincent Square, London, SW1P 2PE (Tel: 020-7834 4333)
Director-General: Dr A. Colquhoun

Royal Hospital for Neuro-disability
West Hill, Putney, London, SW15 3SW (Tel: 020-8780 4500; Fax: 020-8789 3098;
Email: info@neuro-disability.org.uk;
Web: http://www.neuro-disability.org.uk)
Chief Executive: V. J. Beauchamp

Royal Humane Society
Brettenham House, Lancaster Place, London, WC2E 7EP (Tel: 020-7836 8155; Fax: 020-7836 8155)
Secretary: Maj.-Gen. C. Tyler, CB

Royal Institute of British Architects
66 Portland Place, London, W1N 4AD (Tel: 020-7580 5533; Fax: 020-7255 1541; Email: admin@inst.riba.org; Web: http://www.riba.net)
Director-General: A. Reid, Ph.D.

388 Societies and Institutions

Royal Institute of International Affairs
Chatham House, 10 St James's Square, London, SW1Y 4LE (Tel: 020-7957 5700; Fax: 020-7957 5710; Email: contact@riia.org; Web: http://www.riia.org)
Director: C. Gamble, Ph.D.

Royal Institute of Navigation
1 Kensington Gore, London, SW7 2AT (Tel: 020-7591 3130; Fax: 020-7591 3131; Email: info@rin.org.uk; Web: http://www.rin.org.uk)
Director: Gp Capt. D. W. Broughton, MBE

Royal Institute of Oil Painters
17 Carlton House Terrace, London, SW1Y 5BD (Tel: 020-7930 6844; Fax: 020-7839 7830; Email: vnewlandsmallgalleries@dial.pipex.com; Web: http://www.mallgalleries.org.uk)
Secretary: B. Bennett

Royal Institute of Painters in Water Colours
17 Carlton House Terrace, London, SW1Y 5BD (Tel: 020-7930 6844; Fax: 020-7839 7830; Email: vnewlandsmallgalleries@dial.pipex.com; Web: http://www.mallgalleries.org.uk)
Secretary: T. Hunt

Royal Institute of Public Health and Hygiene and Society of Public Health
28 Portland Place, London, W1N 4DE (Tel: 020-7580 2731; Fax: 020-7580 6157; Email: info@riphh.org.uk; Web: http://www.riphh.org.uk)
Chief Executive: Ms N. Wilkins

Royal Institution of Chartered Surveyors
12 Great George Street, London, SW1P 3AD (Tel: 020-7222 7000)
Chief Executive: J. H. A. J. Armstrong

Royal Institution of Great Britain
21 Albemarle Street, London, W1X 4BS (Tel: 020-7409 2992; Fax: 020-7629 3569; Email: ri@ri.ac.uk; Web: http://www.ri.ac.uk)
Director: Prof. S. Greenfield

Royal Literary Fund
3 Johnson's Court, off Fleet Street, London, EC4A 3EA (Tel: 020-7353 7150)
General Secretary: Ms E. M. Gunn

Royal Masonic Benevolent Institution
20 Great Queen Street, London, WC2B 5BG (Tel: 020-7405 8341; Fax: 020-7404 0724; Email: enquiries@rmbi.org.uk)
Chief Executive: Miss J. Reynolds

Royal Medical Benevolent Fund
24 King's Road, London, SW19 8QN (Tel: 020-8540 9194; Fax: 020-8542 0494; Email: rm.bf@virgin.net; Web: http://www.rmbf.co.uk)
Chief Executive Officer: M. Baber

Royal National Institute for Deaf People
19-23 Featherstone Street, London, EC1Y 8SL (Tel: 020-7296 8000; Fax: 020-7296 8199; Email: helpline@rnid.org.uk; Web: http://www.rnid.org.uk)
Chief Executive: J. Strachan

Royal National Institute of the Blind
224 Great Portland Street, London, W1N 6AA (Tel: 0845-766 9999; Fax: 020-7388 2034; Email: helpline@rnib.org.uk; Web: http://www.rnib.org.uk)
Director-General: I. Bruce

Royal Naval Association
82 Chelsea Manor Street, London, SW3 5QJ (Tel: 020-7352 6764; Fax: 020-7352 7385; Email: rna@netcomuk.co.uk; Web: http://www.royal-naval-association.co.uk)
General Secretary: Capt. R. McQueen, CBE, RN

Royal Naval Benevolent Society for Officers
1 Fleet Street, London, EC4Y 1BD (Tel: 020-7427 7471; Fax: 020-7427 7471)
Secretary: Capt. I. B. Sutherland, RN (retd)

Royal Over-Seas League
Over-Seas House, Park Place, St James's Street, London, SW1A 1LR (Tel: 020-7408 0214; Fax: 020-7499 6738; Email: info@rosl.org.uk; Web: http://www.rosl.org.uk)
Director-General: R. F. Newell

Royal Patriotic Fund Corporation
40 Queen Anne's Gate, London, SW1H 9AP (Tel: 020-7233 1894; Fax: 020-7233 1799)
Secretary: Brig. T. G. Williams, CBE

Royal Pharmaceutical Society of Great Britain
1 Lambeth High Street, London, SE1 7JN (Tel: 020-7735 9141; Fax: 020-7735 7629; Email: enquiries@rpsgb.org.uk; Web: http://www.rpsgb.org.uk)
Secretary: Ms A. M. Lewis, OBE

Royal Philatelic Society London
41 Devonshire Place, London, W1N 1PE (Tel: 020-7486 1044; Fax: 020-7486 0803; Web: http://www.rpsl.org.uk)
Hon. Secretary: D. Gurney

Royal School of Needlework
Apartment 12A, Hampton Court Palace, Surrey, KT8 9AU (Tel: 020-8943 1432; Fax: 020-8943 4910; Email: rnwork@intonet.co.uk; Web: http://www.royal-needlework.co.uk)
Principal: Mrs E. Elvin

Royal Society for Asian Affairs
2 Belgrave Square, London, SW1X 8PJ (Tel: 020-7235 5122; Fax: 020-7259 6771; Email: info@rsaa.org.uk; Web: http://www.rsaa.org.uk)
Secretary: D. J. Easton

Royal Society for the Encouragement of Arts, Manufactures and Commerce (RSA)
8 John Adam Street, London, WC2N 6EZ (Tel: 020-7930 5115; Fax: 020-7839 5805; Email: director@rsa-uk.demon.co.uk; Web: http://www.rsa.org.uk)
Chairman: Sir Stuart Hampson

Societies and Institutions 389

Royal Society of Literature
Somerset House, Strand, London, WC2R 0RN (Tel: 020-7845 4676; Fax: 020-7845 4679; Email: rslit@aol.com; Web: http://www.rslit.org)
Secretary: Mrs M. Fergusson

Royal Society of Marine Artists
17 Carlton House Terrace, London, SW1Y 5BD (Tel: 020-7930 6844; Fax: 020-7839 7830)
Secretary: D. Howell

Royal Society of Medicine
1 Wimpole Street, London, W1M 8AE (Tel: 020-7290 2900; Fax: 020-7290 2992; Email: membership@roysocmed.ac.uk; Web: http://www.roysocmed.ac.uk)
Executive Director: Dr A. Grocock

Royal Society of Musicians of Great Britain
10 Stratford Place, London, W1N 9AE (Tel: 020-7629 6137; Fax: 020-7629 6137)
Secretary: Mrs M. Gibb

Royal Society of Chemistry
Burlington House, Piccadilly, London, W1V 0BN (Tel: 020-7437 8656; Fax: 020-7437 8883; Email: rsc1@rsc.org; Web: http://www.rsc.org)
Secretary-General: Dr T. D. Inch

Royal Society of Painter-Printmakers
Bankside Gallery, 48 Hopton Street, London, SE1 9JH (Tel: 020-7928 7521; Fax: 020-7928 2820; Email: bankside@freeuk.com)
President: Prof. D. Carpanini

Royal Society of Portrait Painters
17 Carlton House Terrace, London, SW1Y 5BD (Tel: 020-7930 6844; Fax: 020-7839 7830; Email: vnewlandsmallgalleries@dial.pipex.com; Web: http://www.mallgalleries.org.uk)
Secretary: P. Brason

Royal Society of Tropical Medicine and Hygiene
Manson House, 26 Portland Place, London, W1N 4EY (Tel: 020-7580 2127; Fax: 020-7436 1389; Email: mail@rstmh.org; Web: http://www.rstmh.org)
Hon. Secretaries: Dr D. C. Barker; Dr S. B. Squire

Royal Star and Garter Home for Disabled Sailors, Soldiers and Airmen
Richmond Hill, Richmond-upon-Thames, Surrey, TW10 6RR (Tel: 020-8940 3314; Fax: 020-8940 1953)
Chief Executive: I. A. Lashbrooke

Royal Statistical Society
12 Errol Street, London, EC1Y 8LX (Tel: 020-7638 8998; Fax: 020-7256 7598; Email: rss@rss.org.uk)
Executive Secretary: I. J. Goddard

Royal Television Society
Holborn Hall, 100 Gray's Inn Road, London, WC1X 8AL (Tel: Membership - 020-7691 2460; Events - 020-7691 2470; Fax: 020-7430 0924; Email: info@rts.org.uk; Web: http://www.rts.org.uk)
Executive Director: M. Bunce

Royal Theatrical Fund
11 Garrick Street, London, WC2E 9AR (Tel: 020-7836 3322)
Secretary: Mrs R. M. Foster

Royal United Kingdom Beneficient Association
6 Avonmore Road, London, W14 8RL (Tel: 020-7602 6274; Fax: 020-7371 1807; Email: charity@rukba.org.uk; Web: http://www.charitynet.org/~rukba)
Director: W. Rathbone

Royal United Services Institute for Defence Studies
Whitehall, London, SW1A 2ET (Tel: 020-7930 5854; Fax: 020-7321 0943; Email: defence@rusids.demon.co.uk; Web: http:www.rusi.org/rusi/)
Director: Rear-Adm. R. Cobbold CB

Royal Watercolour Society
Bankside Gallery, 48 Hopton Street, London, SE1 9JH (Tel: 020-7928 7521; Fax: 020-7928 2820)
Secretary: Ms J. Dixey

St Dustan's (For Blind ex-Service Men and Women)
12-14 Harcourt Street, London, W1A 4XB (Tel: 020-7723 5021; Fax: 020-7262 6199)
Chief Executive: G. B. J. Frost

St John Ambulance
1 Grosvenor Crescent, London, SW1X 7EF (Tel: 020-7235 5231)
Executive Director: L. Martin

Sargent Cancer Care for Children
Griffin House, 161 Hammersmith Road, London, W6 8SG (Tel: 020-8752 2800; Fax: 020-8752 2806; Email: care@sargent.org)
Chief Executive: Mrs D. Yeo

Save Britain's Heritage
70 Cowcross Street, London, EC1M 6EJ (Tel: 020-7253 3500; Fax: 020-7253 3400; Email: save@btinternet.com; Web: http://www.savebritainsheritage.org)
Secretary: R. Pollard

Save the Children Fund
17 Grove Lane, London, SE5 8RD (Tel: 020-7703 5400; Fax: 020-7703 2278; Web: http://www.savethechildren.org.uk)
Director-General: M. Aaronson

SCOPE
6 Market Road, London, N7 9PW (Tel: 020-7619 7100; Fax: 020-7619 7399; Web: http://www.scope.org.uk)
Chief Executive: R. P. Brewster

Scout Association
Baden-Powell House, Queen's Gate, London, SW7 5JS (Tel: 020-7584 7030; Fax: 020-7590 5103; Email: baden.powell.house@scout.org.uk; Web: http://www.scoutbase.org.uk/)
Chief Executive: D. M. Twine

390 Societies and Institutions

Sea Cadet Association
202 Lambeth Road, London, SE1 7JF (Tel: 020-7928 8978)
Chief Executive: Cdre R. M. Parker, RN

Selden Society
Faculty of Laws, Queen Mary and Westfield College, Mile End Road, London, E1 4NS (Tel: 020-7882 5136; Fax: 020-8981 8733; Email: selden-society@qmw.ac.uk; Web: http://www.selden-society.qmw.ac.uk)
Secretary: V. Tunkel

Sense (National Deafblind and Rubella Association)
11-13 Clifton Terrace, London, N4 3SR (Tel: 020-7272 7774; Fax: 020-7272 6012; Email: enquiries@sense.org.uk; Web: http://www.sense.org.uk)
Chief Executive: R. Clark

Shadow Strategic Rail Authority
55 Victoria Street, London, SW1H 0EU (Tel: 020-7654 6000; Fax: 020-7654 6010; Web: http://www.sra.gov.uk)
Chief Executive: M. Grant

Shaftesbury Homes and Arethusa
The Chapel, Royal Victoria Patriotic Building, Trinity Road, London, SW18 3SX (Tel: 020-8875 1555; Fax: 020-8875 1954; Email: shaftesbury.homes@virgin.net)
Chief Executive: Ms A. Chesney

Shaftesbury Society
16 Kingston Road, London, SW19 1JZ (Tel: 020-8239 5555; Email: info@shaftesburysoc.org.uk; Web: http://www.shaftesburysoc.org.uk)
Chief Executive: Ms F. Beckett

Shakespeare Globe Trust
21 New Globe Walk, London, SE1 9DT (Tel: 020-7902 1400; Fax: 020-7902 1460; Web: http://www.shakespeare-globe.org)
General Director: P. Kyle

Shellfish Association of Great Britain
Fishmongers' Hall, London Bridge, London, EC4R 9EL (Tel: 020-7283 8305; Fax: 020-7929 1389; Email: sagb@shellfish.org.uk; Web: http://www.shellfish.org.uk)
Director: E. Edwards, OBE, Ph.D

Society for Promoting Christian Knowledge (SPCK)
Holy Trinity Church, Marylebone Road, London, NW1 4DU (Tel: 020-7387 5282; Fax: 020-7388 2352; Email: spck@spck.org.uk; Web: http://www.spck.org.uk)
General Secretary: P. Chandler

Society for Nautical Research
c/o National Maritime Museum, Greenwich, London, SE10 9NF (Web: http://www.snr.org)
Hon. Secretary: Lt.-Cdr. W. J. R. Gardner

Society for Psychical Research
49 Marloes Road, London, W8 6LA (Tel: 020-7937 8984; Fax: 020-7937 8984; Web: http://www.moebius.psy.ed.ac.uk)
Secretary: P. Johnson

Society for the Protection of Ancient Buildings
37 Spital Square, London, E1 6DY (Tel: 020-7377 1644; Fax: 020-7247 5296; Email: info@spab.org.uk; Web: http://www.spab.org.uk)
Secretary: P. Venning, FSA

Society for the Promotion of Roman Studies
Senate House, Malet Street, London, WC1E 7HU (Tel: 020-7862 8727; Fax: 020-7862 8728; Email: romansoc@sas.ac.uk; Web: http://www.sas.ac.uk/icls/roman)
Secretary: Dr H. M. Cockle

Society for the Protection of Unborn Children
Phyllis Bowman House, 5-6 St Matthew Street, Westminster, London, SW1P 2JT (Tel: 020-7222 5845; Fax: 020-7222 0630; Email: enquiry@spuc.org.uk; Web: http://www.spuc.org.uk)
National Director: J. Smeaton

Society of Antiquaries of London
Burlington House, Piccadilly, London, W1V 0HS (Tel: 020-7734 0193; Fax: 020-7287 6967; Email: admin@sal.org.uk; Web: http://www.sal.org.uk)
General Secretary: D. Morgan Evans, FSA

Society of Apothecaries of London
14 Blackfriars Lane, London, EC4V 6EJ (Tel: 020-7236 1189; Fax: 020-7329 3177)
Clerk: R. J. Stringer

Society of Archivists
40 Northampton Road, London, EC1R 0HB (Tel: 020-7278 8630; Fax: 020-7278 2107; Email: societyofarchivists@archives.org.uk; Web: http://www.archives.org.uk)
Executive Secretary: P. S. Cleary

Society of Authors
84 Drayton Gardens, London, SW10 9SB (Tel: 020-7373 6642; Fax: 020-7373 5768; Email: authorsoc@writers.org.uk; Web: http://www.writers.org.uk/society)
General Secretary: M. Le Fanu, OBE

Society of Chiropodists and Podiatrists
53 Welbeck Street, London, W1M 7HE (Tel: 020-7486 3381; Fax: 020-7935 6359; Email: enq@scopd.org; Web: http://www.feetforlife.org)
General Secretary: Ms H. De Lyon

Society of Public Teachers of Law
School of Law, Kings College, Strand, London, WC2R 2LS (Tel: 020-7848 2849; Fax: 020-7848 2788; Email: david.hayton@kcl.ac.uk; Web: http://www.law.warwick.ac.uk/sptl)
Hon. Secretary: Prof. D. Hayton

Society of Scribes and Illuminators
6 Queen Square, London, WC1N 3AR (Tel: 01524-251534; Fax: 01524-251534; Email: scribe@calligraphy.org; Web: http://www.calligraphy.org)
Hon. Secretary: Mrs G. Hazeldine

Societies and Institutions   391

Special Trustees for St Bartholomew's Hospital
57B West Smithfield, London, EC1A 9DS (Tel: 020-7607 6110; Fax: 020-7600 6993)
Chief Executive Officer: J. Dennis

Sport England - London
PO Box 480, Crystal Palace National Sports Centre, London, SE19 2BQ (Tel: 020-8778 8600; Fax: 020-8676 9812; Web: http://www.english.sport.gov.uk)
Regional Director: A. Sutch

SSAFA Forces Help
19 Queen Elizabeth Street, London, SE1 2LP (Tel: 020-7403 8783; Fax: 020-7403 8815; Email: public-awareness@ssafa-forces-help.org.uk; Web: http://www.ssafa.org.uk)
Controller: Maj.-Gen. P. Sheppard, CB, CBE

Standing Conference of National and University Libraries (SCONUL)
102 Euston Street, London, NW1 2HA (Tel: 020-7387 0317; Fax: 020-7383 3197; Email: sconul@sconul.ac.uk; Web: http://www.sconul.ac.uk)
Secretary: A. J. C. Bainton

Standing Council of the Baronetage
3 Eastcroft Road, West Ewell, Epsom, Surrey, KT19 9TX (Tel: 020-8393 6620; Fax: 020-8393 6620)
Chairman: Sir Brian Barttelot, Bt., OBE, DL

Stroke Association
Stroke House, Whitecross Street, London, EC1Y 8JJ (Tel: 020-7566 0300; Fax: 020-7490 2686; Email: stroke@stroke.org.uk; Web: http://www.stroke.org.uk)
Chief Executive Officer: Miss M. Goose

Surrey Archaeological Society
Castle Arch, Guildford, Surrey, GU1 3SX (Tel: 01483 532454; Fax: 01483-532454; Email: surreyarch@compuserve.com; Web: http://ourworld.compuserve.com/homepages/surreyarch)
Hon. Secretary: Miss A. J. Monk

Survival International
11-15 Emerald Street, London, WC1N 3QL (Tel: 020-7242 1441; Fax: 020-7242 1771; Email: info@survival-international.org; Web: http://www.survival-international.org)
Director: S. Corry

Suzy Lamplugh Trust
14 East Sheen Avenue, London, SW14 8AS (Tel: 020-8392 1839; Fax: 020-8392 1830; Email: trust@suzylamplugh.org; Web: http://www.suzylamplugh.org)
Executive Secretary: P. Lamplugh

Swedenborg Society
20-21 Bloomsbury Way, London, WC1A 2TH (Tel: 020-7405 7986; Fax: 020-7831 5848; Email: swed.soc@netmatters.co.uk; Web: http://www.swedenborg.org.uk)
Secretary: Miss M. G. Waters

Theatres Trust
22 Charing Cross Road, London, WC2H 0HR (Tel: 020-7836 8591; Fax: 020-7836 3302; Email: info@theatrestrust.org.uk)
Director: P. Longman

Theosophical Society in England
50 Gloucester Place, London, W1H 4EA (Tel: 020-7935 9261)
National President: C. Price

Tower Hill Improvement Trust
Atlee House, 28 Commercial Street, London, E1 6LR (Tel: 020-7377 6614; Fax: 020-7377 9822)
Secretary and Treasurer: J. Connelly

Toynbee Hall
28 Commercial Street, London, E1 6LS (Tel: 020-7247 6943; Fax: 020-7377 5964; Email: toynbee.hall@talk21.com; Web: http://www.toynbeehall.org.uk)
Chief Executive: A. Prescott

Tree Council
51 Catherine Place, London, SW1E 6DY (Tel: 020-7828 9928; Fax: 020-7828 9060; Web: http://www.treecouncil.org.uk)
Director: R. Osborne

Trust for London
6 Middle Street, London, EC1A 7PH (Tel: 020-7606 6145; Fax: 020-7600 1866; Email: trustforlondon@cityparochial.org.uk; Web: http://www.cityparochial.org.uk)
Secretary: B. Mehta

Turner Society
BCM Box Turner, London, WC1N 3XX (Web: http://www.turnersociety.org.uk)
Chairman: E. Joll

UK Central Council for Nursing, Midwifery and Health Visiting
23 Portland Place, London, W1N 4JT (Tel: 020-7333 6557)
Chief Executive: Ms S. Norman

United Kingdom Alliance
176 Blackfriars Road, London, SE1 8ET (Tel: 020-7928 1538)
General Secretary: D. Sinclair

United Nations Association of Great Britain and Northern Ireland
3 Whitehall Court, London, SW1A 3EL (Tel: 020-7930 2931; Fax: 020-7930 5893; Email: una_uk@compuserve.com; Web: http://www.oneworld.org/una_uk)
Director: M. C. Harper

USPG (United Society for the Propagation of the Gospel)
Partnership House, 157 Waterloo Road, London, SE1 8XA (Tel: 020-7928 8681; Email: enquiries@uspg.org.uk; Web: http://www.uspg.org.uk)
Secretary: Rt. Revd M. Rumalshah

392 Societies and Institutions

Victim Suppport (National Association of Victims Support Schemes)
National Office, Cranmer House, 39 Brixton Road, London, SW9 6DZ (Tel: 020-7735 9166; Helpline: 0845-303 0900; Fax: 020-7582 5712)
Chief Executive: Dame Helen Reeves, DBE

Victorian Society
1 Priory Gardens, Bedford Park, London, W4 1TT (Tel: 020-8994 1019; Fax: 020-8995 4895; Email: admin@victorian-society.org.uk; Web: http://www.victorian-society.org.uk)
Director: Dr W. Filmer-Sankey

Viking Society for Northern Research
Department of Scandinavian Studies, University College London, Gower Street, London, WC1E 6BT (Tel: 020-7380 7176; Fax: 020-7380 7750; Email: cnr@ucl.ac.uk)
Hon. Secretaries: Prof. M. P. Barnes; Dr J. Jesh

VSO (Voluntary Service Overseas)
317 Putney Bridge Road, London, SW15 2PN (Tel: 020-8780 7200; Fax: 020-8780 7300; Web: http://www.vso.org.uk)
Chief Executive: M. Goldring

War on Want
Fenner Brockway House, 37-39 Great Guildford Street, London, SE1 0ES (Tel: 020-7620 1111; Fax: 020-7261 9291; Email: mailroom@waronwant.org; Web: http://www.waronwant.org)
Director: Ms C. Matheson

Waste Watch
Europa House, 13-17 Ironmonger Row, London, EC1V 3QG (Tel: 020-7253 6266; Fax: 020-7253 5962; Web: http://www.wastewatch.org.uk)
Executive Director: R. Georgeson, MBE

The Wellcome Trust
The Wellcome Building, 183 Euston Road, London, NW1 2BE (Tel: 020-7611 8888; Fax: 020-7611 8545; Web: http://www.wellcome.ac.uk)
Director: Dr T. M. Dexter, FRS

WES World-Wide Education Service Ltd
Canada House, 272 Field End Road, Eastcote, Ruislip, Middx, HA4 9NA (Tel: 020-8582 0317; Fax: 020-8429 4838; Email: wes@wesworldwide.com; Web: http://www.wesworldwide.com)
Director: Mrs T. Mulder-Reynolds

Westminster Foundation for Democracy
2nd Floor, 125 Pall Mall, London, SW1Y 5EA (Tel: 020-7930 0408; Fax: 020-7930 0449; Email: wfd@wfd.org; Web: http://www.wfd.org)
Chief Executive: Ms A. Jones

William Morris Society and Kelmscott Fellowship
Kelmscott House, 26 Upper Mall, London, W6 9TA (Tel: 020-8741 3735; Fax: 020-8741 3735; Email: wmsoc@compuserve.com; Web: http://www.ccny.cuny.edu/wmorris/morris.html)
Hon. Secretary: P. Faulkner

Wine and Spirit Association
Five Kings House, 1 Queen Street Place, London, EC4R 1XX (Tel: 020-7248 5377; Fax: 020-7489 0322; Email: wsa@wsa.org.uk; Web: http://www.wsa.org.uk)
Director: Q. Rappoport

Women's Engineering Society
2 Queen Anne's Gate Buildings, Dartmouth Street, London, SW1H 9BP (Tel: 020-7233 1974; Email: info@wes.org.uk; Web: http://www.cant.ac.uk/misc/wes/weshome.html)
Secretary: Mrs C. MacGillivray

Women's Environmental Network
PO Box 30626, London, E1 1TZ (Tel: 020-7481 9004; Fax: 020-7481 9144; Email: wenuk@gn.apc.org; Web: http://www.gn.apc.org/wen)
PR and Information: Ms L. Sutton

Women's Nationwide Cancer Control Campaign
Suna House, 128-130 Curtain Road, London, EC2A 3AQ (Tel: 020-7729 4688; Fax: 020-7613 0771; Email: admin@wnccc.org.uk; Web: http://www.wnccc.org.uk)
Chief Executive: Ms J. Cohen

Workers' Educational Association
Temple House, 17 Victoria Park Square, London, E2 9PB (Tel: 020-8983 1515; Fax: 020-8983 4840; Email: info@wea.org.uk; Web: http://www.wea.org.uk)
General Secretary: R. Lochrie

World Education Fellowship
International Headquarters, 58 Dickens Rise, Chigwell, Essex, IG7 6NY (Tel: 020-8281 7122; Fax: 020-8281 7122; Email: georgejohn@drise.freeserve.co.uk; Web: http://www.itc.glam.ac.uk/wef)
General Secretary: G. John

World Energy Council
5th Floor, Regency House, 1-4 Warwick Street, London, W1R 6LE (Tel: 020-7734 5996; Fax: 020-7734 5926; Email: info@worldenergy.org; Web: http://www.worldenergy.org)
Secretary-General: G. W. Doucet

Yeomanry Benevolent Fund
10 Stone Buildings, Lincoln's Inn, London, WC2A 3TG (Tel: 020-7831 6727)
Secretary: Maj. J. Prince

Young Men's Christian Association (YMCA)
YMCA England, 640 Forest Road, London, E17 3DZ (Tel: 020-8520 5599; Fax: 020-8509 3190; Email: press@england.ymca.org.uk)
National Secretary: E. Thomas

Youth Clubs UK
2nd Floor, Kirby House, 20-24 Kirby Street, London, EC1N 8TS (Tel: 020-7242 4045; Fax: 020-7242 4045; Email: info@youthclubs.org.uk; Web: http://www.youthclubs.org.uk)
Chief Executive: J. Bateman

Zoological Society of London
Regent's Park, London, NW1 4RY (Tel: 020-7722 3333; Fax: 020-7686 5743; Web: http://www.zsl.org)
Director-General: Dr M. Dixon

ASTRONOMY
AND TIDES

ASTRONOMICAL DATA
TIDAL DATA

ASTRONOMY AND TIDES

ASTRONOMICAL DATA

Lighting-up Time

The legal importance of sunrise and sunset is that the Road Vehicles Lighting Regulations 1989 (SI 1989 No. 1796) make use of the front and rear position lamps on vehicles compulsory during the period between sunset and sunrise. Headlamps on vehicles are required to be used during the hours of darkness on unlit roads or whenever visibility is seriously reduced. The hours of darkness are defined in these regulations as the between half and hour after sunset and half an hour before sunrise.

In all laws and regulations, sunset refers to the local sunset, i.e. the time at which the Sun sets at the place in question. This common-sense interpretation has been upheld by legal tribunals. Thus the necessity for providing for different latitudes and longitudes is evident.

Sunrise and Sunset

The times of sunrise and sunset are those when the Sun's upper limb, as affected by refraction, is no the true horizon of an observer at sea-level. Assuming the mean refraction to be 34´, and the Sun's semi-diameter to be 16´, the time given is that when the true zentigh distance of the Sun's centre is 90°+34´+16´ or 90° 50´, or, in other words, when the depression of the Sun's centre below the true horizon is 50´. The upper limb is then 34´ below the true horizon, but is brought there by refraction. An observer on a ship might see the Sun for a minute or so longer, because of the dip of the horizon, while another viewing the sunset over hills or mountains would record an earlier time. Nevertheless, the moment when the true zenith distance of the Sun's centre is 90° 50´ is a precise time dependent only on the latitude and longitude of the place, and independent of its altitude above sea-level, the contour of its horizon, the vagaries of refraction or the small seasonal change in the Sun's semi-diameter; this moment is suitable in every way as a definition of sunset or sunrise for all statutory purposes.

Twilight

Light reaches us before sunrise and continues to reach us for some time after sunset. The interval between darkness and sunrise or sunset and darkness is call twilight. Astronomically speaking, twilight is considered to begin or end when the Sun's centre is 18° below the horizon, as no light from the Sun can then reach the observer. As thus defined, twilight may last several hours; in high latitudes at the summer solstice the depression of 18° is not reached, and twilight lasts from sunset to sunrise. The need for some sub-division of twilight is met by dividing the gatherine darkness into four stages.

(1) Sunrise or sunset, as defined above

(2) Civil twilight, which begins or ends when the Sun's centre is 6° below the horizon. This marks the time when operations requiring daylight may commence or must cease. In England it varies from about 30 to 60 minutes after sunset and the same interval before sunrise

(3) Nautical twilight, which beings or ends when the Sun's centre is 12° below the horizon. This marks the time when it is, to all intents and purposes, completely dark

(4) Astronomical twilight, which begins or ends when the Sun's centre is 18° below the horizon. This marks theoretical perfect darkness. It is of little practical importance, especially if nautical twilight is tabulated

To assist observers the durations of civil, nautical and astronomical twilights are given at intervals of ten days. The beginning of a particular twilight is found by subtracting the duration from the time of sunrise, while the end is found by adding the duration to the time of sunset.

396 Astronomical Data

JANUARY 2001
SUNRISE AND SUNSET (GMT)

	0°		05′ 51° 30′	
	h	m	h	m
1	8	06	16	02
2	8	06	16	03
3	8	06	16	04
4	8	05	16	06
5	8	05	16	07
6	8	05	16	08
7	8	04	16	09
8	8	04	16	11
9	8	03	16	12
10	8	03	16	13
11	8	02	16	15
12	8	02	16	16
13	8	01	16	18
14	8	00	16	19
15	7	59	16	21
16	7	58	16	22
17	7	57	16	24
18	7	56	16	26
19	7	55	16	27
20	7	54	16	29
21	7	53	16	31
22	7	52	16	32
23	7	51	16	34
24	7	50	16	36
25	7	49	16	37
26	7	47	16	39
27	7	46	16	41
28	7	44	16	43
29	7	43	16	45
30	7	42	16	46
31	7	40	16	48

MOON PHASES

	d	h	m
First Quarter	2	22	31
Full Moon	9	20	24
Last Quarter	16	12	35
New Moon	24	13	07

DURATION OF TWILIGHT AT 52°N (MINUTES)

January	1st	11th	21st	31st
Civil	40	39	38	36
Nautical	83	81	79	76
Astronomical	123	121	118	115

FEBRUARY 2001
SUNRISE AND SUNSET (GMT)

	0°		05′ 51° 30′	
	h	m	h	m
1	7	39	16	50
2	7	37	16	52
3	7	35	16	54
4	7	34	16	55
5	7	32	16	57
6	7	30	16	59
7	7	29	17	01
8	7	27	17	03
9	7	25	17	05
10	7	23	17	06
11	7	22	17	08
12	7	20	17	10
13	7	18	17	12
14	7	16	17	14
15	7	14	17	15
16	7	12	17	17
17	7	10	17	19
18	7	08	17	21
19	7	06	17	23
20	7	04	17	25
21	7	02	17	26
22	7	00	17	28
23	6	58	17	30
24	6	56	17	32
25	6	54	17	34
26	6	52	17	35
27	6	50	17	37
28	6	48	17	39

MOON PHASES

	d	h	m
First Quarter	1	14	02
Full Moon	8	07	12
Last Quarter	15	03	24
New Moon	23	08	21

DURATION OF TWILIGHT AT 52°N (MINUTES)

February	1st	11th	21st	28th
Civil	36	35	34	34
Nautical	76	74	73	72
Astronomical	115	113	111	111

Astronomical Data

MARCH 2001
SUNRISE AND SUNSET (GMT)

	0°		05′ 51° 30′	
	h	m	h	m
1	6	46	17	41
2	6	43	17	42
3	6	41	17	44
4	6	39	17	46
5	6	37	17	48
6	6	35	17	49
7	6	32	17	51
8	6	30	17	53
9	6	28	17	55
10	6	26	17	56
11	6	23	17	58
12	6	21	18	00
13	6	19	18	02
14	6	17	18	03
15	6	14	18	05
16	6	12	18	07
17	6	10	18	08
18	6	08	18	10
19	6	05	18	12
20	6	03	18	13
21	6	01	18	15
22	5	59	18	17
23	5	56	18	19
24	5	54	18	20
25	5	52	18	22
26	5	49	18	24
27	5	47	18	25
28	5	45	18	27
29	5	43	18	29
30	5	40	18	30
31	5	38	18	32

MOON PHASES

	d	h	m
First Quarter	3	02	03
Full Moon	9	17	23
Last Quarter	16	20	45
New Moon	25	01	21

DURATION OF TWILIGHT AT 52°N (MINUTES)

January	1st	11th	21st	31st
Civil	34	33	33	34
Nautical	72	72	73	75
Astronomical	111	112	115	119

APRIL 2001
SUNRISE AND SUNSET (GMT)

	0°		05′ 51° 30′	
	h	m	h	m
1	5	36	18	34
2	5	34	18	35
3	5	31	18	37
4	5	29	18	39
5	5	27	18	40
6	5	25	18	42
7	5	22	18	44
8	5	20	18	45
9	5	18	18	47
10	5	16	18	49
11	5	13	18	50
12	5	11	18	52
13	5	09	18	54
14	5	07	18	55
15	5	05	18	57
16	5	03	18	59
17	5	00	19	00
18	4	58	19	02
19	4	56	19	04
20	4	54	19	05
21	4	52	19	07
22	4	50	19	09
23	4	48	19	10
24	4	46	19	12
25	4	44	19	14
26	4	42	19	15
27	4	40	19	17
28	4	38	19	19
29	4	36	19	20
30	4	34	19	22

MOON PHASES

	d	h	m
First Quarter	1	10	49
Full Moon	8	03	22
Last Quarter	15	15	31
New Moon	23	15	26
First Quarter	30	17	08

DURATION OF TWILIGHT AT 52°N (MINUTES)

January	1st	11th	21st	31st
Civil	34	35	37	38
Nautical	75	78	83	88
Astronomical	120	127	137	150

398 Astronomical Data

MAY 2001
SUNRISE AND SUNSET (GMT)

	\\multicolumn{2}{c}{0°}	\\multicolumn{2}{c}{05′ 51° 30′}
	h	m	h	m
1	4	32	19	24
2	4	30	19	25
3	4	29	19	27
4	4	27	19	28
5	4	25	19	30
6	4	23	19	32
7	4	21	19	33
8	4	20	19	35
9	4	18	19	36
10	4	16	19	38
11	4	15	19	40
12	4	13	19	41
13	4	12	19	43
14	4	10	19	44
15	4	09	19	46
16	4	07	19	47
17	4	06	19	49
18	4	04	19	50
19	4	03	19	52
20	4	02	19	53
21	4	00	19	54
22	3	59	19	56
23	3	58	19	57
24	3	57	19	58
25	3	56	20	00
26	3	54	20	01
27	3	53	20	02
28	3	52	20	03
29	3	51	20	05
30	3	51	20	06
31	3	50	20	07

MOON PHASES

	d	h	m
Full Moon	7	13	53
Last Quarter	15	10	11
New Moon	23	02	46
First Quarter	29	22	09

DURATION OF TWILIGHT AT 52°N (MINUTES)

January	1st	11th	21st	31st
Civil	39	41	43	45
Nautical	89	96	103	111
Astronomical	152	175	TAN	TAN

TAN = twilight all night

JUNE 2001
SUNRISE AND SUNSET (GMT)

	\\multicolumn{2}{c}{0°}	\\multicolumn{2}{c}{05′ 51° 30′}
	h	m	h	m
1	3	49	20	08
2	3	48	20	09
3	3	47	20	10
4	3	47	20	11
5	3	46	20	12
6	3	45	20	13
7	3	45	20	14
8	3	44	20	15
9	3	44	20	15
10	3	44	20	16
11	3	43	20	17
12	3	43	20	18
13	3	43	20	18
14	3	43	20	19
15	3	43	20	19
16	3	42	20	20
17	3	42	20	20
18	3	42	20	20
19	3	43	20	21
20	3	43	20	21
21	3	43	20	21
22	3	43	20	21
23	3	43	20	22
24	3	44	20	22
25	3	44	20	22
26	3	45	20	22
27	3	45	20	22
28	3	46	20	21
29	3	46	20	21
30	3	47	20	21

MOON PHASES

	d	h	m
Full Moon	6	01	39
Last Quarter	14	03	28
New Moon	21	11	58
First Quarter	28	03	19

DURATION OF TWILIGHT AT 52°N (MINUTES)

January	1st	11th	21st	31st
Civil	46	47	47	47
Nautical	112	119	122	120
Astronomical	TAN	TAN	TAN	TAN

TAN = twilight all night

JULY 2001

SUNRISE AND SUNSET (GMT)

	0°		05' 51° 30'	
	h	m	h	m
1	3	47	20	21
2	3	48	20	20
3	3	49	20	20
4	3	50	20	19
5	3	50	20	19
6	3	51	20	18
7	3	52	20	18
8	3	53	20	17
9	3	54	20	16
10	3	55	20	16
11	3	56	20	15
12	3	57	20	14
13	3	58	20	13
14	4	00	20	12
15	4	01	20	11
16	4	02	20	10
17	4	03	20	09
18	4	04	20	08
19	4	06	20	07
20	4	07	20	06
21	4	08	20	04
22	4	10	20	03
23	4	11	20	02
24	4	12	20	00
25	4	14	19	59
26	4	15	19	58
27	4	17	19	56
28	4	18	19	55
29	4	20	19	53
30	4	21	19	52
31	4	22	19	50

MOON PHASES

	d	h	m
Full Moon	5	15	04
Last Quarter	13	18	45
New Moon	20	19	44
First Quarter	27	10	08

DURATION OF TWILIGHT AT 52°N (MINUTES)

January	1st	11th	21st	31st
Civil	47	45	43	40
Nautical	120	112	103	95
Astronomical	TAN	TAN	211	170

TAN = twilight all night

AUGUST 2001

SUNRISE AND SUNSET (GMT)

	0°		05' 51° 30'	
	h	m	h	m
1	4	24	19	48
2	4	25	19	47
3	4	27	19	45
4	4	29	19	43
5	4	30	19	41
6	4	32	19	40
7	4	33	19	38
8	4	35	19	36
9	4	36	19	34
10	4	38	19	32
11	4	39	19	31
12	4	41	19	29
13	4	43	19	27
14	4	44	19	25
15	4	46	19	23
16	4	47	19	21
17	4	49	19	19
18	4	50	19	17
19	4	52	19	15
20	4	54	19	13
21	4	55	19	10
22	4	57	19	08
23	4	58	19	06
24	5	00	19	04
25	5	02	19	02
26	5	03	19	00
27	5	05	18	58
28	5	06	18	55
29	5	08	18	53
30	5	10	18	51
31	5	11	18	49

MOON PHASES

	d	h	m
Full Moon	4	05	56
Last Quarter	12	07	53
New Moon	19	02	55
First Quarter	25	19	55

DURATION OF TWILIGHT AT 52°N (MINUTES)

January	1st	11th	21st	31st
Civil	40	38	36	35
Nautical	94	87	82	78
Astronomical	167	147	134	125

400 Astronomical Data

SEPTEMBER 2001
SUNRISE AND SUNSET (GMT)

	0°		05′ 51° 30′	
	h	m	h	m
1	5	13	18	47
2	5	14	18	44
3	5	16	18	42
4	5	18	18	40
5	5	19	18	38
6	5	21	18	35
7	5	22	18	33
8	5	24	18	31
9	5	26	18	29
10	5	27	18	26
11	5	29	18	24
12	5	30	18	22
13	5	32	18	19
14	5	34	18	17
15	5	35	18	15
16	5	37	18	13
17	5	38	18	10
18	5	40	18	08
19	5	42	18	06
20	5	43	18	03
21	5	45	18	01
22	5	46	17	59
23	5	48	17	56
24	5	50	17	54
25	5	51	17	52
26	5	53	17	49
27	5	54	17	47
28	5	56	17	45
29	5	58	17	43
30	5	59	17	40

MOON PHASES

	d	h	m
Full Moon	2	21	43
Last Quarter	10	19	00
New Moon	17	10	27
First Quarter	24	09	31

DURATION OF TWILIGHT AT 52°N (MINUTES)

January	1st	11th	21st	31st
Civil	35	34	33	33
Nautical	77	74	73	72
Astronomical	124	118	114	112

OCTOBER 2001
SUNRISE AND SUNSET (GMT)

	0°		05′ 51° 30′	
	h	m	h	m
1	6	01	17	38
2	6	03	17	36
3	6	04	17	34
4	6	06	17	31
5	6	07	17	29
6	6	09	17	27
7	6	11	17	25
8	6	12	17	22
9	6	14	17	20
10	6	16	17	18
11	6	17	17	16
12	6	19	17	14
13	6	21	17	11
14	6	23	17	09
15	6	24	17	07
16	6	26	17	05
17	6	28	17	03
18	6	29	17	01
19	6	31	16	59
20	6	33	16	57
21	6	35	16	55
22	6	36	16	53
23	6	38	16	50
24	6	40	16	49
25	6	42	16	47
26	6	43	16	45
27	6	45	16	43
28	6	47	16	41
29	6	49	16	39
30	6	50	16	37
31	6	52	16	35

MOON PHASES

	d	h	m
Full Moon	2	13	49
Last Quarter	10	4	20
New Moon	16	19	23
First Quarter	24	2	58

DURATION OF TWILIGHT AT 52°N (MINUTES)

January	1st	11th	21st	31st
Civil	33	33	34	35
Nautical	72	72	73	75
Astronomical	111	111	111	113

Astronomical Data

NOVEMBER 2001
SUNRISE AND SUNSET (GMT)

		0°		05' 51° 30'	
		h	m	h	m
1		6	54	16	33
2		6	56	16	31
3		6	57	16	30
4		6	59	16	28
5		7	01	16	26
6		7	03	16	25
7		7	04	16	23
8		7	06	16	21
9		7	08	16	20
10		7	10	16	18
11		7	11	16	17
12		7	13	16	15
13		7	15	16	14
14		7	17	16	12
15		7	18	16	11
16		7	20	16	10
17		7	22	16	08
18		7	23	16	07
19		7	25	16	06
20		7	27	16	05
21		7	28	16	04
22		7	30	16	02
23		7	32	16	01
24		7	33	16	00
25		7	35	16	00
26		7	36	15	59
27		7	38	15	58
28		7	39	15	57
29		7	41	15	56
30		7	42	15	55

MOON PHASES

	d	h	m
Full Moon	1	05	41
Last Quarter	8	12	21
New Moon	15	06	40
First Quarter	22	23	21
Full Moon	30	20	49

DURATION OF TWILIGHT AT 52°N (MINUTES)

	1st	11th	21st	31st
January				
Civil	35	37	38	39
Nautical	75	77	79	81
Astronomical	113	116	119	121

DECEMBER 2001
SUNRISE AND SUNSET (GMT)

		0°		05' 51° 30'	
		h	m	h	m
1		7	44	15	55
2		7	45	15	54
3		7	46	15	54
4		7	48	15	53
5		7	49	15	53
6		7	50	15	52
7		7	51	15	52
8		7	53	15	52
9		7	54	15	52
10		7	55	15	51
11		7	56	15	51
12		7	57	15	51
13		7	58	15	51
14		7	59	15	51
15		8	00	15	51
16		8	00	15	52
17		8	01	15	52
18		8	02	15	52
19		8	02	15	52
20		8	03	15	53
21		8	04	15	53
22		8	04	15	54
23		8	05	15	54
24		8	05	15	55
25		8	05	15	56
26		8	06	15	56
27		8	06	15	57
28		8	06	15	58
29		8	06	15	59
30		8	06	16	00
31		8	06	16	01

MOON PHASES

	d	h	m
Last Quarter	7	19	52
New Moon	14	20	47
First Quarter	22	20	56
Full Moon	30	10	40

DURATION OF TWILIGHT AT 52°N (MINUTES)

	1st	11th	21st	31st
January				
Civil	39	40	40	40
Nautical	81	83	83	83
Astronomical	122	124	124	124

TIDAL DATA

CONSTANTS

The constant tidal difference may be used in conjunction with the time of high water at London Bridge to find the time of high water at any of the ports or places listed below. These tidal differences are very approximate and should be used only as a guide to the time of high water at the places below. More precise local data should be obtained for navigational and other nautical purposes.

All data allow high water time to be found in Greenwich Mean Time; this applies also to data for the months when British Summer Time is in operation and the hour's time difference should be allowed for. Parts marked with * are in a different time zone and the standard time zone difference also needs to be added/subtracted to give local time. The columns headed Springs and Neaps show the height, in metres, of the tide datum for mean high water springs and nean high water neaps respectively.

Port	Diff.		Springs	Neaps
	h	m	m	m
*Antwerp (Prosperpolder)	+0	50	5.8	4.8
Avonmouth	-6	45	13.2	9.8
Belfast	-2	47	3.5	3.0
*Boulogne	-2	44	8.9	7.2
*Calais	-2	04	7.2	5.9
*Cherbourg	-6	00	6.4	5.0
Cowes	-2	38	4.2	3.5
Dartmouth	+4	25	4.9	3.8
*Dieppe	-3	03	9.3	7.3
Dover	-2	52	6.7	5.3
Dublin	-2	05	4.1	3.4
Dun Laoghaire	-2	10	4.1	3.4
*Dunkirk	-1	54	6.0	4.9
*Flushing	-0	15	4.7	3.9
Folkestone	-3	04	7.1	5.7
Harwich	-2	06	4.0	3.4
*Le Havre	-3	55	7.9	6.6
*Hook of Holland	-0	01	2.1	1.7
Hull (Albert Dock)	-7	40	7.5	5.8
Immingham	-8	00	7.3	5.8
Larne	-2	40	2.8	2.5
Londonderry	-5	37	2.7	2.1
Lowestoft	-4	25	2.4	2.1
Margate	-1	53	4.8	3.9
Newhaven	-2	46	6.7	5.1
*Ostend	-1	32	5.1	4.2
Plymouth	+4	05	5.5	4.4
Portland	+5	09	2.1	1.4
Portsmouth	-2	38	4.7	3.8
Ramsgate	-2	32	5.2	4.1
Richmond Lock	+1	00	4.9	3.7
*Rotterdam	+1	45	2.0	1.7
St Helier	+4	48	11.0	8.1
St Malo	+4	27	12.2	9.2
St Peter Port	+4	54	9.3	7.0
Sheerness	-1	19	5.8	4.7
Shoreham	-2	44	6.3	4.9
Southampton (1st high water)	-2	54	4.5	3.7
Spurn Head	-8	25	6.9	5.5
Swansea	-7	35	9.5	7.2
Tilbury	-0	49	6.4	5.4
Tyne River (North Shields)	-10	30	5.0	3.9
Walton-on-the-Naze	-2	10	4.2	2.8
*Zeebrugge	-0	55	4.8	3.9

TIDAL PREDICTIONS

The data below are daily predictions of the time and height of high water at London Bridge. The time of the data is Greenwich Mean Time; this applies also to data for the months when British Summer Time is in operation and the hour's time difference should be allowed for. The datum of predictions for each port shows the difference of height, in metres from Ordnance data (Newlyn). This tidal information is reproduced with the permission of the UK Hydrographic Office and the Controller of HMSO. Crown copyright reserved.

Tidal Data   403

JANUARY 2001 Highwater GMT

LONDON BRIDGE
Datum predictions 3.20m below

		hr		ht m	hr		ht m
1	Mo	05	17	6.4	17	58	6.3
2	Tu	06	01	6.2	18	45	6.2
3	We	06	52	6.1	19	38	6.1
4	Th	07	50	6.0	20	38	6.0
5	Fr	08	56	6.0	21	45	6.1
6	Sa	10	05	6.1	22	52	6.5
7	Su	11	13	6.4	23	54	6.5
8	Mo	-	-	-	12	14	6.7
9	Tu	00	49	6.8	13	12	7.0
10	We	01	41	7.0	14	05	7.2
11	Th	02	30	7.1	14	56	7.4
12	Fr	03	18	7.2	15	46	7.5
13	Sa	04	04	7.2	16	34	7.5
14	Su	04	49	7.1	17	22	7.3
15	Mo	05	34	6.9	18	11	7.0
16	Tu	06	21	6.6	19	03	6.6
17	We	07	16	6.3	20	01	6.3
18	Th	08	22	6.1	21	06	6.0
19	Fr	09	32	6.0	22	10	6.0
20	Sa	10	38	6.1	23	09	6.1
21	Su	11	38	6.3	-	-	-
22	Mo	00	03	6.3	12	32	6.5
23	Tu	00	52	6.5	13	20	6.6
24	We	01	36	6.6	14	04	6.7
25	Th	02	14	6.6	14	42	6.7
26	Fr	02	47	6.6	15	16	6.6
27	Sa	03	18	6.5	15	47	6.6
28	Su	03	48	6.5	16	19	6.6
29	Mo	04	20	6.5	16	54	6.6
30	Tu	04	56	6.6	17	32	6.6
31	We	05	35	6.5	18	15	6.5

FEBRUARY 2001 Highwater GMT

LONDON BRIDGE
Datum predictions 3.20m below

		hr		ht m	hr		ht m
1	Th	06	20	6.4	19	03	6.3
2	Fr	07	13	6.2	19	58	6.1
3	Sa	08	15	6.1	21	02	5.9
4	Su	09	25	6.0	22	15	6.0
5	Mo	10	42	6.1	23	28	6.2
6	Tu	11	55	6.5	-	-	-
7	We	00	30	6.5	12	57	6.9
8	Th	01	25	6.9	13	52	7.2
9	Fr	02	15	7.1	14	44	7.5
10	Sa	03	03	7.3	15	32	7.6
11	Su	03	47	7.3	16	17	7.6
12	Mo	04	29	7.3	17	01	7.4
13	Tu	05	10	7.1	17	44	7.1
14	We	05	51	6.9	18	26	6.7
15	Th	06	34	6.5	19	11	6.2
16	Fr	07	26	6.1	20	06	5.8
17	Sa	08	41	5.7	21	22	5.6
18	Su	10	06	5.7	22	34	5.6
19	Mo	11	13	5.9	23	34	5.9
20	Tu	-	-	-	12	10	6.2
21	We	00	27	6.2	13	00	6.5
22	Th	01	14	6.5	13	44	6.7
23	Fr	01	55	6.6	14	22	6.7
24	Sa	02	31	6.6	14	56	6.7
25	Su	03	02	6.6	15	27	6.6
26	Mo	03	32	6.6	15	58	6.7
27	Tu	04	01	6.6	16	30	6.7
28	We	04	34	6.7	17	06	6.7

MARCH 2001 Highwater GMT

LONDON BRIDGE
Datum predictions 3.20m below

		hr		ht m	hr		ht m
1	Th	05	11	6.7	17	46	6.6
2	Fr	05	55	6.6	18	32	6.4
3	Sa	06	46	6.3	19	24	6.0
4	Su	07	46	6.0	20	26	5.8
5	Mo	08	57	5.8	21	45	5.7
6	Tu	10	23	5.9	23	08	6.0
7	We	11	42	6.3	-	-	-
8	Th	00	13	6.4	12	45	6.8
9	Fr	01	09	6.8	13	38	7.2
10	Sa	01	58	7.1	14	27	7.5
11	Su	02	43	7.3	15	13	7.6
12	Mo	03	26	7.4	15	55	7.5
13	Tu	04	06	7.4	16	35	7.3
14	We	04	44	7.2	17	12	7.1
15	Th	05	22	7.0	17	47	6.7
16	Fr	06	00	6.6	18	24	6.3
17	Sa	06	44	6.1	19	06	5.9
18	Su	07	42	5.7	20	02	5.5
19	Mo	09	26	5.4	21	49	5.3
20	Tu	10	45	5.6	23	02	5.6
21	We	11	43	6.0	23	58	6.0
22	Th	-	-	-	12	33	6.4
23	Fr	00	46	6.4	13	17	6.6
24	Sa	01	29	6.5	13	56	6.7
25	Su	02	06	6.6	14	30	6.7
26	Mo	02	39	6.6	15	02	6.7
27	Tu	03	10	6.6	15	33	6.8
28	We	03	40	6.7	16	06	6.8
29	Th	04	14	6.8	16	42	6.8
30	Fr	04	53	6.8	17	21	6.6
31	Sa	05	37	6.6	18	06	6.3

APRIL 2001 Highwater GMT

LONDON BRIDGE
Datum predictions 3.20m below

		hr		ht m	hr		ht m
1	Su	06	27	6.3	18	57	5.9
2	Mo	07	28	6.0	20	01	5.6
3	Tu	08	44	5.8	21	27	5.6
4	We	10	16	5.9	22	51	5.9
5	Th	11	31	6.4	23	55	6.4
6	Fr	-	-	-	12	29	6.9
7	Sa	00	48	6.9	13	20	7.3
8	Su	01	36	7.1	14	07	7.5
9	Mo	02	21	7.3	14	50	7.5
10	Tu	03	03	7.3	15	30	7.4
11	We	03	42	7.3	16	07	7.2
12	Th	04	19	7.2	16	40	6.9
13	Fr	04	56	6.9	17	12	6.7
14	Sa	05	34	6.6	17	47	6.4
15	Su	06	16	6.2	18	27	6.0
16	Mo	07	08	5.7	19	18	5.8
17	Tu	08	26	5.4	20	36	5.3
18	We	10	05	5.5	22	19	5.5
19	Th	11	07	5.9	23	20	5.9
20	Fr	11	57	6.3	-	-	-
21	Sa	00	10	6.2	12	42	6.6
22	Su	00	55	6.5	13	22	6.7
23	Mo	01	34	6.6	13	59	6.8
24	Tu	02	10	6.7	14	34	6.8
25	We	02	45	6.8	15	09	6.8
26	Th	03	21	6.8	15	45	6.8
27	Fr	03	59	6.9	16	23	6.8
28	Sa	04	41	6.9	17	03	6.6
29	Su	05	27	6.7	17	48	6.3
30	Mo	06	20	6.4	18	41	5.9

MAY 2001 Highwater GMT

LONDON BRIDGE
Datum predictions 3.20m below

		hr		ht m	hr		ht m
1	Tu	07	23	6.0	19	48	5.7
2	We	08	43	5.9	21	16	5.7
3	Th	10	06	6.2	22	31	6.1
4	Fr	11	12	6.6	23	31	6.5
5	Sa	–	–	–	12	07	7.0
6	Su	00	24	6.9	12	58	7.3
7	Mo	01	13	7.1	13	44	7.4
8	Tu	01	58	7.2	14	26	7.3
9	We	02	41	7.2	15	05	7.2
10	Th	03	21	7.1	15	40	7.0
11	Fr	03	58	7.0	16	11	6.8
12	Sa	04	35	6.8	16	43	6.6
13	Su	05	12	6.5	17	18	6.4
14	Mo	05	54	6.2	17	59	6.1
15	Tu	06	42	5.8	18	48	5.8
16	We	07	42	5.6	19	51	5.5
17	Th	09	00	5.6	21	15	5.5
18	Fr	10	13	5.8	22	27	5.8
19	Sa	11	10	6.1	23	23	6.1
20	Su	11	59	6.5	–	–	–
21	Mo	00	12	6.4	12	44	6.7
22	Tu	00	57	6.6	13	26	6.8
23	We	01	40	6.8	14	07	6.9
24	Th	02	22	6.9	14	47	6.9
25	Fr	03	04	7.0	15	28	6.9
26	Sa	03	48	7.0	16	10	6.8
27	Su	04	34	7.0	16	53	6.7
28	Mo	05	23	6.8	17	40	6.4
29	Tu	06	17	6.5	18	34	6.2
30	We	07	21	6.3	19	41	6.0
31	Th	08	34	6.2	20	57	6.0

JUNE 2001 Highwater GMT

LONDON BRIDGE
Datum predictions 3.20m below

		hr		ht m	hr		ht m
1	Fr	09	44	6.4	22	04	6.2
2	Sa	10	46	6.6	23	04	6.5
3	Su	11	42	6.9	23	59	6.8
4	Mo	–	–	–	12	33	7.1
5	Tu	00	49	7.0	13	20	7.2
6	We	01	37	7.0	14	03	7.1
7	Th	02	22	7.0	14	42	7.0
8	Fr	03	03	6.9	15	17	6.8
9	Sa	03	42	6.8	15	48	6.7
10	Su	04	18	6.6	16	20	6.6
11	Mo	04	54	6.4	16	55	6.4
12	Tu	05	33	6.2	17	35	6.3
13	We	06	17	6.1	18	22	6.0
14	Th	07	08	5.9	19	16	5.8
15	Fr	08	05	5.8	20	19	5.8
16	Sa	09	09	5.9	21	26	5.8
17	Su	10	13	6.1	22	30	6.0
18	Mo	11	12	6.3	23	28	6.3
19	Tu	–	–	–	12	05	6.6
20	We	00	22	6.5	12	55	6.8
21	Th	01	13	6.8	13	43	6.9
22	Fr	02	02	7.0	14	29	7.0
23	Sa	02	51	7.1	15	14	7.0
24	Su	03	39	7.2	16	00	7.0
25	Mo	04	28	7.2	16	45	6.9
26	Tu	05	17	7.1	17	32	6.7
27	We	06	09	6.9	18	23	6.5
28	Th	07	07	6.6	19	22	6.3
29	Fr	08	10	6.4	20	27	6.2
30	Sa	09	15	6.4	21	33	6.2

JULY 2001 Highwater GMT

LONDON BRIDGE
Datum predictions 3.20m below

		hr		ht m	hr		ht m
1	Su	10	16	6.4	22	36	6.4
2	Mo	11	14	6.6	23	34	6.5
3	Tu	–	–	–	12	08	6.7
4	We	00	29	6.7	12	57	6.9
5	Th	01	20	6.8	13	43	6.9
6	Fr	02	06	6.8	14	24	6.8
7	Sa	02	49	6.8	15	00	6.7
8	Su	03	27	6.7	15	31	6.6
9	Mo	04	02	6.5	16	02	6.5
10	Tu	04	35	6.4	16	36	6.5
11	We	05	11	6.4	17	13	6.4
12	Th	05	50	6.3	17	54	6.3
13	Fr	06	33	6.2	18	40	6.1
14	Sa	07	23	6.1	19	33	6.0
15	Su	08	19	6.0	20	33	5.9
16	Mo	09	22	6.0	21	39	6.0
17	Tu	10	28	6.1	22	47	6.1
18	We	11	32	6.4	23	51	6.4
19	Th	–	–	–	12	29	6.6
20	Fr	00	50	6.7	13	23	6.9
21	Sa	01	46	7.0	14	13	7.0
22	Su	02	37	7.3	15	01	7.1
23	Mo	03	27	7.4	15	47	7.2
24	Tu	04	16	7.4	16	32	7.2
25	We	05	03	7.4	17	16	7.1
26	Th	05	51	7.1	18	01	6.9
27	Fr	06	41	6.8	18	51	6.6
28	Sa	07	37	6.4	19	49	6.3
29	Su	08	39	6.2	20	57	6.1
30	Mo	09	43	6.0	22	07	6.0
31	Tu	10	45	6.1	23	12	6.2

AUGUST 2001 Highwater GMT

LONDON BRIDGE
Datum predictions 3.20m below

		hr		ht m	hr		ht m
1	We	11	43	6.3	–	–	–
2	Th	00	10	6.4	12	36	6.5
3	Fr	01	03	6.7	13	23	6.7
4	Sa	01	51	6.8	14	06	6.8
5	Su	02	33	6.8	14	43	6.7
6	Mo	03	10	6.7	15	16	6.6
7	Tu	03	42	6.6	15	45	6.5
8	We	04	13	6.5	16	15	6.5
9	Th	04	44	6.5	16	47	6.5
10	Fr	05	19	6.5	17	23	6.5
11	Sa	05	59	6.4	18	05	6.4
12	Su	06	43	6.2	18	53	6.2
13	Mo	07	35	6.0	19	50	6.0
14	Tu	08	36	5.9	20	56	5.9
15	We	09	47	5.8	22	11	6.0
16	Th	11	02	6.1	23	28	6.3
17	Fr	–	–	–	12	08	6.4
18	Sa	00	33	6.7	13	04	6.8
19	Su	01	31	7.1	13	55	7.1
20	Mo	02	23	7.4	14	43	7.3
21	Tu	03	11	7.6	15	28	7.4
22	We	03	57	7.6	16	11	7.4
23	Th	04	42	7.5	16	52	7.3
24	Fr	05	25	7.2	17	33	7.1
25	Sa	06	08	6.8	18	16	6.8
26	Su	06	54	6.4	19	05	6.3
27	Mo	07	49	5.9	20	13	5.9
28	Tu	09	03	5.6	21	39	5.7
29	We	10	15	5.7	22	51	5.9
30	Th	11	17	6.0	23	51	6.2
31	Fr	–	–	–	12	12	6.3

Tidal Data 405

SEPTEMBER 2001 Highwater GMT

LONDON BRIDGE
Datum predictions 3.20m below

		hr		ht m	hr		ht m
1	Sa	00	43	6.6	13	01	6.6
2	Su	01	30	6.8	13	44	6.7
3	Mo	02	12	6.9	14	22	6.7
4	Tu	02	47	6.8	14	55	6.6
5	We	03	18	6.7	15	23	6.6
6	Th	03	46	6.6	15	50	6.5
7	Fr	04	15	6.6	16	20	6.6
8	Sa	04	47	6.6	16	54	6.6
9	Su	05	24	6.5	17	34	6.5
10	Mo	06	06	6.3	18	21	6.3
11	Tu	06	56	6.0	19	17	6.0
12	We	07	55	5.7	20	24	5.8
13	Th	09	10	5.6	21	46	5.8
14	Fr	10	38	5.8	23	12	6.2
15	Sa	11	48	6.3	–	–	–
16	Su	00	19	6.7	12	45	6.8
17	Mo	01	14	7.2	13	34	7.1
18	Tu	02	04	7.5	14	20	7.3
19	We	02	50	7.6	15	04	7.4
20	Th	03	34	7.6	15	45	7.4
21	Fr	04	15	7.4	16	25	7.4
22	Sa	04	53	7.1	17	04	7.1
23	Su	05	30	6.8	17	43	6.8
24	Mo	06	07	6.3	18	27	6.3
25	Tu	06	47	5.9	19	24	5.8
26	We	07	48	5.4	21	08	5.5
27	Th	09	41	5.4	22	25	5.7
28	Fr	10	48	5.7	23	25	6.1
29	Sa	11	44	6.1	–	–	–
30	Su	00	17	6.5	12	33	6.5

OCTOBER 2001 Highwater GMT

LONDON BRIDGE
Datum predictions 3.20m below

		hr		ht m	hr		ht m
1	Mo	01	03	6.8	13	16	6.7
2	Tu	01	43	6.9	13	54	6.7
3	We	02	17	6.8	14	27	6.7
4	Th	02	48	6.7	14	56	6.6
5	Fr	03	16	6.7	15	24	6.6
6	Sa	03	45	6.7	15	54	6.7
7	Su	04	18	6.7	16	30	6.7
8	Mo	04	54	6.6	17	11	6.6
9	Tu	05	36	6.3	18	00	6.4
10	We	06	25	6.0	18	57	6.0
11	Th	07	24	5.6	20	06	5.8
12	Fr	08	44	5.5	21	34	5.8
13	Sa	10	18	5.8	22	58	6.3
14	Su	11	26	6.3	–	–	–
15	Mo	00	00	6.8	12	21	6.8
16	Tu	00	53	7.3	13	10	7.1
17	We	01	41	7.5	13	55	7.3
18	Th	02	25	7.6	14	38	7.4
19	Fr	03	07	7.5	15	20	7.4
20	Sa	03	46	7.3	16	00	7.3
21	Su	04	22	7.0	16	38	7.1
22	Mo	04	55	6.7	17	17	6.7
23	Tu	05	27	6.4	17	59	6.3
24	We	06	04	6.0	18	50	5.8
25	Th	06	52	5.6	20	14	5.4
26	Fr	08	33	5.3	21	49	5.5
27	Sa	10	09	5.5	22	50	5.9
28	Su	11	07	5.9	23	42	6.3
29	Mo	11	56	6.3	–	–	–
30	Tu	00	27	6.6	12	40	6.5
31	We	01	07	6.8	13	19	6.6

NOVEMBER 2001 Highwater GMT

LONDON BRIDGE
Datum predictions 3.20m below

		hr		ht m	hr		ht m
1	Th	01	42	6.8	13	54	6.7
2	Fr	02	15	6.8	14	27	6.7
3	Sa	02	48	6.8	15	00	6.7
4	Su	03	21	6.8	15	36	6.8
5	Mo	03	55	6.7	16	15	6.8
6	Tu	04	34	6.6	16	59	6.7
7	We	05	16	6.3	17	49	6.4
8	Th	06	04	6.0	18	46	6.1
9	Fr	07	04	5.7	19	57	5.9
10	Sa	08	28	5.6	21	23	6.0
11	Su	09	54	5.9	22	37	6.4
12	Mo	10	59	6.4	23	36	6.8
13	Tu	11	54	6.8	–	–	–
14	We	00	29	7.2	12	44	7.1
15	Th	01	17	7.4	13	31	7.3
16	Fr	02	01	7.4	14	16	7.3
17	Sa	02	42	7.3	14	59	7.2
18	Su	03	20	7.1	15	39	7.1
19	Mo	03	54	6.9	16	18	6.9
20	Tu	04	25	6.6	16	57	6.6
21	We	04	58	6.3	17	37	6.3
22	Th	05	35	6.1	18	23	5.9
23	Fr	06	21	5.8	19	20	5.6
24	Sa	07	22	5.5	20	38	5.5
25	Su	08	56	5.4	21	54	5.7
26	Mo	10	12	5.7	22	51	6.0
27	Tu	11	08	6.0	23	40	6.3
28	We	11	56	6.3	–	–	–
29	Th	00	24	6.6	12	40	6.5
30	Fr	01	06	6.7	13	21	6.7

DECEMBER 2001 Highwater GMT

LONDON BRIDGE
Datum predictions 3.20m below

		hr		ht m	hr		ht m
1	Sa	01	45	6.8	14	01	6.8
2	Su	02	24	6.9	14	42	6.9
3	Mo	03	02	6.8	15	24	7.0
4	Tu	03	42	6.8	16	08	7.0
5	We	04	22	6.7	16	54	6.8
6	Th	05	06	6.5	17	44	6.6
7	Fr	05	54	6.2	18	41	6.4
8	Sa	06	53	6.0	19	47	6.2
9	Su	08	08	5.9	21	00	6.2
10	Mo	09	24	6.1	22	09	6.4
11	Tu	10	30	6.3	23	09	6.6
12	We	11	28	6.6	–	–	–
13	Th	00	03	6.9	12	22	6.9
14	Fr	00	53	7.0	13	11	7.0
15	Sa	01	39	7.1	13	58	7.1
16	Su	02	21	7.0	14	43	7.0
17	Mo	02	59	6.9	15	24	6.9
18	Tu	03	32	6.7	16	03	6.7
19	We	04	03	6.6	16	39	6.5
20	Th	04	36	6.4	17	17	6.3
21	Fr	05	13	6.3	17	57	6.1
22	Sa	05	56	6.1	18	43	5.9
23	Su	06	46	5.9	19	35	5.8
24	Mo	07	47	5.7	20	35	5.7
25	Tu	08	55	5.7	21	41	5.8
26	We	10	03	5.8	22	44	6.0
27	Th	11	05	6.0	23	40	6.3
28	Fr	12	00	6.3	–	–	–
29	Sa	00	31	6.6	12	51	6.6
30	Su	01	19	6.7	13	39	6.8
31	Mo	02	04	6.8	14	27	7.0

FORTHCOMING EVENTS

*Provisional

2000

5 September	Brick Lane Festival
9–10 September	Millennium Festival of Youth **RAF Museum, Hendon**
12–13 September	City of London Flower Show **Guildhall**
17 September	2000 Thames Festival **River Thames from Hampton Court to Canary Wharf**
23 September	London Open House Days; Great River Race **Island Gardens, Richmond**
27 September – 1 October	Horse of the Year Show **Wembley** Twentieth Century British Art Fair **Royal College of Art**
1 October	Pearly Kings and Queens Harvest Festival **St Martin-in-the-Fields Church**
3–28 October	London Festival of Chamber Music
5–8 October	International Festival of Fine Wine and Food **Earl's Court, Olympia**
5 October – 10 December	The Wilde Years: Oscar Wilde and His Times **Barbican Art Gallery**
5 October – 10 December	Rock Style **Barbican Art Gallery**
7 October – 7 January 2001	Correggio and Parmigianino: Master Draughtsmen of the Renaissance **British Museum**
12–15 October	African and Caribbean Writing Festival **Newham**
12 October – 12 November	Terry Frost RA **Royal Academy**
14 October	Ceremony of the Constable's Dues **Tower of London** Supersprints – International Sprint Rowing Challenge **Millharbour**
18 October – 14 January 2001	Telling Time **National Gallery**
20 October – 14 January 2001	Contemporary Japanese Ceramics from Saga **British Museum**
21 October – 21 January 2001	Gladiators and Caesars: The Power of Spectacle in Ancient Rome **British Museum**
22 October	London Antiques Fair **Wembley Exhibition Hall**
26 October – 4 February 2001	Painting the Century **National Portrait Gallery**
28 October	Rugby League World Cup **Twickenham**
28 October – 11 November	London Bach Festival
31 October – 1 November	Royal Horticultural Society Flower Show **RHS Halls**
1 November – 28 January 2001	Impression: Painting Quickly in France, 1860-1890 **National Gallery**
2-16 November	London International Film Festival
5 November	London-Brighton Veteran Car Run
9 November – 11 February 2001	William Blake Exhibition **Tate Britain**
11 November	Lord Mayor's Show Two-minute silence at 11am Commonwealth Fair **Kensington Town Hall**
12 November	Remembrance Sunday service **Cenotaph, Whitehall**
13–16 November	World Travel Market **Earl's Court**
26–29 November	Smithfield Show **Earl's Court**
1–31 December	Bibles Exhibition **British Library**
2 December – 21 November 2001	Turner: The Great Watercolours **Royal Academy**
14–18 December	Olympia International Show Jumping Championships **Earl's Court, Olympia**
17 December	State Parades **Tower of London**

2001

1 January	New Year's Day Parade **Parliament Square to Berkeley Square**
4–14 January	London International Boat Show **Earl's Court**
20 January – 9 April	Caravaggio, Annibale Carracci, Rubens: Painting in Rome 1592-1623 **Royal Academy**
3 March	Women's Head of the River Race (rowing) **Chiswick to Putney**
14 March – 8 April	Ideal Home Exhibition **Earls Court**
17 March – 10 June	Head of the River Race (rowing) **Chiswick to Putney** Botticelli and Dante: Drawings for the Divine Comedy **Royal Academy**
21–27 March	British Antique Dealers' Association Antiques Fair
25–27 March*	London Book Fair **Olympia**
12 May	FA Cup Final
22–25 May	Chelsea Flower Show **Royal Hospital, Chelsea**
6 June	Beating Retreat by the Household Division Massed Bands **Horse Guards Parade**

Forthcoming Events

6–27 June	Spitalfields Festival	25 June – 8 July	Lawn Tennis: All England Championships, **Wimbledon**
*9 June	Trooping the Colour **Horse Guards Parade**	26 June – 19 July	City of London Festival
15–18 June	International Ceramics Fair and Seminar **Park Lane Hotel**	20 July – 15 September	BBC Proms **Royal Albert Hall**
21–24 June	Regent's Park Flower Show	26–27 August	Notting Hill Carnival
23–24 June	Middlesex County Show **Middlesex Showground**		

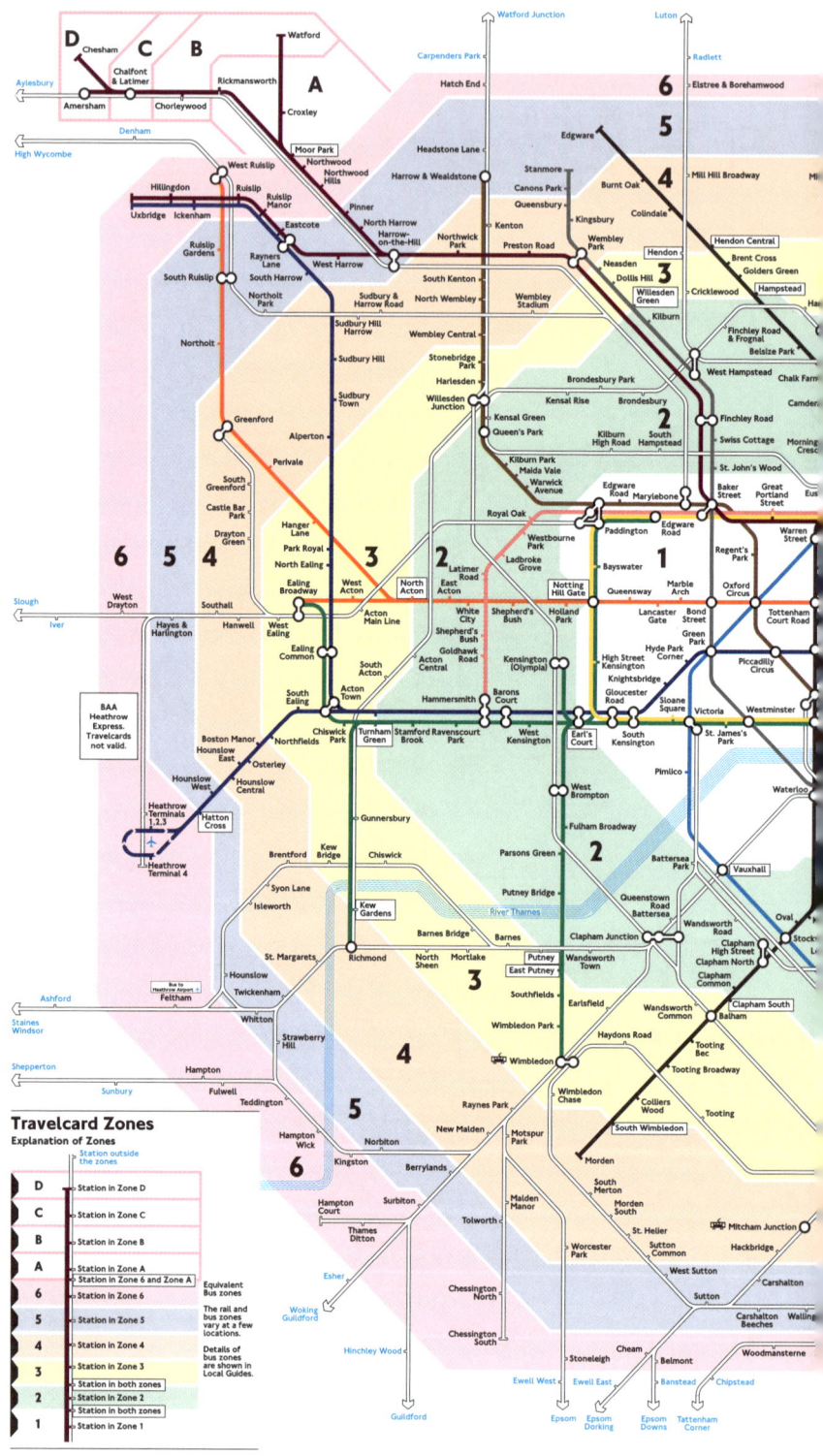

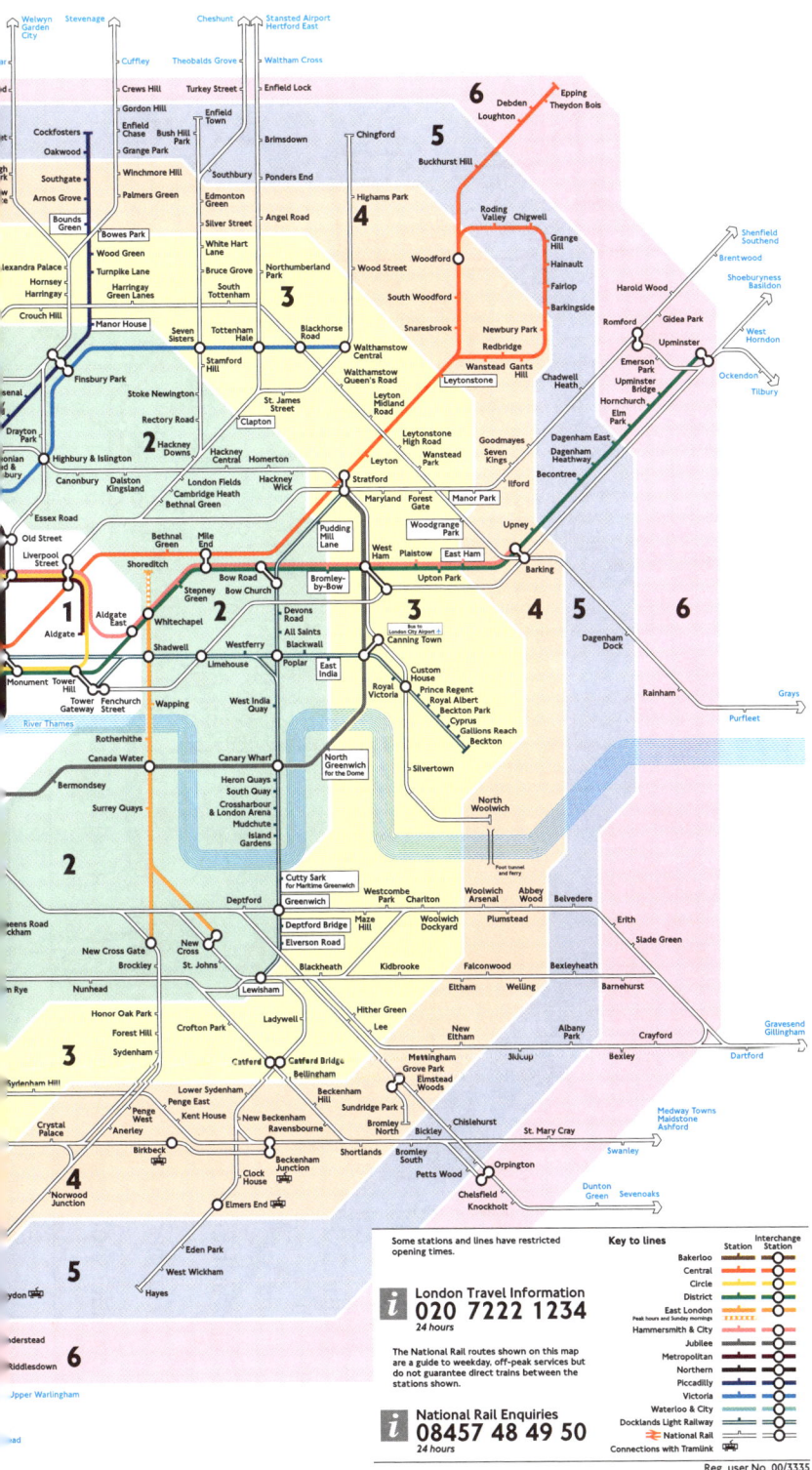

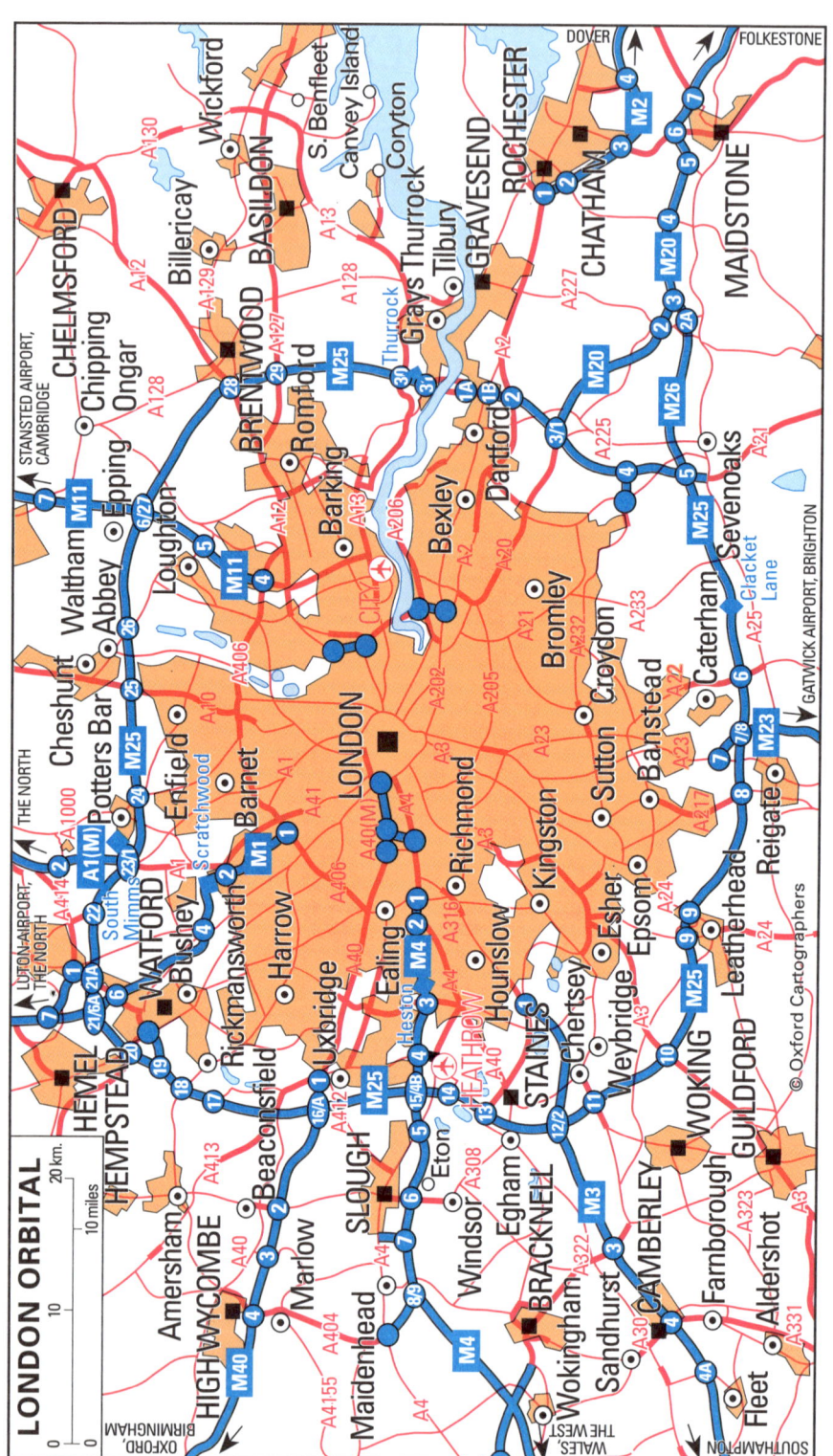

INDEX

A

Accountancy
  education and training 99
  firms 151
Action zones, education 92
Actuarial Science, education and training 99
Adjudicator's Office 155
Adoption 198
Adoption and Fostering, agencies 198
Advertising
  agencies 239-41
  Standards Authority 239
Advisory, Conciliation and Arbitration Service 167
Afghanistan Embassy 340
African and Afro-Caribbean Churches 362-3
Afro-West Indian United Council of Churches 363
Agricultural Land Tribunal 191
Agriculture, Fisheries and Food, Ministry of 81-2
Air travel
  Airlinks 138
  airports 142-4
  Civil Aviation Authority 142
  distances from London 350-1
  statistics 141-2
Albanian Embassy 340
Albert Bridge 299
Albert Hall 296
Aldermen 35
Alexandra, Bridge 298
Alexandra, Palace 262
Algerian Embassy 340
Ambassadors 340-6
Ambulance Service 105
Anglia Railways 135
Angolan Embassy 340
Anguillan Tourist Office 337
Antigua and Barbuda
  Embassy 340
  Tourist Office 337
Apostolic Nuncio of Great Britain 362
Appeals Service, Tribunal 191
Aquaculture, Environment, Fisheries and, Centre for 82
Archbishop of Canterbury 361
Archery 305, 317
Architecture and the Built Environment, Commission for 319
Architecture, education and training 99
Argentinian, Embassy 340
Armenian Embassy 340
Arsenal Football Club 310
Arts Council of England 318
Arya Pratinidhi Sabha 359
Associations
  Amateur Boxing 306, 316
  Amateur Rowing 316
  Amateur Swimming 316
  for Payment Clearing Services 152
  Martial Arts 316
  of Chartered Certified Accountants 154
  of Community Health Councils for England and Wales 116
  of London Government 70
  of South East Asian Nations 347
  of Train Operating Companies 136
Astronomical data 395-401
Athletics Association, South of England 318
Audit Commission for Local Authorities and the National Health Service in England and Wales 70
Australian Embassy 340
Austria
  Embassy 340
  National Tourist Office 337
Azerbaijan, Embassy 340
AZTEC 169

B

BAA plc 142
BACS Ltd 152
Baha'i Faith 358
Bahamas, Embassy 340
Bahrain, Embassy 340
Bangladesh, Embassy 340
Banking 99, 152, 159, 347
Baptist Church 363
  Union of Great Britain 363
Barbados
  High Commission 340
  Tourism Authority 337
Barbados, Antigua and
  Embassy 340
  Tourist Office 337
Barbican Centre 262
Barking, MP 71
Barking and Dagenham
  Borough Council 27-8
  map 27
Barking and Havering, health authorities and trusts 113
Barnes Bridge 299
Barnet
  Borough Council 28-9
  Football Club 310
  map 28
  waste and recycling facilities 330
Bar, The, General Council 195
Battersea
  Bridges 299
  MP 71
BBC 217
  local radio stations 219
  network services 219
  television 217
Bear Baiting 305-6
Beckenham, MP 71
Belarus, Embassy 340
Belgian Embassy 340
Belize, Embassy 340
Benefits Agency 87
Bermondsey, Southwark North and, MP 77
Beth Din, Federation of Synagogues 360
Bethnal Green and Bow, MP 72
Bexley
  Borough Council 29-30

412 Index

map 29
waste and recycling facilities 330
Bexley and Greenwich, health authorities and trusts 114
Bexleyheath and Crayford, MP 72
BFI London Imax Cinema 286
Bharatiya Vidya Bhavan 359
Billiards 306-7
Billingsgate Market 291
Birth statistics 4
Bishops' Conference of England and Wales 362
Black Death, The 256
Blackfriars bridges 298
Blood Service, National 117
Blue plaque sites 262-85
Board of Deputies of British Jews 360
Bolivian Embassy 340
Borough councils
  chief officers 27-69
  council members 27-69
  development of 27
  map 26
  political composition of 27-69
  population 27-69
  tax bands 27-69
Borough Market 291
Bosnia and Herzegovina, Embassy 340
Botswana, Embassy 340
Bow, Bethnal Green and, MP 72
Boxing
  Amateur Association 316
  Board of Control 316
Brazilian Embassy 341
Brent
  Borough Council 30-1
  Business Venture 168
  map 30
  MPs 72
  waste and recycling facilities 330
Brentford and Isleworth, MP 72
Brentford Football Club 310
Bridges 298-9
Britain Burma Buddhist Trust 358
British
  Agencies for Adoption and Fostering 198
  Boxing Board of Control 316
  Broadcasting Corporation 217
  Buddhist Association 358
  Darts Association 317
  Fencing Association 317
  Film Commission 318
  Film Institute 318-19
  Horseracing Board 317
  Library 286
  Olympic Association 317
  Orthodox Church 364
  Property Federation 119
  Railways Board 136
  Sky Broadcasting 218
  Telecom 251
  Tennis Foundation 317
  Tenpin Bowling Association 317
  Tourist Authority 322
  Trade International 160
  Transport Police 106
  Trust for Conservation Volunteers 328

Universities Sports Association 317
British Virgin Islands, Tourist Board 337
Broadcasting 217-19
  Standards Commission 217
Bromley and Chislehurst, MP 72
Bromley
  Borough Council 31-2
  health authorities and trusts 114
  map 31
  waste and recycling facilities 331
Bromley and Harrow, health authorities and trusts 114
Brunei Darussalam, High Commission 341
Brushfield Street Market 291
BT 251
  Cellnet 251
Buddhapadipa Temple 358
Buddhism 358
  Britain Burma Buddhist Trust 358
  British Burma Trust 358
  Buddhist centres 358
  Buddhist Society 358
  Buddhist Vihara, London 358
  origin and development 358
  Soka Gakkai 358
  Thames Buddhist Vihara 358
  Vietnam Society 358
  West London Society 359
Building, education and training 99-100
Building societies
  Commission 153
  Ombudsman 159
Built Environment, Architecture and, Commission for 319
Bulgarian Embassy 341
Bull Baiting 305-6
Burroughs Club 312
Burundi, Embassy 341
Buses
  coach travel 138-9
  companies 138-9
  services 138
  traffic statistics 137
Bushy Park 297
Business
  development of 149-51
  education and training 100
  Links 168-9
  Registration and Deregistration statistics 161
Buying Agency, The 88
Buzzlines 138

C
Cabinet, The 80
  Office 82
Cable and Wireless Communications 251
Cable television 249
Camberwell and Peckham, MP 72
Camden
  Borough Council 32-3
  map 32
  waste and recycling facilities 331
Cameroon, High Commission, Embassy 341
Canada, Embassy 341
Canning Town, Poplar and, MP 76
Capital FM and Gold 219
Caribbean Tourist organisation 337

Index 413

Carlton Television Ltd. 218
Car Parks, National 139
Carshalton and Wallington, MP 72
Catalan Tourist Board 337
Catering, education and training 100
Catford Stadium 310
Cayman Islands, Department of Tourism 337
CBI 160-1
CCTA 88
Cemeteries 286
Cenotaph, The 286
Central Council for Physical Recreation 316
Central Mosque 359
Central Office of Information 83
Central Science Laboratory 82
Chambers of Commerce 168
Channel 5 Broadcasting Ltd. 218
Channel Four Television Corporation 218
Chaps Clearing Company Ltd 153
Charity Commission 171
Charity organisations 170-3
Charlton Athletic Football Club 310
Chartered Certified Accountants, Association of 154
Chartered Institution of Water and Environment Management 328
Charterhouse 286
Cheam, Sutton and, MP 77
Chelsea
    Bridge 299
    Football Club 310
    Physic Garden 286
Chelsea, Kensington and
    map 54
    MP 75-6
    Royal Borough 54-5
    waste and recycling facilities 332
Chelsea, Kensington, Westminster and, health authorities and trusts 115
Chenery Travel (coaches) 138
Cheque and Credit Clearing Company Ltd 153
Chief Rabbinate 360
Children, legal notes 203
Child Support Agency 204
Chilean Embassy 341
Chiltern Railways 135
China, Peoples' Republic, Embassy 341
Chingford and Woodford Green, MP 72
Chipping Barnet, MP 72
Chiropractic, education and training 100
Chislehurst, Bromley and, MP 72
Chiswick Bridge 299
Choice FM radio 219
Christianity 357-8
Christians and Jews, Council for 357
    in London 358
Christian Science Committee on Publication 366
Churches
    African and Afro-Caribbean 362-3
    attendance 357
    Baptist 363
    Christ, Scientist 366
    Church Commissioners 361
    Churches Together in Britain and Ireland 357
    Churches Together in England 357
    Church of Christ, Scientist 366
    Church of England 361-2
    Church of Jesus Christ of Latter-Day Saints 366
    dioceses 361-2
    Jesus Christ of Latter-Day Saints 366
    Lutheran 363
    Methodist 363
    Orthodox 363-4
    Roman Catholic 362
    Seventh-Day Adventist 365
    United Reform 365
Cinemas 286-7
    BFI London Imax 286
Circuit, South Eastern 187
    judges 187
Citizens' Advice Bureaux 174-5
City Airport 142
City, East London and, health authorities and trusts 114-15
City of London
    Aldermen 35
    Common Council 35
    Corporation of 33-40
    guilds 36-40
    map 33
    Police 106
City of London and Westminster, MP 72-3
City Partners, London 169
Civil Aviation Authority 142
Civil Service College 82
Classic FM 219
Clearing House, London, Ltd. 155
Clearing Houses, Recognised 155
Climate change 325
Clubs 287
Coach travel 138-9
Coastguard, Maritime and, Agency 84
Cockfighting 307
Colleges 96-8
Colombian Embassy 341
Commercial Radio Companies Association 219
Commission for Architecture and the Built Environment 319
Commission for Integrated Transport 134
Commonwealth
    Foundation 347
    Games 317
    Institute 347
    Secretariat 347
Communications 248-51
Community Health Councils 116-17
    Association of, for England and Wales 116
Companies House 160
Competition Commission 160
Complementary Medicine, education and training 100
Confederation of British Industry 160-1
Conference centres 176-82
Congo, Democratic Republic, Embassy 341
Connex Rail 135
Conservation, Volunteers, British Trust for 328
Constituencies, parliamentary 71-8
Consumer Law 200
Copyright Tribunal 191
Coroners' courts 186, 191
Corporation of London
    Borough Council 33-40
    map 33
    Records Office 319

414 Index

waste and recycling facilities 331
Costa Rica, Embassy 341
Cote d'Ivoire, Embassy 341
Councils
    for Christians and Jews 357
    for Museums, Archives and Libraries 319, 133
    of African and Afro-Caribbean Churches 363
Countryside Alliance 317
Courts
    Coroners' 186, 191
    county 188-9
    crown 188
    International Arbitration 196
    magistrates 189-90
    Service, The 86
    Supreme Court of Judicature 186
Covent Garden
    Market 291
    Market Authority 319
Crayford, Bexleyheath and, MP 72
Cricket 307-9
Crime Squad, National 107
Criminal Organisation, International 347
Croatia, Embassy 341
Croquet Association 317
Crown
    Court Centres 187
    courts 188
    Estate 319
    Prosecution Service 192-3
Croydon
    Borough Council 40-1
    Buddhist Centre 358
    health authorities and trusts 114
    map 40
    MPs 73
    waste and recycling facilities 331
Crystal Palace 309
    Football Club 310
Cuba
    Embassy 341
    Tourist Board 337
Culture, Media and Sport, Department for 83
Cyprus
    Embassy 341
    tourist offices 337, 338
Czech Republic, Embassy 341

D

Dagenham, MP 73
Dagenham, Barking and
    Borough Council 27-8
    map 27
Dance, education and training 100
Darts, British Association 317
Data Protection Tribunal 191
Death
    legal notes 201-2
    statistics 4
Debt Management Office, United Kingdom 88
Defence
    Ministry of 83
    Studies, Royal College of 100
Denmark
    Embassy 341

Tourist Board 337
Dentistry, education and training 100
Deprivation statistics 5
Derivatives, Securities and, Exchange, 154
Development Agency 10
Dioceses, Church of England 361-2
Dispensing Optics, education and training 103
Distances from London
    air 350-1
    road 137
Divorce, legal notes 202
Docklands Light Railway 137
Dominican Republic
    Embassy 341
    Tourist Office 337
Downing Street 288
Drama, education and training 100
Driver and Vehicle Licensing Agency 83
Driving Standards Agency 83
Dr Johnson's House 289
Dubai, Commerce and Tourism Promotion 337
Dulwich and West Norwood, MP 73

E

Ealing
    Borough Council 42-3
    map 42
    MPs 73
    waste and recycling facilities 331
Ealing Acton and Shepherd's Bush, MP 73
Ealing, Hammersmith and Hounslow, health authorities and trusts 114
Earnings, gross weekly 162
East Ham, MP 73
East London and the City, health authorities and trusts 114-15
East London Mosque Trust 359
Ecuador, Embassy 341
Edmonton, MP 73
Education
    action zones 92
    bodies 98-9
    colleges 96-8
    'Excellence in Cities' 92
    government policy 91
    Local Education Authorities (LEAs) 93-4
    LEA responsibilities 91
    professional 99-104
    statistics 91
    structure 91
    universities 94-6
    urban priorities 92
Education and Employment, Department of 83
Egypt
    Embassy 341
    Tourism Office 337
Electricity
    Association 146
    supply 145
Electricity Markets, Gas and, Office of 146
El Salvador, Embassy 342
Eltham
    MP 74
    Palace 389
Embassies 340-6
Emergency Planning, Fire and, Authority 105

Index

Emergency services 105-12
Emigration 4
Employment
    Appeal Tribunal 191
    by occupation 162
    employer associations 166-7
    legal notes 204
    part-time 162
    Service, The 83
    Tribunal 191
Employment, Education and, Department of 83
Empty Homes Agency 119
Enfield
    Borough Council 43-4
    map 43
    MPs 74
    waste and recycling facilities 331
Engineering, education and training 100-1
English
    Heritage 320
    Sport Council, London and South East Region 316
    Tourism Council 322
Enterprise Agency, London 169
Environment Agency 327
Environmental Education, London Forum 328
Environment, Fisheries and Aquaculture, Centre for 82
Environment, Transport and the Regions, Department of 83-4
Environment, Water and, Management, Chartered Institution of 328
Erith and Thamesmead, MP 74
Eritrean Orthodox Church 364
Esher RFC 314
Estonia, Embassy 342
Ethiopian Orthodox Church 364
European
    Agency for the Evaluation of Medicinal Products 347
    Bank for Reconstruction and Development 347
    Commission Representative Office 347
    Information Centres 347
    Parliament 79
    Union 347
Eurostar 135
Evangelical Alliance 357
Evangelical Lutheran Church of England 363
Environment 13
Exhibition centres 176-82
Expenditure, household 5

F
Family Records Centre 198
Farming and Rural Conservancy Agency 82
Federation of Synagogues 360
Feltham and Heston, MP 73
Fencing Association, British 317
Fiji, High Commission 342
Film
    Commission, British 318
    Council 320
    Institute, British 318-19
Finance
    Financial advisers 151
    Financial Service Authority 154
    Financial Service Compensation Scheme 154
    Financial Services Regulation 153-5

Finchley, MPs 74, 75
Finland
    Embassy 342
    Tourism Board 337
Fire Service
    College 85
    Emergency Planning Authority 105
    Fire Brigade commands 105
First Capital (buses) 138
First Great Eastern (Railway) 135
First North Western (Railway) 135
Fisheries, Agriculture, Food and, Ministry of 81-2
Fisheries, Environment, Aquaculture and, Centre for 82
FLR (radio) 219
Focus Central London 169-70
Food, Agriculture, Fisheries and, Ministry of 81-2
Food and Nutrition Science, education and training 101
Football 309-10
    Association 317
    teams 310
Foreign and Commonwealth Office 84
Forensic Science Service 107
Forthcoming events 406
France
    Embassy 342
    Tourist Office 337
Free Churches' Council 357
Friendly Societies
    Commission 153
    Registry of 153
Friends of the Earth 328
Friends, Religious Society 365
Fuel and Energy Science, education and training 101
Fulham Football Club 310
Fulham, Hammersmith and
    Borough Council 46-7
    MP 74
    waste and recycling facilities 331

G
Gabon, Embassy 342
Galleries 292-6
Gambia
    Embassy 342
    National Tourist Office 337
Gas and Electricity Markets, Office of 146
Gas supply 145
Gatwick
    Airport 142-3
    Express 135
Genealogies, Society of 198
General Council of the Bar 195
General Register Office, The 198
General Synod, Church of England 361
George Inn 289
Georgia, Embassy 342
Germany, National Tourist Office 337
Germany, Federal Republic of, Embassy 342
Ghana, Embassy 342
Gibraltar, Government of 337
GMTV 218
Going for Green 328
Golders Green, Finchley and, MP 74
Government
    Car and Despatch Agency 82

416 Index

Commerce, Office of 88
departments 80-88
ministers 80-1
Offices for the Regions 84
Government of Gibraltar Tourist Office 337
Grand National Archery Society 317
Greater London Authority 8-25
   Constituencies and members 24
   election results 13-23
   elections 9-10
   London List members 24-5
   map 8
   structure 10
Greater London Enterprise 169
Greater London, Magistrates' Courts Authority 190
Great Fire of London 256
Great North Eastern Railway 135-6
Greece
   Embassy 342
   Hellenic Tourism organisation 337
Greenline (coaches) 138
Green Park 297
Greenwich
   Borough Council 44-5
   map 44
   Observatory 289
   Park 297
   Royal Naval College 289
   waste and recycling facilities 332
Greenwich and Woolwich, MP 74
Greenwich, Bexley and, health authorities and trusts 114
Grenada
   High Commission 342
   National Tourist Office 337
Grenadines, St Vincent and
   High Commission 345
   Tourism Office 339
Greyhound Racing 310-11
   National Club 318
Gross Domestic Product 151-2
Grosvenor Bridge 299
Guatemala, Embassy 342
Guildhall, The 289
Guilds 36-40
Guyana, Embassy 342

H
Hackney
   Borough Council 45-6
   map 45
   MPs 74
   waste and recycling facilities 332
Hammersmith and Fulham
   Borough Council 46-7
   map 46
   MP 74
   waste and recycling facilities 332
Hammersmith Bridge 299
Hammersmith, Ealing, Hounslow and, health authorities and trusts 114
Hampstead and Highgate, MP 74
Hampton Court Bridge 299
Harbour Club 312
Haringey
   Borough Council 47-8

Business Link Centre 168
   map 47
   waste and recycling facilities 332
Harlequin FC 314
Harlington, Hayes and, MP 75
Harrow
   Borough Council 48-9
   map 48
   MPs 75
   waste and recycling facilities 332
Harrow, Bromley and, health authorities and trusts 114
Havering
   Borough Council 49-51
   map 49
Havering, Barking and, health authorities and trusts 113
Hayes and Harlington, MP 75
Health
   authorities 113-16
   Department of 84-5
Heart Radio 219
Hendon, MP 75
Heritage of London Trust 320
Heston, Feltham and, MP 74
High Court Centres 187
Highgate, Hampstead and, MP 74
Highways Agency 83-4
Hillingdon
   Borough Council 51-2
   map 51
   waste and recycling facilities 332
Hinduism 359
   Bharatiya Vidya Bhavan 359
   origin and development 359
   Swaminarayan Hindu Mission 359
   Vishnu Hindu Parishad 359
Historic
   buildings 289
   royal palaces 320
Historical Manuscripts, Royal Commission on 320
HM Land Registry 86
Holborn and St Pancras, MP 75
Home Office 85
Honduras, Embassy 342
Hong Kong, Tourism Association 337
Hornchurch, MP 75
Hornsey and Wood Green 75
Horse Guards 290
Horseracing 311
Horseracing Board, British 317
Hotelkeeping, education and training 101
Hounslow
   Borough Council 52-3
   map 52
   waste and recycling facilities 332
Hounslow, Ealing, Hammersmith and, health authorities and trusts 114
Household statistics 5, 6
Houses of Parliament 290
Housing
   average prices 118
   Corporation 119
   Ombudsman 119
   Organisations Mobility and Exchange Service 119
   regulation and provision 119
   Rent Service 120

Index 417

stock by tenure 118
Unit, London 119-20
Hungary
   Embassy 342
   National Tourism Office 338
Hungerford Bridge 298
Hyde Park 297

I
Iceland
   Embassy 342
   Tourism Information Bureau 338
Ice Skating, National Association of the UK 318
Ilford, MPs 75
Illegitimacy, legal notes 206
Imams and Mosques Council 359
Immigration 4
Immigration Appellate Authorities 191
IMRO 153
Independent Radio 219
Independent Television
   Commission 218
   companies 218
   News 218
India
   High Commission 342
   Tourist Office 338
Indonesia, Embassy 342
Industry, Trade and, Department of 87
Information Science, education and training 102
Information Technology Organisation, Police 107
Information Technology Services Group 87
Inland Revenue 155
INMARSAT 347
Institute of Actuaries 154
Institute of Chartered Accountants in England and Wales 154
Institutional Management, education and training 100
Institutions 369-92
Insurance
   companies 151, 156-8
   education and training 101
   London Market 155-6
   Ombudsman 159
Integrated Transport, Commission for 134
Inter-Church and Inter-faith Co-operation 357
Interest rates 152
International
   Development, Department for 85
   Direct Dialling 352-4
   Financial Futures and Options Exchange 154
   Labour Market 347
   Maritime Organisation 347
   Organisations 347
   Petroleum Exchange 154
   Tennis Federation 317
Intestacy 213
Investment
   designated exchanges 155
   Management Regulatory Organisation 153
   Ombudsman 159
Iran, Embassy 342
Iraqi Interests Section 342
Ireland
   Embassy 342
   Tourist Board 338

Islam 359
   Central Mosque 359
   East London Mosque Trust 359
   Imams and Mosques Council 359
   Islamic Cultural Centre 359
   Muslim Council of Britain 359
   origin and development 359
Isleworth, Brentford and, MP 72
Islington
   Borough Council 53-4
   map 53
   MPs 75
   waste and recycling facilities 332
Israel
   Embassy 343
   Government Tourist Office 338
Italy
   Embassy 343
   State Tourist Office 338
ITV Network Centre 218

J
Jainism 360
Jamaica
   High Commission 343
   Tourist Board 338
Japan
   Embassy 343
   National Tourist organisation 338
Jazz FM 219
Jehovah's Witnesses 366
Jersey, Tourism and Information Office 338
Jews, Christians and, Council for 357
Jockey Club, The 317
Jordan, Embassy 343
Journalism, education and training 101
Judaism 360
   Beth Din Federation of Synagogues 360
   Chief Rabbinate 360
   Christians and Jews Council 357
   Federation of Synagogues 360
   Masorti Synagogues 360
   origin and development 360
   Union of Liberal and Progressive Synagogues 360
   United Synagogue 360
Jury service 206

K
Kazakstan Embassy 343
Keep Fit Association 317
Kensington
   Gardens 297
   Palace 289
Kensington and Chelsea
   map 54
   MP 75-6
   Royal Borough Council 54-5
   waste and recycling facilities 332
Kensington, Chelsea and Westminster, health authorities and trusts 115
Kenya
   High Commission 343
   Tourist Office 338
Kew Bridges 299
Kings and Queens, (since 927 AD) 257-60
Kingston and Surbiton, MP 76

Kingston Bridge 299
Kingston upon Thames
  map 55
  Royal Borough Council 55-6
  waste and recycling facilities 333
Kiss 100 FM 219
Korea
  Embassy 343
  National Tourism organisation 338
  Tourist Office 338
Krishna Consciousness, International Society for 359
Kuwait, Embassy 343
Kyrgyz Republic, Embassy 343

L
Labour Force, components 161
Labour Organisation, International 347
Lambeth
  Borough Council 56-7
  Bridge 299
  map 56
  Palace 289
  waste and recycling facilities 333
Land
  Registry, HM 86
  Tribunal 191
  utilisation 327
Language Therapy, education and training 104
Latvia
  Embassy 343
  Lutheran Church 363
  Orthodox Church Abroad 364
Law
  Centres 195
  Centres Federation 195
  Commission 196
  education and training 101-2
  firms 151
  Officers' Department 85-6
  Society 196
  Society, Government Group 196
Lawn Tennis
  Association 317
  Museum 316
LBC Radio 219
Leadenhall Market 291
League of Arab States 347
Leasehold
  Advisory Service 119
  Valuation Tribunal 120
Lebanon
  Embassy 343
  Tourist Office 338
Legal Aid 207-9
Legal notes
  adoption 198
  births 198
  children 203
  citizenship 199
  consumer law 200
  deaths 201-2
  divorce 202
  employment 204
  illegitimacy 206
  intestacy 213
  jury service 206

landlord and tenant 206
legal aid 207
legitimacy 206
marriage 209
tenancy 206
town and country planning 210
voters' qualifications 211
wills 211
Legal Services Commission 196
Legal system
  appointments 186
  barristers 185
  civil cases 186
  criminal cases 186
  solicitors 185
Lesotho, High Commission 343
LETEC 170
Lewisham
  Borough Council 57-8
  map 57
  MPs 76
Leyton and Wanstead, MP 76
Leyton Orient Football Club 310
Liberia, Embassy 343
Liberty Radio 219
Librarianship, education and training 102
Libraries 121-33
Libya, People's Bureau 343
Lithuania
  Embassy 343
  Roman Catholic Church 362
Lloyd's of London 290
Local Education Authorities 93-4
London
  21 Sustainability Network 328
  air distances from 350-1
  Arena 290
  blue plaque sites 262-85
  Bridge 298
  Central (buses) 138
  City Partners 169
  Clearing House Ltd. 155
  Corporation of, waste and recycling facilities 331
  Court of International Arbitration 196
  Dungeon 290
  Enterprise 169
  Eye, The 290-1
  First Centre 161
  Government, Association of 70
  Greek Radio 219
  history 255-7
  Irish RFC 314
  Marathon, The 311-12, 317
  Mayors' Association, The 71
  Metal Exchange 154
  Monument 291
  Rivers Association 328
  River Services Ltd. 141
  Transport 134
  Turkish Radio 219
  walks 303-4
Wasps 314
Weekend Television 218
Welsh RFC 314
Wildlife Trust 328
Zendo 358

Index 419

Lord Chancellor
    Department 86
    Residence 290
Lord Great Chamberlain's Office 320
Lord Mayor's Day 34
Lord Mayor, the first 256
Lord's Cricket Ground 307-8
Lottery Charities Board, National 171
LST Rail 136
Lutheran Church 363
    Council of Great Britain 363
Luton Airport 143-4
Luxembourg
    Embassy 343
    Tourist Office 338

M

Macedonia, Embassy 343
Madame Tussaud's 291
magazines 226-35
Magic Radio 219
Magistrates Courts 189-90
Malankara Orthodox Syrian Church 364
Malawi, Embassy 343
Malaya, Tourism Promotion Board 338
Maldives, Embassy 343
Malta
    High Commission 343
    Tourist Office 338
Management, education and training 100
Marathon, London 311-12, 317
Maritime and Coastguard Agency 84
Markets 291
Marlborough House 291
Marriage, legal notes 209
Marshall's Coaches 138
Martial Arts Association, Amateur 316
Masorti Synagogues, Assembly of 360
Material Studies, education and training 102
Mauritania, Embassy 344
Mauritius
    High Commission 344
    Tourism Promotion Authority 338
Mayoral election
    candidates 11-12
    constituency results 13-23
Mayoralty 34
MCC 318
    Tennis Club 312
Media consultancies 241-7
Media, Culture, Sport and, Department for 83
Medical Devices Agency 85
Medicinal Products, European Agency for Evaluation 347
Medicine
    Complementary, education and training 100
    Control Agency 85
    education and training 102
    supplementary professions 103
Mental Health Review Tribunal 191
MEPs 79
Merchant banks 152
Merton
    Borough Council 58-9
    map 58
    waste and recycling facilities 333

Merton, Sutton and Wandsworth, health authorities and trusts 114-15
Metal Exchange, London 154
Methodist Church 363
    Conference Office 363
Metrobus 138
Metropolitan Police
    Authority 10-11
    RFC 315
    River Division 105
    Service 106
    Special Constabulary 106
Mexico
    Embassy 344
    Ministry of Tourism 338
Midland Mainline 136
Migration 4
Millennium
    Bridge 299
    Commission 320-1
    Dome 291
    Radio 219
Ministry of Defence Police 107
Missing Persons Helpline, National 117
Mitcham and Morden, MP 76
Mobile telephones 250-1
Monaco, Government Tourist and Convention Office 338
Mongolia, Embassy 344
Monuments 291-2
Moon phases 396-401
Morden, Mitcham and, MP 76
Morocco
    Embassy 344
    National Tourist Office 338
Mortality rates 4
Mozambique, Embassy 344
Museums 292-6
Music, education and training 103
Muslim
    Council of Britain 359
    Organisations of the UK and Eire, Union of 359
    World League 359
Myanmar, Embassy 344

N

Namibia
    Embassy 344
    Tourism 338
National Association
    for Councils for Voluntary Service 171
    of Volunteer Bureaux 171
    Blood Service 117
    Car Parks 139
    Centre for Volunteering 171
    Council
        for Voluntary Organisations 171
        for Voluntary Youth Services 171
    Crime Squad 107
    Express 139
    Greyhound Racing Club 318
    Ice Skating Association of the UK 318
    Lottery Charities Board 171
    Missing Persons Bureau 107
    Missing Persons Helpline 117
    Savings 88

National Health Service
    Community Health Councils 116
    regional office 113
    structure 113
    trusts 113-16
Nature Reserves 325-6
NCS Service Authority 107
Nepal, Royal, Embassy 344
Netherlands, Embassy 344
Nevis, St Christopher and, High Commission 345
Nevis, St Kitts and, Tourism Office 339
Newham
    Borough Council 60-1
    map 60
    waste and recycling facilities 333
New Opportunities Fund 172
News Agencies 235
News Direct 219
Newspapers
    national 220-1
    regional 221-6
New Zealand
    High Commission 344
    Tourism 338
NFL Europe League 318
NHS Estates 85
NHS Pensions 85
Nicaragua, Embassy 344
Nigeria, Embassy 344
Northern Ireland, Tourist Board 338
Norway
    Embassy 344
    Tourist Board 338
Nursing, education and training 103
Nutrition Science, Food and, education and training 100

O
Office for National Statistics 88
Office of
    Fair Trading 86
    Gas and Electricity Markets 146
    Passenger Rail Franchising 136
    Telecommunications 248
    the Rail Regulator 136
    Water Service 145
Oftel 248, 251
Old Bexley and Sidcup, MP 76
Olympics 312
    Olympic Association, British 317
Oman, Sultanate of, Embassy 344
Ombudsmen
    Banking 159
    Building Society 159
    Finance 159
    Housing 119
    Insurance 159
    Investment 159
    Pensions 159
    PIA 160
    Prison Service 194
Open Air Theatre 296
Opthalmics, education and training 103
Order of
    Precedence 261-2
    Succession 260-1

Orpington, MP 76
Orthodox Churches 363-4
Osteopathy, education and training 103
Oval Cricket Ground 308, 309
Oxford Express (coaches) 139

P
Pakistan, High Commission 344
Panama, Embassy 344
Papua New Guinea, High Commission 344
Paraguay, Embassy 344
Parcelforce 252
Parking 139-40
    Committee for London 139
Parks 296, 297
    Royal 297
Parliament
    constituencies 71-8
    Houses of 290
Preface iii
Parole Board for England and Wales 194
Passenger Rail Franchising, Office of 136
Patent Office 87
Payment Clearing Services, Association for 152
Peasants Revolt 256
Peckham, Camberwell and, MP 72
Pensions
    Appeal Tribunal 192
    Ombudsman 159
Periodicals
    consumer 230-5
    trade 226-30
Personal Investment Authority 153
Peru, Embassy 344
Petticoat Lane Market 291
Pharmacy, education and training 103
Philippines
    Cultural and Tourist Office 338
    Embassy 344
PIA, Ombudsman 160
Plague, The 256
Planetarium, The 291
Planning Inspectorate 84
Poland, Embassy 345
Police
    British Transport 106
    City of London 106
    Complaints Authority 106
    crime statistics 112
    Forensic Science Service 107
    Information Technology organisation 107
    Metropolitan 10-11, 106
    Ministry of Defence 107
    National Crime Squad 107
    National Missing Persons Bureau 107
    NCS Service 107
    Police Service, the 105-6
    River 106
    Royal Parks Constabulary 107
    stations 108-11
Pollution 325
    Urban Research Centre 329
Poplar and Canning Town, MP 76
Population
    by age 3
    by ethnic groups 3
    trends 3

Index   421

Portobello Road Market 291
Port of London Authority 140-1, 328-9
Portugal
   Embassy 345
   National Tourist Office 339
Postal services 252
Precedence, Order of 261-2
Preface iii
Premier Christian Radio 219
Press, The 220-35
Prime Minister's Office 82
Primrose Hill 297
Printing, education and training 103
Prison Service
   Ombudsman 194
   prisons 194
Prize Ring, London 307
Probation Service, 195
Professional Windsurfing Association 318
Property Advisers to the Civil Service 82
Public
   Mobile Radio 251
   offices 80-8
   relations consultancies 241-7
   Telecommunication Service 248-51
   Trust Office 86
Publishers 235-9
Putney
   Bridges 299
   MP 76-7

Q
Qatar, Embassy 345
Quakers, The 365
Queen Elizabeth II
   Bridge 298
   Conference Centre 84
Queen's Club 312
Queen's House 289
Queens Park Rangers Football Club 310
Queens and Kings (since 927 AD) 257-60

R
Rackets 312
Radio
   Authority, The 218
   BBC 219
   digital 218-19
   independent stations 219
   Public Mobile 251
Rail
   companies 135-7
   Enquiries 136
   Railway Board, British 136
   Regulator, Office of 136
   transport 135-7
Railtrack plc 136
Reach 172
Reading Buses 139
Real Tennis 312
Recognised professional bodies 153
Records Office, Corporation of London 319
Recycling, local authority facilities 330-34
Redbridge
   Borough Council 61-2
   map 61
   waste and recycling facilities 333

Redbridge and Waltham Forest, health authorities and trusts 115-16
Red Crescent 347
Red Cross 347
Reform Synagogues of Great Britain 360
Regent's Park 297
Regent's Park and Kensington North, MP 77
Regions, the, Environment, Transport and, Department of 83-4
Registry of Friendly Societies 153
Religion 357-66
Religious Society of Friends 365
Rent Association Panel 120
Rent Service 120
Retail banks 152
Richmond
   Borough Council 62-3
   Bridges 299
   Gymnastic Association 318
   Lock 299
   map 62
   Park 297
Richmond Park, MP 77
Ritz Radio 219
Rivers Association, London 328
River Services, London Ltd. 141
Road transport 137-9
Roman Catholic Church 362
Romania
   Embassy 345
   National Tourist Office 339
   Orthodox Church in London 364
Roman remains 296
Romans, the 255
Romford
   MP 77
   Stadium 311
Rowing 312-13
   Association, Amateur, The 316
Royal
   Albert Hall 296
   Commission on Historical Manuscripts 320
   Hospital, Chelsea 296
   Mail 252
   Mint 88
   National Theatre Board 321
   Opera House 296
   Parks 297
   Parks Agency 83
   Parks Constabulary 107
   Tennis Court 312
Rugby Football Union 314, 318
Rugby teams 314-15
Ruislip-Northwood, MP 77
Rural Conservancy, Farming and, Agency 82
Russian Federation
   Embassy 345
   Sport and Tourism 339
Rwanda, Embassy 345

S
Salvation Army, London divisions 365
Sanex WTA Tour 318
Saracens FC 315
Saudi Arabia, Royal Embassy 345
Science, education and training 104

Scotland, Tourist Board 339
Scotland Office 86
Securities
　and Derivatives Exchange, Ltd. 154
　and Futures Authority 153
Senegal, Embassy 345
Seventh Day Adventist Church 365
Seychelles
　High Commission 345
　Tourist Office 339
Shelter 120
Shepherd's Bush, Ealing Acton and, MP 73
Shoreditch, Hackney South and, MP 74
Sidcup, Old Bexley and, MP 76
Sierra Leone, High Commission 345
Sikhism 360
　Divine Fellowship 361
　Missionary Society 361
　origin and development 360
　World Fellowship 361
Silverlink 136
Singapore
　High Commission 345
　Tourist Office 339
Slovak Republic, Embassy 345
Slovenia
　Catholic Mission 362
　Embassy 345
　Tourist Office 339
Snooker 306-7
Social Security, Department of 87
Social Work, education and training 104
Societies 369-92
Soka Gakkai UK 358
Solicitors' Disciplinary Tribunal 192
SOLOTEC 170
Somerset House 298
South Africa, High Commission 345
South Bank Centre 298
South East Nations, Association of 347
Southwark
　Borough Council 63-4
　Bridge 298
　Cathedral 298
　map 62
Southwark North and Bermondsey, MP 77
South West Trains 136
Spain, Embassy 345
Spanish and Portuguese Jews' Congregation 360
Special
　Commissioners of Income Tax Tribunal 192
　Constabulary 106
　Immigration Appeals Tribunal 192
Speech Therapy, education and training 104
Spitalfields Market 291
Sport 305-16
　Bodies 316-18
　Culture, Media and, Department for 83
　England 316
Sri Lanka
　High Commission 345
　Tourist Board 339
SSSI sites 326
Stagecoach (buses) 138
Stansted Airport 144
Statistics
　church attendance 357

crime 112
deprivation 5
employment 161-3
finance 151, 155
household expenditure 6
housing 117-18
land utilisation 327
migration 4
mobile phones 250
mortality rates 4
population 3
tourism 322
transport 134
travel 137, 141-2
waste management 329
St Christopher and Nevis, High Commission 345
St James's Palace 297
St James's Park 297
St Kitts and Nevis, Tourism Office 339
St Lucia, High Commission 345
St Matthews Westminster 365
Stock Exchange 154, 158-9
Stoke Newington, Hackney North and, MP 74
St Pancras, Holborn and, MP 75
St Paul's Cathedral 298
Strategic Rail Authority, Shadow 136
Streatham, MP 77
St Vincent and the Grenadines
　High Commission 345
　Tourism Office 339
Succession, Order of 260-1
Sudan, Embassy 345
Sunrise 396-401
Sunrise Radio 219
Sunset 396-401
Supreme Court of Judicature 186
Surbiton, Kingston and, MP 76
Surveying, education and training 104
Sustainable London Trust 329
Sutton
　Borough Council 64-5
　map 64
　waste and recycling facilities 333
Sutton and Cheam, MP 77
Sutton, Merton, Wandsworth and, health authorities and trusts 115
Swaminarayan Hindu Mission 359
Swaziland, High Commission 345
Sweden
　Church 363
　Embassy 346
　Travel and Tourism Council 339
Swimming 313-14
　Amateur Association 316
Switzerland
　Embassy 346
　Travel Centre 339
Synagogues, Federation of 360
Syria, Embassy 346
Syrian Orthodox Church 364-5

T

Takeover Panel 160
Talk Radio 219
Tanzania, High Commission 346
Taxi services 139

Index 423

TECs 169-70
Teddington Lock 299
Telephones
  companies 251
  fixed line 249
  international dialling codes 352-4
  mobile 250-1
  paging 250
Teletext Ltd. 218
Television
  BBC 217
  cable 249
  digital 217
  Independent 218
Tenancy, legal notes 206
Tennis
  International Federation 317
  Tennis and Rackets Association 318
  Tennis Foundation, British 317
Tenpin Bowling Association, British 317
Thailand
  Royal Embassy 346
  Tourism Authority 339
Thames
  21 327
  Buddhist Vihara 358
  Embankments 299
  Estuary Partnership 329
  Flood Barrier 299
  River 298, 327
  Trains 136
  Tunnel 299
  Water Utilities plc 145
Thameslink 136
Thamesmead, Erith and, MP 74
Theatres 299-303
Theological colleges 104
Tidal
  constants 402
  predictions 402-5
Time zones 348-50
Tobago, Trinidad and, High Commission 346
Tonga, High Commission 346
Tooting, MP 77
Tottenham, MP 77
Tottenham Hotspur Football Club 310
Tourism 322
  Information service 322
  statistics 322
  Tourist Boards 337
Tower Bridge 298
Tower Bridge Experience 303
Tower Hamlets
  Borough Council 65-6
  map 66
  waste and recycling facilities 333
Tower of London 289-90
Town and country planning 210
  education and training 104
Trade and Industry, Department of 87
Tradepoint Stock Exchange 154
Trade Unions 164-6
  Trades Union Congress 167
Training and Enterprise Councils 169-70
Train Operating Companies, Association of 136
Transport

air 141-4
bus 138-9
education and training 104
London 134
rail 135-7
taxi 139
Tribunal 192
underground 137
Transport, Environment, the Regions and, Department of 83-4
Treasury 87-8
  Solicitor 88
Tree Officers Association, London 328
Tribunals
  Agricultural Land 191
  Appeals Service 191
  Copyright 191
  Data Protection 191
  Employment 191
  Employment Appeal 191
  Land 192
  Mental Health Review 192
  Pensions Appeal 192
  Solicitors' Disciplinary 192
  Special Commissioners of Income Tax 192
  Special Immigration Appeals 192
  Transport 192
  Valuation 197
  VAT and Duties 192
Trinidad and Tobago, High Commission 346
Tunisia
  Embassy 346
  National Tourist Office 339
Turkey, National Tourist Office 339
Turkmenistan, Embassy 346
Twickenham
  Bridge 299
  MP 77
  Stadium 314
Twilight, duration of 396-401

U
Uganda, High Commission 346
UK
  European Parliament Office 347
  Passport Agency 85
  Sports Council 316
Ukraine, Embassy 346
Underground rail traffic, statistics 137, 257
Union of Liberal and Progressive Synagogues 360
Union of Orthodox Hebrew Congregation 360
Unitarian and Free Christian Churches 366
  General Assembly 366
United
  Arab Emirates, Embassy 346
  Nations 347
  Nations, Office and Information Centre 347
  Reform Church 365
  Synagogue 360
Universities 94-6
Upminster, MP 78
Urban Pollution Research Centre 329
Uruguay, Embassy 346
USA, Embassy 340
Uxbridge, MP 78
Uzbekistan, Embassy 346

424 Index

V
Valuation
  Office 120
  Office Agency 196
  tribunals 120, 197
VAT and Duties Tribunal 192
Vauxhall
  Bridge 299
  MP 78
Vehicle
  Certification Agency 84
  Inspectorate 84
Venezuela
  Embassy 346
  Tourist Office 339
Veterinary
  Laboratory Agency 82
  Medicine Directorate 82
  Medicine, education and training 104
Vietnam
  Buddhist Society 358
  Embassy 346
Vikings, the 255
Virgin Radio 219
Virgin Trains 136
Vishnu Hindu Parishad 359
Vivekananda Centre 359
Voluntary Organisations 170-3
  National Council for 171
Voluntary Service
  Council 171
  councils 172-3
  National Association for Council for, 171
  Voluntary Service Overseas 172
Volunteer Bureaux, National Association of 171
Volunteering, National Centre for 171
Voters' qualifications 211
VSO 172

W
WAGN Railway 136
Wales and West (Railway) 136
Wales Office 88
Walking 303
Wallington, Carshalton and, MP 72
Waltham Forest
  Borough Council 67-8
  map 67
  waste and recycling facilities 333
Waltham Forest, Redbridge and, health authorities and trusts 115-16
Walthamstow
  MP 78
  Stadium 311
Wandsworth
  Borough Council 68-9
  Bridge 299
  map 68
  waste and recycling facilities 334
Wandsworth, Merton, Sutton and, health authorities and trusts 115
Wanstead, Leyton and, MP 76

War Pensions Agency 87
Waste management
  local authority facilities 330-34
  statistics 330
Water and Environment Management, Chartered Institution of 328
Waterloo Bridge 298
Water Services 145
  Office of 145
Water UK 145
Watford Football Club 310
Wembley Stadium 315
West Ham
  Football Club 310
  MP 78
West London Buddhist Society 359
Westminster
  Abbey 303
  Borough Council 69-70
  Bridge 299
  Cathedral 303
  map 69
  waste and recycling facilities 334
Westminster, City of London and, MP 72-3
Westminster, Kensington, Chelsea and, health authorities and trusts 115
West Norwood, Dulwich an, MP 73
Wetlands Centre 303
Wildlife Trust 328
Wills, legal notes 211-13
Wilton Park Conference Centre 84
Wimbledon 315
  All England Tennis Club 316
  Football Club 310
  Lawn Tennis Museum 316
  MP 78
  Stadium 311
Windsurfing Association, National 317
Woodford Green, Chingford and, MP 72
Wood Green, Hornsey and, MP 75
Woolwich, Greenwich and, MP 74
World Bank 347
World Professional Billiards and Snooker Association 318
World Sikh Fellowship 361
World Squares for All 304

X
XFM Radio 219

Y
Yemen, Embassy 346
Youth Services, Voluntary, National Council for 171

Z
Zambia
  High Commission 346
  National Tourist Board 339
Zendo, London 358
Zimbabwe, High Commission 346
Zoological Gardens 291
Zoroastrianism 361